COMBAT FLEETS OF THE WORLD
1978/79

WORKS BY JEAN LABAYLE COUHAT

- French Warships of World War I } Published by Ian Allan, London. Sold in France by Editions Maritimes et d'Outre-Mer
- French Warships of World War II }
- Articles for *La Revue Maritime, Marine, Revue de Défense Nationale,* and *Armées d'aujourdhui*

COMBAT FLEETS OF THE WORLD 1978/79

Their Ships, Aircraft, and Armament

Edited by
JEAN LABAYLE COUHAT

This guide was first published in 1897 by Captain de Balincourt, French Navy. It was continued from 1928 to 1943 by Captain Vincent-Bréchignac, French Navy, and from 1943 to 1974 by Henri Le Masson. The two English-language editions have been prepared under the direction of the staff of the United States Naval Institute.

Naval Institute Press

Published in 1978 by
The United States Naval Institute
Annapolis, Maryland

This second English-language edition is published by
arrangement with Éditions Maritimes et d'Outre-Mer

Library of Congress Catalog Card Number: 78-50192
ISBN 0-87021-121-8

All photographs are official, unless otherwise credited, and have
been issued by the national authorities concerned; new drawings
in this issue are by Henri Simoni, unless otherwise credited.

Printed in the United States of America

CONTENTS

PREFACE

This volume is dedicated to the memory of my eminent predecessor and friend, Henri Le Masson, who died on 27 March 1977.

A number of changes have been made in the 1978 edition of *Flottes de Combat*, notably in the designations of ship classes, even though the English-language edition uses a different nomenclature. Both editions have been re-organized to achieve consistency and ease of reference, and new drawings and photographs have been added or have replaced old ones.

I am indebted to the French Navy, the U.S. Navy, naval and military attachés, and admiralties and ministries that have generously furnished me with valuable information. I am also grateful to Captain John Moore (editor of *Jane's Fighting Ships*), Giorgio Giorgerini (editor of *Almanacco Navale*), Gerhard Albrecht (editor of *Weyers Flottentaschenbuch*), and Ulrich Schulz-Torge (author of a remarkable book on the Soviet Navy, *Die Sowjetische Kriegsmarine*).

As with previous editions, much credit is due to the many ship experts and enthusiasts from near and far who share with me their knowledge and magnificent photographs. It is impossible for me to name them all, but I must express my heartfelt thanks to the following long-time friends of *Flottes de Combat:* Aldo Fraccaroli, G. Arra, J. C. Bellonne, Carlo Martinelli, Norman Polmar, J. F. Pellegrini, J. Taibo, and Stephan Terzibaschitsch.

Many people have given me special assistance in the preparation of the English-language edition. I wish to thank particularly A. D. Baker III for his extensive advice and assistance in translation, as well as S. L. Morison, R. L. Scheina, R. Carlisle, and the staff of the U.S. Navy's Still Photo Branch, Office of the Chief of Information. I am also indebted to Commander James J. McDonald, U.S. Navy (Retired), who translated the first edition, and to Commander J. Bodin, French Navy, who assisted in the translation of this edition.

I have made every effort to avoid mistakes but, if any have crept in, I ask my readers' forgiveness and would appreciate their making any defects known to me through the publisher.

J.LC.

INTRODUCTION

U.S. NAVY

During the two years that have elapsed since the 1976/77 edition of *Combat Fleets of the World* was published, the U.S. Navy has been modernizing its forces; at the same time, its numerical strength has been dwindling. The reason for the shrinkage is that, as ships have been decommissioned, stricken, or scrapped, they have not been replaced on a one-to-one basis. Nevertheless, the U.S. Navy's global offensive, as well as defensive, strength has significantly increased, because the new ships that have been built are more capable than their predecessors. Furthermore, the ambitious shipbuilding program that is under way or being authorized will soon enable the Navy to meet again, in all categories of ships, the minimum numerical level that the Navy's leadership believes to be essential if the service is to execute all the missions assigned to it.

The following major ships have recently been commissioned: two nuclear-powered *Virginia*-class cruisers, ten *Spruance*-class super-destroyers, three *Los Angeles*-class nuclear-powered attack submarines, and two *Tarawa*-class assault ships. One large nuclear-powered aircraft carrier, the *Carl Vinson*, is under construction, her sister ship, the *Dwight D. Eisenhower*, having already joined the fleet. Two sisters of the *Virginia* have been laid down, and a third is under contract. Ten units of the 30-ship *Spruance* program are in service and construction of the remaining 20 is going ahead, as is that of three more *Tarawas*, in spite of significant delays in their schedules. The frigate *Oliver Hazard Perry*, which was commissioned in December 1977, is the prototype of a class that is planned to consist of 76 units.

Four of the 13-unit Trident-class fleet ballistic-missile submarines have been laid down or ordered. The first of this class, the *Ohio*, is to be commissioned at the end of 1979 or in the early 1980s. With an 18,750-ton submerged displacement and 24 missiles with a range of 4,200 miles, she will be the biggest submarine ever commissioned, which means that, in this category, the U.S. Navy will have caught up with the Soviet Navy.

The program to build 31 *Los Angeles*-class submarines is behind schedule, probably because of alterations being made to these boats, which are said to be technically far ahead of the same types built abroad, especially in the U.S.S.R.

Eighty-three combat ships are afloat for final outfitting, laid down, ordered, or approved, for a total of approximately 840,000 tons.* This effort to modernize the fleet itself is being matched in the fields of weaponry and equipment. In fact, something like 30 per cent of its annual budget, which, since 1970, has been the biggest among the three services, goes toward countering the Russian threat: the acquisition of ships, weapons, and equipment (particularly passive detection gear), the development of tactics, and continued research.

Important improvements have been made in fields such as the air defense of surface ships. The AEGIS system, which will change the character of anti-aircraft warfare, is being developed. A number of ships are being equipped with the anti-ship Harpoon missile. Also, the Navy has great hopes for the Tomahawk cruise missile, and is anxious to procure not only the strategic submarine-launched version but also the tactical version that can be fired from surface ships and aircraft.

The U.S. Navy is interested, too, in ships of the future. The hydrofoil program was set aside for a while, mainly, it appears, because of its cost, but now has been partially restored. Controversy has arisen in Congress and in professional circles concerning aircraft carriers of the near future: some people hold that giant nuclear-powered

* Standard displacement, as defined by the Treaty of Washington, 1922. Combatant ships actually under construction total approximately 570,000 tons, including 163,000 tons for aircraft carriers.

ships such as the *Nimitz* class should be built; others favor conventionally powered and cheaper vessels. Two of the latter, whose displacement and main characteristics have not yet been determined, are programmed in the 1977/82 five-year plan submitted to Congress. As of this writing, no decision on this has been reached by Congress, which, because it controls the funding, will, as always, have the last word.

SOVIET NAVY

The Soviet Navy continues to grow rapidly. In categories other than amphibious and logistic ships, it now exceeds the U.S. fleet in tonnage. As in preceding years, special attention is being given to the submarine force, conventional as well as nuclear. The nuclear-powered Delta III, a submarine that can fire 16 missiles at a target 4,800 miles away, has just been commissioned, and is the biggest submarine presently afloat.* The Russians are believed to have attack submarines that can attain high speeds when submerged and can operate at great depths. The newest of such boats are comparable with the best in Western navies.

A significant event for the Soviet Navy was the commissioning of the *Kiev* in 1976. She has characteristics of both a cruiser and an aircraft carrier, and the diversity of her weaponry gives her tremendous offensive and defensive striking power. Her sister ship, the *Minsk*, which is being completed afloat, may, by now, have begun her trials in the Black Sea, and a third is under construction. The delay in the commissioning of the *Minsk*, which was expected to take place soon after that of the *Kiev*, may have been caused by the fact that the experience of the latter indicated the need for some adjustments. Furthermore, the working-up of a ship of this type is not an easy thing for a navy that has no experience in operating aircraft carriers and handling their embarked planes.

The construction of surface combatants is being staggered to some extent, perhaps because the simultaneous need for overhaul or modernization of the many ships in commission has created scheduling difficulties in the shipyards. A few years ago, large numbers of ships were built in record time and now almost all of them need to have their weapons and equipment repaired and updated. Therefore, the Soviet naval command undoubtedly has to choose whether it wants the capacities of the shipyards to be used in continuing to build new ships, which takes time, or in overhauling and modernizing as speedily as possible, for operational reasons, the ships in commission.

The Soviet Navy is engaged in all aspects of naval activity, but at a comparatively low tempo. One reason for this may be that the crews consist mainly of draftees who lack technical qualifications; another may be the poor logistic support provided by the service forces, which, in spite of the help given them by the merchant marine, fall short of the standard set by the combat forces. In spite of its shortcomings, the Soviet Navy, the handiwork of Admiral Gorshkov, manages to support the foreign policy and worldwide ambitions of the U.S.S.R. And, thanks to its nuclear missiles, it is ready to launch a surprise attack about which Admiral Gorshkov has often said "one fatal strike must be considered as the basic form of action."

ROYAL NAVY

The Royal Navy ranks a modest third in the world, behind the Soviet Navy, but it is first in Western Europe and intends so to remain. For that, it can rely on the government in power, whatever its political persuasion. The service can accept, albeit reluctantly, the fact that new construction will be spread out over a long period of time and that, consequently, reconstitution of the fleet will be delayed. Nevertheless, about 100,000 tons of ships are now in different stages of construction.

The 16,000-ton aircraft carrier *Invincible*, for policy reasons designated an antisubmarine cruiser, was launched in May 1977, and her sister ship, the *Illustrious*, was laid down in 1976. A number of guided-missile destroyers and antisubmarine frigates are or soon will be on the ways. Their handy size and large numbers fulfill the formula dear to Britons of building many small units for their navy.

Nuclear-powered attack submarines are being built at a steady pace, and the wire-guided Tigerfish provides them with a suitable torpedo. However, because of the recent cancelation of the Anglo-French Sub-Martel missile and difficulties encountered in acquiring substitute American Sub-Harpoon missiles, they are not yet equipped with an anti-surface tactical missile that can be fired from beneath the ocean's surface. British submarines are said to be exceptionally quiet.

In brief, not as powerful as it once was, but still manned by people who are remarkably well trained and are proud of their job and their traditions, the Royal Navy remains one of the key factors in the security of the Western World. Surveillance of the British 200-mile protected economic zone, which is being added to the navy's traditional missions, will place an additional workload on the service and, since its surface and air assets do not allow for such expansion, the Royal Navy is not likely to have much difficulty in obtaining supplementary appropriations.

FRENCH NAVY

In the past couple of years, the Marine Nationale has been enriched by a few new units: one nuclear-powered, ballistic-missile submarine, *L'Indomptable*, three *Tourville*-class antisubmarine destroyers, five *d'Estienne d'Orves*-class corvettes, two *Agosta*-class 1,200-ton submarines, and one fleet oiler. *Le Tonnant*, the fifth and last SSBN in its class, three *Georges Leygues*-class antisubmarine destroyers, one nuclear-powered attack submarine, two more 1,200-ton submarines, and nine *d'Estienne d'Orves*-class corvettes either are being completed or are in the early stages of construction.

The heart of the 1977/82 program is the laying-down in 1981 of a nuclear-powered helicopter carrier, completion of the six-unit *Georges Leygues* class of destroyers, and, significantly, four more nuclear-powered attack submarines. While this program might seem impressive, the units to be added will fall far short of replacing the approximately 100 ships that will have to be stricken before 1985 on account of their age. Assuming that the service life of a few of the latter might be extended and that the 1977/82 program will be implemented, the French fleet in ten years will include approximately:

5 nuclear-powered, ballistic-missile submarines
5 nuclear-powered attack submarines
6 conventionally powered submarines (including the 4 fairly recent *Agosta* class)
1 nuclear-powered helicopter carrier
2 aging aircraft carriers (the *Clemenceau* and the *Foch*)
1 aging conventionally powered helicopter carrier (the *Jeanne d'Arc*)
1 aging cruiser (the *Colbert*)
38 escort vessels (27 of which relatively new).

If the minehunters, half a score of small patrol boats, and the logistic support ships that might still be in commission are added, the fleet will total roughly 200,000 tons, or 70,000 tons less than today. It will have fallen to its lowest level since World War II.

* Total tonnage of warships under construction is estimated at 300,000 tons, including 140,000 tons in the submarine force.

OTHER EUROPEAN NAVIES

The intermediate and small navies of the world are still upgrading and modernizing their forces, while the countries that have just achieved their independence are acquiring small naval forces in order to elicit recognition of their flag and uphold their economic rights in their own waters.

The Navy of the Federal German Republic has completed its small-combatant building program, which includes small submarines and guided-missile patrol boats. These boats are well suited for operations in the Baltic, the Danish Straits, and the Skagerrak. In order to be able to provide effective support to NATO in the North and Norwegian seas, the Bundesmarine has been authorized by parliament to begin building six large frigates, soon to be followed by a second group of roughly the same size, and to modernize the three *Lütjens*-class guided-missile destroyers. The new frigates will be based on the 3,600-ton *Kortenaer*-class frigates being built for the Netherlands Navy. The new ships will have dual antisubmarine and anti-surface (Harpoon) armament, as well as effective anti-aircraft armament, as does the *Kortenaer* class.

The Royal Netherlands Navy is not only building twelve *Kortenaer*-class frigates, but is preparing to modernize its six *van Speijk*-class frigates. Between now and 1982, these excellent ships will be fitted with Harpoon missiles, in order to give them a strong anti-surface armament. Moreover, in cooperation with Belgium and France, the Netherlands Navy is building fifteen Tripartite-class minehunters. It will build a guided-missile destroyer based on the *Kortenaer* class when the construction of the latter is more advanced. Thus, by 1985 that navy will have a highly effective flotilla of escort ships consisting of eighteen new or modernized ASW frigates, one guided-missile destroyer, and two *Tromp*-class destroyers, the last three being anti-aircraft area-defense and command ships.

Within the next few years, the Royal Danish Navy will be richer by three *Nils Juel*-class corvettes and completion of the ten-unit *Willemoes*-class large, guided-missile patrol boats.

Norway has just created a coast guard to protect its offshore oil rigs and to assert control over its 200-mile economic zone. This force will consist of seven 2,000-ton escort ships, each of which will carry a helicopter. Fourteen guided-missile patrol boats have been ordered, and two minelayers are nearing completion.

Belgium will soon begin building ten Tripartite-class minehunters. By the end of 1978, her small navy should have all four of its largest warships, the 1,860-ton *Westhinder*-class frigates, in service.

In Spain, the five large *Baleáres*-class ASW frigates, derived from the U.S. Navy's *Knox* class, are now operational, as are four submarines based on the French Navy's *Daphné* class. Four 1,200-ton submarines of the French *Agosta*-class design have been ordered. In addition, the first four of the planned eight-ship *Descubierta* class of 1,500-ton frigates are under construction.

Spain's naval program provides for the building of three ASW and anti-surface frigates of the U.S. Navy's *Oliver Hazard Perry* type and a VTOL or V/STOL carrier intended to replace the *Dedalo*, which has been modernized to enable her to carry the Harrier aircraft that Spain has been buying.

A ten-year plan for the modernization of the Italian fleet has been approved by parliament and the funds appropriated. One 12,000-ton VTOL or V/STOL carrier, the *Garibaldi*, six *Maestrale*-class frigates, six guided-missile hydrofoils, two attack submarines, and various other units of less importance have already been ordered.

JAPANESE MARITIME SELF-DEFENSE FORCE

On the other side of the world, Japan, demonstrating a remarkable sense of continuity, is rebuilding her fleet. Her navy will soon rank fifth in the world, immediately behind the French Navy.

LATIN-AMERICAN NAVIES

The countries of Latin America are modernizing their naval forces. The Brazilian Navy already has two of its splendid *Niteroi*-class frigates in commission; four others are building, two of them in Rio de Janeiro. These are Mk-10 frigates designed by the British firm of Vosper Thornycroft.

Argentina, Peru, and Venezuela, having no intention of being left behind, have all ordered new classes of ships, which are building at home or abroad, most notably in Italy. Peru has just ordered six 400-ton PR-72-class patrol boats from France.

NAVIES OF THE THIRD WORLD

Other navies, particularly those of the developing countries, are acquiring expensive modern equipment, thereby creating a new threat that cannot be ignored. The Libyan Navy is being reinforced with submarines and guided-missile patrol boats transferred by the Soviet Union. It has ordered four 550-ton guided-missile corvettes from C.N.T.R., Riva Trigoso, Italy, and ten *La Combattante-II*-class guided-missile patrol boats from Constructions Mécaniques de Normandie, Cherbourg, France. Constructions Mécaniques is in process of building twelve of the same class of patrol boats for Iran. This country, which has great naval ambitions, has ordered from Litton Industries, in the United States, four destroyers based on the *Spruance* class. The first of three *Tang*-class submarines bought from the United States will be delivered toward the end of 1978. The big problem that the Iranian Navy faces is the training of its personnel.

Lastly, India, anxious to maintain her position as the foremost naval power in the Indian Ocean, continues to increase her naval forces. She is doing this, on the one hand, by acquiring materiel from the Soviet Union — two new Nanuchka-class guided-missile patrol boats have recently been delivered — and, on the other, by developing her own naval industry. The Indian-built frigate *Udaygiri*, which participated in Queen Elizabeth's Silver Jubilee Naval Review at Spithead, demonstrates that India has mastered the complexities of naval shipbuilding.

This completes a brief and necessarily selective survey of noteworthy naval developments throughout the world. The reader will acquire a more complete picture by turning the pages of this book.

J.LC.

TERMS AND ABBREVIATIONS

Most ships' characteristics are given in the following form:

	Bldr	Laid down	L	In serv.
D 602 SUFFREN	Lorient	12-62	15-5-65	1967

D: 5,100 tons (6,000 fl) **S:** 34/18 kts
Dim: 157.6 (148 pp) × 15.54 × 6.1
Man: 38 officers, 118 petty officers, 270 men **Range:** 5,000/18
A: 2/100-mm AA (I × 2) — 2/30-mm AA (I × 2) — 2 Masurca (II × 1) — 1 Malafon ASW ML (I × 1) — 4 ASW TT (I × 4)
M: Rateau GT; 2 props; 72,500 hp
Boilers: 4; steam pressure 45 kg/cm^2; superheat 450°

Ships' hull numbers and names are in bold-face capitals. Hull dimensions are in meters, calibers in millimeters, speeds in knots, ranges in nautical miles; speeds and ranges of aircraft are in kilometers/hour and kilometers, unless otherwise indicated.

D: Displacement. In most cases, standard displacement, as defined by the Treaty of Washington (1922), is given. Where possible, full load (fl) is given; otherwise, normal (avg) displacement or trial displacement is given. In the case of most submarines, two displacements are given: the first figure is surfaced displacement; the second is submerged displacement. When available, the figure for standard displacement precedes the surfaced and submerged figures.

Dim: Hull dimensions are given as follows: length overall × beam × draft (full load, unless otherwise stated). Length between perpendiculars is given as "pp"; length at the waterline as "wl." In cases where two figures are given for one of the dimensions, e.g., the beam of the flight deck and of the hull of an aircraft carrier, the hull measurement is given as "h."

S: Speed. This is given in knots and generally refers to maximum speed; in some cases trial speed is given. Where two speeds are given for a surface ship, the top speed is given first, followed by the cruising speed. For submarines, surfaced speed is given first and is followed by submerged speed.

Man: Ship's company.

Range: Cited in nautical miles at a given speed.

A: Armament. Number of guns/caliber; TT/torpedo tubes or launchers with caliber. Figures in parentheses show the number of mounts and whether they are single, double, triple, etc., e.g., (III × 2) indicates two triple mounts.

Armor: Armor protection, thickness given in millimeters.

M: Machinery. Geared turbine is shown as GT; in some cases, the type of turbine is given, e.g., Parsons, etc. COSAG, CODAG/CODOG, COGAG/COGOG are used when such combinations of machinery have to be shown. "Props" indicates propellers.

Electric: Electric generating power.

Boilers: In most cases, number and type are shown. Steam pressure is expressed in kilos/cm^2 (sq cm), and steam superheat in degrees Centigrade.

Dates: Dates are given in the following sequence: day-month-year.

A	Armament
AA	Anti-aircraft
A & C, At & Ch	Shipbuilding yard
ARM	Anti-radiation missile
Ast Nav	Naval shipyard
ASW	Antisubmarine warfare
Author.	Authorized
avg	Average, normal
Bldr	Builder
BPDMS	Base point defense missile system
Ch, Ch Nav	Builder, naval shipyard
C N, Cant Nav	Naval shipyard
COGAG/CODAG/COSAG/ COGOG/CODOG	Combined propulsive machinery systems, gas turbine, diesel, steam. *CO* means *combined, a* means *and, o* means *on.* For example, CODOG means *combined diesel on gas.*
CSGN	Nuclear-powered, guided-missile strike cruiser
D	Displacement
DD, DDM	Dry dock, dry dock company
Dim	Dimensions
DP	Dual-purpose
Electron equipt	Electronic equipment
ELINT	Electronic intelligence
Eng	Engineering
FF, FFG	Frigate, guided-missile frigate
fl	Full load
FR, FRAM	Fleet Rehabilitation and Modernization
fwd	Forward
grt	Gross register tons
GT	Geared turbine
H	Helicopter
h	Hull
HF, MF, LF	High frequency, medium frequency, low frequency
HMDY	Her Majesty's dockyard
hp	Horsepower
kg	Kilogram
Kon. Mij.	Royal company
kt	Kiloton
kts	Knots
kw	Kilowatt
L	Launched
l	Light
loa	Length overall
M	Machinery
m	Mean
MAD	Magnetic Airborne Detection

ABBREVIATIONS

MAP	Military Assistance Program (U.S. and allies)
Man	Manpower on board ship, crew, ship's company
ML	Missile launcher
mm	Millimeters
MSC	Military Sealift Command
N.B.	New Brunswick
N.S.	Nova Scotia
NSY	Naval shipyard
oa	Overall
PLAT	Pilot Landing Air Television
pp	Between perpendiculars
NDY	Naval dockyard
NTDS	Naval Tactical Data System
RDY	Royal dockyard
RL	Rocket launcher
rpm	Revolutions per minute
S	Speed
SAM	Surface-to-air missile
SB	Shipbuilding
S.F.C.N.	Société Française de Construction Navale
SLEP	Service Life Extension Program
SSBN	Nuclear-powered fleet ballistic-missile submarine
SSM	Surface-to-surface missile
STIR	Surveillance Target Indicator Radar Separate Track and Illumination Radar
SY	Shipyard
TT	Torpedo tubes/launchers
VDS	Variable-depth sonar
Wks	Works
wl	Waterline

CONVERSION TABLES

♦ METERS (m.) to FEET (ft.)
based on 1 inch = 25.4 millimeters

m	0	1	2	3	4	5	6	7	8	9
	ft.	ft.	ft.	ft.	ft.	ft.	ft.	ft.	ft.	ft.
—	—	3.28084	6.5617	9.8425	13.1234	16.4042	19.6850	22.9659	26.2467	29.5276
10	32.8084	36.0892	39.3701	42.6509	45.9317	49.2126	52.493	55.774	59.005	62.336
20	65.617	68.898	72.178	75.459	78.740	82.021	85.302	88.583	91.863	95.144
30	98.425	101.706	104.987	108.268	111.549	114.829	118.110	121.391	124.672	127.953
40	131.234	134.514	137.795	141.076	144.357	147.638	150.919	154.199	157.480	160.761
50	164.042	167.323	170.604	173.884	177.165	180.446	183.727	187.008	190.289	193.570
60	196.850	200.131	203.412	206.693	209.974	213.255	216.535	219.816	223.097	226.378
70	229.659	232.940	236.220	239.501	242.782	246.063	249.344	252.625	255.905	259.186
80	262.467	265.748	269.029	272.310	275.590	278.871	282.152	285.433	288.714	291.995
90	295.276	298.556	301.837	305.118	308.399	311.680	314.961	318.241	321.522	324.803
100	328.084	331.365	334.646	337.926	341.207	344.488	347.769	351.050	354.331	357.611
10	360.892	364.173	367.454	370.735	374.016	377.296	380.577	383.858	387.139	390.420
20	393.701	396.982	400.262	403.543	406.824	410.105	413.386	416.667	419.947	423.228
30	426.509	429.790	433.071	436.352	439.632	442.913	446.194	449.475	452.756	456.037
40	459.317	462.598	465.879	469.160	472.441	475.722	479.002	482.283	485.564	488.845
50	492.126	495.407	498.688	501.97	505.25	508.53	511.81	515.09	518.37	521.65
60	524.93	528.22	531.50	534.78	538.06	541.34	544.62	547.90	551.18	554.46
70	557.74	561.02	564.30	567.59	570.87	574.15	577.43	580.71	583.99	587.27
80	590.55	593.83	597.11	600.39	603.67	606.96	610.24	613.52	616.80	620.08
90	623.36	626.64	629.92	633.20	636.48	639.76	643.04	646.33	649.61	652.89
200	656.17	659.45	662.73	666.01	669.29	672.57	675.85	679.13	682.41	685.70
10	688.98	692.26	695.54	698.82	702.10	705.38	708.66	711.94	715.22	718.50
20	721.78	725.07	728.35	731.63	734.91	738.19	741.47	744.75	748.03	751.31
30	754.59	757.87	761.15	764.44	767.72	771.00	774.28	777.56	780.84	784.12
40	747.40	790.68	793.96	797.24	800.52	803.81	807.09	810.37	813.65	816.93
50	820.21	823.49	826.77	830.05	833.33	836.61	839.89	843.18	846.46	849.74
60	853.02	856.30	859.58	862.86	866.14	869.42	872.70	875.98	879.26	882.55
70	885.83	889.11	892.39	895.67	898.95	902.23	905.51	908.79	912.07	915.35
80	918.63	921.92	925.20	928.48	931.76	935.04	938.32	941.60	944.88	948.16
90	951.44	954.72	958.00	961.29	964.57	967.85	971.13	974.41	977.69	980.97
300	984.25	987.53	990.81	994.09	997.38	1000.66	1003.94	1007.22	1010.50	1013.78
10	1017.06	1020.34	1023.62	1026.90	1030.18	1033.46	1036.75	1040.03	1043.31	1046.59
20	1049.87	1053.15	1056.43	1059.71	1062.99	1066.27	1069.55	1072.83	1076.12	1079.40
30	1082.68	1085.96	1089.24	1092.52	1095.80	1099.08	1102.36	1105.64	1108.92	1112.20
40	1115.49	1118.77	1122.05	1125.33	1128.61	1131.89	1135.17	1138.45	1141.73	1145.01
50	1118.29	1151.57	1154.86	1158.14	1161.42	1164.70	1167.98	1171.26	1174.54	1177.82

♦ MILLIMETERS (mm.) to INCHES (in.)
based on 1 inch = 25.4 millimeters

mm	0	1	2	3	4	5	6	7	8	9
	in.	in.	in.	in.	in.	in.	in.	in.	in.	in.
—	—	0.03937	0.07874	0.11811	0.15748	0.19685	0.23622	0.27559	0.31496	0.35433
10	0.39370	0.43307	0.47244	0.51181	0.55118	0.59055	0.62992	0.66929	0.70866	0.74803
20	0.78740	0.82677	0.86614	0.90551	0.94488	0.98425	1.02362	1.06299	1.10236	1.14173
30	1.18110	1.22047	1.25984	1.29921	1.33858	1.37795	1.41732	1.45669	1.49606	1.53543
40	1.57480	1.61417	1.65354	1.69291	1.73228	1.77165	1.81102	1.85039	1.88976	1.92913
50	1.96850	2.00787	2.04724	2.08661	2.12598	2.16535	2.20472	2.24409	2.28346	2.32283
60	2.36220	2.40157	2.44094	2.48031	2.51969	2.55906	2.59843	2.63780	2.67717	2.71654
70	2.75591	2.79528	2.83465	2.87402	2.91339	2.95276	2.99213	3.03150	3.07087	3.11024
80	3.14961	3.18898	3.22835	3.26772	3.30709	3.34646	3.38583	3.42520	3.46457	3.50394
90	3.54331	3.58268	3.62205	3.66142	3.70079	3.74016	3.77953	3.81890	3.85827	3.89764
100	3.93701									

CONVERSION FACTORS

Meter	Yard	Foot	Inch	Centimeter	Millimeter
1	1.093 61	3.280 84	39.370 1	100	1 000
0.914 4	1	3	36	91.44	914.4
0.304 8	0.333 333	1	12	30.48	304.8
0.254	0.027 777 8	0.083 333	1	2.54	25.4 j
0.01	0.010 936 1	0.032 808 4	0.393 701	1	10
0.001	0.001 093 61	0.003 280 84	0.039 370 4	0.1	1

Nautical mile		Statute mile		Meters
1	=	1.151 52	=	1 853.18

♦ Boiler working pressure

Kilogram per square centimeter (atmosphere)		*Pounds per square inch*
1	equivalent →	14.223 3
0.070 307	← equivalent	1

♦ Conversion for Fahrenheit and Centigrade scales

1 degree Centigrade = 1.8 degrees Fahrenheit
1 degree Fahrenheit = 5/9 degree Centigrade
$t\,°F = 5/9(t - 32)°C.$
$t\,°C = (1.8\,t + 32)°F.$

♦ Weights

1 kilogram = 2.204 62 *pounds* (av)
1 *pound* = 0.453 592
1 ton (metric) = 0.984 21 *ton*
1 *ton* = 1.016 05 *metric ton*

♦ Power

1 (CV) = 0.986 32 *horsepower* (HP) 0.735 88 kilowatt (Greenwich) (75 kgm/s)
1 *horsepower* (HP) = 1.013 87 (CV) 0.746 08 kilowatt (Greenwich)

ABU DHABI

The naval branch of the national defense force (Defense Force Sea Wing)

♦ *6 110-foot patrol boats*

Bldr: Vosper-Thornycroft, Portsmouth

		In serv.			In serv.
P 1101	**ARDHANA**	7-3-75	**P 1104**	**AL GHULIAN**	16-9-75
P 1102	**ZURARA**	13-6-75	**P 1105**	**RADOOM**	15-12-75
P 1103	**MURBAN**	15-9-75	**P 1106**	**GHANADHAH**	1-3-76

Ardhana and Zurara 1976

D: 110 tons (140 fl) **Dim:** 33.5 (31.5 pp) × 6.4 × 1.7
S: 29 kts **Man:** 26 total
A: 2/30-mm AA (II × 1), 1/20-mm AA **Range:** 1,800/14
M: 2 Ruston-Paxman Valenta RP200M diesels; 2 props; 5,400 hp
Electron Equipt: Decca RM 916 radar

REMARK: The 30-mm. mount is BMARC/Oerlikon A32 type.

♦ *5 customs patrol craft*, U.S. P-77A design. Bldr: Camcraft, New Orleans. In serv. 9-75

21 through **25**

D: 70 tons (fl) **S:** 25 kts **Dim:** 23.4 × 5.5 × 1.5
A: 2/20-mm AA (I × 2) **Range:** 750/25
M: 2 General Motors 12V-71T diesels; 2 props; 1,400 hp

♦ *3 Kawkab-class patrol craft*

KAWKAB (1-69), **THOABAN** (1-69), **BANIYAS** (7-69)
Bldr: Keith Nelson (G. B.)

Kawkab 1969

D: 25 tons (32 fl) **Dim:** 17.52 (15.84 pp) × 4.72 × 1.37
A: 2/20-mm AA (I × 2) **Man:** 2 officers, 9 men
M: 2 Caterpillar diesels; 2 props; 750 hp **Electron Equipt:** Decca radar
Endurance: 1 week **Range:** 300 miles

REMARKS: Fiberglass hull, 2/12-kw generators, used in coastal patrol, hydrographic surveys, surveillance of petroleum leases. Keith Nelson (division of Vosper) design. Freshwater evaporator provides 900 liters daily.

♦ *6 Dhafeer-class patrol craft*

DHAFEER (2-68) **DURGHAM** (9-68) **GHADUNFAR** (5-68)
HAZZA (5-68) **TIMSAH** (9-68) **MURAYJIB** (2-70)

Bldr: Keith Nelson, Isle of Wight. Fiberglass hull

D: 10 tons **S:** 19 kts **Dim:** 12.50 × 3.65 × 1.10
A: 1/12.7-mm machine gun **Man:** 1 officer, 5 men
M: 2 Cummins diesels; 2 props; 370 hp **Range:** 150

♦ *5 Spear-class police patrol craft, placed in service 8, 9, and 11, 1974 and 1, 1975*

Bldr: Fairey Marine, Hamble

D: 10 tons **S:** 26 kts **Dim:** 9.10 × 2.75 × 0.84
M: 2 T 6-354 Perkins diesels; 2 props; 290 hp
A: 2/12.7-mm machine guns **Man:** 3 men

REMARK: Fiberglass hull.

ALBANIA

PERSONNEL: 3,000 men

MERCHANT MARINE (1976): 20 ships — 57,386 grt

The following are of either Soviet or Chinese origin:

- ♦ *3 W-class submarines* (1,050 tons surfaced, 1,350 submerged, 17/16 kts), two operational
- ♦ *4 Kronstadt-class patrol boats* (310 tons, 18 kts)
- ♦ *6 Shanghai-II-class patrol boats,* 4 transferred in 1974, 2 in 1975

  D: 155 tons (fl) **S:** 28 kts
  A: 4/37-mm AA (II × 2) — 4/25-mm AA (II × 2)
- ♦ *2 T-43-class ocean minesweepers* (500 tons, 14 kts)
- ♦ *6 T-301-class coastal minesweepers* (145.8 tons, 12.5 kts)
- ♦ *4 P-4-class torpedo boats* (19.3 tons, 55 kts)
- ♦ *35 Huchwan-class hydrofoil torpedo boats*
- ♦ *1 Toplevo-class fuel barge*
- ♦ *1 Khobi-class small tanker*
- ♦ *2 small transports*
- ♦ *1 Nyryat-class diving tender*
- ♦ *1 Sekstan-class degaussing ship*
- ♦ *4 tugs*
- ♦ *2 Poluchat-class torpedo-recovery ships*
- ♦ *1 barracks ship*

Huchwan-class hydrofoil torpedo boat 1976

ALGERIA

PERSONNEL (1975): 3,000 men with about 300 to 350 officers, not necessarily on full-time active duty with the navy.

MERCHANT MARINE (1976): 86 ships — 463,094 grt (tankers 9 — 292, 918 grt)

The Algerian Navy is made up of ships from the U.S.S.R. See that section for characteristics.

NAVAL AVIATION: The Algerian Air Force uses 11 twin-engine Fokker F-27 (Maritime) patrol aircraft for maritime surveillance.

MISSILE- AND TORPEDO-LAUNCHING SMALL CRAFT

♦ *6 Komar-class guided missile boats transferred in 1966:* **671** to **676**

♦ *2 Osa-II-class guided missile boats transferred end-1976/beginning 1977*

♦ *3 Osa-I-class guided missile boats transferred in 1967:* **R 167, R 267, R 367**

♦ *10 P-6-class torpedo boats transferred in 1963–68,* of which 4 are armed, 2 without torpedo tubes were transferred to the Coast Guard Service, 2 are hulks, and 2 are unarmed training craft: **623** to **626, 629** to **634**

REMARK: The Komar and Osa-I boats will be re-engined with German MTU diesels.

MINE WARFARE SHIPS

♦ *2 T-43 class transferred in 1968:* **M 221, M 222** (**M 221** in reserve since 1974)

LANDING SHIPS

♦ *1 Polnocny-class medium landing ship transferred in 8–76*

PATROL BOATS

♦ *6 SO-I class transferred from 10–65 to 10–67:* **P 651** to **P 656**

REMARK: Three carry 2 torpedo tubes removed from P-6-class torpedo boats.

♦ *1 or more customs patrol boats.* Bldr: Baglietto, Italy. In serv. 1977
141 . . . . . . ?

D: 175 tons (fl) **S:** 37 kts **Dim:** 36.1 (31.9 pp) × 7.0 × 1.5
A: . . . **Man:** 14 men **Range:** 700/30, 1,000/15
Electron Equipt: 1/SMA-3RM radar
M: 2 MTU MD20V-538TB91 diesels; 2 props; 9,000 hp

REMARK: First unit of a new design delivered early in 1977; more units probably under construction.

PATROL BOATS (*continued*)

Baglietto customs patrol boat C. Martinelli, 1977

♦ *10 Coast Guard patrol craft.* Bldr: Baglietto, Italy
235, 236, 325, 335 . . . . . .

D: 42 tons **S:** 35 kts **Dim:** 22 × 5.24 × . . .
A: 2/20-mm AA **M:** 2 CRM 18DS diesels; 2,700 hp

Remarks: Guns do not appear to have been fitted. The first two entered service in 8-76, the others were delivered at two-month intervals.

Baglietto coast guard patrol craft C. Martinelli, 1977

VARIOUS SHIPS

A 640 VASOUYA, *Sekstan*-class survey ship procured in 1964
A 641, *Poluchat*-class torpedo-recovery ship, 80 tons
VP 650 YAVDEZAN, harbor tug procured in 1965
DJEBEL ANTAR, DJEBEL HONDA, fishery protection and customs vessels

ANGOLA

A small navy was established in 1976 by employing units left behind by the departing Portuguese. Believed operational are:

♦ *5 Argos-class patrol boats* (ex-*Centauro*, ex-*Escorpiao*, ex-*Lira*, ex-*Orion*, ex-*Pegaso*): 180 tons, 18 kts, 2/40-mm AA (I × 2). Blt. 1961-64

♦ *1 Soviet Zhuk-class patrol craft*, transferred 1977

D: 50 tons (60 fl) **S:** 30 kts **Dim:** 26.0 × 4.9 × 1.5
A: 4/14.5-mm machine guns (II × 2) **M:** 2 M50 diesels; 2 props; 2,400 hp

♦ *1 Jupiter-class patrol craft* (ex-*Venus*): 32 tons, 20 kts, 1/20-mm AA. Blt. 1964

♦ *5 Bellatrix-class patrol craft* (ex-*Altair*, ex-*Espiga*, ex-*Fomalhaut*, ex-*Pollux*, ex-*Rigel*): 23 tons, 15 kts, 1/20-mm AA. Blt. 1961-63

♦ *1 Alfange-class landing craft:* 500 tons, 11 kts, 57 × 11.8 × 1.3, 2/20-mm AA

♦ *9 smaller landing craft* (LCM, LCVP types)

ARGENTINA

Personnel: 21,000 men, including 2,300 officers and 3,000 Marines

Merchant Marine (1976): 379 ships — 1,469,754 grt
(tankers: 63 — 546,246 grt)

Naval Program: 4 British *Amazon*-class frigates
2 German *Type-148*-class guided missile boats

Naval Aviation: The air squadron on board the *25 de Mayo* is made up of 12 A-4Q Skyhawk aircraft, 4 SH-3D helicopters, and 6 S-2A Tracker. Land-based naval aircraft are obtained from several sources and include the following types: Macchi, Albatros, Neptune, Alouette III, SNJ, etc.

WARSHIPS IN SERVICE OR UNDER CONSTRUCTION AS OF 1 OCTOBER 1977

	L	Tons	Main armament
♦ *4 submarines*			
2 German 209	1972-73	980	8/533-mm TT
2 Guppy IA, II	1944-45	1,517	10/533-mm TT
♦ *1 aircraft carrier*			
25 de Mayo	1943	15,892	9/40-mm AA, 22 aircraft

♦ *2 cruisers*			
2 BROOKLYN	1936–38	10,800	15/152-mm
♦ *10 destroyers*			
2 SHEFFIELD	1972–74	3,150	1 Sea Dart SAM, 1/114-mm DP, 1 ASW helicopter
1 GEARING, FRAM II	1944	2,400	4 Exocet SSM, 6/127-mm DP
3 ALLEN M. SUMNER, FRAM II	1944	2,200	4 Exocet SSM, 6/127-mm DP
4 FLETCHER	1942–43	2,050	4/127-mm DP, 4/533-mm TT
♦ *2 frigates*			
2 MURATURE	1943–45	1,000	3/105-mm DP
♦ *8 corvettes*			
2 ATF	1944–45	1,235	4/40-mm AA
6 ATA	1944–45	689	1/40-mm AA
♦ *6 patrol boats*			
♦ *6 minesweepers*			
♦ *6 landing ships*			

AIRCRAFT CARRIER

♦ *1 British Colossus-class*

	Bldr	Laid down	L	In serv.	Modernized
25 DE MAYO	Cammell Laird	12-42	30-12-43	5-45	III-1969

(ex-*Venerable*, ex-*Karel Doorman*)

D: 15,892 tons (19,896 fl)
Dim: 212.67 (192.04 pp) × 24.49 (40.66) × 7.50
S: 24.5 kts **Man:** 1,509 men **Range:** 12,000/14
A: 9/40-mm AA — 22 aircraft: 18 planes, 4 helicopters
Electron Equipt: Radars: Dutch: 2/LW 02, 1/SGR 109 (height-finding), 1/SGR 105, 1/SGR 103
M: Parsons GT; 2 props **Electric:** 2,500 kw
Boilers: 4 Admiralty 3-drum type; steam pressure 30.23 kg/cm^2 since refit; 40,000 hp **Fuel:** 3,200 tons

REMARKS: Purchased by The Netherlands from the British Navy in 1948. Rebuilt from 1955 to 1958 by Wilton-Fijenoord, angled flight deck of 165.80 meters, steam catapult, mirror optical landing equipment, new anti-aircraft guns, and new radar equipment of Dutch conception and construction. Modified for service in the tropics. Partially air-conditioned. In 1967 new boilers were installed from the British aircraft carrier *Leviathan* which was never completed. Purchased in 1968 by Argentina. She is equipped with the British C.A.A.I.S. data display system.

25 de Mayo

SUBMARINES

♦ *2 Salta (German 209 class)*

	Bldr	L	In serv.
S 31 SALTA	Howaldtswerke	22-11-72	5-74
S 32 SAN LUIS	Howaldtswerke	7-73	5-74

Salta 1972

D: 980 tons surfaced, 1,230 submerged **Dim:** 55 × 6.60 × 5.90
S: 21 kts submerged; 12 with snorkel **Man:** 5 officers, 26 men
A: 8/533-mm torpedoes forward — 6 reserve torpedoes
M: 4 MTU type 12V-493-TY60 diesels, Siemens electric motor; 3,600 hp; 1 prop
Fuel: 50 tons diesel

REMARKS: Built in four sections at Howaldtswerke in Kiel and assembled at the navy yard in Rio Santiago. Part of the electronic equipment is French. An extension of the German *205/206* class (IKL plans of Professor Ulrich Gabler); submarine is of single-hull construction said to be 1,000 tons. Ordered by the following countries: 4 by Greece, 2 by Ecuador, 2 by Peru, 2 by Colombia, 4 by Turkey, and 2 by Venezuela. The Vickers company is interested in producing this class of submarine with Howaldtswerke.

♦ *2 ex-U.S. Guppy class transferred in 7-71*

	Bldr	L
S 21 SANTA FE (ex-*Catfish*, SS-339)	Electric Boat Co.	19-11-44
S 22 SANTIAGO DEL ESTERO (ex-*Chivo*, SS-341)	Electric Boat Co.	14-1-45

For photograph, see *Murat Reis* in the section on Turkey.

D: 1,517 tons surfaced; 1,870 normal; 2,340 submerged
S: 18/14 kts **Range:** 10,000/10 **Dim:** 93.60 × 8.40 × 5.25
A: 10/533-mm torpedoes (6 forward, 4 aft) **Man:** 9 officers, 76 men
M: 3 (S-22: 4) General Motors 16-278A diesels, each of 1,625 hp, with 2 electric motors of 2,700 hp each; 2 props **Fuel:** 300 tons diesel

REMARK: S-21 is a Guppy II; S-22 is a Guppy IA.

CRUISERS

♦ *2 ex-U.S. Brooklyn class (over age)*

	Bldr	Laid down	L	In serv.
C 4 GENERAL BELGRANO (ex-*Diecisiete de Octubre*, ex-*Phoenix*, CL-46)	New York SB Co.	4-35	12-3-38	10-38
C 5 NUEVE DE JULIO (ex-*Boise*, CL-47)	Newport News	4-35	3-12-36	8-38

D: 10,800 tons (13,680 fl) **Dim:** 185.33 × 20.70 × 7.40
S: 25/24 kts **Man:** 980 men **Range:** 7,600/15
A: *General Belgrano:* 15/152-mm (III × 5) — 8 Sea Cat SAM (IV × 2) — 8/127-mm DP (I × 8) — 20/40-mm AA (IV × 2, II × 6) — 2/20-mm AA
Nueve de Julio: 15/152-mm (III × 5) — 6/127-mm DP (I × 6) — 28/40-mm AA (IV × 4, II × 6) — 12/20-mm AA (II × 6)
Electron Equipt: Radars: SGR-116, SGR-105 or SG-6
Armor: Belt: 102 Decks: 76 Turret: 102 Conning tower: 203
M: Westinghouse GT; 4 props; 100,000 hp; 8 Babcock Express boilers, 31 kg pressure **Fuel:** 2,100 tons

REMARKS: Purchased in the U.S.A., 12-1-51. Ships have two helicopters. Similar to Chilean cruiser that is former American ship. *General Belgrano*'s Sea Cat systems are controlled by 2 Selenia RTN-10. *Nueve de Julio* has only a skeleton crew.

DESTROYERS

♦ *2 Sheffield-class guided missile, ordered 18-5-70*

	Bldr	Laid down	L	In serv.
D 28 HERCULES	Vickers, Barrow	1971	24-10-72	10-5-76
D 29 SANTISIMA TRINIDAD	Ast. Nav. Rio Santiago	2-72	9-11-74	. . .

Hercules 1976

DESTROYERS *(continued)*

D: 3,150 tons (3,600 fl) **Dim:** 125 (119.50 pp) × 14.60 × 5.2
S: 28/18 kts **Range:** 4,000/18 **Man:** 270 men
A: 1/114-mm DP Mk 8 — 2/20-mm AA — 1 Sea Dart (II × 1) — 1 WG 13 Lynx ASW and anti-ship helicopter — 6 ASW torpedo tubes (III × 2)
Electron Equipt: Radars: 1/965M, 1/992, 2/909 — ADA SW4 control
Sonars: 1/177, 1/174, 1/170B, 1/162
Chaff launcher: Knebworth Corvus
M: COGOG propulsion: 2 Olympus TM 3B gas turbines, 27,200 hp each for boost; 2 Tyne RM 1A gas turbines, 4,100 hp each for cruising; 2 controllable-pitch, 5-blade props
Electric: 4,000 kw

REMARK: D-29 was sabotaged on 22-8-75 and will be delayed.

♦ *1 ex-U.S. Gearing class, transferred 1-73*

	Bldr	L	In serv.
D 27 COMODORO PY (ex-*Perkins*, DD-877)	Consolidated Steel	7-12-44	4-45

Comodoro Py 1973

D: 2,400 tons (3,600 fl) **Dim:** 119.17 × 12.45 × 5.80
Man: 15 officers, 260 men **S:** 36 kts **Range:** 2,400/25, 4,800/15
A: 4/MM 38 Exocet — 6/127-mm AA 38-cal. (II × 3) — 2 hedgehogs — 6/324-mm ASW TT (III × 2) Mk 32 for Mk 44 torpedoes
Electron Equipt: Radars: 1/SPS 40, 1/SPS 10 — Sonar: 1/SQS 23
M: Westinghouse GT, 4 Babcock boilers; 2 props; 60,000 hp **Fuel:** 650 tons

REMARK: Had undergone Fram II modernization.

♦ *3 ex-U.S. Allen M. Sumner class, 2 transferred 7-72, 1 in 4-76*

	Bldr	L	In serv.
D 25 SEGUI (ex-*Borie*, DD-704)	Federal SB & DD	21-5-44	8-44
D 26 HIPOLITO BOUCHARD (ex-*Hank*, DD-702)	Federal SB & DD	4-7-44	9-44
D 30 PIEDRABUENA (ex-*Collett*, DD-730)	Bath Iron Works	5-3-44	5-44

Hipolito Bouchard 1975

D: 2,200 tons (3,300 fl) **Dim:** 114.75 × 12.45 × 5.80
Man: 14 officers, 260 men **S:** 30 kts **Range:** 1,260/30, 4,600/15
A: 4/MM 38 Exocet — 6/127-mm DP (II × 3) — D-26 also 4/76-mm AA (II × 2) — 6/324-mm ASW TT Mk32 — 2 hedgehogs
Electron Equipt: Radars: 1/SPS 40, 1/SPS 10 — Sonar: 1/SQS 29 or 30
M: GT; 4 Babcock boilers; 2 props; 60,000 hp **Fuel:** 650 tons

REMARKS: Mansfield (DD-728) was transferred 4-76, for cannibalization. D-26 has SPS 6 vice SPS 40 radar

♦ *4 ex-U.S. Fletcher class, transferred in 1962-63, 1971-72*

	Bldr	L	In serv.
D 20 BROWN (ex-*Heerman*, DD-532)	Bethlehem, San Fran.	5-12-42	7-43
D 22 ROSALES (ex-*Stembel*, DD-644)	Bath Iron Works	8-5-43	7-43
D 23 ALMIRANTE DOMECQ GARCIA (ex-*Braine*, DD-630)	Bath Iron Works	7-3-43	5-43
D 24 ALMIRANTE STORNI (ex-*Cowell*, DD-547)	Bethlehem, San Pedro	18-4-43	8-43

Brown

DESTROYERS *(continued)*

D: 2,050 tons (2,850 fl) **Dim:** 114.85 (wl) × 12.03 × 5.50
Man: 15 officers, 247 men **S:** 30 kts **Range:** 1,260/30, 4,400/15
A: 4/127-mm DP (I × 4) — 6/76-mm AA (II × 3) — 4/533-mm torpedo tubes (IV × 1) — 2 ASW TT racks — 2 hedgehogs — 1 depth-charge rack
Electron Equipt: Radars: 1/SPS 6 and 1/SPS 10. Sonar: 1/SQS 4
M: Gen. Elec. GT; 2 props, 60,000 hp
Boilers: 4 Babcock and Wilcox **Fuel:** 650 tons

REMARK: *Knapp* (DD-653) of this class was purchased for spare parts.

FRIGATES

♦ *4 British Amazon-class (Type 21) ordered July 1975*

Bldr: Navy Yard, Rio Santiago, with Vickers' aid

	L	In serv.		L	In serv.
N . . .	. . .	. . .	**N . . .**	. . .	. . .
N . . .	. . .	. . .	**N . . .**	. . .	. . .

D: 2,300 tons (3,100 fl) **Dim:** . . . × . . . × . . .
A: 4/MM 38 Exocet — 1/114-mm DP Mk 8 — 1 SAM system — 1 WG 13 Lynx ASW and anti-ship helicopter
Electron Equipt: . . .
M: COGOG propulsion: 2 Olympus TM 3 gas turbines, 25,000 hp each for boost; 2 Tyne RB 209 gas turbines, 5,000 hp each for cruise; 2 controllable-pitch props

REMARKS: These ships will take ten years to build. The type of SAM system has not yet been chosen: the U.S. Sea Sparrow, British Sea Wolf, French Crotale, and Italian Aspide are being considered. They may be somewhat enlarged over the British *Amazons* in order to permit installation of both 4 Exocet and the SAM system.

♦ *2 Murature class*

	Bldr	Laid down	L	In serv.
P 20 MURATURE	Ast. Nav. Rio Santiago	6-38	7-45	11-46
P 21 KING	Ast. Nav. Rio Santiago	1939	43	7-46

King

D: 913 tons, 1,000 normal, 1,032 fl **Dim:** 76.80 × 8.85 × 2.50
S: 16 kts **Range:** 6,000/12 **Man:** 140 men

A: 3/105-mm DP — 4/40-mm AA — 4 depth-charge mortars
M: Werkspoor 4-stroke diesels; 2 props; 2,500 hp **Fuel:** 90 tons diesel

REMARK: Both used for training.

CORVETTES (former U.S. tugs used on patrol duties)

	Bldr	L
A 1 COMMANDANTE GENERAL IRIGOYEN (ex-ATF-152)	Charleston SB & DD	2-11-44
A 3 FRANCISCO DE CHURRUCA (ex-*Luiseno*, ATF-156)	Charleston SB & DD	17-3-45

D: 1,235 tons (1,675 fl) **Dim:** 62.50 (59.45 pp) × 11.65 × 4.70
S: 16 kts **Man:** 85 men
A: 4/40-mm AA (II × 1, I × 2) — 2/20-mm AA
M: Diesel-electric propulsion; 1 prop; 3,000 hp

A 5 DIAGUITA (ex-ATA-124), **A 6 YAMANA** (ex-ATA-126), **A 7 CHIRIGUANO** (ex-ATA-227), **A 8 SANAVIRON** (ex-ATA-228), **A 9 ALFEREZ SOBRAL** (ex-ATA-210), **A 10 COMODORO SOMELLERA** (ex-ATA-187)

Bldr: Levingston Shbldg., Texas, 1944-45

D: 689 tons (800 fl) **Dim:** 43.60 (40.75 pp) × 10.37 × 3.65
S: 12 kts **Man:** 49 men **Range:** 16,500
A: 2/20-mm AA
M: Diesel-electric propulsion; 1 prop; 1,850 hp **Fuel:** 154 tons diesel

PATROL BOATS

♦ *2 West German Type 148, ordered 1976 from Lürssen*

Data as for West German units except:

A: 5 Gabriel SSM — 1/76-mm DP

♦ *2 Intrepida class*

	Bldr	L	In serv.
ELPR 1 INTREPIDA	Lürssen (Bremen-Vegesack)	12-12-74	20-7-74
ELPR 2 INDOMITA	Lürssen (Bremen-Vegesack)	5-74	Spring 1975

D: 240 tons **Dim:** 44.90 × (42.30 pp) × 7.10 × 2.50 (prop.)
S: 40 kts **Range:** 1,450/20 **Man:** 34 men

Intrepida Terzibaschitsch, 4-74

PATROL BOATS (*continued*)

A: 1/76-mm AA — 2/40-mm AA — 2/533-mm wire-guided torpedoes
M: 4 MTU diesels; 4 props; 12,000 hp **Electric:** 330 kw

REMARK: Anti-rolling stabilizers.

♦ **ALAKASH, TOWARA** — Bldr: Higgins, New Orleans
Former 24-meter torpedo boats with 2/40-mm AA

MINE WARFARE SHIPS

♦ *6 British "-ton" class* (bought in 1967)

	L		L
M 1 NEUQUEN (ex-*Hickleton*)	26-1-55	**M 4 TIERRA DEL FUEGO** (ex-*Bevington*)	17-3-53
M 2 RIO NEGRO (ex-*Tarlton*)	1954	**M 5 CHACO** (ex-*Rennington*)	27-11-58
M 3 CHUBUT (ex-*Santon*) Transferred in 1968.	18-8-55	**M 6 FORMOSA** (ex-*Ilmington*)	1954

D: 370 tons (425 fl) **Dim:** 46.33 (42.68 pp) × 8.76 × 2.50
S: 15 kts **Man:** 27 men **Range:** 3,000/8
A: 1/40-mm **M:** Diesels; 2 props; 2,500/3,000 hp **Fuel:** 45 tons diesel

M-5 and M-6 are fitted out as minehunters.

HYDROGRAPHIC SHIPS

♦ *2 Puerto Deseado class*

	Bldr	In serv.
Q . . . PUERTO DESEADO	Astarzav, San Fernando	1976
Q . . . ALVARO ALBERTO	Alianza, Avellaneda	1977

D: 2,133 tons **S:** 15 kts **Dim:** 76.81 × 15.75 × 9.50
M: 2 Fiat diesels; 1,800 hp; 1 prop **Man:** 61 men

Q . . . COMODORO RIVADAVIA — Bldr: Mestrina, Argentina
L: 2-12-72. In serv. 1974

D: 655 tons (830 fl) **S:** 12 kts **Dim:** 50.90 × 8.80 × 2.60
M: 2 Werkspoor diesels; 1,200 hp **Man:** 27 men

Q . . . ISLAS ORCADAS (ex-*Eltanin*, T-AGOR-8). Transferred 12-73.
Bldr: Avondale (U.S.A.) 16-1-57

D: 2,040 tons (4,942 fl) **Dim:** 80 × 15.70 × 5.70
S: 13 kts **Man:** 8, plus 38 oceanographers
M: Diesel-electric; 2 props; 3,200 hp

REMARKS: Former small USN cargo ship. Icebreaker hull. Operated for Argentine National Commission for the Antarctic.

♦ *2 ex-U.S. Maritime Commission V-4-class tugs*

Q 17 GOYENA (ex-*Dry Tortugas*)
A 4 THOMPSON (ex-*Sombrero Key*)
Bldr: Pendleton SY, New Orleans, 1943

D: 1,825 tons **Dim:** 58.22 × 11.30 × 5.50 **S:** 11 kts
A: 2/40-mm AA (II × 1) **Man:** 90 men
M: 2 Enterprise diesels; 2 props; 2,250 hp

REMARKS: Q-17 for Antarctic research. A-4 for oceanographic research and patrol.

Q 4 GENERAL SAN MARTIN — Bldr: A.G. Weser, Bremen — L: 24-6-54

D: 4,850 tons (5,300 fl) **Dim:** 84.70 × 18.60 × 6.40
S: 16 kts **Man:** 160 men **Range:** 35,000/10
A: 2/40-mm AA **Cargo Load:** 1,600 tons
M: Diesel-electric propulsion; 2 props; 6,500 hp **Fuel:** 1,100 tons diesel

REMARKS: Oceanographic research vessel with icebreaker configuration. Has a helicopter.

AMPHIBIOUS WARFARE SHIPS

♦ *1 ex-U.S. LSD*

PY 3 CANDIDO DE LASALA (ex-*Gunston Hall*, LSD-5) — Bldr: Moore DD L: 1-5-43.

D: 4,032 tons (8,700 fl) **Dim:** 139 × 21.90 × 4.90
S: 15 kts **Man:** 17 officers, 309 men **Range:** 8,000/15
A: 12/40-mm AA **M:** 2 triple expansion, 7,000 hp

REMARKS: Transferred 24-4-70. Docking well: 103 × 13.30. 2 cranes: 35 tons. Now used as a patrol craft tender.

♦ *1 LST (De Soto County class)*

Q 42 CABO SAN ANTONIO — Bldr: Ast. Nav. Rio Santiago 1966

D: 4,300 tons (8,000 fl) **S:** 17 kts **Dim:** 135 × 18.80 × 5.50
A: 6/76-mm AA (II × 3) **M:** Diesels; 14,000 hp **Man:** 124 men

REMARKS: Never completed; in reserve. Has Stülcken heavy-lift crane.

♦ *4 ex-U.S. LST (1944)* (ex-LST-919, ex-LST-872, ex-LST-1044, ex-LST-1108)

Q 46 CABO SAN ISIDORO **Q 50 CABO SAN PIO**
Q 44 CABO SAN GONZALO **Q . . . CABO SAN VICENTE**

D: 2,370 tons (4,080 fl) **Dim:** 99.98 × 15.24 × 4.25
S: 11 kts **Man:** 80 men **Range:** 9,500/9
M: 2 diesels; 1,800 hp **Fuel:** 700 tons diesel

♦ *2 ex-U.S. LCIL*

Q 56 BDI 4 (ex-LCIL-606), **BDI 15** (ex-LCIL-689)

D: 230 tons (387 fl) **Dim:** 48 × 7.20 × 1.50 **S:** 13 kts

REMARK: Used for training.

♦ *Some LCM and LCVP landing craft*

EDVP 1, 2, 3, 7, 8, 10, 12, 13, 17, 19, 21, 24, 28, 29, 30 (ex-U.S. LCVPs)
LCM-1 to **LCM-4** (1971) Bldr: Argentina

ICEBREAKER

♦ *1 unit ordered 17-12-75 from Wärtsila (Helsinki, Finland)*

Q . . . ALMIRANTE IRIZAR

D: . . . **S:** 16.5 kts **Dim:** 117.3 × 24.6 × 9.4
M: Diesel-electric: 4 SEMT/Pielstick diesels; 2 Stromberg motors; 2 props; 30,000 hp **Range:** 16,200
Electron Equipt: Radar: Plessey AWS-2
Man: 123 crew + 100 scientists

AUXILIARY SHIPS

♦ *3 Bahia Camarones-class transports* Bldr: Principe SY In serv.: . . .

AUXILIARY SHIPS (*continued*)

B . . . BAHIA CAMARONES **B . . . BAHIA SAN BLAS**
B . . . CANAL BEAGLE

D: . . . (7,640 grt) **S:** 15 kts **Dim:** 119.0 × 17.5 × 9.7
M: Diesel; 6,400 hp

♦ *2 Bahia Aguirre-class transports*

	Bldr	L	In serv.
B 2 BAHIA AGUIRRE	Halifax (Canada)	15-5-49	1951
B 6 BAHIA BUEN SUCESO	Halifax (Canada)	15-6-49	1951

D: 3,100 tons (5,255 fl)
Dim: 95.10 × 14.33 × 7.92 (light cruising) × 5.63 **S:** 15 kts
M: 2 Nordberg diesels; 3,750 hp **Fuel:** 400 tons diesel

Bahia Aguirre

Q 7 SAN JULIAN (ex-FS-281) (1-45). Bldr: Wheeler SB Co.

D: 930 tons **Dim:** 55 × 9.95 × 3.40 **S:** 10 kts
M: Diesels; 2 props; 1,000 hp

REMARK: Former U.S. Army cargo ship.

♦ *2 oilers*

	Bldr	L	In serv.
B 18 PUNTA MEDANOS	Swan Hunter	20-2-50	10-50

D: 16,300 tons (fl) **S:** 18 kts **Dim:** 143 × 18.90 × 10.67 (light)
Cargo load: 8,250 tons **Range:** 13,700 **Man:** 99 men
M: Parsons GT; 2 props; 9,500 hp **Fuel:** 1,500 tons
Boilers: 2 Babcock and Wilcox (28 kg/cm^2 pressure)

B 16 PUNTA DELGADA (ex-U.S. AOG-66) — (4-45) — 6,000 tons; 1,400 hp

♦ *7 tugs*

R 33 GUAYACURU and **R 22 QUILMES** (368 tons, 650 hp)
R 29 PEHUENCHE and **R 30 TONOCOTE** (330 tons, 600 hp)
R 4 TOBA (600 tons, 1,200 hp)
R 10 HUARPE (370 tons, 800 hp)
R 1 ONA (560 tons)

♦ *6 former U.S. Navy tugs, transferred between 1965 and 1969*

R 6 CALCHAQUI (ex-YTL-445)
R 16 CAPAYAN (ex-YTL-443)
R 18 CHIQUILLAN (ex-YTL-444)
R 10 CHULUPI (ex-YTL-426)
R 5 MOCOVI (ex-YTL-441)
R 19 MORLOYAN (ex-YTL-448)

D: 70 tons **S:** 10 kts **Dim:** 20.4 × 4.3 × 4.0
M: 1 diesel; 310 hp **Man:** 5 men

♦ *1 sailing training vessel*

Q 2 LIBERTAD — Bldr: Ast. Nav. Rio Santiago. L: 30-5-56. In serv.: 1962.

D: 3,025 tons (3,625 fl) **Dim:** 94.25 × 13.75 × 6.75
S: 12 kts **Man:** 222 men and 140 cadets **Range:** 12,000
A: 1/76-mm — 4/40-mm — 4/47-mm
M: Diesels; 2 props; 2,400 hp

Libertad J. C. Bellonne

COAST GUARD

PATROL CRAFT

GC . . . DELPHIN

D: 1,000 tons **S:** 15 kts **Dim:** 60.0 × 9.0 × 4.7
M: Diesel; 2,300 hp **Man:** 32 men

REMARK: Former trawler, built 1958, acquired 1975 to replace *Bouchard*-class minesweeper *Spiro.*

GC 21 LYNCH, GC 22 TOLL, GC 23 EREZCANO

Bldr: Navy Yard, Rio Santiago (1964-65)

D: 100 tons (117 fl) **Dim:** 27.44 × 5.80 × 1.85
A: 1/20-mm AA **S:** 22 kts **Man:** 16 men
M: 2 Maybach diesels; 2,700 hp

GC 31 — small patrol boat similar to U.S. Navy AVR.

AUSTRALIA

Personnel: approx. 17,000, 2,000 officers

Merchant Marine (1976): 424 ships — 1,247,162 grt
(tankers: 16 — 287,276 grt)

WARSHIPS IN SERVICE OR UNDER CONSTRUCTION AS OF 1 OCTOBER 1977

	L	Tons	Main armament
♦ *1 aircraft carrier*			
MELBOURNE	1945	16,000	17 aircraft
♦ *6 submarines*			
6 OBERON	1965-75	1,610	8/533-mm TT
♦ *6 destroyers*			
3 CHARLES F. ADAMS	1963-66	3,370	1 Tartar system, 2/127-mm, 2 Ikara
3 VENDETTA/DUCHESS	1951-56	2,800	4-6/114-mm
♦ *8 frigates*			
2 OLIVER HAZARD PERRY	1978-79	3,605	1/76-mm, 6 ASW TT
6 RIVER	1958-68	2,100	2/114-mm, 1 Ikara
♦ *3 missile frigates authorized*			
♦ *3 minesweepers*			

Naval Aviation: Only ship-based aircraft belong to the Navy. On 5-12-75 a fire destroyed 12 of the total of 13 S-2E Tracker ASW aircraft. These were to be replaced by 6 ex-U.S. Navy aircraft and 6 other former USN aircraft already on order. Other than these, the Australian Fleet Air Arm operates: 8 A-4G Skyhawk fighter-bombers and 8 Sea King helicopters for shipboard use, and retains 4 Wessex 31-B helicopters formerly used aboard *Melbourne.*

Shore-based aviation is under the direction of the RAAF; it includes a squadron of 12 SP2H Neptunes and another of 10 P3 Orions. Eight P3C are on order to replace the Neptunes. Other land-based aircraft include 7 TA-4G Skyhawk and 7 MB-326H for training, 2 HS-748 transports, and 4 Bell UH-1H and 2 Bell 206B helicopters.

Weapons and Systems: The Australian Navy uses U.S. equipment and systems on its U.S.-built warships and British weapons and systems on its other ships, but some of its air-search and fire-control radars have been purchased in The Netherlands (LWO-2, HSA, etc.)

Except for the U.S.-built ships, the sonars are all of British or Australian (Mulloka) origin. The Australian Navy has perfected an unusual ASW weapon, the Ikara. Similar in basic concept to the French Malafon, it is a Mk 44 or Mk 46 torpedo coupled with a guided missile and guidance equipment, and has a maximum range of about 20,000 yards.

AIRCRAFT CARRIER

	Bldr	Laid down	L	In serv.
R 21 MELBOURNE (ex-*Majestic*)	Vickers-Armstrong	4-43	28-2-45	10-55

D: 16,000 tons (20,000 fl)
Dim: 211.25 (198 wl) × 24.38 hull (39.01 max) × 7.15
S: 23 kts **Man:** 109 officers and 1,100 to 1,120 men
A: 12/40-mm AA (II × 4, I × 4) — about 17 aircraft
Electron Equipt: Radars: 1/LW0-2, 1/293, 1/992
M: Parsons GT; 2 props; 42,000 hp **Range:** 6,200/23, 12,000/14
Boilers: 4 Admiralty, 28 kg pressure **Fuel:** 3,200 tons

Melbourne 1977

Remarks: Steam catapults, 5½° angled flight deck, optical mirror landing equipment. Modernized in 1969 to operate ASW aircraft, and again refitted in 1971 and 1972-73. She is expected to operate well into the 1980s.

SUBMARINES

♦ *6 British Oberon-class torpedo attack submarines*

	Bldr	Laid down	L	In serv.
S 57 OXLEY	Scott's	7-64	24-9-65	3-67
S 59 OTWAY	Scott's	6-65	29-11-66	12-67
S 70 OVENS	Scott's	6-66	5-12-67	1969
S 60 ONSLOW	Scott's	5-67	29-8-68	1970
S 61 ORION	Scott's	1973	16-9-74	6-77
S 62 OTAMA	Scott's	5-73	3-12-75	12-77

Oxley

SUBMARINES (*continued*)

D: 1,610 tons surfaced, 2,410 submerged
Dim: 93.62 (73.45 pp) × 8.07 × 5.48
S: 17.5/15 kts **Man:** 6 officers, 62 men
A: 8/533-mm TT (6 fwd, 2 aft) all contained within pressure hull — 14 torpedoes in reserve
Electron Equipt: Radar: 1/1006
Sonar: 1/187C, 1/197, 1/719, 1/2007
M: Admiralty Standard Range 1 diesel engines; diesel-electric propulsion surfaced

REMARKS: Completion of S-61 and S-62 delayed by deficiencies in the electrical equipment. The four earlier units are being equipped with new U.S. and West German sonars and fire-control equipment. Sub-Harpoon missiles may be purchased from the U.S.

DESTROYERS

♦ *3 U.S. Charles F. Adams-class guided missile*

	Bldr	Laid down	L	In serv.
D 38 PERTH (ex-U.S. DDG-25)	Defoe S.B. Co. (U.S.)	9-62	26-9-63	7-65
D 39 HOBART (ex-U.S. DDG-26)	Defoe S.B. Co. (U.S.)	4-63	9-1-64	8-66
D 41 BRISBANE (ex-U.S. DDG-27)	Defoe S.B. Co. (U.S.)	2-63	5-3-66	1-68

Perth

D: 3,370 tons (4,618 fl) **Dim:** 134.18 (128 pp) × 14.32 × 6
S: 35 kts **Man:** 21 officers, 312 men **Range:** 1,600/30 — 6,000/14
A: 1 Mk 13 Tartar missile (I × 1 aft) — 2/127-mm DP (I × 2) Mk 42 — 6 ASW Mk 32 torpedo tubes (III × 2) — 2 ASW Ikara launching systems, one to each side
Electron Equipt: Radars: 1/SPS 40, 1/SPS 10, 1/SPS 52, 2/SPG 51 — NTDS
Sonar: 1/SQS 23
M: GT; 2 props; 70,000 hp **Fuel:** 900 tons
Boilers: 4 Babcock and Wilcox (84 kg/cm² — superheat 520°)
Electric: 2,000 kw

REMARKS: D-38 modernized in the U.S. 3-9-74 to 2-1-75 with SM-1A Standard missiles, NTDS, and MK 42 mod 10 guns. The other two were to refit to the same standard in Australia. All are scheduled eventually to receive Harpoon anti-ship missiles.

♦ *3 Vendetta/Duchess class*

	Bldr	Laid down	L	In serv.
D 08 VENDETTA	Cockatoo D. & Eng. Co.	7-52	3-5-54	11-58
D 11 VAMPIRE	Williamstown Nav. DY	7-49	27-10-56	6-59
D 154 DUCHESS	J. Thornycroft	7-48	9-4-51	10-52

Vendetta 1975

D: 2,800 tons (3,600 fl) **Dim:** 118.87 (111.55 pp) × 13.10 × 5.10
S: 30 kts **Man:** 327 men **Range:** 3,700/20 (D-154: 3,000/20)
A: 6/114-mm DP Mk 6 (II × 3 — 6/40-mm Bofors AA (II × 2, I × 2) — 1 Limbo Mk 10 ASW mortar
M: Parsons GT; 2 props; 54,000 hp
Boilers: 2 Foster Wheeler **Fuel:** 584 tons
Electron Equipt: D-08, D-11;
Radars: 1/LW0-2, 1/8GR 301, 2/CT HSA M22
Sonars: D-08, D-11: 1/162, 1/170, 1/174 D-154: 1/147, 1/162, 1/164, 1/174

DESTROYERS (*continued*)

REMARKS: D-08 and D-11 modernized from 6-70 to 5-73 with Dutch fire-control and air-search radars. D-154 was loaned by Great Britain until 1971, then purchased by the Royal Australian Navy and modified in 1973 as a school ship. Her 114-mm mount aft and her Squid ASW mortar were removed and replaced by a large deckhouse for extra accommodations. Her sonars are not operable.

FRIGATES

♦ *2 U.S. Oliver Hazard Perry-class guided missile*

	Bldr	Laid down	L	In serv.
F . . . CANBERRA (ex-U.S. FFG-18)	Todd, Seattle (U.S.)	7-77	. . .-78	. . .-80
F . . . ADELAIDE (ex-U.S. FFG-17)	Todd, Seattle (U.S.)	4-78	. . .-79	. . .-80

D: 3,605 tons (fl) **Dim:** 135.6 (126 pp) × 13.7 × 7.5
S: 28.5 kts **Man:** 14 officers, 162 men
A: 1 Mk-13 mod 4 launcher for Standard SM-1A SAM and Harpoon — 1/76-mm DP OTO Melara Compact (U.S. Mk-75) — 6 Mk-32 ASW tubes for Mk-46 torpedoes — 2 helicopters
Electron Equipt: Radars: 1/SPS-55, 1/SPS-49, 1/SPG-60, 1/Mk-92 fire control.
Sonar: 1/SQS-56
M: 2 General Electric LM 2500; 1 controllable-pitch prop; 40,000 hp
Electric: 3,000 kw
Range: 5,000/18

REMARKS: Ordered 27-2-76 in lieu of Australian DDL design. Two drop-down, diesel-electric-driven propellers are located forward beneath the hull for emergency propulsion and maneuvering. No fin stabilizers fitted. Will not have U.S. Vulcan/Phalanx close-defense gun. The type of helicopter to be carried has not been decided between the U.S. Lamps III and the British/French Lynx.

♦ *6 River class, improved versions of the British Rothesay class*

	Bldr	Laid down	L	In serv.
F 45 YARRA	Williamstown Nav. DY	1957	30-9-58	7-61
F 46 PARRAMATTA	Cockatoo D. & Eng. Co.	1957	31-1-59	7-61
F 48 STUART	Cockatoo D. & Eng. Co.	3-59	8-4-61	6-63
F 49 DERWENT	Williamstown Nav. DY	6-59	17-4-61	4-64
F 50 SWAN	Williamstown Nav. DY	2-65	16-12-67	6-70
F 53 TORRENS	Cockatoo D. & Eng. Co.	5-65	28-9-68	1971

Yarra 1974

D: 2,100 tons (2,700 fl) **Dim:** 112.75 (109.75 pp) × 12.50 × 3.90 (avg)
S: 27 kts **Man:** 13 officers, 238 men **Range:** 4,500/12
A: 2/114-mm DP Mk 6 (II × 1 fwd.) — 1 Sea Cat missile launcher — 1 Limbo Mk 10 mortar — 1 ASW Ikara missile launcher
Electron Equipt: Radars: 1/293, 1/LW02, CT HSA M22 on F-50 and F-53, 1/275 on the others
Sonars: 1/162, 1/177, 1/170, 1/199 (except for F-48 and F-49), Mulloka on F-45
M: GT; 2 props; 34,000 hp
Boilers: 2 Babcock & Wilcox

Swan Compare this profile with that of the *Yarra.* 1972

REMARKS: F-50 and F-53 have different profiles than the four others, resembling more the British *Leander* class. The first four are being given a refit, scheduled to be completed in June 1980; they will receive two triple Mk-32 ASW torpedo tubes in place of the Limbo mortar, Mulloka sonar in place of their original suits, HSA M 22 gunfire control systems, have their boilers converted to use diesel fuel, and will have their accommodations improved. The Ikara missile carries a U.S. Mk-44 ASW torpedo as its payload. Variable-depth sonars are being removed, where fitted. F-50 has been used in Mulloka sonar experiments.

Ikara ASW Missile Launcher

MINE WARFARE SHIPS

♦ *3 British "-ton"-class coastal minesweepers*

	Bldr	Laid down	L	In serv.
M 1102 SNIPE (ex-*Alcastan*)	Thornycroft (U.K.)	1952	5-1-53	1953
M 1121 CURLEW (ex-*Chediston*)	Montrose (U.K.)	1952	6-10-53	1954
M 1183 IBIS (ex-*Singleton*)	Montrose (U.K.)	1952	18-11-55	1956

D: 370 tons (425 fl) **Dim:** 46.33 (42.68 pp) × 8.76 × 2.50
S: 15 kts **Man:** 3 officers, 25 men **Range:** 2,300/13, 3,500/8
A: 2/40-mm AA (I × 2)
M: Napier Deltic diesels; 2 props; 3,000 hp **Fuel:** 45 tons diesel

REMARKS: Bought in 1962 after refitting. Air-conditioned and stabilized. M-1102 and M-1121 are equipped as minehunters, with Type 193 sonar. M-1183 has only one gun.

Ibis 1973

HYDROGRAPHIC SHIPS

♦ *2 new hydrographic/oceanographic ships planned.* No details available.

♦ *1 improved Moresby class*

	Bldr	Laid down	L	In serv.
A 291 COOK	Williamstown Nav. DY	30-9-74	1976	. . .

Cook

D: 1,910 tons (2,650 fl) **Dim:** 91.2 × 13.41 × 4.6
S: 17 kts **Range:** 11,000/14 **Man:** 150, with 13 scientists
Electron Equipt: Radar: 1/TM 829 Sonar: 1/Simrad SU 2
M: Diesels; 2 props; 3,400 hp **Fuel:** 640 tons

REMARK: Intended for oceanographic research to replace *Diamantina.*

♦ *1 Moresby class*

	Bldr	Laid down	L	In serv.
A 573 MORESBY	State DY, Newcastle, NSW	1961	7-9-63	3-64

HYDROGRAPHIC SHIPS (*continued*)

Moresby

D: 1,714 tons (2,350 fl) **Dim:** 95.70 (86.70 pp) × 12.80 × 4.60
S: 19 kts **Man:** 13 officers, 133 men
Electron Equipt: Radar: 1/TM 829 Sonar: 1/Simrad SU 2
M: Diesel-electric propulsion; 3 CSVM generators, each 1,330 kw/800 rpm; 2 electric motors, each 2,500 hp/250 rpm; 2 props

REMARKS: A Bell 206B helicopter can be carried on board. Ship is air-conditioned. 2/40-mm AA removed, stack heightened 1973-74.

♦ *1 Flinders class*

	Bldr	Laid down	L	In serv.
A 312 FLINDERS	Williamstown Nav. DY	1971	29-7-72	4-73

D: 750 tons (fl) **Dim:** 49.1 × 10.05 × 3.7
S: 13.5 kts **Range:** 5,000/9 **Man:** 4 officers, 34 men
Electron Equipt: TM 829 radar; Simrad SU 2 sonar
M: 2 Paxman Ventura diesels; 2 props; 1,680 hp

REMARKS: Similar to the Philippine ship *Atyimba*. Replaces the *Paluma* stricken in 1974. Operates along Barrier Reef.

♦ *1 former netlayer*

GOR 314 KIMBLA — Bldr: Walkers (Australia) — L: 23-3-55
D: 762 tons (1,021 fl) **Dim:** 54.55 × 9.75 × 3.7
S: 9.5 kts **Man:** 4 officers, 36 men
M: Triple expansion; 1 prop; 350 hp
Electron Equipt: Type 975 radar and Simrad SU2 sonar

REMARKS: Converted for oceanographic research service in 1959. Will remain in service until 1980.

OILER

♦ *1 tanker*

A0 195 SUPPLY (ex-*Tideaustral*)
Bldr: Harland and Wolf — L: 1-9-54 — In serv. 3-55
D: 15,000 tons (25,941 fl) **Dim:** 177.8 (167.8 pp) × 21.7 × 9.8
S: 17 kts **Range:** 8,500/13 **Man:** 205 men
A: 6/40-mm AA (II × 2, I × 2) **M:** GT; 2 props; 15,000 hp

Supply

REMARKS: 17,600 deadweight tons. Operated in British Navy 1955-62. Plans for a second replenishment ship have been postponed to 1980.

PATROL BOATS

♦ *15 new units are planned as replacements for the boats below*

♦ *12 Acute-class boats for patrol in the coastal waters of Borneo and Australia*

P 81 ACUTE, P 82 ADROIT, P 83 ADVANCE, P 87 ARDENT, P 89 ASSAIL, P 90 ATTACK, P 91 AWARE, P 97 BARBETTE, P 98 BARRICADE, P 99 BOMBARD, P 100 BUCCANEER, P 101 BAYONET

Bldr: Evans Deakin, Ltd. (except P 83, P 97, P 99, P 101: Walkers, Ltd.). Ordered in 1965, delivered 1967-69.

Buccaneer 1972

D: 146 tons (fl) **Dim:** 32.76 (30.48 pp) × 6.20 × 1.90
S: 24/21 kts **Man:** 3 officers, 19 men **Fuel:** 20 tons diesel
A: 1/40-mm AA — 2 machine guns **Radar:** 1/975
M: 2 Davey-Paxman Ventura, 16-cylinder diesels; 2 props; 3,500 hp

REMARKS: Steel hull; light-alloy superstructure; air-conditioned. P-91 is unarmed. Sisters P-84 *Aitape*, P-92 *Lavada*, P-93 *Lae*, P-94 *Madang*, P-85 *Samarai* transferred to Papua, New Guinea, in 1974. P-86 *Archer* and P-95 *Bandolier* sold in 1973 to Indonesia and transferred in 1973 and 1974, respectively. P-88 *Arrow* sunk 25-12-74 in Typhoon Tracey.

AMPHIBIOUS WARFARE SHIPS

♦ *1 modified British Sir Bedivere class*

	Bldr	Laid down	L	In serv.
L 50 TOBRUK	. . .	1977	. . .	1980

D: 6,000 tons (fl) **S:** 17 kts **Dim:** 129.5 × 19.6 × 4.3
A: 2/40-mm Bofors AA **Man:** approx. 18 officers, 50 men
M: 2 diesels; 2 props; 9,400 hp

REMARKS: Construction announced August 1976 as a replacement for *Sydney*. Will carry Wessex Mk-31B troop helicopters operating from platforms amidships and aft, and will be able to carry 300-500 troops, Leopard tanks, and other military vehicles. Bow and stern ramps will be fitted.

♦ *6 LCU ex-U.S. Army landing craft, transferred in 1973*

L 134 BALIKPAPAN, L 127 BRUNEI, L 128 LABUAN, L 129 TARAKAN, L 130 WEWAK, L 133 BETANG

Bldr: Australia, 1972–73

D: 310 tons light (503 fl) **Dim:** 44.50 × 12.20 × 1.90
S: 10 kts **Man:** 2 officers, 11 men
A: 2 machine guns **Range:** 3,000/10
M: 2 General Motors diesels; 2 props; 675 hp

REMARKS: L-131 *Salamaua* and L-132 *Buna* transferred to Papua, New Guinea, in 1974. Can carry three medium tanks.

♦ *1 destroyer tender*

	Bldr	Laid down	L	In serv.
A 215 STALWART	Cockatoo D & E, Sydney	6-64	10-66	2-68

D: 15,500 tons (fl) **Dim:** 157.12 (143.25 pp) × 20.57 × 9.0
S: 20 kts **Man:** 396 men **A:** 4/40-mm AA (II × 2)
M: Scott-Sulzer diesels, (6 cyl) Mk RD 68; 2 props; 14,400 hp
Electric: 3,200 kw **Range:** 12,000/12

REMARKS: Helicopter platform and hangar for two Wessex or Sea King. Workshops and foundry (400 m^2); boiler shop (100 m^2); electric shop; electronic shop (300 m^2); mechanical workshop (500 m^2); and shops for precision equipment and plastic-boat repairs. Four 3-ton and two 6-ton cranes. Carries spare missiles for destroyers and frigates.

Stalwart

VARIOUS SHIPS

♦ *1 training ship*

A . . . JERVIS BAY (ex-*Australian Trader*) Bldr: State DY, Newcastle, 1969

D: 7,005 tons (grt) **Dim:** 135.7 (123.5 pp) × 21.5 × 6.1
S: . . . **A:** . . .
M: 2 SEMT-Pielstick heavy-oil diesels; 2 props; 13,000 hp
Electric: 2,000 kw

REMARKS: A former roll-on/roll-off cargo ferry taken over in 1977 for conversion to a training ship to replace *Duchess*. Name commemorates an armed merchant cruiser of World War II.

♦ **G 247 BASS, G 244 BANKS** — Bldr: Walkers, Ltd., Maryborough, 1960

D: 260 tons (fl) **Dim:** 30.8 × 6.70 × 2.50
S: 10 kts **Man:** 14 men **M:** Diesels

REMARKS: G-247 equipped as a hydrographic ship and G-244 for fisheries protection, but both also used for reserve training.

♦ *2 diving tenders, former British "-ham"-type inshore minesweepers*

Y 298 SEAL (ex-*Wintringham*, 24-5-55)
Y 280 PORPOISE (ex-*Neasham*, 1955)

Bldr: White, Cowes

D: 120 tons (159 fl) **Dim:** 32.43 (30.48 pp) × 6.45 × 1.70
S: 14 kts **Man:** 7 men
M: Davey-Paxman diesels; 2 props; 1,000 hp
Range: 1,500/12 **Fuel:** 15 tons diesel

REMARKS: Transferred in 1966; assigned to the school of diving and underwater demolition, Sydney. Sister Y-299 *Otter* sold 1974. Can support 14 divers.

♦ *3 501-class tugs*

501, 502, 504 (1969, 1972)

D: 47.5 tons **Dim:** 15.4 × 4.6 × . . .
S: 9 kts **Man:** 3 men
M: 2 General Motors diesels; 2 props; 340 hp

REMARK: Sister 503 to Papua, New Guinea, 1974.

♦ *2 ex-U.S. Army wooden-hulled tugs* (1944)

TB 9 SARDIUS **TB 1536**

D: 60 tons (fl) **Dim:** 13.7 × . . . × . . .
S: 10 kts **Man:** 4 men
M: 1 Hercules diesel; 240 hp

♦ *3 torpedo-recovery craft* (1970–71)

TRV 801 **TRV 802** **TRV 803**

D: 91.6 tons **Dim:** 27 × 6.4 × 1.4
S: 13 kts **Man:** 9 men
M: 3 GM diesels; 3 props; 890 hp

REMARK: TRV-802 normally used as a diving tender.

VARIOUS SHIPS (*continued*)

♦ *4 water tenders* (Blt: 1940s)

MRL 253 GAYUNDAH **MWL 254** **MWL 256** **MWL 257**

D: 300 tons (600 fl) **Dim:** 36.5 × 7.3 × . . .
S: 9.5 kts
M: 2 Ruston & Hornsby diesels; 2 props; 440 hp

REMARKS: MRL 253 used as dry-stores carrier. Sisters to hydrographic ship *Paluma*, scrapped in 1974.

♦ *3 stores lighters* (1972)

CSL 01 **CSL 02** **CSL 03**

D: . . . **Dim:** 23.7 × 9.8 × 2
M: 2 GM diesels

REMARKS: Catamarans. One 3-ton electric crane. Based on AWL-304 design but with pilothouse aft.

♦ *1 aircraft lighter* (1967)

AWL 304

REMARKS: Built to service *Melbourne*, can carry 2 Skyhawk or 1 Tracker. Similar to CSL 01 class but with A-frame crane aft and low pilothouse forward.

♦ *1 aircraft-rescue launch* (1960)

Y 256 AIR SPRITE

D: 23.5 tons **Dim:** 19.2 × 4.7 × 1.0
S: 25 kts
M: 2 Hall-Scott gasoline engines

REMARKS: Based on U.S. Navy 63-foot AVR design; sisters are in RAAF service. Two 11.6-m Bertram yachts, 38101 and 38102, purchased as rescue launches, are used as yachts.

NOTE: There are a number of other yard and service craft, including non-self-propelled oil barges, stores lighters, etc., as well as approximately 20 12.2-m motor workboats.

AUSTRIA

MERCHANT MARINE (1976): 15 ships — 3,670 grt

♦ *2 patrol craft for the Danube*

A 604 NIEDERÖSTERREICH

Bldr: Korneuberg, In serv. 4-70

Niederösterreich

D: 71 tons (fl) **Dim:** 29 × 5.4 × 1.1
S: 22 kts **Man:** 9 men
A: 1/20-mm AA — 2 machine guns **M:** 2 diesels; 1,600 hp

A 602 OBERST BRECHT

Bldr: Korneuberg

D: 10 tons **Dim:** 12.3 × 2.5 × 0.7
S: 10 kts **Man:** 5 men
A: 1 machine gun **M:** 2 diesels; 214 hp

♦ *10 U.S.-built M3 class launches* (4 in serv. 1965, 6 in serv. 1976)

D: 2.9 tons **Dim:** 8.3 × 2.5 × . . .
S: 18 kts **M:** 2 gasoline/diesels; 204/184 hp

BAHAMAS

MERCHANT MARINE (1976): 119 ships — 147,817 grt (tankers: 6 — 49,249 grt)

BAHAMAS POLICE MARINE DIVISION

♦ *2 Vosper-Thornycroft 103-ft patrol craft*

N . . . **N . . .**

D: 100 tons (125 fl) **Dim:** 31.5 × 5.9 × 1.6
S: 24 kts **Man:** 3 officers, 16 men
A: 1/20-mm AA **Range:** 2,000/13
M: 2 Paxman Ventura diesels; 2 props; 2,900 hp

REMARKS: Ordered 1977. Fin stabilizers, steel hulls.

♦ *7 patrol craft*

ACKLINS, ANDROS, ELEUTHERA, SAN SALVADOR, N . . . , N . . . , N . . .

Bldr: Keith Nelson (G.B.) First four in serv. 3-71

D: 30 tons **Dim:** 18.68 × 4.77 × 1.40
S: 19.5 kts **Man:** 11 men
M: 2 Caterpillar diesels **A:** 3 machine guns

REMARKS: Fiberglass construction. Keith Nelson is a division of Vosper-Thornycroft. Air-conditioned. Three additional sisters ordered 1977.

Andros 1972

BAHRAIN

MERCHANT MARINE (1976): 25 ships — 25,096 grt (tankers: 2 — 20,640 grt)

♦ *1 Tracker-class patrol craft*

Bldr: Fairey Marine, G.B.

D: 26 tons (fl) **Dim:** 19.6 × 4.9 × 1.5
S: 28 kts **A:** 1/20-mm AA **Range:** 500
M: 2 General Motors diesels; 2 props; 1,120 hp

REMARK: Acquired in 1974.

♦ *2 Spear-class patrol craft*

Bldr: Fairey Marine, G.B.

D: 4.5 tons (10 fl) **Dim:** 9.1 × 2.75 × 0.84
S: 26 kts **A:** 2 machine guns **Man:** 3 men
M: 2 Perkins diesels; 2 props; 290 hp **Range:** 220

REMARK: Acquired in 1974.

♦ *3 27-foot-class patrol craft*

Bldr: Cheverton, Cowes, G.B.

D: 3.3 tons **Dim:** 8.23 × 2.44 × 0.81
M: 2 diesels; 1 prop; 150 hp **S:** 15 kts

REMARKS: Acquired in 1976. For customs and harbor patrol.

♦ *2 Interceptor-class patrol craft*

Bldr: Fairey Marine, G.B.

REMARKS: Catamaran-hulled craft, 7.6 m overall, capable of 30 kts. Powered by 2 outboard motors; 270 hp. Can carry 8 25-man life rafts.

♦ *2 patrol craft*

HOWAR

JIDA

D: 15 tons **Dim:** 13.9 × 6.1 × 1.1
M: 2 diesels; 2 props; 1,080 hp **S:** 23 kts

♦ *1 Loadmaster-class landing craft*

Bldr: Cheverton, Cowes, G.B.

D: 90 tons (fl) **Dim:** 18.23 × 6.1 × 1.0
M: 2 diesels; 2 props; 240 hp **S:** 10 kts

REMARKS: Can carry 40 tons of vehicles or dry cargo, or 60 tons of liquid cargo. Acquired in 1976.

BANGLADESH

Personnel: 3,500 men

Merchant Marine (1976): 127 ships — 146,818 grt

♦ *1 British Salisbury-class frigate*

F 16 UMAR FAROOQ (ex-*Llandaff* F-61)

Bldr: Hawthorn Leslie, G.B. Laid down: 8-53. L: 30-11-55. In serv. 4-58

D: 2,170 tons (2,408 fl) **Dim:** 103.60 (100.58 pp) × 12.19 × 4.8
S: 24 kts **Range:** 2,300/24, 7,500/16 **Man:** 14 officers, 223 men
A: 2/114-mm DP Mk-6 (II × 1) — 2/40-mm AA (II × 1)
Electron Equipt: Radars: 1/985, 1/993, 1/277Q, 1/982, 1/975, 1 CT/275
M: 8 Admiralty Standard Range 1 diesels; 2 props, 12,400 hp
Electric: 1,200 kw **Fuel:** 230 tons diesel

Remark: Former aircraft-direction frigate transferred on 10-12-76.

♦ *2 Yugoslav Kraljevica-class patrol boats, transferred 6-6-75*

P 301 KARNAPHULI (ex-Yugoslav PBR 502)
P 302 TISTA (ex-Yugoslav PBR 505)

D: 190 tons (202 fl) **Dim:** 41.0 × 6.3 × 2.2
S: 18 kts **Man:** 4 officers, 40 men
A: 2/40-mm AA (I × 2) — 4/20-mm AA (I × 4)
M: 2 M.A.N. W8V 30/38 diesels; 2 props; 3,300 hp **Range:** 1,000/12

♦ *2 Ajay-class surveillance patrol boats given by India*

P 201 PADMA (ex-*Akshay*, P 3136)

Bldr: Hooghly D&E, Calcutta (1-62)

P 202 SURMA (ex-*Ajay*, P 3135)

D: 120 tons (160 fl) **Dim:** 35.75 (33.52 pp) × 6.10 × 1.90
S: 12.5 kts **A:** 1/40-mm AA
M: 2 Paxman diesels; 2 props; 1,000 hp
Range: 5,000/10 **Man:** 3 officers, 32 men

♦ *5 river patrol boats*

P 101 PABNA (6-72) **P 102 NOAKHALI** (7-72) **P 103 PATUAKHALI** (11-74)
P 104 BOGRA (6-77) **P 105 RANGAMATI** (6-77)

Bldr: DEW Narayengonj, Dacca

D: 69.5 tons (fl) **Dim:** 22.9 × 6.10 × 1.90
S: 10 kts **Man:** 3 officers, 30 men
A: 1/40-mm AA **Range:** 700/8
M: 2 Cummins diesels; 2 props

♦ *1 training ship*

SHAHEED RUHUL AMIN (ex-Canadian merchant *Anticosti*)

Bldr: Canada (1969). In serv. 12-74

D: 710 tons (fl) **Dim:** 47.5 × 11.1 × 3.1
S: 11.5 kts **Man:** 8 officers, 72 men
A: 1/40-mm AA **Range:** 4,000/10
M: 1 Caterpillar diesel

BARBADOS

Personnel: 61 (4 officers, 57 men)

Merchant Marine (1976): 30 ships — 3,897 grt

♦ *1 Halmatic, 20-meter, Guardian-class police patrol craft*

Bldr: Aquarius Boat, Great Britain. In serv. 12-74

GC 601 GEORGE FERGUSON

D: 30 tons **Dim:** 20 × 5.25 × 1.50
S: 24 kts **A:** 1/20-mm AA **Man:** 11 men
Range: 650/12 **M:** 2 General Motors 12V71 diesels; 1,300 hp

♦ *3 Halmatic, 12-meter, Guardian-class police patrol craft*

Bldr: Aquarius Boat, G.B.

GC 402 COMMANDER MARSHALL
GC 403 T. T. LEWIS
GC 404 J. T. C. RAMSAY

D: 11.5 tons **Dim:** 12.0 × 3.7 × 1.0
S: 21 kts **Man:** 4 men
M: 2 Caterpillar Mk 334 TA diesels; 2 props; 580 hp

PERSONNEL: 4,457, including 300 officers

MERCHANT MARINE (1976): 258 ships — 1,499,431 grt
(tankers: 17 — 302,879 grt)

NAVAL AVIATION: Five helicopters (2 Sikorsky S-58 and 3 Alouette IIIB) used for minehunting. One Alouette may be taken on board the *Zinnia* or the *Godetia*.

FRIGATES

♦ *4 Westhinder class, Type E 71*

	Bldr	Laid down	L	In serv.
F 910 WIELINGEN	Boëlwerf (Temse)	5-3-74	30-3-76	3-76
F 911 WESTDIEP	Cockerill (Hoboken)	2-9-74	8-12-75	6-77
F 912 WANDELAAR	Boëlwerf (Temse)	5-3-75	1-3-77	12-77
F 913 WESTHINDER	Cockerill (Hoboken)	8-12-75	28-1-77	6-78

Wielingen (on trials) 1976

D: 1,860 tons (2,340 fl) **Dim:** 106.38 (103 pp) × 12.30 × 5.30 (over sonar)
S: 28 kts on gas turbine **Range:** 4,500/18, 5,000/14
A: 1/100-mm AA, model 68 — 4 Exocet MM-38 anti-ship missiles — 1 Sea Sparrow BPDMS launcher (8 missiles) — 2/20-mm AA (I × 2) — 1/375-mm Bofors sextuple ASW rocket launcher — 2 launching racks for L 5 torpedoes
Electron Equipt: Radars: 1 air-search, 1 Raytheon navigation, 1 HSA multi-purpose, 2 Knebworth Corvus 8-tube chaff launchers — SEWACO
Sonar: 1 SQS-505A
M: CODOG propulsion, 2 shafts with variable-pitch propellers, 2 Cockerill CO-240 diesels, each 3,000 hp (1,000 rpm); 1 Rolls-Royce Olympus TM 3B gas turbine of 27,500 hp (5,600 rpm) **Man:** 14 officers, 146 men
Fuel: 190 tons diesel **Electric:** 2,000 kw

REMARKS: Welded hull, 2 self-activating Vosper-Thornycroft stabilizers; 15 knots on 1 diesel, 20 knots on 2; for more than 20 kts the gas turbine is brought on the line. Canadian hull sonar. French 100-mm Model 1968. Belgian-Dutch automatic surface and air search radar system, including fire control and an automatic tactical data system.

MINE WARFARE SHIPS

♦ *7 AM/MSO oceangoing minesweepers*

	L
M 902 VAN HAVERBEKE (ex-MSO-522)	29-10-59
M 903 A. F. DUFOUR (ex-*Lagen*, ex-MSO-498)	13-8-54
M 904 DE BROUWER (ex-*Nansen*, ex-MSO-499)	15-10-54
M 906 BREYDEL (ex-AM-504)	25-3-55
M 907 ARTEVELDE (ex-AM-503)	19-6-54
M 908 GEORGES TRUFFAUT (ex-AM-515)	1-11-55
M 909 FRANÇOIS BOVESSE (ex-AM-516)	28-2-56

Artevelde J. C. Bellonne, 1973

D: 720 tons (780 fl) **Dim:** 52.67 (50.30 pp) × 10.67 × 3.20
S: 15/14 kts **Man:** 5 officers, 67 men **A:** 1/40-mm AA Mk 3
Range: 3,000/10, 2,400/12
M: General Motors diesels; 2 variable-pitch props; 1,600 hp
Fuel: 53 tons diesel **Electron Equipt:** SQQ-14 Sonar

REMARKS: Transferred 1955-60, except M-903 and M-904 transferred from Norway in 1966. M-907 has no sonar and serves as divers' clearance ship, rest as minehunters. M-903 and M-904 have no 40-mm gun. Wooden hulls.

MINE WARFARE SHIPS (*continued*)

♦ *6 U.S. AMS/MSC coastal minesweepers*

2 U.S. construction (1953):

M 934 VERVIERS (ex-AMS-259) **M 935 VEURNE** (ex-AMS-260)

REMARK: Converted to minehunters.

Veurne Note the differences in bridge structure between her and *Rochefort*

4 Belgian construction:

	L		L
M 928 STAVELOT	26-3-55	**M 932 NIEUWPOORT**	12-3-55
M 930 ROCHEFORT	5-6-54	**M 933 KOKSIJDE**	4-6-55

Bldr: M-928: Boëlwerf; M-930, M-932, M-933: Béliard, Ostend

Rochefort

D: 330 tons (390 fl) **Dim:** 44 (42.10 pp) × 8.30 × 2.60
S: 13.5/12 kts **A:** 1/40-mm AA **Range:** 2,700/10.5
Man: 4 officers, 17 petty officers, 19 men **Fuel:** 30 m³ diesel
M: General Motors diesels; 2 props; 880 hp

REMARKS: Minehunters have enclosed bridge, deckhouse aft. Three sisters serve as auxiliaries.

♦ *13 Herstal-class inshore minesweepers*

	L		L
M 471 HASSELT	5-68	**M 479 HUY** (ex-MSI-91)	17-11-56
M 473 LOKEREN	18-5-57	**M 480 SERAING** (ex-MSI-92)	16-3-57
M 474 TURNHOUT	7-9-57	**M 482 VISE** (ex-MSI-94)	7-9-57
M 475 TONGEREN	16-11-57	**M 483 OUGRÉE** (ex-MSI-95)	16-11-57
M 476 MERKSEM	5-4-58	**M 484 DINANT** (ex-MSI-96)	5-4-58
M 477 OUDENAERDE	3-5-58	**M 485 ANDENNE** (ex-MSI-97)	3-5-58
M 478 HERSTAL	6-8-56		

Bldr: Mercantile Marine Yard, Kruibeke

D: 160 tons (190 fl) **Dim:** 34.50 (32.50 pp) × 6.70 × 2.10
M: 2 diesels; 2 props; 1,260 hp **S:** 15 kts **Range:** 2,300/10
A: 2/12.7-mm machine guns (II × 1)
Man: 1 officer, 7 petty officers, 9 men **Fuel:** 18 m³ diesel

REMARKS: Wooden hulls. Designed to sweep the Schelde River. Fitted for magnetic, acoustic, and mechanical sweeping to a depth of 4.50 to 10 m. Modified version of British "-ham" class. M-479 to M-485 built with U.S. funds.

Dinant

AUXILIARY SHIPS

♦ *2 mine countermeasures support ships*

	Bldr	Laid down	L	In serv.
A 961 ZINNIA	Cockerill (Hoboken)	11-66	6-5-67	9-67

D: 1,705 tons (2,685 fl) **Dim:** 99.50 (94.20 wl) × 14 × 3.60
S: 18 kts (20 on trials) **Range:** 14,000/12.5

AUXILIARY SHIPS *(continued)*

Zinnia G. Arra, 1976

Man: 13 officers, 46 petty officers, 64 men
A: 3/40-mm AA (I × 3) — 1 Alouette IIIB helicopter with folding hangar
M: Cockerill-Ougrée diesels, V 12 TR 240 CO; 1 controllable-pitch prop; 5,000 hp
Fuel: 150 m^3 diesel, 300 m^3 for supply to minesweepers

REMARK: Anti-rolling devices.

	Bldr	Laid down	L	In serv.
A 960 GODETIA	Boëlwerf (Temse)	1-64	7-12-65	2-66

Godetia J. C. Bellonne, 1973

D: 1,700 tons (2,500 fl) **Dim:** 91.83 (87.85 pp) × 14 × 3.50
Man: 10 officers, 37 petty officers, 48 men
A: 2/40-mm AA (II × 1) **Range:** 2,250/15 **S:** 18 kts
M: 4 ACEC-M.A.N. diesels linked to 2 variable-pitch props; 5,400 hp

REMARKS: Used as fishery protection ship. 15 knots on one diesel engine. Stabilized by liquid anti-rolling devices. Ship can be protected against radioactive fallout by closed-circuit ventilation. Can accommodate oceanographic research personnel on board and has space for laboratory. Cargo hold with crane to unload supplies or small boats. Minesweeping cables are stowed on reels on the former helicopter deck.

PATROL CRAFT

♦ *6 former river gunboats, 1953-54*

P 901 LEIE **P 903 MEUSE** **P 905 SCHELDE**
P 902 LIBÉRATION **P 904 SAMBRE** **P 906 SEMOIS**

Bldr: Theodor (Regensburg)

Libération 1970

D: 30 tons (fl) **Dim:** 23.25 × 3.80 × 0.90
S: 19 kts **Man:** 1 officer, 6 men
M: 2 MWM diesels, 440 hp **A:** 2/12.7-mm machine guns

REMARKS: P-902 is 26 meters in length, 4 meters in beam. P-906 is employed as a diving tender.

VARIOUS SHIPS

A 958 ZENOBE GRAMME — School sailing ship (1961). Fitted out as Bermudian Ketch (240 m^3 sail area)

D: 149 tons **Dim:** 28.15 × 6.85 × . . .
S: 10 kts **M:** 1 MWM diesel; 220 hp

A 950 SUB-LIEUTENANT VALCKE: 110 tons, 600 hp. **A 951 HOMMEL, A 952 WESP:** 22 tons, 300 hp. **A 953 BIJ, A 956 KREKEL:** 71 tons, 400 hp. **A 959 MIER:** 17.5 tons, 90 hp. Tugs.

BELGIUM (*continued*)

VARIOUS SHIPS (*continued*)

A 962 MECHELEN (ex-MSC-class minesweeper). Used as an oceanographic research ship.

A 963 SPA (ex-M-927), **A 964 HEIST** (ex-M-929). Ex-MSC-class minesweepers converted to auxiliary function 1977–78.

Mechelen 1974

BELIZE

PERSONNEL: approx. 50 men

MERCHANT MARINE (1976): 3 ships — 920 grt

♦ *2 Brooke Marine patrol craft (1972)*

D: 15 tons (fl) **Dim:** 12.2 × 3.6 × 0.6
A: 3 machine guns **S:** 22 kts
M: 2 Caterpillar diesels; 2 props; 370 hp

BOLIVIA

PERSONNEL (1977): 1,500

♦ *16 river patrol craft*

♦ *1 transport*

MO 8 CORONEL ABAROA

PERSONNEL: 3,400 officers, 28,000 men, plus 500 officers and 13,000 men in the Fuzileiros Navais (Marine Corps equivalent).

MERCHANT MARINE (1976): 520 ships — 3,096,293 grt (tankers: 56 — 1,128,578 grt)

NAVAL AVIATION: Established in 1965. Uses Westland Whirlwind, U.S. SH3-D Sea King, Westland Wasp, and Bell 206B Jetranger helicopters (Westland WG 13 Lynx on order for *Niteroi* class). The Air Force makes S-2-F Trackers available to the Navy.

MAIN WARSHIPS IN SERVICE OR UNDER CONSTRUCTION AS OF 1 OCTOBER 1977

	L	Tons	Main armament
♦ *1 light aircraft carrier* (ASW)			
MINAS GERAIS	1944	15,890	10/40-mm AA, 20 aircraft
♦ *10 submarines*			
3 HUMAITÁ	1972-75	1,610	8 TT
2 GOIÁS	1945	1,650	10 TT
5 RIO GRANDE DO SUL	1942	1,525	10 TT
♦ *18 destroyers and frigates*			
2 GEARING, FRAM I	1944-45	2,400	2/127-mm DP, 6 ASW TT Asroc
4 ALLEN M. SUMNER, FRAM II	1944	2,200	6/127-mm DP, 6 ASW TT
5 FLETCHER	1942-44	2,050	4-5/127-mm DP, 5/533-mm TT
1 ALLEN M. SUMNER (obsolete)	1944	2,200	6/127-mm DP, 1 Sea Cat SAM 6 ASW TT
4 NITEROI	1974-77	3,200	1/114-mm DP, 2/40-mm AA, 1 Branik missile launcher, 2 Sea Cat missile launchers, 1 Bofors rocket launcher, 6 ASW TT, 1 helicopter
2 INDEPENDÊNCIA	1974-75	3,200	2/114-mm DP, 2/40-mm AA, 4 Exocet missile launchers, 2 Sea Cat missile launchers, 1 Bofors rocket launcher, 6 ASW TT, 1 helicopter
♦ *10 patrol vessels*			
10 IMPERIAL MARINHEIRO	1954	911	1/76-mm DP
♦ *6 coastal patrol craft*			
♦ *5 river patrol craft*			
♦ *6 mine warfare ships*			

LIGHT AIRCRAFT CARRIER (ASW)

♦ *1 British Colossus class*

	Bldr	Laid down	L	In serv.
A 11 **MINAS GERAIS** (ex-*Vengeance*)	Swan Hunter	11-42	23-3-44	1-45

D: 15,890 tons (19,890 fl) **Dim:** 211.25 × 36.44 (24.50 hull) × 7.15
S: 24 kts **Man:** 1,000 ship's company plus 300 aviation personnel
A: 10/40-mm AA (IV × 2, II × 1) — 7 aircraft — 13 helicopters

BRAZIL

Minas Gerais 1973

Range: 12,000/14, 6,200/23
Electron Equipt: Radars: 1/SPS-12, 1/SPS-8B, 1/SPS-4, 1/1402, 2/SPG34FC
M: Parsons GT; 2 props; 42,000 hp **Electric:** 2,500 kw
Boilers: 4/28 kg/cm² pressure **Fuel:** 2,200 tons

REMARKS: Purchased from Great Britain in 12-56; refitted in Rotterdam, completing in 1960 with new weapons, steam catapult, angled flight deck (8.5°), mirror optical landing equipment, new radars, and new elevators. In refit 1976-78.

SUBMARINES

♦ *3 British Oberon-class torpedo attack submarines, ordered 8-69*

	Bldr	Laid down	L	In serv.
S 20 **HUMAITÁ**	Vickers-Barrow	11-70	5-10-71	18-6-73
S 21 **TONELEROS**	Vickers-Barrow	1-71	22-11-72	end-77
S 22 **RIACHUELO**	Vickers-Barrow	1973	6-9-75	mid-77

Humaitá 1973

SUBMARINES (*continued*)

D: 1,610 tons standard, 2,030 surfaced, 2,400 submerged
Dim: 90 × 8.02 × 5.50 **A:** 8/533-mm torpedo tubes, 6 forward, 2 aft
S: 17.5/12 kts **Man:** 6 officers, 66 men
M: Diesel-electric propulsion, surfaced. Admiralty Standard Range 1 16-cyl. diesels; 2 electric generators, each 1,280 kw; 2 electric motors; 2 props; 3,700 surfaced/6,000 submerged hp

REMARKS: S-21 several years late entering active service due to a fire on board during construction. Batteries made up of 224 elements in 2 sections with a 7,240-ampere capacity for 5 hours. Underway cruising with snorkel may be maintained for six weeks at a maximum speed of 11 knots. "One-man control" system for emersion and diving. Digital tactical data system.

♦ *2 ex-U.S. Guppy III class*

	Bldr	L
S 15 GOIÁS (ex-*Trumpetfish,* SS-425)	Wm. Cramp	13-4-45
S 16 AMAZONAS (ex-*Greenfish,* SS-351)	Electric Boat Co.	21-12-45

Goiás 1975

D: 1,650 tons standard, 1,975 surfaced, 2,540 submerged
Dim: 99.40 × 8.20 × 5.20 **S:** 20/13-15 kts
Man: 86 men **Range:** 10,000/10
A: 10/533-mm torpedo tubes, 6 fwd, 4 aft
Electron Equipt: BQG 4 sonar
M: Diesel-electric propulsion; 4 groups of generators (6,400 hp); 2 electric motors (5,400 hp)

REMARKS: S-15 transferred 17-10-73, S-16 on 19-12-73. Both have Puffs passive-ranging fire-control sonar.

♦ *5 ex-U.S. Guppy II class, purchased in 5-72, 7-72, and 1973*

	Bldr	L
S 10 GUANABARA (ex-*Dogfish,* SS-350)	Electric Boat Co.	27-10-45
S 11 RIO GRANDE DO SUL (ex-*Grampus,* SS-523)	Boston NSY	15-12-44
S 12 BAHIA (ex-*Sea Leopard,* SS-483)	Portsmouth NSY	2-3-45
S 13 RIO DE JANEIRO (ex-*Odax,* SS-484)	Portsmouth NSY	10-4-45
S 14 CEARA (ex-*Amberjack,* SS-522)	Boston NSY	15-12-44

D: 1,517 tons standard, 1,950 surfaced, 2,540 submerged
Dim: 93.80 × 8.20 × 5.20 **S:** 18/13-15 kts **Range:** 10,000/10
A: 10/533-mm TT, 6 fwd and 4 aft **Man:** 86 men
M: Diesel-electric propulsion; 3 generator groups; 2 electric motors; 2 props; 4,800/5,400 hp **Fuel:** 300 tons diesel

REMARKS: A fourth group of diesel generators has been removed. Two batteries of 126 elements. Converted in 1952–54. S-11 originally Guppy I.

Rio de Janeiro 1972

DESTROYERS

♦ *2 ex-U.S. Gearing class, FRAM I*

	Bldr	L	In serv.
D 25 MARCILIO DIAZ (ex-*Henry W. Tucker,* DDR-875)	Consolidated Steel Corp.	8-11-44	3-45
D 26 MARIZ E BARROS (ex-*Brinkley Bass,* DD-887)	Consolidated Steel Corp.	26-5-45	10-45

Marcilio Diaz 1974

DESTROYERS (*continued*)

D: 2,400 tons (3,600 fl) **Dim:** 119.17 × 12.45 × 3.80 (light)
S: 30 kts **Range:** 2,400/25 — 4,800/15 **Man:** 14 officers, 260 men
A: 4/127-mm 38 (II × 2) — 1 Asroc ASW system — 6/324-mm ASW TT (III × 2) Mk 32 for Mk 44 torpedoes. Platform and hangar for helicopter
Electron Equipt: Radars: 1/SPS 10, 1/SPS 40
Sonar: 1/SQS 23
M: GT; 4 Babcock & Wilcox boilers; 2 props; 60,000 hp **Fuel:** 650 tons

REMARKS: Transferred in 12-1973 and reached Brazil in 6-1974. Four additional units will not be transferred as planned.

♦ *5 ex-U.S. Allen M. Sumner class (all FRAM II except D-34)*

	Bldr	L
D 34 MATO GROSSO (ex-*Compton*, DD-705)	Federal SB (Kearney)	17-9-44
D 35 SERGIPE (ex-*Buck*, DD-761)	Bethlehem (San Fran.)	11-2-44
D 36 ALAGOAS (ex-*James C. Owens*, DD-776)	Bethlehem (San Pedro)	1-10-44
D 37 RIO GRANDE DO NORTE (ex-*Strong*, DD-758)	Bethlehem (San Fran.)	23-4-44
D 38 ESPIRITO SANTO (ex-*Lowry*, DD-770)	Bethlehem (San Pedro)	6-2-44

Mato Grosso 1975

D: 2,200 tons (3,320 fl) **Dim:** 114.75 × 12.45 × 5.80
S: 30 kts **Man:** 15 officers, 260 men **Range:** 1,260/30, 4,600/15
A: 6/127-mm (II × 3) — (D-34 only: 1 quadruple Sea Cat SAM) — 2 hedgehogs — 6/324-mm ASW TT Mk 32 (III × 2) — platform and hangar for helicopter (except D-34)
Electron Equipt: Radars: 1/SPS 10, 1/SPS 40 (D-34: 1/SPS 6; D-37: 1/SPS 37)
Sonar: 1/SQS 29-32
M: GT; 2 props; 60,000 hp, 4 Babcock & Wilcox boilers **Fuel:** 460 tons

REMARK: D-34 transferred 27-9-72, the others in 1973.

Sergipe Note the variable-depth sonar 1975

♦ *5 ex-U.S. Fletcher class*

	Bldr	L
D 27 PARA (ex-*Guest*, DD-472)	Boston Naval SY	20-2-42
D 28 PARAIBA (ex-*Bennett*, DD-473)	Boston Naval SY	16-4-42
D 29 PARANA (ex-*Cushing*, DD-797)	Bethlehem Steel	30-9-43
D 30 PERNAMBUCO (ex-*Hailey*, DD-556)	Todd SY (Seattle)	9-3-43
D 33 MARANHÃO (ex-*Shields*, DD-596)	Puget Sound B&DD	25-9-44

D: 2,050 tons (2,850 fl) **Dim:** 114.85 × 12.03 × 5.50
S: 30 kts **Man:** 15 officers, 247 men **Range:** 1,260/30, 4,400/15
A: D-27, D-28, D-29, D-33: 5/127-mm DP (I × 5) — 6 or 10/40-mm AA (D-33 none) — D-30: 4/127-mm DP; on all except D-33, 5/533-mm ASW TT (V × 1) — 6/324-mm ASW TT Mk 32 (III × 2) — 2 hedgehogs — 1 depth-charge rack
Electron Equipt: Radars: 1/SPS 10, 1/SPS 6
Sonar: 1/SQS 4, 29, or 32
M: General Electric GT; 2 props; 60,000 hp; 4 Babcock & Wilcox boilers
Fuel: 450 tons

REMARKS: Transferred under Mutual Aid Agreement: D-27 and D-28 in 1959, D-29 and D-30 in 1961, D-33 in 1972.

Maranhão 1975

FRIGATES

♦ *6 Vosper-Thornycroft Mk 10 class, ordered 20-9-70*

	Bldr	Laid down	L	In serv.
ASW type				
F 40 NITEROI	Thornycroft, Woolston	5-1972	8-2-74	11-76
F 41 DEFENSORA	Thornycroft, Woolston	12-1972	11-3-75	4-77
F 44 CONSTITUCÃO	Thornycroft, Woolston	3-1972	3-76	2-78
F 45 LIBERAL	Thornycroft, Woolston	5-1975	7-2-77	8-78
General-purpose type				
F 42 INDEPENDÊNCIA	Ast. Ilha das Cobras (Rio)	6-1972	2-9-74	3-78
F 43 UNIÃO	Ast. Ilha das Cobras (Rio)	6-1972	14-3-75	10-78

D: 3,200 tons (3,800 fl)
S: 30.5 kts (28 cruising on gas turbines, 22 on diesels)
Dim: 129.24 (121.92 pp) × 13.49 × 5.94 (depth includes sonar)
Range: 1,300/28, 4,200/19 (4 diesels), 5,300/17.5 (2 diesels)
A: ASW type: 1/114-mm Mk 8 Vickers automatic DP — 2/40-mm Bofors AA (I × 2) — Branik ASW system — 1 Bofors 375-mm, twin-barrel ASW system — 2 Sea Cat SAM systems (III × 2) — 6/ASW Mk 32 TT (III × 2) — 1 Lynx WG 13 helicopter — 1 depth-charge rack (5 charges)
General-purpose type: similar but without the Branik system and with a second 114-mm Mk 8 aft and 4 launchers (II × 2) for the MM 38 Exocet SSM system
Electron Equipt: Radars: 1/Plessey AWS 2 with Mk 10 IFF (air search), 1/Hollandse Signaalapparaten ZWO-6 with RRA, 2/Selenia RTN-10 X fire control
Sonars: all ships have 1/EDO 610 E; ASW ships also have 1/EDO 700 E VDS
M: CODAG propulsion, 2 Rolls-Royce Olympus TM3B gas turbines, each 28,000 hp; 4 MTU diesels, 16 cylinders in a V, each 3,940 hp coupled to one drive shaft in pairs; 2 variable-pitch Escher-Wyss props
Fuel: 450 tons diesel, 50 tons fresh water, 26 tons helicopter fuel
Endurance: 60 days **Electric:** . . . kw **Man:** 21 officers, 180 men

REMARKS: Fitted with retractable stabilizers. Branik is the name of the system devised for handling the Australian Ikara ASW missile in these ships. All have CAAIS action data system (Ferranti 1600B computers) and are equipped with Decca ECM gear.

Niteroi Vosper-Thornycroft, 1976

FRIGATES *(continued)*

Niteroi Vosper-Thornycroft, 1976

Niteroi Vosper-Thornycroft, 1976

PATROL BOATS AND CRAFT

♦ *10 Imperial Marinheiro class*

V 15 **IMPERIAL MARINHEIRO** (24-11-54)	V 20 **ANGOSTURA** (55)
V 16 **IGUATEMI** (54)	V 21 **BAHIANA** (11-54)
V 17 **IPIRANGA** (29-6-54)	V 22 **MEARIM** (8-54)
V 18 **FORTE DE COIMBRA** (11-6-54)	V 23 **PURUS** (6-11-54)
V 19 **CABOCLO** (28-8-54)	V 24 **SOLIMÕES** (24-11-54)

Imperial Marinheiro 1971

D: 911 tons **Dim:** 55.72 × 9.55 × 4.60
A: 1/76-mm — 4/20-mm AA (I × 4) **Man:** 60 men **S:** 15 kts
M: Sulzer diesels; 2 props; 2,160 hp **Fuel:** 135 tons diesel

REMARKS: Heavy tugs built in Holland. Used in customs and coast guard service. Can be converted for minesweeping or minelaying. The V-15 is used as a submarine tender. Officially designated "corvettes."

♦ *6 Piratini-class patrol craft*

	In serv.		In serv.
P 10 **PIRATINI** (ex-PGM-109)	30-11-70	P 13 **PARATI** (ex-PGM-119)	7-71
P 11 **PIRAJÁ** (ex-PGM-110)	1-71	P 14 **PENEDO** (ex-PGM-120)	9-71
P 12 **PAMPEIRO** (ex-PGM-118)	3-71	P 15 **POTI** (ex-PGM-121)	10-71

Parati 1972

PATROL BOATS AND CRAFT *(continued)*

D:	105 tons (fl)	**S:**	15.5 kts
Dim:	30.50 (29 pp) × 6.05 × 1.90	**Man:**	2 officers, 14 men
A:	1 81-mm mortar — 3 machine guns	**Range:**	1,000/15, 1,700/12
M:	4 Cummins diesels; 2 props; 1,100 hp		

REMARK: These patrol craft are based on the 95-foot WPBs of the U.S. Coast Guard.

MINE WARFARE SHIPS

♦ *6 German Schütze-class (R55) minesweepers, four ordered 4-69, two ordered 11-73*

Bldr: Abeking and Rasmussen (German Federal Republic)

	L		L
M 15 ARATU	27-5-70	**M 18 ARACATUBA**	1971
M 16 ANHATOMIRIM	4-11-70	**M 19 ABROLHOS**	7-5-74
M 17 ATALAIA	14-4-71	**M 20 ALBARDÃO**	9-74

Anhatomirim 1972

Aratu 1971

D:	230 tons (280 fl)	**Dim:**	47.20 × 7.16 × 2.10	**A:**	1/40-mm AA
S:	24 kts	**Range:**	710/20		

M: 4 Maybach diesels; 2 Escher-Wyss variable-pitch props; 4,500 hp
Fuel: 22 tons diesel **Man:** 39 men

REMARKS: Fitted for magnetic, mechanical, and acoustic minesweeping. Wooden hulls.

AMPHIBIOUS WARFARE SHIPS

♦ *2 ex-U.S. LSTs*

G 26 DUQUE DE CAXIAS (ex-*Grant County*, LST-1174) transferred 11-72
Bldr: Avondale. In serv. 11-57

Duque de Caxias

D:	3,860 tons (7,100 fl)	**Dim:**	134.70 × 16.90 × 5.50
S:	16 kts	**A:**	6/76-mm AA (II × 3)

M: 4 Nordberg diesels; 2 variable-pitch props; 14,000 hp

REMARKS: Can carry 700 men. Air-conditioned. 4 LCVP in davits; and 4 causeways (pontoon sections) which can be dropped where needed. Platform for helicopters.

G 28 GARCIA DAVILA (ex-*Outagamie County*, LST-1073) 1944

D:	1,490 tons (4,100 fl)	**Dim:**	100 × 15.25 × 3.36
M:	2 General Motors diesels; 2 props; 1,700 hp	**A:**	8/40-mm AA

REMARK: Transferred 25-5-71.

Garcia Davila 1972

♦ *4 landing craft, U.S. LCU type* — Bldr: Navy Yard, Rio, 1974-77

GUARAPARI, CAMBORIU, TIMBAU, TRAMANDAI

D:	173 tons (396 fl)	**Dim:**	41 × 9.0 × 2.0
S:	11 kts	**Range:**	1,200/10
M:	4 GM 6-71 diesels; 2 props; 1,200 hp		

♦ *28 LCVP built in Japan in 1959-60*

♦ *7 EDVP* (landing craft for vehicles and personnel). Built in Brazil in 1971. Hulls built of synthetic materials.

Dim: 11 × 3.20 × 0.60 (fwd), 1 (aft) **M:** Brazilian Scania diesel

REMARK: Can carry 36 men with full-pack or 1 jeep with trailer and 17 men or 1/105-mm howitzer or an anti-tank gun and 18 men.

RIVER PATROL CRAFT

♦ *3 river patrol craft, Roraima class*

	Bldr	L	In serv.
P 30 RORAIMA	MacLaren, Niteroi	9-11-72	21-2-75
P 31 RONDÔNIA	MacLaren, Niteroi	10-1-73	3-12-75
P 32 AMAPÁ	MacLaren, Niteroi	9-3-73	1-76

D: 340 tons (365 fl) **Dim:** 45 × 8.45 × 1.37
S: 14.5 kts **Man:** 9 officers, 54 men **Range:** 6,000/11
A: 1/40 mm AA — 6 machine guns — 2 81-mm mortars
M: 2 M.A.N. diesels; 912 hp; 2 props

REMARK: In Amazon Flotilla.

♦ *2 river patrol craft ordered in 1970 from Ilha das Cobras Naval Dockyard*

P 20 PEDRO TEIXEIRA L: 11-6-72 **P 21 RAPOSO TAVARES** L: 11-6-72

Raposo Tavares 1974

D: 700 tons **Dim:** 62.0 × 9.35 × 1.65
S: 16 kts **Range:** 5,500/10
A: 1/40-mm AA — 6 machine guns — 2/81-mm mortars
M: 4 MEP-M.A.N. diesels, V6V type; 2 props; 3,840 hp

REMARKS: Platform and hangar for one helicopter. In service 17-12-73.

HYDROGRAPHIC AND OCEANOGRAPHIC SHIPS

♦ *1 new-construction research ship, ordered 1973* — In serv. . . .

ALVARO ALBERTO

D: . . . **Dim:** 60 × 12 × 4.30
S: 13 kts **Man:** 26 men, 17 scientists

♦ *1 ex-U.S. oceanographic ship transferred in 1974*

H 41 ALMIRANTE CAMARA (ex-*Sands*, T-AGOR-6)

D: 1,020 tons (1,370 fl) **Dim:** 70 (63.70 pp) × 11.28 × 6.30 (fl)
S: 13.5 kts **Range:** 12,000/12
Man: 8 officers, 18 men, 15 oceanographers
M: Diesel-electric; 1 prop; 1,000 hp

REMARKS: An auxiliary motor powers a small maneuvering propeller for station-keeping purposes at extremely low rpm. Has echo-sounders capable of measuring 11,000-meter depths.

♦ *2 Sirius class*

	Bldr	Laid down	L	In serv.
H 21 SIRIUS	Ishikawajima	12-56	30-7-57	12-57
H 22 CANOPUS	Ishikawajima	12-56	20-11-57	3-58

Canopus

D: 1,463 tons (1,800 fl) **Dim:** 77.90 × 12.03 × 3.70
S: 15 kts **Range:** 12,000/11
Man: 102 men **M:** Sulzer diesels; 2 props; 2,700 hp

REMARKS: 1 helicopter, 1 LCVP, 3 small survey craft. Fully equipped. Controllable-pitch props. Armament removed.

♦ *6 hydrographic boats (wooden hull)*

	In serv.		In serv.
H 11 PARAIBANO	10-68	**H 15 ITACURUSSÁ**	3-71
H 12 RIO BRANCO	10-68	**H 16 CAMOCIM**	1971
H 14 NOGUEIRA DA GAMA (ex-*Jaceguai*)	3-71	**H 17 CARAVELAS**	1971

Bldr: Bormann (Rio de Janeiro)

Nogueira da Gama 1971

HYDROGRAPHIC AND OCEANOGRAPHIC SHIPS (*continued*)

D: 32 tons (50 fl) **Dim:** 16 × 4.60 × 1.30
S: 11 kts **Man:** 2 officers, 9 men
M: 1 General Motors 6-71 diesel; 165 hp **Range:** 600/11

REMARK: In Amazon Flotilla.

	Bldr	L	In serv.
U 10 ALMIRANTE SALDANHA	Vickers	19-12-33	6-34

Almirante Saldanha

D: 3,225 tons (3,825 fl) **Dim:** 92 × 15.70 × 5.50
S: 11 kts **Man:** 218 men **Range:** 12,000/10

REMARKS: Former 4-masted schooner, refit completed in 7-1961 as an oceanographic research ship. Employed in training.

H 31 ARGUS (6-12-57) — **H 32 ORION** (5-2-58) — **H 33 TAURUS** (7-1-58)
Bldr: Rio de Janeiro SY

Orion

D: 250 tons (300 fl) **Dim:** 44.80 (42.06 pp) × 6.10 × 2.45
S: 17 kts (15 cruising) **Range:** 1,200/15
M: Caterpillar diesels; 2 props; 1,200 hp **Fuel:** 35 tons diesel

REMARKS: Based on the Portuguese *Azevia*-class gunboat. H-32 modernized in 1973/74, with new propulsion machinery, auxiliaries, and electronic equipment.

AUXILIARY SHIPS

♦ *4 transports*

	Bldr	Laid down	L	In serv.
U 26 CUSTÓDIO DE MELLO	Ishikawajima (Tokyo)	12-53	10-6-54	9-54
G 16 BARROSO PEREIRA	Ishikawajima (Tokyo)	12-53	7-8-54	12-54
G 21 ARI PARREIRAS	Ishikawajima (Tokyo)	12-55	24-8-56	12-56
G 22 SOARES DUTRA	Ishikawajima (Tokyo)	12-55	13-12-56	3-57

D: 4,800 tons (8,600 fl) **Dim:** 119.20 × 16 × 6.10
S: 16 kts **Man:** 118 men. Can carry 1,972 troops (497 average)
A: 4/76-mm (U-26) — 2/76-mm and 2/20-mm on the others
Cargo capacity: 4,200 tons **M:** GT; 2 props; 2 boilers; 4,800 hp

REMARKS: Refrigerated storeroom. Living spaces mechanically ventilated and partially air-conditioned. *Custódio de Mello* is used as an underway training ship.

Custódio de Mello 1976

♦ *1 repair ship ex-U.S. LST transferred in 1963*

G 24 BELMONTE (ex-*Helios*, ARB-12, ex-LST-1127)
Bldr: Maryland Dry Dock, Baltimore. In serv. 2-54

Belmonte

AUXILIARY SHIPS (*continued*)

D: 2,030 tons (4,100 fl) **Dim:** 100 × 15.25 × 3.36
S: 9 kts **A:** 8/40-mm AA (IV × 2)
M: General Motors 5-267 diesels; 2 props; 1,800 hp **Range:** 6,000/9

REMARKS: 1/60-ton winch crane, 2/10-ton booms. Used mainly as a transport.

♦ *2 oilers*

G 27 MARAJO (31-1-68) — Bldr: Ishikawajima, Rio do Brasil

D: 7,200 tons **Dim:** 137.10 (127.69 pp) × 19.22 × 7.35
S: 13.6 kts **Range:** 9,200/14.5 **Man:** 80 men
M: 1 Sulzer diesel; 8,000 hp **Cargo capacity:** 10,500 tons

Marajo

G 17 POTENGI (16-3-38) — Bldr: Papendrecht (Holland)

D: 600 tons **Dim:** 54 × 7.20 × 1.80 **S:** 10 kts
M: Diesel; 550 hp **Cargo capacity:** 450 tons

REMARK: In Mato Grosso Flotilla.

♦ *1 submarine-rescue ship* — L: 19-3-46

K 10 GASTÃO MOUTINHO (ex-U.S. *Skylark*, ASR-20; ex-*Yustaga*, ATF-165)

D: 1,780 tons (2,140 fl) **Dim:** 62.48 × 11.73 × 4.70
S: 14.5 kts **A:** 2/76-mm, 2/40-mm AA
M: Diesel-electric; 1 prop; 3,000 hp

REMARKS: Purchased in 6-1973. Employed in hydrographic survey duties.

♦ *3 ex-U.S. ATA-class tugs*

R 21 TRITÃO (ex-ATA-234), **R 22 TRIDENTE** (ex-ATA-235), **R 23 TRIUNFO** (ex-ATA-236) launched in 1944 in U.S.A.; purchased in 1947.

D: 534 tons (835 fl) **Dim:** 43.61 × 10.34 × 4.03
S: 13 kts **A:** 2/20-mm AA
M: Diesel-electric; 1,500 hp

♦ *1 tug*

R 14 LAURINDO PITTA (Vickers, 1910, rebuilt 1969)

D: 514 tons: **Dim:** 39.04 × 7.77 × 3.35 (aft)

♦ *6 tugs* — Bldr: Holland Nautic Yard. In serv. 1953

R 31 AUDAZ, R 32 CENTAURO, R 33 GUARANI, R 34 LAMEGO, R 35 PASSO DE PATRIA, R 36 VOLUNTÁRIO

D: 130 tons **S:** 11 kts **Dim:** 27.6 × 7.2 × 3.1
M: 1 Womag diesel; 765 hp **Man:** 12 men

♦ *3 Isaias de Noronha-class tugs* — In serv. 1972-74

R . . . ISAIAS DE NORONHA **R . . . D.N.O.G.**
R . . . TENIENTE LAHMEYER

D: 1,000 tons (fl) **Dim:** 47 × . . . × . . .

♦ *1 personnel and stores transport* — Bldr: Ebraso, Santa Catarina. L: 29-8-74

R 47 SARGENTO BORGES

D: 108.5 tons **Dim:** 28 × 6.50 × 1.50
S: 10 kts **Range:** 400/10
M: 2 diesels; 2 props; 480 hp

REMARK: Can carry 106 passengers.

♦ *4 passenger ferries*

Ordered in 1974 from Inconav Niteroi Shipbuilders, delivered in 1975-76

U 40 RIO PARDO **U 42 RIO CHUI**
U 41 RIO NEGRO **U 43 RIO OIAPOQUE**

D: 150 tons **Dim:** 35.38 × 6.50 × 1.90
M: 2 diesels; 548 hp **S:** 14 kts

REMARKS: Can carry 600 passengers. Used in and around naval bases.

♦ *6 river transports built in The Netherlands in 1956*

U 20 RIO DOCE **U 23 RIO REAL**
U 21 RIO DAS CONTAS **U 24 RIO TURVO**
U 22 RIO FORMOSO **U 25 RIO VERDE**

D: 150 tons **Dim:** 35 × 6 × 2.10
M: 2 Sulzer diesels; 2 props; 450 hp **S:** 14 kts

REMARK: Can carry 600 passengers.

♦ *7 personnel launches* — Bldr: Brazil. In serv. 1965-67

ACARÁ, AGULHA, ANCHOVA, ARENQUE, ARGENTINA, ARUANA, ATUM

D: 13 tons (fl) **S:** 25 kts **Dim:** 13.0 × 3.8 × 1.2
M: 2 diesels; 280 hp **Man:** 3 men
Cargo: 12 passengers **Range:** 400/20

♦ *1 command transport ship*

G 15 PARAGUASSU

D: 285 tons **S:** 12 kts **Dim:** 40 × 7 × 1.20
M: Diesel; 1 prop **Range:** 2,500/10

REMARKS: Former river transport ship *Guarapuava*, bought in 1971, refitted for the Mato Grosso Flotilla, and used as a river buoy tender.

BRAZIL (*continued*)

AUXILIARY SHIPS (*continued*)

♦ *2 small service transports*

TENENTE FABIO, TENENTE RAUL

D:	55 tons	**S:**	10 kts
Dim:	20.28 × 5.10 × 1.20	**Range:**	350
M:	Diesel; 135 hp; 1/10-ton derrick	**Cargo capacity:**	22 tons

♦ *5 munitions lighters*

SÃO FRANCISCO DOS SANTOS (1964), **UBIRAJARA DOS SANTOS** (1968), **OPERATĨO LUIS LEAL** (1968), **MIGUEL DOS SANTOS** (1968), **APRENDIZ LÉDIO CONCEIÇÃO** (1968)

Remark: Last two for torpedoes.

♦ *2 water tankers* — L: 1957

R 43 PAULO AFONSO **R 42 ITAPURA**

D:	485.3 tons	**Dim:**	42.8 × 7.0 × 2.5
M:	1 diesel	**Cargo:**	389 tons

♦ *3 floating docks*

G 25 ALFONSO PENA (ex-U.S. ARD-14) **D:** 5,200 tons (fl) **Dim:** 150 × 24.7
G 26 ALMIRANTE J. GONCALVES (ex-U.S. AFDL-4) can lift 1,000 tons.
Dim: 60 × . . .
G 27 CIDADE DE NATAL (ex-U.S. AFDL-39) can lift 2,800 tons.
Dim: 119 × . . .

VARIOUS SHIPS

♦ *1 lighthouse and buoy tender*

	Bldr	Laid down	L	In serv.
H 34 GRACA ARANHA	Elbin, Niteroi	End 1970	23-6-74	10-76

D:	1,253 tons	**Dim:**	75.57 × 13 × 3.71
S:	13 kts	**Man:**	101 men
M:	Diesel; 1 variable-pitch prop; 2,000 hp; 1 bow thruster		

♦ *8 130-ton buoy-maintenance ships*

H 13 MESTRE JOÃO DOS SANTOS, H 24 CASTELHANOS, H 28 FAROLEIRO SANTANA, H 27 FAROLEIRO AREAS, H 30 FAROLEIRO NASCIMENTO, H . . . CABO BRANCO, H . . . CABO CALLANHAR, H . . . CABO FRIO

♦ *1 U.S. Navy YMS-type ex-minesweeper (1942)*

H . . . JAVARI (ex-*Cardinal*)

D:	270 tons (350 fl)	**Dim:**	41.45 × 7.45 × 2.45
S:	12 kts	**Range:**	2,300/8.5
M:	2 GM diesels; 2 props; 1,000 hp	**Fuel:**	19 tons diesel

Remarks: Transferred 8-60. Three sisters discarded.

BRUNEI

Personnel: 22 officers, 270 men

Merchant Marine (1976): 2 ships — 899 grt

♦ *3 guided missile patrol boats*

Bldr: Vosper-Thornycroft, Singapore

	L		L		L
N . . .	. . .	**N . . .**	. . .	**N . . .**	. . .

D:	150 tons (fl)	**Dim:**	36.8 × 7.16 × 1.73
S:	30 kts **Range:** 1,350/16	**Man:**	18 men
A:	2 MM 38 Exocet SSM — 1/40-mm Bofors AA		
M:	2 MTU 16 V538 TB90 diesels; 2 props; 7,000 hp		

Remark: To be delivered at the end of 1978.

♦ *1 Vosper Brave-class patrol boat*

Bldr: Vosper Ltd., Portsmouth (5-12-66)

P 01 PAHLAWAN

D:	95 tons (114 fl)	**Dim:**	30.26 (27.44 pp) × 7.30 × 2.15
S:	57 kts	**Man:**	3 officers, 16 men
A:	1/40-mm Bofors AA — 2/20-mm AA (II × 1) — 8 wire-guided SS-12 missiles		
M:	Bristol Marine gas turbines Proteus type; 3 props; 12,750 hp; 2 diesels are used in cruising (10 kts)		
Electron Equipt:	Decca RM 616 radar	**Range:**	450/54, 2,300/10

Remarks: Refitted in 1972 by Vosper-Thornycroft at Singapore. Wooden hull, aluminum superstructure.

♦ *3 patrol craft*

PERWIRA (5-1974) **PEMBURU** (30-1-75) **PENYARANG** (20-3-75)

Bldr: Vosper-Thornycroft, Singapore

D: 38.5 tons **Dim:** 21.40 (pp) × 6.10 × 1.20
S: 32 kts **Range:** 600/20
A: 2/20-mm (I × 2) — 2 machine guns
M: 2 MTU diesels; 2,700 hp **Electron Equipt:** Decca RM 616 radar

♦ *3 Masna-class patrol craft*

P 11 MASNA (19-9-70) **P 12 SALEHA** (18-9-70)
P 13 NORAIN (comm. 11-71)

Bldr: Vosper-Thornycroft Private Ltd., Singapore. In serv: 1971-73

D: 23.5 tons **Dim:** 18.90 × 4.80 × 1.40
S: 25/23 kts **Man:** 8 men
A: 2/20-mm Hispano and machine guns **Range:** 600/23
M: 2 GM diesels 16-cyl. Mk V 71 N; 1,240 hp
Electron Equipt: Decca RM 616 radar

REMARKS: Wooden hull, light-metal superstructure. Manned by the Brunei Malayan Regiment.

♦ *3 small patrol craft*

P 21 BENDAHARA **P 23 KEMAINDERA** **P 22 MAHARAJALELA**

D: 10 tons **Dim:** 14.10 × 3.60 × 0.90
S: 20 kts **Man:** 6 men
A: 2 machine guns **Electron Equipt:** Decca 202 radar
M: 2 General Motors diesels; 334 hp

♦ *3 police patrol craft*

Bldr: Vosper-Thornycroft, Singapore

2 17-meter: **MAKMOR, TENTERAM**

1 11-meter: **AMAN DAMAI**

♦ *25 armed river barges*

Makmor

BULGARIA

PERSONNEL: approximately 4,000 men

MERCHANT MARINE (1976): 176 ships — 933,361 grt
(tankers: 18 — 278,925 grt)

NAVAL AVIATION: 6 Soviet Hound helicopters

NOTE: For additional ships' data, see U.S.S.R. section

SUBMARINES

♦ *2 Soviet Romeo class, transferred 1971-72*

N . . . N . . .

D: 1,400 tons surfaced, 1,800 submerged **Dim:** 76 × 7 × 5.40
S: 17/15 kts **A:** 8/533-mm TT (6 forward, 2 aft)

♦ *2 Soviet Whiskey class, transferred 1958*

SLAVA **POBIEDA**

D: 1,050 tons surfaced, 1,350 tons submerged **Dim:** 76 × 6.30 × 4.80
S: 17/16 kts **A:** 6/533-mm TT (4 forward, 2 aft)

FRIGATES

♦ *2 Soviet Riga class, transferred 1957-58*

DERSKY **SMELY**

D: 1,450 tons (fl) **Dim:** 91.0 × 11.0 × 3.40 **S:** 28 kts
A: 3/100-mm DP — 3/533-mm TT — 2 ASW MBU 2500 rocket launchers

CORVETTES

♦ *3 Soviet Poti class, transferred 1975*

D: 500 tons (fl) **Dim:** 60.30 × 8.0 × 3.0 **S:** 34 kts
A: 2/57-mm AA (II × 1) — 2 MBU 2500A ASW rocket launchers — 2/533-mm ASW TT
Electron Equipt: Radars: 1/Don, 1/Strut Curve, 1/Muff Cob
Sonar: 1 high-frequency
M: CODAG, 2 M503A diesels of 4,000 hp each + 2 gas turbines of 20,000 hp each; 2 props

PATROL BOATS

♦ *3 Soviet Stenka class, transferred . . .*

D: 190 tons (fl) **Dim:** 37.5 × 8.50 × 1.80 **S:** 38 kts
A: 4/30-mm AA (II × 2) — 4/400-mm ASW TT (I × 4) — 2 depth-charge racks
M: 3 M503A diesels; 3 props; 12,000 hp

♦ *7 Soviet SO-1 class, transferred in 1963*

D: 190 tons (215 fl) **Dim:** 42.0 × 6.1 × 1.9 **S:** 25 kts
A: 4/25-mm AA — 4 ASW MBU 1800 rocket launchers — depth charges

♦ *2 Soviet Kronstadt class, transferred in 1957*

D: 300 tons (330 fl) **Dim:** 52.1 × 6.5 × 2.2 **S:** 18 kts
A: 2/37-mm AA — 3 MBU 1800 — mines

GUIDED MISSILE PATROL AND TORPEDO BOATS

♦ *3 Soviet Osa-I-class patrol boats, transferred 1970-71*

D: 175 tons (210 fl) **Dim:** 39.0 × 7.7 × 1.80
S: 36 kts **A:** 4 SS-N-2 Styx systems — 4/30-mm (II × 2)
Electron Equipt: 1/Square Tie, 1/Drum Tilt
M: 2 M503A diesels; 3 props; 12,000 hp

♦ *6 Soviet Shershen-class torpedo boats, transferred 1970*

D: 150 tons (180 fl) **Dim:** 34 × 7.2 × 1.50
S: 45 kts **A:** 4/533-mm TT — 4/30-mm AA (II × 2)
M: 3 diesels; 3 props; 12,000 hp

♦ *8 Soviet P-4-class torpedo boats, transferred 1956*

D: 19.3 tons (22.4 fl) **S:** 55 kts
A: 2/533-mm TT — 2/25-mm AA (II × 1)

MINE WARFARE SHIPS

♦ *4 Soviet Vanya-class minesweepers, transferred 1971-72*

D: 220 tons (245 fl) **Dim:** 40 × 7.6 × 1.8
S: 18 kts **A:** 2/30-mm AA

♦ *2 Soviet T-43-class minesweepers, transferred 1953*

D: 500 tons (580 fl) **Dim:** 58 × 8.4 × 2.3
S: 14 kts **A:** 4/37-mm AA

♦ *4 T-301-class minesweepers*

D: 145.8 tons (160 fl) **Dim:** 38.0 × 5.1 × 1.60
S: 12.5 kts **A:** 2/37-mm AA (I × 2)

♦ *12 small PO-2-class inshore minesweepers, transferred early 1960s*

AMPHIBIOUS WARFARE SHIPS

♦ *10 Soviet Vydra-class LCU*

D: 600 tons (fl) **Dim:** 54.8 × 8.1 × 2.0
M: Diesels; 600 hp **S:** 10.5 kts

♦ *10 German MFP-class LCU* — Bldr: Bulgaria, 1950s

VARIOUS SHIPS — nearly all built in Bulgaria

♦ *3 coastal oilers*

♦ *7 tugs*

♦ *2 salvage ships*

♦ *2 diving vessels*

♦ *6 barracks ships*

BURMA

Personnel: about 6,200, including reserves

Merchant Marine (1976): 39 ships — 68,867 grt (tankers: 2 — 1,478 grt)

FRIGATE

♦ *1 British River class, purchased in 1947*

MAYU (ex-*Fal*) — Bldr: Smith's Dock, Middlesbrough, Eng. (9-11-42)

Mayu

D: 1,460 tons (2,170 fl) **S:** 19 kts **Dim:** 93.50 × 11.16 × 4.40
A: 2/102-mm — 4/40-mm AA **Range:** 4,200/12 **Man:** 140 men
M: Triple expansion; 2 props; 5,500 hp **Boilers:** 2 **Fuel:** 440 tons

CORVETTES

♦ *1 British Algerine class purchased in 1957-58*

YAN MYO AUNG (ex-*Mariner*) — Bldr: Canada (9-5-44)

D: 990 tons (1,237 fl) **S:** 16 kts **Dim:** 68.58 × 10.82 × 3.50
A: 1/102-mm — 4/40-mm AA — fitted to plant 16 mines **Man:** 140 men
M: Triple expansion; 2 props; 2,000 hp **Boilers:** 2 **Range:** 3,000/15

♦ *2 ex-U.S. escort vessels purchased in 1965-66*

YAN GYI AUNG (ex-U.S. *Creddock*, MSF-356) — Bldr: Willamette, U.S.A. (22-7-44)

YAN TAING AUNG (ex-U.S. *Farmington*, PCE-894) — Bldr: Willamette, U.S.A. (1943)

D: 600 tons (903 fl) **Dim:** 56.24 × 10.06 × 2.80
S: 17 kts **A:** 1/76-mm — 6/40-mm AA **Man:** 80/95 men
M: General Motors diesels; 2 props; 2,400 hp

PATROL BOATS

♦ **PGM 401** to **406** (ex-U.S. 43/46 and 51/52) — Bldr: U.S.A. (1959)

D: 100 tons **S:** 16 kts **Dim:** 29 × 5.80 × 1.60
A: 1/40-mm AA — 2 machine guns **Man:** 17 men
M: 4 General Motors diesels; 2 props; 1,000 hp

♦ **MGB 101, 102, 103, 105, 106, 108, 110.** U.S.C.G.-type boats with new hulls built in 1960-61 in Burma.

D: 49 tons (66 fl) **S:** 11 kts **Dim:** 25 × 4.85 × 1.60
Man: 16 men **A:** 1/40-mm AA — 1/20-mm AA
M: 4 General Motors diesels; 2 props; 800 hp

RIVERINE PATROL VESSELS

♦ **Y 311, Y 312** — Bldr: Similak, Burma, 1967

D: 250 tons **S:** 14 kts **Dim:** 37.0 × 7.3 × 1.1
A: 2/40-mm AA (I × 2) — 2/20-mm AA (I × 2)
M: 2 Mercedes-Benz diesels; 2 props; 1,000 hp

♦ **NAWARAT, NAGAKVAY** — Bldr: Dawbon DY, Rangoon, 1961

Nawarat

D: 400 tons (450 fl) **S:** 12 kts **Dim:** 49.70 × 8.23
A: 2/25-pound guns (Army ordnance) — 2/40-mm AA **Man:** 43 men
M: 2 Paxman-Ricardo overhead diesels of 1,160 hp

♦ **Y 301** to **Y 310** — Bldr: Uljanik, Pula, 1957-60

Y-301 class

BURMA (*continued*)

RIVERINE PATROL VESSELS (*continued*)

D: 120 tons **S:** 13 kts **Dim:** 32 × 7.25 × 0.80
A: 2/40-mm AA — 2/20-mm AA **Man:** 29 men
M: 2 Mercedes-Benz diesels; 4 cylinders; 1,100 hp

VARIOUS SHIPS

♦ *8 river transports fitted with gun mounts*

SABAN, SAGU, SEINDA, SETKAYA, SETYAHAT, SHWETHIDA, SHWEPA-ZUN, SINMIN **D:** 98 tons **S:** 12 kts

♦ *10 30-to-40-ton river boats built in Burma in 1951–52*

♦ *25 30-to-40-ton river boats built in Yugoslavia in 1965*

♦ *2 hydrographic ships,* **THU TAY THI** (*1,100 tons*) *built in Yugoslavia in 1965, and* **YAY BO** (*108 tons*) *built in The Netherlands. The first has a helicopter platform.*

Thu Tay Thi

♦ *8 LCM* (*701 to 708*) *built in 1963*

♦ *1 service craft* **AIYAR LULIN** (*ex-U.S. LCU-1620*) *used as a transport*

♦ *1 torpedo transport* **YAN LONG AUNG** (*520 tons*) *built in Japan in 1967. Now used as a diving and repair tender*

CAMBODIA

Kampuchea

Before the Khmer Rouge assumed power, the Cambodian Navy had a number of American-built and French-built ships that had been transferred to it by the United States and France. Because it is difficult to get information out of Cambodia, the fate of most of these vessels is not known. A large number of them, especially the river craft, have probably been broken up or assigned to other tasks. It is known, however, that in April 1975 the corvettes E-311 (ex-*Flamberge*) and E-312 (ex-*Inconstant*) sought refuge in Thailand and Subic Bay, The Philippines, respectively, and that the LSIL landing craft P-111 and P-112 also reached Subic Bay. The ships listed here are those that, because of their value, probably still exist as part of the fleet. China may have transferred a small number of patrol craft to Cambodia in 1975–76.

PATROL CRAFT

♦ *20 U.S. PCF Swift class*

U.S. Navy Swift

Bldr: U.S.A. See South Vietnam section

D: 16 tons (21.7 fl) **Dim:** 15.66 × 4.55 × 1.50
S: 25 kts **Man:** 1 officer, 5 men
A: 2/12.7-mm machine guns — 1/81-mm mortar
M: General Motors diesels 12 V 71; 2 props; 680 hp

REMARKS: 24- to 36-hour endurance. Hull is of aluminum.

AMPHIBIOUS WARFARE VESSELS

♦ **T 916** (French *EDIC*) — Bldr: Franco-Belge, 1968

D: 292 tons (670 fl) **Dim:** 59 × 12 × 1.60 fl
A: 2/20-mm **Man:** 18 men
S: 8 kts **M:** 2 MGO diesels; 1,000 hp

AMPHIBIOUS WARFARE VESSELS (*continued*)

T 916 with PBR on cargo deck 1973

♦ *3 ex-U.S. LCU*

T 917, T 918, T 919

D: 180 tons (360 fl) **Dim:** 36.28 × 10.36 × 1.80
S: 8 kts **Man:** 14 men
A: 2/20-mm **Range:** 700/7
M: 3 diesels; 675 hp

REMARK: Can carry 150 to 400 troops.

RIVER FLOTILLA

NOTE: Numbers reflect units transferred; current status unverified.

♦ *4 small supply ships, ASPB class* — Bldr: Gunderson, U.S.A.

D: 28.7 tons **Dim:** 15.27 × 6.64 × 1.14
S: 20 kts **Man:** 1 officer, 4 men
A: 1/20-mm AA — 1/81-mm mortar aft — 2 machine guns
M: 2 General Motors 12 V 71 diesels; 2 props; 850 hp **Range:** 200/10

♦ *20 ex-U.S. LCM-6 class, AC series* — Bldr: U.S.A.

D: 75 tons (fl) **Dim:** 18.44 × 5.34 × 1.05
S: 8 kts **Man:** 1 officer, 10 men
A: 1/40-mm — 1/81-mm mortar — 1/20-mm — 12.7-mm machine guns. A few have a 105-mm mount forward. **M:** 2 diesels

AC 8 1973

♦ *23 ATC (ex-U.S. LCM 6 or 8) armored troop transports* — Bldr: U.S.A. — Hull number and letter.

D: 66 tons (fl) **Dim:** 17.07 × 5.34 × 1.02
S: 8 kts **Man:** 1 officer, 6 men
A: 1/20-mm — 2/12.7-mm machine guns — 4 grenade launchers
M: 2 diesels

REMARK: Can take a 2.5-ton truck on board, have a platform for a light helicopter.

♦ *4 MSM type river minesweepers (converted LCMs)*

Same characteristics as the ATC class above.

♦ *1 CCB Communication Command Boat* (converted LCM)

A: 1/40-mm — 1/20-mm — radio transmitters and receivers.

♦ *About 50 U.S. PBR type*

AUXILIARY SHIPS

♦ *1 floating dock, 350 tons, transferred by France 1955*

♦ *1 floating dock, 1,000 tons, transferred by U.S.A. 1972*

♦ *1 60-ton floating crane, 2 floating bases MSB class, transferred by U.S.A. 1972*

CAMEROON

PERSONNEL: 600 men

MERCHANT MARINE (1976): 23 ships — 19,445 grt

PATROL BOATS

♦ *2 Chinese Shanghai-II class, transferred 7-76*

101 **102**

D: 155 tons (fl) **S:** 28 kts **Dim:** 38.80 × 5.40 × 1.60
A: 4/37-mm AA (II × 2) — 4/25-mm AA (II × 2) **Man:** 25 men
M: 4 diesels; 4 props; 4,800 hp

♦ *1 French PR-48 class* — Bldr: Soc. Française Constructions Navales. In serv. 11-5-76

L'AUDACIEUX

D: 240 tons (fl) **Dim:** 47.50 (45.50 pp) × 7.10 × 2.50
S: 18.5 kts **Man:** 3 officers, 22 men
A: 2/40-mm AA (I × 2) **Range:** 2,000/15
M: 2 MGO diesels; 2 props; 2,400 hp

PATROL CRAFT

♦ *3 small coastal surveillance craft*

LE VALEUREUX — Bldr: Estérel Naval SY (1970)

D: 45 tons **Dim:** 26.80 × 4.97 × 1.55
S: 25 kts **Range:** . . ./15
A: 2/20-mm AA **Man:** 1 officer, 8 men
M: 2 diesels; 2 props; 960 hp

BRIGADIER M'BONGA TOUNDA — Bldr: Estérel Naval SY (1967)

D: 20 tons (fl) **Dim:** 18.15 (17.03 pp) × 4.03 × 1.10
S: 22.5 kts **Man:** 8 men
A: 1/12.7-mm machine gun
M: Caterpillar diesels D 333 TA; 2 props; 540 hp

REMARKS: Customs ship, manned by the Navy. Same characteristics as the Mauritanian *Imrag'Ni* class.

QUARTIER MAÎTRE ALFRED MOTTO — Bldr: A.C.R.E., Libreville, Gabon

D: 96 tons (fl) **Dim:** 29.10 × 6.20 × 1.85 (aft)
S: 15.5 kts **Man:** 2 officers, 15 men
A: 2/20-mm AA — 2 machine guns **M:** 2 Baudoin diesels; 1,290 hp

AMPHIBIOUS WARFARE CRAFT

♦ *1 LCM*

BAKASI — Bldr: Carena, Abidjan, Ivory Coast, 1973

D: 57 tons (fl) **Dim:** 17.50 × 4.28 × 1.30
S: 9 kts **M:** 2 Baudoin diesels; 490 hp

♦ *5 LCVP type landing craft*

SOUELLABA, INDEPENDANCE, REUNIFICATION, MANOKA, MACHTIGAL

The *Souellaba* built at the A.C.R.E., Libreville, Gabon.

D: 11 tons **S:** 10 kts

SERVICE CRAFT

♦ *2 10-ton harbor launches*

SANAGA, BIMBIA

CANADA

The Canadian Armed Forces have been completely unified. Six operational commands have been set up: Mobile Command, Maritime Command, Air Transport Command, Air Defense Command Training Command, and Material Command. The Maritime Command is in charge of the Navy ships, the ship-based aircraft, and all of the units of the former Maritime Air Command (RCAF). Its principal role is ASW, but it can also be called upon to transport men and equipment for the Mobile Command.

PERSONNEL (1977): about 14,000 men

MERCHANT MARINE (1976): 1,269 ships — 2,638,682 grt
(tankers: 65 — 272,194 grt)

NAVAL AVIATION: Made up of ship-based helicopters on ASW helicopter destroyers (DDH), maritime patrol aircraft, and ASW aircraft, formerly carrier-based but now maintained at land bases.

Identifying letters are as follows: HS (ASW helicopter), HU (supply helicopter), VS (ASW planes), MP (maritime patrol planes), VU (supply planes), VS (experimental planes).

Primary strength as follows:

— 32 ASW CHSS 2 (CH-124) Sea King helicopters (see U.S.A. section). These helicopters are armed with Mk 44 or Mk 46 torpedoes and sensors (AQS 13 sonar, for example) and are used to search for hostile submarines. Upon landing, they are automatically secured and parked in the hangar, thanks to the ingenious Bear Trap recovery system. Several are used in logistics service aboard the three replenishment oilers.

— 26 CS-2F (CP-107) ASW 2-engine Tracker aircraft (see U.S.A. section).

— 16 4-engine CL-28 (CP-121) Argus aircraft.

The CL-28 Argus is an ASW plane with an extended flight radius. **Wingspan:** 43.50. **Length:** 39.20. **Weight:** 67 tons. **Engines:** 4 Wright, each of 3,700 hp. **Speed:** 250 knots. **Search speed:** 163 knots. **Endurance:** 20 hours. **Range:** 3,900 miles. **Ceiling:** 25,000 feet. Radar dome. Can carry mines, torpedoes, depth charges, including an atomic depth charge, and air-to-surface rockets.

As a follow-on for this plane, Canada signed a contract on 25-7-76 with Lockheed for the manufacture of 18 maritime patrol aircraft based on the U.S. Navy's P-3 C Orion. The first plane is to be delivered in 5-80 and the last in 3-81. The Canadian version of the plane is designated Aurora and its equipment will differ considerably from that of the American P-3. It will be fitted not only for reconnaissance, ASW, and electronic warfare, but for detecting atmospheric and maritime pollution and for analyzing oil spills at sea. It will have a crew of twelve.

The Aurora will, of course, be given the Orion's A-NEW system based on the miniaturized computer Univac ASQ 114, which can store 65,000 words of 30 bits and has a retrieval time of 4 microseconds. This equipment integrates all the ASW information put into it. It has 36 launching chutes for dropping active and passive sonobuoys and can carry racks for 120 reserve sonobuoys in the rear of the fuselage.

The Aurora will carry ASW torpedoes or depth charges or a combination of these weapons. Its other principal systems will be:

2 ASN-84 inertial navigation computers
1 Doppler radar
1 tactical recorder flight-control director
1 tactical data link system
1 FLIR (Forward-Looking Infrared)
SLAR (Side-Looking Airborne Radar) antennas
Detectors for lasers
A low-light television pod

WARSHIPS IN SERVICE OR UNDER CONSTRUCTION AS OF 1 OCTOBER 1977

	L	Tons	Main armament
♦ *3 submarines*			
3 OBERON	1962-65	1,610	8/533-mm TT
♦ *4 destroyers*			
4 IROQUOIS	1970-71	3,551	1/127-mm DP, 2 Can. Sea Sparrow, ASW weapons, 2 Sea King helicopters
♦ *16 frigates*			
2 ANNAPOLIS	1961-63	2,400	4/76-mm DP, ASW weapons, 1 Sea King helicopter
4 MACKENZIE	1961-62	2,380	4/76-mm DP, ASW weapons
4 RESTIGOUCHE	1954-57	2,390	2/76-mm DP, Asroc, other ASW weapons
6 ST. LAURENT	1952-56	2,260	2/76-mm DP, ASW weapons, 1 Sea King helicopter

WEAPONS AND SYSTEMS

A. MISSILES

♦ **Surface-to-air missiles.** The Canadian Navy has adopted the short-range surface-air NATO Sea Sparrow for its four *Iroquois*-class destroyers. The missile is designed to attack aircraft or missiles flying at a low altitude or at a transonic speed.

The characteristics are:
Length: 3.660 m. Diameter: 0.200 m. Wingspan: 1.020 m. Weight: 204 kg.
Speed: Mach 3.5. Practical anti-aircraft range: 8,000 to 10,000 m.

The GMLS launching system, designed by Raytheon Canada, is made up of two loaders and two launchers. The launchers are fixed one to port and one to starboard, perpendicular to the axis of the ship. They are retractable and are housed in the structure forward of the bridge. Each launcher has four missiles ready to be fired. The launchers can be trained and elevated.

B. GUNS

The following guns are presently used:

— **76-mm Mk 22.** Twin DP (U.S. Mk 34 mount) mounted behind a plastic spray shield.

— Length: 50 calibers. Muzzle velocity: 822 m/s

— Maximum firing rate: 50 rounds per minute per barrel. Arc of elevation: 15° to +85°

— Maximum effective anti-aircraft range: 4,000 to 5,000 m.

Fitted on the *St. Laurent*, *Restigouche*, *Mackenzie*, and *Annapolis* classes of frigates.

— **76-mm Mk 6.** Twin barrel, automatic (Canadian model).

— Length: 70 calibers. Muzzle velocity: . . . m/s

— Maximum firing rate: 60 rounds per minute per barrel.

B. GUNS *(continued)*

— Maximum effective anti-aircraft range: 5,000 m.
Installed forward on the *Restigouche* and *Mackenzie* classes of frigates.
— **127-mm Oto-Melara-Compact**
Type (see Italy section) installed on the *Iroquois*-class destroyers.

C. ASW WEAPONS

♦ *Depth-charge and torpedo launchers:*

— British Mk 10 Limbo mortar on all destroyers and frigates
— U.S. Asroc on 4 *Restigouche*-class frigates
— U.S. Mk 32 ASW torpedo tubes on all destroyers and 12 frigates
— ASW torpedo side-throwers on 4 frigates

♦ *Torpedoes*

— U.S. Mk 43, 44, and 46 ASW torpedoes aboard ships, and the latter two aboard Sea King helicopters and maritime patrol aircraft

D. ELECTRONICS

Radars: in service:
— SPS 12 long-range air search.
— SPS 501 long-range air search (version of Dutch LWO-2) installed in *Iroquois*-class destroyers.
— SPS 10 and Sperry Mk 2 navigation surface search.
— SPQ 2 D combination search (Italian radar) installed in the *Iroquois* class.
Sonars: in service:
— SQS 501 for detection of submarines lying on the sea bottom.
— SQS 503 hull MF.
— SQS 504 towed MF, Type 503 transducer.
— SQS 505 hull LF installed in the *Iroquois* class.
— SQS 505 towed LF installed in the *Iroquois* class (SQA-502 hoist).
Tactical Data System: Litton CSS 280 system installed in the *Iroquois* class.

Okanagan 1970

SUBMARINES

♦ *3 British Oberon class, Canadian Ojibwa class, ordered 11-4-62*

	Bldr	Laid down	L	In serv.
SS 72 OJIBWA	H.M. Dockyard, Chatham	9-62	29-2-64	9-65
SS 73 ONANDAGA	H.M. DY, Chatham	6-64	25-9-65	6-67
SS 74 OKANAGAN	H.M. DY, Chatham	3-65	17-9-66	6-68

Ojibwa Shbldg. and Sh. Record

Ojibwa

SUBMARINES (*continued*)

D: 1,610 tons standard, 2,030 surfaced, 2,400 submerged
Dim: 89.92 (87.45 pp) × 8.07 × 5.48 **S:** 17.5/15
A: 8/533-mm TT (6 fwd, 2 aft) — 22 torpedoes **Man:** 6 officers, 59 men
M Diesel-electric surface propulsion, Admiralty Standard Range 1, 16-cyl. diesels; 3,700/6,000 hp

REMARKS: Same basic characteristics as the British *Oberon* class. The *Ojibwa* was begun under the name of *Onyx* for the Royal Navy and transferred while still under construction. The living spaces have been modified for Canadian weather conditions.

DESTROYERS

♦ *4 improved Iroquois class (proposed)*

REMARKS: First to be laid down 1980; last to be completed 1988.

♦ *4 Iroquois-class helicopter carriers*

	Bldr	Laid down	L	In serv.
280 IROQUOIS	Marine Industries, Sorel	1-69	28-11-70	8-72
281 HURON	Marine Industries, Sorel	1-69	3-4-71	6-73
282 ATHABASCAN	Davie S.B., Lauzon	6-69	27-11-70	9-73
283 ALGONQUIN	Davie S.B., Lauzon	9-69	23-4-71	6-73

Iroquois 1972

D: 3,551 tons (4,200 fl) **Dim:** 128.92 (121.31 pp) × 15.24 × 4.42
S: 30/29 kts **Man:** 22 officers, 258 men **Range:** 4,500/20
A: 2 BPDMS Sea Sparrow system — 1/127-mm DP — 1 Mk 10 Limbo mortar — 6 Mk 32 TT (III × 2) — 2 ASW Sea King helicopters

Electron Equipt: Radars: 1/SPS 502, 1/SPQ 2 D, 2 W M 22 directors, CSS-280 data system, TACAN
Sonars: 1/SQS 505 (hull), 1 SQS 505 (towed), 1 SQS 501 (bottomed-target)

M: COGOG propulsion; 2 five-bladed reversible-pitch props; 50,000 hp (see Remarks). **Electric:** 2,750 kw

Iroquois 1976

REMARKS: 2 Mk FT4A2 Pratt and Whitney gas turbines, 25,000 hp each, and, for a cruising speed of 18 knots, 2 Mk FT 12 H 3,3700 hp each. Two paired stacks, angled to avoid corrosion of the antennas by stack gases.

FRIGATES

♦ *2 Annapolis-class helicopter frigates*

	Bldr	Laid down	L	In serv.
265 ANNAPOLIS	Halifax Shipyards Ltd	9-61	27-4-63	8-64
266 NIPIGON	Marine Industries, Sorel	7-60	10-12-61	5-64

Annapolis 1970

FRIGATES *(continued)*

D: 2,400 tons (3,000 fl) **Dim:** 113.10 × 12.80 × 4.40 (normal)
S: 28 kts **Man:** 12 officers, 234 men
A: 2/76-mm DP Mk 22 (II × 1) fwd — 1 Mk 10 Limbo mortar — 6 ASW 324-mm TT Mk 32 (III × 2) — 1 Sea King helicopter
Electron Equipt: Radars: 1/SPS 12, 1/SPS 10, 1/Sperry Mk 2, TACAN
Sonar: 1/SQS 503, 1 SQS 504, 1/SQS 501
M: English-Electric GT; 2 props; 30,000 hp **Range:** 4,750/14
Boilers: 2 Babcock & Wilcox **Electric:** 1,400 kw

♦ *4 Mackenzie class*

	Bldr	Laid down	L	In serv.
261 MACKENZIE	Canadian-Vickers	10-58	25-5-61	10-62
262 SASKATCHEWAN	Victoria Machinery	8-59	1-2-61	2-63
263 YUKON	Burrard DD, Vancouver	10-59	27-7-61	5-63
264 QU'APPELLE	Davie S.B., Lauzon	1-60	2-5-62	9-63

Mackenzie 1972

Yukon 1972

D: 2,380 tons (2,890 fl) **Dim:** 111.50 × 12.80 × 4.10 (av)
S: 28 kts **Man:** 12 officers, 233 men
A: 4/76-mm DP (II × 1 Mk 22, II × 1 Mk 6) — 2 Mk 10 Limbo mortars — 2 ASW TT launchers
Electron Equipt: Radars: 1/SPS 12, 1/SPS 10, 1/Sperry Mk 2
Sonars: 1/SQS 503, 1/SQS 501
M: English-Electric GT; 2 props; 30,000 hp **Range:** 4,750/14
Boilers: 2 Babcock & Wilcox **Electric:** 1,400 kw

♦ *4 Restigouche class modified*

	Bldr	Laid down	L	In serv.
236 GATINEAU	Davie S.B., Lauzon	4-53	3-6-57	2-59
257 RESTIGOUCHE	Canadian-Vickers	7-53	22-11-54	6-58
258 KOOTENAY	Burrard DD, Vancouver	8-52	15-6-54	3-59
259 TERRA NOVA	Victoria Machinery	6-53	21-6-55	6-59

Gatineau 1972

D: 2,390 tons (2,900 fl) **Dim:** 113.10 × 12.80 × 4.30 (normal)
S: 28 kts **Man:** 13 officers, 237 men
A: 2/76-mm DP Mk 6 (II × 1) fwd — 1 Asroc system — 1 Mk 10 Limbo mortar
Electron Equipt: Radars: 1/SPS 12, 1/SPS 10, 1/Sperry Mk 2
Sonar: 1/SQS 501, 1/SQS 503, 1/SQS-505 (VDS)

Terra Nova 1970

FRIGATES (*continued*)

M: English-Electric GT; 2 props; 30,000 hp **Range:** 4,750/14
Boilers: 2 Babcock & Wilcox **Electric:** 1,400 kw

REMARK: *Chaudière, Columbia,* and *St. Croix* were reduced to disposal reserve in 1974.

♦ *6 St. Laurent-class helicopter frigates*

	Bldr	Laid down	L	In serv.
206 SAGUENAY	Halifax Shipyards	4-51	30-7-53	12-56
207 SKEENA	Burrard DD, Vancouver	4-51	19-8-52	3-57
229 OTTAWA	Canadian-Vickers	6-51	29-4-53	11-56
230 MARGAREE	Halifax Shipyards	9-51	29-3-56	10-57
233 FRASER	Burrard DD, Vancouver*	12-51	19-2-53	6-57
234 ASSINIBOINE	Marine Industries, Sorel	5-52	12-2-54	8-56

*Completed by Yarrows, Ltd.

Margaree J. Jedrlinic, 1974

D: 2,260 tons (2,800 fl) **Dim:** 111.5 × 12.80 × 4.20 (normal)
S: 28 kts **Man:** 13 officers, 237 men
A: 2/76-mm DP Mk 22 — 1 Mk 10 Limbo mortar — 6 ASW 324-mm Mk 32 TT (III × 2) — 1 Sea King helicopter
Electron Equipt: Radars: 1/SPS 12, 1/SPS 10, 1/Sperry Mk 2
Sonar: 1/SQS 503, 1/SQS 501, 1/SQS 504
M: English-Electric GT; 2 props; 30,000 hp **Range:** 4,750/14
Boilers: 2 Babcock & Wilcox **Electric:** 1,400 kw

REMARKS: *St. Laurent,* 205, taken out of service in 1974. *Fraser* has a lattice mast between her funnels to support a TACAN dome.

Saguenay 1972

Ottawa 1970

SUBMARINE CHASER

♦ *1 experimental hydrofoil ship*

	Bldr	L	Trials
FHE 400 BRAS D'OR	Marine Industries, Sorel	7-68	1969

(FHE for "fast hydrofoil escort")

D: 237.5 tons (fl) **Dim:** (hull) 46 × 6.55 × 5.08 (cruising)
S: 50/60 kts in calm seas **Man:** 17 men
A: 12 ASW TT (III × 4) two groups each side; never actually mounted.
M: Pratt and Whitney Mk FT 4 A gas turbine; 22,000 hp

REMARKS: Outboard length of lifting foils: 27.43 m. Draft hullborne: 7.21; draft foilborne: 1.32. At 15 knots cruising speed, a Davey-Paxman diesel (2,000 hp) drives 2 controllable-pitch props. After experiments, this ship was placed in reserve in 1971.

PATROL CRAFT

♦ *6 Royal Canadian Mounted Police cutters transferred 1975-76*

PBL 191 ADVERSUS, PBL 192 DETECTOR, PBL 193 CAPTOR, PBL 194 ACADIAN, PBL 195 SIDNEY, PBL 196 NICHOLSON (PBL-196 is a sister to AGOR-140, *Fort Steele*)

OCEANOGRAPHIC AND HYDROGRAPHIC SHIPS

	Bldr	Laid down	L	In serv.
AGOR 172 QUEST	Burrard DD, Vancouver	1967	9-7-68	8-69

Quest 1970

D: 2,130 tons **Dim:** 77.20 (71.62 pp) × 12.80 × 4.60
S: 15 kts **Man:** 56 men **Range:** 10,000/12

REMARKS: Modification of the *Endeavour* with the same machinery. Carries a helicopter. See *Endeavour* remarks.

	Bldr	L	In serv.
AGOR 171 ENDEAVOUR	Yarrows Ltd, Victoria	17-8-61	2-65

Endeavour 1970

D: 1,560 tons **Man:** 54 men including 14 scientists
S: 16 kts **Range:** 10,000/12 **Dim:** 71.85 (65.53 wl) × 11.73 × 4
M: Fairbanks-Morse 9-cylinder diesels/General Electric electric drive; 2 props; 2,960 hp

REMARKS (for both ships): Reinforced hulls for navigation in ice fields. Excellent loading equipment, cranes of 5 and 9 tons. Bulb-shaped stems. Anti-rolling and anti-pitching devices. Civilian crews.

AGOR 516 LAYMORE, former small U.S. Army coastal supply ship, modified and reclassified in 1966. L: 1944.

Laymore 1965

D: 560 grt **Dim:** 53.60 × 9.75 × 2.50
S: 10.5 kts **M:** 2 General Motors Diesels; 2 props; 1,000 hp

AGOR 140 FORT STEELE — Bldr: Canadian SB, 1955

D: 85 tons (fl) **S:** 18 kts **Dim:** 36 × 6.4 × 2.1
M: 2 Paxman Ventura diesels; 2 props; 2,800 hp

REMARKS: Acquired 1973 from Royal Canadian Mounted Police. Used mainly for training reserve personnel.

AGOR 114 BLUETHROAT (1955) Former cable ship, minelayer

D: 785 tons (870 fl) **Dim:** 47 × 9.90 × 3 **S:** 13 kts
M: Diesel; 2 props; 12,000 hp

Bluethroat 1969

OCEANOGRAPHIC AND HYDROGRAPHIC SHIPS (*continued*)

AGOR 113 SACKVILLE (1941)

D: 1,085 tons (1,350 fl) **Dim:** 62.5 × 10.1 × 4.30
S: 16 kts **M:** Triple expansion; 1 prop; 2,750 hp

Sackville 1969

REMARK: Former British Flower-class corvette, completed 1941.

REPLENISHMENT OILERS

♦ *2 multi-purpose Protecteur-class supply ships*

	Bldr	Laid down	L	In serv.
AOR 509 PROTECTEUR	St. John SB & DD (NB)	10-67	18-7-68	6-69
AOR 510 PRESERVER	St. John SB & DD (NB)	8-67	20-5-69	9-70

Preserver 1973

D: 9,000 tons (24,000 fl) **Dim:** 172 (166.42 pp) × 23.16 × 9.15
S: 20 kts **Range:** 7,500/11.5 **A:** 2/76-mm DP
Man: 15 officers, 212 men, 57 passengers
M: Canadian General Electric GT; 1 prop; 21,000 hp
Boilers: 2 **Electric:** 3,500 kw
Electron Equipt: Radar: 1/Sperry Mk 2, 1/Decca TM 969, TACAN
Cargo capacity: 13,250 tons, with 12,000 tons of distillate fuel, 600 tons of diesel oil, 400 tons of jet fuel, frozen and dry foods, spare parts, munitions, etc.

REMARKS: Flight deck, hangar space, and repair facilities for 3 Sea King helicopters. Four replenishment-at-sea stations, 1 elevator aft of the navigation bridge, 2/15-ton cranes on the afterdeck. One bow thruster. Daily fresh-water distillation capacity: 80 tons. Was to have gotten Sea Sparrow SAM in place of 76-mm, but never fitted. Can be used to carry military vehicles and troops for commando purposes. Carries four LCVPs.

♦ *1 Provider-class multi-purpose supply ship*

	Bldr	Laid down	L	In serv.
AOR 508 PROVIDER	Davie SB, Lauzon	6-61	5-7-62	9-63

Provider

D: 7,300 tons (22,000 fl) **Dim:** 168 (159.40 pp) × 23.17 × 9.15
S: 20 kts **Man:** 11 officers, 147 men **Range:** 5,000/20
Cargo capacity: 14,700 tons **M:** GT; 1 prop; 21,000 hp
Boilers: 2 **Fuel:** 1,200 tons **Electric:** 2,140 kw

REMARKS: Platform and hangar for 2 Sea King helicopters. Can carry 12,000 tons of distillate fuel, 1,200 tons of diesel, 1,000 tons of aviation gas, 250 tons of provisions, munitions, and various spare parts.

SMALL OILERS

AOC 501 DUNDALK **AOC 502 DUNDURN**

D: 950 tons **Dim:** 54.5 × 9.8 × 3.9 **S:** 10 kts
M: 1 diesel; 700 hp

SMALL OILERS (*continued*)

Dundalk 1969

AUXILIARY SHIPS

♦ *2 repair ships*

ARE 100 CAPE BRETON (ex-*Flamborough*) (7-10-44)
ARE 101 CAPE SCOTT (ex-*Beachy Head*) (27-9-44)

Bldr: Burrard D.D., Vancouver — Decommissioned (see Remarks).

Cape Scott

D: 8,450 tons (11,270 fl) **Dim:** 133.80 × 18.88 × 8.84
M: GT; 2,500 hp; 2 Foster-Wheeler boilers **S:** 11 kts

REMARKS: Purchased from the British Navy in 1951. Refitted (1958-59). Helicopter platform. Equipped as repair ships for pierside service and not expected ever to steam again.

TRAINING SHIPS

♦ *6 Bay class*

PFL	Bldr	Laid down	L	In serv.
159 FUNDY	Davie S.B., Lauzon	3-55	14-6-56	11-56
160 CHIGNECTO	Geo T. Davie Levis	10-55	26-2-57	8-57
161 THUNDER	Port Arthur S.B., Ont.	9-55	27-10-56	10-57
162 COWICHAN	Yarrows Ltd., Victoria	7-56	26-2-57	12-57
163 MIRAMICHI	Victoria Machinery	2-56	22-2-57	10-57
164 CHALEUR	Marine Industries, Sorel	2-56	17-11-56	9-57

Cowichan 1969

D: 370 tons (415 fl) **Dim:** 50 (46.05 pp) × 9.21 × 2.80
S: 15 kts **Man:** 3 officers, 35 men **Range:** 4,500/11
M: General Motors diesels; 2 props; 2,500 hp **Fuel:** 52 tons diesel

REMARKS: Former minesweepers, reclassified as Patrol Escorts in 1972 and used for training reserve personnel. Nos. 159 to 164 have taken the names of minesweepers transferred to France in 1954. Nos. 143 *Gaspé*, 146 *Comox*, 148 *Ungava*, and 157 *Trinity* were transferred to Turkey in 1958. Hull of composite construction. One 40-mm AA removed.

♦ *4 former Gate vessels*

	L		L
YMG 180 PORTE SAINT-JEAN	21-11-50	**YMG 184 PORTE DE LA REINE**	28-12-51
YMG 183 PORTE SAINT-LOUIS	21-7-52	**YMG 185 PORTE QUEBEC**	28-8-51

D: 300 tons (429 fl) **Dim:** 38 × 8.50 × 3.90
S: 11 kts **Man:** 3 officers, 20 men
M: Diesel-electric propulsion; 1 prop; 600 hp

REMARKS: Trawler-like profile; built as auxiliary minesweepers and netlayers. *Porte Dauphine* transferred to the Coast Guard. Armament removed.

♦ **QW3 ORIOLE** — Sailing yacht for training

♦ **YMT 2** — Former 13.7 meter diving tender used for cadet training since 1963.

DIVING TENDERS

♦ *1 former Italian stern trawler, purchased 1975 for conversion*

AXSL 20 . . . (ex-*Aspa Quarto*)

D: 2,500 tons (fl) **S:** 14 kts **Dim:** 72.0 × 11.9 × 5.0
M: Diesel-electric; 1 prop; . . . hp

REMARK: Tender to submersible SDL-1.

♦ **YMT 11, YMT 12** — Bldr: Ferguson, Pictou, NS, 1962-63

D: 110 grt **Dim:** 38.3 × 8 × 4 **Man:** 23 men
S: 11 kts **M:** 1 General Motors diesel; 1 prop; 228 hp

♦ *7 Ville-class former tugs* — Bldr: Russell Bros. In serv. 1944

YTS 582 BURRARD **YTS 583 BEAMSVILLE**
YTS 584 CREE **YTS 586 QUEENSVILLE**
YTS 587 PLAINSVILLE **YTS 588 YOUVILLE**
YTS 589 LOGANVILLE

Dim: 12.2 × 3.2 × 1.5 **M:** 150 hp

REMARKS: Wooden hulled. Used mainly for reserve training.

♦ *7 miscellaneous diving tenders*

YMT 6, YMT 8, YMT 9, YMT 10 — 70 tons;
YMT 1 — 40 tons; **YSD 1, YSD 2**

TUGS

♦ *2 Saint class* — Bldr: St. John DD. In serv. 1967

ATA 531 SAINT ANTHONY **ATA 533 SAINT CHARLES**

D: 600 tons (840 fl) **Dim:** 46.2 × 10.0 × 5.2
S: 14 kts **Man:** 21 men
M: 1 diesel; 1 prop; 1,920 hp

♦ *1 Clifton class* (1944)

ATA 528 RIVERTON

D: 462 tons (fl) **Dim:** 33.9 × 8.5 × 3.4
S: 11 kts **Man:** 17 men
M: 1 Sulzer diesel; 1,000 hp

♦ *5 Glen class* (1975-77)

ATA 640 GLENDYNE **ATA 641 GLENDALE** **ATA 642 GLENEVIS**
ATA 643 GLENBROOK **ATA 644 GLENSIDE**

D: 255 tons (fl) **Dim:** 28.2 × 8.5 × 4.4
S: 11.5 kts **Man:** 7 men
M: 2 diesels; 2 vertical cycloidal props

♦ *5 new Ville class* (1974)

YTS 590 LAWRENCEVILLE **YTS 591 PARKSVILLE**
YTS 592 LISTERVILLE **YTS 593 MERRICKVILLE**
YTS 594 MARYSVILLE

D: 70 tons (fl) **Dim:** 19.5 × 4.7 × 2.7
S: 9.8 kts **Man:** 4 men
M: 1 diesel; 365 hp

♦ *2 Wood class* (1944)

YMT 550 EASTWOOD **YMT 553 WILDWOOD**

D: 65 tons (fl) **Dim:** 18.3 × 4.9 × 1.5
S: 10 kts **Man:** 3 men
M: 1 diesel; 250 hp

TORPEDO-RECOVERY VESSELS

♦ **YMR 1 SONGHEE** **YMR 120 NIMPKISH** (1944)

D: 162 tons (fl) **Dim:** 22.8 × . . . × . . .
S: 8 kts **Man:** 7 men
M: 1 diesel; 400 hp

COAST GUARD

The Canadian Coast Guard is a civilian organization in the Federal Transportation Ministry. It mans some 150 ships, including two weather station cutters, 20 icebreakers, and about 30 helicopters.

♦ *2 weather cutters*

QUADRA (4-7-66) **VANCOUVER** (29-6-65)
Bldr: Burrard DD, Vancouver

Quadra 1969

D: 5,600 tons (fl) **Dim:** 121 × 15.50 × 5.30
S: 18 kts **Man:** 96 men **Range:** 8,400/14. Stabilizers
M: Turbo-electric propulsion; 2 props; 7,500 hp; 2 Babcock boilers

ICEBREAKERS

♦ *1 new construction* (proposed)

D: 33,000 tons (fl) **Dim:** 192.0 × 32.2 × 12.2
S: 20 kts **Man:** 118 men plus 56 cadets
M: CODAG; electric drive; 90,000 hp **Range:** 20,000/15

ICEBREAKERS (*continued*)

♦ 2 R-class new construction — Bldr: Burrards, Vancouver

PIERRE RADISSON L: 6-77 In serv. 1978
N . . . In serv. 1979

Pierre Radisson 1977

D: 8,180 tons (fl) **S:** 13.5 kts **Dim:** 98.15 (87.9 pp) × 19.50 × 9.91
M: Diesel-electric: 6 Montreal Loco MLW 25IV-16F diesels (17,580 hp total); 6 G.E.C. alternators (11,100 kw); 2 G.E.C. motors; 2 props; 13,600 hp
Man: 75 men **Range:** 15,000/13.5

REMARKS: Telescopic hangar and flight deck for one Bell-212 helicopter. Passive tank stabilization. Will be used on St. Lawrence River and Great Lakes in winter, in Arctic in summer.

NORMAN MCLEOD ROGERS (1969) Bldr: Vickers, Montreal

Norman McLeod Rogers 1970

D: 6,320 tons (fl) **Dim:** 90 × 19.5 × 6.1 **S:** 15 kts
M: CODAG: 4 diesels, 2 GT; electric drive; 2 props; 12,000 hp

REMARKS: Also navigation tender. Two helicopters.

LOUIS S. ST. LAURENT (3-12-66)
Bldr: Vickers, Montreal

Louis S. St. Laurent 1970

D: 13,000 tons (fl) **Dim:** 111.80 × 24.39 × 9.45 **S:** 17.5 kts
M: Turbo-electric propulsion; 3 props; 24,000 hp
Range: 16,000/13

REMARKS: Quarters for 216 men. 2 helicopters.

JOHN CABOT (1965)
Bldr: Vickers, Montreal
D: 6,375 tons (fl) **Dim:** 94 × 18 × 6.45 **S:** 15 kts
M: Diesel-electric propulsion: 9,000 hp
Range: 10,000/12 **Man:** 85 men

REMARK: Equipped as a cable layer and repair ship also.

JOHN A. MACDONALD (1959)
Bldr: Davie SB, Lauzon
D: 9,160 tons (fl) **Dim:** 96 × 21.30 × 8.55 **S:** 15.5 kts
M: Diesel-electric propulsion; 15,000 hp

REMARK: One helicopter.

ICEBREAKERS *(continued)*

John Cabot 1969

MONTCALM (1957) **WOLFE** (1959)

D: 3,005 tons (fl) **Dim:** 72.7 × 14.6 × 4.9 **S:** 13 kts
M: Reciprocating steam; 2 boilers; 2 props; 4,000 hp

REMARK: One helicopter.

LABRADOR (1954) Transferred from RCN, 1958

D: 6,490 tons (fl) **Dim:** 88.5 × 19.4 × 8.8 **S:** 16 kts
M: 6 diesels, electric drive; 2 props; 10,000 hp

REMARKS: Patterned after U.S. Coast Guard Wind class. Two helicopters.

D'IBERVILLE (1953)

D: 9,930 tons (fl) **Dim:** 94.6 × 20.3 × 9.2 **S:** 15 kts
M: Reciprocating steam; 2 props; 10,800 hp

REMARK: One helicopter.

VARIOUS SHIPS

♦ *27 navigation tenders* (most also icebreakers)

	In serv.	D	hp
NAMAO	1975	370 tons (fl)	1,350
GRIFFON	1970	3,096 tons (fl)	4,000
BARTLETT	1970	1,620 tons (fl)	1,760
PROVO WALLIS	1970	1,620 tons (fl)	1,760
ROBERT FOULIS	1969	260 tons (fl)	960
TRACY	1968	1,300 tons (fl)	2,000
J. E. BERNIER	1967	3,096 tons (fl)	4,250
NARWHAL	1963	2,064 grt	2,000
MONTMAGNY	1963	565 tons (fl)	1,000
SIMCOE	1962	1,300 tons (fl)	2,000
THOMAS CARLETON	1960	1,532 tons (fl)	2,000
SIMON FRASER	1960	1,876 tons (fl)	2,900
TUPPER	1959	1,876 tons (fl)	2,900
SIR WM ALEXANDER	1959	3,565 tons (fl)	4,250
CAMSELL	1959	3,072 tons (fl)	4,250
SIR H. GILBERT	1959	3,000 tons (fl)	4,250
ALEXANDER HENRY	1959	2,497 tons (fl)	3,550
VERENDRYE	1959	400 tons (fl)	760
MONTMORENCY	1957	1,006 tons (fl)	1,200
SIR JAS. DOUGLAS	1956	720 tons (fl)	1,000
WALTER E. FOSTER	1954	2,715 tons (fl)	2,000
ALEX. MACKENZIE	1950	720 tons (fl)	1,000
EDWARD CORNWALLIS	1949	3,700 tons (fl)	2,800
ERNEST LAPOINTE	1941	1,675 tons (fl)	2,000
N. B. McLEAN	1930	5,034 tons (fl)	6,500
NOKOMIS	—	64 tons (fl)	120
KENOKI	—	270 tons (fl)	940

♦ *11 search and rescue cutters*

ALERT (1969)

D: 2,025 tons (fl) **Dim:** 71.5 × 12.2 × 4.6 **S:** 18.8 kts
M: Diesel-electric; 2 props; 7,716 hp **Range:** 6,000

REMARKS: One helicopter. Was to have been prototype for a class of several.

DARING (ex-*Wood*) (1958) Transferred from RCMP, 1971

D: 600 tons (780 fl) **Dim:** 54.3 × 8.8 × 3.0 **S:** 16 kts
M: 2 Fairbanks-Morse diesels; 2 props; 2,660 hp

RACER, RALLY, RAPID, READY, RELAY, RIDER (all 1963)

Rapid 1969

VARIOUS SHIPS (*continued*)

D: 153 grt **Dim:** 29 × 6.1 × 2.0 **S:** 20 kts
M: 4 Cummins diesels; 2 props; 2,400 hp

REMARK: Patterned after U.S. Coast Guard Cape class

SPINDRIFT, SPRAY, SPUME (1963-64)

D: 57 grt **Dim:** 21.4 × 5.1 × 1.4 **S:** 19 kts
M: 2 Paxman diesels; 2 props; 1,050 hp

♦ *14 motor rescue lifeboats*

CG 101-109, CG 114-118 — 18 tons

REMARK: Patterned after U.S.C.G. craft.

♦ *6 hydrographic survey and soundings vessels*

BEAUPORT, DETECTOR, NICOLET, VILLE MARIE, GLENDALE, JEAN BOURDON — all under 1,000 tons (fl)

♦ *2 cargo ships for northern supply, British LCT(8) class*

EIDER, SKUA (1946)

D: 1,100 grt **Dim:** 70.5 × 11.6 × 2.1 **S:** 9 kts
M: 2 diesels; 2 props; 1,000 hp

REMARK: Former medium landing ships, bought 1957, 1961.

♦ *5 river tenders*

DUMIT, ECKALOO, MISKANAW, TEMBAH, NAHIDIK

♦ *2 training ships*

MIKULA — D: 617 tons (fl) — former lightship
SKIDEGATE — D: 200 tons (fl) — former navigation tender

ROYAL CANADIAN MOUNTED POLICE

About 30 small patrol craft. Most larger units transferred to the Ministry of Defense in 1975-76.

Personnel: 23,800 men, including 3,800 Marines and more than 1,400 officers. Civil Service personnel with a more or less military status number about 6,600.

Merchant Marine (1976): 142 ships — 409,756 grt (tankers: 7 — 84,971 grt)

Naval Aviation: Established in 1923, in 1930 it was merged with the aviation arm of the military, Fuerza Aera de Chile, but re-established in 1953. However, its growth has been restrained by the Air Force, which retains responsibility for the airspace over the ocean. The naval air arm has about 23 aircraft (5 HU-16B, 3 PBY-3A Catalina, 4 SP-2E Neptune, 5 Beech C-45, 5 C-47, 1 Beech D-18S) and about 24 helicopters (4 Bell Jetranger for ASW, 4 UH-19, 2 UH-1D, 14 Bell 47G).

WARSHIPS IN SERVICE OR UNDER CONSTRUCTION AS OF 1 OCTOBER 1977

	L	Tons	Main armament
♦ *2 submarines*			
2 OBERON	1973	1,610	8/533-mm TT
♦ *2 cruisers*			
1 TRE KRONOR	1944	8,200	7/152-mm AA, 4/57-mm AA, 6/533-mm TT
1 BROOKLYN	1937	9,700	15/152-mm, 8/127-mm
♦ *5 destroyers*			
2 ALMIRANTE WILLIAMS	1958	2,730	4/102-mm DP, 4 Exocet
2 ALLEN M. SUMNER	1944	2,200	6/127-mm DP
1 FLETCHER	1943	2,050	4/127-mm DP, 5/533-mm TT
♦ *2 frigates*			
2 LEANDER	1972-73	2,450	2/114-mm DP, 4 Exocet
♦ *4 torpedo boats*	1965-66	134	2/40-mm AA, 4/533-mm TT
♦ *6 patrol ships and boats of various types*			

WEAPONS AND SYSTEMS

The greatest part of the materiel and equipment of the Chilean Navy is of U.S. or British origin. Among the most modern weapons are the guns on board the cruiser *Almirante Latorre* and the *Almirante Williams*-class destroyers.

♦ 152-mm Bofors:

This gun is mounted in twin- or triple-barreled turrets; dates from 1942 and is on board the *Almirante Latorre.*
- — Muzzle velocity: 900 m/sec
- — Arc: +70°
- — Maximum firing rate: 10 rounds/minute/barrel
- — Projectile: 46 kg
- — Maximum range surface target: 26,000 m
- — Maximum range surface target (effective): 15,000 m
- — Maximum range air target (effective): 10,000 m

♦ 102 Vickers AA

Single-barrel automatic mount on the *Almirante Williams* and the *Almirante Riveros.* Dates from 1955. Not used by any other navy.
- — Turret weight: about 26 tons
- — Muzzle velocity: 900 meters/second
- — Arc: +75°
- — Maximum firing rate: 40 rounds/minute

CHILE

- — Projectile: 16 kg
- — Maximum range surface target: 18,500 m
- — Maximum range surface target (effective): 12,000 m
- — Maximum range air target: 12,000 m
- — Maximum range air target (effective): 8000 m

♦ Missiles

The Chilean Navy has adopted the French MM38 Exocet anti-ship system and the British Sea Cat short-range SAM.

SUBMARINES

♦ *2 British Oberon class*

	Bldr	Laid down	L	In serv.
S 22 O'BRIEN	Scott Lithgow	1970	22-12-72	1976
S 23 HYATT	Scott Lithgow	1971	26-9-73	1977

O'Brien Scotts, 1974

D: 1,610 tons standard, 2,030 surfaced, 2,400 submerged
Dim: 89.92 (87.45 pp) × 8.07 × 5.48 **S:** 17.5/15 kts **Man:** 65 men
A: 8/533-mm TT (6 fwd, 2 aft) — 22 torpedoes
M: Diesel-electric propulsion; Admiralty Standard Range 1 diesels; 3,700/6,000 hp

Remark: Delivery of these submarines was a year late because of a number of malfunctions in the electrical equipment.

Note: The former U.S. fleet submarine *Simpson* (ex-*Spot,* SS-413) is retained as a training unit but is not operational.

CRUISERS

♦ *1 Swedish Tre Kronor class purchased in 7-1971*

	Bldr	Laid down	L	In serv.
04 ALMIRANTE LATORRE (ex-*Göta Lejon*)	Eriksberg	9-43	17-11-45	15-12-47

CRUISERS (*continued*)

Almirante Latorre 1972

D: 8,200 tons (10,000 fl) **Dim:** 182 (174 wl) × 16.50 × 6.50
S: 33 kts **Man:** 26 officers, 429 men (peace), 30 officers, 618 men (war)
A: 7/152-mm AA (III × 1, II × 2) — 4/57-mm AA — 11/40-mm AA — 6/533-mm TT (III × 2) — 2 depth charge racks — 120 mines
Electron Equipt: Radars: 1/LW 03 (Dutch), 1/277 and 1/293 (British), Band I fire control
Armor: Belt: 80-100 Main deck: 40 to 60 — Turrets: 135 (fwd), 30 (sides), 50 (top)
M: De Laval GT; 2 props; 100,000 hp
Boilers: 4 Penhoët, 32 kg pressure, superheat to 375°C

♦ *1 U.S. Brooklyn class*

	Bldr	Laid down	L	In serv.
03 CAPITAN PRAT (ex-*Nashville*, CL-43)	New York SB Corp.	5-34	2-10-37	11-38

D: 9,700 tons (13,500 fl) **Dim:** 185.33 × 18.80 × 7
S: 30/25 kts **Man:** 890/970 men
A: 15/152-mm (III × 5) — 8/127-mm (I × 8) — 28/40-mm AA (VI × 4, II × 2) — 24/20-mm AA (II × 12) — 1 Jetranger helicopter
Electron Equipt: Radar: 1/SPS-6, 2/SPS-4
Armor: Belt: 76 to 127. Main Deck: 76. Upper Deck: 52. Turrets: 127.
M: Westinghouse GT; 4 props; 100,000 hp **Range:** 14,500/15
Boilers: 8 Babcock & Wilcox, 31 kg pressure **Fuel:** 2,100 tons

REMARKS: Bought 1951, refitted in U.S.A. 1957-58. Sister *O'Higgins* (ex-*Brooklyn*, CL-40) is an accommodations hulk.

DESTROYERS

♦ *2 Almirante Williams class*

	Bldr	Laid down	L	In serv.
D 18 ALMIRANTE RIVEROS	Vickers-Armstrong	12-4-57	12-12-58	31-12-60
D 19 ALMIRANTE WILLIAMS	Vickers-Armstrong	20-6-56	5-5-58	26-3-60

D: 2,730 tons (3,300 fl) **Dim:** 122.50 (113.99 pp) × 13.10 × 3.90
S: 34.5 kts **Man:** 17 officers, 249 men **Range:** 6,000/16
A: 4/102-mm DP (I × 4) — 6/40-mm AA — 4 MM 38 Exocet — 2 Sea Cat SAM systems (IV × 2) — 6 ASW TT Mk 32 (III × 2) — 2 ASW squid mortars

Almirante Riveros 1976

Electron Equipt: Radar: Plessey AWS-1
M: Parsons-Pamatreda GT; 2 props; 2 Babcock & Wilcox boilers; 50,000 hp

REMARK: Refitted in Great Britain: D-19 in 1971-74; D-18 in 1973-75.

♦ *2 U.S. Allen M. Sumner FRAM II class, delivered 1-74*

	Bldr	L	In serv.
D 17 PORTALES (ex-*Douglas H. Fox*, DD-779)	Federal SB	13-3-44	17-5-44
D 16 ZENTENO (ex-*Charles S. Sperry*, DD-697)	Todd-Pacific	30-9-44	26-12-44

D: 2,200 tons (3,300 fl) **Dim:** 114.75 × 12.45 × 3.80 (light)
S: 30 kts **Range:** 1,260/30 — 4,600/15
A: 6/127-mm DP 38 cal. (II × 3) — 6/324-mm ASW TT Mk 32 (III × 2) — 2 hedgehogs — 1 helicopter
Man: 14 officers, 260 men
Electron Equipt: Radars: 1/SPS-40 (D-17) or SPS-37 (D-16), 1/SPS-10
Sonar: 1/SQS-40 (with VDS)
M: GT; 2 props; 60,000 hp **Boilers:** 4 Babcock **Fuel:** 650 tons

Portales 1975

DESTROYERS *(continued)*

Zenteno 1975

♦ *1 U.S. Fletcher class, transferred in 1962*

	Bldr	L	In serv.
D 14 BLANCO ENCALADA	Bath Iron Wks.	7-8-43	10-43

(ex-*Wadleigh,* DD-689)

D: 2,050 tons (2,850 fl) **Dim:** 114.85 × 12.03 × 5.50
S: 30 kts **Man:** 15 officers, 247 men **Range:** 1,260/30; 4,400/15
A: 4/127-mm DP 38-cal (I × 4) — 6/76-mm AA (II × 3) — 5/533-mm TT (V × 1) — 2 ASW torpedo racks — 2 hedgehogs — 1 depth-charge rack
Electron Equipt: Radars: 1/SPS 6, 1/SPS 10 — Sonar: 1/SQS 29
M: General Electric GT; 2 props; 60,000 hp
Boilers: 4 Babcock & Wilcox

FRIGATES

♦ *2 British Leander class ordered 14-1-70*

	Bldr	Laid down	L	In serv.
PF 06 CONDELL	Yarrow & Co	6-71	6-12-72	21-12-73
PF 07 LYNCH	Yarrow & Co	12-72	12-6-73	1975

D: 2,450 tons (2,900 fl) **Dim:** 113.38 (109.73 pp) × 12.50 × 5.49 (fl)
S: 27 kts **Range:** 4,500/12 **Man:** 263 men
A: 2/114-mm Mk VI DP (II × 1) — 4 MM 38 Exocet — 1 Sea Cat SAM system (IV × 1) — 2/20-mm AA — 6/324-mm ASW TT Mk 32 (III × 2) — 1 helicopter
Electron Equipt: Radars: 1/965, 1/992 Q, 1/978, 1/GWS 22
Sonars: 1/177, 1/170 B, 1/162
M: General Electric GT; 2 props
Boilers: 2 Babcock & Wilcox **Fuel:** 460 tons

Condell J. C. Bellonne, 1974

TORPEDO BOATS

♦ *4 German Lürssen class*

81 FRESIA — 82 GUACOLDA — 83 QUIDORA — 84 TEHUALDA
Bldr: Bazan (Cadiz) (1965-66)

Fresia 1970

D: 134 tons (fl) **Dim:** 36 × 5.60 × 2.20
A: 2/40-mm AA — 4/533-mm TT **Man:** 20 men **S:** 33/32 kts
M: 2 Mercedes-Benz diesels; 2 props; 4,800 hp **Range:** 1,500/15

CORVETTES

63 SERGENTE ALDEA (ex-U.S. tug *Arikara,* ATF-98
D: 1,235 tons (1,675 fl) **Dim:** 61.70 × 11.60 × 4.70
S: 15 kts **Man:** 85 men
A: 1/76-mm DP — 2/20-mm AA
M: Diesel-electric; 1 prop; 3,000 hp
Electron Equipt: 1/SPS-5 radar

REMARKS: Transferred 7-6-71. Used as a patrol ship.

CORVETTES (*continued*)

Sergente Aldea 1975

♦ **60 LIENTUR — 62 LAUTARO** — Bldr: Levingston SB Orange, Texas (1944)

D: 534 tons (835 fl) **Dim:** 43.90 × 10.15 × 5.20
A: 1/76-mm DP — 2/20-mm AA **S:** 12.5 kts **Man:** 46 men
M: General Motors diesels, 2 props, 1,500 hp **Fuel:** 187 tons diesel
Electron Equipt: Radar: 1/SPS-5

Lautaro 1970

♦ *1 U.S. PC-1638 class* — Bldr: ASMAR, Talcahuano, 1971

P 37 PAPUDO

D: 280 tons (350 fl) **S:** 20 kts **Dim:** 54.0 × 7.0 × 3.1
A: 1/40-mm AA — 4/20-mm AA (II × 2) — 1 trainable hedgehog — 4 depth-charge throwers — 2 racks
M: 2 General Motors diesels; 2 props; 4,800 hp

Remark: Identical to the Turkish *Sultanhisar.*

PATROL CRAFT

♦ *2 small trawlers purchased in 1966*

PC 76 CABO ODGER — PC 75 MARINERO FUENTALBAS

Bldr: A.S.M.A.R., Chile (1966-67). Profile of U.S. type trawler.

D: 215 tons **Dim:** 24.40 × 6.40 × 2.75 **S:** 9 kts
A: 1/20-mm **M:** 1 Cummins diesel; 340 hp **Range:** 2,600/9

HYDROGRAPHIC SURVEY AND RESEARCH SHIPS

♦ **AGS 64 YELCHO** (ex-U.S. tug *Tekesta* ATF-93, 1943), transferred 1960

Yelcho 1970

D: 1,235 tons (1,675 fl) **Dim:** 62.50 × 11.65 × 4.70
A: 1/76-mm — 2/20-mm AA **Man:** 5 officers, 59 men
S: 16.5 kts **M:** diesel-electric propulsion; 3,000 hp.

Remarks: Used for oceanographic research in the Antarctic. A new survey ship is planned.

♦ *1 Antarctic patrol ship, transport, and research*

	Bldr	Laid down	L	In serv.
AP 45 PILOTO PARDO	Haarlemsche Scheepsbouw	1957	1958	8-58

D: 1,250 tons (2,545 fl) **Dim:** 83 × 11.90 × 7.40 (fl)
S: 14 kts **Man:** 44 men, 24 passengers **Range:** 6,000
M: Diesel-electric propulsion; 1 prop; 2,000 hp

Remarks: Armament removed; carries 2 Bell 47G helicopters.

PATROL CRAFT *(continued)*

Piloto Pardo

AUXILIARY SHIPS

♦ *3 tankers*

AO 55, N . . .

D: approx. 30,000 (fl) **S:** . . . **Dim:** 176.1 × 25.5 × . . .
M: Diesels; 18,300 hp

Remarks: 19,500 tons deadweight. Ordered 1976 from ASMAR, Talcahuano.

AO 53 ARAUCANO — Bldr: Burmeister and Wain (21-6-66)

Araucano 1969

D: 18,030 tons (fl) **Dim:** 160.93 × 21.95 × 8.80
A: 8/40-mm AA (II × 4) **S:** 17 kts
M: Babcock & Wilcox diesel, type 62 VT 2 BF 140 9-cyl. 1 prop; 10,800 hp

Remark: Can replenish two ships at sea simultaneously.

AOG 54 BEAGLE (ex-U.S. *Genesee*, AOG-8) transferred in 7-72

Beagle 1972

D: 1,850 tons (light) (4,570 fl) **Dim:** 93.50 × 13.60 × 4.75
S: 14 kts **Range:** 6670/10
A: 2/76-mm DP (I × 2) — 2/20-mm AA **M:** Diesel electric; 3,100 hp

♦ *9 transports*

AP 47 AQUILES (ex-Danish *Tjaldur*) — Bldr: Aalborg Vaerft (1953)

Aquiles 1973

D: 1,395 tons **S:** 16 kts **Dim:** 82 × 13.42 × 5.20
A: 1/40-mm AA **Man:** 32 men, 406 passengers
M: B and W diesel; 1 prop; 3,600 hp **Range:** 5,500/16

Remark: Former mixed-cargo ship purchased in 1967.

AUXILIARY SHIPS (*continued*)

AP 91 AGUILA (ex-U.S. *Aventinus*, ARVE-3, ex-LST-1092)
Bldr: U.S.A. (25-3-45)

D: 1,600 tons (fl) **Dim:** 100.04 × 15.24 × 4.35 **S:** 11 kts
M: General Motors diesels; 2 props; 1,800 hp **Range:** 6,000/11

REMARKS: Transferred in 1964. Repair ship fittings dismantled; used as transport.

AP 88 COMMANDANTE HEMMERDINGER (ex-U.S. *New London County*, T-LST-1066)
AP 89 COMMANDANTE ARAYA (ex-U.S. *Nye County*, T-LST-1067)
AP 97 COMMANDANTE TORO (ex-U.S. T-LST-277)
Bldr: U.S.A. 1943-44.

D: 4,080 tons (fl) **Dim:** 100.04 × 15.24 × 4.35 **S:** 11 kts
M: General Motors diesels; 2 props; 1,700 hp. **Range:** 6,000/11

REMARKS: One transferred in February and two in August 1973. No armament; former U.S. Military Sealift Command ships.

AP 94 OROMPELLO — U.S.A. (1963-64) **AP 95 ELICURA** — ASMAR (1968)

D: 290 tons (750 fl) **Dim:** 43.90 (42.05 pp) × 100.37 × 6.90
S: 10.5 kts **Man:** 20 men
A: 3/20-mm AA **Range:** 2,900/9
M: Diesel; 2 props; 900 hp **Fuel:** 77 tons diesel

AP 110 METEORO — Bldr: ASMAR, 1967
AP . . . HUEMEL (1975)

D: 205 tons (fl) **S:** 8 kts **Dim:** 24.4 × 6.7 × . . .
M: Diesel **Man:** 220 passengers (ferries)

♦ *A few U.S.-design LSM and LCVP for logistic support duties*

VARIOUS SHIPS

♦ *1 training ship*

	Bldr	L	In serv.
BE 43 ESMERALDA (ex-*Don Juan de Austria*)	Bazan, Cadiz	12-5-53	9-54

D: 3,673 tons **Dim:** 94.10 × 13.10 × 8.70 **S:** 11 kts
A: 4/47-mm **Man:** 271 men, 80 midshipmen **Range:** 8,000/8
M: Fiat diesel; 1,400 hp

REMARKS: Four-masted schooner, ordered by Spain, sold to Chile in 1953. Similar to the Spanish *Juan Sebastian de Elcano*.

Esmeralda 1973

♦ *1 hospital ship, modified U.S. PGM-59 class*

111 CIRUJANO VIDELA — Bldr: ASMAR, Talcahuano, 1964

D: 140 tons (fl) **S:** 14 kts **Dim:** 31 × 6.5 × 2.0
M: 2 diesels; 2 props; 700 hp

♦ *1 buoy tender and beacon-repair ship*

ATA 73 COLO COLO — Bldr: England (1929)

D: 790 tons **Dim:** 41.38 × 8.72 × 4.07 **S:** 13 kts (11 cruising)
M: Reciprocating 1 prop; 1,500 hp

♦ *6 tugs*

YT . . . GALVEZ — Bldr: Southern Shipbuilders, G.B., 1975

D: 112 grt **S:** . . . **Dim:** 25.5 × 7.3 × 2.8

YT 104 ANCUD, YT 105 MONREAL, YT 120 REYES, YT 127 CAUPOLICAN, YT 128 CORTEZ

♦ *2 3,000-ton-capacity floating docks*

132 MUTILLA (ex-U.S. ARD-32), leased 15-12-60
131 INGENIERO MERY (ex-U.S. ARD-25), bought 20-8-73

D: 5,200 tons **Dim:** 150.1 × 25.6 × 1.7

CHINA

People's Republic of China

Today, the Chinese Navy is the size of a little finger. I hope that in a few years it will be a bit larger than a thumb.

MAO TSE-TUNG

PERSONNEL: 265,000 men in the following categories:
Navy: 207,000
Naval Air Arm: 30,000
Marines: 28,000

MERCHANT MARINE (1976): 551 ships — 3,588,726 grt (tankers: 64 — 895,081 grt)

NAVAL AVIATION: The Naval Air Arm, which is under the control of the Navy, probably consists of more than 700 aircraft, including 500 MIG-17, MIG-19, or F-9 interceptors, 100 light bombers such as the IL-28 and TU-2, and about 100 transport planes, seaplanes, and helicopters. Its principal mission is the defense of the coast and the protection of naval surface forces near the coast. It is believed that a few of the aircraft are equipped for minelaying. Control of naval aircraft is integrated with the continental air defense system. Some of the recently purchased French Super Frélon helicopters may belong to the Navy.

WARSHIPS IN SERVICE OR UNDER CONSTRUCTION AS OF 1 OCTOBER 1977

	L	Tons	Main armament
♦ *62-68 submarines*			
1 HAN CLASS	1971?	. . .	torpedoes
1 SOVIET GOLF	. . .	2,300	3 ballistic missiles, 10/533-mm TT
40-45 SOVIET ROMEO	1964 on	1,400	8/533-mm TT
20-21 SOVIET WHISKEY	1960-64	1,050	6/533-mm TT
♦ *10 destroyers*			
6 LUTA	1970 on	3,500	4/130-mm, 6 Styx
4 SOVIET GORDY	1938-40	1,660	4/130-mm, 4 Styx
♦ *14 frigates*			
3 KIANG HU	1974 on	1,800	2/100-mm, 4 Styx
2 KIANG TUNG	1972 on	1,800	4/100-mm, 2 SAM
5 KIANGNAN	1966-68	1,500	3/100-mm
4 SOVIET RIGA	1953-56	1,450	3/100-mm, 2 Styx
♦ *98-99 guided missile boats*			
♦ *250 torpedo boats*			
♦ *over 650 patrol boats and patrol craft*			
♦ *23 minesweepers*			

SUBMARINES

♦ *1 Han-class nuclear submarine*

	Bldr	In serv.
N . . .	Luta	1974

♦ *1 Soviet Golf-class ballistic missile submarine*

D: 2,300 tons surfaced, 2,750 submerged **Dim:** 98.80 × 8.50 × 6.50
S: 14 kts submerged
A: 3 ballistic missiles — 10/533-mm TT (6 fwd, 4 aft)

REMARKS: Plans furnished by the Soviet Union during that period when relations between the two countries were good. The medium-range missiles are possibly of Chinese origin.

♦ *40 to 45 Soviet Romeo-class submarines, built in China*

Chinese Romeo-class submarine 1975

D: 1,400 tons surfaced, 1,800 submerged **Dim:** 75 × 7 × 5.40
S: 15.5 kts submerged
A: 8/533-mm TT (6 fwd, 2 aft) — 18 torpedoes or 36 mines

♦ *20/21 Soviet W-class submarines*

D: 1,050 tons surfaced, 1,350 submerged **Dim:** 76 × 6.3 × 4.80
S: 17/16 kts
A: 6/533-mm TT (4 fwd, 2 aft) — 14 torpedoes

REMARKS: A few were delivered by the U.S.S.R., the others built in China, probably at the Chiang Nan shipyard at Kao Chang Miao, near Shanghai.

DESTROYERS

♦ *6 Luta-class guided missile destroyers* — In serv. 1972-74

D: ca. 3,500 tons **Dim:** 130 × 13.70 × 4.60 **S:** 32 kts
A: 4/130-mm (II × 2) — 8/57-mm or 37-mm AA (II × 4) — 4/25-mm AA (II × 2) — 6 systems similar to Styx (III × 2)
M: GT; 2 props; 45,000 hp **Range:** 4,000/15 **Man:** 200 men

DESTROYERS (*continued*)

Luta-class destroyer 1974

Remarks: Some systems of Soviet design; superficially resembles Kotlin but is larger and has flat transom stern, larger superstructure, etc.

♦ *4 Gordy-class guided missile destroyers, transferred by the U.S.S.R.* — L: 1936 to 1941

ANSHAN, CHANG CHUN, CHI LIN, FU CHUN (all transferred 1955)

D: 4,500 tons (fl) **Dim:** 13.8 × 4.50 × 5 **Man:** 197 men
S: 38 kts when built, certainly much less today.
A: 4/130-mm (I × 4) — 8/37-mm AA (II × 4) — 4 Styx systems (II × 2)
M: GT; 2 props; 48,000 hp **Boilers:** 3 **Fuel:** 350 tons
Range: 800/38, 3,600/20

Remark: Ex-Soviet *Razyashchy, Reshitelny, Retivy,* and *Resky,* all built in Far East.

FRIGATES

♦ *3 Kiang Hu-class guided missile frigates (1975-)*

D: 1,800 tons (2,200 fl) **S:** 28 kts **Dim:** 103 × 12 × 4.0
A: 2/100-mm DP — 4 systems similar to Styx (II × 2) — 8/37-mm AA (II × 4) — 2 MBU 1800 — 2 depth-charge projectors
M: Diesel; 2 props; 24,000 hp

Remark: A variant of the Kiang Tung class with SSM vice SAM.

♦ *2 Kiang Tung-class guided missile frigates (1974)*

D: 1,800 tons (2,200 fl) **S:** 28 kts **Dim:** 103 × 12 × 4.0
A: 4/100-mm DP (II × 2) — 2 SAM systems — 8/37-mm AA (II × 4) — 2 MBU 1800 — 2 depth-charge projectors
M: Diesels; 2 props; 24,000 hp

Remark: SAM system, of Chinese design, not yet operational.

♦ *5 Kiangnan-class frigates* — Bldr: Chiang Nan SY, Canton, 1967-69

D: 1,500 tons **S:** 28 kts **Dim:** 88 × 10 × 3.90
A: 3/100-mm (I × 3) 1 fwd, 2 aft — 8/37-mm AA (II × 4) — 4/14.5-mm AA (II × 2) — 2 MBU 1800 — 4 depth-charge projectors — 2 depth-charge racks
M: 4 diesels; 2 props; 24,000 hp

Remark: Chinese version of the Soviet Riga class.

Kiangnan-class frigate

♦ *4 Soviet Riga-class frigates* — Bldr: Chiang Nan SY, Canton, 1954-57

CHIENG TU, KUEI LIN, KUEI YANG, K'UN MING

D: 1,450 tons (fl) **S:** 28 kts **Dim:** 91.0 × 11.0 × 3.4
A: 3/100-mm (I × 3) — 4/37-mm AA (II × 2) — 2 Styx systems (II × 1) — 4 depth-charge projectors — 2 depth-charge racks
M: GT; 2 props; 20,000 hp **Range:** 2,000/10

GUIDED MISSILE AND TORPEDO PATROL BOATS

♦ *1 Hola-class patrol boat*

An enlarged version of the Osa-I class armed with 4 surface-to-surface missiles. Equipped with a large radome.

♦ *50 Soviet Osa-I-class patrol boats (ca. 1960)*

D: 175 tons (210 fl) **Dim:** 39 × 7.7 × 1.80 **S:** 40 kts (36 cruising)
Man: 25 men **M:** 3 M503A diesels; 3 props; 12,000 hp
A: 4/25-mm AA (II × 2) — 4 systems similar to Styx

Remarks: The electronic equipment of these ships may be slightly different from that of the Soviet Osa-I ships, and different guns are fitted.

♦ *7/8 Soviet Komar-class patrol boats (ca. 1960)*

D: 71 tons (82 fl) **Dim:** 25.3 × 7.0 × 2.0 **S:** 40 kts
A: 2/25-mm AA (II × 2) — 2 Styx systems **M:** Diesel; 4 props; 4,800 hp

♦ *40 Hoku-class patrol boats*

Chinese version of the Soviet Komar class, 26.8 meters long.

♦ *100 Huchwan-class hydrofoils (since 1966)*

D: 39 tons (fl) **Dim:** 21.8 × 4.90 × 1; foilborne: 7.50 × .31
S: 54 kts **A:** 2/450-mm TT — 2/14.5-mm machine guns (II × 1)
M: 3 diesels; 3 props; 3,600 hp

Remarks: Identical to the hydrofoils delivered to Albania, Pakistan, and Tanzania. Also built in Romania.

♦ *80 Soviet P-6 torpedo boats, built in China since 1960*

D: 56 tons (66.5 fl) **Dim:** 25.30 × 6.1 × 1.7 **S:** 43 kts
A: 4/25-mm AA (II × 2) — 2/533-mm TT
M: 4 M50 diesels; 4 props; 4,800 hp

GUIDED MISSILE AND TORPEDO PATROL BOATS (*continued*)

♦ *70 Soviet P-4 torpedo boats (since 1952)*

D: 19.3 tons (22.4 fl) **Dim:** 19.3 × 3.7 × 1.0 **S:** 55 kts
A: 2/14.5-mm machine guns (II × 1) — 2/450-mm TT
M: 2 M50 diesels; 2 props; 2,400 hp

PATROL BOATS AND PATROL CRAFT

♦ *7 Hainan-class patrol boats*

D: 400 tons **Dim:** 59.0 × 7.3 × 2.4 **S:** 24 kts
A: 4/57-mm AA (II × 2) — 4/25-mm AA (II × 2) — 4 MBU 1800 — 2 depth-charge projectors — 2 racks
M: 4 diesels; 4 props; 8,000 hp

♦ *20 Soviet Kronstadt-class patrol boats (since 1957)*

D: 300 tons (330 fl) **Dim:** 52.1 × 6.5 × 2.2 **S:** 18 kts
A: 1/85-mm — 2/37-mm AA — 6/14.5-mm machine guns (II × 3) — 2 depth-charge projectors — 2 racks
M: 3 diesels; 3 props; 3,300 hp

REMARKS: Six could have been delivered by the U.S.S.R., the others built in Shanghai and Canton. Other information indicates that only two were built in China, the balance in the Soviet Union.

♦ *280 Shanghai-II-class patrol boats*

D: 155 tons (fl) **Dim:** 38.8 × 5.4 × 1.6
S: 28 kts **Man:** 25 men
A: 4/37-mm AA (II × 2) — 4/25-mm AA (II × 2) — in some: 2 recoilless rifles (II × 1)
M: 4 diesels; 4 props; 4,800 hp

REMARKS: See photo in Tanzania section. Shanghai-I was smaller and had 2/57-mm (II × 1) forward.

♦ *Shantung class*

Similar to Swatow class, but with hydrofoils. Very few built. Probably not successful.

♦ *80 Swatow-class patrol boats*

D: 80 tons (fl) **S:** 28 kts **Dim:** 25.10 × 6 × 1.80
A: 4/37-mm AA (II × 2) — 2 heavy machine gun mounts — 8 depth charges
M: 4 diesels; 3,000 hp

REMARK: Similar to P-6, but broader and with a steel hull.

♦ *45 Whampoa-class patrol boats* — Bldr: China (1954–58)

D: 45 tons **S:** 12 kts **Dim:** 27 × 4 × 1.5
A: 2/37-mm AA (II × 1) — 2 machine guns
M: 2 diesels; 2 props; 600 hp

♦ *Several hundred patrol craft of the Yu Lin, Ying Kou, Wu Hsi, Pei Hai, Tai Shan, and Fukien classes, etc.*

Most quite small (10.50 tons) with 14.5-mm machine guns or twin 25-mm AA as armament.

MINE WARFARE SHIPS

♦ *1 Woosung-class minesweeper*

Characteristics not known.

♦ *23 Soviet T-43-class fleet minesweepers*

D: 610 tons (fl) **Dim:** 60 × 8.6 × 2.15 **S:** 14 kts
A: 4/37-mm AA (II × 2) — 4/25-mm AA (II × 2) — 4/14.5-mm machine guns — 2 depth-charge projectors
M: 2 diesels; 2 props; 2,200 hp

REMARKS: A few were transferred from the U.S.S.R., the majority were built in China. A few older units are only 58 meters overall. Several were built or converted as surveying ships and civilian research ships.

AMPHIBIOUS WARFARE SHIPS

♦ *10 or 11 LCUs (ex-LCT)*, of U.S. and U.K. origin

♦ *500 LCMs (300 of the Yunnan class)* built in China

AUXILIARY SHIPS

♦ *20 ex-U.S. LSTs (4,100 tons fl, 11 kts)* transferred before the civil war to the Nationalist Chinese Navy and later captured by the communist forces. Possible names: **CHANG PAI SHAN, TA PIEH SHAN, CHUNG, CHING KANG SHAN, MENG SHAN.** Used as transports or station vessels.

♦ *14 ex-U.S. LSMs dating from 1944–45.* Some used as minelayers.

♦ *1 submarine tender* — Purchased: 4-77

ANGAMOS (ex-merchant *Puerto Monte*)

D: 3,560 (fl) **S:** 16 kts **Dim:** 93.0 × 16.2 × 4.5
M: 2 Pielstick diesels; 3,250 hp

REMARK: Fitted with workshops, spare parts, and ammunition and torpedo magazines.

NOTE: There is no comprehensive information on the logistic support available to the Chinese fleet, but China has designed and built large numbers of auxiliary vessels, reportedly running the entire spectrum of logistics support, repair, hydrographic survey, and research types, including a great many tugs and small oilers.

Some old U.S. (for example, LSTs) and Japanese ships that have no military value today have probably been converted to depot ships, repair ships, etc.

PERSONNEL: 8,000 men, 1,500 of whom are Marines

MERCHANT MARINE (1976): 53 ships — 211,691 grt (tankers: 4 — 11,510 grt)

SHIPS IN SERVICE OR UNDER CONSTRUCTION AS OF 1 OCTOBER 1977

	L	Tons	Main Armament
♦ *4 submarines*			
2 TYPE 209	1974	1,000	8/533-mm TT
2 S.X. 506	1972	58	. . .
♦ *2 destroyers*			
1 HÄLLAND	1956	2,650	6/120-mm DP, 4/533-mm TT
1 ALLEN M. SUMNER, FRAM II	1944	2,200	6/127-mm DP, 6 ASW TT
♦ *2 frigates*			
1 COURTNEY	1956	1,450	2/76-mm DP, 6 ASW TT
1 LPR	1944	1,450	1/127-mm DP, 6 ASW TT
♦ *4 corvettes*			
4 JOÃO ROBY	1973–74	1,252	1/100-mm DP, 6 ASW TT
♦ *2 patrol craft*			
♦ *10 river patrol boats and craft*			

OVERSEAS PURCHASE PROGRAM: Colombia is actively seeking to expand and replenish her aging fleet by the purchase of used naval ships from other nations. In addition to the four Portuguese *João Roby*-class corvettes acquired in 1977, Colombia is reportedly buying the following from the United States, for transfer 1977–78:

♦ *2 Asheville-class patrol boats*

N . . . (ex-*Gallup*, PG-85)
N . . . (ex-*Crockett*, PG-90)

♦ *3 fleet tugs* (for use as patrol boats)

N . . . (ex-*Carib*, ATF-82)
N . . . (ex-*Hidatsa*, ATF-102)
N . . . (ex-*Jicarilla*, ATF-104)

♦ *1 landing ship* (for logistics support)

N . . . (ex-*Duval County*, LST-758)

♦ *1 repair ship*

N . . . (ex-*Midas*, ARB-5)

♦ *1 salvage ship*

N . . . (ex-*Clamp*, ARS-33)

SUBMARINES

♦ *2 German Type 209*

	Bldr:	L	In serv.
SS 28 PIJAO	Howaldtswerke, Kiel	19-6-74	17-4-75
SS 29 TAYRONA	Howaldtswerke, Kiel	. . .	18-7-75

D: 980 tons standard, 105 surfaced, 1,230 submerged
Dim: 56 × 6.2 × 5.90 **Man:** 5 officers, 26 men
S: 22 kts for a few minutes **Endurance:** 30 days

COLOMBIA

A: 8/533-mm TT fwd — 6 reserve torpedoes
M: 4 MTU type 12V-493-TY60 diesels, Siemens electric motor, 3,600 hp; 1 prop **Fuel:** 50 tons diesel

♦ *2 Italian S.X. 506 midget submarines*

SS 20 INTREPIDO, SS 21 INDOMABLE — Bldr: Cosmos, Livorno, Italy (1972–74)

D: 58 tons surfaced, 70 tons submerged **Dim:** 23 × 2 × 4
Man: 5 men **S:** 8.5 kts **Range:** 1,200/7
Cargo capacity: 2,050 kg of explosives; 8 frogmen fully equipped; 2 submarine vehicles (for the frogmen) supported by a fixed system on lower part of the hull, one on each side.

REMARKS: Similar submarines have been bought by the Pakistani and Taiwanese navies. Two additional units, *Roncador* (SS-23) and *Quita Sueno* (SS-24) are no longer in service.

DESTROYERS

♦ *1 Swedish Hälland class*

	Bldr	Laid down	L	In serv.
06 SIETE DE AGOSTO (ex-*13 de Junio*)	Götawerken	11-55	19-6-56	31-10-58

Siete de Agosto (06) Shipbldg. and Sh. Record

D: 2,650 tons (3,300 fl) **Dim:** 121.05 × 12.40 × 4.70 (fl)
S: 25 kts **Range:** 450/25 **Man:** 21 officers, 227 men
A: 6/120-mm AA automatic (II × 3) — 4/40-mm AA (I × 4) — 4/533-mm TT (IV × 1) — 1 ASW Bofors quadruple-barrel 375-mm
Electron Equipt: Radars: 1/LWO-3, 1 DAO-2, HSA fire control (6 sets)
M: De Laval double-reduction GT; 2 props; 55,000 hp
Boilers: 2 Penhoët-Motala-Verkstad **Fuel:** 524 tons

DESTROYERS (*continued*)

REMARKS: Based on the Swedish Hälland class but with a third 120-mm mount and only one torpedo mount and ASW rocket launcher. *Siete de Agosto* completed a major engineering overhaul in the United States in 1975. Her sister, *Veinte de Julio* (05) is in reserve.

♦ *1 ex-Allen M. Sumner class, transferred 16-12-73*

	Bldr	Laid down	L	In serv.
03 SANTANDER (ex-*Waldron*, DD-699)	Federal SB & DD	1943	26-3-44	8-6-44

D: 2,200 tons (3,300 fl) **Dim:** 114.75 × 12.45 (wl) × 5.80
S: 30 kts **Range:** 4,800/15
A: 6/127-mm semi-automatic, 38 cal. (II × 3) — 6/324-mm Mk 32 ASW TT (III × 2) — 2 hedgehogs
Electron Equipt: Radars: 1/SPS-40, 1/SPS-10
Sonar: SQS-30
M: GT; 4 Babcock & Wilcox boilers; 2 props; 60,000 hp **Fuel:** 650 tons

REMARKS: The *Santander* has had FRAM II modernization and can handle a small helicopter. Her sister, *Caldas* (02), was decommissioned in 1976.

FRIGATES

♦ *1 ex-U.S. Courtney class, transferred 8-7-72*

	Bldr	Laid down	L	In serv.
07 BOYACA (ex-*Hartley*, DE-1029)	New York S.B. Corp.	10-55	24-11-56	6-57

D: 1,450 tons (1,914 fl) **Dim:** 95.70 × 11.26 × 4.30
S: 25 kts **Man:** 11 officers, 150 men
A: 2/76-mm DP (II × 1) — 6 ASW Mk 32 TT (III × 2) — 1 depth-charge rack
Electron Equipt: Radars: 1/SPS-6, 1/SPS-10 — Sonar: SQS-23
M: De Laval GT; 2 Foster Wheeler boilers; 1 prop; 20,000 hp
Fuel: 400 tons **Range:** 4,500/15

REMARKS: Twin rudder. Superstructure built of light metal alloy. Flight deck and hangar for small helicopter.

♦ *1 ex-U.S. LPR type, transferred in 1969*

DT 15 CORDOBA (ex-*Ruchamkin*, LPR-89) L: 15-6-44

Cordoba 1973

D: 1,450 tons (2,050 fl) **Dim:** 93.26 × 11.28 × 4.70 **S:** 23 kts
A: 1/127-mm DP — 4/40-mm AA (II × 2) — 6/324-mm Mk 32 ASW TT (III × 2) — 1 depth-charge rack
Electron Equipt: 1/SPS-10 radar
Man: 204 men **Range:** 5,000/15, 2,000/23 **Fuel:** 350 tons
M: Turbo-electric propulsion; 2 props; 12,000 hp; 2 boilers

REMARKS: Can be used as fast transport (100 men). The *Cordoba* had FRAM-II modernization. The *Almirante Tono* was decommissioned 11-76.

CORVETTES

♦ *4 Portuguese João Roby class, purchased 1977*

Bldr: Empresa Nacional Bazan, Cartagena

	Laid down	L	In serv.
F . . . N . . . (ex-*Baptista de Andrade*)	1972	3-73	19-11-74
F . . . N . . . (ex-*João Roby*)	1972	3-6-73	18-3-75
F . . . N . . . (ex-*Alfonso Cerqueira*)	1972	6-10-73	26-6-75
F . . . N . . . (ex-*Oliveira e Carmo*)	1972	2-74	2-75

Oliveira e Camaro (with old number) 1976

D: 1,252 tons (1,348 fl) **Dim:** 84.6 × 10.3 × 3.3
S: 21 kts **Man:** 100 men
A: 1/100-mm DP, French model 1968 — 2/40-mm AA (II × 1) — 6 Mk 32 ASW TT (III × 2) — 2 depth-charge racks
Electron Equipt: Radar: 1/AWS-1, 1 navigation **Range:** 5,900/18
M: 2 SEMT-Pielstick PA6V-280 diesels; 2 props; 10,960 hp

REMARKS: Nearly new ships, surplus to Portuguese needs. Can carry 34 Marines. Small helicopter deck.

PATROL CRAFT

AN 206 CARLOS E. RESTREPO

Bldr: K. G. Bardenfleth, Schurenstedt (1964-65)

D: 123.5 tons **Dim:** 32.77 (pp) × 5.49 × 1.85
S: 25/26 kts **A:** 1/20-mm AA **M:** 2 Maybach diesels; 2,450 hp

AN 208 CARLOS ALBAN — Bldr: Finland. In service since 1971

D: 100 tons **Dim:** 33 × 5.5 × 1.8
S: 19 kts **A:** 2/20-mm
M: 2 Maybach diesels; 2 props; 2,450 hp

REMARK: Similar to Finnish *Ruissalo* class.

RIVER PATROL BOATS AND CRAFT

CF 35 RIO HACHA — CF 37 ARAUCA — Bldr: Unial, Barranquilla (1955)

D: 170 tons (184 fl) **Dim:** 47.25 × 8.23 × 1
S: 13 kts **Range:** 1,000/12
A: 2/76-mm AA (I × 2) — 4/20-mm AA (I × 4) **Man:** 27 to 43 men
M: 2 Caterpillar diesels; 2 props; 800 hp

REMARK: Sister *Leticia* disarmed and equipped as a hospital boat.

Arauca

CF 33 CARTAGENA — Bldr: Yarrow & Co. (Glasgow) 1930

D: 142 tons **Dim:** 41.90 × 7.16 × 0.80
S: 15.5 kts **Range:** 2,100/15 **Man:** 39 men
A: 2/76-mm — 1/20-mm AA — 4/7.7-mm machine guns

Cartagena

Armor: Principal parts of the ship against small arms
M: 2 Gardner diesels; 2 props (in tunnels); 600 hp
Fuel: 24 tons diesel

LR 122 JUAN LUCIO (2-5-53)
LR 123 ALFONSO VARGAS (3-7-52)
LR 124 FRITZ HAGALE (19-7-52)
LR 126 HUMBERTO CORTES (26-11-52)
LR 128 CARLOS GALINDO (1954)

Alfonso Vargas (river gunboat)

Bldr: Cartagena Naval DY

D: 33 tons **Dim:** 25 × 3.66 × 0.85
S: 13 kts **Man:** 13 men
A: 1/20-mm AA — 4 mortars **Fuel:** 3.5 tons diesel
M: 2 General Motors diesels; 260/290 hp

REMARK: LR-123 and LR-124 are slightly smaller: 23.2 meters overall.

LR 131 VENGADORA, LR 132 DILIGENTE

Bldr: Cartagena Naval DY — 1952-54

REMARKS: These are small patrol craft. No other information.

OCEANOGRAPHIC RESEARCH SHIPS

BO 151 SAN ANDRES (ex-*Rockville,* PCER-851) — Bldr: U.S.A. (22-2-44) — Bought 5-6-69.

OCEANOGRAPHIC RESEARCH SHIPS (*continued*)

D: 674 tons (858 fl) **Dim:** 56.20 × 10.05 × 3
S: 15 kts **Man:** 60 men
M: General Motors diesels; 2 props; 1,800 hp

San Andres 1976

BO 153 QUINDIO (ex-U.S. YFR-443, transferred 7-64)
D: 380 tons (600 fl) **Dim:** 40.4 × 9.10 × 2.50
Man: 17 men **M:** 1 Union diesel; 6,000 hp

Remark: Built in 1942 as a refrigerated cargo lighter by Niagara SB, Buffalo, N.Y.

HYDROGRAPHIC SURVEY SHIP

FB 161 GORGONA — Bldr: Lidingo Verken L: 28-5-54
D: 560 tons **Dim:** 41.15 × 9 × 2.83
S: 13 kts **M:** 2 Nohab diesels; 2 props; 900 hp

Remark: Originally intended as a lighthouse tender.

AUXILIARY SHIPS

♦ *1 oiler*

BT 67 TUMACO (ex-U.S. *Chewaucan,* AOG-50), transferred 7-71
Bldr: Cargill, Inc., Savage, Minn. L: 22-7-44
D: 4,570 tons (fl) **S:** 15 kts **Dim:** 94.7 (89.0 pp) × 14.78 × 4.9
A: 2/76-mm DP (I × 2) **Man:** 45 men **Range:** 8,350/11.5
M: 2 General Motors 16-278A diesels; 2 props; 3,300 hp
Cargo capacity: 2,575 tons fuel

Tumaco 1976

♦ *1 small transport/cargo ship*

TM 43 CIUDAD DE QUIBO — Bldr: Sander, Delfzijl, Neth., purchased 1953.
D: 633 tons **Dim:** 50.30 × 7.20 × 2.80
S: 11 kts **Man:** 11 men
M: Diesel; 1 prop; 390 hp **Fuel:** 32 tons

♦ *4 hospital boats*

LETICIA (1955) — Former river patrol boat, see under *Arauca* class. Has 6 beds, surgery facilities, etc.

TF 51 MARIO SERPA (1953) — **TF 52 HERNANDO GUTIERREZ** (1953) — **BD 33 SOCORRO** (1956) — Bldr: Cartagena Naval DY
D: 70 tons **Dim:** 25 × 5.50 × 0.75 **Man:** 10 men
S: 9 kts **M:** 2 General Motors diesels; 270 hp

Remarks: Originally fitted to carry 56 troops on the rivers. BD-33 used for surgery; other pair are mobile dispensaries.

RM 72 PEDRO DE HEREDIA (ex-*Choctaw,* ATF-70) (10-24), transferred 1961

Pedro de Heredia 1975

AUXILIARY SHIPS (*continued*)

D: 1,235 tons (1,765 fl) **S:** 16.5 kts **Dim:** 62.50 × 11.70 × 4.80
M: Diesel-electric propulsion; 3,000 hp, added in 1961.

RM 75 BAHIA UTRIA (ex-*Koka*, ATA-185) — transferred 1-7-71

D: 534 tons (835 fl) **S:** 13 kts **Dim:** 43 × 10 × 4
M: Diesel-electric propulsion; 1 prop; 1,500 hp

REMARK: Sister *Bahia Honda* lost 2-75.

RR 81 CAPITAN CASTRO, RR 82 CANDIDO LEGUIZAMO,
RR 84 CAPITAN ALVARO RUIS,
RR 86 CAPITAN RIGOBERTO GIRALDO,
RR 87 CAPITAN VLADIMIR VALEK, R 88 TENIENTE LUIS BERNAL

D: 50 tons **Dim:** 20 × 4.25 × 0.75 } for river use
S: 10 kts **M:** 2 diesels; 260 hp

RM 71 ANDAGOYA (1928)

D: 117 grt **S:** 12 kts **Dim:** 28 × 6.1 × 3.0
M: Diesel; 400 hp

RM 89 TENIENTE MIGUEL SILVA
RM 90 JOVES FIALLO } for river use

S: 9 kts **M:** Diesel; 260 hp **Dim:** 22.4 × 5.3 × 0.9

VARIOUS SHIPS

♦ *1 school sailing ship*

GLORIA — delivered 7-9-68. Bldr: Celaya (Bilbao)

D: 1,300 tons (fl) **S:** 10.5 kts (on diesel) **Dim:** 64.7 × 10.6 × 6.6
M: 1 diesel; 500 hp

REMARK: Three-masted schooner; fore and main masts are square-rigged.

Gloria 1976

♦ *1 floating dry dock*

JAIME ARIAS

COMORO ISLANDS

♦ *1 landing ship* (ex-LCT-9061), transferred by France, 1976

N . . .

L 9061 C. Limonier, 1975

D: 657 tons (1,000 fl) **S:** 9 kts **Dim:** 70.48 × 11.90 × 1.80
A: 2/20-mm AA (I × 2) — 1/120-mm mortar, Army model
M: 4 Paxman diesels; 2 props; 1,840 hp **Man:** 29 men

REMARK: Ex-British *Buttress,* LCT(8) 4099, bought 7-1965 by France.

CONGO

People's Republic of

PERSONNEL: 180 men

MERCHANT MARINE (1976): 13 ships — 2,453 grt

The naval forces are divided into two groups: the coastal navy and the river navy.

The coastal navy has:

♦ *3 ex-Chinese Shanghai-II-class patrol boats,* delivered in 3-75

P 401 **P 402** **P 403**

D: 155 tons (fl) **S:** 28 kts **Dim:** 38.8 × 5.4 × 1.6
A: 4/37-mm AA (II × 2) — 4/25-mm AA (II × 2) — depth charges
M: 4 diesels; 4 props; 4,800 hp **Man:** 25 men

REMARK: Very unsophisticated boats.

The river navy has:

♦ *4 ex-Chinese Yu Lin-class 10-ton river patrol boats*

♦ *2 locally built small craft*

♦ *10 small craft* with 40-to-75 hp Johnson outboards (probably in poor condition)

COSTA RICA

PERSONNEL: 50 men

MERCHANT MARINE (1976): 15 ships — 6,257 grt

♦ *3 patrol craft,* Coast Guard 40-foot utility Boat class, transferred 1950s

D: 10.6 tons **S:** 19 kts **Dim:** 12.27 × 3.45 × 1.0
A: 1 machine gun **Range:** 280/18 **Man:** 4-5 men
M: 2 General Motors diesels; 2 props; 380 hp

♦ *1 armed tug* — no information

PERSONNEL: approx. 6,000 men

MERCHANT MARINE (1967): 294 ships — 603,650 grt
(tankers: 12 ships — 56,906 grt)

PATROL BOATS

♦ *4 Soviet Kronstadt class, transferred 2-62*

Cuban Kronstadt 1972

D: 300 tons (330 fl) **S:** 18 kts **Dim:** 52.1 × 6.5 × 2.2
A: 1/85-mm DP — 2/37-mm AA (I × 2) — 6/14.5-mm machine guns — 2 MBU 1800 — 2 depth-charge projectors — 2 depth-charge racks
Electron Equipt: Ball End radar **Man:** 50 men
M: 3 diesels; 3 props; 3,300 hp **Fuel:** 20 tons diesel
Range: 1,500/12

REMARK: Two additional believed discarded.

♦ *10 Soviet SO-I class, transferred 1964-67*

Cuban SO-1 1975

CUBA

D: 190 tons (215 fl) **S:** 28 kts **Dim:** 42.0 × 6.1 × 1.9
A: 4/25-mm AA (II × 2) — 4 MBU 1800 ASW rocket launchers — 2 depth-charge racks
Electron Equipt: Pot Head radar **Man:** 30 men
M: 3 diesels; 3 props; 6,000 hp

REMARK: Two units believed discarded.

GUIDED MISSILE BOATS

♦ *2 Soviet Osa-II class, transferred 1976-77*

D: 240 tons (fl) **S:** 36 kts **Dim:** 39.0 × 7.7 × 1.8
A: 4 Styx systems (I × 4) — 4.30-mm AA (II × 2) **Range:** 800/25
Electron Equipt: Radars: 1/Square Tie, 1/Drum Tilt
M: 3 M504 diesels; 3 props; 15,000 hp **Man:** 25 men

♦ *6 Osa-I class, 2 delivered in 1972, 2 in 1973, and 2 in 1974*

D: 175 tons (210 fl) **S:** 36 kts **Dim:** 39.0 × 7.7 × 1.8
A: 4 Styx systems — 4/30 mm AA (II × 2)
Electron Equipt: Radars: 1/Square Tie, 1/Drum Tilt
M: 3 M503A diesels; 3 props; 12,000 hp **Man:** 25 men

TORPEDO BOATS

♦ *18 Komar class (1961-63), 12 delivered in 1962, 6 in 1966*

D: 71 tons (82 fl) **S:** 40 kts **Dim:** 25.3 × 7.0 × 2.0
A: 2 Styx systems — 2/25-mm AA (II × 1)
Electron Equipt: 1 Square Tie radar **Man:** 19 men
M: 4 M50 diesels; 4 props; 4,800 hp **Range:** 650/30

♦ *6 P-6 class (after 1955), delivered in 1962*

D: 56 tons (66.5 fl) **S:** 43 kts **Dim:** 25.31 × 6.1 × 1.7
A: 4/25-mm AA (II × 2) — 2/533-mm TT — depth charges
Electron Equipt: Skin Head radar
M: 4 M50 diesels; 4 props; 4,800 hp **Range:** 450/30

♦ *12 P-4 class (before 1955), delivered 1962-64*

D: 19.3 tons (22.4 fl) **S:** 55 kts **Dim:** 19.3 × 3.7 × 1.0
A: 2/14.5-mm machine guns (aft) — 2/450-mm TT
Electron Equipt: Skin Head radar
M: 2 M50 diesels; 2 props; 2,400 hp

PATROL CRAFT

♦ *8 Soviet Zhuk class, transferred 1975-76*

D: 50 tons (60 fl) **S:** 30 kts **Dim:** 26.0 × 4.9 × 1.5
A: 4/14.5-mm machine guns (II × 2)
M: 2 M50 diesels; 2 props; 2,400 hp

VARIOUS SHIPS

♦ *7 hydrographic survey ships*

H 101 (600 tons) — former trawler, built in Spain, 1972. Also used for training
H 91, H 92, H 93, H 94, H 95, H 96 — Soviet Nyryat-1 class, transferred . . .

D: 120 tons (fl) **S:** 12 kts **Dim:** 29.0 × 5.0 × 1.7
M: 1 diesel **Range:** 1,600/10 **Man:** 15 men

REMARKS: Known as GPB-480 class in U.S.S.R. Same class (with different equipment) also used as diving tenders.

♦ *2 lighthouse and buoy tenders*

ENRIQUE COLLAZO — Bldr: Great Britain (1906)

D: 815 tons **Dim:** 64 × 10.50 × 2.80
M: Triple expansion; 2 props; 680 hp

SF 10 BERTHA (1944)

D: 100 tons **S:** 10 kts **Dim:** 31.50 × 5.75 × 3.40
M: 2 Gray diesels; 2 props; 450 hp

♦ *7 Soviet T-4-class landing craft (LCM), transferred 1967-74*

D: 94 tons (fl) **S:** 9 kts **Dim:** 19.0 × 5.3 × 1.3
M: 2 diesels; 2 props; 400 hp

REMARK: Used as harbor craft.

♦ *1 yacht*

GRANMA — small cabin cruiser in which Fidel Castro returned to Cuba in 1956. Maintained by the Navy as a museum.

♦ *3 small service launches*

A 1, A 2, A 3 — Bldr: U.S., 1949

D: 58 tons **Dim:** 22.50 × 4.60 × 1.60
M: 2 Gray Marine diesels; 2 props; 225 hp

♦ *1 Soviet Okhtenshiy-class tug, transferred 1976*

Caribe

D: 1,000 tons (fl) **S:** 12 kts **Dim:** 46.5 × 9.5 × 3.9
M: 2 diesels; 2 props; 2,000 hp **Man:** 34 men

COAST GUARD

♦ *7 Coast Guard Craft*

GF 528, GF 725, GF 825, GF 720 — similar to 40-foot U.S. Coastal Guard small craft
GF 101, GF 102, GF 701 — similar to 70-foot U.S. Coast Guard small craft

REMARKS: Assigned to the Department of the Interior. Hull numbers painted in red to distinguish these small boats from navy ships.

♦ *1 patrol craft*

GUANABACOA — Bldr: Cadiz, L: . . .

S: 22 kts

♦ *6 fast launches*

MARTI — CAMILO CIENFUEGOS — MACEO — FINLAY — CUARTEL MONCADA — ESCAMBRAY — Bldr: Spain (1971-72)

REMARK: No other information.

CYPRUS

PERSONNEL: 330 men

MERCHANT MARINE (1976): 765 ships — 3,114,263 grt
(tankers: 41 — 497,597 grt)

♦ *2 ex-German R-class minesweepers* (1943)

R class minesweeper in Cypriot service G. Arra, 1971

D: 130 tons (fl) **Dim:** 37.8 × 5.8 × 1.4 **S:** 18 kts
A: 1/40-mm AA — 2/20-mm (I × 2)
M: 2 M.A.N. diesels; 2 props; 1,800 hp

♦ *6 Soviet P-4-class torpedo boats,* four transferred in 10-64 and two in 2-65

D: 19.3 tons (22.4 fl) **S:** 55 kts **Dim:** 19.3 × 3.7 × 1.0
A: 2/14.5-mm machine guns (II × 1) — 2/450-mm TT
Electron Equipt: 1/Skin Head radar **Man:** 12 men
M: 2 M50 diesels; 2 props; 2,400 hp

♦ *10 small former fishing boats*

D: 50 tons **A:** 1 or 2 machine guns

REMARK: Several were probably lost during the crisis of July 1974.

DENMARK

PERSONNEL: 5,800 men, plus 3,100 Home Guard reserves

MERCHANT MARINE (1976): 1,403 ships — 5,143,022 grt
(tankers: 68 ships — 2,485,130 grt)

NAVAL AVIATION: About 15 helicopters, including 8 Alouette III

WARSHIPS IN SERVICE OR UNDER CONSTRUCTION AS OF 1 OCTOBER 1977

	L	Tons	Main armament
♦ *6 submarines*			
2 TYPE 205	1968-69	370	8/533-mm TT
4 DELFINEN	1956-63	595	4/533-mm TT
♦ *2 frigates*			
2 PEDER SKRAM	1965	2,030	4/127-mm DP, 4/40-mm AA
♦ *11 corvettes*			
3 NILS JUEL	. . .	1,320	8 Harpoons, 1 Sea Sparrow, 1/76-mm DP
3 AIRONE	1954-55	760	2/76-mm DP, 1/40-mm AA
1 HVIDBJØRNEN, mod.	1975	1,970	1/76-mm DP, 1 helicopter
4 HVIDBJØRNEN	1961-62	1,345	1/76-mm DP, 1 helicopter
♦ *20 guided missile and torpedo boats*			
10 WILLIMOES	1974-	250	1/76-mm, 4.533-mm TT
6 SØLØVEN	1963-66	95	2/40-mm AA, 4/533-mm TT
4 FALKEN	1961-62	119	1/40-mm AA, 4/533-mm TT
♦ *22 patrol boats and patrol craft*			
2 AGDLEK	1974	330	2/20-mm AA
9 BARSØ	1969-73	155	2/20-mm AA
2 MAAGEN	1960	175	1/40-mm AA
9 DAPHNE	1960-63	150	1/40-mm AA
♦ *6 minelayers*			
2 LINDORMEN	1977	575	2/20-mm AA, mines
4 FALSTER	1962-63	1,880	4/76-mm AA, 400 mines
♦ *8 coastal minesweepers*			

SUBMARINES

♦ *6 German/Norwegian Type 210* — proposed. Denmark is considering construction of six units of this Type 205 replacement design to supplant, first, her existing *Delfinens*, and then, her Type 205s.

♦ *2 German, type 205*

	Bldr	Laid down	L	In serv.
S 320 NARHVALEN	RDY Copenhagen	2-65	10-9-68	2-70
S 321 NORDKAPEREN	RDY Copenhagen	1-66	18-12-69	12-70

SUBMARINES (*continued*)

Narhvalen 1970

D: 370 tons surfaced, 480 submerged **Dim:** 45.41 × 4.60 × 4.58
S: 17/12 kts **A:** 8/533-mm TT, fwd
M: 2 Mercedes-Benz diesels, diesel-electric drive; 1 prop; 1,200/1,700 hp
Man: 22 men

REMARK: Modeled on the German Type 205 and Norwegian Type Type 207 (*Kobben* class)

♦ *4 Delfinen class*

	Bldr	Laid down	L	In serv.
S 326 DELFINEN	RDY Copenhagen	7-54	5-5-56	9-58
S 327 SPÆKHUGGEREN	RDY Copenhagen	12-54	20-2-57	6-59
S 328 TUMLEREN	RDY Copenhagen	5-56	22-5-58	1-60
S 329 SPRINGEREN	RDY Copenhagen	1-61	26-4-63	10-64

Delfinen

D: 595 tons surfaced, 643 submerged **Dim:** 54 × 4.70 × 3.80
S: 13/12 kts **Man:** 33 men
A: 4/533-mm TT, fwd **Range:** 4,000/8.5
M: Burmeister & Wain diesels and motors; 2 props; 1,200 hp

REMARK: S-329 built with U.S. "offshore" funds, as U.S. SS-554.

FRIGATES

♦ *2 Peder Skram (Danish design)*

	Bldr	Laid down	L	In serv.
F 352 PEDER SKRAM	Helsingør Vaerft	9-64	20-5-65	6-66
F 353 HERLUF TROLLE	Helsingør Vaerft	12-64	8-9-65	4-67

Peder Skram St. Steensen, 1970

Herluf Trolle J. C. Bellonne, 1974

D: 2,030 tons (2,720 fl) **Dim:** 112.50 (108 pp) × 12 × 3.60
S: 28 kts **Man:** 200 men
A: 4 (F-353: 2)/127-mm DP (II or I × 2) — 4/40-mm AA (I × 4) — 1 NATO Sea Sparrow system (VIII × 1, F-353 only) — 8 Harpoon SSM (F-353 only) — 4/533-mm TT (IV × 1) — 2 depth-charge racks
Electron Equipt: Radars: 1/CWS-3, 1/CWS-2, 1/NWS-1, 1/NWS-2, 3/M/46
Sonar: 1/MS-26 Plessey
M: CODOG propulsion; 2 diesels (4,800 hp); 2 gas turbines (37,000 hp); 2 Ka-Me-Wa props

REMARKS: Built with U.S. "Offshore" funds. The gas turbines are GG4A-3 Pratt and Whitney Stal-Laval models and the diesels General Motors 567D, V-16 V(800 rpm). Speed with diesels: 16 kts. The 127-mm guns are of the U.S. 38-caliber model. F-353 has been modernized with Sea Sparrow and will get Harpoon shortly in place of one 127-mm mount; F-352 will follow.

CORVETTES

♦ *3 guided missile Nils Juel (Type KV 72) class, ordered 5-12-75*

Bldr: Aalborg Vaerft

CORVETTES (*continued*)

	Laid down	L	In serv.
F . . . NILS JUEL	1977	. . .	1979
F . . . PETER TORDENSKJOLD	1977	. . .	1979
F . . . OLFERT FISCHER	1977	. . .	1980

D: 1,320 tons (fl) **Dim:** 84.0 (80 pp) × 10.30 × 3.10
S: 28 kts **Man:** 90 men
A: 8 Harpoon SSM (IV × 2) — NATO Sea Sparrow systems (VIII × 1) — 1/76-mm DP OTO Melara Compact — ASW system not known
Electron Equipt: Radars: 1/AWS-5, 2/M/46, 2 SCLAR chaff launchers (XX × 2)
M: CODOG: 1 General Electric LM-2500 GT (25,000 hp), 1 MTU 20V-956 diesel (4,800 hp), 2 props

REMARK: Three more may be built later.

♦ *3 Italian Airone class*

	L
F 344 BELLONA	9-1-55
F 346 FLORA	25-6-55
F 347 TRITON	19-9-54

Flora 1970

Orders for U.S. "Offshore" ships given to the Italian shipyards Naval Meccanica (F-344), Tirreno (F-346), and Naval Meccanica, Taranto (F-347); ex-U.S. PC-1622, PC-1624, and PC-1625, respectively.

D: 760 tons (870 fl) **Dim:** 75 (69.49 pp) × 9.50 × 3.00
S: 20 kts (16 cruising) **Man:** 109 men
A: 2/76-mm AA — 1/40-mm — ASW weapons, including 2 hedgehogs
Electron Equipt: Radars: 1/AWS-1, 1/NWS-1; Sonar: QCU-2

REMARKS: Officially classified as "corvettes." The *Diana* was discarded in 1974; others will be scrapped on completion of the *Nils Juel* class.

♦ *1 modified Hvidbjørnen class* — Bldr: Aalborg Vaerft

	Laid down	L	In serv.
F 340 BESKYTERREN	15-12-74	27-5-75	27-2-76

Beskyterren 1976

D: 1970 tons (fl) **Dim:** 74.4 × 11.8 × 4.5
S: 18 kts **Range:** 6,000/13 (one engine)
A: 1/76-mm DP — 1 helicopter **Man:** 60 men
Electron Equipt: CWS-1 radar
M: 4 B & W Alpha diesels; 1 variable-pitch prop; 7,440 hp

REMARKS: Serves as a fisheries protection ship. The helicopter is an Alouette III. An OTO Melara Compact 76-mm gun was originally to have been fitted.

♦ *4 Hvidbjørnen class*

	Bldr	Laid down	L	In serv.
F 348 HVIDBJØRNEN	Aarhus Flydedok	6-61	23-11-61	12-62
F 349 VÆDDEREN	Aalborg SY	10-61	6-4-62	3-63
F 350 INGOLF	Svendborg Skibsvaerft	12-61	27-7-62	6-63
F 351 FYLLA	Aalborg SY	6-62	18-12-62	7-63

Ingolf 1970

CORVETTES (*continued*)

D: 1,345 tons (1,650 fl) **Dim:** 72.60 × 11.60 × 4.90
S: 18 kts **Range:** 6,000/13
A: 1/76-mm DP — 1 helicopter **Man:** 10 officers, 60 men
Electron Equipt: CWS-1 radar
M: 4 G.M. 16-567C diesels linked to a variable-pitch prop; 6,400 hp

REMARKS: Used for fisheries protection. Alouette III helicopter. Reinforced bow. F-350 used for hydrographic survey, has no gun or helicopter but carries four 13-m survey launches on her flight deck.

GUIDED MISSILE BOATS

♦ *10 Willemoes (TB68) class based on the Swedish Spica class (Lürssen design)*

Bldr: Frederikshavn SY (Ordered in 1972).

	L	In serv.		L	In serv.
P 540 BILLE	15-4-74	3-76	**P 545 NORBY**	. . .	. . .
P 541 BREDAL	. . .	2-77	**P 546 RODSTEEN**	. . .	. . .
P 542 HAMMER	. . .	. . .	**P 547 SEHESTED**	. . .	. . .
P 543 HUITFELDT	. . .	. . .	**P 548 SUENSON**	. . .	. . .
P 544 KRIEGER	. . .	. . .	**P 549 WILLEMOES**	5-10-74	7-10-75

Willemoes 1976

D: 250 tons (fl) **Dim:** 46 (42.40 pp) × 7.40 × 2.4
S: 35 kts **Man:** 30 men
A: 1/76-mm OTO Melara Compact — 4/533-mm TT — 4 flare launchers
Electron Equipt: 1/9LV-200 radar
M: CODOG: 2 GM 8V-71 diesels; 3 Rolls-Royce Proteus gas turbines; 3 Ka-Me-Wa props; 12,750 hp/800 hp

REMARKS: In addition to the 76-mm OTO Melara Compact, ultimate armament will include 8 Harpoon and 2/533-mm TT. Harpoon will not be available until at least 1978.

TORPEDO BOATS

♦ *6 Søløven class, modified British Brave class*

	Bldr	Laid down	L	In serv.
P 510 SØLØVEN	Vosper (Portsmouth)	8-62	19-4-63	2-65
P 511 SØRIDDEREN	Vosper (Portsmouth)	10-62	22-8-63	2-65
P 512 SØBJORNEN	RDY Copenhagen	7-63	19-8-74	9-65
P 513 SØHESTEN	RDY Copenhagen	8-63	31-3-65	1966
P 514 SØHUNDEN	RDY Copenhagen	2-64	12-1-66	1-67
P 515 SØULVEN	RDY Copenhagen	6-64	27-4-66	3-67

Søridderen 1970

D: 95 tons (114 fl) **Dim:** 30.26 (27.44 pp) × 7.30 × 2.15 **S:** 50 kts
A: 2/40-mm AA (I × 2) — 4/533-mm TT **Man:** 4 officers, 22 men
M: Rolls-Royce Marine Proteus gas turbines; 3 props; 10,500 hp (12,750 max). Cruising, 2 General Motors 6V-71 diesels (**S:** 10 kts)

REMARKS: Two 533-mm TT removed when after gun is enclosed. P-510 built with U.S. funds as PT-821.

♦ *4 Falken class*

	Bldr	Laid down	L	In serv.
P 506 FALKEN	RDY Copenhagen	11-60	19-12-61	4-10-62
P 507 GLENTEN	RDY Copenhagen	1-61	15-5-62	15-12-62
P 508 GRIBBEN	RDY Copenhagen	5-61	18-7-62	26-4-63
P 509 HØGEN	RDY Copenhagen	9-61	4-10-62	6-6-63

D: 119 tons **Dim:** 35.90 × 5.40 × 2.0
S: 40 **A:** 1/40-mm AA (aft) — 1/20-mm AA (fwd) — 4/533-mm TT
M: 3 Mercedes-Benz diesels; 3 props; 9,000 hp **Man:** 23 men

TORPEDO BOATS *(continued)*

Glenten 1970

REMARKS: Derived from the German *Schnellboote* designs. P-506 and P-507 paid for with U.S. "Offshore" funds as PT-819 and PT-820. Will probably soon be scrapped.

PATROL BOATS AND PATROL CRAFT

♦ *9 Daphne class*

	Bldr	Laid down	L	In serv.
P 530 DAPHNE	RDY Copenhagen	4-60	10-11-60	12-61
P 531 DRYADEN	RDY Copenhagen	7-60	1-3-61	4-62
P 532 HAVMANDEN	RDY Copenhagen	11-60	16-5-61	8-62
P 533 HAVFRUEN	RDY Copenhagen	3-61	4-10 61	12-62
P 534 NAJADEN	RDY Copenhagen	9-61	20-6-62	4-63
P 535 NYMFEN	RDY Copenhagen	4-62	1-11-62	10-63
P 536 NEPTUN	RDY Copenhagen	9-62	29-5-63	12-63
P 537 RAN	RDY Copenhagen	12-62	10-7-63	5-64
F 538 ROTA	RDY Copenhagen	6-63	26-11-63	1-65

Havmanden — disarmed 1970

D: 150 tons (170 fl) **Dim:** 38 × 6.75 × 2
S: 20 kts **Man:** 23 men
A: 1/40-mm AA — 2 depth-charge projectors — 2 depth-charge racks
Electron Equipt: 1/Raytheon 1404 radar
M: 2 Maybach diesels of 1,300 hp and 1 Foden FD 6 diesel of 100 hp; 3 props

REMARKS: The 100-hp engine is used for cruising. P-530, P-532, P-534, and P-536, which were paid for with U.S. "Offshore" funds as PGM-47 to PGM-50, completely disarmed.

♦ *2 Agdlek class* — Bldr: Svendborg

	In serv.
Y 386 AGDLEK	12-3-74
Y 387 AGPA	14-5-74

Agdlek 1976

D: 330 tons (fl) **S:** 12 kts **Dim:** 31.4 × 7.7 × 3.3
A: 2/20-mm AA (I × 2) **Electron Equipt:** 2/Terma 20T48 radars
M: 1 Burmeister & Wain Alpha diesel; 800 hp **Man:** 15 men

REMARKS: For service in Greenland waters. Can carry two survey launches.

♦ *9 Barsø class*

Y 300 BARSØ **Y 301 DREJØ** **Y 302 ROMSØ** **Y 303 SAMSØ**
Y 304 THURØ **Y 305 VEJRØ** **Y 306 FARØ** **Y 307 LAESØ**
Y 308 ROMØ

Bldr: Svendborg, the first six in 1969, the last three from 1972-73.

D: 155 tons (fl) **S:** 11 kts **Dim:** 25.50 × 6 × 2.80
A: 2/20-mm AA (I × 2) **M:** 1 diesel; 1 prop; 385 hp

PATROL BOATS AND CRAFT *(continued)*

Thurø 1970

♦ *2 Maagen class*

	Bldr	In serv.
Y 384 MAAGEN	Helsingør Vaerft	5-60
Y 385 MALLEMUKKEN	Helsingør Vaerft	5-60

Mallemukken 1966

D: 175 tons (190 fl) **Dim:** 27 × 7.20 × 2.75
S: 10 kts **A:** 1/40-mm AA **M:** Diesel; 1 prop; 350 hp

REMARKS: Steel hull; profile of a whale-hunter ship; based in Greenland. Gun normally not carried.

♦ *3 Botved 9.8-meter class (1975)*

Y 377, Y 378, Y 379

D: 9 tons (fl) **S:** 27 kts **Dim:** 9.8 × 3.3 × 0.9
M: 2 Volvo Penta inboard/outboard diesels; 2 props; 600 hp

♦ *2 Botved 13.3-meter class (1974)*

Y 375, Y 376

D: 12 tons (fl) **S:** 26 kts **Dim:** 13.3 × 4.5 × 1.1
M: 2 diesels; 2 props; 680 hp

The following patrol craft are manned by the Home Guard:

♦ *7 MHV-90 class* — In serv. 1974-75

MHV 90 MHV 91 MHV 92 MHV 93 MHV 94 MHV 95 MHV 96

D: 85 tons (130 fl) **S:** 10.7 kts **Dim:** 19.8 × 5.7 × 1.6
A: 1/20-mm AA **M:** 1 Burmeister & Wain diesel; 400 hp

♦ *3 MHV-70 class* — Bldr: Navy Yard, Copenhagen — In serv. 1958

MHV 70 MHV 71 MHV 72

D: 78 tons (130 fl) **S:** 10 kts **Dim:** 20.1 × 5.1 × 2.5
A: 1/20-mm AA **M:** 1 diesel; 200 hp

♦ *6 MHV-80 class* — In serv. 1941

MHV 81 ASKØ MHV 82 ENØ MHV 83 MANØ MHV 84 BAAGØ MHV 85 HJORTØ MHV 86 LYØ

D: 74 tons **S:** 11 kts **Dim:** 24.4 × 4.9 × 1.6
A: 1/20-mm AA **M:** 1 diesel; 350 hp

REMARK: May have been scrapped.

♦ *32 smaller craft, including:*

MHV 1 through **MHV 15; MHV 51, MHV 52, MHV 54, MHV 56** through **MHV 68, MHV 74.** No data known.

MINE WARFARE SHIPS

♦ *4 Falster-class minelayers*

	Bldr	Laid down	L	In serv.
N 80 FALSTER	Nakskov Skibsvaerft	4-62	19-9-62	11-63
N 81 FYEN	Frederikshavn Vaerft	4-62	3-10-62	9-63
N 82 MØEN	Frederikshavn Vaerft	10-62	6-6-63	4-64
N 83 SJÆLLAND	Nakskov Skibsvaerft	1-63	14-6-63	7-64

D: 1,880 tons (fl) **Dim:** 77 (72.50 pp) × 12.50 × 3
S: 16.5 kts **Man:** 10 officers, 108 men
A: 4/76-mm AA (II × 2) — 400 mines — 4 minelaying tracks
Electron Equipt: Radars: 1/CWS-2, 1/NWS-3, 1/M/46
M: General Motors 16-567D diesels; 2 variable-pitch props; 4,800 hp

MINE WARFARE SHIPS (*continued*)

Sjælland 1970

REMARKS: NATO design. The Turkish ship *Nusret* is identical. N-82 is a naval cadet training ship. N-83 converted to submarine tender in 1976, to replace *Henrik Gerner* (can still lay mines). N-80 and N-82 built with U.S. "Offshore" funds as MMC-14 and MMC-15. The *Falster* class may be fitted with BPDM Sea Sparrow.

♦ *2 Lindormen-class minelayers* — Bldr: Svendborg

	L	In serv.
N 43 LINDORMEN	2-77	. . .
N 44 LOUSSEN	2-77	. . .

D: 575 tons (fl) **Dim:** 43.3 (40.0 pp) × 9.0 × 2.65
S: 14 kts **Man:** 27 men
A: 2/20-mm AA (I × 2) — 50 to 60 mines
Electric: 192 kw
M: 2 Wichmann 7AX diesels; 2 props; 4,200 hp

REMARKS: Built to replace the *Lougen* class. In service 1977-78.

♦ *8 coastal minesweepers, U.S. MSC (AMS) type*

M 571 AARØSUND **M 574 GRØNSUND** **M 577 ULVSUND**
M 572 ALSSUND **M 575 GULDBORGSUND** **M 578 VILSUND**
M 573 EGERNSUND **M 576 OMØSUND**

Bldr: U.S.A. (1953-56); transferred in 1955-56

D: 350 tons (376 fl) **Dim:** 43.89 (41.50 pp) × 7.95 × 2.55
S: 13 kts (8 sweeping) **Range:** 2,500/10
A: 2/20-mm AA (II × 1) **Man:** 38 men
Electron Equipt: 1/Decca-12 radar **Fuel:** 40 tons diesel
M: 2 General Motors 8-268A diesels; 2 props; 1,000 hp

REMARKS: Hull entirely of wood. The first three are ex-MSC-127 to MSC-129 and are 405 tons (fl); the others are ex-MSC-256, ex-MSC-257, ex-MSC-221, ex-MSC-263, and ex-MSC-264. M-575 has a charthouse between the stack and bridge so that she can act as a survey ship; she still has minesweeping equipment and carries 1/40-mm AA forward.

Aarøsund 1970

AUXILIARY SHIPS

♦ *2 coastal oilers, transferred 8-1962*

A 568 RIMFAXE, A 569 SKINFAXE (ex-U.S. YO-226 and YO-229) L: 1945

D: 1,390 tons (fl) **Dim:** 53.0 × 9.75 × 4.0
S: 10 kts **Man:** 23 men
M: 1 General Motors 8-278A diesel; 1 prop; 640 hp
Cargo capacity: 900 tons **Range:** 2,000/8

Rimfaxe 1970

DENMARK (*continued*)

AUXILIARY SHIPS (*continued*)

♦ *1 royal yacht* (1931)

A 540 DANNEBROG

D: 1,130 tons **S:** 14 kts **Dim:** 74.9 × 10.4 × 3.7
M: 4 Burmeister & Wain diesels; 2 props; 1,800 hp

♦ *4 icebreakers (owned and manned by the Ministry of Commerce)*

DANBJØRN (1965) **ISBJØRN** (1965)

D: 3,685 tons **S:** 14 kts **Dim:** 75.60 × 16.80 × 6
M: Diesel-electric; 11,880 hp **Man:** 34 men

ELBJØRN (1953)

D: 898 tons (1,400 fl) **S:** 12 kts **Dim:** 47 × 12.10 × 4.35
M: Diesel-electric; 3,600 hp

STOREBJØRN (1931)

D: 2,580 tons **Dim:** 59.10 × 14.75 × 5.70

DJIBOUTI REPUBLIC

On independence in 1977, a small naval/police force was established, employing one patrol craft formerly operated by French colonial police at Djibouti.

PATROL CRAFT

♦ *1 ex-French* — Bldr: Tecimar In serv. 1974

P 472 and P 474 1974 Tecimar

D: 30 tons **S:** 25 kts **Dim:** 13.30 × 4.10 × 1.10
A: 1/12.7-mm and 1/7/5-mm machine gun
M: 2 General Motors diesels; Model V-71; 6 cylinders; 240 hp

REMARK: Molded hull of stratified polyester.

DOMINICAN REPUBLIC

PERSONNEL: 370 officers and 3,630 men

MERCHANT MARINE (1-7-76): 20 ships — 8,469
(tankers: 1 ship — 674 grt)

FRIGATES

♦ *1 Canadian river-class transferred in 1947*

	Bldr	L
451 (ex-F-101) **MELLA** (ex-*Presidente Trujillo*, ex-*Carlplace*)	Davie S.B. (Lauzon)	6-7-44

Mella (now with No. 451 and second tripod mast just forward of original)

D: 1,445 tons (2,300 fl) **S:** 19 kts **Dim:** 92.35 × 11.45 × 4.30
A: 1/102-mm — 1/40-mm AA — 4/20-mm AA — 2/47-mm saluting guns
Man: 15 officers, 135 men **Range:** 7,700/12 **Fuel:** 645 tons
M: Triple expansion; 2 props; 5,500 hp **Boilers:** 2 (3-drum)

REMARKS: Bought in 1947. Serves as a training ship; can carry 50 cadets.

CORVETTES

♦ *2 ex-U.S. Admirable-class minesweeper-escorts, transferred in 1-66*

	Bldr	L
BM 454 PRESTOL BOTELLO (ex-*Separacion*, ex-*Skirmish*, MSF-303)	Assoc. Shbldg.	16-8-43
BM 455 TORTUGERO (ex-*Signet*, MSF-302)	Assoc. Shbldg.	16-8-43

Prestol Botello 1976

D: 600 tons (903 fl) **Dim:** 56.24 × 10.06 × 4.4
S: 15 kts **Man:** 100 men
A: 1/76-mm DP — 2/40-mm AA (I × 2) — 6/20-mm AA (I × 6)
M: General Motors diesels; 2 props; 1,710 hp
Fuel: 260 tons diesel **Range:** 5,600/9

REMARKS: BM-454 renamed 1976. All minesweeping equipment and ASW armament removed from both.

PATROL BOATS

♦ *1 patrol boat, U.S. PGM-71 class*

GC 102 BETELGEUSE (ex-PGM-77) Bldr: Peterson, U.S.A. (1965) Transferred 1-66

D: 130 tons (145.5 fl) **Dim:** 30.80 (30.20 pp) × 6.40 × 1.85
S: 17 kts **Man:** 20 men **Range:** 1,000/12
A: 1/40-mm AA — 4/20-mm AA (II × 2) — 2/12.7-mm machine guns (I × 2)
M: 8 General Motors 6-71 diesels; 2 props; 2,200 hp

REMARK: One of many gunboats of this class transferred to smaller navies by the United States.

♦ *3 patrol boats from the U.S. Coast Guard*

	In serv.
P 203 (ex-P-104) **RESTAURACION** (ex-*Galathea*, PC-108)	1932
P 204 (ex-P-105) **INDEPENDENCIA** (ex-*Icarus*, PC-110)	1931
P 205 (ex-P-106) **LIBERTAD** (ex-*Rafael Atoa*, ex-*Thetis*, PC-115)	1931

D: 235 tons (335 fl) **Dim:** 50.3 × 7.60 × 2.50
S: 14 kts **Man:** 40 men **Fuel:** 25 tons diesel
A: 1/76-mm DP — 1/40-mm AA — 1/20-mm AA
M: 2 Winton diesels; 2 props; 1,280 hp **Range:** 1,300/15

REMARK: All in reserve.

PATROL CRAFT

♦ *4 patrol craft*

	In serv.		In serv.
GC 104 ALDEBARÁN	1972	**GC 106 BELLATRIX**	1967
GC 103 PROCION	1967	**GC 107 CAPELLA**	1968

Bldr: Sewart Seacraft (Berwick, La.)

D: 60 tons **Dim:** 25.9 × 5.7 × 2.1 **Man:** 9 men
S: 21.7 kts **A:** 3/12.7-mm machine guns
M: 2 General Motors 16V71N diesels; 2 props; 1,400 hp **Range:** 800/20

♦ *1 patrol boat, former U.S. Army aircraft rescue launch*

GC 105 CAPITÁN ALSINA — L: 1944

D: 100 tons **S:** 17 kts **Dim:** 31.50 × 5.80 × 1.75
A: 2/20-mm AA **Man:** 20 men
M: 2 G.M. diesels; 2 props; 1,000 hp

REMARK: Wooden hull.

♦ *1 patrol craft, former U.S. 63-ft aircraft rescue launch*

GC 101 RIGEL In serv. 1953

D: 27 tons **S:** 18.5 kts **Dim:** 19.3 × 4.7 × 1.2
A: 2/12.7-mm machine guns **Range:** 450/15
M: 2 G.M. diesels; 2 props; 800 hp **Man:** 9 men

♦ *6 small patrol craft* — Bldr: Navy Yard. In serv. 1975

ALBACORA, ATUN, BONITO, CARITE, MERO, PICUNA

D: 30 tons **S:** 12 kts **Dim:** 13.7 × 4.0 × 1.8
A: 1/7.6-mm machine gun **M:** G.M. diesels; 200 hp

REMARK: Have auxiliary sail power.

AUXILIARY SHIPS

♦ *1 U.S. LSM, converted for cargo-carrying*

301 SIRIO (ex-LSM-483) Bldr: U.S.A., 10-3-45 Transferred in 1960

D: 734 tons (1,100 fl) **Dim:** 62.80 × 10.40 × 2.10
S: 12 kts **Man:** 30 men **Fuel:** 164 tons diesel
M: 2 General Motors diesels; 1,800 hp

DOMINICAN REPUBLIC *(continued)*

AUXILIARY SHIPS *(continued)*

♦ *2 U.S. LCUs, LCT (5) design, for logistics duties*

302 (ex-LA-2) **SAMANA, 303 ENRIQUILLO** (ex-*17 de Julio,* ex-LA 3)
Bldr: Dominican Naval SY, 1957-58

D: 128 tons (310 fl) **Dim:** 36.40 × 11 × 1.15
S: 8/7 kts **A:** 1/12.7-mm machine gun **Man:** 17 men
M: 3 G.M. diesels; 3 props; 450 hp **Fuel:** 80 tons diesel

♦ *3 hydrographic survey and buoy tenders, U.S. Cohoes class, transferred 9-76*

	Bldr	L
N . . . (ex-*Etlah,* AN-79)	Commercial Iron, Portland	16-12-44
N . . . (ex-*Passaconaway,* AN-86)	Marine Iron, Duluth	30-6-44
N . . . (ex-*Passaic,* AN-87)	Leatham D. Smith, Wisc.	29-6-44

D: 650 tons (775 fl) **Dim:** 51.4 (44.5 pp) × 10.3 × 3.3
S: 12.3 kts **Fuel:** 88 tons diesel
A: 1/76-mm DP — 3/20-mm AA
M: 1 Busch-Sulzer 539, electric drive; 1 prop; 1,200 hp

Remark: Former netlayers, purchased for conversion to general-purpose logistics support, navigational tender, and survey duties.

♦ *1 buoy tender, bought in 1949*

1 CAPOTILLO (ex-FB 101, ex-*Camillia*) Bldr: U.S.A., 1911
D: 327 tons **S:** 10 kts

♦ *2 small oilers* — Bldr: Ira S. Bushey, N.Y., loaned 4-1964

BT 4 CAPITÁN W. ARVELO (ex-U.S. YO-215) L: 1945
BT 5 CAPITÁN BEOTEGUI (ex-U.S. YO-213) L: 1944

D: 1,076 tons (fl) **S:** 8 kts **Dim:** 47.6 × 9.3 × 4.0
A: 1/20-mm AA **Cargo:** 6,071 barrels fuel
M: 2 Union diesels; 1 prop; 525 hp **Man:** 25 men

♦ *1 small survey ship*

LA 8 ATLANTIDA

♦ *9 tugs*

RM 21 MACORIX (ex-U.S. *Kiowa,* ATF-73), *transferred in 1973*

D: 1,280 tons (1,700 fl) **Dim:** 62.5 × 11.7 × 4.7
A: 1/76-mm DP **S:** 15 kts
M: 4 diesel-electric groups; 1 prop; 3,000 hp

RM 18 CAONABO (ex-U.S. *Sagamore,* ATA-208)

D: 534 tons (835 fl) **S:** 13 kts **Dim:** 43.6 × 10.3 × 4.0
M: 2 G.M. diesels, electric drive; 1 prop; 1,500 hp

RDM 303 OCOA — Bldr: U.S.A.

D: 50 tons (fl) **S:** 9 kts **Dim:** 17.1 × 4.3 × 1.2
M: 2 diesels; 2 props; 450 hp **Range:** 130/9

Remark: Former USN LCM modified as a tug, circa 1976.

RP 12 HERCULES, RP 13 GUACANAGARIX (500 hp), **RP 20 ISABELA** (300 hp), **PR 14 MAGUANA, RP 16 BOHECHIO, RP 19 CALDERAS** — small coastal tugs

DUBAI

Note: Military forces were formally merged in the United Arab Emirates in May 1976. The following Dubai-manned craft operate with the UAE Coast Guard:

♦ *1 "Spear"-class boat* — Bldr: Fairey Marine, Gt. Br.

D: 10 tons (fl) **S:** 30 kts **Dim:** 9.10 × 2.75 × 0.84
A: 2/7.62-mm machine guns **Range:** 200/26
M: 2 Perkins T-6 diesels; 2 props; 360 hp

♦ *1 "Interceptor"-class launch*

D: 4 tons (fl) **S:** 30 kts **Dim:** 7.6 × . . . × . . .
M: 2 outboard motors; 270 hp

Remark: Can carry a platoon of troops.

ECUADOR

PERSONNEL: 3,450 men, including 700 Marines

MERCHANT MARINE (1976): 46 ships — 180,623 grt
(tankers: 18 ships — 113,969 grt)

NAVAL AVIATION: A small detachment with two French Alouette III helicopters and one Israeli Arava light transport.

WARSHIPS UNDER CONSTRUCTION OR IN SERVICE AS OF 1 OCTOBER 1977

	L	Tons	Main armament
♦ *4 submarines*			
4 TYPE 209-MOD	1976-77	1,100	8/533-mm TT
♦ *3 frigates*			
1 EX-U.S. LPR	1943	1,400	1/127-mm DP, 6/40-mm AA
2 HUNT	1940	1,000	4/102-mm DP, 2/40-mm AA
♦ *2 corvettes*			
2 PCE-821	1943	640	1/76-mm DP, 6/40-mm AA, ASW weapons

♦ *11 missile, torpedo, and patrol boats*

♦ *3 amphibious ships*

SUBMARINES

♦ *4 German 209-Mod (IK-79), ordered in 1974* — Bldr: Howaldtswerke, Hamburg

	L		L
SHYRI	8-10-76	**HUANCAVILCA**	18-3-77
N . . .	. . .	**N . . .**	. . .

D: 1,100 tons standard, 1,260 surfaced, 1,390 submerged
Dim: 59.5 × 6.60 × 5.90
S: 21.5 kts (max. submerged for 5 minutes), 12 kts (with snorkel)
Endurance: 16 days **Man:** 5 officers, 26 men
A: 8/533-mm TT, fwd (plus 6 reserve torpedoes)
M: 4 MTU Type 12V-493-TY60 diesels; Siemens electric motor; 3,600 hp

REMARK: The latest version of a class previously sold to Argentina, Greece, and Peru.

FRIGATES

♦ *1 U.S. fast transport (LPR), transferred 7-67*

	Bldr	L	In serv.
D 01 MORAN VALVERDE (ex-*26 de Julio*, ex-*Enright*, APD-66)	Phila. Navy Yd	29-5-43	21-9-43

D: 1,400 tons (2,130 fl) **S:** 23 kts **Dim:** 93.27 × 11.27 × 4.70
A: 1/127-mm DP — 6/40-mm AA (II × 3) — 2 depth-charge racks
M: GE turbo-electric drive, 2 Foster-Wheeler "D" boilers; 2 props; 12,000 hp
Fuel: 350 tons **Range:** 2,000/23, 5,000/15 **Man:** 212 men
Electron Equipt: Radar: 1/SPS-6, 1/SPS-10

REMARKS: Could carry 162 troops when in USN. Davits can handle four LCPR/LCVP. Now has a raised helicopter deck over the stern area.

Moran Valverde 1974

♦ *2 ex-British Hunt class, bought in 1955*

	Bldr	L
D 02 PRESIDENTE ALFARO (ex-*Quantock*)	Scotts SB & E (Greenock)	22-4-40
D 03 PRESIDENTE VELASCO IBARRA (ex-*Meynell*)	Swan Hunter & Wigham Richardson	9-4-40

Presidente Velasco Ibarra (now D 03) 1970

FRIGATES (*continued*)

D: 1,000 tons (1,490 fl) **Dim:** 83.00 × 8.83 × 4.3
S: 22/21 kts **Man:** 146 men **Range:** 2,000/12, 800/20
A: 4/102-mm DP (II × 2) — 2/40-mm AA (II × 1) — 2/20-mm AA (I × 2) — 2 depth-charge projectors — 2 depth-charge racks
M: Parsons GT; 2 boilers; 2 props; 19,000 hp **Fuel:** 280 tons

CORVETTES

♦ *2 ex-U.S. PCE-821 class, transferred in 1960*

P 21 ESMERALDAS (ex-*Eunice*, PCE-846) L: 20-12-43
P 23 MANABI (ex-*Pascagoula*, PCE-874) L: 11-5-43

Esmeraldas 1973

Bldrs: Pullam Standard Car, Chicago/Albina Eng. Mach., Portland
D: 640 tons (903 fl) **S:** 15 kts **Dim:** 56.24 × 10.08 × 2.90
A: 1/76-mm DP — 6/40-mm AA (II × 3) — 2/20-mm AA (I × 2) — hedgehog — 2 depth-charge projectors — 2 depth-charge racks
Man: 100 men **Range:** 4,300/10
M: 2 General Motors 12-567A diesels; 1,800 hp

GUIDED MISSILE PATROL BOATS

♦ *3 Quito class* — Bldr: Lürssen, Vegasack (F.R.G.)

LM 31 QUITO — L: 20-11-76 **LM 32 CUENCA** — L: 11-76
LM 33 GUAYAQUIL — L: 5-76

D: 250 tons **S:** 40 kts **Dim:** 49.90 (42.50 pp) × 7.0 × 2.40 (prop.)
A: 4/MM 38 Exocet systems — 1/76-mm DP OTO Melara compact — 2/35-mm AA (II × 1)
Electron Equipt: Thomson-CSF fire control **Range:** 700/40, 1,850/16
M: 4 MTU diesels; 4 props; 14,000 hp
Electric: 330 kw **Man:** 34 men

Remark: Another version of the Lürssen Type 148/*La Combattante* basic design.

TORPEDO BOATS

♦ *3 Manta class* — Bldr: Lürssen, Vegesack (F.R.G.)

L 91 MANTA — L: 1-71 **L 92 TULCAN** — L: 12-70
L 93 NUEVA ROCAFUERTE (ex-*Tena*)

Manta 1971

D: 119 tons (134 fl) **Dim:** 36.20 × 5.80 × 1.70
S: 35 kts **Range:** 1,500/15, 700/30 **Man:** 19 men
A: 1/40-mm AA — 2/533-mm TT — 2/81-mm Oerlikon rocket launchers (II × 1)
M: 3 Mercedes-Benz diesels; 3 props; 9,000 hp
Fuel: 21 tons

Remark: Similar to Chilean *Guacolda*, but slower.

PATROL BOATS

♦ *2 ex-U.S. PGM, transferred in 1965*

LC 61 VEINTECINCO DE JULIO (ex-*Quito*, ex-PGM 75)
LC 62 DIEZ DE AGOSTO (ex-*Guayaquil*, ex-PGM 76)

Veintecinco de Julio (now LC 61) 1970

Bldr: Petersen, U.S.A., 1965
D: 130 tons (147 fl) **Dim:** 30.81 (30.20 pp) × 6.45 × 2.30
S: 20 kts **Man:** 15 men
A: 1/40-mm — 4/20-mm (II × 2) — 2/12.7-mm machine guns
M: 4 Mercedes-Benz diesels; 2 props; 2,200 hp **Range:** 1,000/12

AMPHIBIOUS WARFARE SHIPS

♦ *1 former U.S. LST, bought 2-77*

N . . . (ex-*Sutter County*, LST-1158) Bldr: Chicago Bridge, L: 30-5-45

D: 1,650 tons (4,080 fl) **S:** 11.6 kts **Dim:** 100.04 × 15.24 × 4.30
A: 8/40-mm (II × 2, I × 4) **Range:** 7,200/10
M: 2 G.M. 12-567A diesels; 2 props; 1,700 hp **Man:** 119 men

♦ *2 U.S. LSM class, transferred 1958*

T 51 JAMBELLI (ex-LSM-539), **T 52 TARQUI** (ex-LSM-555). Bldr: U.S.A., 1945

D: 513 tons (1,095 fl) **S:** 12.5 kts **Dim:** 62.0 × 10.5 × 2.2
A: 2/40-mm AA **Man:** 60 men **Range:** 2,500/12
M: 2 G.M. 16-278A diesels; 2 props; 2,800 hp

REMARK: Used as transports.

AUXILIARY SHIPS

♦ *2 hydrographic survey ships*

O 112 RIGEL — 50 tons, 10 men — Bldr: Ecuador, L: 1975
O 111 ORION (ex-*Mulberry*, ex-AN-27) — former netlayer, transferred 1965
Bldr: American S.B., Cleveland, Ohio, L: 26-3-41

D: 560 tons (805 fl) **S:** 12.5 kts **Dim:** 49.7 (44.5 pp) × 9.3 × 3.6
M: 1 Busch-Sulzer diesel; electric drive; 800 hp **Man:** 20 men

REMARK: Armament removed, replaced by charthouse.

♦ *1 small cargo ship, U.S. Army FS class, transferred 1963*

T 53 CALICUCHIMA (ex-FS-525) In serv. 1944

D: 650 tons (950 fl) **S:** 11.5 kts **Dim:** 53.7 × 9.8 × 4.3
M: 2 G.M. diesels; 2 props; 500 hp

REMARK: Used to supply Galápagos Islands.

♦ *1 small water tanker, U.S. YW class, transferred 1963*

T 62 ATALHUAPA (ex-YW 131) Bldr: Leatham D. Smith, Wisc., 1945

D: 415 tons (1,235 fl) **S:** 11.5 kts **Dim:** 53.1 × 9.8 × 4.6
M: 1 G.M. diesel; 1 prop; 640 hp **Cargo:** 200,000 gallons fresh water

♦ *4 tugs*

R 101 CAYAMBE (ex-*Los Rios*, ex-*Cusabo*, ex-ATF-155), transferred 1960
Bldr: Charleston SB&DD, L: 26-2-45

D: 1,235 tons (1,675 fl) **S:** 16.5 kts **Dim:** 62.5 × 11.7 × 4.7
A: 1/76-mm DP — 2/40-mm AA (I × 2) — 2/20-mm AA **Man:** 85 men
M: 4 G.M. 12-278A diesels, electric drive; 1 prop; 3,000 hp

Cayambe (now R 101) 1966

R 102 SANGAY (ex-*Losa*) L: 1952, bought 1964

D: 295 tons (390 fl) **S:** 12 kts **Dim:** 32.6 × 7.9 × 4.25
M: 1 Fairbanks-Morse diesel

R 103 COTOPAXI (ex-*R. T. Ellis*) L: 1945, bought from U.S.A., 1947

D: 150 tons **S:** 9 kts **Dim:** 25.0 × 6.62 × 2.90
M: Diesel; 1 prop; 650 hp

R 104 ANTIZANA — Small tug; no other information

VARIOUS SHIPS

♦ *1 sail training ship*

BE 01 GUAYAS — Bldr: Celaya SY, Bilbao, Spain — L: 22-10-76

D: 934 grt **S:** 10.5 kts **Dim:** 76.2 × 10.6 × 4.2
M: G.M. 12V-149 diesel; 700 hp

REMARK: Three-masted bark.

♦ *1 repair barge, transferred 7-62*

BT 123 PUTAMAYO (ex-YR-34) Bldr: New York Navy Yard, 1944

D: . . . **Dim:** 45.7 × 10.4 × . . .

♦ *1 floating dry dock, transferred 1961*

DF 121 AMAZONAS (ex-ARD 17) Bldr: U.S.A., 1944

Dim: 149.9 × 24.7 × 10.0 **Capacity:** 3,500 tons

EGYPT

PERSONNEL: approx. 17,500 men with more than 1,500 officers

MERCHANT MARINE (1976): 157 ships — 376,066 grt
(tankers: 22 ships — 126,449 grt)

NAVAL AVIATION: A branch of the Air Force which includes a few IL-28 torpedo attack planes, a few Badgers, and about 24 MI-4 ASW helicopters, all of these aircraft from the U.S.S.R.

WARSHIPS IN SERVICE OR UNDER CONSTRUCTION AS OF 1 OCTOBER 1977*

	L	Tons	Main armament
♦ *12 submarines*			
6 ROMEO	1957	1,400	8/533-mm TT
6 WHISKEY	1955	1,050	6/533-mm TT
♦ *5 destroyers*			
4 SKORY	1950-54	2,400	4/130-mm, 2/85-mm or 4/57-mm AA, 10/533-mm TT
1 Z	1944	1,730	4/102-mm DP, 6/40-mm AA, 8/533-mm TT
♦ *3 frigates*			
♦ *16 guided missile boats*			
6 OSA-I	...	175	4 Styx systems
4 KOMAR	1961-63	71	2 Styx systems
6 EGYPTIAN KOMAR	...	71	2 surface-to surface systems, type unknown
♦ *30 torpedo boats*			
♦ *12 patrol boats*			
♦ *12 minesweepers*			
♦ *17 amphibious ships*			

SUBMARINES

♦ *6 Soviet R class (transferred 1966-69)*

D: 1,400 tons surfaced, 1,800 submerged **Dim:** 76.0 × 7.0 × 5.40
S: 17/15 kts **Range:** 7,000/5 snorkel

* Although various schemes to build or acquire European warships and submarines have been discussed since the Soviet withdrawal, no firm commitments have been announced.

A: 8/533-mm TT (6 fwd, 2 aft) — 18 torpedoes or 36 mines
M: Diesel propulsion and electric motors; 2 props; 4,000/2,500 hp
Endurance: 45 days **Man:** 60 men

♦ *6 Soviet W class (transferred from 6-57 to 8-62)*

D: 1,050 tons surfaced, 1,350 submerged **Dim:** 74 × 6.6 × 4.8
S: 17/16 kts **Man:** 60 men **Range:** 6,000/5
A: 6/533-mm TT (4 fwd, 2 aft) — 14 torpedoes or 28 mines
M: Diesels and electric motors; 2 props; 4,000/2,500 hp
Endurance: 40-45 days

REMARK: Reported in poor condition.

DESTROYERS

♦ *4 Soviet Skory class*

	Bldr	Transferred
6 OCTOBER (ex-*El Nasser*)	U.S.S.R.	1956
EL ZAFFER	U.S.S.R.	1967
DAMIET	U.S.S.R.	1967
SUEZ	U.S.S.R.	1956

Egyptian Skory class

D: 2,400 tons (3,200 fl) **Dim:** 121.50 × 12.50 × 4.60
S: 34 kts **Man:** 250 men **Range:** 900/32, 3,500/15
A: *El Zaffer, Suez:* 4/130-mm DP (II × 2) — 2/85-mm AA (II × 1) — 8/37-mm AA (II × 4) — 4/25-mm AA (II × 2) — 10/533-mm TT (V × 2) — 2 depth-charge projectors — 2 depth-charge racks — 80 mines

DESTROYERS (*continued*)

6 October, Damiet: 4/130-mm DP (II × 2) — 4/57-mm AA (IV × 1) — 4/37-mm AA (II × 2) — 4/25-mm AA (II × 2) — 10/533-mm TT (V × 2) — 2 MBU-2500 — 2 depth-charge racks — 80 mines

M: GT; 2 props; 62,000 hp

REMARK: The ex-*El Zaffer* and the *Damiet* were replaced in 1968 by two ships of the same class and with the same names.

♦ *1 British Z class*

	Bldr	Laid down	L	In serv.
EL FATEH (ex-*Zenith*)	Wm. Denny	19-5-42	5-6-44	22-12-44

El Fateh 1975

D: 1,730 tons (2,575 fl) **Dim:** 110.6 × 10.9 × 5.2
S: 31 kts **Range:** 2,800/20 **Man:** 250 men
A: 4/102-mm DP (I × 4) — 6/40-mm AA (II × 1, I × 4) — 8/533-mm TT — 4 depth-charge projectors
M: GT; 2 props; 2 boilers; 40,000 hp **Fuel:** 580 tons

FRIGATES

♦ *1 British Black Swan class, bought in 12-49*

	Bldr	Laid down	L	In serv.
EL TARIK (ex-*El Malek Farouk*, ex-HMS *Whimbrel*)	Yarrow & Co.	10-41	25-8-42	1-43

D: 1,470 tons (1,925 fl) **Dim:** 91.30 × 11.73 × 3.45
S: 14 kts **Man:** 180 men **Range:** 4,500/12
A: 6/102-mm DP (II × 3) — 4/40-mm AA — 4 depth-charge projectors
M: Parsons GT; 2 props; 2 boilers; 4,300 hp **Fuel:** 370 tons

♦ *1 British River class, bought 12-49.* Used as submarine tender

	Bldr	Laid down	L	In serv.
RACHID (ex-HMS *Spey*)	Smith's Dock Co., Ltd.	7-41	18-21-41	3-42

D: 1,460 tons (2,175 fl) **Dim:** 91.85 × 11.17 × 4.34 (fl)
S: 19 kts **Range:** 7,700/12, 5,000/16
A: 1/102-mm — 4/40-mm AA (II × 2) — 2/12.7-mm machine guns
M: Triple expansion; 2 props; 2 boilers; 5,500 hp **Fuel:** 640 tons

♦ *1 British Hunt class, transferred 7-50*

Rachid 1974

	Bldr	L
PORT SAID (ex-*Mohamed Ali El Kebit*, ex-*Cottesmore*)	Yarrow & Co.	5-9-40

D: 1,000 tons (1,490 fl) **Dim:** 85.3 × 8.8 × 4.3
S: 25 kts **Man:** 146 men **Range:** 2,000/12, 800/25
A: 4/102-mm DP (II × 2) — 2/25-mm AA — 2/12.7-mm machine guns
M: Parsons GT; 2 props; 2 boilers; 19,000 hp **Fuel:** 280 tons

PATROL BOATS

♦ *12 Soviet SO-1 class, transferred since 1962-63*

D: 190 tons (215 fl) **S:** 28 kts **Dim:** 42.0 × 6.1 × 1.9
A: 4/25-mm AA (II × 2) — 4/MBU-1800 rocket launchers — 2 depth-charge racks — mines. Some are armed with 2/533-mm TT as well
M: 3 diesels; 3 props; 6,000 hp **Man:** 30 men
Electron Equipt: Radar: Pot Head

REMARK: Some carry SA-N-5 SAMs.

GUIDED MISSILE BOATS

♦ *6 ex-Soviet Osa-I class, transferred since 1966*

Soviet Osa-I

GUIDED MISSILE BOATS (*continued*)

D: 175 tons (210 fl) **S:** 36 kts **Dim:** 39 × 7.7 × 1.80
A: 4 Styx systems (I × 4) — 4/30-mm AA (II × 2) — some carry SA-7 Grail
Electron Equipt: 1/Square Tie, 1/Drum Tilt
M: 3 M503A diesels; 3 props; 12,000 hp **Endurance:** 450/34, 700/20

♦ *4 ex-Soviet Komar class, transferred since 1966*

D: 71 tons (82 fl) **S:** 40 kts **Dim:** 25.3 × 7.0 × 2.0
A: 2 Styx systems (I × 2) — 2/25-mm AA **Endurance:** 650/30
M: 4 M50 diesels; 4 props; 4,800 hp
Electron Equipt: Radar: Square Tie

♦ *6 built in Egypt, based on the Komar class*

REMARKS: May be fitted with 2 European surface-to-surface missiles. Still incomplete.

Egyptian Komar (Soviet-built) 1976

TORPEDO BOATS

♦ *6 Soviet Shershen class, transferred from 1967 on*

D: 150 tons (180 fl) **S:** 45 kts **Dim:** 34 × 7.2 × 1.5
A: 4/30-mm AA (II × 2) — 4/533-mm TT (I × 4)
Electron Equipt: 1/Square Tie, 1/Drum Tilt
M: 3 diesels; 3 props; 12,000 hp

REMARKS: Three are armed with two 40-tubed 122-mm rocket launchers instead of torpedoes. Some carry SA-N-5 missiles as well.

♦ *20 ex-Soviet P-6 class, transferred since 1960*

D: 56 tons (66.5 fl) **S:** 43 kts (cruising) **Dim:** 25.3 × 6.1 × 1.7
A: 4/25-mm AA (II × 2) — 2/533-mm TT
M: 4 M50 diesels; 4 props; 4,800 hp

REMARKS: A few are armed with one 40-tubed 122-mm rocket launcher, have no TT, and the after 25-mm mount removed; these carry 2/12.7-mm machine guns. Some of these boats were built in Egypt. At least two have 4/533-mm TT.

Egyptian P-6 equipped with multiple rocket launcher 1975

♦ *4 ex-Soviet P-4 class*

D: 19.3 tons (22.4 fl) **S:** 55 kts **Dim:** 19.3 × 3.7 × 1.0
A: 2/14.5-mm AA (II × 1) — 8/122-mm rockets (VIII × 1)
M: 2 M50 diesels; 2 props; 2,400 hp

P-4 with octuple rocket launcher mounted on bow 1974

PATROL CRAFT

♦ *30 fiberglass-hulled DC-35 class* — Bldr: Dawncraft, Wroxham, G.B. Delivered 1977

D: 4 tons **S:** 25 kts **Dim:** 10.7 × 3.5 × 0.8
M: 2 Perkins T-6-354 diesels; 2 props; 290 hp **Man:** 4 men

REMARK: For police service.

♦ *3 or more NISR class, for Coast Guard* — Bldr: De Castro, Port Said, 1963

D: 110 tons (fl) **M:** 2 Maybach diesels **A:** 1/20-mm

♦ *20 launches* — Bldr: Bertram, Miami, U.S.A., 1963

D: 8 tons (fl) **S:** 24 kts **Dim:** 8.5 × . . . × . . .
A: 2/12.7-mm machine guns — 4/122-mm rockets (I × 4)
M: Diesels; 2 props

MINE WARFARE SHIPS

♦ *4 ex-Soviet Yurka-class minesweepers, delivered in 1969*

ASSUAN, GUIZEN, QENA, SUHAG

D: 460 tons (fl) **Dim:** 52.0 × 8.8 × 2.0
S: 18 kts **A:** 4/30-mm AA (II × 2) — 20 mines
M: Diesels; 2 props; 4,000 hp **Electron Equipt:** 1/Don

♦ *6 ex-Soviet T-43-class minesweepers*

BAHAIRA CHARKIEH GHARBIA
ASSIUT DAQHALA SINAI

Bldr: U.S.S.R. (1953). Transferred since 1956, 1 in 1970

D: 500 tons (580 fl) **Dim:** 58.0 × 8.4 × 2.3
S: 14 kts **M:** 2 diesels; 2 props; 2,200 hp
A: 4/37-mm AA (II × 2) — 8/12.7-mm machine guns — depth charges

♦ *2 Soviet T-301-class minesweepers, delivered in 1962–63*

EL FAYOUD, EL MANUFIEH

D: 145.8 tons (160 fl) **S:** 12.5 kts **Dim:** 38.0 × 5.1 × 1.6
A: 2/45-mm — 2 machine guns **M:** 3 diesels; 3 props; 1,440 hp

AMPHIBIOUS WARFARE SHIPS

♦ *3 Soviet Polnocny-class Type I LSM, transferred in 1974*

D: 900 tons (fl) **S:** 18 kts **Dim:** 72.5 × 8.5 × 2.0
A: 2/30-mm AA (II × 1) — 2/140-mm multiple rocket launchers (XVIII × 2)
M: 2 diesels; 2 props; 4,000 hp

♦ *9 ex-Soviet Vydra-class LCUs, transferred 1967–69*

D: 750 tons (fl) **S:** 10 kts **Dim:** 54.8 × 8.1 × 2.0
A: 4/40-mm AA (II × 2) — 8 15-tube rocket launchers
M: 2 diesels; 2 props; 800 hp

♦ *5 ex-Soviet SMB-I-class LCUs, transferred 1965*

D: 335 tons (fl) **S:** 10 kts **Dim:** 48.5 × 6.5 × 2.0
A: . . . **M:** 2 diesels; 2 props; 600 hp
Cargo: 200 tons **Man:** 16 men

♦ *10 to 12 LCMs of various origins*

Egyptian Vydra with rocket launchers 1976

AUXILIARY SHIPS

♦ *4 Soviet Okhtenshiy-class tugs, transferred in 1966*

AL ISKANDARAN, EL AGAMI, EL MEY, N . . .

♦ *2 Soviet Nyryat-class diving tenders, transferred in 1964*

♦ *2 Soviet Poluchat-class torpedo-recovery boats*

♦ *2 PO-2-class tenders (70 ton)*

♦ *1 Soviet Sekstan-class degaussing ship*

TRAINING SHIP

EL HORRIA (ex-*Mahroussa*) Bldr: Samuda, Scotland, 1865

D: 4,561 tons (fl) **S:** 16 kts **Dim:** 145.6 (121.9 pp) × 13.0 × 5.3
A: Several machine guns **M:** GT; 3 props; 5,500 hp

REMARKS: Visited U.S.A. during July 1976. World's oldest active naval ship.

El Horria G. Garier, 1976

EL SALVADOR

PERSONNEL: 130 officers and men

MERCHANT MARINE (1976): 3 ships — 2,128 grt

PATROL CRAFT

♦ *3 aluminum-hulled, ordered 1976* — Bldr: Camcraft, New Orleans

GC 6, GC 7, GC 8

D: . . . **S:** . . . **Dim:** 30.5 × . . . × . . .

♦ *1 aluminum-hulled, transferred 9-67* — Bldr: Sewart Seacraft, Berwick, La.

GC 5

D: 33 tons (fl) **S:** 25 kts **Dim:** 19.8 × 4.9 × 1.5
A: 3/12.7-mm machine guns
M: 3 G.M. 8V71 diesels; 3 props; 1,590 hp

♦ *2 ex-U.S. Coast Guard utility boats* L: 1950

GC 3, GC 4

D: 10.6 tons **S:** 18 kts **Dim:** 12.3 × 3.4 × 1.0
A: 1/12.7 machine gun **Range:** 160/18
M: 2 diesels; 2 props; 400 hp

♦ *1 ex-British HMDL, bought 1959*

GC 2 (ex-*Nohaba*, ex-*HDML* . . .) In serv. 1942

D: 46 tons (54 fl) **S:** 11.5 kts **Dim:** 21.9 × 4.8 × 1.7
A: 1/12.7-mm machine gun **M:** 2 diesels; 2 props; 300 hp

♦ *25 small launches with outboard motors*

EQUATORIAL GUINEA

PERSONNEL: 100 men

♦ *1 P-6-class torpedo boat, delivered in 1974*

D: 56 tons (66.5 fl) **S:** 43 kts **Dim:** 25.3 × 6.1 × 1.7
A: 4/25-mm AA (II × 2) — 2/533-mm TT (I × 2) **Man:** 12 men
M: 4 M50 diesels; 4 props; 4,800 hp **Endurance:** 400/32, 700/15
Electron Equipt: Radar: Skin Head

♦ *1 Poluchat-class patrol boat, delivered in 1974*

D: 80 tons (90 fl) **S:** 18 kts **Dim:** 29.6 × 5.8 × 1.5
A: 2/14.5-mm machine guns **Man:** 20 men
M: 2 M50 diesels; 2 props; 2,400 hp

♦ *2 small patrol craft*

ETHIOPIA

PERSONNEL: 1,200 men including 230 officers

MERCHANT MARINE (1976): 23 ships — 24,593 grt
(tankers: 1 ship — 2,051 grt)

PATROL BOATS

♦ *4 aluminum-hulled boats, ordered 1976* — Bldr: Swiftships, Morgan City, Louisiana

P 201, P 202, P 203, P 204

D: 118 tons (fl) **S:** 32 kts **Dim:** 32.0 × 7.2 × 2.1
A: 4/30-mm Emerlec AA (II × 2) **Man:** 21 men
M: 2 MTU MB 16V538 TB90 diesels; 2 props; 7,000 hp
Electron Equipt: Radar: Decca RM 916 **Range:** 1,200/18

REMARK: Four were delivered in 4-77; two were canceled by the U.S. arms embargo.

P 202

PATROL BOATS (*continued*)

♦ *4 ex-U.S. Coast Guard Cape design*

PC 12 (ex-CG-WPB-95310) **PC 14** (ex-U.S. PGM-54)
PC 13 (ex-U.S. PGM-53) **PC 15** (ex-U.S. PGM-58)

Bldr: Petersen (U.S.A.) — 1955-62

PC 14

D: 80 tons (101 fl) **S:** 20 kts **Dim:** 28.80 × 5.80 × 1.55
A: 1/40-mm AA — 1/20-mm AA **Man:** 15 men
M: 4 diesels; 2 props; 2,200 hp **Range:** 1,500/10

REMARKS: Transferred in 1958 (3), 1961 (1) and 1962 (1). PC-11 lost in action, 4-77.

♦ *1 ex-Dutch minesweeper, bought in 1970*

MS 41 (ex-M-829 *Elst*) Bldr: Netherlands (21-3-56)

D: 373 tons (417 fl) **S:** 14 kts **Dim:** 46.62 × 8.78 × 2.30
A: 2/40-mm AA (I × 2) **Man:** 40 men
M: 2 Werkspoor diesels; 2 props; 2,500 hp **Range:** 2,500/10

REMARKS: For profile, see *Wildervank* class, Netherlands section. All minesweeping gear removed.

♦ *1 ex-Yugoslav Kraljevica-class subchaser, donated 1975*

N . . . (ex-509) In serv. 1953

D: 190 tons (202 fl) **S:** 18 kts **Dim:** 41.0 × 6.3 × 2.2
A: 2/40-mm AA (I × 2) — 4/20-mm AA (I × 4)
M: 2 M.A.N. diesels; 2 props; 3,300 hp

PATROL CRAFT

♦ *4 aluminum-hulled patrol craft*

GB 21, GB 22, GB 23, GB 24 (ex-*John, Caroline, Patrick, Jacqueline*)

Bldr: Sewart Seacraft, Berwick, La., 1966-67

D: 15 tons **S:** 20 kts **Dim:** 13.1 × 3.9 × 0.9
A: 2/12.7-mm machine guns **Man:** 7 men
M: 2 G.M. diesels; 2 props; 500 hp

GB 23 1976

AMPHIBIOUS SHIPS

♦ *2 LCU, French EDIC class* — Bldr: SFCN, Villeneuve la Garronne, 5-1977

L 1035 **L 1036**

D: 250 tons (670 fl) **S:** 8 kts **Dim:** 59.0 × 11.95 × 1.3
A: 2/20-mm AA (I × 2) **Range:** 1,800/8
M: 2 MGO diesels; 2 props; 1,000 hp **Man:** 1 officer, 15 men

♦ *2 ex-USN LCM and 2 LCVP transferred, two in 1962 and two in 1971*

TRAINING SHIP

	Bldr	L
A 01 ETHIOPIA (ex-*Orca*, AVP-49)	Lake Washington SY	4-10-42

Ethiopia

D: 1,766 tons (2,800 fl) **Dim:** 94.70 (91.50 pp) × 12.52 × 3.65
S: 18 kts **Man:** 215 men **Range:** 15,000/12
A: 1/127-mm DP — 5/40-mm AA
M: 2 Fairbanks-Morse 38D diesels; 2 props; 6,000 hp

REMARK: Transferred in 1-62.

FIJI

A small naval force was established in 6-74 for coastal patrol, anti-smuggling, and local hydrographic surveying duties.

PERSONNEL (1976): 159 men (19 officers)

PATROL BOATS

♦ *3 ex-U.S. Navy Bird-class minesweepers*

Bldr: Bellingham SY, Washington

	In serv.
205 KULA (ex-*Vireo*, MSC-205)	6-55
206 KIRO (ex-*Warbler*, MSC-206)	7-55
209 KIKAU (ex-*Woodpecker*, MSC-209)	2-56

D: 370 tons (fl) **S:** 13 kts **Dim:** 43.9 × 8.5 × 2.6
A: 1/20-mm AA — 2/12.7-mm machine guns **Range:** 2,500/10
M: 2 G.M. 8-268A diesels; 2 props; 880 hp **Man:** 39 men

REMARKS: The first two were transferred 10-75, the third 6-76. Most minesweeping gear removed.

SURVEY SHIP

♦ **RUVE** (ex-*Volasiga*, ex-*Marinetta*), transferred 6-76 from Maritime Department.

Dim: 28.7 × 5.3 × 2.3

FINLAND

The naval force, limited to 10,000 tons and 4,500 men by the Treaty of Paris, is a separate establishment under the orders of the chief of the armed forces. Submarines and torpedo boats are excluded from the fleet and there is no naval aviation.

PERSONNEL (1977): about 2,500, including 200 officers.

MERCHANT MARINE (1976): 350 ships — 2,115,322 grt
(tankers: 52 ships — 1,127,954 grt)

NAVAL PROGRAM

Present plans are to bring the Finnish navy to the following strength by 1988, having passed 8,000 tons in 1983 and reaching 8,600 at the later date, the warships being divided as follows:

♦ 6 frigates/corvettes (4 currently)

♦ 24 fast small boats (19 currently)

♦ 2 minelayers (1 currently)

♦ 14 minesweepers (6 currently)

♦ 8 patrol boats (5 currently) with minesweeping capability.

This goal will require considerable effort because by 1980 many of the ships in today's Finnish forces will be at best obsolescent.

WARSHIPS IN SERVICE OR UNDER CONSTRUCTION AS OF 1 OCTOBER 1977

	L	Tons	Main armament
♦ *2 frigates*			
2 RIGA	1955	1,600	3/100-mm, 2/40-mm AA, 3/533-mm TT
♦ *2 corvettes*			
2 TURUNMAA	1967	650	1/120-mm AA, 2/40-mm AA
♦ *5 guided missile patrol boats*			
4 OSA-II			
1 ISKU			
♦ *20 patrol boats, including 13 Nuoli and 2 Vasama*			
♦ *2 minelayers*			
♦ *6 minesweepers*			

WEAPONS

The *Turunmaa*-class corvettes have a single barrel automatic Bofors 120-mm gun with the following characteristics:

- weight without munitions: 28.5 tons
- length: 46 calibers
- muzzle velocity: 800 m/sec
- training speed: 40°/sec
- elevation speed: 30°/sec
- arc of elevation: −10° to +80°
- maximum rate of fire: 80 rounds/min
- projectile weight: 35 kg
- maximum effective range, surface fire: 12,000 m

FRIGATES

♦ *2 Soviet Riga class, transferred in the spring of 1964*

HAMEENMAA, USIMAA — Bldr: U.S.S.R.

Hameenmaa prior to rearmament

FRIGATES (*continued*)

D: 1,600 (fl) **S:** 28/27 kts **Dim:** 91.0 × 11.0 × 3.4
A: 3/100-mm AA — 2/40-mm AA (I × 2) — 2/30-mm AA (II × 1) — 3/533-mm TT (III × 1) — 1 hedgehog, 4 depth-charge projectors, 2 depth-charge racks
Man: 175 men **Range:** 2,000/10
Electron Equipt: Radars: 1/Neptune, 1/Slim Net, 1/Sun Visor B
M: GT; 2 props; 2 boilers; 20,000 hp

REMARK: The twin 30-mm mount is carried at the extreme bow.

CORVETTES

♦ *2 Finnish Turunmaa class*

	Bldr	Laid down	L	In serv.
TURUNMAA	Wärtsilä, Helsinki	3-67	11-7-67	8-68
KARJALA	Wärtsilä, Helsinki	3-67	16-8-67	10-68

Karjala

D: 650 tons (770 fl) **S:** 35 kts **Dim:** 74.10 × 7.80 × 2.60 (light)
A: 1/120-mm Bofors automatic, 2/40-mm AA (I × 2) — 2/30-mm (II × 1) — depth charges
M: CODOG propulsion: 1 Bristol-Siddeley Olympus gas turbine; 3 Mercedes-Benz diesels; 3 props; 22,000 hp
Electron Equipt: Radars: 1/HSA M22, 1/navigational **Man:** 70 men

REMARKS: Flush-deck hull; closed bridge; sharp profile. Cruises on the diesel engines (3 × 1,100 hp) at 17 knots. Ka-Me-Wa controllable-pitch propellers. Have Vosper fin stabilizers.

GUIDED MISSILE PATROL BOATS

♦ *4 Soviet Osa-II class, transferred in 1975*

TUIMA, TUISKU, TUULA, TYRSKY

D: 210 tons (240 fl) **S:** 36 kts **Dim:** 39.0 × 7.7 × 1.8
A: 4 SS-N-2 Styx — 4/30-mm AA (II × 2) **Range:** 450/34
Electron Equipt: Radars: 1/Square Tie, 1/Drum Tilt, 1/navigation
M: 3 M504 diesels; 3 props; 15,000 hp

REMARK: Some Western electronic equipment has been added.

♦ **ISKU** — Bldr: Reposaaren Konepaja, Pori, 1969

D: 115 tons (140 fl) **S:** 15 kts **Dim:** 26.35 × 8.70 × 2.0
A: 2/30-mm AA — 4 Styx missiles
M: Soviet M50 diesels; 4 props; 3,600 hp

REMARK: Bargelike hull.

PATROL BOATS

♦ *13 Nuoli class*

NUOLI 1 to **13** (1961-63)

D: 64 tons (fl) **S:** 40 kts **Dim:** 22.0 × 6.65 × 1.50
A: 1/40-mm — 1/20-mm **Electron Equipt:** Band X radars
M: 3 Soviet M50 diesels; 2,700 hp

♦ *2 British Dark class*

VASAMA I, VASAMA II — Bldr: Saunders Roe Anglesey Ltd., 1955-57

D: 70 tons (fl) **S:** 42 kts **Dim:** 21.75 (20.42 pp) × 5.85 × 1.85
A: 2/40-mm AA — mines **Man:** 13 men
M: Napier-Deltic diesels; 2 props; 5,000 hp

♦ *5 Rihtniemi and Ruissalo class convertible patrol boat/minesweepers*

R 1 RIHTNIEMI **R 3 RUISSALO** **R 5 RÖYTTA**
R 2 RYMÄTTYLÄ **R 4 RAISIO**

Bldr: Rauma SY, 1956-59

Ruissalo 1972

D: 110 tons (130 fl) **S:** 18 kts **Dim:** 34.0 × 6.0 × 1.8
A: 1/40-mm — 1/20-mm AA Madsen — mines **Man:** 20 men
M: Mercedes-Benz diesels; 2 variable-pitch props; 2,500 hp

REMARKS: R-1 and R-2 are 90 tons, Dim: 31.0 × 5.7 × 1.7, and have only 1,400 hp for 15 knots. R-3 to R-5 can carry one Squid triple ASW mortar.

MINE WARFARE SHIPS

♦ *1 800-ton, 70-meter minelayer/training ship under construction to replace Matti Kurki and Ruotsinsalmi — planned for 1978-79*

MINE WARFARE SHIPS (*continued*)

♦ **KEIHÄSSALMI** — Bldr: Valmet Oy, Helsinki — L: 16-3-57

Keihässalmi prior to rearmament

D: 290 tons (360 fl) **S:** 15 kts **Dim:** 56.0 × 7.7 × 2.0
A: 4/30-mm AA (II × 2) — 2/20-mm AA — 100 mines
M: 2 Wärtsilä diesels; 2 props; 2,000 hp **Man:** 60 men
Electron Equipt: Radar: Drum Tilt added 1976

♦ *6 Kuha-class inshore minesweepers* — Bldr: Laivateollisuus, Turku

	In serv.		In serv.
KUHA 21	28-6-74	**KUHA 24**	7-3-75
KUHA 22	-74	**KUHA 25**	17-6-75
KUHA 23	-75	**KUHA 26**	13-11-75

Kuha type inshore minesweeper 1975

D: 90 tons (fl) **S:** 12 kts **Dim:** 26.6 × 6.9 × . . .
A: 3/20-mm AA (II × 1, I × 1) **Man:** 15 men
M: 2 Cummins NT-380M diesels; 2 outboard drive props; 600 hp

REMARKS: Plastic hulls. Funds for eight additional provided.

AMPHIBIOUS WARFARE SHIPS

♦ *6 Kala-class LCU* — Bldr: Rauma-Repola. In serv. 1956-59

KALA 1-6

D: 60 tons (200 fl) **S:** 9 kts **Dim:** 27.0 × 8.0 × 1.8
A: 1/20-mm AA — 34 mines **Man:** 10 men
M: 2 Valmet diesels; 2 props; 360 hp

♦ *5 Kave-class LCM* — In serv. 1956-60

KAVE 1-4, 6

D: 27 tons (60 fl) **S:** 9 kts **Dim:** 18.0 × 5.0 × 1.3
A: 1/20-mm AA **Man:** 3 men
M: 2 Valmet diesels; 2 props; 360 hp

AUXILIARY SHIPS

♦ *2 headquarters tenders*

LOUHI (ex-*Sisu*) — Bldr: Wärtsilä, Helsinki — L: 24-9-38

D: 2,075 tons **S:** 16 kts **Dim:** 64.1 × 14.2 × 5.1
A: 2/40-mm AA (I × 2) **Man:** 100 men
M: 2 Atlas diesels, electric drive; 2 props; 4,000 hp

REMARK: Former icebreaker, converted 1975.

KORSHOLM (ex-*Korsholm III*, ex-*Öland*) — In serv. 1931

D: 650 tons **S:** 11 kts **Dim:** 48.0 × 8.5 × 2.9
A: 2/20-mm AA **M:** Reciprocating steam; 1 prop; 865 hp

REMARK: Former car ferry, bought 1967 for use as staff headquarters and small-craft tender.

♦ *1 cable ship*

PIRTSAARI — Bldr: Rauma-Repola — L: 15-12-65

D: 430 tons **S:** 10 kts **Dim:** 45.5 × 8.9 × 2.3
M: 1 Wärtsilä diesel; 1 prop; 450 hp **Man:** 20 men

♦ *6 tugs*

PIRTTISAARI, PYHTÄÄ, PURHA — Bldr: U.S.A., 1943-44

D: 150 tons **S:** 8 kts **Dim:** 21.3 × 6.2 × 2.6
A: 1/20-mm AA **Man:** 10 men
M: 1 Wärtsilä or Atlas diesel; 1 prop; 400 hp

REMARKS: Used as miscellaneous transports. *Pyhtää* belongs to the Coast Artillery.

PUKKIO, PORKKALA, PANSTO — Bldr: Valmet, Helsinki — In serv. 1939, 40, 47

D: 162 tons **S:** 10 kts **Dim:** 28.5 × 6.0 × 2.7

AUXILIARY SHIPS (*continued*)

A: 1/40-mm — 1/20-mm — 20 mines **Man:** 10 men
M: 1 Wärtsilä diesel; 1 prop; 300 hp

REMARK: Used as tugs, transports, and minelayers.

♦ *57 service launches, K, Y, L, YM, and H classes,* 2 to 34 tons, 7 to 10 kts, for local service transport

---

COAST GUARD

Operated by the Ministry of the Interior

PATROL BOATS

N . . . — Bldr: Laivateollisuus, Turku, ordered 1976

D: 550 tons

REMARK: An improved *Valpas.*

♦ **VALPAS** — Bldr: Laivateollisuus, Turku — L: 22-12-70

D: 545 tons **S:** 15 kts **Dim:** 48.3 × 8.7 × 4.0
A: 1/20-mm AA **Man:** 22 men
M: 1 Werkspoor TMABS-398 diesel; 1 controllable-pitch prop; 2,000 hp

REMARK: Ice-strengthened, equipped with sonar.

♦ **VIIMA** — Bldr: Laivateollisuus, Turku — L: 20-7-64

D: 135 tons **S:** 23 kts **Dim:** 35.7 × 6.6 × 2.0
A: 1/40-mm AA **Man:** 12 men
M: 3 Mercedes-Benz diesels; 3 props; 4,050 hp

♦ **SILMA** — Bldr: Laivateollisuus, Turku — L: 25-3-63

D: 530 tons **S:** 15 kts **Dim:** 48.3 × 8.3 × 4.3
A: 1/20-mm AA **Man:** 22 men
M: 1 Werkspoor diesel; 1 prop; 1,800 hp

♦ **UISKO** — Bldr: Valmet, Helsinki — In serv. 1959

Uisko

D: 370 tons **S:** 15 kts **Dim:** 43.4 × 7.3 × 3.83
A: 1/20-mm AA **Man:** 20 men
M: 1 Werkspoor diesel; 1 prop; 1,800 hp

♦**KAAKKURI**	**KOSKELO**	**KUOVI**	**TAVI**
KIISLA	**KUIKKA**	**KURKI**	**TELKKÄ**

Bldr: Valmet, Helsinki, 1956-59

D: 75 tons (97 fl) **S:** 23 kts **Dim:** 29.42 × 5.02 × 1.5
A: 1/20-mm AA **Man:** 11 men
M: Mercedes-Benz diesels; 2 props; 2,700 hp

REMARKS: Steel hull, ice-strengthened. *Kuikka, Kaakkuri:* 1,000 hp, 16 kts, 90 tons full load.

PATROL CRAFT

♦ *89 small patrol craft of the RV, NV, and PV series,* 1.1 to 19 tons, most 9-13 kts, 8 to 14 meters overall

♦ *1 training ship*

ECKERO — Bldr: Kone & Silta, Helsinki, 1903; rebuilt 1954

D: 55 tons **S:** 10 kts **Dim:** 40.7 × 7.2 × 4.4
M: 1 Mercedes-Benz diesel; 1 prop; 225 hp

♦ *1 small cargo ship*

TURJA — Bldr: Wärtsilä, Helsinki, 1928

D: 65 tons **S:** 11 kts **Dim:** 22.6 × 4.5 × 2.5
M: 1 Mercedes-Benz diesel; 1 prop; 225 hp

ICEBREAKERS (Under Board of Navigation)

♦ *2 Urho class* — Bldr: Wärtsilä, Helsinki

URHO, SISU — In serv. 1975-76

D: 7,500 tons (9,500 fl) **S:** 18 kts **Dim:** 104.6 × 23.8 × 8.3
M: 5 SEMT-Pielstick diesels, electric drive; 4 props; 22,000 hp

REMARKS: Sisters to Swedish *Atle.* One helicopter. Two props forward, two aft.

♦ *3 Tarmo class* — Bldr: Wärtsilä, Helsinki

	In serv.		In serv.		In serv.
TARMO	1963	**VARMA**	1968	**APU**	1970

D: 4,890 tons **S:** 17 kts **Dim:** 85.7 × 21.7 × 6.8
M: 4 Sulzer diesels, electric drive; 4 props; 10,000 hp

REMARK: Two props forward, two aft.

♦ *3 Karhu class* — Bldr: Wärtsilä, Helsinki

	In serv.		In serv.		In serv.
KARHU	1958	**MURTJALA**	1959	**SAMPO**	1960

D: 3,540 tons **S:** 16 kts **Dim:** 74.2 × 17.4 × 6.4
M: Diesel-electric; 4 props; 7,500 hp

FRANCE

For the first time in its history, the Navy is among the most important components in the military might of France and its contribution will become more significant every day.

General Charles DE GAULLE (1965)

This strategic nuclear strength . . . the completion of this force and of certain of its components, especially the submarine, is without question a great scientific and technical exploit.

Valéry GISCARD D'ESTAING (1974)

The two important elements of the French Navy

The aircraft carrier, keystone of general-purpose forces

The SSBN, nucleus of the strategic deterrent forces

PERSONNEL (1977): 68,285 on active duty including 4,357 officers, 28,134 chief petty officers and petty officers, and 35,794 other enlisted personnel. These budgetary figures include female (458) regulars and 26 volunteers, and among the drafted personnel 26 ensigns, 814 midshipmen and petty officers, and 16,553 petty officers and other enlisted personnel.

MERCHANT MARINE (1-7-76): 1,388 ships — 11,278,016 grt
(tankers: 128 ships — 7,406,329 grt)

WARSHIPS IN SERVICE OR UNDER CONSTRUCTION AS OF 1 OCTOBER 1977

	L	Tons	Main armament
♦ *3 aircraft carriers*			
2 CLEMENCEAU (fixed-wing)	1957-60	22,000	8/100-mm DP, 40 aircraft
1 JEANNE D'ARC (helicopter)	1961	10,000	4/100-mm DP, 6/MM38 Exocet, 8 heavy helicopters
♦ *31 submarines*			
5 LE REDOUTABLE (nuclear)	1967-77	7,500	16 missiles, 4 TT
1 GYMNOTE	1964	3,000	2 missiles
2 SNA 72 (nuclear)	. . .	2,265	4 TT
4 AGOSTA	1974-76	1,200	4 TT
9 DAPHNÉ	1959-67	700	12 TT
4 ARÉTHUSE	1957-58	400	4 TT
6 NARVAL	1954-58	1,320	6 TT
♦ *1 guided missile cruiser*			
1 COLBERT	1956	8,500	1 Masurca, 2/100-mm DP 12/57-mm AA
♦ *23 destroyers*			
4 GEORGES LEYGUES	1975-	3,800	1/100-mm, 4/MM38, 2 WG 13 Lynx helicopters
3 TOURVILLE	1972-74	4,580	1 Malafon, 6/MM38, 3/100-mm DP, 2 TT, 2 WG 13 Lynx helicopters
2 SUFFREN	1965-66	5,090	1 Masurca, 2/100-mm DP, 1 Malafon
1 ACONIT	1970	3,500	2/100-mm DP, 1 Malafon, ASW mortar, 2 TT
1 LA GALISSONIÈRE	1960	2,750	2/100-mm DP, 1 Malafon, 1 helicopter
1 DUPERRÉ	1956	3,900	1/100-mm DP, 4/MM38
5 D'ESTRÉES	1954	3,900	2/100-mm DP, 1 Malafon ASW weapons
4 KERSAINT	1953-54	2,750	1 Tartar, 6/57-mm AA, 1 rocket launcher, 6 TT
2 LA BOURDONNAIS	1955	2,750	4 or 6/127-mm DP, 4 or 6/57-mm AA, 6 TT, 1 rocket launcher
♦ *18 frigates*			
1 BALNY	1962	1,750	2/100-mm DP, ASW mortar
8 COMMANDANT RIVIÈRE	1958-63	1,750	4/MM38, 2/100-mm DP, 1 ASW mortar, 6 TT
3 L'ALSACIEN	1957	1,250	4/57-mm AA, 12 TT, 1 ASW mortar
6 LE NORMAND	1954-56	1,250	4 or 6/57-mm AA, 12 TT 1 rocket launcher
♦ *41 escorts, patrol boats and craft or station vessels*			
14 D'ESTIENNE D'ORVES	1973-80	1,170	1/100-mm DP, 1 rocket launcher, ASW weapons
4 LE FOUGUEUX	1957-59	325	2/40-mm AA, ASW weapons
4 TRIDENT	1976-77	115	1/40-mm, 6/SS 12 SSM
1 LA COMBATTANTE	1963	180	2/40-mm AA, 4/SS 12 SSM
4 LA LORIENTAISE	1952-54	370	1/40-mm AA
9 SIRIUS	1953-57	400	1/40-mm AA, 1 or 2/20-mm
5 "-HAM"	1954-55	140	1/20-mm AA
♦ *31 minehunters and minesweepers*			
5 CIRCÉ (minehunters)	1970-72	465	1/20-mm AA, 2 remotely controlled sleds
10 U.S. MSO (5 minehunters)	1953-54	700	1/40-mm AA
1 MERCURE	1957	365	2/20-mm AA
5 "-TON"	1955-56	400	1/40-mm AA
15 U.S. MSC	1953-54	300	2/20-mm AA

NOTE: The total tonnage of all units in active service approaches 320,000 metric tons.

SHIPS ENTERING ACTIVE SERVICE DURING 1977

1 frigate: *De Grasse;* 2 corvettes: *Détroyat* and *Jean Moulin;* 2 submarines: *Agosta* and *Beveziers;* 1 fleet replenishment ship: *Durance;* 2 local service tenders: *Élan* and *Chevreuil.*

SHIPS RETIRED FROM SERVICE DURING 1977

1 destroyer: *Jauréguiberry;* 1 frigate: *Le Gascon;* 3 coastal escorts: *L'Effronté, Le Hardi* and *Le Frondeur;* 1 patrol boat: *La Malouine.*

SHIPS EXPECTED TO ENTER SERVICE DURING 1978

2 corvettes: *Quartier Maître Anquetil, Commandant de Pimodan;* 2 submarines: *La Praya* and *Ouessant;* 2 local service tenders: *Gazelle Isard.*

SHIPS EXPECTED TO RETIRE FROM SERVICE DURING 1978

1 destroyer: *Tartu;* 2 frigates: *L'Agenais* and *Le Béarnais;* 1 coastal escort: *L'Alerte.*

NEW CONSTRUCTION PROGRAMMED UNDER THE "FOURTH PLAN" (1977-82)

1 nuclear aircraft carrier, PA 75
3 ASW frigates, Type C-70
3 AA frigates, Type C-70
4 nuclear attack submarines
6 patrol boats
13 minesweepers

During the same period the Naval Aviation service will receive 40 *Super Etenard* fighter-bombers and 13 WG 13 *Lynx* helicopters (the remainder of an original order for 80 and 40 machines, respectively).

WEAPONS AND SYSTEMS

(A) MISSILES

♦ *Strategic ballistic missiles*

M 2:

Two-stage engine, not stabilized aerodynamically, solid propulsion
— total height: 10.40 m
— first stage height: 5.20 m
— second stage height: 2.60 m
— diameter: 1.50 m
— total weight: 20,000 kg
— warhead: 500 kilotons
— range: about 3,000 km

Le Terrible, Le Redoutable and *Le Foudroyant* carry the M 2.

WEAPONS AND SYSTEMS *(continued)*

M 20:

This missile is designed to replace the M 2 on board *Le Terrible, Le Foudroyant,* and *Le Redoutable.* It carries a thermonuclear warhead and its new equipment is more refined than that in the M 2 missile. The chief elements controlling re-entry and the terminal flight are in the upper part of the missile. These may include a thermonuclear warhead in the megaton range, new systems to protect against anti-missile efforts, and a greater penetration capability. The M 20's range, about 3,000 km, will be almost the same as the M 2. *L'Indomptable* carries the M 2.

M 4:

Beginning in 1980, the M 20 will be replaced by the M 4, which will have greater range and will carry six multiple warheads of about 150 kilotons. Submarine launching tubes will have to be enlarged before the M 4 enters service.

♦ *Surface-to-air missiles*

Masurca

Medium range system (30 nautical miles, can intercept between 100-75,000 ft) launched by means of a solid propellant booster which in a few seconds brings it to a speed close to Mach 3; a slower burning solid propellant maintains this speed for the duration of the flight.

Characteristics:

	Missile only	*Booster*
— Length	5.380 m	3.320 m
— Diameter	0.406 m	0.570 m
— Span of fins		1.500 m
— Weight	950 kg	1,148 kg
— Warhead	100 kg	—

— Missile and booster: length 8.600 m — weight 2,098 kg

The MOD 2 beam-riding missile is no longer used, and the MOD 3, a homing missile, is the only system still in service (semi-active homing).

The missile follows a trajectory determined by proportional navigation, keeping its antenna pointed at the target, which is illuminated by the launching ship's radar transmitter.

The Masurca system is made up of:

* A target designator and weapon assignment console, including a computer. This system employs the shipboard search radar and the Senit automatic tactical data system.

* Two guidance systems, each with:

— a DRBR 51 tracking radar
— a director carrying the rear reference beam and illumination beam for the control system
— an illumination beam
— a twin launcher
— storage and maintenance facilities including 2 horizontal ready service drums containing 18 missiles in addition to reserve missiles in the magazines
— IFF and control equipment.

The system is installed in the *Suffren*-class guided missile destroyers and in the *Colbert* guided missile cruiser.

Tartar

An American system of short range (15 nautical miles), with interception altitudes between 100 and 75,000 ft in the ITR and SM 1A version, and of medium range (25 nautical miles) with air interception from 100 to 75,000 feet in the SM 1 version. These 3 types can be used in surface warfare (range 25,000 m max.).

In its complete form the system has:

— the missile (1 stage solid propulsion)
  length: 4.600 m
  diameter: .410 m
  weight: 590 kg
  semi-active homing guidance proximity fuze
— 1 single MK 13 GMLS
— 1 vertical stowage-loading system containing 40 missiles
— various computers
— height-finding SPS 39 B radar
— 2 tracking radars SPG 51

The system is mounted on T-47 type destroyers modified for Tartar. It will be installed in the planned C-70 AA type destroyers.

Crotale

Air Force missile adapted for naval use

— Length: 2.930 m
— Diameter: 0.156 m
— Span: cruciform (0.540 m with wings extended), anti-pitching ailerons mounted forward.
— Weight: 85.1 kg
— Range: 8,000 m
— Interception ranges: 150 to 12,000 feet
— Guidance system: Beam riding, then detonation by infrared fuze incorporated in the missile.
— Octuple missile launcher: The system to be installed on the F-67 and C-70 types destroyers and will be used with the DRBV 51 C radar and will have a special extractor and a Thomson tracking radar in the KU band. Additional missiles will be carried in a separate magazine. The prototype was installed in the test ship *Ile d'Oléron* during May 1977.

♦ *Surface-to-surface missiles*

MM 38 Exocet (built by SNIAS)

Homing missile (solid fuel propellant): Weight: about 700 kg (explosive charge more than 150 kg); Speed: Mach 1; Range more than 37 km.

Usual missile silhouette, cylindrical body with a pointed nose, cruciform wings with arrow shape.

Length: 5.20 m; Diameter: .35 m.; Wing span: 1 m.

The fire control solution requires a fix on the target provided by the surface radar of the firing ship and uses the necessary equipment for launching the missile and determining the correct range and height bearing of the target.

The missile is launched at a slight elevation (about 15°). After the boost phase, it reaches its flight altitude and is stabilized between 3 and 15 meters. Stabilization is maintained by a radar altimeter.

During the first part of the flight, the missile is automatically guided by an inertial device which has received the azimuth of the target. When within a certain distance from the target, an automatic homing radar begins to seek the target, picks it up and directs the missile. Great effort has been made to protect the missile from enemy countermeasures during this phase.

Detonation takes place upon impact or by proximity fuze, according to interception conditions, size of the target ship and the condition of the sea.

WEAPONS AND SYSTEMS *(continued)*

MM 38 ramps on board the Tourville 1975

The MM 38 is mounted (1-10-77) on board the *Jeanne d'Arc*, the 3 *Tourville* class, the *Duperré*, 8 *Commandant Rivière* class, 1 *Suffren* class, 6 A-69-type corvettes, and will be aboard the C-70 AA and ASW frigates.

MM 40 Exocet (Bldr: SNIAS)

An offshoot of the MM 38 and the AM 39, the MM 40 will be an over-the-horizon, surface-to-surface missile with the range adapted to the radar performance but able to use fire control data relayed by a third means. Maximum range will be at least 65 km. The missile introduces a new fiberglass cylindrical launcher to replace the conventional metal launcher, which reduces the weight and fittings of the launcher and therefore yields an increase in fire power because of the greater number of missiles that can be carried on board.

The MM 40 is still being developed.

SS 11

Wire guided system with line-of-sight alignment on the target.
Length: 1.215 m
Diameter: 0.164 m
Wingspan: 0.500
Weight: 30.4 kg
Range: 3,000 m

SS 12 M

Similar system to SS 11
Length: 1.870 m
Diameter: 0.210 m
Wingspan: 0.650
Weight: 75 kg (upon firing)
Warhead: 30 kg (about)
Range: 5,500 m

Mounted on the missile patrol boat *La Combattante* and on the *Trident* class.

♦ *Air-to-surface missiles*

AM 39 (Bldr: SNIAS)

Anti-ship missile fired by airplane or helicopter. This is the air-sea version of the MM 38; after detachment by gravity, and with a retro-firing booster motor, the missile acquires a trajectory similar to that of the MM 38. Thereupon it has the same flight characteristics as the MM 38.
Length: 4.633 m
Diameter: 0.348 m
Wingspan: 1.004 m
Weight: 65 kg (before launching)
Range: 50 to 70 km according to altitude and speed at launching.
Radar: Active homing seeker head (EMD)*

This is known as a "fire and forget" missile which permits the aircraft to renew its attack after having fired, or to seek a new target. This system may be used with the Atlantic and the Super Étendard aircraft. It is equally appropriate for such heavy or medium weight helicopters as the Super Frélon.

(B) AVIATION MISSILES

♦ *Air-to-ground missiles*

AS 11

Bldr: SNIAS
Length: 1.210 m
Diameter: 0.164 m
Wingspan: 0.50 m
Weight: 29.900 kg
Wire-guided system with optical alignment on the target.

Used for training for the CM 175 and the HSS 1.

AS 12

Bldr: SNIAS
Length: 1.870 m
Diameter: 0.210 m
Wingspan: 0.650 m
Weight: 75 kg
Range: Maximum 7,500 to 8,000 m; minimum 1,500 m
Wire-guided system with optical alignment on the target.

Used by the BR 1150 Atlantic and the BR 1050 Alizé.

AS 20

Bldr: SNIAS
Length: 2.60 m
Diameter: 0.25 m
Wingspan: 0.80 m
Weight: 140 kg
Radio command
Range: 4,000 m to 8,000 m

Used in firing training of the AS 30 on the Étendard IV M.

*EMD = Electronique Marcel Dassault

WEAPONS AND SYSTEMS (*continued*)

AS 30

System developed for firing from a maneuvering aircraft at middle, low, or very low altitude. Used by the Étendard IV M.

Bldr: SNIAS
Length: 3.785 m
Diameter: 0.342 m
Wingspan: 1.000 m
Total weight: 528 kg
Range: maximum 9 to 12,000 m.; minimum 1,500 m.
Radio command

AS 37 Martel

Bldr: Matra and Hawker Siddeley Dynamics
2 types, television and anti-radar. Only the latter is used in the French Navy.
Length: 4.122 m
Diameter: 0.40 m
Wingspan: 1.192 m
Total weight: 531 kg
Range: over 20,000 m

Passive homing head (EMD); the missile homes on the radar emissions of the enemy vessel. Immediately after firing, the missile is on its own, permitting the aircraft to depart or evade. To be used with BR 1150 Atlantic.

♦ *Air-to-air missiles*

R 530

Bldr: Matra
2 types, infrared and radar homing
Length: IR type: 3.198 m; EM type: 3.284 m
Diameter: 0.263 m
Wingspan: 1.103 m
Weight: IR type: 193.5 kg, EM type: 192 kg
Range: maximum 10,000 m: minimum 5,000 m
Semi passive: homing EMD or infrared homing

Sidewinder

The French Navy also uses this air-to-air American missile (see U.S.A. section).

Magic

Bldr: Matra
Length: 2.900 m
Diameter: 0.157 m
Wingspan: 0.660 m
Weight: 89 kg
Range: 300/8,000 m
Infrared homing

(C) GUNS

100-mm, Models 1953 and 1968

Single barrel automatic, for use against aircraft, surface vessels, or land targets. The Model 1968 is a lighter version of the Model 1953. The ammunition is the same.

Characteristics of the Model 1968:
Weight of the gun mount: 22 tons
Length of barrel: 55 calibers
Range at 40° elevation: 17,000 m
Maximum effective range for surface fire: 15,000 m
Maximum effective range for anti-aircraft fire: 8,000 m
Maximum rate of fire: 60 rounds/minute
Arc of elevation: −15° to +80°
Maximum Speed: training, 40°/sec., elevation, 25°/sec

The 100 M (1953) uses an analog fire control system with electro-mechanical and electronic equipment for the fire control solution. The director can be operated in optical and radar modes.

The 100 M (1968) uses a digital fire control system, with central units, and memory disks, or magnetic tape for data storage. Light radar gun director. Optical direction equipment can be added.

57-mm Model 1951

Twin barrel automatic mount:
Length of barrel: 60 calibers
Muzzle velocity: 865 m/sec
Maximum range: 13,000 m
Effective anti-aircraft range: 5,000 m
Maximum rate of fire: 60 rounds/min per barrel
Arc of elevation: −8° to 90°
Maximum rate of fire: 60 rounds per minute, per barrel.

127-mm Model 1948

Twin-barrel semi-automatic for use against aircraft, surface vessels, or land targets. The French model can use American ammunition, as used in the U.S. Mk 39 version.

Length of barrel: 54 calibers
Muzzle velocity: 810 m/sec
Maximum anti-aircraft range: 14,000 m
Effective anti-aircraft range: 9,000 m
Maximum surface range: 22,400 m
Effective surface range: 18,000 m
Weight: 48 tons
Weight of mount: 14 tons
Maximum rate of fire: 18 rounds per minute

30-mm

Single automatic barrel:
Length: 2.440 m/m
Weight: 4 tons
Muzzle velocity: 1,000 m/sec
Maximum effective range: 2,800 m
Maximum rate of fire: 650 rounds per minute

Also in service are typical **40-mm** guns based on Bofors designs and **20-mm** guns of Oerlikon design.

(D) ANTISUBMARINE WEAPONS (surface vessels)

♦ **Malafon** (Bldr: Latécoère in partnership with St. Trôpez) L 4 torpedo-carrying glider launched with the assistance of a double booster, stabilization by automatic pilot, radio command guidance. *Glider:* speed 230 m/sec. *Range:* 12,000 m. *Missile:* length 6.15 m, diameter 0.65 m., span 3.30 m, total weight, including torpedo, 1,500 kg. The Malafon is installed in the 2 *Suffren*-class destroyers, the *La Galissionnière*, the ASW T 47, the *Aconit* and the *Tourville* class destroyers.

1. Masurca

2. Tartar

3. Automatically loaded 305-mm ASW and bombardment mortar (with three flare rails)

4. Automatically loaded, six-barreled 325-mm ASW rocket launcher (with six flare rails)

WEAPONS AND SYSTEMS (*continued*)

♦ **375-mm Rocket Launchers, Models 1964 or 1972:** Sextuple mount. Automatic loading in vertical position. Firing rate, 1 rocket/second. Range: 1,600 m. Time or proximity fuze. Based on Bofors quadruple mounting.

♦ **305-mm Mortar:** Quadruple mount. Automatic loading, ASW projectile weight, 230 kg; range: 400 to 3,000 m. Can also fire a 100 kg projectile against land targets; range 6,000 m.

(E) TORPEDOES

♦ *For surface ships*

Class	Weight in kg	Diameter in mm	Speed in kts
K 2	1,100	550	50
L 3	900	550	25
L 4	500	533	30
L 5 mod 1 and mod 4	1,000	533	35
♦ *For submarines*			
Z 13	1,700	550	30
E 12	1,600	550	25
E 14	900	550	25
L 5 mod 3	1,300	533	35
F 17	1,300	533	35

♦ *For aircraft*

In addition to the U.S. torpedoes **Mk 44** and **46,** French naval aircraft use the **L 4** torpedo.

(F) SONARS

♦ *Surface ships*

	Type	Frequency	Average range
DUBA 1	Hull	HF	2,500 m
DUBA 3	Hull	HF	3,000 m
DUBV 24	Hull	LF	6,000 m
DUBV 23	Bow	LF	see remarks
DUBV 43	Towed	LF	see remarks
DUBA 25	Hull	MF	see remarks
DUBA 26	Hull	MF	see remarks
DUBM 20	Hull — on *Circé*-class minehunters		
DUBM 21	Hull — on new Tripartite minehunters		
DUBM 41	Towed — on modernized *Berlaimont*-class MSO		

REMARKS: **DUBV 23** and **DUBV 43** are used simultaneously and under normal sound propagation conditions achieve ranges of 8,000 to 10,000 meters, and in certain bathymetric conditions, 20,000 meters.
The **DUBA 25** is a new sonar designed for the A-69 corvettes.
DUBA 26 is under development.

♦ *Submarines* — Carry listening devices, active-passive sonars, and telemetric equipment.

♦ *Helicopters*	AQS 13	MF	U.S. sonar
	DUAV 1	HF	
	HS 71	HF	equips the WG 13 Lynx helicopter

(G) COMBAT INFORMATION SYSTEMS

SENIT — This system has 4 principal roles:

— establishing the combat situation from manual collection of information coming from detection equipment on board and automatic or manual collection of information coming from external sources;

— dissemination of this combat situation data to the ship and other vessels by automatic means (Links 11 and 14);

— decision-making assistance;

— transmission of all required information to the target designation console.

Although their general concept is similar, there are several versions of the Senit System which differ in construction and, for each type, programming, to assure fulfillment of the various missions assigned each type of ship.

— *Senit 1:* system with 1 or 2 computers found in the *Duquesne*, the *Suffren*, and the *Colbert*.

— *Senit 2:* single computer system found in the T-47 type *Kersaint*-class destroyers as well as the *Duperré*.

— *Senit 3:* built around a central computer system consisting of 2 computers and 2 memory banks, the entire group designed for control of various weapons (guns, Malafon ASW system, torpedoes). Installed in the *Aconit* and the 3 F-67 class ships.

These three systems are based on equipment of American origin, some built in France under license.

— *Senit 4:* a system conceived by the French Navy programming center and designed around the French Iris 55 N computer. Will be fitted in the C-70 class.

— *Senit 5:* also designed by the French Navy programming center, it will be fitted on small ships. It uses the 15 M minicomputer, which is of French origin.

(H) RADARS

♦ *Air search*

DRBV 20 A: Metric
DRBV 20 C: Metric, long-range. Mounted on aircraft carriers.
DRBV 22 A: Mounted in *T 47 ASW* version, *T 53* class, fast frigates, patrol vessels.
DRBV 22 C: *Ile d'Oléron*
DRBV 22 D: *Jeanne d'Arc, Henri Poincaré*
DRBV 23 B: Mounted in aircraft carriers.
DRBV 23 C: Mounted in the *Colbert;* transistorized model of the 23 B
DRBV 26: Mounted in the *Tourville*, the *Georges Leygues*, and the *Duperré*
DRBV 13: Doppler pulse radar. Has several uses, installed in the *Aconit.*

♦ *Height-finding/three-dimensional*

DRBI 10: Mounted in aircraft carriers, *T 53* destroyers, the *Colbert*, the *Jeanne d'Arc*, the *Ile d'Oléron*
DRBI 23: Mounted in the *Duquesne* and *Suffren*
SPS 39: American radar. Mounted on Tartar-equipped *T 47* class destroyers
DRBJ 11: Pulse coded radar for the *C 70 AA* class guided missile destroyers

♦ *Surface and low-altitude air search*

DRBV 50: Mounted on aircraft carriers, *Jeanne d'Arc*, *T 47 ASW* class destroyers, the *Rhin*, the *Ile d'Oléron*, *Victor Schoelcher*, *Commandant Bourdais*, the *Colbert*, the *La Galissonnière*.

WEAPONS AND SYSTEMS (*continued*)

DRBV 51: Mounted on C 70 and F 67 destroyers, on A 69 corvettes, and the *Duperré*

♦ *Navigation*

DECCA RM-416
DRBN 31: Mounted on certain minesweepers and coastal patrol craft.
DRBV 31: Mounted on the Tartar-equipped T 47 class destroyers, as well as the T 53 class, and some frigates

♦ *Fire control*

DRBC 31: 57-mm, 100-mm of the aircraft carriers and *Duperré*
DRBC 32 A: Mounted on ASW modified T 47 class destroyers. For 100-mm guns of the *Suffren* class guided missile destroyers, some frigates, and the *Jeanne d'Arc*
DRBC 32 B: 100-mm guns on *Aconit*
DRBC 32 C: Mounted on the *Colbert*, and the C 70 guided missile destroyers
DRBC 32 D: Mounted on the *Tourville* destroyers
DRBC 32 E: Mounted on the A 69 class corvettes
SPG 51: U.S. tracking radar used with the Tartar system on the type T 47 AA destroyers
DRBR 51: Tracking radar for the Masurca

(I) COUNTERMEASURES

The French Navy uses the 8-barreled Syllex chaff launcher which will eventually be replaced by the Dagaie, an improved system. Syllex is essentially identical to the British Knebworth/Corvus.

AIRCRAFT CARRIERS

	Budget	Bldr	Laid down	L	In serv.
R 98 CLEMENCEAU	1953	Brest	11-55	21-12-57	11-61
R 99 FOCH	1955	Ch. de l'Atlantique	2-57	28-7-60	7-63

D: 22,000 tons (17,307 mean) (32,780 fl)
Dim: 265 (238 pp) × 31.72 beam × 51.20 flight deck × 7.50 draft light × 8.60 fl
S: 32 kts (33 on trials) **Range:** 7,500/18 — 4,800/24
A: 8/100-mm DP Model 1953 (I × 8) — 40 aircraft (see remarks)
Armor: Reinforced flight deck, armored bulkheads in engine room and magazines, bridge superstructure in reinforced steel
Man: Peacetime: As aircraft carriers: 64 officers, 476 petty officers, 798 other enlisted. Total: 1,338 men
As helicopter carriers: 45 officers, 392 petty officers, 547 other enlisted. Total: 984 men
M: Two Parsons GT; two props; 126,000 hp
Boilers: 6 (45 kg/cm²) — superheat: 450° **Fuel:** 3,720 tons
Electron Equipt: Radars: 1/DRBV 20 C, 1/DRBV 23 B, 2/DRBI 10, 1/DRBV 50, 1/DRBC 31
Sonars: 1/SQS 505

REMARKS: Flight deck 257 m in length; deck angled at 8°, 165.50 × 29.50; deck forward of the angled deck: 93 × 28; width of the deck abeam the island: 35. Hangar dimensions, 180 × 22 to 24 × 7 (height). Two elevators 16 m long, 11 m in width, one forward on the main flight deck, one slightly abaft the island, able to raise a 15-ton aircraft 8.50 m in 9 seconds. Two 50-meter Mitchell-Brown type BS5 steam catapults, able to launch 15/20-ton aircraft at 110 knots, one forward, another on the angled deck. Optical mirror landing equipment of French manufacture.

The propulsion machinery was built by the Chantiers de l'Atlantique. Living spaces are air-conditioned. Island medium-sized with 3 bridges: flag, navigation, aviation. Communication systems, especially with fighter aircraft, are a significant aspect of the ships' capabilities.

The *Foch*, built in a special drydock at St. Nazaire, was towed to Brest for the installation of its armament.

Aviation fuel: 1,800 m³ of jet fuel and 109 m³ of aviation gasoline carried by the *Foch*. 1,200 m³ of jet fuel and 400 m³ of aviation gasoline by the *Clemenceau*. Work

Clemenceau (R 98) Guiglini, 1974

Clemenceau (R 98) J. C. Bellonne, 1974

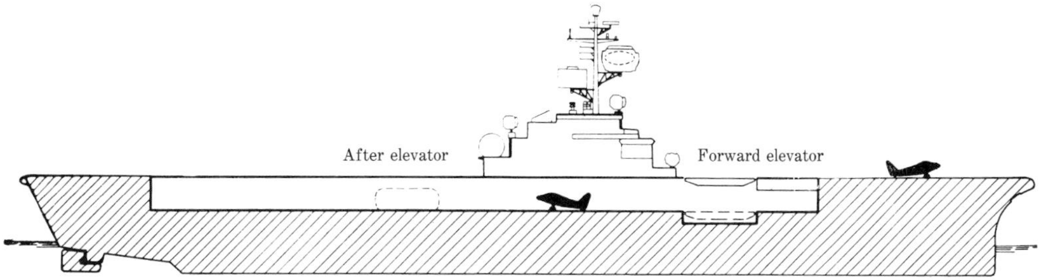

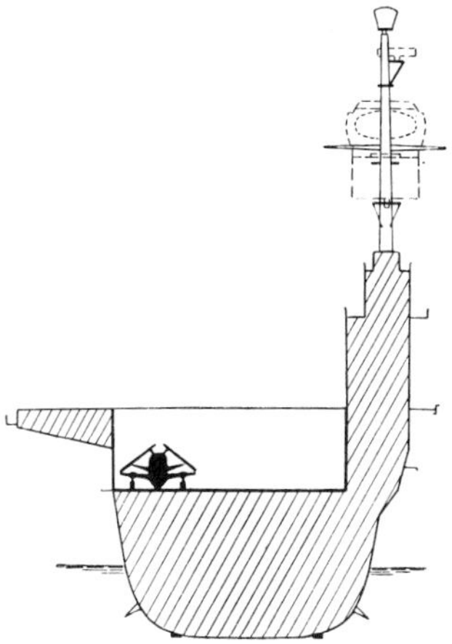

Starboard and stern profiles *Clemenceau* (R 98)

Foch (R 99)

AIRCRAFT CARRIERS (*continued*)

is being carried on to adapt these ships for the Super Étendard aircraft and for the carriage of tactical nuclear munitions.

Aircraft complement: During 1977, *Clemenceau* carried 16 Étendard IVM strike fighters, 4 Étendard IVP reconnaissance fighters, 10 F-8 Crusader interceptors, 6 Alizé ASW aircraft, 2 Super Frélon ASW helicopters, and 2 Alouette II utility helicopters on operations in the Indian Ocean.

HELICOPTER CARRIER

♦ *1 nuclear propulsion, Type PA 75 (ASW and amphibious assault)*

	Bldr	Laid down	In serv.
N . . .	Brest Navy Yard	1981	. . .

D: 16,400 tons (18,400 fl)
Dim: 208 × 202 flight deck × 26.4 (wl.) × 46 flight deck × 6.5
S: 28 kts **Man:** 840 men, 50 staff
Range: Under nuclear power, unlimited — 3,000/18 diesel engines
A: 2 BPDM systems (Crotale VIII × 2) — 2/100-mm DP Model 1968 (I × 2) — helicopters (see Remarks)
Electron Equipt: Radars: 1/DRBV 26, 1/DRBV 51 C, 2/Decca, 2/DRBC 32
Sonars: 1/DUBA 25 — 2 Dagaie systems — SENIT
M: 1 CAS 230 reactor furnishes steam to 2 turbo-reduction-condenser groups; 65,000 hp; 2 props; 2 AGO standby diesels
Electric: 9,400 kw

REMARKS: The installations for aircraft operation include the following: 1 hangar 84 × 21 × 6.50, 2 deck-edge elevators (15 tons in 11 seconds), 1 fixed crane, 1 mobile crane, munition-handling rooms, magazines, workshops, fuel tanks for 1,000 m^3 of TR jet fuel.

Originally, the ship was to be able to launch about 25 WG 13 Lynx, about 10 Super Frélon, or 15 Army type Puma helicopters, or a combination of these, space being available for all of them on the hangar deck. It is now planned to carry fixed-wing aircraft of the V/STOL or V/TOL type as well — hence the change in designation from PH (Porte-Hélicoptères) to PA (Porte Aéronefs). Due to budgetary restrictions, the laying down of the ship has been postponed from 1976 until 1981. It is entirely possible that, by that date, the design may have been considerably modified.

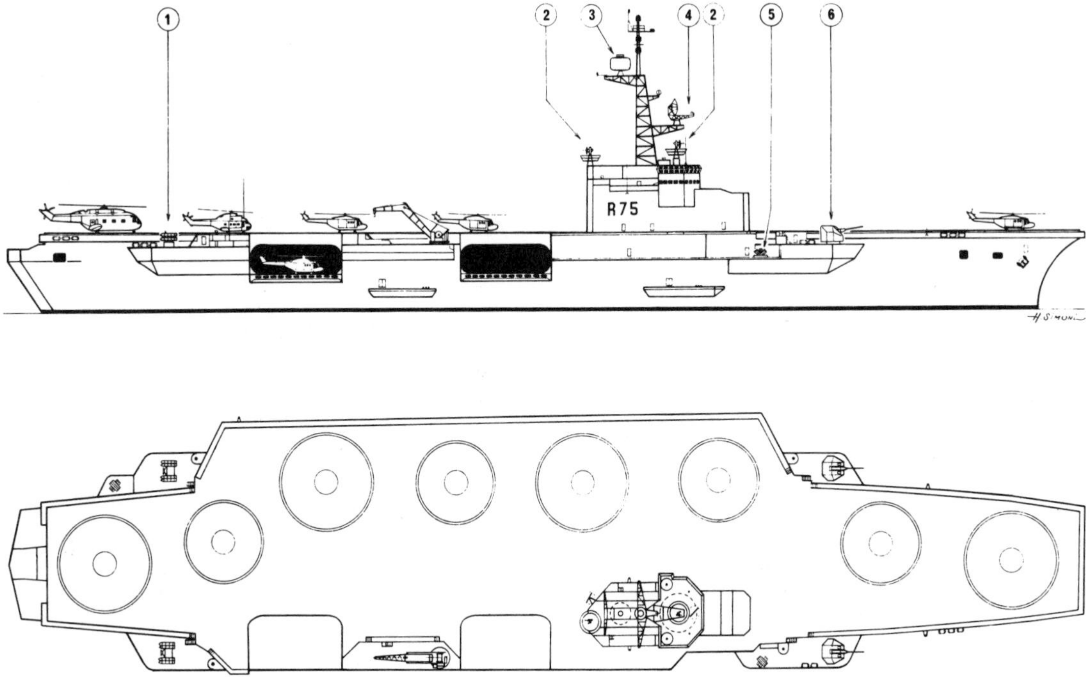

1: Crotale — 2: Radar DRBC 32 — 3: Radar DRBV 51 C — 4: Radar DRBV 26 — 5: Dagaie System — 6: 100-mm Model 1968

HELICOPTER CARRIER (*continued*)

♦ *1 cruiser helicopter-carrier (1957 Budget)*

	Bldr	Laid down	L	Trials	In serv.
R 97 JEANNE D'ARC (ex-*La Résolue*)	Brest	7-60	30-9-61	7-63	7-64

Jeanne d'Arc (R 97) 1975

D: 10,000 tons (12,365 fl) **S:** 26.5 kts (cruising)
Dim: 182 (172 wl) × 24 × 22 (wl) × 7.32 (fl)
A: 6/MM 38 Exocet — 4/100-mm DP, Model 1953 (I × 4) — 8 helicopters (see Remarks)
Electron Equipt: Radars: 1/DRBV 22 D, 1/DRBV 50, 1/DRBN 32, 1/DRBI 10, 3/DRBC 32 A
Sonar: 1/SQS 503 — 2 Syllex installations
Man: Regular ship's company. 30 officers, 183 petty officers, + 404 other enlisted
M: Two Rateau-Bretagne GT; two props; 40,000 hp **Eletric:** 4,400 kw
Boilers: 4 dissymmetric multitube type rated at 45 kg/cm^2 — superheat: 450°C.
Fuel: 1,360 tons **Range:** 6,800/16, 5,500/20, 3,750/25, 3,000/26.5

REMARKS: Has replaced the former cruiser *Jeanne d'Arc* as a training vessel for officer cadets. When on this mission, the ship carries only 4 heavy helicopters. In wartime she would be used as an antisubmarine helicopter carrier, amphibious assault helicopter carrier, or as a troop transport. The number of heavy helicopters embarked can be quickly augmented by simple structural changes. The hull is welded throughout. Landing platform: 62 × 21 m.

The aircraft installations include:

— Aft of the island structure the flight deck permits simultaneous takeoff of 2 Super Frélon helicopters while 2 machines can be stationed forward of the takeoff area and 2 others astern, one on each side of the elevator.

— A 12-ton capacity elevator is located aft on the flight deck and the hangar deck.

— The hangar deck can accommodate 8 helicopters during wartime, taking some of the living quarters used by midshipmen. At the after end of the hangar is an inspection area for the helicopters as well as all necessary machine shops for maintenance and repair, including helicopter electronic equipment. Here also are located the handling rooms for the weapons and ammunition for the helicopters (torpedoes, rockets, etc.).

There are three fire control directors for the 100-mm guns, each served by three automatically controlled radar directors.

On the superstructure, in addition to the navigation bridge, may be found:
— the helicopter control bridge
— a modular type information and operations center
— a combined control center for amphibious landing operations

The engine spaces are divided into two rooms, each with two boilers and a turbine, and are completely separated by a bulkhead.

Jeanne d'Arc (R 97) 1975

NAVAL AVIATION

1. The Naval Air establishment which is part of the Navy, is made up of combatant flotillas, maintenance squadrons or sections, bases, schools, and special services necessary to insure the efficient operation of the flight components.

Naval air is manned by naval personnel.

Administration naval air problems are handled by the Aeronautical Division of the Naval General Staff and the Central Service Branch of Naval Air, both headed by a flag officer.

Operational and training matters concerning Naval Air are directed by the Navy Staff, which includes in its various bureaus, aviation officers.

Primary training in fixed-wing planes is provided by the Air Force; helicopter pilots are given initial training by the Army as well as the Air Force. Specialization of these pilots in multi-engine aircraft or in carrier-based fixed-wing and rotary aircraft is provided by Naval Air. The latter also trains navigators and maintenance crews (Naval Air School at Rochefort).

2. The combat flotillas are:

(a) those embarked which, flying from aircraft or helicopter carriers, carry out intercept, attack, reconnaissance, or CAP missions and engage in antisubmarine warfare.

(b) maritime patrol flotillas and antisubmarine warfare flotillas that are land-based.

3. The service support squadrons and sections have various missions: schools, training exercises, transportation, logistical support for seagoing forces, experimental and salvage operations.

4. Authority over the embarked flotillas and squadrons is assigned to a rear admiral, the Commander Aircraft Carriers and seagoing aviation. (ALPA)

Maritime patrol squadrons are commanded by a rear admiral. (ALPATMAR)

Shore-based flotillas, squadrons and sections are commanded by the Préfets Maritimes (Naval District Commandants) through the regional aviation commanders.

5. Bases: Nîmes-Garon, Saint-Mandrier (helicopters), Saint-Raphaël (experimental station), Hyères, Cuers (maintenance), Ajaccio-Aspretto (training), Lorient-Lann Bihoué, Lanvéoc-Poulmic (helicopters), Landivisiau.

There were approximately 115 aircraft in service during 1977: 24 Étendard-IV-M, 20 F-8-E Crusader, 24 Alizé, 25 Atlantic, 10 P2-H Neptune, 12 Étendard-IV-P photo reconnaissance, 15 Super Frélon, 23 Sikorsky HSS-1, over 18 Alouette III, over 13 Alouette II, plus unspecified numbers of C-54, C-47, Nord 262, Piper Navajo, MS 760, Falcon X, and Fouga Magister. Eighteen WG 13 Lynx helicopters and 40 Super Étendard jet fighter-bombers are on order to replace earlier Alouette II and III helicopters and Étendard-IV-M fighter-bombers.

Units	Shipboard or landbased	Missions	Aircraft
Combat Flotillas			
12-F, 14-F	Ship	All-weather interception	**Crusader (F-8-E)**
11-F, 17-F	Ship	Attack	**Étendard-IV-M**
16-F	Ship	Reconnaissance	**Étendard-IV-P**
4-F, 6-F	Ship	Surveillance	**Alizé**
31-F, 32-F	Ship	Antisubmarine warfare (helicopter)	**HSS-1, (31-F), Super Frélon (32-F)**
33-F	Ship	Troop transport	**HSS-1**
34-F	Ship	Antisubmarine warfare (helicopter)	**Alouette III**
25-F	Land	Maritime patrol and antisubmarine warfare	**Neptune (P2-H)**
21-F, 22-F, 23-F, 24-F	Land	Maritime patrol and antisubmarine warfare	**Atlantic**
Support Squadrons			
2-S, 3-S	Land	All-weather Instruction	**Piper Navajo** **Nord 262**
9-S		Reconnaissance	**C-47, C-54, Neptune (P2-H)**
12-S	Land	General service	**Neptune (P2-H)**
55-S	Land	Multi-engine pilot training	**Nord 262**
56-S	Land	Navigation (non-pilot) personnel training	**C-47**
59-S	Ship	Carrier qualification training	**CM-175, Étendard IV-M, Alizé**
20-S	Land	Experimental aircraft (planes, helicopters)	**Alouette II and III, HSS 1, Super Frélon**
22-S, 23-S	Land and ship	Liaison, salvage Search and Rescue	**Alouette II and III**
27-S	Land	General services	**Super Frélon**
Sections			
	Land or ship	General services	**C-47, CM 175, MS 760** **C-54, Nord 262** **Alouette III, HSS-1** **Falcon X, etc.**

Prototype Super Étendard (ground attack aircraft)

Étendard IV M (ground attack aircraft)

Crusader (interceptor) taking off

Étendard IV P (reconnaissance aircraft)

Alizé (early-warning and ASW aircraft, carrier-based)

Lynx WG 13 (ASW, close-support, and logistic-support helo)

Super Frélon (ASW helo, carrier-based)

Super Frélon (ASW helo, carrier-based)

Alouette III (search and rescue, utility helo)

Atlantic (ASW and long-range patrol and reconnaissance)

Atlantic (ASW and long-range patrol and reconnaissance)

P2-H Neptune (ASW and long-range patrol and reconnaissance)

Type	Mission	Wingspan	Length	Height	Weight (max.) kilos	Engine	Maximum speed in mach or in knots	Maximum ceiling	Range	Weapons	Remarks
SHIP-BASED PLANES:											
CRUSADER F8 E (FN) (Ling-Temco-Vought)	All-weather interceptor	10.72	16.61	4.80	13,000	1 J57 P20 *A* Pratt and Whitney jet with after-burner	Mach 1.8	50,000 ft	1,500 miles 2 hr 30	20-mm guns, Air to air missiles	(1) May be outfitted with a small photo pod for reconnaissance missions.
SUPER-ÉTENDARD	Fleet air defense, attack, reconnaissance photo	9.60	14.35	3.85	11,500	1 8 K 50 SNECMA jet developing 5 tons of thrust	Mach 1 (11,000 kts) Mach 0.97 low altitude			2/30-mm guns, bombs, rockets, combination or AM 39	The MK II Atlantic which will enter service at the beginning of the 1980s will have the same airframe, engines, and characteristics as the Mk I but its weapon system will be entirely new, built around a digital tactical computer. It will be able to transport 3 tons of weapons, e.g., 4 Martel under the wings or 2 AM 39 inboard.
ÉTENDARD IV M (Dassault)	Attack aircraft	9.60	14.35	3.85	10,200	1 SNECMA jet Atar 8	Mach 1.3	35,000 ft	750 miles 1 hr 45 or 2 hr 15 with supplemental reserve tank	2/30-mm guns, air surface missiles (or air-to-air), 68-mm rockets, various bombs of 50 to 400 kg	
ÉTENDARD IV P	Reconnaissance photo	9.60	14.50	3.85	10,200	1 SNECMA jet Atar 8	Mach 1.3	35,000 ft	750 miles 1 hr 45 or 2 hr 15 with supplemental reserve tank	100-mm rockets, 68-mm rockets, photo-flash bombs	
ALIZÉ (BR 1050) (Bréguet)	AEW, anti-submarine warfare	15.60	13.66	5	8,200	1 Rolls-Royce Dart 21 turbo-prop (1,925 hp + 230 kg of thrust)	240 kts	11,000 ft	685 miles 3 hr 45	Air-to-surface missiles, Mk 44 torpedoes, 100-mm rockets, ASW depth charges, 50 to 250 kg bombs, acoustic buoys, mortar type projectiles	(2) Localization, classification and attack of contacts picked up by an anti-submarine ship.
LAND-BASED PLANES: **P2-H NEPTUNE** (Lockheed)	Patrol, anti-submarine warfare	31.50	31.70	10.80	34,280	2 R 3350 32 *Wa* Wright engines × 3,250 hp + 2 Westinghouse turbojets type J34 × 1,540 kg	240 kts	25,000 ft	3,200 miles 16 hr	L 4 or Mk 44 or 46 torpedoes, ASW depth charges, sono-buoys, mortar type projectiles (ASW), photo flash bombs	(3) Detection, identification and neutralization of small surface vessels with weak anti-aircraft defense.
ATLANTIC MK1 (BR 1150) (Bréguet)	Patrol, anti-submarine warfare (1)	36.30	31.75	11.33	43,500	2 Rolls-Royce Tyne 20 turbo-props × 6,000 hp	300 kts	30,000 ft	4,300 miles 17 hr	Air-to-surface missiles, L 4 or Mk 44 or 46 torpedoes, ASW depth charges, sono-buoys, mortar type projectiles (ASW), photo flash bombs	(4) Equipped with retractable MAD gear.
HELICOPTERS: HSS-1 (Sikorsky)	Antisubmarine warfare, troop carrier	17.07 (rotor diameter)	20.06	4.73	6,000	1 R 1820.84 Wright, 1,525 hp	110 kts	9,000 ft	380 miles 4 hr 30	Mk 44 and Mk 46 torpedoes, air-to-surface missiles, ASW depth charges	
SUPER-FRÉLON (SNIAS)	Antisubmarine warfare	18.90 (rotor diameter)	23	6.35	13,000	3 C3 Turboméca III turboshafts, each with 1,500 hp	145 kts	10,000 ft	420 miles 3 hr 30	Mk 44 and Mk 46 torpedoes, ASW torpedoes	
LYNX (WG 13) (Westland-SNIAS)	Antisubmarine warfare (2) Surface attack aircraft (3)	12.80 (rotor diameter)	15.2	3.20	4,150	2 BS 360 Rolls-Royce turboshafts, each with 900 hp	150 kts	12,000 ft	1 hr 30, half hovering, half in flight 2 hr 30 with 3 men and 4 missiles	Mk 44 and Mk 46 torpedoes, air-to-surface missiles	
ALOUETTE III	Antisubmarine warfare (4)	11.02 (rotor diameter)	12.8	3.0	2,200	1 Turbomeca Astazou turboshaft, 870 hp	110 kts	10,000 ft	325 miles 2 hr 30	Mk 44 torpedoes	

SUBMARINES

♦ *5 nuclear-powered, ballistic missile* (SSBN)

	Bldr	Laid down	L	Trials	In serv.
S 611 (Q 252) LE REDOUTABLE	Cherbourg	1964	29-3-67	1969	1-12-71
S 612 (Q 253) LE TERRIBLE	Cherbourg	1967	12-12-69	1971	1-1-73
S 610 (Q 257) LE FOUDROYANT	Cherbourg	1969	4-12-71	5-73	6-6-74
S 613 (Q 258) L'INDOMPTABLE	Cherbourg	1971	8-74	12-75	12-76
S 614 (Q 259) LE TONNANT	Cherbourg	1973	17-9-77	. . .	5-80

Le Redoutable (S 611) E.C.P.A., 1970

Le Redoutable (S 611) E.C.P.A., 1971

D: 7,500 tons surfaced, 9,000 submerged **S:** 20 kts maximum
Dim: 128.0 × 10.6 × 10.0
A: (a) strategic weapons: 16 M2 ballistic missiles (except S-613 with M20 missiles);
(b) tactical weapons: 4 TT, 18 torpedoes
Man: twin crews of 15 officers and 120 men for each ship, manning in rotation
M: 1 nuclear reactor producing pressurized steam for propulsion; 1 prop

Le Terrible (S 612) E.C.P.A., 1971

Remarks: The *Redoutable* (authorized in March 1963) and other submarines of this class are the principal elements of the French naval deterrent. The pressure hull is of great strength and the ship can submerge more than 200 meters.

The propulsion system consists of a reactor with enriched uranium and distilled water under pressure giving the required heat energy for the production of steam to produce the power of two turbine installations and two turbo-alternators. An auxiliary main engine with electrical energy can substitute for the main engines in an emergency. The range of the auxiliary propulsion engine is about 5,000 nautical miles.

Construction of the sixth unit, *L'Inflexible,* has been postponed until at least 1982.

♦ *1 experimental*

	Bldr	Laid down	L	In serv.
S 655 GYMNOTE	Cherbourg	3-63	17-3-64	10-66

Gymnote (S 655) E.C.P.A., 1972

D: 3,000 tons surfaced, 3,250 submerged **S:** 11/10 kts
Dim: 84.0 × 10.6 × 7.6
M: 4 diesel-electric motors × 620 kw and 2 electric engines; 2 props; 2,600 hp
Man: 8 officers, 35 petty officers, 35 other enlisted

Remarks: Used for testing missiles designed for the SSBNs, 2 vertical missile launching tubes. Bow diving planes do not fold.

SUBMARINES (*continued*)

♦ *5 Type SNA 72 nuclear attack*

	Bldr	Laid down	L	In serv.
S 616 N . . . (Q 265)	Cherbourg	11-12-76	. . .	10-81
S . . . N . . .	Cherbourg	. . .	. . .	. . .
S . . . N . . .	Cherbourg	. . .	. . .	. . .
S . . . N . . .	Cherbourg	. . .	. . .	. . .
S . . . N . . .	Cherbourg	. . .	. . .	. . .

D: 2,265 tons, 2,385 surfaced, 2,670 submerged (fl)
Dim: 72.1 × 7.6 × 6.4
A: 4/533-mm TT fwd (14 torpedoes or mines) **S:** 25 kts
Man: 9 officers, 35 chief petty officers, 22 other enlisted
M: A nuclear power system made up of an integrated reactor-exchanger able to deliver constant power of 48 MW for the necessary steam to two turbo-alternators. A single electric motor drives a single shaft, and an emergency diesel generator group can be cut into the propulsion line in case of nuclear breakdown.

REMARKS: New class of nuclear attack submarines. Fire control, torpedo-launching, and submarine detection systems are the same as the *Agosta* class. The first SNA-72 was financed under the Third Military Equipment Plan. The second (ordered 9-76) through fifth come under the Fourth Plan (1977-82).

♦ *4 Agosta-class attack* (Authorized in the 1970-75 Program)

	Bldr	Laid down	L	In serv.
S 620 AGOSTA	Cherbourg	1972	19-10-74	7-77
S 621 BÉVÉZIERS	Cherbourg	17-5-73	14-6-75	10-77
S 622 LA PRAYA	Cherbourg	1974	15-5-76	1978
S 623 OUESSANT	Cherbourg	1974	23-10-76	1978

Agosta (S 620) 1976

SNA 72 — Longitudinal Cutaway

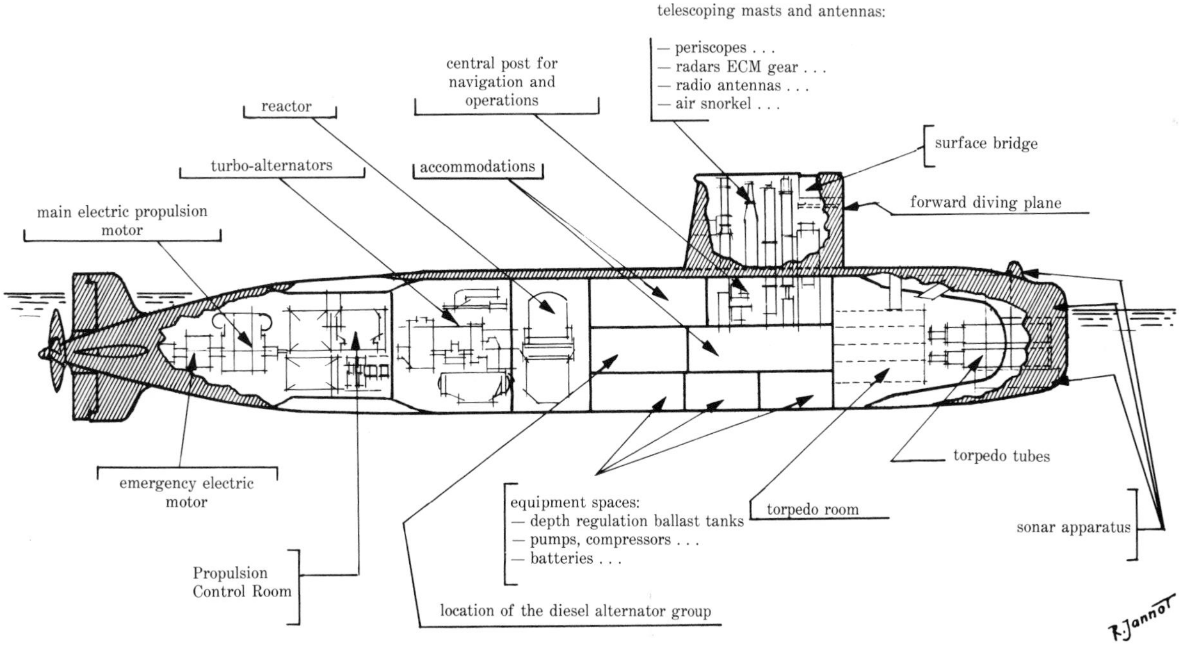

SUBMARINES (*continued*)

Agosta (S 620) 1976

D: 1,200 tons, 1,450 surfaced, 1,725 submerged (fl)
Dim: 67.57 × 6.80 × 5.40 **S:** 20 kts (submerged)
A: 4/550-mm TT forward — 20 torpedoes (rapid-loading)
Man: 7 officers, 43 men **Endurance:** 45 days
M: 1 drive shaft; a 3,500-kw main engine; a cruising engine of 23 kw; 2 generating plants (SEMT-Pielstick A 16 PA 4 185 of 850 kw each)
Range: 8,500 nautical miles with snorkel at 19 knots

REMARKS: Oceangoing submarines. Weapons and equipment similar to the refitted *Daphné*-class submarine. Fire control centralized in one computer bank. Air-conditioned. Retractable deck fittings on hull exterior. Advanced silencing techniques for quiet operations both inboard and outboard. The torpedo tubes will accept torpedoes of either 550 or 533 mm in diameter. This class of submarine is also building for Spain (4) and South Africa (2).

Agosta (S 620) E.C.P.A., 1976

♦ *9 Daphné class attack*

	Budget	Bldr	Laid down	L	In serv.
S 641 DAPHNÉ	1955	Dubigeon	3-58	20-6-59	6-64
S 642 DIANE	1955	Dubigeon	7-58	4-10-60	6-64
S 643 DORIS	1955	Cherbourg	19-58	14-5-60	8-64
S 645 FLORE	1956	Cherbourg	19-58	21-12-60	5-64
S 646 GALATÉE	1956	Cherbourg	19-58	22-9-61	7-64
S 648 JUNON	1960	Cherbourg	7-61	11-5-64	2-66
S 649 VÉNUS	1960	Cherbourg	8-61	24-9-64	1-66
S 650 PSYCHÉ	1964	Brest	5-65	28-6-67	7-69
S 651 SIRÈNE	1964	Brest	5-65	28-6-67	3-70

Vénus J. C. Bellonne, 1972

D: 700 tons, 869 surfaced, 1,043 submerged (fl)
Dim: 57.75 × 6.76 × 4.62 **S:** 13.5/16 kts
A: 12/550-mm; 8 forward, 4 aft **Man:** 6 officers, 39 men
M: Diesel-electric propulsion (SEMT-Pielstick), 2 props; 1,600 hp
Range: 4,500 nautical miles/5 knots with snorkel

REMARKS: Development of the *Aréthuse*-class submarine. Superquiet when submerged. Modernized, beginning in 1971, with special attention given to detection equipment and weapons. Can submerge to more than 300 meters. No spare torpedoes are carried. This class of submarine has been purchased by the following countries: Portugal, four in 1964; Pakistan, four in 1966; South Africa, three in 1967; and Spain has built 4 submarines of this type with French technical assistance. One Portuguese unit was sold to Pakistan in 1976.

Doris (S 643) 1975

SUBMARINES (*continued*)

Flore (S 645) J. C. Bellonne, 1975

♦ *4 Aréthuse class attack*

	Budget	Bldr	Laid down	L	In serv.
S 635 ARÉTHUSE	1953	Cherbourg	3-55	9-11-57	10-58
S 636 ARGONAUTE	1953	Cherbourg	3-55	29-6-57	2-59
S 639 AMAZONE	1954	Cherbourg	End of 1955	3-4-58	7-59
S 640 ARIANE	1954	Cherbourg	End of 1955	12-9-58	3-60

Aréthuse (S 635) Martinelli, 1976

D: 400 tons, 543 surfaced, 669 submerged (fl)
A: 4/550-mm TT forward, 4 torpedoes in reserve
Man: 6 officers, 34 men **S:** 12.5 kts (surfaced), 16 kts (submerged)
M: Diesel-electric propulsion; 12-cylinder SEMT-Pielstick motors; 1 prop; 1,060/1,300 hp

REMARKS: Ballast tanks reduced to a minimum, can submerge to more than 200 meters. Quiet and maneuverable, handy submarines.

Aréthuse (S 635) G Arra, 1972

♦ *6 Narval class attack*

	Author	Bldr	Laid down	L	In serv.
S 631 NARVAL	1949	Cherbourg	6-51	11-12-54	12-57
S 632 MARSOUIN	1949	Cherbourg	9-51	21-5-55	10-57
S 633 DAUPHIN	1950	Cherbourg	5-62	17-9-55	8-58
S 634 REQUIN	1950	Cherbourg	6-52	3-12-55	8-58
S 637 ESPADON	1954	A. Normand	12-55	15-9-58	4-60
S 638 MORSE	1954	Seine Maritime	2-56	10-12-58	5-60

D: 1,320 tons, 1,635 surfaced, 1,910 submerged
Dim: 77.63 × 7.82 × 5.40 **A:** 6/550-mm TT forward
Man: 7 officers, 56 men **S:** 15/18 kts
Range: 15,000 with snorkel at 8 knots **M:** 2 props — see remarks.

REMARKS: Exceptionally strong hull welded throughout, streamlined sail. Endurance at sea 45 days. Rebuilt from 1966 to 1970 with special attention to the machinery spaces. They now have diesel-electric propulsion (two main engines of 1,500 hp, two electric cruising motors of 40 hp, three diesel-electric generators (SEMT-Pielstick 12 PA 4). Complete modernization of detection devices, weapons (6 TT forward, 14 torpedoes in reserve, and mines), and sail (streamlined). Considered to be very good diesel submarines.

Narval (S 631)

GUIDED MISSILE CRUISER

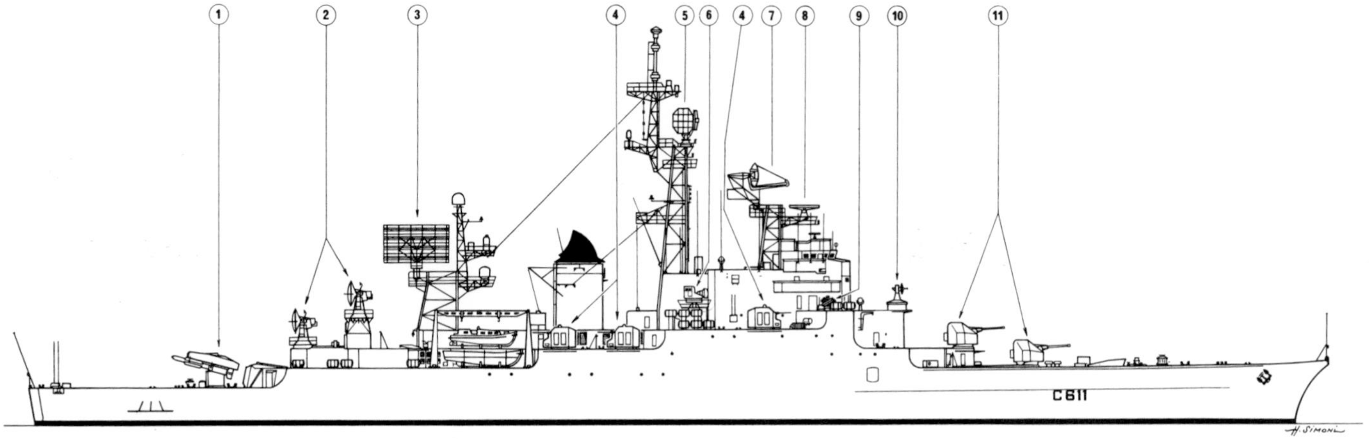

Scale 1/1000

1: Masurca launcher — 2: DRBR 51 radars — 3: DRBV 20 radar — 4: 57-mm mounts — 5: DRBI 10D radar — 6: 57-mm fighting director (DRBC 31) — 7: DRBV 23C radar — 8: DRBV 50 radar — 9: Syllex system — 10: DRBC 32C radar — 11: 100-mm (Model 1968) gun mounts

♦ *1 guided missile cruiser* (1953 Budget)

	Bldr	Laid down	L	In serv.
C 611 COLBERT	Brest	12-53	24-3-56	5-59

D: 8,500 tons (11,300 fl)
Dim: 180 (175 pp) × 19.7 (20.2 max) × 7.66
S: 31.5 kts **Range:** 4,000/25
A: 1 Masurca system — 2/100-mm DP Mod 1968 (I × 2) — 12/57-mm AA (II × 6)
Electron Equipt: Radars: 1 Decca RM 416, 1/DRBV 50, 1/DRBV 23 C, 1/DRBV 20, 2/DRBR 51, 1/DRBR 32 C, 1/DRBC 31, 1/DRBI 10 D — SENIT 1 — countermeasures consist of 2 Syllex systems
Armor: Deck: 50 Belt: 50 to 80
M: C.E.M. — Parsons GT; 2 props; 86,000 hp **Electric:** 4,920 kw
Boilers: 4 dissymmetric multi-tubular, 45 kg/cm², superheat 450°C
Man: (after refitting) 24 officers, 190 petty officers, 346 men

REMARKS: Converted into a surface-to-air guided missile cruiser between 4-70 and 10-72. Together with the guided missile destroyers *Duquesne* and *Suffren*, this ship, thanks to the power and precision of the Masurca system, provides a high degree of anti-aircraft protection to ships at sea at a medium range. The capability of the SENIT tactical data system enables the ship to maintain real time control of the surface and air situation at the center of a widely dispersed formation, which makes this an excellent command ship, able as well to coordinate the air defense of the formation. If necessary the ship can be used as a command post for an inter-service operation overseas. During the refit the bridge superstructure was rebuilt, the electronic equipment for command and control was modernized, the electric power increased, and living spaces were improved, including air-conditioning. Four MM 38 Exocet anti-ship missiles have not been installed as was earlier planned.

Colbert (C 611) E.C.P.A., 1976

Machinery and boilers are installed in two separate compartments, each with two boilers and a turbine, separated by an 18-meter-long watertight bulkhead.

Colbert (C 611) J. C. Bellonne, 1974

Colbert (C 611) E.C.P.A., 1976

Colbert (C 611) E.C.P.A., 1973

DESTROYERS

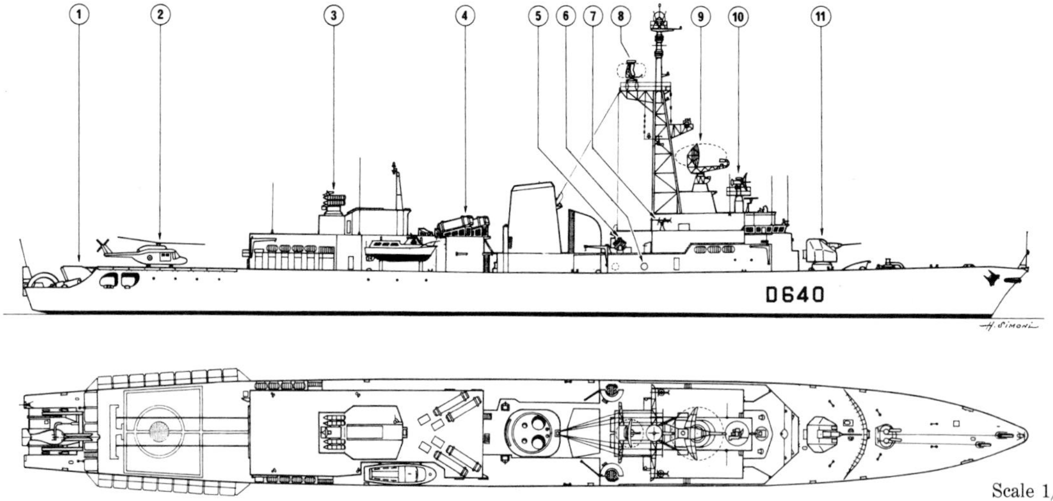

Scale 1/1000

1: DUBV 43 sonar — 2: Lynx helicopter — 3: Crotale — 4: Exocet launchers — 5: Dagaie system — 6: 20-mm AA — 7: DRBV 51 radar — 8: DRBV 26 radar — 9: DRBC 32E radar — 10: 100-mm mount (Model 1968)

♦ *3 Type C-70 AA guided missile* (1977-82 Plan)

	Bldr:	Laid down	L	In serv.
D . . . N . . .	. . .	. . .	. . .	. . .
D . . . N . . .	. . .	. . .	. . .	. . .
D . . . N . . .	. . .	. . .	. . .	. . .

A: 4/MM38 Exocet — 1 Tartar SM1 SAM system (40 missiles) — 2/100-mm DP Model 1968 (I × 2) with Vega fire control system — 2/20-mm AA (I × 2) — 2 catapults for L-5 ASW torpedoes (10 torpedoes)

Electron Equipt: Radars: 1/DRBJ 11, 1/DRBV 26, 2/SPG-51C
Sonar: 1/DUBV 25 or 26

Remarks: This design, of which the first is scheduled to be laid down in 1978 or 1979, has the maximum possible commonality with the C-70 ASW version. The armament scheme centers around the SM1 version of the Tartar surface-to-air missile and a new phased-array three-dimensional radar, the DRBJ 11, which is under development by Thomson/CSF.

♦ *6 Type C-70 ASW guided missile* (3 under the 1970-75 Plan, 3 under the 1977-82 Plan)

	Bldr	Laid down	L	Trials	In serv.
D 640 GEORGES LEYGUES	Brest	6-74	6-9-75	1977	1978
D 641 DUPLEIX	Brest	9-75	. . .	1978	1979
D 642 MONTCALM	Brest	9-75	. . .	1978	1979
D . . .	Brest	. . .	. . .	. . .	. . .
D . . . N . . .	Brest	. . .	. . .	. . .	. . .
D . . . N . . .	Brest	. . .	. . .	. . .	. . .

D: 3,800 tons (4,100 fl) **Dim:** 139.0 (129 pp) × 14.0 × 5.73 (fl)
S: 29.75 kts (GT), 19.5 kts (diesels) **Range:** 9,500/18 on diesels
Man: Peacetime: 15 officers, 90 petty officers, 111 men
A: 4/MM38 Exocet — 1/100-mm DP Model 1968, with Vega fire control system — 1 Crotale BPDM — 2/20-mm AA (I × 2) — 2 catapults for L-5 ASW torpedoes (10 torpedoes) — 2 WG 13 Lynx helicopters with sonar and torpedoes; by replacing these, the helicopters can be used in an anti-surface role using 4 AS 12.
M: CODOG propulsion system, 2 Rolls-Royce Olympus TM3B gas turbines; 2 SEMT-Pielstick 16 PA 6 diesels; 2 variable-pitch props; 42,000 hp (gas turbine); 10,000 hp (diesel)
Electric: 3,400 kw **Fuel:** 600 tons distillate
Electron Equipt: Radars: 1/DRBV 26, 1/DRBV 51, 1/DRBC 32 E, 2/Decca 1226 — SENIT 4, 2 Dagaie systems
Sonars: 1/DUBV 23, 1/DUBV 43

Remarks: The *Georges Leygues* is the first of a series of destroyers that is divided into two principal categories, one antisubmarine, the other anti-aircraft. They will have the same hull and propulsion system and also the same general surface-to-surface armament. Living spaces in the *Georges Leygues* are designed for 250 men, including 21 officers. Special efforts have been made to improve living conditions by giving rooms to petty officers, improving watch conditions, cutting the number of men living in division compartments, and improving the sanitary facilities. This should result in an acceptable resolution of the problems of habitability. The fourth unit will be funded from the 1977 Budget.

DESTROYERS (*continued*)

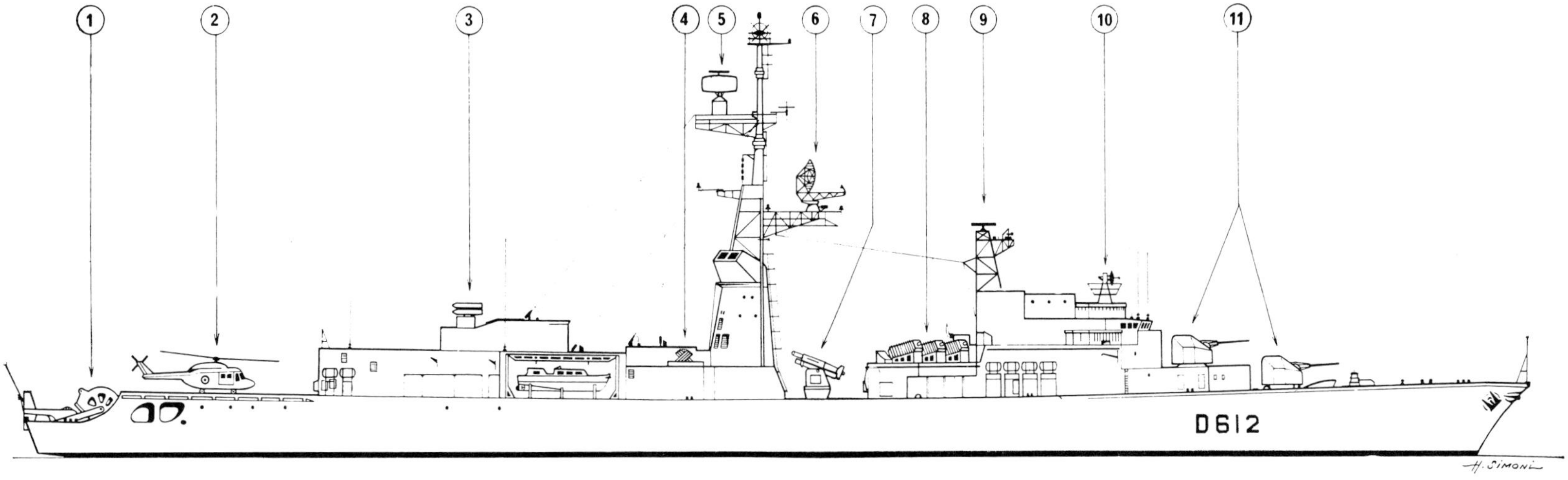

1: DUBV 43 sonar — 2: Lynx helicopters — 3: Crotale — 4: Syllex system — 5: DRBV 51 radar — 6: DRBV 26 radar — 7: Malafon launcher — 8: Exocet launchers — 9: navigation radar — 10: DRBC 32D radar — 11: 100-mm mounts (Model 1968)

♦ *3 Type F-67 (ex-C-67 A) guided missile* (Built under the 1965-70 Plan)

	Author	Bldr	Laid down	L	In serv.
D 610 TOURVILLE	1967	Lorient	3-70	13-5-72	21-6-74
D 611 DUGUAY TROUIN	1967	Lorient	1-71	1-6-73	17-9-75
D 612 DE GRASSE	1970	Lorient	1972	30-11-74	1977

D: 4,580 tons (5,800 fl) **Dim:** 152.75 (142 pp) × 15.30 × 5.70
S: 32 kts **Range:** 5,000/18, 4,550/20, 3,600/24, 1,900/30
A: 3/100-mm DP (1968 model) — 6/MM38 Exocet — 1 Malafon missile launcher (13 missiles) — 2 catapults for L-5 antisubmarine torpedoes — 2 WG 13 Lynx helicopters
Man: 17 officers, 111 petty officers, 155 men
M: 2 Rateau double reduction GT; 2 props; 54,400 hp **Electric:** 4,400 kw
Boilers: 4 dissymmetrical multitubular boilers; steam pressure 45 kg/cm^2 superheat 450°C
Electron Equipt: Radars: 1/DRBV 26, 1/DRBV 51, 1/DRBC 32 D, 2 Decca 1226 — SENIT 3 — 2 Syllex systems
Sonars: 1/DUBV 23, 1/DUBV 43

***De Grasse* on trials, Crotale not yet aboard** 1976

DESTROYERS *(continued)*

Duguay Trouin (D 611) G. Arra, 1976

Duguay Trouin (D 611) J. C. Bellonne, 1976

Duguay Trouin (D 611) J. C. Bellonne, 1976

Tourville (D 610) G. Arra, 1976

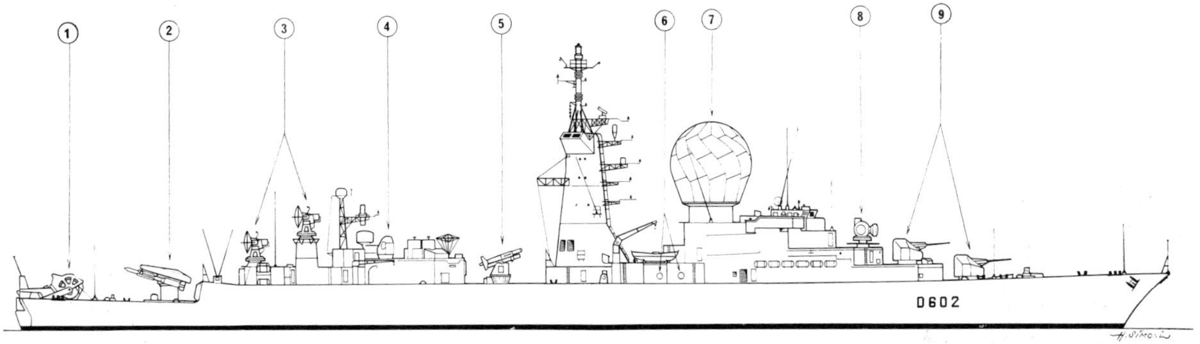

1: DUBV 43 sonar — 2: Masurca launcher — 3: DRBR 51 radars — 4: 30-mm AA — 5: Malafon launcher — 6: catapults for L-5 torpedoes — 7: DRBI 23 radar — 8: 100-mm director with DRBC 32A radar — 9: 100-mm mounts (Model 1953)

REMARKS: These ships are designed for antisubmarine warfare and can operate in formation in a high air threat environment. Trials on the *Tourville* indicated that these ships will have good sea-keeping qualities, similar to those of the *Suffren* class. The *De Grasse* has a Crotale BPDMS in place of the after 100-mm gun mount; the other two will be similarly armed during their next refits. *De Grasse* also has 2/20-mm AA (I × 2). Endurance of *De Grasse*, whose boilers burn distillate fuel, is 4,500 nautical miles at 18 knots.

GUIDED MISSILE DESTROYERS

♦ *2 Suffren class* (Built under the 1960-65 Plan)

	Bldr	Author	Laid down	L	Trials	In serv.
D 602 SUFFREN	Lorient	1960	12-62	15-5-65	12-65	1967
D 603 DUQUESNE	Brest	1960	11-64	11-2-66	7-68	4-70

D: 5,090 tons (6,090 fl) **Dim:** 157.60 (148 pp) × 15.54 × 7.25 (fl)
S: 34 kts **Range:** 5,000/18
Man: 23 officers, 164 petty officers, 163 men
A: 1 Masurca system — 4/MM38 Exocet on *Duquesne* — 2/100-mm (I × 2) Model 1953 — 2/20-mm AA (I × 2) — 2/30-mm AA (I × 2) on *Suffren* — 1 Malafon system — 2 launchers for L-5 torpedoes
Electron Equipt: Radars: 1/DRBI 23, 1/DRBV 50, 2/DRBR 51, 1/DRBC 32 A, 1/DRBN 32 — SENIT 1
Sonars: 1/DUBV 23, 1/DUBV 43 — 2 Syllex systems
M: 2 double reduction Rateau turbines; 2 props; 72,500 hp
Boilers: 4 multitubular automatically controlled; steam pressure 45 kg/cm^2 superheat 450°C **Electric:** 4,000 kw

REMARKS: The French Navy has returned to the term "frigate" to designate guided missile ships of medium tonnage. Three pairs of non-retractable, anti-rolling stabilizers are installed, energized by 2 central gyroscopes, only one of which is normally in use. Living and operational spaces are air-conditioned.

These ships are extremely seaworthy; they roll very little and pitch only slightly; there is little vibration.

Suffren will receive MM38 Exocet missile launchers like *Duquesne* at next refit.

Duquesne (D 603) with MM 38 Exocet E.C.P.A., 1977

Suffren (D 602)

Suffren (D 602)

Suffren (D 602)

DESTROYERS

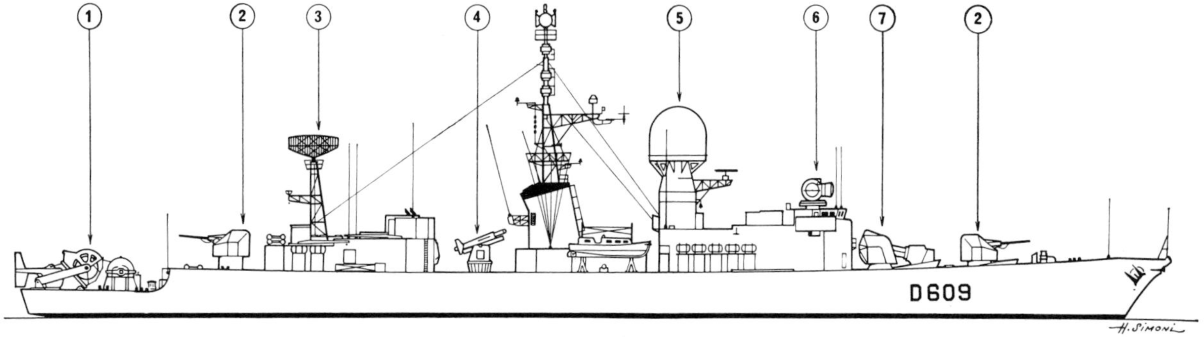

1: DUBV 43 sonar — 2: 100-mm (1968 model) mounts — 3: DRBV 22A — 4: Malafon launcher — 5: DRBV 13 radar — 6: 100-mm director with DRBC 32B radar — 7: 305-mm mortar

Aconit (D 609) Martinelli, 1974

Aconit (D 609) Martinelli, 1974

♦ *1 C-65 class ASW* (1965-1970 Program)

	Bldr	Laid down	L	In serv.
D 609 ACONIT	Lorient	1967	7-3-70	30-3-73

D: 3,500 tons (3,900 fl) **Dim:** 127 × 13.40 × 4.05 (5.80 fl)
S: 27 kts **Range:** 5,000/18
Man: 15 officers, 89 petty officers, 125 men
A: 2/100-mm DP Model 1968 (I × 2) — 1/305-mm ASW mortar — 1 Malafon system (13 missiles) — 2 catapults for L-5 ASW torpedoes
M: Double reduction Rateau GT; 1 prop
Boilers: 2 multitubular, automatic asymetric boilers; steam pressure 45 kg/cm^2, superheat 450°C; 28,650 hp (31,500 hp max)
Electric: 2,960 kw
Electron Equipt: Radars: 1/DRBV 13, 1/DRBN 32, 1/DRBV 22 A, 1/DRBC 32 B — SENIT 3 — 2 Syllex systems
Sonars: 1/DUBV 23, 1/DUBV 43

REMARKS: *Aconit* is a predecessor of the F-67 Type destroyer but does not carry a helicopter. One computer center controls the SENIT functions and the weapons. Propulsion machinery is very compact. Ship is equipped with stabilizers.

DESTROYERS (*continued*)

♦ *1 T-56 class ASW*

	Bldr	Laid down	L	In serv.
D 638 LA GALISSONNIÈRE	Lorient	11-58	12-3-60	7-62

La Galissonnière (D 638) with hangar open J. C. Bellonne, 1973

D: 2,750 tons (3,740 fl) **Dim:** 132.80 × 12.70 × 5.40 (fwd)
S: 34 kts (32 fl) **Range:** 5,000/18
A: 2/100-mm DP Model 1954 (I × 2) — 6/550-mm TT (III × 2) for K-2 and L-3 torpedoes — 1 Malafon ASW missile system — 1 Alouette III ASW helicopter (the hangar overhead folds down to become the helicopter platform)
Electron Equipt: Radars: 1/DRBV 22 A, 1/DRBV 50, 1/DRBN 32, 1/DRBC 32 A
Sonars: 1/DUBV 23, 1/DUBV 43
M: Rateau GT; 2 props; 63,000 hp **Fuel:** 800 tons oil
Boilers: 4 boilers, steam pressure 35 kg/cm^2; superheat 385°C
Electric: 1,740 kw **Man:** Peace: 15 officers, 92 petty officers, 165 men

La Galissonnière (D 638)

REMARKS: Formerly ASW sonar experimental vessel with two bow-mounted sonars. Has U.S. URN-22 TACAN beacon for helicopter. A quadruple 305-mm ASW mortar and six torpedo tubes (III × 2) have been removed. *La Galissonnière* was the final unit in the *Surcouf* series and is the last ship to be typed "destroyer" (escorteur d'escadre) built for France.

♦ *1 modified T-53 class ASW (1972)*

	Bldr	Laid down	L	In serv.
D 633 DUPERRÉ	Lorient	11-54	23-6-56	10-57

Duperré (D 633) Guiglini, 1974

D: 3,900 tons (fl)
Dim, S, Range, M, and **Boilers** are the same as for the *La Galissonnière.*
A: 1/100-mm DP Model 1968 — 4 MM38 launcher — 2 catapults for ASW TT (L-5 model, 8 in number) — 1 WG 13 Lynx helicopter
M: 15 officers, 257 men **Electric:** 1,640 kw
Electron Equipt: Radars: 1/DRBV 22 A, 1/DRBV 51, 1/DRBC 32 E — 2 Decca (1 navigation, 1 surface search) — SENIT 2
Sonars: 1/DUBV 23, 1/DUBV 43

Duperré (D 633) Guiglini, 1974

DESTROYERS (*continued*)

REMARKS: From 1967 to 1971, ship was disarmed and used for sonar experimentation. Conversion in Brest from 1972 to 21-5-74 in the most final evolution of the ASW version of the T-47 Type destroyer. Hangar has maintenance facilities. Flight deck has a helicopter-recovery system similar to that found on F-67 and C-70 destroyers, but simpler. DRBC 32E fire control radar still not mounted in 1977.

♦ *5 Type T-47 converted ASW*

	Bldr	Laid down	L	In serv.
D 627 MAILLE BRÉZÉ	Lorient	10-53	26-9-54	5-57
D 628 VAUQUELIN	Lorient	3-54	26-9-54	11-56
D 629 D'ESTRÉES	Brest	5-53	27-11-54	3-57
D 631 CASABIANCA	F.C. de la Gironde	10-53	13-11-54	5-57
D 632 GUÉPRATTE	A.C. de Bretagne	8-53	8-11-54	6-57

Guépratte (D 632)

D: 3,900 tons (fl) **Dim:** 132.50 × 12.72 × 5.90 **S:** 32 kts
Range: 5,000/18 **Man:** 15 officers, 104 petty officers, 151 men
A: 2/100-mm DP Model 53 (I × 2) — 2/20-mm AA — 1 Malafon ASW (13 missiles) — 1/375-mm ASW rocket launcher — 6 TT (III × 2) for K-2 or L-3 ASW torpedoes
Electron Equipt: Radars: 1/DRBV 22 A, 1/DRBV 50, 1/DRBN 32, 2/DRBC 32 A
Sonars: 1/DUBV 23, 1/DUBV 43
M: GT; 2 props; 63,000 hp **Electric:** 1,440 kw **Fuel:** 800 tons
Boilers: 4 boilers; steam pressure 35 kg/cm^2; superheat 385°C

D'Estrées (D 629) with British SCOT satellite communication antennas 1977

REMARKS: Successful conversion between 1-1968 and 1-1971; weapon system renewed, air-conditioned living spaces. Electrical system and safety installations completely redesigned. These ships do not have the SENIT system.

♦ *4 Type T-47 with Tartar*

	Bldr	Laid down	L	In serv.
D 622 KERSAINT	Lorient	6-51	3-10-53	3-56
D 624 BOUVET	Lorient	11-51	3-10-53	5-56
D 625 DUPETIT THOUARS	Brest	3-51	4-3-54	9-56
D 630 DU CHAYLA	Brest	7-53	27-11-54	6-57

D: 2,750 tons (4,000 fl) **Dim:** 128.5 × 12.96 × 6.30 fwd/5.00 aft
S: 32 kts (at 3,800 tons) **Range:** 1,200/32, 3,500/20, 4,100/14
A: Single Mk 13 Tartar launcher (40 SM1 or SM1 A missiles) — 6/57-mm AA (II × 3) — 1/375-mm RL (Model 1954) mounted forward — 6/550-mm TT (III × 2) for K 2 or L 3 ASW torpedoes

Bouvet (D 624) G. Arra, 1972

DESTROYERS (*continued*)

Dupetit Thouars (D 625) J. C. Bellonne, 1974

Dupetit Thouars (D 625) J. C. Bellonne, 1974

Kersaint (D 622) J. C. Bellonne, 1974

Electron Equipt: Radars: 1/DRBV 20, 1/SPS 39 A or B, 1/DRBV 31, 2/SPG 51 B, 1/DRBC 31 — SENIT
Sonars: 1/DUBA 1, 1/DUBV 24

Man: Peace: 17 officers, 83 petty officers, 177 men **Electric:** 1,600 kw
War: 24 officers, 83 petty officers, 216 men

M: As for T-47 ASW group

♦ *2 T-53 type*

	Bldr	Laid down	L	In serv.
D 635 FORBIN	Brest	8-54	15-10-55	2-58
D 636 TARTU	A.C. de Bretagne	11-54	2-12-55	2-58

Forbin (D 635) E.C.P.A.

D: 2,750 tons (3,740 fl) **Dim:** 128.60 × 12.70 × 5.40 fwd
S: 34 kts (32 fl) **Range:** 5,000/18
Man: 15 officers, 261 men
A: 6/127-mm DP (II × 3) — 6/57-mm AA (II × 3) — 6/550-mm TT for ASW K 2 and L 3 torpedoes — 1/375-mm ASW rocket launcher, Model 1954 — URN-22 TACAN
Electron Equipt: Radars: 1/DRBV 22 A, 1/DRBI 10 A, 1/DRBV 31
Sonars: 1/DUBA, 1/DUBV 24
M: GT; 2 props; 63,000 hp **Electric:** 1,160 kw **Fuel:** 800 tons
Boilers: 4 boilers, steam pressure 35 kg/cm²; superheat 385°C

REMARKS: Fitted for aircraft direction and detection. ASW rocket-launcher aft of the second stack. *Forbin* attached as school ship (1973), forward 57-mm mount removed, aftermost 127-mm mount removed and helicopter platform substituted. *La Bourdonnais* (D-634) stricken 1976. *Jauréguiberry* (D-637) stricken 1977.

FRIGATES

♦ *1 Balny type*

	Budget	Bldr	Laid down	L	In serv.
F 729 BALNY	1956	Lorient	3-60	17-3-62	2-70

Main characteristics the same as for the *Commandant Rivière* class except: maximum draft: 5 meters and: **D:** 1,650 tons

A: 2/100-mm DP, Model 1953 (I × 2) — 2/20-mm AA — 1/305-mm ASW mortar — 6 tubes (III × 2) for K-2 or L-3 ASW torpedoes
M: Experimental CODAG: 2 AGO V-16 diesels (3,600 hp) plus 1 Turbomeca M38 GT (11,800 sust./14,700 max. hp); 1 controllable-pitch prop

REMARK: Will *not* receive Exocet.

FRIGATES *(continued)*

Balny (F 729) E.C.P.A., 1975

Protet (F 748) E.C.P.A., 1975

♦ *8 Commandant Rivière Class*

	Budget	Bldr	Laid down	L	In serv.
F 733 COMMANDANT RIVIÈRE	1955	Lorient	4-57	11-10-58	12-62
F 725 VICTOR SCHOELCHER	1956	Lorient	10-57	11-10-58	10-62
F 726 COMMANDANT BORY	1956	Lorient	3-58	11-10-58	3-64
F 727 AMIRAL CHARNER	1956	Lorient	11-58	12-3-60	12-62
F 728 DOUDART DE LAGRÉE	1956	Lorient	3-60	15-4-61	3-63
F 740 COMMANDANT BOURDAIS	1956	Lorient	4-59	15-4-61	3-63
F 748 PROTET	1957	Lorient	9-61	7-12-62	5-64
F 749 ENSEIGNE DE VAISSEAU HENRY	1957	Lorient	1962	14-12-63	1-65

D: 1,750 tons (2,250 fl) **S:** 25 kts (26.6 on trials)
Dim: 103.0 (98 pp) × 11.50 × 3.80 (average) × 4.30 fl
Man: 9 officers, 61 petty officers, 96 men **Fuel:** 210 tons
A: 4 MM38 Exocet — 2/100-mm DP Model 1953 (I × 2) — 2/30- or 40-mm AA — 1/305-mm mortar — 6 TT for K-2 and L-3 ASW torpedoes (III × 2)
Electron Equipt: Radars: 1/DRBV 22 A, 1/DRBV 50, 1/DRBN 32, 1/DRBC 32 C
Sonars: 1/DUBA 3, 1/SQS 17
Range: 4,500/15, 6,000/10-12 **Electric:** 1,280 kw
M: 4 SEMT-Pielstick diesels, 12 cylinders in V; 2 props; 16,000 hp

Protet (F 748) J. C. Bellonne, 1975

FRIGATES *(continued)*

Commandant Bory (F 726) J. C. Bellonne, 1976

REMARKS: Designed for escort duty in different climates; air-conditioned; 45 days' storage space for fresh food. Can embark a flag officer and staff or an 80-man commando unit on board. These ships are very maneuverable and particularly successful. *Commandant Bory* was originally equipped with free-piston generators driving turbines — replaced with a standard diesel plant in 1974-75. All are now refitted to a generally identical standard.

♦ *3 Type E-52, late version*

	Bldr	Laid down	L	In serv.
F 776 L'ALSACIEN	Lorient	7-56	26-1-57	8-60
F 777 LE PROVENÇAL	Lorient	2-57	5-10-57	11-59
F 778 LE VENDÉEN	F.C. de la Mediterranée	3-57	27-7-57	10-60

Le Provençal (F 777) J. C. Bellonne, 1976

D: 1,250 tons (1,528 trials, 1,702 fl)
Dim: 99.80 (95 pp) × 10.30 × 5.45 (fwd)
S: 27 kts **Range:** 4,500/15
A: 4/57-mm AA (II × 3) — 2/20-mm AA — 12 TT (III × 4) for K-2 and L-3 ASW torpedoes — 1/305-mm mortar
Man: 10 officers, 51 petty officers, 110 men
Electron Equipt: Radars: 1/DRBV 22 A, 1/DRBV 31, 1/DRBC 32
Sonars: 1/DUBV 24, 1/DUBA 1
M: GT; 2 props; 20,000 hp **Electric:** 790 kw.
Boilers: 2 boilers, steam pressure 35 kg/cm²; superheat 385°C

REMARK: Very narrow funnel of Strombos-Valensi type.

Le Vendéen (F 778) J. C. Bellonne, 1972

♦ *6 Type E-52, early version*

	Bldr	Laid down	L	In serv.
F 765 LE NORMAND	F.C. de la Mediterranée	7-53	13-2-54	11-56
F 766 LE PICARD	A.C. Loire	11-53	31-5-54	9-56
F 771 LE SAVOYARD	F.C. de la Mediterranée	11-53	7-5-55	8-57
F 733 LE BASQUE	Lorient	12-54	25-2-56	10-57
F 774 L'AGENAIS	Lorient	9-55	23-6-56	5-58
F 775 LE BÉARNAIS	Lorient	12-55	23-6-56	10-58

Le Savoyard (F 771) J. C. Bellonne, 1974

FRIGATES (*continued*)

D: 1,250 tons (1,528 trials, 1,702 fl)
Dim: 99.80 (95 pp) × 10.30 × 5.80 (max)
S: 27 kts (29 kts on trials) **Range:** 4,500/15
A: 6/57-mm AA (II × 3) — F-771 and F-773 only; 4/57-mm AA — 2/20-mm AA — 12 TT (III × 4) for K-2 and L-3 ASW torpedoes — 1/375-mm ASW rocket launcher, Model 1954
Electron Equipt: Radars: 1/DRBV-22A, 1/DRBV-31, 1/DRBC 31 or 32
Sonars: 1/DUBV-24, 1/DUBA-1, except F-771 and F-773 with 1/DUBV-1, 1/DUBA-1
Man: 10 officers, 51 petty officers, 110 men
M: GT; 2 props; 20,000 hp **Electric:** 720 kw
Boilers: 2 boilers, steam pressure 35 kg/cm^2; superheat 385°C

REMARKS: *Le Lorrain* (F-768) and *Le Champenois* (F-770) stricken 1975. *Le Gascon* (F-767) stricken 1967. *L'Agenais, Le Béarnais,* and *Le Normand* will be placed in reserve in 1978. *Le Basque* and *Le Savoyard* operate with Group M (the Atlantic Missile Range) as missile tracking ships.

Le Basque (F 773) E.C.P.A., 1973

CORVETTES

♦ *14 A-69 Type.* All built at Lorient.

	Laid down	L	In serv.
F 781 D'ESTIENNE D'ORVES	8-72	1-6-73	10-9-76
F 782 AMYOT D'INVILLE	9-73	30-11-74	30-7-76
F 783 DROGOU	10-73	30-11-74	30-9-76
F 784 DÉTROYAT	12-74	31-1-76	24-3-77
F 785 JEAN MOULIN	12-74	31-1-76	5-77
F 786 QUARTIER MAITRE ANQUETIL	8-75	7-8-76	2-78
F 787 COMMANDANT DE PIMODAN	9-75	7-8-76	4-78
F 788 SECOND MAITRE LE BIHAN	11-76	8-77	4-79
F 789 LIEUT. DE VAISS. LE HENAFF	3-77	6-78	12-79
F 790 LIEUT. DE VAISS. LAVALLÉE	10-77	4-79	3-80
F 791 COMMANDANT L'HERMINIER	12-77	4-79	5-80
F 792 PREMIER MAITRE L'HER	7-78	12-79	12-80
F 793 COMMANDANT BLAISON	9-78	12-79	3-81
F 794 ENSEIG. DE VAISS. JACOUBET	4-79	6-80	10-81

Amyot D'Inville (F 782) E.C.P.A., 1975

D: 1,170 tons **S:** 24 kts **Dim:** 80.0 (76 pp) × 10.30 × 3.00
A: 2/MM38 Exocet — 1/100-mm DP Model 1968 — 2/20-mm AA — 1/375-mm ASW rocket launcher — 4 fixed TT for L-3 and L-5 ASW torpedoes
Man: 5 officers, 29 petty officers, 41 men **Endurance:** 15 days
Electron Equipt: Radars: 1/DRBV 51, 1/DRBC 32 E, 1/DRBN 32
Sonar: 1PDUBA 25
M: 2 SEMT-Pielstick 12 PC 2 diesels; 2 controllable-pitch props; 11,000 hp
Electric: 840 kw

Drogou (F 783) J. C. Bellonne, 1976

CORVETTES (*continued*)

Drogou (F 783) J. C. Bellonne, 1976

Drogou (F 783) E.C.P.A., 1976

REMARKS: Designed for coastal antisubmarine warfare. They are also available for scouting missions, instruction, and showing the flag overseas. Can carry a troop detachment of 1 officer and 17 men. The 100-mm gun fire control system consists of a monopulse band X radar and semi-analog, semi-digital computer, and has an optical sight. Only ships destined for the Mediterranean Squadron will carry 2/MM38 missiles but the foundations for the missile containers will be installed on all units. Very economical and seaworthy ships. F-793 and F-794 will have a hanger and flight deck for a Dauphin light helicopter; these two units will also have a stabilization system. A fifteenth ship will be ordered. Stacks and masts have been modified from F785 onward.

SUBMARINE CHASERS

♦ *4 Le Fougueux class*

	Bldr	L
P 635 L'ARDENT	Normand	17-7-58
P 640 LE FRINGANT	F.C. Méditerranée	6-2-59
P 644 L'ADROIT	Lorient	5-10-57
P 645 L'ALERTE	Lorient	5-10-57

L'Ardent (P 635) M.N., 1975

D: 325 tons (400 fl) **Dim:** 53.03 × 7.26 × 3.10 fl
A: 2/40-mm AA — 1/120-mm mortar fwd — 2 depth-charge projectors — 2 depth-charge racks
Man: 4 officers, 42 men
S: 18.7 kts (22 under trials) **Range:** 3,000/12, 2,000/15
M: 4 SEMT-Pielstick diesels built by S.G.C.M.; 2 props; 3,240 hp
Electron Equipt: 1 Decca radar and 1 QCU-2 sonar

REMARKS: *Le Fougueux* (P-641), *L'Opiniatre* (P-642), and *L'Agile* (P-643) stricken in 1975. *L'Intrepide* (P-630), *L'Étourdi* (P-637), *L'Attentif* (P-646), and *L'Enjoué* (P-647) were stricken in 1976. *L'Effronté* (P-638), *Le Hardi* (P-648), and *Le Frondeur* (P-639) were stricken in 1977.

PATROL BOATS

♦ *6 scheduled in the 1977-1982 equipment plan*

♦ *4 Trident class*

	Bldr	In serv.
P 670 TRIDENT	Auroux, Arcachon	17-12-76
P 671 GLAIVE	Auroux, Arcachon	3-77
P 672 EPEE	C.N.M. Cherbourg	9-10-76
P 673 PERTUISANE	C.N.M. Cherbourg	20-1-77

D: 115/130 tons **S:** 26 kts **Dim:** 37 × 5.50 × 1.60
A: 1/40-mm AA — 6/SS 12 missiles — 1/12.7-mm machine gun

PATROL BOATS *(continued)*

Épée (P 672) E.C.P.A., 1976

Man: 2 officers, 5 petty officers, 12 men **Range:** 750/20, 1,750/10
M: 2 AGO V 12 CZSHR diesels; 2 controllable-pitch props; 4,000 hp

REMARK: Originally 30 were planned, then 14, but only these four are to be built.

Trident (P 670) E.C.P.A., 1976

♦ *1 Combattante-I class*

	Laid down	L	In serv.
P 730 LA COMBATTANTE	4-62	20-6-63	3-64

Bldr: Const. Méc. de Normandie

D: 180 tons (202 fl) **Dim:** 45 × 7.35 × 2.45 fl
S: 23 kts **Man:** 3 officers, 22 men
A: 4 SS 12 (IV × 1) — 2/40-mm AA
Range: 2,000/12 **Electric:** 120 kw
M: SEMT-Pielstick diesels; 2 variable pitch props; 3,200 hp

La Combattante (P 730) M.N., 1974

REMARKS: Antimagnetic hull of laminated wood and plastic. Can carry a commando group of 80 men and equipment for a short passage.

♦ *4 former coastal minesweepers, Canadian-built*

P 652 LA LORIENTAISE (ex-*Miramichi*)
P 653 LA DUNKERQUOISE (ex-*Fundy*)
P 655 LA DIEPPOISE (ex-*Chaleur*)
P 657 LA PAIMPOLAISE (ex-*Thunder*)

La Dieppoise (P 655) J. C. Bellonne

Bldrs: Port Arthur SB, St. John Drydock, Marine Industries, Davie SB, Canadian Vickers. Launched from 11-51 to 1953

D: 370 tons (470 fl) **Dim:** 50 (46.05 pp) × 9.21 × 2.80
S: 15 kts **Range:** 4,500/11
A: 1/40-mm AA **Man:** 4 officers, 31 men
M: General Motors Diesels; 2 props; 2,500 hp **Fuel:** 52 tons

PATROL BOATS (*continued*)

REMARKS: Minesweeping equipment removed. Transferred in 1954 under the Mutual Assistance Pact (MAP). Wooden hull, with duralumin used throughout. Used as station vessels overseas. Air-conditioned. *La Bayonnaise* (P-654) stricken 1976, *La Malouine* (P-651) stricken 1977.

♦ *9 Sirius-class ex-coastal minesweepers*

	Bldr	L
P 650 ARCTURUS	C.N. Caen	12-3-54
P 656 ALTAIR	C.M.N., Cherbourg	27-3-56
P 658 CROIX DU SUD	Seine Maritime	13-6-56
P 659 CANOPUS	Augustin Normand	31-12-55
P 660 ÉTOILE POLAIRE	Seine Maritime	5-3-57
P 707 VEGA	Normand	14-1-53
P 741 ERIDAN	Penhoët	18-5-54
P 743 SAGITTAIRE	Seine Maritime	12-1-55
P 759 LYRE	Penhoët	3-5-56

D: 400 tons (440 fl) **Dim:** 46.40 (42.70 pp) × 8.55 × 2.50
S: 15 kts **Man:** 3 officers, 35 men **Fuel:** 48 tons
A: 1/40-mm AA and 1/20-mm or 2/20-mm **Range:** 3,000/10
M: SEMT-Pielstick diesels, 16 cylinders constructed by S.G.C.M.; 2 props; 2,000 hp

REMARKS: Minesweeping equipment removed. P-707, P-741, and P-743 are in reserve. French-built version of British "-*ton*" class.

Altair (P 656)

♦ *5 ex-minesweepers, English "-ham" class* — Built in Great Britain 1954-55

P 742 PAQUERETTE (ex-*Kingham*)
P 661 JASMIN (ex-*Stedham*)
P 662 PETUNIA (ex-*Pineham*)
P 784 GÉRANIUM (ex-*Tibenham*)
P 787 JONQUILLE (ex-*Sulham*)
P 788 VIOLETTE (ex-*Mersham*)

Petunia (P 662) M.N., 1975

D: 140 tons (170 fl) **Dim:** 33.43 × 6.45 × 1.70
A: 1/20-mm AA **Man:** 2 officers, 10 men
S: 14 kts **Endurance:** 4 days
M: 2 Paxman YHAXM diesels; 2 props; 550 hp **Fuel:** 15 tons

REMARK: Except for P-662, which is used by the Navy as a buoy tender, all are manned by the Gendarmerie.

PATROL CRAFT

♦ *3 or 4 Tecimar Type* — In serv. 1974

P 770 **P 771** **P 772** and/or **P 774**

P 772 and P 774 Tecimar, 1974

D: 30 tons **S:** 25 kts **Dim:** 13.30 × 4.10 × 1.10
A: 1/12.7-mm machine gun — 1/7.5-mm machine gun
M: 2 G.M. 6-71 diesels; 2 props; 670 hp

REMARKS: Hull moulded of stratified polyester. Manned by the Gendarmerie. One unit was to be transferred to Djibouti on independence.

MINE WARFARE SHIPS

♦ *3 Tripartite-design minehunters* (1 in 1976 Budget, 2 in 1977)

Bldr: Lorient

M . . . N . . .   M . . . N . . .   M . . . N . . .

D: 544 tons (fl) **Dim:** 47.10 (pp) × 8.90 × 2.60 (max.)
A: 1/20-mm AA **Man:** 49 men **Range:** 3,000/12
M: 1 Werkspoor diesel; 1 controllable-pitch prop; 1,870 hp; 2 electric maneuvering props of 120 hp each; bow-thruster
S: 15 kts on main engine; 7 kts while hunting
Electron Equipt: Radar: Decca 1229, 1 automatic track-plotter with numerical calculator, automatic pilot, Toran and Syledis radio navigation systems
Sonar: DUBM 21, 2 PAP 104 remote-controlled mine locators

REMARKS: Hull composite-built of glass and polyester resin. Will have one mechanical drag sweep. These minehunters will be constructed in cooperation between Belgium, France, and The Netherlands for the requirements of the three countries. Thirteen are programmed for construction for France under the 1977-82 Plan.

♦ *5 Circé-class minehunters*

	Laid down	L	In serv.
M 712 CYBELE	15-9-70	2-3-72	28-9-72
M 713 CALLIOPE	4-4-70	20-10-71	28-9-72
M 714 CLIO	4-9-69	10-6-71	18-5-72
M 715 CIRCÉ	30-1-69	15-12-70	18-5-72
M 716 CÉRÈS	2-2-71	10-8-72	8-3-73

Bldr: Const. Méc. de Normandie (Cherbourg)

D: 465 tons (normal) **Dim:** 50.90 (46.50 pp) × 8.90 × 3.40
S: 15 kts **Man:** 4 officers, 15 petty officers, 29 men
A: 1/20-mm — 2 remotely controlled sleds with charges
M: 1 MTU diesel; 1 prop; 1,800 hp **Range:** 3,000/12

REMARKS: Designed for the detection and destruction of mines laid as deep as 60 meters. Hull made of laminated wood; anti-magnetic and silent aspects stressed. Two independent propulsion systems, one for navigation at sea, the other for minesweeping, both with remote control. Special rudders with small screw-propellers mounted at the base of the after end of the rudder and powered by a 260-hp electric motor, giving a speed of 7 knots and permitting exceptional maneuverability. Detection and identification of mines by DUBM 20 sonar. The destruction of the mines is accomplished either by divers (six in each crew), or by the P.A.P. (*posisson auto-propulsé*) wireguided sled device. It is 2.70 m long, 1.10 m in diameter, weighs 700 kg, and is moved by two lateral electric batteries linked to electric motors which drive it at 6 knots for a distance of 500 m. It has a television camera and projector and sends an image of the mine to the ship; it can deposit its explosive charge of 100 kg near the mine. After the sled has been recovered, the charge is detonated by ultra-sonic waves. These ships do not have minesweeping gear.

Calliope (M 713) J. C. Bellonne, 1974

Clio 1972

♦ *5 minehunters, ex-ocean minesweepers, U.S. MSO type*

L: 1953-54 under the U.S. numbers in parentheses

M 616 DOMPAIRE (ex-MSO-434)
M 617 GARIGLIANO (ex-MSO-432)
M 618 MYTHO (ex-MSO-475)
M 615 CANTHO (ex-MSO-476)
M 619 VINH-LONG (ex-MSO-477)

D: 700 tons (780 fl) **Dim:** 50.29 × 10.67 × 3.15
S: 13.5 (14 trials) **Man:** peace: 4 officers, 13 petty officers, 35 men
A: 1/40-mm AA **Range:** 3,000/10
M: 2 G.M. 8-278A diesels; 2 controllable-pitch props; 1,600 hp; bow thruster

MINE WARFARE SHIPS (*continued*)

Dompaire 1977

Electron Equipt: Sonar: DUBM 21, 2 PAP 104 remote-controlled mine locator, EVEC automatic plotting table

REMARKS: Conversion to minehunters completed between 1976 and 1979. Mechanical minesweeping capability retained.

♦ *5 ocean minesweepers, ex-U.S. MSO type* — L: 1953-54

M 610 OUISTREHAM (ex-MSO-513)
M 612 ALENÇON (ex-MSO-453)
M 613 BERNÉVAL (ex-MSO-450)
M 620 BERLAIMONT (ex-MSO-500)
M 623 BACCARAT (ex-MSO-503)

Alençon (M 612) J. C. Bellonne, 1975

D: 700 tons (780 fl) **Dim:** 50.29 × 10.67 × 3.15
S: 13.5 kts (14 trials) **Range:** 3,000/10 **Man:** 5 officers, 53 men
A: 1/40-mm AA **Fuel:** 47 tons
M: 2 G.M. diesels; 2 controllable-pitch props; 1,600 hp

REMARKS: Due to budget restrictions, modernization of these five ships to minehunters has been abandoned. They will, however, receive the new DUBM 41 sonar beginning in 1978. *Narvik* (*M-609*) was reclassified 1-1-76 as a trials ship for the AP-4 sweep drag and a new lens-type sonar.

♦ *1 special coastal minesweeper, Type DB-1*

	Bldr	Laid down	L	In serv.
M 765 MERCURE	Const. Méc. de Normandie	1-55	21-2-57	12-58

D: 365 tons (400 fl) **Dim:** 44.35 (42 pp) × 8.27 × 4.04
S: 15 kts **A:** 2/20-mm AA (II × 1) (removed)
M: 2 Mercedes-Benz diesels MB 820 EB; 2 Ka-Me-Wa controllable-pitch props; 4,000 hp

REMARKS: In reserve. Her conversion from minesweeper to fisheries protection ship has been under study for some time. Six sisters built for West Germany have been transferred to Turkey.

Mercure (M 765)

♦ *5 coastal minesweepers, French-built versions of the British "-ton" class*

	L		L
M 737 CAPRICORNE	8-8-56	**M 756 CÉPHÉE**	3-1-56
M 749 PHÉNIX	23-5-55	**M 757 VERSEAU**	26-4-56
M 755 CAPELLA	6-10-55		

Bldr: Constructions Mécaniques de Normandie, Cherbourg

D: 400 tons (440 fl) **Dim:** 46.40 (42.70 pp) × 8.55 × 2.50
S: 15 kts (11.5 sweep.) **Man:** 3 officers, 35 men
A: 1/40-mm AA, 1 or 2/20-mm AA **Range:** 3,000/10 **Fuel:** 48 tons

MINE WARFARE SHIPS (*continued*)

REMARKS: Hull is laminated wood and light aluminum which produces a strong, rigid, and light body. Keel and stem in heavy wood. Have mechanical, magnetic, and acoustic minesweeping gear. The *Capricorne* has been given greater degaussing treatment than the other ships. All have one diesel sweep generator (500 hp). The *Aries* was loaned to Morocco in 1975. *Bételgeuse* (A-747) reclassified 1-5-77 as a trials ship and used for experiments with the DUBM 41 sonar and its computer. *Algol* (M-704) and *Cassiopée* (M-740) stricken 1976. *Vega* (M-707), *Antares* (M-703), *Eridan* (M-741), *Sagittaire* (M-743), and *Lyre* (M-759) have been reclassified as patrol boats (1977).

Capricorne (M 737) E.C.P.A., 1973

♦ a) *9 coastal minesweepers, U.S. Navy MSC (ex-AMS) class*

M 632 PERVENCHE (ex-MSC-141)
M 633 PIVOINE (ex-MSC-125)
M 639 ACANTHE (ex-MSC-70)
M 671 CAMÉLIA (ex-MSC-68)
M 679 GLYCINE (ex-MSC-118)
M 681 LAURIER (ex-MSC-86)
M 682 LILAS (ex-MSC-93)
M 687 MIMOSA (ex-MSC-99)
M 688 MUGUET (ex-MSC-97)

Camélia (M 671) M.N., 1974

Lilas J. C. Bellonne, 1972

♦ b) *6 coastal minesweepers, for which antimagnetic standards are no longer maintained:*

M 635 RÉSÉDA (ex-MSC-126)
M 638 ACACIA (ex-MSC-69)
M 668 AZALÉE (ex-MSC-67)
M 674 CYCLAMEN (ex-MSC-119)
M 675 EGLANTINE (ex-MSC-117)
M 684 LOBELIA (ex-MSC-96)

Bldr: U.S.A. (1951-54) Transferred between 6-1953 and 1955.

D: 300 tons (372 fl) **Dim:** 43.00 (41.50 pp) × 7.95 × 2.55
S: 13 kts (8 sweep.) **Man:** 3 officers, 35 men

MINE WARFARE SHIPS (*continued*)

A: 2/20-mm AA (II × 1) **Range:** 2,500/10
M: 2 G.M. 8-268A diesels; 2 props; 1,200 hp (cruising)
Fuel: 40 tons

REMARKS: These minesweepers are the survivors of a series of 27 transferred under the Mutual Assistance Pact. The hulls are constructed entirely of wood. Four have been converted into auxiliaries: *Ajonc* as a tender to the diving school, *Gardenia* and *Magnolia* as base ships for underwater demolition teams, and *Jacinthe* as a trials ship and minelayer. The others have been stricken or transferred abroad: *Coquelicot* and *Marjolaine* to Tunisia, *Marguerite* to Uruguay, and *Pavot* and *Renoncule* to Turkey.

AMPHIBIOUS WARFARE SHIPS

♦ *2 TCD Dock Landing Ships*

	Author	Bldr	Laid down	L	In serv.
L 9021 OURAGAN	1960	Brest	6-62	9-11-63	6-65
L 9022 ORAGE	(22-7-65)	Brest	6-66	22-4-67	3-68

Orage (L 9022); she is now armed J. C. Bellonne, 1973

D: 5,800 tons (8,500 fl) **S:** 17.3 kts **Range:** 4,000/15
Dim: 149 (144.50 pp) × 21.50 × 4.90 (8.70 flooded-down)
A: 6/40-mm AA — 2/120-mm mortars — landing areas for 4 helicopters
Electron Equipt: Radars: 1/DRBN-32 — Sonars: 1/SQS 17 on 9021
M: SEMT-Pielstick diesels; 2 controllable-pitch props; 8,640 hp
Electric: 2,650 kw
Man: *Orage:* 10 officers, 46 petty officers, 145 men
Ouragan: 9 officers, 54 petty officers, 144 men

REMARKS: Assault transports whose mission it is to carry and place in operation far from home bases:

(a) helicopters which can land a full commando, sustain troops already ashore, and provide fire support and communication liaison.

Ouragon (L 9021) J. C. Bellonne, 1975

(b) landing craft carrying personnel or material (tanks, vehicles, supplies, etc.). 349 troops including 14 officers can be carried on board, or 470 for a short distance.

A floodable well 120 meters long can be sunk under 3 meters of water and has a stern gate 14 × 5.5 meters. When ballasted down, displacement reaches 14,400 tons. Movement of the water control sluices and valves is automatic using pumps (3,000 m^3/h) controlled from a central post. A removable deck in six sections covers the after part of the well for 36 meters and allows the landing and takeoff of heavy

Ouragon (L 9021) J. C. Bellonne, 1975

AMPHIBIOUS WARFARE SHIPS *(continued)*

helicopters. Another temporary deck 90 meters in length (15 sections) increases if necessary the stowage space for cargo or vehicles, but reduces the number of landing craft which can be carried, inasmuch as the original well is then diminished by half.

If used as transports, they can carry either two EDIC landing craft for infantry and tanks, carrying 11 light tanks or trucks, or 18 LCM Mk-6 with tanks; or, vehicles, and, in addition, heavy helicopters on a landing platform. If employed as cargo carriers, they can carry 1,500 tons of material. Power-lifting equipment includes two 35-ton cranes. Combined command center permits the simultaneous direction of helicopter and amphibious operations.

♦ *5 Type BDC Tank Landing Ships*

	Bldr	Laid down	L	In serv.
L 9003 ARGENS (BDC-2)	A.C. de Bretagne	10-58	7-4-59	6-60
L 9004 BIDASSOA (BDC-5)	Seine Maritime	1-60	30-12-60	7-61
L 9007 TRIEUX (BDC-1)	A.C. de Bretagne	12-58	6-12-58	3-60
L 9008 DIVES (BDC-4)	Seine Maritime	5-59	29-6-60	4-61
L 9009 BLAVET (BDC-3)	A.C. de Bretagne	4-59	15-1-60	1-61

Argens (L 9003) G. Arra, 1972

Trieux (L 9007) with hangar, and **Blavet (L 9009)** M. N., 1970

D: 1,400 tons, 1,750 (av), 4,225 (fl)
Dim: 102.12 (96.60 pp) × 15.54 × 3.20
A: 3/40-mm AA (I × 3) — 1/120-mm mortar mounted fwd
Man: 6 officers, 69 men **Range:** 18,500/10 **S:** 11 kts
M: 2 SEMT-Pielstick 16PA1 diesels; 2 props; 2,000 hp

Remarks: Design derived from U.S. LST1 class. Can carry 1,800 tons of cargo, 4 LCVP landing craft, and a maximum of 807 passengers (normally 170 troops). MacGregor type loading hatches. *Trieux* and *Blavet* have been modified with a hangar for two Alouette III helicopters.

♦ *2 Batral-class LSM*

	Bldr	Laid down	L	In serv.
L 9030 CHAMPLAIN	Brest	1973	17-11-73	5-10-74
L 9031 FRANCIS GARNIER	Brest	1973	17-11-73	21-6-74

Francis Garnier (L 9031) M.N., 1975

D: 750 tons (1,330 fl) **Dim:** 80 (68 pp) × 13 × 3 (max.)
S: 16 kts (13 cruising) **Man:** 4 officers, 35 men
M: 2 diesels; 2 props; 1,800 hp **Range:** 4,500/13

Remarks: Bow-door design, embarkation ramp and helicopter platform aft. Living quarters for a landing team (5 officers, 15 non-commissioned officers, 118 men) and its 12 vehicles, including Leopard armored personnel carriers. Can carry 2/40-mm AA, 2/81-mm mortars as defensive armament.

♦ *12 EDIC-class LCU*

L 9091 (7-1-58)	**L 9094** (24-7-58)	**L 9072** (1968)	**L 9082** (1964)
L 9092 (2-12-58)	**L 9096** (11-10-58)	**L 9073** (1968)	**L 9083** (1964)
L 9093 (17-4-58)	**L 9070** (30-3-67)	**L 9074** (22-7-69)	**L 9084** (. . .)

Bldrs: 7 Ch. Franco-Belges; 2 Toulon Naval DY; 2 Ch. de La Perrière; 1 Lorient

L 9096 D.C.A.N., 1974

AMPHIBIOUS WARFARE SHIPS (*continued*)

D: 250 tons (670 fl) **Dim:** 59 × 11.95 × 1.30 (1.62 fl)
S: 8 kts **M:** 2 MGO diesels; 2 props; 1,000 hp
A: 2/20-mm AA **Man:** 1 officer, 15 men

REMARKS: Can carry 11 trucks or 5 LVTs. L-9095 transferred 1-7-74 to Senegal. L-9071 stricken 19-4-77. Two each can be carried aboard the *Ouragan* and the *Orage*.

♦ *16 U.S. LCM (8) class* — Bldr: France

D: 56 tons (150 fl) **Dim:** 23.80 × 6.35 × 1.17
Man: 6 men **S:** 9.5 kts **Cargo capacity:** 90 tons. Bow door.
M: 2 Hispano-HS 103 S diesels; 2 props; 450 hp **Fuel:** 3.4 tons diesel

♦ *about 20 U.S. LCM (3) and LCM (6)*

D: 26/52 tons **Dim:** 15.25 or 17.0 × 4.30 × 1.20 **S:** 8 kts
Load: 1 30-ton tank **M:** 2 diesels

SPECIAL DUTY SHIPS

♦ *1 trials and measurement ship*

	Bldr	L	In serv.
A 603 HENRI POINCARÉ (ex-*Maina Morasso*)	Adriatico	10-60	3-68

Henri Poincaré (A 603) D.C.A.N., 1974

D: 24,000 (fl) **Dim:** 180 (160 pp) × 22.20 × 9.40 **A:** 2/20-mm AA
Man: 11 officers, 70 petty officers, 136 men, and several civilian technicians.
Electron Equipt: Radar: 1/DRBV 22 D, 1/*Savoie*, 2/*Bearn*
M: Parsons GT; 10,000 hp; 1 prop; 1 bow prop. **S:** 15 kts
Boilers: 2 Foster-Wheeler (48 kg/cm²; superheat 445°C) **Range:** 11,800/13.5

REMARKS: Flagship of the Naval Test and Measurement Group (Group "M"), for making at-sea tests, measurements, and conducting various experiments as may be requested by the Navy on any other organization, civil as well as military.

The chief mission of the *Henri Poincaré* is to measure as closely as possible the trajectory of ballistic missiles (MSBS and SSBS) fired from the experimental station at Landes or by missile-carrying nuclear submarines and to compute their flight characteristics, especially from re-entry until impact.

The secondary mission of the ship is to help the flag officer to control the naval and air elements in the test area especially in recovery and security functions.

A former Italian tanker, the ship was entirely rebuilt by DCAN at Brest from 1964 and 1967 and received specific equipment: 3 radars (tracking and trajectory measuring for ballistic tests) and a sonar dome. Automatic tracking station. Astro-observatory. Camera-equipped theodolite. Infrared equipment. Transit navigational system. Aerology, meteorologic, and oceanographic equipment. Excellent communication equipment. Programming and transcribing center for all experiments and installations. Heavy helicopter platform and hangar for 2 heavy and 5 light helicopters.

♦ *1 experimental guided missile ship*

A 610 ILE D'OLÉRON (ex-*München*) — Bldr: Germany (1939)

D: 5,500 tons (6,500 fl) **Dim:** 115.05 × 15.24 × 6.50
S: 14.5 kts **Range:** 7,200/12, 5,900/14 **Electric:** 1,240 kw
M: 2 MAN 6-cylinder diesels; 1 prop; 3,500 hp **Fuel:** 340 tons
Electron Equipt: 1/DRBV 22 C, 1/DRBV 50, 1/DRBI 10

REMARKS: Taken from the Germans as a war prize. Converted in 1957–58 to an experimental ship for missiles. In addition to the radars listed, she also carries guidance radars for the systems under test. Recently used for Exocet trials and, from 1977 on, for crotale.

Ile d'Oléron (A 610) C. Martinelli, 1974

♦ *1 Sirius-class ex-coastal minesweeper*

A747 BETELGEUSE

REMARK: For trials with the DUBM 41 minehunting sonar.

♦ *1 electronics experimental ship (former stores ship)*

A 644 BERRY (ex-*Medoc*) — Bldr: Roland Werft, Bremen — L: 10-9-58

D: 2,700 tons (fl) **S:** 15 kts **Dim:** 86.70 (78.50 pp) × 11.60 × 4.60
M: 2 MWM diesels; 2 props; 2,400 hp **Range:** 7,000/15

REMARKS: Converted 1976–77 at Toulon, recommissioning 2-77. Former sister *Aunis* is a sonar trials ship (see later page).

SPECIAL DUTY SHIPS (*continued*)

Berry (A 644) J. C. Bellonne, 1976

♦ *1 ex-ocean minesweeper (MSO)*

A 769 NARVIK (ex-M-609)

REMARK: Experiments with Type AP-4 drag sweep and with a new lenticular sonar.

♦ *1 ex-coastal minesweeper*

A 680 JACINTHE (ex-M-680)

REMARK: Equipped as a minelayer and trials ship.

♦ *1 deep-diving submarine*

A 648 ARCHIMÈDE — Bldr: Toulon Dockyard

D: 200 tons (submerged) **Weight:** 60 tons (light)
Dim: 21 × 5 × 5.20

Archimède J. C. Bellonne, 1972

REMARKS: Painted bright yellow. Can reach 11,000 meters in depth.

♦ *1 underwater research ship*

	Author	Bldr	Laid down	L	In serv.
A 646 TRITON	1967	Lorient	1967	7-3-70	1972

Triton (A 646) J. C. Bellonne, 1971

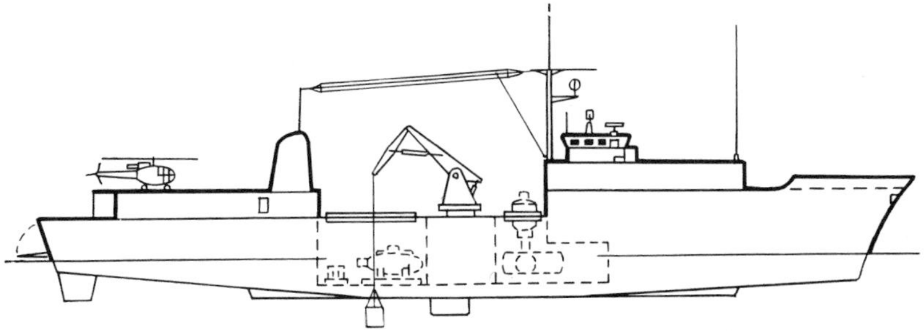

D: 1,410 tons (1,510 fl) **Dim:** 74 (68 pp) × 11.85 × 3.65 (aver)
S: 13 kts **Range:** 4,000/13
Man: 4 officers, 41 men. Divers: 5 commissioned and 12 enlisted
M: 2 MGO V 12 ASHR diesels generating 660 kw which are linked by reduction gear to a Voith-Schneider 30 G cycloidal propeller at the stern; forward a Voith-Schneider 26 G cycloidal propeller is powered by two electric motors, generating 400 kw through a reduction gear.

REMARKS: Assigned to the GISMER (*Groupe d'Intervention Sous la Mer*), for deep sea diving and observation. Decompression chamber, laboratories; underwater television, etc., have all been provided. Extremely maneuverable at very slow speeds; can stay positioned above a point 300 meters deep. Helicopter platform; can be used in submarine rescue operations. **Electric:** 960 kw (propulsion plant), 640 kw (auxiliary). Navigational radar, sonar for deep water area search.

Using a 15-ton crane, can lift (a) a 13.5-ton submersible chamber which can be sunk to 250 meters and which can carry two 4-man diving teams (this bell does not float but is wire-tethered); (b) the two-man submarine *Griffon* for underwater exploration to 600 meters. *Griffon* has a manipulator arm; her characteristics are: **D:** 14.2 to 16.7 tons. **Dim:** 7.80 × 2.30 × 3.10 (height), 1 electric motor. **Range:** 24 hours/ 4 knots. (c) diving devices, sleds (troika, automatically guided). *Triton* is painted white.

SPECIAL DUTY SHIPS (*continued*)

A 643 AUNIS (ex-*Regina Pacis*) — Bldr: Roland Werft — 1956

Aunis (A 643) 1974

D: 2,900 tons **S:** 12 kts **Dim:** 94.43 × . . . × 11.60
M: 2 MAN diesels; 1 prop; 2,400 hp
Man: 3 officers, 47 men **Range:** 4,500/12

REMARKS: Former Italian cargo ship purchased as a transport ship in 1966. Modified at Toulon, 1972-74. Used in the Cormoran deep-submerged-sonar project, using equipment formerly carried by the Duperré (D-633).

OCEANOGRAPHIC RESEARCH SHIPS

	Bldr	Laid down	L	In serv.
A 757 D'ENTRECASTEAUX	Brest	7-69	30-5-70	1971

D: 2,400 tons (fl) **S:** 15 kts **Dim:** 89 × 13 × 3.90
Man: 6 officers, 73 men, up to 38 scientists and technicians
Electron Equipt: Radar: 1/DRBV 50
Range: 10,000/12 **M:** 2 diesel-electric main engines × 1,000 kw; 2 controllable-pitch props. For extremely slow maneuvering, 2 retractable Schöttel propellers, one fwd, one aft.

D'Entrecasteaux (A 757) J. C. Bellonne, 1974

REMARKS: For oceanographic research and hydrographic duties. Can take soundings and surveys to a depth of 6,000 meters. 2 radars, 1 sonar; helicopter platform and hangar (Alouette type helicopter). Booms, one LCPS, three hydrographic launches. Painted white.

A 640 ORIGNY

Origny (A 640) 1974

D: 780 (fl) **S:** 13.5 kts **Dim:** 50.29 × 10.67 × 3.15
M: 2 General Motors 8-278A diesels; 2 controllable-pitch props; 1,600 hp

REMARKS: Ex-MSO class minesweeper. Painted white.

HYDROGRAPHIC SURVEY SHIPS

♦ *2 modified trawlers*

	Bldr	L	In serv.(1)
A 756 L'ESPERANCE (ex-*Jacques Coeur*)	Gdynia, Poland	1962	1969
A 766 L'ESTAFETTE (ex-*Jacques Cartier*)	Gdynia, Poland	1962	1972

(1) for the French Navy

L'Estafette (A 766) 1973

HYDROGRAPHIC SURVEY SHIPS (*continued*)

D: 956 tons (1,360 fl) **Dim:** 63.45 (59.75 pp) × 9.82 × 5.85 fl
S: 13.5 kts **Man:** 3 officers, 29 men; 14 hydrographic service personnel
M: MAN diesels; 1 prop; 1,870 hp **Range:** 7,500/13

REMARKS: Former ocean-going fishing trawlers, purchased in 1968-69. Painted white. Large oceanographic winch on stern, articulated crane amidships.

	Bldr	L	In serv.
A 758 LA RECHERCHE (ex-*Guyane*)	Ziegler, Dunkerque	4-51	3-62

La Recherche (A 758) J. C. Bellonne, 1972

D: 810 tons (910 fl) **Dim:** 67.50 (62 pp) × 10.40 × 4.50
S: 13.5 kts **Range:** 3,100/10
Man: 2 officers, 21 men; 43 hydrographic personnel
M: 1 Werkspoor MABS 398 diesel, 8 cylinders 4 t.; 1,535 hp

REMARKS: Operated for the French Overseas Ministry. Bought in 1960. Hull bulged for stability. Painted white.

♦ *2 specially constructed coastal survey ships*

	Bldr	Laid down	L	In serv.
A 780 ASTROLABE	Seine Maritime	1962	27-5-63	7-64
A 781 BOUSSOLE	Seine Maritime	6-62	11-4-63	7-64

Astrolabe (A 780) 1968

D: 330 tons (440 fl) **Dim:** 42.70 (36.65 pp) × 8.45 × 2.90
S: 12.5 kts **Man:** 1 officer, 32 men **Range:** 4,000/12
A: (*780*): 1/40-mm — 2/12.7-mm machine guns (not normally mounted)
M: 2 Beaudoin DV 8 diesels; 1 controllable-pitch prop; 800 hp

REMARKS: Authorized in 1961. Air conditioned. Carries two radio-equipped survey launchers of 4.5 tons each. Painted white.

♦ *2 coastal survey ships* (ex-fishing boats, modified in 1962-63)

A 683 OCTANT (ex-*Michel Marie*, 1955)

D: 128 tons (133 fl) **S:** 9 kts **Dim:** 24 × 6.10 × 3.23
M: 2 diesels; 1 variable-pitch prop; 200 hp **Range:** 2,000
Man: 1 officer, 12 men

REMARKS: Endurance 12 days. Painted white. Sister *Alidade* (A-682) stricken 4-77.

Alidade (A 682) — Octant (A 683) similar G. Arra, 1972

A 794 CORAIL (ex-*Marc Joly*) — Bldr: Thuin, Belgium (1967)

Corail (A 794) 1975

HYDROGRAPHIC SURVEY SHIPS *(continued)*

D: 54.78 tons (light) **Dim:** 17.80 × 4.92 × 1.83
M: 1 Caterpillar diesel; 250 hp **S:** 10.3 kts

REMARKS: Painted white. Operates from New Caledonia.

SUPPORT TENDERS

♦ *1 Jules Verne class*

	Budget	Bldr	Laid down	L	In serv.
A 620 JULES VERNE (ex-*Achéron*)	1961	Brest	1969	30-5-76	3-76

D: 6,485 tons (10,250 fl) **S:** 18 kts **Dim:** 147.00 × 21.56 × 6.50
A: 2/40-mm AA (I × 2) **Range:** 9,500/18 **Electric:** 3,800 kw
M: 2 SEMT-Pielstick T2PC diesels; 1 props; 11,200 hp

REMARKS: Six years after being launched as an ammunition ship, the *Jules Verne* was completed as a multi-purpose floating workshop intended to provide prolonged support to a force composed of from three to six surface warships, without shore assistance. Significant repair capabilities, both for voyage repairs and for battle-damage repairs: general mechanical, engine, electrical, sheet-metal, electronic workshops, etc. She also carries a stock of torpedoes and other munitions.

Jules Verne (A 620) E.C.P.A., 1976

♦ *5 medium tonnage ships, each specializing in a particular area for the maintenance of different ships of the fleet*

	Budget	Purpose	Bldr	Laid down	L	In serv.
A 621 RHIN	1959	electronics	Lorient	5-61	17-3-62	3-64
A 622 RHÔNE	1960	submarines	Lorient	2-62	8-12-62	10-64

Rhin (A 621)

D: 2,075 tons (2,445 fl) **Dim:** 101.05 (92.05 pp) × 13.10 × 3.65
S: 16.5 kts **Man:** (*621, 622*): 6 officers, 142 men
A: 3/40-mm AA (I × 3) **Range:** 13,000/13
Electron Equipt: Radar: 1/DRBV 50 **Electric:** 920 kw
M: 2 SEMT-Pielstick 16 PA 2V diesels; 1 prop; 3,200 hp

Rhin (A 621) J. C. Bellonne, 1974

REMARKS: The *Rhin* is equipped to maintain two or three large ships or a dozen patrol boats, minesweepers, or landing craft for two months under operational conditions; she has 1,700 m³ of storerooms and 700 m³ of workshops, many air-conditioned. She has a hangar and flight deck for one helicopter.

The *Rhône* is fitted out for the surveillance and assistance of fishing vessels in the North Atlantic. She has a flight deck, but no hangar.

SUPPORT TENDERS *(continued)*

Rhône (A 622) G. Arra, 1972

	Budget	Purpose	Bldr	Laid down	L	In serv.
A 618 RANCE	1964	experimental	Lorient	8-64	5-5-65	2-66

Rance (A 168)

Different profile from the other BSL-class ships. An additional deck has been fitted between the navigating bridge and the stack; laboratory ship; radioactive decontamination chambers. Carries up to three Alouette helicopters. **Man:** 10 officers, 140 men, 118 passengers. DRBV-22C radar. No armament. SEMT-Pielstick 12 PA 4 diesels.

	Budget	Purpose	Bldr	Laid down	L	In serv.
A 615 LOIRE	1962	minesweepers	Lorient	7-65	1966	6-67
A 617 GARONNE	1964	repair ship	Lorient	11-63	8-8-64	9-65

Loire (A 615)

D: 2,320 tons **S:** 15 kts **Dim:** 101.50 (92.05 pp) × 13.80 × 3.70
A: (A-615) 3/40-mm AA; (A-617) 1/40-mm AA — 2/20-mm AA
Range: 13,000/13
Man: (A-615) 9 officers, 44 petty officers, 87 men
(A-617) 10 officers, 211 men
M: 2 SEMT-Pielstick 12 PA 4 diesels, 1 prop, 3,600 hp

Garonne (A 617) J. C. Bellonne, 1974

REMARKS: (615) helicopter platform; 5-ton crane and 12-meter radius. (617) designed for overseas service; metal-working and carpenter shops; extra deck with lower overhead; no helicopter facilities; fantail has a crane mounted in the center.

The *Loire* is fitted out as a tender for minehunters and minesweepers.

FLEET REPLENISHMENT SHIPS

♦ *3 Durance-class fleet oilers*

	Bldr	Laid down	L	In serv.
A 629 DURANCE	Brest	1973	6-9-75	1-12-76
A 607 MEUSE	Brest	. . .	. . .	1-81
A . . . N . . .				

D: 17,800 tons (fl) **Dim:** 157.30 (149 pp) × 21.20 × 8.65 (10.80 fl)
S: 19 kts (fl) **Man:** 149 men, 45 passengers
A: 2/40-mm AA (I × 2) **Range:** 9,000/15
M: 2 SEMT-Pielstick 16 PC 2-5 diesels; 1 controllable-pitch prop; 20,000 hp
Electric: 5,400 kw **Fuel:** 750 tons

REMARKS: Two underway replenishment kingposts. Can supply two ships alongside and one astern. Capacity — *Durance:* 7,500 tons fuel oil, 1,500 tons diesel fuel, 500 tons JP-5, 130 tons distilled water, 170 tons fresh provisions, 150 tons munitions, 50 tons spare parts; *Meuse:* 5,000 tons fuel oil, 3,200 tons diesel, 1,800 tons JP-5, the remainder identical. Hangar for one Alouette III and flight deck for larger helicopters.

Durance (A 629) E.C.P.A., 1976

FLEET REPLENISHMENT SHIPS (*continued*)

Durance (A 629) E.C.P.A., 1976

A 675 ISÈRE (ex-*Caltex Strasbourg*) — Bldr: A.C. Seine Maritime (22-6-59)

D: 7,440 tons (26,700 fl) **Dim:** 170.38 (167 pp) × 21.72 × 10.27 (max.)
S: 16 kts **Man:** 6 officers, 86 men **Cargo capacity:** 18,200 tons
M: Parsons GT; 1 prop; 2 boilers; 8,260 hp

Isère (A 675) J. C. Bellonne, 1977

REMARK: French tanker purchased in 1965 and refitted with 2 underway fueling stations as well as an astern fueling station.

♦ *1 La Seine class*

A 628 LA SAÔNE (ex-*Stormarn*) — Bldr: A.C. de France — L: 27-2-48

La Saône (A 628) E.C.P.A., 1976

D: 7,250 tons (8,390 light, 23,410 fl) **A:** 3/40-mm AA
Dim: 160.0 × 22.0 × 10.75 (aft, fl) × 8.75 (fwd, fl)
S: 18 kts (14 cruising) **Man:** 10 officers, 42 petty officers, 127 men
M: Parsons GT; 2 props; 15,800 hp **Range:** 6,400/12.5, 11,000/10
Boilers: 3/37 kg/cm^2, superheat 350°C

REMARKS: Originally laid down 1940 and taken over for Germany. Modernized 1962-63. Carries 9,100 tons black oil, 1,800 tons jet fuel, 730 tons diesel fuel, 200 tons fresh provisions, including 83,165 liters wine. Five transfer positions, one with automatic constant-tension rig, two light transfer stations, two stations for heavy loads. Sister *La Seine* stricken 13-10-76.

TRANSPORT OILERS

♦ *1 La Charente class*

A 626 LA CHARENTE (ex-*Beaufort*) — Bldr: Haldnes, Tönsberg (1957)

La Charente (A 626) M.N., 1974

La Charente (A 626) M.N., 1974

TRANSPORT OILERS (*continued*)

D: 7,440 tons (26,000 fl) **Dim:** 179 × 21.90 × 9.25 × 10.40 (fl)
S: 17.5 kts **Man:** 6 officers, 94 men
Cargo capacity: 19,000 tons
A: 4/40-mm AA (I × 4).
M: General Electric GT; 1 prop; 2 boilers; 12,000 hp

REMARKS: Norwegian tanker purchased in 5-64. Modified to serve as flagship in the Indian Ocean. Helicopter platform and hangar on stern. Capability for astern refueling only.

♦ *2 Punaruu class*

A 625 PAPENOO (ex-*Bow Queen*) **A 632 PUNARUU** (ex-*Bow Cecil*)
Bldr: Built in Norway in 1969

Punaruu (A 632) M.N., 1975

D: 1,195 tons (2,927 fl) **S:** 12 kts **Dim:** 83 × 13.85 × 5.50
M: 2 diesels; 1 controllable-pitch prop; 2,050 hp; 1 bow thruster

REMARKS: Former Norwegian tankers purchased at the end of 1969, highly automated ships. 2,500 m³ capacity. Ten washable "inox" cargo tanks which can accept any liquid. Astern fueling capability.

A 638 SAHEL (1951) — fuel carrier — Bldr. C.N. de Caen

Sahel (A 638) Guiglini, 1974

D: 630 tons (1,450 fl) **Dim:** 53.70 × 9 × 4.40
S: 12 kts **Cargo capacity:** 646 tons
A: 2/20-mm AA **M:** 2 Sulzer diesels; 2 props; 1,400 hp

REMARKS: One of eleven units of a class begun for Germany during World War II. Three sisters are in East German Navy. Carries fuel and water.

♦ *1 ex-U.S. YO-55-class, transferred 1945*

A 630 LAC TONLÉ SAP (ex-*Pumper*, YO-56) — Bldr: R.T.C. Shipbuilding, Camden, N.J.; L: 9-42

Lac Tonlé Sap (A 630) J. C. Bellonne, 1972

D: 800 tons (2,700 fl) **S:** 11 kts **Dim:** 71.65 × 11.30 × 4.80
A: 3/20-mm AA **Range:** 6,300/11 **Man:** 2 officers, 35 men
M: 2/5-cyl. Fairbanks-Morse 37E14-5 diesels; 2 props; 1,150 hp

REMARKS: Will be retained until 1981. 1,700 tons cargo capacity. Capable of replenishing at sea. *Lac Chambon* scrapped in 1975.

LIGHT FUELS TANKER

	Bldr	Laid down	L	In serv.
A 619 ABER WRACH	C.N.M., Cherbourg	11-62	11-63	1966

Aber Wrach (A 619) E.C.P.A., 1972

LIGHT FUELS TANKER (*continued*)

D: 1,220 tons (3,500 fl) **Dim:** 86.55 (80 pp) × 12.20 × 4.80
S: 12 kts **Man:** 3 officers, 45 men
A: 1/40-mm AA **Range:** 5,000/12
M: 1 SEMT-Pielstick 6 PL diesel; 1 controllable-pitch prop; 2,000 hp
Cargo capacity: 2,200 tons

REMARKS: Carries diesel oil, jet fuel, gasoline in point-to-point service. Capable of underway fueling (astern) or anchored alongside.

PROVISIONS SHIP

♦ **A 733 SAINTONGE** (ex-*Santa Maria*) — Bldr: Duchèsne et Bossière (1956)

Saintonge (A 733) M. N.

D: 300 tons (990 fl) **Dim:** 54 × 8.50 × 3.22 **S:** 10 kts
Man: 2 officers, 13 men **M:** 1 MAK diesel; 760 hp
Fuel: 51 tons **Cargo capacity:** 500 tons

MISCELLANEOUS AUXILIARY SHIPS

♦ *4 coastal support tenders*

Bldr: Ch. de la Perrière, Lorient

	In serv.
A 767 CHAMOIS	1976
A 768 ELAN	1977
A 774 CHEVREUIL	1977
A 775 GAZELLE	1978

D: 400 tons **Dim:** 41.50 (36.96 pp) × 7.50 × 3.18
S: 14.5 kts **Man:** 10 men
M: 2 SACM MGO V 16 diesels; 2 controllable-pitch props; 1,100 hp

REMARKS: Identical to the 14 civilian-manned F.I.S.H. class designed for the supply of petroleum platforms, except for provision of a 5.6-ton crane. Hydraulic 50-ton stern crane mounted. Can be used for coastal towing and oil-spill cleanup. Bow prop and 2 rudders. After winch with 28-ton bollard pull. Can be used to transport 28 passengers, as minelayers, or as torpedo retrievers.

Chamois (A 767) 1976

♦ *8 ex-shore minesweepers, "-ham" class, used in base-support duties*

A 710 MYOSOTIS (ex-*Riplingham*)
A 735 HIBISCUS (ex-*Sparham*)
A 736 DAHLIA (ex-*Whippingham*)
A 737 TULIPE (ex-*Frettenham*)
A 738 CAPUCINE (ex-*Petersham*)
A 739 ŒILLET (ex-*Isham*)
A 740 HORTENSIA (ex-*Mileham*)
A 741 ARMOISE (ex-*Vexham*)

D: 140 tons (170 fl) **Dim:** 32.43 × 6.45 × 1.70
S: 14 kts (9 sweeping) **Man:** 2 officers, 10 men
A: 1/20-mm AA or none **Endurance:** 4 days
M: 2 Paxman YHAXM diesels; 2 props; 550 hp **Fuel:** 15 tons

Myosotis (with her old number) M.N., 1974

NET TENDERS

♦ *1 seagoing net tender*

	Bldr	Laid down	L	In serv.
A 731 TIANÉE	Brest	1-4-73	1-11-73	1975

NET TENDERS (*continued*)

Tianée (A 731) M.N., 1974

D: 842 tons (905 fl) **S:** 12 kts **Dim:** 54.30 × 10.60 × . . .
Man: 1 officer, 12 petty officers, 24 men **Range:** 5,200/12
M: 2 diesels; 1 prop; 1,200 hp

REMARK: Living quarters air-conditioned, transverse bow thruster.

♦ *5 Cigale-class tenders, U.S. AN-93 class*

	Bldr	L
A 760 CIGALE (ex-AN-98)	A.C. de la Rochelle-Pallice	23-9-54
A 761 CRIQUET (ex-AN-96)	A.C. Seine Maritime	3-6-54
A 762 FOURMI (ex-AN-97)	A.C. Seine Maritime	6-7-54
A 763 GRILLON (ex-AN-95)	Penhoët	18-2-54
A 764 SCARABÉE (ex-AN-94)	Penhoët	21-11-53

Criquet (A 761) G. Arra, 1972

D: 770 tons (850 fl) **Dim:** 46.28 (44.50 pp) × 10.20 × 3.20
A: 1/40-mm AA — 4/20-mm AA **Range:** 5,200/12
Man: 1 officer, 36 men **Fuel:** 125 m^3 diesel oil
M: Diesel-electric propulsion; 2 SEMT PA-1 diesels; 1 prop; 1,600 hp

REMARKS: U.S. "Offshore" mutual assistance. One sister built for Spain, two others built in Italy.

♦ *1 ex-German seaplane tender*

	Bldr	In serv.	In serv. In France
A 759 MARCEL LE BIHAN (ex-*Greif*)	Lübecker Flender-werke	1937	8-48

Marcel Le Bihan (A 759) J. C. Bellonne, 1973

D: 800 tons (1,250 fl) **S:** 13 kts **Dim:** 72 × 10.60 × 3.20 (fl)
A: 4/20-mm AA (II × 2) **Range:** 2,500/13
Man: 3 officers, 47 men, + 22 spaces for additional men
M: 2 G.M. 16-278A diesels; 2 Voith-Schneider props; 2,800 hp

REMARKS: Transferred from the U.S.A., Feb. 1948; 13-ton crane. Tender for Bathyscape Research Group in 1961. The similar *Robert Giraud* (A-755) was stricken in 1976.

♦ *5 port netlayers*

	Bldr	L
Y 749 LA PRUDENTE	A.C. de la Manche	13-5-68
Y 750 LA PERSÉVÉRANTE	A.D. de la Rochelle-Pallice	14-5-68
Y 751 LA FIDÈLE	A.C. de la Manche	26-8-68

D: 446 tons (626 fl) **Dim:** 43.50 (42 pp) × 10 × 2.80
S: 10 kts **Range:** 4,000/10
Man: 1 officer, 8 petty officers, 21 men **Electric:** 440 kw
M: Diesel-electric propulsion; 2 Baudoin diesels; 1 prop; 620 hp

NET TENDERS (*continued*)

Prudente (Y 749) 1976

REMARK: Lifting power: 25 tons

Y 667 TUPA — 292 tons, 210-hp motor
Y 688 CALMAR — Converted into an anchorage maintenance barge

DIVING TENDERS

♦ *1 base tender for frogman commando training*

A 722 POSEIDON — Bldr: SIGNAV, Saint-Malo — L: 5-12-74, In serv. 14-1-77

Poseidon (A 722) J. C. Bellonne, 1977

D: 220 tons (fl) **Dim:** 40.50 (38.50 pp) × 7.20 × . . .
S: 13 kts **Man:** 42 men
M: 1 diesel; 600 hp **Endurance:** 8 days

♦ *4 ex-coastal minesweepers, U.S. MSC class*

A 701 AJONC **A 723 LISERON**
A 711 GARDENIA **A 770 MAGNOLIA**

Liseron (A 723) M.N., 1974

REMARK: *Ajonc* is tender to the French Navy diving school; the remainder support mine-clearance divers.

TORPEDO-RECOVERY SHIPS

♦ **A 698 PÉTREL** (ex-*Cap Lopez*, ex-*Yvon Loic II*) — Bldr: Dubigeon — 1960

Pétrel (A 698) Yves Grangeon

D: 277 tons (318 fl) **Dim:** 30 × 7.80 × 3.50
S: 10 kts **Man:** 5 petty officers, 14 men
M: 2 Baudoin DV 6 diesels; 1 controllable-pitch prop; 600 hp

TORPEDO-RECOVERY SHIPS *(continued)*

♦ **A 699 PÉLICAN** (ex-*Kerfany*) — Bldr: Avondale (U.S.A.) — 1951

Pélican (A 699) J. C. Bellonne, 1972

D: 362 tons (425 fl) **Dim:** 37 × 8.55 × 4
S: 11 kts **Man:** 5 petty officers, 14 men
M: Burmeister and Wain diesel; 1 prop; 650 hp

REMARKS: Purchased 1965. Former tunny fishing boat. Torpedo tube at stern.

COASTAL TRANSPORTS

♦ *13 small personnel transports for port service*

Y 604 ARIEL (1963)	**Y 698 ALPHÉE** (10-6-69)	**Y 613 FAUNE** (8-9-71)
Y 661 KORRIGAN (1964)	**Y 741 ELFE** (14-4-70)	**Y 622 DRYADE** (1973)
	Y . . . NEREIDE	**Y . . . ONDINE**

Bldr: Soc. Française de Constr. Navale (formerly Franco-Belges), except D.C.A.N., Brest for *Nereide* and *Ondine*

Alphée (Y 696) 1976

D: 195 tons (225 fl) **S:** 15 kts **Dim:** 40.50 × 7.45 × 3.30
M: MGO diesels (1,640 hp) or Poyaud diesel; (1,730 hp); 2 props
Man: 9 men, 400 passengers (250 seated)

Y 735 MERLIN — **Y 736 MÉLUSINE** — **Y 671 MORGANE** — Bldr: C.N. Franco-Belges (1967-68) — **Y 671** — Bldr: A. du Mourillon

Mélusine 1968

D: 170 tons **S:** 11 kts **Dim:** 31.50 × 7.06 × 2.40
M: MGO diesels; 2 props; 960 hp **Man:** 400 passengers

Y 664 LUTIN (ex-small craft *Georges Clemenceau*, purchased in 1965)

D: 68 tons **S:** 10 kts **M:** 400 hp

REMARK: Assigned to the Sonar School, Toulon.

Y 710 SYLPHE — Bldr: C.N. Franco-Belges — (1959-60)

D: 171 tons (189 fl) **Dim:** 38.50 (36.75 pp) × 6.90 × 2.50
S: 12 kts **Man:** 9 men **M:** 1 MGO diesel; 1 prop; 425 hp

REMARK: Operates at Toulon.

Sylphe (Y 710) 1976

COASTAL TRANSPORTS (*continued*)

♦ *1 self-propelled port fuel barge*

Y 641 FORMÈNE

D: 280 tons light (1,400 fl) **S:** 5 kts **Capacity:** 1,000 m³ of fuel

♦ *3 launches*

A 702 GIRELLE

Girelle (A 702) E.C.P.A., 1976

D: . . . **S:** . . . **M:** . . .

Y 760 (ex-P-9786) — Bldr: Bodanwerft-Kressbronn — In serv. 1954

D: 45 tons **S:** 18 kts **Dim:** 24.18 × 4.50 × 1.25
A: 8/12.7-mm machine guns (IV × 2) **Fuel:** diesel oil, 4,000 liters
M: 2 Daimler-Benz diesels (model Mb 836 Bb); 2 props; 1,000 hp

A 714 TOURMALINE — 37/45 tons — Bldr: C.M.N. Cherbourg

Tourmaline (A 714) 1974

D: 45 tons fl **S:** 15 kts **Dim:** 26.8 × 4.97 × 1.53
M: 2 diesels; 2 props; 480 hp

♦ *6 fireboats*

Y 745 AIGUIÈRE — Y 618 CASCADE — Y 746 EMBRUN — Y 645 GAVE — Y 646 GEYSER — Y 684 OUED

D: 70 tons (85 fl) **S:** 11.3 kts **Dim:** 23.8 × 5.3 × 1.7
M: 2 Poyaud 6 PZM diesels; 2 props; 405 hp

TRAINING CRAFT

♦ *2 ex-trawlers for Petty Officers' Navigation School*

A 772 ENGAGEANTE (ex-*Cayolle*) **A 774 VIGILANTE** (ex-*Iseran*)

D: 286 tons fl (156 grt) **Dim:** 30 (25 pp) × 6.7 × 3.8 (aft)
M: 1 Deutz diesel; 1 prop; 560 hp **S:** 11 kts

REMARKS: Built 1964; purchased 1975. Decca radar.

♦ *2 tenders to the Naval Academy* — Bldr: Bayonne, 1971

Y 706 CHIMÈRE **Y 711 FARFADET**

D: 100 tons **S:** 11 kts **M:** 1 diesel; 200 hp

REMARK: Used for maneuvering training; sail-equipped.

♦ *2 auxiliary barkentines, assigned to the Naval Academy*

A 649 L'ÉTOILE (1932)
A 650 LA BELLE POULE (1932)

D: 227 tons (275 fl) **Dim:** 32.25 × 7.0 × 3.2
M: Sulzer diesel; 125 hp **S:** 6 kts

La Belle Poule E.C.P.A., 1974

TRAINING CRAFT (*continued*)

A 653 LA GRANDE HERMINE (ex-*La Route Est Belle*, ex-*Menestrel*)

REMARK: 14-meter yawl (1932) purchased in 1964 for the Reserve Officers School

A 652 MUTIN Assigned to the Dundee annex — Seamanship School

Bldr: Chauffeteau, les Sables (1927)

D: 57 tons **Dim:** 22 × 6.30 × 3.40 (1.50 fwd)
M: 1 Deutz diesel; 120 hp **Sails:** 240 m^2

SEAGOING TUGS

♦ *3 Tenace class*

A 664 MALABAR — Bldr: Oelkers, Hamburg (L. 16-4-75; in serv: 3-2-76)
A 669 TENACE — Bldr: Oelkers, Hamburg, 1971-73
A 674 CENTAURE — Bldr: de la Rochelle-Pallice, 1972-74

Tenace (A 669) E.C.P.A., 1975

Malabar (A 664) J. C. Bellonne, 1976

D: 1,080 tons (trials) — 1,454 (fl) **Dim:** 51 × 11.50 × 5.70
S: 15 kts at 1,080 tons **Man:** 42 men **Range:** 9,500/15
M: diesel; 1 prop **Fuel:** 500 tons

REMARKS: Living quarters air-conditioned. Bollard pull: 60 tons.

♦ **A 666 ELEPHANT**

D: 880 tons **S:** 11 kts **M:** 2,000 hp

♦ *2 ex-U.S. Sotoyomo class*

A 668 RHINOCEROS (ex-ATA-226) **A 660 HIPPOPOTAME** (ex-*Utrecht*)

D: 640/940 tons **S:** 12 kts **Dim:** 43.7 (38.7 pp) × 10.3 × 4.4 (aft)
M: 2 G.M. 12-278A diesels, electric drive; 1 prop; 1,500 hp — A-660: 1,850 hp

REMARKS: Slightly different ships, both built by Levingstron Brothers, Texas. A-668, launched 5-45, sold to France 7-47. A-660, sold commercial postwar, bought by France in 1964.

Rhinoceros (A 668) 1976

COASTAL TUGS

♦ *12 Actif class (1960–74)*

A 693 ACHARNE	**A 667 HERCULE**	**A 685 ROBUSTE**
A 686 ACTIF	**A 687 LABORIEUX**	**A 692 TRAVAILLEUR**
A 706 COURAGEUX	**A 671 LE FORT**	**A 672 UTILE**
A 694 EFFICACE	**A 673 LUTTEUR**	**A 688 VALEUREUX**

D: 230 tons (300 fl) **S:** 11.8 kts **Dim:** 28.3 (25.3 pp) × 7.9 × 4.3
M: 1 MGO ASHR diesel; 1,100 to 1,450 hp **Range:** 2,400/11

REMARKS: 17-ton bollard pull. Four completed in 1960, four in 1962-63, two in late 1960s, and A-693 and A-694 in 1974.

COASTAL TUGS *(continued)*

Lutteur (A 673) D.C.A.N., 1974

♦ *2 of 200 tons (fl) and 11 kts*

Y 608 BAMBOU **Y 652 HAUR BARR**

HARBOR TUGS

NOTE: Two-letter contractions of names used on bows instead of official pendant numbers.

♦ *2 new construction*

Y 634 ROUGET (1974) **Y 630 BONITE** (1975)

Bonite (Y 630) J. C. Bellonne, 1975

D: 93 tons (fl) **S:** 11 kts **M:** 380 hp

REMARK: 7-ton bollard pull.

♦ *29 Acajou class*

Y 601 ACAJOU, Y 607 BALSA, Y 612 BOULEAU, Y 623 CHARME, Y 620 CHATAIGNER, Y 624 CHÊNE, Y 629 CORMIER, Y 717 ÉBÈNE, Y 618 ÉRABLE, Y 635 EQUEURDREVILLE, Y 644 FRÊNE, Y 654 HÊTRE, Y 655 HEVEA, Y 663 LATANIER, Y 666 MANGUIER, Y 638 MARRONIER, Y 668 MÉLÈZE, Y 669 MERISIER, Y 739 NOYER, Y 682 OKOUMÉ, Y 719 OLIVIER, Y 686 PALÉTUVIER, Y 740 PAPAYER, Y 688 PEUPLIER, Y 689 PIN, Y 695 PLATANE, Y 720 SANTAL, Y 708 SAULE, Y 704 SYCOMORE

Mélèze (Y 668) 1975

D: 105 tons (fl) **S:** 11 kts **Dim:** 21 × 6.9 × 3.2
M: 1 diesel; 700 hp

REMARK: 10-ton bollard pull.

♦ *32 Oiseau class*

Y 602 AIGRETTE, Y 720 ALOUETTE, Y 730 ARA, Y 611 BENGALI, Y 625 CIGOGNE, Y 628 COLIBRI, Y 632 CYGNE, Y 729 EIDER, Y 723 ENGOULE-VENT, Y 687 FAUVETTE, Y 748 GELINOTTE, Y 648 GOELAND, Y 728

Bengali (Y 611) D.C.A.N., 1975

HARBOR TUGS (*continued*)

GRAND DUC, Y 653 HÉRON, Y 658 IBIS, Y 747 LORIOT, Y 727 MACREUSE, Y 725 MARABOUT, Y 675 MARTIN PÊCHEUR, Y 636 MARTINET, Y 670 MERLE, Y 621 MÉSANGE, Y 673 MOINEUA, Y 617 MOUETTE, Y 687 PASSEREAU, Y 690 PINGOUIN, Y 691 PINSON, Y 694 VERT, Y 724 SARCELLE, Y 726 TOUCAN, Y 643 TOURTERELLE, Y 722 VANNEAU

D: 200 tons (fl) **S:** 9 kts **Dim:** 18.4 × 5.7 × 2.5
M: 1 Poyaud diesel; 250 hp **Range:** 1,700/9

REMARKS: 3.5-ton bollard pull. *Ibis* (Y-658) on loan to Senegal.

♦ *1 tug (no data)*

Y 680 MURENE

VARIOUS SHIPS

♦ *1 underwater archeological research ship*

A 789 ARCHÉONAUTE — Bldr: Auroux, Arcachron (25-8-67)

Archéonaute J.C. Bellonne, 1972

D: 120 tons (fl) **S:** 12 kts **Dim:** 29.30 × 6 × 1.70
M: Baudoin diesels; 600 hp; 2 variable pitch props
Man: 2 officers, 4 men, 3 scientific research personnel, 6 divers

REMARKS: Ordered by the Office of Cultural Affairs, manned by Navy personnel. Laboratory and workshops, decompression chamber, underwater television.

♦ *1 radiological surveillance ship*

Y 743 PALANGRIN — Commissioned in 1969

D: 44 tons **M:** 1/220-hp diesel

Y 743

GABON

Republic of

PERSONNEL: 100 men

MERCHANT MARINE (1976): 14 ships — 98,285 grt
(tankers: 2 ships — 74,471 grt)

GUIDED MISSILE PATROL BOATS

♦ *2 fiberglass-hulled on order* — Bldr: Intermarine, Sarzana, Italy

GC . . . N . . . **GC . . . N . . .**

D: 165 tons (fl) **S:** 35 kts **Dim:** 37.3 × 8.0 × 1.6
A: 4/Otomat missiles — 1/76-mm DP Oto Melara — 1/40-mm AA
M: 3 MTU 20V 562TY90 diesels; 3 props; 4,000 hp **Man:** 24 mm

♦ *1 wooden-hulled* — Bldr: de l'Esterel, Cannes — In serv. 1977

D: 155 tons (fl) **S:** 33 kts **Dim:** 42.0 × 7.8 × 1.9
A: 4/SS-12 missiles — 2/40-mm Bofors AA
M: 2 MTU 16V538TB91 diesels; 2 props; 7,200 hp
Range: 1,000/18 **Man:** 25 men **Radar:** Decca RM1226

PATROL BOATS

♦ *4 N'Golo class* — Bldr: Intermarine, Sarzana, Italy

	In serv.		In serv.
GC 05 N'GOLO	1976	**GC . . . N . . .**	1977
GC . . . N . . .	1977	**GC . . . N . . .**	1977

D: 65 tons (88 fl) **S:** 43 kts **Dim:** 27.3 × 6.8 × 2.1
A: 1/40-mm AA — 2/20-mm AA **Man:** 13 men
M: 2 MTU diesels; 2 props; 7,000 hp

♦ *6 U.S. design* — Bldr: Swiftships, Morgan City

	In serv.		In serv.
GC 03 N'GUENE	2-76	**GC . . . N . . .**	. . .
GC . . . N . . .	. . .	**GC . . . N . . .**	. . .
GC . . . N . . .	. . .	**GC . . . N . . .**	. . .

D: 118 tons (fl) **S:** 35 kts
Dim: 32.17 (29.18 pp) × 6.80 × 2.3 (props)
A: 2/40-mm AA (I × 2) — 2/20-mm AA (I × 2) — 2/12.7-mm machine guns
M: 3 G.M. 16V 149TE diesels; 3 props; 4,800 hp **Range:** 825/25
Electron Equipt: Radar: Decca RM916 **Electric:** 80 kw **Man:** 21 men

REMARKS: Aluminum. Five additional ordered 1977.

♦ **GC 02 PRESIDENT ALBERT BONGO** — Bldr: de l'Esterel — In serv. 3-72

D: 80 tons **S:** 30 kts **Dim:** 32 × 5.80 × 1.50
A: 2/20-mm **Man:** 17 men **M:** 2 MTU diesels; 2,700 hp

REMARK: Wooden hull treated with résorcine (anti-boring worm product).

PATROL CRAFT

	Bldr	Laid down	L	In serv.
♦ **GC 01 PRESIDENT LÉON M'BA**	Gabon	1967	6-1-68	1968

President Léon M'Ba 1968

D: 85 tons **S:** 12.5 kts **Dim:** 28 × 6.20 × 1.54
M: diesel; 1 prop **A:** 1/75-mm recoilless rifle — 12.7-mm machine gun
Range: 1,000/12 **Man:** 1 officer, 3 petty officers, 12 men

♦ *7 small Arcoa patrol craft* — 15 to 25 kts

♦ *2 SRN 6 hovercraft, delivered 1977*

♦ *1 small buoy tender*

THE GAMBIA

MERCHANT MARINE (1967): 3 ships — 1,337 tons grt

PATROL CRAFT

♦ *1 Lance class* — Bldr. Fairey Marine, G.B. (1976)

SEA DOG

D: 17 tons (fl) **S:** 24 kts **Dim:** 14.81 × 4.65 × 1.30
A: 1/20-mm AA — 3/7.62-mm machine guns (I × 3)
M: 2 G.M. 8V-71 TI diesels; 2 props; 850 hp
Range: 500/15 **Man:** 6 men plus 10-man boarding party

♦ *1 Keith Nelson 75-foot class* — Bldr. Camper and Nicholson, G.B. (1974)

MANSA KILA IV

D: 70 tons (fl) **S:** 24.5 kts **Dim:** 22.9 × 6.0 × 1.6
A: 2/20-mm AA (I × 2) **Range:** 800/20
M: 2 diesels; 2 props; 1,840 hp **Man:** 11 men

PERSONNEL: 15,500 men, about 5,000 on board ship

MERCHANT MARINE (1976): 446 ships — 1,437,054 grt
(tankers: 19 ships — 294,406 grt)

NAVAL AVIATION: About 15 Soviet MI-4 Hound helicopters used for ASW and assault operations.

WEAPONS AND SYSTEMS: Nearly all of Soviet design. See U.S.S.R. section for details.

WARSHIPS IN SERVICE OR UNDER CONSTRUCTION AS OF 1 OCTOBER 1977

	L	Tons	Main armament
♦ *2 frigates*			
2 RIGA (Soviet)	1953-58	1,450	3/100-mm, 2/533-mm TT
♦ *12 corvettes*			
12 HAI-III	1962-70	350	4/30-mm AA, 4 ASW RL
♦ *4 submarine chasers*			
4 SO-I (Soviet)	1960-63	190	4/25-mm AA, 4 ASW RL
♦ *63 to 66 missile and torpedo boats*			
15 OSA-I (Soviet)	1964-	175	4 Styx systems, 4/30-mm AA
15 SHERSHEN (Soviet)	1966-	150	4/30-mm AA, 4/533-mm TT
26 LIBELLE	1975-	30	2/533-mm TT
7 to 10 ILTIS-II	1962	17	2/533-mm TT
♦ *53 minesweepers*			
3 KRAKE	1956-58	650	1/85-mm DP, 10/25-mm AA
50 KONDOR-I, II	1968-71	225/310	2 or 6/25-mm AA

FRIGATES

♦ *2 Soviet Riga class*

121 ERNST THAELMANN — 122 KARL MARX
Bldr: U.S.S.R., 1953-58

D: 1,450 tons (fl) **Dim:** 91.0 × 11.0 × 3.4
S: 28 kts **Man:** 15 officers, 160 men
A: 3/100-mm DP (I × 3) — 4/37-mm AA (II × 2) — 2/533-mm TT (II × 1) — 4 MBU-1800 RL — 4 depth-charge projectors — 2 depth-charge racks — 50 mines
M: GT; 2 props; 2 boilers; 20,000 hp
Fuel: 300 tons **Range:** 2,000/10
Electron Equipt: Radars: 1/Don, 1/Slim Net, 1/Sun Visor B

GERMANY

Democratic Republic

CORVETTES

♦ *12 Hai III class (hull numbers, 400 series)*

Possible names: **BAD DOBERAN, BÜTZOW, DIRNA, GADEBUSCH, GREVES MUEHLEN, LUDWIGSLUST, LÜBZ, PERLEBERG, RIBNITZ-DAMGARTEN, STERNBERG, TETEROW, WISMAR**
Bldr: Peenewerft, Wolgast (1962-70)

Hai-III class 1976

D: 350 tons (400 fl) **S:** 32 kts **Dim:** 51.0 × 6.2 × 2.4
A: 4/30-mm (II × 2) — 4/ASW MBU 1800 rocket launchers, depth-charge racks — mines **Man:** 28 men
Electron Equipt: Radars: 1/Pot Head, 1/Drum Tilt
Sonar: 1/Tamir
M: CODOG propulsion system; 1 gas turbine × 10,000 hp; 2 diesels, total of 4,800 hp **Range:** 1,000/18

SUBMARINE CHASERS

♦ *4 Soviet SO-I class*

Possible names: **421 FALKE, 422 TIGER, 423 LEOPARD, 424 PANTHER**
Bldr: U.S.S.R., 1960-63

SUBMARINE CHASERS (*continued*)

SO-1 class 1975

D: 190 tons (215 fl) **S:** 28 kts **Dim:** 42.0 × 6.1 × 1.9
A: 4/25-mm (II × 2) — 4/MBU 1800 rocket launchers — 2 depth-charge racks — mines
Electron Equipt: 1/Pot Head **Man:** 30 men
M: 3 diesels; 3 props; 7,500 hp **Fuel:** 20 tons

GUIDED MISSILE AND TORPEDO PATROL BOATS

♦ *15 Soviet Osa-1-class missile boats*

Possible names: **ALBERT GAST, ALAIN KÖBIS, A. SAEFKOW, FRIEDRICH SCHULZE, FRITZ GAST, KARL MESEBERG, MAX REICHPIETSCH, PAUL WIEKZOREK, RICHARD SORGE, RUDOLF EGLHOFER, AUGUST LÜTTGENS, PAUL EISENSCHNEIDE, PAUL SCHULZ, WALTER KRÄMER, N . . .**

Bldr: U.S.S.R. — 1964

1970

D: 175 tons (205 fl) **Dim:** 39.0 × 7.6 × 1.8
A: 4/Styx (SS-N-2) systems — 4/30-mm AA (II × 2) **S:** 35 kts
M: 3 M503A diesels; 3 props; 12,000 hp
Electron Equipt: 1 Square Tie, 1/Drum Tilt

♦ *15 Soviet Shershen-class torpedo boats (hull numbers, possibly 800 series)*

Bldr: U.S.S.R., since 1966

EDGAR ANDRÉ, WILLI BÄNSCH, BERNHARD BÄSTLEIN, ARTHUR BECKER, FRITZ BEHN, RUDOLF BREITSCHEID, ERNST GRUBE, ARVID HARNACK, HEINZ KAPELLE, FRITZ HECKERT, ADAM KUCKHOFF, BRUNO KÜHN, ERNST SCHNELLER, N . . . , N . . .

D: 150 tons (fl) **S:** 45 kts **Dim:** 34 × 7.2 × 1.5
A: 4/533-mm torpedoes (2 on each side) — 4/30-mm AA (II × 2) — 2 depth-charge racks
M: 3 M503A diesels; 3 props; 12,000 hp
Electron Equipt: Radars: 1/Pot Drum, 1/Drum Tilt

Shershen class (training squadron hull number) 1976

♦ *26 Libelle-class light torpedo boats*

Libelle class 1976

GUIDED MISSILE AND TORPEDO PATROL BOATS *(continued)*

D: 30 tons (fl) **S:** 50 kts **Dim:** 19.6 × 4.5 × 2.0
A: 2/533-mm TT (aft-launching) — 2/23-mm AA (II × 1)
M: 3 diesels; 3 props; 3,600 hp

REMARKS: Completed since 1975. Can quickly convert to commando/frogman carriers.

♦ *7 to 10 Iltis-II-class light torpedo boats (hull numbers, possibly 900 series)*

Bldr: Schiffswerft-Rosslau, since 1962

Iltis-II 1970

D: 17 tons (fl) **S:** 56 kts **Dim:** 15 × 3.2 × 0.8
A: 2,533-mm TT (aft-firing) **M:** 2 M50 diesels; 2 props; 2,400 hp
Man: 3 men

REMARKS: The torpedoes are fired from the stern as was done by British CMB torpedo craft in 1917-18. Two or three *Iltis-III* also survive: larger version with three torpedoes or racks for nine mines, 23 tons (fl), 17.4 × 3.2 × 0.9.

PATROL CRAFT

♦ *19 Bremse class*

D: 25 tons **S:** 14 kts **Dim:** 23.0 × 5.0 × . . .
A: Small arms only **M:** 2 diesels; 2 props; . . . hp

REMARK: Operated by the Border Guard on rivers and inland waterways.

♦ *7 "fishing cutter" class*

G 91 to **G 97**

REMARK: Wooden-hulled former fishing boats operated by the Border Guard.

Bremse class

MINE WARFARE SHIPS

♦ *3 Krake-class minesweepers*

Bldr: Peenewerft, Wolgast (1956-68)

BERLIN, LEIPZIG, POTSDAM

Krake class 1970

D: 650 tons **S:** 18 kts **Dim:** 70 (65 pp) × 8.10 × 3.60
A: 1/85-mm DP — 10/25-mm AA (II × 5) — 4 depth-charge projectors — 30 mines
M: 2 DMR diesels; 2 props; 3,400 hp **Man:** 82 men

REMARKS: Hull numbers S-11 to S-13. In training squadron. Seven sisters scrapped.

MINE WARFARE SHIPS (*continued*)

♦ *28 Kondor-II-class inshore minesweepers (hull numbers in 300 series)*

Bldr: Peenewerft, Wolgast (Since 1971)

ALTENBURG, BERNAU, BITTERFELD, BOLTENHAGEN, DESSAU, EILENBURG, FREIBERG, GENTHIN, GREIZ, GUBEN, KAMENZ, KLÜTZ, KYRITZ, MEININGEN, NEURUPPIN, POESSNICK, RATHENOW, RIESA, ROBEL, ROSSLAU, SCHOENEBECK, STRALSUND, STRASBURG, TANGERHUETTE, TIMMENDORF, TORGAU, WITTSTOCK, ZERBST

Kondor II class 1976

Kondor II class (training squadron hull number) 1976

D: 310 tons (fl) **S:** 20 kts **Dim:** 55.0 × 7.0 × 1.7
A: 6/25-mm AA (II × 3) — mines **M:** 2 diesels; 2 props; 5,000 hp

♦ *23 Kondor-I-class inshore minesweepers*

Bldr: Peenewerft, Wolgast (1968–1970)

AHRENSHOOP, ANKLAM, BERGEN, DEMMIN, GRAAL-MÜRITZ, GREIFSWALD, HETTSTED, KUHLUNGSBORN, MEISSEN, NEUSTRELITZ, PASEWALK, PRENZLAU, PREROW, RERIK, STENDAL, UECKERMÜNDE, VITTE, WEISSWASSER, WOLGAST, ZINGST, ZWICKAU

Kondor I class 1976

D: 225 tons (275 fl) **S:** 20 kts **Dim:** 52 × 7.0 × 1.7
A: 2/25-mm AA (II × 1) — mines **M:** 2 diesels; 2 props; 5,000 hp

REMARKS: Eighteen units attached to Border Guard as patrol boats, G-11-16, G-21-26, G-41-46. Two were converted as target torpedo-recovery craft; 2 others altered as intelligence collectors, *Komet, Meteor;* another is the state yacht *Ostseeland.*

AMPHIBIOUS SHIPS AND CRAFT

♦ *6 French class tank landing ships* — Bldr: Peenewerft, Wolgast, 1976–77

N . . . N . . . N . . .
N . . . N . . . N . . .

Frosch class 1976

AMPHIBIOUS SHIPS AND CRAFT *(continued)*

Frosch class 1976

D: 2,000 tons (fl) **S:** 18 kts **Dim:** 98 × 12.5 × . . .
A: 4/57-mm AA (II × 2) — 4/30-mm AA (II × 2) — mines
M: 2 diesels; 2 props; . . . hp
Electron Equipt: 1 Strut Curve, 1 Muff Cob, 1 German TSR-333 (navigation)

REMARKS: Cargo capacity 800 to 1,000 tons. Similar in general form to new Soviet *Ropucha* class but smaller and with a blunt bow, different, heavier armament, etc. Has a large number of communications antennas, possibly indicating an ability to act as command ships in amphibious operations.

♦ *6 Robbe class*

Bldr: Peenewerft, Wolgast

EBERSWALDE	**GRIMMEN**	**LÜBBEN**
EISENHÜTTENSTADT	**HOYERSWERDA**	**SCHWEDT**

D: 500 tons (1,100 fl) **Dim:** 64 × 12 × 1.50 × 2.20 (aft)
S: 13/12 kts **M:** 2 diesels; 2 props; 5,000 hp
A: 2/57-mm AA (II × 1) — 2/25-mm AA (II × 1) — mines
Range: 2,000 (econ.)

REMARK: Utility load 500 tons.

♦ *7 Labo-100 class*

Bldr: Peenewerft, Wolgast — 1961-63

Including: **GERHARD PRENZLER, HEINZ WILKOWSKI, ROLF PETERS, N . . .**

Type Labo

AMPHIBIOUS SHIPS AND CRAFT (*continued*)

D: 150 tons (285 fl) **Dim:** 40 × 7.50 × 1.50
S: 13 kts **Man:** 5 men
A: 4/25-mm AA (II × 2) **M:** 4 diesels; 1,080 hp

REMARKS: Can carry 100 tons of freight or 1 or 2 tanks, trucks, etc. Five have been scrapped.

INTELLIGENCE GATHERING VESSELS

♦ *2 modified Kondor-I class*

KOMET, METEOR

Komet 1974

REMARKS: No armament. Collection antennas added, otherwise as for *Komet-I* class.

♦ **HYDROGRAPH** (1958)

Hydrograph

D: 700 tons (fl) **Dim:** 50.80 × 8.80 × 3.40
S: 10 kts **Man:** 32 men
M: 1 diesel; 540 hp **Range:** 7,900/11

REMARKS: — Soviet Okean-class trawler equipped with Sigint collection devices.

HYDROGRAPHIC SURVEY SHIPS

NOTE: All survey ships, buoy tenders, and the cable tender *Dornbusch* are operated under the SHD, Naval Hydrographic Service, and are civilian-manned.

♦ *1 Soviet Kamenka class (1972)* — Bldr: Szczecin SY, Poland

BUK

D: 703 tons (fl) **S:** 13.7 kts **Dim:** 53.5 × 9.1 × 2.6
M: 2 Zgoda diesels; 2 props; 1,765 hp **Range:** 4,000/10

♦ *3 Arkona class, also buoy tenders (1965–70)*

ARKONA **DARSSER ORT** **STUBBENKAMMER**

D: 55 tons **S:** 10 kts **M:** diesel

♦ *2 Karl F. Gauss class*

KARL F. GAUSS (1952) — **ALFRED MERZ** (1955)

D: 200 tons **S:** 9.5 kts

♦ *1 cable and buoy tender*

DORNBUSCH

D: 700 tons (fl)

REMARK: Bow cable sheaves, large crane, superstructure aft.

♦ *8 buoy tenders (1971–72)*

BREITLING, ESPER ORT, GOLWITZ, GRASS ORT, LANDTIEFF, PALMER ORT, RAMZOW, ROSEN ORT

D: 158 tons (fl) **S:** 11.5 kts **Dim:** 29.6 × 6.2 × 1.9
M: 1 diesel; 1 prop; 580 hp

EXPERIMENTAL SHIPS V = *Versuch* (Research)

♦ *1 ex-civilian research ships*

V 71 1976

EXPERIMENTAL SHIPS (*continued*)

V 71 (ex-*Meteor*)

REMARK: Built as a fishing boat.

♦ *1 ex-corvette, Hai-II class (1964)*

V 81 PARCHIM

Parchim 1976

REMARK: Used in minesweeping research.

♦ *1 Kondor-II-class minesweeper*

V 32

OILERS

♦ *1 Soviet Baskunchak class*

C 27 USEDOM

D: 2,500 tons **S:** 13 kts **Dim:** 70 × 8.9 × 3.8

♦ *3 Hiddensee class*

C 37 (ex-*Hiddensee*), **C 76** (ex-*Riems*), **C . . .** (ex-*Poel*)
Bldr: Peenewerft, Wolgast, 1960–61

Hiddensee class (prior to arming)

D: 1,450 tons (fl) **S:** 12 kts **Dim:** 53.7 × 9.0 × 4.5
A: 4/25-mm (II × 2) **Man:** 26 men
M: 2 diesels; 1,400 hp **Cargo:** 650 tons

REMARKS: Laid down during World War II. *Sahel* in French Navy is a sister.

GENERAL SUPPORT SHIPS

♦ *3 Kuemo class*

RUDEN, VILM, RÜGEN — Bldr: Matthias Thiesen Werft, Wismar, 1955–57

Ruden 1976

D: 585 tons (fl) **S:** 9 kts **Dim:** 36.0 × 7.3 × 2.7
M: 1 diesel; 1 prop; 300 hp

REMARK: *Ruden* is a cargo ship, *Vilm* is an oiler, and *Rügen* is a torpedo trials ship.

TRAINING SHIP S = *Schulschiff* (Schoolship)

♦ *1 Polish Wodnik class* — Bldr: Gdansk SY — In serv. 6-7-76

S 61 WILHELM PIECK

Wilhelm Pieck 1976

D: 2,000 tons (fl) **S:** 17 kts **Dim:** 73.0 × 12.0 × 4.0
A: 4/30-mm AA (II × 2) — 4/25-mm AA (II × 2)
M: 2 Zgoda diesels; 2 props; 3,600 hp **Electric:** 530 kw
Electron Equipt: Radar: 3/TSR-333

REMARKS: Sister to *Wodnik* and *Gryf* in Polish Navy. Design developed from *Moma*-class surveying ships.

NOTE: In addition to *Wilhelm Pieck*, the following are used for training (data earlier): 3 *Krake*-class minesweepers; 3 *Osa-I* class; 3 *Shershen* class; 3 *Kondor-II* class; 3 *Kondor-I* class.

SALVAGE SHIP

♦ *1 Polish Piast class* — Bldr: Gdansk SY, 1977

A 46 OTTO VON GUERICKE

D: 1,560 tons (1,732 fl) **S:** 16.5 kts **Dim:** 73.2 × 10.0 × 4.0
M: 2 Zgoda GTD48 diesels; 2 props; 3,800 hp
Range: 3,000/12

REMARKS: Sister to Polish *Piast* and *Lech*. Can mount 8/25-mm AA (II × 4). Has diving bell. Built on *Moma* survey ship hull and propulsion plant.

VARIOUS SHIPS

♦ *2 torpedo retriever/target ships, converted Kondor-I class*

B 73, B 74

B 74 1976

REMARKS: Characteristics basically similar to *Kondor-I* minesweeper. No armament. Ramp at stern for torpedo recovery. Radar reflector array on mast.

♦ *1 yacht*

OSTSEELAND

REMARKS: Used for the head of state. *Kondor-I* hull with large, rakish superstructure.

♦ *several small diving tenders*

♦ *up to 11 barracks barges, Jugend class*

♦ *1 small cable tender*

FREESENDORF (1963)

1 seagoing tug (also salvage tug)

A 14 — 800 tons, 12 knots

♦ *11 harbor tugs*

♦ *6 or more harbor fuel lighters*

GERMANY

Federal Republic

PERSONNEL: approx. 35,000 men

MERCHANT MARINE (1976): 1,957 ships — 9,264,671 grt
(tankers: 141 ships — 3,306,034 grt)

SHIPS IN SERVICE, UNDER CONSTRUCTION, OR ORDERED AS OF 1 OCTOBER 1977

	L	Tons	Main armament
♦ *24 submarines*			
18 TYPE 206	1972-74	450	8/533-mm TT
6 TYPE 205	1961-68	370	8/533-mm TT
♦ *11 destroyers*			
3 LÜTJENS	1967-69	3,370	1 Tartar system, 2/127-mm DP, 1 Asroc
4 HAMBURG	1960-63	3,400	4/mm38, 3/100-mm, 8/40-mm AA, 4 ASW TT
4 Z	1942-43	2,050	4/127-mm DP, 6/76-mm AA, 5/533-mm TT
♦ *12 frigates*			
6 TYPE 122	. . .	3,750	8/Harpoon, 2 ML, 1/76-mm 6/ASW TT
6 KÖLN	1958-62	1,750	2/100-mm DP, 6/40-mm AA, 2 ASW RL, 4 ASW TT
♦ *5 corvettes*			
5 THETIS	1960-62	604	2/40-mm AA, 1 ASW RL, 4 ASW TT
♦ *30 guided missile boats*			
10 TYPE 143	1973-76	370	4/MM38, 2/76-mm AA, 2/533-mm TT
20 TYPE 148	1972-75	234	4/MM38, 1/76-mm DP, 1/40-mm AA
♦ *10 torpedo boats*			
10 TYPE 142	1961-63	160	2/40-mm AA, 2/533-mm TT
♦ *59 minesweepers*			

Bréguet Atlantic 1973

NAVAL AVIATION: The Navy has the following units:

- 2 groups of Starfighter (F-104G) all-weather interceptor attack and reconnaissance airplanes (110–120 planes). Starfighter features are:
  length: 16.61 meters
  wingspan: 6.68 meters
  takeoff weight: 9.900 kg
  motor: 1 GE S79 GE 11A turbojet, 7,170 kg thrust
  max. speed: Mach 2
  altitude: 50,000 feet
  range: 250 to 600 nautical miles, depending on equipment
  weapons: 4,000 kg maximum (bombs, rockets, Bullpup, etc.)
- 1 squadron of 20 Bréguet Atlantic 1150 aircraft, 5 of which have been modified for electronic warfare.
- 1 squadron of 22 Mk 41 Sea King helicopters for search and rescue operations.

On 7-4-76 the German government decided to begin fabrication of a series of 112 MRCA Tornado variable-geometry fighter-bombers for the Navy. Their entry into service is scheduled for late 1979. Characteristics are:

length: 16.70 meters
wingspan: 13.90 meters max./8.60 meters min.
maximum takeoff weight: 24,500 kg.
maximum speed: mach 2.2

WEAPONS AND SYSTEMS

With few exceptions, West German ships have weapons and systems of foreign navies.

(A) MISSILES

Surface-to-air: Standard Tartar SM 1 A or SM 1 on board the 3 *Lütjens*-class destroyers.

Surface-to-surface: MM38 Exocet on board *Hamburg*-class destroyers and Types 143 and 148 guided missile patrol boats.

(B) GUNS

— Automatic 100-mm French Model 1953 on board the *Hamburg*-class destroyers, *Köln*-class frigates, and 9 Rhein-class tenders
— OTO Melara compact 76-mm guns on board Types 143 and 148 guided missile patrol boats
— 40-mm (70-caliber) Bofors, in single or twin mounts
— 40-mm/70 Breda
— 20-mm Oerlikon

(C) ANTISUBMARINE WARFARE

— Quadruple 375-mm Bofors rocket launchers, similar to French models automatically loaded in a vertical position
— Torpedoes:
U.S. Mk 37 on submarines
U.S. Mk 44 and Mk 46 on *Lütjens* guided missile destroyers and Bréguet Atlantic

WEAPONS AND SYSTEMS (*continued*)

1150 ASW patrol aircraft

Wire-guided Seal type (20,000 m range) on Type 143 missile boats, Type 142 torpedo boats, and submarines.

(D) ELECTRONICS

In addition to the U.S. radars mounted in the *Lütjens* DDGs, the West German Navy uses the following Dutch radars (Hollandse Signaal-apparaaten):

LW 02 long-range air search (Band D)
SGR 105 multi-purpose search (Band E-F)
SGR 103 surface search (Band I)
Band X for 100-mm and 40-mm fire control

Type 148 missile patrol boats have a Thomson-CSF Triton target-designation radar and Vega fire-control system with Pollux radar. Type 143 missile patrol boats carry the AGIS fire-control system combined with the Dutch HSA Mk 27 M radar. AGIS employs two UNIVAC computers, one for fire control and the other for real-time threat-processing. WM 27 has two antennas within its dome, one for search and one for tracking. An automatic data link permits AGIS to relay information with other units of the Type 143, *Lütjens* DDGs, and with future combatants destined for service with the fleet operating from Glücksberg-Meierwik.

SUBMARINES

♦ . . . *Type 210*

A 750-ton (submerged) submarine replace the Norwegian *Kobben* (Type 207) and German 205 classes in the 1980s is under study by IKL Lübeck in conjunction with the Norwegian Navy.

♦ *18 Type 206*

	L		L		L
S 192 U 13	28-10-71	**S 198 U 19**	15-12-72	**S 174 U 25**	25-5-73
S 193 U 14	1-3-72	**S 199 U 20**	16-1-73	**S 175 U 26**	24-11-73
S 194 U 15	15-6-72	**S 170 U 21**	9-3-73	**S 176 U 27**	21-8-73
S 195 U 16	29-8-72	**S 171 U 22**	27-3-73	**S 177 U 28**	22-1-74
S 196 U 17	10-10-72	**S 172 U 23**	22-5-73	**S 178 U 29**	5-9-73
S 197 U 18	31-10-72	**S 173 U 24**	24-6-73	**S 179 U 30**	26-3-74

Bldrs: Howaldtswerke-Deutsche Werft, Kiel; Rheinstahl Nordseewerke, Bremen

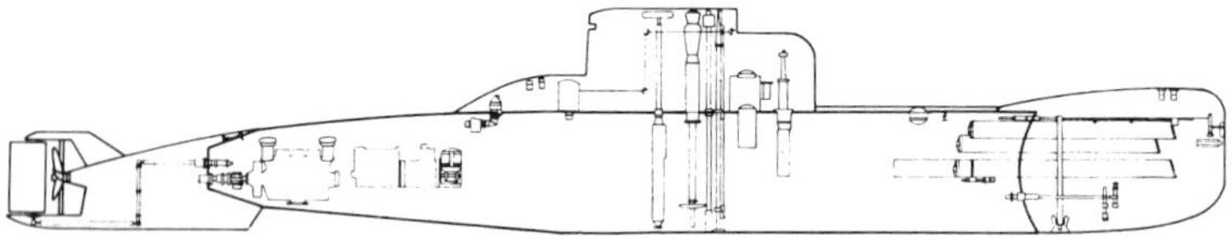

Type 206

D: 450 tons surfaced, 600 submerged **S:** 17 kts (5 cruising)
Man: 22 men **Range:** 4,500/5 **Dim:** 48.6 × 4.50 × 4.0
A: 8/533-mm TT — 16 wire-guided Seal or Mk 37 torpedoes, or 12 to 18 mines
M: 2 MTU diesels; 750 hp each, 2 500-kw generators; 1 1,500-hp electric motor

REMARK: *U-13* to *U-24* authorized in 1969, *U-25* to *U-30* in 2-70.

♦ *6 type 205*

	L		L		L
S 180 U 1	21-10-61	**S 188 U 9**	20-10-66	**S 190 U 11**	2-9-68
S 181 U 2	25-1-62	**S 189 U 10**	20-7-67	**S 191 U 12**	10-9-68

Bldrs: Howaldtswerke-Deutsche Werft, Kiel; Rheinstahl Nordseewerke, Bremen

Submarine type 206 (S 192) Marineamt, 1974

Submarine type 205

D: 370 tons surfaced, 450 submerged **Dim:** 43.50 × 4.60 × 3.80
A: 8/533-mm TT **S:** 17/10 kts **Man:** 21 men
M: 2 MTU 820Db diesels; 2 electric motors; 1 prop; 1,200 — 1,500 hp

REMARKS: The poor quality of the anti-magnetic steel used in the first six of this class (serious pitting) made it necessary to rebuild *U-1* and *U-2* with regular steel. Beginning with the *U-9* laid down in 1964, these submarines were built with a new anti-magnetic steel. The *U-1* and *U-2* are now training ships, the *U-3* was stricken in 1968, the *U-4* and *U-8* in 1974.

♦ *1 Type XXI submarine, for experimental service*

Y 880 WILHELM BAUER (ex-*U-2540*) — Bldr: Blohm and Voss — L: 13-1-45

D: 1,620 tons surfaced, 1,820 submerged **Dim:** 77 × 6.60 × 6.20
S: 17.5/15.5 kts **Man:** 57 men **Range:** 11,000/12

SUBMARINES *(continued)*

A: 4/533-mm TT forward
M: M.A.N. diesels and electric motor; 2 props; 4,000/5,000 hp

REMARKS: Sank in shallow water in 1945; raised and returned to service as an experimental ship in 9-60. Officially removed from service for scrapping 26-4-68, but rebuilt and put back in service 15-5-70 as an experimental ship. Not considered a combatant unit.

GUIDED MISSILE DESTROYERS

♦ *3 Lütjens (Charles F. Adams)-class guided missile destroyers (author. 1964)*

	Bldr	Laid down	L	In serv.
D 185 LÜTJENS	Bath Iron Works	3-66	11-8-67	3-69
D 186 MOLDERS	Bath Iron Works	4-66	13-4-68	9-69
D 187 ROMMEL	Bath Iron Works	8-67	1-2-69	4-70

Lütjens (D 185) 1974

D: 3,370 tons (4,500 fl) **Dim:** 134.11 (131.56 pp) × 14.32 × 6.1 (fl)
S: 35 kts **Man:** 21 officers, 319 men
A: 1 Tartar Mk 13 missile launcher (40 SM 1A or SM 1 missiles) — 2/127-mm Mk 42 DP (I × 2) — 6 ASW Mk 32 TT (III × 2) — 1 Asroc ASW missile launcher
Electron Equipt: Radars: 1/SPS 40, 1/SPS 10, 1/SPS 52, 2/SPG 51 — 1/Mk 68 FC
Sonar: 1/SQS 23 — ECM: Satir-I system — URN/22 TACAN
M: Geared turbines; 2 props; 70,000 hp **Range:** 1,600/30, 6,000/14
Boilers: 4 Combustion Engineering with steam pressure 84 kg/cm²
Fuel: 900 tons

REMARKS: American numbers DDG 28, 29, 30; have several differences, especially in profile, from the *Charles F. Adams* design on which they are based. Installation of the SM 1 system and digitalization of some computer equipment completed on the D-187 and being completed on the other two.

♦ *4 Hamburg class (Type 101 Modified)*

	Bldr	L	In serv.
D 181 HAMBURG	H. C. Stülcken, Hamburg	26-3-60	5-64
D 182 SCHLESWIG-HOLSTEIN	H. C. Stülcken, Hamburg	20-8-60	10-64
D 183 BAYERN	H. C. Stülcken, Hamburg	14-8-62	7-65
D 184 HESSEN	H. C. Stülcken, Hamburg	4-5-63	10-68

D: 3,400 tons (4,400 fl) **S:** 35 kts **Man:** 280 men
Dim: 133.80 (128 pp) × 13.40 × 5.20 (fl)
A: 4/MM38 Exocet SSM — 3/100-mm automatic (III × 1) — 8/40-mm Breda AA (II × 4) — 2/533-mm ASW TT — 2 4-barreled 375-mm Bofors ASW rocket launchers — can carry 60 to 80 mines
Electron Equipt: Radars: 1/DA-08, 1/SGR 105, 1/SGR 103 — 3 M45 FC
Sonar (German Atlas): 1 medium-frequency, hull — 2 Breda SCLAR 20-cell chaff launchers
M: M.A.N. GT; 2 props; 68.000 hp **Electric:** 5,400 kw
Boilers: 4 with steam pressure 64 kg/cm², 460°C superheat

REMARKS: Between the beginning of 1975 and the end of 1977, refitted with 4/MM38 to replace mount C, in the following order: D-184, D-181, D-182, and D-183. Five fixed anti-ship torpedo tubes (3 in bows, 2 aft) removed, 40-mm replaced by later model, new air search radar.

Hessen (D 184) 1976

DESTROYERS

♦ *4 Z (ex-U.S. Fletcher)-class*

	Bldr	L
D 171 Z 2 (ex-*Ringgold* DD-500)	Federal SB&DD	11-11-42
D 172 Z 3 (ex-*Wadsworth* DD-516)	Bath Iron Works	10-1-43
D 178 Z 4 (ex-*Claxton* DD-571)	Consolidated Steel	1-4-42
D 179 Z 5 (ex-*Dyson* DD-572)	Consolidated Steel	15-4-42

D: 2,050 tons (2,750 fl) **Dim:** 114.85 × 12.03 × 5.50
S: 30/32 kts **Man:** 350 men **Range:** 1,260/35, 4,400/15
Electron Equipt: Radars: 1/SPS-6, 1/SPS-10 — Fire control: Mk 37 and Mk 56
Sonar: SQS-29
A: 4/127-mm DP 38-cal (I × 4) — 6/76 MM AA (II × 3) — 5/533-mm TT (V × 1) — 2 ASW TT (I × 2) — 2 hedgehogs — 1 depth-charge rack — mines

DESTROYERS (*continued*)

Z 4 (D 178) 1974

M: General Electric GT; 2 props; 4 Babcock boilers, 60,000 hp
Fuel: 650 tons

REMARKS: Loaned by the U.S.A., later transferred: the *Z-1* in 1958, the *Z-2* in 1959, the others in 1960. *Z-6* removed from service in 1968, *Z-1* in 1972. *Z-4* does not have after twin 76-mm mount.

GUIDED MISSILE FRIGATES

♦ *6 Type 122 (to complete 1981-86)*

	L	In serv.		L	In serv.
F . . . N . . .	. . .	. . .	**F . . . N . . .**	. . .	. . .
F . . . N . . .	. . .	. . .	**F . . . N . . .**	. . .	. . .
F . . . N . . .	. . .	. . .	**F . . . N . . .**	. . .	. . .

Bldrs: Two by Blohm & Voss, one each by Ag Weser, Bremen-Vulcan, Howaldtswerke, and Rheinstahl-Nordseewerke

D: 3,750 tons (fl) **S:** 30 kts **Dim:** 128.0 × 14.8 × 6.0
A: 8/Harpoon SSM — 1/NATO Sea Sparrow SAM (8-cell) — 1/Stinger SAM (8-cell) — 1/76-mm OTO Melara DP — 6/305-mm ASW TT Mk 32 (III × 2) — 2 LAMPS III ASW helicopters
Range: 4,000/18 **Man:** 185 men
M: CODOG: 2 Rolls-Royce Olympus TM3BGT (53,200 hp); 2 MTU diesels (16,000 hp); 2 controllable-pitch props
Electron Equipt: Radars: 1/DA-08, 1 WM25 with STIR
Sonar: Atlas 80 (bow-mounted) — 2 Breda SCLAR 20-cell chaff launchers

REMARKS: Germanized version of Dutch *Kortenaer* class. First six ordered 7-77; six additional may eventually be authorized.

FRIGATES

♦ *6 Köln class*

Bldr: H. C. Stülcken, Hamburg

	L	In serv.
F 220 KÖLN	6-12-58	4-61
F 221 EMDEN	21-3-59	10-61
F 222 AUGSBURG	15-8-59	4-62
F 223 KARLSRUHE	24-10-59	12-62
F 224 LÜBECK	23-7-60	7-63
F 225 BRAUNSCHWEIG	3-2-62	6-64

Karlsruhe (F 223) 1974

D: 1,750 tons (2,100 normal, 2,500 fl)
Dim: 109.0 (105.0 pp) × 10.56 × 3.70 (fl)
S: 30 kts (20 on diesels) **Man:** 212 men
A: 2/100-mm French Model 1953 DP (I × 2) — 6/40-mm AA (II × 2, I × 2) — 2/4-barreled 375-mm Bofors ASW rocket launchers — 4/533-mm ASW TT (I × 4) — mines
Electron Equipt: Radars: 1/DA-02, 1/SGR 3M45 FC
Sonar: 1 PAE/CWE M/F hull-mounted
M: CODAG: 4 M.A.N. V-16-cylinder diesels (each 3,000 hp); 2 Brown-Boveri GT (each 13,000 hp) a total of 38,000 hp; 2 controllable-pitch props
Electric: 2,700 kw **Fuel:** 333 tons **Range:** 900/30

REMARKS: The rocket launchers carry 72 projectiles. Two diesels and one gas turbine on each of the two shafts. Made 33 kts. on trials.

CORVETTES

♦ *5 Thetis class, former torpedo-recovery boats converted and designated "corvettes"*

P 6052 THETIS (21-3-60)
P 6053 HERMES (9-8-60)
P 6054 NAJADE (6-12-60)
P 6055 TRITON (5-8-61)
P 6056 THESEUS (20-3-62)

Bldr: Roland Werft (Bremen-Hemelingen)

CORVETTES (*continued*)

Najade (P 6054) 1974

D: 564 tons (650 fl) **S:** 23.5 kts **Dim:** 69.70 × 8.50 × 4.2
A: 2/40-mm AA (II × 1 aft) — 1/4-barreled Bofors 375-mm rocket launcher (fwd) — 4/533-mm ASW TT (I × 4)
M: 2 M.A.N. diesels; 2 props; 6,800 hp **Man:** 5 officers, 43 men
Electron Equipt: Radar: Kelvin-Hughes 14/9, TRS-N
Sonar: ELAC 1BV

REMARKS: Well-designed ships for operations in the Belts and the Baltic. May receive OTO Melara 76-mm in place of 40-mm.

NOTE: Former corvette *Hans Bürkner* is now listed under experimental auxiliaries.

GUIDED MISSILE HYDROFOILS

♦ *4 Type 162* — Bldr: Boeing, Seattle

NOTE: Program in abeyance due to enormous rise in price of U.S. *Pegasus* class, upon which this design is based. Details for reference only, as class is unlikely to be built:

D: 202 tons (235 fl) **S:** 50 kts (12 on diesel)
Dim: 40.2 × 8.9 × 1.6 (hull mode)
A: 4/MM38 Exocet — 1/76-mm OTO Melara DP
M: CODOG: 1 G.E. LM2500 GT (26,200 hp) or 2 MTU diesels (1,340 hp)

GUIDED MISSILE PATROL BOATS

♦ *10 type 143 (composite construction hull)*

	L	In serv.		L	In serv.
P 6111 S 61	22-10-73	1-11-76	**P 6116 S 66**	5-9-75	25-11-76
P 6112 S 62	21-3-74	13-4-76	**P 6117 S 67**	6-3-75	1-77

S 62 (P 6112) 1976

S 62 (P 6112) 1976

GUIDED MISSILE PATROL BOATS (*continued*)

S 62 (P 6112) 1976

P 6113 S 63	18-9-74	2-6-76		**P 6118 S 68**	17-11-75	2-77
P 6114 S 64	14-4-75	14-8-76		**P 6119 S 69**	5-6-75	4-77
P 6115 S 65	15-1-74	27-9-76		**P 6120 S 70**	14-4-76	6-77

Bldrs: **S-65, S-67, S-69:** Kröger, Rendsburg; remainder: Lürssen, Vegasack

D: 295 tons (378 fl) **S:** 36 kts (32 fl)
Dim: 57.45 (54.40 pp) × 7.62 × 2.82
A: 4/MM38 Exocet — 2/76-mm OTO Melara AA (I × 2) — 2/533-mm TT (aft-launching, for Seal wire-guided torpedoes)
M: 4 MTU 16V956 diesels; 4 props; 16,000 hp **Fuel:** 116 tons
Range: 600/30, 2,600/16 **Man:** 40-42 men **Electric:** 540 kw
Electron Equipt: Radar: HSA WM-27 with AGIS data system

♦ *20 Type 148* (steel hulls)

	L		L
P 6141 S 41	27-9-72	**P 6143 S 43**	7-3-73
P 6142 S 42	12-12-72	**P 6144 S 44**	5-5-73

S 41 (P 6141) 1973

P 6145 S 45	3-7-73	**P 6153 S 53**	4-7-74
P 6146 S 46	21-5-73	**P 6154 S 54**	8-7-74
P 6147 S 47	20-9-72	**P 6155 S 55**	25-3-74
P 6148 S 48	10-9-73	**P 6156 S 56**	30-10-74
P 6149 S 49	11-1-74	**P 6157 S 57**	13-2-75
P 6150 S 50	10-12-73	**P 6158 S 58**	26-2-75
P 6151 S 51	25-4-74	**P 6159 S 59**	15-5-75
P 6152 S 52	25-3-74	**P 6160 S 60**	26-5-75

Bldr: Constructions Mécaniques de Normandie (Cherbourg) with Lürssen (Vegesack), who built the boats carrying even number designations from number P-6146. All were fitted out at Lorient.

S 41 (P 6141) 1973

S 41 (P 6141) 1973

GUIDED MISSILE PATROL BOATS (*continued*)

D: 234 tons (265 fl) **Dim:** 47.0 (44.0 pp) × 7.1 × 2.5 (fl)
S: 35.5 kts **Man:** 4 officers, 17 petty officers, 9 men
A: 4/MM38 Exocet — 1/76-mm DP OTO Melara (fwd) — 1/40-mm Bofors AA (aft) — 8 mines in place of the 40-mm AA
Electron Equipt: Radars: 1 3 RM 20 navigation, 1 Triton target designation, 1 Vega FC system with Pollux
M: 4 MTU MD 872 type diesels; 4 props; 14,400 hp (12,000 sust.)
Fuel: 39 tons **Electric:** 270 kw **Range:** 900/30

TORPEDO BOATS

♦ *10 Type 142 Zobel-class (modernized early 1970s)*

P 6092 ZOBEL (21-8-61)
P 6093 WIESEL (16-3-61)
P 6094 DACHS (10-6-61)
P 6095 HERMELIN (5-8-61)
P 6096 NERZ (5-9-61)
P 6097 PUMA (26-10-61)
P 6098 GEPARD (14-4-62)
P 6099 HYÄNE (31-3-62)
P 6100 FRETTCHEN (20-11-62)
P 6101 OZELOT (4-2-63)

Frettchen (P 6100) 1974

D: 160 tons (225 fl) **S:** 42 kts **Dim:** 42.80 × 7.14 × 2.20
A: 2/40-mm AA (I × 2) — 2/533-mm TT (aft-launching for Seal wire-guided torpedoes) **Man:** 42 men
M: 4 MTU 20V 538 diesels; 4 props; 12,000 hp
Electron Equipt: Radars: H.S.A. M 20 FC, Kelvin Hughes 14/9 navigational

REMARKS: Wooden hull, light-alloy superstructure. Four mines can be carried in lieu of torpedoes. Not all have M 20 radar.
NOTE: All the Type 141 (*Jaguar*) torpedo boats have been retired; seven were transferred to Greece and seven to Turkey.

MINE WARFARE SHIPS

♦ . . . *Type 331*

A design study for a new minehunter class to replace the Type 320 in the 1980s

♦ *18 Type 320 — 10 minehunters and 8 minesweepers*

* **M 1070 GÖTTINGEN** (14-4-57)
* **M 1071 KOBLENZ** (6-5-57)
* **M 1072 LINDAU** (16-2-57
M 1073 SCHLESWIG (1-10-57)
* **M 1074 TÜBINGEN** (12-8-57)
* **M 1075 WETZLAR** (24-6-57)
M 1076 PADERBORN (5-12-57)
* **M 1077 WEILHEIM** (4-2-58)
* **M 1078 CUXHAVEN** (10-4-58)
M 1079 DÜREN (12-6-58)
* **M 1080 MARBURG** (4-4-58)
M 1081 KONSTANZ (30-10-58)
M 1082 WOLFSBURG (10-2-59)
M 1083 ULM (10-2-59)
M 1084 FLENSBURG (7-4-59)
* **M 1085 MINDEN** (9-6-59)
M 1086 FULDA (19-8-59)
* **M 1087 VÖLKLINGEN** (20-10-59)

Bldr: Burmeister, Bremen-Burg

Marburg (M 1080) 1974

D: 365 tons (524 fl) **Dim:** 44.70 × 8.30 × 2.50
S: 16 kts **Man:** 46 men
A: 1/40-mm AA **M:** Maybach diesels, 2 props; 4,000 hp
Fuel: 40 tons diesel **Range:** 850/16

REMARKS: Units marked * fitted out as minehunters between 1975 and 1977 (Sonar: Plessey Type 193 and French PAP-104 wire-guided hunting sleds). The eight others will be fitted with the Troika remote-controlled minehunting system between 1978 and 1980. Units converted to minehunters have extended superstructure in place of the magnetic-sweep cable reel and can no longer sweep.

♦ *22 Type 340 and Type 341 patrol minesweepers*

M 1051 CASTOR (12-7-62)
M 1054 POLLUX (15-9-60)
M 1055 SIRIUS (15-3-61)
M 1056 RIGEL (2-4-62)
M 1057 REGULUS (18-12-61)
M 1063 WAAGE (9-4-59)
M 1058 MARS (1-12-60)
M 1064 DENEB (11-9-61)
M 1065 JUPITER (15-2-61)
M 1067 ALTAIR (20-4-61)
M 1069 WEGA (10-10-62)
M 1090 PERSEUS (22-9-60)
M 1092 PLUTO (9-8-60)
M 1093 NEPTUN (9-6-60)

MINE WARFARE SHIPS (*continued*)

M 1059 SPICA (25-5-60)
M 1060 SKORPION (29-5-63)
Y 849 STIER (30-10-58)
M 1062 SCHUTZE (20-5-58)
M 1094 WIDDER (13-3-59)
M 1095 HERKULES (25-8-60)
M 1096 FISCHE (14-7-59)
M 1097 GEMMA (6-10-59)

Bldr: Schlichting, Travemünde; Schürenstedt, Bardenfleth; Abeking and Rasmussen, Lemwerde (1958-63)

Herkules (M 1095) 1974

Waage (M 1063) in patrol boat configuration Terzibaschitsch

D: 230 tons (280 fl) **S:** 24.6 kts **Dim:** 47.20 × 6.80 × 2.20
Man: 39 men **A:** 1/40-mm AA (see Remarks)
M: Maybach or Mercedes-Benz diesels; 2 Escher-Wyss cycloidal props; 3,600 hp
Fuel: 22 tons

REMARKS: Multi-purpose ships that can be employed as minesweepers, coastal patrol craft (2/40-mm AA), and minelayers (2 mine rails), the minesweeping gear having been removed in the latter two instances. *Stier* (former M-1061), used as a submarine-rescue ship, has been given a new hull number and is disarmed; decompression chamber on new stern deckhouse.

♦ *1 Type 300, converted inshore minesweeper*

	Bldr	Laid down	L	In serv.
Y 836 HOLNIS	Abeking	1964	20-5-66	1966

D: 180 tons **Dim:** 35.60 × 7.40 × 2.10

Holnis (now carries number Y836) Terzibaschitsch

S: 14.5 kts **Man:** 21 men
A: None **M:** MB diesels; 2 props; 2,00 hp **Fuel:** 13.tons

REMARKS: Now used as trials ship for Troika pressure/acoustic minesweeping system, which uses three radio-controlled launches about 18 meters long. *Holnis* now has a deckhouse aft and bulwarks around her stern, no armament. Nineteen projected sisters were cancelled.

♦ *18 Type 343 (a) and 344 (b) inshore minesweepers*

(*a*) **M 2650 ARIADNE** (23-4-60)
M 2651 FREYA (25-6-60)
M 2652 VINETA (17-9-60)
M 2653 HERTHA (18-2-61)
M 2654 NYMPHE (20-9-62)
M 2655 NIXE (3-12-62)
M 2656 AMAZONE (27-2-63)
M 2657 GAZELLE (14-8-63)

(*b*) **M 2658 FRAUENLOB** (8-4-65)
M 2659 NAUTILUS (19-5-65)
M 2660 GEFION (16-9-65)
M 2661 MEDUSA (25-1-66)
M 2662 UNDINE (16-5-66)
M 2663 MINERVA (25-8-66)
M 2664 DIANA (15-12-66)
M 2665 LORELEY (14-3-67)
M 2666 ATLANTIS (20-6-67)
M 2667 ACHERON (11-10-67)

Minerva (Y 1657) 1974

MINE WARFARE SHIPS (*continued*)

Bldr: Kröger, Rendsburg

D: (*a*) 185 tons (210 fl) (*b*) 204 tons (230 fl)
Dim: (*a*) 34.60 × 6.50 × 7.10 (*b*) 37.90 × 7.20 × 2
S: 14 kts **Man:** 4 officers, 24 men **Range:** 740/14
A: 1/40-mm AA **Fuel:** 30 tons
M: MB diesels; 2 props; 1,900 hp

REMARKS: Wooden hulls. Formerly had Y-series hull numbers, and earlier W-series.

♦ *2 Hansa-class converted inshore minesweepers*

Y 806 HANSA (1958) **Y 1653 NIOBE** (1958)

Bldr: Kröger, Rendsburg

D: 150 tons (180 fl) **S:** Y-806: 14 kts Y-1653: 16 kts
Dim: 35.1 × 6.5 × 1.7
A: 1/40-mm AA **Range:** 1,100/max. speed **Man:** 19/22 men
M: Y-806: 1 MTU diesel; 1 prop; 950 hp Y-1653: 2 MTU diesels; 2 props; 1,900 hp

REMARKS: *Hansa* now tender for mine-clearance divers, *Niobe* is used for minesweeping experiments. Wood hulls.

AMPHIBIOUS WARFARE CRAFT

♦ *19 Type 520 utility landing craft*

L 760 FLUNDER	**L 767 TUMMLER**	**L 791 DELPHIN**
L 761 KARPFEN	**L 768 WELS**	**L 792 DORSCH**
L 762 LACHS	**L 769 ZANDER**	**L 793 FELCHEN**
L 763 PLÖTZE	**L 788 BUTT**	**L 794 FORELLE**
L 764 ROCHEN	**L 789 BRASSE**	**L 796 MAKRELE**
L 765 SCHLEI	**L 790 BARBE**	**L 797 MÜRÄNE**
L 766 STÖR		

Bldr: Howaldtswerke, Hamburg, 1965-66

Butt Terzibaschitsch, 1971

D: 197 tons (397 fl) **Dim:** 41.45 (39.93 pp) × 8.84 × 1.60
S: 11 kts **M:** 4 GM 6-71 diesels; 1,200 hp
A: 1/20-mm AA **Man:** 17 men **Range:** 1,200/11

REMARKS: Design based on the American LCU-1646 class. Carries 160 tons. Will get 2/20-mm AA of a new type. *Renke* (L-798), *Salm* (L-799) discarded; *Inger* (L-95) used for training.

♦ *28 U.S. LCM-8 landing craft* — Bldr: Blohm & Voss

LCM 1-28 (1965-67)

D: 116 tons (140 fl) **S:** 11 kts **Dim:** 23 × 6.41 × 1.3
M: 4 G.M. diesels; 1,200 hp **Cargo capacity:** 60 tons

AUXILIARY SHIPS

♦ *11 Type 401 and Type 402 B Rhein-class tenders*

(*a*) *For small combatants*

A 58 RHEIN (10-12-59) **A 66 NECKAR** (26-6-61)
A 61 ELBE (5-5-60) **A 68 WERRA** (26-3-63)
A 63 MAIN (23-7-60) **A 69 DONAU** (26-12-60)

(*b*) *For minesweepers*

A 54 ISAR (14-7-62) **A 65 SAAR** (11-3-61) **A 67 MOSEL** (15-12-60)

Mosel (A 67) 1975

(*c*) *For submarines*

A 55 LAHN (21-11-61) **A 56 LECH** (4-5-62)

Laid down: 1959/61 — In serv: 1961/64

D: (*a*) 2,370 tons (2,540 fl) (*b*) and (*c*) 2,460 tons (2,680 fl)
Dim: 98.60 × 11.80 × 3.70 (light) 5.20 (fl)
S: 21/20 kts (trials, 22) **Range:** 1,625/15
Man: 98 men (space for 40 officers, 40 petty officers, 130 non-rated men)
A: 2/100-mm AA (I × 2) (not in A-55, A-56) — 4/40-mm AA (I × 4, except A-55, A-56: II × 2) — mines

AUXILIARY SHIPS (*continued*)

Electron Equipt: Radars: 1/SGR 105, 1/SGR 103, 2 M45 fire control
M: 6 Maybach diesels (Mercedes-Benz in A-55 and A-56); 2 controllable-pitch props; 11,400 hp **Fuel:** 334 tons

Lech (A 56) 1975

REMARKS: A-54, A-55, A-56, A-65, A-67 have electric drive. Tenders carry 200 tons of fuel oil, 40 reserve torpedoes; A-55, A-56, and A-58 have an additional 200 tons of stores; A-66, A-68, and A-69 can be used as training ships. A-62 *Weser* and A-64 *Ruhr* transferred to the Greek and Turkish navies in 1975 and 1976, respectively.

Neckar (A 66) Kowark, 1976

UNDERWAY REPLENISHMENT SHIPS

NOTE: These ships are grouped together here because, despite their dissimilar functions, they are variations on the same basic design.

♦ *8 Type 701 and Type 701C multi-purpose supply ships*

A 1411 LÜNEBURG (5-3-65)
A 1412 COBURG (15-12-65)
A 1413 FREIBURG (15-4-66)
A 1414 GLÜCKSBURG (3-5-66)
A 1415 SAARBURG (15-7-66)
A 1416 NIENBURG (26-7-66)
A 1417 OFFENBURG (10-9-66)
A 1418 MEERSBURG (22-3-67)

Bldr: Flensburger Schiffbau; Vulkan, Vegesack; Blohm & Voss, Hamburg

Saarburg (A 1415) lengthened 1976

Coburg (A 1412) unmodified Terzibaschitsch

D: 3,254 tons (fl) — except A-1411, A-1415, A-1418: 3,450 tons (fl)
Dim: 103.5 × 13.2 × 4.2 — except A-1411, A-1415, A-1418: 115.0 (oa)
S: 17 kts **A:** 4/40-mm AA (II × 2) in preservation **Man:** 103 men
M: 2 Maybach MD 874 diesels; 2 controllable-pitch props; 5,600 hp
Range: 3,500/17

UNDERWAY REPLENISHMENT SHIPS (*continued*)

REMARKS: Originally configured to carry over 1,100 tons cargo, including 640 tons fuel oil, 200 tons ammunition, 100 tons spare parts (10,000 separate items), and 130 tons fresh water. A-1415 lengthened 11.5 meters in 1974-75 to carry spare Exocet missiles and other supplies for the new Type 143 and Type 148 classes; stowage for spare parts increased to 30,000 items with inventory management by the Nixdorf computer system. A-1411 and A-1418 also converted to Type 702C standard, 1975-77.

♦ *2 Type 760 ammunition ships*

A 1435 WESTERWALD (25-2-66) **A 1436 ODENWALD** (5-5-66)

Bldr: Lübecker Flenderwerke (*W*), Orenstein & Koppel, Lübeck

Westerwald (A 1435) 1974

D: 3,460 tons (fl) **S:** 17 kts **Dim:** 106.0 × 14.0 × 3.7
A: 4/40-mm AA (II × 2) in preservation **Man:** 58 men
M: 2 Maybach MD 874 diesels; 2 controllable-pitch props; 5,600 hp
Range: 3,500/17

REMARK: Similar to Type 701 but carry only ammunition.

♦ *2 Type 762 mine-supply ships* — Bldr: Blohm & Voss, Hamburg

A 1437 SACHSENWALD (10-12-66) **A 1438 STEIGERWALD** (10-3-67)

Steigerwald (A 1438) 1974

D: 3,850 tons (fl) **S:** 17 kts **Dim:** 111.0 × 13.9 × 3.4
A: 4/40-mm AA (II × 2) **Man:** 65 men **Range:** 3,500/17
M: 2 Maybach MD 864 diesels; controllable-pitch props; 5,600 hp

REMARKS: Official typing as "supply ships" is something of a euphemism as these ships have mine ports at the stern and are actually minelayers. Construction of a torpedo transport version of this class was canceled.

REPAIR SHIPS

♦ *2 former U.S. Aristaeus class*

A 512 ODIN (ex-*Ulysses*, ARB-9) **A 513 WOTAN** (ex-*Diomedes*, ARB-11)

Transferred by the U.S.A. in 6-61.

Odin (A 512)

D: 1,625 tons (3,455 fl) **Dim:** 100 × 15.20 × 2.80
S: 11 kts **Man:** 187 men (civil personnel)
M: 2 General Motors diesels; 2 props; 1,800 hp
Range: 20,000/9 **Fuel:** 438 tons

REMARK: Modified former LST-1119 and LST-967, respectively.

OILERS

♦ *2 former merchant tankers, converted while building* — L: 1974-75

A 1443 RHÖN (ex-*Okapi*) **A . . . SPESSART** (ex-*Okene*)

Bldr: Kröger, Rendsburg

D: approx. 14,500 tons (fl) — 6,107 grt/10,950 dwt
Dim: 130.0 × 19.6 × 8.20 **S:** 16 kts
M: 1 MAK 12-cyl. diesel; 8,000 hp

REMARKS: Purchased from Bulk Acid Carriers, Monrovia, in 1976. Will replace *Emsland* (A-1440) and *Münsterland* (A-1441), which were scheduled to be stricken in 1977-78.

♦ *4 Type 703* — Bldr: Lindenau, Friedrichsort

A 1424 WALCHENSEE (10-7-66) **A 1426 TEGERNSEE** (27-10-66)
A 1425 AMMERSEE (22-9-66) **A 1427 WESTENSEE** (8-4-67)

OILERS (*continued*)

Ammersee (A 1425) 1975

D: 2,060 tons **Dim:** 71 × 11.20 × 4.10
Cargo capacity: 1,130 tons **S:** 12.5 kts
M: Diesels; 2 props; 1,400 hp

♦ *1 former merchant tanker, purchased 29-3-59*

A 1407 WITTENSEE (ex-*Sioux*) (23-9-58)

Wittensee (A 1407) 1975

D: 2,000 tons (fl) — 985 grt/1,250 hp **Dim:** 63.55 × 9.90 × 4.57
Man: 21 men **M:** Diesel; 1,250 hp **S:** 12 kts

REMARK: Sister *Bodensee* has been stricken.

♦ *1 former merchant tanker, purchased 1963*

A 1429 EIFEL (ex-*Friedrich Jung*) — Bldr: Norderwerft, Hamburg, 29-3-58

D: 7,200 tons (fl) — 2,279 grt/4,720 dwt **Dim:** 102.0 × 14.4 × 7.1
M: 2 diesels; 1 prop; 3,360 hp **S:** 13 kts

REMARK: Equipped for underway replenishment.

♦ *1 former merchant tanker, purchased 1963*

A 1428 HARZ (ex-*Clare Jung*) — Bldr: Norderwerft, Hamburg, 1953

D: 5,300 tons (fl) — 1,308 grt/3,696 dwt **S:** 12 kts
Dim: 92.4 × 13.2 × 6.6 **M:** Diesel; 1 prop; 2,520 hp

REMARK: Equipped for underway replenishment.

SEAGOING TUGS

♦ *6 Baltrum-class tugs*

Bldr: Schichau, Bremerhaven, 1965-68

A 1451 WANGEROOGE **A 1453 LANGEOOG** **A 1455 NORDERNEY**
A 1452 SPIEKEROOG **A 1454 BALTRUM** **A 1456 JUIST**

Langeoog (A 1453) 1969

D: 854 tons (1,138 fl) **S:** 13.5 kts **Dim:** 51 × 11.50 × 4.0
A: 1/40-mm AA **M:** 2 MWM diesels; electric motors; 1 prop; 2,400 hp
Range: 5,000/10 **Man:** 24 men

REMARKS: Also employed as salvage tugs and port icebreakers. The *Baltrum* has been employed as a diving training tender since 1974.

♦ *2 Helgoland-class salvage tugs*

A 1457 HELGOLAND (8-4-65) — **A 1458 FEHMARN** (1965)

D: 1,643 tons (fl) **Dim:** 68 × 12.70 × 4.40 **S:** 16.5 kts
A: 2/40-mm (II × 1) **Man:** 36 men **Range:** 6,000/10
M: 4 MWM diesels; 2 props; 3,600 hp

SEAGOING TUGS *(continued)*

Fehmarn (A 1458) 1974

♦ *2 Eisvogel-class icebreaking tugs* — Bldr: Hitzler, Laurenburg

A 1401 EISVOGEL (5-5-60) **A 1402 EISBAR** (9-6-60)

D: 560 tons (650 fl) **S:** 13 kts **Dim:** 38.2 × 9.5 × 4.6
M: 2 Maybach diesels; 2 props; 2,400 hp **Man:** 14 men

HARBOR TUGS

♦ *3 Neuende-class tugs* — Bldr: Schichau, Bremerhaven — In serv. 1971

Y 1680 NEUENDE **Y 1681 HEPPENS** **Y 1682 ELLERBEK**

Ellerbek (Y 1682) Terzibaschitsch

D: 122 tons **S:** 12 kts **Dim:** 26.6 × 7.4 × 2.6
M: 1 MWM diesel; 800 hp **Man:** 6 men

♦ *4 Sylt-class tugs, 1963* — Bldr: Schichau, Bremerhaven

Y 820 SYLT **Y 822 AMRUM**
Y 821 FOHR **Y 823 NEUWERK**

D: 266 tons **S:** 12 kts **Dim:** 30.60 × 7.50 **M:** 800 hp

♦ *1 prewar coastal tug* — Bldr: Schichau, Konigsberg, 1939

Y 801 PELLWORM

D: 500 tons (fl) **S:** 12 kts **Dim:** 38.7 × 8.5 × 1.2
M: 1 MW diesel; 800 hp **Range:** 2,900/8

♦ *10 tugs, from 36 to 100 tons, 1958-60*

Y 812 LÜTJE HÖRN **Y 817 NORDSTRAND**
Y 813 MELLUM **Y 818 TRISCHEN**
Y 814 KNECHTSAND **Y 819 LANGENESS**
Y 815 SCHARNHORN **Y 802 PLON**
Y 816 VOGELSAND **Y 803 BLAUORT**

WATER TANKERS

♦ *5 FW-1 class, 1963-64*

Y 864 FW 1 **Y 866 FW 3** **Y 868 FW 5**
Y 865 FW 2 **Y 867 FW 4**

D: 600 tons (fl) — 350 dwt **S:** 9.5 kts **Dim:** 44.1 × 7.8 × 2.5
M: 1 MWM diesel; 230 hp

REMARK: Sister FW-6 sold to Turkey in 1975.

FW 5 (Y 868) Terzibaschitsch

TORPEDO-RECOVERY BOATS

♦ *14 boats*

Y 851, Y 852, Y 853, Y 854, Y 855, Y 856, Y 872, Y 873, Y 874, Y 882, Y 883, Y 884, Y 885, Y 886.

S: 17 kts **Dim:** 24.5 × . . . × . . .
M: 950 hp for Y-851 to 856, 872 to 874.

REMARKS: Y-883 to 886 are much older. Stern ramps to recover torpedoes.

TF 5 (Y 855) 1975

INTELLIGENCE COLLECTORS

♦ *2 converted trawlers* — Bldr: Unterweser, Bremen, 1962

A 50 ALSTER (ex-*Mellum*) **A 53 OKER** (ex-*Hoheweg*)

D: 1,187 tons **S:** 15 kts **Dim:** 72.5 × 10.5 × 4.9
M: Diesel-electric; 1 prop; . . . hp

♦ *1 converted tug* — Bldr: Akers, Oslo, 1943

A 52 OSTE (ex-U.S. 101, ex-*Puddefjord*)

Oste Terzibaschitsch, 1969

D: 567 grt **S:** 11 kts **Dim:** 49.0 × 8.8 × 5.2
M: 1 Akers diesel; 1,600 hp **Man:** 30 men

AIR-SEA RESCUE CRAFT

♦ *1 FL-10 class*

Y 864 FL 11 — Bldr: Kroger, Rendsburg, 1955

D: 70 tons **S:** 30 **Dim:** 29.0 × 5.0 × 1.3
M: 2 MTU diesels; 2 props; 3,200 hp **Range:** 600/25

REMARK: Sister FL-10 now in Uruguayan Navy.

♦ *6 KW series, 1951–53*

Y 827 KW 15	**Y 832 KW 18**	**Y 845 KW 17**
Y 830 KW 16	**Y 833 KW 19**	**Y 846 KW 20**

D: 45 tons (60 fl) **S:** 25 kts **Dim:** 28.9 × 4.9 × 1.5
M: 2 MTU diesels; 2 props; 1,600–2,000 hp **Man:** 14 men

TRAINING SHIPS

♦ *1 cruiser-type*

	Bldr	Laid down	L	In serv.
A 59 DEUTSCHLAND	Nobiskrug, Rendsburg	1958	5-11-60	5-63

Deutschland (A 59) 1974

D: 4,880 tons (5,400 fl) **Dim:** 145.00 (137.90 pp) × 17.98 × 4.80 (fl)
S: 22 kts (18 cruising) **Man:** 33 officers, 521 men (250 cadets)
A: 4/100-mm AA (I × 4) — 8/40-mm AA (II × 2, I × 4) — 4/533-mm ASW TT — 2 ASW rocket launchers
Electron Equipt: Radars: 1/LWO 3, 1/SGR 114, 1/SGR 105, 1/SGR 103, 4 M 45 fire control
Sonar: 1 ELAC 1BV (M/F)
M: 4 diesels (2 Maybach and 2 Mercedes-Benz), each of 1,670 hp; 1 Wahodag GT 8,000 hp; 3 props, 2 controllable-pitch **Electric:** 1,500 kw
Range: 6,000/17 **Fuel:** 640 tons

REMARKS: Quarters for 7 instructors and 250 cadets. Can be used as a minelayer.

TRAINING SHIPS (*continued*)

♦ *1 sail training ship*

A 60 GORCH FOCK — Bldr: Blohm & Voss, Hamburg — L: 23-8-58

D: 1,760 tons (1,880 fl) **Dim:** 81.26 × 12.02 × 4.85
S: 10 kts **M:** 1 M.A.N. diesel; 880 hp

REMARKS: 1,964 m^2 of sail area; living spaces for 200 cadets.

♦ *1 ex-KW class patrol cutter, now ketch-rigged*

Y 834 NORDWIND (1944) **D:** 110 tons **Dim:** 24.0 × 6.4 × 2.5

♦ *70 smaller sail training craft*

EXPERIMENTAL AND TRIALS SHIPS

♦ *1 former corvette* — Bldr: Atlaswerke, Bremen — L: 16-7-61

A 1449 HANS BÜRKNER

Hans Bürkner (A 1449) 1975

D: 950 tons (1,000 fl) **S:** 24 kts **Dim:** 81.0 × 9.4 × 2.8
A: 1/375-mm Bofors 4-barreled ASW rocket launchers (see Remarks)
M: 4 M.A.N. diesels; 2 props; 13,600 hp **Man:** 50 men

REMARKS: Employed as ASW trials ship. Has recently carried a small variable-depth sonar. Position for 2/40-mm AA (II × 1) retained, and has previously carried 2/533-mm ASW torpedo tubes.

♦ *2 net tenders, used in experimental trials*

Y 837 SP 1 (21-6-66) **Y 838 WILHELM PULLWER** (16-8-66)

Bldr: Schürenstedt K.G., Bardenfleth

D: 132 tons **S:** 12.5 kts **Dim:** 31.75 × 6.35 × 2
M: Daimler-Benz diesels; 2 Voith-Schneider cycloidal props; 580 hp

SP 1 (Y 837) Terzibaschitsch

♦ *3 former U.S. YMS-class minesweepers*

Y 847 OT 2, Y 881 ADOLF BESTELMEYER, Y 889 RUDOLF DIESEL

D: 270 tons (350 fl) **S:** 15 kts **Dim:** 41.5 × 7.5 × 2.4
M: 2 MTU diesels; 2 props; 1,000 hp

REMARKS: Two sisters, *H. C. Oersted* and *Herman von Helmholtz*, used as degaussing tenders.

♦ *1 British Isles-class ex-trawler* — In serv. 1942

Y 1663 EIDER (ex-*Catherine*, ex-*Dochet*) — Bldr: Davie, Lauzon, Can.

D: 480 tons (750 fl) **S:** 12 kts **Dim:** 53.9 × 8.4 × 4.0
A: Mines **Range:** 3,700/10 **Man:** 45 men
M: Triple-expansion; 1 prop; 750 hp

REMARKS: Civilian-manned mine-trials ship and exercise minelayer. Guns removed.

DEGAUSSING TENDERS

♦ *1 special magnetic research ship* — L: 30-6-66

Y 841 WALTHER VON LEDEBUR — Bldr: Burmeister, Bremen

D: 725 tons **S:** 19 kts **Dim:** 63.0 × 10.6 × 2.7
M: 2 MTU diesels; 2 props; 5,000 hp **Man:** 10 men (plus 11 technicians)

REMARKS: One of the largest wooden ships built in modern times. Used in mine-warfare research.

♦ *2 former U.S. YMS-class minesweepers, bought 1962*

Y 877 H. C. OERSTED **Y 878 HERMAN VON HELMHOLTZ**

REMARK: See date under Experimental and Trials Ships.

DEGAUSSING TENDERS (*continued*)

H. C. Oersted (Y 877) Terzibaschitsch

DIVING TENDERS

♦ *1 former water tanker*

Y 1662 EMS (ex-U.S. 104, ex-*Harle*) — Bldr: Kremer, Elmshorn, 1941

D: 660 grt **S:** 12 kts **Dim:** 56.6 × 8.8 × 4.7
M: 2 Sulzer diesels; 2 props; 1,000 hp **Range:** 2,400/12

REMARKS: Resembles a tug. *Baltrum* (A-1454), see under Seagoing Tugs, is used as divers' training ship.

♦ **Y 1678 TB 1** (1972), 70 tons, 14 kts

♦ **Y 882 OTTO MEYCKE** (1944), 112 tons

VARIOUS SHIPS

♦ *1 torpedo workshop*, 270 tons

Y 805 MEMMERT (ex-U.S. 106, ex-*India*) (1941)

Memmert (Y 805) 1975

♦ *2 floating barracks*

Y 811 KNURRHAN — 261 tons
Y 809 ARCONA (ex-*Royal Prince*) — former liner

♦ *2 tank-cleaning craft* (1967) — Bldr: Deutsche Werft, Hamburg

Y 1641 FÖRDE **Y 1642 JADE**

D: 600 grt **S:** 8 kts **Dim:** 59.0 × 10.4 × 4.1
M: 1 MWM diesel; 390 hp

REMARKS: For steam-cleaning fuel tanks and sludge-removal. Resemble small tankers.

HYDROGRAPHIC SHIPS

NOTE: Listed separately, because they are civilian-manned units operated for the Ministry of Communications.

A 1450 PLANET — Bldr: Norderwerft, Hamburg — L: 23-9-65

Planet A. and J. Pavia

D: 1,950 tons **S:** 13.9 kts **Dim:** 80 × 12.60 × . . .
Man: 40 men and 22 civilian specialists
M: Diesel-electric propulsion; 1 prop; 1,350 hp

A . . . PASSAU

Passau (as a minesweeper)

HYDROGRAPHIC SHIPS *(continued)*

Former French *Mercure*-class minesweeper, placed in the reserve group in 1963, then refitted as an oceanographic research vessel in 1975.

D: 378 tons (fl) **S:** 15 kts **Dim:** 44.2 × 8.0 × 2.7
M: 2 MTU diesels; 2 controllable-pitch props; 1,500 hp

REMARK: Sisters transferred to Turkey.

COAST GUARD

NOTE: A separate paramilitary force of 1,000 men (*Bundesgrenzschutz-See*)

PATROL BOATS

♦ *8 Neustadt class* — Bldrs: Lürssen, Vegesack, except B-613: Schlichting, Travemünde — In serv. 1969–70

BG 611 NEUSTADT **BG 615 ESCHWEGE**
BG 612 BAD BRAMSTEDT **BG 616 ALSFELD**
BG 613 UELTZEN **BG 617 BAYREUTH**
BG 614 DUDERSTADT **BG 618 ROSENHEIM**

D: 140 tons (203 fl) **S:** 30 kts **Dim:** 38.6 × 7.0 × 1.8
A: 2/40-mm AA (I × 2) **Man:** 27 men
M: 3 MTU diesels; 3 props; 7,885 hp

♦ *a number of smaller craft plus helicopters*

♦ *1 tug*

BG 5 RETTIN (1976)

Bldr: Mützelbeldt-Werft, Cuxhaven, 12-76

D: 99.9 grt **S:** 9 kts **Dim:** 22.5 (20.0 pp) × 6.6 × 2.9
M: 2 MWM diesels; 1 prop; 590 hp

PERSONNEL: 1,300 men

MERCHANT MARINE (1976): 84 ships — 183,089 grt

CORVETTES

♦ *2 Vosper Mk 1*

	Bldr	L	In serv.
F 17 KROMANTSE	Vosper Ltd	5-9-63	9-64
F 18 KETA	Vickers-Armstrong	18-1-65	8-65

Keta (F 18) G. Arra, 1975

D: 435 tons (590 fl) **Dim:** 53.95 (49.38 pp) × 8.70 × 3.05
S: 18 kts **Man:** 5 officers, 49 men
A: 1/102-mm — 1/40-mm AA — 1 Squid
M: 2/16-cyl. Bristol Siddeley-Maybach diesels; 2 props; 5,720 hp
Fuel: 60 tons **Range:** 2,900/14, 1,100/18
Electric: 360 kw
Electron Equipt: Radars: 1/Type 978 navigational, 1/Plessey ASW-1

REMARKS: Stabilizers. Quarters are air-conditioned. Both refitted 1974-75.

GUIDED MISSILE PATROL BOATS

♦ *2 Jaguar-III class* — Bldr: Lürssen, Vegesack

N . . . N . . .

D: 400 tons (fl) **S:** 35 kts **Dim:** 58.1 × 7.6 × 2.8
A: 2/76-mm DP OTO Melara compact — missiles (?)
M: 4 MTU diesels; 4 props; . . . hp

REMARK: Ordered at the end of 1976.

♦ *2 Jaguar-II class* — Bldr: Lürssen, Vegesack

N . . . N . . .

D: 255 tons (fl) **S:** 40 kts **Dim:** 44.3 × 7.0 × 1.8
A: 4/anti-ship missiles — 1/76-mm DP OTO Melara
M: 4 MTU diesels; 4 props; 14,000 hp

REMARK: Ordered at the end of 1976.

GHANA

PATROL BOATS

♦ *2 Sahene class* — Bldr: Ruthoff, Mainz, Germany, 1976

P 24 SAHENE **P 25 DELA**

Dela (P 25) 1976

D: 160 tons (fl) **S:** 30 kts **Dim:** 35.2 × 6.5 × 1.8
A: 1/40-mm AA (with flare launchers attached) **Man:** 32 men
M: 2 MTU MD16V538 TB90 diesels; 2 props; 3,000 hp **Range:** 1,000/30

REMARKS: Ordered 1973; builder went bankrupt and four others not delivered. Designed for rescue and fisheries protection.

♦ *2 British Ford class* — Seaward Defense Boats

P 13 ELMINA (18-10-62) **P 14 KOMENDA** (17-5-62) Bldr: Yarrow

D: 120 tons (160 fl) **S:** 15 kts **Dim:** 35.7 × 6.2 × 2.1
A: 1/40-mm — depth charges **Man:** 19 men
M: 2 Paxman YHAXM diesels; 2 props; 1,100 hp **Fuel:** 23 tons

MINE WARFARE SHIPS

♦ *1 British "-ton"-class coastal minesweeper* — Loaned 1964, bought 1974

M 16 EJURA (ex-*Aldington*) — Bldr: Camper & Nicholson, 1955

♦ *2 British "-ham"-class inshore minesweepers* (1959)

M 11 YOGADA (ex-*Malham*) **M 12 AFADZATO** (ex-*Ottringham*)

NOTE: For characteristics, see classes in Great Britain section. "-ham" class fitted with funnel and have no magnetic sweep gear.

REPAIR SHIP

♦ **ASUANTSI** (ex-MRC-1122) — British LCT(4) class

D: 657 tons (fl) **S:** 9 kts **Dim:** 70.5 × 11.9 × 1.5

REMARKS: Landing craft converted to floating workshop. Purchased 1965.

PERSONNEL (1977-78):

	Officers	Non-officers	Total
Royal Navy	9,216	55,268	64,484
Royal Marines	620	6,939	7,559
Women's Royal Naval Service	277	2,891	3,168
Total	10,113	65,098	75,211

MERCHANT MARINE (1976): 3,549 ships — 32,923,308 grt (tankers: 513 — 16,146,592 grt)

NAVAL PROGRAM: There is no publicly announced long-range construction program. However, as of 1 October 1977, there were on order or under construction 4 nuclear-powered attack submarines, 2 small aircraft carriers, 7 guided missile destroyers, 5 guided missile frigates, 1 patrol boat, 2 minehunters, 2 fleet replenishment ships, and a number of smaller auxiliaries.

NOTE: Most British shipyards were nationalized on 30-4-77 but, since they continue to be operated as though they were separate entities, the original names are used in this book.

WARSHIPS IN SERVICE, UNDER CONSTRUCTION, OR PROJECTED AS OF 1 OCTOBER 1977

	L	Tons	Main armament
♦ *1 attack aircraft carrier*			
1 ARK ROYAL	1950	43,840	39 aircraft
1 HERMES	1953	23,900	24 aircraft
1 BULWARK	1948	23,300	20 helicopters
♦ *34 submarines*			
4 Fleet ballistic-missile			
4 RESOLUTION (nuclear)	1966-68	7,500	16 Polaris A-3, 6/533-mm TT
♦ *30 Attack*			
1 TRAFALGAR (nuclear)	...	...	...
6 SWIFTSURE (nuclear)	1971-	4,000	5/533-mm TT
5 VALIANT (nuclear)	1963-70	3,500	6/533-mm TT
1 DREADNOUGHT	1960	3,000	6/533-mm TT
17 PORPOISE/OBERON	1956-66	1,610	6/533-mm TT
♦ *5 cruisers*			
3 INVINCIBLE	1977	16,000	1 Sea Dart system, 5 Sea Harrier, 10 Sea King
2 TIGER	1945	9,550	2/152-mm DP, 2/76-mm DP, 2 Sea Cat systems, 3 helicopters
♦ *18 guided missile destroyers*			
10 SHEFFIELD	1971-	3,150	1 Sea Dart, 1/114-mm DP, 1 helicopter
1 BRISTOL	1969	6,100	1 Sea Dart system, 1 Limbo, 1 Ikara, 1/114-mm DP
7 COUNTY	1960-67	5,440	1 Sea Slug, 2 Sea Cat, 4/114-mm DP, 1 helicopter
♦ *61 frigates*			
4 B	1976-	3,500	2 Sea Wolf systems, 2/40-mm AA, 2 helicopters
8 AMAZON	1971-75	2,750	4 have Exocet, 1 Sea Cat system, 1/114-mm DP, 1 helicopter
26 LEANDER	1961-71	2,450	1 or 2 Sea Cat systems, 2/114-mm or 40-mm, 1 ASW helicopter, MM38 Exocet or Ikara in 16
7 TRIBAL	1959-62	2,300	2/114-mm DP, ASW weapons, 1 helicopter
9 ROTHESAY	1957-60	2,380	2/114-mm DP, 1 Sea Cat system, 1 helicopter
1 WHITBY	1954	2,150	2/114-mm DP, ASW weapons
2 SALISBURY	1953-59	2,170	2/114-mm DP, 1 Sea Cat system, ASW weapons
2 LEOPARD	1955-57	2,300	4/114-mm DP, 1/40-mm AA, ASW weapons
2 BLACKWOOD	1953	1,180	2/40-mm AA, ASW weapons

GREAT BRITAIN

We can no longer afford to patrol the World's sea lanes.

ROY MASON
Ministry of Defense (1975)

FORCE LEVEL BUDGET (1977-78): 133 operational ships; 28 in reserve, undergoing major overhaul, or modernization.

Type	Ships in service, about to enter service, or used for training	In reserve, major overhaul, or conversion
SSBN (Fleet Ballistic Sub.)	*Repulse, Renown, Revenge*	*Resolution*
Aircraft carriers	*Ark Royal, Hermes*	
Cruisers	*Blake, Tiger*	
Guided missile destroyers	9	2
Frigates	43	13
Fleet submarines	*Dreadnought, Conqueror, Churchill, Swiftsure, Superb, Valiant*	*Warspite, Sovereign, Courageous*
Patrol Submarines	15	3
Minesweepers/minehunters	34	4
Patrol boats	18	
Amphibious:		
Support aircraft carriers		*Bulwark*
LPD	*Fearless*	*Intrepid*

WEAPONS AND SYSTEMS

(A) MISSILES

♦ *strategic ballistic missiles*

The Royal Navy uses the U.S. Polaris A3, but the 3 non-maneuverable re-entry warheads, 200 kilo tons each, are of British design and construction.

♦ *surface-to-air missiles*

Sea Dart (GWS 30): Builder: Hawker Siddeley Dynamics
Medium range system (25 miles, interception altitudes from 100 to 60,000 ft).

Length: 4.400 m — Wingspan: 0.910 m
Diameter: 0.420 m — Weight: 550 kgs
Solid propellant then ramjet. Semi-active homing. Fitted on the *Bristol*, the *Sheffield*, and the *Invincible*. Type 909 fire control radar.
Mk 30 Mod 0 launcher on the *Bristol*, the lighter Mk 30 Mod 2 on the *Sheffield* class.

Sea Slug Mk 1 and Mk 2: Builder: Hawker Siddeley Dynamics
Short-range system (15 miles slant range, 500 to 50,000 feet).

Length: 5.940 m — Weight: 900 kg (2,000 kg with boosters)
Diameter: 0.410 m — Speed: Mach 1.8
Wingspan: 1.420 m (1.600 with fins)
Solid propulsion system with four solid boosters
Type 901, a beam-riding radar
Fitted on the *County*-class DDG

Sea Wolf (GWS 25): Builder: BAC
Short-range missile system (5,000 m)

Length: 1.900 m — Diameter: 0.300 m
Wingspan: 0.450 m — Weight: 82 kg
Radar guidance
The launcher contains 6 missiles (total weight with missiles: 3,500 kg).

Will be fitted on weapon-class frigates.

Sea Cat (GWS 20, 21 and 22): Builder: Short and Harland

Length: 1.470 m — Wingspan: 0.650 m
Diameter: 0.200 m — Weight: 68 kg
2-stage solid propellant. Launcher contains 4 missiles.
Guidance by GWS 21, GWS 22, or GWS 24, radar or GWS 20 optical system.

♦ *surface-to-surface missiles*

The Royal Navy has purchased the MM38 Exocet (see section on France) and builds it under license.

In August 1977, it was announced that the U.S. Harpoon system would be bought for use from submarines.

♦ *air-to-surface missiles*

AS 11 (see section on France) — used on helicopters on frigates

Bull Pup: Builder: Martin (U.S.A.)
Solid propellant

Length: 3.200 m — Weight: 260 kg (75 kg of explosive)
Diameter: 0.300 m — Speed: Mach 2.0
Wingspan: 0.940 m — Range: 12,000 m
Radio command, guided by sight

Skua: Builder: BAC
Solid propellant

Length: 2.830 m — Weight: 210 kg (20 kg of explosive)
Diameter: 0.200 m — Speed: . . .
Wingspan: 0.600 m — Range: 9,000 m
Guidance: semi-active

Martel: Builder: Matra and Hawker Siddeley Dynamics
See section on France. The Royal Navy uses the television-guided version.

♦ *air-to-air missiles*

Firestreak: Builder: Hawker Siddeley Dynamics.

Length: 3.200 m — Weight: 136 kg
Diameter: 0.930 m — Speed: Mach 2
Wingspan: 0.750 m — Range: 6,000 m
Infrared guidance

Red Top: Builder: Hawker Siddeley Dynamics.

Length: 3.500 m — Speed: Mach 3
Wingspan: 0.910 m — Range: 10,000 m
Infrared guidance

The Royal Navy used U.S. Sparrow and Sidewinder missiles (see U.S.A. section).

(B) GUNS

114 Mk 5
Single barrel, semi-automatic, deck-installed, hand-loaded.

Maximum effective range in surface fire: 11,000 m
Maximum effective range in anti-aircraft fire: 5,000 m
Rate of fire: 8/10 rounds/minute.

Fitted on the *Tribal*-class frigates.

114 Mk 6
Double-barreled, semi-automatic, triple-purpose (air, surface, and land targets)

Muzzle velocity: 850 m/sec
Maximum effective range in surface fire: 13,000 m
Maximum effective range in anti-aircraft fire: 6,000 m
Rate of fire: 10/12 rounds/minute per barrel.

114 Mk 8
Single-barreled, automatic, triple-purpose (air, surface, and land targets); muzzle brake

Length of barrel: 55 calibers
Maximum effective range in surface fire: 13,000 m

WEAPONS AND SYSTEMS (*continued*)

Maximum effective range in anti-aircraft fire: 6,000 m
Rate of fire: 25 rounds/minute.
Arc of elevation: $-10° +53°$
Light gun mount in synthetic resin reinforced with fiberglass.
Installed on the *Bristol*, *Sheffield*-class destroyers, and *Amazon*-class frigates.

152 Mk 26
Twin-barreled automatic, triple-purpose (air, surface, and land targets)
Length of tube: 50 calibers
Muzzle velocity: 800 m/sec
Maximum effective range in surface fire: 15,000 m
Maximum effective range in anti-aircraft fire: 8,000 m
Rate of fire: 25 rounds/min
Turret weight: 156 tons
Fitted in the cruisers *Blake* and *Tiger*. Fire control MRS 3.

76 Mk . . .
Twin-barreled automatic anti-aircraft
Length of tube: 70 calibers
Muzzle velocity: 1,400 m/sec
Maximum effective range in surface fire: 5,000 m
Rate of fire: 120 rounds/min/barrel.
Fitted in the cruisers *Blake* and *Tiger*.

Bofors 40-mm
70-caliber equipment is used on single mounts; all twin mounts have now been discarded (except on the *Bulwark*, which is in reserve)

Oerlikon 20-mm
Standard 80-caliber single mountings are used in many classes

(C) ANTISUBMARINE WEAPONS

Mk 10 Mortar (Limbo)
Triple-barreled mortar based on the Squid of World War II. Range: 700 to 1,000 m.

Ikara
Mk 44 or Mk 46 torpedo in a glider launched by a solid-fuel rocket motor. Maximum range: 18,000 m. Fitted on the *Bristol* and seven *Leander*-class frigates.

(D) TORPEDOES

U.S. Mk 44 and Mk 46 ASW torpedoes
The principal torpedoes of British origin are:
the wire-guided, submarine-launched ASW Mk 23
the wire-guided Mk 24 Tigerfish (ex-Ongar). This torpedo is designed for use by nuclear attack submarines.
a new torpedo designated NST 75 11 is scheduled to enter service in 1980

(E) SONARS

On surface ships:

No.	Type	Frequency band	Average range (above layer)
170B	Hull	High	2,500 m
174	Hull	High	2,500 m
177	Hull, 360° scan	Medium	6,000 m
184	Hull, 360° scan	Medium	7,000 m
199	Towed	Medium	7,000 m
2016	Hull, 360° scan	Multiple	. . .

REMARKS: **199** is the British version of the Canadian SQS 504. Most VDS have been removed from *Leander*- and *Tribal*-class frigates (Ikara *Leander*s retain them), the reason being given that the equipment is not needed in the normal Eastern Atlantic operating area for RN ships. But the real reason is insufficient mastery of VDS employment techniques, plus a preference for development of a towed passive linear array like the U.S. Tass.

On submarines:

186	Passive	Low	
187	Active-Passive	Low-Medium	
2001	Active-Passive	Low	
2007	Passive	Low-Medium	

On helicopters:

195	Dipping	Medium	3,000 m

(F) DATA SYSTEMS

The data systems outlined below are either in service or will soon enter service:

ADA (Action Data Automation)
ADA WS 1 Aerial defense system. Fitted on County-class destroyers.
ADA WS 2 Integrated AAW and ASW defense system. Fitted on the *Bristol*.
ADA WS 4 Integrated AAW and ASW defense system. Fitted on the *Sheffield*-class destroyers.
ADA WS 5 Aerial and ASW defense. Fitted on the *Invincible*-class support aircraft carriers.

CAAIS (Computer Assisted Action Information System)
In *Amazon*-class frigates for tactical data-handling — linked to WSA 4 fire control system.

(G) RADARS

Navigation

975 (3 cm, I band)
978 (3 cm, I band)
1002 (9,650 MHz) — for *Porpoise*-class submarines
1006 (9,445 MHz) — in newest surface ships

Air-search

965 Metric radar (long-range)
965M The **M** is composed of 2/965 antennas, one placed on top of the other with the Mk 10 IFF interrogator built in

WEAPONS AND SYSTEMS *(continued)*

966 **STIR (Surveillance Target Indicator Radar)** is new radar designed for the *Invincible* and can operate in a strong electronic countermeasures environment

Surface-to-air, low-altitude search (combination):

992, 992 Q, and **993** (E-F bands)

967 } Pulse doppler: combination of radar bands H, G, and I, found in the Sea Wolf
968 } system (GWS 25)

Height-finding

277 and **982** (E-F bands)
278 and **983** (E-F bands)

Gun-direction

275 (F band), **903** (I band) built into the MRS 3 fire-control radar. **275** is used in the older FC system for Mk 6 twin 114-mm gun mounts in the *Whitby, Leopard,* and *Salisbury* frigates; **903** is used in all other Mk 6 and Mk 5 114-mm directors (MRS 3), as well as with the 152-mm and 76.2-mm guns on the *Tiger*-class cruisers

Missile-guidance

901 Sea Slug system (I band)
903 MRS 3 and GWS 22 fire control for the Sea Cat
909 Sea Dart system (also 114-mm Mk 8 gun in the *Sheffield*-class destroyers)
910 Tracking radar used with the Sea Wolf (GWS 25) system
RTN-10X used for Sea Cat and 114-mm control in *Amazon*-class frigates

Ark Royal (R 09) Terzibaschitsch, 1977

Ark Royal (R 09) Terzibaschitsch, 1977

(H) COUNTERMEASURES

A launched decoy system (chaff) called Knebworth/Corvus is used on major combat units. All ships so equipped have 2 eight-tubed launchers, except the *Ark Royal,* which has 4 six-tubed launchers

AIR IDENTIFICATION

British carriers use the following deck letters for identification from the air:
R Ark Royal **B Bulwark** **H Hermes**

3 AIRCRAFT CARRIERS

	Bldr	Laid down	L	In serv.
R 09 ARK ROYAL	Cammell Laird	5-43	3-5-50	2-55

D: 43,840 tons (53,840 fl)
Dim: 263.50 (overall), 257.6 (flight deck), 244.68 (wl), 219.45 (pp) × 50.12 (flight deck), 34.40 (wl) × 11 (fl)
S: 31/30 kts **A:** None
Aircraft: 12 Phantom FG-1, 14 Buccaneer S-2, 4 Gannet, 7 Sea King, 1 Wessex
Armor: Flight deck and belt: 203 mm max
Electron Equipt: Radars: 2/965M, 1/993, 1/978, 1/983, 1/982 — 4 Corvus chaff launchers. The radar used for carrier-controlled landing of aircraft is covered by a radar dome.
Man: 1,745, with the flying squadrons embarked; quarters available for 2,750.
M: Parsons GT; 4 props; 152,000 hp
Boilers: 8 Admiralty at 28 kg/cm²; superheat to 385°C
Electric: 8,250 kw **Fuel:** 5,500 tons

REMARKS: Flight-deck angle 8.5°. Hull 90 per cent welded. Air-conditioned. Was modernized between 1967 and 1970 but, owing to rigorous budget cuts, this

AIRCRAFT CARRIERS (*continued*)

Ark Royal (R 09) with USN F4 and A7 aircraft aboard 1975

modernization was limited to strict necessities, although it provided for the landing and take-off of Phantom and Buccaneer aircraft:

waist catapult able to launch the largest aircraft without wind across the deck;
arresting gear capable of receiving the largest aircraft with just 25 knots of wind on deck.

Has no air defense weapons or modern radars. Nevertheless, with her present air group of Phantoms and Buccaneers, the *Ark Royal* is the most powerful surface ship of the West European navies. She will be withdrawn from service in 1979.

The aircraft carrier *Eagle* (1946, 44,100 tons) was stricken in 1972; her stripped hull is retained at Devonport.

	Bldr	Laid down	L	In serv.
R 12 HERMES	Vickers, Barrow	6-44	16-2-53	11-59

Hermes (R 12) Terzibaschitsch, 1977

D: 23,900 tons (28,700 fl) **Dim:** 226.85 (198.12 pp) × 27.43 (wl) × 8.80
S: 28 kts **A:** 2 Sea Cat systems (IV × 2) — up to 24 helicopters
Electron Equipt: Radars: 1/965, 1/978, 1/993, 2/GWS 22 FC — TACAN
M: Parsons GT; 2 props; 83,000 hp **Boilers:** 4 Admiralty
Fuel: 3,860 tons **Electric:** 5,400 kw **Man:** 980 men

REMARKS: Converted 1971-73 by the Devonport Naval Dockyard into a helicopter-carrying commando carrier (LPH). Converted again 1976/1-77 as an ASW carrier for Sea King, and Wessex helicopters and, by 1980, will be converted for operational employment of the first of some 24 Sea Harrier V/STOL strike aircraft now on order. She will apparently continue in service well into the 1980s as an interim version of the *Invincible* class. *Hermes* retains the ability to embark a commando group (750 men) and continues to carry 4 LCVP in davits. Catapults and arresting gear removed 1971. Flight deck angled 6.5° and strengthened for Harriers.

Hermes (R 12) 1977

Hermes (R 12) 1977

AIRCRAFT CARRIERS (*continued*)

	Bldr	Laid down	L	In serv.
R 08 BULWARK	Harland & Wolff	5-45	22-6-48	10-54

D: 23,300 tons (27,705 fl) **S:** 28 kts
Dim: 224.9 (198.12 pp) × 37.49 × 27 (wl) × 8.5
A: 8/40-mm AA (II × 4) — 20 Wessex Mk-5 helicopters
Electron Equipt: Radars: 1/983, 1/993, 1/978
Man: 980 men + one Royal Marine commando (battalion)
Armor: Flight deck: 50 mm — Watertight bulkheads on each side below the waterline: 25 mm
M: Parsons GT; 2 props; 83,000 hp **Boilers:** 4 Admiralty
Electric: 3,200 kw

Bulwark (R 08) J. C. Bellonne, 1972

REMARKS: Converted in 1959-60 to commando carrier. She was reduced to reserve in 4-1976 but is to remain in ready-reserve with a caretaker crew in order to act as an ASW support and/or commando carrier until the *Illustrious* (CAH 2) completes in the early 1980s. She is equipped to handle Harrier V/STOL strike aircraft as well as Wessex helicopters. Two centerline elevators. The commando (750 men) can be put ashore by helicopter or by 4 LCVP landing craft, which are hung in davits aft, two on each side. For short distances, two commandos can be carried. Living quarters air-conditioned. Sisters *Albion* and *Centaur* stricken in 1972.

NAVAL AVIATION

Ship-based aviation, the Fleet Air Arm, is the only air component in the Royal Navy.

Except at the level of formation commanders, there is no naval air command. Land-based ASW aircraft belong to the RAF and, since the reorganization of the latter, have constituted the Eighteenth, or Maritime, Group of Strike Command. While the group is part of the RAF as regards personnel and equipment, its employment is determined by the Royal Navy.

The Fleet Air Arm consists of:

— first-line squadrons (designation characterized by a group of three figures beginning with an 8) whose missions are: all-weather interception and attack, ASW, electronic warfare, and helicopter assault. Altogether some 150 aircraft.

— second-line squadrons (designation characterized by a group of three figures beginning with a 7) that are used in schools, tests, and maintenance. Altogether some 150 aircraft.

Phantom FG1 (Interception)

Nimrod (Maritime Group of the RAF) 1970

The total of operational aircraft available to the Royal Navy includes 12 Phantom FG-1, 14 Buccaneer S-2, and 8 Gannet-30 fixed-wing planes, plus 30 Sea King, 7 Wessex Mk-3, and 40 Wasp ASW helicopters, and about 20 Wessex Mk-5 troop-carrying helicopters. For short-based training and other duties, Sea King, Wessex MK-3, Wasp, and Gazelle helicopters are available, as well as Sea Prince, Canberra, and Hunter fixed-wing aircraft. As of 1-10-77, 13 Sea King, 30 Lynx, 6 Gazelle, and 24 Sea Harrier were on order.

BASES

Fleet Air Arm bases are given ships' names. The Royal Navy now mans only helicopter bases. They are:

RNAS, Yeovilton (HMS Heron)
RNAS, Culdrose (HMS Sea Hawk)
RNAS, Prestwick (HMS Gannet)
RNAS, Lee-on-Solent (HMS Daedalus)
RNAS, Portland (HMS Osprey)

Fixed-wing aircraft that are not ship-based are stationed at RAF bases at Honington, Leuchars, and Lossiemouth.

COMBAT AIRCRAFT

Type and builder	Mission	Wingspan	Length	Height	Weight	Engine	Max. speed in mach or in knots	Practical maximum ceiling in feet	Range	Weapons	Remarks
FIXED-WING											
PHANTOM II (FG-1K) (McDonnell) 2-man	All-weather attack, interception	11.70 8.36 wings folded	17.75	4.96	24,700	2 Rolls-Royce Spey 25 R engines with 5,670 kg of thrust each, 9,640 with afterburners	Mach 2	70,000	780 miles (interception) 870 miles (troop support)	Sparrow, Sidewinder, Martel, Bull Pup	On board the *Ark Royal.*
BUCCANEER S-2 (Bristol Siddeley)	Attack	13.41 6.10 wings folded	19.32	5.05 wings folded	28,000	2 Rolls-Royce RB 168 turbofans with 5,105 kg of thrust each	Mach 0.85	45,000	900 miles	4/1,000-lb bombs, or 4/Martel	Can carry a tactical nuclear bomb. On board the *Ark Royal.*
SEA HARRIER (Hawker Siddeley)	Attack	7.60	14.10	3.35	10,500	1 Rolls-Royce Pegasus turbojet with 9,750 kg of thrust	Mach 0.96 Mach 1.2 (diving)	50,000	VTOL: 50 miles STOL: 250 miles	2,270 kg	For the *Invincible* class and *Hermes.* The Sea Harrier plane will have a more corrosion resistant Pegasus 104 engine in place of the 103 which is used by RAF aircraft. In defense missions the Sea Harrier will have air-to-air missiles and Aden guns.
NIMROD (Hawker Siddeley)	ASW detection and engagement	35.10	38.03	9	79,000	4 Rolls-Royce Spey (RB 168-20) Mk 250 jet engines, 5,200 hp thrust each	450 kts	40,000	11 hours	Bomb bay for 15-m weapons (6 torpedoes + 10 buoys) 2 Martel or 4 AS 12	Can carry nuclear depth charges.
GANNET-30 (Westland)	Electronic warfare	16.56	13.57	4.19	9,800	1 Bristol-Siddeley turboprop	275 kts	25,000	840 miles	None	Also used for air early warning and utility transports on *Ark Royal.*
HELICOPTERS											
WASP (Westland)	ASW, anti-surface	Rotor diam. 9.82	12.23	3.27	1,370	1 Blackburn Nimbus 102 turboshaft, 1,050 hp	109 kts 96 kts (cruising)	12,000		1 Mk 44 torpedo or 2 AS 11	On board the *Tribal, Whitby; Rothesay,* and *Leander* frigate classes.
LYNX WG-13 (Westland)	ASW, anti-surface	12.80	15.20	3.20	4,150	2 Rolls-Royce BS 360 turboshafts, 900 hp each	150 kts	12,000	1 hr, 30 min., (half hovering, half cruising)	2 Mk 44 or Mk 46 torpedoes Skua air-surface missiles	Franco-British helicopter. Will be on board the *Sheffield*-class guided missile destroyers and the type *Amazon* and weapon-class frigates. Anti-surface version has priority.
WESSEX Mk-3 Mk-5 (Westland)	ASW transport assault	17.06	20.05	4.82	5,700	1 Napier Gazelle 161 NGA 13 turboshaft with 1,650 hp (Mk 3). 2 linked Bristol-Siddeley Gnome H 1400 turbo-shafts with 1,400 hp each (Mk 5)	120 kts	6,000 hovering 14,000 cruising	3 hours	2 Mk 44 or 46 torpedoes or 4 depth charges. Sonar	On board the *County*-class destroyers, *Ark Royal,* and *Hermes.*
SEA KING (Westland)	ASW	19	22		9,300	2 Rolls-Royce Gnome H turboshafts, 1,500 hp each driving a 5-bladed rotor and a tail rotor	124 kts	10,000	3 hr. 15 min.	4 Mk 44 torpedoes or 4 depth charges. Sonar, radar	US SH3D Sikorsky, built under license. On board the *Ark Royal, Hermes* and to be on *Invincible.*

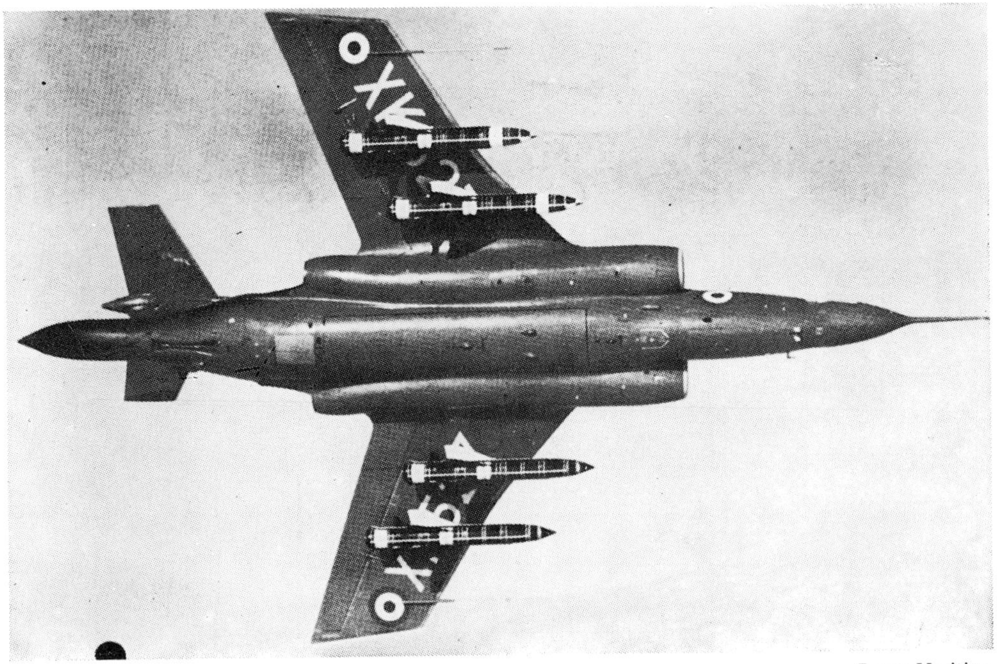

Buccaneer S-Z (Assault) Revue Maritime

Westland Lynx WG 13 France/British 1975

Westland Wessex Mk 3 1972

NAVAL AVIATION (*continued*)

Westland Sea King 1972

Buccaneer S-2 1972

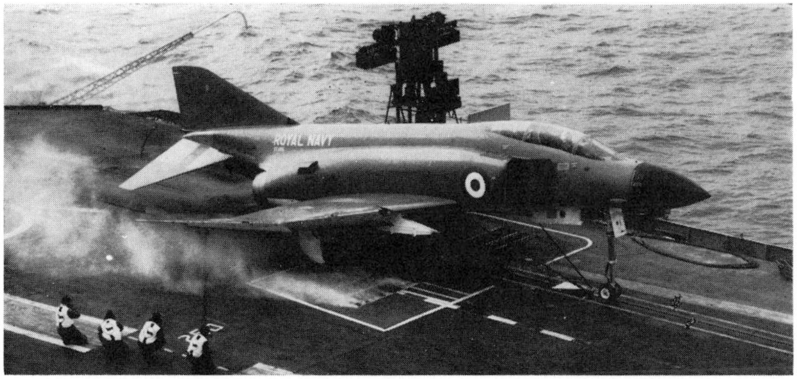

Phantom II F 4 K 1971

DESIGNATION OF AIRCRAFT

Classes of aircraft are, in general, designated by a conventional name (Phantom, etc.) followed by two designators of the version (Mk — for Mark — 1, 2, etc. and Mod — for Modified). To specify the exact missions of an aircraft with special modifications or weapon suits, an indicator is inserted into the designation of the series.

Note: Royal Navy submarines no longer wear hull numbers. The assigned numbers are included here for reference only.

BALLISTIC MISSILE SUBMARINES

♦ *4 Resolution-class*

	Bldr	Laid down	L	In serv.
S 22 RESOLUTION	Vickers-Armstrong	26-2-64	15-9-66	10-67
S 23 REPULSE	Vickers-Armstrong	12-3-65	4-11-6	7-69
S 26 RENOWN	Cammell Laird	25-6-64	25-2-67	2-69
S 27 REVENGE	Cammell Laird	19-5-65	15-3-68	7-6

Resolution (S 22) Vickers

D: 7,500 tons surfaced, 8,100 submerged) **S:** 25/20 kts
Dim: 129.54 × 10.05 × 9.15 **Man:** 13 officers, 130 men
A: 16 Polaris A3 — 6/533-mm TT
Electron Equipt: Sonars: 2001, 2007
M: 1 Rolls-Royce pressurized-water reactor; 1 English-Electric turbine; 1 prop

BALLISTIC MISSILE SUBMARINES (*continued*)

Renown (S 22) 1968

REMARKS: Characteristics are very similar to those of the U.S. *Lafayette* class, including the propulsion machinery, the launching and guidance systems, and the inertial navigation. The A3 missiles with 3 MRV warheads of 200 kilotons each were furnished by the U.S., but the re-entry vehicles are of British conception and construction. Substitution of the Polaris A3 by the Poseidon or the Trident I is no longer being considered.

NUCLEAR-PROPELLED ATTACK SUBMARINES

♦ *1 Trafalgar class* — Ordered 1977 — Bldr: Vickers, Barrow

S 113 TRAFALGAR

REMARKS: No details available; will be an enlarged and improved *Swiftsure*.

♦ *6 Swiftsure class* — Bldr: Vickers, Barrow

	Laid down	L	In serv.
S 107 SWIFTSURE	6-6-69	7-9-71	17-4-73
S 108 SOVEREIGN	18-9-70	22-2-73	22-7-74
S 109 SUPERB	16-3-72	30-11-74	13-11-76
S 110 SCEPTRE	25-10-73	20-11-76	1978
S 111 SPARTAN	-74	...	...
S 112 SPLENDID (ex-*Severn*)	-76	...	...

D: 4,000 tons light, 4,200 surfaced, 4,500 submerged
Dim: 82.90 × 10.12 × 8.2 **S:** 28/30 kts
A: 5/533-mm bow TT (20 torpedoes)
Electron Equipt: Radar: 1003 — Sonars: 2001, 2007, 197, 183
M: 1 reactor; 1 turbine; 1 prop; 20,000 hp

REMARKS: High-performance, very quiet submarines. Carry the wire-guided Mk 24 Tigerfish torpedo. Will carry the U.S. Sub-Harpoon missile. Intended for ASW defense of surface forces.

Revenge (S 27) 1976

NUCLEAR-PROPELLED ATTACK SUBMARINES (*continued*)

Superb (S 109) 1976

Sovereign (S 108) 1975

♦ *5 Valiant class*

	Bldr	Laid down	L	In serv.
S 102 VALIANT	Vickers, Barrow	22-1-62	3-12-63	7-66
S 103 WARSPITE	Vickers, Barrow	12-63	25-9-65	4-67
S 104 CHURCHILL	Vickers, Barrow	6-67	20-12-68	7-70
S 105 CONQUEROR	Cammell Laird	12-67	29-8-69	11-71
S 106 COURAGEOUS (ex-*Superb*)	Vickers, Barrow	10-68	7-3-70	10-71

Valiant (S 102) 1974

NUCLEAR-PROPELLED ATTACK SUBMARINES (*continued*)

D: 3,500 tons standard, 4,000 surfaced, 4,500 submerged
Dim: 86.87 × 10.12 × 8.25 **S:** 25/20 kts **Man:** 13 officers, 90 men
A: 6/533-mm TT fwd (26 torpedoes)
Electron Equipt: Radar: 1003 — Sonars: 2001, 2007, 197, 183
M: 1 pressurized-water reactor; English-Electric GT; 1 prop; 20,000 hp

REMARKS: The propulsion plant of the *Valiant* and the *Warspite* (20,000 hp) is of entirely British design and construction (Admiralty, Vickers, Rolls-Royce, and English-Electric). The hull form of this class is a development of the *Dreadnought*. In 1967 the *Valiant* made a nonstop, submerged cruise from Singapore to Great Britain in 28 days (12,000 miles).

Churchill (S 104) 1970

Courageous (S 106) 1972

♦ *1 Dreadnought class*

	Bldr	Laid down	L	In serv.
S 101 DREADNOUGHT	Vickers, Barrow	12-6-59	21-10-60	4-63

D: 3,000 tons standard, 3,500 surfaced, 4,000 submerged
Dim: 81.08 × 9.75 × 7.80
S: 25/15 kts **A:** 6/533-mm TT fwd **Man:** 11 officers, 77 men
Electron Equipt: Radar: 1003 — Sonars: 2001/2007, 197, 183
M: 1 U.S./S5W reactor; GT; 1 prop

REMARKS: Authorized in 1956. The first Admiralty studies for the ship were entrusted to the nuclear branch of the Vickers Company, including Rolls-Royce for the reactor, Foster-Wheeler for the heat exchanger, and Vickers for the turbines.

Dreadnought (S 101)

NUCLEAR-PROPELLED ATTACK SUBMARINES *(continued)*

Finally, however, a Westinghouse S5W engine, furnished by the U.S. (1958), was adopted. The hull shape is similar to the U.S. nuclear submarine *Skipjack* except for the forward one-third. Endurance: 70 days. During major overhaul from 5-68 to 9-70, the core was renewed. Later in 1970 the ship made a cruise under the North Pole.

TORPEDO ATTACK SUBMARINES

♦ *4 Porpoise class*

	Bldr	Laid down	L	In serv.
S 01 PORPOISE	Vickers-Armstrong	6-54	25-4-56	4-58
S 05 FINWHALE	Cammell Laird	9-56	21-7-59	8-60
S 07 SEALION	Cammell Laird	6-58	31-12-59	7-61
S 08 WALRUS	Scott's SB, Greenock	2-53	22-9-59	2-61

♦ *13 Oberon class*

	Bldr	Laid down	L	In serv.
S 09 OBERON	HM Dockyard, Chatham	11-57	18-7-59	2-61
S 10 ODIN	Cammell Laird	3-59	4-11-60	5-62
S 11 ORPHEUS	Vickers-Armstrong	4-59	17-11-59	11-60
S 12 OLYMPUS	Vickers-Armstrong	3-60	14-6-61	7-62
S 13 OSIRIS	Vickers-Armstrong	1-62	20-11-62	1-64
S 14 ONSLAUGHT	HM Dockyard, Chatham	4-59	24-9-60	8-62
S 15 OTTER	Scott's SB, Greenock	1-60	15-5-61	8-62
S 16 ORACLE	Cammell Laird	4-60	26-9-61	2-63
S 17 OCELOT	HM Dockyard, Chatham	11-60	5-5-62	8-63
S 18 OTUS	Scott's SB, Greenock	5-61	17-10-62	10-63
S 19 OPOSSUM	Cammell Laird	12-61	23-5-63	6-64
S 20 OPPORTUNE	Scott's SB, Greenock	10-62	14-2-64	12-64
S 21 ONYX	Cammell Laird	11-64	16-8-66	11-67

Onslaught (S 14) G. Arra, 1976

D: 1,610 tons, 2,030 surfaced, 2,400 submerged
Dim: 89.92 (87.45 pp) × 8.07 × 5.48 **S:** 17.5/15 kts
Man: 6 officers, 65 men (62 beginning with the S-09, 57 in the S-19, S-20, S-21)
A: 6/533-mm TT fwd, 2 aft (22 torpedoes)
Electron Equipt: Sonars: 186, 187
M: Diesel-electric propulsion surfaced; Admiralty Standard Range I 16-cyl. diesel engines; 3,700/6,000 hp

Remarks: Conventional propulsion and hull form. Streamlined sail. Maximum depth: 200 m. Snorkel. Air-conditioned. Excellent living spaces. Long endurance. Plastics used throughout in the design of the superstructure of the second series (*Oberon, Odin, Onslaught,* for example) as well as light alloys (*Orpheus*). *Onyx* transferred to Canada (1-64) and renamed the *Ojibwa;* another ship was built and given the same name. Canada ordered 3 more ships of this class, Australia 6, Chile 2, and Brazil 3. The *Porpoise* is used as a submarine target. The *Grampus* (S-04) of the same class was stricken in 1976, the *Rorqual* (S-02) was stricken in 1976, and the *Narwhal* (S-03) in 1977.

Sea Lion (S 07) G. Arra

Sea Lion G. Arra

Note: In 1974 it was said that the Royal Navy would resume building conventional diesel-engine submarines, but this project does not yet seem to have been followed up.

TORPEDO ATTACK SUBMARINES (*continued*)

NOTE: The four MM38 Exocet launchers are still present to starboard on the forecastle in this view; they were subsequently deleted from the armament scheme, although "cut-out" in the flight deck remains, denying valuable deck park space for aircraft. The Sea Dart launcher on the ship's centerline protrudes into the aircraft flight space and is an obvious hazard.

ANTISUBMARINE CRUISERS

♦ *3 Invincible class* (designated for the moment an "antisubmarine cruiser," formerly "through-deck cruiser")

	Bldr	Laid down	L	In serv.
CAH 1 INVINCIBLE	Vickers, Barrow	20-7-73	3-5-77	1980-81
CAH 2 ILLUSTRIOUS	Swan Hunter	1976	. . .	. . .
CAH 3 INDOMITABLE	. . .	. . .	. . .	. . .

Invincible (at launching) 1977

D: 16,000 tons (19,500 fl) **S:** 28 kts
Dim: 206.60 (loa) × 192.87 (wl) × 31.89 (max.) × 27.50 (wl) × 6.40 (avg)
A: 1/Sea Dart system — **Aircraft:** 5 Sea Harrier, 10 Sea King
Electron Equipt: Radars: 1/965M, 1/992, 2/209, 1/1006 — ADA WS 5 — 2 Knebworth/Corvus
Sonars: 1/184
M: 4 Rolls-Royce Olympus TM3 B gas turbines, each 23,500 hp; 2 controllable-pitch props
Electric: 9,000 kw **Range:** 5,000/18
Man: 900 men — living spaces for 1,000 men (plus air crew)

REMARKS: Flight deck of about 180/190 meters long with a 4° to 5° angle, 170 × 13 meters. Three hangar bays on the same level, hangars 1 and 3 practically as wide as the hull, but the central hangar is narrower because of the gas turbine exhausts to starboard and a workshop to port. Two elevators, one forward of the middle hangar bay midships, the other on the port side forward of the after hangar bay. The 965M air-search radar will eventually be replaced by a 966 STIR. A contract to build the *Illustrious* was announced on 14-5-76. The intention of the government to order a third ship of this class (reportedly to be named *Indomitable*) was officially confirmed on 15-5-75, but no order for the ship, CAH 3, has yet been announced.

CRUISERS

♦ *2 Tiger class*

	Bldr	Laid down	L	In serv.
C 99 BLAKE (ex-*Tiger*)	J. Brown, Clydebank	1-42	20-12-45	3-61
C 20 TIGER (ex-*Bellerophon*)	Fairfield SB, Govan	6-43	25-10-45	3-59

D: 9,550 tons (12,100 fl) **Dim:** 172.8 (164 pp) × 19.5 × 7.0
S: 31.5 kts (29.5 cruising) **Man:** 85 officers, 800 men
A: 2/152-mm DP (II × 1) — 2/76-mm DP (II × 1) — 2 Sea Cat systems (IV × 2) — 3 Sea King ASW helicopters
Electron Equipt: Radars: 1/965, 1/992Q, 1/978, 1/278, 4/903
Armor: Belt: 90 Conning tower: 100 Deck: 52 Turrets: 26/52
M: Parsons GT; 4 props; 72,500 hp **Electric:** 4,000 kw
Boilers: 4 Admiralty 28.5 kg/cm² pressure; superheat to 355°C
Range: 2,100/29, 4,000/20, 6,500/13 **Fuel:** 1,850 tons

REMARKS: Survivors of a series of eight cruisers of the *Swiftsure* class laid down during World War II. Converted into helicopter cruisers, the *Blake* from 1965 to 1968, and the *Tiger* from 1969 to 1972. The after 152-mm and 76-mm gun mounts were replaced by a hangar and a flight deck. The port and starboard 76-mm gun mounts were replaced by two Sea Cat launchers. The conversion of the cruiser *Lion* was canceled and the ship was stricken.

Blake (C 99) G. Arra, 1976

Blake (C 99) 1974

Bristol (D 23) British Crown Copyright, 1972

Blake (C 99) 1974

GUIDED MISSILE DESTROYERS

NOTE: The prototype, *Sheffield* (shown in the drawing), had an experimental funnel design with the uptakes bent sideways in a form referred to as "Loxton Bends." This feature was intended to keep the exhaust gases away from the after paft of the ship, but it was found to be unnecessary, and the remainder of the class have reverted to a normal configuration. In D-86 and later units, the Mk 32 torpedo tubes are on the deckhouse at the base of the after mast.

♦ *10 Sheffield class (Type 42)*

		Bldr	Laid down	L	In serv.
D 80	**SHEFFIELD**	Vickers, Barrow	1-70	10-6-71	16-2-75
D 86	**BIRMINGHAM**	Cammell Laird	3-72	30-7-73	3-12-76
D 118	**COVENTRY**	Cammell Laird	3-73	21-6-74	1978
D 108	**CARDIFF**	Vickers, Barrow	11-72	22-2-74	1978
D 87	**NEWCASTLE**	Swan Hunter	2-73	24-4-75	1978
D 88	**GLASGOW**	Swan Hunter	3-74	14-4-76	1978
D . . .	**EXETER**	Swan Hunter	5-76	. . .	. . .
D . . .	**SOUTHAMPTON**	Vosper Thornycroft	10-76	. . .	. . .
D . . .	**N . . .**	Vosper Thornycroft	. . .	. . .	. . .
D . . .	**N . . .**	Cammell Laird	. . .	. . .	. . .

Birmingham (D 86) 1976

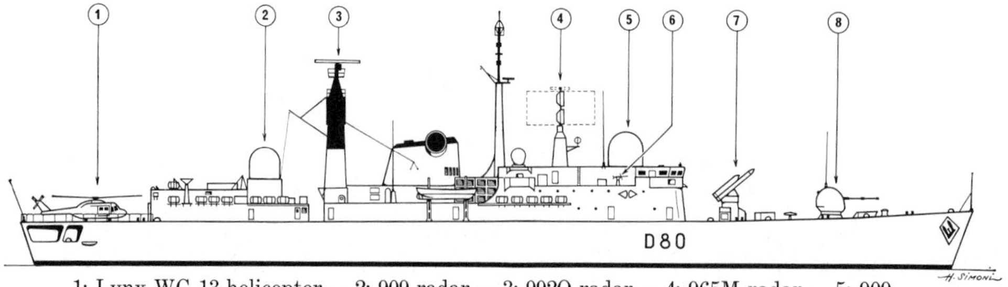

Scale 1/1000

1: Lynx WG 13 helicopter — 2: 909 radar — 3: 992Q radar — 4: 965M radar — 5: 909 radar — 6: 20-mm AA — 7: Sea Dart launcher — 8: 114-mm AA mount Mk 8

GUIDED MISSILE DESTROYERS *(continued)*

Sheffield (D 80) 1975

Birmingham (D 86) 1976

GUIDED MISSILE DESTROYERS *(continued)*

D: 3,150 tons (4,100 fl) **Dim:** 125.0 (119.50 pp) × 14.34 × 5.0
S: 28 kts (18 cruising) **Man:** 299 men
A: 1/114-mm Mk 8 DP — 2/20-mm AA — 1 Sea Dart GWS 30 (II × 1) (20 missiles) — 1 Lynx WG 13 ASW and anti-surface helicopter — 6 MK 32 ASW TT (III × 2) (not in D-80)
Electron Equipt: Radars: 1/965M, 1/992Q, 2/909, 1/1006 — ADA WS 4 — 2 Knebworth/Corvus
Sonars: 1/184, 1/174, 1/170B, 1/162
M: COGOG propulsion; 2 Olympus TM3B gas turbines × 27,200 hp for high speed; 2 Tyne RM1A gas turbines × 4,100 hp for cruising; 2 five-bladed controllable-pitch props
Range: 650/30, 4,500/18 **Electric:** 4,000 kw

REMARKS: First ordered 11-68. The cruising and high-speed turbines are not linked to each other; each shaft must be driven by one or the other. Mk 30 Mod 2 launcher for the Sea Dart system. The *Sheffield* does not have any ASW torpedo tubes; later units do. The *Cardiff,* delayed by labor problems, is being completed by Swan Hunter. Completion of the *Glasgow* delayed by fire 9-76. Ninth unit ordered on 1-3-77, tenth on 27-5-77; more are contemplated. All will receive two Scot radomes for Skynet satellite communications system.

♦ *1 Type 82*

	Bldr	Laid down	L	In serv.
D 23 BRISTOL	Associated Shipbuilders, Wallsend-on-Tyne	15-11-67	30-6-69	3-73

D: 6,100 tons (7,100 fl) **Dim:** 154.60 (149.90 wl) × 16.77 × 7.0
S: 28 kts **Man:** 29 officers, 378 men
A: 1 Sea Dart system (II × 1) (40 missiles) — 1/114-mm Mk 8 DP — 1 Mk 10 Limbo ASW mortar — 1 Ikara ASW system (32 missiles)
Electron Equipt: Radars: 1/965M, 1/992Q, 1/978, 2/909, 1/1006 — ADA WS 2
Sonars: 1/162, 1/170, 1/182, 1/184, 1/185, 1/189
M: COSAG propulsion; 2 props. On each shaft, 1 A.E.I. GT (15,000 hp) and 1 Rolls-Royce Olympus TMIA gas turbine (22,300 hp): 74,600 hp total
Boilers: 2 **Electric:** 7,000 kw **Range:** 5,000/18

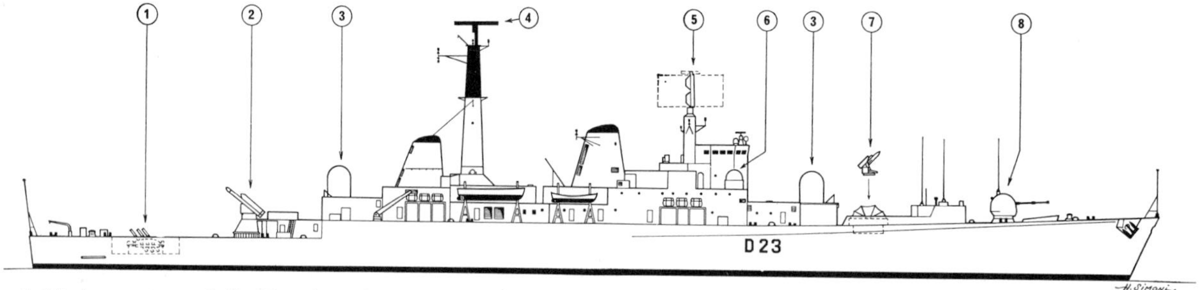

Scale 1/1000

1: Limbo mortar — 2: Sea Dart launcher — 3: 909 radar — 4: 992Q radar — 5: 965M radar — 6: Ikara fire-control radar — 7: Ikara — 8: 114-mm DP Mk 8

Bristol (D 23) J. C. Bellonne

GUIDED MISSILE DESTROYERS (*continued*)

REMARKS: Designed as an escort for the 50,000-ton aircraft carrier *Furious* when construction of the latter was being considered. There were to be eight in the class, but this ship, ordered in 10-66, is the only one built. Stabilizers and air-conditioning. The Sea Dart launcher is Mk 3 Mod 0. Storage areas aft, where missiles are stowed in a vertical position, are two-decks deep. Although nominally "commissioned" in 1973, she had not been accepted for active service by the time of her first refit in 1976-77. Unlike fully operational units, she carries no electronic warfare equipment and no chaff rocket launchers. Generally considered an expensive failure.

Bristol (D 23) J. C. Bellonne, 1974

♦ *7 County class*

Authorized: 2 in 1955-56, 2 in 1956-57, 2 in 1961-62, 2 in 1964-65, 2 in 1965-66

		Bldr	Laid down	L	In serv.
(*a*)	**D 02 DEVONSHIRE**	Cammell Laird	3-59	10-6-60	11-62
	D 12 KENT	Harland & Wolff	3-60	27-9-61	8-63
	D 16 LONDON	Swan Hunter	2-60	7-12-61	11-63
(*b*)	**D 19 GLAMORGAN**	Fairfield SB&E	5-62	9-7-64	10-66
	D 18 ANTRIM	Fairfield SB&E	2-66	19-10-67	3-71
	D 20 FIFE	Vickers-Armstrong	9-62	9-7-64	6-66
	D 21 NORFOLK	Swan Hunter	2-66	16-11-67	3-70

Kent (D 12) G. Arra, 1976

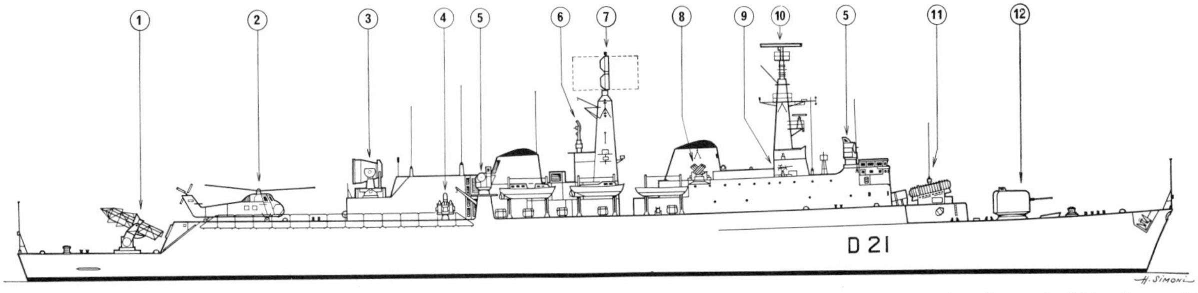

Scale 1/1000

1: Sea Slug launcher — 2: Wessex Mk 3 helicopter — 3: 901 radar — 4: Sea Cat — 5: MRS 3 fire-control radar — 6: 278 radar — 7: 965M radar — 8: Corvus — 9: 20-mm AA — 10: 992Q radar — 11: Exocet launchers — 12: 114-mm DP Mk 6 mount

GUIDED MISSILE DESTROYERS *(continued)*

London (D 16) G. Arra, 1976

Antrim (D 18) G. Arra, 1976

D: 5,440 tons (6,200 fl) **Dim:** 158.55 (153.90 pp) × 16.46 × 6.10 (fl)
S: 32.5 kts (30 cruising) **Range:** 3,500/28
A: (*a*) 4/114-mm Mk 6 DP (II × 2) fwd — 2/20-mm AA — 1 Sea Slug Mk-1 surface-to-air (30 missiles) — 2 Sea Cat systems (one on each side) (IV × 2) — 1 Wessex Mk-3 ASW helicopter. See Remarks
(*b*) 4/MM38 Exocet — 2/114-mm Mk 6 DP (II × 1) — 2/20-mm AA — 1 Sea Slug Mk-2 system (30 missiles) — 2 Sea Cat systems (IV × 2) — 1 Wessex Mk-3 ASW helicopter
Electron Equipt: Radars: 1/965 (965M on the (*b*) group), 1/992Q, 1/901, 1/278, 3/MRS-3 fire control — 2 Knebworth/Corvus — ADA WS 1
Sonars: 1/184 or 177, 1/170B, 1/174, 1/162
Man: 33 officers, 438 men
M: COSAG propulsion; 2 props. On each shaft, 1 A.E.I.GT (15,000 hp) and 2 linked G 6 gas turbines (7,500 hp each): 60,000 hp total
Boilers: 2 Babcock & Wilcox, 49.21 kg/cm² pressure; superheat to 510°C
Fuel: 600 tons **Electric:** (*a*) 3,750 kw (*b*) 4,750 kw

Remarks: Stabilizers. Twin rudders. Air-conditioned. Remote control of the boilers and engines from a command post that is completely protected from radioactive contamination. The Sea Slug launcher is on the stern and its fire-control radar is forward of the helicopter hangar. Missile stowage extends to the midships area and is more than 100 meters long; it is inboard, along the axis of the ship, and contains two parallel rows of 15 missiles, which can also be used against surface targets. The Sea Cat system is now GWS 22 in all units. The (*b*) group has its mast slightly farther aft than the (*a*) group. All (*b*) group units were fitted with four Exocet anti-ship missiles in 1974-76. The *Hampshire* (D-08) was stricken 4-76; the *Devonshire* (D-02) may follow in 1978.

GUIDED MISSILE DESTROYERS (*continued*)

Norfolk (D 21) with MM 38 launchers forward

FRIGATES

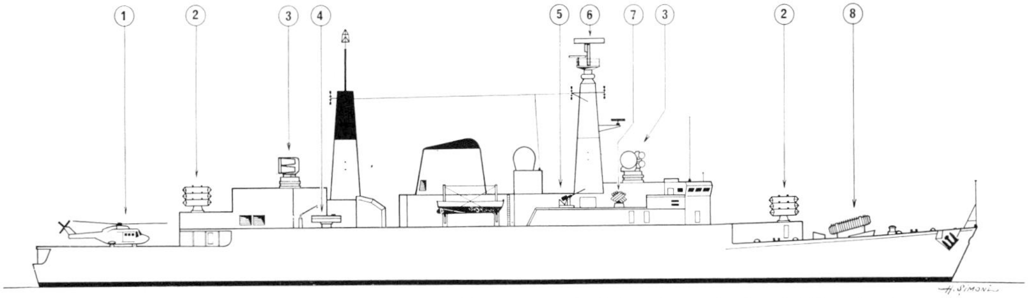

Scale 1/1000

1: Lynx WG 13 helicopter—2: Sea Wolf system—3: 910 radar—4: Mk 32 TT—5: 40-mm AA—6: 967/968 radar—7: Knebworth Corvus—8: Exocet launchers

♦ *4 B class (Type 22)*

	Bldr	Laid down	L	In serv.
F 88 BROADSWORD	Yarrow, Scotstoun	7-2-75	12-5-76	1978
F . . . BATTLEAXE	Yarrow, Scotstoun	1976	18-5-77	1979
F . . . BRILLIANT	Yarrow, Scotstoun	24-3-77	. . .	. . .
F . . . BOXER	. . .	. . .	. . .	. . .

D: 3,500 tons (4,000 fl) **S:** 29 kts **Dim:** 131.2 × 14.8 × 4.3 (av)

A: 4/MM38 Exocet — 2 Sea Wolf GWS 25 systems (VI × 2) — 2/40-mm AA — 6 Mk 32 ASW TT (III × 2) — 2 Lynx WG 13 helicopters

Electron Equipt: Radars: 1/967-968, 2/910 (GWS 25), 1/1006
Sonar: 1/2016 — CAAIS — 2 Knebworth/Corvus

M: COGOG propulsion; 2 Olympus TM3B gas turbines × 27,300 hp for high speed; 2 Tyne RM1A × 4,100 hp for cruising; 2 controllable-pitch props

Electric: 4,000 kw **Range:** 4,500/18 (on Tyne GT)

Broadsword model

FRIGATES (*continued*)

Broadsword (F 88) Yarrow, 1976

REMARKS: The class is expected to number at least 14 ships. The fourth was to be ordered during 1977. The 2016 is a new multiple-frequency sonar. All will receive Scot radomes for the Skynet communications satellite system. The Lynx WG 13 can carry both ASW and anti-ship weapons. The 967-968 radar is a back-to-back array with track-white-scan features.

♦ *8 Amazon class* (*Type 21*)

		Bldr	Laid down	L	In serv.
(*a*)	**F 169 AMAZON**	Vosper Thornycroft	11-69	26-4-71	11-5-74
	F 170 ANTELOPE	Vosper Thornycroft	3-71	16-3-72	19-7-65
	F 172 AMBUSCADE	Yarrow, Scotstoun	9-71	18-1-73	5-9-75
(*b*)	**F 171 ACTIVE**	Vosper Thornycroft	23-7-71	23-11-72	17-6-77
	F 173 ARROW	Yarrow, Scotstoun	9-72	5-2-74	29-7-76
	F 174 ALACRITY	Yarrow, Scotstoun	3-73	18-9-74	2-4-77
	F 175 ARDENT	Yarrow, Scotstoun	2-74	9-5-75	1977
	F 176 AVENGER	Yarrow, Scotstoun	10-74	20-11-75	1978

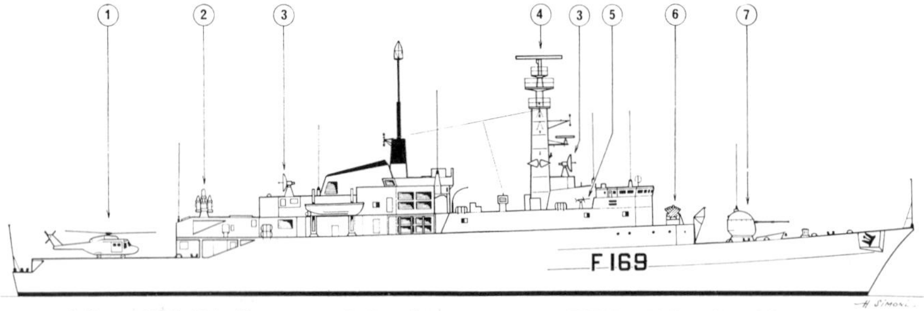

1: Lynx WG 13 helicopter — 2: Sea Cat system — 3: RTN-10X Sea Cat guidance radar (GWS 22) — 4: 992Q radar — 5: 20-mm AA — 6: Knebworth Corvus — 7: 114-mm Mk 8 mount

Scale 1/1000

D: 2,750 tons (3,250 fl) **Dim:** 117.04 × 12.80 × 4.4
S: 32 kts (18 on cruising turbines) **Man:** 13 officers, 164 men
A: (*b*) only: 4/MM38 Exocet — all: 1/114-mm Mk 8 DP — 2/20-mm AA — 1 Sea Cat system GWS 24 (IV × 1) — 1 Lynx WG 13 helicopter — 6 Mk 32 ASW TT (III × 2)
Electron Equipt: Radars: 1/992Q, 1/978, 2 RTN-10X — WSA 4 CAAIS — 2 Knebworth/Corvus
Sonars: 1/184, 1/170B, 1/174, 1/162
Range: 1,200/30, 4,500/18 **Electric:** . . .
M: COGOG propulsion: 2 Olympus TM3 gas turbines × 25,000 hp each; 2 Tyne RB209 gas turbines × 4,250 hp each; 2 controllable-pitch props

Antelope (F 170) G. Arra, 1976

REMARKS: Frigate designed jointly by Vosper Thornycroft and Yarrow. Remote control of engine room from the bridge. Supplies on board for 60 days. Ferranti WSA 4 digital system used in fire control, employing two Selenia RTN-10X radar directors for both Sea Cat and the 114-mm gun. The CAAIS is a separate entity, whose data are automatically transmitted to WSA 4; both use a single FM-1600B computer.

The Exocet launchers in the (*b*) group are paired, toed-in, forward of the bridge. It was originally intended to replace Sea Cat with Sea Wolf in the later units but, as the ships are overweight, this may not be done; fitting Sea Wolf would necessitate deletion of Exocet. The Knebworth/Corvus chaff launchers are before the bridge on the (*a*) group and abaft the bridge, one deck higher, on the (*b*) group. All are to receive two Scot radomes for the Skynet communications satellite system.

FRIGATES *(continued)*

Amazon (F 169) Vickers, 1974

Amazon (F 169) 1975

Amazon (F 169) 1975

FRIGATES *(continued)*

Antelope (F 170) — Group A G. Arra, 1976

Arrow (F 173) — Group B 1976

♦ *26 Leander class*

Programs (starting with F-10): 3 in 1960-61, 3 in 1961-62, 3 in 1962-63, 3 in 1963-64, 3 in 1964-65, 3 in 1965-66, 2 in 1966-67, 2 in 1967-68

		Bldr	Laid down	L	In serv.
(*a*)	**F 109 LEANDER** (ex-*Weymouth*)	Harland & Wolff	4-59	28-6-61	3-63
	F 114 AJAX (ex-*Fowey*)	Cammell Laird	10-59	16-8-62	12-63
	F 10 AURORA	John Brown	6-61	28-11-62	4-64
	F 15 EURYALUS	Scotts SB&E	11-61	6-6-63	9-64
	F 18 GALATEA	Swan Hunter	12-61	23-5-63	4-64
	F 38 ARETHUSA	J. Samuel White	9-62	5-11-63	11-65
	F 39 NAIAD	Yarrow, Scotstoun	10-62	4-11-63	3-65
(*b*)	**F 28 CLEOPATRA**	HMDY, Devonport	6-63	25-3-64	1-66
	F 104 DIDO (ex-*Hastings*)	Yarrow, Scotstoun	12-59	22-12-61	9-63
	F 45 MINERVA	Vickers-Armstrong	7-63	19-12-64	5-66
	F 42 PHOEBE	Alex Stephen & Sons	6-63	8-7-64	4-66
	F 40 SIRIUS	HMDY, Portsmouth	8-63	22-9-64	6-66
	F 56 ARGONAUT	Hawthorn Leslie	11-64	8-2-66	8-67
	F 52 JUNO	Thornycroft	7-64	24-11-65	7-67
	F 47 DANAE	HMDY, Devonport	12-64	31-10-65	9-67
	F 127 PENELOPE (ex-*Coventry*)	Vickers-Armstrong	3-61	17-8-62	10-63
(*c*)	**F 58 HERMIONE**	Stephen/Yarrow	12-65	26-4-67	7-69
	F 60 JUPITER	Yarrow, Scotstoun	10-66	4-9-67	8-69
	F 57 ANDROMEDA	HMDY, Portsmouth	5-66	24-5-67	12-68
	F 69 BACCHANTE	Vickers-Armstrong	10-66	29-2-68	10-69
	F 71 SCYLLA	HMDY, Devonport	5-67	8-8-68	2-70
	F 75 CHARYBDIS	Harland & Wolff	1-67	28-2-68	6-69
	F 12 ACHILLES	Yarrow, Scotstoun	12-67	21-11-68	7-70
	F 16 DIOMEDE	Yarrow, Scotstoun	1-68	15-4-69	4-71
	F 70 APOLLO	Yarrow, Scotstoun	5-69	15-10-70	5-72
	F 72 ARIADNE	Yarrow, Scotstoun	11-69	10-9-71	2-73

Hermione (F 58) — Broad-beamed *Leander* G. Arra, 1975

FRIGATES (*continued*)

D: (*a*) and (*b*): 2,450 tons (2,860 fl); (*c*): 2,500 tons (2,962 fl)
Dim: (*a*) and (*b*): 113.38 (109.73 pp) × 12.50 × 5.49
(*c*): 113.38 (109.73 pp) × 13.12 × 5.49
S: 27 kts (30 on trials) **Man:** av. 17 officers, 245 enlisted
A: (*a*): 2/40-mm AA (I × 2) — 2/Sea Cat systems (IV × 2) — 1/Ikara ASW system — 1 Limbo Mk. 10 ASW mortar (III × 1) — 1 Wasp ASW helicopter
(*b*): 4/MM38 Exocet — 2/40-mm AA — 3/Sea Cat systems — 6 Mk. 32 ASW TT (III × 2) — 1/Wasp ASW helicopter; F-127: 1/Sea Wolf system (VI × 1), see remarks
(*c*): 2/114-mm DP Mk 6 (II × 1) — 2/20-mm AA (I × 2) — 1/Sea Cat system — 1 Limbo Mk. 10 ASW mortar — 1 Wasp ASW helicopter
Electron equipt: Radars: 1/965 (not on (*a*) group), 1/993, 1/978 or 975, 1 or 2/903 (on MRS 3 FC) — CAAIS on (*a*) group — 2 Knebworth/Corvus
Sonars: 1/177 or 184, 1/170B, 1/162 (1/199 on (*a*) group only)
M: White-English Electric GT; 2 5-bladed props; 30,000 hp
Boilers: 2 Babcock & Wilcox 3-drum; 38.7 kg/cm²; superheat 450°C
Electric: (*a*) group plus F-28, F-104: 1,600 kw; other (*b*) group: 1,900 kw; (*c*) group: 2,500 kw
Range: approx. 4,500/12 **Fuel:** 460 tons — (*c*) group: 500 tons

Achilles (F 12) 1975

REMARKS: Improvement on the *Rothesay* class. Hull entirely welded; quarters air-conditioned; twin rudders; excellent sea-keeping qualities. Successive improvements to the propulsion and auxiliary machinery. All are gradually being fitted with Scot radomes.

The (*a*) group, or "Ikara *Leander*" class, have been modernized, completions coming from 12-72 to 11-76. The Ikara system replaced the 114-mm twin mount, while the number of Sea Cat launchers was doubled and 2/40-mm AA were mounted abreast the bridge. These ships have the Ikara guidance radar in a radome atop the bridge and only one MRS 3 director, aft for the GWS 22 Sea Cat. All have VDS, and the 965 radar has been removed.

The (*b*) group, or "Exocet *Leander*" class, have had the 114-mm mount replaced by 4 MM38 Exocet and a Sea Cat launcher. The Limbo mortar was removed and two triple ASW TT were mounted abreast the hangar, which now has two Sea Cat launchers atop it; two MRS 3 directors are carried, and single 40-mm mounts were placed abreast the bridge. The VDS well was plated up. F-28 completed conversion 11-75; the others (except F-127) were scheduled to complete 1977-78. F-127, otherwise disarmed, is serving as Sea Wolf system trials ship, with a six-celled launcher on the stern, the 910 radar director atop deckhouse on the former helicopter deck, and a 967-968 tracking radar atop her after mast. Originally scheduled to be an Ikara conversion on completion of Sea Wolf trials, she will now be given the Exocet conversion.

The (*c*) group, or "Broad-Beamed *Leander*" class, are .61-meters greater in beam to improve seaworthiness, provide larger fuel tanks, and permit installation of a more powerful electrical generator plant. All carried 1 Sea Cat GWS 22 system — unlike many of the earlier (*a*) and (*b*) groups, which did not get Sea Cat prior to modernization. The (*c*) group are also scheduled for modernization in the early 1980s, possibly with Sea Wolf and Exocet.

Naiad (F 39) — Ikara *Leander* with Scot domes G. Arra, 1976

Ajax (F 114) — Ikara *Leander* 1974

FRIGATES (*continued*)

Ariadne (F 72) — Broad-beamed *Leander* G. Arra, 1976

Apollo (F 70) G. Arra, 1976

Cleopatra (F 28) — Exocet *Leander* 1976

FRIGATES (*continued*)

Penelope (F 127) — Sea Wolf trials ship 1975

♦ *7 Tribal class* (*Type 81*)

Authorized: 3 in 1955-56, 4 in 1956-57

	Bldr	Laid down	L	In serv.
F 117 ASHANTI	Yarrow, Scotstoun	1-58	9-3-59	11-61
F 119 ESKIMO	J. Samuel White	10-58	20-3-60	2-63
F 122 GURKHA	Thornycroft, Woolston	11-58	11-7-60	2-63
F 125 MOHAWK	Vickers-Armstrong	12-60	5-4-62	11-63
F 131 NUBIAN	HMDY, Portsmouth	10-59	6-9-60	10-62
F 133 TARTAR	HMDY, Devonport	9-60	19-9-60	2-62
F 124 ZULU	Alex Stephen & Sons	12-60	3-7-62	4-64

Tartar (F 133) G. Arra, 1975

Mohawk (F 125) with a Wasp on the helo deck 1968

Eskimo (F 119) 1976

FRIGATES (*continued*)

D: 2,300 tons (2,700 fl) **S:** 24/23 kts (actual)
Dim: 109.73 (106.68 pp) × 12.95 × 5.30 (fl)
A: 2/114-mm Mk 5 DP (I × 2), 1 fwd, 1 aft — 2/20-mm AA (I × 2) — 2 Sea Cat GWS 22 systems (IV × 2) — 1 Mk 10 Limbo ASW mortar — 1 Wasp ASW helicopter
Electron Equipt: Radars: 1/965, 1/978, 1/993, 1/903, 2/262 — 2 Knebworth/Corvus
Sonars: 1/177, 1/170B, 1/162 (1/199 on F-117 and F-122)
Man: 13 officers, 237-240 men **Range:** 4,500/12
M: COSAG propulsion: 1 Metrovik GT (15,000 hp) and 1 A.E.I.G6 (7,500 hp) gas turbine geared to a single prop
Boiler: 1 Babcock & Wilcox 38 kg/cm², 450°C **Electric:** 1,500 kw

REMARKS: Living quarters air-conditioned. Remote control of propulsion machinery. The gas turbine permits almost instantaneous cold starts but is used only when high speeds are required. Denny-Brown stabilizers and twin rudders. Flush deck and welded hull, which had to be reinforced after the trials of the F-117. Despite its heavy appearance, the tripod mast is made of light metal and weighs only two tons. These ships will not be modernized. F-117 was seriously damaged by a fire in her engine room on 3-3-77; she will be repaired but will be placed in ready-reserve status.

♦ *9 Rothesay class* (*Type 12*)

	Bldr	Laid down	L	In serv
F 107 ROTHESAY	Yarrow, Scotstoun	11-56	9-12-57	4-60
F 108 LONDONDERRY	Thornycroft	11-56	20-5-58	7-60
F 115 BERWICK	Harland & Wolff	6-58	15-12-59	6-61
F 106 BRIGHTON	Yarrow, Scotstoun	7-57	30-10-59	9-61
F 113 FALMOUTH	Swan Hunter	11-57	15-12-59	7-61
F 126 PLYMOUTH	HMDY, Devonport	7-58	20-7-59	5-61
F 129 RHYL	HMDY, Portsmouth	1-58	23-4-59	10-60
F 101 YARMOUTH	John Brown (Clyde)	11-57	23-3-59	3-60
F 103 LOWESTOFT	Alex Stephen & Sons	6-58	23-6-60	10-61

D: 2,380 tons (2,800 fl) **Dim:** 112.77 (109.73 pp) × 12.50 × 5.30
S: 30 kts (26/25 actual) **Man:** 15 officers, 220 men
A: 2/114-mm Mk 6 DP (II × 1) — 2/20-mm AA (I × 2) — 1 Sea Cat GWS 20 system (IV × 1) — 1 Mk 10 Limbo ASW mortar — 1 Wasp ASW helicopter
Electron Equipt: Radars: 1/978, 1/993, 1/903
Sonars: 1/174, 1/170, 1/162
M: Same as *Whitby* class **Electric:** 1,460 kw **Fuel:** 400 tons
Range: 4,500/12

REMARKS: Improved version of the *Whitby* class. All modernized 1966-72 with Sea Cat GWS 20 system and helicopter facility in place of one Limbo ASW mortar. MRS 3 fire-control system replaced the original Mk 6 director, and new electronics and air-conditioning were installed. F-108 began conversion 11-75 to serve as trials ship for the Admiralty Surface Weapons Establishment, and will probably be greatly altered in appearance when recommissioned in late 1978.

Rothesay (F 107) refueling a Wessex III helicopter 1972

Rhyl (F 129) G. Arra, 1976

FRIGATES (*continued*)

♦ *1 Whitby class* (*Type 12*)

	Bldr	Laid down	L	In serv.
F 43 TORQUAY	Harland & Wolff	3-53	1-7-54	5-56

Torquay (F 43) 1975

D: 2,150 tons (2,560 fl) **S:** 30 kts (26/25 usual)
Dim: 112.77 (109.73 pp) × 12.50 × 5.26
A: 2/114-mm Mk 6 DP (II × 1) — 1 Mk 10 Limbo ASW mortar
Electron Equipt: Radars: 1/978, 1/993, 1/275
Sonars: 1/174, 1/170, 1/162 — CAAIS
M: English-Electric GT; 2 props; 30,000 hp
Boilers: 2 Babcock, 38.7 kg/cm² pressure; superheat 450°C
Fuel: 370 tons **Range:** 4,500/12 **Electric:** 1,140 kw

REMARKS: Welded hull, air-conditioned, twin rudders. Cruising turbines for normal underway passage, with automatic shift to high-speed turbines. Bridge spacious and comfortable. Excellent sea-keeping qualities. In trials, 30 knots were attained with 75 per cent of anticipated power. Assigned to Navigation and Aircraft Division Training at Portsmouth. The *Eastbourne* (F-73), formerly assigned to the Machinists' School (weapons removed), was relegated to status of harbor training hulk in 1976. The *Blackpool* (F-77), discarded in 1974, is retained as a target. The *Scarborough* (F-63) and *Tenby* (F-65) of the same class, purchased in 1974 by Pakistan, were sold for scrap. The *Whitby* (F-36) was discarded in 1975.

♦ *2 Salisbury class* (*Type 61*) — Aircraft Direction

	Bldr	Laid down	L	In serv.
F 32 SALISBURY	HMDY, Devonport	1-52	25-6-53	2-57
F 99 LINCOLN	Fairfield SB & E	5-55	6-4-69	7-60

D: 2,170 tons (2,400 fl) **Dim:** 103.63 (100.58 pp) × 12.19 × 4.80 (fl)
S: 23 kts (operational) **Man:** 14 officers, 223 men
A: 2/114-mm Mk 6 DP (II × 1) — 2/20-mm AA (I × 2) — 1/Sea Cat GWS 20 system
Electron Equipt: Radars: 1/965M, 1/982, 1/278, 1/993, 1/275
Sonars: 1/174, 1/170B
M: 8 Admiralty Standard Range I, fast diesels with reduction gear, hydraulically linked, 4 by 4, on two propeller shafts; 12,400 hp
Fuel: 230 tons **Range:** 2,300/23, 7,500/16 **Electric:** 1,200 kw

REMARKS: Both in ready-reserve. *Llandaff* (F-61) sold to Bangladesh 1-12-76. *Chichester* (F-59) stricken 7-77.

Salisbury (F 32). Lincoln is nearly identical Terzibaschitsch, 1977

♦ *2 Leopard class* (*Type 41*) — Anti-Aircraft

	Bldr	Laid down	L	In serv.
F 27 LYNX	J. Brown (Clydebank)	1953	12-1-55	3-57
F 37 JAGUAR	Wm. Denny (Dumbarton)	11-53	30-7-57	12-59

Jaguar (F 37) G. Arra, 1972

D: 2,300 tons (2,520 fl) **Dim:** 103.63 (100.58 pp) × 12.19 × 4.80 (fl)
S: 23 kts **Man:** 10 officers, 195-205 men
A: 4/114-mm Mk 6 DP (II × 2) — 1/40-mm AA
Electron Equipt: Radars: 1/965, 1/978, 1/993, 1/262
Sonars: 1/174, 1/170B

FRIGATES (*continued*)

M: 8 Admiralty Standard fast diesels with reduction gear, hydraulically linked, 4 by 4, on two propeller shafts; 12,400 hp
Fuel: 230 tons diesel **Electric:** 1,200 kw **Range:** 2,300/23, 7,500/16

REMARKS: Type 61 and Type 41 classes have the same welded hull and the same machinery. Anti-rolling stabilizers except on the F-32. Four 300-kw diesel generators as auxiliary machinery. The original lattice masts have been replaced by mast-stacks, or "macks" (contraction of mast and stack). F-99 has controllable-pitch propellers. In trials, these ships reached 25 knots. *Panther* of this series sold to India in 1956 and renamed *Brahmaputra*. *Puma* (F-34) stricken in 1973, *Leopard* (F-14) in 1976. The two survivors are in ready-reserve.

♦ *2 Blackwood Class* (*Type 14*) — Utility ASW frigates

	Bldr	Laid down	L	In serv.
F 48 DUNDAS	J. Samuel White	10-52	23-9-53	3-56
F 54 HARDY	Yarrow	2-53	25-11-53	12-55

Dundas (F 48) G. Arra, 1976

D: 1,180 tons (1,460 fl) **Dim:** 94.50 (91.44 pp) × 10.05 × 4.70
S: 25 kts (23 actual) **Man:** 8 officers, 132 men
A: 2/40-mm AA (I × 2) — 2 Mk 10 Limbo mortars mounted in echelon
Electron Equipt: Radar: 1/978 — Sonars: 1/174, 1/170 B 1/162
M: GT; 1 prop; 15,000 hp
Boilers: 2 Babcock & Wilcox, 38.7 kg/cm², 450°C **Range:** 4,500/12
Electric: 1,108 kw

REMARKS: Survivors of a class of 12 (plus 3 for India). F-48 is active, F-54 to ready-reserve 7-77. Sisters *Russell* (F-97) and *Duncan* (F-80) are retained as harbor training hulks. The *Exmouth* (F-84), converted as gas-turbine propulsion trials ship, stricken 4-77. These ships essentially had one half a *Whitby*-class propulsion plant. The lightly constructed hulls required reinforcement at the forecastle "break." A third 40-mm AA aft and two twin 533-mm ASW torpedo tubes were removed early in the ships' careers.

NOTE: *Mermaid* (F-76), ordered for Ghana in 1965 and incorporated in the Royal Navy in 1972, was sold to Malaysia 4-77.

PATROL BOATS

♦ *5 Isles class* — Bldr: Hall Russell, Aberdeen

	L	In serv.
P 295 JERSEY	18-3-76	15-10-76
P 297 GUERNSEY	17-2-77	7-77
P 298 SHETLAND	22-11-76	25-5-77
P 299 ORKNEY	29-6-76	25-2-77
P 300 LINDISFARNE	. . .	1977

D: 1,000 tons (1,280 fl) **S:** 16 kts **Dim:** 59.51 (51.97 pp) × 10.90 × 4.26
A: 1/40-mm AA Mk 3 — 2/7.6-mm machine guns **Range:** 7,000/15
M: 2 Ruston 12-RK 3 CM diesels (750 rpm); 1 controllable-pitch prop; 4,380 hp
Man: 7 officers, 32 men (plus Marine Detachment) **Fuel:** 310 tons

Orkney (P 299) 1976

REMARKS: Near duplicates of the Scottish Department of Fisheries ships *Jura* and *Westra*. The *Jura* (as P-296) was loaned to the Royal Navy from 1975 to 1-77 for use in patrolling off-shore oil rigs and the 200-nautical-mile economic zone, the purpose for which the Isles class were built.

♦ *4 Kingfisher class* — Bldr: Dunston, Hessle

	Laid down	L	In serv.
P 260 KINGFISHER	7-73	20-9-74	8-10
P 261 CYGNET	10-73	26-10-75	1-7-76
P 262 PETEREL	11-73	14-5-76	23-12-76
P 263 SANDPIPER	12-73	20-1-77	1977

PATROL BOATS *(continued)*

Kingfisher (P 260) 1975

D: 187 tons **S:** 25 kts **Dim:** 36.6 (33.8 pp) × 7.0 × 2.0
A: 1/40-mm AA — 2/7.6-mm machine guns **Man:** 4 officers, 10 men
M: 2 Paxman 16 YJCM diesels (1,500 rpm); 2 props; 4,000 hp

REMARKS: RAF *Seal*-class air-sea rescue craft. A large number of additional sisters were canceled. P-262 and P-263 are used for Naval Reserve training; the other pair are employed in patrol work in the North Sea. Have fin stabilizers; evidently have stability problems.

♦ *5 ex-"-ton"-class minesweepers* — all employed at Hong Kong

P 1007 BEACHAMPTON **P 1055 MONKTON** **P 1089 WASPERTON**
P 1093 WOLVERTON **P 1096 YARNTON**

D: 360 tons (425 fl) **S:** 15 kts **Dim:** 46.3 (42.7 pp) × 8.8 × 2.5
A: 2/40-mm AA (I × 2) — 2/7.6-mm machine guns **Range:** 2,300/13
Electron Equipt: Radar: 978 **Fuel:** 45 tons
M: 2 Deltic diesels; 2 props; 3,000 hp **Man:** 5 officers, 25 men

REMARKS: Originally completed 1953-57. Modified, 1971-72. All sweep gear removed, light armor added around bridge.

Beachampton (P 1007) G. Arra, 1976

PATROL CRAFT

♦ *1 prototype, purchased 25-1-72*

P 276 TENACITY — Bldr: Vosper Thornycroft, 18-2-69

D: 165 tons (220 fl) **S:** 39 kts **Dim:** 44.1 × 8.10 × 2.40
A: 2/7.6-mm machine guns **Range:** 2,500/15 **Man:** 4 officers, 28 men
M: CODOG propulsion: 3 Rolls-Royce Proteus gas turbines, 12,750 hp; 2 Paxman diesels, 1,200 hp; 3 props

REMARKS: Built as a private-venture experimental missile boat, dummy weapons only. Employed for fisheries protection in the Irish Sea, for anti-smuggling patrol, and as a target craft.

♦ *3 Scimitar class*

P 271 SCIMITAR (4-12-69) **P 274 CUTLASS** (19-2-70) **P 275 SABRE** (21-4-70)
Bldr: Vosper Thornycroft, Portsmouth

Scimitar (P 271)

D: 102 tons (fl) **S:** 40 kts **Dim:** 30.50 × 8.10 × 1.95
Man: 2 officers, 10 men **Range:** 425/35, 1,500/21.5
M: CODOG propulsion: 2 Rolls-Royce Proteus gas turbines (9,000 hp); 2 Fodens diesels (180 hp) for cruising; 2 props

REMARKS: Designed for anti-missile-boat training. Hull of laminated and glued wood. A third gas turbine allowed for in design. Can carry two 7.6-mm machine guns if required for patrol duties.

MINE WARFARE SHIPS

♦ *2 Brecon-class minehunters*

	Bldr	L	In serv.
M . . . BRECON	Vosper Thornycroft	. . .	1978
M . . . LEDBURY	Vosper Thornycroft	. . .	. . .

D: 615 tons (725 fl) **S:** 17 kts **Dim:** 60.00 (56.60 pp) × 9.85 × 2.20
A: 1/40-mm AA Mk 9 **Man:** 45 men

MINE WARFARE SHIPS *(continued)*

Brecon (artist's rendering) 1974

Electron Equipt: Radar: 1/1006 — Sonar: 1/193
M: 2 Ruston-Paxman Deltic 59K diesels (1,600 rpm); 2 props; 3,540 hp
Electric: 1,080 kw (3 diesel alternators of 200 kw each for ship's service plus one 480 kw diesel alternator for magnetic minesweeping)

REMARKS: Equipped for both hunting and sweeping mines. Hull constructed of glass-reinforced plastic. Up to 12 may be built, with Yarrow cooperating in the program. Will carry divers and 2 French PAP 104 wire-guided, remote-controlled mine-locators.

♦ *1 prototype glass-reinforced plastic minehunter*

M 1116 WILTON — Bldr: Vosper Thornycroft — Ordered 11-2-70 — L: 18-2-72 — In serv: 25-4-73

Wilton (M 1166) 1973

D: 450 tons (fl) **S:** 15 kts **Dim:** 46.33 × 8.76 × 2.60
A: 1/40-mm AA Mk 7 **Man:** 5 officers, 32 men
M: As for "-ton" class

REMARKS: First large warship with an all-glass-reinforced plastic hull. Machinery and fittings are from the *Derriton,* scrapped in 1970.

♦ *15 "-ton"-class minehunters* — Bldr: Various

M 1110 BILDESTON	**M 1140 GAVINTON**	**M 1157 KIRKLISTON**
M 1133 BOSSINGTON	**M 1147 HUBBERSTON**	**M 1165 MAXTON**
M 1113 BRERETON*	**M 1151 IVESTON**	**M 1166 NURTON**
M 1114 BRINTON*	**M 1153 KEDLESTON****	**M 1181 SHERATON**
M 1115 BRONINGTON	**M 1154 KELLINGTON***	**M 1182 SHOULTON**

Nurton (M 1166) — Minehunter G. Arra, 1976

♦ *17 "-ton"-class minesweepers* — Bldr: Various

M 1103 ALFRISTON*	**M 1158 LALESTON**	**M 1204 STUBBINGTON***
M 1109 BICKINGTON*	**M 1208 LEWISTON**	**M 1187 UPTON****
M 1124 CRICHTON**	**M 1173 POLLINGTON***	**M 1188 WALKERTON**
M 1216 CROFTON**	**M 1167 REPTON****	**M 1175 WISTON****
M 1141 GLASSERTON	**M 1180 SHAVINGTON***	**M 1195 WOTTON***
M 1146 HODGESTON**	**M 1200 SOBERTON***	

D: 370 tons (425 fl) **Dim:** 46.33 (42.68 pp) × 8.76 × 2.50
S: 15 kts (cruising) **Man:** 29 men sweepers/38 hunters
A: 1/40-mm AA Mk 7 — plus 2/20-mm AA (II × 1) in some sweepers (M-1141, M-1158, M-1182, M-1188 disarmed)

* Fisheries protection. ** Naval Reserve training. M 1158 mine-clearance diving tender; M 1188 navigational training ship at Royal Naval College, Dartmouth.

MINE WARFARE SHIPS (*continued*)

Walkerton (M 1188) — no guns or sweep gear G. Arra, 1975

M: 2 Paxman Deltic 18A-7A diesels; 2 props; 3,000 hp — except M-1141, M-1158, M-1167: 2 Mirrlees JVSS 12 diesels; 2 props, 2,500 hp
Range: 2,300/13, 3,000/8 **Fuel:** 45 tons
Electron Equipt: Radar: 1/978 — Sonar: 1/193 (hunters only)

REMARKS: Survivors of a class of 118; five others are equipped as patrol boats. All minehunters are equipped with active rudders for low-speed operations, have a Type 193 sonar, and carry mine-clearance divers (divers not in Fisheries Patrol units). All hunters and M-1216, M-1208, M-1173, M-1167, M-1204, M-1188, and M-1175 have enclosed bridges. M-1182, as the prototype minehunter, was given pump-jet propulsion and a bow-thruster. M-1141 carries the Osbourne multiple sweep array. M-1188 is to be replaced by M-1103 shortly. The three units still with Mirrlees diesels will likely soon be stricken. M-1136, in collision with the frigate *Mermaid* 21-9-76, was salvaged but scrapped.

All have wooden hulls, most sheathed with nylon below the waterline. Fin stabilizers are fitted.

MINE COUNTERMEASURES SUPPORT SHIP

♦ *1 exercise minelayer and tender*

	Bldr	Laid down	L	In serv.
N 21 ABDIEL	Thornycroft (Woolston)	5-66	22-1-67	10-67

D: 1,375 tons (1,460 fl) **Dim:** 80.42 (74.67 pp) × 11.74 × 2.85
S: 16 kts **A:** 44 mines **Man:** 77 men
Electron Equipt: Radar: 1/978 **Electric:** 1,225 kw
M: Paxman Ventura 16-YSCM diesels; 2 props; 2,690 hp

REMARKS: Carries and repairs spare sweeping equipment and cable.

Abdiel (N 21) 1967

Abdiel (N 21) G. Arra, 1976

AMPHIBIOUS WARFARE SHIPS

ASSAULT SHIPS

♦ *2 Fearless class*

	Author	Bldr	Laid down	L	In serv.
L 10 FEARLESS	1961-62	Harland & Wolff	7-62	19-12-63	11-65
L 11 INTREPID	1962-63	J. Brown (Clyde)	1-63	26-6-64	3-67

Fearless (L 10) 1976

D: 11,060 tons (12,120 fl) (16,950 tons, draft 9.15, with well deck flooded)
S: 21 kts **Dim:** 158.50 (152.40 pp) × 24.38 × 6.20
A: 4/Sea Cat GWS 20 systems (IV × 4) — 2/40-mm AA (I × 2)
Electron Equipt: Radars: 1/978, 1/993 — CAAIS — 2 Knebworth/Corvus
Man: 36 officers, 520 men, 380-700 troops **Range:** 5,000/20
M: English-Electric GT; 2 props; 22,000 hp
Boilers: 2 Babcock & Wilcox 38.66 kg/cm² pressure; superheat 454°C
Electric: 4,000 kw

Remarks: These ships are equivalent to U.S. LPD and French TCD types, and have excellent command and communication facilities for amphibious operations. They can launch 4 to 6 Wessex Mk 5 assault helicopters (landing platform but no hangar), and have quarters for troop contingents of various sizes, depending on the duration and distance of operations, but usually a single light infantry battalion and an artillery battery. On board are four LCA landing craft, which can transport 35 men or a half-ton vehicle and 4 LCM(9) landing craft carrying two Chieftain or Centurion tanks, or four vehicles, or 100 tons of supplies; four additional tanks can be carried on the tank deck. The vehicles are divided between the tank deck, a lower deck, and a half-deck reserved for jeeps. The Skynet satellite communications system (now removed) had experiments carried out on board the *Intrepid. Intrepid,* placed on reserve in 1976, will refit during 1978 and replace the *Fearless* in 1979. The active unit is normally assigned as officer cadet training ship at the Royal Naval College, Dartmouth, but is immediately available for amphibious operations as required.

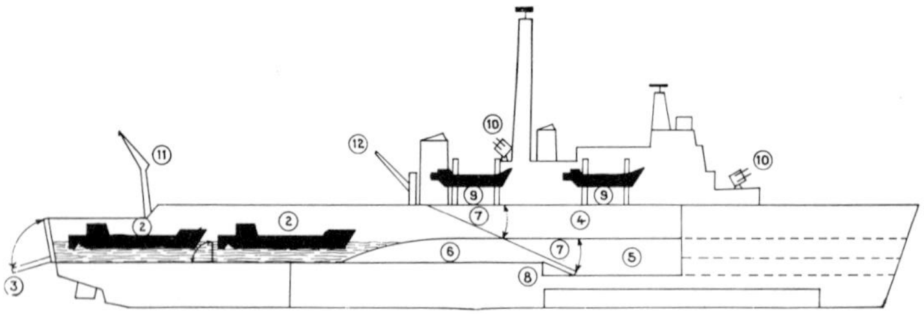

1: well deck — 2: LCM 9 — 3: stern well gate — 4: tank deck — 5: lower deck (light vehicles) — 6: half-deck — 7: mobile ramps — 8: fixed ramp — 9: LCA — 10: Sea Cat system — 11, 12: cranes

LANDING SHIPS, TANK

♦ *6 Sir Bedivere class*

	L	Bldr
L 3004 SIR BEDIVERE	20-7-66	(3)
L 3005 SIR GALAHAD	19-4-66	(2)
L 3027 SIR GERAINT	26-1-67	(2)
L 3029 SIR LANCELOT	6-63	(1)
L 3036 SIR PERCIVAL	4-10-67	(3)
L 3505 SIR TRISTRAM	12-12-66	(3)

Bldrs: (1) Fairfield, (2) Alexander Stephen, (3) Hawthorn Leslie

Sir Geraint (L 3027) 1972

D: 5,550 tons (fl) **S:** 17 kts **Dim:** 126.45 × 17.70 × 3.80
Man: 18 officers, 51 men **Range:** 8,000/15
M: 2 diesels; 2 props; 9,400 hp (L-3029: 9,520 hp)
A: 2/40-mm (not installed) **Fuel:** 811 tons

Remarks: In 1963 the Ministry of Transportation ordered the first of six specially designed LST-class ships for the Army, chartered in peacetime to various private maritime firms. In 1970 these ships came under the control of the Royal Fleet Auxiliary Service, which mans them today. Beaching cargo capacity is 340 tons (military lift). Built into the bow and the stern are ramps and doors for the handling of vehicles (roll-on/roll-off system); interior ramps connect the two decks. Quarters are provided in the after superstructure for 402 men. The ships have a helicopter platform, and three cranes (two 4.5, one 8.5 tons); landing craft may be carried in cradles normally used for lifeboats. L-3029 has four cranes.

♦ *1 LST (3) class*

L 3513 EMPIRE GULL (ex-*Trouncer,* ex-LST(3)-3513) — Bldr: Davie SB, Quebec, 9-7-45

AMPHIBIOUS WARFARE SHIPS (*continued*)

D: 2,260 tons (4,960 fl) **S:** 10 kts **Dim:** 105.8 × 16.5 × 3.7
M: 2 triple-expansion steam; 2 props; 5,500 hp **Fuel:** 950 tons
Boilers: 2 Scotch-type **Man:** 63 men (plus 80 troops)

REMARKS: Last operational British survivor of a steam-driven version of the U.S. LST. Manned by the Royal Fleet Auxiliary Service.

MEDIUM LANDING SHIPS

♦ *2 Ardennes-class logistic landing craft* — Bldr: Brooke Marine

	Laid down	L	In serv.
L 4001 ARDENNES	8-75	29-7-76	1977
L 4003 ARAKAN	-76	23-5-77	1978

D: 870 tons (1,413 fl) **S:** 10.3 kts **Dim:** 73.1 × 14.4 × 1.8
M: 2 Mirrlees-Blackstone GWSL 8-MGR2 diesels; 2 props; 2,000 hp
Range: 4,000/10 **Man:** 36 men (plus 34 troops)

REMARKS: Replacements for the LCT(8) class, will be operated by the Royal Corps of Transport. Can carry five 70-ton tanks or 24 standard 20-ft. containers (340 dwt).

♦ *2 LCT (8) class*

L 4041 ABBEVILLE **L 4061 AUDEMER**

D: 657 tons (895 to 1,075 fl) **Dim:** 70.18 × 11.90 × 1.80
S: 12 kts (9 cruising) **Man:** 33 men
M: 4 Paxman diesels; 2 props; 1,840 hp

Audemer (L 4061) Terzibaschitsch, 1977

REMARKS: Operated by the Army's Royal Corps of Transport. The following have been scrapped since 1974: *Aachen* (L-4062), *Andalnes* (L-4097), *Akyab* (L-4037), *Antwerp* (L-4071), *Arezzo* (L-4128), and *Arakan* (L-4164). *Agheila* (L-4002) was to be stricken on completion of *Ardennes*, 1977.

LANDING CRAFT

♦ *14 LCM (9) class*

LCM (9) 700 to **711, LCM (9) 3507** and **LCM (9) 3508**

The prototype of this new series, L-3507, was delivered in 1963. The *Fearless* (L-10) and the *Intrepid* (L-10) can each carry four of these.

Bldrs: 2 by Vosper, 6 by Richard Dunston, 4 by Brooke Marine Ltd., 2 by Bolson & Sons, 1964-66

1966, Shipbuilding and Shipping Record

D: 75 tons (176 fl) **Dim:** 25.7 × 6.5 × 1.7
M: 2 Paxman YHXAM diesels; Kort nozzle props; 624 hp **Man:** 6 men

REMARK: Can carry 2 Centurion tanks or 100 tons of cargo.

♦ *11 Avon class*

RPL 01 AVON
RPL 02 BUDE
RPL 03 CLYDE
RPL 04 DART
RPL 05 EDEN
RPL 06 FORTH
RPL 07 GLEN
RPL 08 HAMBLE
RPL 10 KENNET
RPL 11 LODDEN
RPL 12 MEDWAY

D: 61 tons **S:** 8 kts **Dim:** 22.0 × 6.10
M: 2 diesels; 2 props, 870 hp

REMARKS: Two-deck superstructure aft. Used in U.K. coastal service. Operated by the Army's Royal Corps of Transport.

♦ *2 LCM (7) class*

L 7037 **L 7100**

D: 28 tons (63 fl) **S:** 9.8 kts **Dim:** 18.4 × 4.9 × 1.2
M: 2 Gray Marine diesels; 2 props; 290 hp

REMARKS: Wartime construction, used as stores tenders; survivors of a once-numerous class.

LANDING CRAFT *(continued)*

♦ *26 LCVP*

LCVP (1): 102, 112, 118, 120, 123, 127, 128, 134, 136
LCVP (2): 142–149
LCVP (3): 150–158

D: 8.5 tons (13.5 fl) **S:** 8–10 kts **Dim:** 12.7 or 13.1 × 3.1 × 0.8
M: 2 diesels; 2 props; 130 or 200 hp

REMARKS: Eight of the LCVP (2) are carried in *Fearless* and *Intrepid.*

♦ *3 LCP(L) (3)*

501, 503, 556

D: 6.5 tons (10 fl) **S:** 12 kts **Dim:** 11.3 × 3.4 × 1.0
M: 225 hp

♦ *3 smaller craft:* **LCR 5507, LCR 5508, LCN 604**

AUXILIARY SHIPS

Most auxiliary and supply vessels are responsible to the Royal Fleet Auxiliary (RFA), an organization peculiar to the Royal Navy. Built to the specifications of Lloyds of London (compartmentation, security, habitability), they also meet the standards of the Shipping Naval Acts of 1911 and of the Ministry of Transportation. Manned by the Civil Service, they fly the blue flag of the reserve, rather than the white ensign. In addition, about 40 tugs, salvage vessels, cable-layers, research vessels, etc. are assigned to the Royal Maritime Auxiliary Service (RMAS), whose personnel are also civil servants. The former Port Auxiliary Service (PAS) was absorbed by the RMAS on 1-10-76. Ships not listed below as either RFA or RMAS are manned by the Royal Navy. RMAS ships have black hulls and gray upperworks. They do not normally display hull numbers; most former PAS ships never had any. Former numbers, listed hereafter in parentheses for these ships, are for reference only.

HYDROGRAPHIC SHIPS

NOTE: All British survey ships, except the *Waterwitch,* are painted white, with buff-colored stacks and masts.

♦ *1 improved Hecla class*

(A 138) HERALD — Bldr: Robb, Caledon — L: 4-10-73 — In serv. 31-10-74

Herald (A 138) 1976

D: 2,125 tons (2,945 fl) **S:** 14 kts **Dim:** 79.3 × 14.9 × 4.7
Man: 128 men **Range:** 12,000/11, 20,000/9
M: Diesel-electric propulsion (identical to the *Hecla* class); 1 prop

REMARKS: Improved version of the *Hecla* class. Carries one Wasp helicopter. Replaces the *Vidal,* stricken in 1972.

♦ *3 Hecla class*

A 133 HECLA (21-12-64) **A 137 HECATE** (31-3-65) **A 144 HYDRA** (14-7-65)

Bldr: Yarrow; two hulls overhauled at the Blythswood Shbldg Co.

D: 1,915 tons (2,733 fl) **Dim:** 79.25 (71.63 pp) × 14.94 × 4.0
S: 14 kts **Range:** 12,000/11, 20,000/9
Man: 14 officers, 104 men **Fuel:** 450 tons
M: Diesel-electric propulsion: 3 Paxman Ventura diesels (12 cyl), each 1,280 hp; 2 electric motors for propulsion (2,000 hp, 190 rpm) linked to a single prop

REMARKS: Based on the oceanographic research vessel *Discovery.* Air-conditioned hull, reinforced against ice; bow propeller for navigation in narrow waters. Hangar and platform for 1 Wasp helicopter. Wide range and endurance. Excellent scientific laboratories; usually carries 7 civilian scientists in addition to crew.

Hecla (A 133) 1965

♦ *4 Bulldog-class coastal survey ships*

(A 317) BULLDOG (12-7-67)
(A 319) BEAGLE (ex-*Barracuda*) (7-9-67)
(A 320) FOX (6-11-67)
(A 335) FAWN (29-2-68)

Bldr: Brooke Marine (Lowestoft)

D: 800 tons (990 avg), (1,030 fl) **Dim:** 60.95 × 11.43 × 3.60
S: 15 kts **Man:** 4 officers, 34 men **Range:** 4,000/12
M: 4 Lister Blackstone ERS 8 M diesels; 2 Ka-Me-Wa controllable-pitch props; 2,000 hp
Electric: 720 kw

REMARKS: New class coastal ships; operate in pairs; air-conditioned; hulls built to commercial specifications and reinforced against ice damage.

HYDROGRAPHIC SHIPS *(continued)*

Fawn 1972

♦ *3 Echo-class inshore survey craft*

(A 70) ECHO (1-5-57) — **(A 71) ENTERPRISE** (20-9-58) — **(A 72) EGERIA** (13-9-58)

Bldr: J. Samuel White, (Cowes) 1957-59

Echo (A 70) Terzibaschitsch, 1977

D: 160 tons (fl) **S:** 13/12 kts **Dim:** 32.55 × 6.98 × 2.10
Man: 2 officers, 16 men **Range:** 1,600/10 **Fuel:** 15 tons
M: 2 Paxman diesels; 2 controllable-pitch props; 700 hp

REMARKS: Built of laminated wood. Quarters for 22. Mount for 1/40-mm. Two echo-sounders; sonar for detecting shipwrecks. Modified version of "-ham" class

♦ *2 "-ham"-class minesweepers, modified as inshore survey craft* — RMAS

(M 2720) WATERWITCH (ex-*Powderham*) **M 2780 WOODLARK** (ex-*Yaxham*)

Bldr: J. Samuel White, Cowes, 11-57 and 1-58

Waterwitch G. Arra, 1972

D: 160 tons (fl) **Dim:** 32.43 (30.48 pp) × 6.45 × 1.70
S: 13/12 kts **Man:** 2 officers, 16 men
Fuel: 15 tons **Range:** 1,500/12
M: 2 Paxman YHAXM diesels; 2 props; 1,100 hp

EXPERIMENTAL SHIPS

♦ *1 sonar-research ship* — RMAS

A 367 NEWTON — Bldr: Scott Lithgow, Greenock — L: 26-6-75

Newton (A 367) Terzibaschitsch, 1977

EXPERIMENTAL SHIPS (*continued*)

D: 3,940 tons (fl) **S:** 15 kts **Dim:** 98.60 (88.70 pp) × 16.15 × 4.70
Range: 5,000/13 **Man:** 61 men (including 12 technicians)
M: 3 Mirrlees-Blackstone diesels, electric drive; 1 Kort nozzle prop; 4,350 hp

REMARKS: Intended for sonar-propagation trials and also fitted to lay cable over the bows. Equipped with bow thruster and passive tank stabilization system. Propulsion plant extremely quiet. Has four laboratories and seven special winches.

NOTE: The sonar-trials ship, former destroyer *Matapan* (D-43), was stricken 7-77 after only 4½ years of service.

♦ *1 torpedo-research vessel* — RMAS

A 364 WHITEHEAD — Bldr: Scotts SB, Greenock — L: 5-5-70

D: 3,040 tons (fl) **S:** 15.5 kts **Dim:** 97.23 (88.70 pp) × 14.63 × 5.20
A: 1/533-mm TT (bow, submerged) — 3/380-mm Mk 32 ASW TT (III × 1)
Man: 10 officers, 47 men and scientists **Range:** 4,000/12
M: 2 Paxman 12 YLCM diesels; 1 prop; 3,400 hp

REMARKS: Designed not only to launch and recover exercise torpedoes but also to perform precision tracking in three dimensions, using passive hydrophone arrays, and post-firing checkout and maintenance on torpedoes.

Whitehead (A 364) 1971

♦ *1 sonar-research barge* — RMAS

(RDV 01) CRYSTAL — Bldr: HMDY, Devonport — L: 5-5-70

D: 3,040 tons (fl) **Dim:** 126.0 × 17.0 × 1.7

REMARKS: No propulsion plant. Assigned to test new sonars at Portland.

♦ *1 weapons-research ship* — RMAS

A 179 WHIMBREL (ex-MRC-1012) (1944)

D: 600 tons (fl) **S:** 10.5 **Dim:** 58.5 × 9.5 × 1.4
M: 2 Paxman diesels; 2 props; 920 hp
Man: . . . **Range:** 1,900/9 **Fuel:** 25 tons

REMARKS: Former repair-configured landing craft employed since 1964 by the Admiralty Underwater Weapons Establishment, Portland. Has a 3-dimensional underwater tracking system.

♦ *1 Miner-class stabilization-systems trials ship* — RMAS

. . . **STEADY** (ex-*Miner VII*) — Bldr: Philip, Dartmouth, 1944

D: 300 tons (355 fl) **S:** 10 kts **Dim:** 33.6 × 8.1 × 2.4
M: 2 Ruston & Hornsby diesels; 2 props; 360 hp

REMARKS: Former minelayer employed in testing gyro systems at Portsmouth. Sister *Britannic* is now a cable-layer.

REPAIR SHIPS

♦ *1 converted Colossus-class aircraft carrier*

	Bldr	Laid down	L	In serv.
A 108 TRIUMPH	Hawthorn Leslie	1-43	2-10-44	4-46

Triumph (A 108) 1970

D: 13,500 tons (17,500 fl) **Dim:** 213.11 (198.17 wl) × 24.39 × 7.15
S: 24 kts **Man:** 27 officers, 472 men
A: 4/40-mm AA (removed) **Range:** 5,500/23, 10,000/14
M: Parsons GT; 2 props; 40,000 hp
Fuel: 3,000 tons **Boilers:** 4 Admiralty; 28 kg/cm², 371°C

REMARKS: Conversion to repair ship 1958 to 1965. Landing and takeoff platform, 3 Wessex helicopters in one hangar, 4 cranes on the flight deck. In reserve at Chatham since 1970.

♦ *1 Head class*

	Bldr	Laid down	L	In serv.
A 134 RAME HEAD	Burrard, Vancouver	7-44	22-11-44	8-45

D: 9,000 tons (11,270 fl) **S:** 10 kts **Dim:** 134.6 (126.8 pp) × 17.5 × 6.9
A: 11/40-mm AA (I × 11) **Man:** 425 men
M: Triple-expansion steam; 1 prop; 2,500 hp
Boilers: 2 Foster-Wheeler; 17 kg/cm², 330°C **Fuel:** 700 tons

REMARKS: Former escort maintenance ship employed as an accommodations ship at Portsmouth since 6-76. Repair equipment maintained on board in preservation since 1972. Has one 12-ton and two 5-ton cranes.

NOTE: Former submarine tenders *Maidstone* and *Forth* stricken 1977-78. *Maidstone* had been an accommodations hulk at Belfast, while *Forth* had been non-operational as a repair hulk at Devonport.

REPAIR SHIPS *(continued)*

Rame Head (A 134) Terzibaschitsch, 1977

FLEET REPLENISHMENT SHIPS

♦ *2 Fort-class* — RFA

	Bldr	Laid down	L	In serv.
A 385 FORT GRANGE	Scotts	9-11-73	9-12-76	1978
A 386 FORT AUSTIN	Scotts	9-12-75	-77	1978

Fort Class — Artist's rendering 1972

D: 17,200 tons **Dim:** 183.8 (170.0 pp) × 24.1 × 9.0
S: 20 kts **Electric:** 4,120 kw
M: 1 8-cyl. Sulzer RND 90 diesel; 1 prop; 23,000 hp

Remarks: Ordered 11-71. Will carry ammunition, provisions, and combat stores. In addition to the flight deck on the stern, the roof of the hangar can land helicopters. Two Wessex will be carried, and the ships will have ASW torpedoes and other ASW stores for their use if needed. The design is a combination of features of the *Resource* and *Lyness* classes. There will be three sliding-stay, constant-tension, alongside-replenishment stations on each beam.

♦ *2 Resource-class* — RFA

	Bldr	Laid down	L	In serv.
A 480 RESOURCE	Scott's SB (Greenock)	6-64	11-2-66	5-67
A 486 REGENT	Harland & Wolff	9-64	9-3-66	6-67

Resource (A 480) J. C. Bellonne, 1972

D: 19,000 tons (fl) (18,029 light) **S:** 17 kts
Dim: 195.07 (182.88 pp) × 23.47 × 7.95
Man: 182 men, including 11 RN
M: Assoc. Electric Industries GT; 1 prop; 20,000 hp
Boilers: 2 Foster-Wheeler

♦ *3 Lyness class* — RFA

	Bldr	Laid down	L	In serv.
A 339 LYNESS	Swan Hunter	4-65	7-4-66	12-66
A 344 STROMNESS	Swan Hunter	10-65	16-9-66	3-67
A 345 TARBATNESS	Swan Hunter	4-66	22-2-67	8-67

Lyness (A 339) 1972

FLEET REPLENISHMENT SHIPS (*continued*)

D: 9,010 tons, light (16,792 fl) **Dim:** 159.76 (149.39 pp) × 21.95 × 6.70
S: 17 kts **Man:** 25 officers, 126 men
Tonnage: 7,782 dwt, 12,359 grt, 4,744 nrt
M: Sulzer 8-cyl. RD.76 diesel; 1 prop; 11,520 hp

REMARKS: Platform for two helicopters. Improved holds with hoists. Closed-circuit TV provided to monitor handling of stores. A-339 is especially configured to act as air-stores support ship. The others carry food and stores, but not ammunition.

♦ *2 Retainer-class ammunition ships* — RFA

	L
A 329 RETAINER (ex-*Chungking*)	19-1-50
A 280 RESURGENT (ex-*Changchow*)	31-7-50

Bldr: Scott's — Completed in 1950-51. Bought and modified 1952-1956

Retainer (A 329) British Crown Copyright, 1972

D: 14,400 tons (fl) **Dim:** 145.80 × 18.92 × 8.83 (fl)
S: 14 kts **Man:** 107 men
M: 1 Doxford diesel; 1 prop; 6,500 hp **Fuel:** 925 tons

REMARKS: A-280: 9,357 grt; A-329: 9,498 grt. Former mixed-cargo ships of the China Line. Carry mainly ammunition, but also some combat stores. May be replaced by the new *Fort*-class.

♦ *2 Bacchus-class cargo ships* — RFA

A 404 BACCHUS, A 406 HEBE — Bldr: Henry Robb, Ltd., 1962

D: 2,740 tons light (8,173 fl) **Dim:** 115.52 (106.70 pp) × 16.76 × 6.40
S: 17 kts **Man:** 57 men
M: 2 Sulzer SRD 68 diesels; 1 prop; 5,500 hp
Fuel: 720 tons **Range:** 14,000/15

REMARKS: 4,823 grt, 5,318 dwt. Chartered for 19 years upon completion. Living spaces and machinery area aft. Transportation of cargo and provisions. Three holds. Refrigerated compartments. Can carry 800 tons fuel oil, 200 tons lube oil, 240 tons of fresh water. Not intended for underway replenishment.

Hebe (A 406) Guiglini, 1974

FLEET OILERS

♦ *3 Olwen class* — RFA

	Bldr	L	In serv.
A 122 OLWEN (ex-*Olynthus*)	Hawthorn Leslie	10-7-64	6-65
A 123 OLNA	Hawthorn Leslie	28-7-75	4-66
A 124 OLMEDA (ex-*Oleander*)	Swan Hunter	19-11-64	10-65

Olmeda (A 124) 1974

D: 10,890 tons light (36,000 fl)
S: 20 kts
Dim: 197.51 (185.92 pp) × 25.60 × 10.50
Man: 87 men
M: Pamatreda GT; 1 prop; 26,500 hp
Boilers: 2 Babcock & Wilcox, 60 kg/cm^2, superheat 510°C

REMARKS: Hull reinforced against ice, living spaces air-conditioned; advanced automation, excellent facilities for replenishment at sea. Helicopter platform. Hangar to port recently enlarged to hold 3 Wessex helicopters. 25,000 dwt, 18,600 grt. Can carry 18,400 tons fuel oil, 1,720 tons diesel, 3,730 tons aircraft fuel, 130 tons lube oil.

FLEET OILERS (*continued*)

♦ *2 later Tide class* — RFA

	Laid down	L	In serv.
A 75 TIDESPRING	7-61	3-5-62	1-63
A 76 TIDEPOOL	12-61	11-12-62	6-63

Bldr: Hawthorn Leslie, Hebburn-on-Tyne

Tidespring (A 75)

D: 8,531 tons light (27,400 fl) **Dim:** 177.60 (167.65 pp) × 21.64 × 9.75
S: 18.3 kts **Man:** 110 men
M: 1 Pamatreda GT; 1 prop; 15,000 hp
Boilers: 2 Babcock & Wilcox, 60 kg/cm^2, 510°C

REMARKS: 18,900 dwt, 14,130 grt. As built, carried 17,400 tons fuel oil and 700 tons diesel, but with RN dependence on gas-turbine propulsion, proportions may have changed. Hangar and flight deck for 2 Wessex helicopters.

NOTE: Older Tide-class ships discarded 1975-78.

SMALL FLEET OILERS

♦ *5 Rover class* — RFA

A 268 GREEN ROVER (19-12-68), **A 269 GREY ROVER** (17-4-69), **A 270 BLUE ROVER** (11-11-69), **A 271 GOLD ROVER** (7-3-73), **A 273 BLACK ROVER** (30-8-73)

Bldr: Swan Hunter

Blue Rover (A 270) 1970

D: 4,700 tons light (11,522 fl) **Dim:** 140.50 × 19.20 × 7.30
S: 18 kts **Man:** 47 men
M: 2 SEMT-Pielstick 16PA 4 diesels (V-16); 1 controllable-pitch prop; 15,300 hp

REMARKS: 7,060 dwt, 7,510 grt. Carry 6,600 tons fuel plus water, dry stores, and provisions. Helicopter deck but no hangar.

SUPPORT OILERS

♦ *1 mobile reserve tanker* — RFA

A 219 DEWDALE (ex-*Edenfield*) — Bldr: Harland & Wolff, 1965

D: 77,519 tons (fl) **S:** 15 kts **Dim:** 236.2 (227.8 fl) × 32.9 × 12.7
M: 1 Burmeister & Wain 884-VTT2BF180 diesel; 16,800 hp **Man:** 51 men

REMARKS: Chartered 7-67. No underway replenishment capability. 63,588 dwt; 35,640 grt.

♦ *4 Leaf group support oilers* — all on charter to RFA

A 82 CHERRYLEAF (ex-*Overseas Adventurer*) — Bldr: Rheinstal FRG, 1963

D: 28,000 tons (fl) **S:** 16 kts **Dim:** 170.5 × 22.0 × 9.2
M: 1 7-cyl. M.A.N. diesel; 1 prop; 8,400 hp

REMARKS: No underway replenishment capability. 19,700 dwt; 13,700 grt.

A 78 PLUMLEAF — Bldr: Blyth — L: 15-10-59

Plumleaf (A 78) G. Arra, 1976

D: 26,480 tons (fl) **S:** 15.5 kts **Dim:** 170.8 × 22.0 × 9.2
M: 1 6-cyl. Doxford diesel; 1 prop; 9,500 hp

REMARKS: 19,430 dwt, 12,459 grt. Can refuel at sea alongside (2 stations) or astern.

A 77 PEARLEAF — Bldr: Blythwood, Glasgow — L: 15-10-59

D: 25,790 tons (fl) **S:** 16 kts **Dim:** 173.2 (162.7 pp) × 21.9 × 9.2
M: 1 Rowan-Doxford 6-cyl. diesel; 1 prop; 8,800 hp

REMARKS: 18,711 dwt, 12,353 grt. Can refuel at sea alongside (2 stations) or astern.

SUPPORT OILERS (*continued*)

A 80 ORANGELEAF (ex-*Southern Satellite*) — Bldr: Furness SB — L: 8-2-55

D: 24,000 tons (fl) **S:** 14 kts **Dim:** 169.7 (160.1 pp) × 21.9 × 9.3
M: 1 Doxford 6-cyl. diesel; 1 prop; 6,800 hp **Fuel:** 1,610 tons

REMARKS: 18,222 dwt, 12,146 grt. Chartered 25-5-59. Can refuel at sea alongside (2 stations) or astern.

♦ *1 Eddy-class coastal tanker* — RFA

A 261 EDDYFIRTH — Bldr: Lobnitz, Renfrew — In serv. 2-54

Eddyfirth (A 261)

D: 1,960 tons light (4,160 fl) **Dim:** 87.65 (82.30 pp) × 13.44 × 5.26
S: 12.5 kts **Man:** 26 men
M: Triple-expansion; 1 prop; 1,750 hp **Boilers:** 2 Scotch-type, 17 kg/cm^2
Range: 7,550/11 **Fuel:** 515 tons

REMARKS: Last of a class of eight. 2,200 dwt, 2,222 grt. Carries 1,500 tons light petroleum products, 246 tons dry cargo, 50 tons lube oil. No underway replenishment capability.

MISCELLANEOUS AUXILIARY SHIPS

♦ *1 helicopter training ship* — RFA

	Bldr	Laid down	L	In serv.
K 08 ENGADINE	Henry Robb Ltd.	8-65	16-9-66	12-67

D: 3,640 tons light (9,000 fl) **S:** 16 kts
Dim: 129.31 × 17.86 × 6.73
Man: 61 RFA plus 14 RN (and 113 air group with 29 officers)
M: 1 Sulzer 5RD68, 5-cyl. diesel; 1 prop; 5,500 hp
Electric: 1,200 kw

REMARKS: Intended to train flight crews in ASW helicopter procedures at sea. The hangar can hold either 4 Wessex or 2 Sea King and 2 Wasp. A smaller hangar atop the superstructure serves a target drone launch facility. Equipped with Denny-Brown fin stabilizers and has remote bridge control for all engineering plant. Much internal space is void.

Engadine (K 08) G. Arra, 1976

♦ *1 patrol ship*

H 171 ENDURANCE (ex-*Anita Dan*)
Bldr: Kröger-Werft, Rendsburg, 25-5-56

Endurance (A 171) G. Arra, 1975

D: 3,600 tons (fl) **Dim:** 93.58 (82.90 pp) × 14.03 × 5.03
S: 14.5 kts **Man:** 13 officers, 106 men, up to 12 scientists
A: 2/20-mm AA (I × 2) **Range:** 12,000/14
M: 1 Burmeister & Wain 550VTBF, 5-cyl. diesel; 1 prop (plus a bow prop); 3,220 hp

MISCELLANEOUS AUXILIARY SHIPS (*continued*)

REMARKS: Hull painted red, superstructure white. Carries two Whirlwind-9 helicopters and two survey launches. Converted 1967-68 by Harland & Wolff, Belfast, to support the British Antarctic Survey and act as guard ship in the Falkland Islands. 2,641 grt.

♦ *1 royal yacht*

	Bldr	Laid down	L	In serv.
BRITANNIA	J. Brown (Clydebank)	7-52	16-4-53	1-54

A. and J. Pavia

D: 3,990 tons (4,961 fl) **Dim:** 125.90 (115.82 pp) × 16.76 × 4.86
S: 21 kts **Man:** 270 men
Fuel: 490 tons **Range:** 2,100/20, 3,000/15
M: GT; 2 props; 12,000 hp **Boilers:** 2

REMARKS: In wartime, would become a hospital ship (200 beds and 60 medical personnel) and have a helicopter platform. Gyro-stabilizer.

♦ *1 submarine-support ship*

A 236 WAKEFUL (ex-*Dan*, ex-*Herakles*) — Bldr: Cochrane, Selkirk, 1965

D: 1,100 tons (fl) **S:** . . . **Dim:** 44.43 (38.86 pp) × 10.7 × 4.74
M: Ruston & Hornsby 9-cyl. diesels; 1 prop; . . . hp **Man:** 14 men
Fuel: 247 tons **Electric:** 380 kw

REMARKS: Purchased 1974 from Sweden to act as submarine target ship and safety vessel at Faslane; subsequently, also used occasionally on fisheries patrol duties. Former commercial tug, 492 grt.

♦ *1 submarine rescue and salvage ship*

A 231 RECLAIM (ex-*Salverdant*) — Bldr: Simons, Renfrew — L: 12-3-48

Reclaim (A 231) Terzibaschitsch, 1977

D: 1,200 tons (1,800 fl) **S:** 12 kts **Dim:** 66.4 × 11.6 × 4.7
M: Triple-expansion; 1 prop; 1,500 hp **Boilers:** 2 Scotch, 17 kg/cm²
Range: 3,000/10 **Fuel:** 310 tons **Man:** 100 men

REMARKS: Equipped for general-purpose salvage, wreck-location, tending divers, and submarine rescue. Carries sonar. Due for replacement.

♦ *1 cable-layer and repair ship* — RMAS

(A 259) ST. MARGARETS — Bldr: Swan Hunter, 1944

D: 1,300 tons (2,500 fl) **Dim:** 76.8 (69.7 pp) × 10.9 × 4.8
S: 12 kts **Boilers:** 2 Scotch, 17 kg/cm²
M: Triple-expansion; 2 props; 1,250 hp

REMARKS: 1,200 dwt, 1,524 grt. Lays and recovers cables over the bow. Sister *Bullfinch* stricken 1975.

MOORING, SALVAGE, AND NET TENDERS

♦ *2 Pochard class* — RMAS

(P 196) POCHARD (L: 21-6-73) **(P 197) GOOSANDER** (L: 12-4-73)
Bldr: Robb Caledon

Goosander (P 197) Robb Caledon, 1974

MOORING, SALVAGE, AND NET TENDERS *(continued)*

D: 750 tons (1,200 fl) **Dim:** 55.4 (48.8 pp) × 12.2 × 5.5
S: 10 kts **Man:** 26 men
M: 2 Paxman RPHXM 16-cyl. diesels; 550 hp
Range: 3,000/10

REMARKS: All mooring, salvage, and boom vessels are multi-purpose and are capable of transporting and servicing moorings, performing salvage duties, and, in wartime, handling harbor-defense nets.

♦ *4 Wild Duck class* — RMAS

	Bldr	L	In serv.
(P 192) MANDARIN	Cammell Laird	17-9-63	2-64
(P 193) PINTAIL	Cammell Laird	3-12-63	3-64
(P 194) GARGANEY	Brooke Marine Ltd	13-12-65	9-66
(P 195) GOLDENEYE	Brooke Marine Ltd	31-3-66	12-66

Goldeneye G. Arra, 1975

D: 850 tons (1,300 fl) (P-192, P-193: 941/1,622 tons)
Dim: 57.86 (47.24 pp) × 13.0 × 3.20 (P-192, P-193: 60.23 × 12.22 × 4.21)
S: 10.8 kts
Man: 7 officers, 18 men
M: 2 Davey-Paxman diesels, 16 cyl.; controllable-pitch prop; 550 hp (P-192, P-193: 750 hp)
Electric: P-194, P-195: 640 kw; P-192, P-193: 405 kw

♦ *2 Lay class* — RMAS

(P 190) LAYMOOR (6-8-59)
(P 191) LAYBURN (14-4-60)

Bldr: Wm. Simons & Co.

D: 800 tons (1,050 fl) **Dim:** 58.83 (48.77 pp) × 10.36 × 3.50
S: 14 kts **Man:** 4 officers, 26 men
M: Triple-expansion; 1 prop, 1,300 hp
Boilers: 2 Foster-Wheeler, 17 kg/cm²

Layburn, now painted black & gray 1960

♦ *4 Kin class (1944–45)* — RMAS

(A 281) KINBRACE **(A 482) KINLOSS**
(A 232) KINGARTH **(A 507) UPLIFTER**

D: 950 tons (1,050 fl) **S:** 9 kts
M: 1 Atlas Polar M44M diesel; 630 hp
Dim: 54.0 × 10.6 × 3.6
Man: 34 men

REMARKS: 200 tons lift. Originally had reciprocating steam engines; diesels fitted 1964–67.

NOTE: The Insect-class fleet tender *Scarab* is also equipped as a moorings tender (10-ton lift).

SEAGOING TUGS

♦ *3 Roysterer class* — RMAS

		L	In serv.
	ROYSTERER	20-5-70	4-72
A 502	**ROLLICKER**	29-1-71	2-73
	ROBUST	7-10-71	4-74

Roysterer 1972

SEAGOING TUGS (*continued*)

D: 1,630 tons (fl) **S:** 15 kts **Dim:** 54.8 (49.4 pp) × 11.6 × 5.5
M: 2 Mirrlees KMR6 diesels; 2 props; 4,500 hp **Range:** 13,000/12
Man: 31 men (plus 10-man RN salvage party if needed)

REMARKS: 50-ton bollard pull. Although designed for long-distance towing, have been used primarily in port service.

♦ *1 Typhoon class* — RMAS

A 95 TYPHOON — Bldr: H. Robb, Leith — L: 14-10-58

D: 800 tons (1,380 fl) **S:** 17 kts **Dim:** 60.5 × 12.3 × 4.0
M: 2 12-cyl. diesels; 1 controllable-pitch prop; 2,750 hp

REMARK: 32-ton bollard pull.

Typhoon (A 95) G. Arra, 1975

♦ *5 Confiance class* — RMAS

A 88 AGILE, A 89 ADVICE, A 90 ACCORD, A 289 CONFIANCE, A 290 CONFIDENT

Bldr: Inglis, Glasgow, except A-88: Goole — In serv. 1956-59

D: 760 tons (fl) **Dim:** 47.2 (42.7 pp) × 10.7 × 3.4
S: 13 kts **Man:** 29 men (plus 13 salvage)
M: 4 Paxman HAXM diesels; 2 controllable-pitch props; 1,800 hp

♦ *2 Samson class* — RMAS

A 288 SEA GIANT — SUPERMAN — Bldr: A. Hall, Aberdeen, 1954-55

D: 1,200 tons (fl) **S:** 15 kts **Dim:** 54.9 × 11.3 × 4.3
M: 2 sets triple-expansion; 2 props; 3,000 hp **Boilers:** 2

REMARKS: *Superman* in reserve. Sister *Samson* stricken 1974.

♦ *1 Bustler class* — RMAS

A 111 CYCLONE (ex-*Growler*) — Bldr: H. Robb, Leith — L: 10-9-42

D: 1,118 tons (1,630 fl) **S:** 16 kts **Dim:** 62.5 (58.0 pp) × 12.3 × 5.1
Man: 42 men **Fuel:** 405 tons
M: 2 Polar 8-cyl. diesels; 1 prop; 4,000 hp **Range:** 17,000/14

REMARKS: Last of a class of four, in reserve. Sister *Reward* rammed and sunk 1976 while serving as North Sea patrol ship; salvaged and scrapped.

SERVICE CRAFT
AMMUNITION LIGHTERS — RMAS

♦ *1 new construction* — Bldr: Cleland, Wallsend, 1977

THROSK

D: 1,800 tons (fl) **S:** 14 kts **Dim:** 64.3 × 11.9 × 4.6
M: 2 Mirrlees Blackstone diesels; 1 prop; 3,000 hp

REMARKS: 1,150 dwt. Two holds, two 5-ton cranes. Ordered 12-75.

♦ *1 Kinterbury class* — Bldr: Philip and Son, 1943

(A 378) KINTERBURY

D: 1,490 tons (1,770 fl) **Dim:** 60.90 (56.39 pp) × 10.46 × 3.96
S: 11 kts **Man:** 21 men
Range: 2,600/11 **Fuel:** 154 tons coal
M: Triple-expansion; 1 prop; 900 hp **Boilers:** 2 Scotch, 17 kg/cm^2

REMARKS: 600 dwt. Converted 1959 to transport Sea Slug missiles. Sister *Throsk* stricken 1977.

♦ *1 Gun class* — RMAS

(A 377) MAXIM — Bldr: Lobnitz, 1944

D: 383 tons (707 fl) **Dim:** 44.0 (40.8 pp) × 7.9 × 2.4
S: 10.5 kts **Man:** 13 men **Fuel:** 60 tons
M: Triple-expansion; 1 prop; 490 hp **Range:** 1,200/10

REMARKS: 340 dwt. In reserve.

DEGAUSSING TENDERS

♦ *3 converted "-ham" class* — RMAS

(M 2717) FORDHAM (M 2790) THATCHAM (M 2737) WARMINGHAM

REMARKS: Details as for "-ham"-class tenders. Deckhouse greatly enlarged, cable reel at stern.

TORPEDO RETRIEVERS

♦ *2 Torrent class, seagoing* — RMAS

(A 127) TORRENT — (A 128) TORRID — In serv.: 9-71 and 1-72

Bldr: Cleland, Wallsend

D: 468 tons (685 fl) **Dim:** 49.55 (44.20 pp) × 9.72 × 3.05
S: 11.5 kts **Man:** 19 men
M: Paxman 16 RPHM diesel; 1 prop; 700 hp **Fuel:** 49 tons
Range: 1,500/11 **Electric:** 300 kw

TORPEDO RETRIEVERS (*continued*)

Torrent 1972

Remarks: Can stow 32 torpedoes on deck and perform post-firing maintenance. Stern ramp for recovery.

♦ *6 converted "-ham" class* — RMAS

(M 2614) BUCKLESHAM (M 2622) DOWNHAM (M 2626) EVERINGHAM
(M 2630) FRITHAM (M 2635) HAVERSHAM (M 2636) LASHAM

Remarks: Details as for "-ham"-class tenders. Ramp in stern for torpedo recovery.

♦ *1 former cargo lighter, converted 1968* — RMAS

THOMAS GRANT — Bldr: Chas. Hill, Bristol, 11-5-53

D: 209 tons (460 fl) **Dim:** 34.59 (31.85 pp) × 7.77 × 3.05
S: 9 kts **Fuel:** 10 tons
M: 2 Mirrlees Blackstone diesels; 2 props; 590 hp

Remark: 252 dwt; 218 grt.

DIVING TENDERS

♦ *4 modified Cartmel class* — RMAS

(A 389) CLOVELLY ILCHESTER INSTOW (A 310) INVERGORDON
In serv.: 1972–74

Remark: Details and appearance as for Cartmel-class tenders, except for decompression chamber on deck forward.

♦ *1 Datchet class* — RMAS

DATCHET — Bldr: Vosper, Singapore — In serv.: 1968

D: 70 tons (fl) **S:** 12 kts **Dim:** 22.86 × 5.79 × 1.22
M: 2 Gray Marine diesels; 2 props; 500 hp
Range: 500/12

TRAINING CRAFT

♦ *3 "-ham"-class former inshore minesweepers*

M 2621 DITTISHAM M 2628 FLINTHAM M 2793 THORNHAM
In serv.: 1954–57

D: 120 tons (157 fl) **Dim:** 32.47 (30.48 pp) × 6.61 × 1.75
S: 14 kts **Man:** 15 men
A: 1/20-mm AA **Range:** 2,350/9
M: 2 Paxman YHAXM 12-cyl. diesels; 2 props; 1,100 hp **Fuel:** 15 tons

Remarks: M-2621 and M-2628 employed for enlisted basic training; M-2793 attached to Aberdeen University naval training unit. All minesweeping gear removed.

♦ *2 Ley-class former inshore minehunters*

M 2002 AVELEY (1953) **M 2010 ISIS** (ex-*Cradley*)

Aveley (M 2002) G. Arra, 1976

D: 123 tons (140 fl) **Dim:** 32.44 (30.48 pp) × 6.10 × 1.68
S: 14 kts **Man:** 15 men
A: M-2010 only: 1/40-mm AA **Electric:** 108 kw
M: 2 Paxman YHAXM 12-cyl. diesels; 2 props; 1,100 hp

Remarks: Survivors of 10 built. Had sonars vice magnetic sweep gear; otherwise similar to "-ham" class but with larger superstructure. M-2010 attached to Southampton University; M-2002 is tender at Plymouth.

♦ *2 Ford-class former submarine chasers*

P 3104 DEE (ex-*Beckford*) (1953) **P 3113 DROXFORD** (1954)

D: 115 tons (138 fl) **Dim:** 35.76 (33.53 fl) × 6.10 × 1.68
S: 18 kts **Man:** 19 men
A: Removed **Range:** 500/12; 1,000/8 (cruise diesel) **Fuel:** 23 tons
M: 2 Paxman YHAXM diesels (500 hp each), 1 Foden FD 6 diesel (100 hp); 3 props

Remarks: Survivors of a class of 20, some transferred abroad. P-3104 attached to Liverpool University, P-3113 to Glasgow University for naval cadet training.

CABLE TENDER

♦ *1 converted Miner class* — RMAS

BRITANNIC (ex-*Miner V*) — Bldr: Philip & Son — L: 2-11-40

Britannic G. Arra, 1972

D: 300 tons (355 fl) **S:** 10 kts **Dim:** 33.6 × 8.1 × 2.4
M: 2 Ruston & Hornsby diesels; 2 props; 360 hp

REMARKS: Former minelayer now used for harbor service as a cable tender. Sister *Steady* is a trials ship.

FUEL LIGHTERS

♦ *6 Oil class* — RMAS

(Y 21) OILPRESS	**(Y 23) OILWELL**	**(Y 25) OILBIRD**
(Y 22) OILSTONE	**(Y 24) OILFIELD**	**(Y 26) OILMAN**

Bldr: Appledore, 1969

Oilwell G. Arra, 1976

D: 250 tons (535 fl) **Dim:** 42.26 (39.62 pp) × 7.47 × 2.51
S: 10 kts **Man:** 4 officers, 7 men
Range: 1,500/10 **Fuel:** 15 tons
M: 1 Lister-Blackstone ES6MGR diesel; 405 hp **Electric:** 225 kw

REMARK: First three carry diesel fuel and are 247 tons (527 fl); other three carry fuel oil.

WATER LIGHTERS

♦ *6 Water class* — RMAS

(Y 15) WATERCOURSE	**(Y 17) WATERFALL**	**(Y 19) WATERSPOUT**
(Y 16) WATERFOWL	**(Y 18) WATERSHED**	**(Y 20) WATERSIDE**

Bldr: Drypool, Hull, 1966-73

D: 344 tons (478 fl) **Dim:** 40.02 (37.5 pp) × 7.50 × 2.44
S: 11 kts **Man:** 11 men
Range: 1,500/11 **Electric:** 155 kw
M: 1 Lister-Blackstone ERS8MGR diesel; 600 hp

REMARKS: Carry 150 tons water cargo. Resemble Oil class. Y-15 and Y-16 (L: 1973) have deckhouse over cargo tanks.

♦ *2 Spa class* — RMAS

	Bldr	In serv.
(A 222) SPAPOOL	Chas. Hill, Bristol	1947
(A 224) SPABROOK	Philip, Dartmouth	1946

D: 1,219 tons (fl) **S:** 9 kts **Dim:** 52.43 × 9.14 × 3.66
Fuel: 90 tons coal **Cargo:** 500 tons water
M: Triple-expansion, 1 boiler; 1 prop; 675 hp

♦ *2 Fresh class* — RMAS

FRESHLAKE, FRESHSPRING

D: 594 tons (fl) **S:** 9 kts **Dim:** 38.47 × 7.77 × 3.28
Fuel: 42 tons coal (*Freshspring:* oil) **Cargo:** 236 tons water
M: Triple-expansion, 1 boiler; 1 prop; 450 hp

TANK-CLEANING CRAFT

♦ *6 Isles-class converted escorts*

(A 334) BERN	**(A 340) GRAEMSAY**	**(A 338) SKOMER**
(A 332) CALDY	**(A 336) LUNDY**	**(A 346) SWITHA**

All in serv. 1942-43

D: 560 tons (770 fl) **Dim:** 49.99 (45.72 pp) × 8.43 × 4.19
S: 12 kts **Range:** 4,200/8 **Fuel:** 183 tons coal
M: Triple-expansion, 1 boiler; 1 prop; 850 hp

REMARKS: Survivors of 155 built as ASW trawlers or minesweepers. Converted 1951-57 for cleaning fuel tanks of other ships. *Coll* stricken 1977. Sister *Mull* serves Army as a cargo ship.

GENERAL-PURPOSE TENDERS

♦ *7 100-foot Insect class* — RMAS

BEE	**COCKCHAFER**	**GNAT**	**SCARAB**
CICALA	**CRICKET**	**LADYBIRD**	

Bldr: C. D. Holmes, 1970-73

GENERAL-PURPOSE TENDERS (*continued*)

D: 213 tons (450 fl) **Dim:** 34.06 (30.48 pp) × 8.53 × 3.20
S: 10.5 kts **Man:** 10 men
M: 1 Lister-Blackstone ERS8HGR diesel; 660 hp

REMARKS: 200 tons cargo, one 3-ton crane. *Scarab,* with 5-ton winch and bow horn, is used as a moorings tender.

♦ *3 Loyal class* — RMAS

LOYAL CHANCELLOR, (A 220) LOYAL MODERATOR, (A 1771) LOYAL PROCTOR

Bldr: R. Dunston, Thorne, 1974-75

Loyal Moderator (A 220) Terzibaschitsch, 1977

REMARKS: Details as for *Cartmel* class but equipped to carry up to 200 personnel in cargo hold for short distances (except A-220, RMAS training craft, 12 extra berths instead). Five additional units were ordered 1976.

♦ *2 Loyal-class fleet tenders*

A 382 VIGILANT (ex-*Loyal Factor*)
A 510 ALERT (ex-*Loyal Governor*)

REMARKS: Details as for other units of the class. Used for patrol duties off Ulster and commissioned with Royal Navy crews. May carry machine guns.

♦ *29 75-foot Cartmel class* — RMAS

CARTMEL, CAWSAND, CRICCIETH, CRICKLADE, CROMARTY, DENMEAD, DORNOCH, (A 393) DUNSTER, (A 353) ELKSTONE, (A 277) ELSING, (A 352) EPWORTH, (A 274) ETTRICK, (A 384) FELSTED, FINTRY, FOTHERBY, (A 354) FROXFIELD, FULBECK, GLENCOVE, GRASMERE, HAMBLEDON, HARLECH, HEADCORN, HEVER, (A 1772) HOLMWOOD, (A 1773) HORNING, (A 318) IXWORTH, LAMLASH, LECHLADE, LLANDOVERY

Bldrs: Various, 1971-74

D: 143 tons (fl) **Dim:** 24.38 (22.86 pp) × 6.40 × 1.98
S: 10.5 kts **Man:** 6 men
M: 1 Lister-Blackstone ERS4MGR diesel; 330 hp
Range: 700/10
Electric: 106 kw

REMARKS: Improved version of *Aberdovey* class; 25 tons cargo. First two, 5.49-m beam Carry stores, personnel, food. Can tow.

♦ *12 75-foot Aberdovey class* — RMAS

ABERDOVEY, ABINGER, ALNESS, ALNMOUTH, APPLEBY, ASHCOTT, (A 99) BEAULIEU, (A 100) BEDDGELERT, (A 101) BEMBRIDGE, (A 103) BIBURY, (A 104) BLAKENEY, (A 105) BRODICK

Bldrs: First 6: I. Pimblott, Norwich, 1963-68; others: I. S. Doig, Grimsby, 1966-71

D: 117.5 tons (fl) **Dim:** 24.16 (22.86 pp) × 5.79 × 1.68
S: 10.5 kts **Range:** 700/10
M: 1 Lister-Blackstone ER4MGR diesel; 225 hp

REMARKS: Carry 25 tons cargo. *Alnmouth* used for Sea Cadet Corps training.

♦ *6 "-ham"-class former inshore minesweepers* — RMAS

(M 2716) PAGHAM, (M 2781) PORTISHAM, (M 2784) PUTTENHAM, (M 2726) SHIPHAM, (M 2733) THAKEHAM, (M 2735) TONGHAM (1953-57)

Pagham (M 2716) Terzibaschitsch, 1977

REMARKS: Details as for "-ham"-class training craft; no armament, all sweep gear removed. Carry passengers and stores.

LARGE HARBOR TUGS

♦ *19 Dog class* — RMAS

(A 102) AIREDALE, (A 106) ALSATIAN, (A 327) BASSET, (A 394) . . . , (A 126) CAIRN, (A 328) COLLIE, (A 330) CORGI, (A 129) DALMATIAN, (A 155) DEERHOUND, (A 162) ELKHOUND, (A 169) HUSKY, (A 168) LABRADOR, (A 180) MASTIFF, (A 188) POINTER, (A 182) SALUKI, (A 187) SEALYHAM, (A 189) SETTER, (A 250) SHEEPDOG, (A 201) SPANIEL (1962–72)

D: 206 tons (248 fl) **Dim:** 28.65 (25.91 pp) × 7.72 × 3.51
S: 10.5 kts **Man:** 8 men **Electric:** 80 kw
M: 2 Lister-Blackstone ERS86MGR diesels; 1 prop; 1,320 hp

Remark: 18.7-ton bollard pull.

Setter G. Arra, 1975

♦ *7 Dexterous-class paddle tugs* — RMAS

(A 93) DEXTEROUS, (A 94) DIRECTOR, (A 85) FAITHFUL, (A 86) FORCEFUL, (A 87) FAVOURITE, (A 92) GRINDER, (A 91) GRIPER

Bldrs: Yarrow (except A-87): Ferguson), 1957–59

D: 710 tons (fl)
S: 13 kts
M: 4 Paxman diesels (500 hp each), 2 electric motors; 2 paddles; 1,600 hp
Dim: 47.91 (44.20 pp) × 18.24 × 3.04
Man: 21 men

Remarks: Built to handle aircraft carriers; world's only naval paddle tugs. Hull beam 9.14 m.

Director

MEDIUM HARBOR TUGS

♦ *5 Felicity-class water tractors* — RMAS

FELICITY, FIONA, GEORGINA, GWENDOLINE, HELEN

Bldr: Hancock, Pembroke, except *Felicity:* Dunston — In serv. 1973

D: 220 tons (fl) **S:** 8 kts **Dim:** 21.95 (20.73 pp) × 6.4 × 2.97
M: 1 Lister-Blackstone ERS8MGR diesel; cycloidal propeller; 615 hp

♦ *9 modified Girl class* — RMAS

(A 206) CELIA, (A 210) CHARLOTTE, (A 217) CHRISTINE, (A 288) CLARE, (A 145) DAISY, DAPHNE, (A 252) DORIS, DOROTHY, (A 177) EDITH

Bldrs: First four: I. Pimblott, others: R. Dunston — In serv. 1972

D: 100 tons (fl) **S:** 10.5 kts **Dim:** 20.57 × 6.25 × 2.90
M: 1 Lister-Blackstone ERS6MGR diesel; 495 hp **Range:** 900/10

Remarks: 50 grt. 6.5-ton bollard pull

♦ *8 Girl class* — RMAS

(A 116) AGATHA, (A 121) AGNES, (A 113) ALICE, (A 117) AUDREY, (A 324) BARBARA, (A 232) BETTY, (A 335) BRENDA, (A 322) BRIDGET

Bldrs: First four: P. Harris; others: R. Dunston, 1962–72

D: 66.5 tons (81 fl) **S:** 10 kts **Dim:** 18.75 (17.30 pp) × 5.11 × 2.36
M: 1 Lister-Blackstone ERS6MGR diesel; 495 hp **Range:** 980/9.8

Remarks: 40 grt; 6.5-ton bollard pull

SMALL HARBOR TUGS

♦ *12 Triton-class water tractors* — RMAS

IRENE, ISABEL, JOAN, JOYCE, KATHLEEN, KITTY, LESLEY, LILAH, MARY, MYRTLE, NANCY, NORAH

Bldr: R. Dunston, 1972–74

D: 107.5 tons (fl) **S:** 7.75 kts **Dim:** 17.65 (16.76 pp) × 5.26 × 2.80
M: 1 Lister-Blackstone ERS4M diesel; cycloidal prop; 330 hp

Remarks: 50 grt; 3-ton bollard pull. Voith vertical cycloidal prop to provide instant mobility and full power in any direction.

GREECE

PERSONNEL: About 16,500 men, including 1,900 officers

MERCHANT MARINE (1976): 2,921 ships — 25,034,585 grt
(tankers: 406 ships — 8,910,322 grt)

NAVAL AVIATION: The Greek Navy has 4 Alouette III ASW helicopters fitted with AS 12. These aircraft are the first of the future Greek naval aviation arm, which began when these helicopters were placed in service in April 1975. The Air Force has a dozen Albatross amphibian planes for antisubmarine warfare.

NAVAL PROGRAM: The following long- and short-term projects are planned:
- Modernization of the *Gearing*-class destroyers
- Purchase of 6 *La Combattante-III*-class missile boats, for a total of 10 in that class
- Purchase of 4 additional Type-209 submarines, for a total of 8
- Purchase of 4 medium-tonnage frigates

WARSHIPS IN SERVICE OR UNDER CONSTRUCTION AS OF 1 OCTOBER 1977

	L	Tons	Main armament
♦ *10 submarines*			
8 TYPE 209	1970–71	980	8/533-mm TT
1 GUPPY III	1945	1,660	10/533-mm TT
1 GUPPY II	1944	1,500	10/533-mm TT
♦ *12 destroyers*			
5 GEARING	1944–45	2,425	4-6/127-mm, Asroc (in 4), 6 ASW TT
1 ALLEN M. SUMNER	1944	2,200	6/127-mm, 6 ASW TT
6 FLETCHER	1942–43	2,050	4/127-mm, 6/76-mm AA, 10/40-mm AA
♦ *4 frigates*			
4 CANNON	1942–43	1,300	3/76-mm AA, ASW weapons
♦ *3 corvettes*			
3 173-FT	1943–44	325	1/76-mm, ASW weapons
♦ *35 guided-missile and torpedo patrol boats*			
4 LA COMBATTANTE III	1976–77	400	4 MM 38, 2/76-mm
10 LA COMBATTANTE II	1971–79	234	4 MM 38 or 6 Penguin, 4/35-mm AA
2 KELEFSTIS STAMOU	1975	80	2/20-mm AA, 4/SS-12 SSM
5 TJELD	1966–67	69	4/533-mm TT
1 FEROCITY	1961	75	2/40-mm AA, 2/533-mm TT
1 BRAVE	1962	95	2/40-mm AA, 2/533-mm TT
7 S-141	1958	160	2/40-mm AA, 4/533-mm TT
5 SILBERMÖWE	1951–56	110	1/40-mm AA, 2/533-mm TT
♦ *15 minesweepers*			
♦ *2 minelayers*			

SUBMARINES

♦ *8 German type 209* — Bldr: Howaldtswerke, Kiel

	Laid down	L	In serv.
S 110 GLAVKOS	1969	1970	1972
S 111 NEREUS	1969	1970	1972
S 112 TRITON	1969	1971	8-1972
S 113 PROTEUS	1970	1971	11-1972
S	1975	. . .	. . .

Glavkos (S 110) 1973

Glavkos (S 110) 1977

SUBMARINES (*continued*)

S	1975	. . .	. . .
S	1975	. . .	. . .
S	. . .	. . .	. . .

D: 980 tons, 1,105 surfaced, 1,230 submerged **Dim:** 55.0 × 6.6 × 5.9
S: 21 kts (max. submerged for 5 min), 12 kts with snorkel
A: 8/533-mm TT fwd (+6 reserve torpedoes) **Man:** 5 officers, 26 men
M: Diesel-electric propulsion; 4 Maybach diesels, each linked to an AEG generator of 420 kw; a single Siemens electric motor of 3,600 hp; 1 prop

REMARKS: Similar to the submarines ordered by Argentina, Peru, and other countries. Submersion depth better than 200 m. See Remarks under *Salta* class, Argentina section. The eighth unit may not be a firm order.

♦ *1 ex-U.S. Guppy III class, transferred in 10-73*

	Bldr	L	In serv.
S 115 L. KATSONIS (ex-*Remora,* SS-487)	Portsmouth NSY	12-7-45	3-1-46

Katsonis (S 115)

D: 1,660 tons, 1,975 surfaced, 2,540 submerged **Dim:** 99.4 × 8.2 × 5.2
S: 20/13-15 kts
A: 10/533-mm TT (6 fwd, 4 aft) **Electron Equipt:** Sonar: BQG 4
M: Diesel-electric propulsion; 4 groups of generators (6,000 hp); 2 electric motors (5,400 hp)

♦ *1 ex-U.S. Guppy II class, transferred 26-7-72*

	Bldr	L
S 114 PAPANIKOLIS (ex-*Hardhead,* SS-365)	Manitowoc SB	12-12-44

D: 1,500 tons, 1,840 surfaced, 2,245 submerged **Dim:** 93.2 × 8.2 × 5.2
S: 18/15 kts **Man:** 86 men
A: 10/533-mm TT (6 fwd, 4 aft) **Range:** 10,000/10
M: Diesel-electric propulsion; 3 groups of generators; 2 electric motors; 2 props; 4,800/5,200 hp
Fuel: 300 tons diesel

REMARKS: Originally the *Balao* type, but the fourth group of generators has been removed to permit the sonar compartment to be enlarged. Two batteries of 126 cells. *Poseidon* (S-115), ex-*Blackfin* (SS-322) is now used for pierside training.

DESTROYERS

♦ *5 ex-U.S. Gearing class*

Transferred: D-210 in 1971, D-212 in 1972, D-213 and D-214 in 1973, D-215 in 1977

	Bldr	In serv.
D 210 THEMISTOCLES (ex-*Frank Knox,* DD-742)	Bath Iron Works	17-9-44
D 212 KANARIS (ex-*Stickell,* DD-888)	Consolidated Steel	16-6-45
D 213 KONTOURIOTIS (ex-*Rupertus,* DD-851)	Bethlehem, Quincy	21-9-45
D 214 SACHTOURIS (ex-*Arnold J. Isbell,* DD-869)	Bethlehem, Quincy	6-8-45
D 215 TOUMBAZIS (ex-*Gurke,* DD-783)	Todd SY, Seattle	15-4-45

Sachtouris (D 214) 1977

D: 2,425 tons (3,500 fl) **S:** 30 kts **Dim:** 119.72 × 12.55 × 5.50
Man: 14 officers, 260 men **Range:** 2,400/25, 4,800/15
A: D-210: 6/127-mm, 38-cal (II × 3) — 2/40-mm AA (I × 2) — 6/20-mm AA (I × 6) — 6 ASW Mk 32 TT (III × 2); Others: 4/127-mm, 38-cal. (II × 2) (D-214 also 1/76-mm OTO Melara) — 1 Asroc system — 6 ASW Mk 32 TT (III × 2)
Electron Equipt: Radars: 1/SPS 10, 1/SPS 37 or 40
Sonar: SQS 23
M: GT; 4 Babcock & Wilcox boilers; 2 props; 60,000 hp
Fuel: 650 tons

REMARKS: D-212, D-213, D-214, and D-215 modernized under FRAM I program, D-210 under FRAM II. D-210 given modest modernization 1976-77; others may receive more extensive improvements, including Albatros BPDMS, 4/40-mm Breda AA (II × 2), NA-10 fire control, etc. D-213 has an enlarged hangar and flight deck for an Alouette-III ASW helicopter.

♦ *1 ex-U.S. Allen M. Sumner class, transferred 16-7-71*

	Bldr	L
D 211 MIAOULIS (ex-*Ingraham,* DD-694)	Federal SB & DD	16-1-44

D: 2,200 tons (3,320 fl) **S:** 30 kts **Dim:** 114.75 × 12.45 × 5.80

DESTROYERS (*continued*)

Man: 14 officers, 260 men **Range:** 2,400/25, 4,800/15
A: 6/127-mm 38-cal (II × 3) — 2/40-mm AA (I × 2) — 6/20-mm AA (I × 6) — 2 hedgehogs — 6 ASW Mk 32 TT (III × 2)
Electron Equipt: Radar: 1/SPS 10, 1/SPS 40
Sonar: SQS 29
M: GT; 4 Babcock & Wilcox boilers; 2 props; 60,000 hp **Fuel:** 650 tons

REMARKS: Modernized in U.S. under FRAM II program. Now has AA guns on former helicopter platform.

♦ *6 ex-U.S. Fletcher class*

	Bldr	L	In serv.
D 06 ASPIS (ex-*Conner*, DD-582)	Boston NSY	18-7-42	6-43
D 16 VELOS (ex-*Charette*, DD-581)	Boston NSY	3-6-42	5-43
D 28 THYELLA (ex-*Bradford*, DD-545)	Bethlehem, San Pedro	12-12-42	6-43
D 58 LONCHI (ex-*Hall*, DD-583)	Boston NSY	18-7-42	7-43
D 85 SPHENDONI (ex-*Aulick*, DD-569)	Consolidated SB	2-3-42	10-42
D 63 NAVARINON (ex-*Brown*, DD-546)	Bethlehem, San Pedro	22-2-43	7-43

D: 2,050 tons (2,850 fl) **S:** 32/30 kts **Dim:** 114.85 × 12.03 × 5.50
Range: 1,260/30, 4,400/15 **Man:** 350 men
Electron Equipt: Radar: 1/SPS 10, 1/SPS 6
A: D-06, D-16, D-58, D-85: 4/127-mm, 38-cal. (I × 4) — 6/76-mm AA 50-cal (II × 3) — 5/533-mm TT (V × 1); D-28, D-63: 5/127-mm AA (I × 5) — 10/40-mm AA (IV × 2, II × 1). No tubes. All: ASW torpedoes, hedgehog, and depth charges.
M: General Electric GT; 2 props; 60,000 hp
Boilers: 4 Babcock & Wilcox **Fuel:** 650 tons

REMARKS: Transferred under the Military Assistance Program, three in 1959, D-58 in 1960, D-28 and D-63 in 9-62. Loan renewed in 3-70.

FRIGATES

♦ *4 ex-U.S. Cannon class, transferred in 1951*

	Bldr	L
D 01 AETOS (ex-*Ebert*, DE-768)	Tampa Shipbldg	23-5-44
D 31 HIERAX (ex-*Slater*, DE-766)	Tampa Shipbldg	13-2-44
D 54 LEON (ex-*Garfield Thomas*, DE-193)	Federal, Port Newark	12-12-43
D 67 PANTHIR (ex-*Eldridge*, DE-173)	Federal, Port Newark	25-6-43

Aetos (D 01) 1971

D: 1,300 tons (1,750 fl) **Dim:** 93 (91.50 pp) × 11.17 × 3.25
S: 19 kts **Range:** 5,500/19, 11,500/11
Man: 150 men (peace), 185 men (war)
A: 3/76-mm AA — 6/40-mm AA (II × 3) — 14/20-mm AA — 2 hedgehogs — 8 depth-charge projectors — 2 ASW torpedo racks
M: Diesel-electric propulsion; 4 General Electric diesels and 2 electric motors; 2 props; 6,000 hp
Fuel: 300 tons

CORVETTES

♦ *2 ex-U.S. 173-ft coastal patrol vessels* — Bldr: U.S.A., 1943-44

P 14 PLOTARCHIS ARSANOGLOU (ex-PGM-25, ex-PC-1556)
P 70 ANTIPLOIARCHOS PEZOPOULOS (ex-PGM-21, ex-PC-1552)

Plotarchis Arsanoglou (P 14)

D: 325 tons (400 fl) **S:** 18 kts **Dim:** 52.95 × 7.05 × 3.25
Man: 65 men **Range:** 2,300/18, 6,000/10
A: 1/76-mm — 6/20-mm AA Oerlikons — 1 hedgehog — 2 ASW torpedo racks
M: General Motors diesels; 2 props; 3,600 hp

GUIDED-MISSILE PATROL BOATS

♦ *4 La Combattante III class* — Bldr: Constr. Méc. de Normandie, Cherbourg

	L	In serv.
P 50 ANTIPLIARCHOS LASCOS	6-7-76	2-4-77
P 51 ANTIPLIARCHOS BLESSAS	10-11-76	7-77
P 52 ANTIPLIARCHOS TROUPAKIS	6-1-77	. . .
P 53 ANTIPLIARCHOS MYKONIOS	5-5-77	. . .

D: 400 tons (fl) **S:** 32.6 kts **Dim:** 56.0 × 7.9 × 2.5
A: 4 MM 38 — 2/76-mm AA OTO Melara (I × 2) — 4/30-mm Emerlec AA (II × 2) — 2/533-mm wire-guided TT
Electron Equipt: Radar: Thomson: 1 Castor, 1 Pollux, 1 Triton
Range: 700/32.5, 2,000/15 **Man:** 6 officers, 36 men
M: MTU 205 538TB91 diesels; 4 props; 15,000 hp **Electric:** 520 kw

GUIDED MISSILE PATROL BOATS (*continued*)

Antipliarchos Lascos (P 50) 1976

Antipliarchos Lascos (P 50) 1976

Antipliarchos Lascos (P 50) 1976

♦ *10 La Combattante II class*

	L
P 53 IPOPLIARCHOS KONIDIS (ex-*Kimothoi*)	26-1-71
P 54 IPOPLIARCHOS BATSIS (ex-*Kalypso*)	27-4-71
P 55 IPOPLIARCHOS ANNINOS (ex-*Evniki*)	8-9-71
P 56 IPOPLIARCHOS ARLIOTIS (ex-*Navsithoi*)	12-71

Bldrs: P-53 to P-56 plus one: Constr. Méc. de Normandie, Cherbourg; others: Skaramanga SY, Greece

Ipopliarchos Konidis (P 53) 1976

Ipopliarchos Batsis (P 54) 1976

D: 234 tons (255 fl) **S:** 36.5 kts **Dim:** 47.0 (44 pp) × 7.1 × 2.5 (fl)
A: 4 MM 38 Exocet missiles — 2 ASW wire-guided TT aft — 4/35-mm AA (II × 2)
Electron Equipt: Radars: Thomson CSF: 1 Castor, 1 Pollux, 1 Triton
Range: 850/25, 2,000/15 **Man:** 4 officers, 36 men
M: 4 MTU 872 high-speed diesels; 4 props; 12,000 hp **Fuel:** 39 tons

GUIDED-MISSILE PATROL BOATS (*continued*)

REMARKS: Steel hull, light-steel superstructure. In service in 1972. Contract for six more with 6 Penguin SSM, 1/76-mm OTO Melara, 4/30-mm Emerlec AA (II × 2) signed 22-12-76; will have Decca TM 626 and Thomson D-1280 radars.

NOTE: Transfer of the *Beacon* (PG-99) and *Douglas* (PG-100) has been discussed with the U.S. Navy, but the transfer had not been made as of 1 October 1977, nor had any date been set.

♦ *2 Kelefstis Stamou class* — Bldr: de l'Esterel, Cannes

P 28 KELEFSTIS STAMOU (1975) **P 29 DIOPOS ANTONIOU** (1975)

D: 80 tons (115 fl) **S:** 30 kts **Dim:** 32.0 × 5.8 × 1.5
A: 4/SS-12 SSM — 2/20-mm AA
Man: 17 men **Range:** 1,500/15
M: 2 MTU 12V331 TC81 diesels; 2 props; 2,700 hp

REMARK: These wooden-hulled ships were ordered by Cyprus but acquired by Greece.

TORPEDO PATROL BOATS

♦ *7 ex-German S-141 class* — Bldr: Lürssen or Kroger

P 196 ESPEROS (ex-*Seeadler*)
P 197 KATAIGIS (ex-*Falke*)
P 198 KENTAUROS (ex-*Habicht*)
P 199 KYKLON (ex-*Greif*)
P 228 LAIAPS (ex-*Kondor*)
P 229 SCORPIOS (ex-*Kormoran*)
P 230 TYFON (ex-*Geier*)

D: 160 tons (190 fl) **S:** 40 kts **Dim:** 42.5 × 7.2 × 2.4
A: 2/40-mm AA (I × 2) — 4/533-mm TT (I × 4)
M: 4 diesels; 4 props; 12,000 hp

REMARKS: Transferred 1976-77. Three others (ex-*Albatros, Bussard, Sperber*) were sent to be cannibalized for spares.

♦ *5 Norwegian Tjeld class*

P 21 ANDROMEDA
P 23 KASTOR
P 24 KYKONOS
P 25 PIGASSOS
P 26 TOXOTIS

Bldr: Mek. Verks. Mandal, Norway, 1966-67

Andromeda (P 21) 1971

D: 69 tons (76 fl) **Dim:** 24.50 (22.86 pp) × 7.50 × 1.95
S: 43 kts (40 cruising) **Man:** 22 men **Range:** 450/40, 600/25
A: 2/40-mm AA (I × 2) — 4/533-mm TT (I × 4)
M: 2 Napier-Deltic diesels Mk T 1827K with turbo compressors; 2 props; 6,280 hp
Fuel: 10 tons

♦ *1 Ferocity class*

P 19 AIOLOS (ex-*Pfeil*) — Bldr: Vosper — L: 26-10-61 — In serv. 6-62

Aiolos (P 19) 1971

D: 75 tons (85 fl) **Dim:** 28.95 (28.03 wl) × 7.22 × 2.00
S: 54/50 kts **A:** Same as the *Astrapi* **Man:** 14 men
M: 2 Bristol-Siddeley Proteus gas turbines; 7,500 hp

♦ *1 Brave class*

P 20 ASTRAPI (ex-*Strahl*) — Bldr: Vosper — L: 10-1-62 — In serv.: 11-62

D: 95 tons (100 fl) **S:** 50 kts **Dim:** 30.17 (29.26 wl) × 7.62 × 2.15
Range: 400/45 **Man:** 3 officers, 19 men
A: 2/40-mm AA — 2/533-mm TT or 1/40-mm AA and 4/533-mm TT — or mines
M: 3 Bristol-Siddeley Proteus gas turbines; 12,500 hp

REMARKS: P-19 and P-20 were bought in Germany in January 1968. Their hulls are made of wood and light metal. Welded superstructure in light alloys.

♦ *5 ex-German Silbermöwe class*

P 15 DELPHIN (ex-*Sturmmöwe*)
P 16 DRAKON (ex-*Silbermöwe*)
P 17 POLIKOS (ex-*Raubmöwe*)
P 18 POLYDEYKIS (ex-*Wildschwan*)
P 27 PHOINIX (ex-*Eismöwe*)

Bldr: Lürssen, Vegesäck (1951-56)

Polydeykis (P 18) 1971

TORPEDO PATROL BOATS (*continued*)

D: 110 tons (155 fl) **S:** 35 kts **Dim:** 35.4 × 5.1 × 1.8
A: 1/40-mm AA or 4/20-mm AA — 2/533-mm TT **Range:** 600/30
Man: 19 men **Fuel:** 12.5 tons
M: 3 Mercedes-Benz diesels, 20 cylinders; 3 props; 9,000 hp

REMARKS: Purchased from West Germany in 1968.

PATROL CRAFT

♦ *5 Goulandris class* — Bldr: Neozioh (Syros) and Skaramanga

	In serv.
P 14 ARSANOGLOU	. . .
P 22 N.I. GOULANDRIS I	25-6-75
P 24 N.I. GOULANDRIS II	1977
P 61 E. PANAGOPOULOS	23-6-76
P 70 PEZOPOULOS	. . .

D: 75 tons (86 fl) **S:** 30 kts **Dim:** 29.0 × 6.2 × 1.1
A: . . . **Range:** 1,600/25 **M:** 2 MTU diesels; 2 props; 2,700 hp

♦ *2 ex-German KFK class*

P 290 ARCHIKELEFSTIS MALLIOUPOULOS (ex-W-8)
P 288 ARCHIKELEFSTIS STASIS (ex-W-2)

REMARKS: Built in World War II. For data, see sister *Anemos* (A-469), now a survey ship.

MINE WARFARE SHIPS

♦ *15 U.S. Adjutant and Falcon minesweepers classes*

M 202 ATALANTI (ex-MSC-169)*
M 205 ANTIOPI (ex-MSC-153)*
M 206 PHEDRA (ex-MSC-154)
M 210 THALIA (ex-MSC-170)*
M 211 ALKYON (ex-MSC-319)
M 240 PLEIAS (ex-MSC-314)
M 241 KICHLI (ex-MSC-308)
M 242 KISSA (ex-MSC-309)
M 245 DORIS (ex-MSC-298)
M 246 AIGLI (ex-MSC-299)
M 247 DAPHNI (ex-MSC-307)
M 248 AIDON (ex-MSC-310)
M 213 ARGO (ex-MSC-317)
M 214 AVRA (ex-MSC-318)
M 254 NIOVI (ex-MSC-171)*

Antiopi (M 205) J. C. Bellonne, 1972

Bldr: U.S.A., *1954-55; others 1964-69
D: 300 tons (372 fl) **Dim:** 43.0 (41.50 pp) × 7.95 × 2.55
S: 13 (8 sweeping) **Man:** 4 officers, 27 men
A: 2/20-mm (II × 1) **Range:** 2,500/10
M: General Motors diesels; 2 props; 880/1,000 hp **Fuel:** 40 tons

REMARKS: Transferred, beginning in 1964, under M.A.P. The M-202, M-205, M-206, M-210, and M-254 of the *Adjutant* class (D: 330/402 fl) are the former Belgian ships *St. Truiden, Herne, Malmédy, Blankenbergue,* and *Laroche,* returned to the U.S.A. on 7-9-69 and then transferred to Greece. M-202 is fitted as a hydrographic survey ship.

♦ *2 minelayers*

N 04 AKTION (ex-LSM-301), **N 05 AMVRAKIA** (ex-LSM-303) — Bldr: Charleston NY, 1943

Amvrakia (N 05)

D: 720 tons (1,100 fl) **S:** 13 kts **Dim:** 61.87 × 10.36 × 2.40
Man: 65 men **Range:** 3,500/12
A: 8/40-mm AA (II × 4) — 6/20-mm AA (I × 6) — 100 to 300 mines, depending upon type
M: 2 General Motors 16-278A diesels; 2 props; 2,800 hp

REMARKS: Transferred in 1953; four derricks, two forward and two aft, for handling mines. Two minelaying rails. Four 30-cm searchlights, 1 of 60 cm. Twin rudders. Three of the same class ships were transferred to Turkey, and two to Norway, who passed them on to Turkey in 1961.

AMPHIBIOUS WARFARE SHIPS

♦ *1 ex-U.S. LSD*

L 153 NAFKRATOUSSA (ex-*Fort Mandan,* LSD-21) — Bldr: U.S.A. — L: 2-6-45

Nafkratoussa (L 153) A. and J. Pavia

AMPHIBIOUS WARFARE SHIPS (*continued*)

D: 4,790 tons (9,375 fl) **S:** 15 kts **Dim:** 139.0 × 21.9 × 4.9
Man: 254 men **Range:** 8,000/15
A: 8/40-mm AA — helicopter platform
M: GT; 2 water-tube boilers, 3 drums; 2 props; 9,000 hp

REMARKS: Modernized under the FRAM program (see U.S.A. section) and transferred 1-71. Flagship of the amphibious forces. Well deck: 103 × 13.3; two 35-ton cranes. Can carry eighteen LCMs, each with an LCVP nested in it.

♦ *2 U.S. Terrebonne Parish-class LSTs*

	Bldr	In serv.
L 104 OINOUSSAI (ex-*Terrell County,* LST-1157)	Bath Iron Works	19-3-53
L 116 KOS (ex-*Whitfield County,* LST-1169)	Christy Corp.	14-9-54

D: 2,590 tons (5,800 fl) **S:** 15 kts **Dim:** 117.1 × 16.7 × 5.2
A: 6/76-mm AA (II × 3) **Man:** 115 men plus 395 troops
M: 4 G.M. diesels; 2 controllable-pitch props; 6,000 hp

REMARKS: Transferred 1976. Two more may follow.

♦ *8 ex-U.S. LST-1 and LST-511 classes* — Bldr: U.S.A., 1943-45

L 144 SYROS (ex-LST-325)
L 179 SAMOS (ex-LST-33)
L 195 CHIOS (ex-LST-35)
L 158 LEMNOS (ex-LST-36)
L 171 KRITI (ex-LST-1076)
L 154 IKARIA (ex-LST-1068)
L 157 RODOS (ex-LST-391)
L 172 LESBOS (ex-LST-389)

Syros (L 144) 1972

D: 4,080 tons (fl) **S:** 11 kts **Dim:** 100.04 × 15.24 × 4.30
A: 10/40-mm AA or 8/40-mm — 6/20-mm
M: 2 G.M. 16-278A diesels; 1,700 hp **Cargo:** 2,100 tons

REMARKS: Transferred in 1944, 1947, 1960, 1964, and 1971. L-144 was transferred 29-5-64 after a complete refit and modernization; L-171 in 3-71.

♦ *5 ex-U.S. LSMs*

LSM-227, LSM-45, LSM-399, LSM-102, and LSM-541, transferred in 1958.

L 161 GRIGOROPOULOS, L 162 TOURNAS, L 163 DANIOLOS, L 164 ROUSEN, L 165 KRYSTALLIDIS — all names prefixed by **IPOPLIARCHOS**

REMARK: Same characteristics as the *Aktion*-class minelayers, except 2/40-mm (II × 1).

♦ *10 ex-LCU-501 class, transferred 1960-72* — Bldr: U.S.A., 1944

L 145 KASSOS (ex-LCU-1382)
L 146 KARPATHOS (ex-LCU-1379)
L 147 KIMONOS (ex-LCU-971)
L 148 KEA
L 149 KYTHNOS (ex-LCU-763)
L 150 SIFNOS (ex-LCU-677)
L 151 SKOPELOS
L 152 SKYATOS (ex-LCU-827)
L 185 KYTHIRA
L 189 MILOS

D: 143 tons (309 fl) **S:** 8 kts **Dim:** 36.30 × 10.05 × 1.50
A: 2/20-mm **Man:** 13 men **M:** 3 diesels; 440 hp

♦ *13 LCM*

♦ *34 LCVP*

HYDROGRAPHIC SHIPS

♦ **A 478 NAFTILOS** — Bldr: Annastadiades Tsortanides (Perama) — In serv. 3-76

Naftilos (A 478)

D: 1,480 tons **S:** 15 kts **Dim:** 64.0 × 11.4 × 4.0
A: 1 helicopter **M:** . . .

REMARK: Sisters *St. Lykoudis* (A-481) and *I. Theophilopoulos Karavoyiannos* (A-485) are lighthouse tenders.

♦ **HEPHAISTOS** (ex-U.S. *Josiah Willard Gibbs,* AGOR-1)

D: 2,800 tons (fl) **S:** 17 kts **Dim:** 94.70 × 12.52 × 3.65
Man: 150 men **M:** Diesels; 2 props; 6,000 hp

REMARKS: Transferred in 12-71, she was a *Barnegat*-class seaplane tender (*San Carlos,* AVP-51), built in 1942.

♦ **A 469 ANEMOS** — Bldr: Germany

D: 112 tons **S:** 9 kts **Dim:** 22.6 × 5.8 × 2.5
M: 1 diesel; 135 hp

HYDROGRAPHIC SHIPS (*continued*)

Anemos (A 469) 1971

Remark: Small, wooden-hulled KFK-class survey ship commissioned in 1944.

♦ *1 modified minesweeper*

M 202 ATALANTI

For data, see under minesweepers.

AUXILIARY SHIPS

♦ *5 ex-British Algerine-class transports*

	Bldr	L
A 12 ARMATOLOS (ex-*Aries*)	Toronto SY	19-9-42
A 58 MAHITIS (ex-*Postillion*)	Redfern Construction Co.	18-3-43
A 64 NAVMACHOS (ex-*Lightfoot*)	Redfern Construction Co.	14-11-42
A 74 POLEMISTIS (ex-*Gozo*)	Redfern Construction Co.	27-1-43
A 76 PYRPOLITIS (ex-*Arcturus*)	Redfern Construction Co.	31-8-43

Mahitis (A 58) G. Arra, 1972

D: 990 tons (1,237 fl) **S:** 16 kts **Dim:** 68.58 × 10.82 × 3.50
Man: 85 to 90 men **Range:** 3,000/15 **Fuel:** 270 tons
A: 2/76-mm — 4/20-mm — 2 machine guns; A-58: no weapons
M: Triple-expansion; 2 props; 2,000 hp; 2 boilers

Remarks: A-58 is a training ship; A-76 is a command ship for amphibious operations; the other three are now designated "fleet auxiliary transports."

♦ *2 small transports*

A 419 PANDORA, A 420 PANDROSOS — D: 350 tons — **S:** 11 kts

♦ *1 ex-German Rhein-class tender* — Bldr: Elsflether, 1960

A 215 AEGEON (ex-*Weser*, A-62)
D: 2,370 tons **S:** 20 kts **Dim:** 98.6 × 11.8 × 5.2 (fl)
A: 2/100-mm DP (I × 2) — 4/40-mm AA (I × 4) — mines
Man: 110 men **Range:** 1,625/15
M: 6 Maybach diesels; 2 controllable-pitch props; 11,400 hp

Remarks: Transferred 1976.

♦ *1 netlayer*

A 307 THETIS (ex-U.S. AN-103) transferred in 1960
D: 560 tons (805 fl) **S:** 13 kts **Dim:** 49.00 × 9.25 × 3.10

♦ *4 oilers and tankers*

A 377 ARETHOUSA (ex-U.S. *Natchaug*, AOG-54) — L: 6-12-44; transferred 7-59
A 414 ARIADNI (ex-U.S. *Tombigbee*, AOG-11) — L: 18-11-45; transferred 7-92

Arethousa (A 377) wearing old number 1968

D: 1,850 tons (4,335 fl) **S:** 13 kts **Dim:** 94.0 × 14.6 × 4.7
Man: 46 men **Cargo capacity:** 2,040 tons
A: 4/76-mm AA (I × 4); A-414: 2/76-mm (I × 2) — 4/20-mm AA (I × 4)
M: General Motors diesels; 2 props; 3,300 hp

A 372 ZEUS (ex-U.S. YOG-98), 1944
D: 1,390 tons **Dim:** 53.0 × 9.8 × 3.1
S: 9 kts **Cargo capacity:** 900 tons

A 345 SIRIOS (ex-*Poseidon*, ex-*Empire Faun*), built 1943, bought 1958
D: 846 grt/850 dwt **S:** 9.5 kts **Dim:** 59.8 × 9.5 × . . .

AUXILIARY SHIPS (*continued*)

♦ *1 ammunition ship* — Bldr: Dubigeon, Nantes, 1957

A 415 EVROS (ex-German *Schwarzwald*, ex-French *Amalthée*)

D: . . . **S:** 14 kts **Dim:** 85.0 × 13.0 × 6.1
A: 4/40-mm AA (II × 2) **M:** 1 Sulzer diesel; 3,000 hp

REMARKS: Flight deck: 210 × 34; one hangar; two elevators. Fitted with angled flight to Greece on 6-6-76.

♦ *8 motorized water vessels*

A 474 ILIKI
A 467 VOLVI
A 470 KASTORIA
A 472 STYMPHALIA
A 473 TRICHONIS
A 484 KERKINI (ex-German FW-3, transferred 1976)
A . . . PRESPA (built 1976; 600 tons)
A 468 KALLIROI (built 1976; 600 tons)

♦ *14 tugs*

A 406 AIAS
A 407 ANTAIOS
A 408 ATLAS
A 409 ACHILLEUS
A 410 ATROMITIS
A 411 ADAMASTOS
A 418 ROMALEOS
A 421 MINOTAURUS
A 426 KIKLOPS
A 427 PATRAIKOS
A 429 PERSEUS
A 430 SAMSON
A 431 TITAN
A 432 GIGAS

♦ *1 salvage ship*

A 384 SOTIR (ex-HMS *Salventure*, 24-11-42) — **D:** 700 tons (fl)

♦ *2 lighthouse tenders*

A 481 ST. LYKOUDIS
A 485 I. THEOPHILOPOULOS KARAVOYIANNOS

REMARK: Sisters to hydrographic survey ship *Naftilos*.

GUATEMALA

PERSONNEL: approx. 600 men

MERCHANT MARINE (1976): 6 ships — 8,197 grt

♦ *1 U.S. Broadsword class* — Bldr: Halter Marine, New Orleans, Louisiana, 1976

P 1051 KUKOLKAN

D: . . . **S:** 32 kts **Dim:** 32.0 × 6.3 × 1.9
A: 1/75-mm recoilless rifle — 1/81-mm mortar — 1/12.7-mm machine gun (atop mortar) — 4/7.6-mm machine guns (I × 4)
Man: 5 officers, 15 men **Electric:** 60 kw
M: 2 G.M. 16V-149TI diesels; 3,200 hp

REMARK: Additional units may be on order.

♦ *2 U.S. 85-ft class, transferred 5-67, 1972* — Bldr: Sewart Seacraft, Berwick, Louisiana

P 851 UTATLAN **P 852 SUBTENIENTE USORIO SARAVIA**

D: 60 tons **S:** 23 kts **Dim:** 25.9 × 5.8 × 1.0
A: 2 machine guns **Man:** 7 officers, 10 men
M: 2 G.M. diesels; 2,200 hp **Range:** 400/12

♦ *5 U.S. Cutlass class* — Bldr: Halter Marine, New Orleans, Louisiana, 1972, 1976

P 651 TECUNUMAN **P 654 TZACOL**
P 652 KAIBILBALAM **P 655 BITOL**
P 653 AZUMANCHE

D: 32 tons (fl) **S:** 25 kts **Dim:** 19.7 × 5.2 × 0.9
A: 1/12.7-mm machine gun — 3/7.6-mm machine guns (I × 3)
M: 2 G.M. 12V-71 diesels; 2 props; 960 hp **Man:** 28 men

♦ *2 ex-U.S. aircraft rescue boats (AVR), 1945*

P 632 HUNAHPU, transferred in 1964
P 631 CABRAKAN, transferred in 1965

D: 328 tons **S:** 25 kts **Dim:** 19.0 × 4.7 × 0.9
A: 2/12.7-mm machine guns **M:** 2 G.M. diesels; 2 props

♦ *2 ex-U.S. Coast Guard 12-m boats*

P 401 TIKAL, P 402 IXINCHE, transferred in 1962

♦ *2 Strikecraft class*

P 281 XUCUXUY, P 282 CAMALOTE, transferred in 1961

D: 6.5 tons **S:** 30 kts **D:** 8.6 × . . . × . . .
M: 1 G.M. diesel

♦ *2 U.S. Machete class* — Bldr: Halter Marine, New Orleans, Louisiana, 1976

P 361 PICUDA **P 362 BARRACUDA**

D: 6 tons **S:** 36 kts **Dim:** 11.0 × . . . × . . .
M: 2 G.M. 6V-53PI diesels; 2 water jets

REMARKS: Troop carriers, square bows; aluminum construction.

♦ *1 ex-U.S. LCM(6) class*

561 CHINALTENANGO, transferred in 12-1965

♦ *1 ex-U.S. repair barge*

YR 40, transferred in 1952 — **D:** 2,200 tons (fl)

GUIANA

MERCHANT MARINE (1976): 69 ships — 19,105 grt (tankers: 3 ships — 818 grt)

♦ *2 103-ft-class British patrol boats* — Bldr: Vosper Thornycroft, Portsmouth

DF 1010 PECCARI (3-77) **DF 1011 N . . .**

D: 96 tons (109 fl) **S:** 27 kts **Dim:** 31.4 × 6.0 × 1.6
A: 2/20-mm AA (I × 2) **Man:** 22 men **Range:** 1,400/14
M: 2 Paxman Ventura diesels; 2 props; 3,500 hp

REMARK: Second unit ordered 1976.

♦ *3 patrol boats, delivered 1971* — Bldr: Vosper Thornycroft

JAGUAR, MARGAY, OCELOT

D: 10 tons **S:** 20 kts **Dim:** 14.0 × 3.4 × 2.0
A: 1/7.62-mm machine gun **Man:** 6 men
M: 2 Cummins D 366A diesels; 2 props; 270 hp **Range:** 150/12

REMARKS: Fiberglass hull; light alloy superstructure.

♦ *3 U.S. 45-ft class*

CAMOUDIE, LABANA, RATTLER

NOTE: Under AID, Guiana has also received the ex-U.S. Navy tug YTM-190 and the converted lighter YFN-960.

GUINEA

PERSONNEL: 350 men

MERCHANT MARINE (1976): 11 ships — 15,280 grt

♦ *6 Shanghai-class patrol boats*
P-733 to **P-736** transferred by the People's Republic of China in 1974, with two others in 1976. For data, see China section.

♦ *2 Soviet Poluchat-I-class patrol boats* For data, see U.S.S.R. section

♦ *4 Soviet P-6-class torpedo boats* For data, see U.S.S.R. section; no torpedo tubes

HAITI

PERSONNEL: 250 men

COAST GUARD

♦ *2 ex-U.S. Coast Guard Cape-class patrol craft*

MH 8 LA CRETE A PIERROT, transferred 1956
MH 9 VERTIERES, transferred 1960

D: 100 tons **S:** 21 kts **Dim:** 29.0 × 5.80 × 1.55
M: 4 Cummins diesels; 2 props

♦ *3 U.S. 65-ft Commercial Cruiser class* — Bldr: Sewart, Louisiana, 1976

MH 21, MH 22, MH 23

D: 33 tons (fl) **S:** 25 kts **Dim:** 21.3 × 5.2 × 1.0
A: 2/12.7-mm machine guns
M: 3 G.M. 8V71 diesels; 3 props; 1,590 hp

♦ *2 U.S. Enforcer class* — Bldr: Bertram, Miami

MH 5, MH 6 9.5 m, inboard/outboard motor

♦ *1 presidential yacht* — Bldr: U.S.A.

SANS SOUCI (ex-*Captain James Taylor*)

D: 161 tons **S:** 10 kts **Dim:** . . . × . . . × . . .
M: 2 Winton, 8-cyl diesels; 2 props; 300 hp

HONDURAS

MERCHANT MARINE (1976): 57 ships — 71,042 grt (tankers: 1 ship — 609 grt)

♦ *1 U.S. 105-ft class* — Bldr: Swiftships, 4-77

N . . .

D: 103 tons (fl) **S:** 32 kts **Dim:** 31.5 × 6.6 × 2.1
A: . . . **Man:** 16 men **Range:** 1,200/18
M: 2 MTU diesels; 2 props; 7,000 hp

♦ *2 U.S. 65-ft Commercial Cruiser class* — Bldr: Swiftships

GC 6501 GRAL, GC 6502 J. T. CABANA

D: 32 tons (fl) **S:** 27 kts **Dim:** 21.3 × 5.2 × 1.0
A: . . . **Man:** 5 men
M: 3 G.M. diesels; 3 props; 1,590 hp

HONG KONG

British Crown Colony

MERCHANT MARINE (1976): 98 ships — 423,218 grt
(tankers: 19 ships — 32,307 grt)

PATROL BOATS AND CRAFT

♦ *2 34-meter patrol boats* — Bldr: Hong Kong Dockyard

N . . . **N . . .**

D: 222 tons **S:** 11.8 kts **Dim:** 33.9 × 7.3 × 3.2
A: . . . **Man:** 29 men **M:** 2 diesels; 340 hp

♦ *7 24-meter patrol craft* — Bldr: Vosper, Singapore

D: 82 tons (fl) **S:** 20 kts **Dim:** 24.0 × 5.3 × 1.7
A: 1 12.7-mm machine gun **Man:** 16 men **Range:** 700/15
M: 2 Cummins diesels; 1,500 hp

REMARK: These ships are armed for the police.

HUNGARY

♦ *10 river patrol craft*

A: 1/14.5-mm machine gun

♦ *5 LCM*

ICELAND

PERSONNEL: 150 men
MERCHANT MARINE (1976): 370 ships — 162,268 grt
(tankers: 4 ships — 2,434 grt)

♦ *7 fishery-protection patrol boats*

	L	In serv.	D	Length	HP	S
AEGIR	1968	1968	1,150 tons	63 m	8,000 (2 props)	19 kts
TYR	1974	1975	1,150 tons	63 m	8,000 (2 props)	19 kts
ODINN	1959	1960	1,000 tons	57 m	4,400 (2 props)	18 kts
ARVAKUR	1962	1962	716 tons	32 m	1,000	12 kts
ALBERT	1956	1957	200 tons	35 m	650	12 kts
THOR	1951	1951	920 tons	56 m	3,200 (2 props)	17 kts
BALDUR	1974	1975	740 tons	62 m	3,000 (1 prop)	15 kts

A: All have 1/57-mm gun, except *Arvakur*, which has 1/12.7-mm machine gun

ICELAND (*continued*)

Aegir J. Meister, 1971

Tyr 1974

Odinn J. Meister, 1971

REMARK: All but *Albert* and *Arvakur* have helicopter hangar and flight deck.

INDIA

PERSONNEL: approx. 46,000 men

MERCHANT MARINE (1976): 526 ships — 5,093,984 grt
(tankers: 37 ships — 1,130,983 grt)

NAVAL AVIATION: A few airplanes (18 Sea Hawk and 4 Bréguet Alizé) on board the carrier *Vikrant*, and some helicopters, including the Alouette III, belong to the Navy. Soviet Ka-25 Hormone A are to be delivered for the newly transferred Kashin-class missile destroyers. The Indian Air Force has turned over 10 Lockheed Constellations to the Navy for long-range reconnaissance, while the U.S.S.R. has delivered at least 3 IL-38 May aircraft. 12 Sea King helicopters have been delivered by Great Britain.

WARSHIPS IN SERVICE, UNDER CONSTRUCTION, OR PROJECTED AS OF 1 OCTOBER 1977

	L	Tons	Main armament
♦ *1 aircraft carrier*			
1 GLORY	1945	15,700	15 aircraft
♦ *8 submarines*		Tons (submerged)	
8 FOXTROT	1965	2,400	10/533-mm TT
♦ *2 cruisers*		Tons	
1 FIJI	1939	8,700	9/152-mm, 8/102-mm
1 LEANDER/AJAX	1932	7,030	6/152-mm
♦ *2 destroyers*			
2 KASHIN	1963-72	3,500	2 Goa SAM, 4/76-mm, ASW weapons
♦ *25 frigates*			
6 LEANDER	1968-74	2,250	4/115-mm, 1 helicopter
10 PETYA II	1963-. . .	950	4/76-mm DP, 3/533-mm TT
3 LEOPARD	1957-59	2,300	4/114-mm
2 WHITBY	1958	2,150	2/144-mm, 2 Limbo
2 BLACKWOOD	1958	1,180	3/40-mm, 2 Limbo
2 BLACK SWAN	1943	1,470	4/102-mm
♦ *4 corvettes*			
4 NANUCHKA	1969-7 . . .	780	4/SS-N-11, 1/SA-N-4, 2/57-mm
♦ *16 guided-missile patrol boats*			
8 OSA II	1960-70	240 (fl)	4/SS-N-2, 4/30-mm
8 OSA I	1960-70	175	4/SS-N-2, 4/30-mm
♦ *8 minesweepers*			
4-"Ton"	1955-56	370	1/40-mm
4-"Ham"	1954-69	120	1/20-mm

AIRCRAFT CARRIER

♦ *1 Glory class,* bought in Great Britain 1-57 — Bldr: Vickers-Armstrong

	Laid down	L	In serv.
R 11 VIKRANT (ex-*Hercules*)	10-43	22-9-45	3-61

D: 15,700 tons (19,500 fl) **Dim:** 211.25 (198 wl) × 24.29 × 7.15
S: 24 kts (fl) (17 cruising) **Range:** 6,200/23, 12,000/14
A: 15/40-mm (II × 4, I × 7) — 15 aircraft (maximum capacity)
M: Parsons GT; 2 props; 40,000 hp **Man:** 1,075 (peace) 1,340 (war)
Boilers: 4 Admiralty, 28-kg pressure **Fuel:** 3,000/3,200 tons

REMARKS: Flight deck: 210 × 34; one hangar; two elevators. Fitted with angled flight deck, steam catapult, air-conditioning.

SUBMARINES

♦ *8 Soviet Foxtrot class*

S 20 KURURA **S 40 VELA**
S 21 KARANJ **S 41 VAGIR**
S 22 KANDHERI **S 42 VAGLI**
S 23 KALVARI **S 43 VAGSHEER**

Kalvari (S 23) wearing old number 1973

D: 2,000 tons surfaced, 2,500 submerged **S:** 18/16 kts
Dim: 96.5 × 7.5 × 6.0 **Man:** 8 officers, 70 men
A: 10/533-mm TT (6 fwd, 4 aft) — 22 torpedoes
M: Diesels and electric motors; 3 props **Range:** 20,000

REMARKS: S-20 and S-21 were transferred in 4-68 and 1-69; S-22 and S-23 at the end of 1970; S-40 and S-41 in 9-73; S-42 in 12-73; and S-43 in 2-75.

CRUISERS

♦ *1 British Fiji class*

	Bldr	Laid down	L	In serv.
C 60 MYSORE (ex-*Nigeria*)	Vickers-Armstrong	8-2-38	18-7-39	23-9-40

D: 8,700 tons (11,000 fl) **S:** 31 kts **Dim:** 169.32 × 18.88 × 6.49 (fl)
A: 9/152-mm (III × 3) — 8/102-mm AA (II × 4) — 12/40-mm AA (II × 5, I × 2)
Man: 800 men
M: Parsons GT; 4 props; 72,000 hp **Boilers:** 4 Admiralty

REMARK: Bought in 1954, refitted from 1954-57.

Mysore (C 60)

♦ *1 British Leander/Ajax class*

	Bldr	Laid down	L	In serv.
C 74 DELHI (ex-*Achilles*)	Cammell Laird	6-31	1-9-32	10-33

Delhi (C 74) A. and J. Pavia

D: 7,030 tons (9,750 fl) **S:** 32.5 kts
Dim: 169 (161.55 pp) × 16.80 × 4.87
Man: 800 men **Range:** 12,000/14
A: 6/152-mm (II × 3) — 10/40-mm Bofors AA (I × 10)
Armor: Belt: 76-mm — Main deck (partial): 80 — Turret: 25 — Bridge: 25
M: Parsons GT; 4 props; 72,000 hp
Boilers: 6 Admiralty, 3-drum, 21-kg pressure **Fuel:** 1,800 tons

REMARKS: The oldest cruiser still in service. Bought and transferred in October 1948; modernized in 1960. Employed as a cadet training ship, with deckhouses for extra accommodations in the spaces formerly occupied by 8/102-mm AA (II × 4).

DESTROYERS

NOTE: It has been reported in the European press that two Soviet Kashin-class guided-missile destroyers will be delivered to India during 1978 and that, unlike their Soviet sisters, they will be equipped with Ka-25 Hormone A antisubmarine helicopters.

FRIGATES

♦ *6 British Leander class* — Bldr: Mazagon, Bombay

	Laid down	L	In serv.
F 33 NILGIRI	10-66	23-10-68	6-72
F 34 HIMGIRI	1967	6-5-70	23-11-74
F 35 UDAYGIRI	9-70	24-10-72	1975
F 36 DUNAGIRI	1-73	9-3-74	1976
F 37 TARAGIRI	...	...	...
F 38 UINDHYAGIRI	...	...	...

Udaygiri (F 35) 1977

D: 2,250 tons (2,800 fl) **S:** 30 kts
Dim: 113.38 × 13.10 × 4.27 (aver.)
A: 2/115-mm AA (II × 1) — 1 or 2 Sea Cat launchers — 1 ASW Limbo mortar Mk 10 — 1 ASW Alouette-III helicopter.

Udaygiri (F 35) 1977

REMARKS: For other characteristics, see section on Great Britain. F-35 and later have 2 Sea Cat launchers and Dutch instead of British electronics.

♦ *10 Soviet Petya-II class*

P 68 ARNALA
P 69 ANDROTH
P 73 ANJADIP
P 74 ANDAMAN
P 75 AMINI
P 77 KAMORTA
P 78 KADMATH
P 79 KILTAN
P 80 KAVARATTI
P 81 KATCHAL

Transferred in 1969, 1972, and 1975

Kavaratti (P 80) 1970

Andaman (P 74) wearing old hull number

FRIGATES (*continued*)

D: 950 tons (1,100 fl) **S:** 30 kts **Dim:** 82.0 × 9.1 × 3.2
A: 4/76-mm DP — 4 MBU 2500 rocket launchers — 3/533-mm ASW TT (III × 1) — 2 depth-charge racks — mine rails
Man: 130 men
Electron Equipt: Radars: 1 Slim Net, 1 Hawk Screech
Sonar: 1 Hercules
M: CODOG propulsion: 1 diesel × 6,000 hp + 2 gas turbines × 15,000 hp; 3 props; 36,000 hp

♦ *3 British Leopard class*

	Bldr	Laid down	L	In serv.
F 31 BRAHMAPUTRA (ex-*Panther*)	J. Brown, Clydebank	1956	15-3-57	3-58
F 37 BEAS	Vickers-Armstrong	1957	9-10-58	5-60
F 38 BETWA	Vickers-Armstrong	1957	15-9-59	12-60

Brahmaputra (F 31) A. and J. Pavia

REMARK: For characteristics, see Great Britain section.

♦ *2 British Whitby class*

	Bldr	Laid down	L	In serv.
F 40 TALWAR	Cammell Laird	1957	18-7-58	4-60
F 43 TRISHUL	Harland & Wolff	1957	18-6-58	1-60

REMARKS: For characteristics, see Great Britain section. F-40 has 3 SS-N-2 Styx in place of the twin 114-mm mount; both mount 4/40-mm AA (II × 1; I × 2).

♦ *2 British Blackwood class*

	Bldr	Laid down	L	In serv.
F 44 KIRPAN	Alex Stephen & Sons	1957	19-8-58	7-59
F 46 KUTHAR	J. Samuel White, Cowes	1957	14-10-58	1960

REMARKS: For characteristics, see Great Britain section. Transferred to the new Indian Coast Guard 1-7-77; painted white. Carry 3/40-mm AA (I × 3) instead of 2 in Royal Navy. Sister ship *Khukri* sunk by a Pakistani *Daphné*-class submarine during the Indo-Pakistani conflict.

♦ *2 British Black Swan class*

F 46 KISTNA (22-4-43), **F 10 KAVERI** (15-6-43)

D: 1,470 tons (1,925 fl) **S:** 18 kts **Dim:** 91.3 × 11.7 × 3.4
A: 4/102-mm — 4/40-mm AA (I × 4) **Man:** 210 men
M: Parsons GT; 2 props; 2 boilers; 4,300 hp **Range:** 4,500/12

REMARK: Both used for training.

GUIDED-MISSILE CORVETTES

♦ *4 Soviet Nanuchka class (modified)* — Delivered 1977-

K 71 VISAYDURG, K 72 SINDHURDURG, K 73 HOSDURG, K 74 N . . .

D: 780 tons (930 fl) **S:** 30 kts **Dim:** 60.0 × 12.0 × 2.7
A: 4/SS-N-2C (II × 2) — 1/SA-N-4 system — 2/57-mm AA (II × 1)
Electron Equipt: Radars: 1 Band Stand, 1 Pop Group, 1 Muff Cob, 1 Don-2
M: 3 M507 twin diesels; 3 props; 24,000 hp **Man:** 60 men

GUIDED-MISSILE PATROL BOATS

♦ *8 Soviet Osa-II class*

K . . . PRALAYA **K . . . PRACHAND** **K . . . PRATAP** **K . . . PRABAL**
K . . . CHAPAL **K . . . CHAMAK** **K . . . CHATAK** **K . . . N . . .**

Transferred from U.S.S.R.: 7 in 1976, 1 in 1977

D: 240 tons (fl) **S:** 36 kts **Dim:** 39.0 × 7.7 × 1.8
A: 4/SS-N-2 Styx (I × 4) — 4/30-mm AA (II × 2)
Electron Equipt: Radars: 1 Square Tie, 1 Drum Tilt
M: 3 M-504 diesels; 3 props; 15,000 hp

REMARK: Two of these craft bear the numbers K-90 and K-96.

♦ *8 Soviet Osa-I class*

K 82 AZVA **K 83 VIDYUT** **K 84 VIJETA** **K 85 VINASH**
K 86 NIPAT **K 87 NASHAT** **K 88 NIRBNIK** **K 89 NIRGHAT**

Transferred in 1971

D: 175 tons (210 fl) **S:** 36 kts **Dim:** 39.0 × 7.7 × 1.8
A: 4/SS-N-2 Styx (I × 4) — 4/30-mm AA (II × 2)
Electron Equipt: Radars: 1 Square Tie, 1 Drum Tilt
M: 3 M 503A diesels; 3 props; 12,000 hp

REMARKS: K-84 had three of her missile launchers remounted on the frigate *Talwar* (F-40); she may therefore be considered to be out of service.

PATROL CRAFT — all in or for the new Indian Coast Guard

♦ *8 SDB Mk 2 class* — Bldr: Garden Reach DY, Calcutta

T . . . (31-12-76) T . . . T . . . T . . .
T . . . T . . . T . . . T . . .

GUIDED-MISSILE PATROL BOATS (*continued*)

D: 160 tons (fl) **S:** 24 kts **Dim:** 37.5 × 7.5 × 1.8
A: 1/40-mm AA **M:** 2 Deltic diesels; 2 props; 5,500 hp

♦ *1 Ajay class* — Bldr: Hooghly D & E, Calcutta

T 35 ABHAY (11-61)

D: 120 tons (160 fl) **Dim:** 35.75 (33.52 pp) × 6.10 × 1.53
S: 18 kts **A:** 1/40-mm AA **M:** 2 diesels

REMARKS: Flight deck: 210 × 34; one hangar; twp elevators. Fitted with angled flight deck, steam catapult, air-conditioning.

T 46 PANVEL, T 47 PAMBAN, T 48 PURI, T 49 PANAJI, T 50 PULICAT

Transferred 1967-69

D: 80 tons (90 fl) **S:** 18 kts **Dim:** 29.8 × 5.8 × 1.5
M: 2 M 50 diesels; 2 props; 2,400 hp

♦ *2 Sharada class* — Bldr: Yugoslavia

P 3132 SUKANYA (12-59), **P 3133 SHARADA** (12-59)

D: 86 tons **S:** 18 kts **Dim:** 31.5 × . . . × . . .

♦ *4 ex-British HDML,* 1943

SPC 3110 (ex-HDML-1110) **SPC 3117** (ex-HDML-1117)
SPC 3112 (ex-HDML-1112) **SPC 3118** (ex-HDML-1118)

D: 48 tons (54 fl) **S:** 12 kts **Dim:** 21.6 × 4.8 × 1.3
A: 2/20-mm AA **Man:** 14 men **M:** 1 diesel; 320 hp

MINE WARFARE SHIPS

♦ *4 British "-Ton"-class minesweepers*

	L		L
M 90 CUDDALORE (ex-*Wennington*)	6-4-55	**M 91 CANNAMORE** (ex-*Whitton*)	30-1-56
M 97 KARWAR (ex-*Overton*)	28-1-56	**M 1201 KAKINADA** (ex-*Durweston*)	18-8-55

D: 370 tons (425 fl) **Dim:** 46.33 (42.68 pp) × 8.76 × 2.50
S: 15 kts **Man:** 27 men
A: 1/40-mm — 2/20-mm AA **Range:** 3,000/8
M: Diesels; 2 props; 2,500 hp **Fuel:** 45 tons

♦ *4 British "-Ham"-class minesweepers*

M 89 BHATKAL (5-67), **M 90 BULSAR** (17-5-69) — Built at Mazagon Docks, Bombay

2705 BIMLIPATHAM (ex-*Hildersham*) (5-2-54) — **2707 BASSEIN** (ex-*Littleham*) (4-5-54)

D: 120 tons (159 fl) **Dim:** 32.43 (30.48 pp) × 6.45 × 1.70
S: 14 kts (9 sweeping) **A:** 1/20-mm AA
Man: 2 officers, 13 men **Fuel:** 25 tons
M: Davey-Paxman YHAXM diesels; 2 props; 1,000 hp

REMARKS: 2705 and 2707 transferred in 1955. The Indian-built units have teakwood hulls.

AMPHIBIOUS WARFARE SHIPS

♦ *4 Soviet Polnocny-III class*

L 14 GHORPAD, L 15 KESARI, L 16 SHARDUL, L 17 SHARABH

Transferred: 3 in 1975, 1 in 1976

D: 1,150 (fl) **S:** 18 kts **Dim:** 82.0 × 10.0 × 2.0
A: 4/30-mm AA (II × 2) — 2/140-mm rocket launchers (XVIII × 2)
M: 2 diesels; 2 props; 5,000 hp **Cargo:** 350 tons

Shardul (L 16) 1976

♦ *2 Soviet Polnocny-I class*

L 13 GULDAR **L 14 GHARIAL**

Transferred 1966

D: 900 tons (fl) **S:** 18 kts **Dim:** 72.5 × 8.5 × 2.0
A: 2/25-mm AA (II × 1) — 2/140-mm rocket launchers (XVIII × 2)
M: 2 diesels; 2 props; 4,000 hp **Cargo:** 200 tons

AUXILIARY SHIPS

♦ *1 hydrographic survey ship* — Bldr: Hindustan SY, India

J 14 DARSHAK — L: 2-11-59 — In serv. 12-64

D: 2,790 tons **S:** 16 kts **Dim:** 97.30 × 14.94 × 5.80
M: Diesel-electric propulsion; 3,000 hp **Man:** 150 men

REMARK: Carries one helicopter.

AUXILIARY SHIPS (*continued*)

♦ *2 British Egret-class hydrographic survey ships*

J 15 SUTLEJ (1-10-40) **J 16 JUMNA** (16-11-40)

D: 1,300 tons (1,735 fl) **Dim:** 89.15 × 11.43 × 3.10
S: 18 kts **Man:** 160 men **Range:** 4,500/12
A: J-16: 6/102-mm AA (II × 3) — 6/20-mm AA — 4 depth-charge launchers
M: Parsons GT; 2 props; 2 boilers; 3,600 hp **Fuel:** 370 tons

♦ *2 Gaveshani-class small inshore survey craft, 2-76*

J . . . GAVESHANI **J . . . N . . .**

♦ *1 Soviet Ugra-class submarine tender* — Bldr: U.S.S.R.

A 54 AMBA

Amba (A 54) 1978

D: 9,500 tons (fl) **Dim:** 144.0 × 17.6 × 5.4
S: 20/17 kts **A:** 4/76-mm AA (II × 2)
Electron Equipt: Radars: 1 Slim Net, 2 Hawk Screech
M: Diesels; 2 props; 14,000 hp

REMARKS: Purchased in 1968. Helicopter platform. Quarters for 750 men. Two 6-ton cranes, one 10-ton crane.

♦ *1 Soviet T-58-class submarine rescue ship*

A 55 NISTAR

D: 850 tons **S:** 18 kts **Dim:** 71.7 × 9.1 × 2.5
Electron Equipt: Radar: 1 Don **M:** 2 diesels; 2 props; 4,000 hp

REMARKS: Purchased at the end of 1971. Two rescue chambers, port and starboard sides of the stern. Decompression chamber, diving bells.

♦ *1 repair ship*

	L (Canada)	In serv.
A 52 DHARINI	25-7-44	5-60

(ex-*La Petite Hermine*, ex-*Ketowna Park*)

D: 4,625 dwt **S:** 9 kts **Dim:** 99.0 × 13.9 × 4.0
M: Triple-expansion; 800 hp **Fuel:** 620 tons

♦ *1 training ship, former British frigate*

F 256 TIR (ex-*Bann*) 29-12-42

D: 1,450 tons (2,100 fl) **Dim:** 91.90 × 11.07 × 4.10
S: 19/18 kts **Man:** 100-120 men
A: 1/102-mm — 1/40-mm AA — 2/20-mm AA (I × 2)
Range: 9,500/12 **Fuel:** 540 tons
M: Triple-expansion; 2 props; 2 boilers; 5,500 hp

REMARK: The cruiser *Delhi* (C-74) and the frigates *Kistna* (F-46) and *Kaveri* (F-10) are also used for training.

OILERS

♦ *2 Deepak class* — Bldr: Bremen Vulkan Schiffbau, Bremen-Vegesäck

Shakti (A 57) 1975

A 50 DEEPAK (1972), **A 57 SHAKTI** (In serv. 31-12-75)

D: 22,000 tons (fl) **S:** 20 kts **Dim:** 168.5 × 23.0 × 9.2
A: 3/40-mm AA (I × 3) — 2/20-mm AA (I × 2) **M:** GT; 1 prop; . . . hp

REMARKS: 12,690 grt/15,800 dwt. Two liquid replenishment stations per side with British-style rigs. Telescoping hangar and flight deck for one helicopter. Also carry dry cargo.

♦ **LOK ADHAR** (ex-*Hooghly*) — 9,231-dwt tanker taken over in 1972

♦ **DESH DEEP** — 11,000-dwt tanker taken over in 1972

YARD CRAFT

NOTE: Most of the Indian Navy's service craft are of local design and construction. Oilers of up to 1,000 dwt have been built at Bombay, while a new class of 1,200-hp tug is in series production. No data are available on any of these craft.

PERSONNEL: 40,000 men, including 5,000 Marines

MERCHANT MARINE (1976): 882 ships — 1,046,198 grt
(tankers: 60 ships — 96,618 grt)

WARSHIPS IN SERVICE OR UNDER CONSTRUCTION AS OF 1 OCTOBER 1977

	L	Tons (submerged)	Main armament
♦ *5 submarines*			
2 TYPE 209	. . .	1,356	8/533-mm TT
3 WHISKEY	1958	1,350	6/533-mm TT
		Tons	
♦ *15 frigates*			
3 . . .	. . .	1,200	1/127-mm, 1/40-mm
4 CLAUD JONES	1958-59	1,450	1 or 2/76-mm, 6 Mk 32 TT
2 PATTIMURA	1956-57	950	2/85-mm
2 ALMIRANTE CLEMENTE	1956	1,150	4/102-mm, 3/533-mm TT
4 RIGA	1954-57	1,200	3/100-mm, 3/533-mm TT
♦ *11 guided-missile patrol boats*			
4 PSSM MK 5	. . .	. . .	SSM, 1/76-mm
7 KOMAR	1955	75	2/SS-N-2
♦ *4 torpedo patrol boats*			
♦ *20 patrol boats*			
♦ *7 minesweepers*			
♦ *11 amphibious warfare ships*			

NOTE: The names of Indonesian ships are preceded by the designation KRI (Kapal perang Republik Indonesia, or warship of the Republic of Indonesia).

SUBMARINES

♦ *2 West German Type 209* — Bldr: Howaldtswerke

Ordered: 2-4-77

D: 980 tons surfaced, 1,356 submerged **Dim:** 60.0 × 6.2 × 5.2
S: 10/22 kts **Man:** 32 men
A: 8/533-mm TT fwd **M:** 4 MTU diesels, electric drive; 3,600 hp

♦ *3 Soviet Whiskey class*

403 NAGABANDA, 410 PASOPATI, 412 BRAMASTRA

Pasopati (410) 1976

INDONESIA

D: 1,050 tons surfaced, 1,350 submerged **S:** 17/16 kts
Dim: 76.0 × 6.3 × 5.0
A: 6/533-mm TT (4 fwd, 2 aft) — 14 torpedoes or 28 mines
Man: 60 men **Endurance:** 40 to 45 days **Range:** 6,000/5
M: 2 diesels (4,000 hp), electric drive; 2 props; 2,500 hp

REMARKS: The 403 serves as an alongside training ship. The 412, which was thought to have been removed from the active list, has been refitted and returned to service.

FRIGATES

3 . . . class — Bldr: Wilton-Fijenoord, Schiedam, The Netherlands

	Laid down	L	In serv.
N . . .	8-76	. . .	1979
N . . .	31-1-77	. . .	1980
N . . .	. . .	. . .	1980

Ordered: 8-75

D: 1,200 tons (1,500 fl) **S:** 30 kts **Dim:** 84.0 × 11.3 × 3.3
A: 1/127-mm OTO Melara — 1/40-mm AA — helicopter
M: CODOG: 1 Rolls-Royce Olympus gas turbine (28,000 hp); 2 MTU diesels (6,000 hp); 2 controllable-pitch props

REMARKS: Details of armament uncertain. Considering their small size, a 76-mm vice a 127-mm gun may be fitted. May carry anti-ship missiles.

♦ *4 ex-U.S. Claud Jones class*

	L	In serv.
341 SAMADIKUN (ex-*John R. Perry*, DE-1034)	29-7-58	5-5-59
342 MARTADINATA (ex-*Charles Berry*, DE-1035)	17-3-59	25-11-60
343 MONGINDISI (ex-*Claud Jones*, DE-1033)	27-5-58	10-2-59
344 NGURAH RAI (ex-*McMorris*, DE-1036)	26-5-59	4-3-60

Martadinata (342) 1974

FRIGATES *(continued)*

Transferred: 2-73 and 2-74

D: 1,450 tons (1,750 fl) **Dim:** 95.0 × 11.3 × 5.5
S: 22 kts **Man:** 15 officers, 160 men
A: 1 or 2/76-mm AA (I × 1 or 2) — 0 or 2/37-mm AA (II × 1) — 2/25-mm AA (II × 1) — 6/ASW Mk 32 TT (III × 2)
Electron Equipt: Radars: 1 SPS 10, 1 SPS 6
Sonar: 1 SQS 29
M: 4 Fairbanks-Morse 38D81/8 diesels; 1 prop; 9,200 hp

REMARK: The 341 and 342 have twin 37-mm AA in place of one 76-mm on fantail.

♦ *2 Pattimura class*

	Bldr	Laid down	L	In serv.
801 PATTIMURA	Ansaldo, Livorno	1-56	1-7-56	28-1-58
802 SULTAN HASANUDIN	Ansaldo, Livorno	1-56	24-3-57	8-3-58

Pattimura — number has been changed 1974

D: 950 tons (1,200 fl) **S:** 21.5 kts **Dim:** 82.37 × 10.30 × 2.80
Man: 119 men **Range:** 2,400/18
A: 2/85-mm DP — 4/25-mm AA (II × 2) — 4/14.5-mm AA (II × 2) — 2 hedgehogs — 4 depth-charge launchers
M: Diesels; 2 props; 7,000 hp **Fuel:** 100 tons diesel

REMARKS: Rearmed 1976-77 with Soviet guns removed from discarded units of Kronstadt, P-6, and Komar classes.

♦ *2 Italian-built Almirante Clemente class*

	Bldr	Laid down	L	In serv.
355 IMAN BONDJOL	Ansaldo, Genoa	1-56	5-5-56	19-5-58
358 SURAPATI	Ansaldo, Genoa	1-56	5-5-56	28-5-58

D: 1,150 tons (1,500 fl) **S:** 31.5 kts **Dim:** 97.60 × 10.84 × 2.60
A: 4/102-mm (II × 2) — 6/30-mm AA (II × 3) — 6/20-mm — 3/533-mm TT (III × 1) — 2 hedgehogs — 4 depth-charge projectors
Fuel: 350 tons black oil **Man:** 200 men **Range:** 2,800/22
M: GT; 2 props; 2 Foster-Wheeler boilers; 24,000 hp

REMARKS: Similar to the frigates ordered in Italy by Venezuela. May have been rearmed with Soviet 85-mm and 25-mm guns. Have been in poor condition for some years.

Iman Bondjol (355) Ansaldo, 1958

♦ *4 ex-Soviet Riga class* — Bldr: U.S.S.R., 1954-57

351 JOS SUDARSO, 360 NUKU, 357 LAMBUNG MANEGURAT

Transferred: 1964

D: 1,200 tons (1,450 fl) **S:** 28 kts **Dim:** 91.0 × 10.0 × 3.4
A: 3/100-mm — 4/37-mm AA — 3/533-mm TT (III × 1) — 1 MBU 600 hedgehog — 4 depth-charge projectors — 50 mines (fitted)
Electron Equipt: Radars: 1 Don, 1 Slim Net, 1 Sun Visor A fire control
M: GT; 2 props; 20,000 hp **Man:** 150 men

GUIDED-MISSILE PATROL BOATS

♦ *4 PSSM Mk 5 class* — Bldr: Korea — Tacoma SY

D: 250 tons (280 fl) **S:** 40 kts **Dim:** 50.3 × 7.3 × 2.0
A: SSM (type ?) — 1/76-mm OTO Melara DP — 1/40-mm AA — 2/12.7-mm machine guns (I × 2)
M: 1 G.E.-Fiat LM 2500 gas turbine (25,000 hp); 2 MTU 12V331 TC81 diesels (1,120 hp each); 2 controllable-pitch props
Range: 2,000/17 (diesels)

REMARKS: Building in South Korea to a U.S. design based on the *Asheville*-class hull. Up to 18 may ultimately be built. First units to be delivered 1979-80.

♦ *7 Soviet Komar class*

601 KALAPLINTAH	**605 PULANGGENI**	**611 NAGAPASA**
602 KALAMISANI	**608 SAROTAMA**	**612 GRIWIDJAJA**
603 SARPAWISESA		

D: 71 tons (82 fl) **S:** 40 kts **Dim:** 25.5 × 5.0 × 2.0
A: 2 SS-N-2 Styx — 2/25-mm AA (II × 1) **Range:** 400/30
M: 4 diesels; 4,800 hp

TORPEDO PATROL BOATS

♦ *4 German TNC-45 class* — Bldr: Lürssen, Vegesack, 1959-60

P 652 BERUANG **P 653 MADJAN KUMBANG**
P 654 HARIMAU **P 655 ANOA**

Harimau (P 654) 1976

D: 140 tons (180 fl) **S:** 40 kts **Dim:** 42.0 × 7.6 × 1.8
A: 2/40-mm AA — 4/533-mm TT **Man:** 42 men
M: 4 Mercedes-Benz diesels; 4 props; 12,000 hp

REMARKS: Similar to German Jaguar class. Several had steel vice wooden hulls.

SUBMARINE CHASERS

♦ *3 Soviet Kronstadt class* — Bldr: U.S.S.R., 1951-52

811 KATULA, 814 PANDRONG, 816 KAKAP

D: 300 tons (330 fl) **S:** 18 kts **Dim:** 52.1 × 6.5 × 2.2
A: 1/85-mm — 2/37-mm AA (I × 2) — 6/14.5-mm — 2 MBU 1200 ASW rocket launchers — 2 depth-charge projectors — 2 depth-charge racks — mines
M: 3 diesels; 3 props; 3,300 hp **Fuel:** 20 tons **Man:** 50 men

REMARKS: Transferred 1958-59. A number of others have been stricken.

♦ *6 ex-Yugoslav PBR-500 class*

819 KAYANG **821 KRAPU** **823 TODAK**
820 LEMADANG **822 DORANG** **830 SEMBILANG**

Transferred: spring, 1959

Kayang (819) 1976

D: 190 tons (235 fl) **S:** 20 kts **Dim:** 41.0 × 6.3 × 2.1
A: 1/76-mm — 1/40-mm AA — 6/20-mm AA (II × 3) — 2 Mousetraps — 2 depth-charge projectors — 2 depth-charge racks
Man: 54 men **Range:** 1,500/12 **Fuel:** 15 tons
M: 2 M.A.N. diesels; 2 props; 3,300 hp

PATROL BOATS

♦ *3 Kelabang class* — Bldr: Surabaya DY, 1966-70

KALAHITAM, KELEBANG, KOMPAS

D: 147 tons (fl) **S:** 21 kts **Dim:** 36.0 × 5.0 × 2.0
A: 1/40-mm AA — 4-12.7-mm machine guns (II × 2)
M: 2 M.A.N. diesels; 2 props; . . . hp

♦ *3 U.S. PGM-53 class* — Transferred 1-62

570 BENTANG KALAKUANG (ex-PGM-57) **572 BENTANG SILUNGKANG**
571 BENTANG WAITATIRE (ex-PGM-55)

D: 122 tons (fl) **S:** 17 kts **Dim:** 30.5 × 6.4 × 2.6
A: 2/20-mm AA (I × 2) — 2/12.7-mm machine guns
M: 2 MTU MB820dB diesels; 2 props; 1,600 hp

♦ *2 Australian Attack class* — Transferred in 1973

846 SULIMAN (ex-*Archer*), **847 SIBARU** (ex-*Bandolier*)

D: 146 tons (fl) **S:** 24/21 kts **Dim:** 32.76 × 6.20 × 1.90
A: 1/40-mm — 2 machine guns **Man:** 3 officers, 19 men
M: 2 Davey-Paxman diesels; 3,460 hp **Fuel:** 20 tons

REMARKS: Superstructure of light alloys. Air-conditioned.

♦ *3 ex-U.S. PC class* — Transferred 1959-60

805 HIU (ex-*Malvern*, PC-580) (29-4-42)
806 TORANI (ex-PC-581) (8-7-42)
807 TJAKALANG (ex-*Pierre*, PC-1141) (22-6-43)

D: 335 tons (400 fl) **S:** 19 kts **Dim:** 52.95 × 7.25 × 3.25
A: 1/37-mm — 4/25-mm (II × 2) **Man:** 55 men **Range:** 4,800/9
M: 2 G.M. diesels; 2 props; 2,880 hp **Fuel:** 60 tons

MINE WARFARE SHIPS

♦ *5 ex-Soviet T-43-class minesweepers* — Transferred 1962-64

701 PULAU RANI **703 PULAU ROON** **715 PULAU RADJA**
702 PULAU RATEWO **704 PULAU RORBAS**

D: 500 tons (580 fl) **S:** 14 kts **Dim:** 58.0 × 8.4 × 2.3
A: 4/37-mm AA (II × 2) — 8/12.7-mm machine guns (II × 4) — 2 depth-charge projectors — 2 mine rails
M: 2 diesels; 2 props; 2,200 hp **Range:** 3,200/10

REMARK: Used on patrol duties.

♦ *2 German Raum Boote-class inshore minesweepers* — Bldr: Abeking & Rasmussen, 1954-56

708 PULAU RUPAT **712 PULAU RENGATI**

D: 130 tons **S:** 24 kts **Dim:** 39.00 × 5.70 × 1.58
A: 1/40-mm AA — 2/12.7-mm machine guns **Man:** 26 men
M: 2 M.A.N. diesels; 2 props; 2,800 hp

MINE WARFARE SHIPS *(continued)*

Pulau Rupat (708)

REMARKS: Frame and inner hullwork of metal alloy; planked in wood.

AMPHIBIOUS WARFARE SHIPS

503 TELUK AMBOINA — Bldr: Sasebo HI, 17-3-61

D: 4,145 tons (fl) **S:** 13 kts **Dim:** 99.9 × 15.2 × 4.6
A: 4/40-mm AA — 1/37-mm AA **Man:** 88 men + 212 passengers
M: 2 M.A.N. diesels, 2 props; 2,850 hp
Range: 4,000/13 **Fuel:** 1,200 tons

REMARK: Similar to the U.S. LSTs listed below.

♦ *8 ex-U.S. LSTs bought since 1961* — Bldr: U.S.A., 1943

501 TELUK LANGSA (ex-LST-1128)
502 TELUK BAJUR (ex-LST-616)
504 TELUK KAU (ex-LST-652)
505 TELUK MENADO (ex-LST-657)
508 TELUK TOMINI (ex-*Middlesex County,* LST-983)
509 TELUK RATAI (ex-*Polk County,* LST-1084)
510 TELUK SALEN (ex-LST-601)
511 TELUK BONE (ex-LST-639)

D: 1,650 tons (4,080 fl) **S:** 11 kts **Dim:** 100.04 × 15.24 × 4.30
Man: 119 men + 264 passengers
A: 7/40-mm or 37-mm AA **Fuel:** 600 tons **Range:** 7,200/10
M: General Motors diesels; 2 props; 1,800 hp

REMARKS: Can carry 2,100 tons of cargo. Transferred in 3-60, 1961, and 7-70 (510, 511) under the Military Assistance Program.

♦ **TELUK DORE, TELUK AMURANG**

D: 182 tons (275 fl) **S:** 8 kts **Dim:** 38.3 × 10.0 × 1.8
M: 2 diesels; 420 hp **Man:** 17 men

REMARK: Several others built for merchant service.

HYDROGRAPHIC SHIPS

♦ **1006 BURUDJULASAD** — Bldr: Schlichtingwerft, Travemünde, 1966

Burudjulasad (1006)

D: 1,470 tons **S:** 19 kts
Dim: 82.0 × 11.4 × 3.5
Man: 78 men
M: 4 M.A.N. high-speed diesels; 2 props; 6,850 hp

REMARK: Carries one helicopter.

♦ **1002 BURDJAMHAL** — Bldr: De Waal Scheepswerf, Nijmegen, 6-9-52 (manned in 7-53)

D: 1,200 tons **S:** 10 kts **Dim:** 65.0 × 12.0 × 4.5
M: Werkspoor diesels; 2 props; 1,160 hp

♦ **1005 JALAN NIDI, 1006 ARIES** (ex-*Samudera*), **1008 PARIT**
Bldr: Ferus Smit, 28-5-52 (manned in 8-52)
D: 35 tons **S:** 8 kts **Dim:** 21.0 × 3.8 × 2.0
M: 2 Werkspoor diesels; 450 hp **Man:** 13 men

AUXILIARY SHIPS

♦ *1 ex-Soviet Don-class submarine tender* — Bldr: U.S.S.R., 1960 — Transferred in 1962

4101 RATULANGI (ex-441)

D: 6,000 tons (fl) **Dim:** 137.20 × 14.95 × 5.20
S: 20 kts **Man:** 300 men
A: 4/100-mm — 12/37-mm AA **M:** Diesels; 2 props

♦ *1 command ship built in Japan* — Bldr: Ishikawajima, 13-6-61

561 MULTATULI

D: 4,500 tons (fl) **S:** 18.5 kts
Dim: 111.35 (103 pp) × 16.00 × 6.98
Man: 134 men **Range:** 6,000/16
A: 8/37-mm AA (II × 2, I × 4) — 4/14.5-mm AA (II × 2) — 1 Alouette II helicopter
M: 1 Burmeister & Wain diesel; 5,500 hp **Fuel:** 1,400 tons

AUXILIARY SHIPS (*continued*)

Multatuli (561) 1974

REMARKS: Originally a submarine support ship, converted as fleet command ship late 1960s. Helicopter platform aft.

♦ *1 ex-U.S. Achelous-class repair ship* — Transferred 31-8-71

. . . JAJA WIDJAJA (ex-*Askari*, ARL-30)

D: 1,625 tons (4,100 fl) **S:** 11 kts **Dim:** 100.0 × 15.3 × 13.4
A: 8/40-mm AA (IV × 2) **Man:** 280 men
M: 2 G.M. diesels; 2 props; 1,800 hp

♦ *1 replenishment oiler* — Bldr: Yugoslavia, 1965

911 SORONG

D: 5,100 (dwt) **S:** 15 kts **Dim:** 112.0 × 15.4 × 6.6
A: 8/12.7-mm machine guns (II × 4)
M: 1 diesel

REMARK: Cargo: 3,000 tons fuel/300 tons water.

♦ *1 Soviet Uda-class replenishment oiler* — Transferred 1962

. . . BALIKPAPAN

D: 7,100 tons (fl) **S:** 17 kts **Dim:** 122.0 × 16.0 × 6.3
A: 6/25-mm AA (II × 3) **Range:** 4,000/15
M: 2 diesels; 2 props; 8,000 hp

REMARK: Two sisters discarded.

♦ *1 Soviet-built oiler* — Transferred 1964

906 SUNGAI GERONG

D: 1,300 (dwt) **S:** 13 kts **Dim:** . . . × . . . × . . .
A: 4/14.5-mm machine guns (II × 2)
M: 1 diesel; 1 prop; . . . hp

Sungai Gerong (906) 1976

♦ *1 ex-Soviet Khobi-class oiler*

960 PAKANBBARU

D: 1,525 tons (fl) **S:** 12.7 kts **Dim:** 67.4 × 10.0 × 4.4
M: 2 diesels; 2 props; 1,600 hp

♦ *1 buoy and cable tender* — Bldr: J. and K. Smit, 30-10-51 (put in service 7-52)

1003 BIDUK

D: 1,250 tons **S:** 12 kts **Dim:** 65.0 × 12.0 × 4.5
M: Triple-expansion; 1 prop; 1,600 hp **Man:** 66 men

♦ *5 tugs*

922 RAKATA (ex-U.S. *Menominee*, ATF-73) Transferred in 1961

REMARK: For characteristics, see U.S. *Cherokee* class

934 LAMPO BATANG — Bldr: Japan, 4-61

D: 250 tons **S:** 11 kts **M:** 1,200 hp

935 TAMBORA, 936 BROMO — Bldr: Japan, 6-61

D: 150 tons **M:** 600 hp

KARIMAJA

♦ *1 sail training ship*

DEWARUTJI — Bldr: Stülcken, Hamburg, 21-1-52

D: 810 tons (1,500 fl) **Dim:** 58.30 (41.50 pp) × 9.50 × 4.23
S: 9 kts **Man:** 110 men, 78 cadets
M: 1 M.A.N. diesel; 575 hp

REMARKS: Sail area: 1,091 m². Armed in 7-53

INDONESIA *(continued)*

AUXILIARY SHIPS *(continued)*

Dewarutji 1977

♦ *14 police-manned Bango-class ships* — Bldr: The Netherlands

BANGO, BETTET, BABUT, BEKALLA, BEO, BLEKOK, BIDO, BLIBIS, 1952
BALAM, BARAU, BEKAKA, BELATIK, BENDALU, BOGA, 1953

D: 194 tons **S:** 11 kts **Dim:** 38.18 × 6.53 × 2.95
A: 1/40-mm — 4 machine guns **M:** 1 Werkspoor diesel; 450 hp

NOTE: The Indonesian Customs Service, Army, and Air Force also operate sizeable seagoing contingents.

IRAN

PERSONNEL: 12,500 men, including 1,100 officers

MERCHANT MARINE (1976): 168 ships — 683,329 grt
(tankers: 17 ships — 217,452)

MARITIME AVIATION: 8 AB-204 or AB-206 helicopters, 8 Sea King helicopters, 6 P3-F Orion patrol planes

SUBMARINES

♦ *3 U.S. Tang class* — Bldrs: 101: Portsmouth NSY; 102 and 103: Gen. Dynamics, Groton

	Laid down	L	In serv.
101 **KUSSEH** (ex-*Wahoo*, SS-565)	24-10-49	16-10-51	30-5-52
102 **NAHANG** (ex-*Trout*, SS-566)	1-12-49	21-8-51	27-6-52
103 **DOLFIN** (ex-*Gudgeon*, SS-567)	20-5-50	11-6-52	21-11-52

D: 2,100 tons surfaced, 2,700 submerged **S:** 16/16 kts
Dim: 87.4 × 8.3 × 6.2 **A:** 8/533-mm TT (6 fwd, 2 aft)
M: 3 Fairbanks-Morse diesels, electric drive; 2 props; 5,600 hp
Man: 8 officers, 79 men

REMARKS: Transfers to take place after periods of thorough overhaul and training, 1978, 1980, and 1982.

GUIDED-MISSILE DESTROYERS

♦ *4 modified U.S. Spruance class* — Bldr: Litton, Pascagoula, Mississippi

	Laid down	L	In serv.
11 **KOUROUSH**	. . .	. . .	. . .
12 **DARYUSH**	. . .	. . .	. . .
14 **NADER**	. . .	. . .	. . .
16 **ANDUSHIRVAN**	. . .	. . .	. . .

D: 8,500 tons (fl) **S:** 30 kts **Dim:** 171.1 × 17.6 × 8.8
A: 2 Mk 26 twin launchers for Standard-MR and Asroc — 2/127-mm Mk 45 (I × 2) — 6 ASW TT Mk 32 (III × 2) — 2 helicopters
Electron Equipt: Radars: 1 SPS 55, 1 SPS 48, 2 SPG 60 fire control, 1 SPQ 9 fire control
Sonar: SQS 23 — TACAN
Man: 13 officers, 232 men **Range:** 6,000/20
M: 4 General Electric LM 2500 gas turbines; 2 controllable-pitch props; 80,000 hp

REMARKS: Ordered from the U.S. Navy in 1974 but not contracted for until late 1977. Two sisters canceled due to rapidly rising costs.

♦ *1 ex-British Battle class* — Bldr: Cammell Laird

	Laid down	L	In serv.
51 **ARTEMIZ** (ex-*Sluys*, D-60)	11-43	28-2-45	9-46

Artemiz, now 51 Thornycroft, 1969

GUIDED MISSILE DESTROYERS (*continued*)

D: 2,325 tons (3,360 fl) **Dim:** 115.32 (108.20 pp) × 12.95 × 5.20 (fl)
S: 31 kts **Man:** 260 men
Range: 3,200/20 **Fuel:** 680 tons
A: Standard ASM launchers (8 missiles) — 4/114-mm (II × 2, fwd) — 4/40-mm AA (I × 4) — 4 Sea Cat (IV × 1) — 1 Squid ASW mortar
Electron Equipt: Radars: 1 Plessey AWS-1 air search, 1 Plessey surface search
M: Parsons GT; 2 props; 50,000 hp **Boilers:** 2 Admiralty

REMARKS: Modernized prior to transfer on 20-1-67. Anti-ship missiles added after refit in South Africa, 1975-76.

♦ *2 ex-U.S. Allen M. Sumner class*

	Bldr	L
61 **BABR** (ex-*Zellars*, DD-777)	Todd, Pacific	18-7-44
62 **PALANG** (ex-*Stormes*, DD-780)	Federal SB, Kearny	4-11-44

Babr (61) 1976

D: 2,200 tons (3,320 fl) **Dim:** 114.75 × 12.45 × 5.60
S: 30 kts **Man:** 14 officers, 260 men
A: 4 anti-surface Tartar systems — 4/127-mm DP (II × 2) — 6/ASW TT Mk 32 — 2 hedgehogs — AB-204 ASW helicopter
Electron Equipt: Radars: 1 SPS 10, 1 SPS 37, Mk 37 fire control
Sonars: 1 SQS 29, 1 SQS 11 towed
M: GT; 4 Babcock & Wilcox boilers; 2 props; 60,000 hp
Range: 1,260/30, 4,600/15 **Fuel:** 650 tons

REMARKS: Assigned in 3-71 and delivered in 10-73 and 1974. The *Gainard* (DD-706) and the *Kenneth D. Bailey* (DD-713) were transferred for cannibalization.

FRIGATES

♦ *4 Saam Mk 5 class*

	Bldr	Laid down	L	In serv.
71 **SAAM**	Thornycroft	5-67	25-7-68	20-5-71
72 **ZAAL**	Vickers, Newcastle	3-68	25-7-68	1-3-71
73 **ROSTAM**	Vickers, Barrow	12-67	4-3-69	26-5-72
74 **FARAMARZ**	Thornycroft	7-68	30-7-69	28-2-72

Saam (71) 1977

D: 1,100 tons (1,350 fl) **S:** 40/30 kts (17.5 with diesel)
Dim: 94.50 (88.40 pp) × 11.07 × 3.25 **Man:** 135 men
A: 1/114-mm DP Mk 8 — 2/35-mm AA (II × 1) — 1 surface-surface Sea Killer missile system — 1 Sea Cat system — 1 ASW Limbo Mk 10
M: CODOG; 2 Rolls-Royce Olympus TM 8A gas turbines; 2 Paxman 16-cyl. diesels for cruising; 2 controllable-pitch props; 48,000 hp (turbines), 3,800 hp (diesels)
Range: 5,000/15 **Fuel:** 150 tons (250 with overload)

Zaal (72) 1977

REMARKS: Air-conditioned. Retractable stabilizers. Plessey radars. All now carry Mk 8 guns in place of original Mk 6 guns.

♦ *4 U.S. PF-103 class* — Bldr: Levingston SB, Orange, Texas

	L	In serv.
81 **BAYANDOR** (ex-PF-103)	7-7-63	5-64

FRIGATES *(continued)*

82 NAGHDI (ex-PF-104)	10-10-63	7-64
83 MILANIAN (ex-PF-105)	4-1-68	12-68
84 KAHNAMOIE (ex-PF-106)	4-4-68	2-69

Naghdi (82) wearing old number

D: 900 tons (1,135 fl) **S:** 20 kts **Dim:** 83.82 × 10.05 × 3.05
A: 2/76-mm (I × 2) — 2/40-mm AA (II × 1) — 2/20-mm AA (II × 1) — 1 hedgehog — 4 depth-charge projectors — 2 depth-charge racks
Electron Equipt: Radars: 1 SPS 10, 1 SPS 6
M: Fairbanks-Morse diesels; 2 props; 5,600 hp
Range: 3,000/15 **Man:** 133 men

REMARKS: Transferred under M.A.P. One of them may receive a 76-mm AA OTO Melara Compact gun. Twin 20-mm AA have been added forward of the bridge. 83 and 84 have tripod masts.

GUIDED-MISSILE PATROL BOATS

♦ *12 La Combattante-II class* — Contracted 19-2 and 14-10-74

Bldr: Constr. Méc. de Normandie, Cherbourg

	L		L		L
P 221 KAMAN	1-76	**P 225 JOSHAN**	2-77	**P 229 GARDOUNEM**	10-77
P 222 ZOUBIN	4-76	**P 226 FALAKHON**	6-77	**P 230 KHANSAR**	78
P 223 KHADAN	7-76	**P 227 SHAMSHIR**	8-77	**P 231 NEYZAH**	78
P 224 PEYKAN	10-76	**P 228 GORZ**	9-77	**P 232 TABARZIN**	78

D: 249 tons (275 fl) **S:** 36 kts **Dim:** 47.0 × 7.1 × 1.9
A: 4 Harpoon SSM (II × 2) — 1/76-mm OTO Melara AA — 1/40-mm AA

Zoubin (P 222) Terzibaschitsch, 1977

Electron Equipt: Radar: WM 28 fire control **Range:** 700/30
M: 4 MTU diesels; 4 props; 14,000 hp **Fuel:** 41 tons

PATROL BOATS

♦ *3 U.S. PGM-71 class, 1967-70* — Bldrs: P-211: Peterson, Sturgeon Bay; P-212, P-213: Tacoma Boat

P 211 PARVIN **P 212 BAHRAM** **P 213 NAHID**

D: 105 tons (146 fl) **S:** 17 kts **Dim:** 30.5 × 6.7 × 3.1
A: 1/40-mm AA — 4/20-mm AA (II × 2) — 4/12.7-mm machine guns (II × 2) — 2 Mk 22 Mousetrap — 2 depth-charge racks
M: 8 G.M. 6-71 diesels; 2 controllable-pitch props; 2,000 hp

♦ *4 U.S. Coast Guard Cape class, 1956-59* — Bldr: U.S. Coast Guard Yard, Curtis Bay, Maryland

P 201 KEYVAN **P 202 TIRAN** **P 203 MEHRAN** **P 204 MAHVAN**

D: 85 tons (107 fl) **S:** 20 kts **Dim:** 29.0 × 6.2 × 2.0
A: 1/40-mm AA — 2 Mk 22 Mousetrap — 2 depth-charge racks
M: 4 Cummins diesels; 2 props; 2,200 hp **Range:** 1,500/15

PATROL CRAFT

♦ *20 + 50 U.S. 64-ft Mk III class* — Bldr: Peterson, U.S.A.

D: 28.6 tons (37.4 fl) **S:** 30 kts **Dim:** 19.8 × 5.6 × 2.0
A: 3/20-mm AA (I × 3) — 1/12.7-mm machine gun **Man:** 5 men
M: 3 G.M. 8V71-TI diesels; 3 props; 2,050 hp **Range:** 500/30

REMARKS: Twenty ordered 1973; up to fifty more ordered 1976. Some may be built under license in Iran; some may be in the Iranian Coast Guard.

♦ *20 U.S. 50-ft Mk II class* — Bldr: Peterson, U.S.A., 1976-77

D: 22 tons (fl) **S:** 26 kts **Dim:** 15.3 × 4.8 × 1.9
A: 4/12.7-mm machine guns (II × 2) **Man:** 6 men
M: 2 G.M. 12V71 diesels; 2 props; 900 hp

REMARK: Some or all to be operated by the Iranian Coast Guard.

♦ *12 U.S. 40-ft class* — Bldr: Sewart, Louisiana, 1963, 197. . .

MAHMAVI-HAMRAZ, MAHMAVI-TAHERI, MAHMAVI-VANEDI, MARDJAN, MORDARID, SADAF, 6 others

D: 10 tons **S:** 30 kts **Dim:** 12.2 × 3.4 × 1.1
A: 2/7.6-mm machine gums **M:** 2 G.M. diesels; 2 props; 600 hp

REMARKS: Operate under Iranian Coast Guard. Hull numbers in 1200 series.

NOTE: The Iranian Coast Guard also operates:

♦ *Over 40 U.S. Bertram Enforcer harbor patrol craft* (9.5 and 6.1 oa)

♦ *10 British Fairey Marine Medina-class motor lifeboats*

MINE WARFARE SHIPS

♦ *3 U.S. Falcon-class minesweepers*

	Bldr	L
301 SHAHROKH (ex-MSC-276)	Peterson	1958
302 SIMORGH (ex-MSC-291)	Bellingham SY	3-3-61
303 KARKAS (ex-MSC-292)	Tacoma Boat	1962

D: 320 tons (378 fl) **Dim:** 43.0 (41.5 pp) × 7.95 × 2.55

MINE WARFARE SHIPS (*continued*)

Simorgh (302) 1961

S: 12.5 kts (8 sweeping) **Man:** 3 officers, 35 men
A: 2/20-mm AA (II × 1) **Range:** 2,500/10
M: 2 General Motors diesels; 2 props; 890 hp **Fuel:** 27 tons

REMARKS: Sister *Shabaz* lost through fire in 1975. *Shahrokh* is the largest unit of the Iranian Navy in the Caspian Sea.

♦ *2 U.S. Cape-class inshore minesweepers* — Bldr: Tacoma Boatbuilding, 1964

311 HARISCHI (ex-*Kahnamuie*, ex-MSI-13) **312 RIAZI** (ex-MSI-14)

Harischi (311) 1964

D: 180 tons (235 fl) **S:** 13 kts **Dim:** 34.0 × 7.0 × 1.8
A: 1/12.7-mm machine gun **Man:** 5 officers, 18 men
M: 2 diesels; 650 hp **Fuel:** 20 tons **Range:** 1,000/9

AMPHIBIOUS WARFARE SHIPS

♦ *6 Hengam-class LSTs* — Bldr: Yarrow & Co., Glasgow

	L	In serv.		L	In serv.
511 HENGAM	27-9-73	12-8-74	**514 TONB**	...	1979
512 LARAK	7-5-74	12-11-74	**515 N . . .**	...	1980
513 LAVAN	...	1979	**516 N . . .**	...	1981

Larak (512) wearing old hull number 1976

D: 2,500 tons **S:** 16 kts **Dim:** 91.5 × . . . × . . .
M: 2 Paxman diesels; 2 controllable-pitch props; 5,600 hp

REMARKS: Bow door. Helicopter platform on stern. 513 laid down 4-77; sixth unit ordered 7-77.

♦ *1 ex-U.S. LCU* — Transferred in 1964

GHESHNE (ex-LCU-1431)

D: 160 tons (320 fl) **S:** 10 kts **A:** 2/20-mm
M: 2 diesels; 675 hp

HOVERCRAFT

♦ *6 BH-7 Wellington class*

101 to **106**

D: 50 tons **S:** 60 kts **Dim:** 23.4 × 12.6 × 12.7 (h)
M: 1 Rolls-Royce Proteus gas turbine

♦ *8 SR-N6 Winchester class*

01 to **08**

D: 10 tons **S:** 58 kts **Dim:** 14.4 × 8.0 × 4.8
A: 2/7.6-mm machine guns **M:** 1 Gnome Mk 1050 gas turbine

AUXILIARY SHIPS

♦ *1 large replenishment oiler*

	Bldr	Laid down	L	In serv.
91 KHARG	Swan Hunter, G.B.	1-76	3-2-77	1978

AUXILIARY SHIPS (*continued*)

Kharg (at launch) Swan Hunter, 1977

D: 33,014 tons (fl) **Dim:** 207.1 (195.0 pp) × 25.5 × 9.1
S: 21.5 kts **Man:** 248 men
A: 1/76-mm OTO Melara AA — 4/40-mm Breda AA (II × 2) — 3 helicopters
M: Westinghouse GT; 1 prop; 26,870 hp
Electric: 7,000 kw **Boilers:** 2 Babcock & Wilcox

REMARKS: 21,100 grt/20,000 dwt Design is a greatly modified version of the Royal Navy's *Olwen* class.

♦ *2 Bandar Abbas-class small replenishment oilers*

422 BANDAR ABBAS (L: 14-8-73) **441 BOOSHEHR** (L: 22-3-74)
Bldr: Lühring, German Federal Republic

Bandar Abbas (422) 1976

Bandar Abbas 1975

D: 5,000 tons (fl) **S:** 15 kts **Dim:** 108.0 × 16.6 × 4.5
A: 2/40-mm AA (I × 2) — 1 helicopter
M: 2 M.A.N. diesels; 2 props; 6,000 hp

REMARKS: 3,250 dwt. Telescoping hangar.

♦ *1 modified U.S. 174-ft-class yard oiler* — Bldr: Nav. Mec. Castellammare, 1956

43 HORMUZ
D: 1,700 tons (fl) **S:** 9 kts **Dim:** 54.4 × 9.8 × 4.3
A: 2/20-mm AA (I × 2) **M:** 1 Ansaldo diesel

Hormuz (43) 1974

♦ *2 water tankers* — Bldr: Mazagon Dock, India, 1978-79

411 KANGAN **412 TAHERI**
D: 9,430 tons (fl) **S:** 15 kts **Dim:** 140.0 (pp) × 21.5 × 5.0
M: 1 M.A.N. 7L-52/55A diesel; 7,385 hp

♦ *1 U.S. 174-ft-class water tanker* — Purchased 1964

46 HENGEH (ex-YW-88)
D: 1,250 tons **S:** 10 kts **Dim:** 54.3 × 9.8 × 4.3

♦ *1 U.S. Amphion-class repair ship* — Bldr: Tampa SB, Florida, 15-5-45

CHAH BAHAR (ex-*Amphion,* AR-13)

IRAN (*continued*)

AUXILIARY SHIPS (*continued*)

D: 14,450 tons (fl) **S:** 16 kts **Dim:** 150.0 × 21.4 × 8.4
A: 2/76-mm (I × 2) **M:** 1 GT; 8,500 hp
Man: Quarters for 921 men

REMARKS: Transferred in 10-71. Primarily stationary, but can steam.

♦ *2 imperial yachts*

CHAH SEVAR — Bldr: Boele's SW, Bolnes, The Netherlands, 1936

D: 530 tons **S:** 15 kts **Dim:** 53.0 × 7.65 × 3.2
M: Stork diesels; 2 props; 1,300 hp

REMARK: In the Caspian Sea.

KISH — Bldr: West Germany, 1970

D: 175 tons **Dim:** 37.0 × 7.6 × 2.2 **M:** 2 MTU diesels; 2,920 hp

REMARK: In the Persian Gulf.

♦ *2 barracks ships* — Purchased 12-12-76

	Bldr	L	In serv.
MICHELANGELO	Ansaldo	9-62	. . .
RAFFAELLO	CRDA, Monfalcone	. . .	7-7-65

D: 42,000 tons (fl) **S:** 29 kts
Dim: 275.8 (244.0 pp) × 31.0 × 9.3
M: GT; 4 props; 65,000 hp **Boilers:** 4 Foster-Wheeler

REMARKS: Former cruise liners. Arrived July/August 1977 at Bandar Abbas for use as floating barracks for Iranian naval personnel and their families. Apparently will retain original names.

♦ *1 ex-U.S. Army tug* — Transferred 1962

45 BAHMAN SHIR (ex-ST-1002) — **D:** 150 tons

♦ *2 ex-German tugs* — Transferred 6-74

1 (ex-*Karl*) — 2 (ex-*Ise*) — **D:** 134 tons

REMARK: Built 1962-63

IRAQ

PERSONNEL: 3,000 men, including 300 officers

MERCHANT MARINE (1976): 87 ships — 748,774 grt
(tankers: 22 ships — 638,596 grt)

PATROL BOATS

♦ *3 ex-Soviet SO-1 class* — Delivered in 1962

D: 190 tons (215 fl) **S:** 28 kts **Dim:** 42.0 × 6.1 × 1.9
A: 4/25-mm AA (II × 2) — 4 MB 1800 ASW rocket launchers — 2 depth-charge racks — mines
Electron Equipt: Radar: 1 Pot Head — Sonar: High-frequency
M: 3 diesels; 3 props; 6,000 hp **Man:** 3 officers, 27 men
Range: 1,500/12

GUIDED-MISSILE PATROL BOATS

♦ *6 ex-Soviet Osa-I and 8 Osa-II classes* — Delivered in 1972, 1973, 1974, 1975, 1976, and 1977

D: 175 tons (210 fl, Osa-II: 240 fl) **S:** 36 kts
Dim: 39.0 × 7.7 × 1.8 **Man:** 25 men
A: 4/30-mm AA (II × 2) — 4 SS-N-2 Styx
Electron Equipt: Radars: 1 Square Tie, 1 Drum Tilt
M: 3 diesels; 3 props; 12,000 hp (Osa-II: 15,000 hp)

TORPEDO BOATS

♦ *12 ex-Soviet P-6 class* — Transferred in 1960-62

14 RAMADAN	**ALEF. AL ADRISI**	**N . . .**
AL TAMI	**AL BAHI**	**N . . .**
LAMAKI BIN ZIHYAD	**AL SHAAB**	**N . . .**
TAMOUR	**TAREQ BEN ZOID**	**N . . .**

D: 65 tons (66.5 fl) **S:** 43 kts **Dim:** 25.3 × 6.1 × 1.7
A: 4/25-mm AA (II × 2) — 2/533-mm TT (I × 2)
M: 4 M50 diesels; 4 props; 4,800 hp
Range: 650/26 **Man:** 2 officers, 12 men

PATROL CRAFT

♦ *3 Soviet Zhuk class* — Transferred in 1975

D: 50 tons (60 fl) **S:** 30 kts **Dim:** 26.0 × 4.9 × 1.5
A: 4/14.5-mm AA (II × 2) **M:** 2 M50 diesels; 2 props; 2,400 hp

♦ *2 Soviet Poluchat-I class* — Transferred in 1966

D: 80 tons (90 fl) **S:** 18 kts **Dim:** 29.6 × 5.8 × 1.5
A: 2/14.5-mm AA **M:** 2 diesels; 2 props; 2,400 hp

REMARK: May in fact be torpedo-recovery versions of the Poluchat class.

♦ *4 river patrol craft* — Bldr: Thornycroft, 1937

D: 67 tons **S:** 12 kts **Dim:** 30.5 × 5.2 × 0.9
A: 1/90-mm howitzer — 4/12.7-mm machine guns
M: 2 diesels; 2 props; 280 hp

MINE WARFARE SHIPS

♦ *2 Soviet T-43-class fleet minesweepers* — Transferred in 1969

N . . . **N . . .**

D: 500 tons (580 fl) **S:** 14 kts **Dim:** 58.0 × 8.4 × 2.3
A: 4/37-mm AA (II × 2) — 8/12.7-mm machine guns (II × 4) — 2 depth-charge projectors — mines
M: 2 diesels; 2 props; 2,200 hp **Range:** 3,200/10

♦ *3 Yevgenya-class inshore minesweepers* — Transferred in 1975

D: 80 tons (90 fl) **S:** 12 kts **Dim:** 26.0 × 6.0 × 1.5
A: 2/25-mm AA **M:** 2 diesels; 2 props; 600 hp

REMARKS: Transferred as "oceanographic research craft." Have heavier guns than their Soviet Navy sisters.

IRAQ (*continued*)

AMPHIBIOUS WARFARE SHIPS

♦ *2 Soviet Polnocny-C class* — Bldr: Poland — Transferred in 1977

ATIKA GANDA

D: 1,150 tons (fl) **S:** 18 kts **Dim:** 82.0 × 10.0 × 2.0
A: 4/30-mm AA (II × 2) — 2/122-mm rocket launchers (XL × 2)
M: 2 diesels; 2 props; 5,000 hp

REMARK: Have a helicopter platform forward of the superstructure.

VARIOUS SHIPS

♦ *4 Soviet Nyryat-2-class diving tenders* — Transferred . . .

D: 60 tons (fl) **S:** 10 kts **Dim:** 21.3 × . . . × . . .
M: 1 diesel; 300 hp

REMARK: May also be used as tugs.

♦ *1 Soviet Pozharney-I-class fireboat*

D: 180 tons (fl) **S:** 17 kts **Dim:** 35.0 × 6.2 × 2.0
M: 2 diesels; 2 props; 1,800 hp

CUSTOMS SERVICE

♦ *1 yacht used as a patrol boat*

AL THAWRA (1929)

D: 746 tons **S:** 14 kts **M:** Diesels; 2 props; 1,800 hp

♦ *8 pilot launches* — Bldr: Thornycroft, 1961-62

D: 10 tons **S:** . . . **Dim:** 11.0 × . . . × . . .
M: 1 diesel; 125 hp

♦ *4 pilot launches* — Bldr: Thornycroft
Dim: 6.4 × . . . × . . . **M:** 40 hp

IRELAND

Eire

PERSONNEL: 500 men (53 officers)

MERCHANT MARINE (1976): 96 ships — 201,965 grt
(tankers: 4 ships — 5,060 grt)

♦ *2 fishery protection ships*

	Bldr	L	In serv.
FP 20 DEIRDRE	Verolme, Cork DY	29-12-71	4-72
FP 21 EMER	Verolme, Cork DY	. . .	9-1-78

Deirdre (FP 20) Batenian, 1972

D: 972 tons **Dim:** 62.50 (56.20 pp) × 10.40 × 4.35
S: 18 kts (15.5 cruising) **Man:** 5 officers, 41 men
Range: 3,000/15.5 (on one engine)
A: 1/40-mm — 2/52-mm flare launchers
M: 2 British Polar SF 112 VS-F diesels; 1 controllable-pitch prop; 4,200 hp

REMARKS: Vosper fin stabilizers. FP-21: 64.5 m overall; 2 SEMT-Pielstick 6PA6-L280 diesels; 1 prop; 4,800 hp for 20 kts maximum.

♦ *3 fishery protection ships, ex-British "-ton"-class minesweepers*
Transferred in 1971

	Bldr	In serv.
CM 10 GRAINNE (ex-*Oulston*)	Thornycroft	. . .
CM 11 BANBA (ex-*Alverton*)	Camper & Nicholson	1953
CM 12 FOLA (ex-*Blaxton*)	Thornycroft	1956

D: 370 tons (425 fl) **Dim:** 46.33 (42.68 pp) × 8.76 × 2.50
S: 15 kts **Man:** 33 men

Grainne (CM 10) 1972

IRELAND (*continued*)

A: 1/40-mm AA — 2/20-mm AA (II × 1) **Range:** 2,300/13, 3,000/8
M: Diesels; 2 props; 2,500/3,000 hp **Fuel:** 45 tons

♦ *1 training ship* — Bldr: Liffey, Dublin, 1953

A 15 SETANTA (ex-*Isolde*)

D: 1,173 tons (fl) **S:** 11.5 kts **Dim:** 63.5 × 11.6 × 4.0
A: None **Man:** 44 men **Range:** 3,500/10
M: Reciprocating steam; 2 props; 1,500 hp **Fuel:** 276 tons

Remark: Taken over in 1976 from the Irish Lighthouse Commission.

♦ *1 stores tender* — Bldr: R. Dunston, G.B., 1934

JOHN ADAMS

D: 3.4 grt **S:** 10 kts **Dim:** 25.9 × 5.6 × 2.1
M: 1 diesel; 216 hp

ISRAEL

Personnel: Active: 3,500, of whom 250 officers and 500 men are especially trained as commandos and frogmen. In reserve: 500 men.

Merchant Marine (1976): 68 ships — 481,594 grt
(tankers: 2 ships — 368 grt)

SHIPS IN SERVICE OR UNDER CONSTRUCTION AS OF 1 OCTOBER 1977

	L	Tons	Main armament
♦ *3 submarines*			
3 GERMAN TYPE 206	1975	600 (submerged)	8/533-mm TT
♦ *at least 24 guided-missile patrol boats*			
12 RESHEV	1973-. . .	415	2/76-mm, Gabriel missile system
12 SA'AR II and III	1967-68	220	1/40-mm or 1/76-mm, Gabriel missile system

♦ *53 or more patrol craft*

WEAPONS AND SYSTEMS

The Israeli Navy uses foreign equipment such as 76-mm OTO Melara Compact, Breda 40-mm, and Oerlikon guns, and it has perfected the Gabriel anti-ship missile system.

Gabriel is a 400-kg, solid-propellant, surface-to-surface missile. After being fired, it climbs about 100 meters, then, at 7,500 meters from the launcher, descends slowly to an altitude of 20 meters. Optical or radar guidance is provided in azimuth, and a radio altimeter determines altitude. At a distance of 1,200 meters from the target, the missile descends to 3 meters, under either radio command or semi-active homing. The explosive charge is a 75-kg conventional warhead. In the Yom Kippur War of 1973, 85 per cent of the Gabriel missiles fired reached their targets.

Triple trainable Gabriel missile launcher

In order to have an even more effective surface-to-surface missile for sale on the international market, the Israeli Navy has introduced an improved version of the Gabriel system, Gabriel II. This missile carries a television camera and a transceiver for azimuth and altitude commands. The television is energized when the missile has attained a certain height and sends to the firing ship a picture of the areas that cannot be picked up by shipboard radar. The operator then can send any necessary corrections during the middle and final phases of the missile's flight, and thus find a target that cannot be seen either by the naked eye or on radar. The range of the Gabriel II is about 40,000 meters. The need to increase the range of the Gabriel is one of the lessons the Israeli learned from the Yom Kippur War.

The Israeli Navy hopes to re-equip its *Reshev*-class guided-missile patrol boats with U.S.-built Harpoon missiles (IV × 2).

WEAPONS AND SYSTEMS (*continued*)

Chaff launchers on a Reshev-class guided-missile patrol boat 1975

SUBMARINES

♦ *3 German Type 206* — Ordered from Vickers, Barrow, in 1972

GAL (1977) **TANNIN** (1977) **RAHAV** (1978)

D: 420 tons surfaced, 600 submerged **S:** 17/11 kts
Dim: 45.0 × 4.7 × 3.8 **Man:** 22 men **A:** 8/533-mm TT, fwd

M: 2 MTU 12V-493-TY60 diesels (600 hp each); AEG generators; 1 prop; 1,800 hp

REMARKS: May have British SLAM missile system installed. Carry two spare torpedoes. First unit ran aground on delivery voyage, but has been repaired.

GUIDED-MISSILE PATROL BOATS

♦ *12 Reshev (Sa'ar IV) class* — Bldr: Haifa SY

	L	In serv.		L	In serv.
. . . **RESHEV**	19-2-73	4-73	. . . **KIDON**	7-74	9-74
. . . **KESHET**	23-8-73	10-73	. . . **TARSHISH**	1-75	3-75
. . . **ROMACH**	1-74	3-74	. . . **YAFO**	2-75	4-75
. . . N . . .	. . .	1-77	. . . N . . .	. . .	. . .
. . . N . . .	. . .	. . .	. . . N . . .	. . .	. . .
. . . N . . .	. . .	. . .	. . . N . . .	. . .	. . .

Yafo Terzibaschitsch, 1976

GUIDED-MISSILE PATROL BOATS (*continued*)

Yafo Terzibaschitsch, 1976

D:	415 tons (450 fl)	**S:**	32 kts	**Dim:**	58.1 × 7.6 × 2.4
Man:	45 men	**Range:**	1,500/30		

A: 7 Gabriel missile launchers (II × 3, I × 1) — 2/76-mm OTO Melara Compact — 4/12.7-mm machine guns (II × 2) or 2/20-mm and 2/12.7-mm machine guns — 4 large and 72 small chaff launchers

M: 4 MTU MD871 diesels; 4 props; 14,000 hp

Keshet 1974

Remarks: The second group of six ships are reportedly 2-meters longer than the first group. The final three will be fitted with U.S. Harpoon missiles (IV × 2). Quarters air-conditioned. Can launch chaff for long-distance cluttering of radar screens. Three being built for the Republic of South Africa, and three more are building at Durban.

♦ *6 Sa'ar I and II classes*

	L		L
MIVTACH	11-4-67	**EILATH**	14-6-68
MIZNAG	1967	**HAIFA**	14-6-68
MIFGAV	1967	**AKKO**	1968

Bldr: Constr. Méc. de Normandie, Cherbourg

D:	220 tons (250 fl)	**S:**	40 kts	**Dim:**	45.0 × 7.0 × 1.8 (2.5 fl)
Range:	1,000/30, 1,600/20, 2,500/15	**A:**	See Remarks		
Man:	5 officers, 30 to 35 men	**Fuel:**	30 tons		

M: 4 MTU MD 871 diesels; 4 props; 14,000 hp

Sa'ar II type 1970

Sa'ar I type 1970

GUIDED-MISSILE PATROL BOATS (*continued*)

REMARKS: Excellent sea qualities and endurance. Two weapon variations are now in use. Reading from forward to aft: 1/40-mm AA Breda, 2 single fixed Gabriel launchers, bridge, 1 triple trainable Gabriel launcher, 1/40-mm AA, or, the same but with a second triple trainable Gabriel launcher replacing the after 40-mm AA gun. Single U.S. Mk 32 ASW torpedo tubes can be bolted on at the stern. *Sa'ar I* was the name used for these ships in all-gun configuration.

♦ *6 Sa'ar III class*

	L		L
331 SA'AR	25-11-69	**341 HEREV**	20-6-69
332 SOUFA	4-2-69	**342 HANIT**	1969
333 GAASCH	24-6-69	**343 HETZ**	14-12-69

Bldr: Constr. Méc. de Normandie, Cherbourg

Sa'ar III type

REMARKS: Same characteristics as the *Sa'ar II* class but armament as follows: 1/76-mm AA OTO Melara Compact, bridge, 2 triple trainable Gabriel launchers or 1 triple trainable and 2 fixed launchers.

PATROL CRAFT

♦ *25 Dabur class*

Bldrs: 12 by Sewart Seacraft, U.S.A., others by Israeli Aircraft Industries, 1973–77

D: 25 tons (35 fl) **S:** 25 kts **Dim:** 19.8 × 5.8 × 0.8
A: 2/20-mm (I × 2) — 4/12.7-mm machine guns (II × 2)
M: 2 GM diesels; 2 props; 960 hp
Range: 1,200/17 **Man:** 1 officer, 5 men

REMARKS: Quarters air-conditioned and spacious. Five given to Lebanon in 1976. An enlarged version, nicknamed Dvora, has been offered for export and may be built also for the Israeli Navy. Of 47 tons full-load displacement, the craft is 21.6 × 5.5 × 1.0 and would be armed with 2 Gabriel missiles, 2/20-mm AA (I × 2), and 2/12.7-mm machine guns (I × 2).

Dabur class 1973

♦ *4 Kedma, or Winds, class*

46 KEDMA, 48 YAMA, 50 TZAFONA, 52 NEGBA — Bldr: Japan, 1968

Negba 1974

D: 32 tons **S:** 25 kts **Dim:** 20.50 × 4.60 × 1.45
A: 2/20-mm **Man:** 10 men **M:** 2 diesels; 1,540 hp

REMARK: Actually operated by the Port Police Forces, rather than the Navy.

♦ *28 Yatush class (U.S. PBR type)*

D: 6.5 tons **S:** 25 kts **Dim:** 9.8 × 3.4 × 0.8
A: 2 machine guns **Man:** 5 men **M:** 2 diesels; water jets

REMARKS: Early units bought in the United States in 1968, later ones built in Israel. Several may be stationed in the Red Sea. Two given to Lebanon in 1975–76.

AMPHIBIOUS WARFARE SHIPS

♦ **BAT SHEVA,** 1967

Bat Sheva 1969

D: 900 tons (1,150 fl) **S:** 10 kts **Dim:** 95.1 × 11.2 × . . .
A: 4/20-mm — 4/12.7-mm machine guns **Man:** 26 men
M: Diesels; 2 props

REMARK: Built in Germany and bought in 1968 in South Africa.

♦ *3 LCT type*

61 ASHDOD, 63 ASHKELON, 65 AHZIV — Bldr: Haifa, 1966–67

Ashdod (61) — now has helicopter deck amidships 1971

D: 400 tons (730 fl) **S:** 10.5 kts **Dim:** 62.7 × 10.0 × 1.8
A: 2/20-mm AA (I × 2) **Man:** 20 men **Fuel:** 37 tons
M: 3 MWM diesels; 3 props; 1,900 hp

♦ **51 ETZION GUEBER, 53 SHIKMONA, 55 . . .** — Bldr: Haifa, 1965

Etzion Gueber

D: 182 tons (230 fl) **S:** 10 kts **Dim:** 30.5 × 5.9 × 1.3
A: 2/20-mm AA (I × 2) **Man:** 10 men
M: Diesels; 2 props; 1,280 hp

♦ *3 ex-U.S. LSM-1 class* — Built 1944–45, bought 1972

N . . . **N . . .** **N . . .**

D: 1,095 (fl) **S:** 12.5 kts **Dim:** 62.1 × 10.5 × 2.2
A: 1/20-mm AA — several machine guns
M: 2 GM diesels; 2 props; 2,800 hp

VARIOUS SHIPS

♦ **BAT YAM** — Small cargo ship fitted out as a transport and based at Eilath. Former Dutch motorized barge, refitted in Israel in 1967.

♦ **NOGAH** — Former small cargo ship equipped as a training ship for the merchant marine.

♦ **NAHARYA** — Base ship for the missile craft stationed at Eilath.

♦ **MA'OZ** — 4,000-ton oilfield supply ship type used as a missile-boat tender in the Mediterranean. Built by Todd, Seattle, 1976.

ITALY

PERSONNEL (1976): 42,000, including 5,200 officers

MERCHANT MARINE (1976): 1,719 ships — 11,077,549 grt
(tankers: 311 ships — 4,727,846 grt)

NAVAL AVIATION: Fixed-wing ASW aircraft belong to the Air Force, which puts them at the disposal of the Navy. For some time, American two-engined S-2A Trackers were the primary planes in use, but, following a contract entered into in October 1968, the BR-1150 Atlantic became the principal type, the last 18 units being delivered in 1973.

Helicopters, of which there are about 80 (AB-204B, etc.), are under the control of the Navy. They are used mainly for ASW, but could be used in an anti-ship role; they carry such missiles as the AS-12. For antisubmarine warfare, the Italian Navy has favored a light, weapon-carrying helicopter working in combination with another helicopter of the same size equipped with ASW sensors. Because this limits the ships that can participate in ASW operations to those that are fitted to carry both types of helicopter, future orientation in ASW operations appears to be towards the use of a heavier helicopter (SH-3D) that carries both weapons and sensors. These helicopters, several of which have been ordered from the United States, may be based ashore or on such ships as can handle them (*Giuseppe Garibaldi, Vittorio Veneto,* the two *Andrea Doria*-class cruisers, and the two *Audace*-class destroyers).

At present the most widely used helicopter is the Bell 204B built under American license in Italy. Its principal characteristics are:

Ceiling: 10,800 feet	Length: 17.4 m
Range: 2 hours 5 min without torpedoes	Rotor: 14.6 m
1 hour 15 min with torpedoes	Max. weight at takeoff: 3,600 kg
Armament: 2 Mk 44 torpedoes or 4 AS-12	Motor: 1 turbo shaft, 1,200 hp
Electronics: 1 ASQS 13 sonar	Max. speed: 120 kts
Crew: 3	Cruising speed: 90 kts

WARSHIPS IN SERVICE, UNDER CONSTRUCTION, OR AUTHORIZED AS OF 1 OCTOBER 1977

	L	Tons	Main armament
♦ *1 VTOL carrier*			
GIUSEPPE GARIBALDI	. . .	10,043	6 Otomat, 3 Albatros, 16 helicopters and VTOL aircraft
		Tons (submerged)	
♦ *12 submarines*			
4 NAZARIO SAURO	1976-. . .	1,613	6/533-mm TT
4 ENRICO TOTI	1967-68	591	4/533-mm TT
2 TANG	1951	2,700	8/533-mm TT
2 GUPPY III	1944-46	2,540	10/533-mm TT
		Tons	
♦ *3 cruisers*			
1 VITTORIO VENETO	1967	7,500	2 missile launchers, 8/76-mm, 9 helicopters
2 ANDREA DORIA	1962-63	6,500	2 missile launchers, 8/76-mm, 4 helicopters
♦ *6 destroyers*			
2 AUDACE	1971	3,950	1 Tartar system, 2/127-mm, ASW weapons
2 IMPAVIDO	1962	3,201	1 Tartar system, 2/127-mm, ASW weapons
2 IMPETUOSO	1955-56	2,775	4/127-mm, ASW weapons
♦ *33 frigates and corvettes*			
8 MAESTRALE	Bldg	2,650	4 Otomat, 1 Albatros, 1/127-mm, ASW weapons
4 LUPO	1976-. . .	2,500	8 Otomat, 1 Albatros, 1/127-mm, ASW weapons
2 ALPINO	1967	2,000	6/76-mm, ASW weapons
4 CARLO BERGAMINI	1960	1,410	2/76-mm, ASW weapons
4 CANOPO	1954-56	1,680	3/76-mm, ASW weapons
4 PIETRO DE CRISTOFARO	1964-65	940	2/76-mm, ASW weapons
4 ALBATROS	1954	800	4/40-mm, ASW weapons
3 APE	1942-44	670	4/40-mm

NAVAL PROGRAM: In 1974 the Italian Navy presented parliament with a White Paper, which indicated that the Navy needed 160,000 tons of ships to carry out its tasks. Present tonnage is only about 105,000 and most of the vessels, especially the small ones, are aged. Funds now allotted the Navy do not allow for the renewal of any equipment and, according to the document, if this situation continues the fleet will be reduced to 45,000 tons by 1984 and will be unable to carry out even its essential peacetime missions. To correct the situation, the White Paper stated that it was vital to begin a ten-year building program.

WEAPONS AND SYSTEMS

(A) MISSILES

♦ *Surface-to-air*

American Terrier, Tartar, SM 1, and SM 1 A (see U.S.A. section).

Sea Indigo — Builder: CONTRAVES

Length: 3.2 m	Diameter: 0.200 m
Wingspan: 0.8 m	Weight: 110 kg
Range: 10,000 m	Guidance system: beam-rider

Albatros Aspide (Italian version of the Sea Sparrow) — Builder: SELENIA

Ceiling: mini: 15 m, maxi: 5,000 m

Length: 3.7 m	Diameter: 0.2 m
Wingspan: 1.02 m	Weight: 204 kg
Range: 10,000 m	Guidance system: semi-active homing

♦ *Surface-to-surface*

Nettuno (also known as Sea Killer Mk 1) — Builder: CONTRAVES

Length: 3.9 m	Diameter: 0.2 m
Wingspan: 0.85 m	Weight: 168 kg
Range: 10,000 m	Guidance system: beam-rider

Vulcano (also known as Sea Killer Mk 2) — Builder: CONTRAVES

Length: 4.5 m	Diameter: 0.2 m
Wingspan: 0.85 m	Weight: 270 kg
Range: 25,000 m	Guidance system: beam-rider

Otomat Mk 1 — Builder: OTO MELARA/MATRA

Length: 4,820 m

WEAPONS AND SYSTEMS (*continued*)

Diameter: 1,060 m (with boosters) — 460 m
Wingspan: 1.19 m Weight: 750 kg
Range: 60-80 km Guidance system: Thomson/CSF active homing

This missile flies almost at sea level after firing, climbs at a steep angle to a predetermined height, and strikes its target during descent.

Otomat Mk 2 (also known as Teseo)

This model differs from the Mk 1 in having an Italian (SMA) active radar homing head, instead of a French one. It is also a sea-skimmer: that is, it flies close to the water after firing. Its explosive charge is about 200 kg, and its ramjet propulsion system allows it to be used at ranges limited only by its guidance system and its target designation. It will be mounted in the *Lupo*-class destroyers.

♦ *Air-to-surface*

Marte (system using the Vulcano missile still under development)

In the meantime the French AS-12 has been adopted.

(B) GUNS

With the exception of some old American guns, such as the 127-mm twin-barrel 38-cal. semi-automatic, the following Italian systems are used:

♦ 76 Brescia

Single- or twin-barrel, automatic, air, surface, and land targets

Length: 62 calibers
Max. effective range, surface fire: 8,000 m
Max. effective range, anti-aircraft fire: 4,000-5,000 m
Muzzle velocity: 850 m/sec.
Rate of fire: 60 rounds/min./barrel

♦ 76 OTO Melara Compact

Single-barrel light anti-aircraft automatic fire; entirely remote control with muzzle brake and cooling system

Length: 62 calibers
Muzzle velocity: 925 m/sec
Max. effective range, surface fire: 8,000 m
Max. effective range, anti-aircraft fire: 4,000-5,000 m
Rate of fire: 85 rounds/min.
Weight of mount: 7.35 tons, because of the use of light alloys and fiberglass; 80 ready-service rounds in the drum, which permits at least one minute of fire before reloading. There are no personnel in the mount; the ammunition-handlers in the magazine have only to feed the drum.

The gun has been purchased by many navies.

♦ 127 OTO Melara Compact

Single-barrel automatic, triple-purpose, remote control

Length: 54 calibers
Muzzle velocity: 808 m/sec
Max. effective range, surface fire: 15,000 m
Max. effective range, anti-aircraft fire: 7,000 m
Rate of fire: 45 rounds/minute, automatic setting
Weight of the mount: 32 tons because of the use of light alloys and a fiberglass shield. The gun has a muzzle brake; it can fire, if desired, 66 rounds thanks to 3 loading drums, each with 22 rounds. Two hoists serve two loading trays with rounds coming from the magazine, and a drum may be loaded even while the gun is firing. An automatic selection system allows a choice of ammunition (anti-aircraft, surface target, pyrotechnics, chaff for cluttering radar).

This equipment has been purchased by the Canadian Navy for its *Iroquois*-class destroyers.

(C) ANTISUBMARINE WEAPONS

♦ Menon triple-barreled mortar

The system has a launcher carrying three 4.6-m barrels. These tubes fire a 160-kg rocket at a fixed elevation of 45°. The range (400 to 900 m) is reached by varying the quantity of gas admitted into the tubes from three powder chambers. The tubes are reloaded at a 90° elevation from a drum containing the projectiles.

♦ Menon single-barreled mortar

The system has a single barrel with automatic loading. Fire control is usually directed in the underwater battery plot. The mortar is fired at a 45° angle with the range fixed by a system similar to that of the triple-barrel Menon; firing 160-kg grenades round by round; the gas relief valves have adjustable vents. The weapon is automatically reloaded from the magazine by hoist and a loading drum.

♦ Torpedoes

American Mk 44 and Mk 46 torpedoes are used on ships and helicopters.

The A-184 wire-guided torpedo is now in use, with a carrier torpedo that ejects a Mk 46.

(D) RADARS

The following American radars, either bought or built under license, are in use:

SPQ 2 combined search
SPS 6, SPS 12 long-range air search
SPS 39, SPS 52 height-finding
SPG 51 Tartar guidance system on *Audace* and *Impavido* destroyers
SPG 55B Terrier guidance system on board *Vittorio Veneto* and *Andrea Doria* cruisers

For fire control of the 76-mm and 127-mm guns, the Italians use the Argo system, which is made up of an optical target-selection and a tracking radar (Orion) of Italian design.

(E) SONARS

Most of the newest equipment is American or Dutch.

	Type	Frequency		Type	Frequency
SQS 23	Hull	MF	SQS 4	Hull	MF
SQS 29	Hull	MF	SQA 10	Towed	MF
SQS 11A	Hull	MF	SQS 36	Towed	HF
SQS 10	Hull	MF	CWE 610	Hull	LF (Dutch)

(F) TACTICAL INFORMATION SYSTEM

The Italian Navy has perfected the SADOC system, which is compatible with the American NTDS and the French SENIT.

VTOL CARRIER

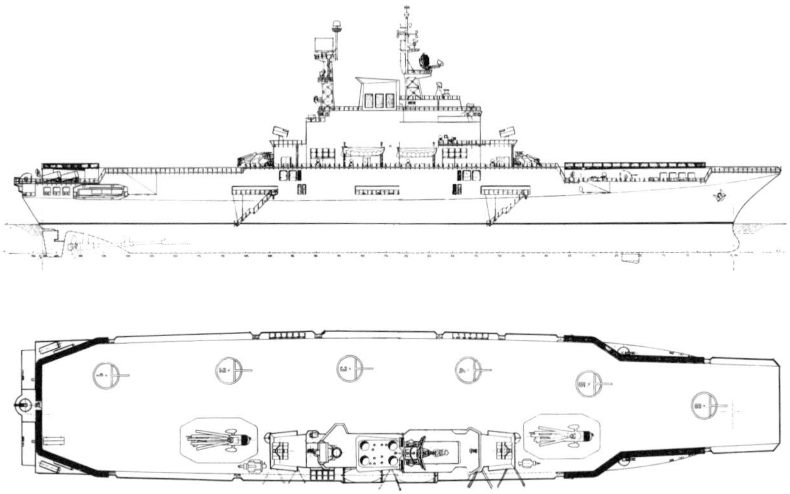

Giuseppe Garibaldi Rivista Marittima, 1977

♦ *1 Giuseppe Garibaldi class*

	Bldr	Authorized
C . . . GIUSEPPE GARIBALDI	C. Nav. del Monfalcone	29-7-77

D: 10,043 tons (12,000 fl) **Dim:** 179.0 × 23.4 × 30.4 (flight deck) × 6.0
S: 29 kts **Man:** 560 crew + 250 troops
A: 6 Otomat (I × 6) — 24 Albatros (VIII × 3) — 6/40-mm 70 cal. AA Breda (II × 3) — 6 TT Mk 32 (III × 2) (Mk 44 or 46 torpedoes) — 16 SH-3D Sea King helicopters and VTOL aircraft
Electron Equipt: Radars: NA 10, RAN 3L, RAN 10S, SPQ 2D, 1 PN 10 Dardo — NTDS
Sonar: hull-mounted
Range: 7,000/20
M: 4 General Electric/Fiat LM 2500 gas turbines; electric: 4 GMT A 230.12M diesels of 1,560 kw capacity each; 2 props; 80,000 hp

Remarks: The flight deck will be 174 × 30.4, and there will be two elevators on each side of the island on the starboard side. The embarked complement of aircraft will be a mix of helicopters and STOL or VTOL fixed-wing aircraft. The ship is designated a helicopter cruiser by the Italian Navy, and its primary mission will be antisubmarine warfare.

SUBMARINES

♦ *4 Nazario Sauro class* — Bldr: C.R.D.A., Monfalcone

	Laid down	L	In serv.
S . . . NAZARIO SAURO	1971	9-10-76	12-77
S . . . CARLO FECIA DI COSSATO	1973	4-77	10-78
S . . . GUGLIELMO MARCONI	. . .	. . .	. . .
S . . . LEONARDO DA VINCI	. . .	. . .	. . .

D: 1,456 tons surfaced, 1,631 submerged **Dim:** 63.85 × 6.83 × 5.70
S: 12/20 kts **A:** 6/533-mm TT (6 reloads) **Man:** 45 men
M: 3 Fiat diesels (3,210 hp), electric drive; 1 prop; 3,650 hp
Range: 7,000/12, 12,500/4 **Endurance:** 45 days

Remarks: Can travel 20 knots submerged for one hour, or 100 hours at 4 knots. Diving depth is 300 m. Second pair approved 1977.

♦ *4 Enrico Toti class* — Bldr: C.R.D.A., Monfalcone

	Laid down	L	In serv.
S 505 ATTILIO BAGNOLINI	15-4-65	26-8-67	16-6-68
S 506 ENRICO TOTI	15-4-65	12-3-67	22-1-68
S 513 ENRICO DANDOLO	10-3-67	16-12-67	25-9-68
S 514 LAZZARO MOCENIGO	12-6-67	20-4-68	11-1-69

Enrico Dandolo (S 513) Martinelli, 1976

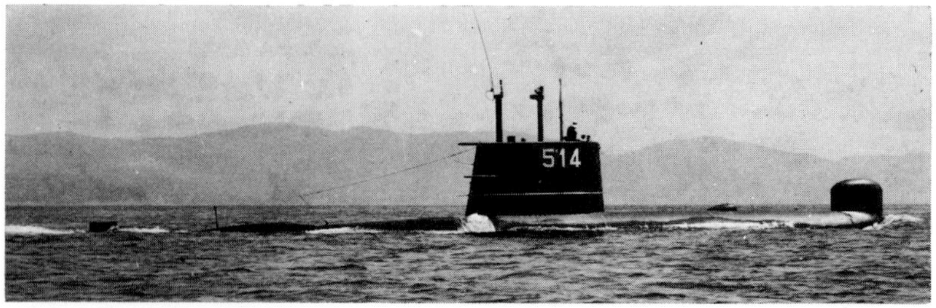

Lazzaro Mocenigo (S 514) 1974

SUBMARINES (*continued*)

D: 535 tons surfaced, 591 submerged **Dim:** 46.2 × 4.7 × 3.99
S: 14/20 kts **Man:** 4 officers, 22 men
A: 4/533-mm TT (6 torpedoes) **Range:** 7,500/4.5 (surf.), 180/4 (sub.)
M: Diesel-electric propulsion; 2 Fiat MB 820 diesels; 1 electric motor; 1 prop; 2,200 hp

♦ *2 U.S. Tang class* — Bldr: Electric Boat

	Laid down	L	In serv.
S 515 LIVIO PIOMARTA (ex-*Trigger*, SS-564)	24-9-49	14-6-51	31-3-52
S 516 ROMEO ROMEI (ex-*Harder*, SS-568)	30-6-50	3-12-51	19-8-52

Transferred in 7-73 and 3-74

Romeo Romei (S 516) G. Arra, 1976

D: 2,100 tons surfaced, 2,700 submerged **Dim:** 87.5 × 8.3 × 6.2
S: 20/17 kts **Man:** 8 officers, 73 men
A: 8/533-mm TT (6 fwd, 2 aft)
M: Diesel-electric propulsion: 3 Fairbanks-Morse diesels; 2 props; 5,600 hp

REMARK: The S-515 arrived in Italy in 4-75.

♦ *2 U.S. Guppy-III class*

	Bldr	Laid down	L	In serv.
S 502 GIANFRANCO GAZZANA PRIAROGGIA (ex-*Volador*, SS-490)	Portsmouth NSY	15-6-45	17-1-46	10-1-48
S 501 PRIMO LONGOBARDO (ex-*Pickerel*, SS-524)	Boston NSY	8-2-44	15-12-44	4-9-49

Transferred in 1972

D: 1,650 tons, 1,975 surfaced, 2,540 submerged **S:** 20/13-15 kts
Dim: 99.4 × 8.2 × 5.2 **Man:** 86 men **Range:** 10,000/10
A: 10/533-mm TT (6 fwd, 4 aft) **Electron Equipt:** Sonar: BQR 2
M: Diesel-electric propulsion, 4 groups of generators, 2 electric motors; 6,400/5,200 hp

Primo Longobardo (S 501) 1972

REMARKS: Originally *Balao*-class submarines. Underwent FRAM II modernization in 1961-63: a 1.5-m compartment was added to the sail to make room for an "attack center" operations area, and a 3.5-m battery compartment was added. Two 126-cell batteries.

NOTE: The two surviving *Balao*-class submarines. *Alfredo Cappellini* (S-507) and *Evangelista Torricelli* (S-512), were stricken in 1977.

CRUISERS

♦ *1 Vittorio Veneto class*

	Bldr	Laid down	L	In serv.
C 550 VITTORIO VENETO	Nav. Mec. Castellammare	6-65	5-2-67	3-69

D: 7,500 tons (9,500 fl) **Dim:** 179.6 (170.61 pp) × 19.4 × 6.0
S: 32 kts **Range:** 3,000/28, 6,000/20 **Man:** 72 officers, 493 men
A: 1 Aster system (II × 1, fwd) — 8/76-mm OTO Melara AA — 6/324-mm MK 32 TT (III × 2) — 9 AB-204B ASW helicopters or 6 HSS or 4 SH-3D

Vittorio Veneto (C 550) J. C. Bellonne, 1972

CRUISERS (*continued*)

Vittorio Veneto (C 550) A. Fraccaroli

Electron Equipt: Radars: 1 SPS 40, 1 SPS 52, 1 SPQ 2B, 2 SPG 55B, 4 Argo systems
Sonar: 1 SQS 23
M: Tosi GT; 2 props; 73,000 hp
Fuel: 1,200 tons
Boilers: 4 Foster-Wheeler, 43 kg/cm^2 pressure
Electric: . . .

REMARKS: The flight deck (40 × 18.5) is on the stern and is served from a hangar immediately below by two elevators (18 × 5.3). The hangar (27.5 × 15.3) is two decks in depth. Anti-rolling stabilizers. The Aster system can launch either Asroc or Terrier.

♦ *2 Andrea Doria class*

	Bldr	Laid down	L	In serv.
C 553 **ANDREA DORIA**	C. Nav. Tirreno, Riva Trigoso	5-58	27-2-63	2-64
C 554 **CAIO DUILIO**	Nav. Mec. Castellammare	5-58	22-12-62	4-64

D: 6,500 tons (7,300 fl) **Dim:** 149.3 (144 pp) × 17.25 × 4.96 (7.5 fl)
S: 30 kts **Range:** 6,000/15 **Man:** 54 officers, 460 men
A: 2 Terrier (II × 1) fwd — 8/76-mm AA (I × 8) — 6/324-mm ASW TT Mk 32 (III × 2) — 4 AB-204B helicopters
Electron Equipt: Radars: 1 SPS 12 (1 SPS 40 on C-554), 1 SPQ 2, 1 SPS 39 (1 SPS 52 on C-554), 2 SPG 55, 4 Argo systems
Sonar: 1 SQS 23

M: GT; 2 props; 60,000 hp **Boilers:** 4 Foster-Wheeler, 43 kg/cm^2 pressure
Fuel: 1,100 tons **Electric:** 4,700 kw

REMARKS: Officially designated escort cruisers, these ships are really small helicopter carriers with a 30 × 16 m platform. Their helicopters work in tandem: one carries a sonar system, the other two Mk 44 ASW torpedoes. Anti-rolling stabilizers. The

Andrea Doria (C 553) G. Arra, 1976

CRUISERS *(continued)*

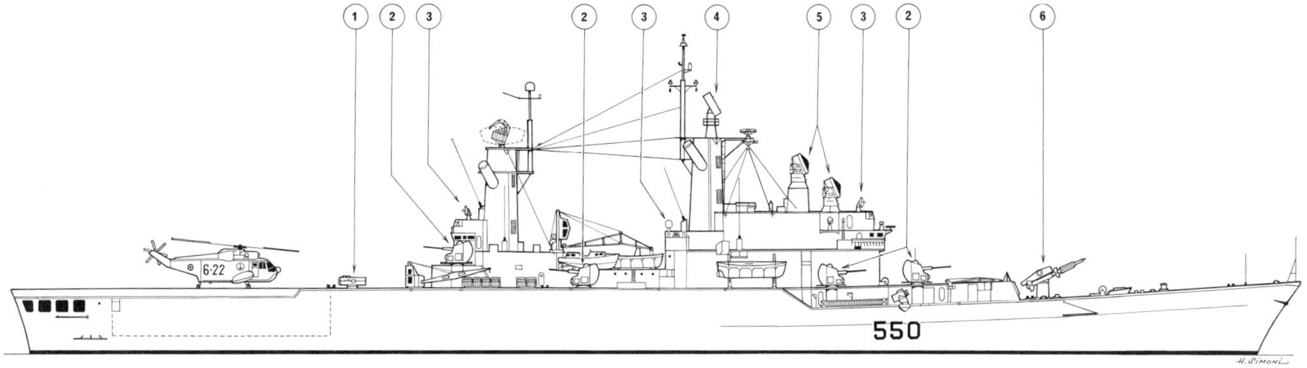

Vittorio Veneto

1: Mk 32 ASW TT — 2: 76-mm AA — 3: Argo fire control — 4: SPS 52 radar — 5: SPG 55 radars — 6: Mk 20 launcher (Aster system)

Note — The radar above the after stack is an SPS 40

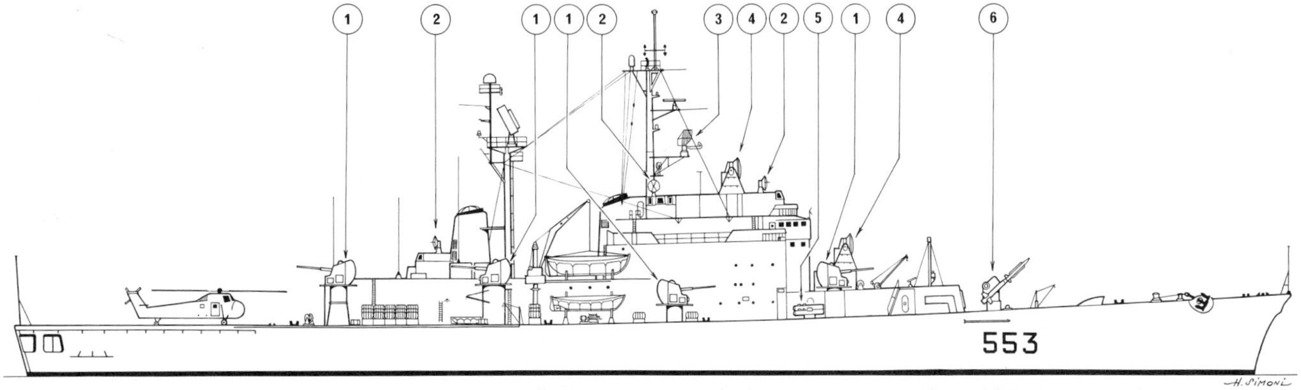

Andrea Doria

1: 76-mm AA — 2: Argo fire control — 3: SPS 12 radar — 4: SPG 55 radars — 5: Mk 32 ASW TT — 6: Mk 20 launcher (Terrier system)

Note — The radar on the after mast is an SPS 39

CRUISERS (*continued*)

Andrea Doria (C 553) G. Arra, 1976

engineering spaces are divided in two groups, forward and aft: each has a boiler room with two boilers and a turbine compartment separated by living spaces. In each turbine space are two turbo-alternators of 1,000 kw each; there are also two emergency diesel alternators of 350 kw each. The engineering groups are automatic and remote-controlled. The C-554 will be fitted with SM-1 "Extended Range" missiles and will have the Sadoc system installed.

DESTROYERS

♦ *2 Audace class*

		Bldr	Laid down	L	In serv.
D 550	**ARDITO**	Nav. Mec. Castellammare	7-68	27-11-71	9-72
D 551	**AUDACE**	C. Nav. del Tirreno	4-68	2-10-71	4-72

D: 3,950 tons (4,559 fl) **Dim:** 136.6 × 14.23 × 4.6 (aver.)
S: 33/34 kts **Range:** 4,000/25 **Man:** . . . officers . . . men
A: 1 Tartar Mk 13 missile launcher aft (40 SM-1) — 2/127-mm OTO Melara Compact — 4/76-mm AA OTO Melara Compact — 6/324-mm ASW Mk 32 TT (III × 2) — 4 single TT for wire-guided torpedoes — 2 AB-204B ASW helicopters or 1 SH-3D Sea King

Audace (D 551) J. C. Bellonne, 1975

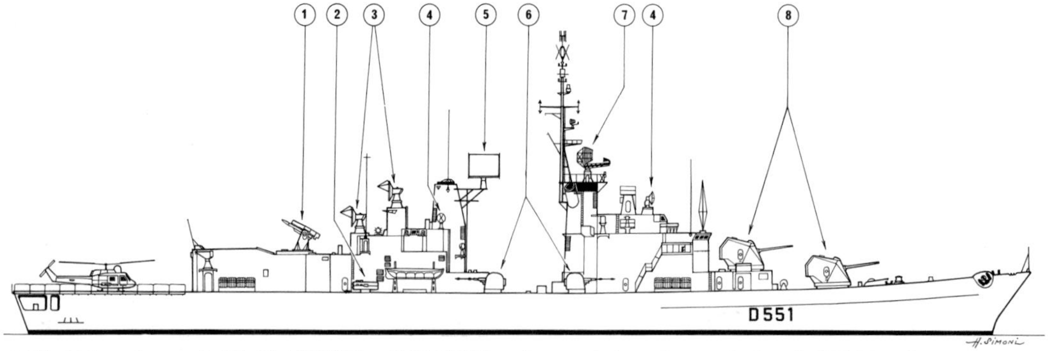

Audace Scale: 1/1,000

1: Mk 13 launcher — 2: Mk 32 ASW TT — 3: SPG 51B radars — 4: Argo fire control — 5: SPS 52 radar — 6: 76-mm AA — 7: SPS 12 radar — 8: 127-mm AA

DESTROYERS *(continued)*

Audace (D 551) J. C. Bellonne, 1975

Electron Equipt: Radars: 1 SPS 12, 1 SPQ 2, 1 SPS 52, 2 SPG 51B, 3 Argo systems
Sonar: 1 CWE 610

M: GT; 2 props; 73,000 hp **Boilers:** 4 Foster-Wheeler
Electric: . . . kw

REMARK: Habitability has been given much attention in the design of these very fine ships.

♦ *2 Impavido class*

	Bldr	Laid down	L	In serv.
D 570 IMPAVIDO	C. N. del Tirreno, Riva Trigoso	6-57	25-5-62	11-63
D 571 INTREPIDO	Ansaldo, Livorno	5-59	21-10-62	7-64

Impavido (D 570)

Intrepido (D 571) G. Arra, 1976

D: 3,201 tons (3,990 fl) **Dim:** 131.30 × 13.65 × 4.43
S: 33.5 kts **Range:** 4,000/25 **Man:** 22 officers, 312 men
A: 1 Tartar Mk 13 missile launcher aft (40 missiles Tartar (IT) or SM-1) — 2 U.S. 127-mm 38-cal. (II × 1) fwd — 4/76-mm Brescia AA (I × 4) — 6/324-mm Mk 32 TT (III × 2) — 1 AB-204B ASW helicopter
Electron Equipt: Radars: 1 SPS 12, 1 SPQ 2, 1 SPS 39 (1 SPS 52 on the D-570), 2 SPG 51, 3 Argo systems
Sonar: 1 SQS 23
M: Tosi GT; 2 props; 70,000 hp
Boilers: 4 Foster-Wheeler, 43 kg/cm² pressure

♦ *2 Impetuoso class*

	Bldr	Laid down	L	In serv.
D 558 IMPETUOSO	C. Nav. del Tirreno, Riva Trigoso	5-52	16-9-56	1-58
D 559 INDOMITO	Ansaldo, Livorno	4-52	9-8-55	2-58

D: 2,775 tons (3,811 fl) **Dim:** 127.6 (123.4 pp) × 13.15 × 4.5

Indomito (D 559) G. Arra, 1976

DESTROYERS *(continued)*

S: 34 kts (32 fl) **Range:** 3,460/20 **Man:** 24 officers, 330 men
A: 4/127-mm U.S. (II × 2) — 16/40-mm AA (IV × 2, II × 4) — 1 Menon triple mortar fwd — 6/324-mm ASW Mk 32 TT (III × 2)
Electron Equipt: Radars: 1 SFS 60, 1 SG 6B
Sonar: 1 SQS 11 or 1 SQS 4
M: Tosi GT; 2 props; 65,000 hp
Boilers: 4 Foster-Wheeler, 43 kg/cm² pressure **Electric:** 3,100 kw

FRIGATES

♦ *8 Maestrale class*

	L		L
F 570 MAESTRALE		**F 574 ALISEO**	
F 571 GRECALE		**F 575 EURO**	
F 572 LIBECCIO		**F 576 ESPERO**	
F 573 SCIROCCO		**F 577 ZEFFIRO**	

D: 3,400 tons (fl) **S:** 30 kts **Dim:** 116.4 × 12.28
A: 1/127-mm OTO Melara — 4/Otomat Mk 2 Teseo — 1 Albatros — A-184 torpedoes — 2 AB-212 helicopters
Electron Equipt: Sonar: 1 hull-mounted, 1 towed (VDS)
M: CODOG: 2 General Electric gas turbines/Fiat LM 2500 of 20,000 hp; 2 diesels of 3,900 hp; 2 variable-pitch props

REMARK: This program will be financed by appropriations allocated under the 10-year building program approved in 1975.

♦ *4 Lupo class* — Bldr: C. N. del Tirreno, Riva Trigoso

	Laid down	L	In serv.
F 564 LUPO	8-10-74	29-7-76	20-9-77
F 565 SAGITTARIO	4-2-76	22-6-77	. . .
F 566 PERSEO	18-1-76	. . .	. . .
F 567 ORSA	. . .	. . .	. . .

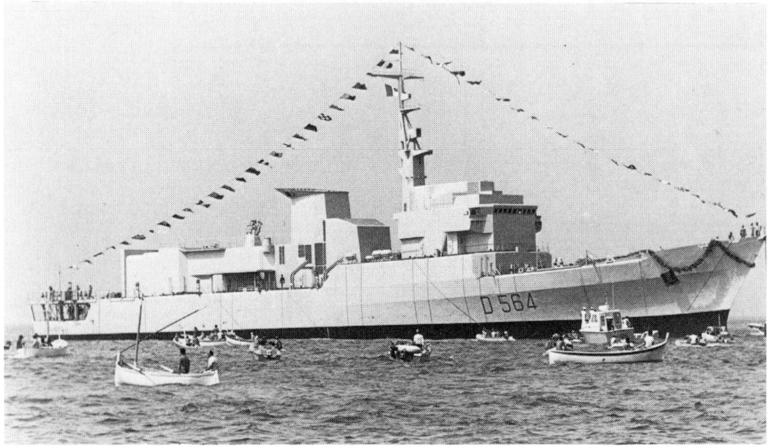

Lupo (F 564) Martinelli, 1976

D: 2,500 tons (2,900 fl) **Dim:** 113.2 (106 pp) × 11.3 × 3.7
S: 35 kts **Man:** 16 officers, 169 men
A: 8/Otomat Mk 2 Teseo systems — 1/127-mm OTO Melara Compact AA — 1/Albatros — 6/324-mm Mk 32 TT (III × 2) — 4/40-mm Breda-Bofors (II × 2) — 1 helicopter
Electron Equipt: Radars: 1 SPQ 2F, 1 Selenia long-range air search, 1 Argo Mk 10 fire control
Sonar: 1 medium-frequency, hull-mounted
M: CODOG, with 2 General Electric gas turbines/Fiat LM 2500 of 25,000 hp, 2 GMT diesels of 3,900 hp (1,140 rpm); 2 variable-pitch props
Electric: 3,120 kw (4 diesels, 780-kw alternator) **Range:** 5,000/12 (1 diesel)

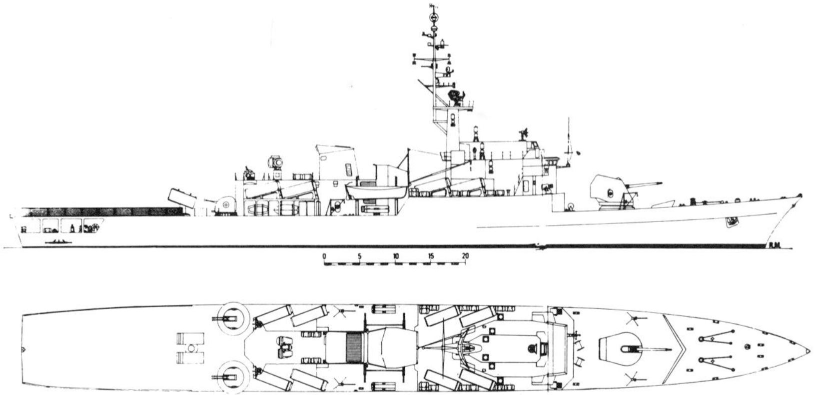

Lupo

REMARKS: Principal mission: surface-to-surface warfare; secondary mission: fire support. Machinery compartments are divided into four parts: auxiliaries, turbines, reduction gears, diesels. The diesels exhaust through two tubes leading to the after section of the stacks, whereas the hot gas turbines exhaust through the forward part of the stack. Air intake for the turbines is through ports forward and on the sides of the stacks. Maximum speed on the diesels is 22.5 knots. Reclassed as frigates in 1977. Four frigates based on the *Lupo* class have been ordered by Peru.

♦ *2 Alpino class* — Bldr: C. N. del Tirreno, Riva Trigoso

	Laid down	L	In serv.
F 580 ALPINO (ex-*Circe*)	2-63	14-6-67	1-68
F 581 CARABINIERE (ex-*Climene*)	1-65	30-9-67	4-68

D: 2,000 tons (2,700 fl) **Dim:** 113.3 (106.4 pp) × 13.3 × 3.76
S: 29 kts **Range:** 4,200/18 **Man:** 20 officers, 244 men
A: 6/76-mm 62-cal AA (I × 6) — 1/single-barrel Menon mortar — 6/324-mm Mk 32 TT (Mk 44 torpedoes) — 2/ASW AB-204B helicopters
Electron Equipt: Radars: 1 SPS 12, 1 SPQ 2, 3 Argo systems
Sonars: 1 SQS 29, 1 SQA 10 (towed)
M: CODAG propulsion: 4 Tosi diesels, 4,200 hp each; Tosi-Metrovik gas turbines, 7,700 hp each; 2 props; 31,800 hp
Electric: 2,400 kw

REMARKS: Stabilizers. 22 knots cruising on diesels.

FRIGATES (*continued*)

Alpino (F 580) G. Arra, 1976

Carabiniere (F 581) G. Arra, 1976

♦ *4 Carlo Bergamini class*

	Bldr	Laid down	L	In serv.
F 593 CARLO BERGAMINI	C.R.D.A., Trieste	7-59	16-6-60	6-62
F 594 VIRGILIO FASAN	Castellammare	3-60	9-10-60	6-62
F 595 CARLO MARGOTTINI	Castellammare	5-57	12-6-60	5-62
F 596 LUIGI RIZZO	Castellammare	5-57	6-3-60	12-61

Virgilio Fasan (F 594) Molinari, 1971

Virgilio Fasan (F 594)

FRIGATES (*continued*)

D: 1,410 tons (2,100 fl) **Dim:** 93.95 (86.51 pp) × 11.35 × 3.10
S: 24 kts **Man:** 155 men **Range:** 3,600/18, 4,500/16
A: 2/76-mm automatic 62-cal (I × 2) — 1/single-barrel Menon — 6/324-mm Mk 32 ASW TT (III × 2) — 1 ASW helicopter
Electric: 204 kw
Electron Equipt: Radars: 1 SPS 12, 1 SPQ 2
Sonar: 1 SQS 11
M: 4 high-speed Fiat CB/LR or Tosi diesels; 2 props; 16,000 hp

REMARKS: Denny-Brown anti-rolling stabilizers. Rolling can be reduced from 20° to 3°. Enlargement of the helicopter platform required the removal of the after 76-mm gun. Telescopic hangar.

♦ *4 Canopo class*

	Bldr	Laid down	L	In serv.
F 552 CANOPO	C. Nav. di Taranto	5-52	20-2-55	5-58
F 553 CASTORE	C. Nav. di Taranto	3-55	8-7-56	7-57
F 554 CENTAURO	Ansaldo, Livorno	5-52	4-4-54	5-57
F 555 CIGNO	C. Nav. di Taranto	2-54	14-3-55	4-57

Centauro (F 554) G. Arra, 1976

D: 1,680 tons **S:** 26 kts **Dim:** 93.3 × 12.0 × 7.8
Range: 2,600/20 **Man:** 160 men
A: 3/76-mm Brescia AA (1 fwd, 2 aft) — 1/triple-barrel Menon mortar — 6/324-mm Mk 32 TT (III × 2)
Electron Equipt: Radars: 1 SPS 6, 1 SPQ 2
Sonar: 1 SQS 11
M: Tosi GT; 2 props; 22,000 hp **Boilers:** 2 Foster-Wheeler 43 kg/cm^2 pressure
Fuel: 400 tons **Electric:** . . . kw

REMARK: Refitted after 1965.

CORVETTES

♦ *4 Pietro de Cristofaro*

	Bldr	Laid down	L	In serv.
F 540 PIETRO DE CRISTOFARO	C. N. del Tirreno	4-63	29-5-65	12-65
F 541 UMBERTO GROSSO	Ansaldo, Livorno	10-62	12-12-64	4-66
F 546 LICIO VISINTINI	C.R.D.A., Monfalcone	9-63	30-5-65	8-66
F 550 SALVATORE TODARO	Ansaldo, Livorno	10-62	24-10-64	4-66

Pietro de Cristofaro (F 540) 1974

D: 940 tons (1,050 fl) **S:** 23/24 kts **Dim:** 80.2 × 10.0 × 2.5
Range: 4,600/18 **Man:** 8 officers, 123 men
A: 2/76-mm Brescia AA (I × 2) — 1/single-barrel Menon mortar — 6/324-mm Mk 32 TT (III × 2)
Electron Equipt: Radars: 1 SPQ 2, 2 Argo systems
Sonar: 1 SQS 36 (towed)
M: Diesels (see Remarks); 2 props; 8,400 hp

REMARKS: High-speed diesels: Fiat on P de C, ST and UG, Tosi on LV with reduction gears and Tosi-Vulcan hydraulic linkage.

♦ *4 Albatros class*

	Bldr	Laid down	L	In serv.
F 542 AQUILA (ex-*Lynx hollandais*)	Breda, Marghera	7-53	31-7-54	10-56
F 543 ALBATROS	Nav. Mec. Castellammare	1953	18-7-54	6-55
F 544 ALCIONE	Nav. Mec. Castellammare	1953	19-9-54	15-55
F 545 AIRONE	Nav. Mec. Castellammare	1953	21-11-54	10-55

D: 800 tons (950 fl) **Dim:** 76.3 (69.49 pp) × 9.65 × 2.8
S: 19 kts **Range:** 2,988/18 **Man:** 7 officers, 111 men
A: 4/40-mm 70-cal. AA (II × 2) — 6/324-mm ASW Mk 32 TT — 2 hedgehogs — 1 depth-charge projector
M: 2 Fiat diesels; 2 props; 5,200 hp **Fuel:** 100 tons

CORVETTES *(continued)*

Alcione (F 544) G. Arra, 1972

REMARKS: Ships built with U.S. "offshore" funds (ex-U.S. PC-1626, PC-1919, PC-1920, PC-1921). One similar ship was delivered to The Netherlands (returned to Italy in 10-61) and four to Denmark, one of which has been scrapped.

♦ *3 Ape class* (1942-43)

F 549 BOMBARDA, F 569 CHIMERA, F 579 SFINGE

Chimera (F 569) G. Arra, 1976

D: 670 tons (771 fl) **S:** 15 kts **Dim:** 64.8 × 8.7 × 2.7
A: 4/40-mm — 2/20-mm **Man:** 56 men
M: 2 Fiat diesels; 2 props; 3,500 hp

REMARKS: These ships have little military value. F-569 is equipped to launch aerial targets. Sister *Ape* (F-567) serves as a support ship for divers.

GUIDED-MISSILE PATROL BOATS

♦ *1 hydrofoil*

	Bldr	Laid down	L	In serv.
P 420 SPARVIERO	Alinavi, Naples	4-71	3-73	1974

Sparviero (P 420) Martinelli, 1976

Sparviero (P 420) G. Arra, 1976

D: 63 tons (fl) **S:** 42 kts (heavy sea), 50 kts (calm sea)
Dim: 24.6 × 12.1 × 1.5
Man: 10 men **Range:** 325/42, 1,050/8 (diesel)
A: 1/76-mm automatic OTO Melara Compact — 2/Otomat surface-to-surface missiles

GUIDED-MISSILE PATROL BOATS (*continued*)

M: Water-jet propulsion while foilborne; 1 Proteus Rolls-Royce gas turbine; 4,500 hp

REMARKS: Prototype studied by the Alinavi Society, which was formed in 1964 by Boeing, U.S.A., the Italian government's I.R.I., and Carlo Rodriguez of Messina, builder of commercial hydrofoils. Her three hydrofoils are raised when she is cruising and the diesel engine is engaged (1 propeller). Project based on U.S. *Tucumcari* experiments, but improved.

♦ *2 Freccia class*

	Bldr	Laid down	L	In serv.
P 493 FRECCIA (ex-MC-590)	C. Nav. di Taranto	4-63	9-1-65	7-65
P 494 SAETTA (ex-MC-591)	C.R.D.A., Monfalcone	6-63	11-4-65	1966

Freccia (P 493) G. Arra, 1972

D: 175 tons (205 fl) **S:** 40 kts **Dim:** 46.10 × 7.20 × 1.54
A: As guided-missile patrol boat: 2 or 3/40-mm 70-cal AA — 1 missile launcher
As torpedo boat: 1/40-mm 70-cal AA — 4/533-mm TT
M: 2 Fiat diesels, 3,800 hp each; 1 Metrovik-Nuove Reggiane gas turbine, 4,250 hp; 3 props; 11,860 hp

REMARKS: Two more that had been planned will not be built. P-494 has served in the Nettuno trials.

♦ *2 Lampo class* — Bldr: C. Nav. di Taranto

	Laid down	L	In serv.
P 491 LAMPO	1-58	22-11-60	7-63
P 492 BALENO	1-58	10-5-64	7-65

D: 197 tons (210 fl) **S:** 39 kts **Dim:** 43.0 × 6.3 × 1.5
A: As guided-missile patrol boat: 2 or 3/40-mm 70-cal AA — 1 missile launcher
As torpedo boat: 1/40-mm 70-cal AA — 2/533-mm TT
M: 2 Fiat diesels, 3,600 hp each; 1 Metrovik-Nuove Reggiane gas turbine, 11,700 hp

Lampo (P 491) G. Arra, 1972

TORPEDO BOATS

♦ *1 Folgore class* — Bldr: C.R.D.A., Monfalcone

	Laid down	L	In serv.
P 490 FOLGORE (ex-MC-490)	1953	21-1-54	31-7-55

Folgore (P 490) G. Arra, 1972

D: 160 tons (190 fl) **S:** 38 kts **Dim:** 39.4 × 6.0 × 1.5
M: 4 diesels; 2 rudders; 4 props; 10,000 hp

♦ *3 ex-Higgins type PTs* (1943)

MS 441 (ex-841), **MS 443** (ex-843), **MS 453** (ex-853)

D: 43 tons (64 fl) **Dim:** 23.77 × 6.09 × 1.70
S: 29 kts (practical max.) **Man:** 12 men
Range: 1,000/20 **Fuel:** 8 tons gasoline
A: 1/40-mm — 2 or 4/20-mm (II or IV × 1) — 2/450-mm torpedoes (no tubes)
M: 3 Isotta-Fraschini, 12 cyl. 4 M 2500; 3 props; 4,050 hp

REMARKS: Accepted in 1951. Four stricken in 1958, four in 1964. Transferred to the customs administration.

TORPEDO BOATS (*continued*)

♦ *2 German Schnellboote, Italian design* — Bldr: C.R.D.A., Monfalcone, 1942-43

MS 474, MS 481 (ex-MS/MV 614/615)

D: 63 tons (72 fl) **S:** 27 kts **Dim:** 28.0 × 4.3 × 1.5
A: 1 or 2/40-mm AA — 2/450-mm torpedoes without tubes **Man:** 17 men
M: 3 Isotta-Fraschini; 3 props; 3,450 hp **Range:** 600/16

REMARK: MS-473 retained as a museum.

MINE WARFARE SHIPS

♦ *4 ex-U.S. fleet minesweepers* — Transferred 1956-57

M 5340 SALMONE (ex-MSO-507)
M 5431 STORIONE (ex-MSO-506)
M 5432 SGOMBRO (ex-MSO-517)
M 5433 SQUALO (ex-MSO-518)

Bldr: Martinolich, San Diego (Calif.) 1955-56

Storione (M 5431) G. Arra, 1972

D: 665 tons (750 fl) **S:** 14 kts **Dim:** 52.7 × 10.7 × 4.0 (fl)
A: 1/40-mm AA **Man:** 104 men **Range:** 3,000/10
M: Diesels; 2 props; 1,600 hp **Fuel:** 46 tons

REMARK: American *Agile* class, similar to the French *Alençon* class.

♦ *13 ex-U.S. coastal minesweepers (Abete series, AMS/MSC)*

M 5504 CASTAGNO
M 5505 CEDRO
M 5507 FAGGIO
M 5508 FRASSINO
M 5509 GELSO
M 5510 LARICE
M 5511 NOCE
M 5512 OLMO
M 5513 ONTANO
M 5514 PINO
M 5516 PLATANO
M 5517 QUERCIA
M 5519 MANDORLO

D: 375 tons (405 fl) **Dim:** 43.9 × 8.2 × 2.5
S: 13.5 kts **Range:** 2,500/10
A: 2/20-mm AA **Fuel:** 25 tons
Man: 36/38 men **M:** Diesels; 2 props; 1,200 hp

REMARKS: Transferred in 1953-54. M-5519 has a large, tall stack and her detection and sweeping equipment differs from that of the others.

Mandorlo (M 5519) Nani

♦ *17 MSC-type, Italian-built, coastal minesweepers*

M 5521 BAMBU (26-6-55)
M 5522 EBANO (15-4-56)
M 5523 MANGO (19-4-56)
M 5524 MOGANO (3-5-56)
M 5525 PALMA (8-11-56)
M 5527 SANDALO (9-1-57)
M 5531 AGAVE (27-6-55)
M 5532 ALLORO (11-7-55)
M 5533 EDERA (25-7-55)
M 5534 GAGGIA (15-12-55)
M 5535 GELSOMINO (5-3-55)
M 5536 GIAGGIOLO (29-1-56)
M 5537 GILICINE (25-5-56)
M 5538 LOTO (19-12-54)
M 5540 TIMO (19-12-55)
M 5541 TRIFOGLIO (10-5-55)
M 5542 VISCHIO (20-5-56)

Bldrs: Monfalcone; Costaguta, Voltri; Baglietto, Varazze; Picchiotti, Viareggio; Mediterraneo Piera. The last seven were built with U.S. "offshore" funds.

Sandalo (M 5527) G. Arra, 1972

REMARK: Same silhouette and characteristics as the French *Acacia* class.

♦ *10 Aragosta-class inshore minesweepers*

M 5450 ARAGOSTA (8-56)
M 5462 PINNA (4-57)

MINE WARFARE SHIPS (*continued*)

M 5452 ASTICE (1-57)
M 5457 GAMBERO (5-57)
M 5458 GRANCHIO (5-57)
M 5459 MITILO (6-57)
M 5463 POLIPO (5-57)
M 5464 PORPORA (6-57)
M 6465 RICCIO (5-57)
M 5466 SCAMPO (5-57)

Bldrs: Monfalcone; Baglietto, Varazze; Viareggio; Celle, Venice; Costaguta, Voltri; C. N. Carrera; Ancona; Breda, Venice

D: 119 tons (188 fl) **S:** 14 kts **Dim:** 32.5 × 6.4 × 1.9
A: 1/20-mm AA **Man:** 14 men **Range:** 2,000/9
M: Diesels; 2 props; 550 hp **Fuel:** 15 tons

Scampo (M 5466) G. Arra, 1972

REMARK: Based on British "-ham" class.

AMPHIBIOUS WARFARE SHIPS

♦ *2 ex-U.S. LSTs* Transferred in 7-72

	Bldr	L
L 9890 GRADO (ex-*de Soto County*, LST-1171)	Boston NSY	28-2-57

Grado (L 9890) G. Arra, 1972

L 9891 CAORLE Newport News SB & DD 5-9-57
(ex-*York County*, LST-1175)

D: 3,680 tons (7,100 fl) **S:** 16/15 kts **Dim:** 134.7 × 16.8 × 3.7
A: 6/76-mm AA 50-cal. (II × 3) **Man:** 15 officers, 173 men
M: 6 Fairbanks-Morse diesels; 2 variable-pitch props; 14,000 hp

REMARKS: See *Lorain County* class, U.S.A. section. Quarters for 634 troops, including 30 officers.

♦ *1 experimental LST*

	Bldr	Laid down	L	In serv.
L 9881 QUARTO	C. Nav. di Taranto	3-66	18-3-67	6-68

D: 764 tons (980 fl) **S:** 13 kts **Dim:** 96.0 × 9.55 × 1.81
Range: 1,300/13 **A:** 4/40-mm AA (II × 2) **M:** 3 diesels; 2,300 hp

Quarto (L 9881) G. Arra, 1972

REMARKS: Bow door. Sister ships *Marsala* and *Caprera* were planned but not completed. The *Marsala* hull is used as a pontoon.

♦ *1 assault transport* — Bldr: Todd, Tacoma, 14-2-44

A 9871 ANDREA BAFILE (ex-*St. George*, AV-16)

D: 13,380 tons (fl) **S:** 17 kts **Dim:** 163.0 × 23.0 × 8.5
Range: 13,400/13 **A:** 2/127-mm — 12/40-mm
M: 1 GT; 2 boilers, 8,500 hp

REMARK: Former U.S. aviation supply ship, modified and transferred 12-68.

♦ *55 landing craft*

MTM 9909 to **MTM 9925** (less **MTM 9910)** — ex-U.S. LCMs (1943-44)

D: 20 tons **S:** 10 kts

MTP 9701 to **MTP 9741** (less **MTP 9716** and **MTP 9725)** — ex-U.S. LCVPs (1943-44)

D: 8 tons **S:** 11 kts

HYDROGRAPHIC SHIP

♦ *1 Ammiraglio Magnaghi class* — 1972 program — Bldr: C. N. del Tirreno, Riva Trigoso

	Laid down	L	In serv.
A 5303 AMMIRAGLIO MAGNAGHI	1973	11-9-74	. . .

D: 1,700 tons (fl) **S:** 15 kts **Dim:** 82.70 × 13.6 × 4.45

HYDROGRAPHIC SHIP (*continued*)

Ammiraglio Magnaghi (A 5303) G. Arra, 1976

A: 1/40-mm — 1 helicopter **Man:** 145 men
M: 2 diesels; 1 prop; 3,400 hp

AUXILIARY SHIPS

♦ *2 Stromboli-class oilers* — Bldr: C. N. del Tirreno, Riva Trigoso

	Laid down	L	In serv.
A 5327 STROMBOLI	10-73	20-2-75	10-75
A 5329 VESUVIO	. . .	4-6-77	. . .

Stromboli (A 5327) Martinelli, 1976

Stromboli (A 5327) Martinelli, 1976

D: 8,706 tons (fl) **S:** 19 kts **Dim:** 129.0 (118.5 pp) × 18.0 × 6.5
A: 1/76-mm AA — 2/40-mm AA (II × 1) **Man:** 9 officers, 106 men
Electron Equipt: Radars: 1 navigation, 1 fire control
M: 2 Fiat diesels; 1 prop; 9,600 hp
Range: 4,000/19 **Electric:** 2,350 kw

REMARKS: Cargo capacity: 3,000 tons fuel oil, 1,000 tons diesel oil, 400 tons jet fuel, 300 tons spare parts. Lifting equipment: double booms, one crane.

♦ *1 supply ship* — Bldr: Lake Washington SY

	L
A 5301 PIETRO CAVEZZALE (ex-AGP-6, ex-*Oyster Bay*, AVP-28)	23-5-43

Pietro Cavezzale (A 5301) Martinelli, 1973

AUXILIARY SHIPS (*continued*)

D: 1,766 tons (2,800 fl) **S:** 16 kts **Dim:** 94.6 × 12.58 × 3.7
A: 2/40-mm AA **Man:** 210 men **Range:** 10,000/11
Electron Equipt: Radar: ASP/SN 6
M: 2 diesels; 2 props; 6,000 hp **Fuel:** 400 tons

REMARKS: Transferred at the end of 1957. Serves amphibious ships and small boats.

♦ *1 support ship for frogmen and divers* — Bldr: Nav. Mec. Castellammare, 22-11-42

A 5328 APE

D: 771 tons (fl) **S:** 15 kts **Dim:** 64.80 × 8.70 × 2.72
A: 2/20-mm AA **Man:** 108 men **Range:** 2,445/15
M: 2 Fiat diesels; 2 props **Fuel:** 63 tons

♦ *3 netlayers*

	Bldr	Laid down	L	In serv.
A 5304 ALICUDI (AN-99)	Ansaldo, Livorno	4-54	11-7-54	1955
A 5305 FILICUDI (AN-190)	Ansaldo, Livorno	5-54	26-7-54	1955
A 5309 RAMPINO	. . .	. . .	. . .	. . .

Filicudi (A 5305) G. Arra, 1972

D: 680 tons (832 fl) A-5309: 350 tons **S:** 13 kts
Dim: 46.28 × 10.26 × 3.20
A: 1/40-mm AA — 4/20-mm AA
M: Diesel-electric; 1 prop; 1,200 hp

REMARK: A-5309 now used as a lighthouse tender.

♦ *1 Magnaghi-class salvage ship* — Bldr: Monfalcone

D: 3,000 tons **S:** . . . **Dim:** . . . × . . . × . . .

REMARKS: Based on the U.S. Navy's submarine-rescue ships (ASRs). She positions herself over the submarine and anchors, then lowers her two McCann rescue chambers to the submarine.

♦ *8 water carriers*

A 5354 PIAVE, A 5355 TEVERE — Bldr: Italy, 1970-71

Piave (A 5354)

D: 4,973 tons **Dim:** 88.0 × 13.4 × 5.9
S: 13.6 kts **Range:** 1,500/12
M: 2 diesels; 2,560 hp **Cargo capacity:** 3,500 tons

A 5356 BASENTO, A 5357 BRADANO, A 5358 BRENTA, 1970-71

Basento (A 5356)

D: 1,914 tons **Dim:** 66.1 × 1.0 × 3.9
S: 12.5 kts **Range:** 1,650/12.5
M: 2 diesels; 1,730 hp **Cargo capacity:** 1,200 tons

A 5376 TANARO (ex-YM-99) **A 5369 ADIGE** (ex-YM-92)
A 5377 TICINO (ex-YM-79)

D: 1,517 tons **S:** 8 kts **M:** 2 diesels; 315 hp

REMARK: Carry 300 tons of water.

♦ *7 motorized barges*

A 5331 (ex-MOC-1201) **A 5335** (ex-MOC-1205)

AUXILIARY SHIPS (*continued*)

A 5332 (ex-MOC-1202)
A 5333 (ex-MOC-1203)
A 5334 (ex-MOC-1204)
A 5336 (ex-MOC-1207)
A 5337 (ex-MOC-1208)

D: 640 tons **S:** 10 kts **Dim:** 48.0 × 7.7 × 1.7
A: 2/40-mm AA

REMARKS: A-5336 and A-5337 fitted as ammunition carriers. A-5331 is a supply ship for small craft. A-5333 is a minesweeper supply ship.

♦ *10 motorized barges*

MTC 1001, MTC 1004 to **MTC 1010, MTC 1101, MTC 1102**
D: 240 tons **S:** 10 kts **Dim:** 50.0 × 6.5 × 1.7
A: 3/20-mm AA **M:** 2 or 3 diesels; 500 hp

REMARK: Former wartime Italian or German landing craft.

♦ *1 tug* — Bldr: C. N. del Tirreno, Ancona, 1944

A 5310 PROTEO

Proteo (A 5310) 1968

D: 1,865 tons (2,178 fl) **S:** 16 kts **Dim:** 76.7 × 11.7 × 6.1
A: 1/100-mm — 2/20-mm **Range:** 7,500/13
M: 2 diesels; 4,800 hp

REMARKS: Used as a salvage ship. Will be replaced by the Magnaghi-class salvage ship.

♦ *2 oceangoing tugs* — Bldr: Visintini Donada, 1974–75

A 5317 ATLANTE **A 5318 PROMETEO**
D: 750 tons **Dim:** 39.0 × 9.6 × 4.1
M: 1 diesel; 1 prop; 2,600 hp

♦ *19 harbor tugs*

A 5319 CICLOPE, 1948 — **D:** 1,200 tons — **M:** Triple-expansion, 1,000 hp
A 5320 COLOSSO, A 5321 FORTE (ex-U.S., 1943) — **D:** 835 tons — **M:** Diesel-electric; 700 hp
A 5326 SAN GIUSTO, 1941 — **D:** 486 tons — **M:** 900 hp
A 5322 GAGLIARDO, A 5323 ROBUSTO, 1939 — **D:** 506 tons — **M:** 1,000 hp
A 5388 ERCOLE, A 5394 VIGOROSO
A 5378 PORTO D'ISCHIA, A 5379 RIVA TRIGOSO — **D:** 296 tons — **S:** 12 kts — **M:** 850 hp
AUSONIA, PANARIA — **D:** 240 tons — **S:** 9 kts — **M:** 500 hp
MISENO, MONTECRISTO — Bldr: U.S.A. — **D:** 285 tons
A 5376 PORTO RECANATI, A 5386 PORTO PISANO, A 5391 SALVORE, A 5392 TINO
D: 226 tons — **S:** 9 kts — **M:** 600 hp
VINTIMIGLIA — **D:** 230 tons — **S:** 10 kts — **M:** 500 hp

Forte (A 5321) G. Arra, 1974

♦ *30 small harbor tugs, including:*

RP 101 to **RP 112**
D: 75 tons **S:** 12 kts **Dim:** 18.8 × 4.5 × 1.9
M: 1 diesel; 1 prop; 431 hp

VARIOUS SHIPS

♦ *1 fishery protection vessel* — Bldr: Brest, 1955

F 597 VEDETTA
D: 325 tons (450 fl) **S:** 19 kts **Dim:** 51.9 × 7.0 × 3.1

VARIOUS SHIPS (*continued*)

A: 2/40-mm — 2/20-mm — 1 hedgehog — 4 mortars
M: 4 diesels; 2 props; 3,500 hp

REMARK: Ex-submarine chaser.

♦ *5 training ships*

	Bldr	Laid down	L	In serv.
D 562 SAN GIORGIO (ex-*Pompeo Magno*)	C. N. del Tirreno Ancona	9-39	28-8-41	6-43

San Giorgio (D 562) G. Arra, 1972

D: 3,950 tons (4,450 fl) **Dim:** 142.18 (138.75 pp) × 14.40 × 6.40
S: 27 kts **Man:** 314 men, 130 midshipmen
A: 4 U.S. 127-mm 38-cal AA (II × 2) — 3/76-mm AA (I × 3) OTO Melara — Menon triple mortar — 6 U.S. 324-mm ASW Mk 32 TT (III × 2) with Mk 44 torpedoes
Electron Equipt: Radar: 1/SPS 6
Sonar: 1/SQS 10
M: 4 Fiat-Tosi diesels, 4,500 hp each; 2 AEI/G 6/2 gas turbines, 7,500 hp each; combined on 2 shafts (CODAG apparatus); 2 props; 31,200 hp

REMARKS: Sister ship of the *San Marco* which was stricken from the active list in 1970. Converted into a school ship for the naval academy at Livorno in 1964-65. New engine fittings; armament renewed.

A 5312 AMERIGO VESPUCCI — Bldr: Nav. Mec. Castellammare — L 22-3-30

D: 3,545 tons (4,186 fl) **Dim:** 82.38 (70.72 pp) × 15.54 × 6.70
S: 10 kts **Range:** 5,450/6.5
A: 4/76-mm — 1/20-mm **Man:** 400 men, 150 cadets
M: 2 Fiat diesels with electric transmission; 1 prop; 1,900 hp

REMARK: Sail area: 2,100 m^2.

Amerigo Vespucci (A 5312) Lionel Fava

A 5311 PALINURO (ex-*Cdt Louis Richard*) — Bldr: Dubigeon, 1920

D: 1,042 tons (1,351 fl) **Dim:** 59.0 × 9.7 × 4.8
A: 2/76-mm (saluting battery) **Range:** 5,300/7.5
M: 1 diesel; 450 hp

Palinuro (A 5311) Aldo Fraccaroli

REMARK: Former French cod-fishing craft bought in 1951. Steel hull.

A 5316 CORSARO II — Bldr: Costaguta, Genoa, 1960

D: 41 tons **Dim:** 20.90 × 4.70 **M:** 1 auxiliary engine; 96 hp

REMARK: Sailing ship, rigged as a yawl.

A 5313 STELLA POLARE — Bldr: Sant. Germ., Chiavari, 1965

REMARK: 47-ton, RORC-class cruising yacht.

IVORY COAST

PERSONNEL: 140 to 150 men

MERCHANT MARINE (1976): 53 ships — 114,191 grt

PATROL BOATS AND CRAFT

♦ *2 PR-48 patrol boats* — Bldr: S.F.C.N.

	Laid down	L	In serv.
VIGILANT	2-67	23-5-67	1968
LE VALEUREUX	28-10-75	8-3-76	25-9-76

D: 240 tons (avg) **Dim:** 47.5 (45.5 pp) × 7.0 × 2.5
S: 23 kts **Man:** 3 officers, 22 men
A: 2/40-mm AA — 8 SS-12 missiles **Range:** 2,000/15
M: 2 MGO diesels with Masson reduction gear; 2 props; 4,200 hp

♦ *1 Perseverance-class patrol craft* (25-2-58)

PERSEVERANCE (ex-P-759, VC-9)

D: 70 tons (80 fl) **S:** 28 kts **Dim:** 31.77 × 4.70 × 1.70
A: 2/20-mm AA **Man:** 15 men **Range:** 1,500/15
M: 2 Mercedes-Benz diesels; 12 cyl; 2 props; 2,700 hp **Fuel:** 4 tons

AMPHIBIOUS WARFARE SHIPS

♦ *1 LSM*

	L	In serv.
ELEPHANT	. . .	2-2-77

REMARK: Similar to the *Francis Garnier* of the French Navy.

♦ *2 LCVP recently built in Abidjan*

M: Mercedes-Benz motors

VARIOUS SHIPS

♦ *1 training and support ship*

LOCODJO — Built in West Germany in 1953, delivered in 1970

D: 450 tons

♦ *4 small craft, 7 to 10 meters*

♦ *1 Arcoa-class small craft*

♦ *1 small Barracuda-type transport (25 men)*

JAMAICA

MERCHANT MARINE (1976): 6 ships — 6,892 grt

A military force similar to the U.S. Coast Guard. Material furnished by the U.S.A. under the Military Assistance Program. British personnel.

PATROL BOATS AND CRAFT

♦ *1 Fort Charles-class patrol boat* — Bldr: Teledyne Sewart, U.S.A., 1974

P 7 FORT CHARLES

D: 100 tons **S:** 32 kts **Dim:** 31.5 × 5.7 × 2.1
A: 2/30-mm AA — 3/12.7-mm machine guns — 1/81-mm mortar
M: 2 MTU diesels; 6,000 hp **Man:** 15 men

REMARK: Can carry 24 soldiers and serve as a floating hospital.

♦ *3 Discovery Bay-class patrol craft*

P 4 DISCOVERY BAY, P 5 HOLLAND BAY, P 6 MANATEE BAY

Bldr: Sewart Seacraft, Berwick, La., U.S.A., 1966-68

D: 60 tons **S:** 30 kts **Dim:** 25.90 × 5.68 × 1.83
A: 3/12.7-mm machine guns **Man:** 10 men **Range:** 500/12
M: General Motors Mk 16 V71N diesels; 2 props; 700 hp

Discovery Bay (P 4)

PERSONNEL: approximately 46,500 men, 13,000 of whom are assigned to naval aviation.

MERCHANT MARINE (1976): 9,748 ships — 41,663,188 grt
(tankers: 1,470 ships — 19,046,436 grt)

The Maritime Self-Defense Force (MSDF), or Kaiso Jeitai, was created in 1954. In Article 9 of her constitution, Japan waived the right of belligerence and declared her peaceful intentions. As a result her armed forces are designed to carry out purely defensive tasks. The duties of the MSDF involve essentially the protection of coastal traffic and of Japan's sea lines of communication, both of which are vital to the economic survival of one of the world's most industrialized nations. For some years now, however, the MSDF has tended to look more and more like an ocean-going navy, as is evidenced by the construction of more important ships.

In addition to the MSDF, Japan has a maritime safety agency (Kaijo Hoancho) that is comparable to the U.S. Coast Guard. Its ships are listed at the end of this section.

FIFTH DEFENSE PLAN: The Fifth Defense Plan, which covers the period from 1-4-77 to 31-3-82, calls for:

- 4 destroyers based on Nos. 143 and 144 of the Fourth Plan
- 6 to 8 guided-missile destroyers, 2,500 to 3,000 tons, armed with Harpoon surface-to-surface missiles
- 6 to 8 *Chikugo*-class frigates
- 6 to 8 2,200-ton submarines

This plan has not yet been adopted by parliament.

FOURTH DEFENSE PLAN: The Fourth Defense plan, which covered the period from 1-4-72 to 31-3-77 and was adopted 9-10-72, called for:

- 2 5,200-ton destroyers (DDH), Nos. 143 and 144
- 1 3,850-ton destroyer (DDG) armed with medium-range, surface-to-air missiles
- 1 2,900-ton destroyer (DDG) armed with surface-to-surface missiles
- 3 2,500-ton antisubmarine destroyers (DD)
- 3 1,500-ton *Chikugo*-class frigates
- 3 1,470-ton *Chikugo*-class frigates
- 2 2,200-ton submarines

This plan will probably be completed in another two or three years.

NAVAL AVIATION: Naval air is an integral part of the Navy. The MSDF does not have any aircraft carriers; some 20 helicopters serve on board the destroyers and frigates. As of August 1, 1977, the naval air arm consisted of:

- 187 planes, most of them P-2s and S2-Fs
- 18 PS-1 ASW seaplanes
- 84 helicopters, most of them Bell and Sikorsky models

Naval aviation is divided into two commands:

The Fleet Air Force, which consists of the regular forces (140 aircraft and 8,000 men). It has its headquarters at Atsugi and twelve bases along the coasts of Japan;

The Air Training Command, which has several centers at Shimofusa.

Plans center on the acquisition of 50 U.S. P3-C Orion ASW patrol planes. The first ones are to be delivered in 1982, the others will be built under license in Japan, beginning in 1981. However, the uneasiness created in Japan by the recent Lockheed scandal has resulted in that plan being postponed.

A new large ASW seaplane, possibly a replacement beginning in 1985 for the PS-1s now in service, is being studied.

JAPAN

WARSHIPS IN SERVICE AND UNDER CONSTRUCTION AS OF 1 OCTOBER 1977

	L	Tons	Main armament
♦ *17 submarines*			
2 573 TYPE	. . .	2,200	6/533-mm TT
7 UZUSHIO	1970–75	1,850	6/533-mm TT
5 OSHIO/ASASHIO	1964–68	1,650	8/533-mm TT
3 HAYASHIO/NATSUSHIO	1961–63	750	3/533-mm TT
♦ *37 destroyers*			
2 MODIFIED HARUNA	. . .	5,200	2/127-mm AA, 2/35-mm AA
1 DDG	. . .	2,900	Harpoon missiles, Sea Sparrow
2 TACHIKAZE	1974–77	3,850	1 Tartar launcher, 2/127-mm, Asroc, 6 TT
2 HARUNA	1971–73	4,700	2/127-mm AA, 6/324-mm TT, Asroc, 3 helicopters
8 YAMAGUMO	1965–77	2,066	4/76-mm AA, 4/324-mm TT, 1 helicopter
3 MINEGUMO	1967–69	2,066	4/76-mm AA, 1 rocket launcher, 6/324-mm TT, 2 helicopters
4 TAKATSUKI	1966–69	3,050	2/127-mm, Asroc
1 AMATSUKAZE	1963	3,050	1 Tartar missile launcher 4/76-mm AA, Asroc
2 AKIKUZI	1959	2,300	3/127-mm AA, 4/76-mm AA, 1 Weapon Able launcher
3 MURASAME	1958–59	1,800	3/127-mm AA, 4/76-mm AA, 4/305-mm TT
7 AYANAMI	1957–60	1,700	6/76-mm AA, 4/533-mm TT, 4/ASW TT
2 HARUKAZE	1955	1,600	3/127-mm AA, 8/40-mm AA, ASW weapons
♦ *18 frigates*			
13 CHIKUGO	1970–76	1,470	2/76-mm AA, 2/40-mm AA, Asroc
4 ISUZU	1961–63	1,490	4/76-mm AA, 1 Weapon Able launcher
1 IKAZUCHI	1955	1,080	2/76-mm AA, 2/40-mm AA, ASW weapons
♦ *19 corvettes*			
12 MIZUTORI	1959-65	420/440	2/40-mm, 6/ASW TT
1 HAYABUSA	1957	380	4/40-mm AA, ASW weapons
3 KARI	1956	310	2/40-mm, ASW weapons
3 KAMOME	1956	330	2/40-mm, ASW weapons

WEAPONS AND SYSTEMS

Most weapons and detection gear are of American design, built under license in Japan. However, the latest ships are being equipped with a long-range, air-search radar of Japanese design, which has a short-pulse feature, and the 76-mm OTO Melara has been adopted. The latter will be built under license and will replace most of the old 76-mm guns currently mounted.

SUBMARINES

♦ *2 new type* — 4th Plan

	Bldr	Laid down	L	In serv.
573 N . . .	Mitsubishi, Kobe	3-12-76	. . .	. . .
574 N . . .	. . .	. . .	. . .	. . .

D: 2,200 tons **S:** 20/13 kts **Dim:** 69 × 9 × . . .
A: 6/533-mm TT **M:** Diesel-electric: 2 diesels V8/V24; 7,200 hp

♦ *7 Uzushio class* — 566 to 570: 3rd Plan — 571: 4th Plan

	Bldr	Laid down	L	In serv.
566 UZUSHIO	Kawasaki, Kobe	9-68	11-3-70	1-71
567 MAKISHIO	Mitsubishi, Kobe	1969	1-2-71	2-72
568 ISOSHIO	Kawasaki, Kobe	7-70	3-72	25-11-72
569 NARUSHIO	Mitsubishi, Kobe	1972	24-11-72	28-9-73
570 KUROSHIO	Kawasaki, Kobe	5-7-72	22-2-74	27-11-74
571 TAKASHIO	Kawasaki, Kobe	6-7-73	30-6-75	30-1-76
572 YAESHIO	Kawasaki, Kobe	. . .	19-5-77	. . .

Narushio (569) 1974

D: 1,850 tons **S:** 20/12 kts **Dim:** 72 × 9.9 × 7.5
A: 6/533-mm TT (fwd) **Man:** 10 officers, 70 men
M: Diesel-electric propulsion; Kawasaki M.A.N. diesels; V8V24/30; 1 prop; 3,400/7,200 hp

REMARKS: Tear-drop hull. Maximum depth: 200 m.

♦ *5 Oshio/Asashio class*

	Bldr	Laid down	L	In serv.
561 OSHIO	Shin-Mitsubishi, Kobe	6-63	30-4-64	4-65
562 ASASHIO	Kawasaki, Kobe	10-64	27-10-65	10-66
563 HARUSHIO	Shin-Mitsubishi, Kobe	10-65	25-2-67	3-68
564 MICHISIO	Kawasaki, Kobe	7-66	5-12-67	8-68
565 ARASHIO	Shin-Mitsubishi, Kobe	7-67	27-10-68	9-69

D: 1,650 tons **S:** 18/14 kts **Dim:** 88.0 × 8.2 × 4.9
A: 8/533-mm TT (6 fwd, 2 aft) **Man:** 80 men
M: 2 Kawasaki diesels, 2,900 hp each; 2 electric motors, 3,150 hp each; 2 props

REMARK: Since the *Oshio*, built during the 1961 program, was the prototype for the other four, it can be considered a separate class.

♦ *3 Hayashio/Natsushio class*

	Bldr	Laid down	L	In serv.
522 WAKASHIO	Kawasaki, Kobe	6-60	2-8-61	6-62
523 NATSUSHIO	Shin-Mitsubishi, Kobe	12-61	18-9-62	6-63
524 FUYUSHIO	Kawasaki, Kobe	12-61	14-12-63	1-64

Arashio (565)

SUBMARINES (*continued*)

Natsushio (523) Mitsubishi, 1963

D: 522: 750 tons; 523 and 524: 780 tons **S:** 14/11 kts
Dim: 59.2 (523 and 524: 61) × 6.5 × 4.1
A: 3/533-mm TT **Man:** 43 men
M: 2 Sulzer-Mitsubishi diesels, 850 hp each; 2 electric motors, 650 hp each; 2 props

REMARK: Considered to be a successful design; subdivided into two classes.

DESTROYERS

♦ *2 modified Haruna class* — 4th Plan

	Bldr	Laid down	L	In serv.
143 N . . .	. . .	1974	. . .	. . .
144 N . . .	. . .	1976	. . .	. . .

D: 5,200 tons **S:** 32 kts **Dim:** 155.0 × 17.5 × . . .
A: 2/127-mm AA Mk 2 (I × 2) — 2/35-mm AA (II × 1) — 1 Sea Sparrow — 1 Asroc — 6 ASW TT Mk 32 (III × 2) — 6 ASW helicopters
Electron Equipt: Japanese and American radars

REMARKS: Modification of the *Haruna* class. May be fitted with Harpoon surface-to-surface missile.

♦ *1 DDG* — 4th Plan

	Bldr	Laid down	L	In serv.
N . . .	. . .	1975	. . .	. . .

D: 2,900 tons **S:** . . . **Dim:** . . . **A:** . . .
Electron Equipt: . . . **M:** COGOG system

REMARK: Will be equipped with Harpoon missiles and Sea Sparrow.

♦ *2 Tachikaze class* — 1 from the 3rd Plan, 1 from the 4th Plan

	Bldr	Laid down	L	In serv.
168 TACHIKAZE	Mitsubishi	. . .	17-12-74	2-76
169 ASAKAZE	Mitsubishi	. . .	1977	1978

D: 3,850 tons **S:** 32 kts **Dim:** 143.0 × 14.3 × 4.6
A: 1 Mk 13 missile launcher (40 Tartar SM-1) — 2/127-mm AA Mk 42 (I × 2) — 1 Asroc system — 6/ASW TT Mk 32 (III × 2)
Electron Equipt: Radars: 1 Japanese air-search, 1 SPS 52, 2 SPG 51
M: GT; 2 props; 70,000 hp

Tachikaze (168)

Tachikaze (168) Ships of the World, 1976

♦ *2 Haruna class* — 3rd Plan

	Bldr	Laid down	L	In serv.
141 HARUNA	Mitsubishi, Nagasaki	3-70	12-71	22-2-73
142 HIEI	Ishikawajima-Harima	. . .	13-8-73	27-12-74

Haruna (141) Ships of the World, 1973

DESTROYERS (*continued*)

Haruna (141) 1973

D: 4,700 tons **S:** 32 kts **Dim:** 153.0 × 17.5 × 5.1
A: 2/127-mm AA Mk 42 (I × 2) — 6/324-mm Mk 32 ASW TT (III × 2) — 1 Asroc ASW system — 3 HSS-2 helicopters
Man: 36 officers, 304 men **M:** GT; 2 props; 70,000 hp
Electron Equipt: Radars: Japanese and U.S. fire-control

Hiei (142) 1975

♦ *8 Yamagumo class* — 3rd Plan and 4th Plan

	Bldr	Laid Down	L	In serv.
113 YAMAGUMO	Mitsui, Tamano	3-64	27-2-65	3-66
114 MAKIGUMO	Uraga, Yokosuka	6-64	26-7-65	3-66
115 ASAGUMO	Maizuru, H.I.	6-65	25-11-66	8-67
119 AOKUMO	Sumitomo, Uraga	11-70	30-3-72	25-11-72
120 AKIGUMO	Sumitomo, Uraga	7-71	19-10-73	31-4-74
121 YUGUMO	. . .	4-2-76	5-77	. . .
122 . . .	. . .	. . .	. . .	. . .
123 . . .	. . .	. . .	. . .	. . .

D: 2,066 tons (2,204 fl) **S:** 26 kts **Dim:** 114.9 × . . . × . . .
A: 4/76-mm AA — 4 or 6/324-mm ASW TT — 4 Bofors ASW rocket launchers (IV × 1) — 1 Asroc — 1 helicopter
Electron Equipt: Radar: 1 Japanese air-search
Sonar: *Akigumo:* towed
M: 6 Mitsubishi diesels; 2 props; 26,500 hp **Range:** 7,000/20

Aokumo (119) J. C. Bellonne, 1974

REMARK: Improvement on the *Minegumo* class.

Asagumo (115) 1974

♦ *3 Minegumo class*

	Bldr	Laid down	L	In serv.
116 MINEGUMO	Mitsui, Tamano	3-67	16-12-67	8-68
117 NATSUGUMO	Uraga, Yokosuka	6-67	25-7-68	4-69
118 MURAKUMO	Maizuru, H.I.	10-68	15-11-69	8-70

Minegumo (116) 1975

DESTROYERS (*continued*)

D: 2,066 tons (2,204 fl) **Dim:** 114.0 × 11.8 × 3.9
S: 28/27 kts **Man:** 19 officers, 196 men
A: 4/76-mm AA (II × 2) — 4 Bofors 375-mm ASW rocket launchers (IV × 1) — 6/324-mm ASW TT (III × 2) — 2 helicopters
Electron Equipt: Sonar: VDS **Range:** . . .
M: 6 Mitsubishi diesels; 12 VEV3/40 linked, 3 by 3, on 2 props; 26,500 hp

REMARK: The Italian 76-mm OTO Melara Compact has been tested on the *Murakumo.*

♦ *4 Takatsuki class* — 2nd Plan

	Bldr	Laid down	L	In serv.
164 TAKATSUKI	Ishikawajima, Tokyo	10-64	7-1-66	3-67
165 KIKUZUKI	Mitsubishi	3-66	25-3-67	3-68
166 MOCHIZUKI	Ishikawajima, Tokyo	11-66	15-3-68	3-69
167 NAGATSUKI	Ishikawajima, Tokyo	3-67	19-3-69	2-70

D: 3,050 tons (4,000 fl) **Dim:** 136.0 (131 pp) × 13.0 × 4.5
S: 32 kts **Range:** 7,000/20 **Man:** 270 men

Takatsuki (164)

Kikuzuki (165) 1974

A: 2/127-mm AA 54-cal. (I × 2) — 1 Asroc system — 4 Bofors ASW rocket launchers (IV × 1, fwd) — 6/324-mm Mk 32 TT (III × 2) — 2 ASW helicopters
M: General Electric GT; 2 props; 60,000 hp
Fuel: 900 tons **Boilers:** 2 Foster-Wheeler

REMARKS: This series is named after the phases of the moon. The first Japanese destroyers to have "macks" (masts and stacks combined). Same hull and engineering spaces as the *Amatsukaze.* American equipment built under license. Japanese search radar; the sonar is a Japanese copy of the U.S. SQS 23. The *Mochizuki* has TACAN. The Dash helicopters will be replaced by SH-2F Kamans, which are pilot-operated, and aerial equipment will be modified accordingly.

♦ *1 Amatsukaze class* — Bldr: Mitsubishi, Nagasaki

	Laid down	L	In serv.
163 AMATSUKAZE	11-62	5-10-63	2-65

Amatsukaze (163) Ships of the World, 1974

DESTROYERS (*continued*)

D: 3,050 tons (4,000 fl) **S:** 33 kts **Dim:** 131.0 × 13.4 × 4.2
Range: 7,000/18 **Man:** 290 men **Fuel:** 900 tons
A: 1 Mk 13 missile launcher (40 Tartars) (I × 1, aft) — 4/76-mm AA 50-cal. (II × 2) — 1 Asroc system — 2 fixed ASW TT — 2 hedgehogs
Electron Equipt: Radars: 1 SPS 39, 1 SPS 37, 2 SPG 51
M: Ishikawajima General Electric GT; 2 props; 60,000 hp
Boilers: 2 Foster-Wheeler **Electric:** 2,750 kw

♦ *2 Akizuki class*

	Bldr	Laid down	L	In serv.
161 **AKIZUKI**	Mitsubishi, Nagasaki	7-58	26-6-59	2-60
162 **TERUZUKI**	Shin-Mitsubishi, Kobe	8-58	24-6-59	2-60

Akizuki (161) 1970

D: 2,300 tons (2,890 fl) **Dim:** 118.0 (115 pp) × 12.0 × 4.02
S: 32 kts **Man:** 330 men
A: 3/127-mm 54-cal. AA (I × 3) — 4/76-mm 50-cal. AA (II × 2) — 4/533-mm TT (IV × 1) — 2 ASW torpedo launchers — 2 hedgehogs — 1 ASW Weapon Able Mk 108 rocket launcher — 2 depth-charge projectors
M: 161: Mitsubishi-Escher-Wyss GT, 162: Westinghouse; 2 props; 4 boilers; 45,000 hp

REMARKS: Would be used as flotilla leaders or convoy-escort command ships in wartime.

♦ *3 Murasame class*

	Bldr	Laid down	L	In serv.
107 **MURASAME**	Mitsubishi, Nagasaki	12-57	31-7-58	2-59
108 **YUDACHI**	Ishikawajima, Tokyo	12-57	29-7-58	3-59
109 **HARUSAME**	Uraga, Yokosuka	6-58	18-6-59	12-59

D: 1,800 tons (2,400 fl) **Dim:** 109.73 × 10.97 × 3.70 (light)
S: 30 kts **Man:** 229 men
A: 3/127-mm AA (I × 3) — 4/76-mm 50-cal. (II × 2) — 2 fixed ASW TT — 1 hedgehog — 2 depth-charge projectors

Harusame (109) Uraga Dock

M: 107 and 108: Kampon GT, 109: Mitsubishi-Escher-Wyss; 2 props; 2 boilers; 35,000 hp

REMARKS: This series is named for the winds. Hull and machinery spaces similar to those of the *Ayanami* class. 109 has Mitsubishi CE boilers, 107 and 108 have Foster-Wheeler D boilers. 107 has two Mk 32 ASW triple TT.

♦ *7 Ayanami class*

	Bldr	Laid down	L	In serv.
103 **AYANAMI**	Mitsubishi, Nagasaki	11-56	1-6-57	2-58
104 **ISONAMI**	Mitsubishi, Kobe	12-56	30-9-57	3-58
105 **URANAMI**	Kawasaki, Kobe	2-57	29-8-57	2-58
106 **SHIKINAMI**	Mitsui, Tamano	12-56	25-9-57	2-58
110 **TAKANAMI**	Mitsui, Maizuru	11-58	8-8-59	1-60
111 **ONAMI**	Ishikawajima, Tokyo	3-59	13-2-60	8-60
112 **MAKINAMI**	Iino, Maizuru	3-59	25-4-60	10-60

Isonami (104)

DESTROYERS (*continued*)

Onami (111) Isikawajima

D: 1,700 tons (2,400 fl) **Dim:** 109.0 × 10.7 × 8.7 (light)
S: 32 kts **Man:** 220/230 men
A: 6/76-mm AA (II × 3) — 4/533-mm TT (IV × 1) — 4 fixed ASW TT (2 each side) — 2 hedgehogs — 2 depth-charge projectors
M: Mitsubishi Escher-Wyss GT; 2 props; 2 boilers; 35,000 hp

REMARKS: This series is named after the waves. The two hedgehogs, which are forward of the bridge, are trainable. 106 and 110 have Hitachi-Babcock boilers, the others have Mitsubishi. 111 has a Hitachi-General Electric geared turbine. 104 and 106 are fitted as training ships; their trainable TT have been replaced by a classroom.

♦ *2 Harukaze class*

	Bldr	Laid down	L	In serv.
101 HARUKAZE	Mitsubishi, Nagasaki	12-54	20-9-55	4-56
102 YUKIKAZE	Mitsubishi, Kobe	12-54	20-8-55	7-56

Harukaze (101) Akura Nakumo

D: 1,600 tons (2,300 fl) **Dim:** 106.3 × 10.5 × 4.4 (fl)
S: 30 kts **Man:** 187 men **Range:** 6,000/18
A: 3/127-mm 38-cal. AA (I × 3) — 8/40-mm AA (IV × 2) — 2 hedgehogs — 8 depth-charge projectors — ASW torpedo launchers
M: 101: Mitsubishi-Escher-Wyss GT, 102: Westinghouse; 2 props; 101: 2 Hitachi-Babcock boilers, 102: Combustion Engineering; 30,000 hp
Fuel: 557 tons

REMARKS: This series is named after the winds. Most of the hull is electric-welded; light alloys are widely used in the superstructure. The guns are American; refitted in 1959-60. 102 received a VDS in 1976.

FRIGATES

♦ *13 Chikugo class*

	Bldr	Laid down	L	In serv.
215 CHIKUGO	Mitsui, Tamano	12-68	13-1-70	7-70
216 AYASE	Ishikawajima, Tokyo	12-69	16-9-70	7-71
217 MIKUMO	Mitsui, Tamano	3-70	2-71	8-71
218 TOKACHI	Mitsui, Tamano	12-70	11-71	5-72
219 IWASE	Mitsui, Tamano	1971	4-72	12-12-72
220 CHITOSE	Hitachi, Maizuru	1971	25-1-73	21-8-73
221 NIYODO	Mitsui, Tamano	1972	28-8-73	8-2-74
222 TESHIO	Hitachi, Maizuru	. . .	28-5-74	10-1-75
223 YOSHINO	Mitsui, Tamano	. . .	8-74	6-2-75
224 KUMANO	Hitachi, Maizuru	. . .	24-2-75	19-11-75
225 NOSHIRO	Mitsui, Tamano	. . .	23-12-76	6-77
226 N . . .	. . .	. . .	. . .	. . .
227 N . . .	. . .	. . .	. . .	. . .

Chitose (220) Ships of the World, 1975

D: 1,470 tons (1,700 fl) **S:** 25 kts **Dim:** 93.0 × 10.8 × 3.5
A: 2/76-mm AA (II × 1) — 2/40-mm AA (II × 1) — 6/324-mm ASW TT — 1 Asroc ASW system
Electron Equipt: Radar: 1 Japanese air-search
Sonars: 1 hull-mounted, 1 towed
M: 4 Burmeister & Wain diesels, Mitsui Mk 1628 V3B U38V; 2 props; 16,000 hp

REMARK: 225-227 are registered under the 4th Plan, which also provides for three somewhat larger ones.

FRIGATES *(continued)*

Teshio (222) 1975

Tokachi (218) Ships of the World, 1973

♦ *4 Isuzu class*

	Bldr	Laid down	L	In serv.
211 **ISUZU**	Mitsui, Tamano	5-60	17-1-61	7-61
212 **MOGAMI**	Mitsubishi, Nagasaki	8-60	13-3-61	11-61
213 **KITAKAMI**	Ishikawajima, Tokyo	1962	21-6-63	2-64
214 **OHI**	Maizuru H.I.	1962	15-6-63	2-64

Mogami (212) Ships of the World, 1975

D: 1,490 tons (1,700 fl) **Dim:** 94.0 × 10.4 × 3.5
S: 25 kts **Man:** 180 men
A: 4/76-mm AA 50-cal. (II × 2) — 1 quadruple Bofors 375-mm rocket launcher — 6 ASW TT (III × 2) on 213 and 214 — 1 depth-charge projector
M: 4 Burmeister & Wain Mitsubishi diesels; 2 props; 16,000 hp

CORVETTES

♦ *12 Mizutori class*

309 **UMITAKA** (25-7-59)
310 **OTAKA** (3-9-59)
311 **MIZUTORI** (22-9-59)
312 **YAMADORI** (22-10-59)
313 **OTORI** (27-5-60)
314 **KASASAGI** (31-5-60)
315 **HATSUKARI** (24-6-60)
316 **UMIDORI** (15-10-62)
317 **WAKATAKA** (13-11-62)
318 **KUMATAKA** (21-10-63)
319 **SHIRATORI** (8-10-64)
320 **HIYODORI** (25-9-65)

Bldrs: Kawasaki, Kobe; Kure; Fujinagata, Osaka; Sasebo

Yamadori (312)

CORVETTES (*continued*)

D: 420/440 tons (450/480 fl) **Dim:** 60.0 × 7.10 × 2.35
S: 20 kts **Man:** 75 men **Fuel:** 24 tons
A: 2/40-mm AA (II × 1) — 6 ASW TT — 1 hedgehog — 1 depth-charge rack
M: 309 and 310: Mitsui-Burmeister & Wain diesels, others: Kawasaki M.A.N. V-8-V; 2 props; 3,800/4,000 hp

♦ *1 gas-turbine experimental ship*

308 HAYABUSA (10-6-57) — Bldr: Mitsubishi

Hayabusa (308) Mitsubishi

D: 380 tons **Dim:** 58.0 × 7.8 × 2.0
S: 26 kts **Range:** 2,000/12
Man: 80 men **Fuel:** 22 tons
A: 4/40-mm AA (II × 2) — 1 hedgehog — 2 depth-charge projectors
M: 14,000-hp gas turbine; 2 Burmeister & Wain diesels (4,000 hp)

♦ *3 Kari class*

302 KIJI (11-9-56), **303 TAKA** (17-11-56), **304 WASHI** (12-11-56)

Washi (304)

D: 310 tons **S:** 21 kts **Dim:** 54.0 × 6.5 × 2.0
Man: 74 men **Range:** 2,000/12 **Fuel:** 21.5 tons
A: 2/40-mm AA (II × 1) — 1 hedgehog — 2 depth-charge projectors — 2 depth-charge racks
M: Kawasaki-M.A.N. diesels; 2 props; 4,000 hp

REMARKS: Four of these ships were built, two by Fujinagata and two by Maizuru. The *Kari* (301) has been stricken and the above three were retired from active service 15-3-77.

♦ *2 Kamome class*

305 KAMOME (3-9-56), **307 MISAGO** (1-11-56)
Bldrs: Uraga; Kure

Kamome (305) Uraga

D: 330 tons **S:** 20 kts **Dim:** 54.0 × 6.6 × 2.1
A: 2/40-mm AA (II × 1) — 1 hedgehog — 2 depth-charge racks
M: Mitsui-Burmeister & Wain diesels; 2 props; 4,000 hp
Fuel: 21.5 tons

TORPEDO BOATS

♦ *3 PT type* — 4th Plan

N . . . **N . . .** **N . . .**

D: 160 tons **S:** . . . **Dim:** . . .

REMARK: May be fitted with Harpoon surface-to-surface missiles.

♦ *6 PT type* — 3rd Plan and 4th Plan — Bldr: Mitsubishi

	L	In serv.		L	In serv.
811 PT 11	10-70	. . .	**814 PT 14**	. . .	10-7-73
812 PT 12	7-72	8-72	**815 PT 15**	. . .	8-1-75
813 PT 13	7-72	12-72	**816 PT 16**	. . .	. . .

812 PT 12 Ships of the World, 1973

TORPEDO BOATS *(continued)*

D: 100 tons **S:** 50 kts **Dim:** 35.0 × 9.2 × 1.2
A: 2/40-mm — 4/533-mm torpedoes **Man:** . . .
M: CODAG: 2 gas turbines, 2/24W2 diesels; 3 props; 10,500 hp

PATROL CRAFT

♦ *9 PB type*

PB 19 to **PB 27**

D: 18 tons **S:** 20 kts **Dim:** 17.0 × 4.3 × 0.8
A: 1/20-mm **Man:** 5 men **M:** 2 diesels; 760 hp

REMARK: These craft are used for rescue.

♦ **KOSOKU 6**

D: 40 tons **S:** 30 kts

REMARK: This boat has an experimental aluminum hull.

MINE WARFARE SHIPS

♦ *2 Hayase-class minelayers*

	Bldr	Laid down	L	In serv.
462 HAYASE (MST)	Ishikawajima	9-70	6-71	6-11-71
951 SOYA (MMC)	Maizuru, H.I.	7-70	31-3-71	30-9-71

D: 2,150 tons (3,050 fl) **S:** 18 kts **Dim:** 99.0 × 15.0 × 4.2
A: 2/76-mm AA (II × 1) — 2/20-mm AA — 6/324-mm ASW TT (III × 2) — 200 mines

Hayase (462) 1974

Soya (951) Ships of the World, 1973

M: Diesels; 2 props; 4,000 hp **Man:** 185 men

REMARKS: 462 is a support ship for minesweepers. Platform for minesweeping helicopter (type V 107). 462 has a 13-m beam and a 3.8-m draft.

♦ *1 coastal mine- and cable-layer* — Bldr: Mitsubishi, Yokohama

	Laid down	L	In serv.	Modernized
481 TSUGARU	12-54	19-7-55	12-55	1969-70

Tsugaru (481) 1970

MINE WARFARE SHIPS (*continued*)

D: 1,000 tons **S:** 16 kts **Dim:** 66.8 × 10.4 × 3.35
M: Diesels; 2 props; 3,200 hp **Man:** 105 men
A: 1/76-mm — 2/20-mm — 4 depth-charge projectors — 4 minelaying rails for 40 mines

♦ *3 coastal minesweepers* — 4th Plan

N . . . **N . . .** **N . . .**

D: 420 tons **S:** 14 kts **Dim:** 54.0 × 9.4 × 4.2
A: 1/20-mm **M:** 2 diesels; 2 props; 1,400 hp

REMARK: Will be fitted for minehunting as well as minesweeping.

♦ *19 Takami-class minehunters*

630 TAKAMI (15-7-69)
631 IOU (12-8-69)
632 MIYAKE (3-6-70)
633 UTONE (6-4-70)
634 AWAJI (11-12-70)
635 TOOSHI (13-12-70)
636 TEURU (10-72)
637 MUROTSU (10-72)
638 TASHIRO (2-4-73)
639 MIYATO (3-4-73)
640 TAKANE (8-3-74)
641 MUZUKI (5-4-74)
642 YOKOSE (21-7-75)
643 SAKATE (5-8-75)
644 OUMI (28-5-72)
645 FUKUE (12-7-76)
646 OKITSU (4-3-77)
647 N . . .
648 N . . .

Bldrs: Nippon Kokan, Tsurumi, and Hitachi, Kanagawa

D: 380 tons **S:** 14 kts **Dim:** 52.0 × 8.8 × 2.4
A: 1/20-mm AA **Man:** 45/47 men
M: Mitsubishi YV12ZC diesels; 2 props; 1,440 hp

Takami (630) Ships of the World

♦ *14 Kasada-class minesweepers*

	L		L
615 KOSHIKI	(6-11-61)	**623 RISHIRI**	(22-11-65)
617 KARATO	(10-12-62)	**624 REBUN**	(7-12-65)
618 HARIO	(10-12-62)	**625 AMAMI**	(31-10-66)
619 MUTSURE	(16-12-63)	**626 URUME**	(12-11-66)
620 CHIBURI	(29-11-63)	**627 MINASE**	(10-1-67)
621 OTSU	(5-11-64)	**628 IBUKI**	(2-12-67)
622 KUDAKO	(8-12-64)	**629 KATSURA**	(18-9-67)

Bldrs: Nippon Kokan, Tsurumi, and Hitachi, Kanagawa

Hario (618) Shbldg and Sh. Record

D: 330 tons **S:** 14 kts **Dim:** 45.7 × 8.38 × 2.3
A: 1/20-mm AA **Man:** 40 men
M: Mitsubishi YV 10 Z-DE diesels; 2 props; 1,200 hp

REMARK: *Hotaka* (616) now serves as a support ship.

♦ *6 inshore minesweepers*

	In serv.		In serv.
MSB 707	30-3-73	**MSB 710**	29-3-74
MSB 708	27-3-73	**MSB 711**	10-5-75
MSB 709	28-3-74	**MSB 712**	24-4-75

MSB 708 Ships of the World, 1973

MINE WARFARE SHIPS *(continued)*

Bldrs: Hitachi and Tsurumi

D: 58 tons (fl) **S:** 10 kts **Dim:** 22.5 × 5.4 × 1.1
Man: 10 men **M:** Diesels; 2 props; 960 hp

AMPHIBIOUS WARFARE SHIPS

♦ *3 LSTs* — 4th Plan — Bldr: Ishikawajima

	Laid down	L	In serv.
4151 MIURA	1972	13-8-74	29-1-75
4152 OJIKA	1973	2-9-75	3-76
4153 SATSUMA	26-5-75	12-5-76	17-2-77

Miura (4151) 1975

D: 2,000 tons **S:** 14 kts **Dim:** 98 × 14 × 3
A: 2/76-mm (II × 1) — 2/40-mm (II × 1) **Man:** 118 men
M: 2 diesels; 2 props; 4,400 hp **Range:** . . .

♦ *3 Atsumi-class LSTs* — Bldr: Sasebo H.I.

	Laid down	L	In serv.
4101 ATSUMI	1971	13-6-72	27-11-72
4102 MOTOBU	1972	3-8-73	21-12-73
4103 NEMURO	1973	5-77	10-77

Atsumi (4101) 1973

D: 1,480 tons **S:** 14 kts **Dim:** 89 × 13 × 2.7
A: 2/40-mm AA **Man:** 100 men **Range:** 4,300/12
M: 2 Kawasaki M.A.N. diesels; 2 props; 4,400 hp

REMARK: The *Atsumi* can carry 20 vehicles and 120 men.

AUXILIARY SHIPS

♦ *2 submarine-rescue ships*

402 FUSHIMI — Bldr: Sumitomo, Uraga, 10-9-69

Fushimi (402) 1970

D: 1,430 tons **S:** 16 kts **Dim:** 76.0 × 12.5 × 3.8
M: 2 Mitzu V622/30 diesels; 1 prop; 3,000 hp **Man:** 102 men

401 CHIHAYA — Bldr: Mitsubishi, 4-10-60

D: 1,340 tons **S:** 15 kts **Dim:** 73.0 × 12.0 × 3.9
M: Diesel; 2,700 hp **Man:** 90 men

REMARKS: Same profile as the 402. Salvage diving bell for six persons.

♦ *1 oiler* — 4th Plan

	Laid down	L	In serv.
N . . .	1975	. . .	. . .

D: 5,000 tons **Dim:** 140 × 19 × 10.8
M: 2 diesels; 2 props; 20,000 hp

♦ *1 Hamana-class oiler* — Bldr: Uraga, 24-10-61

411 HAMANA

Hamana (411) Uraga

AUXILIARY SHIPS (*continued*)

D: 2,900 tons (7,550 fl) **S:** 16 kts **Dim:** 128.0 × 15.7 × 6.3
A: 2/40-mm **Man:** 100 men **M:** 1 diesel; 1 prop; 5,000 hp

♦ *1 target support ship*

	Bldr	Laid down	L	In serv.
ATS 4201 AZUMA	Maizuru H.I.	7-68	14-4-69	11-69

Azuma (4201) 1970

D: 1,950 tons **S:** 18 kts **Dim:** 98 × 13 × 3.8
A: 1/76-mm AA — 2/324-mm ASW TT **Man:** 185 men
M: Kawasaki-M.A.N. diesels; 2 props; 4,000 hp

REMARKS: Has 10 KD-2R and 3 RQM-34 drones.

♦ *10 support ships, ex-Kasada-class minesweepers*

YAS 56 ATADA (ex-MSC-601)
YAS 57 ITSUKI (ex-MSC-602)
YAS 58 YASHIRO (ex-MSC-603)
YAS 62 SHISAKA (ex-MSC-605)
YAS 63 KOSHIKI (ex-MSC-615)
YAS 64 SAKITO (ex-MSC-607)
YAS 65 KANAWA (ex-MSC-606)
YAS 66 MIKURA (ex-MSC-612)
YAS 67 TSUKUMI (ex-MSC-619)
YAS 70 HOTAKA (ex-MSC-616)

REMARK: YAS-66 and YAS-67 are designated gunnery school ships.

♦ *5 target support craft*

	In serv.		In serv.		In serv.
YAS 101	30-3-68	**YAS 103**	9-71	**YAS 105**	1974
YAS 102	31-3-69	**YAS 104**	9-72		

D: 550 tons (fl) **S:** 14 kts **Dim:** 51.5 × 10.0 × 2.6
M: 2 diesels; 2 props; 1,600 hp **Man:** 26 men + 14 passengers

YAS 105 1974

♦ *1 submarine tender* — 4th Plan — Bldr: . . .

N . . . Laid down: 1976

♦ *1 icebreaker* — Bldr: Nippon Kokan, Tsurumi

	Laid down	L	In serv.
5001 FUJI	8-64	18-3-65	7-65

Fuji (5001) J. C. Bellonne, 1974

D: 8,500 tons (fl) **S:** 17 kts **Dim:** 99.0 × 27.8 × 8.9
M: Diesel-electric propulsion; 12,000 hp **Range:** 15,000/15

REMARKS: Carries three helicopters. Can make way through 5.4-m ice.

♦ *1 gunnery school ship (ex-coastal escort)*

YAS 69 ERIMO — Bldr: Uraga Dock Co. — L: 12-7-55

AUXILIARY SHIPS *(continued)*

Erimo (YAS 69)

D: 630 tons **S:** 18 kts **Dim:** 64 × 7.93 × 2.95
A: 2/40-mm AA — 2/20-mm
M: Diesel; 1 prop; 2,500 hp **Man:** 74 men

♦ *1 Ikazuchi class (ex-frigate)*

	Bldr	Laid down	In serv.
IKAZUCHI	Mitsui, Tamano	4-8-55	2-56

D: 1,070 tons (1,300 fl) **S:** 25 kts **Dim:** 87.5 × 8.7 × 3.1 (light)
A: 2/76-mm AA — 2/40-mm AA — 1 hedgehog — 4 depth-charge projectors
M: Diesels; 2 props; 18,000 hp **Boilers:** 2 Foster-Wheeler

♦ *1 training ship*

	Bldr	Laid down	L	In serv.
3501 KATORI	Ishikawajima	12-67	19-11-68	9-69

Katori (3501) J. C. Bellonne, 1974

D: 3,372 tons (4,100 fl) **S:** 25 kts **Dim:** 127.50 (122 pp) × 15 × 4.35
A: 4/76-mm AA (II × 2) — 1/375-mm Bofors quadruple ASW rocket launcher — 6/324-mm ASW TT (III × 2) for Mk 44 torpedoes
M: Ishikawajima GT; 2 props; 20,000 hp **Range:** 7,000/18

REMARKS: Helicopter platform. Can be used as an ASW frigate if required.

HYDROGRAPHIC SHIPS

♦ *1 AGS* — 4th Plan

N . . . Bldr: . . . Laid down: 1976

D: 2,000 tons **Dim:** 90 × 15 × 7.6
M: 2 diesels; 2 props; 4,000 hp

♦ *1 Akashi class*

5101 AKASHI — Bldr: Nippon Kokan, Tsurumi, 5-69

D: 1,420 tons **S:** 16 kts **Dim:** 74 × 12.9 × 4.3
M: 2 V8V 20/32 Kawasaki diesels; 2 props (1 bow prop); 3,800 hp
Man: 70 men + 10 hydrographic research personnel

REMARK: One 5-ton crane and one 1-ton crane.

♦ *4 ex-coastal minesweepers*

5111 ICHI-GO (ex-*Kasada*, MSC-604)
5112 NI-GO (ex-*Habuchi*, MSC-608)
5113 SAN-GO (ex-*Tatara*, MSC-630)
5114 YON-GO (ex-*Hirado*, MSC-614)

D: 340 tons **S:** 14 kts **Dim:** 46 × 8.5 × 2.3
M: 2 diesels; 2 props; 1,200 hp

MARITIME SAFETY AGENCY
(Kaijo Hoancho)

PERSONNEL: Approximately 11,000 men

The Maritime Safety Agency, a force modeled on the U.S. Coast Guard, is directed by the Department of Transportation in peacetime. Although its ships are armed, they are not considered part of the Navy and fly only the national colors (a red disk on a white background), not the flag flown by naval ships. In wartime, the ships would be under naval control.

DISPATCH VESSELS

♦ *2 Izu class*

PL 31 IZU — Bldr: Hitachi Zosen, 1-67 **PL 32 MIURA** — Bldr: Maizuru, 11-68

Miura (PL 32) 1970

D: 2,081 tons **Dim:** 95.5 (86.45 pp) × 11.6 × 3.8
S: 20.5 kts **Range:** 5,000/20.5, 14,500/12.7
M: 2 diesels, 2 props; 10,400 hp **Man:** 72 men

DISPATCH VESSELS (*continued*)

♦ *1 Kojima class*

PL 21 KOJIMA — Bldr: Kure Zosen — In serv.: 5-64

Kojima (PL 21) E. Aoki

D: 1,201 tons **S:** 17.2 kts **Dim:** 69.6 × 10.3 × 5.4
A: 1/76-mm — 1/40-mm AA — 1/20-mm AA
M: Uraga Sulzer diesel engine; 1 prop; 2,600 hp
Range: 6,000/13 **Man:** 59 men and 55 midshipmen

REMARK: Used as a training ship.

♦ *4 Erimo class* — Bldr: Hitachi Zosen

PL 13 ERIMO (14-8-65) **PL 14 SATSUMA** (4-66) **PL 15 DAIO** (19-6-73)
PL 16 MUROTO (15-3-74)

Daio (PL 15) 1974

D: 1,009 tons **S:** 19.5 kts **Dim:** 73.0 (wl) × 9.2 × 3.0
A: 1/76-mm — 1/20-mm AA **Range:** 6,000/18
M: Diesels; 2 props; 4,800 hp

REMARK: Hull reinforced against ice.

♦ *2 Nojima class* — Bldr: Uraga Dock Company Ltd

PL 11 NOJIMA (12-2-62) **PL 12 OJIKA** (In serv.: 6-64)

Nojima (PL 11) E. Aoki

D: 984 tons **S:** 17.5 kts **Dim:** 69.0 × 9.18 × 5.4
A: . . . **Man:** 51 men **Range:** 6,000/14
M: Uraga Sulzer diesels, 6 MD 42; 2 props; 3,000 hp

REMARK: Used for meteorological purposes.

♦ *1 Soya class*

PL 107 SOYA

D: 4,818 tons (fl) **S:** 14 kts **Dim:** 79.0 × 15.75 × 5.25
M: Diesels; 2 props; 4,800 hp **Range:** 10,000/12

Soya (PL 107) Tsurumi

REMARKS: Refitted in 1956, she serves as a hydrographic research ship for the Southern Hemisphere. Reinforced bow for navigation in ice 1-m thick. Four helicopters. Should be retired from active service shortly.

PATROL BOATS

♦ *21 Bihoro class* — Bldrs: Various

	In serv.		In serv.
PM 73 BIHORO	28-2-74	**PM 81 KIKUCHI**	2-76
PM 74 KUMA	28-2-74	**PM 82 KUZURYU**	18-3-76
PM 75 FUJI	2-75	**PM 83 HOROBETSU**	27-1-77
PM 76 KABASHINA	25-3-75	**PM 84 SHIRAKAMI**	3-3-77
PM 77 SADO	2-75	**PM 85 SAGAMI**	30-11-76
PM 78 ISHIKARI	13-3-76	**PM 86 TONE**	30-11-76
PM 79 ABUKUMA	30-1-76	**PM 87 YOSHINO**	28-1-77
PM 80 ISUZU	10-3-76	**PM 88 KUROBE**	15-2-77

D: 636 tons **S:** 18 kts **Dim:** 63.4 × 7.8 × 4.3
A: 1/20-mm **Man:** 34 men **Range:** 3,200/18
M: 2 diesels; 2 variable-pitch props; 3,000 hp

REMARK: PM-89 to PM-93 are being built.

♦ *3 Miyake class*

PM 70 MIYAKE **PM 71 AWAJI** **PM 72 YAEYAMA**

D: 574 tons **S:** 17.8 kts **Dim:** 58.1 × 7.4 × 2.5
A: 1/20-mm AA **Man:** 40 men **Range:** 3,580/16
M: 2 diesels; 2 props; 3,200 hp

♦ *4 Kunashiri class* — Bldrs: Maizuru; Usuki Iron Works, 1968-72

PM 65 KUNASHIRI (12-68) **PM 66 MINABE** (3-70)
PM 67 SAROBETSU (71) **PM 68 KAMISHIMA** (72)

D: 498 tons **S:** 17.5 kts **Dim:** 58.0 × 7.4 × 2.4
A: 1/20-mm AA **Man:** 40 men **Range:** 3,000/16.9
M: Diesels; 2 props; 2,600 hp

♦ *5 Matsuura class* — Bldrs: 60 and 61: Osaka SB; Others: Hitachi Zosen

PM 60 MATSUURA (24-12-60) **PM 63 NATORI** (8-65)
PM 61 SENDAI (18-1-62) **PM 64 KARATSU** (1-67)
PM 62 AMAMI (1964)

D: 420 tons **Dim:** 55.3 × 7.01 × 2.3
S: 16.5 kts PM-64: 18 kts
A: 1/20-mm AA **Man:** 37-40 men **Range:** 3,500/12
M: Diesels; 2 props; 1,400 hp PM-63: 1,800 hp PM-64: 2,600 hp

♦ *7 Yahagi class* — Bldr: Niigata

PM 54 YAHAGI (19-5-56) **PM 57 SORACHI** (3-59) **PM 69 OKINAWA**
PM 55 SUMIDA (6-57) **PM 58 YUBARI** (3-60)
PM 56 CHITOSE (24-2-58) **PM 59 HORONAI** (2-61)

D: 400-430 tons **S:** 15 kts **Dim:** 52.0 × 6.6 × 3.4 (fl)
A: 1/40-mm AA **Man:** 37 men **Range:** 3,600-4,000/12
M: Diesels; 2 props; 1,400 hp

♦ *1 Teshio class* — Bldr: Uraga

PM 53 TESHIO (12-1-55)

D: 420 tons **S:** 15.7 kts **Dim:** 58.0 × 7.9 × 2.5
A: 1/40-mm AA **Man:** 37 men **Range:** 3,800/12
M: 2 diesels; 1,400 hp

♦ *2 Tokachi class*

PM 51 TOKACHI (8-5-54) **PM 52 TATSUTA** (8-54)

D: 370 tons (380 fl) **S:** 15-16 kts **Dim:** . . .
A: 1/40-mm AA **Man:** 37 men **M:** 2 diesels; 1,400-5,000 hp

♦ *14 Rebun class* — Bldr: Japan, 1950-52

PM 04 REBUN **PM 09 AMAKUSA** **PM 14 HEKURA**
PM 05 IKI **PM 10 OKUSHIRI** **PM 15 MIKURA**
PM 06 OKI **PM 11 KUSAKAKI** **PM 16 KOSHIKI**
PM 07 GENKAI **PM 12 RISHIRI** **PM 17 HIRADO**
PM 08 HACHIJO **PM 13 NOTO**

Genkai (PM 07) Shizuo Fukui

D: 450-510 tons **S:** 14.6 kts **Dim:** 52.0 (47.5 pp) × 8.1 × 2.9
A: 1/76-mm — 1/20-mm AA **Range:** 3,340/12 **Man:** 40 men
M: 2 diesels; 1,300 hp

♦ *5 Chifuri class*

PM 18 CHIFURI **PM 20 KOZU** **PM 22 DAITO**
PM 19 KUROKAMI **PM 21 SHIKINE**

D: 483 tons **S:** 16.1 kts **Dim:** 51.1 × 7.6 × 2.6
A: 1/76-mm AA — 1/20-mm AA **Man:** 45 men
M: 2 diesels: 1,300 hp **Range:** 4,450/12

♦ *4 Sagami class* — Bldr: Japan

PS 11 MOGAMI (9-51) **PS 16 CHIKUGO** (1-52)
PS 15 SHINANO (12-51) **PS 17 KUMANO** (2-52)

D: 280 tons **S:** 13.5 kts **Dim:** 40.3 × 7.0 × 2.2
A: 1/40-mm AA **Man:** 35 men **Range:** 2,000/12
M: Diesels; 2 props; 800 hp

♦ *13 Hidaka class* — Bldr: Japan

PS 32 HIDAKA (2-3-62) **PS 39 TAKATSUKI** (1966)
PS 33 HIYAMA (3-63) **PS 41 KAMUI** (1966)
PS 34 TSURUGI (3-63) **PS 43 ASHITAKA** (1967)
PS 35 ROKKO (1964) **PS 44 KURAMA** (1968)

PATROL BOATS (*continued*)

PS 36 TAKANAWA (1964)
PS 37 AKIYOSHI (1964)
PS 38 KUNIMI (19-12-64)
PS 45 IBUKI (1969)
PS 46 TOUMI (1970)

Akiyoshi (PS 37) E. Aoki

D: 169.4 tons **Dim:** 33.72 (30.5 pp) × 6.3 × 1.8
S: 13.5 kts **Man:** 17 men
Range: 1,200/12 **M:** 1 diesel; 700 hp

♦ *1 Nagara class* — Bldr: Japan, 1952

PS 20 KITAKAMI

D: 260 tons **S:** 13.5 kts **Dim:** 49.4 × 6.9 × 2.2
A: 1/40-mm AA **Man:** 35 men **Range:** 2,000/12
M: 2 diesels; 800 hp

SMALL BOATS

♦ *8 Isayuki class*

	In serv.		In serv.
PC 64 AKIZUKI	2-74	**PC 75 HATAYUKI**	2-75
PC 65 SHINONOME	3-74	**PC 76 HAMAYUKI**	2-76
PC 72 YURAYUKI	5-75	**PC 77 HAMAZUKI**	11-76
PC 73 ISAYUKI	7-75	**PC 78 ISOZUKI**	3-77

Hatayuki Capt. F. Lauga, 1976

♦ *17 Shikinami class* — Bldr: Japan

	In serv.		In serv.
PC 54 SHIKINAMI	25-2-71	**PC 63 URAZUKI**	30-1-73
PC 55 TOMONAMI	20-3-71	**PC 66 URANAMI**	12-73
PC 56 WAKANAMI	30-10-71	**PC 67 TAMANAMI**	12-73
PC 57 ISENAMI	29-2-72	**PC 68 MINEGUMO**	11-73
PC 58 TAKANAMI	30-11-71	**PC 69 KIYONAMI**	10-73
PC 59 MUTSUKI	18-12-72	**PC 70 OKINAMI**	2-74
PC 60 MOCHIZUKI	18-12-72	**PC 71 WAKAGUMO**	3-74
PC 61 HARUZUKI	30-11-72	**PC 74 ASOYUKI**	6-75
PC 62 KIYOZUKI	18-12-72		

D: 44 tons **S:** 26.5 kts **Dim:** 21.0 × 5.3 × 1.0
M: MTU diesels; 2,200 hp **Range:** 280/26 **Man:** 10 men

♦ *5 aircraft rescue boats* — Bldr: Mitsubishi-Shimonoseki

PS 42 BIZAN (3-66)
PS 47 ASAMA (2-69)
PS 48 SHIRAMINE (12-69)

D: 83-130 tons; PS-48: 48 tons **Dim:** 26.0 × 5.6 × 1.0
S: 21-25 kts **A:** 1 machine gun **Man:** 14 men
M: 2 diesels; 1,140 hp; PS-48: 2 Benz diesels; 2,200 hp
Range: 400/18; PS-48: 250/25

PS 40 AKAGI (3-65) — Bldr: Hitachi Zosen, Kanagawa

D: 42 tons **S:** 28 kts **Dim:** 23.5 × 5.3 × 1.0
M: 2 Mercedes-Benz diesels; 2,200 hp **Range:** 350/21

PS 31 TSUKUBA (3-62) — Bldr: Hitachi Zosen, Kanagawa

D: 65 tons **S:** 18 kts **Dim:** 23.0 × 6.5 × 1.0
M: 2 Niigata diesels; 1,800 hp **Range:** 230/15

♦ *2 Makigumo class*

PC 34 ASAGUMO **PC 35 NATSUGUMO**

D: 42 tons **S:** 20.5 kts **Dim:** 21.0 × 5.2 × 1.0
M: 2 diesels; 1,400 hp

♦ *3 Mineyuki class*

PC 37 HANAYUKI **PC 38 MINEYUKI** **PC 39 ISOYUKI**

D: 46 tons **S:** 21 kts **Dim:** 22.0 × 5.4 × 1.0
M: 3 diesels; 1,500 hp

♦ *14 Matsuyuki class* — Bldr: Japan

	In serv.		In serv.
PC 40 MATSUYUKI	28-3-64	**PC 47 ASAGIRI**	. . .
PC 41 SHIMAYUKI	31-1-66	**PC 48 HAMAGIRI**	15-3-68
PC 42 TAMAYUKI	7-2-66	**PC 49 SAGIRI**	. . .
PC 43 HAMAYUKI	24-3-66	**PC 50 SETOGIRI**	. . .
PC 44 YAMAYUKI	15-3-67	**PC 51 HAYAGIRI**	. . .
PC 45 KOMAYUKI	15-3-67	**PC 52 HAMANAMI**	23-3-71
PC 46 UMIGIRI	. . .	**PC 53 MATSUNAMI**	30-3-71

D: 40-55 tons **S:** 26 kts **Dim:** 21.0 × 5.1 × 1.0
M: 2 MTU diesels; 2,200 hp

SMALL BOATS (*continued*)

REMARKS: PC-48: 15 kts, 1,140 hp; PC-53: 59 tons, 21.6 kts, 25.0 × 6.0 × 2.75. Reserved for the emperor's scientific work.

♦ *more than 150 15-meter craft*

D: 20 tons **S:** 19 kts **M:** Diesels; 530 hp

HYDROGRAPHIC SHIPS

♦ **HL 01 SHOYO** (1973)

D: 2,000 tons **S:** 17.4 kts **Dim:** 78.6 × 12.0 × 4.2
M: 2 diesels; 4,000 hp **Man:** 73 men

♦ **HL 02 TAKUYO** — Bldr: Niigata, 19-12-56

D: 930 tons **S:** 14 kts **Dim:** 58.75 × 9.50 × 3.25
M: Diesels; 2 props; 1,300 hp **Man:** 42 men
Range: 8,000/12

♦ **HL 03 MEIYO** — Bldr: Nagoya Zosen — In serv: 3-63

Meiyo (HL 03)

D: 486 tons **S:** 12 kts **Dim:** 40.5 × 8.05 × 3.8
M: Diesel; 1 prop; 700 hp **Range:** 5,280/11

♦ **HM 04 HEIYO** (1955)

D: 77 tons **S:** 10.6 kts **Dim:** 23.3 × 4.4 × 1.6
Man: 9 men **Range:** 670/9 **M:** Diesel; 1 prop; 130 hp

♦ **HM 05 TENYO** (1961)

D: 171 tons **S:** 10 kts **Dim:** 28.0 × 5.8 × 2.0
Man: 28 men **Range:** 3,160/10 **M:** 1 diesel; 1 prop; 230 hp

♦ **HM 06 KAIYO** — Bldr: Isikawajima-Harima — In serv: 3-64

D: 378 tons **S:** 12 kts **Dim:** 44.53 × 8.05 × 3.8
M: 1 diesel; 1 prop; 450 hp **Range:** 6,100/11

♦ **HU 06 SHINKAI** (5-68)

D: 85 tons **S:** 10/3.5 **Dim:** 15.3 × 5.5 × 4.0
M: 1 electric motor **Range:** 3 h (submerged) **Man:** 4 men

REMARK: Deep-diving submarine (600 m).

♦ *18 small craft + 3 planned*

VARIOUS SHIPS

♦ *1 lighthouse supply ship*

LL 01 WAKAGUSA — Bldr: Hitachi Zosen, 1946

D: 1,760 tons **S:** 14.7 kts **Dim:** 69.0 × 10.5 × 5.8
M: Diesel; 2 props; 1,200 hp

♦ *3 buoy tenders*

LL 11 HOKUTO **LL 12 GINGA** **LL 13 KAIO**

D: 500 tons **S:** 11.2 kts **Dim:** 38.6 × 9.4 × 4.2
M: 2 diesels; 420 hp **Range:** 2,800/10

♦ *1 buoy tender*

LM 11 MIYOJO

D: 318 tons **S:** 11 kts **Dim:** 26.10 × 13.60 × 2.65
M: 2 diesels; 600 hp **Range:** 3,680/10

Miyojo (LM 11) Capt. F. Lauga, 1976

REMARK: Has catamaran hull.

JAPAN (*continued*)

VARIOUS SHIPS (*continued*)

♦ *2 catamarans for measuring radioactive fallout*

MS 01 KINUGASA (9-10) **MS 02 SAIKAI** (9-70)

D: 23 tons **S:** 8.5 kts
Dim: 10.02 × 5.0 × 0.63 (beam of each hull: 2 m)
M: Diesels; 90 hp **Man:** 3 men

♦ *1 radioactive-fallout measurement boat*

MS 03 KATSUREN (11-12-75)

D: 30 tons **S:** 14 kts **Dim:** 16.5 × 5.0 × 2.2

♦ *1 catamaran for anti-pollution patrol*

SOKAI

D: . . . **S:** 11 kts **Dim:** 27.4 × 13.6 × 2.0
M: 2 diesels; 2 props; 1,080 hp

♦ *4 fireboats*

FL 01 HIRYU (3-69) **FL 03 NANRYU** (3-71)
FL 02 SHORYU (2-70) **FL 04 KAYRIU** (In serv: 18-3-77)

D: 250 tons **S:** 13.5 kts **Dim:** 27.5 × 10.4 × 2.2

Hiryu (FL 01) Capt. F. Lauga, 1976

Remarks: Catamarans, intended for fighting fires on large oilers

♦ *7 Nunobiki-class fireboats*

FM 01 NUNOBIKI **FM 02 YODO** **FM 03 OTOWA**
FM 04 SHIRAITO **FM 05 KOTOBIKI** **FM 06 NACHI** **FM 07 KEGON**

D: 89 tons **S:** 14 kts **Dim:** 23.0 × 6.0 × 3.2
M: Diesels **Man:** 12 men **Range:** 230/13.5

Remark: Four hoses.

JORDAN

Personnel: 300 men, including the personnel of the base at Aqaba and the frogmen.

♦ *1 12-m wooden small craft*

HUSSEIN ABDALLAH

♦ *4 7.5-meter small craft*

♦ *4 5- or 6-meter small craft (unarmed)*

♦ *6 14-m U.S. Bertram-class small craft*

D: 6.5 tons **S:** 25 kts **Dim:** 9.26 × 3.26 × 0.46
A: 1/12.7-mm machine gun — 1/7.62-mm machine gun **Man:** 8 men

KENYA

Personnel: 360 men

Merchant Marine (1976): 19 ships — 15,469 grt
(tankers: 2 ships — 3,706 grt)

PATROL BOATS

♦ *3 Simba-class coastal security craft* — Bldr: Vosper, 1965-66

P 3110 SIMBA (9-9-65) **P 3112 CHUI** (25-11-65)
P 3117 NDOVU (ex-*Twigg*) (22-12-65)

Simba (P 3110) Vosper

KENYA *(continued)*

PATROL BOATS *(continued)*

D: 96 tons (109 fl) **Dim:** 31.25 (28.95 pp) × 5.95 × 1.65
S: 24/23 kts **Man:** 3 officers, 21 men
A: 2/40-mm AA Mk 7 (I × 2)
Range: 1,500/16 **Fuel:** 14 tons
M: 2 Paxman-Ventura 12-cyl. diesels; 2 props; 2,900 hp

REMARKS: Welded hull, similar to the Malaysian SRI class.

♦ *1 37.5-m coastal surveillance craft* — Bldr: Brooke (Gt. Br.) — (L: 6-11-73)

P 3100 MAMBA

Mamba (P 3100) 1975

D: 130 tons (160 fl) **S:** 25 kts **Dim:** 37.5 × 6.9 × 1.6
A: 2/40-mm AA **Man:** 3 officers, 22 men **Range:** 3,500/13
M: 2 16-cyl. Ruston diesels; 4,000 hp

♦ *3 32-m coastal surveillance craft*

P 3121 MADARAKA (28-1-75) **P 3122 JAMHURI** (14-3-76)
P 3123 HARAMBEE (2-5-75)

D: 120 tons (145 fl) **S:** 25.5 kts **Dim:** 32.6 × 6.1 × 1.7
A: 2/40-mm AA **Man:** 21 men **Range:** 2,300/12
M: 2 Ruston-Paxman-Valenta diesels; 5,400 hp

♦ *3 port-service craft*

KOREA
North

PERSONNEL: Approximately 9,000 men

MERCHANT MARINE (1976): 19 ships — 89,482 grt
(tankers: 3 — 21,734 grt)

The North Korean Navy is composed mainly of ships received from the U.S.S.R. and the People's Republic of China. See those sections for ship characteristics.

SUBMARINES

♦ *4 Soviet Whiskey class, transferred by the U.S.S.R.*

♦ *9 Soviet Romeo class, transferred by China:* 2 in 1973, 2 in 1974, 3 in 1975, and 2 built locally with Chinese assistance.

FRIGATES

♦ *3 Najin class* — Bldr: North Korea 1973, 1975, 1977

D: 1,200 tons **S:** 25 kts **Dim:** 70.2 × 7.9 × 2.7
A: 2/100-mm AA — 4/57-mm AA (II × 2) — 4/25-mm AA (II × 2) — 4 depth-charge projectors — 30 mines
M: 2 diesels; 2 props; 5,000 hp **Man:** 55 men

CORVETTES

♦ *4 Sariwan class* — Bldr: North Korea, 1965

D: 600 tons **S:** 21 kts **Dim:** 62.1 × 7.3 × 2.4
A: 1/100-mm AA — 4/37-mm AA (II × 2) — 4/25-mm AA (II × 2) — depth-charge projectors

GUIDED-MISSILE PATROL BOATS

♦ *8 Soviet Osa-I class*

♦ *10 Soviet Komar class*

PATROL BOATS

♦ *8 Chinese Shanghai class,* acquired since 1967

♦ *8 Soviet SO-1 class*

♦ *8 Chinese Swatow class,* transferred in 1968

♦ *4 Chodo class* — Bldr: North Korea

D: 130 tons **S:** 24 kts **Dim:** 42.7 × 5.8 × 2.6
A: 1/76-mm AA — 3/37-mm AA (I × 3) — 4/25-mm AA (II × 2)
M: Diesels, 2 props, 6,000 hp **Man:** 24 men

TORPEDO BOATS

♦ *4 Soviet Shershen class*

♦ *80 Soviet P-4 class and P-6 class*

KOREA
South

PERSONNEL: Approximately 27,000 men, including Marines

MERCHANT MARINE (1976): 936 ships — 1,796,106 grt
(tankers: 52 ships — 652,025 grt)

DESTROYERS

♦ *2 ex-U.S. Gearing class, FRAM I*

Transferred: 25-2-77

	Bldr	L
D 90 KUANG JU (ex-*Richard E. Kraus*, DD-849)	Consolidated Steel	18-8-45
D 99 TAEJON (ex-*New*, DD-818) (ex-*Richard E. Kraus*, DD-849)	Bath Iron Works	2-3-46

D: 2,425 tons **S:** 34 kts **Dim:** 119.0 × 12.4 × 5.8
A: 4/127-mm AA Mk 28 (II × 2) — 6 ASW TT Mk 32 (III × 2)
Electron Equipt: Radars: 1 SPS 10, 1 SPS 40
Sonar: SQS 23
Man: 274 men **Range:** 2,400/25, 4,800/15 **Fuel:** 640 tons
M: GT; 4 Babcock & Wilcox boilers; 2 props; 60,000 hp

♦ *2 ex-U.S. Gearing class, FRAM II*

Transferred: 7-72 and 10-72

95 CHUNG BUK (ex-*Chevalier*, DDR-805)
96 JEONG BUK (ex-*Everett F. Larson*, DDR-830)

D: 2,400 tons (3,500 fl) **Dim:** 119.17 × 12.45 × 5.8
S: 30 kts **Man:** 14 officers, 260 men
Range: 2,400/25, 4,800/15 **Fuel:** 640 tons
A: 6/127-mm AA (II × 3) — 4/40-mm AA (II × 2) — ASW weapons
M: GT; 4 Babcock & Wilcox boilers; 2 props; 60,000 hp

♦ *2 ex-U.S. Allen M. Sumner class, FRAM II*

Transferred: 12-73

97 DAE GU (ex-*Wallace L. Lind*, DD-703)
98 INCHON (ex-*De Haven*, DD-727)

D: 2,350 tons (3,320 fl) **S:** 34 kts **Dim:** 114.8 × 12.4 × 5.2
A: 6/127-mm AA (II × 3) — 4/40-mm AA (II × 2) — 6/324-mm TT Mk 32 (III × 2)
Electron Equipt: Radars: 1 SPS 10, 1 SPS 40
Sonars: 1 SQS 29 series, IVDS
M: GT; 4 Babcock & Wilcox boilers; 2 props; 60,000 hp

♦ *3 ex-U.S. Fletcher class*

Transferred: 91 in 1963, 92 and 93 in 1968

91 CHUNG MU (ex-*Erben*, DD-631) Bath Iron Works, 21-3-43
92 SEOUL (ex-*Halsey Powell*, DD-686) Bethlehem, 30-6-43
93 PUSAN (ex-*Hickox*, DD-673) Federal SB, 4-7-43

D: 2,050 tons (2,850 fl) **Dim:** 114.85 (wl) × 12.03 × 5.5
S: 35 kts **Man:** 303 men
Range: 900/35, 4,500/12 **Fuel:** 650 tons
A: 5/127-mm 38-cal. (I × 5) — 6/40-mm AA (II × 3) — 6 ASW TT
Electron Equipt: Radars: 1 SPS 10 and 6
M: General Electric GT; 4 boilers; 2 props; 60,000 hp

Chung Mu (former USS Erben; shown with USN hull number) 1955

FRIGATE

♦ **DE 73 CHUNG NAM** (ex-*Holt*, DE-706) — Bldr: Defoe SB, 15-12-43

Transferred: 5-63

D: 2,230 tons (fl) **S:** 24/23 kts **Dim:** 92.3 × 11.2 × 4.3
A: 2/127-mm — 2/40-mm AA — 6/20-mm AA — 6 ASW TT (III × 2)
Electron Equipt: Radars: 1 SPS 5 and 6
M: Turbo-electric; 2 boilers; 2 props; 12,000 hp **Range:** 5,000/15

CORVETTES

♦ *3 Raven/Auk class*

Transferred: 7-63, 5-66, and 1967

PCE 1001 SHIN SONG (ex-*Ptarmigan*, MSF-376), 15-7-44
PCE 1002 SUN CHONKE (ex-*Speed*, MSF-116), 1944
PCE 1003 KOJE HO (ex-*Dextrous*, MSF-341), 1944

D: 890 tons (1,250 fl) **Dim:** 67.2 (65 pp) × 9.75 × 3.3
S: 18 kts **Man:** 100 men
A: 2/76-mm AA — 4/40-mm AA — 4/20-mm AA — hedgehog — 3 ASW TT (III × 1)
M: Diesel-electric propulsion; 2 props; 3,500 hp

♦ *4 ex-U.S. PCE type*

Transferred since 1955

CORVETTES (*continued*)

PCE 53 HAN SAN (ex-PCE-873)
PCE 57 PYOK PA (ex-PCE-870)
PCE 58 RYUL PO (ex-PCE-892)
PCE 59 SA CHON (ex-PCE-903)

D: 970 tons (fl) **S:** 17 kts **Dim:** 56.24 × 10.06 × 2.75
A: 1/76-mm — 3/40-mm — 8/20-mm **Man:** 80-95 men
M: General Motors diesels; 2 props; 2,400 hp **Range:** 4,300/10

PATROL BOATS

♦ *7 PGF type* — Bldrs: PGM-102 to PGM-105: Tacoma Boatbuilding Co.; Others: South Korea

	Laid down	In serv.
PGM 102 (ex-Paek Ku-12)	1-75	9-10-75
PGM 103 (ex-Paek Ku-13)	2-75	1976
PGM 105 (ex-Paek Ku-15)	. . .	8-77
PGM 106 (ex-Paek Ku-16)	. . .	1977
PGM 107 (ex-Paek Ku-17)	. . .	1977
PGM 108 (ex-Paek Ku-18)	. . .	1977
PGM 109 (ex-Paek Ku-19)	. . .	1977

Paek Ku

D: 220 tons (250 fl) **S:** 40 kts **Dim:** 49.5 × . . . × . . .
A: 1/76-mm AA — 1/40-mm AA — 2/12.7-mm machine guns
M: 6 gas turbines; 2 props **Man:** 5 officers, 7 men

REMARK: These multi-purpose boats could be fitted with Tartar or Harpoon anti-surface missiles.

♦ *1 ex-U.S. Asheville class*

Transferred: 1972

PGM 101 PAEK KU 11 (ex-*Benicia*, PG-96)

D: 225 tons (240 fl) **S:** 40 kts **Dim:** 50.14 × 7.28 × 2.9
A: 1/76-mm AA, Mk 64 fire control — 1/40-mm AA — 4/12.7 machine guns
M: CODAG propulsion: 1 General Electric turbine; 2 Cummins diesels

♦ *2 PGF type built in Korea*

PKM 121 **PKM 122**

D: 120 tons **S:** 40 kts **Dim:** 30.0 × 7.5 × 1.1
A: 1/40-mm AA — 1/20-mm AA
M: 2 Mercedes-Benz diesels; 3 props; 10,200 hp

♦ *9 ex-U.S. Sewart class*

Transferred: 1967

FB 1 to **FB 10**

D: 33 tons **S:** 25 kts **Dim:** 20.0 × 4.9 × . . .
A: 2/20-mm — 3/12.7-mm machine guns **Range:** 1,200/17
M: 2 General Motors diesels; 1,590 hp

♦ *1 PGF U.S. CPIC type*

Ordered: 1972

PKM 123

PKM 123 Tacoma Boatbuilding Co.

D: 70 tons (fl) **S:** 40 kts **Dim:** 30.5 × 5.0 × 1.8
A: 2/30-mm Emerlec AA (II × 1) — 1 recoilless rifle
M: 3 gas turbines; 3 props; 5,400 hp

♦ *20 PK type* — Bldr: South Korea

PK 151 to **PK 170**

D: 78 tons **S:** . . . **Dim:** . . .
A: 1/20-mm Vulcan — 3/20-mm Mk 56, MO 5 — 8 rocket launchers (IV × 2)
M: . . .

♦ *8 ex-USCG Cape class*

Transferred: 1968-69

PB 3 (ex-*Cape Rosier*, WPB-95333)
PB 5 (ex-*Cape Sable*, WPB-95334)
PB 6 (ex-*Cape Providence*, WPB-95335)
PB 8 (ex-*Cape Porpoise*, WPB-95327)
PB 9 (ex-*Cape Falcon*, WPB-95330)
PB 10 (ex-*Cape Trinity*, WPB-95331)
PB 11 (ex-*Cape Darby*, WPB-95323)
PB 12 (ex-*Cape Kiwanda*, WPB-95329)

D: 101.95 tons (fl) **S:** 20-21 kts **Dim:** 28.95 × 5.8 × 1.55

PATROL BOATS (*continued*)

A: 1/40-mm or 2/20-mm AA **Man:** 15 men
M: 4 diesels; 2 props; 2,200 hp **Range:** 1,500

REMARK: PB-7 (ex-*Cape Florida*) was lost in 1971.

MINE WARFARE SHIPS

♦ *8 ex-U.S. minesweepers*

Transferred: 6 in 1959-68, 2 in 1974

MSC 522 KUM SAN (ex-MSC-284)
MSC 523 KO HUNG (ex-MSC-285)
MSC 525 KUM KOK (ex-MSC-286)
MSC 526 NAM YANG (ex-MSC-295)
MSC 527 HA-DONG (ex-MSC-296)
MSC 528 SHAM CHOK (ex-MSC-316)
MSC 529 YONG-DONG (ex-MSC-320)
MSC 530 OKCHEON (ex-MSC-321)

REMARK: Characteristics of the French *Acacia* class. **A:** 2/20-mm

♦ *1 small ex-U.S. minesweeper*

Transferred: 1961

MSB 1 (ex-MSB-2)

D: 39 tons (fl) **Dim:** 17.5 × 4.6 × 1.25
M: 2 Packard diesels; 2 props, 600 hp

AMPHIBIOUS WARFARE SHIPS

♦ *6 ex-U.S. APD type employed as frigates*

Transferred: 1960-67

81 KYONG NAM (ex-*Cavallaro*, APD-128) (15-6-44)
82 AH SAN (ex-*Harry L. Corl*, APD-108) (1-3-44)
83 UNGPO (ex-*Julius A. Raven*, APD-110) (3-3-44)
85 KYONG PUK (ex-*Kephart*, APD-61) (6-9-43)
86 JONNAM (ex-*Hayter*, APD-80) (11-2-44)
87 CHE JU (ex-*W.M. Hobby*, APD-95) (11-11-43)

Kyong Nam

D: 2,114 tons (fl) **Range:** 2,300/22, 4,800/12
A: 2/127-mm (I × 2) — 6/40-mm AA (II × 3)

♦ *8 ex-U.S. LSTs*

Transferred: 1955-58

LST 807 UN-BONG (ex-LST-1010)
LST 808 TUK-BONG (ex-LST-227)
LST 809 BI-BONG (ex-LST-218)
LST 810 KAE-BONG (ex-LST-288)
LST 812 WEE-BONG (ex-*Johnson County*, LST-849)
LST 813 SU-YONG (ex-*Kane County*, LST-853)
LST 815 BUK-HAN (ex-*Linn County*, LST-900)
LST 816 HWA-SAN (ex-*Pender County*, LST-1080)

Tuk-Bong

D: 1,653 tons (4,080 fl) **S:** 10 kts **Dim:** 100.04 × 15.24 × 4.3
A: 7/40-mm — 2/20-mm **Man:** 70 men
M: General Motors diesels; 2 props; 1,800 hp

♦ *10 ex-U.S. LSMs*

Transferred: 1956

LSM 601 TAE CHO (ex-LSM-546)
LSM 602 TYO TO (ex-LSM-268)
LSM 605 KA TOK (ex-LSM-462)
LSM 606 KO MUN (ex-LSM-30)
LSM 607 PIAN (ex-LSM-96)
LSM 609 WOLMI (ex-LSM-57)
LSM 610 KI RIN (ex-LSM-19)
LSM 611 NUNG RA (ex-LSM-84)
LSM 612 SIN MI (ex-LSM-316)
LSM 613 UL RUNG (ex-LSM-17)

Bldr: U.S.A., 1943-44

D: 520 tons (1,095 fl) **S:** 13 kts **Dim:** 62.0 × 10.52 × 3.0
A: 1/40-mm AA — 4/20-mm AA **Man:** 75 men
M: Diesels; 2 props; 2,880 hp

♦ *1 ex-U.S. LSMR*

Transferred: 1960

SI HUNG (ex-*St. Joseph River*, LSMR-527)

D: 944 tons **S:** 12.6 kts **Dim:** 67.6 × 11.3 × 3.3
A: 2/40-mm AA — 4/20-mm AA — 1/12.7 machine gun
M: 2 diesels; 2 props; 2,800 hp

♦ *1 ex-U.S. LCU*

LCU 1 (ex-LCU-531)

HYDROGRAPHIC SHIPS

♦ *2 ex-Belgian-U.S. MSI type*

Bought: 1970

SURO 5 (ex-*Temse*) **SURO 6** (ex-*Tournai*), 1956-57

KOREA — SOUTH (*continued*)

HYDROGRAPHIC SHIPS (*continued*)

D: 160 tons (190 fl) **S:** 15 kts **Dim:** 34.5 × 6.6 × 2.1
A: 2/20-mm AA (II × 1) **Man:** 17 men **Fuel:** 18 m³ diesel
M: Diesels; 2 props; 630 hp **Range:** 2,300/10

AUXILIARY SHIPS

♦ *1 LST-type repair ship*

R 1 TUK-SU (ex-*Minotaur*, ARL-15)

Loaned by the U.S.A.

D: 2,225 tons (3,640 fl) **S:** 10 kts **Dim:** 99.98 × 15.34 × 4.27
A: 2/40-mm AA — 6/20-mm AA **Man:** 277 men
M: Diesels; 2 props; 1,000 hp

♦ *1 ex-Norwegian oiler*

AO 2 CHUN JI (ex-*Birk*)

D: 2,225 tons **Dim:** 84.0 × 13.5 × 5.6
A: 1/40-mm AA — 2/20-mm AA **Man:** 73 men

REMARKS: Bought in 1951. The *Puchon* of the same class was lost 5-71.

♦ *2 ex-U.S. oilers*

Transferred: 1960

YO 1 KU RYONG (ex-YO-118)

D: 1,126 tons (fl) **S:** 7 kts **Dim:** 53.0 × 10.0 × 4.0
M: Diesel; 1 prop; 700 hp **Man:** 36 men

YO 5 HWA CHON (ex-YO-59)

D: 2,700 tons (fl) **S:** 10 kts **Dim:** 72.0 × 11.6 × 4.6
M: Diesel; 1 prop; 1,150 hp **Man:** 46 men

♦ *6 ex-U.S. supply ships*

Transferred: Since 1956

AKL 902 IN CHON (ex-FS-198)
AKL 905 CHIN NAM (ex-FS-356)
AKL 907 MOK PO (ex-WAK-170)
AKL 908 KUN-SAN (ex-AKL-10)
AKL 909 MA-SAN (ex-AKL-35)
AKL 910 UL-SAN (ex-AKL-28)

D: 520 tons **S:** 12 kts **Dim:** 53.95 × 10.06 × 3.1
A: 1/40-mm AA — 2/20-mm AA — 2 machine guns
M: Diesels; 2 props; 1,000 hp **Man:** 43-49 men

♦ *2 ex-U.S. tugs, 1944*

DO BANG (ex-ATA-206), **YUNG MUNG** (ex-ATA-138)

D: 835 tons **M:** 1,500 hp

KUWAIT

PERSONNEL: 200 men

MERCHANT MARINE (1976): 182 ships — 1,106,816 grt
(tankers: 9 ships — 706,030 grt)

PATROL BOATS

♦ *10 coastal boats* — Bldrs: Thornycroft, Woolston, 2; Vosper Thornycroft, 8

AL SALEMI (30-6-66)
AL MUBARAKI (16-7-66)
MAYMOON (4-68)
AMAN (3-68)
AL SHURTI (1972)
MARZOOK (1969)
MASHHOOR (1969)
MURSHED (1970)
WATHAH (1970)
INTISAR (1972)

Intisar Vosper, 1972

D: 40 tons **S:** 20 kts **Dim:** 27.78 × 4.73 × 1.38
Man: 5 officers, 7 men **Range:** 700/15
M: Rolls-Royce 8-cyl. diesels; 2 props; 1,340 hp

♦ *2 56-foot boats* — Bldr: Vosper Thornycroft Private Ltd. Singapore, 1974

DASTOR **KASAR**

D: 25 tons **S:** 21 kts **Dim:** 16.8 × . . . × . . .
A: 1/20-mm — 2 machine guns **Man:** 8 men
M: 2 MTU MB-6 diesels; 1,350 hp **Range:** 320/20

♦ *7 50-foot craft* — Bldr: Thornycroft Ltd., Singapore

♦ *1 45-foot craft* — Bldr: Thornycroft Ltd., Singapore

MAHROOS

Mahroos Vosper, 1975

KUWAIT (*continued*)

PATROL BOATS (*continued*)

D: . . . **S:** 21 kts **Dim:** 14.0 × . . . × . . .
A: 2/20-mm — 2 machine guns
M: 2 Rolls-Royce C8M-410 diesels; 780 hp

♦ *8 35-foot craft* — Bldr: Vosper Thornycroft Private Ltd., Singapore

S: 24 kts **M:** 2 Perkins diesels

♦ *3 landing craft* — Bldr: Vosper Thornycroft Private Ltd., Singapore, 1971

WAHEED **REGGA** **FAREED**

Regga

D: 88 tons **S:** 10 kts **Dim:** 27.0 × 6.9 × 1.3
M: 2 Rolls-Royce C8M-410 diesels; 752 hp **Man:** 8 men

LEBANON

Personnel: 200 men

Merchant Marine (1976): 136 ships — 213,752 grt

PATROL BOATS

	Bldr	L
TARABLOUS	Estérel NSY	6-59

Tarablous

D: 105 tons **S:** 27 kts **Dim:** 38.0 × 5.5 × 1.75
A: 2/40-mm **Range:** 1,500 **Man:** 3 officers, 16 men
M: Mercedes-Benz diesels; 2 props; 2,700 hp

♦ *3 Biblos-class* — Bldr: Estérel NSY, 1954-55

11 BIBLOS **12 SIDON** **13 BEYROUTH** (ex-*Tir*)

D: 28 tons **S:** 18 kts **Dim:** 20.1 × 4.1 × 1.3
A: 1/20-mm AA — 2 machine guns
M: General Motors diesels; 2 props; 530 hp

Remark: In poor condition.

AMPHIBIOUS CRAFT

♦ *1 ex-U.S. landing craft*

Transferred: 11-58

SOUR (ex-LCU-1474)

D: 180 tons (360 fl) **S:** 10 kts **Dim:** 35.05 × 10.36 × 1.85
A: 2/20-mm AA **M:** Diesels; 3 props; 675 hp

LIBERIA

Personnel: Approximately 120 men

Merchant Marine (1976): 2,600 ships — 73,477,326 grt
(tankers: 953 ships — 47,253,363 grt)

♦ **ALERT** (ex-PGM-102) — Bldr: U.S.A., 1967

Remark: Same type as the PGMs transferred to South Vietnam, Thailand, etc.

LIBERIA (*continued*)

♦ **LIBERIAN** (ex-*Virginian*) — Bldr: Wm. Beardmore & Co., Dalmuir, 1930
D: 1,200 tons **S:** 14 kts **Dim:** 63.7 × 9.05 × 4.0
M: 2 diesels

REMARK: Yacht with sharply raked bow bought in 1957 and modified.

♦ **ML 4001 to ML 4002** (1957) — Former USCG craft
D: 12 tons **S:** 22 kts

LIBYA

PERSONNEL: Approximately 1,200 men

MERCHANT MARINE (1976): 36 ships — 458,805 grt
(tankers: 8 ships — 431,602 grt)

SUBMARINE

♦ *1 Soviet Foxtrot class*

BADR

D: 1,950 tons surfaced, 2,400 submerged **Dim:** 96.0 × 7.5 × 6.0
S: 18/16 kts **Man:** 10 officers, 70 men
A: 10/533-mm TT (6 fwd, 4 aft) — 22 torpedoes or 44 mines
Range: 9,000/7 **Endurance:** 70 hours, submerged
M: Diesels and electric motors; 3 props

REMARKS: Arrived at Tripoli 27-12-76. Three or four more are expected.

FRIGATE

♦ *1 Vosper Mk 7*

	Bldr	Laid down	L	In serv.
DAT ASSAWARI	Vosper Thornycroft	1968	10-69	1973

Dat Assawari (F 01) Vosper, 1972

Dat Assawari (F 01) 1976

D: 1,325 tons (1,650 fl) **Dim:** 101.6 (94.5 pp) × 11.08 × 3.36
S: 37 kts (17 cruising) **Man:** 132 men **Range:** 5,700/17
A: 1/114-mm AA — 2/40-mm (II × 1) — 3 Sea Cat (III × 1) — 1 helicopter — 1 depth-charge projector
M: CODOG propulsion; 2 Rolls-Royce TM 2A Olympus gas turbines, 24,000 hp each; 2 Paxman-Ventura diesels 1,900 hp each; 2 variable-pitch props
Fuel: 300 tons

CORVETTES

♦ *4 550-ton ships* — Bldr: C.N.T.R. Riva Trigoso, Italy

N . . . **N . . .**
N . . . **N . . .**

Ordered: 1974

D: 550 tons (fl) **S:** . . . **Dim:** 61.7 × 9.3 × 2.7
A: 4 Otomat missiles — 2/76-mm AA OTO Melara Compact
Electron Equipt: . . . **M:** . . .

♦ *1 Vosper Mk 1B* — Bldr: Vosper Ltd, Portsmouth, 29-4-65

TOBRUK

D: 440 tons (500 fl) **Dim:** 53.95 (48.77 pp) × 8.68 × 4.0
S: 18 kts **Man:** 5 officers, 58 men
A: 1/102-mm — 4/40-mm AA **Range:** 2,900/14
M: Paxman-Ventura 16-cyl. diesels; 1,500 rpm; 2 props; 3,800 hp
Fuel: 60 tons

REMARKS: Anti-rolling devices, living quarters air-conditioned.

CORVETTES (*continued*)

Tobruk Shbldg. and Sh. Record

GUIDED-MISSILE PATROL BOATS

♦ *10 La Combattante-II class* — Bldr: C.M.N., Cherbourg

REMARK: Will be similar to the units ordered by Iran, but will have Otomat missiles.

♦ *1 Soviet Osa-II class*

REMARKS: Delivered in 1977. More are expected.

♦ *3 Sölöven type*

	Bldr	L	In serv.
P 01 SUSA	Vosper Ltd, Portsmouth	31-8-67	8-68
P 02 SIRTE	Vosper Ltd, Portsmouth	10-1-68	4-68
P 03 SEBHA (ex-*Sokna*)	Vosper Ltd, Portsmouth	29-2-68	1-69

D: 95 tons (115 fl) **S:** 50 kts **Dim:** 30.38 (27.44 pp) × 7.3 × 2.15
A: 8/SS 11 or 12 (II × 4) — 2/40-mm **Man:** 20 men
M: 3 Bristol-Siddeley Proteus gas turbines; 2 General Motors cruising diesels, 190 hp; 3 props; 12,750 hp

REMARK: These are modeled on the Danish *Sölöven* class.

Susa (P 01) Vosper, 1968

PATROL BOATS AND CRAFT

♦ *4 Brooke type* — Bldr: Brooke Marine, Lowestoft, G.B., 1968–70

PC 1 GARIAN **PC 3 MERAWA**
PC 2 KHAWLAN **PC 4 SABRATHA**

Khawlan (PC 2) 1970

D: 100 tons (125 fl) **S:** 23.5 kts **Dim:** 36.58 × 7.16 × 1.75
A: 1/40-mm — 1/20-mm **Man:** 22 men **Range:** 1,800/13
M: Paxman-Ventura 16-cyl. diesels; 2 props; 3,600 hp

REMARKS: Have the same engines as the *Tobruk* and the *Zeltin*. At least one is equipped with one BM-21 multiple rocket launcher.

♦ *6 security craft*

AR RAKIB, FARWA — Bldr: John I. Thornycroft, Woolston, 1966–67
BENINA, MISURATA, AKRAMA, HOMS — Bldr: Vosper Thornycroft, Portsmouth, 1967–69

D: 100 tons **S:** 20/18 kts **Dim:** 30.5 × 6.4 × 1.7
A: 1/20-mm **Man:** 15 men **Range:** 1,800/14
M: 3 Rolls-Royce diesels; 1,740 hp

REMARK: Used for customs and fishery protection.

AMPHIBIOUS WARFARE SHIPS

♦ *2 Ibn Ouf-class LSTs* — Bldr: C.N.I.M., La Seyne

	Laid down	L	In serv.
130 IBN OUF	1-4-76	5-77	. . .
131 IBN HARISSA	. . .	3-78	. . .

D: 2,800 tons (fl) **S:** 15 kts **Dim:** 100.0 × 15.65 × 2.6
A: 4/40-mm AA (I × 4) — 1 81-mm mortar
M: 2 diesels; 2 props; 5,340 hp

AMPHIBIOUS WARFARE SHIPS *(continued)*

Ibn Ouf J. C. Bellonne, 1977

AUXILIARY SHIPS

♦ *2 support ships for small craft*

	Bldr	Laid down	L	In ser.
ZELTIN	Vosper Thornycroft, Woolston	1967	29-2-68	1-69

Zeltin 1968

D: 2,200 tons (2,470 fl) **Dim:** 98.72 (91.44 wl) × 14.64 × 3.05
S: 15 kts **Man:** 15 officers, 86 men
A: 2/40-mm AA **Range:** 3,000/14
M: 2 Paxman-Ventura 16 cyl, diesels, 1,750 hp each; 1,350 rpm

Zeltin 1972

REMARKS: The well deck, 41 × 12, can receive small craft drawing 2.3 m. Hydraulically controlled stern gate. A moveable crane (3-ton loading capacity) is available for the well deck, and a 9-ton crane on the port side is available for the workshops. Electricity furnished by four diesel alternators, 200 kw Ac, 450 volts.

ZLEITEN (ex-British MRG-1013)

D: 650 tons (900 fl) **S:** 10/11 kts **Dim:** 70.4 × 11.8 × 1.6
M: 4 Paxman diesels; 2 props; 1,840 hp

REMARK: Former LCT bought and modified in 1968.

♦ *1 ex-Italian Expresso-class ro-ro carrier*

EL TIMSAH

D: 3,100 tons (fl) **Dim:** 117.5 (108.7 pp) × 17.5 × 4.9
S: 20 kts **M:** 2 Fiat diesels, 18 cyl. in V; 9,000 hp

REMARK: Has stabilizers.

MALAGASY REPUBLIC

PERSONNEL: Approximately 300 men

MERCHANT MARINE (1976): 49 ships — 49,738 grt
(tankers: 4 ships — 10,236 grt)

PATROL BOATS

♦ *1 PR-48 type coastal patrol boat*

	Bldr	Laid down	L	In serv.
MALAIKA	C. N. Franco-Belges	11-66-72	22-3-67	12-67

D: 240 tons (avg) **S:** 18.5 kts **Dim:** 47.5 (45.5 pp) × 7.1 × 2.5
A: 2/40-mm AA **Range:** 2,000/15 **Man:** 3 officers, 22 men
M: 2 MGO diesels with Masson reduction gears (1/3); 2 props; 2,400 hp

♦ *1 transport*

	Bldr	L
FANANTENANA (ex-*Richelieu*)	A.G. Weser, Bremen	1959

D: 1,040 tons (1,200 fl) **Dim:** 62.9 (56 pp) × 9.15 × 4.52
S: 12 kts **A:** 2/40-mm AA **Man:** . . .
M: 2 Deutz diesels ("father-mother" system); 1 prop; 1,060 + 500 hp

REMARKS: Former trawler, bought and modified 1966-67. Can carry 300 tons of freight and up to 120 military passengers.

AMPHIBIOUS WARFARE SHIPS

♦ *1 LSM*

	Bldr	Laid down	L	In serv.
TOKY	Diego Suarez SY	1972	1973	10-74

D: 810 tons (avg) **S:** 13 kts **Dim:** 66.37 (56 pp) × 12.5 × 1.9
Range: 3,000/12 **Electric:** 240 kw **Man:** 27 men
A: 1/76-mm — 2/20-mm AA — 1/81-mm mortar
M: 2 M-60 diesels; 2 props; 2,400 hp

REMARKS: Similar to a French EDIC. Used as a transport and support ship. Forward ramp can be folded upon itself. Transport capacity: 250 tons; quarters for 30 passengers; 120 soldiers can be carried for short distances. Financed by the French government under the military cooperation pact.

MARITIME POLICE

♦ *5 coast surveillance craft*

Delivered by the West German Republic in 1962

D: 46 tons **S:** 22 kts **Dim:** 24.0 × . . . × . . .
A: 1/40-mm **M:** 2 diesels; 2 props

MALAYSIA

PERSONNEL: Approximately 5,500 men

MERCHANT MARINE (1976): 150 ships — 442,746 grt
(tankers: 14 ships — 61,740 grt)

FRIGATES

	Bldr	Laid down	L	In serv.
♦ **F 24 RAHMAT**	Yarrow, Glasgow	2-66	18-12-67	3-71

Rahmat (F 24) Yarrow, 1970

D: 1,550 tons (fl) **S:** 27 kts (16.5 on diesels alone)
Dim: 93.87 (91.44 pp) × 10.36 × 3.05 **Range:** 1,000/27, 5,200/16.5
A: 1/114-mm AA Mk 4 — 2/40-mm 70-cal. Bofors AA — 4 Sea Cat (IV × 1) — 1 ASW Mk 10 triple mortar — helicopter platform
M: CODOG propulsion: 8 cyl. Pielstick-Crossley diesels, 3,850-hp; Rolls-Royce Olympus gas turbine; 2 Stone Ka-Me-Wa props; 22,000 hp
Man: 120 men

REMARKS: Advanced automation. Mk 22 fire-control radar atop the mast for the 114-mm and Mk 44 on the stern for the Sea Cat.

♦ *1 British-built*

	Bldr	Laid down	L	In serv.
HANG TUAH II (ex-*Mermaid*, F-76)	Yarrow	1965	29-12-66	4-72

D: 2,300 tons (2,520 fl) **Dim:** 103.4 × 12.2 × 4.8
S: 24/23 kts **Man:** 200-210 men
A: 2/102-mm AA (II × 1) — 2/40-mm AA (I × 2) — 1 Limbo
Range: 4,800/15 **Fuel:** 230 tons
Electron Equipt: Radars: 1 Plessey AWS-1 air-search
M: 8 16-cyl. Admiralty Standard Range-I high-speed diesels with reduction gear hydraulically linked, 4 by 4, on 2 props; 12,400 hp

REMARKS: In 1964 the Royal Navy ordered for Ghana a ship conforming to the specifications of the 41 type. Because of the political situation, the ship was not delivered and was purchased at the end of 1971 by the British government. Transferred to Malaysia in 1977.

GUIDED-MISSILE PATROL BOATS

♦ *4 Swedish Spica Class* — Bldr: Karlskrona

N . . . N . . . N . . . N . . .

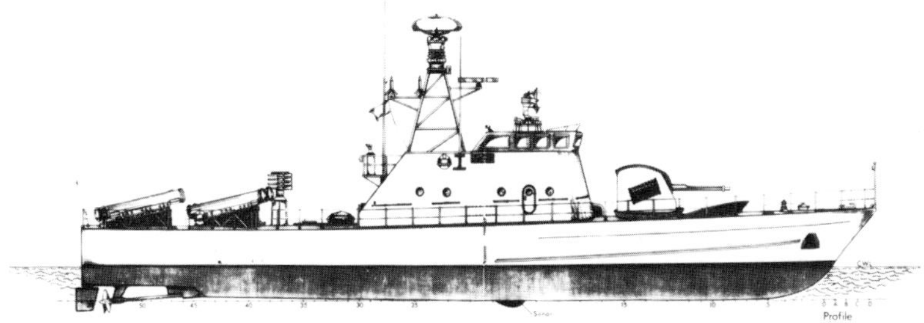

D: 240 tons (fl) **Dim:** 43.6 × 7.0 × 2.4 (aft)
S: 34.5 kts (37.5 max.) **Man:** . . .
A: 4 MM 38 Exocet missiles — 1/57-mm Bofors
Electron Equipt: Radars: 1 DO Philips air-search, 1 CT Saab-Scania
Range: 1,850/14 **Electric:** 200 kw
M: 3 MTU MD16V538TB91 diesels; 3 props; 10,800 hp

REMARK: Contract signed 13-8-76.

♦ *4 Serang class*

	L	In serv.		L	In serv.
SERANG	22-12-71	31-2-73	**GANYANG**	16-3-72	20-3-73
GANAS	26-10-72	28-2-73	**PERDANA**	31-5-72	31-12-72

Bldr: S.F.C.N., 2. Constr. Méc. de Normandie, Cherbourg, 2. Delivered in 1973

Ganyang M. N., 1973

Serang 1973

D: 234 tons (265 fl) **Dim:** 47.0 × 7.1 × 2.5 (fl)
S: 36.5 kts **Range:** 800/25
Man: 5 officers, 30 men **Fuel:** 39 tons
A: 2 MM 38 Exocet missiles — 1/57-mm Bofors — 1/40-mm Bofors L 70
M: 4 MTU MB 870 diesels; 4 props; 14,000 hp

REMARKS: *La Combattante II* (A4L) class of the French Navy. Steel hull. Superstructure in alloyed metal. Similar type ships have been ordered by Greece and West Germany.

PATROL BOATS

♦ *6 Jerong class* — Bldr: Leong Lürssen, Butterworth, Singapore

	L	In serv.		L	In serv.
P 3505 JERONG	28-7-75	23-3-76	**P 3508 YU**	. . .	. . .
P 3506 TUDAK	16-3-76	. . .	**P 3509 BAUNG**	5-10-76	. . .
P 3507 PAUS	2-6-76	9-76	**P 3510 PARI**	. . .	. . .

D: 240 tons (fl) **S:** 38 kts **Dim:** 45.0 × 5.0 × . . .
A: 1/57-mm AA — 1/40-mm AA **Man:** 35 men **Range:** . . .
M: Diesels

REMARK: Will replace the six *Sri Kedah* class, which have been condemned.

♦ *4 Perkasa class* — Bldr: Vosper, Ltd., Portsmouth

P 150 PERKASA (26-10-65) **P 152 GEMPITA** (6-4-66)
P 151 HANDALAN (18-1-66) **P 153 PENDEKAR** (24-6-66)

Perkasa (P 150) Shbldg. and Shipping Record

PATROL BOATS (*continued*)

D: 95 tons (114 fl) **S:** 54 kts; P-150: 57, on trials
Dim: 30.4 (27.43 pp) × 7.3 × 2.15 **Man:** 22 men
A: 1/40-mm — 1/20-mm AA — 8/SS-12 missiles (IV × 2)
M: 2 Rolls-Royce gas turbines; for cruising at 10 kts, 2 General Motors V-71 diesels; 12,750 hp
Fuel: 25 tons

REMARKS: Quarters air-conditioned. Can be armed with torpedoes or fitted as minelayers (10). Equipped with SS-12 missiles in 1972.

♦ *24 103-foot Vosper type* — Bldr: Vosper Ltd., Portsmouth

Ordered in September 1961

P 3138 SRI KEDAH (4-6-62)
P 3139 SRI SELANGOR (17-7-62)
P 3140 SRI PERAK (30-8-62)
P 3141 SRI PAHANG (15-10-62)
P 3142 SRI KELANTAN (8-1-63)
P 3143 SRI TRENGGANU (12-12-62)

Ordered in March 1963

P 3114 SRI SABAH (30-12-63)
P 3145 SRI SARAWAK (20-1-64)
P 3146 SRI NEGRI SEMBILAN (17-9-64)
P 3147 SRI MELAKA (25-2-64)

Ordered in 1965

P 34 KRIS (11-3-66)
P 36 SUNDANG (22-5-66)
P 37 BADEK (8-5-66)
P 38 RENCHONG (22-6-66)
P 39 TOMBAK (20-6-66)
P 40 LEMBING (22-8-66)
P 41 SERAMPANG (15-9-66)
P 42 PANAH (10-10-66)
P 43 KERAMBIT (20-11-66)
P 44 BALADAU (11-1-67)
P 45 KELEWANG (31-1-67)
P 46 RENTAKA (15-3-67)
P 47 SRI PERLIS (26-5-67)
P 48 SRI JOHORE (21-8-67)

Sri Kedah (P 3138)

D: 96 tons (109 fl) **Dim:** 31.39 × 5.95 × 1.65
S: 27 kts (23 cruising) **Man:** 3 officers, 20 men
A: 2/40-mm (I × 2) — 2 machine guns **Range:** 1,500/17.5
M: 2 Bristol-Siddeley or Maybach MD 655/18 diesels; 2 props; 3,550 hp

REMARKS: Vosper anti-rolling stabilizers. Decca radar. Welded hull. The Malaysian prototype was delivered in February 1963 and was quickly followed by many others. Patrol boats of this type are found in the navies of Peru, Kenya, Libya, Singapore, and Trinidad and Tobago. They differ somewhat according to the engines installed — Maybach, Davey-Paxman or Napier-Deltic. Those of Peru and Singapore are 110 feet instead of 103. This type of Vosper patrol boat has been produced by several other British shipbuilders, such as Brooke Marine, who built similar ships for Pakistan.

MINE WARFARE SHIPS

♦ *6 British "-ton"-class coastal minesweepers*

Transferred: 1963-65

M 1127 MAHAMIRU (ex-*Darlaston*) (25-9-53)
M 1143 LEDANG (ex-*Keston*) (1954)
M 1134 KINABALU (ex-*Essington*) (9-54)
M 1163 TAHAN (ex-*Lullington*) (31-8-55)
M 1168 JERAI (ex-*Dilston*) (15-11-54)
M 1172 BRINCHANG (ex-*Thankerton*) (4-9-56)

For characteristics, see Great Britain section. **A:** 1/40-mm — 2/20-mm

AMPHIBIOUS WARFARE SHIPS

♦ *3 ex-U.S. LSTs*

N . . . (ex-*Henry County*, LST-824)
N . . . (ex-*Sedgwick County*, LST-1123)
A 1500 SRI LANGKAWI (ex-*Sutter County*, LST-1150)

D: 1,653 tons (4,080 fl) **S:** 11 kts **Dim:** 99.85 × 15.25 × 4.36
A: 8/40-mm AA (II × 2, I × 4) **M:** GM diesels; 2 props; 1,700 hp

REMARK: Transferred in 7-71.

HYDROGRAPHIC SHIP

♦ **A 151 PERANTAU** (ex-HMS *Myrmidon*)

D: 360 tons (420 fl) **S:** 15 kts **Dim:** 46.33 × 8.75 × 2.5
M: 2 diesels **Man:** 26 men **Range:** 2,300/13

REMARK: Former "-ton"-class minesweeper modified as a hydrographic ship in 1964.

VARIOUS SHIPS

♦ *1 support ship for divers*

DUYONG (18-8-71)

D: 140 tons (fl) **S:** 10 kts **Dim:** 33.0 × 6.3 × 1.7
A: 1/20-mm AA **Man:** 23 men **M:** 2 Cummins diesels; 500 hp

♦ *6 police small boats built in Malaysia with the assistance of the Lürssen shipyards*

♦ *18 PX-type police boats*

ARAU, BENTARA, HULUBULANG, KELANG, KUALA KANGSAR, LAKSAMANA, MAHAKOTA, MAHARAJASETIA, MAHARAJALELA, PAHLAWAN, PEKAN, PERTANDA, PERWIRA, SANGSETIA, SHAHBANDAR, SRI GUMANTONG, SRI LABUAN, TEMENGGONG

D: 80 tons **S:** 29 kts **Dim:** 26.29 × 5.7 × 1.45
A: 2/20-mm **Man:** 15 men **Range:** 700/15
M: 2 Mercedes-Benz diesels; 2 props; 2,700 hp

MALAYSIA *(continued)*

VARIOUS SHIPS *(continued)*

PX 10 and PX 11 1975

♦ *6 improved PX*

ALOR STAR, JOHORE BAHRU, KOTA BAHRU, KUALA TRENGGANU, KUCHING, SRI MENANTI

D: 92 tons **S:** 25 kts **Dim:** 27.3 × 5.8 × . . .
A: 2/20-mm **Man:** 18 men **Range:** 750/15
M: 2 diesels; 2,460 hp

REMARKS: The PX and improved PX boats were built between 1963 and 1970 and between 1972 and 1973 by the Vosper shipyards of Singapore.

MALTA

MERCHANT MARINE (1976): 32 ships — 39,140 grt (1 tanker — 18,324 grt)

♦ *2 ex-U.S. Swift-class PCF* — Bldr: Sewart Seacraft, 1967

Transferred: 1-1971

C 23 and **C 24**

D: 22.5 tons (fl) **S:** 25 kts **Dim:** 15.6 × 4.12 × 1.5
Range: 24 to 36 hours **Man:** 6-8 men
A: 3/12.7-mm machine guns (II × 1 and 1 combined with an 81-mm mortar)
M: General Motors 12-V-71T diesels; 2 props; 960 hp

♦ *1 ex-customs service craft* — Bldr: Malta Drydock, 1969

Acquired 1973

C 21

C 21

D: 20 tons **S:** 19 kts **Dim:** 16.3 × 4.1 × 2.3 (light)
A: 2 mounts for machine guns **Man:** 8 men
M: 2 Fiat 521-SH diesels; 2 props; 500 hp

♦ *3 ex-German craft used on border patrol*

C 27 (ex-*Brunsbüttel* 1)	**D:** 95 tons	**Dim:** 31.7 × 5.18 × . . .
C 28 (ex-*Geier*)	**D:** 90 tons	**Dim:** 28 × 5.49 × . . .
C 29 (ex-*Kondor*)	**D:** 85 tons	**Dim:** 28 × 5.25 × . . .

A: 1 machine gun **M:** Diesels (added in 1972)

C 27

♦ *2 small support craft (ex-Libyan 1967-68) acquired in 1974*

No other information.

Personnel: 200 men

Merchant Marine (1976): 4 ships — 1,113 grt

PATROL BOATS AND CRAFT

♦ *2 ex-Soviet Mirnyi-class whaling ships* — Bldr: Ivan Nosenko, Nikolaev, 1956

IDINI **BOULANOUAR**

Idini 1975

D: 1,200 tons **S:** 17.5 kts **Dim:** 63.6 × 9.5 × 4.5
A: 2/25-mm AA (II × 1) — 1/12.7-mm machine gun
M: 4 Penza 6-cyl. diesel-electric engines; 3,100 hp

Remark: Used for fisheries protection and as tenders for the *Tichitt* class and smaller craft.

♦ *2 Spanish ex-trawlers* — Bldr: Astano, El Ferrol, 1953

N . . . (ex-*Centinela,* W-33) **N . . .** (ex-*Serviola,* W-34)

D: 280 tons (fl) **S:** 12 kts **Dim:** 36.0 × 6.8 × 3.0
A: 2/37-mm **M:** Diesel; 450 hp

♦ *2 Spanish Barcelo class* — Bldr: Bazán, Cadiz

N . . . **N . . .**

D: 139 tons **S:** 40 kts **Dim:** 36.2 × 5.8 × 2.5
A: 1/40-mm — 2/20-mm **Man:** 3 officers, 16 men
M: 2 MTU MD-16 TB-90 diesels; 6,000 hp **Range:** 1,200/17

Remark: Scheduled to be delivered in the spring of 1978.

MAURITANIA

♦ *2 Tichitt-class craft*

	Bldr	In serv.
TICHITT	Estérel NSY	4-69
DAR EL BARKA	Estérel NSY	4-69

Tichitt Ch. de l'Estérel, 1969

D: 80 tons (fl) **S:** 28 kts **Dim:** 31.45 × 5.75 × 1.7
A: 1/20-mm — 1/12.7-mm machine gun **Range:** 1,500/15
M: 2 Maybach-Mercedes diesels; 2,700 hp

Remark: Identical to the Tunisian *Istiklal* and the Moroccan *El Sabiq* classes of patrol craft.

♦ *2 security craft*

	Bldr	In serv.
IMRAG'NI	Estérel NSY	11-65
SLOUGHI	Estérel NSY	5-68

D: 20 tons (fl) **S:** 21 kts (22.7 trials)
Dim: 18.15 (17.03 pp) × 4.03 × 1.1 **Man:** 8 men
A: 1/12.7-mm machine gun **Range:** 860/12
M: General Motors 7-71-M diesels; 2 props; 512 hp

♦ *1 coastal patrol craft*

CHINGUETTI

Remark: Practically inoperative. Used as a support ship.

MAURITIUS

Merchant Marine (1976): 32 ships — 39,140 grt

♦ *1 ex-Indian Ajay-class patrol boat* — Bldr: Calcutta, 1961

N . . . (ex-*Amar*)

D: 120 tons (160 fl) **Dim:** 35.7 (33.52 pp) × 6.1 × 1.5
S: 18 kts **A:** 1/40-mm **M:** 2 diesels

1976

MEXICO

Personnel: 11,000 men, including 1,300 Marines

Merchant Marine (1976): 290 ships — 593,875 grt
(tankers: 26 ships — 305,515 grt)

Maritime Aviation: Approximately 20 aircraft (helicopters and flying boats)

DESTROYERS

♦ *2 ex-U.S. Fletcher class*

Transferred: 8-70

	Bldr	L
F 1 CUITLAHUAC (ex-*John Rodgers*, DD-574)	Consolidated Steel	7-5-43
F 2 CUAUHTEMOC (ex-*Harrison*, DD-573)	Consolidated Steel	7-5-43

D: 2,050 tons (2,850 fl) **Dim:** 114.85 (wl) × 12.03 × 5.5
S: 30 kts **Man:** 262 men **Range:** 1,260/30, 4,400/15
A: 5/127-mm (I × 5) — 14/40-mm — 5/533-mm TT (V × 1) — 2 hedgehogs
M: General Electric GT; 2 props; 60,000 hp
Boilers: 4 Babcock & Wilcox **Fuel:** 650 tons

FRIGATES

♦ **A 06 MANUEL AZUETA** (ex-*Hurst*, DE-250)

Bldr: Brown SB, Houston, Texas — Transferred: 1-10-73

D: 1,200 tons (1,850 fl) **S:** 21 kts **Dim:** 93.3 × 11.3 × 3.4
A: 3/76-mm AA — 2 hedgehogs — 2 depth-charge racks
M: 4 diesels; 2 props; 6,000 hp

♦ *4 ex-U.S. amphibious transports*

	L
B 5 TEHUANTEPEC (ex-*Begor*, APD-127, ex-DE-711)	5-2-44
B 6 USUMACINTA (ex-*Don O. Woods*, APD-118, ex-DE-721)	19-2-44
B 7 COAHMUILA (ex-*Barber*, APD-57)	20-5-43
B 8 CHIHUAHUA (ex-*Rednour*, ADP-102)	12-2-44

Transferred: 1964 and 1970

California (B 3)

D: 1,450 tons (2,130 fl) **Dim:** 93.26 × 11.28 × 4.7
S: 23 kts (fl) **Man:** 204 men, 162 military
A: 1/127-mm (fwd) — 6/40-mm AA (II × 3) **Range:** 5,000/15
M: Turbo-electric propulsion; 2 boilers; 2 props; 12,000 hp

Remarks: Modified destroyer escorts. The *California* (B-3, ex-*Belet*, APD-109) was lost at sea in 1972, and the *Papaloapan* (B-4) was lost in 1976.

PATROL BOATS

♦ *17 ex-U.S. minesweepers* — Bldr: U.S.A., 1943-44

ID 1 DM 01 (ex-MSF-255)
ID 2 DM 02 (ex-MSF-241)
ID 3 DM 03 (ex-MSF-232)
ID 4 DM 04 (ex-MSF-306)
ID 5 DM 05 (ex-MSF-298)
ID 6 DM 06 (ex-MSF-224)
ID 0 DM 10 (ex-MSF-252)
ID 11 DM 11 (ex-MSF-220)
IE 2 DM 12 (ex-MSF-283)
IE 3 DM 13 (ex-MSF-256)
IE 4 DM 14 (ex-MSF-284)
IE 5 DM 15 (ex-MSF-214)
IE 6 DM 16 (ex-MSF-223)
IE 7 DM 17 (ex-MSF-221)
IE 8 DM 18 (ex-MSF-254)
IE 9 DM 19 (ex-MSF-253)
IE 10 DM 20 (ex-MSF-365)

Transferred: Since 1-10-62

ID 3

D: 650 tons (945 fl) **S:** 15 kts **Dim:** 56.24 × 10.06 × 2.8
A: 1/76-mm AA — 2/40-mm AA — 4 to 6/20-mm AA
Man: 80-104 men **Fuel:** Diesel
M: 2 General Motors diesels; 2 props; 1,700/1,800 hp

♦ *18 ex-U.S. Auk/Raven-class minesweepers* — Bldr: U.S.A., 1942-45

IG 01 LEANDRO VALLE (ex-*Pioneer*, MSF-105)
IG 02 GUILLERMO PRIETO (ex-*Symbol*, MSF-123)
IG 03 MARIANO ESCOBEDO (ex-*Champion*, MSF-314)
IG 04 PONCIANO ARRIAGA (ex-*Competent*, MSF-316)
IG 05 MANUEL DOBLADO (ex-*Defense*, MSF-317)
IG 06 SEBASTIAN LEIDO DE TEJADA (ex-*Devastator*, MSF-318)
IG 07 SANTOS DEGOLLADO (ex-*Gladiator*, MSF-319)
IG 08 IGNACIO DE LA LLAVE (ex-*Spear*, MSF-322)
IG 09 JUAN N. ALVAREZ (ex-*Ardent*, MSF-340)
IG 10 MELCHIOR OCAMPO (ex-*Roselle*, MSF-379)
IG 11 VALENTIN G. FARIAS (ex-*Starling*, MSF-64)
IG 12 IGNACIO ALTAMIRANO (ex-*Sway*, MSF-120)
IG 13 FRANCISCO ZARCO (ex-*Threat*, MSF-124)
IG 14 IGNACIO L. VALLARTA (ex-*Velocity*, MSF-128)
IG 15 JÉSUS G. ORTEGA (ex-*Chief*, MSF-315)
IG 16 GUTIERRIEZ ZAMORA (ex-*Seater*, MSF-381)
IG 18 JUAN ALDARMA (ex-*Pilot*, MSF-104)
IG 19 HERMENEGILDO GALEANA (ex-*Sage*, MSF-111)

Transferred: 1972 and 1973

D: 890 tons (1,250 fl) **Dim:** 67.4 (65 pp) × 9.75 × 4.1
S: 16/15 kts **Man:** 9 officers, 86 men
A: 1/76-mm — 4/40-mm AA (II × 2) — 4/20-mm (II × 2)
M: Diesel-electric propulsion: 2 General Motors diesels; 2 props, 3,500 hp

♦ *22 Azteca class*

	Bldr	In serv.
P 01 ANDRES QUINTANA ROO	Ailsa	1-11-74
P 02 MATIAS DE CORDOVA	Scott	22-10-74
P 03 MIGUEL RAMOS ARIZPE	Ailsa	23-12-74
P 04 JOSÉ MARIA IZAZAGO	Ailsa	19-12-74
P 05 JUAN BAUTISTA MORALES	Scott	19-12-74
P 06 IGNACIO LOPEZ RAYON	Ailsa	19-12-74
P 07 MANUEL CRESCENCIO REJON	Ailsa	4-7-75
P 08 ANTONIO DE LA FUENTE	Ailsa	4-7-75
P 09 LEON GUZMAN	Scott	7-4-75
P 10 IGNACIO RAMIREZ	Ailsa	17-7-75
P 11 IGNACIO MARISCAL	Ailsa	23-9-75
P 12 HERIBERTO JARA CORONA	Ailsa	7-11-75
P 13 JOSÉ MARIA MATA	Lamont	13-10-75
P 14 FELIX ROMERO	Scott	23-6-75
P 15 FERNANDO LIZARDI	Ailsa	12-75
P 16 FRANCISCO J. MUJICA	Ailsa	12-75
P 17 PASTOR ROUAIX JOSÉ MARIA	Scott	7-11-75
P 18 DEL CASTILLO VELASCO	Lamont	14-1-75
P 19 LUIS MANUEL ROJAS	Lamont	6-76
P 20 JOSÉ NATIVIDAD MACIAS	Lamont	6-76
P 21 ESTEBAN BACA CALDERON	Lamont	. . .
P 22 IGNACIO ZARAGOZA	Vera Cruz	6-76

Andres Quintana Roo (P 01) 1975

MEXICO (*continued*)

PATROL BOATS (*continued*)

D: 130 tons **S:** 24 kts **Dim:** 34.06 (30.94 pp) × 8.6 × 2.0
A: 1/40-mm — 1/20-mm **Man:** 2 officers, 22 men **Electric:** 80 kw
M: 2 Ruston-Paxman-Ventura 12-cyl. diesels; 7,200 hp

REMARK: At least ten more will be built in Mexico.

♦ **G 6 VILLAPANDO** (1960) **G 9 AZUETA** (8-59) — Bldr: Astilleros, Tampico

D: 80 tons (85 fl) **S:** 12/10 kts **Dim:** 26.0 × 4.9 × 2.5
A: 2/13-mm machine guns (II × 1) **M:** 1 Superior diesel; 600 hp

♦ **G 1** to **G 4 POLIMAR 1, 2, 3, 4** (1960-68) — Bldr: Astilleros, Tampico

Polimar (G 1)

D: 57 tons **S:** 16 kts **Dim:** 20.5 × 4.5 × 1.3
M: Diesel; 2 props; 450 hp

♦ *7 river patrol boats*

AM 4, AM 5, AM 6, AM 7, AM 8, AM 9, AM 10 (1960-62) — Bldr: Astilleros Tampico and Vera Cruz

D: 35 tons **S:** 10 kts **M:** Diesel

AMPHIBIOUS WARFARE SHIPS

♦ *2 ex-U.S. LSTs*

Transferred: 1971 and 1972

RIO PANUCO (ex-*Park County*, LST-1077)
RIO MANZANILLO (ex-*Clearwater County*, LST-602)

D: 4,080 tons (fl) **S:** 11 kts **Dim:** 100.04 × 15.24 × 4.3
M: General Motors diesels; 2 props; 1,800 hp

AUXILIARY SHIPS

♦ *2 small oilers*

A 5 AGUASCALIENTES (ex-YOG-6) **A 6 TLAXCALA** (ex-YO-107)

D: 440 tons (1,800 fl) **S:** 8 kts **Dim:** 52.5 × 10.0 × 4.0
M: Fairbanks-Morse diesel; 1 prop; 500 hp **Man:** 62 men

REMARK: Ex-U.S. motorized water barges, bought in 1964.

♦ *1 ex-U.S. repair ship, bought in 10-73*

VICENTE GUERRERO (ex-*Megata*, ARV-6)

D: 1,625 tons (4,100 fl) **S:** 11.6 kts **Dim:** 98.4 × 15.0 × 4.2
A: 8/40-mm AA **M:** 2 General Motors diesels; 2 props; 1,800 hp

♦ *1 transport*

B 2 ZACATECAS — Bldr: Ulua, Vera Cruz, 1959

D: 780 tons **S:** 10 kts **Dim:** 47.5 × 8.2 × 2.8
A: 1/40-mm AA — 2/20-mm AA **Man:** 50 men
M: M.A.N. diesel; 1 prop; 560 hp

♦ *4 ex-U.S. tugs transferred in 1971*

R 1 (ex-*Farallon*), **R 2** (ex-*Montauk*), **R 3** (ex-*Point Vicente*), **R 5** (ex-*Burnt Island*)

♦ *2 tugs acquired in 1973*

PRAGMAR **PATRON**

♦ *1 ex-U.S. drydock*

N . . . (ex-ARD-11)

REMARK: Transferred 17-6-74.

MOROCCO

PERSONNEL: 1,800 men, including 58 officers and 260 petty officers

MERCHANT MARINE (1976): 67 ships — 136,596 grt
(tankers: 3 ships — 2,536 grt)

PATROL BOATS

♦ *2 PR 72 type*

	L	In serv.
OKBA	10-10-75	12-76
TRIKI	2-2-76	2-77

Okba S.F.C.N., 1976

PATROL BOATS (*continued*)

D: 370 tons (440 fl) **S:** 28 kts **Dim:** 57.0 (54 pp) × 7.6 × 2.5
A: 1/76-mm OTO Melara — 1/40-mm Bofors **Man:** 5 officers, 48 men
Range: 2,500/16 **Electric:** 360 kw
M: 2 AGO diesels; 2 props; 2,760 hp

REMARKS: Ordered in 6-73 from the Societé Française de Construction Navale (ex-C.N. Franco-Belges). The second might be equipped with SSM.

♦ *1 boat based on French Fougueux class* — Bldr: Constr. Méc. de Normandie

	Laid down	L	In serv.
32 LIEUTENANT RIFFI	5-63	1-3-64	5-64

D: 311 tons (light) (374 fl) **Dim:** 52.95 (51.82 pp) × 7.04 × 2.01
S: 19 kts **Man:** 4 officers, 55 men
Range: 2,000/15, 3,000/12
A: 1/76-mm — 2/40-mm — 2 depth-charge projectors
M: 2 SEMT-Pielstick diesels; 2 KMW-CMN variable-pitch props; 3,600 hp

♦ *1 Al Bachir class* — Bldr: Constr. Méc. de Normandie

	Laid down	L	In serv.
22 AL BACHIR	6-65	25-2-67	4-67

Al Bachir, wearing old number

D: 124.5 tons (light) (153.50 fl) **Dim:** 40.6 (38 pp) × 6.35 × 1.4
S: 25.5 kts **Man:** 3 officers, 20 men
A: 2/40-mm — 2 machine guns **Range:** 2,000/15
M: 2 SEMT-Pielstick 12 PA diesels; 2 props; 3,600 hp **Fuel:** 21 tons

♦ *1 El Sabiq class*

	Bldr	L	Transferred
11 EL SABIQ (ex-P-762, VC-12)	Estérel NSY	13-8-57	1960

D: 60 tons (80 fl) **S:** 28 kts **Dim:** 31.77 × 4.7 × 1.7
A: 2/20-mm AA **Man:** 17 men **Range:** 1,500/15
M: 2 Mercedes-Benz diesels, 4 tons, 12-cyl; 2 props; 2,700 hp

REMARK: For profile, see the *Istiklal* in the Tunisian section.

♦ *6 type P-92* — Bldr: C.M.N. Cherbourg (contract 2-74)

	L	In serv.		L	In serv.
EL WACIL	12-6-75	9-10-75	**EL KHAFIR**	21-1-76	16-4-76
EL JAIL	10-10-75	3-12-75	**EL HARIS**	31-3-76	30-6-76
EL MIKDAM	1-12-75	30-1-76	**ESSAHIR**	2-6-76	16-7-76

El Wacil CMN, 1975

D: 89 tons **S:** 28 kts **Dim:** 32.0 × 4.7 × 1.7
A: 2/20-mm AA **Range:** 1,200/15
M: 2 M GO 12 V BZSHR diesels; 1,270 hp

REMARKS: Laminated-wood hull. One Decca radar. One fathometer.

MINESWEEPER

♦ **TAWFIC** (ex-*Aries*)

REMARK: Loaned by the French Navy 28-11-74 for a period of four years.

AMPHIBIOUS WARFARE SHIPS

♦ *3 LSMs based on French Champlain class* — Bldr: Dubigeon, Normandy

	In serv.
DAOUD BEN AICHA	5-77
AHMED ES SAKALI	9-77
ABOU ABDALLAH EL AYACHI	3-78

D: 1,305 tons **S:** . . . **Dim:** 80 × . . . × . . .
A: 2/40-mm AA (I × 2) — 1/81-mm mortar **Man:** 30 officers, 54 men
M: . . . **Range:** 3,500/13

REMARK: The *Daoud Ben Aicha* was commissioned 28-5-77 at Brest.

♦ *1 LSM based on French EDIC*

21 LIEUTENANT MALGHAGH — Bldr: C.N. Franco-Belges — In serv: 1965

D: 292 tons (642 fl) **S:** 8 kts **Dim:** 59.0 × 11.95 × 1.3
A: 2/20-mm AA — 1/120-mm mortar (fwd) **Man:** 16 men
M: MGO diesels; 2 props; 1,000 hp

TRAINING SHIP

♦ **ESSAOUIRA**

D: 60 tons

REMARK: Yacht presented by Italy in 1967, and used for training watchstanders.

PERSONNEL: Approximately 18,000 men, including 3,000 Marines

MERCHANT MARINE (1976): 1,325 ships — 5,919,892 grt
(tankers: 101 ships — 2,845,142 grt)

NAVAL AVIATION: The Navy has approximately 80 aircraft, P2-H Neptune, BR-1150 Atlantic, and S2-A Tracker antisubmarine patrol planes, Westland Lynx and Wasp helicopters, the latter two carried on board the *Kortenaer* and *Van Speijk*-class frigates. Support aircraft such as the UH-1 Bell helicopters and others of various types are included in this total.

WARSHIPS IN SERVICE OR UNDER CONSTRUCTION OR AUTHORIZED AS OF 1 OCTOBER 1977

	L	Tons (surfaced)	Main armament
♦ *6 submarines*			
2 ZWAARDVIS	1970–71	2,300	6 TT
4 DOLFIJN	1959–60	1,140	8 TT
		Tons	
♦ *12 destroyers*			
2 TROMP	1973–74	3,665	1 Tartar missile launcher, 8 Harpoon, 8 Sea Sparrow, 2/120-mm, 6 TT, 1 ASW helicopter
8 FRIESLAND	1953–56	2,406	4/120-mm AA — ASW weapons
2 HOLLAND	1953	2,215	4/120-mm AA — ASW weapons
♦ *18 frigates*			
12 KORTENAER	1976–	3,600	8 Harpoon, 8 Sea Sparrow, 2/76-mm AA, 6 TT
6 VAN SPEIJK	1965–67	2,200	8 Sea Cat, 2/114-mm, ASW weapons
♦ *11 corvettes*			
6 WOLF	1954	808	1/76-mm AA
5 BALDER	1954	150	1/40-mm AA

WEAPONS AND SYSTEMS

(A) MISSILES

surface-to-air

U.S. SM-1 on the *Tromp*-class destroyers.
U.S. Sea Sparrow and Harpoon on the *Tromp*-class destroyers and *Kortenaer*-class frigates.
British Sea Cat on the *Van Speijk*-class frigates.

(B) GUNS

120-mm twin-barreled automatic in the *Friesland*- and *Holland*-class destroyers:
Weight: 65 tons
Arc of elevation: 10° to +85°
Muzzle velocity: 850 m/sec.
Direction rate: 25°/s in train, 40°/s in elevation
Rate of fire: 45 rounds/min/barrel
Maximum effective range in surface fire: 13,000 m
Maximum effective range in anti-aircraft fire: 7,000 m

NETHERLANDS

114-mm Mk 6 (see section on Great Britain) on the *Van Speijk*-class frigates
76-mm OTO Melara Compact
40-mm Bofors automatic

(C) ANTISUBMARINE WEAPONS

375-mm Bofors quadruple rocket launchers
U.S. Mk 44 and Mk 46 torpedoes on ships and aircraft

(D) RADARS

LWO-1: height-finding
LWO-2: long-range, air-search
LWO-6: long-range, air-search
SGR-103: surface search
SGR-105: combination search
M-20 HSA, band X type: fire-control

All of the above are of Dutch manufacture (HSA). The *Tromp*-class destroyers are fitted with a new type of three-dimensional radar.

(E) SONARS

CWE-610, LF: hull
PDE-700, LF: towed

Both of the above are of Dutch design and manufactured in the U.S. British 170-B and 162 are also used.

(F) DATA PROCESSING

Sewaco, a system built by Hollandse Signaal Apparaaten (a subsidiary of Philips) and centrally directed by a digital computer.

SUBMARINES

♦ *2 Zwaardvis class*

Ordered: 24-12-65 and 14-7-66

	Bldr	Laid down	L	In serv.
S 806 ZWAARDVIS	Rotterdam DDM	7-67	2-7-70	1972
S 807 TIJGERHAAI	Rotterdam DDM	7-67	25-5-71	1972

Tijgerhaai (S 807) 1973

SUBMARINES (*continued*)

D: 2,300 tons surfaced, 2,572 submerged — **Dim:** 66.9 × 8.4 × 8.0
S: 15/18 kts — **Man:** 8 officers, 60 men
A: 6/533-mm TT fwd — 12 torpedoes
M: Diesel-electric propulsion; 1 prop linked to 3 diesel generators of 900 kw each, and 1 3,800-kw motor

REMARKS: In general, these submarines are based on the U.S. Navy's diesel-electric *Barbel,* which has a teardrop hull design. For economic reasons, equipment of Dutch manufacture was used and this necessitated some rather important modifications to the original design. These ships can carry 18 torpedoes. The torpedo-firing system uses a digital computer that permits the simultaneous launching of two torpedoes, one of which may be wire-guided. All noise-producing machinery is mounted on a false deck with spring suspension for silent running.

♦ *4 Dolfijn class*

	Bldr	Laid down	L	In serv.
S 804 POTVIS	Wilton-Fijenoord	17-9-62	12-1-65	11-65
S 805 TONIJN	Wilton-Fijenoord	28-11-62	14-6-65	2-66
S 808 DOLFIJN	Rotterdam DDM	12-54	20-5-59	12-60
S 809 ZEEHOND	Rotterdam DDM	12-54	20-2-60	3-61

Authorized: S-804 and S-805 in 1962, S-808 and S-809 in 1949

Tonijn (S 805) 1968

Dolfijn (S 808) 1974

D: 1,140 tons, 1,494 surfaced, 1,826 submerged — **Dim:** 79.5 × 8.84 × 4.8
S: 14.5/17 kts — **Man:** 7 officers, 57 men
A: 8/533-mm TT
M: Diesel-electric propulsion; 2 M.A.N. 12-cyl. diesels, 1,550 hp each; 2 electric motors; 2 props; 2,200 hp

REMARKS: Profile and sail similar to the U.S. *Guppy* class. Designed by M. T. Gunning; the thick hull is made up of an exterior hull and three parallel interior pressure cylinders: one is placed on top of a pair of slightly shorter ones. The crew and the armament occupy the top cylinder, and the batteries and diesel engines are mounted in the other two.

DESTROYERS

♦ *2 Tromp class* — Bldr: Kon. Mij. De Schelde, Flushing

	Laid down	L	In serv.
F 801 TROMP	8-71	2-6-73	1975
F 806 DE RUYTER (ex-*Heemskerck*)	1-71	9-3-74	1975

D: 3,665 tons (4,300 fl) — **Dim:** 138.6 (131 pp) × 14.8 × 4.6
S: 28 kts — **Man:** 34 officers, 267 men

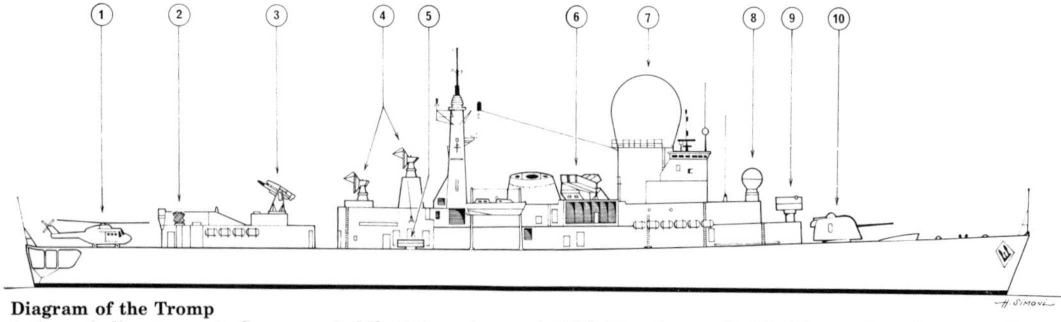

Scale 1/1000

Diagram of the Tromp
1: Lynx helicopter — 2: Corvus — 3: Mk 13 launcher — 4: SPG 51 radars — 5: Mk 32 torpedo tubes — 6: Harpoon launchers — 7: 3 D radar — 8: M 25 fire control radar — 9: Sea Sparrow system — 10: 120-mm mount.

DESTROYERS *(continued)*

Tromp (F 801) 1976

Tromp (F 801) 1976

Tromp (F 801)

A: 8 Harpoon missiles — 1 Tartar Mk 13 missile launcher aft (I × 1, 40 SM-1 missiles) — 8 Sea Sparrow (VIII × 1, 60 missiles) — 2/120-mm Bofors DP (II × 1) — 6/324-mm ASW Mk 32 TT (III × 2) — WG-13 Lynx ASW helicopter

Electron Equipt: Radars: 1 3-D, 2 Decca, 1 M-25, 2 SPG-51
Sonars: 1 CWE-610, 1 162. 2 Knebworth Corvus. Sewaco system

M: COGOG propulsion: 2 Rolls-Royce Olympus gas turbines, 27,000 hp each; 2 Tyne gas turbines, 4,100 hp each, for economical cruising (18 kts); 2 reversible-pitch props; 54,000 hp

Range: 5,000/18 **Electric:** 4,000 kw

REMARKS: Although the Dutch Navy designates them as frigates, these ships are more closely related to guided-missile destroyers, by virtue of their armament. They are equipped with stabilizers and have excellent sea-keeping qualities.

♦ *8 Friesland class (47-B type)*

Authorized: 2 in 1947, 6 in 1949

	Bldr	Laid down	L	In serv.
D 812 FRIESLAND	Nederlandsche DSM	17-12-51	21-2-53	3-56
D 813 GRONINGEN	Nederlandsche DSM	4-2-52	9-1-54	9-56
D 814 LIMBURG	Kon. Mij. De Schelde	28-11-53	5-9-55	10-56

DESTROYERS (*continued*)

D 815 OVERIJSSEL	Wilton-Fijenoord	15-10-53	8-7-56	10-57
D 816 DRENTHE	Nederlandsche DSM	9-1-54	26-3-55	8-57
D 817 UTRECHT	Kon. Mij. De Schelde	15-2-54	2-6-56	10-57
D 818 ROTTERDAM	Rotterdam DDM	7-4-54	26-1-56	2-57
D 819 AMSTERDAM	Nederlandsche DSM	26-3-55	25-8-56	4-58

Friesland (D 812)

Limburg (D 814) G. Arra, 1976

D: 2,406 tons (3,150 fl) **S:** 36 kts (trials: up to 42.8)
Dim: 116.0 × 11.77 × 5.1 (light) **Man:** 280 men
A: 4/120-mm AA (II × 2) — 4/40-mm AA (I × 4) — 2 Bofors rocket launchers — 1 depth-charge rack
Electron Equipt: Radars: 1 LWO-2, 1 SGR-105, 1 SGR-103, 3 HSA band X for fire control
Sonars: 1 170-B, 1 CWE-610 (?), 1 162
M: Parsons GT; 3 Babcock boilers; 2 props; 60,000 hp
Range: 4,000/18 **Electric:** 1,350 kw

REMARK: Same building program as the *Holland* class, of which they are an improved version.

Drenthe (D 816) G. Arra, 1972

♦ *2 Holland class (47-A type)*

Authorized: 1947

	Laid down	L	In serv.
D 808 HOLLAND	21-4-50	11-4-53	12-54
D 809 ZEELAND	12-1-51	27-6-53	3-55

Zeeland Terzibaschitsch, 1968

Bldrs: D-808: Rotterdam DDM — D-809: Kon. Mij. De Schelde

D: 2,215 tons (2,765 fl) **S:** 32 kts (trials: up to 40.3)
Dim: 111.3 × 11.3 × 4.86 (light) **Man:** 247 men
A: 4/120-mm (II × 2) — 1/40-mm — 2 Bofors rocket launchers — 1 depth-charge rack

DESTROYERS *(continued)*

Electron Equipt: Radars: 1 LWO 2, 1 SGR 105, 1 SGR 103, 3 HSA band X for fire control
Sonars: 1 170-B, 1 CWE-610 (?), 1 162
M: Parsons GT; 2 props; 45,000 hp **Boilers:** 4 Babcock, 28 kg/cm^2
Electric: 1,350 kw **Range:** 4,000/18

REMARKS: The 45,000-hp engines were ordered in 1939 by the Germans for the *Gerard Callenburg*, T-61, series of destroyers, which was never built. The *Nord Brabant* (D-810) was scrapped following severe damage suffered in a collision on 19-1-74. The *Gelderland* (D-811), her guns and radars removed, is now a school ship at Den Helder.

FRIGATES

♦ *8 Kortenaer class* — Bldr: Kon. Mij. De Schelde, Flushing

	L		L
F 807 KORTENAER	18-12-76	**F 811 PIET HEIN**	. . .
F 808 CALLENBURGH	3-77	**F 812 PIETER FLORISZ**	. . .
F 809 VAN KINSBERGEN	16-4-77	**F 813 WITTE DE WITH**	. . .
F 810 BANCKERT	. . .	**F 816 ABRAHAM CRIJNSSEN**	. . .

D: 3,600 tons **S:** 30 kts **Dim:** 121.8 × 14.8 × . . .
Man: 185 men **Range:** 4,000/18
A: 8 Harpoon missiles — 8 Sea Sparrow (VIII × 1) — 1 or 2/76-mm AA OTO Melara — 2/35-mm AA (II × 1) — 6/324-mm MK 32 ASW TT (III × 2) — 2 WG-13 Lynx ASW helicopters
Electron Equipt: Radars: 1 ZWO-6 navigation, 1 DO surface-search, 1 WW-25 fire-control, 1 LWO-8. 2 Knebworth Corvus. Sewaco system
M: COGOG propulsion: 2 Rolls-Royce Olympus gas turbines, 27,000 hp each; 2 Tyne gas turbines, 4,100 hp each, for economical cruising; 2 props

Model of a Kortenaer-class frigate

REMARK: Four more to be built. An anti-aircraft version may be ordered.

♦ *6 Van Speijk class*

	Bldr	Laid down	L	In serv.
F 802 VAN SPEIJK	Nederlandsche DSM	10-63	5-3-65	2-67
F 803 VAN GALEN	Kon. Mij. De Schelde	7-63	19-6-65	3-67
F 804 TJERK HIDDES	Nederlandsche DSM	6-64	17-12-65	8-67
F 805 VAN NES	Kon. Mij. De Schelde	7-63	26-3-66	8-67
F 814 ISAAC SWEERS	Nederlandsche DSM	5-65	10-3-67	12-67
F 815 EVERTSEN	Kon. Mij. De Schelde	7-65	18-6-66	5-68

D: 2,200 tons (2,835 fl) **Dim:** 113.58 (109.81 pp) × 12.5 × 4.57 (fl)

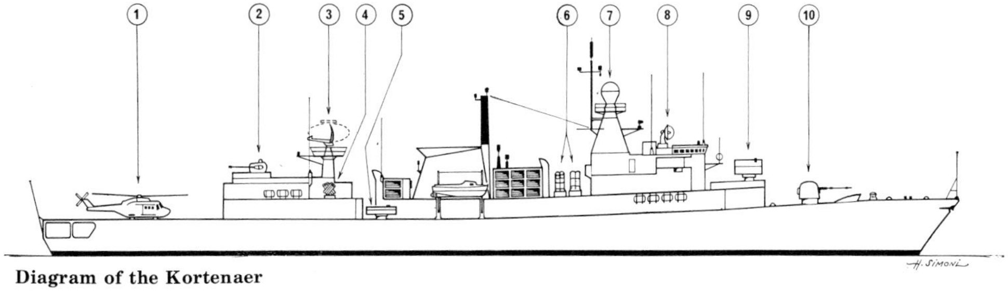

Scale 1/1000

Diagram of the Kortenaer

1: Lynx helicopter — 2: 35-mm AA twin mount — 3: LW 08 radar — 4: Corvus — 5: Mk 32 torpedo tubes — 6: Harpoon launchers — 7: WW 25 fire-control radar — 8: Sea Sparrow system fire-control radar — 9: Sea Sparrow — 10: 76-mm OTO Melara Compact gun.

FRIGATES (*continued*)

Evertsen (F 815) J. C. Bellone, 1974

S: 28.5 kts **Man:** 19 officers, 228 men **Range:** 4,500/12
A: 8 Sea Cat (IV × 2) — 2/114-mm DP Mk 6 (II × 1) — 1 Limbo — 1 Wasp ASW helicopter
Electron Equipt: Radars: 1 Kelvin Hughes, 1 LWO-3, 1 SGR-105
Sonars: 1 CWE-610, 1 170-B, 1 PDE-700, 1 162
M: Double-reduction Werkspoor-English Electric GT; 2 props; 30,000 hp
Boilers: 2 **Electric:** 1,900 kw

REMARKS: Derived from the British *Leander* class with a few modifications and with Dutch electronic equipment. Radar for the 114-mm fire control is an HSA Mk 45, and for the Sea Cat a Mk 44. Between 1977 and 1982, these frigates will be refitted: the 114-mm mount will be replaced by a 76-mm AA OTO Melara Compact; 8 Harpoon missiles will be installed in two launchers, as will new radars and a Sewaco system.

CORVETTES

♦ *6 Wolf class (ex-U.S. submarine chasers, 1952–53)*

	In serv. in Netherlands
F 817 WOLF (ex-PCE-1607)	3-54
F 818 FRET (ex-PCE-1604)	5-54
F 819 HERMELIJN (ex-PCE-1605)	8-54
F 820 VOS (ex-PCE-1606)	12-54
F 821 PANTHER (ex-PCE-1608)	6-54
F 822 JAGUAR (ex-PCE-1609)	6-54

D: 808 tons (945 fl) **S:** 15 kts **Dim:** 56.2 × 10.3 × 2.95
A: 1/76-mm AA — 6/40-mm — 1 hedgehog — 2 depth-charge projectors
M: Diesels; 2 props; 1,600 hp **Man:** 96 men

Vos (F 820)

REMARKS: Built with U.S. "offshore" funds. They are used as fisheries protection vessels. F-821 and F-822 have four 40-mm AA in place of the listed six, and four depth-charge projectors instead of two.

♦ *5 Balder class* — Bldr: Rijkswerf Willemsoord, Den Helder

	Laid down	L	In serv.
P 802 BALDER	8-53	24-2-54	7-54
P 803 BULGIA	10-53	24-4-54	8-54
P 804 FREYR	2-54	17-7-54	12-54
P 805 HADDA	4-54	2-10-54	2-55
P 806 HEFRING	8-54	1-12-54	3-55

Hefring (P 806) S. Terzibaschitsch, 1971

D: 150 tons (170 fl) **Dim:** 36.35 (35 pp) × 6.21 × 1.8
S: 15.5 kts **Man:** 3 officers, 24 men
A: 1/40-mm AA — 3/20-mm AA — 2 mousetrap, fwd (4 ASW rockets) — 2 depth-charge projectors — 1 depth-charge rack, aft
M: Diesels; 2 props; 1,050 hp **Range:** 1,000/13

REMARKS: Built with U.S. "offshore" funds. All but the last two are in reserve.

MINE WARFARE SHIPS

♦ *15 Tripartite-class minehunters*

ALKMAAR	**HELLEVOETSLUIS**	**URK**
DELFZIJL	**MAKKUM**	**VEERE**
DORDRECHT	**MIDDELBURG**	**VLAARDINGEN**
HAARLEM	**SCHEVENINGEN**	**WILLEMSTAD**
HARLINGEN	**SCHIEDAM**	**MAASLUIS**

D: 544 tons (fl) **S:** 15 kts **Dim:** 47.1 (pp) × 8.9 × 2.6
A: 1/20-mm **Range:** 3,000/12 **Man:** 49 men
M: 1 Werkspoor diesel, 1,400 kw; 1 variable-pitch prop; 1 bow thruster; 2 electric maneuvering props
Electric: 750 kw

REMARKS: Hull made of a glass and polyester-resin compound. DUBM 21 sonar; automatic scanning system linked to a digital computer; 2 PAP 104 remote-controlled mine locators, automatic pilot; automatic track-plotter with numerical calculator; Toran and Sydelis radio navigation systems; mechanical drag sweep.

♦ *20 Dokkum-class minesweepers and minehunters* — Bldr: The Netherlands

Coastal minesweepers

M 802 HOOGEZAND	**M 813 OMMEN**	**M 827 HOOGEVEEN**
M 809 NAALDWIJK	**M 815 GIETHOORN**	**M 830 SITTARD**
M 810 ABCOUDE	**M 817 VENLO**	**M 841 GEMERT**
M 812 DRACHTEN	**M 823 NAARDEN**	

Minehunters

M 801 DOKKUM	**M 828 STAPHORST**
M 818 DRUNEN	**M 842 VEERE**

Support ships for underwater demolition

M 806 ROERMOND	**M 820 WOERDEN**	**M 844 RHENEN**
M 807 WALWIJK	**M 822 LEERSUM**	

D: 373 tons (417 fl) **S:** 14 kts **Dim:** 46.62 × 8.78 × 2.28
A: 2/40-mm AA **Man:** 40 men
M: 2 Werkspoor diesel engines; 2 props; 2,500 hp

Dokkum (M 801) 1970

REMARKS: Similar to the French *Sirius* and British "-ton" classes. The highly automated minehunters are equipped with the Arnas system, which displays dropped marker buoys on the radar screen.

♦ *16 Van Straelen-class inshore minesweepers*

	Bldr	Laid down	L	In serv.
M 868 ALBLAS	Noord	2-58	26-9-59	12-3-60
M 869 BUSSEMAKER	DVL	8-58	27-2-60	19-8-60
M 870 LACOMBLE	ASM	9-58	6-2-60	22-8-60
M 871 VAN HAMEL	DVL	4-59	28-5-60	14-10-60
M 872 VAN STRAELEN	ASM	11-58	17-5-60	20-12-60
M 873 VAN MOPPES	Noord	4-59	10-5-60	19-12-60
M 874 CHÖMPFF	Noord	6-59	10-5-60	19-12-60
M 875 VAN WELL GROENEVELD	ASM	12-59	1-10-60	28-4-61
M 876 VAN DER WELL	DVL	5-60	5-61	6-10-61
M 877 VAN VERSENDAAL	Noord	3-61	8-61	11-4-62
M 878 SCHUILING	DVL	6-59	30-6-60	5-4-61
M 879 VAN'T HOFF	Noord	6-60	15-3-61	6-10-61
M 880 MAHU	Noord	6-60	15-3-61	6-10-61
M 881 STAVERMAN	DVL	7-60	7-61	21-2-62
M 882 HOUTEPEN	ASM	9-60	6-61	21-3-62
M 883 ZOMER	ASM	5-60	4-3-61	6-10-61

Bldr: Werf de Noord, Alblasserdam; De Vries-Lentsch, Amsterdam; Arnhem Scheepsbouw Mij.

Van't Hoff (M 879) S. Terzibaschitsch, 1971

D: 151 tons (169 fl) **S:** 13 kts **Dim:** 33.1 × 6.65 × 1.75
A: 1/20-mm AA **Man:** 12 men
M: Werkspoor diesels; 2 props; 1,100 hp

REMARKS: Eight of these ships were built with U.S. "offshore" funds. The Dutch designs differ from the French A.M.I. and the British "-ham" classes. They have wooden hulls. Named for officers, petty officers, and non-rated men who died for their country during World War II.

AMPHIBIOUS WARFARE SHIPS

♦ *11 landing craft (LCA)* — Bldr: Rijkswerf Willemsoord, Den Helder, 1962-64

L 9526

D: 20 tons **S:** 8 kts **M:** 1 diesel; 150 hp

L 9510	**L 9512**	**L 9514**	**L 9517**	**L 9520**
L 9511	**L 9513**	**L 9515**	**L 9518**	**L 9522**

D: 8.5 tons (13.6 fl)
S: 12 kts
Dim: 14.45 × 3.8 × 1.3
M: 1 diesel; 1 Schottel prop; 300 hp

HYDROGRAPHIC SHIPS

♦ *1 Tydeman class* — Bldr: B. V. De Merwede Hardinxveld

	Laid down	L	In serv.
A 906 TYDEMAN	29-4-75	18-12-75	1-9-76

Tydeman (A 906)

D: 3,000 tons **S:** 15 kts **Dim:** 90.0 × 14.4 × 4.75
M: Diesel-electric; 1 prop; 3,690 hp **Man:** 63 men, 15 civilians

Remark: Assigned to civilian and military research.

♦ *2 Blommendal class* — Bldr: Boele S.M., Bolnes

A 904 BUYSKES (11-7-72) **A 905 BLOMMENDAL** (22-11-72)

D: 1,050 tons **S:** 13 kts **Dim:** 59.0 × 11.0 × 3.7
M: Diesel-electric propulsion: 3 engines, 700 hp each **Man:** 45 men

Remark: Helicopter platform.

Buyskes 1973

AUXILIARY SHIPS

♦ *2 oilers*

	Bldr	Laid down	L	In serv.
A 832 ZUIDERKRUIS	Verolme, Alblasserdam	16-7-73	15-10-74	27-6-75

D: 16,910 tons **Dim:** 169.6 × 20.3 × 8.3 (max.)
S: 21 kts **Man:** 17 officers, 26 petty officers, 130 men
A: 4/20-mm AA (II × 2)
Electron Equipt: Radar: 1 navigation. 2 Corvus. **Electric:** 3,000 kw
M: 2 16-cyl. Werkspoor TM 410 diesels, 10,500 hp each; 2 props
Cargo capacity: 9,000 tons fuel, 400 tons TR-5, 200 tons fresh water, spare parts, ammunition

Zuiderkruis (A 832)

AUXILIARY SHIPS (*continued*)

Zuiderkruis refueling Tromp

	Bldr	Laid down	L	In serv.
A 835 POOLSTER	Rotterdam DDM	18-9-62	16-10-63	9-64

Authorized: 1961

Poolster (A 835)

D: 16,800 tons (fl) **S:** 18 kts (trials: 21)
Dim: 168.3 (157 pp) × 20.3 × 8.2 **A:** 2/40-mm AA
M: GT; 1 prop; 22,500 hp
Cargo capacity: 10,300 tons, including 8,000 tons of fuel

REMARKS: Hangar for three HSS-2 helicopters. This replenishment tanker is also a combat supply ship capable of participating effectively in antisubmarine warfare with a hunter/killer group, thanks to her ability to handle five helicopters. These helicopters can, for example, replace a frigate in a screen when the latter has to replenish. The *Poolster* has a wide-scan sonar and depth-charge racks. For short distances, she can carry 300 soldiers as well as her own crew.

♦ *3 supply and command ships (ex-U.S. minesweepers)*

A 855 ONBEVREESD (ex-AM-491) (9-1954)
A 858 ONVERVAARD (ex-AM-482) (3-1955)
A 859 ONVERDROTEN (ex-AM-485) (11-1954)

♦ *2 torpedo-recovery ships*

	Laid down	L	In serv.
A 856 MERCUUR	7-35	26-2-36	7-36

Bldr: Peterson Builders, Wisconsin
D: 735 tons (790 fl) **S:** 15.5 kts **Dim:** 50.3 × 11.0 × 2.1
Man: 70 men **A:** 1/40-mm AA **M:** 2 diesels; 2 props; 1,600 hp

REMARK: Sister to the ships listed above.

A 923 VAN BOCHOVE (1967)
D: 140 tons (fl) **Dim:** 29.8 × 5.53 × 1.8 **M:** 1 diesel; 140 hp

♦ *4 coastal tugs*

A 870 WAMANDAI (1959-61)
D: 155 tons (185 fl) **S:** 10.5 kts **M:** 500 hp

A 871 WAMBRAU (1955-56)
D: 154 tons (184 fl) **S:** 10.5 kts **M:** 500 hp

A 872 WESTGAT — **A 873 WIELINGEN** (1967-68) — Bldr: Den Helder
D: 185 tons **S:** 12 kts **Dim:** 27.6 × 6.4 × 2.35
A: 2/20-mm **M:** 720 hp

♦ *13 harbor tugs*

Y 8037 BERKEL **Y 8038 DINTEL**
Y 8039 DOMMEL **Y 8040 IJSSEL** (1956-57)
D: 139 tons (163 fl) **S:** 10.5 kts **Dim:** 25.0 × 6.2 × 2.2
M: Werkspoor diesel; 500 hp

A 847 ARGUS (1967)
D: 44.5 (fl) **S:** 8 kts **Dim:** 23.0 × 4.68 × 1.05
M: 144 hp

REMARK: Training ship for deep-sea divers, as are the three *Triton*-class tugs.

A 848 TRITON **A 849 NAUTILUS** **A 850 HYDRA** (1967)
D: 69.3 (fl) **S:** 9 kts **Dim:** 23.3 × 5.15 × 1.34
M: 105 hp

Y 8014 **Y 8016** **Y 8017** **Y 8022** **Y 8028** (built since 1960)

♦ *1 sail training ship*

Y 8050 URANIA (1928)
D: 38 tons **Dim:** 22.0 × 5.0 × 3.1 **Man:** 15 men
M: 65 hp

REMARK: Assigned to the naval academy.

NEW ZEALAND

PERSONNEL: Approximately 2,800 men

MERCHANT MARINE (1976): 102 ships — 164,192 grt
(tankers: 2 ships — 32,442 grt)

NAVAL AVIATION: The Wasp helicopters carried on the frigates and five P3-B Orion patrol planes belong to the Royal New Zealand Air Force.

FRIGATES

♦ *2 British Leander class*

	Bldr	Laid down	L	In serv.
F 55 WAIKATO	Harland & Wolff	1964	18-2-65	9-66
F 421 CANTERBURY	Yarrow	1969	6-5-70	8-72

Canterbury (F 421) Wright and Logan, 1972

A: 2/114-mm AA — 2/20-mm AA — 1/Sea Cat system — 2 triple Mk 32 ASW TT — 1 Wasp helicopter

REMARK: For other characteristics, see the *Leander* class in the section on Great Britain.

♦ *2 British Rothesay class*

	Bldr	Laid down	L	In serv.
F 111 OTAGO (ex-*Hastings*)	J. Thornycroft	1957	11-12-58	6-60
F 148 TARANAKI	J. Samuel White	1957	19-8-59	3-61

Taranaki (F 148)

A: 2/114-mm AA — 2/20-mm AA — 1/Sea Cat system — 6/324-mm ASW TT (III × 2) — 2/Limbo Mk 10 ASW mortars

REMARK: For other characteristics, see the *Rothesay* class in the section on Great Britain. F-148 may become a training ship, losing some armament.

PATROL BOATS

♦ *4 Pukaki class* — Bldr: Brooke Marine Ltd., 1974-75

P 3568 PUKAKI **P 3570 TAUPO**
P 3569 ROTOITI **P 3571 HAWEA**

D: 140 tons **S:** 12 kts **Dim:** 32.0 (30 pp) × 6.1 × 3.5
A: 3/12.7-mm machine guns — 1/81-mm mortar **Man:** 18 men
M: 2 Paxman diesels; 2,500 hp

REMARK: The *Pukaki* and the *Taupo* reached Auckland early in 1975, the other two in 6-75.

♦ *4 British HDML type (1943)*

P 3563 KUPARU **P 3565 HAKU**
P 3564 KOURA **P 3567 MANGA**

D: 54 tons **S:** 12 kts **Dim:** 22.0 × 4.9 × 1.7
M: 2 diesels; 320 hp

HYDROGRAPHIC SHIPS

♦ *1 ex-U.S. oceanographic research ship*

A 2 TUI (ex-*Sands*, AGOR-6) — L: 16-9-63

D: 1,020 tons (1,370 fl) **Dim:** 70.0 (63.7 pp) × 11.28 × 6.3 (fl)
S: 12.5 kts **Man:** 8 officers, 18 men, 15 technicians
Range: 12,000/12
M: Diesel-electric propulsion; 1 prop; 1,100 hp; bow-thruster

♦ **MONOWAI** (ex-*Moana Roa*)

D: 2,900 tons **S:** 13.5 kts **Dim:** 90.4 × 11.0 × 5.2
M: 2 Sulzer diesels; 3,080 hp **Man:** 120 men

REMARK: Former steamer, acquired in 1974. Carries a helicopter.

TUGS

♦ **ARATAKI** **MANAWANUI** (320 hp)

NICARAGUA

PERSONNEL: Approximately 200 men

MERCHANT MARINE (1976): 27 ships — 26,415 grt
(tankers: 3 ships — 4,026 grt)

♦ *1 Sewart-type patrol boat*

GC 7 RIO KURINGWAS

D: 60 tons **S:** 26.5 kts **Dim:** 25.9 × 5.6 × 1.8
A: 3/7.62-mm machine guns **Man:** 10 men
M: 3 General Motors diesels; 3 props; 2,000 hp

NIGERIA

PERSONNEL: 120 officers, 1,700 men

MERCHANT MARINE (1976): 92 ships — 181,765 grt
(tankers: 5 ships — 2,469 grt)

NAVAL PROGRAM: 6 *La Combattante-III-class guided-missile patrol boats ordered in September 1977.*

FRIGATES

♦ *2 Mk 9* — Bldr: Vosper Thornycroft, Portsmouth

Ordered: 1975

	L	In serv.		L	In serv.
ERIN'MI	20-1-77	1979	**N . . .**	. . .	1980

Erin'mi

D: 850 tons **S:** 27 kts **Dim:** 71.6 × 10.5 × 3.6
A: 1/76-mm AA OTO Melara Compact — 1 triple Sea Cat system — 1 Bofors ASW rocket launcher — 1/40-mm Bofors AA
M: 4 MTU 20V-956-TB 92 diesels; 2 props; 19,740 hp **Range:** 2,200/14

♦ *2 Mk 3 Hippopotamus class* — Bldr: Vosper Thornycroft, Portsmouth

F 81 DORINA (16-9-70) **F 82 OTOBO** (25-5-71)

Dorina (F 81) Vosper, 1972

D: 650 tons **Dim:** 61.57 (55.4 pp) × 7.45 × 3.35
S: 22/23 kts **Man:** 7 officers, 13 petty officers, 46 men
A: 2/102-mm Mk 19 (II × 1) — 2/40-mm 60 cal. Bofors AA — 2/20-mm Mk 7
Electron Equipt: Radars: Dutch HSA-22 fire-control with a Plessey Mk AWS-1, 1 Decca TM-626
M: M.A.N. V-8 V 24/30-B diesels; 2 props; 3,400 hp (4,430 max)
Fuel: 68 tons **Electric:** 176 kw **Range:** 3,500/14

REMARKS: Can carry a flag officer and his staff; living spaces air-conditioned; Vosper stabilizers. The 102-mm guns are hand-loaded. Can be fitted with sonar. Twelve compartments. Refitted in 1976.

	Bldr	Laid down	L	In serv.
♦ **F 87 NIGERIA**	Wilton-Fijenoord, Netherlands	4-64	9-65	9-66

Nigeria (F 87) 1966

FRIGATES (*continued*)

D: 1,724 tons (2,000 fl) **Dim:** 109.85 (104 pp) × 11.3 × 3.35
S: 25 kts **Man:** 216 men
A: 2/102-mm (II × 1) — 4/40-mm AA — 1 triple squid ASW mortar
M: 4 M.A.N. V-8 diesels; 2 props; 15,500 hp

REMARKS: Helicopter platform. Refit by Cammell Laird, 1970-71.

PATROL BOATS

♦ *4 Makurdi class* — Bldr: Brooke Marine Ltd., Lowestoft

	In serv.		In serv.
P 167 MAKURDI	14-8-74	**169 JEBBA**	3-77
P 168 HADEJIA	14-8-74	**170 OGUTA**	3-77

Hadejia (P 168) 1975

D: 115 tons (143 fl) **S:** 20.5 kts **Dim:** 32.6 × 6.1 × 3.5
A: 2/40-mm AA **Man:** 4 officers, 20 men **Range:** . . .
M: 2 Ruxton-Paxman YJCM diesels; 2 props; 3,000 hp

♦ *4 Argundu class* — Bldr: Abeking & Rasmussen

	L	In serv.		L	In serv.
P 165 ARGUNDU	4-7-73	10-74	**P . . . BRAS**	. . .	3-76
P 166 YOLA	12-6-73	10-74	**P . . . EPE**	. . .	3-76

Argundu (P 165) 1975

D: 90 tons **S:** 20 kts **Dim:** 32.0 × 6.0 × 1.7
A: 1/40-mm AA — 1/20-mm AA **Man:** 25 men **Range:** . . .
M: 2 MTU diesels; 2,070 hp

♦ *4 British SBD type*

ENUGU (1961)	**BONNY** (ex-*Difford*)
BENIN (ex-*Hinksford*)	**SAPELE** (ex-*Dubford*)

D: 120 tons (160 fl) **S:** 15 kts **Dim:** 35.7 × 6.1 × 2.1
A: 1/40-mm — 2/20-mm — depth charges **Man:** 19 men
M: 2 Davey-Paxman diesels; 1,100 hp

REMARKS: The *Enugu* was built specifically for Nigeria; three of the others were transferred in September 1966 and two in 1968. The original *Ibadan,* which was seized in May of 1967 by the Biafrans and renamed *Vigilance,* was sunk in September of that year, refloated, and later scrapped. *Ibadan II* and *Sapele* were bought in 1967-68 and 1968-69.

HYDROGRAPHIC SHIPS

♦ *1 British Bulldog class* — Bldr: Brooke Marine Ltd., Lowestoft
Ordered: end 1973

	L	In serv.
LANA	4-3-76	9-76

Lana 1976

D: 800 tons (1,100 fl) **S:** 15 kts **Dim:** 57.8 × 11.4 × 3.7
M: 4 diesels; 2 props; 2,000 hp **Range:** 4,000/12 **Man:** 38 men

NIGERIA *(continued)*

HYDROGRAPHIC SHIPS *(continued)*

♦ *1 AGSC*

P 11 PENELOPE (30-9-58)

D: 79 tons **S:** 10 kts **Dim:** 24.2 × 2.4 × 1.4

VARIOUS SHIPS

♦ *1 training ship* — Bldr: The Netherlands

A 497 RUWAN YARO (ex-*Ogina Bereton*)

Ruwan Yaro

D: 600 tons **S:** 18 kts **Dim:** 50 × 7 × . . .
A: None **Man:** 90 men, 11 of whom are in officers' training
Electron Equipt: Radar: Decca TM-626
M: 2 diesels; 1 variable-pitch prop; 4,000 hp

REMARK: A former yacht with a plastic hull and a bow-thruster for maneuvering in shallow water.

♦ *1 tug*

RIBADU (1973)

D: 147 tons **S:** 12 kts **Dim:** 28.5 × 7.2 × 3.7

NORWAY

PERSONNEL: Approximately 8,000 men, including 1,600 men in the Coast Artillery.

MERCHANT MARINE (1976): 2,759 ships — 27,943,834 grt
(tankers: 287 ships — 14,891,231 grt)

NAVAL AVIATION: The Norwegian Navy does not have a naval air arm, as such. However, two Air Force formations are assigned to naval missions, usually reconnaissance and ASW patrol:
— a squadron consisting of about 12 SH-3 Sea King and 12 UH-1 helicopters;
— a smaller group with about 6 P-3 Orion patrol aircraft.

NAVAL PROGRAM: The long-term program drawn up in 1973 by the Norwegian government was to replace the following ships before the end of the 1980s:
— the German 207-type submarines
— the *Oslo*-class frigates and *Sleipner*-class corvettes
— the *Tjeld*-class torpedo boats
— the *Sauda/Tana*-class minesweepers

The first new construction was scheduled for 1974–78. To be built or converted during this period were:
— 14 *Snögg*-class guided-missile patrol boats
— 2 minelayers
— 2 logistic-support ships for submarines and small craft
— 1 training ship, also assigned to coastal protection
— 1 fisheries-protection ship
— conversion of one minesweeper into a minehunter

This program is likely to be modified now that the Norwegian government has decided to create a coast guard to protect offshore oil installations and patrol the 200-mile economic zone. The coast guard program provides for seven 2,000-ton escort ships, each carrying a helicopter, and three Orion-type patrol aircraft.

WARSHIPS IN SERVICE OR UNDER CONSTRUCTION AS OF 1 OCTOBER 1977

	L	Tons (surfaced)	Main armament
♦ *15 submarines*			
15 GERMAN 207 TYPE	1964–67	370	8 533-mm TT
♦ *5 frigates*		Tons	
5 OSLO	1964–66	1,450	4/76-mm, 1 Penguin system, 1 Sea Sparrow system, 1 Terne rocket launcher
♦ *2 corvettes*			
2 SLEIPNER	1963–65	600	1/76-mm, 1 Terne rocket launcher, 6 ASW TT
♦ *60 missile and torpedo boats*			
14 HAUK	. . .	129	1/40-mm AA, 1 Penguin system, 4/533-mm TT
6 SNÖGG	1970–71	140	1/40-mm AA, 1 Penguin system, 4 533-mm TT

WARSHIPS (*continued*)

20 STORM	1963–67	100	1/76-mm, 1 Penguin system
20 TJELD	1960–64	70	1 or 2/40-mm AA, 2 or 4 533-mm TT

WEAPONS AND SYSTEMS

The Norwegian Navy uses mostly British, American, and Swedish weapons and systems, but it has built two interesting systems of its own, the Terne automatic ASW defense system and the Penguin surface-to-surface missile, which are described below. Submarines are equipped with Swedish M 61 (45 kts, 20,000 m) or American Mk 37 (20,000 m) wire-guided torpedoes.

Terne

Maximum range: 900 m
1 search sonar
1 attack sonar
1 computer
1 fixed rocket-launcher mount with a rapid-reloading system.

The sextuple mount weighs a little less than 3 tons. Firing is done between 45° and 75° of elevation, the latter for maximum range. Six rounds are fired at a time. Reloading is done automatically in 40 seconds, as the carriage is returned to a vertical position, in which ready-service racks reload the launchers. The rocket is 1.97 m in length, 0.2 m in diameter, 120 kg in weight (warhead: 48 kg), and has a combination timed and proximity fuse.

Penguin

Length: 0.3 m	Maximum range: 20,000 m
Wingspan: 1.4 m	Speed: Mach 0.7
Diameter: 0.28	Guidance: infrared homing
Weight: 330 kg	

The system is mounted in an enclosure to protect it from the weather.

76-mm Bofors gun

Single-barrel automatic gun mounted on the *Storm*-class patrol boats.
Turret weight (no ammunition): 6.5 tons
Length: 50 calibers
Muzzle velocity: 825 m/sec
Rate of train: 25°/sec
Rate of elevation: 25°/sec
Arc of elevation: −10° to +30°
Rate of fire: 30 rounds/min — 100 rounds immediately available in the ready-firing station
Cartridge weight: 11.3 kg
Shell weight: 5.9 kg
Warhead weight: 0.54 kg
Maximum range, surface mode: 8,000 m

SUBMARINES

♦ *15 German 207 Type* — Bldr: Rheinstahl-Nordseewerke, Emden

	L	In serv.
S 300 ULA	19-12-64	7-5-65
S 301 UTSIRA	11-3-65	1-7-65
S 302 UTSTEIN	19-5-65	9-9-65
S 303 UTVAER	30-6-65	1-12-65
S 304 UTHAUG	8-10-65	16-2-66
S 305 SKLINNA	21-1-66	27-5-66
S 306 SKOLPEN	24-3-66	17-8-66
S 307 STADT	10-6-66	15-11-66
S 308 STORD	2-9-66	9-2-67
S 309 SVENNER	27-1-67	1-7-67
S 315 KAURA	16-10-64	5-2-65
S 316 KINN	30-11-63	8-4-64
S 317 KYA	20-2-64	15-6-64
S 318 KOBBEN	25-4-64	17-8-64
S 319 KUNNA	16-7-64	1-10-64

Kya (S 317) 1975

D: 370 tons surfaced, 482 submerged **Dim:** 45.41 × 4.6 × 4.58
S: 13.5/17 kts **Man:** 17 men
A: 8/533-mm TT, fwd **M:** Diesel electric; 1,200/1,700 hp

REMARKS: These submarines are based on the West German Navy's type 205, but they have a stronger hull. They will be fitted with new sensors, new batteries, and wire-guided torpedoes.

NOTE: JKL, Lübeck, has received a contract from the West German Navy to study a 750-ton submarine, to be designated type 210. This boat is expected eventually to replace the above submarines.

FRIGATES

♦ *5 Oslo class* — Bldr: Marinens Hovedverft, Horten

	Laid down	L	In serv.
F 300 OSLO	1963	17-1-64	29-1-66
F 301 BERGEN	1963	23-8-65	15-6-67
F 302 TRONDHEIM	1963	4-9-64	2-6-66
F 303 STAVANGER	1964	4-2-66	1-12-67
F 304 NARVIK	1964	8-1-65	30-11-66

D: 1,450 tons (1,850 fl) **Dim:** 96.62 (93.87 pp) × 11.17 × 4.4
S: 25 kts **Man:** 11 officers, 19 petty officers, 120 men
A: 4/76-mm AA automatic (II × 2) — 6 launchers for Penguin missiles — 1 Sea Sparrow — 1 Terne ASW rocket launcher — 2 Mk 32 ASW TT for Mk 44 torpedoes

FRIGATES (*continued*)

Penguin launchers and Sea Sparrow aboard the Bergen

Bergen (F 301) 1975

Electron Equipt: Radars: 1 DRBV 22, 1 HSA fire-control
Sonars: 1 Terne attack, 1 AN SQS 36
M: STAL-Laval PN 20 GT; 1 prop; 20,000 hp
Boilers: 2 Babcock, 42.18 kg/cm^2, superheat 454°
Electric: 1,100 kw **Range:** 4,500/15

REMARK: Based on the U.S. *Dealey*-class destroyer escorts.

CORVETTES

♦ *2 Sleipner class* — Bldr: Nylands Verksted, Oslo

F 310 SLEIPNER (9-11-63) — In serv. 29-4-65
F 311 AEGER (24-9-65) — In serv. 31-3-67

Authorized: 1960

D: 600 tons (790 fl) **S:** over 20 kts **Dim:** 69.33 × 7.9 × 2.5
A: 1/76-mm — 1/40-mm AA — 1 Terne ASW rocket launcher — 6/324-mm Mk 32 TT (III × 2) — depth charges

Sleipner, wearing her old number H.L.M.

Electron Equipt: Radar: 1 V-DO
Sonars: 1 Terne attack, 1 AN SQS 36
M: 4 Maybach diesels; 2 props; 9,000 hp **Man:** 61 men

GUIDED-MISSILE PATROL BOATS

♦ *14 Hauk class* — Bldr: Bergens Mekaniske Verksteder

	L		L		L
P 986 HAUK	. . .	**P . . . N . . .**	. . .	**P . . . N . . .**	. . .
P . . . N . . .	. . .	**P . . . N . . .**	. . .	**P . . . N . . .**	. . .
P . . . N . . .	. . .	**P . . . N . . .**	. . .	**P . . . N . . .**	. . .
P . . . N . . .	. . .	**P . . . N . . .**	. . .	**P . . . N . . .**	. . .
P . . . N . . .	. . .	**P . . . N . . .**	. . .		

Ordered: 6-75

D: 129 tons (150 fl) **S:** 34 kts **Dim:** 36.5 × 6.2 × 1.6
A: 1/40-mm AA — 4 Penguin missiles — 4/533-mm TT
M: 2 3,500-hp diesels **Range:** 440/34 **Man:** 22 men

REMARKS: Based on the Swedish Jägaren class. Four will be subcontracted to Westermöen, Alta. MSI-805 fire-control system developed by Kongsberg.

♦ *6 Snögg class* — Bldr: Båtservice Verft, Mandal, 1970-71

P 980 SNÖGG **P 982 SNARR** **P 984 KVIK**
P 981 RAPP **P 983 RASK** **P 985 KJAPP**

Snarr (P 982) J. C. Bellonne, 1974

GUIDED-MISSILE PATROL BOATS *(continued)*

D: 140 tons (fl) **S:** 36 kts **Dim:** 36.58 × 6.2 × 1.65
A: 1/40-mm AA — 4 533-mm TT for wire-guided torpedoes and, usually, one single launcher on each side for Penguin missiles
Man: 3 officers, 17 men **Range:** 550/36
M: Maybach diesels; 2 props; 7,200 hp

♦ *20 Storm class* — Bldr: Norway

	L		L
P 960 STORM	19-3-63	**P 970 BRANN**	3-7-66
P 961 BLINK	28-6-65	**P 971 TROSS**	29-9-66
P 962 GLIMT	27-9-65	**P 972 HVASS**	20-12-66
P 963 SKJOLD	17-2-66	**P 973 TRAUST**	18-11-66
P 964 TRYGG	25-11-65	**P 974 BROTT**	27-1-67
P 965 KJEKK	27-1-66	**P 975 ODD**	7-4-67
P 966 DJERV	28-4-66	**P 976 PIL**	29-3-67
P 967 SKUDD	25-3-66	**P 977 BRASK**	27-5-67
P 968 ARG	24-5-66	**P 978 ROKK**	1-6-67
P 969 STEIL	20-9-66	**P 979 GNIST**	15-8-67

Blink (P 961) without her Penguin missiles

D: 100 tons (125 fl) **Dim:** 37.0 (35.98 pp) × 5.87 × 1.55
S: over 30 kts **Man:** 4 officers, 9 petty officers, 13 men
A: 1/76-mm Mk 76 automatic — 1/40-mm — 6 Penguin launchers
M: Maybach MB 872A diesels; 2 props; 7,200 hp

Traust (P 973) 1970

TORPEDO BOATS

♦ *20 Tjeld class* — Bldr: Westermoen, Mandal

	In serv.		In serv.
P 343 TJELD	6-60	**P 381 HAI**	7-64
P 344 SKARV	11-60	**P 382 SEL**	5-63
P 345 TEIST	12-60	**P 383 HVAL**	3-64
P 346 JO	2-61	**P 384 LAKS**	5-64
P 347 LOM	4-61	**P 385 KNURR**	1966
P 348 STEGG	6-61	**P 386 DELFIN**	5-66
P 349 HAUK	8-61	**P 387 LYR**	1966
P 350 FALK	9-61	**P 388 GRIBB**	3-62
P 357 RAVN	12-61	**P 389 GEIR**	8-62
P 380 SKREI	1962	**P 390 ERLE**	6-62

Lom (P 347)

Teist, Tjeld, Skarv (P 345, P 343, P 344) Shbldg. and Sh. Record

TORPEDO BOATS *(continued)*

D: 70 tons (82 fl) **Dim:** 24.5 × 7.5 × 1.95
S: 45 kts (40 cruising) **Range:** 450/40, 600/25
A: As a torpedo boat: 1/40-mm AA — 1/20-mm AA — 4/533-mm TT
As a gunboat: 2/40-mm AA — 2/533-mm TT
Modified as a minelayer: fitted with a rocket launcher as well
Man: 4 officers, 4 petty officers, 12 men **Fuel:** 10 tons
M: 2 Napier-Deltic T 18-37 diesels with turbo-compressors; 2 props; 6,280 hp

REMARKS: Designed by Jan H. Linge of Boat Service, Ltd., Oslo. Mahogany hull, engines and fittings imported from Great Britain. Two were delivered in 1962 to the West German Navy, which later sold them to Turkey. Two were transferred to the U.S.A. in 1963. Six have been ordered by Greece. The oldest ones will soon be retired from active service, the name of one of them, *Hauk*, having already been chosen for the first of the *Hauk*-class guided-missile boats.

MINE WARFARE SHIPS

♦ *2 Vidar-class minelayers* — Bldr: Mjellem & Karlsen, Bergen

N 53 VIDAR **N 52 VALE**

D: 1,673 (fl) **S:** 15/16 kts **Dim:** 64.8 (60 pp) × 12.0 × 4.0
A: 2/40-mm AA (II × 1) **Man:** 32 men
M: 2 Wichman diesels; 2 props; 1 bow prop; 2,100 hp **Electric:** 1,000 kw

REMARKS: Will be able to serve as minelayers (320 mines carried on three decks with an automatic hoist, 3 minelaying rails), torpedo-recovery boats, personnel and cargo transports, and fisheries protection boats.

♦ *2 ex-U.S. Auk-class minesweepers*

	Bldr	L	In serv.
N 49 BRAGE (ex-*Triumph*, MMC-3)	Associated SB, Seattle	25-2-43	3-2-44
N 50 ULLER (ex-*Sneer*, MSF-112)	American SB, Lorain	23-5-42	21-10-42

Tyr (N 47)

D: 890 tons (1,250 fl) **S:** 18 kts **Dim:** 67.2 (65 pp) × 9.75 × 3.4
A: 1/76-mm AA — 4/20-mm AA — 2 hedgehogs — 2 depth-charge projectors — mines
Man: 105 men
M: Diesel-electric propulsion with General Motors diesels; 2 props; 2,070 hp

REMARKS: Transferred in 1959-60. N-49 has for armament: 1/40-mm AA, 1/Terne ASW rocket launcher, 6/324-mm Mk 32 ASW TT (III × 2). Will be discarded on completion of the *Vidar* and *Vale*.

	Bldr	L
♦ **N 51 BORGEN**	Marinens Hovedverft, Horten	29-4-60

D: 282 tons **S:** 9 kts **Dim:** 31.28 × 8.0 × 3.35
M: 2 General Motors diesels; Voith-Schneider prop; 330 hp

♦ *1 prototype Swedish Gasten-class minesweeper*

D: 135 tons (fl) **S:** 11 kts **Dim:** 23.0 × 6.6 × 2.0
A: 1/40-mm AA **M:** Diesels

REMARK: Experimental plastic and fiberglass ship.

♦ *10 Sauda/Tana-class coastal minesweepers (U.S. Falcon class)*

M 311 SAUDA (ex-AMS-131)
M 312 SIRA (ex-AMS-132)
M 313 TANA (ex-*Roseelaere*, ex-MSC-103)
M 314 ALTA (ex-*Arlon*, ex-MSC-104)
M 315 OGNA (18-6-54)
M 316 VOSSO (16-6-54)
M 317 GLOMMA (ex-*Bastogne*, ex-MSC-151)
M 331 TISTA (1-6-54)
M 332 KVINA (21-7-54)
M 334 UTLA (2-3-55)

Bldrs: M-315, M-332, M-334: Båtservice Verft, Mandal; M-331: Forenede Båtbyggeri, Risŏr; M-316: Skåluren, Rosendal; M-311 to M-314 and M-317: U.S.A.

D: 370 tons (465 fl) **S:** 14/13 kts **Dim:** 43.9 × 8.23 × 2.55
A: 1/12.7-mm AA **Man:** 38 men **Range:** 2,500/12
M: 2 General Motors diesels; 2 props; 1,600 hp **Fuel:** 40 tons

REMARK: M-313, M-314, and M-317 were transferred by Belgium in 1966 in exchange for two ocean minesweepers, the *Lagen* and the *Namsen*.

AMPHIBIOUS WARFARE SHIPS

♦ *5 560-ton LSMs* — Bldr: Mjellem & Karlsen, Bergen

A 33 REINSØYSUND (1-72) **A 36 ROTSUND** (1973)
A 34 SØRØYSUND (6-72) **A 37 BORGSUND** (1973)
A 35 MAURSUND (9-72)

D: 560 tons **S:** 11 kts **Dim:** 51.4 × 10.3 × 1.85
A: 3/20-mm — 4/12.7-mm machine guns — rails for 120 mines
Cargo capacity: 5 Leopard tanks, 80-180 men
M: 2 MTU diesels; 2 props **Man:** 2 officers, 7 men

REMARK: Double-folding bow ramp door.

♦ *2 500-ton LCUs*

A 31 KVALSUND **A 32 RAFTSUND**

NORWAY (*continued*)

AUXILIARY SHIPS

♦ *1 supply ship* — Bldr: Horten (contract signed 30-3-76)

A . . . HORTEN

D: 2,500 tons (fl) **Dim:** 87.0 (82 pp) × 13.7 × 8.7
S: 16.5 kts **Man:** 86 men, quarters for 60 additional men
M: 2 Wichman diesels; 2 props; bow thruster

REMARK: Used to support submarines and patrol and torpedo boats.

♦ *2 tenders for combat divers*

DRAUG (2-72) **SARPEN**

D: 250 tons **S:** . . . **Dim:** . . . **M:** . . .

VARIOUS SHIPS

♦ *1 Nornen-class fisheries-protection ship* — Bldr: Mjellem & Karlsen, Bergen

A 538 NORNEN (20-8-62)

Nornen (P 950)

D: 1,000 tons **S:** 17 kts **Dim:** 61.5 × 10.0 × 3.8
A: 1/76-mm, fwd — 1/40-mm, aft — 1 Terne ASW rocket launcher
M: 4 diesels; 1 prop; 3,700 hp **Man:** . . .

♦ *2 fisheries-protection ships*

A 532 FARM (22-2-62) **A 534 HEIMDAL** (7-3-62)

Bldrs: *Farm:* Ankerlokken Verft, Frederikstad; *Heimdal* Bolsones Verft, Molde

D: 488 tons (600 fl) **S:** 16.5 kts **Dim:** 54.3 × 8.2 × 2.8
A: 1/76-mm **M:** 2 diesels; 2 props; 2,400 hp

♦ *3 fisheries-protection ships* — Bldr: The Netherlands, 1957

A 539 ANDENES **A 531 NORDKAPP** **A 536 SENJA**

Nordkapp (A 531) 1969

D: 500 tons **S:** 16 kts **Dim:** 56.7 × 9.45 × 4.9
A: 1/76-mm **Man:** 29 men **M:** M.A.N. diesel; 2,300 hp

REMARK: Modified whale-hunters, purchased in 1965.

♦ *1 royal yacht* — Bldr: Camper & Nicholson, Ltd.

A 533 NORGE (ex-*Philante*) (1-2-37)

D: 1,686 tons **S:** 14 kts **Dim:** 76.27 × 8.53 × 4.56
M: 1 8-cyl. diesel; 2 props; 2,600 hp

OMAN

MERCHANT MARINE (1976): 6 ships — 3,374 grt

PATROL BOATS

♦ *7 37.5-meter class* — Bldr: Brooke Marine Ltd., Lowestoft, 1972-76

	In serv.		In serv.
B 1 AL BUSHRA	22-1-73	**B 5 AL FULK**	4-77
B 2 AL MANSUR	26-3-73	**B 6 ALAUL**	8-77
B 3 AL NEJAH	13-5-73	**B 7 N . . .**	8-77
B 4 AL WAFI	1976		

OMAN (*continued*)
PATROL BOATS (*continued*)

D: 135 tons (153 fl) **S:** 25 kts **Dim:** 37.5 × 6.65 × 1.65
A: 2/40-mm AA; B-4 to B-7: 1/76-mm OTO Melara Compact
Man: 29 men **Range:** 3,250/12
M: 2 Paxman-Ventura, 16-cyl. diesels; 2 props; 4,800 hp

	Bldr	In serv.
♦ **AL SAID**	Brooke Marine Ltd., Lowestoft	1971

D: 785 tons (930 fl) **S:** 17 kts **Dim:** 57.4 × 10.7 × 3.05
A: . . . **Man:** 11 officers, 23 men, quarters for 37
M: 2 Paxman Mk 12 YJCM diesels; 1,500 rpm; 2 props; 3,350 hp

REMARK: Also used as a yacht.

♦ *2 ex-Dutch coastal minesweepers*

P 1 AL NASSIRI (ex-*Axel*, M-808) (5-3-55)
P 2 AL SALIHI (ex-*Aalsmeer*, M-811) (23-4-55)

D: 373 tons (417 fl) **S:** 14 kts **Dim:** 46.63 × 8.78 × 2.28
A: 2/40-mm AA **Man:** 40 men
M: 2 Werkspoor diesels; 2 props; 2,500 hp

REMARKS: Purchased in 1974, air conditioned, and fitted out as patrol boats. Similar to the British "-ton" class. Their minesweeping equipment has been removed.

AUXILIARY SHIPS

♦ *1 repair ship* — Bldr: Conoship, Groningen, The Netherlands

AL SULTANA In serv: 4-6-75

D: 900 tons (1,380 dwt) **S:** 11 kts **Dim:** 65.4 × 10.7 × 4.2
M: 1 Mirrless-Blackstone diesel; 1,150 hp

♦ *1 logistic support ship* — Bldr: Brooke Marine, G.B., ordered in 1977

D: 2,000 grt

♦ *7 landing craft*

♦ *1 training ship, ex-cargo ship*

DHOFAR — **D:** 1,500 tons

PAKISTAN

PERSONNEL: Approximately 11,000 men

MERCHANT MARINE (1976): 83 ships — 483,333 grt
(1 tanker — 15,941 grt)

NAVAL AVIATION: The naval air arm consists of:
- 3 Atlantic patrol aircraft
- 6 Sea King helicopters (1976) armed with AM-39
- 4 Alouette III helicopters
- 2 Albatros amphibians
- 2 Cessna liaison aircraft

WARSHIPS IN SERVICE AS OF 1 OCTOBER 1977

	L	Tons (surfaced)	Main armament
♦ *4 submarines*			
4 HANGOR	1969–70	869	12 550-mm TT
		Tons	
♦ *1 cruiser*			
1 BABUR	1942	5,900	8 133.5-mm AA
♦ *6 destroyers*			
2 GEARING CLASS	1944–46	2,400	
1 BATTLE CLASS	1945	2,325	4 114-mm AA, 8 533-mm TT
3 CR CLASS	1944–45	1,710	3 114-mm AA, 4 533-mm TT
♦ *2 frigates*			
2 O CLASS	1941	1,800	2 102-mm, 4 533-mm TT
♦ *24 patrol boats*			

SUBMARINES

♦ *4 Hangor class*

	Bldr	Laid down	L	In serv.
S 131 HANGOR	Arsenal de Brest	12-67	30-6-69	1971
S 132 SHUSHUK	C. N. Ciotat, Le Trait	12-67	30-7-69	1971
S 133 MANGRO	C. N. Ciotat, Le Trait	6-68	7-2-70	1971
S 134 GHAZI (ex-Portuguese *Cachalote*)	Dubigeon, Normandy	10-66	16-2-68	1-69

Shushuk (S 132) J. C. Bellonne, 1970

SUBMARINES (*continued*)

D: 869 tons surfaced, 1,043 submerged **S:** 13.5/16 kts
Dim: 57.75 × 6.76 × 4.62 **A:** 12/550-mm TT (8 fwd, 4 aft)
M: Diesel-electric: SEMT-Pielstick engines, 450 kw; 2 props; 1,300/1,600 hp
Man: 5 officers, 45 men

Mangro (S 133) 1970

REMARKS: See *Daphné* class in French section. One of the above submarines sank the Indian frigate *Kukri* during the Indo-Pakistani conflict.

♦ *5 Italian-built Cosmos submarines*

D: 70 tons **S:** 11/6.5 kts **Dim:** 16.0 × 1.80 × . . .
Man: 4 men **Range:** 1,200 surface

REMARKS: Unarmed. Used for the transport of raiders. A sixth sank 27-12-76 following an accident at sea.

CRUISER

	Bldr	Laid down	L	In serv.
♦ **84 BABUR** (ex-*Diadem*)	Hawthorn Leslie	11-39	26-8-42	1-44

D: 5,900 tons (7,560 fl) **Dim:** 156.05 (154.23 pp) × 15.7 × 5.7
S: 20 kts **Man:** 590 (peacetime)
Range: 1,300/29, 2,900/20, 4,000/13
A: 8/133.5-mm AA (II × 4) — 14/40-mm AA — 4/47-mm (saluting battery) — 6/533-mm TT (III × 2)
Armor: Belt: 52 to 76 — Deck: 52 — Turret: 25 — Conning tower: 25
M: Parsons GT; 4 props; 62,000 hp
Boilers: 4 Admiralty **Fuel:** 1,000 tons

REMARKS: Sold to Pakistan in 2-56. Modernized. Used as a training ship.

DESTROYERS

♦ *2 ex-U.S. Gearing class*

N . . . (ex-*Epperson*, DD-719) In serv. 18-3-44
N . . . (ex-*Wiltsie*, DD-716) In serv. 11-1-46
Transferred: 1977

♦ *1 ex-British Battle class*

	Bldr	Laid down	L	In serv.
161 BADR (ex-*Gabbard*)	Swan Hunter	2-44	16-3-45	12-46

Transferred: 1957

Badr (161) 1974

D: 2,325 tons (3,360 fl) **Dim:** 115.32 (108.2 pp) × 12.95 × 4.1
S: 31 kts **Man:** 300 men
Range: 3,000/20 **Fuel:** 680 tons
A: 4/114-mm AA (II × 2) — 10/40-mm AA — 8/533-mm TT (IV × 2) — 1 squid — depth charges
Electron Equipt: Radars: 1/275, 1/293, 1 Marconi
Sonars: 1/170, 1/174
M: 2 Parsons GT; 2 props; 50,000 hp **Boilers:** 2 3-drum Admiralty

REMARK: Sister ship *Khaibar* was sunk during the Indo-Pakistani conflict, 1971.

♦ *3 ex-British CR class* — Transferred: 1958

	Laid down	L	In serv.
160 ALAMGIR (ex-*Creole*)	8-44	22-11-45	10-46
162 JAHANGIR (ex-*Crispin*)	2-44	23-6-45	7-46
164 SHAH JAHAN (ex-*Charity*)	7-43	30-11-44	11-45

Bldrs: 160 and 162: J. Samuel White, Cowes; 164: J. I. Thornycroft, Woolston

D: 1,710 tons (2,500 fl) **Dim:** 110.55 (106.07 pp) × 10.88 × 3.8
S: 31 kts **Man:** 200 men
Range: 1,000/30, 2,800/20 **Fuel:** 580 tons
A: 3/114-mm AA (I × 3) — 6/40-mm AA — 4/533-mm TT (IV × 1) — 2 squid — depth charges

DESTROYERS (*continued*)

Shah Jahan (164)

Electron Equipt: Radars: 1/293, 1/275 fire-control
Sonars: 1/174, 1/170
M: 2 Parsons GT; 2 props; 40,000 hp **Boilers:** 2 3-drum Admiralty

FRIGATES

♦ *2 ex-British O-class destroyers*

	Bldr	Laid down	L	In serv.
260 TIPPU SULTAN (ex-*Onslow*)	John Brown, Clydebank	7-40	31-3-41	10-41
261 TUGHRIL (ex-*Onslaught*)	Fairfield, Glasgow	1-41	9-10-41	6-42

Tippu Sultan (260) 1973

D: 1,800 tons (2,300 fl) **Dim:** 103.2 (wl) × 10.68 × 4.7
S: 35 kts (31 fl) **Range:** 1,700/20, 2,700/12
A: 2/102-mm — 5/40-mm AA — 4/533-mm TT (IV × 1) — 2 squid
Electron Equipt: Radar: 1/293
Sonars: 1/174, 1/170
M: Parsons GT; 2 props; 40,000 hp
Boilers: 2 3-drum Admiralty **Fuel:** 430 tons

REMARKS: Transferred at the end of 1949, rebuilt as Type 16 frigates, 1958-59. 261 is used for instructing midshipmen from the naval academy. No longer gets underway.

PATROL BOATS

♦ *5 Chinese Hainan class*

301 SIND **303 N . . .** **305 N . . .**
302 BALUCHISTAN **304 N . . .**

D: 400 tons **S:** 24 kts **Dim:** 59.0 × 7.3 × 2.4
A: 4/57-mm AA (II × 2) — 4/25-mm AA (II × 2) — copies of Soviet MBU 1800 rocket launcher — depth-charge rack
M: Diesels

REMARK: Undoubtedly very rugged ships.

♦ *12 Chinese Shanghai-II class* — Bldr: People's Republic of China

P 141 LAHORE	**P 145 PISHIN**	**P 149 SAHIVAL**
P 142 MULTAN	**P 146 KALAT**	**P 150 BANNU**
P 143 GUILGIT	**P 147 SUKKUR**	**P 151 LARKANA**
P 144 MARDAN	**P 148 QUETTA**	**P 152 BAHAWALPUR**

Transferred: 8 in 1972, 4 in 1973

Quetta (P 148) 1974

D: 155 tons (fl) **S:** 28 kts **Dim:** 38.8 × 5.4 × 1.6
A: 4/37-mm AA (II × 2) — 4/25-mm AA (II × 2) athwartships
M: 4 diesels; 4 props; 4,800 hp **Man:** 28 men

Photo Requested

Multan (P 142)

PATROL BOATS (*continued*)

♦ **P 140 RAJSHAHI** — Bldr: Brooke Marine, Lowestoft, 1965

D: 115 tons (143 fl) **Dim:** 32.62 (30.48 pp) × 6.1 × 1.55
S: 24 kts **Man:** 19 men
A: 2/40-mm 70-cal AA **M:** 2 Mercedes-Maybach, 1,700 hp each

REMARKS: Welded construction, light metal used in the superstructure. Sister ships *Jessore, Comilla,* and *Sylhet* were sunk during the Indo-Pakistani conflict, 1971.

♦ *6 Chinese Huchwan-class hydrofoils*

HDF 01, HDF 02, HDF 03, HDF 04, HDF 05, HDF 06

1973

D: 39 tons (fl) **S:** 54 kts
Dim: 21.8 × 4.9 × 1.0; foilborne: 7.5 × .31
A: 2 machine guns (II × 1) — 2 torpedoes
M: 3 diesels; 3 props; 3,600 hp

REMARKS: In dry dock to prevent corrosion.

MINE WARFARE SHIPS

♦ *7 ex-U.S. minesweepers*

M 160 MAHMOOD (ex-MSC-267)
M 161 MOMIN (ex-MSC-293)
M 162 MURABAK (ex-MSC-262)
M 164 MUJAHID (ex-MSC-261)
M 165 MUKHTAR (ex-MSC-274)
M 166 MUNSIF (ex-MSC-373)
M 167 MOSHAL (ex-MSC-294)

Mukhtar (M 165) 1974

REMARKS: Same characteristics as the French *Acacia* class. Transferred under MAP: 5 in 1956–58, 2 in 1963. Sister ship *Muhafiz* sunk during the Indo-Pakistani conflict, 1971.

AUXILIARY SHIPS

♦ *1 fleet replenishment oiler*

A 41 DACCA (ex-U.S. *Mission Santa Clara*, AO-132) — Transferred: 1-63

D: 22,380 tons (fl) **S:** 15 kts **Dim:** 159.4 × 20.73 × . . .
Cargo capacity: 20,000 tons

♦ *1 harbor oiler*

A 298 ATTOCK (ex-U.S. YO-249) (1960)

D: 1,225 tons (fl) **S:** 8 kts

♦ *1 hydrographic ship* — Bldr: Smith's Dock, Great Britain

	Laid down	L	In serv.
262 ZULFIQUAR (ex-F-265)	4-42	12-10-42	3-43

D: 1,370 tons (2,100 fl) **Dim:** 91.84 × 11.17 × 4.34
S: 19 kts **Man:** 150 men
A: 1/102-mm, fwd — 2/40-mm **Range:** 3,000/12
M: Triple-expansion; 2 props; 5,500 hp **Boilers:** 2

REMARK: Former River-class frigate.

♦ *1 rescue ship*

A 42 MADADGAR (ex-U.S. ATF-94) (7-43)

D: 1,575 (fl) **S:** 16 kts **M:** 3,000 hp

♦ *1 tug* — Bldr: The Netherlands, 1955

RUSTOM — **S:** 9 kts — **M:** 1,000 hp

♦ *2 floating docks*

PESHAWAR (ex-U.S. ARD-6)
FD 11 — Bldr: West Germany, 1974 — Lifting power: 1,200 tons

♦ *1 water carrier*

YW 15 ZUM ZUM — Bldr: Italy, 1957

PANAMA

MERCHANT MARINE (1976): 2,680 ships — 15,631,180 grt
(tankers: 260 ships — 5,925,127 grt)

PATROL BOATS AND CRAFT

♦ *2 103-foot Vosper boats*

GC 10 PANQUIACO (22-7-70) **GC 11 LIGIA ELENA** (25-8-70)

PANAMA (*continued*)

REMARKS: Same characteristics and appearance as the *Trinity* class of Trinidad and Tobago. Manned by the Panamanian National Guard.

♦ *2 ex-U.S. patrol craft* — Transferred: 1962

D: 35 tons **S:** 13 kts **Dim:** 21.0 × 4.27 × 1.55
A: 1 machine gun **Man:** 10 men **M:** 400 hp

PAPUA
New Guinea

PATROL BOATS

♦ *5 ex-Australian river-surveillance boats* — Transferred: 1975

P 84 AITAPE P 92 LAVADA P 93 LAE P 94 MADANG P 85 SAMARAI

D: 146 tons (fl) **Dim:** 32.76 (30.48 pp) × 6.2 × 1.9
S: 21/24 kts **A:** 1/40-mm — 2 machine guns
M: 2 Davey-Paxman Ventura 16 cyl. diesels; 3,460 hp

AMPHIBIOUS WARFARE SHIPS

2 ex-Australian LCUs — Transferred: 1975

L 131 SALAMAUA L 132 BUNA

D: 180 tons (360 fl) **S:** 8 kts **Dim:** 44.5 × 12.2 × 1.9
M: Diesel; 675 hp

PARAGUAY

MERCHANT MARINE (1976): 26 ships — 21,390 grt
(tankers: 3 ships — 2,935 grt)

♦ *3 ex-Argentinian minesweepers* — Transferred: 1964-67

CAPITAN MESA (ex-*Parker*) **NANAVA** (ex-*Bouchard*)
TENIENTE FARINA (ex-*Py*)

Bldr: Argentina, 1937-38

D: 450 tons (650 fl) **S:** 16 kts **Dim:** 59.5 × 7.3 × 2.6
A: 4/40-mm AA — 2 machine guns **Man:** 170 men
M: 2 M.A.N. diesels; 2,000 hp **Range:** 3,000/12

♦ *2 obsolete gunboats* — Bldr: Odero, Genoa, 1930

C 1 PARAGUAY (ex-*Comodoro Meya*) **C 2 HUMAITA** (ex-*Capitan Cabral*)

D: 636 tons, 745 avg (865 fl) **Dim:** 70.15 × 10.7 × 1.65
S: 17.5 kts **Man:** 86 men
Range: 1,700/16 **Fuel:** 170 tons
A: 4/120-mm — 3/76-mm AA — 2/40-mm AA — 6 mines
M: Parsons GT; 2 props; 3,800 hp

♦ *2 ex-U.S. coastal patrol craft*

P 1 (ex-USCGC-20417) **P 2** (ex-USCGC-20418)

D: 16 tons **S:** 19 kts **Dim:** 14.0 × 4.1 × 1.0
A: 2/20-mm AA **M:** Gasoline engines; 190 hp

♦ **A 1 CAPITAN CABRAL**

D: 206 tons (fl) **S:** 9 kts **Dim:** 30.5 × 7.0 × 2.9
A: 1/76-mm — 2/37-mm **Man:** 47 men **M:** Reciprocating; 300 hp

REMARK: Wooden hull, former tug, used for riverine patrol.

♦ *2 ex-U.S. tugs*

YLT 599 A 4 (ex-YTL-211) **. . . A 5 . . .** (ex-YTL-567)

♦ *1 ex-U.S. floating dry dock* (ex-AFDL-26) — Lifting capacity: 1,000 tons

♦ *1 ex-U.S. floating workshop* (ex-YR-37)

♦ *1 dredge*

TENIENTE O CARRERAS SAGUIER

♦ *6 small craft*

P 101 to **P 106**

PERU

PERSONNEL: Approximately 14,000 men, including 1,200 officers

MERCHANT MARINE (1976): 681 ships — 525,137 grt
(tankers: 12 ships — 70,272 grt)

NAVAL AVIATION: The air arm consists of a dozen helicopters (Bell and Alouette III) and some fixed-wing aircraft (S-2 Tracker, DC-3, and Cessna).

WARSHIPS IN SERVICE AND UNDER CONSTRUCTION AS OF 1 OCTOBER 1977

	L	Tons (surfaced)	Main armament
♦ *8 submarines*			
2 ISLAY	1973-74	980	8/533-mm TT
4 DOS DE MAYO	1953-57	825	6/533-mm TT
2 PEDRERA	1944	1,870	10/533-mm TT

WARSHIPS (*continued*)

		Tons	
♦ *1 helicopter cruiser*			
AGUIRRE	1950	9,850	4/152-mm, 6/57-mm AA, 4/40-mm
♦ *3 cruisers*			
1 ALMIRANTE GRAU	1944	9,529	8/152-mm AA, 8/57-mm AA
2 CORONEL BOLOGNESI	1941-42	8,800	9/152-mm, 8/102-mm AA
♦ *4 destroyers*			
2 PALACIOS	1949-52	2,800	8 MM 38 Exocet, 6/114-mm
2 VILLAR	1942-43	2,050	4/127-mm, 6/76-mm AA, 5/533-mm TT
♦ *4 frigates*			
4 LUPO TYPE	1976-. . .	2,500	8 Otomat, 1 Albatros, 1/127-mm DP
♦ *2 corvettes*			
2 GALVEZ	1944-45	890	1/76-mm, 2/40-mm

SUBMARINES

♦ *2 Islay class, German Type 209* — Bldr: Howaldtswerke, Kiel

	L	In serv.
S 45 ISLAY	1973	23-1-75
S 46 ARICA	8-74	4-4-75

Islay (S 45) 1975

D: 980 tons surfaced, 1,230 submerged **Dim:** 55.0 × 6.6 × 5.9
S: 21 kts for 5 minutes, submerged, 12 with snorkel
A: 8/533-mm TT — 6 torpedoes in reserve **Man:** 5 officers, 26 men
M: 4 MTU Type 12V-493-TY60 diesels, each linked to a 450-kw AEG generator, single Siemans electric motor; 3,600 hp

REMARK: Similar to the Argentinian *Salta* class.

♦ *4 Dos de Mayo class* — Bldr: U.S.A., 1953-57

S 41 DOS DE MAYO
S 42 ABTAO
S 43 ANGAMOS
S 44 IQUIQUE

Angamos (S 43)

D: 825 tons surfaced, 1,400 submerged **S:** 16/10 kts
Dim: 74.0 × 6.7 × 4.2 **A:** 6/533-mm TT (except S-41 and S-43)
M: 2 General Motors diesels; 2 electric motors; 2,400 hp

REMARKS: S-41 and S-42 were refitted in 1965, S-43 and S-44 in 1968. Now obsolete.

♦ *2 Pedrera class* (ex-U.S. *Guppy-IA* class, purchased in 7-74 and 1-74)

	Bldr	L
S 47 PEDRERA (ex-*Sea Poacher*, SS-406)	Portsmouth NSY	20-5-44
S 48 PACOCHA (ex-*Atule*, SS-403)	Portsmouth NSY	6-3-43

D: 1,870 tons surfaced, 2,400 submerged **S:** 18/15 kts
Dim: 93.8 × 8.2 × 5.2 **Man:** 84 men
A: 10/533-mm TT (6 fwd, 4 aft)
M: 3 diesels; 2 electric motors; 2 props; 4,800 hp

REMARK: A third submarine of this class was towed out in 11-76 to be cannibalized for the S-47 and S-48.

CRUISERS

♦ *1 ex-Dutch cruiser* — Bldr: Rotterdam DDM — Purchased: 1976

	Laid down	L	In serv.
AGUIRRE (ex-*De Zeven Provincien*)	5-39	22-8-50	12-53

D: 9,850 tons (12,250 fl) **Dim:** 185.7 (182.4 pp) × 17.25 × 6.7
S: 32 kts **Man:** 940 men
A: 4/152-mm AA (II × 2) — 6/57-mm AA (II × 3) — 4/40-mm AA
Electron Equipt: Radars: 1 LWO-1, 1 LWO-2, 1 SGR-103, 1 SGR-104, 1 SPS-39, 2 SPG-55
Armor: Belt: 76 to 102 — 2 Decks: 20 to 25
M: Parsons GT; 2 props; 80,000 hp **Boilers:** 4 3-drum Yarrow

REMARK: The Terrier missile has been replaced by a hangar and a helicopter platform.

♦ *1 ex-Dutch cruiser* — Bldr: Wilton-Fijenoord — Purchased: 1973

	Laid down	L	In serv.
81 ALMIRANTE GRAU (ex-*de Ruyter*)	9-39	24-12-44	11-53

CRUISERS (*continued*)

Almirante Grau (81) 1977

Almirante Grau wearing her Dutch number G. Arra, 1972

D: 9,529 tons (11,850 fl) **Dim:** 187.32 (182.4 pp) × 17.25 × 6.7
S: 32 kts **Man:** 920 men
A: 8/152-mm AA (II × 4) — 8/57-mm AA (II × 4) — 8/40-mm AA (II × 4)
Electron Equipt: Radars: 1 LWO-1, 1 LWO-2, 1 SGR-105, 1 SGR-103, 1 SGR-104
Armor: Belt: 76 to 102 — 2 Decks: 20 to 25
M: Parsons GT; 2 props; 80,000 hp **Boilers:** 4 3-drum Yarrow

♦ 2 *Coronel Bolognesi class* (ex-British Colonies class)

	Bldr	L
82 **CORONEL BOLOGNESI** (ex-*Ceylon*)	Alex Stephen & Son	30-7-42
83 **CAPITÁN QUIÑONES** (ex-*Almirante Grau*, ex-*Newfoundland*)	Swan Hunter	19-12-41

D: 8,800 tons (11,100 fl) **Dim:** 169.31 × 18.31 × 6.3
S: 29 kts (max) **Man:** 776 to 800 men
Range: 7,000/14 **Fuel:** 2,000 tons

Capitán Quiñones (83) 1977

A: 9/152-mm (III × 3, 2 fwd, 1 aft) — 8/102-mm AA (II × 4) — 12/40-mm
Armor: Belt: 76 to 102 — Deck: 52 — Turret: 25 to 52 — Conning tower: 102
M: Parsons GT; 4 props; 80,000 hp **Boilers:** 4 Admiralty

REMARKS: Purchased in 1959, transferred in 12-59 and 1-60. The 102-mm guns of the *Coronel Bolognesi* have radar fire control. The *Capitán Quiñones* has two trellis masts, the *Coronel Bolognesi* has a tripod mast aft.

DESTROYERS

♦ 2 *Palacios class* (ex-British D class) — Bldr: Yarrow, Glasgow

	L	In serv. after refit
73 **PALACIOS** (ex-*Diana*)	8-5-52	11-73
74 **FERRÉ** (ex-*Decoy*)	29-3-49	7-73

Palacios (73) 1973

D: 2,800 tons (3,700 fl) **Dim:** 118.87 (111.55 pp) × 13.1 × 5.5
S: 30 kts **Man:** 250 to 300 men
Range: 4,400/20

DESTROYERS (*continued*)

A: 8/MM 38 Exocet SSM launchers — 1 squid — 6/114-mm AA (II × 3) — 2/40-mm AA
Electron Equipt: Radars: 1 combination surface-to-air search, 1 Decca, 1 Plessey AWS-1 air-search
M: Pamatreda GT; 2 props **Boilers:** 2 Foster-Wheeler, 60 kg/cm²

REMARKS: Welded hull. Purchased in 1969. Refit by Cammell Laird completed at the end of 1973. A helicopter deck has been added over the stern.

♦ *Villar class* (ex-U.S. *Fletcher* class) — Bldr: Bethlehem Steel, Staten Island

	L	Transferred
71 **VILLAR** (ex-*Benham*, DD-796)	29-8-43	12-60
72 **GUISE** (ex-*Isherwood*, DD-520)	24-11-42	10-61

Villar (71)

D: 2,050 tons (3,050 fl)
Dim: 114.85 (wl) × 12.03 × 5.5
S: 30 kts
Man: 15 officers, 260 men
Range: 1,260/30, 4,400/15
A: 4/127-mm 38-cal. (I × 4) — 6/76-mm 50-cal. AA (II × 3) — 5/533-mm TT (V × 1) — 2 hedgehogs
M: General Electric GT; 2 props; 60,000 hp
Fuel: 650 tons
Boilers: 4 Babcock & Wilcox, 42 kg/cm², superheat 455°

REMARKS: Transferred in 1961 under MAP. Two sister ships, *La Vallette* (DD-448) and *Terry* (DD-513) were transferred in 1974 for cannibalization.

FRIGATES

♦ *4 Italian Lupo type* — Bldr: 51 and 52: CNTR, Riva Trigoso; 53 and 54: CNTR, Callao

	Laid down	L	In serv.
51 **CARVAJAL**	8-10-74	17-11-76	. . .
52 **VILLAVICENCIO**	6-10-76	11-77	. . .
53 **MELITON**	. . .	. . .	. . .
54 **MANUEL**	. . .	. . .	. . .

Carvajal (51) 1976

D: 2,500 tons (fl) **S:** 30 kts **Dim:** 113 × 12 × . . .
A: 8 Otomat Mk 2 Teseo — 1/127-mm DP — 1 BPDMS Albatros — 4/40-mm AA (II × 2) — 6 ASW TT (III × 2) — 1 AB-212 helicopter
Electron Equipt: Radars: 1 RAN 10 air-search, 1 RAN 11 surface-search, 2 CT NA 10 Elsag — technical data system
Sonar: hull
M: CODOG: 2 Fiat GE LM-2500 gas turbines; 2 GMT diesels, 3,100 hp; 2 variable-pitch props; 20,000 hp
Electric: 3,120 kw

REMARK: Italian technicians will assist in the building of the 53 and the 54 at Callao.

CORVETTES

♦ *2 Galvez-class ex-U.S. minesweepers*

	Bldr	L
68 **GALVEZ** (ex-*Ruddy*, MSF-380)	Gulf SB Corp.	29-10-44
69 **DIEZ CANSECO** (ex-*Shoveler*, MSF-382)	Gulf SB Corp.	10-21-45

D: 890 tons (1,250 fl)
Dim: 67.36 (65.9 pp) × 10.51 × 3.3
S: 17 kts
Man: 100 men
A: 1/76-mm — 2/40-mm AA — 2 depth-charge projectors — 1 hedgehog
M: Diesel-electric propulsion; General Motors diesels; 2 props; 3,500 hp

CORVETTES *(continued)*

Diez Canseco (69)

REMARK: Transferred under MAP in 12-60, and now in Coast Guard.

PATROL BOATS

♦ *6 French PR-72* ordered 8-76 for delivery 1979-80 — Bldr: Soc. Française Navale

	Laid down		Laid down
N . . .	. . .	N . . .	. . .
N . . .	. . .	N . . .	. . .
N . . .	. . .	N . . .	. . .

D: . . . **S:** . . . **Dim:** . . .
A: . . . **M:** . . .

♦ *6 Rio Cañete class* — Bldr: SIMA, Callao

	L	In serv.		L	In serv.
P 234 RIO CAÑETE	8-10-74	31-3-76	**P . . . N . . .**	. . .	. . .
P . . . N . . .	. . .	. . .	**P . . . N . . .**	. . .	. . .
P . . . N . . .	. . .	. . .	**P . . . N . . .**	. . .	. . .

D: 300 tons **Dim:** 50.62 (49.1 pp) × 7.4 × 1.7
S: 21 kts **Man:** 6 officers, 33 men
A: 1/40-mm — 1/20-mm **Endurance:** 20 days
M: 4 MTU 8V diesels; 5,640 hp **Electric:** 170 kw

REMARKS: Only the first one had been laid down by 5-76. They are intended for use in port security and coastal patrol.

♦ *6 Vosper boats* — Bldr: Vosper, Ltd., Portsmouth

	L		L
21 VELARDE	10-7-64	**24 HERRERA**	26-10-64
22 SANTILLANA	24-8-64	**25 LARREA**	18-2-65
23 DE LOS HEROES	18-11-64	**26 SANCHEZ CARRION**	18-2-65

Santillana Shbldg. and Sh. Record

D: 100 tons (130 fl) **Dim:** 33.4 (31.46 wl) × 6.4 × 2.15
S: 25 kts **Man:** 4 officers, 27 men
A: 2/20-mm AA (II × 1)
M: 2 Napier Deltic diesels; 6,200 hp

REMARKS: Modification of the *Sri* class built for Malaysia. Welded hull, light-metal superstructure, air-conditioned living spaces. Being fitted with SS-12 missiles. They have sonar and in time of war could be modified to carry four torpedoes or to lay mines. Fitted for fisheries protection and for rescue missions. Went into service in 10-65.

♦ *2 ex-U.S. boats* — Bldr: U.S.A., 1965 — Transferred: 9-66 and 6-72

PC 11 RIO SAMA (ex-PGM-78) **PC 12 RIO CHIRA** (ex-PGM-111)

D: 100 tons (147 fl) **S:** 18.5 kts **Dim:** 31.1 × 4.9 × 2.0
A: 1/40-mm AA — 4/20-mm AA (II × 2) **Man:** 27 men
M: 8 diesels; 2 props; 1,800 hp

REMARK: Since 1966 the U.S.A. has transferred a great many of these boats to various navies.

♦ *3 Rio-class river patrol boats* — Bldr: Viareggio, Italy — In serv. 5-60

01 RIO ZARUMILLA **02 RIO TUMBES** **04 RIO PIURA**

D: 37 tons (fl) **S:** 18 kts **Dim:** 20.27 × 5.25 × 2.75
A: 2/40-mm **Range:** 1,000/14
M: General Motors diesels; 2 props; 1,200 hp

PATROL BOATS (*continued*)

Rio Zarumilla

♦ *4 La Punta-class river patrol boats*

230 LA PUNTA **232 RIO SANTA**
231 RIO CHILLON **233 RIO MAJES**

D: 16 tons **Man:** 5 men **A:** 2 machine guns

RIVER GUNBOATS (Amazon Flotilla)

♦ *2 Marañon class* — Bldr: John I. Thornycroft

	Laid down	L	In serv.
13 MARAÑON	4-50	23-4-51	7-51
14 UCAYALI	4-50	7-3-51	7-51

Marañon Thornycroft

D: 350 tons (365 fl) **S:** 12 kts **Dim:** 47.22 × 9.75 × 1.22
Man: 4 officers, 36 men **Range:** 5,000/10
A: 2/76-mm — 7/20-mm **M:** Polar diesels; 2 props; 800 hp

REMARKS: Based at Iquitos and in service on the Upper Amazon. Forced ventilation. Superstructure of light metal.

♦ *2 Amazonas class* — Bldr: Electric Boat Co., Groton, 1934

11 AMAZONAS **12 LORETO**

Amazonas

D: 250 tons **S:** 15 kts **Dim:** 46.7 × 6.7 × 1.2
A: 4/76-mm — 1/47-mm — 2/20-mm AA **Man:** 5 officers, 20 men
Range: 4,000/10 **M:** Diesels; 1 prop; 750 hp

♦ **14 AMERICA** (1902-04)

D: 185 tons (240 fl) **S:** 12 kts **Dim:** 40.5 × 5.9 × 1.4
A: 2/47-mm — 4/AA machine guns **Man:** 26 men
M: Reciprocating; 1 prop; 350 hp **Fuel:** 42 tons coal

♦ **301** (ex-16) **NAPO** — Bldr: Yarrow, 1920

D: 98 tons **S:** 12 kts **Dim:** 29.5 × 3.05 × 0.9
A: 3/47-mm — 2/AA machine guns **Man:** 22 men
M: Reciprocating; 1 prop; 45 hp **Boilers:** Yarrow **Fuel:** oil

REMARK: Modified as a hospital ship.

♦ *2 10-ton lagoon patrol boats*

PA 11 LAVE **PA 12 RAMIS**

Photo Requested

AMPHIBIOUS WARFARE SHIPS

♦ *2 ex-U.S. landing ships*

34 CHIMBOTE (ex-LST-283) **35 PAITA** (ex-LST-512)

D: 1,625 tons (4,088 fl) **A:** *Chimbote:* 1/76-mm — *Paita:* 6/40-mm AA

REMARKS: *Chimbote* purchased in 1951, *Paita* in 1957. The latter is assigned to the naval academy.

♦ *2 ex-U.S. landing ships* — Bldr: U.S.A., 1945

36 LOMAS (ex-LSM-396) **37 ATICO** (ex-LSM-554)

D: 513 tons (913 fl) **S:** 12 kts **Dim:** 61.5 × 10.4 × 2.15
A: 2/40-mm AA — 4/20-mm AA **Fuel:** 165 tons
M: Diesels; 3,600 hp

REMARKS: Living spaces for 116 men. Purchased in the U.S.A. and transferred in 7-59.

AUXILIARY SHIPS

♦ *7 oilers*

TALARA BAYORAN — Bldr: SIMA, Callao — L: 8-7-76 and 1977

D: 25,000 tons (fl) **S:** 15.5 kts **Dim:** 171.0 × 25.0 × 9.5
M: Diesel; 12,000 hp

151 MOLLENDO — Bldr: Japan, 1962

D: 6,084 tons (25,670 fl) **S:** 14 kts **Dim:** 163.0 × 22.0 × 9.15
M: 1 B & W diesel; 7,500 hp

REMARK: Bought in 1967 and now in reserve.

155 PARINAS (12-6-67) **156 PIMENTAL** (5-4-68) — Bldr: Ars, Callao

Pimental (156) 1977

D: 13,600 tons (fl) **S:** 14 kts **Dim:** 125.0 × 18.9 × 7.3
M: B & W diesel; 5,400 hp **Cargo capacity:** 7,000 tons

158 ZORRITOS (8-10-58) **159 LOBITOS** — Bldr: Ars, Callao

D: 8,700 tons **S:** 12 kts **Dim:** 115.37 × 15.85 × 6.5
M: B & W diesel; 2,400 hp **Man:** 60 men
Cargo capacity: 6,000 tons

REMARK: Fitted for replenishment at sea.

♦ *1 transport*

31 INDEPENDENCIA (ex-*Bellatrix*, AKA-3)

D: 6,200 tons (14,225 fl) **Dim:** 140.0 × 19.2 × 7.95
S: 15 kts **Man:** 19 officers, 220 men
A: 1/127-mm — 4/76-mm 50-cal. AA — 10/20-mm AA
M: Nordberg diesel; 1 prop; 6,000 hp **Range:** 18,000/14

REMARKS: Former U.S. C2-T-class cargo ship, built in 1940, refitted in 1954, and transferred under MAP in 2-63. Used as a training ship for midshipmen.

♦ *1 Ilo-class transport* — Bldr: SIMA, Callao

131 ILO — In serv. 15-12-71

D: 18,000 tons fl **Dim:** 153.85 (144.53 pp) × 20.4 × 9.2
S: 19.4 kts **A:** 4/40-mm AA (II × 2)
M: 1/BW 6 K-74 EF class diesel; 1 prop; 11,600 hp

♦ *2 ex-U.S. tugs*

123 GUARDIAN RIOS (ex-*Pinto*, ATF-90, *Apache* class) (5-1-43)

D: 1,235 tons (1,675 fl) **S:** 16 kts **Dim:** 62.5 × 11.7 × 4.8
M: Diesel-electric; 3,000 hp **Man:** 85 men

136 UNANUE (ex-*Wateree*, ATA-174) (1943)

D: 534 tons (835 fl) **S:** 13 kts **Dim:** 43.58 × 10.3 × 4.1
M: Diesel-electric propulsion; 1,500 hp

♦ *2 tugs*

SELENDON — Bldr: West Germany, 1968

D: 1,000 tons **S:** . . . **Dim:** . . . **M:** . . .

CONTRAESTRE NAVARRO

D: 50 tons

REMARK: In the Amazon Flotilla. Added to the fleet in 2-73.

VARIOUS SHIPS

♦ *3 water carriers*

141 MANTILLA (ex-U.S. YW-122) — Modified: 3-63

D: 1,800 tons **S:** 8 kts **Dim:** 53.0 × 9.75 × 2.9
M: 1 diesel

ABA 113 (330 tons) built in Peru (1972)

ABA 001 800-ton barge for the Amazon Flotilla (1972)

♦ *2 floating docks*

ADF 111 (1,900 tons)
ADF 112 (5,000 tons)

♦ *1 floating training center*

61 CASTILLA (ex-*Bangust*, DE-739)

REMARKS: Pontoon ship at Iquitos.

Personnel (1976): 17,000 men, including a brigade of Marines

Merchant Marine (1976): 457 ships — 1,018,065 grt
(tankers: 46 ships — 293,790 grt)

Naval Aviation (1975): In the process of being established with helicopters and transport and liaison aircraft.

FRIGATES

♦ *1 ex-U.S. escort ship* — Transferred: to Vietnam, 1971, to the Philippines, 1975

PS 4 RAJAH LAKANDULA (ex-*Camp*, DER-251)

Rajah Lakandula (PS 4) 1977

D: 1,590 tons (2,100 fl) **Dim:** 93.26 × 11.22 × 4.0
S: 19 kts **Man:** 150 men
Range: 11,500/11 **Fuel:** 300 tons
A: 2/76-mm AA — 6 TT — 1 hedgehog
M: Fairbanks-Morse diesels; 2 props; 6,000 hp

♦ *6 ex-U.S. Coast Guard cutters* — Transferred: 4 on 1-1-71, 2 on 25-7-72

PS 7 ANDRES BONIFACIO (ex-*Chincoteague*, WHEC-375)
PS 8 GREGORIO DE PILAR (ex-*McCulloch*, WHEC-386)
PS 9 DIEGO SILANG (ex-*Bering Strait*, WHEC-382)
PS 10 FRANCISCO DAGAHOY (ex-*Castle Rock*, WHEC-383)
PS . . . N . . . (ex-*Yakutat*, WHEC-380)
PS . . . N . . . (ex-*Cook Inlet*, WHEC-384)

D: 1,766 tons (2,800 fl) **Dim:** 94.5 × 12.52 × 3.7
S: 17 kts **Man:** 160 men
A: 1/127-mm — machine guns **Range:** 18,000/15
M: Diesels; 2 props; 6,000 hp **Fuel:** 400 tons

Remarks: These ships served with the Vietnamese Navy and escaped to the Philippines in 1975. They were transferred to the Philippine Navy 5-4-76.

PHILIPPINES

Andres Bonifacio (PS 7) 1977

♦ *1 ex-U.S. destroyer escort* — Transferred: 12-67

PS 76 DATU KALANTIAW (ex-*Booth*, DE-170)

D: 1,240 tons (1,908 fl) **Dim:** 93.3 (91.5 pp) × 11.22 × 4.0
S: 21 kts **Man:** 165 men
Range: 11,600/11 **Fuel:** 300 tons
A: 3/76-mm — 6/40-mm AA (I × 6) — 2/20-mm AA — 6/533-mm TT
M: Diesels; 6,000 hp

CORVETTES

♦ *2 ex-U.S. Raven/Auk-class minesweepers*

	L	Transferred
PS 69 RIZAL (ex-*Murrelet*, MSF-372)	24-12-44	5-65
PS 70 QUEZON (ex-*Vigilance*, MSF-324)	5-4-43	8-67

D: 890 tons (1,250 fl) **Dim:** 67.2 (65.0 pp) × 9.75 × 3.3
S: 18 kts **Man:** 100 men
A: 2/76-mm AA — 4/40-mm AA — 4/20-mm AA — 1 hedgehog — 3/324-mm TT
M: Diesel-electric; 2 props; 3,500 hp

♦ *8 ex-U.S. patrol escorts* — Transferred: 8-48

	L
PS 19 MIGUEL MALVAR	. . .
PS 22 SULTAN KURADAT	. . .

CORVETTES (*continued*)

PS 23 DATU MARIKUDO	. . .
PS 28 CEBU (ex-PCE-881)	10-11-43
PS 29 NEGROS OCCIDENTAL (ex-PCE-884)	24-2-44
PS 30 LEYTE (ex-PCE-885)	30-4-45
PS 31 PANGASINAN (ex-PCE-891)	15-6-44
PS 32 ILOILO (ex-PCE-897)	3-8-45

D: 640 tons (850 fl) **S:** 15 kts **Dim:** 59.95 × 7.05 × 3.25
A: 1/76-mm — 6/40-mm AA — 4/20-mm AA **Man:** 100 men
M: Diesel; 2 props; 2,000 hp

♦ *2 ex-U.S. minesweepers*

PS 18 MAGAT SALAMAT (ex-*Gayety*, MSF-239)
PS 20 MAGAL CAPAZ (ex-*Shelter*, MSF-301)

Magal Capaz (PS 20)

D: 640/650 tons (900/950 fl) **Dim:** 56.24 × 10.06 × 2.75
S: 14/15 kts **Man:** 7 officers, 90 men
A: 1/76-mm AA — 2/40-mm — 8/20-mm
M: General Motors diesels; 2 props; 1,800/2,400 hp

REMARKS: These ships had been transferred to Vietnam and escaped to the Philippines in 1975. They were acquired by the latter in 1976.

PATROL BOATS AND CRAFT

♦ *4 ex-U.S. patrol boats* — Transferred: 1947-48 and 1976

PS 25 NUEVA ECIJA (ex-PC-1241)	24-12-42
PS 27 CAPIZ (ex-PC-1564)	19-4-44
PS 80 NUEVA VISCAYA (ex-PCE-568)	24-4-42
PS . . . N. . . (ex-Cambodian E-312)	15-5-43

D: 280 tons (450 fl) **S:** 18 kts **Dim:** 52.95 × 7.05 × 3.25
A: 1/76-mm — 1/40-mm AA — 3 or 5/20-mm AA **Man:** 70 men
M: Diesel; 2 props, 2,880 hp **Fuel:** 60 tons

REMARK: The E-312 escaped from Cambodia to the Philippines and was acquired by the latter in 1976.

♦ *5 ex-U.S. motor gunboats* — Transferred: 1960-61 and 1976

	L
P 60 BASILAN (ex-PGM-83)	. . .
P 61 AGUSAN (ex-PGM-39)	3-60
P 62 CATANDUANES (ex-PGM-40)	3-60
P 63 ROMBEOM (ex-PGM-41)	6-60
P 64 PALAWAN (ex-PGM-42)	6-60

D: 122 tons (fl) **S:** 17 kts **Dim:** 30.6 × 6.5 × 2.6
A: 2/20-mm AA **M:** Diesel; 2 props; 950 hp

REMARKS: P-62 is manned by the coast guard. P-60 escaped from Vietnam to the Philippines in 1975 and was acquired by the latter in 1976.

Palawan (P 64)

♦ *2 Italian-built hydrofoils* — Bldr: Cant. Nav. Leopoldo Rodriguez, Messina, 1965

M 72 CAMIGUIN **M 73 SIQUIJOR**

Camiguin

PATROL BOATS AND CRAFT (*continued*)

D: 28 tons **S:** 38 kts **Dim:** 27.0 × 4.7/7.5 × 2.1
A: 1/20-mm AA **Man:** 15 men **Range:** 400
M: 1 Mercedes-Benz diesel; 1,250 hp

REMARKS: Based on the commercial PT 20-type hydrofoil.

♦ *2 Japanese-built hydrofoils* — Bldr: Hitachi Zosen, Osaka, 1966

M 74 BONTOC **M 75 BALEK**

D: 32 tons (fl) **S:** 38 kts **Dim:** 21.0 × 4.8/7.5 × 2.1
A: 2/AA machine guns **Man:** 15 men **Range:** 400
M: 1 Mercedes-Benz diesel; 1,100 hp

♦ *18 ex-U.S. Swift boats* — Bldr: U.S.A., 1965

PCF 300 to **PCF 317**

PCF 302

D: 22.5 tons (fl) **S:** 25 kts **Dim:** 15.6 × 4.12 × 1.5
A: 3/12.7-mm machine guns — 1/81-mm mortar **Man:** 6 men
M: Diesel; 2 props; 960 hp

♦ *6 improved Swift boats* — Bldr: Sewart, U.S.A., 1975

PCF 332 to **PCF 337**

D: 33 tons (fl) **S:** 25 kts **Dim:** 21.3 × 5.2 × 1.1
A: 2/12.7 machine guns — 2/7.62 machine guns
M: 3 diesels; 3 props; 1,590 hp

MINE WARFARE SHIPS

♦ *2 ex-U.S. ocean minesweepers* — Transferred: 1972

	L
M 91 DAVAO DEL NORTE (ex-*Firm*, MSO-444)	9-53
M 92 DAVAO DEL SUR (ex-*Energy*, MSO-436)	9-53

♦ *2 ex-U.S. coastal minesweepers* — Transferred: 1956

	L
M 55 ZAMBALES (ex-MSC-218)	1955
M 56 ZAMBOANGA DEL NORTE (ex-MSC-219)	1955

AMPHIBIOUS WARFARE SHIPS

♦ *22 ex-U.S. landing ships*

	L
LT 38 BULACAN (ex-LST-843)	29-11-44
LT 39 ALBAY (ex-LST-865)	22-11-44
LT 40 MISAMIS ORIENTAL (ex-LST-875)	29-11-44
LT 85 BATAAN (ex-LST-515)	21-12-43
LT 86 CAGAYAN (ex-LST-825)	11-11-44
LT 87 ILOCOS NORTE (ex-LST-905)	30-12-44
LT 93 MINDORO OCCIDENTAL (ex-LST-222)	17-8-43
LT 94 SURIGAO DEL NORTE (ex-LST-488)	5-3-43
LT 95 SURIGAO DEL SUR (ex-LST-546)	16-2-44
LT N . . . (ex-LST-975)	6-1-45
LT N . . . (ex-LST-529)	17-1-44
LT N . . . (ex-LST-848)	2-1-43
LT N . . . (ex-LST-47)	24-9-43
LT N . . . (ex-LST-230)	12-10-43
LT N . . . (ex-LST-287)	31-10-43
LT N . . . (ex-LST-491)	23-9-43
LT N . . . (ex-LST-566)	11-5-44
LT N . . . (ex-LST-607)	7-4-44
LT N . . . (ex-LST-692)	31-3-44
LT N . . . (ex-LST-822)	1-11-44
LT N . . . (ex-LST-1069)	7-3-45
LT N . . . (ex-LST-1072)	20-3-45

D: 1,620 tons (4,080 fl) **S:** 11.6 kts **Dim:** 100.04 × 14.24 × 4.3
A: 8/40-mm AA — 2/20-mm **M:** General Motors diesels; 2 props

REMARKS: Ex-LST-975, ex-LST-529, and ex-LST-848 escaped from Vietnam to the Philippines in 1975 and were acquired by the latter in 1976. The ships listed above, from ex-LST-47 on, are used as local transports.

♦ *5 ex-U.S. landing ships*

	L	Transferred
LP 41 ISABELA (ex-LSM-463)	1944-45	3-61
LP 65 BATANES (ex-LSM-175)	3-8-44	. . .
LP 66 WESTERN SAMAR (ex-LSM-335)	10-11-44	. . .
LP 68 MINDORO ORIENTAL (ex-LSM-320)	1944-45	4-62
LP . . . N . . . (ex-LSM-110)	28-10-44	. . .

D: 743 tons (912 fl) **S:** 12 kts **Dim:** 62.18 × 10.52 × 2.6
A: 2/40-mm AA — several 20-mm AA **Man:** 39 men
M: 2 diesels; 2,800 hp

♦ *3 ex-U.S. landing ships*

CAMARINES SUR (ex-LSSL-129)
N . . . (ex-LSSL-101)
N . . . (ex-LSSL-9)

D: 250 tons (387 fl) **Dim:** 48.8 × 7.1 × 1.75

AMPHIBIOUS WARFARE SHIPS (*continued*)

S: 14 kts **Man:** 6 officers, 54 men
A: 1/76-mm — 4/40-mm — 4/20-mm AA — 4 mortars
M: General Motors diesels; 2 props; 1,600 hp **Range:** 5,000/12

REMARK: These are ex-Vietnamese ships that took refuge in the Philippines and were acquired by the latter in 1976.

♦ *3 ex-U.S. landing ships*

	L
SERGOSON (ex-LSIL-872)	4-10-44
CAMARINES (ex-LSIL-699)	21-6-44
MISAMIS OCCIDENTAL (ex-LSIL-871)	3-10-44

D: 227 tons (383 fl) **S:** 14.4 kts **Dim:** 57.8 × 7.6 × 1.7
A: 1/76-mm AA — 1/40-mm AA — 2/20-mm AA — depth-charge projectors
M: Diesels; 2 props; 1,600 hp **Man:** 55 men

REMARKS: Ex-Vietnamese ships that took refuge in the Philippines in 1975 and were acquired by the latter in 1976.

♦ *12 ex-U.S. LCVPs* — Transferred: 1-70

♦ *1 ex-U.S. landing craft repair ship*

AKLAN (ex-*Krishna*, ARL-38), 1943 — Transferred: 30-10-71

D: 1,650 tons (3,700 fl) **S:** 10 kts
Dim: 99.85 × 15.25 × 4.36 **M:** 2 diesels; 1,500 hp

HYDROGRAPHIC SHIPS

♦ *2 Arinya class* — Bldr: Walkers Ltd., Australia — In serv: 1962-64

ARINYA **ARLUNYA**

D: 245 tons **S:** 10 kts **Dim:** 33.0 × 6.6 × 3.15
M: 2 diesels; 336 hp

♦ **ATYIMBA** — In serv. 1969

D: 611 tons (fl) **S:** 11 kts **Dim:** 43.5 × 9.9 × 4.5
M: 2 diesels; 2 props; 720 hp

AUXILIARY SHIPS

♦ *7 ex-U.S. tankers*

YO 43 LAKE MAUJAN (ex-YO-173)
YO 78 LAKE BOHI (ex-YOG-73)
N . . . (ex-YOG-80)
N . . . (ex-YOG-33)
N . . . (ex-YOG-61)
N . . . (ex-YO-115)
N . . . (ex-YO-116)

D: 520 tons (1,400 fl) **S:** 8 kts **Dim:** 53.0 × 9.7 × 4.7
A: 2/20-mm AA **M:** Diesel; 1 prop; 560 hp

♦ *4 ex-U.S. water carriers*

YW 42 LAKE LANAO, YW 33 LAKE BULAN, YW 39 LAKE PAOAY, N . . .

D: 1,235 tons (fl) **S:** 11 kts **Dim:** 53.0 × 9.7 × 3.0
M: 2 diesels; 1,000 hp

♦ *1 ex-U.S. cargo ship* — Transferred: 3-72

TK 90 MACTAN (ex-AK-174) (1945)

D: 4,900 tons (5,636 fl) **S:** 11.5 kts **M:** Diesel; 1,750 hp

♦ *1 rescue tug* — Transferred: 7-48

AQ 44 IFUGAO (ex-HMS *Emphatic*, ex-U.S. AKR-96)

D: 852 tons **S:** 13 kts **Dim:** 43.6 × 10.06 × 4.15
A: 1/76-mm — 2/20-mm AA **M:** Diesel-electric; 1,800 hp

♦ *6 ex-U.S. harbor tugs*

YQ 221 MARANAO (ex-YTL-554)
YQ 222 IGOROT (ex-YTL-572)
YQ 223 TAGBANUA (ex-YTL-429)
YQ 224 AETA (ex-YTL-449)
YQ 225 ILONGOT (ex-YTL-427)
YQ 226 TASADAY (ex-YTL-425)

VARIOUS SHIPS

♦ **TP 777 ANG PANGULO** (ex-*The President*, ex-*Rosax*, ex-*Lapu-Lapu*) — Bldr: Japan, 1958

D: 2,000 tons **S:** 18 kts **Dim:** 83.9 × 12.95 × 6.4
A: 2/20-mm AA **Man:** 90 men
M: B & W diesels; 5,000 hp; 2 props

REMARK: Former presidential yacht.

♦ **TK 21 MOUNT SAMAT** (ex-*Pagasa*, ex-*Santa Maria*, ex-APO-21, ex-*Quest*, AM-281)

L: 16-3-44 — Transferred: 7-48

D: 650 tons (945 fl) **S:** 14 kts **Dim:** 56.24 × 10.06 × 2.75
A: 1/76-mm — 4/40-mm AA **Man:** 100 men
M: Diesel; 2 props; 1,800 hp

REMARK: Former American minesweeper.

♦ *1 ex-USCG buoy tender*

D: 935 tons **S:** 13 kts **Dim:** 59.0 × 12.1 × 4.3
M: Diesel-electric; 1 prop; 1,200 hp

♦ *4 ex-U.S. buoy tenders*

L 45 LAUIS LEDGE (ex-FS-185)
L 46 BOJEADUR (ex-FS-203)
L 48 LIMASAWA (ex-FS-169)

D: 470 tons (811 fl) **S:** 11 kts **Dim:** 54.5 × 9.6 × 3.1
M: Diesel; 2 props

L 47 PEARL BANK (1944) — Transferred: 1953

D: 162 tons (300 fl) **S:** 6 kts **Dim:** 37.0 × 7.27 × 2.45
M: Diesel; 2 props; 1,000 hp

POLAND

PERSONNEL (1976): 25,000 men

MERCHANT MARINE (1976): 733 ships — 3,263,206 grt
(tankers: 25 ships — 557,553 grt)

NAVAL AVIATION: About 40 fixed-wing aircraft, including MIG-17 Fresco fighters and IL-28 Beagle bombers, and about 20 Hare and Hound helicopters. All are of Soviet origin.

WARSHIPS IN SERVICE OR UNDER CONSTRUCTION AS OF 1 OCTOBER 1977

	L	Tons	Main armament
♦ *4 submarines*			
4 WHISKEY	1962	1,050 (surfaced)	6/533-mm TT
♦ *1 destroyer*			
1 KOTLIN SAM	1958	2,850	1 SA-N-1 system, 2/130-mm
♦ *13 patrol boats*			
13 OSA-I	1960	165	4 SS-N-2, 4/30-mm
♦ *10 torpedo boats*			
10 WISLA	1970	70	2/30-mm AA, 4/533-mm TT

WEAPONS AND SYSTEMS

Most weapons and systems in use in the Polish Navy are of Soviet origin.

SUBMARINES

♦ *4 ex-Soviet Whiskey class* — Transferred: Since 1962

ORZEL **SOKOL** **KONDOR** **BIELIK**

Orzel

D: 1,050 tons surfaced, 1,350 submerged **S:** 17/16 kts
Dim: 76.0 × 6.3 × 4.8 **Man:** 60 men **Range:** 13,000
A: 6/533-mm TT (4 fwd, 2 aft) — 18 torpedoes
M: 2 diesels; diesel-electric drive; 2 props; 4,000/2,500 hp

REMARK: Snorkel on the after end of the sail.

GUIDED-MISSILE DESTROYER

♦ *1 ex-Soviet Kotlin SAM class* — Bldr: U.S.S.R., 1958 — Transferred: 1970

275 WARSZAWA

D: 2,850 tons (3,500 fl) **Dim:** 127.0 × 12.75 × 4.0
S: 34 kts **Man:** 360 men
Range: 3,000/18, 5,500/16

Warszawa 1973

A: 2 SA-N-1 missile launchers (II × 1) — 2/130-mm (II × 1, fwd) — 4/45-mm AA (IV × 1) — 2/MBU-2500A ASW rocket launchers — 5/533-mm TT (V × 1)
Electron Equipt: Radars: 1 Head Net C, 1 Don, 1 Sun Visor, 1 Hawk Screech, 1 Peel Group
Sonar: Herkules or Pegas
M: GT; 2 props; 60,000 hp **Boilers:** 4

GUIDED-MISSILE PATROL BOATS

♦ *13 Osa-I class* — Bldr: U.S.S.R., 1960 — Transferred: Since 1966

D: 165 tons (210 fl) **S:** 36 kts **Dim:** 39.0 × 7.7 × 1.8
A: 4/30-mm AA (II × 2) — 4 SS-N-2 missile launchers (I × 4)
Electron Equipt: Radars: 1 Square Tie, 1 Drum Tilt **Man:** 25 men
M: 3 M503A diesels; 3 props; 12,000 hp

TORPEDO BOATS

♦ *10 Wisla class* — Bldr: Poland, 1970

Wisla class

Wisla class

D: 70 tons **S:** 34 kts **Dim:** 25.0 × 5.4 × 1.8
A: 2/30-mm AA — 4/533-mm TT **Range:** . . . **M:** Gas turbines

MINE WARFARE SHIPS

♦ *12 Krogulec-class minesweepers* — Bldr: Stocznia Gdynska, Gdynia, 1963-67

PELIKAN	JASTRAB	JASKOLKA
KROGULEC	ALBATROS	ZURAW
ORLIK	KANIA	CZAPLA
KORMORAN	TUKAN	CZALDA

Krogulec class

D: 450 tons **S:** 16 kts **Dim:** 58.0 × 8.4 × 2.5
A: 6/25-mm AA (II × 3) **M:** Diesels

REMARK: Some of these ships have 4/25-mm rapid-fire AA mounted aft.

♦ *12 Soviet T-43-type minesweepers* — Bldr: Stocznia Gdynska, Gdynia, 1955-60

ZUBR	BIZON	FOKA
TUR	BOBR	MORS
LOZ	ROZMAK	RYS
DZIK	DELFIN	ZBIK

T-43 class

MINE WARFARE SHIPS (*continued*)

D: 500 tons (580 fl) **S:** 17 kts **Dim:** 61.0 × 8.4 × 2.7
A: 4/37-mm AA (II × 2) — 8/15-mm machine guns **M:** Diesels

♦ *28 K-8-class inshore minesweepers*

D: 39/41 tons **S:** 18 kts **Dim:** 17.0 × 3.5 × 2.2
A: 2/25-mm AA — 2 machine guns **M:** Diesels

AMPHIBIOUS WARFARE SHIPS

♦ *23 Soviet Polnocnyi-type landing ships* — Bldr: Poland

D: 800/850 tons **S:** 18 kts **Dim:** 75.0 × 8.9 × 2.6 (max)
A: 2/30-mm AA (II × 1)
Electron Equipt: Radars: 1 Drum Tilt, 1 Don
M: Diesels; 4,000 hp **Cargo capacity:** 350 tons

REMARKS: Some have 18-barrel fire-support rocket launchers. There are variations in profile (bow and masts).

♦ *15/16 landing craft*

HYDROGRAPHIC SHIPS

♦ *2 Soviet Moma class*

KOPERNIK **HYDROMETR**

Kopernik 1976

D: 1,300 tons **S:** 16 kts **Dim:** 67.0 × 10.8 × 4.0
M: Diesels

REMARK: One of them can be used for intelligence-collecting.

AUXILIARY SHIPS

♦ *5 coastal oilers*

Z 5 **Z 6** **Z 7** **Z 8** **Z 9 (MOSKIT)**

Z 8 1973

D: 300 tons (fl) **A:** 4/25-mm AA (II × 2) **M:** Diesel

♦ *3 coastal transports*

Z 1 KRAB **Z 2 MEDUSA** **Z 3 SLIMAK**
D: 300 tons (fl)

♦ *2 salvage ships (1974)*

PIAST **LECH**

Piast 1974

D: 1,860 tons **S:** 14.5 kts **Dim:** 72.6 (67.2 pp) × 11.0 × 4.0
A: . . . **M:** Diesel; 1 prop

REMARK: Carry a diving bell.

VARIOUS SHIPS

♦ *1 intelligence collector*

BALTYK

Baltyk 1970

D: 1,200 tons **S:** 11 kts **Dim:** 58.3 × 8.75 × 4.2
M: Steam; 1,200 hp

♦ *2 training ships*

WODNIK — L: 29-11-75 **GRYF** — L: 13-3-76

Wodnik 1976

D: 1,800 tons **S:** 20 kts **Dim:** 74.0 × 10.8 × 4.2
A: 4/30-mm AA (II × 2) — 4/29-mm AA (II × 2)
Electron Equipt: Radar: 1 Drum Tilt
M: Diesels; 2 props; 4,000 hp

REMARK: Identical to the East German Navy's *Wilhelm Pieck.*

♦ *3 Briza-class training ships*

ELEW **KADET** **PODCHORAZY**

Podchorazy 1976

D: 150 tons **S:** 10 kts **Dim:** 30 × 7 × 2
Man: 11 men, 26 midshipmen **M:** Diesels

♦ *1 three-masted sail training ship* — Bldr: The Netherlands, 1917

IOKTA (ex-*Iskra*)

D: 460 tons **S:** 7.5 kts **Dim:** 39.0 × 7.6 × 2.95
Man: 38 men **M:** 1 diesel

♦ *1 ex-Polnocnyi Mod. repair ship*

♦ *2 Pajak-class torpedo-recovery ships*

♦ *18 tugs of various types*

♦ *3 Mrowka-class degaussing ships*

♦ *8 diving tenders*

PATROL BOATS MANNED BY BORDER GUARDS

♦ *4 Oksywie class* — Bldr: Poland, 1962–64

OP 301 to **OP 304**

D: 170 tons **S:** 20 kts **Dim:** 41 × 6 × 2
A: 2/37-mm AA (I × 2) — 4/25-mm AA (II × 2) **M:** Diesels

POLAND (*continued*)

PATROL BOATS — BORDER GUARDS (*continued*)

OP 303 1972

♦ *13 Obluze class* — Bldr: Poland, 1965

OP . . . to **OP** . . .

Obluze class 1976

D: 170 tons **S:** 20 kts **Dim:** 40.0 × 6.0 × 2.1
A: 4/30-mm AA (II × 2) **M:** Diesels
Electron Equipt: Radars: 1 Don, 1 Drum Tilt

♦ *9 Gdansk class* — Bldr: Poland, 1960

OP 311 to **OP 319**

Gdansk class

D: 120 tons **S:** 20 kts **Dim:** 35.0 × 5.8 × 1.5
A: 2/37-mm AA **M:** Diesels

♦ *7 Pilica class* — Bldr: Poland, 1973

KP 162 to **KP 168**

D: 100 tons **S:** 15 kts **Dim:** . . .
A: 2/25-mm AA (II × 1) **M:** 2 diesels

♦ *5 Wisloka class*

D: 100 tons **S:** 10 kts **Dim:** . . .
A: 2/14.5-mm (II × 1) **M:** Diesels

PORTUGAL

Personnel: Approximately 12,000, including 3,000 Marines.

Merchant Marine (1976): 431 ships — 1,173,710 grt
(tankers: 24 ships — 503,148 grt)

Naval Aviation: A few Air Force P2-V Neptune maritime patrol aircraft are at the disposal of the Navy.

WARSHIPS IN SERVICE OR UNDER CONSTRUCTION AS OF 1 OCTOBER 1977

	L	Tons	Main armament
♦ *3 submarines*			
3 DAPHNÉ	1966–68	869 (surfaced)	12/550-mm TT
♦ *13 frigates*			
6 JOÃO COUTINHO	1969–70	1,252	2/76-mm AA, ASW weapons

WARSHIPS (*continued*)

4 COMMANDANT RIVIÈRE	1966-68	1,650	3/100-mm, ASW weapons
3 ALMIRANTE PEREIRA DA SILVA	1964-65	1,450	4/76-mm AA, ASW weapons

WEAPONS AND SYSTEMS

Most of the recently acquired systems are of French origin.

SUBMARINES

♦ *3 Daphné class* — Bldr: Dubigeon, Normandy — Purchased: 1964

	Laid down	L	In serv.
S 163 ALBACORA	9-65	15-10-66	10-67
S 164 BARRACUDA	10-65	24-4-67	5-68
S 166 DELFIM	5-67	23-9-68	10-69

Albacora (S 163)

D: 689 tons surfaced, 1,043 submerged **S:** 13.5/16 kts
Dim: 57.75 × 6.76 × 4.62 **Man:** 5 officers, 45 men
A: 12/550-mm TT (8 fwd, 4 aft)
M: Diesel-electric propulsion: SEMT-Pielstick diesels (450 kw); 2 props; 1,300/1,600 hp

REMARKS: See Remarks on the *Daphné* class in French section. The *Cachalote* (S-165) has been purchased by the Pakistani Navy.

FRIGATES

♦ *6 João Coutinho class*

	Laid down	L	In serv.
F 475 JOÃO COUTINHO	9-68	2-5-69	3-70
F 476 JACINTO CANDIDO	4-68	16-6-69	6-70
F 477 GENERAL PEREIRA D'ECA	10-68	26-7-69	10-70
F 484 AUGUSTO CASTILHO	8-68	5-7-69	11-70
F 485 HONORIO BARRETO	7-68	11-4-70	5-71
F 471 ANTONIO ENES	4-68	1-8-69	7-71

Bldrs: F-475 to F-477: Blohm & Voss, Germany; F-484 to F-471: Bazan, Spain

João Coutinho (F 475) 1971

D: 1,252 tons (1,348 fl) **Dim:** 84.6 × 10.3 × 3.3
S: 21 kts **Man:** 9 officers, 84 men
A: 2/76-mm Mk 33 AA (II × 1) — 2/40-mm AA (II × 1) — 1 hedgehog — 2 depth-charge projectors — helicopter platform
Electron Equipt: Radar: 1 MLA-1B scan
Sonar: 1 QCU 2
M: SEMT-Pielstick PA6V-280 diesels; 2 props; 10,960 hp
Range: 5,900/18 **Electric:** 600 kw

REMARKS: The engines for these ships were ordered from Chantiers de l'Atlantique, St. Nazaire, France, in 1967. The ships can carry 34 Marines. Made more than 22 knots in trials; the F-475 made more than 25 knots. Designated "corvettes."

♦ *4 Commandant Rivière class* — Bldr: A. C. de Bretagne

	Laid down	L	In serv.
F 480 COMMANDANTE JOÃO BELO	5-65	22-3-66	7-67
F 481 COMMANDANTE HERMEGILDO CAPELO	5-66	29-11-66	4-68
F 482 COMMANDANTE ROBERTO IVENS	1-67	11-8-67	11-68
F 483 COMMANDANTE SACADURA CABRAL	8-67	15-3-68	11-69

D: 1,760 tons (2,250 fl) **Dim:** 103.0 (98 pp) × 11.5 × 3.8
S: 25 kts (26.6 max) **Man:** 214 men
Range: 4,500/15, 6,000/10-12

Commandante João Belo (F 480)

FRIGATES (*continued*)

A: 3/100-mm automatic AA (I × 3) — 2/40-mm AA — 305-mm ASW mortar (IV × 1) — 6 ASW TT (III × 2)
Electron Equipt: Radars: 1 DRBV 22, 1 DRBV 50, DRBR-C 31
Sonars: 1 DUBA, 1 SQS 17
M: 4 SEMT-Pielstick diesels; 2 props, 16,000 hp **Electric:** 1,280 kw

REMARK: See Remarks on *Commandant Rivière* class in French section.

♦ *3 Almirante Pereira da Silva class*

	Laid down	L	In serv.
F 472 ALMIRANTE PEREIRA DA SILVA	6-62	2-1-64	12-66
F 473 ALMIRANTE GAGO COUTINHO	9-63	30-8-65	11-67
F 474 ALMIRANTE MAGALHAES CORREA	1963	26-4-65	11-68

Bldrs: F-472 and F-473: Est. Nav. Lisnave, Lisbon; F-474: Est. Nav de Viana do Castelo

Almirante Gago Coutinho (F 473) J. C. Bellonne, 1973

D: 1,450 tons (1,950 fl) **S:** 25 kts **Dim:** 95.7 × 11.26 × 4.3
Man: 11 officers, 154 men **Range:** 4,500/15
A: 4/76-mm AA (II × 2) — 2/375-mm Bofors ASW rocket launchers — 6/ASW TT (III × 2) for Mk 44 torpedoes
Electron Equipt: Radars: 1 978 (band X), 1 MLA-1B (band L), 1 Mk 34 fire-control
Sonars: SQS 29, SQS 35 (towed)
M: GT; 1 prop; 20,000 hp **Boilers:** 2 **Fuel:** 400 tons

REMARK: Based on the U.S. *Dealey*-class escorts.

PATROL BOATS AND CRAFT

♦ *10 Cacine class*

P 1140 CACINE
P 1141 CUNENE
P 1142 MANDOVI
P 1143 ROVUMA
P 1144 QUANZA (30-5-69)
P 1145 GEBA (21-5-69)
P 1146 ZAIRE (28-11-70)
P 1147 ZAMBEZE (1971)
P 1160 LIMPOPO (9-4-73)
P 1161 SAVE

Cacine (P 1140) 1970

Bldrs: P-1140 to P-1143: Arsenal do Alfeite; Others: Est. Nav. do Mondego

D: 310 tons (fl) **S:** 20 kts **Dim:** 44.0 × 7.67 × 2.2
A: 2/40-mm AA — 1/37-mm rocket launcher **Man:** 3 officers, 30 men
M: 2 Maybach diesels; 2 props; 4,400 hp

♦ *6 Albatroz class* — Bldr: Arsenal do Alfeite, 1975

P 1162 ALBATROZ
P 1163 ACOR
P 1164 AGUIA
P 1165 ANDORHINA
P 1166 CONDOR
P 1167 CISNE

D: 45 tons (fl) **S:** 20 kts **Dim:** 21.88 × 5.25 × . . .
A: 1/20-mm AA — 1/12.7-mm machine gun **Range:** 450/18
M: Diesels

♦ *2 Dom Aleixo class* — Bldr: San Jacintho Aveiro

P 1148 DOM ALEIXO (12-67) **P 1149 DOM JEREMIAS** (12-67)

Dom Aleixo (P 1148)

D: 60 tons **S:** 16 kts **Dim:** 25.0 × 5.2 × 1.6
A: 1/20-mm or 2 machine guns **Man:** 1 officer, 9 men
M: Cummins diesels; 2 props; 1,600 hp

MINE WARFARE SHIPS

♦ *4 São Roque-class minesweepers* — Bldr: Estaleiros Navais da C.U.F., Lisbon

M 401 SÃO ROQUE (15-9-55)
M 402 RIBEIRA GRANDE (14-10-55)
M 403 LAGOA (15-9-55)
M 404 ROSARIO (29-11-55)

MINE WARFARE SHIPS *(continued)*

D: 370 tons (425 fl) **Dim:** 46.33 (42.68 pp) × 8.75 × 2.5
S: 15 kts **Man:** 4 officers, 43 men
A: 1/40-mm AA — 2/20-mm AA (II × 1)
M: Diesels; 2 props; 2,500 hp

REMARKS: Ordered early in 1954, two built with U.S. "offshore" funds. Similar in appearance to the British "-ton" class.

AMPHIBIOUS WARFARE CRAFT

♦ *1 landing craft*

LDG 202 ALABARDA (1969-71)

D: 500 tons **S:** 11 kts **Dim:** 57.0 × 11.8 × 1.27
Man: 2 officers, 18 men **M:** Diesels; 2 props; 1,000 hp

♦ *3 100-class landing craft*

LDM 119 **LDM 120** : **LDM 121**

♦ *8 400-class landing craft*

LDM 406 (1967-68) **LDM 419** **LDM 421** **LDM 423**
LDM 418 (1971-72) **LDM 420** **LDM 422** **LDM 424**

D: 56 tons (101 fl) **S:** 9 kts **Dim:** 17.0 × 5.0 × 1.2
A: 1/20-mm **M:** Diesels; 2 props; 450 hp

HYDROGRAPHIC SHIPS

♦ *1 ex-U.S. survey ship* — Bldr: Marietta SB, U.S.A., 1969 — Transferred: 21-1-72

A 526 COMMANDANTE ALMEIDA CARVALHO (ex-*Kellar*, AGS-25)

D: 1,200 tons **S:** 15 kts **Dim:** 57.5 × 11.7 × 4.5
Man: 5 officers, 25 men **M:** Diesel-electric; 1 prop; 1,200 hp

REMARKS: Sister ship of the U.S. Navy's *S. P. Lee* (AGS-31). Has hull and machinery characteristics of *Robert D. Conrad* (AGOR-3) — see U.S.A. section.

♦ *1 ex-British frigate* — In serv. 2-49

A 527 ALFONSO DE ALBUQUERQUE

D: 1,590 tons (2,230 fl) **Dim:** 93.6 (87.2 pp) × 11.7 × 4.3
S: 19.5 kts **Range:** 7,000/9
M: Triple-expansion; 2 props; 5,500 hp **Boilers:** 3

♦ *1 survey ship*

A 5200 MIRA (ex-*Fomalhaut*, ex-*Arrabile*)

D: 23 tons **S:** 15 kts **Dim:** 18.9 × 4.6 × 1.2
M: 3 Perkins diesels; 300 hp **Man:** 16 men

AUXILIARY SHIPS

♦ *1 oiler* — Bldr: Arsenal do Alfeite

	Laid down	L
A 523 SAM BRAS	1939	17-5-42

D: 5,766 tons (6,374 fl) **S:** 12 kts **Dim:** 102.5 × 15.6 × 5.5
Man: 11 officers, 90 men **Range:** 11,000/12 **Fuel:** 568 tons

Sam Bras (A 523) 1970

A: 1/76-mm — 2/40-mm — 1/20-mm AA
M: B & W diesel; 1 prop; 2,700 hp

REMARKS: Former tanker modified as a logistics support ship. Platform for three helicopters. Cargo capacity: oil, 3,000 tons; gasoline, 49 tons; lubricating oil, 50 tons; distilled water, 100 tons. In special reserve since 13-8-75.

♦ *1 tanker* — Bldr: Est. Nav. de Viana do Castelo

	L	In serv.
A 5206 SÃO GABRIEL	1961	3-63

São Gabriel (A 5206)

D: 14,200 tons (fl) **Dim:** 146.0 (138 pp) × 18.22 × 8.0
S: 17 kts **Man:** 9 officers, 93 men
Range: 6,000/15 **Cargo capacity:** 9,000 tons
M: Pametrada GT; 1 prop; 9,500 hp **Boilers:** 2

♦ *1 netlayer* — Bldr: Arsenal do Alfeite

	Laid down	L	In serv.
A 54 SCHULTZ XAVIER	2-70	1972	1973

D: 900 tons **S:** 14 kts **Dim:** . . .
Man: . . . **Range:** 3,000/12.5
M: Diesels; 1 prop; 2,400 hp **Fuel:** Diesel

PORTUGAL (*continued*)

AUXILIARY SHIPS (*continued*)

Schultz Xavier (A 54) J. C. Bellonne, 1973

REMARK: Fitted for servicing lighthouses.

♦ *1 sail training ship* — Bldr: Blöhm & Voss, Hamburg, 1937

A 520 SAGRES (ex-*Guanabara*, ex-*Alberto Leo Schlageter*)

D: 1,425 tons (1,869 fl) **S:** 10 kts **Dim:** 75.9 × 12.0 × 4.6
Sail area: 20,793 sq. ft. **Fuel:** 52 tons
M: M.A.N. diesel; 1 prop; 750 hp

Sagres (A 520)

REMARKS: Three-masted schooner. Former school sailing ship of the German Navy. Assigned to the U.S.A. in 1945, sold to Brazil in 1948, sold to Portugal in 1960. Early in 1961 she replaced the training ship *Sagres* (1896), which was removed from the active list, renamed *Santo Andre* (A-5207), and now serves as a depot ship.

QATAR

MERCHANT MARINE (1976): 14 ships — 75,747 grt

PATROL BOATS AND CRAFT

♦ *6 103-foot patrol boats* — Bldr: Vosper Thornycroft, 1975-76

Q 11 BARZAN **Q 14 AL WUSSAIL**
Q 12 HWAR **Q 15 AL KHATAB**
Q 13 THAT ASSUARI **Q 16 TARIQ**

D: 120 tons **S:** 27 kts **Dim:** 32.4 (31.1 pp) × 6.3 × 1.6
A: 2/40-mm AA **Man:** 25 men
M: 2 diesels; 4,000 hp **Range:** . . .

♦ *2 75-foot patrol craft* — Bldr: Whittingham and Mitchell, Chertsey, 1969

D: . . . **A:** 2/20-mm **Dim:** 22.5 × . . . × . . .
M: 2 diesels; 1,420 hp

♦ *3 45-foot patrol craft* — Bldr: Vosper

D: 13 tons **S:** 26 kts **Dim:** 13.5 × 3.8 × 1.1
A: 1/12.7-mm machine gun

♦ *15 Spear-class patrol craft*

D: 4 tons **S:** 26 kts **Dim:** 9.1 × 2.8 × 0.8
A: 3/7.62-mm machine guns

ROMANIA

PERSONNEL: 9,000 men, 3,000 of whom are seagoing

MERCHANT MARINE (1976): 161 ships — 994,134 grt
(tankers: 9 ships — 246,095 grt)

NAVAL AVIATION: 4 to 6 ASW helicopters

WARSHIPS IN SERVICE OR UNDER CONSTRUCTION AS OF 1 OCTOBER 1977

	L	Tons	Main armament
♦ *3 corvettes*			
3 POTI	1964-67	500 (fl)	2/57-mm, 2 rocket launchers, 4 TT
♦ *45 patrol boats*			
17 SHANGHAI-II	1971-74	120	1/57-mm, or 1/37-mm, rocket launchers
5 OSA-I	post 1960	175	4 SS-N-2
14 P-4	pre 1954	19.3	2/25-mm AA, 2 TT
3 KRONSTADT	1950	300	1/85-mm, 2/37-mm
6 HUCHWAN	. . .	39 (fl)	2 TT

CORVETTES

♦ *3 ex-Soviet Poti class* — Transferred: 1964–67

V 31 **V 32** **V 33**

D: 500 tons (fl) **S:** 34 kts **Dim:** 60.3 × 8.0 × 3.0
A: 2/57-mm AA (II × 1) — 2 MBU 2500A rocket launchers — 2 or 4/400-mm ASW TT (I × 2 or II × 2)
Electron Equipt: Radars: 1 Don, 1 Strut Curve, 1 Muff Cob
M: CODAG: 2 M503A diesels (4,000 hp each) plus 2 GT (20,000 hp each); 2 props
Man: 50 men

PATROL BOATS

♦ *17 Shanghai-II class* — Bldr: Mangolia, Romania, 1972–74

VS 41 to **VS 44** **VS 52** **VP 20** to **VP 31**

D: 120 tons (155 fl) **S:** 30 kts **Dim:** 39.6 × 5.5 × 1.7
A: VS-41 to VS-44, VS-52: 1/37-mm — 2/14.5-mm machine guns (II × 1) — 2 MBU 1800 rocket launchers
VP-30 to VP-31: 1/57-mm — 4/25-mm (II × 2) — 2 MBU 1800 (?)
M: 4 diesels; 4 props; 5,000 hp

♦ *5 ex-Soviet Osa-I class* — Transferred: Since 1960

Osa-I type 1974

D: 175 tons (210 fl) **S:** 36 kts **Dim:** 39.0 × 7.7 × 1.8
A: 4 SS-N-2 — 4/20-mm AA (II × 2)
Electron Equipt: Radars: 1 Square Tie, 1 Drum Tilt
M: 3 M503A diesels; 3 props; 12,000 hp

♦ *14 ex-Soviet P-4 class* — Launched: Prior to 1954

D: 19.3 tons (22.4 fl) **S:** 55 kts **Dim:** 19.3 × 3.7 × 1.0
A: 2/25-mm AA — 2/450-mm TT (one on each side)
M: 2 M50 diesels; 2 props; 2,400 hp

P-4 class

REMARK: The torpedoes have been removed from some of these ships.

♦ *3 ex-Soviet Kronstadt class* — Bldr: U.S.S.R., 1950

V 1 **V 2** **V 3**

D: 300 tons (330 fl) **S:** 18 kts **Dim:** 52.1 × 6.5 × 2.2
A: 1/85-mm — 2/37-mm AA **Man:** 40 men **Fuel:** 20 tons
M: 3 diesels; 3 props; 3,300 hp

♦ *6 Huchwan-class hydrofoils*

VT 51 to **VT 56**

VT 53

D: 39 tons (fl) **Dim:** 21.8 × 4.9 × 1.0; foilborne: 7.5 × 0.31
S: 54 kts **Range:** 500/20
A: 4/25-mm AA (II × 2) — 2/533-mm TT
M: 3 diesels; 3 props; 3,600 hp

ROMANIA (*continued*)

MINE WARFARE SHIPS

♦ *4 Democratia-class minesweepers (German M-40 class)* — Bldr: Galatz, 1943

DB 13 DEMOCRATIA **DB 15 DESROBIREA**
DB 14 DESCATUSARIA **DB 16 DREPTATEA**

German M 40 class minesweeper

D: 643 tons (775 fl) **S:** 17 kts **Dim:** 62.3 × 8.5 × 2.6
Man: 80 men **Range:** 4,000/10 **Fuel:** 152 tons coal
A: 6/37-mm AA (II × 3) — 2 depth-charge projectors
M: 2 triple-expansion engines, each driving an exhaust turbine; 2 props; 2 boilers; 2,400 hp

♦ *18 ex-Soviet T-301-class minesweepers*

DR 4 to **DR 9** **DR 17** to **DR 19** **DR 21** to **DR 29**

D: 145.7 tons (160 fl) **S:** 12.5 kts **Dim:** 38.0 × 5.1 × 1.6
A: 1/45-mm AA or 2/20-mm AA — 4 machine guns **Man:** 32 men
M: 3 diesels; 3 props; 1,440 hp

♦ *8 TR-40-class inshore minesweepers*

VD 241 to **VD 248**

D: 60 tons (fl) **S:** 18 kts **Dim:** 17.0 × 3.5 × 1.2
A: 2/29-mm AA **M:** 2 diesels; 2 props; 600 hp

AMPHIBIOUS WARFARE SHIPS

♦ *8 to 10 Braila-class utility landing craft*

AUXILIARY SHIPS

♦ *3 coastal tankers*

♦ *4 ocean tugs*

D: 450 tons **M:** 1,200 hp

VARIOUS SHIPS

♦ *1 sail training ship* — Bldr: Blohm & Voss — Launched: 9-38

MIRCEA

D: 1,630 tons **S:** 10 kts **Dim:** 82 × 12 × 5
M: 1 diesel **Sail area:** 1,750 m^2

REMARK: Refitted in Germany, 1966-67.

♦ *2 to 3 small hydrographic ships*

♦ *3 Sontu-class gunboats*

GHICULESCU **N . . .** **N . . .**

Ghiculescu 1972

D: 330 tons **S:** 12 kts **Dim:** 60.9 × 7.0 × 2.5
A: 2/100-mm (I × 2) **Man:** 50 men
M: 2 Sulzer diesels, 900 hp each

REMARKS: Former World War I French *Friponne*-class gunboats sold to Romania in 1920. Appear to be used for coastal surveillance.

DANUBE FLOTILLA

♦ *7 monitors*

VB 76 to **VB 82**

A: 1/57-mm — 4/25-mm AA (II × 2) — 2 mortars

♦ *60 patrol boats*

VD series: **D:** approx. 30 tons **A:** 4/25-mm AA (II × 2)
VG series: **D:** approx. 20 tons **A:** 2 machine guns

SABAH

PATROL BOATS

♦ *2 55-foot boats* — Bldr: Vosper Thornycroft, Singapore

SRI SEMPORNA **SRI BANGJI**

D: 50 tons **S:** 20 kts **Dim:** 16.5 × 5.5 × 1.0
A: 1 machine gun **Man:** 11 men
M: Diesels; 1,200 hp **Range:** 300/15

SABAH *(continued)*

PATROL BOATS *(continued)*

♦ *2 91-foot boats*

SRI GUMANGTONG **SRI LABUAN**

D: . . . **S:** . . . **Dim:** . . .
A: . . . **Range:** . . . **Man:** . . . **M:** Diesels

♦ *1 ex-yacht*

PUTRI SABAH

D: 117 tons **S:** 22 kts **Dim:** 27.3 × 9.5 × 1.65

♦ *2 PX-class small craft transferred by Malaysia*

ST. LUCIA

MERCHANT MARINE (1976): 2 ships — 904 grt

♦ *1 small craft* — Bldr: Brooke Marine Ltd, Lowestoft, Great Britain

CHATOYER

D: 15 tons **S:** 22 kts **Dim:** 12.0 × 3.6 × 0.65
A: 2 machine guns **M:** 2 diesels; 370 hp

ST. VINCENT

MERCHANT MARINE (1976): 18 ships — 5,663 grt

♦ *1 small craft* — Bldr: Brooke Marine Ltd, Lowestoft, Great Britain

HELEN

D: 15 tons **S:** 22 kts **Dim:** 12.0 × 3.6 × 0.6
A: 2 machine guns **M:** 2 diesels; 370 hp

SAUDI ARABIA

PERSONNEL: 750 men + 350 coast guard

MERCHANT MARINE (1976): 84 ships — 588,745 grt
(tankers: 21 ships — 426,200 grt)

CORVETTES

♦ *6 U.S.-built ships*

D: 720 tons (fl) **Dim:** 71.4 × 8.4 × 2.65
S: 30 kts gas turbines/20 diesels **Man:** 53 men
A: 8/Harpoon (IV × 2) — 1/76-mm OTO Melara Compact — 2/20-mm AA — 1/81-mm mortar — 2/40-mm army grenade launchers — 6/TT Mk 32 (III × 2)
Electron Equipt: Radars: 1 SPS 40A, 1 SPS 60
Sonar: 1 SQS 56
M: CODOG: 1 General Electric gas turbine (16,500 hp); 2 diesels (2,000 hp); 2 props

PATROL BOATS

♦ *6 U.S.-built boats*

D: 320 tons (fl) **Dim:** 56.2 × 4.6 × 1.75
S: 38 kts gas turbines/18 diesels **Man:** 35 men
A: 4/Harpoon (II × 2) — 1/76-mm OTO Melara Compact — 2/20-mm AA — 1/81-mm mortar — 2/40-mm army grenade launchers
M: CODOG: 1 General Electric gas turbine (16,500 hp); 2 diesels (1,500 hp)

♦ *1 ex-U.S.C.G. Cape class* — Transferred: 1969

RIYADH

D: 102 tons **S:** 20 kts **Dim:** 28.95 × 5.80 × 1.85
A: 1/40-mm **Man:** 15 men **Range:** 1,500/12
M: 4 diesels; 2 props; 2,200 hp

♦ *2 Badr class* — Bldr: Bayerische Schiffbau, Erlenbach/Main — In serv. 1976

BADR
AL YARMOUK

D: 110 tons

TORPEDO BOATS

♦ *3 ex-German Jaguar class* (Type 141) — Bldr: Lürssen, Vegesack, 1969

DAMMAM **KHABAR** **MACCAH**

SAUDI ARABIA (*continued*)

TORPEDO BOATS (*continued*)

1975

D: 170 tons	**S:** 40 kts	**Dim:** 42.8 × 7.15 × 2.2	
A: 2/40-mm — 4/533-mm TT			
M: 4 diesels; 4 props; 12,000 hp		**Man:** 3 officers, 33 men	

MINE WARFARE SHIPS

♦ *4 MSC-type coastal minesweepers* — Being built

Ordered: 30-9-75 — Bldr: Peterson, Sturgeon Bay, Wisconsin

AMPHIBIOUS WARFARE SHIPS

♦ *4 medium landing ships*

Remarks: Being built in the U.S.A. Two delivered in 1976.

VARIOUS SHIPS

♦ *1 training ship* — Bldr: Bayerische Schiffbau, Erlenbach/Main

D: . . . **S:** . . . **Dim:** 60 × 10 × . . .
M: 2 MTU diesels; 2,630 hp

Remark: Delivered late 1977.

♦ *1 yacht* — Bldr: C. Van Lent & Zonen, The Netherlands

D: . . . **S:** . . . **Dim:** 64.0 × 9.6 × 3.0
M: Diesels; 6,300 hp **Man:** 26 men

♦ *8 British SRN-6 air-cushion vehicles* — Delivered: 1970-72

♦ *2 harbor tugs* — Delivered: late 1975

♦ *Approximately 30 coast guard patrol boats of different makes and dimensions*
Most in poor condition.

SENEGAL

Personnel: 180 men

Merchant Marine (1976): 65 ships — 26,621 grt
(tankers: 4 ships — 3,876 grt)

PATROL BOATS AND CRAFT

♦ *3 PR-48 class* — Bldr: S.F.C.N. Villeneuve-la-Garenne

	Laid down	L	In serv.
ST. LOUIS	4-70	5-8-70	3-71
POPENGUINE	1972	1973	10-8-74
PODOR	. . .	20-7-76	2-77

St. Louis 1971

D: 240 tons (avg.) **Dim:** 47.5 (45.5 pp) × 7.1 × 2.5
S: 23 kts **Man:** 3 officers, 22 men
A: 4/40-mm AA — 8/SS-12 missiles **Range:** 2,000/15
M: 2 MGO diesels; 2 props; 4,200 hp

♦ *3 coastal surveillance small craft* — Transferred by France: 1963, 1966

CASAMANCE (ex-P-755, ex-VC-5)
SINÉ SALOUM (ex-P-754, ex-VC-4) (17-8-57)
Bldr: Constr. Méc. de Normandie, Cherbourg

D: 70 tons (80 fl) **S:** 28 kts **Dim:** 31.77 × 4.7 × 1.7
A: 2/20-mm AA **Man:** 15 men **Range:** 1,500/15
M: 2 4-ton, 12 cyl. Mercedes-Benz diesels; 2 props; 2,700 hp

LES ALMADIES — Former fisheries protection vessel

♦ *1 small craft* — Bldr: Fairey Marine, Great Britain, 1974

D: 4.25 tons **S:** 28 kts **Dim:** 9.0 × 2.7 × 0.8
A: 2 machine guns **Man:** 4 men **Range:** 200/24
M: Perkins diesels; 2 props; 290 hp

AMPHIBIOUS WARFARE SHIPS

♦ *1 ex-French landing craft* — Transferred: 7-1-74

FALEME (ex-Edic-9095) (11-4-58)

SENEGAL (*continued*)
AMPHIBIOUS WARFARE SHIPS (*continued*)

D: 250 tons (670 fl) **S:** 8 kts **Dim:** 59.0 × 11.95 × 4.62
A: 2/20-mm **Man:** 16 men **M:** MGO diesels; 2 props; 1,000 hp

REMARK: Can carry 11 trucks or 5 LVT landing craft.

♦ *2 ex-U.S. 26-ton medium landing craft* — Transferred: 1968

DJOMBOSS **DOULOULOU**

VARIOUS SHIPS

♦ *1 training ship*

CRAME JEAN — Former fishing vessel — In serv. 1970 — **D:** 18 tons

♦ *1 tug* (ex-*Ibis*, Y-658) — On loan from the French Navy

SIERRA LEONE

Shanghai II: 001 and 002

PATROL BOATS

♦ *2 Shanghai-II class*

001 N . . . **002 N . . .**

D: 120 tons **S:** 30 kts **Dim:** 39.6 × 5.5 × 1.7
A: 4/37-mm AA (II × 2) — 4/25-mm AA (II × 2)
M: 4 diesels; 5,000 hp **Man:** 28 men

SINGAPORE

PERSONNEL (1976): 3,000 men

MERCHANT MARINE (1976): 722 ships — 5,481,720 grt
(tankers: 114 ships — 2,650,038 grt)

GUIDED-MISSILE PATROL BOATS

♦ *6 Lürssen type* — Ordered: 1970

P 76 SEA WOLF **P 79 SEA TIGER**
P 77 SEA LION **P 80 SEA HAWK**
P 78 SEA DRAGON **P 81 SEA SCORPION**

Bldrs: P-76 and P-77: Lürssen, Bremen; Others: Jurong, Singapore, with German technical assistance

Sea Scorpion (P 81) 1976

GUIDED-MISSILE PATROL BOATS (*continued*)

Sea Lion (P 77) without missiles 1976

D: 280 tons **S:** 34 kts **Dim:** 48.0 × 7.0 × 2.9
A: 5 Israeli Gabriel missiles (III × 1, I × 2) — 1/57-mm AA — 1/40-mm AA
M: 4 MTU diesels; 4 props; 14,400 hp **Man:** 40 men

REMARK: Not all are armed with Gabriel missiles.

GUNBOATS

♦ *3 110-ft type Vosper Thornycroft*

	L		L
P 69 INDEPENDENCE	15-7-69	**P 72 JUSTICE**	15-5-70
P 70 FREEDOM	18-1-69		

Independence (P 69) Vosper, 1970

Bldrs: P-69: Vosper Thornycroft, Portsmouth; P-70 and P-72: Vosper Thornycroft Private Ltd., Tanjong Rhy, Singapore

D: 100 tons (130 fl) **Dim:** 33.4 (31.46 pp) × 6.4 × 1.71
S: 30 kts **Man:** 4 officers, 27 men
A: 1/40-mm AA Bofors — 1/20-mm Oerlikon Mk 15 SLA/204 GK (1,000 rounds/min, muzzle velocity 1,050 m/sec)
M: 2 Maybach MD 872 diesels, 3,100 hp each (2,400 cruising), with 2,100 rpm and 1,800 rpm, respectively
Electric: 100 kw

REMARK: Ordered 21-5-68.

♦ *3 120-ft type Vosper Thornycroft*

P 71 SOVEREIGNTY **P 73 DARING** **P 74 DAUNTLESS**

Sovereignty (P 71) Thornycroft, 1971

D: 100 tons (130 fl) **S:** 32 kts **Dim:** 33.4 × 6.4 × 1.71
A: 1/76-mm Bofors (for characteristics, see section on Norway) — 1/20-mm Oerlikon
M: 2 MTU diesels; 7,200 hp **Man:** 4 officers, 27 men

♦ *1 British Ford class* — Bldr: United Engineers, Singapore, 1956

P 48 PANGLIMA

D: 119 tons (131 fl) **S:** 14 kts **Dim:** 35.66 × 6.1 × 1.85
A: 1/40-mm **Man:** 15 men
M: 2 Paxman diesels **Fuel:** 15 tons

REMARK: Transferred by Malaysia in 1967.

MINE WARFARE SHIPS

♦ *2 ex-U.S. Bluebird-class minesweepers* — Transferred: 5-12-75

JUPITER (ex-*Thrasher*, MSC-203)
MERCURY (ex-*Whippoorwill*, MSC-207)

D: 370 tons (fl) **S:** 12 kts **Dim:** 43.9 × 8.5 × 2.5
A: 2/20-mm (II × 1) **Range:** 1,500/12 kts **Man:** 39 men
M: 2 General Motors diesels; 2 props; 1,760 hp

AMPHIBIOUS WARFARE SHIPS

♦ *6 ex-U.S. LSTs* — Transferred: 1 in 7-71; the last three in 1973

A 81 ENDURANCE (ex-*Holmes County*, LST-836)
A . . . N . . . (ex-LST-579)
A . . . N . . . (ex-LST-613)
A . . . N . . . (ex-LST-623)

SINGAPORE (*continued*)

AMPHIBIOUS WARFARE SHIPS (*continued*)

A . . . N . . . (ex-LST-629)
A . . . N . . . (ex-LST-649)

D: 1,653 tons (4,080 fl) **S:** 11.6 kts **Dim:** 98.4 × 15.0 × 4.2
A: 8/40-mm (II × 2, I × 4) **Man:** 120 men
M: 2 General Motors diesels; 2 props; 1,700 hp

VARIOUS SHIPS

♦ *3 transports (ex-U.S. LSTs)*

N . . . (ex-LST-117)
N . . . (ex-LST-276)
N . . . (ex-*Chase County,* LST-532)

SOMALI REPUBLIC

Merchant Marine (1976): 255 ships — 1,792,900
(tankers: 14 ships — 246,094 grt)

GUIDED-MISSILE PATROL BOATS

♦ *3 ex-Soviet Osa-II class* — Transferred: 1975

Osa-II class 1976

D: 205 tons (240 fl) **S:** 36 kts **Dim:** 39.0 × 7.7 × 1.8
A: 4/SS-N-2 Styx — 4/30-mm AA (II × 2)
M: 3 M504 diesels; 3 props; 15,000 hp

TORPEDO BOATS

♦ *4 ex-Soviet MOL-class boats* — Transferred: 1976

MOL class

MOL class with TT

D: 170 tons (210 fl) **S:** 40 kts **Dim:** 39.9 × 7.6 × 1.8
A: 4/30-mm AA (II × 2) — 4/533-mm TT (I × 4)
M: 3 diesels; 13,500 hp

♦ *4 ex-Soviet P-6 class*

D: 73 tons **S:** 43 kts **Dim:** 25.3 × 6.1 × 1.7
A: 4/25-mm AA (II × 2) — 2/533-mm TT

PATROL BOATS

♦ *5 ex-Soviet Poluchat class*

D: 100 tons **S:** 19 kts **Dim:** 29.57 × 6.1 × 1.9
A: 4/25-mm AA (II × 2) **M:** Diesels; 2 props

AMPHIBIOUS WARFARE SHIP

♦ *1 ex-Soviet Polnocnyi-class landing ship* — Transferred: 12-76

PERSONNEL: 4,500, including 420 officers

MERCHANT MARINE (1976): 279 ships — 477,011 grt
(tankers: 3 ships — 27,355 grt)

NAVAL AVIATION: An Air Force detachment is available to the Navy. Shackleton and Piaggio aircraft are used for patrol and Wasp helicopters are embarked on the ships.

WARSHIPS IN SERVICE OR UNDER CONSTRUCTION AS OF 1 OCTOBER 1977

	L	Tons (Surfaced)	Main armament
♦ *5 submarines*			
2 AGOSTA	...	1,450	4/533-mm TT
3 DAPHNÉ	1969-70	869	12/550-mm TT
		Tons	
♦ *1 destroyer*			
JAN VAN RIEBEECK	1943	2,105	4/102-mm, 1 helicopter
♦ *9 frigates*			
3 A-69	1977-	1,250 (fl)	1/100-mm
3 WHITBY	1960-62	2,250	2/114-mm, 1 helicopter
2 LOCH	1944	1,610	1/102-mm
1 ALGERINE	1943	1,040	2/102-mm
♦ *12 patrol boats*			
♦ *10 minesweepers*			

SUBMARINES

♦ *2 Agosta class* — Bldr: Dubigeon, Nantes

	Laid down	L	In serv.
S . . . N . . .	15-9-76	...	...
S . . . N . . .	...	...	...

D: 1,200 tons standard, 1,450 surfaced, 1,725 submerged
S: 20 kts (submerged) **Dim:** 67.57 × 6.8 × 5.4
Man: 7 officers, 43 men
A: 4/533-mm TT (fwd) — 20 reloads **Endurance:** 45 days
M: 2 SEMT-Pielstick A16 PA4 185 diesels, 850 kw; 1 3,500-kw main engine; 1 cruising electric engine of 23 kw; 1 prop

REMARKS: Very quiet, long-range boats. Armament based on the modernized *Daphné* class. Central digital fire-control computer. Contract signed in 1975 but a recent embargo by the French government may prevent delivery.

♦ *3 Daphné class* — Bldr: Dubigeon, Nantes

	Laid down	L	In serv.
S 97 MARIA VAN RIEBEECK	3-68	18-3-69	1971
S 98 EMILY HOBHOUSE	12-68	10-69	1971
S 99 JOHANNA VAN DER MERWE	5-69	4-70	1971

D: 869 tons surfaced, 1,043 submerged **S:** 13/15.5 kts
Dim: 57.75 × 6.75 × 4.5 **Man:** 6 officers, 41 men
A: 12/550-mm TT (8 fwd, 4 aft)
M: Surfaced: diesel-electric propulsion: SEMT-Pielstick 450-kw diesels; 2 props; 1,300/1,600 hp

SOUTH AFRICA

Republic of

Emily Hobhouse (S 98) Marius Bar, 1971

REMARK: See French *Daphné* class.

DESTROYER

♦ *1 ex-British W class* — Bldr: Fairfield SB & E — Transferred: 1950

	Laid down	L	In serv.
D 278 JAN VAN RIEBEECK (ex-*Wessex*, ex-*Zenith*)	10-42	2-9-43	5-44

D: 2,105 tons (2,750 fl) **Dim:** 110.55 × 10.88 × 5.2 (fl)
S: 31 kts **Man:** 186 men (peacetime), 215 (wartime)
Range: 1,000/30, 2,800/20 **Fuel:** 580 tons
A: 4/102-mm AA (II × 2) — 2/40-mm AA — 4/533-mm TT (IV × 1) — 2 Wasp ASW helicopters — 2 depth-charge projectors
M: Parsons GT; 2 props; 40,000 hp **Boilers:** 2 Admiralty

REMARKS: Refitted 1964-66. Will soon be stricken.

FRIGATES

♦ *3 A-69 class* — Bldr: Lorient

	Laid down	L	Trials
F 432 GOOD HOPE	...	5-3-77	15-11-77
F 602 TRANSVAAL	...	...	1-5-78
F . . . N . . .	...	...	...

D: 1,250 tons (fl) **S:** 24 kts **Dim:** 80.5 × 10.3 × 5.2 (fwd)
A: 1/100-mm Mod. 68 — 1/40-mm AA — 1/20-mm AA — 3 ASW Mk 32 TT (III × 1)
Electron Equipt: Radars: 1 DRBV 51A, 1 Decca navigation, 1 DRBC 32E
Sonar: Diodon
Range: 3,000/18, 4,500/15 **Electric:** 840 kw
M: 2 SEMT-Pielstick diesels; 2 4-bladed controllable-pitch props; 8,800 hp

FRIGATES (*continued*)

REMARK: A recent embargo by the French government may prevent delivery.

♦ *3 British Whitby class* — Bldrs: F-145 and F-150: Yarrow; F-147: Alex. Stephen

	Laid down	L	In serv.
F 145 PRESIDENT PRETORIUS	1960	28-9-62	3-64
F 147 PRESIDENT STEYN	1960	23-11-61	4-63
F 150 PRESIDENT KRUGER	1959	20-10-60	10-62

President Kruger (F 150) 1970

D: 2,250 tons (2,800 fl) **Dim:** 112.77 (100.73 pp) × 12.5 × 5.2 (fl)
S: 27 kts **Man:** 190 men **Range:** 2,100/26, 4,500/12
A: 2/114-mm AA Mk 6 (II × 1) — 2/40-mm AA (I × 2) — 6/ASW TT (II × 3) — 1 Mk 10 Limbo mortar — 1 Wasp helicopter (Mk 44 torpedoes)
Electron Equipt: Radars: 1 974 GB navigation, 1 air-search band D, 1 scan DO band C, 1 275 fire-control
Sonars: 1 177 GB, 1 174 GB
M: 2 double-reduction GT; 2 props; 30,000 hp **Boilers:** 2 Babcock

REMARKS: F-147 and F-150 modernized at Simonstown, 1968-70 and 1969-71.

♦ *2 ex-British Loch class* — Transferred: 1945

	Bldr	Laid down	L	In serv.
F 432 GOOD HOPE (ex-*Loch Boisdale*)	Blyth DD & SB	11-43	5-7-44	12-44
F 602 TRANSVAAL (ex-*Loch Ard*)	Harland & Wolff	1-44	2-8-44	5-45

Good Hope (F 432) 1970

D: 1,610 tons (2,400 fl) **Dim:** 93.57 (87.2 pp) × 11.25 × 4.4
S: 19 kts **Man:** 140 men
Range: 2,500/19, 6,400/10 **Fuel:** 720 tons
A: 1/102-mm — 2/40-mm AA, 6 on the F-602 — 4 depth-charge projectors
M: Triple-expansion; 2 props; 5,500 hp **Boilers:** 2 Admiralty

REMARKS: A large number of these oceangoing frigates were built during World War II. Both have had refits. F-432 has been modified to accommodate the staff of the commander in chief. Will be disarmed when the two A-69 frigates that have been given their names go into service.

♦ *1 ex-British Algerine class* — Bldr: Lobnitz & Co., Renfrew — Bought: 1947

	Laid down	L	In serv.
M 291 PIETERMARITZBURG (ex-*Pelorus*)	10-42	13-6-43	10-43

D: 1,040 tons (1,330 fl) **Dim:** 68.58 (64.8 pp) × 10.82 × 3.5
S: 17 kts **Man:** 8 officers, 107 men
Range: 3,000/15 **Fuel:** 270 tons
A: 2/102-mm (II × 1) — 2/40-mm AA — 4 depth-charge projectors
M: Triple-expansion; 1 prop; 3,000 hp **Boilers:** 2

REMARKS: Belongs to a minesweeper class built in large numbers during World War II. Used as a training ship.

NOTE: The frigate *Vrijstaat* (F-157) was sunk as a gunnery target in 1975.

GUIDED-MISSILE PATROL BOATS

♦ *6 Israeli Reshef type*

	L	In serv.		L	In serv.
N . . .			**N . . .**		
N . . .			**N . . .**		
N . . .			**N . . .**		

REMARKS: Three building in Haifa and three in Durban. May be armed with Gabriel missiles.

PATROL BOATS AND CRAFT

♦ *5 British Ford class*

P 3105 GELDERLAND (ex-*Brayford*)
P 3120 NAUTILUS (ex-*Glassford*)
P 3125 RIJGER
P 3126 HAERLEM
P 3127 OOSTERLAND

Haerlem (P 3126) as a hydrographic ship

PATROL BOATS AND CRAFT (*continued*)

D: 160 tons (fl) **S:** 15 kts **Dim:** 35.7 × 6.1 × 2.1
A: 1/40-mm **Man:** 19 men
M: 2 Paxman diesels; 1,100 hp **Fuel:** 23 tons

REMARK: The *Haerlem* (P-3126) has been fitted as a hydrographic ship.

♦ *1 British SDML type small craft* (1943)

SDML 1204

D: 46 tons (54 fl) **S:** 11 kts **Dim:** 21.95 × 4.82 × 1.62
Man: 11 men **M:** 2 Gardner diesels; 130 hp

REMARK: Assigned to the naval college.

MINE WARFARE SHIPS

♦ *10 British "-ton"-class minesweepers*

	L		L
M 1142 KAAPSTAD (ex-*Hazleton*)	6-2-54	**M 1213 MOSSELBAAI** (ex-*Oakington*)	10-12-58
M 1144 PRETORIA (ex-*Dunkerton*)	8-3-54	**M 1214 WALVISBAAI** (ex-*Packington*)	3-7-58
M 1207 JOHANNESBURG (ex-*Castleton*)	26-8-58	**M 1215 EAST LONDON** (ex-*Chilton*)	15-7-57
M 1210 KIMBERLEY (ex-*Stratton*)	29-7-57	**M 1498 WINDHOEK**	28-6-57
M 1212 PORT ELIZABETH (ex-*Dumbleton*)	8-11-57	**M 1499 DURBAN**	12-6-57

D: 370 tons (425 fl) **Dim:** 46.33 (42.68 pp) × 8.76 × 2.5
S: 15 kts (cruising) **Man:** 27 men
A: 1/40-mm AA — 2/20-mm AA **Range:** 2,300/13, 3,000/8
M: Mirrlees diesels in M-1142 and M-1144; Deltic diesels in others; 2 props; 3,000 hp
Fuel: 45 tons

REMARKS: M-1142 and M-1144 have an open bridge and a lattice mast; M-1498 and M-1499 have a frigate-type bridge and a tripod mast.

AUXILIARY SHIPS

♦ *1 British Hecla-class hydrographic ship*

	Bldr	Laid down	L	In serv.
PROTEA	Yarrow	7-70	14-7-71	12-71

D: 2,750 tons (fl) **S:** 15.5 kts **Dim:** 71.6 × 14.9 × 4.6
Man: 123 men **Range:** 12,000/11 **Fuel:** 500 tons
M: 4 Paxman-Ventura diesels; 1 variable-pitch prop; 4,800 hp

REMARK: Hull reinforced for navigating in ice.

♦ *1 fleet replenishment ship*

A 243 TAFELBERG (ex-Danish tanker *Annam*) (20-6-58)

Tafelberg (A 243) 1970

D: 12,499 grt **S:** 15 kts **Cargo capacity:** 18,430 tons
M: 1 B & W diesel; 8,420 hp **Man:** 100 men

REMARK: Purchased and refitted in Durban in 1967.

♦ *1 British "Bar-" class net-tender*

P 285 SOMERSET (ex-*Barcross*) (21-10-41)

♦ *1 torpedo-recovery and diver-training ship* — Bldr: Dorman Long, Durban, 1969

P 3148 FLEUR

Fleur (P 3148) 1970

D: 257 tons (fl) **Dim:** 35.0 × 7.5 × 3.4
M: 2 Paxman-Ventura diesels; 1,400 hp

♦ *2 tugs*

DE NEYS (180 tons), **DE NOORDE** (170 tons)

♦ *2 air-sea rescue boats* — Bldr: Fairey Marine Corporation, 1973

P 1554 **P 1555**

SPAIN

Personnel (1977): 46,000, including 4,000 officers and 6,500 Marine officers and men

Merchant Marine (1976): 2,792 ships — 6,027,763 grt
(tankers: 112 ships — 3,028,307 grt)

WARSHIPS IN SERVICE OR UNDER CONSTRUCTION AS OF 1 OCTOBER 1977

	L	Tons	Main armament
♦ *1 helicopter carrier*			
DEDALO	1943	13,000	26/40-mm, 20 aircraft
		Tons (surfaced)	
♦ *15 submarines*			
4 AGOSTA	. . .	1,450	4/533-mm TT
4 DAPHNÉ	1972–75	870	12/TT
4 GUPPY II	1943–44	1,840	10/533-mm TT
1 CORSAIR	1944	1,825	10/TT
2 TIBURON	1963–64	76.8	2/533-mm TT
		Tons	
♦ *17 destroyers*			
2 ROGER DE LAURIA	1967–68	3,000	6/127-mm, ASW weapons, 1 helicopter
1 FIER	1961	1,227	2/76-mm, ASW weapons
1 OQUENDO	1956	2,342	4/120-mm, ASW weapons
2 ALAVA	1946–47	1,841	3/76-mm, ASW weapons
5 GEARING (FRAM I)	1945	2,400	4/127-mm, 1 Asroc system
5 FLETCHER	1942–44	2,050	4 or 5/127-mm, 6 TT
♦ *15 frigates*			
8 DESCUBIERTA	. . .	1,500 (fl)	1/76-mm, 1 Sea Sparrow, 1/rocket launcher, 6/TT
5 BALÉARES	1970–72	2,900	1/127-mm, 1 Asroc system, 1 Tartar system, 6/ASW TT
2 PIZARRO	1945	1,685	2/127-mm, ASW weapons
♦ *4 corvettes*			
4 ATREVIDA	1952–56	977	1/76-mm, 3/40-mm, ASW weapons
♦ *14 torpedo and patrol boats*			
2 LÜRSSEN			
6 LAZAGA			
6 BARCELO			
♦ *19 minesweepers*			

Naval Program: The fleet program has two phases:

1. The modernization of several units currently in commission and completion of the following ships, whose construction has begun:
   - 5 *Baléares*-class frigates
   - 4 *Daphné*-class submarines
2. The construction of the following ships, which is either in hand or anticipated:
   - 4 *Agosta*-class submarines
   - 8 *Descubierta*-class frigates
   - 6 *Lazaga*-class patrol boats
   - 6 *Barcelo*-class patrol boats

Proposals to replace the helicopter carrier *Dedalo* are still being studied.

Naval Aviation: ASW fixed-wing aircraft, about ten Grumman Albatros amphibians, and two P-3 Orions that were transferred by the U.S. Navy in 1973 belong to the Air Force. Helicopters, whether ASW or transport, belong to the Navy (Arma Aera de la Armada). They include Bell 47-G (assault), Sikorsky S-55 (training), Agusta Bell 204-B, Sikorsky SH3-D, and Hughes 369-HM (all ASW), for a total of about 40 craft.

Five Harrier AV-8A VTOL aircraft, bought in the U.S.A. for the *Dedalo*, were delivered in 1976. They are named Matador in the Spanish Navy. Eight or twelve more of these aircraft might be ordered and, if the carrier being considered in the naval program is indeed built, the order could go as high as twenty-four.

WEAPONS AND SYSTEMS

Except for naval guns, which are domestically designed and manufactured, most of the weapon systems in use are of American or French make. However, an advanced anti-aircraft/anti-missile point-defense system of Spanish origin is about to be introduced. Called Meroka, it consists of:

Two six-barreled 20-mm Oerlikon R TG guns
Length: 120 calibers
Muzzle velocity: 1,250 m/sec
Maximum rate of fire: 2,700/3,600 rounds/minute
Maximum effective range: 2,000 m
Fire control: Lockheed Electronics "sharp shooter" with Doppler radar and stabilized optical sights

Two prototypes are undergoing firing tests, and 20 units may be produced to equip the helicopter carrier *Dedalo*, the *Roger de Lauria*-class destroyers, and the *Beléares*-class and *Descubierta*-class frigates.

HELICOPTER CARRIER

♦ *1 ex-U.S. light aircraft carrier* — Bldr: New York SB — Transferred: 1967

	Laid down	L	In serv.
PH 01 DEDALO (ex-*Cabot*, CVL-28)	8-42	4-4-43	7-43

Dedalo (PH 01) 1974

HELICOPTER CARRIER (*continued*)

D: 13,000 tons (16,416 fl) **S:** 32 kts (trials) **Man:** 1,112 men
Dim: 188.35 (182.9 wl) × {20.11 (hull) / 31.7 (flight deck)} × 7.2 **Range:** 7,200/15
A: 26/40-mm (IV × 2, II × 9) — about 20 aircraft, 5 of which are Harriers
Electron Equipment: Radars: 1 SPS 10, 1 SPS 40
Armor: Partial belt: 37 to 127 **Fuel:** 1,800 tons
M: GT; 4 props **Boilers:** 8 Babcock & Wilcox

REMARKS: Ended service in the U.S. Navy as an aviation transport (AVT-3). Loaned for five years by law of 30-8-67, acquired in 12-73. Will be equipped with an air defense system built around the three-dimensional AN/SPS 52B radar, which combines a fixed electronic azimuthal sweep with the usual mechanical rotating sweep. She is supposed to be given the Meroka point-defense gun system.

SUBMARINES

♦ *4 Agosta class* — Bldr: Bazan, Cartagena

	Laid down	L		Laid down	L
S 70 N . . .	1975	. . .	**S 72 N . . .**	. . .	. . .
S 71 N . . .	1975	. . .	**S 73 N . . .**	. . .	. . .

D: 1,200 tons standard, 1,450 surfaced, 1,725 submerged
S: 20 kts (submerged) **Dim:** 67.57 × 6.8 × 5.4
Man: 7 officers, 43 men **Range:** 8,500/9 (snorkeling)
A: 4/533-mm TT (rapid reload) — 20 reloads
M: 2 SEMT-Pielstick diesels; 1 3,500-kw main engine; 1 35-kw cruising engine; 1 prop

REMARKS: See Agosta class in section on France. As with the *Daphné* class, will be built with French technical assistance. Agreement signed 6-2-74; first two ordered 4-74.

♦ *4 Daphné class* — Bldr: E. N. Bazan, Cartagena

	Laid down	L	In serv.
S 61 DELFIN	8-68	25-3-72	5-73
S 62 TONINA	1969	3-10-72	7-73
S 63 MARSOPA	1971	6-74	12-75
S 64 NARVAL	1972	1-75	11-75

Tonina (S 62) J. C. Bellonne, 1973

D: 870 tons surfaced, 1,040 submerged **S:** 13/15.5 kts
Dim: 57.75 × 6.75 × 4.56
A: 12 TT (8 fwd, 4 aft) **Man:** 5 officers, 45 men
M: Diesel-electric propulsion: SEMT-Pielstick motors; 2 props; 1,300/1,600 hp

REMARKS: Built with French technical assistance. Agreement of 16-7-66.

♦ *4 ex-U.S. Guppy-II class* — Transferred: 1971, 1972, and 1974

	Bldr	L
S 32 ISAAC PERAL (ex-*Ronquil*, SS-396)	Portsmouth NSY	27-1-44
S 33 NARCISO MONTURIOL (ex-*Picuda*, SS-382)	Portsmouth NSY	12-7-43
S 34 COSME GARCIA (ex-*Bang*, SS-385)	Portsmouth NSY	30-8-43
S 35 N . . . (ex-*Jallao*, SS-368)	Manitowoc SY	12-3-44

Isaac Peral (S 32) 1971

D: 1,500 tons standard, 1,840 surfaced, 2,240 submerged
S: 18/13-15 kts **Dim:** 93.2 × 8.2 × 5.2
Man: 86 men **Range:** 10,000/10 **Fuel:** 300 tons
A: 10/533-mm TT (6 fwd, 4 aft)
M: Diesel-electric propulsion: 3 groups of generators; 2 electric motors; 2 props; 4,800/5,200 hp

REMARKS: Built as the *Balao* class, but the fourth generator group was removed to allow enlargement of the sonar compartment. Two 126-cell batteries. Modernized in 1952-54. Purchased by Spain.

♦ *1 ex-U.S. Corsair class* — Bldr: Manitowoc SY — Transferred: 10-59

	L	In serv.
S 31 ALMIRANTE GARCIA DE LOS REYES (ex-*Kraken*, SS-370)	30-6-44	9-44

D: 1,525 tons standard, 1,825 surfaced, 2,300 submerged **S:** 20/10 kts
Dim: 95.0 (92.72 pp) × 8.25 × 5.2 **Man:** 8 to 9 officers, 66 men

SUBMARINES *(continued)*

Almirante Garcia de los Reyes (S 31) 1971

A: 6/533-mm TT — 4/ASW TT **Range:** 10,000/10 **Fuel:** 300 tons
M: Diesel-electric propulsion: 4 groups of General Electric, 1,625 hp each; 2 2,700-hp electric motors

REMARKS: Complete modernization in Philadelphia, 1965-66. Probably will be stricken soon because of her poor condition.

♦ *2 Tiburon class, 1963-64*

SA 51 **SA 52**

SA 51 1972

D: 76.8 tons surfaced, 79.3 submerged **S:** 10/14.5 kts
Dim: 21.15 (19.8 pp) × 2.4 × 2.4 **A:** 2/533-mm TT
Range: 2,040/6 (surfaced), 150/2 (submerged) **Man:** 5 men
M: Pegaso diesels and electric motors; 2 props; 400 hp

REMARKS: Received new batteries in 1966-67. Such small combat craft are also operated by the Pakistani, Taiwanese, and Colombian navies.

DESTROYERS

♦ *2 Roger de Lauria class* — Bldr: Cartagena

	Laid down	L	In serv.
D 42 ROGER DE LAURIA	9-51	22-8-67	5-69
D 43 MARQUES DE LA ENSENADA	9-51	22-2-68	8-70

Roger de Lauria (D 42) 1970

D: 3,000 tons (3,775 fl) **S:** 30 kts **Dim:** 119.0 × 13.0 × 5.5
A: 6/127-mm (II × 3) — 6/324-mm ASW TT Mk 32 (III × 2) for Mk 44 torpedoes — 2/ASW fixed Mk 25 TT for Mk 37 torpedoes — 1 ASW helicopter
Electron Equipt: Radars: 1 SPS 40, 1 SPS 10
Sonars: 1 SQS 29, 1 SQS 10 towed, middle-frequency
Man: 20 officers, 235 men **Fuel:** 673 tons
M: Rateau-Bretagne GT; 2 props **Boilers:** 3 35-kg/cm², superheat 375°

REMARKS: Modified (widened and lengthened) during construction in order to eliminate defects found in the *Oquendo* prototype, which delayed their completion. U.S. semiautomatic, 38-caliber guns. Will be fitted with the Meroka system.

♦ *1 Fier class* — Bldr: S.E. Constr. Nav., El Ferrol

	Laid down	L	In serv.	Modified
D 38 INTREPIDO	14-7-45	15-2-61	1961	3-65

D: 1,227 tons (1,484 fl) **Dim:** 93.93 (90.0 pp) × 9.37 × 3.05
S: 33 kts **Man:** 7 officers, 138 men
Range: 900/max., 1,500/25, 3,800/15
A: 2/76-mm AA 50-cal. (II × 1) — 2/40-mm AA 70-cal. — 2 fixed ASW TT (6 torpedoes) — 8 depth-charge projectors
Electron Equipt: Radars: 1 MLA-1b, 1 SPS 5B, 1 SPG 34 fire-control
Sonar: 1 QHB-a
M: Rateau-Bretagne GT; 2 props; 30,800 hp (32,500 max.)
Boilers: 3 F.C.M., 35 kg/cm², superheat 375° **Fuel:** 290 tons

REMARKS: Hull and machinery have the same characteristics as the French Le Fier destroyers of 1939-40, none of which was completed because of the war. The 105-mm and 37-mm guns originally mounted have been replaced with American weapons. The two boiler compartments are separated by the engine compartment. Trials indicated a top-heavy superstructure. The *Osado* (D-32) was stricken in 1972, the *Audaz* (D-31), *Meteoro* (D-33), *Furor* (D-34), and *Rayo* (D-35) in 1974. The *Temerario* (D-37) and *Relampago* (D-39) were stricken at the end of 1975.

DESTROYERS (*continued*)

♦ *1 Oquendo class* — Bldr: S.E. Constr. Nav., El Ferrol

	Laid down	L	In serv.
D 41 OQUENDO	15-6-51	5-9-56	1964

Oquendo (D 41) J. C. Bellonne, 1972

D: 2,342 tons (3,004 fl) **Dim:** 116.47 (110.8 pp) × 11.0 × 3.85
S: 32 kts **Man:** 15 officers, 252 men
Range: 5,000/15
A: 4/120-mm AA (II × 2) — 6/40-mm AA (I × 6) — 2 hedgehogs — 4 depth-charge projectors
Electron Equipt: Radars: (British) 1 275 and 1 262 fire-control, 1 293-Q, 1 SNW 10
Sonar: 1 QHB high-frequency
M: Rateau-Bretagne GT; 2 props; 60,000 hp
Boilers: 3 35-kg/cm², superheat 375° **Fuel:** 660 tons

REMARKS: Based on the German *Narvik*-class destroyers of 1942. Trials indicated a tendency to instability. The 120-mm 50-caliber semiautomatic guns are Spanish.

♦ *2 Alava class* — Bldr: Cartagena NSY

	Laid down	L	In serv.
D 51 LINIERS	1-45	5-46	1-51
D 52 ALAVA	12-44	6-47	1-51

D: 1,841 tons (2,270 fl) **Dim:** 101.15 (97.52 pp) × 9.65 × 3.1
S: 28 kts **Man:** 201 men **Range:** 4,500/14
A: 3/76-mm AA (I × 3) — 3/40-mm AA — 2 hedgehogs — 8 depth-charge projectors — 2 fixed ASW TT (6 Mk 32 torpedoes)
Electron Equipt: Radars: 1 SPS 6, 1 MLA-1b
Sonar: 1 QHB-a high-frequency or 1 SQS 4 middle-frequency
M: Parsons GT; 2 props; 42,000 hp **Boilers:** 4 Yarrow
Fuel: 540 tons

Alava (D 52) 1976

REMARKS: Rearmed with U.S. weapons in 1964.

♦ *5 ex-U.S. Gearing FRAM I* — Transferred: 2 in 8-72; 3 in 8-73

	Bldr	L
D 61 CHURRUCA (ex-*Eugene A. Greene*, DDR-711)	Federal SB	18-3-45
D 62 GRAVINA (ex-*Furze*, DDR-882)	Consolid. Steel	9-3-45
D 63 MENDEZ NUÑEZ (ex-*Leary*, DDR-879)	Consolid. Steel	20-1-45
D 64 LANGARA (ex-*O'Hare*, DDR-889)	Consolid. Steel	22-6-45
D 65 BLAS DE LEZO (ex-*Noa*, DD-841)	Bath Iron Works	30-7-45

Churruca (D 61) 1974

D: 2,400 tons (3,600 fl) **S:** 30 kts **Dim:** 119.17 × 12.45 × 5.8
Man: 14 officers, 260 men **Range:** 2,400/25, 4,800/15

DESTROYERS (*continued*)

A: 4/127-mm 38-cal (II × 2) — 1 Asroc ASW system — 6/324-mm ASW TT (III × 2) Mk 32 for Mk 43 or Mk 44 torpedoes
Electron Equipt: Radars: 1 SPS 10, 1 SPS 40
Sonar: 1 SQS 23
M: GT; 2 props; 60,000 hp **Boilers:** 4 Babcock **Fuel:** 650 tons

REMARK: D-65 has 2/127-mm mounts.

♦ *5 ex-U.S. Fletcher class* — Transferred: 2 in 1957, 1 in 1959, 2 in 1960

	Bldr	L
D 21 LEPANTO (ex-*Capps*, DD-550)	Gulf SB	31-5-42
D 22 ALMIRANTE FERRANDIZ (ex-*David W. Taylor*, DD-551)	Gulf SB	4-7-42
D 23 ALMIRANTE VALDES (ex-*Converse*, DD-509)	Bath Iron Works	30-8-42
D 24 ALCALA GALIANO (ex-*Jarvis*, DD-799)	Todd Pacific	14-2-44
D 25 JORGE JUAN (ex-*McGowan*, DD-678)	Federal SB	14-11-43

Almirante Valdes (D 23) 1976

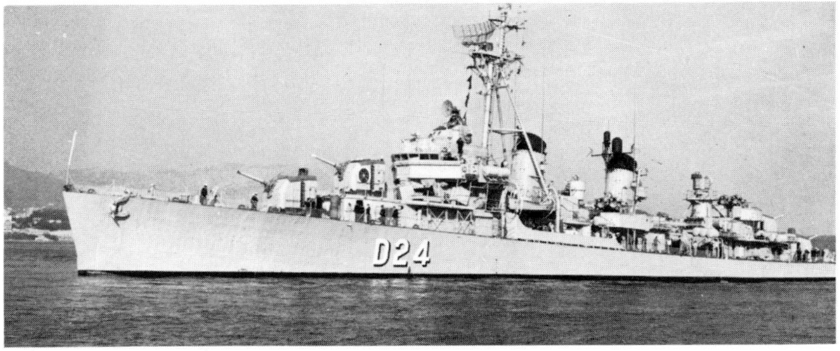

Alcala Galiano (D 24) 1976

D: 2,050 tons (2,750 fl) **S:** 30/32 kts **Dim:** 114.85 × 12.03 × 5.5
Man: 350 men **Range:** 1,260/32, 4,400/15
A: D-21 and D-22: 5/127-mm (I × 5) — 6/40-mm AA (II × 3) — 6/20-mm AA — 6/324-mm ASW torpedo tubes (III × 2) — 2 hedgehogs — 6 mortars — 2 depth-charge racks
D-23: 4/127-mm (I × 4) — 6/76-mm AA (II × 3) — 5/533-mm TT (V × 1) — 6/324-mm ASW TT (III × 2) — 4 mortars — 1 depth-charge rack
D-24: Same as D-25 but single ASW tubes and 1 hedgehog
D-25: Same guns as D-23 but 3/533-mm TT (III × 1) — 6/324-mm ASW TT (III × 2)
Electron Equipt: Radars: 1 SPS 6, 1 SPS 10
Sonars: 1 SQS 4, or 1 SQS 29, or 1 SQS 32, all middle-frequency
M: General Electric GT; 2 props; 60,000 hp **Boilers:** 4
Fuel: 650 tons

FRIGATES

♦ *8 Descubierta class* — Bldrs: First 4: Bazan, Cartagena; last 4: Bazan, El Ferrol

	L	In serv.		L	In serv.
F 31 DESCUBIERTA	8-7-75	. . .	**F 35 N . . .**	. . .	. . .
F 32 DIANA	26-1-75	. . .	**F 36 N . . .**	. . .	. . .
F 33 INFANTA ELENA	14-9-76	. . .	**F 37 N . . .**	. . .	. . .
F 34 INFANTA CRISTINA	25-4-77	. . .	**F 38 N . . .**	. . .	. . .

Ordered: 23-5-76

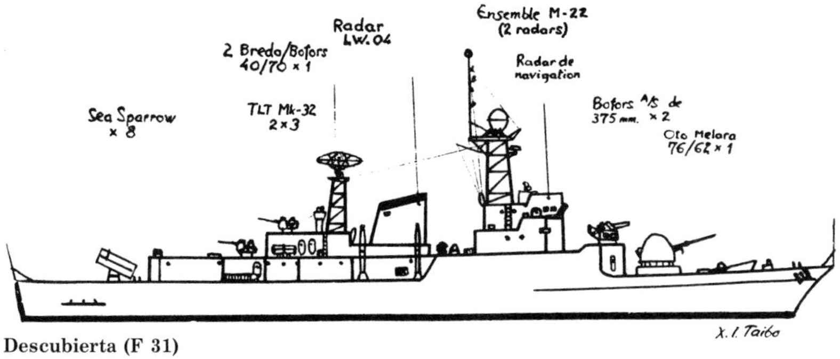

Descubierta (F 31)

D: 1,500 (fl) **S:** 26 kts **Dim:** 88.8 × 10.4 × 3.4
A: 1/76-mm OTO Melara — 2/40-mm AA — 1/Sea Sparrow — 2/375-mm Bofors rocket launchers (II × 1) — 6/324-mm TT Mk 32 (III × 2) — Meroka (expected to be fitted)
Electron Equipt: Radars: 1 LWO-4 (Dutch), 1 navigation, 1 CT-DO M-22 fire-control (Dutch)
M: 4 Bazan MTU 16V856 TB91 diesels, 4,380 hp each; 2 variable-pitch props; 17,520 hp
Electric: 2,150 kw

REMARK: Twin stacks inclined outboard, as on the Canadian *Iroquois*-class destroyers.

FRIGATES (*continued*)

♦ *5 Baléares class* — Bldr: E. N. Bazan, El Ferrol

	Laid down	L	In serv.
F 71 BALÉARES	31-10-68	20-8-70	24-9-73
F 72 ANDALUCIA	2-7-69	30-3-71	23-5-74
F 73 CATALUÑA	20-8-70	3-11-71	16-1-75
F 74 ASTURIAS	30-3-71	13-5-72	2-12-75
F 75 EXTREMADURA	3-11-71	21-11-72	10-11-76

D: 2,900 tons (4,177 fl) **S:** 27/28 kts
Dim: 133.6 (126.5 pp) × 14.25 × 5.6 (7.5 with sonar)
Man: 14 officers, 39 petty officers, 250 men **Range:** 4,500/20
A: 1/127-mm Mk 42 — 1 Tartar SAM — 1 ASW Asroc system — 4/324-mm ASW TT for Mk 44 torpedoes — 2/fixed TT for Mk 37 torpedoes

Cataluña (F 73) G. Arra, 1976

Baléares (F 71) 1976

FRIGATES (*continued*)

Baléares (F 71) 1974

Cataluña (F 73) 1975

Electron Equipt: Radars: 1 SPS 10, 1 SPS 52, 1 SPG 51
Sonars: 1 SQS 23 (hull), 1 SQS 35 (towed)
M: 1 GT; 1 prop; 35,000 hp **Boilers:** 2 84-kg/cm² pressure

REMARKS: Built with American aid (agreement of 31-5-66). May have one or two ASW helicopters. The ships have a high-pressure steam propulsion plant, as do their U.S. counterparts, the *Knox* class. Fire control Mk 68. The Mk 32 torpedo tubes are built into the port and starboard sides of the after superstructure and are oriented to a 45-degree angle outboard of the centerline. The 2 Mk 37 tubes are built into the stern, facing aft, on the centerline. Eventually, these ships will be fitted with a digital Mk 152 fire-control computer console in the place of the Analog Mk 111. They will also be equipped with NTDS and the Meroka point-defense system.

♦ *2 Pizarro class* — Bldr: S.E. Constr. Nav., El Ferrol

	Laid down	L	In serv.
F 41 VICENTE YANEZ PINZON	9-44	8-8-45	5-8-49
F 42 LEGAZPI	9-44	8-8-45	8-8-51

Legazpi (F 42) 1971

D: 1,685 tons (2,123 fl) **S:** 18.5 kts (trials: 20)
Dim: 95.2 (87.54 pp) × 12.15 × 3.4 **Man:** 13 officers, 238 men
A: 2/127-mm 38-cal — 4/40-mm AA — 2 hedgehogs — 8 depth-charge projectors — 2 fixed ASW TT (6 Mk 32 torpedoes)
Electron Equipt: Radars: 1 SPS 5-B, 1 MLA 1b
Sonar: QHB-a
M: Parsons GT; 2 props; 5,000 hp **Range:** 3,000/15
Boilers: 2 Yarrow, 25 kg/cm² superheat pressure
Fuel: 402 tons (max), 386 (avg)

REMARKS: Exceptionally seaworthy ships, modernized in 1960. Six that were not modernized have been taken out of service since 1965, the *Hernan Cortes* (F-32) and *Sarmiento de Gamboa* (F-36) in 1971 and 1973.

CORVETTES

♦ *4 Atrevida class* — Bldrs: F-61 and F-62: Cartagena; F-64 and F-65: Cadiz

	Laid down	L	In serv.
F 61 ATREVIDA	26-6-50	2-12-52	4-55
F 62 PRINCESA	18-3-53	31-3-55	10-59
F 64 NAUTILUS	27-7-53	23-8-56	12-59
F 65 VILLA DE BILBOA (ex-*Favorita*)	18-3-53	19-2-58	7-60

D: 977 tons (1,136 fl) **Dim:** 75.5 (68 pp) × 10.2 × 2.64
S: 18 kts **Man:** 10 officers, 122 men
A: 1/76-mm AA — 3/40-mm AA — 2 hedgehogs — 8 depth-charge projectors
Electron Equipt: Radar: 1 SPS 5-B combination search
M: 2 diesels; 2 props; 3,000 hp **Fuel:** 100 tons

CORVETTES (*continued*)

Princesa (F 62) 1971

REMARKS: Tandem machinery arrangement. Electronic equipment and weapons modernized with U.S. aid. Can carry 20 mines. The *Diana* (F-63) stricken in 1972.

TORPEDO BOATS

♦ *2 Lürssen type* — Bldr: La Carraca, Cadiz

	In serv.		In serv.
LT 30	1954	**LT 31**	1957

D: 120 tons **S:** 40 kts **Dim:** 34.8 × 5.1 × 1.4
Man: 22 men **Range:** 700-800/30
A: 2/20-mm AA — 2/533-mm TT **Fuel:** 20 tons
M: Mercedes-Benz diesels; 3 props; 7,500 hp

REMARKS: Based on German torpedo boats of World War II. LT-32 has been converted into a target drone (**S:** 12 kts). LT-27, LT-28, and LT-29 were stricken 1963-64.

PATROL BOATS

♦ *6 Lazaga class* — Bldrs: P-01: Lürssen; others: Bazan, Cadiz

	L	In serv.		L	In serv.
P 01 LAZAGA	30-9-74	16-7-75	**P 04 VILLAMIL**	24-5-74	. . .
P 02 ALSEDO	8-1-75	5-76	**P 05 BONIFAZ**	24-5-74	. . .
P 03 CADARSO	8-1-75	10-7-76	**P 06 RECALDE**	9-11-75	. . .

Alsedo (P 02) 1976

D: 400 tons (fl) **Dim:** 58.1 (54.4 wl) × 7.6 × 2.8
S: 29.5 kts **Man:** 30 men
Range: 2,260/27, 4,200/17
A: 1/76-mm AA OTO Melara — 1/40-mm AA Breda-Bofors — 6/20-mm AA — 6/324-mm ASW TT Mk 32 (III × 2) — 2 ASW mortars
Electron Equipt: Radars: 1 navigation, 1 Dutch M 22 air-surface search
Sonar: 1 hull-mounted, high-frequency
M: 2 MTU diesels; 2 props; 8,760 hp

REMARKS: Installation of SSM is planned. The P-01 was commissioned with a 40-mm AA instead of a 76-mm AA.

♦ *6 Barcelo class* — Bldrs: P-11: Lürssen; others: E. N. Bazan, La Carraca

	L	In serv.
P 11 BARCELO	10-10-75	26-3-75
P 12 LAYA	16-12-75	21-12-76
P 13 JAVIER QUIROGA	. . .	. . .
P 14 ORDONEZ	10-9-76	. . .
P 15 ACEVEDO	10-9-76	. . .
P 16 CANDIDO PEREZ	. . .	. . .

D: 150 tons (fl) **S:** 36 kts **Dim:** 36.2 × 5.8 × 2.5

PATROL BOATS (*continued*)

A: 1/40-mm Breda-Bofors — 1/20-mm AA — 2/12.7-mm machine guns
Man: 3 officers, 16 men **Range:** 1,200/17
M: 2 Bazan MTU MD 16 TB-90 diesels; 2 props; 6,000 hp

♦ *3 ex-tugs, 1941–42*

RR 19 **RR 20** **RR 29**

D: 454 tons **S:** 11.5 kts **Dim:** 38.0 × 8.4 × 3.0
A: 1/37-mm AA — 1/20-mm AA **Range:** 1,000/10
M: Triple-expansion; 1 prop; 800 hp
Boiler: 1 drum type, 13 kg/cm^2 pressure **Fuel:** 200 tons coal

PATROL CRAFT

♦ *1 ex-trawler, 1948* — Purchased: 1952

W 32 SALVORA

D: 270 tons (fl) **S:** 12 kts **Dim:** 31.0 × 6.1 × 2.5
A: 1/20-mm AA **M:** Diesel; 400 hp

♦ **W 01 GAVIOTA**

D: 104.2 tons

REMARK: This captured boat had been used for smuggling.

♦ *5 LPI class*

LPI 1 **LPI 2** **LPI 3** **LPI 4** **LPI 5**

D: 25 tons **Dim:** 14.0 × 4.7 × 1.0 **A:** 2 machine guns

♦ *3 83-foot craft* — Bldr: Bazan, Cadiz, 1962–64

LAS 10 **LAS 20** **LAS 30**

D: 49 tons (63 fl) **S:** 15 kts **Dim:** 25.4 (23.8 pp) × 4.9 × 2.0
A: 1/20-mm AA — 1 machine gun — 2 Mk 20 mortars
M: Diesel; 800 hp **Man:** 15 men

REMARKS: Wooden hull. Based on U.S.C.G. WPBs.

♦ *3 Aguilucho class* — Bldr: Roberto Rodriguez, Vigo, 1973–76

AGUILUCHO **GAVILAN I** **GAVILAN II**

D: 45 tons **S:** 30 kts **Dim:** 26.1 × 5.1 × 1.3
M: Diesels; 2 props; 2,750 hp **Range:** 750/30

♦ *1 river craft* — Bldr: Bazan, La Carraca, 1966

CABO FRADERA

D: 28 tons (fl) **S:** 16 kts **Dim:** 14.05 × 4.67 × 0.99
A: 2 machine guns **M:** Diesel; 280 hp

REMARK: For use on the Miño River.

♦ *8 craft*

V 4	**D:** 65 tons	**S:** 9 kts
V 5	**D:** 4.5 tons	**S:** 5 kts
V 6	**D:** 42 tons	**S:** 19.5 kts
V 9	**D:** 16.5 tons	**S:** 9 kts
V 10	**D:** 12 tons	**S:** 9.5 kts
V 11	**D:** 12 tons	**S:** 9.5 kts
V 33		
V 36		

MINE WARFARE SHIPS

♦ *4 ex-U.S. minesweepers* — Bldr: U.S.A., 1952–56 — Transferred: since 7-71

M 41 GUADELETE (ex-*Dynamic*, MSO-432)
M 42 GUADALMEDINA (ex-*Pivot*, MSO-463)
M 43 GUADALQUIVIR (ex-*Persistent*, MSO-491)
M 44 GUADIANA (ex-*Vigor*, MSO-473)

Guadelete (M 41)

D: 637 tons (735 fl) **S:** 14 kts **Dim:** 52.3 × 10.36 × 4.15
Man: 6 officers, 70 men **Range:** 2,000/12, 3,000/10
A: 2/20-mm AA (II × 1) — 2/12.7-mm machine guns
M: 4 Packard diesels linked to 2 variable-pitch props; 2,280 hp

REMARKS: Modernized, 1969–70. Equipped for mechanical, magnetic, and acoustic sweeping. SQQ 14 sonar mine detector.

♦ *12 ex-U.S. minesweepers*

M 21 NALON (ex-MSC-139)
M 22 LLOBREGAT (ex-MSC-143)
M 23 JUCAR (ex-MSC-220) — In serv. 24-6-55
M 24 ULLA (ex-MSC-265)
M 25 MIÑO (ex-MSC-266)
M 26 EBRO (ex-MSC-269) — In serv. 8-11-57
M 27 TURIA (ex-MSC-130)
M 28 DUERO (ex-MSC-200)
M 29 SIL (ex-MSC-202)
M 30 TAJO (ex-MSC-287)
M 31 GENIL (ex-MSC-279)
M 32 ODIEL (ex-MSC-288)

D: 370 tons (405 fl) **S:** 13 kts (8 sweeping)
Dim: 43.0 (41.5 pp) × 7.95 × 2.55 **Man:** 2 officers, 35 men
A: 2/20-mm AA (II × 1) **Range:** 2,500/10
M: General Motors diesels; 2 props; 1,200 hp **Fuel:** 40 tons

REMARKS: Transferred under MAP: 2 in 1954, 1 in 1955, 3 in 1956, 1 in 1958, 2 in 1959, 3 in 1960. M-21 through M-25 and M-27 through M-29 have a mast well astern of the stack. The others have only a small davit behind the stack.

MINE WARFARE SHIPS (*continued*)

Ebro (M 26) 1977

♦ *5 German wartime M-40 type minesweepers*

	L	In serv.
M 13 EUME	27-7-53	5-54
M 14 ALMANZORA	27-7-53	11-54
M 15 NAVIA	28-7-53	3-55
M 16 GUADALHORCE	18-2-53	1953
M 17 EO	22-9-53	3-53

Bldrs: M-13: Bazan, Cadiz; others: Bazan, Cartagena

D: 670 tons (770 fl) **S:** 13 kts **Dim:** 74.26 × 10.17 × 3.7
A: 2/20-mm AA **Man:** 65 to 80 men **Range:** 3,000/10
M: Reciprocating and BP turbines; 2 props; 2,400 hp
Boilers: 2-tube (3 manifolds) **Fuel:** 90 tons

REMARKS: 1948 program. Modernized, 1959-61. Each shaft is powered by a triple-expansion engine with hydraulic linkage to a low-pressure turbine. The *Lerez* (M-03) taken out of service in 1971, the *Nervion* (M-02) and *Ter* (M-06) in 1972; the *Bidasoa* (M-01), *Tambre* (M-04), and *Segura* (M-05) in 1974. The *Guadiaro* (M-11) and *Tinto* (M-12) were stricken on 31-1-76. The remaining ships will be stricken when the *Lazaga*-class and *Barcelo*-class patrol boats are commissioned.

Eo (M 17) 1970

AMPHIBIOUS WARFARE SHIPS

♦ *1 personnel transport*

TA 11 ARAGON (ex-*Noble*, APA-218) (18-10-44)

Aragon (TA 11)

D: 6,970 tons (14,900 fl) **S:** 17 kts **Dim:** 133.0 × 18.9 × 8.6
A: 12/40-mm AA (IV × 1, II × 4) **Range:** 14,700/16
Electron Equipt: Radars: 1 SPS 6, 1 SPS 10 **Fuel:** 1,150 tons
M: GT; 1 prop; 8,500 hp **Boilers:** 2 Babcock

REMARKS: Victory-class ships fitted out for troop transport (1,560 men, 3,000 tons of cargo), transferred by the U.S.A. in 1964. Carries 19 LCVPs, 2 LCMs, 1 LCPR, 2 LCPs.

♦ *1 ex-U.S. cargo carrier*

TA 21 CASTILLA (ex-*Achernar*, AKA-53)

D: 7,430 tons (13,050 fl) **S:** 15.5 kts **Dim:** 140.0 × 19.2 × 7.4
A: 1/127-mm — 8/40-mm AA (II × 4)
M: GT; 1 prop; 6,000 hp **Boilers:** 2 Foster-Wheeler

Castilla (TA 21) Aguilera

AMPHIBIOUS WARFARE SHIPS (*continued*)

REMARKS: C-2 cargo ship of the Maritime Commission, built in 1943 and transferred early in 1965. Can carry 7,200 tons of cargo, including 2,000 tons of oil in ballast. Has 14 LCVPs, 8 LCMs, and 2 LCPs embarked.

♦ *1 ex-U.S. landing ship, dock* — Bldr: Newport News SB & DD

TA 31 GALICIA (ex-*San Marcos*, LSD-25)

Galicia (TA 31) 1972

D: 4,790 tons (9,375 fl) **S:** 15 kts **Dim:** 139.0 × 21.9 × 4.0
Man: 17 officers, 237 men **Range:** 8,000/15
A: 12/40-mm AA (IV × 2, II × 2) **M:** GT; 2 props; 9,000 hp

REMARKS: Built in 1945, transferred 1-7-71. Well deck 103 × 13.3. Platform for three helicopters. Carries 18 LCMs with 1 LCVP nested in each.

♦ *3 ex-U.S. tank landing ships* — Transferred: 2 in 10-71 and 1 in 1972

L 11 VELASCO (ex-*Terrebonne Parish*, LST-1156)
L 12 MARTIN ALVAREZ (ex-*Wahkiakum County*, LST-1162)
L 13 CONDE DEL VENADITO (ex-*Tom Green County*, LST-1159)

Martin Alvarez (L 12) 1972

D: 2,590 tons (5,786 fl) **S:** 13 kts **Dim:** 117.35 × 16.7 × 3.7
A: 6/76-mm AA (II × 3) **Man:** 115 men **Range:** 6,000/9
M: 4 General Motors diesels; 2 props; 6,000 hp **Fuel:** 1,060 tons

REMARK: Accommodations for 395 troops.

♦ *3 French EDIC-type landing craft* — Bldr: E. N. Bazan, La Carraca, 1965-67

BDK 6 **BDK 7** **BDK 8**

BDK 6 1970

D: 279 tons (665 fl) **Dim:** 59.0 (52.9 pp) × 11.9 × 1.3
S: 9.5 kts **Range:** 1,500/9
A: 2/12.7-mm machine guns — 1/81-mm mortar
M: Diesels; 2 props; 1,040 hp

♦ *3 landing ships* — Bldr: Bazan, El Ferrol

BDK 3 **BDK 4** **BDK 5**

D: 902 tons (fl) **S:** 8.5 kts **Dim:** 56.6 × 11.6 × 1.7
A: 2/20-mm AA **Range:** 1,000/7 **M:** 2 diesels; 2 props; 1,000 hp

AUXILIARY SHIPS

♦ *4 Castor-class hydrographic ships* — Bldr: Bazan, La Carraca

	L	In serv.		L	In serv.
A 21 CASTOR	5-11-65	10-11-66	**A 23 ANTARES**	3-73	21-11-74
A 22 POLLUX	5-11-65	15-12-66	**A 24 RIGEL**	3-73	21-11-74

Antares (A 23) 1974

AUXILIARY SHIPS (*continued*)

D: 355 tons (383.4 fl) **Dim:** 38.36 (33.84 pp) × 3.85 × 2.75
S: 11.5 kts **Man:** 36 men
Range: 3,600 **M:** Sulzer diesel; 1 prop; 720 hp

♦ *2 Malaspina-class hydrographic ships* — Bldr: Bazan, La Carraca

	L	In serv.		L	In serv.
A 31 MALASPINA	15-8-73	21-2-75	**A 32 TOFIÑO**	21-12-73	1-5-75

D: 820 tons (1,090 fl) **S:** 15 kts **Dim:** 57.6 × 11.7 × 3.64
A: 2/20-mm AA **Man:** 63 men **Range:** 3,140/14.5, 4,000/12
M: 2 diesels; 2 variable-pitch props; 3,240 hp

♦ *1 oiler* — Bldr: E. N. Bazan, Cartagena, 1955

BP 11 TEIDE

Teide (BP 11)

D: 2,750 tons (8,030 fl) **S:** 12 kts **Dim:** 117.5 × 14.78 × 6.2
M: Diesels

REMARK: Fitted for underway replenishment.

♦ *13 auxiliary tankers* — Bldr: Ast. de Santander, 1939

PP 1

D: 470 tons **S:** 10 kts **Dim:** 45.0 × 7.6 × 2.9
M: 1 Deutz diesel; 220 hp

PP 3 **PP 4** **PP 5** (300 tons)
PB 1 **PB 2** **PB 3** **PB 4** **PB 5** **PB 6** **PB 20** **PB 21** **PB 22** (100 tons)

♦ *1 netlayer* — Bldr: Penhoët-Loire, 1954

CR 1 (ex-G-6)

D: 770 tons (850 fl) **S:** 12 kts **Dim:** 46.28 (44.5 pp) × 10.2 × 3.2
A: 1/40-mm AA — 1/20-mm AA **Man:** 45 men **Range:** 5,200/12
M: Diesel-electric propulsion (2 SEMT-Pielstick diesels); 1 prop; 1,600 hp
Fuel: 125 m³ diesel

CR 1

REMARKS: Same characteristics as the French *Scarabée.* Transferred in 1955 under MAP.

♦ *1 transport* — Bldr: Ast. Echevarrieta, Cadiz, 1953

A 41 ALMIRANTE LOBO (ex-cargo *Torrelaguna*) — In serv. 4-10-54

D: 7,750 tons **S:** 12 kts **Dim:** 103.0 × 14.6 × 6.8
A: 1/37-mm **M:** 1 reciprocating engine; 1 prop; 2,300 hp

♦ *6 ocean tugs*

RA 1 **RA 2** — Bldr: E. N. Bazan, Cartagena, 1954

D: 1,023 tons (fl) **S:** 14.5 kts **Dim:** 56.1 (49.8 pp) × 10.0 × 3.9
A: 2/20-mm (II × 1) — 24 mines **Man:** 60 men **Range:** 5,500/14
M: 2 Sulzer diesels; 1 reversible-pitch prop; 3,200 hp
Fuel: 142 tons

RA 4 **RA 5** **BS 1 POSEIDON** — Bldr: E. N. Bazan, Cadiz, 1962–63

D: 1,050 tons (fl) BS-1: 1,098 (fl) **Dim:** 55.9 (49.8 pp) × 10.0 × 4.0

Poseidon (BS 1) 1971

SPAIN (*continued*)

AUXILIARY SHIPS (*continued*)

REMARKS: Other characteristics same as the RA-1. BS-1 is equipped for salvage and frogman support. Can carry and lay 24 mines.

RA 3 (ex-British merchant *Metinda III*)

D: 1,050 tons (fl) **S:** 10 kts **Dim:** 41.75 × 10.1 × 3.95
M: Triple-expansion; 1 prop; 3,200 hp

REMARK: Joined the fleet in 5-61.

♦ *19 harbor tugs*

RR 53 **RR 54** **RR 55** — In serv. 1967

D: 227 tons (fl) **S:** . . . **Dim:** 27.8 × 7.0 × 3.4
M: Diesels; 1,400 hp

RR 50 **RR 51** **RR 52** — In serv. 1963

D: 227 tons (fl) **S:** . . . **Dim:** 27.8 × 7.0 × 3.4
M: Diesels; 800 hp

RP 1 RP 2 RP 3 RP 4 RP 5 RP 6 RP 7 RP 8 RP 9 RP 10 RP 11 RP 12 (In serv. 1965-67 **M:** 200 hp)
RP 40 (In serv. 1961 **M:** 600 hp)

♦ *1 royal yacht* — Bldr: Bazan, El Ferrol, 1949

AZOR

Azor **J. Taibo, 1970**

D: 442 tons (486 fl) **S:** 12 kts **Dim:** 47.0 × 7.7 × 3.8
M: 2 diesels; 1,200 hp

♦ *1 training ship* — Bldr: Ast. Echevarrieta, Cadiz

	Laid down	L	In serv.
JUAN SEBASTIAN DE ELCANO	1925	5-3-27	8-28

Juan Sebastian de Elcano 1972

D: 3,420 tons (3,714 fl) **S:** 11 kts **Dim:** 94.11 × 13.6 × 6.95
A: 4/57-mm **Man:** 224 men, 80 cadets **Range:** 13,000/8
M: 1 Sulzer diesel; 1 prop; 1,500 hp **Fuel:** 230 tons

REMARKS: Four-masted schooner, 2,467 m^2 sail area. School ship for the Coast Guard. Similar to the Chilean training ship *Esmeralda*.

SRI LANKA

Ceylon

PERSONNEL (1976): 2,310 men, including 189 officers

MERCHANT MARINE (1976): 36 ships — 91,031 grt
(tankers: 5 ships — 19,805 grt)

FRIGATE

♦ *1 ex-Canadian River class*

F 232 GAJABAHU (ex-Israeli *Misnak*, ex-Canadian *Hallowell*) (8-8-44)

D: 1,445 tons (2,360 fl) **Dim:** 91.9 × 11.07 × 3.65
S: 19.5 kts **Man:** 106 men **A:** 1/102-mm — 3/40-mm AA
Range: 6,000/12 **M:** Triple expansion; 2 props; 5,500 hp
Boilers: 2 **Fuel:** 645 tons

REMARKS: Bought from Israel in 1959. Immobile.

SRI LANKA — CEYLON (*continued*)

PATROL BOATS

♦ *1 Soviet MOL class (1975)*

SAMUDRA DEVI

Samudra Devi

D: 170 tons (210 fl) **S:** 40 kts **Dim:** 39.9 × 7.6 × 1.8
A: 4/30-mm AA (II × 2)
M: 3 diesels; 3 props; 12,000 hp

REMARKS: Does not have 4/533-mm TT or Drum Tilt gun fire-control radar, as on Soviet and Somali units. Hull and propulsion same as Osa-I-class missile boat.

♦ *6 Chinese Shanghai-II class* — Transferred: 2-72 and 75

SURAYA, WEERAYA, BALAWATHA, DAKSAYA, RAMAKAMI, N . . .

D: 155 tons (fl) **S:** 28 kts **Dim:** 38.8 × 5.4 × 1.6
A: 4/37-mm AA (II × 2) — 4/25-mm AA (II × 2)
M: 4 diesels; 4 props; 4,800 hp **Man:** 28 men

PATROL CRAFT

♦ *1 patrol craft* — Bldr: Colombo DY — In serv. 1977

D: 44 tons (fl) **S:** 19 kts **Dim:** 19.5 × 4.9 × 1.1
A: 2/20-mm AA (I × 2) **Man:** 12 men **Range:** 1,200/14
M: 2 G.M. 8V-71TI diesels; 2 props; 1,240 hp

♦ *3 patrol craft* — Bldr: Colombo DY — In serv. 1976-77

D: 15 tons (fl) **S:** 16 kts **Dim:** 12.7 × . . . × . . .
A: 1/12.7-mm machine gun
M: 2 G.M. 6-71M diesels; 2 props; 530 hp

REMARK: Additional units may be built.

♦ *5 British Cheverton customs craft* — In serv. 4-77

No. 421 to **No. 425**

D: . . . **S:** 23.6 kts **Dim:** 17.0 × 4.5 × 1.2
M: 2 G.M. 8V-71TI diesels; 2 props; 800 hp
Range: 790/18, 1,000/12.2

REMARKS: Plastic; additional units may replace 101 class.

♦ *4 customs craft* — Bldr: Italy

DIYAKAWA, KORAWAKKA, SERUWA, TARAWA

D: 13 tons **Dim:** 15 × 3.70 × 0.95 **S:** 15 kts
M: 2 Foden diesels; 240 hp

REMARK: *Seruwa* and *Tarawa* are hydrographic craft.

♦ *20 101-class patrol craft (1966-68)* — Bldr: Thornycroft, Singapore

No. 102 to **No. 110**, **No. 201** to **No. 211**

D: 15 tons **Dim:** 13.86 × 3.65 × 0.92 **S:** 25 kts
A: 1 machine gun **Man:** 6 men
M: 2 General Motors or Thornycroft engines

SUDAN

PERSONNEL: About 800 men

MERCHANT MARINE (1976): 14 ships — 45,578 grt

PATROL BOATS

♦ *2 Yugoslav Kraljevica class* — Bldr: Yugoslavia, 1968-69

522 EL FASHER **523 EL KHARTOUM**

El Khartoum (523) 1974

D: 190 tons (245 fl) **S:** 20 kts **Dim:** 41.0 × 6.3 × 2.1
A: 2/40-mm AA — 4/20-mm AA — depth charges **Range:** 2,500/10
M: Diesels; 2 props; 3,300 hp

SUDAN (*continued*)

PATROL BOATS (*continued*)

♦ *4 El Gihad class* — Bldr: Mosor, Yugoslavia, 1961

PB 1 EL GIHAD **PB 3 EL ISTIQLAL**
PB 2 EL HORRIYA **PB 4 EL SHAAB**

El Horriya (PB 2) L. V. Pujo

D: 86 tons **S:** 20 kts **Dim:** 31.4 × 4.9 × 1.45
A: 1/40-mm — 1/20-mm — 2 machine guns **Man:** 17 men
M: 2 Mercedes-Benz diesels, 910 hp each **Range:** 1,200/12

♦ *6 ex-Yugoslav modified 308 class* — Transferred: 4-70

D: 60 tons (fl) **S:** 36 kts **Dim:** 23.8 × 6.5 × 2.4
A: 2/40-mm — 2/20-mm **Man:** 14 men **Range:** 1,500/10
M: 2 diesels; 3 props; 5,000 hp

AMPHIBIOUS CRAFT

♦ *2 ex-Yugoslav DTK-221-class LCUs* — Transferred: 1969

SOBAT **DINDER**

D: 410 tons **S:** 10 kts **Dim:** 44.0 × 6.0 × 2.1
A: 1/20-mm — 2 machine guns

REMARK: See section on Yugoslavia.

♦ *3 utility landing craft* — Transferred by Yugoslavia: end 1970

D: 40 tons (80 fl)

VARIOUS SHIPS

♦ *1 supply ship* — Bldr: Yugoslavia — Transferred: 1969

FASHODA

D: 200 tons

♦ *1 self-propelled barge* — Bldr: Yugoslavia — Transferred: 1969

BARAKA

D: 100 tons

♦ *1 survey ship*

TIENAGA

SURINAM

MERCHANT MARINE (1976): 4 ships — 4,890 grt

♦ *3 patrol craft ordered from The Netherlands*

N . . . **N . . .** **N . . .**

D: . . . **S:** . . . **Dim:** . . .
A: . . . **M:** . . .

SWEDEN

PERSONNEL:
Peacetime: 9,200 men of the regular Navy, including officers, petty officers, enlisted men, and civilians with a permanent status, plus 7,000 men available for immediate service.
Wartime: With the mobilization of the reserve, the number of men could reach 80,000.

MERCHANT MARINE (1976): 764 ships — 7,971,246 grt
(tankers: 128 ships — 3,673,684 grt)

NAVAL AVIATION: Consists of some 40 helicopters: Alouette II (HKP-2) for minesweeping, sea rescue, and ASW missions, a few Agusta Bell 206-A (HKP-6), and some Vertol 107 (HKP-4).

WARSHIPS IN SERVICE OR UNDER CONSTRUCTION AS OF 1 OCTOBER 1977

	L	Tons	Main armament
♦ *23 submarines*			
3 NACKEN	. . .	980	8/533-mm TT
5 SJÖBJÖRNEN	1967–68	800 (surfaced)	4/533-mm TT, 2 ASW TT
12 HAJEN	1954–61	770	4/533-mm TT
3 U	1943–44	430 (surfaced)	4/533-mm TT
♦ *6 destroyers*			
4 ÖSTERGÖTLAND	1956–57	2,150	4/120-mm, 1 Sea Cat, 5/533-mm
2 HÅLLAND	1952	2,650	4/120-mm, SSM system
♦ *6 frigates*			
2 ÖLAND	1945–46	1,990	4/120-mm, 6/533-mm
4 VISBY	1942–43	1,150	3/120-mm, 3/40-mm
♦ *3 corvettes*			
3 R	. . .	700	2 SSM, 2/57-mm

WARSHIPS (*continued*)

♦ *16 guided-missile patrol boats*

16 STORM/SNÖGG	. . .	145	1/57-mm, 4 Penguin

♦ *45 patrol boats*

12 SPICA II	1972-76	230	1/57-mm, 6/533-mm or SSM
6 SPICA	1966-67	190	1/57-mm, 6/533-mm TT
11 PLEJAD	1954-58	155	2/40-mm, 6/533-mm
11 T-42	1956-59	44.5	1/40-mm, 2/533-mm TT
1 JAGAREN	1972	145	1/57-mm, mines
4 EX-T-42	1956-59	44.5	1/40-mm

In peacetime, the fleet is used primarily for training recruits, and not all the ships are manned.

WEAPONS AND SYSTEMS

Most of the electronic equipment in use in the Swedish Navy is Dutch (for example, LWO-2 air-search radars, HSA fire-control radars).

(A) MISSILES

The SAAB 08-A, a surface-to-surface missile based on the CT-30 of the SNIAS, is in use on both the 2 *Hålland*-class destroyers and in the coastal batteries.

Length: 5.70 m
Diameter: 0.650 m
Wingspan: 3.600 m
Weight: 9,000 kg
Maximum range: 30 nautical miles (on destroyers), 70 nautical miles (in coastal batteries)

The Norwegian Penguin missile is in use on board the *Storm/Snögg*-class patrol boats.

(B) GUNS

The Swedish Bofors firm furnishes the guns, the principal ones being:

120-mm twin automatic

Installed on the *Hålland*-class destroyers
Mount weight: 55 tons
Length of barrel: 46 calibers
Muzzle velocity: 850 m/sec (projectile weight 23.5 kg)
Elevation: +80°
Firing rate: 40 rounds/min/barrel
Maximum effective range, surface target: 12,000 to 13,000 m
Maximum effective range, anti-aircraft fire: 7,000 to 8,000 m

Each barrel can fire 26 rounds at a time, after which the magazine must be reloaded. Water-cooled. Used with LA-01 fire-control radar of Hollandse Signaal Apparaten (HSA).

120-mm twin semi-automatic

Installed on the *Östergötland* and *Öland* classes of destroyers
Mount weight: . . . tons
Length of barrel: 46 calibers
Muzzle velocity: 850 m/sec
Elevation: +80°
Firing rate: 20 rounds/min/barrel

57-mm twin automatic

Installed on the *Hålland*-class destroyers
Mount weight: 20 tons
Muzzle velocity: 850 m/sec
Maximum rate of fire: 120/rounds/barrel
Maximum effective range, surface target: 13,000 m
Maximum effective range, anti-aircraft fire: 5,000 m

57-mm single-barrel automatic

Installed on *Spica* and *Spica II* torpedo boats
Mount weight (without ammunition): 6 tons
Train speed: 55°/sec
Elevation speed: 20°/sec
Elevation: −10° +75°
Maximum rate of fire: 200/rounds/min

Used on the *Spica* with S-62 HSA fire control made up of two radars in a dome, one for search, the other for target designation and, if required, the firing of the gun. On the *Spica II* class, these radars are separated.

(C) ASW WEAPONS

The 375-mm Bofors ASW rocket launcher in triple or quadruple mount.

The M-41 400-mm ASW torpedo with homing guidance system and the M-61 500-mm wire-guided torpedo are the most recent torpedo models in use.

SUBMARINES

♦ *3 Nacken* (*type A-14*) *class* — Bldr: Kockums, Malmö

	L	In serv.
NACKEN	. . .	1977
NAJAD	. . .	1978
NEPTUN	. . .	1978

D: 980 tons **S:** 20 kts **Dim:** 49.5 × 5.7 × . . .
A: 8/533-mm TT **Man:** 5 officers, 12 men
M: Diesel-electric propulsion: generator group of engines with 2,100 hp; 1/1,100-kw motor; 1 prop

REMARKS: Ordered at the end of 1972. The electric battery installation is mounted on shock absorbers. Single periscope. A central computer furnishes, in addition to tactical information, data on the main engines. Will be able to lay mines.

♦ *5 Sjöbjörnen* (*type 11-B*) *class* — Bldrs: 3 by Kockums Mek. Verk. A.B., Malmö; 2 by Karlskronavarvet

SJÖBJÖRNEN	9-1-68	**SJÖHUNDEN**	21-3-68
SJÖHÄSTEN	6-8-68	**SJÖLEJONET**	29-6-67
SJÖORMEN	25-1-67		

D: 800 tons surfaced, 1,125 submerged **Dim:** 51.0 × 6.1 × 5.1
S: 20 kts (submerged) **Man:** 7 officers, 11 men
A: 4/533-mm, fwd — 2 TT fwd for torpedoes or mines
Endurance: 21 days
M: Propulsion by an Asea electric motor, 3,500 hp, which runs at slow speeds and is virtually noiseless, plus 2 Hedemora-Pielstick diesel-electric groups on the surface (4 generators) and, submerged, four batteries; 1 five-bladed prop

REMARKS: Hull and sail of the U.S. *Barbel* class; two decks; advanced compartmentation. Diving depth of up to 150 m (the Baltic Sea is quite shallow).

SUBMARINES (*continued*)

Sjöormen

♦ *12 Hajen (A-11) class* — Bldrs: Kockums; *Valen* and *Gripen:* Karlskronavarvet

	L		L
A. **HAJEN**	11-12-54	**BÄVERN**	3-2-58
SÄLEN	3-10-55	**ILLERN**	14-11-57
VALEN	21-4-55	**UTTERN**	14-11-58
B. **DRAKEN**	9-1-60	**NORDKAPAREN**	8-3-61
GRIPEN	31-5-60	**SPRINGAREN**	31-8-61
VARGEN	20-5-60	**DELFINEN**	7-3-61

Sälen 1972

D: 770 tons, 835 normal (A type: 720) **S:** 14/17 kts
Dim: A type: 66 B type: 70 × 5.1 × 5.1 **Man:** 44 men
A: 4/533-mm TT fwd
M: Diesel-electric propulsion surfaced (SEMT-Pielstick diesels); 1,700 hp

REMARKS: Snorkel, streamlined sail, derived from the German XXI class. The A type has 2 props; the more recent B type, 1 prop. Eight reserve torpedoes are stored in a ready-service rack abaft the torpedo tubes.

♦ *3 U class* — Bldr: Kockums or Karlskronavarvet

	L		L
ABBORREN (ex-**U-5**)	8-7-43	**MAKRILLEN** (ex-**U-9**)	23-5-44
LAXEN (ex-**U-8**)	25-4-44		

Abborren

D: 420/430 tons surfaced, 460 submerged **S:** 14/9 kts
Dim: 49.8 (pp) × 5.3 × 4.3 **Man:** 23 men
A: 4/533-mm TT (3 fwd, 1 aft)
M: 2 M.A.N. diesels; electric motor; 1,500/750 hp

REMARKS: One-piece hull, snorkel, and streamlined sail. Rebuilt 1960-63. The *Gäddan* taken out of service in 1974, and the *Siken* in 1975.

DESTROYERS

♦ *4 Östergötland class*

	Bldr	Laid down	L	In serv.
J 20 ÖSTERGÖTLAND	Götaverken, Göteborg	9-55	8-5-56	3-58
J 21 SÖDERMANLAND	Eriksbergs, Göteborg	6-55	28-5-56	6-58
J 22 GÄSTRIKLAND	Götaverken, Göteborg	10-55	6-6-56	1-59
J 23 HÄLSINGLAND	Kockums, Malmö	10-55	14-1-57	6-59

Södermanland (J 21) 1970

D: 2,150 tons (2,600 fl) **Dim:** 115.8 (112 pp) × 11.2 × 3.7
S: 35 kts **Man:** 18 officers, 226 men
Range: 2,200/20 **Fuel:** 330 tons

DESTROYERS (*continued*)

A: 4/120-mm AA (II × 2) — 4/40-mm AA (J-20: 7) — J-21, J-22, and J-23: 1 Sea Cat system — 5/533-mm TT (V × 1) — 1 squid — 60 mines
Electron Equipt: Radars: Similar to the *Hålland* class
Sonars: 1 search, 1 attack
M: Laval GT; 2 props; 40,000 hp **Boilers:** 2 Penhoet

REMARK: These ships may be converted into frigates.

♦ *2 Hålland class*

	Bldr	Laid down	L	In serv.
J 18 HÅLLAND	Götaverken, Göteborg	1949	16-7-52	4-55
J 19 SMÅLAND	Eriksbergs, Göteborg	1949	23-10-52	1-56

Hålland (J 18) 1970

Småland (J 19) 1970

D: 2,650 tons (3,300 fl) **Dim:** 121.0 (116 pp) × 12.6 × 4.5
S: 35 kts **Man:** 18 officers, 272 men
Range: 3,000/20 **Fuel:** 500 tons
A: 1 twin launcher for SAAB 08-A SSM — 4/120-mm AA (II × 2) — 2/57-mm AA (II × 1) — 6/40-mm AA — 8/533-mm TT (IV × 2) — 2 quadruple Bofors ASW rocket launchers
Electron Equipt: Radars: 1 LWO-2, 1 VC/DO HSA fire-control
Sonars: 1 search, 1 attack
M: GT; 2 props; 55,000 hp **Boilers:** 2 Penhoet

FRIGATES

♦ *2 Öland class*

	Bldr	Laid down	L	In serv.
J 16 ÖLAND	Kockums, Malmö	1943	15-12-45	12-47
J 17 UPPLAND	Karlskronavarvet	1943	15-11-46	1-49

Uppland (J 17)

D: 1,990 tons (2,400 fl) **Dim:** 111.0 (107 pp) × 11.2 × 3.4
S: 35 kts **Man:** 210 men
Range: 2,500/20 **Fuel:** 300 tons
A: 4/120-mm AA (II × 2) — 6/40-mm AA (II × 3) — 6/533-mm TT (III × 2) — 60 mines
Electron Equipt: Radars: 2 Thomason-CSF Saturn type air-search, 2 M-45 fire-control
Sonars: 1 search, 1 attack
M: Laval GT; 2 props; 40,000 hp **Boilers:** 2 Penhoet
Electric: . . . kw

♦ *4 Visby class* — Authorized: 1941

	Bldr	L	In serv.
F 11 VISBY	Götaverken, Göteborg	16-10-42	10-8-43
F 12 SUNDSVALL	Götaverken, Göteborg	20-10-42	17-9-43
F 13 HÄLSINGBORG	Karlskronavarvet	23-3-43	30-11-43
F 14 KALMAR	Eriksbergs, Göteborg	20-7-43	3-2-44

FRIGATES (*continued*)

Visby (F 11)

D: 1,150 tons (1,320 fl) **S:** 35 kts **Dim:** 98.0 × 9.1 × 3.8
Man: 140 men **Range:** 1,600/20
A: 3/120-mm (I × 3) — 3/40-mm AA — depth-charge projector
M: 2 Laval GT; 2 props; 36,000 hp **Boilers:** 3

REMARKS: F-11 and F-12 have only 2/57-mm AA (I × 2) with HSA fire-control radar, and a helicopter platform.

CORVETTES

♦ *3 R class (building)*

R 01 **R 02** **R 03**

D: 700 tons **S:** 35 kts **Dim:** 80.6 × 8.6 × 2.6
A: 2 SSM — 2/57-mm AA (I × 2) — 1/ASW rocket launcher
M: CODOG **Man:** 70 men

GUIDED-MISSILE PATROL BOATS

♦ *16 Storm/Snögg class* — Bldr: Båtservice Verft, Mandal, Norway

HUGIN	**MODE**	**SPEJAREN**	**TORDON**
KAPAREN	**MUNIN**	**STAKKODER**	**VAKTAREN**
MAGNE	**MYSING**	**STYRBJORN**	**VALE**
MJOLNER	**SNAPHARREN**	**TIRFING**	**VIDAR**

D: 145 tons **S:** 35 kts **Dim:** 37.0 × 6.0 × 1.5
A: 1/57-mm AA — 4 improved Penguin SSM
M: 2 MTU 3082 diesels, 2,900 hp each, at 1,600 rpm or 3,500 hp at 1,700 rpm; 2 props

TORPEDO BOATS

♦ *12 Spica-II class* — Bldrs: Karlskronavarvet and Götaverken

	L	In serv.
T 131 NÖRRKÖPING	16-11-72	5-11-73
T 132 NYNÄSHAMN	24-4-73	9-73
T 133 NORTÄLJE	18-9-73	1-8-74
T 134 VARGERG	21-3-74	10-74
T 135 VÄSTERAS	15-5-74	20-10-74
T 136 VÄSTERVIK	3-9-74	2-9-74
T 137 UMEA	. . .	15-5-75
T 138 PITEA	12-5-73	12-9-75
T 139 LULEA	19-8-75	28-11-75
T 140 HALMSTAD	28-11-75	9-4-76
T 141 STRÖMSTAD	26-4-76	13-9-76
T 142 YSTAD	3-9-76	10-12-76

D: 230 tons **S:** 40.5 kts **Dim:** 43.6 × 7.1 × 1.6
A: 1/57-mm AA — 6/533-mm wire-guided torpedoes — 2 illumination rocket launchers — 1 chaff launcher
M: 3 Rolls-Royce gas turbines, 3,860 hp each

REMARKS: Some of this class will probably be armed with SSMs. The fire-control system is not the same as in the *Spica* class. It and the search radar are separated and no longer enclosed in a dome.

Nörrköping (T 131) 1974

Västeras (T 135) 1975

TORPEDO BOATS (*continued*)

♦ *6 Spica class* — Bldrs: T-121 to T-123: Götaverken; T-124 to T-126: Karlskronavarvet

	L		L
T 121 SPICA	26-4-66	**T 124 CASTOR**	7-6-67
T 122 SIRIUS	26-4-66	**T 125 VEGA**	7-6-67
T 123 CAPELLA	26-4-66	**T 126 VIRGO**	7-6-67

D: 190 tons (235 fl) **S:** 40 kts **Dim:** 42.5 × 7.3 × 1.6
Man: 4 officers, 10 petty officers, 14 men
A: 1/57-mm, fwd — 6/533-mm wire-guided torpedoes
M: 3 Bristol-Siddeley Proteus 1274 gas turbines, 3,860 hp each; 3 Ka-Me-Wa props

REMARKS: Automatic 57-mm Bofors gun with S-62 fire-control radar. Can carry mines.

Sirius (T 122) 1970

Port-quarter view of a Spica-class torpedo boat

Bow view of a Spica-class torpedo boat

♦ *11 Plejad class* — Bldr: Lürssen-Vegesack, Germany

	L		L
T 102 PLEJAD	1954	**T 108 ALTAIR**	1957
T 103 POLARIS	1954	**T 109 ANTARES**	1958
T 104 POLLUX	1954	**T 110 ARCTURUS**	1958
T 105 REGULUS	1954	**T 111 ARGO**	1958
T 106 RIGEL	1954	**T 112 ASTREA**	1958
T 107 ALDEBARAN	1954		

Polaris (T 103) 1970

TORPEDO BOATS (*continued*)

D: 155 tons (170 fl) **Dim:** 48.15 (45 pp) × 5.8 × 1.61
S: 37 kts **Man:** 3 officers, 40 men
Range: 600/30
A: 2/40-mm — 6/533-mm TT for wire-guided torpedoes
M: 3 Mercedes-Benz diesels; 3 props; 7,800 hp (T-108 to T-112: 9,000)

Argo (T 111) 1970

REMARKS: The 40-mm have remote control. Launchers for illumination and short-range rockets. Can be used for minelaying when the torpedo tubes have been removed. The West German *Jaguar* class is derived from the *Plejad* class.

♦ *11 T-42 class* — Bldrs: T-46 to T-52: Kockums; T-53 to T-56: Karlskronavarvet

T 46 to **T 56**

T 46 torpedo boat

D: 44.5 tons **S:** 40 kts **Dim:** T-46 to T-52: 22.5 × 5.68 × 1.6
A: 1/40-mm — 2/533-mm TT **M:** 2 gasoline engines

REMARKS: Built, 1956-59. Steel hull, welded construction. One illumination rocket.

PATROL BOATS

♦ *1 Storm/Snögg class* — Bldr: Båtservice Verft, Mandal, Norway

P 151 JAGAREN (8-6-72)

Jagaren (P 151) 1974

D: 145 tons **S:** 35 kts **Dim:** 37.0 × 6.0 × 1.5
A: 1/57-mm AA — minelaying capability
M: 2 MTU 3082 diesels, 900 hp each at 1,600 rpm, 3,500 hp at 1,700 rpm; 2 props

♦ *4 ex-T-42 class torpedo boats* — Bldr: Kockums, 1956-59

V 01 SKANÖR **V 02 SMYGE** **V 03 ARILD** **V 04 VIKEN**

D: 22.5 × 6.68 × 1.6 **A:** 1/40-mm AA

REMARKS: Ex-T-42 to ex-T-45. Speed reduced to 27 knots.

MINE WARFARE SHIPS

♦ *1 M 04-class minelayer*

M 04 N . . .

Artist's concept of R-01 corvette.
See page 385.

MINE WARFARE SHIPS (*continued*)

D: 3,100 tons **S:** . . . **Dim:** 100 × . . . × . . .
A: 2/57-mm AA (I × 2) — 2/40-mm AA

♦ *2 Älvsborg-class minelayers* — Bldr: Karlskronavarvet

	Laid down	L	In serv.
M 02 ÄLVSBORG	11-68	11-11-69	4-71
M 03 VIBORG	1973	22-1-74	1976

Älvsborg (M 02) 1971

D: 2,650 tons **S:** 15 kts **Dim:** 92.4 (83.8 pp) × 14.7 × 4.0
A: 3/40-mm AA — 1 helicopter **Man:** 97 men + quarters for 210
M: 2 Nohab-Polar 12-cyl. diesels; 1 Ka-Me-Wa prop; 4,200 hp
Electric: 1,200 kw

REMARK: Used as a submarine tender.

♦ *1 Älvsnabben-class minelayer* — Bldr: Eriksbergs, Göteborg

	Laid down	L	In serv.
M 01 ÄLVSNABBEN	11-12	19-1-43	5-43

Älvsnabben (M 01) 1970

D: 4,250 tons **S:** 14 kts **Dim:** 102.0 (96.8 pp) × 13.6 × 4.9
A: 2/152-mm, aft (I × 2) — 2/57-mm AA — 2/40-mm AA — at least 300 mines
M: Diesel; 1 prop; 3,000 hp **Man:** 255 men

REMARKS: Cargo ship modified while under construction. Also used as a supply ship for minesweepers and submarines. Will be replaced by the M-04. Used as a training ship.

♦ *9 minehunters ordered in 1976–77*

The Karlskrona shipyards will build a fiberglass half-scale model of the prototype of this class, whose only known characteristics are:

D: 140 tons (fl) **Dim:** 25.3 × 6.64 × 3.65

♦ *18 Hanö/Arkö-class coastal minesweepers*

	L		L
M 51 HANÖ	1953	**M 60 IGGÖ**	1958
M 52 TÄRNÖ	1953	**M 61 STYRSÖ**	1961
M 53 TJURKÖ	1954	**M 62 SKAFTÖ**	1961
M 54 STURKÖ	1954	**M 63 ASPÖ**	1962
M 55 ORNÖ	1954	**M 64 HASSLÖ**	1962
M 56 UTÖ	1954	**M 65 VINÖ**	1962
M 57 ARKÖ	21-1-57	**M 66 VALLÖ**	1962
M 58 SPÅRÖ	1957	**M 67 NÅMDÖ**	1964
M 59 KARLSÖ	1957	**M 68 BLIDÖ**	1964

M-51 to M-56:
D: 270 tons **Dim:** 42.0 (40 pp) × 7.0 × 2.7
A: 1/40-mm AA **S:** 14.5 kts
M-57 to M-68:
D: 285 tons **Dim:** 44.0 × 7.0 × 2.5
A: 1/40-mm AA **S:** 14.5 kts **Man:** 25 men
M: 2 Mercedes-Benz diesels; 1,000 hp

Utö (M 56) 1976

MINE WARFARE SHIPS (*continued*)

Aspö (M 63)

REMARKS: The six Hanö-class ships, M-51 to M-56, have steel hulls: the twelve Arkö-class have wooden hulls. Excellent antimagnetic features.

♦ *3 Gasten-class inshore minesweepers*

	L	In serv.
M 31 GASTEN	. . .	11-73
M 32 NORSTEN	. . .	10-73
M 33 VIKSTEN	18-4-74	. . .

Viksten (M 33)

D: 120 tons **S:** 9 kts **Dim:** 23.0 × 6.6 × 3.7
A: 1/40-mm AA **M:** Diesel

REMARK: The hull of M-31 is made of a fiberglass and plastic compound.

♦ *8 M-15-class inshore minesweepers*

M 15 **M 16** **M 21** to **M 26**

M 25

D: 70 tons **S:** 13 kts **Dim:** 26.0 × 5.05 × 1.4
A: 1/20-mm AA **Man:** 10 men
M: Diesels; 1 prop; 600 hp

REMARKS: Wooden hulls. M-21, M-22, and M-25 are used as tenders for divers.

♦ *2 Örust-class inshore minesweepers*

M 41 ÖRUST **M 42 TJÖRN**

D: 110 tons **S:** . . . **Dim:** 19.0 × 6.0 × 2.4

♦ *7 Hisingen-class inshore minesweepers*

M 43 HISINGEN (1960)
M 44 BLACKAN (1960)
M 45 DAMMAN (1960)
M 46 GALTEN (1960)
M 47 GILLÖGA (1964)
M 48 RÖDLÖGA (1964)
M 49 SVARTLÖGA (1964)

Hisingen (M 43)

D: 140 tons **S:** 9 kts **Dim:** 22.0 × 6.4 × 1.4
A: 1/40-mm **M:** Diesel; 600 hp

AMPHIBIOUS WARFARE CRAFT

♦ *3 landing craft*

GRIM (1961) **BORE** (9-66) **HEIMDAL** (12-66)
D: 380 tons **S:** 12 kts **Dim:** 36.0 × 8.5 × 2.6

♦ *2 landing craft*

A 333 SKAGUL (1960) **A 335 SLEIPNER** (1959)
D: 355 tons **S:** 12 kts **Dim:** 36.0 × 8.5 × 2.6

♦ *55 landing craft*

L 201 to **L 255** (1957-64)
D: 31 tons **S:** 18 kts **Dim:** 20.0 × 4.2 × 1.3

♦ *24 landing craft under construction*

L 256 to **L 279**
D: 20 tons **S:** 18 kts **Dim:** 18.0 × . . . × . . .

♦ *5 landing craft*

L 51 to **L 55** (1948)
D: 32 tons **S:** 8 kts **Dim:** 14.0 × 4.8 × 0.9

AUXILIARY SHIPS

♦ *2 surveying ships*

JOHAAN MÅNSSON (14-1-66)

Johaan Månsson

D: 900 tons **S:** 15 kts **Dim:** 56.0 × 11.0 × 2.6
M: Nohab-Polar diesel; 3,300 hp

GUSTAF AF KLINT (1941) — Rebuilt in 1963
D: 750 tons (fl) **S:** 10 kts **Dim:** 52.0 × 8.7 × 4.7
M: Diesel; 300 hp

♦ *2 coastal surveying ships*

NILS STRÖMKRONA (1894) — Rebuilt in 1952
D: 140 tons **S:** 9 kts **Dim:** 26.6 × 5.1 × 2.5
M: Diesel; 300 hp

ANDERS BURE (ex-*Rali*)
D: 54 tons **S:** 11 kts **Dim:** 24.6 × 5.9 × 2.0

REMARK: Former trawler dating from 1968 and bought in 1971.

♦ *1 coastal tanker*

A 228 BRANNAREN (ex-*Indio*) (1965)
D: . . . **S:** 11 kts **Dim:** 62.0 × . . . × . . . **Cargo:** 857 tons

REMARK: Small commercial tanker assigned at the end of 1972.

♦ *1 salvage ship*

A 211 BELOS (1961)

Belos (A 211) 1970

D: 1,000 tons **S:** 13 kts **Dim:** 62.3 × 11.2 × 3.65
M: Diesel; 1 prop; 1,200 hp

REMARKS: Carries a helicopter, and is well equipped for underwater search: decompression chamber, active rudder, and television.

♦ *3 Finnish Urho-class icebreakers* — Bldr: Wärtsilä, Helsinki

	L	In serv.
ATLE	. . .	21-10-74
FREJ	. . .	30-9-74
YMER	3-9-76	1977

Atle 1975

AUXILIARY SHIPS (*continued*)

D: 7,800 tons **S:** 19 kts **Dim:** 104.0 (99 pp) × 23.8 × 7.8
M: Diesel-electric; 1 prop; 22,000 hp

♦ *1 Ale-class icebreaker* — Bldr: Wärtsilä, Helsinki

ALE — In serv. 12-12-73

D: 1,488 tons **S:** 14 kts **Dim:** 46.0 × 13.0 × 5.0
M: Diesels; 2 props; 4,750 hp **Man:** 21 men

♦ *4 icebreakers*

NJORD — Bldr: Wärtsilä, Helsinki — L: 2-10-68 — In serv. 10-69

Njord 1970

D: 5,626 tons **S:** 18 kts **Dim:** 86.45 (79.45 pp) × 21.18 × 6.9
M: Diesel-electric propulsion: 4 Sulzer 9MH-51 diesels; Stromber electric motors, 2 fwd (3,400 kw each), 2 aft (2,200 kw each); 4 props; 13,620 hp (330 rpm)

TOR — Bldr: Sandviken, Finland — L: 25-5-63

D: 5,260 tons **S:** 18 kts **Dim:** 84.4 × 20.42 × 6.2
M: Diesel-electric propulsion; 4 props; 11,200 hp. Same motors as the *Njord.*

ODEN — Bldr: Wärtsilä, Helsinki — L: 16-10-56 — In serv. 1958

D: 4,950 tons (3,370 light) **Dim:** 83.35 (78 pp) × 19.4 × 6.9
S: 17 kts **Man:** 75 men **Fuel:** 740 tons
M: Diesel-electric; 4 props (2 fwd, 2 aft); 10,500 hp

THULE — Bldr: Karlskronavarvet — In serv. end 1953

D: 2,200 tons **S:** 16 kts **Dim:** 57.0 × 16.07 × 5.9
M: Diesel-electric; 3 props (1 fwd, 2 aft); 4,800 hp **Man:** 43 men

♦ *2 icebreaker tugs*

A 251 ACHILLES (1962) **A 252 AJAX** (1963)

D: 450 tons **Dim:** 33.15 × 8.8 × 4.9

♦ *3 ex-M-15-class minesweepers*

A 231 LOMMEN (ex-M-37), **A 232 SPOVEN** (ex-M-18), **A 254 SKULD** (ex-M-20)

♦ *1 water carrier*

A 216 UNDEN (1946)

D: 500 tons **S:** 10 kts **Dim:** 36.5 × 7.1 × 4.3

♦ *1 water carrier*

A 217 FRYKEN (1959)

D: 307 tons **S:** 10 kts **Dim:** 32.0 × 5.8 × 2.75

♦ *1 fresh-water supply ship* (1953)

A 221 FREJA

D: 300 tons (450 fl) **S:** 11 kts **Dim:** 49.0 × 8.4 × 3.0
M: 1 diesel

♦ *3 torpedo-recovery vessels*

A 246 HAGERN (1951)

D: 50 tons **S:** 10 kts **Dim:** 28.0 × 5.0 × 1.2

A 247 PELIKANEN (1964)

D: 100 tons **S:** 15 kts **Dim:** 33.0 × 5.8 × 1.8

A 248 PINGVINEN L: 26-9-73

D: 189 tons **S:** 11 kts **Dim:** 33.0 × . . . × . . .

VARIOUS SHIPS

♦ **A 253 HERMES** (1958) **A 321 HECTOR** **A 322 HEROS**

D: 185 tons **S:** 11.5 kts **Dim:** 23.0 × 6.8 × 4.0

♦ **A 324 HERA** **A 323 HERKULES**

D: 127 tons **Dim:** 19.6 × 6.4 × 3.7

♦ *1 laundering ship*

A 256 SIGRUN (1961)

D: 250 tons **S:** 10 kts **Dim:** 32.0 × 6.8 × 2.5

♦ *2 mine transports*

A 236 FALLAREN **A 237 MINOREN**

D: 165 tons **S:** 9 kts **Dim:** 31.5 × 6.1 × 2.1

♦ *2 sail training ships* (1946-47)

FALKEN **GLADAN**

D: 220 tons **Dim:** 28.3 × 7.27 × 4.2
M: 1 diesel auxiliary engine; 50 hp

COASTAL ARTILLERY SERVICE

♦ *1 patrol craft*

V 57 (1954)

D: 115 tons (135 fl)
S: 13.5 kts
A: 1/20-mm AA
Dim: 29.9 × 5.3 × 2.2
Man: 12 men
M: Nohab-Polar diesel; 1 prop; 500 hp

♦ *22 patrol craft*

Nos. **61** to **70** (1960–61)

D: 30 tons **S:** 19 kts **Dim:** 21.0 × 4.6 × 1.2
A: 1/20-mm

66

Nos. **71** to **77** (1966–67)

72 197(

D: 28 tons **S:** 18 kts **Dim:** 21.0 × 4.6 × 1.5
A: 1/20-mm

SVK 1 to **SVK 5** (1944)

D: 19 tons **S:** 11 kts **Dim:** 17.0 × 3.65 × 1.2
A: 1/20-mm

REMARK: At one time assigned to the Sjövarnkären (Volunteer Naval Reserve), but have been reassigned to the naval list.

♦ *9 coastal minelayers*

MUL 12 to **MUL 19** (1952–56)

MUL 19 1970

D: 245 tons **S:** 10.5 kts **Dim:** 31.18 × 7.62 × 3.1
A: 1/40-mm

SWEDEN (*continued*)

COASTAL ARTILLERY SERVICE (*continued*)

MUL 11 (1946)

D: 200 tons **S:** 10 kts **Dim:** 30.1 × 7.21 × 3.65
A: 2/20-mm

Remark: MUL-12 to MUL-19 have 1 diesel-electric engine and 360 hp.

♦ *4 service craft, 1943-45*

J 324 ANE **J 325 BALDER** **J 326 LOKE** **J 327 RING**

D: 135 tons **S:** 8.5 kts **Dim:** 28.0 × 8.0 × 1.8
A: 1/20-mm

SYRIA

Personnel: Approximately 2,500

Merchant Marine (1976): 17 ships — 10,192 grt

FRIGATES

♦ *2 ex-Soviet Petya class* — Transferred: 1975

D: 1,100 tons (fl) **Dim:** 82.0 × 9.1 × 3.2
S: 30 kts **Man:** 80 men
A: 4/76-mm AA (II × 2) — 4/MBU 4500 rocket launchers — 5/400-mm TT (V × 1)
Electron Equipt: Radars: 1 Don, 1 Spin Net, 1 Hawk Screech
Sonar: 1 HF system
M: CODAG: 2 gas turbines (15,000 hp each); 1 diesel (6,000 hp); 3 props; 36,000 hp

GUIDED-MISSILE PATROL BOATS

♦ *6 ex-Soviet Osa-I class*

OSA-I boat 1976

D: 175 tons (210 fl) **S:** 36 kts **Dim:** 39.0 × 7.7 × 1.8
A: 4/SS-N-2 Styx — 4/30-mm AA (II × 2)
Electron Equipt: Radars: 1 Square Tie, 1 Drum Tilt
M: 3 M503A diesels; 3 props; 12,000 hp **Range:** 450/34, 700/20

Remark: Two transferred earlier were sunk during the Arab-Israeli War, October 1973.

♦ *6 ex-Soviet Komar class*

D: 71 tons (82 fl) **S:** 40 kts **Dim:** 25.3 × 7.0 × 2.0
A: 2/SS-N-2 Styx — 2/25-mm AA (II × 1) **Man:** 20 men
Electron Equipt: Radar: 1 Square Tie
M: 4 M50 diesels; 4 props; 4,800 hp

Remark: Survivors of a group, three of which were sunk in the Arab-Israeli War, October 1973.

TORPEDO BOATS

♦ *8 ex-Soviet P-4 class* — Transferred: 1958-60

D: 19.3 tons (22.4 fl) **S:** 55 kts **Dim:** 19.3 × 3.7 × 1.0
A: 2/14.5-mm machine guns (II × 1) — 2/533-mm TT (I × 2)

P 4 1972

Remark: The remaining units in service of a group of at least 17; one was sunk during the Arab-Israeli War, October 1973.

PATROL BOATS

♦ *3 ex-French submarine chasers* — Bldrs: First 2: Seine Maritime; third: A.C. de France

	Laid down	L	In serv.
ABDULLAH IBN ARISSI (ex-CH-19)	1938	1-40	4-40
TAREK IBN ZAYED (ex-CH-13)	1938	1939	1940
AKABEH IBN NEFEH (ex-CH-10)	1938	1939	1940

D: 107 tons (131 fl) **S:** 16 kts **Dim:** 37.1 (35.5 pp) × 5.34 × 1.95
A: 1/75-mm — 2/20-mm AA — depth charges **Man:** 28 men
Range: 680/13.5, 1,200/8
M: M.A.N. diesels; 2 props; 1,130 hp **Fuel:** 5.4 tons

Remarks: Rebuilt, 1955-56. Not in service.

SYRIA (*continued*)

MINE WARFARE AND VARIOUS SHIPS

♦ *1 Soviet-T-43-class fleet minesweeper*

YARMOUK

REMARK: For characteristics, see section on U.S.S.R.

♦ *2 Soviet Vanya-class coastal minesweepers* — Transferred: December 1972

♦ *1 Soviet Nyryat-class diving tender*

TAIWAN

Republic of China

PERSONNEL (1976): 64,000 men, including 29,000 Marines

MERCHANT MARINE (1976): 438 ships — 1,483,981 grt
(tankers: 17 ships — 364,902 grt)

SUBMARINES

♦ *2 ex-U.S. Guppy class* — Transferred: 2-73 and 4-73

	L
S 91 HAI CHIH (ex-*Cutlass*, SS-478)	5-11-44
S 92 HAI PAO (ex-*Tusk*, SS-426)	8-7-45

D: 1,517 tons standard, 1,870 surfaced, 2,240 submerged
S: 15-18/13 kts **Dim:** 93.8 × 8.2 × 5.2
A: 10/533-mm TT **Range:** 10,000/10 **Man:** 82-86 men
M: Diesel-electric propulsion: 3 groups of generators; 2 electric motors; 4,800/5,200 hp

DESTROYERS

♦ *10 ex-U.S. Gearing class* — Transferred: 1971-73, 1977

	Bldr	L
DD 7 FU YANG (ex-*Ernest G. Small*, DD-838)	Bath Iron Works	9-6-45
DD 11 DANG YANG (ex-*Lloyd Thomas*, DD-764)	Bethlehem, San Fran.	5-10-45
DD 12 CHIEN YANG (ex-*James E. Kyes*, DD-787)	Todd, Seattle	4-8-45
DD 15 HAN YANG (ex-*Herbert J. Thomas*, DD-833)	Bath Iron Works	25-3-45
DD 20 LAO YANG (ex-*Shelton*, DD-790)	Todd, Seattle	8-3-46
DD 21 LIAO YANG (ex-*Hanson*, DD-832)	Bath Iron Works	25-2-45

D: 2,425 tons (3,500 fl) **S:** 30 kts **Dim:** 119.17 × 12.55 × 5.5
A: 4/127-mm AA (II × 2) — 1 Asroc system — 6/Mk 32 ASW TT (III × 2)
Electron Equipt: Radars: SPS 10, SPS 6 or SPS 40
Sonars: SQS 23 or SQS 29
M: GT; 2 props; 60,000 hp **Boilers:** 4 Babcock **Fuel:** 650 tons

REMARK: The last four ships, as yet unnamed, were transferred on 1-10-77.

♦ *8 ex-U.S. Allen M. Sumner class* — Transferred: Since 1969

	Bldr	L
DD 1 HSIANG YANG (ex-*Brush*, DD-745)	Bethlehem, Staten I.	28-12-43
DD 2 HENG YANG (ex-*Samuel N. Moore*, DD-747)	Bethlehem, Staten I.	23-2-44
DD 3 HUA YANG (ex-*Bristol*, DD-857)	Bethlehem, San Pedro	29-10-44
DD 5 YUEH YANG (ex-*Hainsworth*, DD-700)	Federal SB & DD	15-4-44
DD 6 HUEI YANG (ex-*English*, DD-696)	Federal SB & DD	27-2-44
DD 10 PO YANG (ex-*Maddox*, DD-731)	Bath Iron Works	19-3-44
DD 14 LO YANG (ex-*Taussig*, DD-746)	Bethlehem, Staten I.	25-1-44
DD 17 NAN YANG (ex-*John W. Thomason*, DD-760)	Bethlehem, San Fran.	30-9-44

Heng Yang (DD 2) 1972

D: 2,200 tons (3,320 fl) **S:** 30 kts **Dim:** 114.75 × 12.45 × 5.8
A: 6/127-mm AA (II × 3) — 6/76-mm AA or 12/40-mm AA — 6/Mk 32 ASW TT (III × 2) — 2 hedgehogs or, on some ships, depth-charge racks
Electron Equipt: Radars: SPS 10, SPS 6 or SPS 40, DD-17: SPS 37
M: GT; 2 props; 60,000 hp **Boilers:** 4 Babcock **Fuel:** 650 tons

♦ *4 ex-U.S. Fletcher class* — Transferred: 6-67, 4-68, 1972

	Bldr	L
DD 8 KWEI YANG (ex-*Twining*, DD-540)	Bethlehem, San Fran.	11-7-43
DD 9 CHING YANG (ex-*Mullany*, DD-528)	Bethlehem, San Fran.	12-10-42
DD 18 AN YANG (ex-*Kimberly*, DD-521)	Bethlehem, Staten I.	4-2-43

DESTROYERS (*continued*)

DD 19 KUEN YANG Bethlehem, San Fran. 25-7-43
(ex-*Yarnall*, DD-541)

Kuen Yang (DD 19) 1970

D: 2,050 tons (2,850 fl) **Dim:** 114.85 (wl) × 12.03 × 5.5
S: 33 kts **Man:** 350 men
Range: 1,260/30, 4,400/15 **Fuel:** 650 tons
A: 5/127-mm semiautomatic 38-cal. — 6/40-mm AA — 6/20-mm AA — 5/ASW TT
M: 2 General Electric GT; 60,000 hp **Boilers:** 4 Babcock

FRIGATES

♦ *1 ex-U.S. escort* — Transferred: 1946

27 TAI YUAN (ex-*Riley*, DE-579) — L: 29-12-43

D: 1,150 tons (1,360 fl) **S:** 19 kts **Dim:** 88.22 × 10.69 × 3.25
A: 2/127-mm DP (I × 2) — 4/40-mm (II × 2) — 4/20-mm — 6/ASW TT — 1 hedgehog — depth charges
M: Diesel-electric **Range:** 5,500/19

♦ *11 ex-U.S. fast transports* — Bldr: U.S.A., 1942-44 — Transferred: Between 4-65 and 8-69

315 YU SHAN (ex-*Kinzer*, APD-91)
316 HUA SHAN (ex-*Scribner*, APD-122)
317 WEN SHAN (ex-*Gantner*, APD-42)
318 FU SHAN (ex-*Truxtun*, APD-98)
319 LU SHAN (ex-*Bull*, APD-78)
320 SHOU SHAN (ex-*Kline*, APD-120)
321 TAI SHAN (ex-*Register*, APD-92)
322 HENG SHAN (ex-*Ray W. Herndon*, APD-121)
323 KANG SHAN (ex-*George W. Ingram*, APD-43)
324 CHUNG SHAN (ex-*Blessman*, APD-48)
325 LUNG SHAN (ex-*Schmitt*, APD-76)

Shou Shan (320) 1970

D: 1,450 tons (2,049 fl) **Dim:** 93.26 × 11.28 × 4.7
S: 22 kts (fl) **Man:** 214 men
Range: 5,000/15
A: 2/127-mm — 6/40-mm AA — 6/324-mm ASW TT Mk 32 (III × 2) or 1 or 2 hedgehogs
M: Turbo-electric propulsion; 2 props; 12,000 hp **Boilers:** 2

Hua Shan (316) 1969

Remarks: Hull numbers were changed in 1970; previously they were PF-32 to PF-44. Used as escort vessels.

CORVETTES

♦ *3 ex-U.S. Raven-class minesweepers* — Transferred: 1964 and 3-68

	L
66 WU CHENG (ex-*Redstart*, MSF-378)	18-10-44
67 CHU YUN (ex-*Waxwing*, MSF-389)	10-3-45
70 MO LING (ex-*Steady*, MSF-118)	. . .

CORVETTES (*continued*)

D: 890 tons (1,250 fl) **Dim:** 67.2 (65 pp) × 9.75 × 3.3
S: 18 kts **Man:** 80-100 men
A: 1/76-mm — 4/40-mm AA (II × 2) — depth-charge projectors
M: Diesel-electric propulsion; 2 props; 3,500 hp

PATROL BOATS AND CRAFT

♦ *2 Japanese-built boats* — Bldr: Mitsubishi, Zosen — Delivered: 6-57 and 11-57

PT 511 FU CHOU **PT 512 HSUEH CHIH**

D: 30 tons **S:** 30 kts **A:** 1/40-mm AA — 2/457-mm torpedoes

♦ *1 U.S. 79-foot boat* — Bldr: U.S.A., 1957

PT 515 FUH KWO

D: 50 tons **S:** 32 kts **A:** 1/40-mm AA

♦ *2 U.S. 71-foot craft* — Bldr: U.S.A., 1957

PT 513 FAAN KONG **PT 514 SAO TANG**

D: 46 tons (fl) **S:** 32 kts **A:** 1/20-mm AA — 2 torpedoes

MINE WARFARE SHIPS

♦ *2 ex-U.S. minesweepers* — Transferred: 1975

N . . . (ex-*Bold*, MSO-424) **N . . .** (ex-*Bulwark*, MSO-425)

D: 750 tons (fl) **S:** 15 kts **Dim:** 56.4 × 12.8 × 4.5
A: . . . **M:** 2 diesels; 2 variable-pitch props; 2,280 hp

♦ *12 ex-U.S. Bluebird-class minesweepers*

	Transferred		Transferred
155 YUNG PING (ex-MSC-140)	6-55	**161 YUNG LO** (ex-MSC-306)	6-66
156 YUNG AN (ex-MSC-240)	6-55	**162 YUNG FU** (ex-Belgian *Diest*)	1970
157 YUNG NIEN (ex-MSC-277)	12-58	**163 YUNG CHING** (ex-Belgian *Eeklo*)	1970
158 YUNG CHOU (ex-MSC-278)	7-59	**164 YUNG SHAN** (ex-Belgian *Lier*)	1970
159 YUNG HSIN (ex-MSC-302)	3-65	**165 YUNG CHENG** (ex-Belgian *Maaseik*)	1970
160 YUNG JU (ex-MSC-300)	4-65	**168 YUNG SUI** (ex-Belgian *Diksmuide*)	1970

D: 370 tons **S:** 13.5 kts **Dim:** 47.2 × 9.2 × 2.8
A: 2/20-mm (II × 1) **Man:** 40 men
M: General Motors diesels; 2 props

AMPHIBIOUS WARFARE SHIPS

♦ *1 command ship*

AGC 1 KAO HSIUNG (ex-*Chung Hai*, LST-229, ex-U.S. LST-735)

D: 1,650 tons (4,080 fl) **S:** 11 kts **Dim:** 160.0 × 16.4 × 4.6
M: General Motors diesels; 2 props; 1,700 hp **Range:** 15,000/9

Remark: Modified in 1968.

♦ *1 ex-U.S. landing ship* — Bldr: Moore, Oakland, 1943 — Transferred: 11-60

191 CHUNG CHENG (ex-*Tung Hai*, ex-*Whitemarsh*, LSD-8)

Chung Cheng (191)

D: 4,032 tons (8,700 fl) **S:** 15.5 kts **Dim:** 139.0 × 21.9 × 4.9
A: 12/40-mm **M:** 2 triple-expansion; 2 props; 7,000 hp

♦ *2 ex-U.S. landing ships* —

N . . . (ex-*Comstock*, LSD-19) **N . . .** (ex-*Fort Marion*, LSD-22)

D: 4,790 tons (9,375 fl) **S:** 15 kts **Dim:** 155.8 × 24.9 × 5.9
A: 12/40-mm AA (IV × 2, II × 2) **M:** GT; 2 props; 7,000 hp

♦ *22 ex-U.S. landing ships*

	Transf.		Transf.
201 CHUNG HAI (ex-LST-755)	4-46	**221 CHUNG CHUAN** (ex-LST-640)	2-48
203 CHUNG TING (ex-LST-537)	3-46	**222 CHUNG SHENG** (ex-LST-1033)	12-47
204 CHUNG HSING (ex-LST-557)	3-46	**223 CHUNG FU** (ex-LST-840)	7-58
205 CHUNG CHIEN (ex-LST-716)	6-46	**224 CHUNG CHENG** (ex-LST-859)	8-58
206 CHUNG CHI (ex-LST-1017)	12-46	**225 CHUNG CHIANG** (ex-LST-1110)	8-58
208 CHUNG SHUN (ex-LST-732)	3-46	**226 CHUNG CHIH** (ex-LST-1091)	10-58
209 CHUNG LIEN (ex-LST-1050)	1-47	**227 CHUNG MING** (ex-LST-1152)	10-58
210 CHUNG YUNG (ex-LST-574)	3-59	**228 CHUNG SHU** (ex-LST-520)	9-58
216 CHUNG KUANG (ex-LST-503)	6-60	**229 CHUNG WAN** (ex-LST-535)	9-58
217 CHUNG SUO (ex-LST-400)	9-58	**230 CHUNG PANG** (ex-LST-587)	9-58
218 CHUNG CHIH (ex-LST-279)	6-60	**231 CHUNG YEH** (ex-LST-1144)	9-61

AMPHIBIOUS WARFARE SHIPS (*continued*)

D: 1,653 tons (4,080 fl) **Dim:** 100 × 15.24 × 4.36
A: 10/40-mm AA (II × 2, I × 6) **Man:** 100–125 men
M: General Motors diesels; 2 props; 1,700 hp

♦ *4 ex-U.S. landing ships*

	Transf.		Transf.
341 MEI CHIN (ex-LSM-155)	9-46	**353 MEI PING** (ex-LSM-471)	11-56
347 MEI SUNG (ex-LSM-431)	6-46	**356 MEI LO** (ex-LSM-362)	5-62

D: 1,095 tons (fl) **S:** 12.5 kts **Dim:** 62.0 × 10.5 × 2.2
A: 2/40-mm AA (II × 1) — 4 to 8/20-mm AA **Man:** 65–75 men
M: Diesels; 2 props; 2,800 hp **Range:** 2,500/12

♦ *21 ex-U.S. landing craft*

481 HO CHEN (ex-LCU-892)
482 HO CH'UNG (ex-LCU-1213)
484 HO CHUNG (ex-LCU-849)
485 HO CHANG (ex-LCU-512)
486 HO CHENG (ex-LCU-1145)
488 HO SHAN (ex-LCU-1596)
489 HO CHUAN (ex-LCU-489)
490 HO SENG (ex-LCU-1598)
491 HO MENG (ex-LCU-1599)
492 HO MOU (ex-LCU-1600)
493 HO SHOU (ex-LCU-1601)
494 HO CHUN (ex-LCU-1225)
495 HO YUNG (ex-LCU-1271)
496 HO CHIEN (ex-LCU-1278)
501 HO CHI (ex-LCU-1212)
502 HO HOEI (ex-LCU-1218)
503 HO YAO (ex-LCU-1244)
504 HO DENG (ex-LCU-1367)
505 HO FENG (ex-LCU-1397)
506 HO CHAO (ex-LCU-1429)
507 HO TENG (ex-LCU-1452)

D: 143 tons (285 fl) **S:** 8 kts **Dim:** 37.0 × 9.7 × 1.2
A: 2/20-mm AA **Man:** 11 men
M: Diesels; 3 props; 675 hp **Range:** 700/7

AUXILIARY SHIPS

♦ *3 hydrographic ships*

563 CHIU LIEN (ex-*Geronimo*, ATA-207)
D: 838 tons (fl) **S:** 11.5 kts **M:** 2 diesels; 1,750 hp

REMARK: Former ocean tug.

564 CHU WA (ex-*Sgt. George Keathley*, AGS-35) (1944)
D: 2,460 tons **S:** 10 kts

REMARK: Former auxiliary hydrographic ship.

466 LIEN CHANG (ex-LSIL-1017) (1944)
D: . . . **S:** 14 kts **Dim:** 52.1 × 7.7 × 1.8
A: 2/40-mm (II × 1)
M: General Motors diesels; 2 props; 2,320 hp

♦ *1 ex-U.S. repair ship* — Transferred: 1975

YU TAI (ex-*Cadmus*, AR-14)
D: 13,900 tons **S:** 16 kts **Dim:** 142.7 × 19.0 × 8.5
M: 2 GT; 8,500 hp

♦ *1 tanker* — Bldr: Japan, 1969

AOG 512 WAN SHOU
D: 4,150 tons (fl) **S:** 13 kts **Dim:** 86.0 × 16.5 × 5.4
A: 2/40-mm AA **M:** Diesel; 1 prop; 2,100 hp

♦ *3 ex-U.S. tankers* — Transferred: 4-61, 6-71, and 1972

307 CHANG PEI (ex-*Pecatonica*, AOG-57) (1945)
515 LUNG CHUAN (ex-*Namakagon*, AOG-53) (1944)
517 HSING LUNG (ex-*Elkhorn*, AOG-7) (1944)
D: 4,335 tons (fl) **S:** 14 kts **Dim:** 95.0 × 14.6 × 4.7
M: General Motors diesels; 2 props; 3,300 hp

♦ *2 ex-U.S. fuel-oil barges*

504 SZU MING (ex-YO-188)
510 TAI YUN (ex-YO-175)
D: 1,600 tons (fl) **S:** 10.5 kts **M:** Diesel; 1 prop; 560 hp

♦ *2 transports*

514 YUNG KANG (ex-*Mark*, AKL-12)
D: 700 tons **S:** 10 kts **M:** Diesel; 1 prop; 1,000 hp

REMARK: Former cargo ship transferred by the U.S.A. in 9-47.

520 TAI WU (ex-*Agenor*, ARL-3, ex-LST-490)
D: 4,100 tons (fl) **S:** 11 kts **Dim:** 107.5 × 16.4 × 3.6
M: Diesels; 2 props; 1,800 hp

REMARK: Former U.S. repair ship.

♦ *2 ex-U.S. ocean tugs* — Transferred: 1-66 and 4-71

548 TA TUNG (ex-*Chickasaw*, ATF-83)
D: 1,700 tons (fl) **S:** 16 kts **M:** 3,000 hp

550 TA WAN (ex-*Cahoka*, ATA-186)
A: 1/76-mm AA — 4/40-mm AA

♦ *3 ex-U.S. ocean tugs* — Transferred: 4-66 and 4-72

547 TA SUEH (ex-*Tonkawa*, ATA-176)
549 TA PENG (ex-*Mahopac*, ATA-196)
TA AN (ex-ATA-186)
D: 435–835 tons **S:** 13 kts **M:** 1,500 hp

♦ *5 ex-U.S. floating docks*

AFDL 1 HAY TAN (ex-AFDL-36)
AFDL 2 KIM MEN (ex-AFDL-5)
AFDL 3 HAN JIH (ex-AFDL-34)
} capacity: 1,000 tons

ARD 5 FO WU 5 (ex-ARD-9)
ARD 6 FO WU 6 (ex-*Windsor*, ARD-22)
} capacity: 3,000 tons

TANZANIA

PERSONNEL: Approximately 150 men

MERCHANT MARINE (1976): 20 ships — 34,934 grt
(1 tanker — 239 grt)

PATROL BOATS

♦ *7 Shanghai-II class* — Transferred: 1970-71

JW 9861 to **JW 9867**

JW 9862 1975

D: 120 tons (fl) **S:** 33 kts **Dim:** 39.6 × 5.5 × 1.7
A: 4/37-mm AA (II × 2) — 4/25-mm (II × 2) **Man:** 28 men
M: 4 diesels; 5,000 hp

TORPEDO BOATS

♦ *2 ex-Soviet P-6 class* (no torpedoes)

♦ *4 ex-Soviet P-4 class*

JW 9841 to **JW 9844**

JW 9842 1976

D: 30 tons (fl) **S:** 32 kts **Dim:** 16.8 × 3.75 × 1.0
A: 4/14.5-mm machine guns (II × 2) — 2/533-mm TT (I × 2)
M: 2 diesels; 2 props; 2,200 hp

REMARK: Some units do not have torpedoes.

COASTAL PATROL CRAFT

♦ *3 craft based on the East German Schwalbe class*

ARAKA **SALAAM** **N . . .**

D: 70 tons (fl) **S:** 17 kts **Dim:** 26.0 × 4.5 × 1.4
A: 2/37-mm AA — 2 machine guns **M:** Diesel; 300 hp

REMARK: Transferred by East Germany in 1-66 and 1-67.

♦ *4 Chinese craft* — Transferred by the Chinese People's Republic: 11-66

D: 20 tons **S:** 20 kts **Dim:** 13.0 × . . . × . . .
A: 1/12.7-mm machine gun **Man:** 10 men

♦ *2 East German craft* — Bought: 1967

RAFIKI **UHURU**

D: 50 tons **A:** 1/40-mm AA — 4 machine guns

♦ *1 Soviet Poluchat class*

THAILAND

PERSONNEL (1976): Navy: approximately 13,000 men — Marines: 7,000 men

MERCHANT MARINE (1976): 90 ships — 194,983 grt
(tankers: 23 ships — 93,485 grt)

FRIGATES

	Bldr	Laid down	L	In serv.
♦ **MAKUT RAJAKUMARN**	Yarrow	1970	18-11-71	8-73

FRIGATES (*continued*)

Makut Rajakumarn Yarrow, 1975

D: 1,900 tons (fl) **S:** 25 kts (gas turbine), 18 kts (diesel)
Dim: 97.56 (93 pp) × 11.0 × 5.5 **Man:** 16 officers, 124 men
A: 2/114-mm Mk 8 — 1 Sea Cat, aft — 2/40-mm AA — 1 ASW Limbo Mk 10 mortar — 1 depth-charge projector
Electron Equipt: Radars: 1/LWO-4 (Band L), 1/Decca 626, 1/WM 22 (band X), 1 WM 44 (Band X)
Sonars: 1/170 high-frequency, hull-mounted, 1/162
M: CODOG system including one Rolls-Royce Olympus TBM-3-B gas turbine (23,125 hp), Crossley-Pielstick diesel; 2 props; 60,000 hp
Range: 1,000/25, 4,000/18

REMARKS: Excellent automatic features. Dutch radars and British sonars.

♦ *1 ex-U.S. escort* — Bldr: Western Pipe and Steel — Transferred: 1959

	L	Delivered
3 **PIN KLAO** (ex-*Hemminger*, DE-746)	12-9-43	5-44

Pin Klao (3)

D: 1,240 tons (1,900 fl) **Dim:** 93.26 × 11.22 × 4.0
S: 19 kts **Man:** 200 men **Range:** 11,500/11
A: 3/76-mm (I × 3) — 6/40-mm AA (II × 3) — 6/324-mm ASW TT (III × 2) — 8 depth-charge projectors
M: Diesel-electric propulsion; 2 props; 6,000 hp **Fuel:** 300 tons

REMARK: Original armament modified in 1966.

♦ *2 ex-U.S. patrol frigates* — Bldr: Consolidated Steel — Transferred: 1951

	L	In serv.
1 **PRASAE** (ex-*Gallup*, PF-47)	17-9-43	2-44
2 **TAHCHIN** (ex-*Glendale*, PF-36)	28-5-43	10-43

D: 1,430 tons (2,100 fl) **Dim:** 92.61 × 11.43 × 4.4
S: 19 kts **Man:** 180 men **Range:** 5,600/16, 7,800/12
A: 3/76-mm (I × 3) — 2/40-mm AA — 9/20-mm AA — 8 ASW mortars
M: Triple-expansion; 2 props; 5,500 hp **Boilers:** 2 **Fuel:** 685 tons

CORVETTES

♦ *2 U.S.-built patrol frigates* — Bldr: American SB, Toledo, Ohio

	L	Delivered
5 **TAPI** (ex-PF-107)	1970	1972
6 **KHIRIRAT** (ex-PF-108)	18-2-72	10-8-73

D: 900 tons (1,135 fl) **S:** 20 kts **Dim:** 83.32 × 10.05 × 3.05
A: 2/76-mm (I × 2) — 2/40-mm AA (II × 1) — ASW mortar and torpedoes — 1 hedgehog
M: Fairbanks-Morse diesels; 2 props; 5,600 hp **Man:** 150 men

REMARK: Similar to the Iranian *Bayandor.*

GUIDED-MISSILE PATROL BOATS

♦ *3 Prabrarapak class* — Bldr: Jurong, Singapore

	L	In serv.		L	In serv.
PRABRARAPAK	29-7-75	. . .	**SUPHAIRIN**	20-2-76	. . .
HANHAKSATTRU	28-10-75	. . .			

D: 230 tons **S:** 40 kts **Dim:** 48.0 × 7.0 × 2.3
A: 5/Gabriel surface-to-surface missiles — 1/57-mm AA — 1/40-mm AA
M: 4 MTU diesels; 4 props; 14,000 hp **Man:** 40 men

REMARK: Similar to the Singapore Navy's Lürssen type boats.

♦ *3 Italian-built boats* — Bldr: Breda, Venice

N . . . **N . . .** **N . . .**

D: 230 tons normal (260 fl) **S:** 40 kts **Dim:** 49.8 × 7.5 × . . .
A: 4/MM-38 Exocet — 1/76-mm OTO Melara Compact — 2/40-mm AA Breda (II × 1)
Man: 35 men **Range:** 500/40, 2,000/20 **M:** 4 MTU diesels; 4 props

REMARKS: Contract signed 23-7-76. The first two are to be delivered in late 1979 or early 1980.

PATROL BOATS AND CRAFT

♦ *10 U.S.-built boats*

	L		L
T 11 (ex-PGM-71)	22-5-65	**T 16** (ex-PGM-115)	24-4-69
T 12 (ex-PGM-79)	18-12-65	**T 17** (ex-PGM-116)	3-6-69

PATROL BOATS AND CRAFT *(continued)*

T 13 (ex-PGM-107)	13-4-67	**T 18** (ex-PGM-117)	24-6-69
T 14 (ex-PGM-113)	3-6-69	**T 19** (ex-PGM-123)	4-5-70
T 15 (ex-PGM-117)	24-6-69	**T 20** (ex-PGM-124)	22-6-70

D: 130 tons (147 fl) **Dim:** 30.8 (30.2 pp) × 6.4 × 1.85
S: 18.5 kts **Man:** 30 men
A: 1/40-mm AA — 4/20-mm AA — 2/12.7-mm machine guns
M: Diesels; 2 props; 1,800 hp

REMARK: Built in the U.S.A. for export and transferred as follows: 1 in 1966, 1 in 1967, 1 in 1968, others 1969–71.

♦ *3 Thai-built boats* — Bldr: Royal Thai Naval Dockyard, Bangkok

T 91 (1965) **T 92** (1973) **T 93** (1973)

D: 87.5 tons **S:** 25 kts **Dim:** 30.8 × 6.4 × 1.85
A: 1/40-mm — 1/20-mm **Man:** 21 men
M: Diesels; 2 props; 1,600 hp

♦ *7 Italian-built boats* — Bldr: Cantieri Riuniti del Adriatico

	L		L
11 **TRAD**	26-10-35	22 **CHANDABURI**	6-12-36
12 **PHUKET**	28-9-35	23 **RAYONG**	11-1-37
13 **PATTANI**	16-10-36	31 **CHUMPORN**	1937
21 **SURASDRA**	28-11-36		

D: 318 tons (470 fl) **S:** 25 kts **Dim:** 68.0 × 6.4 × 2.1
Man: 11 officers, 112 men **Range:** 850/14.5
A: 2/20-mm AA (II × 1) — 4 machine guns — 4/457-mm TT (II × 2)
M: Parsons GT; 2 props; 9,000 hp **Boilers:** Yarrow
Fuel: 102 tons

Trad (11)

REMARK: These ships are in poor condition and will soon be scrapped.

♦ *3 Klongyai class*

	Bldr	Laid down	L	In serv.
5 **KLONGYAI**	Ishikawajima	1936	26-3-37	6-37
7 **KANTANG**	Ishikawajima	1936	26-3-37	6-37
8 **SATTAHIP**	Bangkok NDY	11-56	28-10-57	1958

D: 110 tons (135 fl) **S:** 18 kts **Dim:** 42.0 × 4.6 × 1.5
A: 1/76-mm AA — 2/20-mm AA (II × 1) — 2/457-mm TT
Man: 51 men **Range:** 475/15 **Fuel:** 18 tons
M: GT; 2 props; 1,000 hp **Boilers:** Yarrow

REMARK: These ships are in very poor condition.

♦ *7 ex-U.S. boats*

1 **SARASIN** (ex-PC-495)
2 **THAYANCHON** (ex-PC-575)
4 **PHALI** (ex-PC-1185) (1942–43)
5 **SUKRIP** (ex-PC-1218)
6 **TONGPLIU** (ex-PC-616)
7 **LIULCOM** (ex-PC-1253)
8 **LONGLOM** (ex-PC-570)

D: 280 tons (400 fl) **S:** 19 kts **Dim:** 53.0 × 7.0 × 3.3 (fl)
A: 1/76-mm AA — 1/30-mm AA — 5/20-mm AA **Man:** 62–71 men
M: General Motors diesels; 2 props; 3,600 hp **Range:** 6,000/10
Fuel: 60 tons

REMARK: In poor condition.

♦ *1 ex-U.S. submarine chaser*

SC 8 (ex-8, ex-SC-1633) (1945)

D: 125 tons (fl)
S: 16 kts
Dim: 33.85 × 5.2 × 1.85
A: 1/40-mm — 3/20-mm — 1 hedgehog — depth charges
M: Diesels; 2 props

REMARK: Wooden boats, in poor condition.

♦ *4 ex-U.S.C.G. Cape-class patrol craft* — Bldr: U.S.A., 1953

CGC 3 **CGC 4** **CGC 5** **CGC 6**

D: 105 tons (fl) **S:** 19/18 kts **Dim:** 28.95 × 5.8 × 1.55

PATROL BOATS AND CRAFT (*continued*)

A: 1/20-mm — 2 hedgehogs — 2 depth-charge racks **Man:** 15 men
M: 4 diesels; 2 props; 2,200 hp **Range:** 1,500

REMARK: Transferred in 1954.

♦ *5 ex-U.S. Swift-type inshore patrol craft* — Transferred: 1966–70

T 23 (ex-PCF-696) **T 25** (ex-PCF-698) **T 27** (ex-PCF-691)
T 24 (ex-PCF-697) **T 26** (ex-PCF-699)

D: 20-22 tons (fl) **S:** 25 kts **Dim:** 15.6 × 4.12 × 1.5
A: 3/12.7-mm machine guns (II × 1, and 1 combined with an 81-mm mortar)
M: Diesels; 2 props; 960 hp **Man:** 1 officer, 7 men

♦ *30 ex-U.S. river patrol boats* — Transferred: 20 in 1965-67; 10 in 1972

D: 10 tons **Dim:** 9.75 × 3.53 × . . .
S: 14 kts **Man:** 1 officer, 6 men
A: Same as the Swift boats, but with a 60-mm mortar
M: Water-jet propulsion; 2 Detroit 6-V-53 diesels, 220 hp each

MINE WARFARE SHIPS

♦ *2 Bangrachan-class minelayers* — Bldr: C. R. del A., Monfalcone

	Laid down	L	In serv.
1 **BANGRACHAN**	1936	1936	1937
2 **NHONG SARHAI**	1936	7-36	1936

D: 319 tons (408 fl) **S:** 12 kts **Dim:** 49.0 × 7.96 × 2.2
Man: 55 men **Range:** 2,690/10 **Fuel:** 33.5 tons
A: 1/76-mm AA — 1/40-mm AA — 2/20-mm AA (II × 1) — 142 mines
M: 2 B & W diesels; 2 props; 540 hp

♦ *2 ex-U.S. ocean minesweepers* — Transferred: 1974

N . . . (ex-*Prime*, MSO-466) **N . . .** (ex-*Reaper*, MSO-467)

D: 750 tons (fl) **S:** 15.5 kts **Dim:** 56.4 × 11.8 × 4.5
A: 1/40-mm — 2/20-mm **M:** 4 diesels, 2 props; 2,280 hp

♦ *4 ex-U.S. coastal minesweepers*

TADINDENG (ex-MSC-301) (8-65) **LADYA** (ex-MSC-297) (12-63)
BANGKEO (ex-MSC-303) (7-65) **DON CHEDI** (ex-MSC-313) (1-66)

REMARKS: Transferred upon completion. For characteristics, see the U.S. coastal minesweepers transferred to France, page 129.

♦ *10 river minesweepers*

MSM 1 to **MSM 10**

D: 30 tons **S:** 9/10 kts **Dim:** 17.0 × 5.3 × 1.4
A: 2/20-mm — 1/12.7-mm machine gun — 2/40-mm grenade launchers
M: 2 diesels **Man:** 7 men

REMARK: Modified ex-U.S. landing craft.

AMPHIBIOUS WARFARE SHIPS

♦ *5 ex-U.S. landing ships*

ANTHONG (ex-LST-294) **LANTA** (ex-*Stone County*, LST-1141)
CHANG (ex-*Lincoln County*, LST-898) **N . . .** (ex-*Dodge County*, LST-722)
PANGAN (ex-*Stark County*, LST-1134)

Pangan (ex-*LST 1134*, transferred in 5-66)

D: 1,615 tons (4,080 fl) **S:** 11 kts **Dim:** 100.0 × 15.24 × 4.36
A: 6/40-mm AA — 4/20-mm **M:** General Motors diesels; 1,700 hp

♦ *3 ex-U.S. landing ships*

KUT (ex-LSM-333) **PHAI** (ex-LSM-338) **KRAM** (ex-LSM-469)

D: 743 tons (1,095 fl) **S:** 12.5 kts **Dim:** 62.0 × 10.5 × 2.2
A: 2/40-mm AA **Range:** 2,500/12 **M:** Diesels; 2 props; 2,800 hp

♦ *2 ex-U.S. landing ships*

PRAB **SATAKUT**

D: 230 tons (387 fl) **S:** 10 kts **Dim:** 47.0 × 7.0 × 1.7
A: 2/20-mm **M:** Diesels; 3 props; 675 hp

REMARK: The *Prab* is not operational.

♦ *6 ex-U.S. landing craft*

1 **MATAPHON** 3 **ARDANG** 5 **KOLUM**
2 **RAWI** 4 **PHETRA** 6 **TALIBONG**

D: 134 tons (280 fl) **S:** 8 kts **Dim:** 37.0 × 9.7 × 1.2
M: Diesels; 3 props; 675 hp **Range:** 700/7

♦ *8 landing craft (LCVP)*

♦ *26 landing craft (LCM)*

HYDROGRAPHIC SHIP

CHANDHARA — Bldr: Lürssen, Vegesack, West Germany — L: 17-12-60

THAILAND (*continued*)

HYDROGRAPHIC SHIP (*continued*)

D: 870 tons (990 fl) **S:** 12 kts **Dim:** 70.0 (61 pp) × 10.5 × 3.0
M: Deutz diesels; 2 props; 1,000 hp **Man:** 90 men (50 cadets)

REMARKS: Used in oceanography but built as a training ship.

TRAINING SHIPS

♦ *1 ex-British Algerine class* — Bldr: Redfern Constr. Co. — L: 5-10-44

MSF 1 PHOSAMTON (ex-*Minstrel*)

D: 1,040 tons (1,350 fl) **S:** 16 kts **Dim:** 68.58 × 10.82 × 2.36
A: 1/102-mm — 6/20-mm AA — 2 depth-charge projectors **Man:** 113 men
Range: 3,000/15, 5,000/10 **M:** Triple-expansion; 2 props; 3,000 hp
Boilers: 2 to 3 fireboxes **Fuel:** 270 tons

REMARKS: One of the very few survivors of a long series of escort minesweepers built during World War II.

♦ *1 ex-Japanese frigate* — Bldr: Uraga SY — In serv. 6-37

MAEKLONG

D: 1,400 tons **S:** 14 kts **Dim:** 32.0 × 10.4 × 3.2
A: 4/76-mm (I × 4) — 3/40-mm — 3/20-mm **Man:** 155 students + crew
M: Reciprocating steam; 2 props; 2,500 hp

VARIOUS SHIPS

♦ *1 patrol boat tender* — Transferred: 1966

3 NAKA (ex-U.S. LSSL-102)

D: 287 tons (fl) **S:** 15 kts **Dim:** 47.5 × 7.0 × 1.4
A: 1/76-mm — 4/40-mm — 4/81-mm mortars
M: Diesels; 2 props; 1,320 hp

REMARK: Used as a base for small patrol boats.

♦ *1 minesweeper maintenance ship* — Bldr: Japan, 1944 — Purchased: 1967

RANG KWIEN (ex-*Muhimari Maru*)

D: 586 tons **S:** 10 kts **Dim:** 49.0 × 9.5 × 4.0
M: Triple-expansion

REMARK: Former tug.

♦ *6 tankers and fuel-oil or gasoline carriers*

AO 2 CHULA (ex-Japanese *Seisyo Maru*) — Tanker

D: 2,395 tons **Dim:** 100.0 × 13.2 × 7.6 **M:** GT

AO 3 MATRA (ex-Japanese *Waka Kosa Maru*) — Tanker

D: 4,750 tons **Dim:** 100.0 × 14.0 × 6.1 **M:** GT

YO 4 SAMUI (ex-U.S. YOG) (1944) — Barge

D: 420 tons **S:** 8 kts **Dim:** 53.2 × 9.75 × 4.6
M: Diesels; 2 props; 600 hp **Man:** 63 men

YO 5 PRONG (1938) — Barge

D: 150 tons **S:** 10 kts **Dim:** 29.0 × 5.49 × 4.5
M: Diesel; 1 prop; 150 hp **Man:** 26 men

YO 6 PROET (1970)

D: 360 tons (485 fl) **S:** 9 kts **Dim:** 37.4 × 6.0 × 2.65
M: Diesel; 1 prop; 500 hp

YO . . . SAMED — Bldr: Bangkok Dockyard, 1970

D: 465 (fl) **S:** 9 kts **Dim:** 39.0 × 6.1 × 3.1
M: Diesel; 500 hp

♦ *2 small water carriers*

YW 6 CHARN **YW 8 CHUANG**

D: 355 tons **Dim:** 42.0 × 7.5 × . . . **M:** Diesel

♦ *2 small transports* — Bldr: Harima SB&E, Tokyo, Japan — L: 10-11-37

AKL 1 SICHANG

D: 815 tons (1,369 fl) **S:** 15 kts **Dim:** 48.77 × 8.54 × 4.9
M: Diesels; 2 props; 550 hp **Man:** 66 men

AKL 7 KLED KEO

D: 450 tons (fl) **S:** 11 kts **Dim:** 46.0 × 7.6 × 4.3
M: Diesel; 1 prop **Man:** 54 men

♦ *4 tugs*

YTB SAMAESAN **D:** 503 tons (fl) **S:** 10.5 kts **M:** 850 hp
YTL KLUEN BADAN **YTL MARN VICHAI** **D:** 63 tons
YTL RAD **D:** 52 tons

TOGO

PERSONNEL: 200 men

MERCHANT MARINE (1976): 1 ship — 134 grt

PATROL BOATS

♦ *2 32-meter boats* — Bldr: Estérel, 1976

KARA **MONO**

D: 90 tons (fl) **S:** 30 kts **Dim:** 32.0 × 5.8 × 1.5
A: 1/40-mm — 1/20-mm **Man:** 1 officer, 17 men
M: 2 diesels; 5,400 hp

Kara 1976

TRINIDAD AND TOBAGO

PERSONNEL: 280 men

MERCHANT MARINE (1976): 33 ships — 13,603 grt
(1 tanker — 1,766 grt)

♦ *4 Trinity-class coastal patrol boats* — Bldr: Vosper, Portsmouth

CG 1 TRINITY (14-4-64)
CG 2 COURLAND BAY (20-5-64)
CG 3 CHAGUARAMAS (29-3-71)
CG 4 BUCCO REEF (1971)

D: 96-100 tons (123-125 fl) **Dim:** 31.29 (28.95 pp) × 5.94 × 1.68
S: 23 kts **Man:** 3 officers, 14 men
Range: 1,800/13.5 **Fuel:** 18 tons
A: CG-1 and CG-2: 1/40-mm CG-3 and CG-4: 1/20-mm AA
M: Davey-Paxman 12-cyl. diesels; 2 props; 2,300 hp

REMARKS: In the coast guard service. Living spaces air-conditioned. The engines can be pushed to 1,400 hp (1,500 rpm) and the speed raised to 25 knots in certain conditions. CG-1 and CG-2 entered service in 1965, the other two in 1972.

♦ *4 patrol craft*

CG 6 to **CG 9**

Dim: 12-18 × . . . × . . . **S:** 18 kts

Courland Bay (CG 2) 1968

TUNISIA

PERSONNEL: 2,000 men

MERCHANT MARINE (1976): 31 ships — 62,941 grt
(tankers: 2 ships — 26,827 grt)

FRIGATE

♦ *1 ex-U.S. radar picket escort* — Bldr: Consolidated Steel

E 7 PRESIDENT BOURGUIBA (ex-*Thomas J. Gary,* DER-326)

President Bourguiba (E 7) J. C. Bellonne, 1974

D: 1,590 tons (2,100 fl) **Dim:** 93.26 (91.5 pp) × 11.22 × 4.0
S: 19 kts **Man:** 160-170 men
A: 2/76-mm AA — 2/20-mm AA — ASW hedgehog **Range:** 11,500/11
M: 4 Fairbanks-Morse diesels; 2 props; 6,000 hp

REMARKS: Modified as a radar picket ship in 1957. Transferred in October 1973.

PATROL BOATS AND CRAFT

♦ *3 Bizerte class*

P 301 BIZERTE (20-11-69)
P 302 EL HORRIA (19-2-70)
P 304 MONASTIR — L: 25-6-74 — In serv. 2-75

PATROL BOATS AND CRAFT (*continued*)

El Horria J. C. Bellonne, 1973

D: 250 tons **S:** 22 kts **Dim:** 48.0 (45.5 pp) × 7.1 × 2.25
A: 2/40-mm 60-cal. AA — 8/SS-12 missiles
M: 2 MGO MB-839 Bb diesels, 2,000 hp each

♦ *1 French Le Hardi class* — Bldr: Dubigeon, 1956 — Purchased: 12-69

P 303 SAKIET SIDI YOUSSEF (ex-UW-12)

Sakiet Sidi Youssef (P 303) 1970

D: 325 tons (440 fl) **S:** 18.7 kts **Dim:** 53.03 × 7.26 × 3.1 (fl)
Man: 4 officers, 59 men **Range:** 2,000/15, 3,000/12
A: 1/40-mm — 2/20-mm — 1 hedgehog — 4 depth-charge projectors
M: 4 SEMT-Pielstick diesels; 2 props; 3,240 hp

♦ *2 ex-French coastal minesweepers* — Loaned: 1973 and 1977

P . . . HANNIBAL (ex-*Coquelicot*, ex-AMS-84) (1955)
P . . . N . . . (ex-*Marjolaine*)

D: 300 tons (372 fl) **Dim:** 43.0 (41.5 pp) × 7.95 × 2.55

Hannibal J. C. Bellonne, 1973

S: 13 kts **Man:** 3 officers, 35 men
A: 2/20-mm AA (II × 1) **Range:** 2,500/10
M: 2 General Motors diesels; 2 props; 1,200 hp **Fuel:** 40 tons

REMARK: Minesweeping gear removed.

♦ *2 Menzel Bourguiba class* — Bldr: Vosper, Portchester

	L
P 205 TAZARKA	. . .
P 206 MENZEL BOURGUIBA	19-7-76

D: 120 tons **S:** 27 kts **Dim:** 31.25 (28.95 pp) × 6.02 × 1.98
A: 1/40-mm **Man:** 24 men **M:** 2 MTU diesels; 4,000 hp

♦ *4 Istiklal class* — Bldr: Estérel

P 201 ISTIKLAL (ex-French V-11) — L: 25-5-57 — Transferred: 3-59
P 202 JOUMHOURIA — Delivered: 1-61
P 203 AL JALA — Transferred: 11-63
P 204 REMADA — Delivered: 7-67

Istiklal (P 201) 1970

TUNISIA (*continued*)

PATROL BOATS AND CRAFT (*continued*)

D: 60 tons (80 fl) **S:** 28 kts **Dim:** 31.45 × 5.75 × 1.7
A: 2/20-mm **Man:** 3 officers, 14 men **Range:** 1,400/15
M: 2 supercharged Mercedes-Benz diesels; 2 props; 2,700 hp

REMARK: Similar to the Moroccan *El Sabiq* class.

♦ *2 Shanghai-II class* — Transferred: 2-5-77

P . . . GAFSA **P . . . AMILCAR**

♦ *6 coastal patrol craft* — Bldr: Estérel

V 101 to **V 106**

V 101 class

D: 38-39 tons **S:** 23 kts **Dim:** 25.0 × 4.75 × 1.25
A: 1/20-mm **Man:** 10 men **Range:** 900/16
M: 2 General Motors twin diesels; 2 props; 940 hp

REMARK: The V-107 and V-108 were delivered without armament to the fisheries administration.

VARIOUS SHIPS

♦ *1 tug* — Bldr: The Netherlands, 1939

RAS ADAR (ex-*Zeeland*)

D: 450 tons **Dim:** 43 × 10 × 4

♦ *2 small tugs* — Bldr: Estérel

T 1 JAQUEL EL BAHR **T 2 SABBACK EL BAHR**

TURKEY

PERSONNEL (1976): 36,000 men, including 3,000 officers and 5,000 petty officers

MERCHANT MARINE (1976): 405 ships — 1,079,347 grt
(tankers: 54 ships — 331,483 grt)

NAVAL AVIATION: A small naval air arm, organized in 1972, consists of 4 S-2A and 12 S-2E Tracker ASW airplanes and 3 AB-204 helicopters.

WARSHIPS IN SERVICE OR UNDER CONSTRUCTION AS OF 1 OCTOBER 1977

	L	Tons (surfaced)	Main armament
♦ *18 submarines*			
4 TYPE 209	1974-75	980	8/533-mm TT
4 GUPPY III	1945-47	1,975	10/533-mm TT
7 GUPPY II-A	1943-44	1,825	10/533-mm TT
2 GATO	1944-45	1,829	10/533-mm TT
1 GUPPY I-A	1944	1,840	10/533-mm TT
♦ *10 destroyers*		Tons	
5 GEARING	1945-46	2,400	4/127-mm, 1 Asroc, 6/324-mm TT
2 ALLEN M. SUMNER	1944	2,200-2,250	6/127-mm, mines or 324-mm TT
3 FLETCHER	1942-43	2,050	4/127-mm, 6/76-mm, 5/533-mm TT
♦ *8 frigates and corvettes*			
2 BERK	1971-72	1,450	4/76-mm, 6/ASW TT
6 SULTAN HISAR	1964-65	280	1/76-mm, 1/40-mm
♦ *36 patrol and torpedo boats*			

WEAPONS AND SYSTEMS

Most weapons and systems are furnished by the U.S.A. but some by West Germany. For characteristics, see the sections on the U.S.A. and West Germany.

SUBMARINES

♦ *4 German 209 type* — Bldrs: S-347 and S-348: Howaldtswerke, Kiel
S-349 and S-350: Gölçük

	Laid down	L	In serv.
S 347 ATILAY	1972	23-10-74	1975
S 348 SALDIRAY	1972	1-2-75	1976
S 349 YILDIRAY	1975	. . .	. . .
S 350 N . . .	. . .	. . .	. . .

D: 980 tons surfaced, 1,230 submerged **S:** 21 kts max. (submerged)
Dim: 55.0 × 6.6 × 5.9 **Man:** 3 officers, 26 men
A: 8/533-mm TT — 6 torpedoes in reserve
M: 4 MTU type 12V-493-TY60 diesels; Siemens electric motor, 3,600 hp

REMARKS: For further details, see sections on Argentina and Greece. S-349 and S-350 are being built in Turkey with German assistance.

♦ *4 ex-U.S. Guppy III* — Bldrs: First 3: Electric Boat Co.; other: Mare Island NSY

	L	Transferred
S 333 IKINCI INONU (ex-*Corporal*, SS-346)	1-4-45	11-73
S 341 CANAKKALE (ex-*Cobbler*, SS-344)	1-4-45	11-73
S . . . N . . . (ex-*Clamogore*, SS-343)	25-2-45	. . .
S . . . N . . . (ex-*Tiru*, SS-410)	16-9-47	. . .

D: 1,975 tons surfaced, 2,450 submerged **S:** 20/15 kts
Dim: 99.4 × 8.2 × 5.2 **Range:** 10,000-12,000/10 and 95/5 (submerged)

SUBMARINES (*continued*)

A: 10/533-mm TT (6 fwd, 4 aft)
M: Diesel-electric propulsion: 4 diesels, 1,625 hp each; 2 electric motors, 2,750 each; 2 props

REMARKS: The transfer of SS-343 and SS-410 was delayed by the U.S. embargo on arms to Turkey imposed by Congress in 1975. The embargo having been lifted in 4-76, they may now have been delivered.

♦ *7 ex-U.S. Guppy II-A* — Bldrs: Portsmouth NSY, except S-345, Electric Boat Co.

	L	Transferred
S 335 BURAK REIS (ex-*Sea Fox*, SS-402)	28-3-44	1970
S 336 MURAT REIS (ex-*Razorback*, SS-394)	27-1-44	1970
S 337 ORUÇ REIS (ex-*Pomfret*, SS-391)	27-10-43	1971
S 338 ULUÇ ALI REIS (ex-*Thornback*, SS-418)	7-7-44	1971
S 340 CERBE (ex-*Trutta*, SS-421)	18-8-44	7-72
S 345 PREVESE (ex-*Entemedor*, SS-340)	17-12-44	7-72
S 346 BIRINCI INÖNÜ (ex-*Threadfin*, SS-410)	26-6-44	8-72

Murat Reis (S 336)

D: 1,525 tons, 1,825 surfaced, 2,400 submerged
S: 20/10 kts (19/9 cruising)
Dim: 95.0 (92.72 pp) × 8.25 × 5.20 **Man:** 8-9 officers, 66 men
Range: 10,000-12,000/10 and 95/5 (submerged)
A: 10/533-mm TT (6 fwd, 4 aft) — 24 torpedoes or 40 mines, which can be laid through the tubes
M: Diesel-electric propulsion (surface): 3 or 4 groups of diesel engines 1,625 hp each; 2 electric motors of 2,750 hp; 2 props
Fuel: 300 tons

♦ *2 ex-U.S. Gato class* — Bldrs: S-342: Electric Boat Co.; S-344: Manitowoc SB

	L	Transferred
S 342 TURGUT REIS (ex-*Bergall*, SS-320)	16-2-44	1958
S 344 HIZIR REIS (ex-*Mero*, SS-378)	17-1-45	1960

Hizir Reis (S 344)

D: 1,525 tons, 1,829 surfaced, 2,424 submerged **S:** 20/10 kts
Dim: 95.0 × 8.3 × 4.2 **Range:** 12,000/10
A: 10/533-mm TT (6 fwd, 4 aft) **Man:** 85 men
M: Diesel-electric; 4 General Motors diesels, 6,400 hp; 2 electric motors, 5,400 hp

♦ *1 ex-U.S. Guppy 1-A* — Bldr: Electric Boat Co.

	L	Transferred
S 339 DUMLUPINAR (ex-*Caiman*)	30-3-44	6-72

D: 1,840 tons surfaced, 2,445 submerged **S:** 17/15 kts
Dim: 93.2 × 8.2 × 5.2
A: 10/533-mm TT (6 fwd, 4 aft) **Range:** 12,000/10 **Man:** 85 men
M: Diesel-electric; 3 General Motors diesels, 4,800 hp; 2 electric motors, 5,400 hp

DESTROYERS

♦ *5 ex-U.S. Gearing class* — Transferred: 1971-72-73-75

Bldrs: D-351 and D-353: Bethlehem, Staten I.; D-354: Bethlehem, San Pedro; D-352: Todd Pacific; D-355: Bethlehem, San Francisco

	L	In serv.
D 351 M. F. KAKMAK (ex-*Charles H. Roan*, DD-853)	15-5-46	9-46
D 352 GAYRET (ex-*Eversole*, DD-789)	8-1-46	7-46
D 353 ADATEPE (ex-*Forrest Royal*, DD-872)	17-1-45	6-46
D 354 KOCATEPE (ex-*Norris*, DD-859)	4-2-45	9-6-45
D 355 TINAZTEPE (ex-*Keppler*, DD-765)	24-6-46	5-47

D: 2,400 tons (3,600 fl) **S:** 30 kts **Dim:** 119.17 × 12.45 × 5.8
Man: 14 officers, 260 men **Range:** 2,400/25, 4,800/15
A: 4/127-mm 38-cal. AA (II × 2) — 6/324-mm ASW Mk 32 TT (III × 2) — 1/ASW Mk 108 rocket launcher or 2 hedgehogs, D-352: 1 Asroc system — helicopter platform
Electron Equipt: Radars: SPS 10, SPS 40 (or 37)
Sonar: SQS 23
M: GT; 2 props; 60,000 hp **Boilers:** 4 Babcock **Fuel:** 560 tons

DESTROYERS (*continued*)

Adatepe (D 353) G. Arra, 1973

REMARKS: A first *Kocatepe* (D-354) was accidentally sunk by the Turkish Air Force 21-7-74 during the Cyprus conflict. She was replaced by the *Norris* (DD-859), modernized with FRAM II, which was renamed *Kocatepe*.

♦ *1 ex-Allen M. Sumner* — Bldr: Bethlehem, San Pedro — Transferred: 10-71

	L	In serv.
D 357 MUAVENET (ex-*Gwin*, DD-772)	9-4-44	9-44

D: 2,250 tons (3,375 fl) **S:** 30 kts **Dim:** 114.74 × 12.45 × 5.8
Man: 15 officers, 260 men **Range:** 1,260/30, 4,600/15
A: 6/127-mm AA (II × 3) — 6/76-mm AA — 80-100 mines
Electron Equipt: Radars: 1 SPS 10, 1 SPS 6
Sonar: 1 SQS 29
M: GT; 2 props; 60,000 hp **Boilers:** 4 Babcock **Fuel:** 650 tons

REMARK: One of a dozen *Allen M. Sumner* class built in 1944 and modified as minelayers.

♦ *1 ex-Allen M. Sumner class* — Bldr: Federal SB & DD — Transferred: 7-72

	L	In serv.
D 356 ZAFER (ex-*Hugh Purvis*, DD-709)	17-12-44	3-45

D: 2,200 tons (3,300 fl) **S:** 30 kts **Dim:** 114.65 × 12.45 × 5.8
A: 6/127-mm (38-cal.) AA (II × 3) — 6/324-mm ASW Mk 32 TT (III × 2)
Electron Equipt: Radars: 1 SPS 10, 1 SPS 40
Sonar: 1 SQS 29
M: GT; 2 props; 60,000 hp **Boilers:** 4 Babcock **Fuel:** 650 tons
Range: 1,260/30, 4,600/15

REMARK: Has a helicopter platform.

♦ *3 ex-U.S. Fletcher class* — Transferred: D-342 and D-343, 10-69; D-344, 3-70
Bldrs: D-342: Bath Iron Works; D-343 and D-344: Bethlehem, San Pedro

	L	In serv.
D 342 IZMIT (ex-*Cogswell*, DD-651)	5-6-43	8-43
D 343 ISKENDERUN (ex-*Boyd*, DD-544)	29-10-42	5-43
D 344 ICEL (ex-*Preston*, DD-795)	12-12-43	3-44

Istanbul (D 340) 1970

D: 2,050 tons (3,000 fl) **Dim:** 114.85 (wl) × 12.03 × 5.5
S: 34 kts **Man:** 15 officers, 247 men
Range: 1,260/30, 4,400/15 **Fuel:** 650 tons
A: 4/127-mm (38-cal.) AA (I × 4) — 6/76-mm (50-cal.) AA (II × 3) — 5/533-mm TT — 2 fixed ASW TT — depth charges
Electron Equipt: Radars: 1 SPS 10, 1 SPS 6
Sonar: 1 SQS 4
M: General Electric GT; 2 props; 60,000 hp **Boilers:** 4 Babcock

REMARK: The *Istanbul* (D-340) and *Izmir* (D-341) were scrapped in 1972 for spare parts to ensure the maintenance of the other three.

FRIGATES

♦ *2 Berk class* — Bldr: Gölçük

	Laid down	L	In serv.
D 358 BERK	3-67	7-71	2-74
D 359 PEYK	1968	1-72	24-7-75

Berk (D 358) J. C. Bellonne, 1976

FRIGATES (*continued*)

D: 1,450 tons (1,950 fl) **Dim:** 95.15 × 11.82 × 4.4
S: 25 kts **Man:** . . . **Range:** . . .
A: 4/76-mm AA (II × 2) — 6/ASW Mk 32 TT (III × 2)
Electron Equipt: Radars: 1 SPS 10, 1 SPS 40
Sonar: 1 SQS 11
M: 4 Fiat-Tosi high-speed 3-016-RSS diesels (800 rpm) linked, 2 by 2, to a single propeller shaft; 24,000 hp

REMARKS: Based on the U.S. *Claude Jones* class. The 16-cylinder diesel engines (300 mm × 610 mm) are similar to those installed in the Italian *San Giorgio.* No hangar but can carry a helicopter.

CORVETTES

♦ *6 Sultan Hisar class* — Bldrs: Gunderson, Portland, U.S.A., 1964-65, except P-116, Gölçük NSY

P 111 SULTAN HISAR (ex-PC-1638) (1964)
P 112 DEMIRHISAR (ex-PC-1639) (9-7-64)
P 113 YARHISAR (ex-PC-1640) (14-5-64)
P 114 AKHISAR (ex-PC-1641) (14-5-64)
P 115 SIVRIHISAR (ex-PC-1642) (5-11-64)
P 116 KOCHISAR (ex-PC-1643) (12-65)

Demirhisar (P 112) 1970

D: 280 tons (412 fl) **Dim:** 54.0 × 7.0 × 3.1
S: 25 kts **Man:** 5 officers, 60 men
A: 1/76-mm — 1/40-mm — 4 depth-charge projectors
M: Alcoa diesels; 2 props; 4,800 hp

REMARK: Based on the World War II type of patrol craft.

GUIDED-MISSILE PATROL BOATS

♦ *4 S-143 type* — Bldrs: P-340: Lürssen, Vegesack; others: Tazkizak, Istanbul

	L	In serv.		L	In serv.
P 340 DOGAN	7-76	1977	**P 342 TAYFUN**	. . .	. . .
P 341 MARTI	. . .	. . .	**P 343 VOLKAN**	. . .	. . .

D: 400 tons (fl) **S:** 27 kts **Dim:** 58.1 (54.6 pp) × 7.62 × 2.79
A: 8 Harpoon — 1/76-mm AA OTO Melara Compact — 2/35-mm AA (II × 1)
M: 2 diesels, 4,500 hp each **Electric:** 500 kw

♦ *9 guided-missile or torpedo boats* — Bldr: Lürssen, Vegesack, 1967-71

P 321 DENIZKUSU **P 324 KARTAL** **P 327 ALBATROS**
P 322 ATMACA **P 325 MELTEN** **P 328 SIMSEK**
P 323 SAHIN **P 326 PELIKAN** **P 329 KASIRGA**

Kartal (P 324) 1970

D: 160 tons (180 fl) **S:** 42 kts **Dim:** 42.8 × 7.14 × 2.2
A: 2/40-mm (70-cal.) AA — 4/533-mm TT, two on each side — 4 torpedoes P-325 to P-328: 4 Norwegian Penguin missiles and only 2 TT
M: Maybach 20-cyl. diesels; 4 props; 12,000 hp **Man:** 39 men

REMARKS: Similar to the German *Zobel* class. Wooden hull; steel and light-metal keel and frames; light-metal superstructure. Can be fitted as fast gunboats or minelayers (4 mines).

TORPEDO BOATS

♦ *7 ex-German Jaguar S-141* — Bldr: Lürssen, Vegesack, 1962

P 330 FIRTINA (ex-*Pelikan*, P-6086)
P 331 TUFAN (ex-*Storch*, P-6085)
P 332 KILIÇ (ex-*Pinguin*, P-6090)
P 333 MIZRAK (ex-*Löwe*, P-6065)
P 334 YILDIZ (ex-*Alk*, P-6084)
P 335 KALKAN (ex-*Wolf*, P-6062)
P 336 KARAYEL (ex-*Tiger*, P-6063)

D: 160 tons (190 fl) **S:** 40 kts **Dim:** 42.5 × 7.2 × 2.4
A: 2/40-mm AA (I × 2) — 4/533-mm TT or 2 TT and mines
M: 4 MTU diesels; 4 props; 12,000 hp

REMARKS: Transferred in 1976. The *Häher, Fuchs,* and *Reiher* were transferred at the same time to be cannibalized for the maintenance of the seven in service.

PATROL BOATS AND CRAFT

♦ *2 ex-U.S. Asheville class* — Bldr: Peterson, U.S.A. — Transferred: 2-73 and 6-73

P 339 BORA (ex-*Surprise*, PG-97) L: 15-11-68
P 340 YLDIRIM (ex-*Defiance*, PG-95) L: 24-8-68

D: 225 tons (240 fl) **Dim:** 50.14 (46.94 pp) × 7.28 × 2.9
S: 40 kts **Range:** 325/35, 1,700/16
A: 1/76-mm fwd — 1/40-mm AA — 4/12.7 machine guns
M: CODAG propulsion: 1 General Electric gas turbine; 2 Cummins diesels; 2 props
Fuel: 50 tons

PATROL BOATS AND CRAFT (*continued*)

REMARK: See *Asheville* class in section on U.S.A.

♦ *10 AB 25/34 type* — Bldrs: Gölçük NSY and Turkish merchant shipyard, 1967-70

P 1225 AB 25 **P 1229 AB 29** **P 1232 AB 32**
P 1226 AB 26 **P 1230 AB 30** **P 1233 AB 33**
P 1227 AB 27 **P 1231 AB 31** **P 1234 AB 34**
P 1228 AB 28

AB 26 (Hull number changed) 1969

D: 170 tons **S:** 22 kts **Dim:** 40.24 × 6.4 × 1.65
A: 2/40-mm **M:** SACM-AGO diesels; 2 props; 4,800 hp

REMARK: Six others are assigned to the police.

♦ *4 ex-U.S. motor gunboats* — Bldr: Peterson, Sturgeon Bay

	L	In serv.
P 1221 (ex-P-117) **AB 21** (ex-PGM-104)	4-5-67	8-67
P 1222 (ex-P-118) **AB 22** (ex-PGM-105)	25-5-67	9-67
P 1223 (ex-P-119) **AB 23** (ex-PGM-106)	7-7-67	10-67
P 1224 (ex-P-120) **AB 24** (ex-PGM-108)	14-9-67	5-68

AB 23 (Hull number changed) 1969

D: 130 tons (147 fl) **Dim:** 30.8 (30.2 pp) × 6.4 × 1.85
S: 18.5 kts **Man:** 15 men
A: 1/40-mm — 4/20-mm — 2 hedgehogs **M:** Diesels; 2 props; 1,800 hp

♦ *4 ex-U.S. patrol craft* — Transferred: 25-6-53

P 1209 LS 9 **P 1211 LS 11**
P 1210 LS 10 **P 1212 LS 12**

LS 12 (Hull number changed) 1969

D: 63 tons **S:** 18 kts **Dim:** 25.3 × 4.25 × 1.55
A: 1/20-mm AA — 2 ASW hedgehogs **M:** 2 Cummins motors; 1,100 hp

REMARK: Former hull numbers P-339, P-308, P-309, P-310.

MINE WARFARE SHIPS

♦ *1 coastal minelayer* — Bldr: Denmark

	Laid down	L	In serv.
N 110 NUSRET (ex-N-108, ex-MMC-16)	1962	1964	1966

Nusret (Hull number changed)

D: 1,880 tons **S:** 16 kts **Dim:** 77.0 × 12.8 × 3.4
A: 4/76-mm AA (II × 2) — 400 mines **Man:** 130 men
M: General Motors diesels; 2 props; 4,800 hp

REMARKS: Ordered by the U.S.A. under MAP. Similar to the Danish *Falster* class.

MINE WARFARE SHIPS (*continued*)

♦ *5 coastal minelayers*

N 101 MORDOGAN (ex-MMC-11, ex-LSM-484)
N 102 MERIC (ex-MMC-12, ex-LSM-481)
N 103 MARMARIS (ex-MMC-10, ex-LSM-490)
N 104 MERSIN (ex-MMC-13, ex-LSM-42, ex-Norwegian *Vale*)
N 105 MUREFTE (ex-MMC-14, ex-LSM-493, ex-Norwegian *Vidar*)

Mersin (N 104)

D: 743 tons (1,100 fl) **S:** 12/13 kts **Dim:** 61.87 × 10.52 × 2.4
A: 2/40-mm AA — 2/20-mm AA **Man:** 70 men **Range:** 2,500/12
M: 2 diesels; 2 props; 2,800 hp **Fuel:** 60 tons

REMARKS: Ex-U.S. landing ships, transferred in 1952 after a complete overhaul. The first three were transferred to Turkey, the other two to Norway. They were returned to the U.S.A. in 1960, then reassigned to Turkey. Four booms, two forward, two aft, for the loading of mines; two minelaying rails.

♦ *2 coastal minelayers* — Bldr: U.S.A., 1942-43

Sankaktar (Hull number changed)

L 403 BAYRAKTAR (ex-*Bottrop*, ex-LST-1101)
L 404 SANKAKTAR (ex-*Bochum*, ex-LST-1089)

D: 1,650 (4,080 fl) **S:** 11 kts **Dim:** 100.04 × 15.24 × 4.3
A: 6/40-mm AA (II × 3) **Range:** 15,000/9 (max)
M: General Motors diesels; 2 props **Fuel:** 600 tons

REMARKS: Ex-U.S. landing ships that were transferred to the West German Navy in 1964 and modified as minelayers. Used also as amphibious ships.

♦ *1 ex-U.S. coastal minelayer* — Bldr: Higgins — L: 1958

N 115 MEHMETCIK (ex-YMP-3)

D: 540 tons (fl) **S:** 10 kts **Dim:** 39.62 × 10.6 × 1.9
A: 1/40-mm AA **Man:** 22 men **M:** Diesels; 2 props

REMARK: Transferred in 1958 under MAP.

♦ *12 ex-U.S. coastal minesweepers* — Bldr: U.S.A.

	L
M 507 SEYMEN (ex-MSC-131)	1952
M 508 SELÇUK (ex-MSC-124)	1952
M 509 SEYHAN (ex-MSC-142)	1952
M 510 SAMSUN (ex-MSC-268)	6-9-57
M 511 SINOP (ex-MSC-270)	4-1-58
M 512 SÜRMENE (ex-MSC-271)	1958
M 513 SEDDUL BAHR (ex-MSC-272)	1958
M 514 SILIFKE (ex-MSC-304)	21-11-64
M 515 SAROS (ex-MSC-305)	1-5-65
M 516 SIGAÇIK (ex-MSC-311)	12-6-64
M 517 SAPANCA (ex-MSC-312)	14-9-64
M 518 SARIYER (ex-MSC-315)	21-4-66

Selçuk (M 508) J. C. Bellonne, 1970

MINE WARFARE SHIPS (*continued*)

D: 300 tons (392 fl) **Dim:** 43.0 (41.5 pp) × 7.95 × 2.55
S: 14 kts **Man:** 4 officers, 34 men
A: 2/20-mm AA **Range:** 2,500/10
M: 2 diesels; 2 props; 1,200 hp

REMARKS: M-507 was returned by Belgium in 1970. M-508 and M-509 are the former French *Pavot* and *Renoncule*. They were returned to the U.S.A. 23-3-70 and then transferred to Turkey.

♦ *4 ex-Canadian coastal minesweepers*

	L
M 530 TRABZON (ex-*Gaspé*)	20-5-53
M 531 TERME (ex-*Trinity*)	31-7-53
M 532 TIREBOLU (ex-*Comax*)	24-4-52
M 533 TEKIRDAG (ex-*Ungava*)	12-11-51

Trabzon (Hull number changed) 1969

D: 390 tons (412 fl) **S:** 16 kts **Dim:** 50.0 × 9.21 × 2.8
A: 1/40-mm **Man:** 44 men **Range:** 4,500/11
M: General Motors diesels; 2 props; 2,500 hp **Fuel:** 52 tons

REMARK: Transferred in 1958 under MAP.

♦ *5 French Mercure-class coastal minesweepers*

M 520 KARAMÜRSEL (ex-*Worms*)
M 521 KEREMPE (ex-*Detmold*)
M 522 KILIMLI (ex-*Siegen*)
M 523 KOZLU (ex-*Hameln*)
M 524 KUSAKASI (ex-*Vegesack*)

D: 362 tons **S:** 15 kts **Dim:** 44.2 × 8.0 × 2.1
A: 2/20-mm AA (II × 1) **Man:** 40 men
M: Mercedes-Benz MB-820-EB diesels; 2 props; 4,000 hp

REMARKS: These ships were built for the German Navy. They were placed in reserve in 1963 and transferred to Turkey in 1976. A sister, the *Passau*, is serving in the German Navy as an oceanographic ship.

Kilimli (M 522) 1976

♦ *4 ex-U.S. inshore minesweepers* — Bldr: Peterson, U.S.A.

	L
M 500 FOCA (ex-MSI-15)	23-8-66
M 501 FETHIYE (ex-MSI-16)	7-12-66
M 502 FATSA (ex-MSI-17)	11-4-67
M 503 FINIKE (ex-MSI-18)	11-67

Fethiye (M 501) 1970

MINE WARFARE SHIPS (*continued*)

D: 180 tons (235 fl) **S:** 10 kts **Dim:** 34.1 × 7.14 × 2.4
A: 1/12.7-mm machine gun **Man:** 20 men
M: Diesels; 2 props; 960 hp

AMPHIBIOUS WARFARE SHIPS

♦ *2 ex-U.S. landing ships* — Bldr: U.S.A., 1954 — Transferred: 6-73 and 8-74

L 401 ERTOGRUL (ex-*Windham County*, LST-1170)
L 402 SERDAR (ex-*Westchester County*, LST-1167)

D: 2,590 tons (5,786 fl) **S:** 13 kts **Dim:** 117.35 × 16.76 × 3.7
A: 4/76-mm AA **Man:** 116 men
M: 4 General Motors diesels; 2 variable-pitch props; 6,000 hp

♦ *5 ex-U.S. tank landing craft*

C 101 **C 103** to **C 106**

D: 500 tons (700 fl) **S:** . . . **Dim:** 55.2 × 8.4 × 1.6

♦ *12 landing ships* — Bldr: Tazkizak, Istanbul

C 107 to **C 118**

D: 400 tons (600 fl) **S:** 10.5 kts **Dim:** 55.2 × 11.2 × 1.4
A: 2/20-mm **Man:** 15 men

Remark: Based on the French EDIC design.

♦ *12 utility landing craft* — Bldr: Tazkizak, Istanbul, 1965-66

C 205 to **C 216**

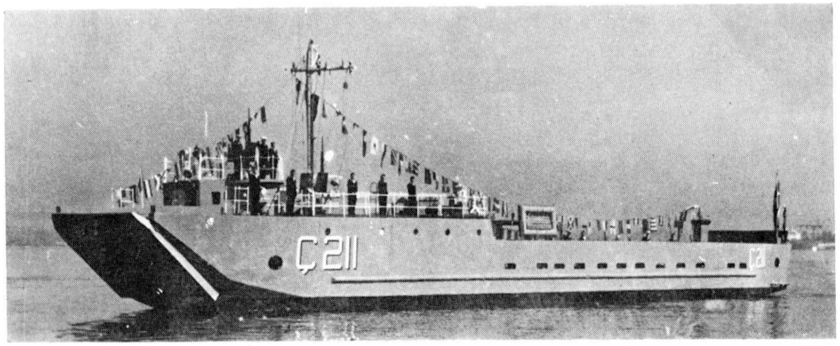

C 211 1973

D: 320 tons (405 fl) **S:** 10 kts **Dim:** 43.3 × 8.5 × 1.7
A: 2/20-mm **M:** General Motors diesels; 2 props; 600 hp

♦ *4 ex-U.S. utility landing craft*

C 201 to **C 204**

D: 160 tons (320 fl) **S:** 10 kts **Dim:** 36.3 × 10.0 × 1.8
A: 2/20-mm **M:** 3 diesels; 675 hp

C 201 1976

♦ *20 mechanized landing craft* — Bldr: Turkey, 1965

C 301 to **C 320**

D: . . . **S:** 9.5 kts **Dim:** 22.0 × 6.3 × 1.4
A: 2 machine guns **Man:** 9 men **M:** Diesels; 2 props; 600 hp

AUXILIARY SHIPS

♦ *2 ex-U.S. Raven-class survey ships* — Bldr: Gulf SB, U.S.A.

	L		L
A 593 CANDARLI (ex-*Frolic*)	1943	**A 594 CARSAMBA** (ex-*Tattoo*)	4-10-42

Candarli (A 593) G. Arra, 1972

AUXILIARY SHIPS (*continued*)

D: 1,010 tons (1,250 fl) **Dim:** 67.31 × 9.75 × 2.95 (light)
A: 1/76-mm AA — 6/40-mm AA **Man:** 105 men
M: Diesel-electric propulsion: Fairbanks or General Motors diesels; 2 props; 3,500 hp

REMARK: While under construction, transferred to Great Britain; given to Turkey in 4-47.

♦ *3 submarine tenders*

A 591 ERKIN (ex-*Trabzon*, ex-*Imperial*)

Erkin (A 591) G. Arra, 1972

D: 10,990 tons (fl) **Dim:** 133.0 × 17.5 × 7.0

REMARK: Former liner, built in 1938, added to the Navy List in 1960.

A 583 DONATAN (ex-*Anthedon*, AS-24) — Bldr: U.S.A., 1943

Donatan (A 583) 1970

D: 8,100 tons (16,100 fl) **S:** 16.6 kts **Dim:** 149.96 × 21.18 × 8.05
A: 1/127-mm AA — 4/65-mm AA **M:** GT; 1 prop; 8,500 hp

REMARKS: Former C3-S-A2 cargo ship. Transferred on 7-2-69.

A 579 GASI HASAN PAÇA (ex-*Ruhr*, A-64) (18-8-60)

D: 2,370 tons (2,430 fl) **S:** 20 kts **Dim:** 98.8 × 11.8 × 5.2 (fl)
A: 2/100-mm AA Mk 53 (I × 2) — 4/40-mm AA (I × 4)
M: 6 Maybach diesels, 1,900 hp each

REMARK: Ex-German replenishment ship, transferred 9-11-76.

♦ *1 submarine repair ship* — Transferred by U.S.A.: 1953

A 582 BASARAN (ex-*Patroclus*, ex-LST-955) (22-10-44)

♦ *1 small-craft repair ship* — Transferred by U.S.A.: 1948

A 581 ONARAN (ex-*Alecto*, ex-LST-558) (14-4-44)

Onaran (A 581) G. Arra, 1971

D: 1,490 tons (4,080 fl) **S:** 10.5 kts **Dim:** 99.98 × 15.24 × 4.36
A: 2/40-mm AA — 8/20-mm AA **Range:** 6,000/9
M: Diesels; 2 props; 1,800 hp **Fuel:** 1,060 tons

♦ *2 ex-U.S. salvage ships* — Bldr: U.S.A., 1945

A 584 KURTARAN (ex-*Bluebird*, ASR-19)

Kurtaran (A 584) 1970

D: 1,735 tons (fl) **S:** 16 kts **Dim:** 62.5 × 12.2 × 3.0
A: 1/76-mm — 2/40-mm AA **M:** Diesel-electric; 1 prop; 3,600 hp

A 585 AKIN (ex-*Greenlet*, ASR-10) (12-7-42) — Transferred: 1970

D: 1,740 tons (2,140 fl) **S:** 14 kts **Dim:** 75.5 × 12.7 × 4.3
M: Diesel-electric; 1 prop; 3,000 hp **Man:** 85 men

AUXILIARY SHIPS (*continued*)

♦ *5 oilers*

A 571 YUSBASI TOLÜNAY (ex-*Tazkizak*)
Bldr: Istanbul Naval DY — L: 22-8-50

D: 3,500 tons (fl) **S:** 14 kts **Dim:** 79.0 × 12.4 × 5.9
M: Diesels; 1,900 hp

A 572 ALBAY HAKKI BURAK — Bldr: Gölçük Naval DY, 1964

D: 1,800 tons (3,740 fl) **S:** 16 kts **Dim:** 83.73 × 12.25 × 5.5
A: 2/40-mm **Man:** 18-20 men
M: Diesel-electric propulsion; 4,000 hp

A 573 BINBASI SAADETIN GÜRLAN — Bldr: Tazkizak Naval DY

D: 1,505 tons (4,680 fl) **S:** . . . **Dim:** 89.7 × 11.8 × 5.4
M: Diesels; 4,400 hp

A 574 AKPINAR (ex-AOG-26) — Bldr: U.S.A., 1944

D: 4,335 tons (fl) **S:** 14 kts **Dim:** 95.0 × . . . × . . .
M: Diesel-electric propulsion; 3,300 hp

Y 1207 GÖLÇÜK — Bldr: Gölçük Naval DY, 1935

D: 1,250 tons **S:** 12 kts **Dim:** 57.0 × . . . × . . .
M: Diesel; 700 hp **Cargo capacity:** 750 tons

♦ *2 water carriers* — Bldr: Gölçük Naval DY, 1968-70

Y 1208 VAN **Y 1209 ULABAT**

D: 900 tons **S:** 14.5 kts **M:** Diesels

♦ *9 netlayers*

P 301 AG 1 (ex-*Barbarian*) (21-10-37) **P 303 AG 3** (ex-*Barfair*) (21-5-38)
P 302 AG 2 (ex-*Barbette*) (15-12-37)

Bldrs: P-301 and P-302: Blyth DD & SB, Great Britain; P-303: John Lewis & Sons, Aberdeen

D: 730 tons **S:** 11.7 kts **Dim:** 52.93 × 9.4 × 2.7
M: Triple-expansion; 1 prop; 850 hp **Boilers:** 2 drum
Man: 32 men

REMARKS: Former British boom-defense vessels, the first one transferred in 1944, the others in 2-46.

P 304 AG 4 (ex-*Larch*, AN-21) — Bldr: American SB, Cleveland, 1941

D: 500 tons (700 fl) **S:** 12.5 kts **Dim:** 49.69 (44.5 pp) × 9.3 × 3.2
A: 1/76-mm **Man:** 48 men **M:** Diesel-electric; 1,000 hp

REMARKS: Identical to the French Navy's *Cigale* class. Transferred in 7-48.

P 305 AG 5 (ex-AN-104) — Bldr: Kröger, Germany (20-10-60)

D: 680 tons (960 fl) **S:** 12 kts **Dim:** 52.5 × 10.5 × 4.05
A: 1/40-mm AA — 3/20-mm AA **Man:** 48 men
M: 4 M.A.N. diesels; 2 props; 1,450 hp

P 307 AG 6 (ex-Dutch *Cerberus*, ex-AN-93) (1952) — Transferred: 1970

D: 855 tons **S:** 12.5 kts **Dim:** 50.8 × 10.4 × 4.0
A: 1/76-mm — 6/20-mm AA **Man:** 48 men
M: Diesel-electric; 1,500 hp

Y 1201 **Y 1202** **Y 1203**

D: 360 tons **Dim:** 30.8 × 10.2 × 1.3

♦ *2 ex-German transports* — Bldr: A. & Ch. de Bretagne

A 586 ULKÜ (ex-*Angeln*) — L: 9-10-54
A 588 UMUR BEY (ex-*Ditmarshen*) — L: 7-7-54

Ulkü (with German hull number)

D: 2,100 tons (2,600 fl) **Dim:** 90.5 (84.5 pp) × 13.3 × 6.2
S: 17 kts **Man:** 57 men
M: 2 SEMT-Pielstick diesels; 1 prop; 3,000 hp

REMARKS: Small but fast cargo ships bought by the West German Navy from the Société Navale Caennaise at the end of 1959, and transferred to Turkey in 1972. Bulbous bow.

♦ *1 fleet ocean tug* — Transferred: 30-10-72

A 587 GAZAL (ex-*Sioux*, ATF-75)

D: 1,700 tons (fl) **S:** 16 kts **Dim:** 60.7 × 11.6 × 4.7
A: 1/76-mm — 4/40-mm AA **Man:** 85 men
M: 4 diesel-electric groups; 2 props; 3,000 hp

♦ *5 harbor tugs*

Y 1128 AKBAS **Y 1129 KEPEZ**

D: 971 tons **S:** 12 kts **Dim:** 44.7 × 10.17 × 4.2

Y 1123 ÖNCU **Y 1124 ÖNDER**

D: 500 tons **S:** 12 kts

Y 1122 KUVVET

D: 390 tons **S:** . . . **Dim:** 32.1 × 7.95 × 3.6

VARIOUS SHIPS

♦ *1 training ship* — Bldr: Blohm & Voss, 1930 — Purchased: 1938

A 578 SAVARONA (ex-*Gunes Dil*)

Savarona (A 578) J. C. Bellonne, 1973

D: 5,750 tons **S:** 18 kts **Dim:** 123.0 × 16.1 × 5.6
A: 2/75-mm — 2/40-mm AA — 2/20-mm AA
Man: 132 men, 80 midshipmen
M: GT; 2 props; 8,000 hp **Boilers:** 4 **Range:** 9,000/15

REMARK: Former state yacht, converted into a training ship for student officers in 1952.

♦ *7 floating docks*

Y 1081 (16,000 tons) **Y 1084** (4,500 tons) **Y 1086** (3,000 tons)
Y 1082 (12,000 tons) **Y 1085** (4,000 tons) **Y 1087** (3,500 tons)
Y 1083 (2,500 tons)

POLICE FORCE

PATROL CRAFT

♦ **J 12** to **J 16** — Bldr: U.S.A., 1960-62

J 16 1970

♦ **J 18** to **J 20** — Bldr: Turkey

D: 70 tons (101.75 fl) **S:** 25/27 kts **Dim:** 29.0 × 5.8 × 1.55
A: 1/40-mm AA — 2/20-mm AA **Man:** 15 men **Range:** 1,500/20
M: 4 Mercedes-Benz diesels; 2 props; 5,400 hp

♦ **J 21** to **J 28** — Bldr: Gölçük Naval DY

D: 170 tons **S:** 22 kts **Dim:** 40.24 × 6.4 × 1.65
A: 2/40-mm **M:** SACM-AGO diesels; 2 props; 4,800 hp

J 28 1976

REMARK: AB 25/34 type of the Turkish Navy.

♦ **J 29** **J 30** **J 41** to **J 49**

REMARK: Similar to the preceding ships, but with a depth-charge rack in place of the 40-mm gun aft.

♦ *1 SAR-33 class* — Bldr: Abeking & Rasmussen

D: . . . **S:** 40 kts **Dim:** 33.0 × 8.6 × . . .
A: . . . **M:** 3 SACM diesels; 3,725 hp

REMARK: Twelve units are planned, the remaining eleven to be built in Turkey.

URUGUAY

PERSONNEL: 3,500 + 300 civilians

MERCHANT MARINE (1976): 43 ships — 151,255 grt
(tankers: 7 ships — 92,757 grt)

NAVAL AVIATION: The small naval air arm is under the direct administration of the Navy and uses American equipment.

FRIGATES

♦ *1 ex-U.S. destroyer escort* — Bldr: Bath Iron Works — Transferred: 1972

	Laid down	L	In serv.
DE 3 18 DE JULIO (ex-*Dealey*, DE-1006)	12-52	8-11-53	6-54

D: 1,450 tons (1,914 fl) **S:** 25 kts **Dim:** 95.7 × 11.26 × 4.3
Man: 11 officers, 150 men **Range:** 4,500/15 **Fuel:** 400 tons
A: 2/76-mm (II × 1) — 1 ASW Mk 108 Weapon Able rocket launcher — 6/ASW Mk 32 TT (III × 2)
M: Laval GT; 1 prop; 20,000 hp **Boilers:** 2 Foster-Wheeler

♦ *2 ex-U.S. destroyer escorts* — Bldr: Federal SB & DD, Newark

	L	In serv.
DE 1 URUGUAY (ex-*Baron*, DE-166)	9-5-43	7-43
DE 2 ARTIGAS (ex-*Bronstein*, DE-189)	14-11-43	12-43

D: 1,240 tons (2,000 fl) **S:** 19 kts
Dim: 93.16 (91.5 pp) × 11.22 × 3.25 (avg) **Man:** 175 men
A: 3/76-mm AA — 2/40-mm AA — 2 depth-charge projectors — 2 depth-charge racks — 1 hedgedog
Range: 5,500/19, 11,500/11
Electron Equipt: Radar: 1 U/SP 6
M: Diesel-electric propulsion; 2 props; 6,000 hp **Fuel:** 340 tons

REMARKS: Same profile as the Greek *Aetos* class. Transferred in 1951. DE-1 refitted in Norfolk in 1955; DE-2 refitted 1954-56.

CORVETTES

♦ *1 ex-U.S. minesweeper* — Bldr: Defoe SB, Michigan, 1942 — Transferred: 1966

MSF 1 COMMANDANTE PEDRO CAMPBELL (ex-*Chickadee*, MSF-59)

D: 890 tons (1,250 fl) **Dim:** 67.45 (65.53 pp) × 9.82 × 3.45
S: 18 kts **A:** 1/76-mm — 2/40-mm AA **Man:** 100 men
M: Diesel-electric; 2 props; 3,200 hp

♦ *1 ex-U.S. ocean minesweeper* — Transferred: 1970

MALDONADO (ex-French *Bir Hakeim*, ex-MSO-451) (1953)

D: 780 tons (fl)

PATROL BOATS AND CRAFT

♦ *1 ex-U.S. coastal minesweeper* — Transferred: 11-69

RIO NEGRO (ex-French *Marguerite*, ex-MSC-94) (1952)

REMARK: Characteristics of the French *Acacia*.

♦ *1 Italian-built ship* — Bldr: Riuniti NSY, Ancona

	L	In serv.
PR 2 SALTO	11-8-35	1936

Salto C. de Rysky

D: 150 tons (180 fl) **S:** 17 kts **Dim:** 42.1 × 5.8 × 1.58
A: 1/40-mm AA — ASW depth charges **Man:** 26 men
M: Germania-Krupp diesels; 2 props; 1,000 hp **Range:** 4,000/10

REMARK: Used as a buoy tender.

♦ *3 patrol craft*

PR 12 PAYSADU — Bldr: Sewart Seacraft, U.S.A., 1968

D: 42 tons **S:** 22 kts **Dim:** 25.5 × 5.6 × 1.7
A: 3 machine guns **Range:** 400/12 **M:** 2 MG; 1,100 hp

PR 11 CARMELO — Bldr: Lürssen, West Germany, 1957

D: 70 tons **S:** 25 kts **Dim:** 28.5 × 5.9 × 2.0

PR 10 COLONIA

D: 34 tons (fl) **S:** 33 kts **Dim:** 20.6 × 4.9 × 1.2
A: 2 machine guns

AUXILIARY SHIPS

♦ *1 ex-U.S. netlayer* — Bldr: U.S.A., 1945 — Delivered: 4-69

HURACAN (ex-*Nahant*, AN-83)

AUXILIARY SHIPS (*continued*)

D: 775 tons (fl) **S:** 12 kts **Dim:** 51.35 × 10.23 × 3.35
A: 4/20-mm AA **Man:** 48 men
M: Diesel-electric; 1 prop; 1,000 hp

Remark: Can be used for netlaying or for salvage.

♦ *1 hydrographic ship* — Bldr: Cadiz NSY, 1930

ACS 10 CAPITÁN MIRANDA

D: 516 tons (550 fl) **S:** 10 kts **Dim:** 45.0 × 8.4 × 3.0
M: M.A.N. diesel; 1 prop; 500 hp **Fuel:** 45 tons

♦ *2 tankers*

AO 28 PRESIDENTE RIVERA — Bldr: Spain, 1971

D: 19,350 tons **S:** 16.5 kts **Dim:** 191.0 × 25.4 × . . .

AO 9 PRESIDENTE ORIBE — Bldr: Ishikawajima, Japan, 1962

D: 17,900 tons **S:** 16 kts **Dim:** 189.0 (179 pp) × 25.7 × 10.05
Man: 76 men **Range:** 16,000/16 **Cargo capacity:** 28,270 tons
M: Ishikawajima-Harima GT; 1 prop; 12,500 hp

♦ *1 training ship*

TACOMA

Remark: Ex-merchant cargo ship.

A. Barrilli, 1969

U.S.S.R.

Being at sea is being at home.

Admiral Makarov (1900)

Henceforth, the flag of the Soviet Navy will float proudly on all the oceans of the world. Sooner or later, the United States will have to understand that it is no longer master of the sea.

Admiral Gorshkov
Commander in Chief of the Soviet Navy

Demonstrating economic and military power abroad; showing readiness for action; deterring potential enemies and encouraging friends; being so equipped that probable enemies see the futility of combat — this is a situation that has often in the past led to the settlement of political ends without recourse to military operations.

Admiral Gorshkov
Commander in Chief of the Soviet Navy

SOVIET MARITIME AREAS

The Soviet Union has nearly 20,000 km of coastline, half of which is in the Arctic and nearly all the rest on inland seas. Only from the Kola Peninsula, whose coast is kept ice-free by the Gulf Stream, can ships gain access to the Atlantic. In the Far East the Soviets have access to the Pacific from the Soviet-held Kurile Islands and from Petropavlovsk, on the east coast of Kamchatka.

The Northern Sea Route, which links the White Sea with the Pacific, is open only from the beginning of July until the end of September, and even then ships can navigate only with the help of icebreakers. The White Sea, the Gulf of Finland in the Baltic, and all the interior navigational waterways are closed each winter by ice.

In the Pacific, the Bering Sea, the Sea of Okhotsk, and the Tatar Strait are icebound in winter. Even Vladivostok, the great base on the Sea of Japan, sometimes has to be opened by icebreakers. Only the Petropavlovsk region, on the east coast of Kamchatka, is open all year.

Exit from the Black Sea is via the Turkish straits, where the passage of ships is controlled by the Montreux Convention.

The Baltic Sea is dominated by the Baltic straits which are only 7 meters deep in the Öresund and 10 meters in the Great Belt, making it impossible for submerged submarines to pass and limiting the size of surface vessels that can transit them.

These geographic characteristics indicate why it is essential for the Soviet Union to have four fleets.

Kiev R.A.F., 1976

SOVIET FLEETS

The Northern Fleet

This fleet is the most important by far because of its strength in nuclear submarines. Its headquarters are at Severomorsk. Surface forces are stationed and supported at numerous bases along the Kola, or Murmansk, Fjord. Murmansk itself is a commercial and fishing port. Submarines, especially the nuclear types, are based at various points along the Murmansk coast in areas that are well protected and ice-free all year.

For industrial support, Northern Fleet submarines depend on the great complex of Severodvinsk near Arkhangelsk. This is the largest naval shipyard in the Soviet Union, specializing in the construction and, no doubt, the maintenance of atomic submarines. Surface ships are maintained at Rosta, near Murmansk.

The Baltic Fleet

The Soviets have assured themselves control of the Baltic by extending their naval bases westward.

Originally, the Baltic Fleet was limited to the Leningrad area and stationed at Kronstadt, but it now has bases in the former Baltic states (at Tallin in Estonia, Riga and Lepaya in Latvia), former East Prussia (Baltiisk, ex-Pillau), and even some facilities on the German-Polish frontier (Świnoujście, ex-Swinemünde).

Numerous shipyards are scattered along the coast, but those especially designed for

naval ships (Zhdanov, Baltic, Admiralty, Sudomekh, etc.) are concentrated in the Leningrad port area.

Of special note are the following conditions:

In general, the rather shallow approaches to the Baltic ports limit submarine activity. Boats have to surface in order to travel by way of the Danish straits.

For at least two months during the winter, the Gulf of Finland, the Gulf of Bothnia, and the Gulf of Riga are partially blocked by ice.

The Black Sea Fleet

Headquarters of the Black Sea Fleet are at Sevastopol. This fleet is stronger than the requirements of the area where it is home-ported, but it helps to maintain the squadron that the Soviets now have permanently in the Mediterranean. In order to keep a squadron in that sea, the Soviets have developed expertise in conforming to the regulations of the Montreux Convention, which controls the Turkish straits.

There is only one really important naval seaport on the Black Sea, Sevastopol, with its submarine base, but the support areas of Odessa and Poti can be used by the fleet.

There are two important shipyards: Nikolaev at the mouth of the Bug River, which specializes in large commercial and naval vessels, and Kamych Burun in the Kerch Strait, which has the capacity to build naval ships in series.

The Pacific Fleet

Nearly as important as the Northern Fleet, the Pacific Fleet has two naval-base complexes: one in the area of Vladivostok, where its headquarters are, and the other in the area of Petropavlovsk, these two sectors being the least affected by winter conditions.

Defense of the approaches seems to depend on a well developed network of sensors and a number of air bases on some of the Kurile Islands and on Sakhalin Island.

Lack of strength in the Pacific area arises from poor port communication facilities and the vulnerability of the Trans-Siberian Railroad. On the other hand, the fleet can be maintained by the heavy industrial shipyards in the Amur Valley and by the large naval shipyards at Komsomolsk, at the headwaters of the Amur River.

SOVIET RIVER SYSTEM

The U.S.S.R. has the best system of interior waterways in the world. The most significant unit in this network has been called by the Soviets the "Canal of Five Seas." It links together the Black Sea, the Sea of Azov (Rostov-on-the-Don), the Caspian Sea (Astrakhan), the Baltic (Leningrad), and the White Sea (Belomorsk).

Aside from its economic advantages, this system has obvious military importance. It permits the passage of small surface ships and — thanks to specially built facilities — the transfer of submarines, including certain nuclear classes, between the three European areas. It has made it possible for shipyards on the Volga River, notably the large one at Gorki, to build warships and even nuclear submarines.

The great weaknesses of this system are the vulnerability of its locks and the interruption of navigation from the beginning of November until mid-April because of winter weather and the breaking up of drift ice.

THE NORTHERN SEA ROUTE

The Northern Sea Route shortens considerably passage between Murmansk and Vladivostok (5,700 miles instead of 13,000 or 14,000 miles by the Suez or Panama canals).

The advantage of this routing is not so much strategic as it is economic. In effect, however, the route consists of three separate sectors, uninterrupted passage being assured for only four to eight weeks in August and September, when the most difficult passages (the Straits of Vilkitskii, Sannikov, and Dimitri Laptev) are ice-free.

Navigation of this route requires the help of icebreakers and aerial reconnaissance and can be accomplished only by ships of 9,000 tons or less.

Some warships, notably submarines, have, at certain periods of the year, been able to make the passage from the White Sea to the Pacific.

PERSONNEL (1977): 425,000 men; 51,000 officers, 84,000 petty officers, and 290,000 sailors (nearly all conscripts). 170,000 are on board ship, 65,000 belong to the naval air arm, 190,000 are part of the shore establishment (10,000 in the Naval Infantry).

MERCHANT MARINE (1976): 7,945 ships — 20,667,882 grt (tankers: 499 ships — 4,149,915 grt). All these ships are available to the Soviet Navy as needed.

WARSHIPS IN SERVICE OR UNDER CONSTRUCTION AS OF 1 OCTOBER 1977

	L	Tons (fl)	Main armament
♦ *3 VTOL carriers*			
3 KIEV	1973-75(?)	37,000	Missile launchers, guns, helicopters, VTOL aircraft
♦ *319-323 submarines*		Tons (submerged)	
83 Ballistic-missile			
1+ DELTA III (nuclear)	. . .	. . .	16 SS-N-18
5 DELTA II (nuclear)	1975-77	11,300	16 SS-N-8, 6 TT
13 DELTA I (nuclear)	1973-76	9,700	12 SS-N-8, 6 TT
34 YANKEE (nuclear)	1967-75	9,500	16 SS-N-6, 6 TT
1 HOTEL III (nuclear)	1965	5,500	3 SS-N-8, 8 TT
8 HOTEL II (nuclear)	1960-63	5,500	3 SS-N-5, 8 TT
13 GOLF II (diesel)	1958-61	2,700	3 SS-N-5, 10 TT
8 GOLF I (diesel)	1958-61	2,700	3 SS-N-4, 10 TT
238-240 Attack			
2 PAPA (nuclear)	1972-	7,000	10 SS-N-7, 8 TT
3 CHARLIE II (nuclear)	. . .	5,100	8 SS-N-7, 6 TT
12 CHARLIE I (nuclear)	1968-75	4,900	8 SS-N-7, 6 TT
28 ECHO II (nuclear)	1960-68	5,800	8 SS-N-3, 8 TT
1 ALFA (nuclear)	1972	4,250	TT
5 VICTOR II (nuclear)	. . .	5,700	8 TT
16 VICTOR I (nuclear)	1967-74	5,100	8 TT
5 ECHO (nuclear)	1960-68	5,600	10 TT
14 NOVEMBER (nuclear)	1959-64	4,800	12 TT
16 JULIETT (diesel)	1961-68	3,400	4 SS-N-3, 10 TT
5 WHISKEY LONG BIN (diesel)	1961-63	1,500	4 SS-N-3, 4 TT
4 TANGO (diesel)	1973	2,200	TT
4 BRAVO (diesel)	1970-72	2,900	None
56-58 FOXTROT (diesel)	1959-7 . .	2,400	10 TT
15 ZULU IV (diesel)	1952-57	2,300	10 TT
10 ROMEO (diesel)	1960	1,800	8 TT
34 WHISKEY (diesel)	1950-57	1,350	6 TT
4 WHISKEY CANVAS BAG (diesel)	1950-57	1,350	. . .
4 QUEBEC (diesel)	1950-57	540	4 TT

		Tons (fl)	
♦ *38 cruisers*			
2 Helicopter			
2 MOSKVA	1965-66	20,000	4 SA-N-3, 1 SUW-N-1, 16 helicopters
24 Guided-missile			
5 KARA	1971-75	10,000	8 SS-N-14, 4 SA-N-3, 2 SA-N-4, 4/76-mm DP, 10 TT, 1 helicopter
10 KRESTA II	1967-72	7,600	8 SS-N-14, 4 SA-N-3, 4/57-mm AA, 10 TT, 1 helicopter
4 KRESTA I	1964-67	7,500	4 SS-N-3, 4 SA-N-1, 4/57-mm AA, 10 TT, 1 helicopter
4 KYNDA	1959-61	5,700	8 SS-N-3, 2 SA-N-1, 4/76-mm AA, 6 TT
1 DZERZHINSKY	1954	20,000	1 SA-N-2, 9/152-mm, 12/100-mm DP, 16/37-mm AA
12 Conventional			
11 SVERDLOV	1950-58	20,000	6, 9, or 12/152-mm, 12/100-mm DP
1 CHAPAEV	1949	15,000	12/152-mm, 8/100-mm DP
♦ *96 destroyers*			
57 Guided-missile			
18 KRIVAK II, I	1970-7 . .	3,600	4 SS-N-14, 4/76-mm or 2/85-mm DP, 2 SA-N-4, 8 TT
5 MOD. KASHIN	1963-72	4,900	4 SS-N-11, 4 SA-N-1, 4/76-mm DP, 5 TT
14 KASHIN	1963-72	4,750	4 SA-N-1, 4/76-mm DP, 5 TT
8 KANIN	1958-60	4,500	2 SA-N-1, 8/57-mm AA, 10 TT
3 MOD. KILDIN	1958-59	3,800	4 SS-N-11, 4/76-mm AA, 16/45 or 57-mm AA
1 KILDIN	1959	3,800	1 SS-N-1, 16/57-mm AA, 4 TT
8 SAM KOTLIN	1955-57	3,500	1 SA-N-1, 2/130-mm DP, 12/45-mm AA
39 Conventional			
19 KOTLIN	1955-57	3,800	4/130-mm DP, 16/45-mm AA, 4 to 8/25-mm AA, 10 TT
20 SKORY, MOD. SKORY	1949-53	3,200	4/130-mm DP, 2/85-mm or 5/57-mm AA, 10 or 5 TT
♦ *106 frigates*			
1 KONI	1977-	1,800	2 SA-N-4, 4/76-mm DP
47 PETYA II, I	1962-64	1,100	2-4/76-mm DP, 5 or 10 TT
20 MIRKA I, II	1964-67	1,100	4/76-mm DP, 5 or 10 TT
35 RIGA	1955-58	1,450	3/100-mm DP, 3 TT
3 KOLA	1953-57	1,700	4/100-mm DP, 3 TT
♦ *119-121 corvettes*			
12 Guided-missile			
12 NANUCHKA	1969-7 . .	930	6 SS-N-9, 2 SA-N-4, 2/57-mm AA
109 Conventional			
5 GRISHA II	1973-75	900	4/57-mm AA, 4 TT
20-22 GRISHA I, III	1968-7 . .	900	2/57-mm AA, 2 SA-N-4, 4 TT
65 POTI	1961-67	500	2/57-mm AA, 4 TT
17 KRONSTADT	1948-56	300	1/85-mm DP, 2/37-mm AA

NOTE ON SOVIET VESSELS

Submarines

Although the noise factor has been reduced in the newest units, all classes of Soviet nuclear submarines are said to be noisier than their Western counterparts. They can go deep but, according to American sources, their detection systems cannot compare with those of Western submarines.

The SSBNs carried by the Delta class are the biggest in the world, and their range is far greater than that of the Polaris or Poseidon. However, they do not have individually targeted, multiple warheads.

Submarines equipped with tactical missiles, particularly those capable of submerged launching, are a very serious threat. Foxtrot submarines, the most numerous of the modern conventional classes, are known for their high endurance.

Surface Ships

A striking feature of Soviet surface ships is the large number of weapon systems with which they are equipped. The objective seems to be to build ships capable of dealing with any threat. Soviet ships carry far more weapons than do ships of comparable displacements in other navies. This multi-purpose capability can be achieved only at the expense of habitability and fuel capacity, the disadvantage of the latter being the need for frequent refueling. Furthermore, the great number of magazines that the multiplicity of weapons entails increases vulnerability, and damage control is not as well developed as it is in Western navies. Another hazard is that the strategic ballistic missiles in submarines and the majority of tactical anti-surface weapons use liquid fuels.

Most cruisers and destroyers have excellent sea-keeping qualities, the newest ones being fitted with fixed or active anti-rolling stabilizers. The use of gas turbines alone or in conjunction with another system is becoming widespread.

In short, Soviet naval engineers and architects build satisfactory ships of innovative design and continue to improve them.

WEAPONS AND SYSTEMS

(A) MISSILES

Ballistic Missiles

NOTE: All have liquid-fuel propulsion, except perhaps the SS-N-17 and 18, which may have solid-fuel propulsion.

SS-N-4

Range: 300 nautical miles. Nuclear warhead. Fitted in Golf-I diesel-powered fleet ballistic-missile submarines. Can be launched only from the surface.

WEAPONS AND SYSTEMS (*continued*)

1

3

1. Top, left: Launching of a surface-air Goa missile (SA-N-1), from a Kynda-class cruiser.
2. Below, left: Goa twin launcher with missiles ready.
3. Top right: The MBU 1800 ASW rocket launchers on board an SO-I-class patrol boat.
4. Below, right: launching of a Styx missile from an Osa-I-class missile patrol boat.

2

4

WEAPONS AND SYSTEMS (*continued*)

French Navy, 1969

On board the *Moskva:* At left the twin SUW-N-1 launcher with a FRAS-1 ASW missile on its left arm; at right the forwardmost twin SA-N-3 system launcher with a Goblet surface-to-air missile on its left arm.

WEAPONS AND SYSTEMS (*continued*)

SS-N-5

Range: 700 nautical-miles. Nuclear warhead of about 800 kilotons. Fitted in Hotel II nuclear-powered submarines and in Golf-II diesel-powered strategic submarines. Can be launched while submerged. Range may have been increased to 900 nautical miles.

SS-N-6

Range: 1,300 nautical miles. Nuclear warhead of about 1 megaton. Fitted in Yankee-class nuclear submarines. Can be launched while submerged. A more recent version has a 1,600 nautical-mile range and a MRV-type warhead.

SS-N-8 (NATO code name: Sawfly)

Range: 4,200 miles. Nuclear warhead of about 1 megaton. Fitted in Delta I and Delta II nuclear submarines.

SS-N-13

Range: 370 nautical miles. Nuclear warhead. Tactical ballistic missile. Program suspended in 1973 due to inadequate technology.

SS-N-17

Range: 1,800 nautical miles. Nuclear warhead. First ballistic missile with possible solid-fuel propulsion. May be aboard Yankee-class submarines.

SS-N-18

Range: 4,800 nautical miles. Nuclear MRV-type warhead. Believed to be aboard Delta-III submarines.

Surface-to-Surface Cruise Missiles

NOTE: Liquid-fuel propulsion, except for SS-N-7, which has a solid-propellant engine.

SS-N-1 (NATO code name: Scrubber)

Range: 25 nautical miles on surface targets, 120 to 130 miles on land targets. Subsonic turbojet engine. Radio-directed for initial trajectory, then active automatic radar guidance to the target. Nuclear or conventional warhead. Fitted in the remaining Kildin-class destroyer *Neulovimy.* No longer produced.

SS-N-2 (NATO code name: Styx)

Maximum range: 25 nautical miles. Practical range: 16 nautical miles. Liquid propulsion. I-band active radar guidance in targeting, possibly with infrared homing in the most recent version, SS-N-2b. Flight altitude pre-set: 100, 150, 200, 250, or 300 m. 400 to 450 kg conventional warhead. Installed in Osa-I and Osa-II guided-missile boats.

SS-N-3 (NATO code name: Shaddock)

On surface ships:
Maximum range: 30 nautical miles on surface targets, but can reach 170 nautical miles with an aerial relay (aircraft fitted with a Video Data Link system).

On submarines:
Maximum range: 30 nautical miles on surface targets, 250 nautical miles on land targets. Inertial guidance with mid-course correction by radio, active radar homing to target. Turbojet propulsion. Conventional or nuclear warhead. Fitted in Kynda (quadruple launcher) and Kresta-I (twin launcher) cruisers, and Whiskey Long Bin, Juliett, and Echo-II submarines. Launched from the surface by submarines.

SS-N-7

Maximum range: 30 nautical miles. Conventional warhead, can be launched while submerged. Fitted in Charlie-I and Charlie-II (8 per ship) and Papa (10 per ship) nuclear-powered attack submarines.

SS-N-9

Maximum range: 30 miles, but can reach 150 miles with an aerial relay (aircraft fitted with a Video Data Link system), inertial guidance, and active radar homing to the target. Ramjet propulsion. Conventional or nuclear warhead. Installed in Nanuchka-class guided-missile corvettes.

SS-N-11

Maximum range: 26 nautical miles. Improvement on the SS-N-2 Styx. Fitted in Mod. Kashin and Mod. Kildin destroyers. May not exist.

SS-N-12

Maximum range: 270 nautical miles. Conventional or nuclear warhead. Will replace the SS-N-3 on submarines and is aboard the *Kiev.*

SS-N-14

The missile, thought to have a range of 20 miles, carries a torpedo. Introduced in the late 1960s, this missile was long regarded as a surface-to-surface missile and was fitted in the *Kiev*, Kresta-II and Kara cruisers as well as on the Krivak guided-missile destroyers. It was first called the SS-N-10. Although the SS-N-14 is primarily an ASW weapon, it can undoubtedly be employed against surface ships.

Surface-to-Air Missiles

SA-N-1 (NATO code name: Goa)

Twin launchers. Range: 30,000 m, interception altitudes: 1,000 to 50,000 feet. Guidance: radar/command. Conventional warhead, 60 kg. Fitted on Kynda and Kresta-I cruisers, as well as on Kashin, Kanin, and Kotlin destroyers. Also has a surface-to-surface capability.

SA-N-2 (NATO code name: Guideline)

Twin launchers. Range: 40,000 m, interception altitude: 1,000 to 80,000 feet. Guidance: radar/command. Conventional warhead, 150 kg. Fitted on the cruiser *Dzerzhinsky* only.

SA-N-3 (NATO code name: Goblet)

Twin launchers. Range: 30,000 m, interception altitudes: 500 to 80,000 feet. Guidance: radar/command. Conventional warhead, 60 kg. Fitted on Kresta-II and Kara cruisers as well as the *Moskva*-class helicopter cruisers. An improved version has a range of 55,000 m and is employed on the *Kiev.* Goblet has an anti-surface target capability.

SA-N-4 (short-range system)

Twin launcher, retracting into a vertical drum. Range: 9,000 m, interception altitude: 30 to 10,000 feet. Guidance: radar command. Conventional warhead. Fitted in Kara cruisers, two *Sverdlov* cruisers, Krivak guided-missile destroyers, Grisha and Nanuchka guided-missile, corvettes, and the Sarancha hydrofoils.

SA-N-5 (very short range)

Naval version of SA-7 Strela. Fitted on some Osa-class guided-missile patrol boats and some Polnocny-class landing ships.

WEAPONS AND SYSTEMS (*continued*)

Air-to-Surface Missiles

AS 1 (NATO code name: Kennel)

Range: 50 to 55 nautical miles. Turbojet propulsion. Semi-active radar guidance. Conventional warhead. Obsolescent.

AS 2 (NATO code name: Kipper)

Range: 100 nautical miles. Solid-fuel propulsion. Inertial guidance or automatic pilot with radar homing head. Conventional or nuclear warhead. Placed in service on Badger-C aircraft.

AS 4 (NATO code name: Kitchen)

Range: 170 nautical miles. Nuclear warhead. Inertial guidance with radar terminal homing. In service on Backfire aircraft.

AS 5 (NATO code name: Kelt)

Range: 100 nautical miles. Solid-fuel propulsion. Inertial or autopilot guidance with radar terminal homing. Conventional and nuclear warheads. In service on Badger-C and -G aircraft.

AS 6

Range: over 100 nautical miles. Conventional or nuclear warhead. In service on Badger-C aircraft, two on each.

AS 7

Range: 6 nautical miles. Mach 1. Tactical weapon. Solid-fuel propulsion. Pencil-beam radar terminal homing. 100 kg. Conventional warhead. Used on Forger aircraft aboard the *Kiev*.

AS 9

Range: 55 nautical miles. Anti-radar missile. Turbojet propulsion. Passive homing on electromagnetic radiation. 150 kg. Conventional warhead. In use on Badger and Backfire aircraft.

(B) GUNS

152-mm

Fitted in triple turrets on *Sverdlov* and *Chapaev* cruisers. Individual barrels can be loaded and elevated separately.

barrel length: 57 calibers
muzzle velocity: 915 m/sec
altitude arc: −5° to +50°
maximum rate of fire: 4 to 5 rounds/min/barrel
maximum range: 27,000 m
effective range: 18,000 m
projectile weight: 50 kg
fire control: Top Bow and Egg Cup radars in the upper turrets forward and aft
8-m range-finder in each turret

130-mm twin

Semi-automatic for surface and air targets. Fitted on Kotlin and SAM-Kotlin destroyers. Tri-axially stabilized. Twin mount with electric or hydraulic-electric pointing system.

barrel length: 58 calibers
muzzle velocity: 900 m/sec
arc of elevation: −5° to +80°
maximum rate of fire: 10 rounds/min/barrel
maximum range, surface target: 28,000 m
effective range, surface target: 16,000 to 18,000 m
maximum vertical range: 13,000 m
projectile weight: 27 kg
target designation by stabilized Wasp Head director with a Sun Visor radar
Egg Cup radar in each mount (being removed)

130-mm twin

Semi-automatic type fitted on *Skory*-class destroyers.

barrel length: 50 calibers
muzzle velocity: 875 m/sec
arc of elevation: −5° to +45°
maximum rate of fire: 10 rounds/min/barrel
maximum range: 24,000 m
effective range: 14,000 to 15,000 m
projectile weight: 27 kg

100-mm twin

Mounted on three axes installed on *Sverdlov* and *Chapaev* cruisers.

barrel length: 50 calibers
weight: approx. 40 tons
muzzle velocity: 900/sec
arc of elevation: −15° to 85°
maximum rate of fire: 15 rounds/min/barrel
maximum range, surface target: 20,000 m
effective range, surface target: 10,000 to 12,000 m
maximum range, AA fire: 15,000 m
effective range, AA fire: 8,000 to 9,000 m
projectile weight: 16 kg
target designation by stabilized director with a Top Bow or Post Lamp radar
Egg Cup radar in each mount (being removed)

100-mm single

Gun mount with a shield. Installed on *Kola* and *Riga* frigates, and Don-class submarine tenders.

barrel length: 56 calibers
muzzle velocity: 850 m/sec
arc of elevation: −5° to +40°
maximum rate of fire: 15 rounds/min
maximum range: 16,000 m
effective range: 10,000 m
projectile weight: 13.5 kg
target designation by stabilized Wasp Head director fitted with Sun Visor radar

85-mm automatic AA

A single-barreled, water-cooled gun in an enclosed mounting found on the most recent units of Krivak-class destroyers. Rate of fire: 30 rounds/min. Maximum effective range: 8,000 m.

85-mm AA

Twin-barreled gun mount on some *Skory* destroyers; single barrel on Kronstadt-class corvettes.

barrel length: 50 calibers

WEAPONS AND SYSTEMS (*continued*)

muzzle velocity: 850 m/sec
arc of elevation: −5° to +70°
maximum rate of fire: 10 rounds/min/barrel
maximum range, surface target: 15,000 m
effective range, surface target: 8,000 to 9,000 m
practical maximum range, AA fire: 6,000 m

76-mm twin

Installed on *Kara* and *Kynda* cruisers, *Kashin* and *Krivak* destroyers, *Petya* and *Mirka* frigates, and the training ship *Smolny.*

length of barrel: 60 calibers
muzzle velocity: 900 m/sec
maximum rate of fire: 60 rounds/min/barrel
arc of elevation: +80°
maximum range, AA fire: 10,000 m
effective range, AA fire: 6,000 to 7,000 m
projectile weight: 16 kg
target designation with Owl Screech radar director and automatic tracking

57-mm automatic

Single-barrel gun mount (Mod. *Skory* destroyers), twin-barrel (several classes), or quadruple on *Kanin* and *Kildin* destroyers; in the latter case, the guns are mounted in superimposed pairs.

length of barrel: 70 calibers
muzzle velocity: 900 to 1,000 m/sec
arc of elevation: 0° to +90°
maximum rate of fire: 150 rounds/min/gun
effective vertical range: 4,500 m
target designation by Hawk Screech and Muff Cob tracking radars

57-mm twin

This equipment, which appears to be entirely automatic from the ammunition-handling room to the gun mount, is installed on *Moskva,* Kresta-I, and Kresta-II cruisers, Poti and Grisha corvettes, Nanuchka guided-missile corvettes, Turya torpedo boats, Ropucha LSTs, and Ugra submarine tenders. Now removed from *Boris Chilikin* replenishment ships and *Manych* oilers.

length of barrel: 70 calibers?
water-cooling system
maximum rate of fire: 120 rounds/min/barrel
maximum effective vertical range: 5,000 to 6,000 m
target designation by Muff Cob radar

45-mm

Quadruple-barreled installations in Tallin, Sam Kotlin, and Kotlin destroyers; single ones on some Sasha minesweepers. The guns are in two superimposed pairs on a single mount.

length of barrel: 85 calibers
muzzle velocity: 900 m/sec
arc of elevation: 0° to +90°
rate of fire: 300 rounds/min/mount
effective maximum vertical range: 4,000 m
target designation by Hawk Screech tracking radar (visually in Sasha)

37-mm Model 39

Installed in twin-barreled mounts in *Sverdlov* and *Chapaev* cruisers, *Skory* destroyers, Riga frigates, and various other ships; singly in Kronstadt corvettes.

length of barrel: 60 calibers?
muzzle velocity: 900 m/sec
arc of elevation: 0° to +80°?
maximum rate of fire: 160 rounds/min/gun
optical tracking

30-mm twin automatic

Installed in a light mount on several classes of ships — cruisers, destroyers, guided-missile boats, supply ships, etc. Water-cooling system.

length of barrel: 60 calibers
muzzle velocity: 1,000 m/sec
maximum rate of fire: 240 rounds/min/barrel
effective maximum range, AA fire: 2,500 to 3,000 m
target designation by Drum Tilt tracking radar

25-mm twin

Found on many ships and made up of two superimposed guns.

length of barrel: 60 calibers
muzzle velocity: 900 m/sec
maximum rate of fire: 500 rounds/min/mount
optical tracking

Anti-missile gun

This gun is in service on *Kiev* carriers, Kara and Kresta-II cruisers, and several other smaller classes. It is installed in mounts similar to those of the 30-mm AA double-barreled automatic guns. It is a Gatling machine gun designed to fire a great number of rounds at an extremely high rate in order to intercept a cruise missile at a comparatively short distance. It has six 23-mm barrels. Rate of fire is at least 3,000 rounds/min/mount. Target designation is by Bass Tilt radar or visual.

(C) ANTISUBMARINE WEAPONS

Missiles

SS-N-15

ASW missile similar to the U.S. Navy's Subroc. Maximum range: 25 miles. Nuclear warhead. A version with a torpedo payload is called SS-N-16.

FRAS 1

Rocket-propelled weapon similar to the U.S. Navy's Asroc. Installed on *Kiev* carriers and *Moskva* helicopter cruisers. Maximum range: 16 miles. Nuclear warhead. Twin launcher.

SS-N-14

Similar to the Australian Ikara. Maximum range: 20 miles. It is carried by Kara and Kresta-II cruisers, and Krivak destroyers. It may also have an anti-ship capability. Fras 1 and SS-N-14 are launched from the SUW-N-1 on the *Moskva* and *Kiev* classes.

Rockets

MBU 1800

Made up of two horizontal rows of short barrels superimposed, two below and three in the upper row. Tube diameter: 0.250 m; length: 1.400 m; the rocket is somewhat

WEAPONS AND SYSTEMS (*continued*)

shorter. Range: 1,800 m. Fixed tubes. Installed in SO-I patrol boats, Kronstadt corvettes, and Natya and T-58 minesweepers.

MBU 2500

Made up of two horizontal rows of 8 barrels each, approximately 1.600 m in length. Trainable. Manual reloading. Range: 2,500 m.

MBU 2500A

Made up of 12 barrels, approximately 1.600 m long, arranged in a ring and fired in sequence. Vertical automatic loading system, barrel by barrel. Can be trained and elevated. Range: 6,000 m. Installed on the *Kiev* carrier, *Moskva, Kynda,* Kresta-I and Kresta-II cruisers, Krivak, Kashin, and Kanin guided-missile destroyers, the smaller Mirka and Petya frigates, and Poti and Grisha corvettes.

MBU 4500

Made up of 6 barrels, 0.300 m in diameter and 1.500 m long, superimposed in two rows and fired simultaneously. Trainable. Range: 2,500 m.

MBU 4500A

Made up of 6 barrels, arranged in a ring and fired in order, with vertical automatic reloading. Trainable. Tube diameter: approx. 0.300 m. Length: approx. 1.800 m. Range: 2,500 m. Installed in Kara, Kresta-I, and Kresta-II cruisers and Kashin destroyers.

Torpedoes

The Soviet Navy uses anti-surface and ASW torpedoes that are 533 mm in diameter, and short ASW torpedoes that are 400 mm in diameter.

(D) RADARS (NATO code names)

Navigation

The most widely used are the I-band Neptun, Ball End and various Don types.

Long-range air search

Head Net A
Head Net B, consisting of 2 Head Net A antennae, mounted back-to-back in a horizontal plane
Head Net C, consisting of 2 Head Net A antennae, mounted back-to-back, one in a horizontal plane, the other inclined
These radars use a band that gives a 60- to 70-mile detection range on an attack bomber flying at high altitude
Big Net, a large C-band radar fitted on Kresta-I and a few *Sverdlov* cruisers, and some Kashin destroyers. Its detection range on an aircraft is probably over 100 miles
Slim Net (E band), early model radar fitted on some cruisers and destroyers
Hair Net (E band), early model radar now only on one Riga frigate
Top Trough (C band), on some *Sverdlov* cruisers
Sea Gull (A band), copy of British WW2
Knife Rest (A band), antenna resembles a knife rest
Strut Curve (F band), mounted on the Petya and Mirka frigates and Poti and Grisha corvettes
Strut Pair (F band), mounted on one Mod. Kildin. Employs pulse-compression

Height-finding

Top Sail (C band), three-dimensional radar installed on *Moskva,* Kresta-II, and Kara cruisers.
Top Steer, three-dimensional radar found with Top Sail on the *Kiev;* possibly for air-controlling.

Tracking

Trap Door, in a retractable mount. Used for SS-N-12.
Peel Group, mounted on Kynda and Kresta-I cruisers as well as Kashin, Kanin and Sam Kotlin destroyers. Consists of a tracking radar for high altitudes (I-band) and a missile-guidance radar at lower altitudes (E-band). The assembly is made up of two groups of large and small reflectors, in both horizontal and vertical position, with parabolic design. Maximum range approximately 30 to 40 miles. Used for missile guidance for the Goa in the SA-N-1 system.
Head Lights (F, G, H, and D bands), mounted in *Kiev* carriers and *Moskva,* Kresta-II and Kara cruisers. Similar to the Peel Group with an assembly of tracking radar for the target and guidance radar for the missile. Used for guidance in the Goblet missile of the SA-N-3 system and for the surface-to-underwater missiles of the SS-N-14 system.
Scoop Pair (E band), missile-guidance radar for the Shaddock missile of the SS-N-3 system on board Kynda and Kresta-I cruisers
Pop Group (F, H, and I bands), missile guidance for the SA-N-4 system
Eye Bowl (F band), smaller version of Head Lights, installed on Krivak destroyers, missile-guidance radar for the SS-N-14 system
Fan Song E, installed on the *Dzerzhinsky;* used with the Guideline missile of the SA-N-2 system. Consists of two antennae made up of parabolic reflectors in the form of troughs, one vertical and one horizontal, plus three circular reflectors, two side-by-side, and a third mounted on an arm at the extreme end of the horizontal reflector. Detection range: at least 80 miles on a bomber-size aircraft
Band Stand, on Nanuchka corvettes and Sarancha hydrofoils for missile-tracking and control. In large radome.

Surface search

The most common are Pot Head, Square Tie, Snoop Plate (I Band), High Sieve, Low Sieve, Skin Head, and Pot Head (E band)

Fire Control

Half Bow, **Post Lamp**, **Long Bow** } (I band) mounted on various older classes of ships
Top Bow, 152-mm gun
Sun Visor, 130-mm AA, 100-mm AA guns
Hawk Screech, 45-mm and 76-mm AA guns
Owl Screech, 76-mm DP
Muff Cob (H Band), used for 57-mm AA twin automatic guns
Egg Cup (E band), installed in turrets for 152-mm, 130-mm, and 100-mm AA guns
Drum Tilt (H and I bands), installed on Osa patrol boats and ships fitted with 30-mm twin-barrel AA
Bass Tilt (H band), used with the Gatling-type gun fitted in *Kiev* carriers, Kara and Kresta-II cruisers, and Mod. Kashin destroyers, as well as in Grisha-III corvettes, where it also controls twin 57-mm

(E) SONARS

Until a few years ago, the Soviet Navy evinced little interest in antisubmarine warfare or, of course, submarine detection. Most of its ships were equipped with high-frequency sonar (Tamir, Pegas, Hercules). New or modernized ships appear to be equipped with better sensors:

WEAPONS AND SYSTEMS (*continued*)

hull sonars of mid-frequency (Kresta-II cruisers, Krivak and Kanin destroyers, Grisha corvettes)
towed sonars of mid-frequency (*Kiev* carriers, *Moskva* and Kara cruisers, Krivak and Mod. Kashin destroyers)
hull sonars of low frequency (*Kiev* carriers, *Moskva* cruisers)
helicopter dipping sonars (Mirka frigates, Stenka and Pchela patrol boats, Turya torpedo boats, and others)

Most submarines still have old detection equipment (active-passive Hercules, passive Feniks), but recent nuclear submarines have a modern 10w-frequency sonar.

Soviet literature has also expressed interest in the use of towed passive sonar arrays.

(F) ELECTRONIC WARFARE

The Soviet Navy has always taken a great interest in electronic warfare. The increasing number of radomes of every description that can be seen on Soviet ships, especially on the newest and most important types (helicopter and guided-missile cruisers, for example) indicates the attention and consideration being given to this aspect of modern warfare.

VTOL CARRIERS

♦ *3 Kiev class*

	Bldr	Laid down	L	In serv.
KIEV	Nikolaev	1971	1973	1976
MINSK	Nikolaev	1972	1974	1977–78
KHARKOV	Nikolaev	1973?	1975?	1978–79?

Kiev French Navy, 1976

D: 35,000 tons (37,000 fl)
Dim: 273.0 (249.0 pp) × 48.0 (3.20 wl) × 7.6–9.1
S: 30 kts
Range: 4,000/30, 13,000/18

A: 8/SS-N-12 (II × 4) — 4/SA-N-3 (II × 2) (72 Goblet missiles) — 4/SA-N-4 (II × 2) (60 missiles?) — 4/76-mm DP (II × 2) — 8/6-barrel Gatling guns (VI × 8) — 10/533-mm TT (V × 2) — 2/SUW-N-1 (II × 1) — 2/MBU-2500A rocket launchers — 15 Hormone A&B helicopters — 10 Forger aircraft
Electron Equipt: Radars: 1/Don Kay, 2/Don-2, 1/Top Sail, 1/Top Steer, 2/Head Lights, 2/Pop Group, 2/Owl Screech, 4/Bass Tilt, 1/Trap Door
Sonars: 1 low-frequency, hull mounted, 1 medium-frequency, towed — ECM: numerous systems.
M: Steam turbines (see Remarks); 4 props; 140,000 hp
Fuel: 7,000 tons
Man: 1,700 men?

Kiev French Navy, 1976

REMARKS:
Propulsion: Reportedly, the *Kiev* has too small a stack for gas turbine propulsion. According to observers, she emits black smoke — indicative of conventional propulsion — and does not have the characteristic "whine" of gas turbines.
Aviation installations: The flight-deck portion of the upper deck is inclined about 4.5° to port of the centerline axis of the ship and is about 180 m long. It is partially covered with a mosaic of refractory tiles (to protect against the hot exhaust of the Forger aircraft). There are two elevators to the hangar deck: one (19.20 m × 10.35 m) beside the stack; the other (18.50 × 4.70) abaft the island. Five small ammunition elevators are connected by an on-deck rail system.
Armament: The SS-N-12 missiles are launched from four twin elevating tubes that are fixed in train. In order to use the full range of the missiles over the horizon, it is necessary to use a forward-located, target-designation platform. On the *Kiev*, that requirement is met by the Hormone-B which carries a long-range radar giving a range of 100 nautical miles with the helicopter at an altitude of 4,000 feet. Alternatively, it may be possible to use target designation from the Forger aircraft. It is also not impossible that the ship uses target information relayed by a satellite. There are 8 missiles in the launch tubes, plus 16 reloads.

VTOL CARRIERS (*continued*)

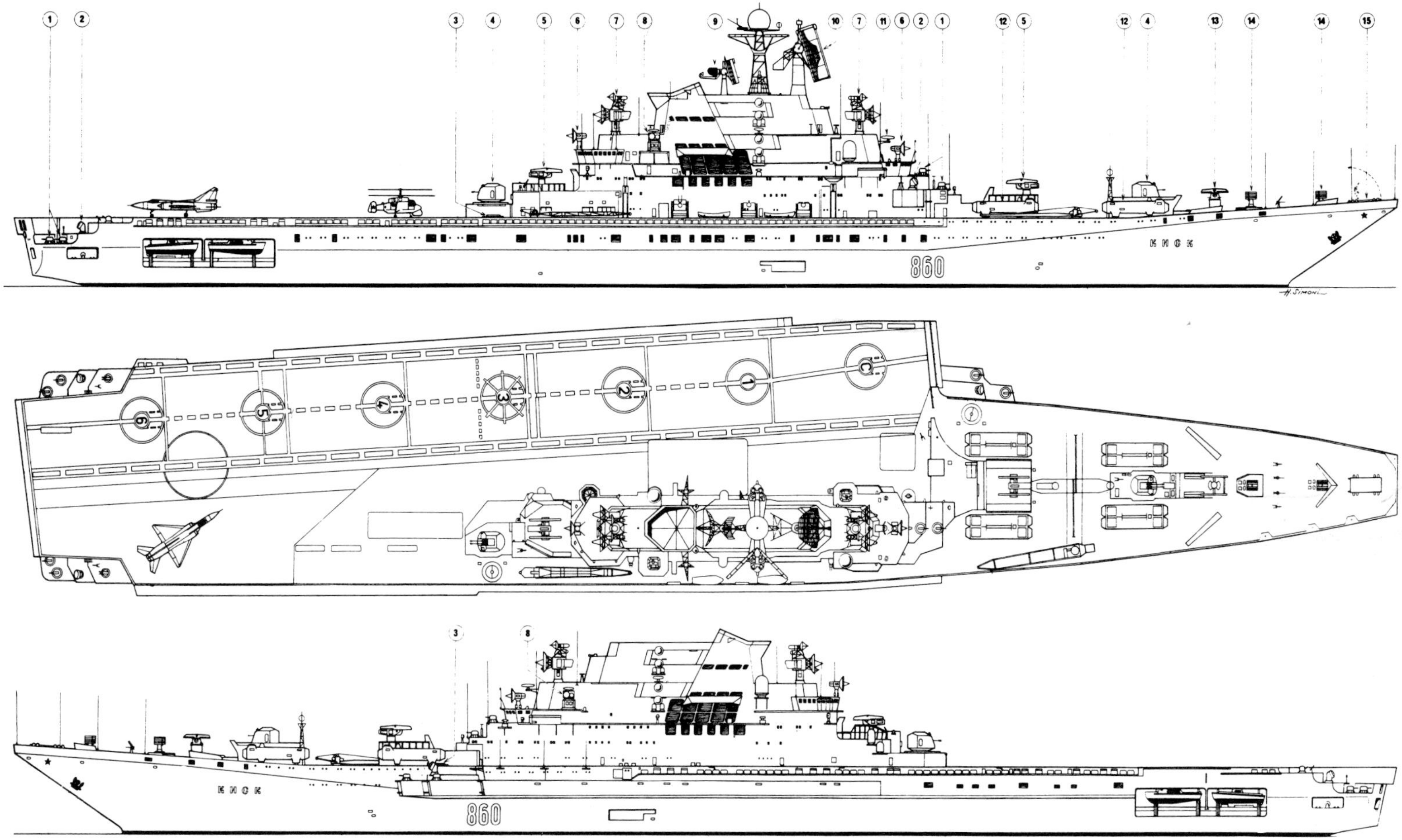

1: 23-mm gatling guns (VIII × 1) — 2: Bass Tilt radar — 3: SA-N-4 system — 4: twin 76-mm DP gun mount — 5: SA-N-3 system — 6: Owl Screech radar — 7: Head Lights radar — 8: Pop Group radar — 9: Top Steer radar — 10: Top Sail radar — 11: Don-2 radar — 12: twin launchers for the SS-N-12 system — 13: SUW-N-1 system twin launcher — 14: MBU 2500A — 15: Trap Door.

VTOL CARRIERS (*continued*)

Kiev (island) French Navy, 1976

Kiev French Navy, 1976

Kiev U.S. Navy, 1976

NAVAL AVIATION

Naval aviation, which dates from 1919, is an integral part of the Soviet Navy, but its organization and ranks are those of the air forces. With the possible exception of a few helicopters, land-based aircraft are part of the four naval fleets (Northern, Baltic, Black Sea, and Pacific) and are under the direct control of the commanders of those fleets. The air arm has approximately 1,200 aircraft, including:

- ♦ 75 Bear, C, D, and F
- ♦ 60 Badger, E, F, and J
- ♦ 60 Blinder-A, fitted for reconnaissance, electronic warfare, etc.
- ♦ 35-40 Fitter-C interceptors
- ♦ 300 Badger, A, C, and G, bombers
- ♦ 35-40 Backfire bombers
- ♦ 70-80 Badger-A for aerial refueling
- ♦ 100 Mail ASW amphibians
- ♦ 50-60 May ASW patrol bombers
- ♦ 270 helicopters (Haze, Hound, and Hormone-A and -B)

Approximately 65,000 men are involved in naval aviation.

Forger

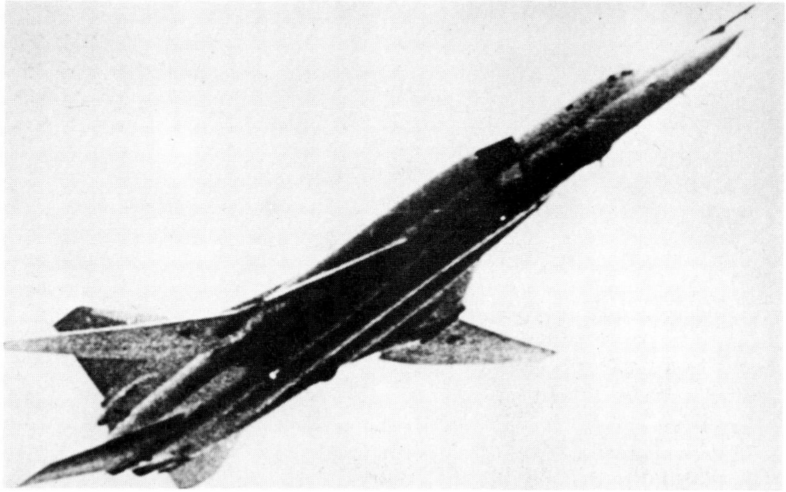

Backfire

Bear D (reconnaissance) French Navy, 1972

Badger A (tanker) French Navy, 1972

NAVAL AVIATION (*continued*)

Badger C (bomber) French Navy, 1972

Mail (Beriev BE 12) **ASW seaplane** 1972

May (Ilyushin I1 38) **ASW patrol** 1972

Bear D (Tupolev Tu 20) U.S. Navy, 1970

Badger (Tupolev Tu 16)

COMBAT AIRCRAFT

NATO code name and builder	Mission	Year put in serv.	Weight	Wing-span	Length	Engine	Speed max. cruising	Operational radius (1)	Armament	Fitted with	Remarks
Fixed-wing											
BACKFIRE	Reconnaissance, Ship attack	1975	130 t	34 m	38 m	2 Kuznetsov NK 144 turbo-jets of 20,000 kg thrust each	Mach 2.2 at 50,000 ft; Mach 1.3 at 3,000 ft	Supersonic: 3,485/2,250 km with/without refueling Subsonic: 6,300/5,320 km with/without refueling	4/23-mm cannon 9 tons of bombs (nuclear or conventional) 2 AS 4 Kitchen or AS 9	1 navigation bombing radar 1 optical bomb sight. 1 tail radar. IFF	The Backfire-B naval version has ECM and ECCM equipment.
BEAR D TU 20 (Tupolev)	Reconnaissance and electronic warfare	1955	165 t	50 m	44 m	4 turboprops 12,500 hp each 2 props with 4 blades, contrarotating	550 kts at 25,000 ft 440 kts	8,000 km without refueling 9,500 km with	6/23-mm cannon	Radomes and tail radar. Well equipped with electronic countermeasures.	An ASW Bear-F version is fitted with sonar buoys, depth charges and torpedoes.
BADGER A TU 16 (Tupolev)	Bombardment Ship attack	1953	75 t	33 m	35 m	2 turbojets RD 3 M 9,550-kg thrust each	540 kts at 22,000 ft 445 kts	3,000 km without refueling 4,500 km with	7/23-mm cannon 9 tons of bombs	1 navigation/bomb. radar. 1 tail radar. Some electronic warfare equipment.	A modified version is used for in-flight fueling.
BADGER C TU 16 (Tupolev)	Ship attack		75 t	33 m	35 m	2 turbojets RD 3 M 9,550-kg thrust each	540 kts at 22,000 ft 445 kts	3,000 km without refueling 4,500 km with	6/23-mm cannon, 1 AS 2 Kipper or 2 AS 6	1 navigation/bomb. radar. 1 Doppler radar. 1 tail radar.	
BADGER G TU 16 (Tupolev)	Ship attack		75 t	33 m	35 m	2 turbojets RD 3 M 9,550-kg thrust each	540 kts at 22,000 ft 455 kts	3,000 km without refueling 4,500 km with	8/23-mm cannon 2 AS 5 Kelt or 2 AS 6	1 navigation/bomb. radar. 1 Doppler radar. 1 tail radar	
BADGER E, D, E, F, J. TU 16 (Tupolev)	Reconnaissance and electronic warfare		75 t	33 m	35 m	2 turbojets RD 3 M 9,550-kg thrust each	540 kts at 22,000 ft 455 kts	3,000 km without refueling 4,500 km with	6-7/23-mm cannon	1 navigation/bomb. radar. Electronic warfare equipment. 1 tail radar. IFF.	Different versions for ELINT, photo reconnaissance, etc.
BLINDER TU 22 (Tupolev)	Reconnaissance	1963	84 t	24 m	38 m	2 turbojets. 20,000-kg thrust each, with 13,000-kg thrust without using after burners	Mach 1,6 at 36,000 ft	Supersonic F speeds: 1,000 km without refueling, 1,600 km with Subsonic speeds: 1,500 km without refueling, 2,000 km with	1/23-mm cannon	1 navigation radar. 1 tail radar. IFF. 7 cameras.	

COMBAT AIRCRAFT (*cont.*)

NATO code name and builder	Mission	Year put in serv.	Weight	Wing-span	Length	Engine	Speed max. cruising	Operational radius (1)	Armament	Fitted with	Remarks
FORGER YAK-36 (Yakolev)	Attack and reconnaissance	1976	10 t	7 m	15 m	1/7,650 kg thrust main engine; 2/2,520 kg lift engines	Mach 1.1 at 30,000 ft	125 nautical miles low-low-low; 240 n.m. low-high-low	16 or 32 rockets, 2/23-mm cannon, 2/AS-7 missiles	Ranging radar, passive warning system, Inertial navigation, Laser range finder	The two-seat version is Forger B.
FITTER C SU-20 (Sukhoi)	Ship attack	1976	18 t	14 m	18 m	1 turbojet 12,000 kg thrust	Mach 2.6 at 50,000 ft	220 nautical miles low-low-low; 435 n.m. high-low-high	32/57-mm rockets, 2/30-mm cannon, 727 kg bombs, nuclear or conventional	Ranging radar, tail warning radar	
MAY (Ilyushin)	ASW	1969	64 t	37 m	40 m	4 turboprops. 4,000 hp each	380 kts at 30,000 ft 315 kts	3,000 km endurance 12 hours	4 tons of bombs, depth charges, torpedoes	Radomes. MAD (2). Sonar buoys.	
MAIL BE 12 (Beriev) (Amphibian)	ASW	1967	38 t	27 m	25 m	2 turboprops. AI 20 K 4,000 hp each	310 kts at 30,000 ft 240 kts	1,300 km land version 1,000 km amphibian	Bombs, charges, mines	Radomes and MAD. Sonar buoys.	
Helicopters											
HAZE MI 14	ASW	1976	12 t	rotor dia. 21 m	24 m	2 Isotov TV 2 117A turboprops, 1,500 hp each	140 kts 122 kts	305 km endurance 2.5 hours	Depth bombs and torpedoes 2,000 kg total	Sonobuoys and dipping sonar	Based (initially) in the Baltic
HORMONE KA 25 (Kamov)	ASW	1967	7.3 t	rotor diam. 16 m	10 m	2 turboshafts. GTD 3 F 906 hp each	120 kts 105 kts	300 km endurance 1.5 to 2 h.	Depth charges or torpedoes 1,000 kg total	Sonar buoys and dipping sonar.	Carried on board Kiev, Moskva, Kara and Kresta classes. The B version is fitted with Video Data Link system.
HOUND MI 4 (Mil)	ASW	1953	7.2 t	rotor diam. 21 m	17 m	1 piston engine ASH 82 V 1,700 hp	97 kts 86 kts	230 km	1/12.7-mm machine gun, Depth charges, 4 × 16 depth charges, 57-mm rockets.	Sonar buoys and towed MAD	Land-based

(1) The operational radius is roughly 60% of the radius given by one-half of the range
(2) MAD = Magnetic Anomaly Detection

BALLISTIC-MISSILE SUBMARINES

NOTE: Nuclear-powered submarines are built or modified in the Severodvinsk (former Molotovsk) Naval Shipyard on the White Sea, near Arkhangelsk; at Komsomolsk-on-Amur (Far East); in the Gorki Shipyard on the Volga; and at the Admiralty Shipyard in Leningrad.

♦ *1 or more Delta-III class* — Bldr: Severodvinsk, 1976

Identical to Delta-II but equipped to launch 16 SS-N-18

♦ *5 Delta-II class* — Bldr: Severodvinsk, 1975-77

D: 9,700 tons surfaced, 11,300 submerged **Dim:** 152.5 × 12.0 × 8.7
S: 24 kts **Man:** 100 men
A: 16/SS-N-8 — 6/533-mm TT (18 torpedoes)
M: 1 nuclear reactor, steam turbines; 2 props (5-bladed)

♦ *13 Delta-I class* — Bldr: Severodvinsk and Komsomolsk/Amur, 1973-76

Delta-I class 1973

D: 8,100 tons surfaced, 9,700 submerged **Dim:** 137.0 × 12.0 × 8.7
S: 25 kts **Man:** 100 men
A: 12/SS-N-8 — 6/533-mm TT (18 torpedoes)
M: 1 nuclear reactor, steam turbines; 2 props (5-bladed)

♦ *34 Yankee class* — Bldr: Severodvinsk and Komsomolsk/Amur, 1967-75

D: 7,900 tons surfaced, 9,500 submerged **Dim:** 128.0 × 11.5 × 9.0
S: 27 kts **A:** 16/SS-N-6 — 6/533-mm TT (18 torpedoes or 36 mines)
M: 1 nuclear reactor, steam turbines; 2 props (5-bladed)
Man: 100 men

REMARK: SS-N-6 may be being replaced by SS-N-17.

♦ *1 Hotel-III class* — Bldr: Severodvinsk

D: 4,500 tons surfaced, 5,500 submerged **Dim:** 116.0 × 9.0 × 7.0
S: 20/25 kts **A:** 3/SS-N-8 — 6/533-mm TT — 2/400-mm TT
M: 1 nuclear reactor, steam turbines; 2 props (6-bladed) **Man:** 80 men

REMARK: Used as trial ship for SS-N-8 missiles.

Yankee class U.S. Navy, 1971

Yankee class U.S. Navy

BALLISTIC MISSILE SUBMARINES (*continued*)

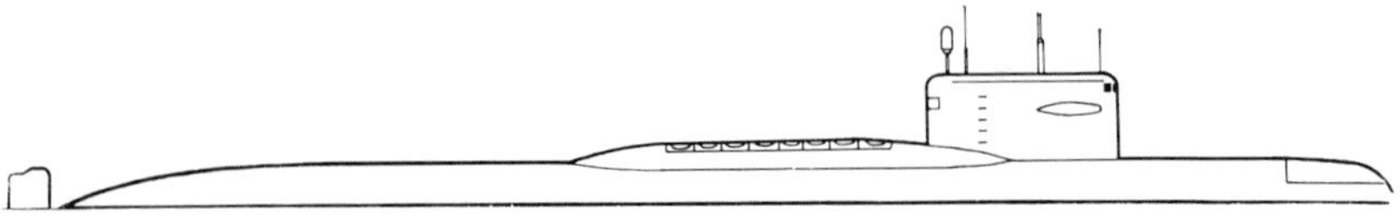

♦ *8 Hotel-II class* — Bldr: Severodvinsk and Komsomolsk/Amur, 1960-63

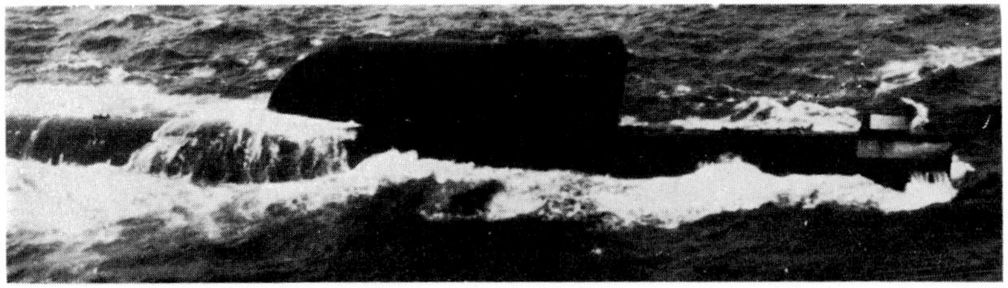

Hotel-II class 1972

Hotel-II class 1972

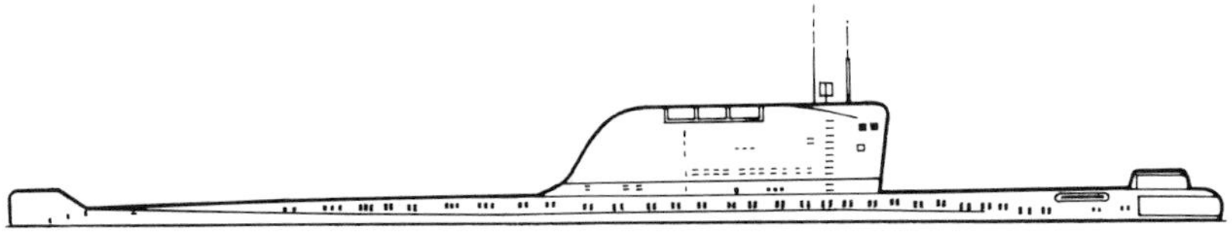

D: 4,500 tons surfaced, 5,500 submerged **Dim:** 116.0 × 9.0 × 7.0
S: 20/23 kts **A:** 3/SS-N-5 — 6/533-mm TT — 2/400-mm TT
M: 1 nuclear reactor, steam turbines; 2 props (6-bladed)

♦ *13 Golf II class* — Bldr: Severodvinsk, 1958-61

Golf II class 1976

Golf II class 1976

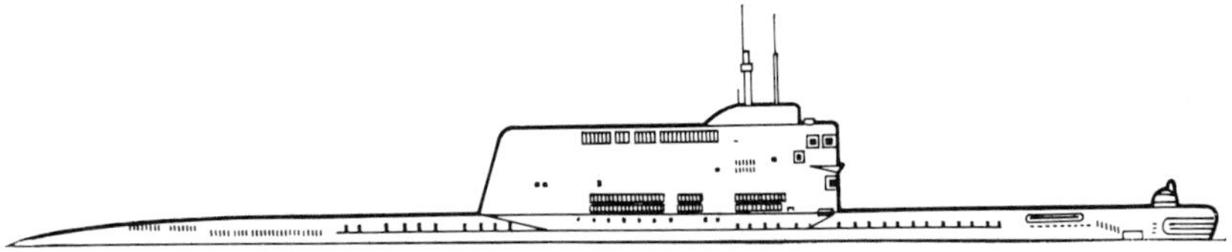

D: 2,300 tons surfaced, 2,700 submerged **Dim:** 100.0 × 8.50 × 6.60
A: 3/SS-N-5 — 10/533-mm TT (6 fwd, 4 aft)
S: 12 kts (submerged) **Range:** 9,000/5 **Endurance:** 70 days
M: Diesels and electric motors; 3 props **Man:** 75 men

BALLISTIC MISSILE SUBMARINES (*continued*)

♦ *8 Golf-I class* — Bldr: Severodvinsk, 1958–61

Same characteristics as the Golf-II class but, in place of the 3/SS-N-5, the armament is 3/SS-N-4, which can only be surface-fired.

ATTACK SUBMARINES

♦ *2 Papa class* — Bldr: ?

D: 7,000 tons (submerged) **Dim:** 109.0 × 11.5 × 7.6
S: 28 kts **Man:** 85 men
A: 10/SS-N-7 — 8/533-mm TT
M: 1 reactor, steam turbines; 2 props (5-bladed)

REMARK: Possible prototypes for submerged-launch cruise-missile submarines of the future

♦ *3 Charlie-II class* — Bldr: ?

D: 4,300 tons surfaced, 5,100 submerged **Dim:** 103.0 × 10.0 × 8.0
S: 26 kts **Man:** 80 men
A: 8/SS-N-7 — 6/533-mm TT — SS-N-15
M: 1 reactor, steam turbines; 1 prop (5-bladed)

♦ *13 Charlie-I class* — Bldr: Gorki, 1968–75

D: 4,000 tons surfaced, 4,900 submerged **Dim:** 94.0 × 10.0 × 8.0
S: 27 kts **Man:** 80 men **A:** 8/SS-N-7 — 6/533-mm TT
M: 1 reactor; steam turbines; 1 prop (5-bladed)

Charlie I class U.S. Navy, 1971

Charlie I class U.S. Navy, 1970

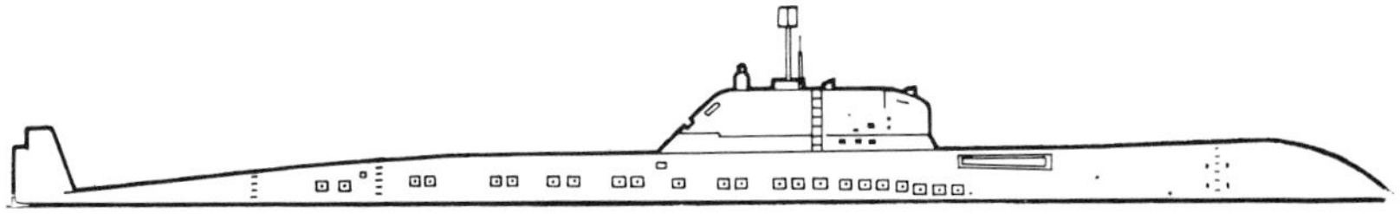

Charlie-I class U.S. Navy, 1974

ATTACK SUBMARINES *(continued)*

Victor-I class

U.S. Navy, 1974

Foxtrot class

French Navy, 1974

ATTACK SUBMARINES (*continued*)

♦ *28 Echo-II class* — Bldr: Severodvinsk and Komsomolsk/Amur, 1960-68

Echo-II class U.S. Navy

Echo-II class 1968

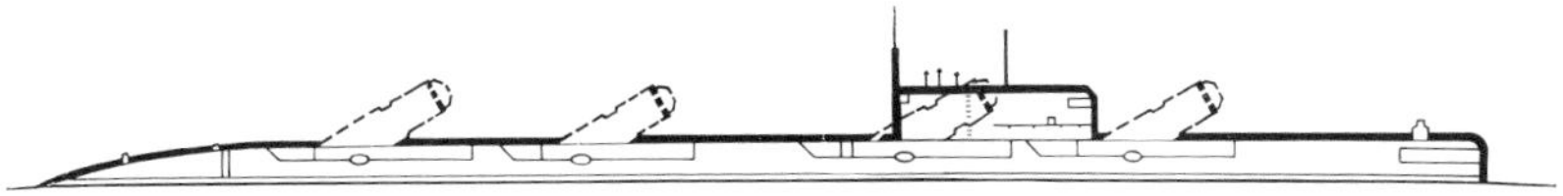

D: 4,800 tons surfaced, 5,800 submerged **Dim:** 120.0 × 9.0 × 7.5
S: 20/23 kts **A:** 8/SS-N-3 — 8/533-mm TT (fwd) — 4/400-mm TT (aft)
M: 1 nuclear reactor, steam turbines; 2 props (4-bladed) **Man:** 80-85 men

♦ *1 Alfa class* — Bldr: Sudomekh, Leningrad, 1972

Alfa class

D: 3,900 tons surfaced, 4,250 submerged **Dim:** 80 × 10 × . . .
S: 30 kts **A:** Torpedoes
M: 1 nuclear reactor, steam turbines **Man:** 75 men

REMARK: Probably has advanced automation and is a prototype.

♦ *5 Victor-II class* — Bldr: Leningrad

D: 4,500 tons surfaced, 5,700 submerged **Dim:** 100.0 × 10.0 × 7.0
S: 28 kts **A:** 8/533-mm TT — SS-N-15
M: 1 nuclear reactor, steam turbines; 1 prop (5-bladed) **Man:** 80 men

♦ *16 Victor-I class* — Bldr: Leningrad, 1967-74

D: 4,300 tons surfaced, 5,100 submerged **Dim:** 93.0 × 10.0 × 7.0
S: 30 kts **A:** 8/533-mm TT — SS-N-15
M: 1 nuclear reactor, steam turbines; 1 prop for slow cruising, plus 2 props for normal speeds

Victor-I class U.S. Navy, 1975

ATTACK SUBMARINES *(continued)*

Sail of a Victor I U.S. Navy

D: 4,000 tons surfaced, 4,800 submerged **Dim:** 109.0 × 9.0 × 7.7
S: 30 kts **Man:** 75-80 men
A: 8/533-mm TT (fwd) — 4/400-mm TT (aft) — 32 torpedoes or mines
M: 1 nuclear reactor, steam turbines; 2 props (4 or 6 blades)

♦ *5 Echo class* — Bldr: . . ., 1960-68

Echo class U.S. Navy

D: 4,600 tons surfaced, 5,600 submerged **Dim:** 114.0 × 9.0 × 7.5
S: 25/20 kts **A:** 6/533-mm TT (fwd) — 4/400-mm TT (aft)
M: 1 nuclear reactor, steam turbines; 2 props (5-bladed) **Man:** 75 men

REMARK: Formerly, cruise-missile submarines that carried 6/SS-N-3.

♦ *14 November class* — Bldr: Severodvinsk, 1959-64

November class U.S. Navy

♦ *16 Juliett class* — Bldr: Leningrad, 1961-68

Juliett class French Navy, 1970

Juliett class French Navy, 1972

D: 2,800 tons surfaced, 3,400 submerged **Dim:** 87.0 × 10.0 × 7.0
S: . . ./14 kts **Range:** 9,000/7 **Man:** 80 men
A: 4/SS-N-3 — 6/533 mm TT (fwd) — 4/400-mm TT (aft)
M: Diesels and electric motors; 2 props
Endurance: 70 days

♦ *5 Whiskey Long Bin class* — Bldr: Leningrad, 1961-63 (converted)

D: 1,200 tons surfaced, 1,500 submerged **Dim:** 83.0 × 6.1 × 5.0
S: 13.5/8 kts **Range:** 6,000/5 **Man:** 60-65 men
A: 4/SS-N-3 — 4/533-mm TT
M: Diesels and electric motors; 2 props
Endurance: 40 days

ATTACK SUBMARINES (*continued*)

Whiskey Long Bin class 1968

REMARKS: Modified Whiskey class. Hull has been lengthened. Four fixed missile launchers

NOTE: The Whiskey Twin Cylinder class have been stricken.

♦ *4 Tango class* — Bldr: . . .

Tango class French Navy, 1976

Tango class French Navy, 1976

D:	1,700 tons surfaced, 2,200 submerged	**Dim:**	90.0 × 7.5 × . . .
S:	. . .	**Man:**	72 men
A:	. . ./533-mm TT		
M:	Diesels and electric motors		

♦ *4 Bravo class* — Bldr: . . . , 1970-72

D:	2,400 tons surfaced, 2,900 submerged	**Dim:**	70.0 × 9.7 × . . .
S:	. . .	**Man:**	65 men
A:	. . .		
M:	Diesels and electric motors; 1 prop; 4,000 hp		

REMARK: Training and target submarines for use with surface ASW forces.

♦ *56-58 Foxtrot class* — Bldr: Leningrad, 1959-7. . .

Foxtrot class French Navy, 1976

Foxtrot class French Navy, 1973

ATTACK SUBMARINES *(continued)*

A Foxtrot alongside a Don-class tender 1974

D: 1,950 tons surfaced, 2,400 submerged **Dim:** 96.0 × 7.5 × 6.0
S: 18/16 kts **Endurance:** 70 days **Range:** 9,000/7
A: 10/533-mm TT (6 fwd, 4 aft) — 22 torpedoes or 44 mines
M: Diesels and electric motors; 3 props **Man:** 8 officers, 70 men

REMARKS: These submarines seem to be strongly built. Eight have been transferred to the Indian Navy and one to Libya, with additional units apparently to follow.

♦ *15 Zulu-IV class* — Bldr: Various, 1952-57

D: 2,000 tons surfaced, 2,300 submerged **Dim:** 90.0 × 7.5 × 6.0
S: 18/16 kts **Endurance:** 70 days **Range:** 12,000/5

Sail of a Foxtrot French Navy

Zulu-IV class French Navy, 1969

ATTACK SUBMARINES *(continued)*

Zulu-IV class French Navy, 1974

A: 10/533-mm TT (6 fwd, 4 aft) — 22 torpedoes or 44 mines
M: Diesels and electric motors; 3 props (?); 10,000/3,500 hp

REMARK: Nine of this class have been stricken.

♦ *10 Romeo class* — Bldr: Leningrad, 1960

Romeo class 1967

D: 1,400 tons surfaced, 1,800 submerged **Dim:** 76.0 × 7.0 × 5.40
S: 17/15 kts **Endurance:** 45 days **Range:** 7,000/5
A: 8/533-mm TT (6 fwd, 2 aft) — 18 torpedoes or 36 mines
M: Diesels and electric motors; 2 props; 4,000/2,500 hp **Man:** 60 men

♦ *34 Whiskey class* — Bldr: Various, 1950-57

D: 1,050 tons surfaced, 1,350 submerged **Dim:** 76.0 × 6.3 × 4.8
S: 17/16 kts **Endurance:** 40/45 days **Man:** 60 men
A: 6/533-mm TT (4 fwd, 2 aft) — 14 torpedoes or 28 mines
M: Diesels and electric motors; 2 props; 4,000/2,500 hp

REMARKS: Strong, uncomplicated boats, built in prefabricated sections, that have proven quite satisfactory. Twelve were converted to cruise-missile boats. Some have been transferred to Egypt, Poland, Albania, Communist China, and Indonesia. Four were modified as radar picket submarines. Most of the Whiskey class are now in reserve; the others are used for training. Many of the more than 200 built have been stricken.

Whiskey class

♦ *4 Whiskey Canvas Bag class* — radar picket conversions

Whiskey Canvas Bag radar picket U.S. Navy, 1965

♦ *4 Quebec class* — Bldr: Leningrad, 1950-57

Quebec class

D: 460 tons surfaced, 540 submerged **Dim:** 57.0 × 5.1 × 3.8
S: 18/16 kts **Endurance:** 30 days
A: 4/533-mm TT (fwd) — 8 torpedoes or 16 mines **Range:** 4,500/6
Man: 30 men
M: Diesels and electric motors: 2 props; 3,000/2,500 hp

REMARKS: Especially designed for Baltic and Black Sea operations. Most now stricken.

HELICOPTER CRUISERS

♦ *2 Moskva class*

	Bldr	Laid down	L	In serv.
MOSKVA	Nikolaev (Black Sea)	1963	1965	7-67
LENINGRAD	Nikolaev (Black Sea)	1964	1966	1968

Leningrad French Navy, 1974

D: 20,000 tons (fl) **Dim:** 190 × 34 (flight deck) (26 wl) × 7.6
S: 30 kts **Man:** 850 men
A: 4/SA-N-3 (II × 2) with 44 Goblet missiles — 2/SUW-N-1 — 4/57-mm AA (II × 2) — 2 MBU 2500A rocket launchers — 10/533-mm TT (V × 2) (removed from *Moskva*) — 16 Hormone-A helicopters

Electron Equipt: Radars: 3 Don-2, 1 Top Sail, 1 Head Net-C, 2 Head Lights, 2 Muff Cob
Sonars: 1 low-frequency hull-mounted, 1 medium-frequency towed

M: GT; 2 props; 100,000 hp **Range:** 2,500/30, 7,000/15

REMARKS: (Appears to be based on the French *Jeanne d'Arc.*) Three elevators, two on the flight deck and one forward of and interior to the superstructure. The *Moskva* was modified for a time to permit the testing of VTOL Yak-36 aircraft, which were to go aboard the *Kiev* carriers. Notice the ASW SUW-N-1 system just aft of the bow, the two SA-N-3 mounts used with Head Lights guidance radars, and the three-dimensional Top Sail radar.

Moskva French Navy, 1964

Hormone helicopter U.S. Navy, 1971

HELICOPTER CRUISERS *(continued)*

Leningrad French Navy, 1974

HELICOPTER CRUISERS (*continued*)

Flight deck of Hormone A helicopters aboard Moskva Tass

Ochakov French Navy, 1977

GUIDED MISSILE CRUISERS

♦ *5 Kara class*

	Bldr	Laid down	L	In serv.
NIKOLAEV	Nikolaev	1969	1971	1973
OCHAKOV	Nikolaev	1970	1972	1975
KERCH	Nikolaev	1971	1973	1976
AZOV	Nikolaev	1972	1974	. . .
PETROPAVLOVSK	Nikolaev	1973	1975	. . .

D: 9,500–10,000 tons (fl) **S:** 30 kts **Dim:** 170.0 × 18.8 × 7.0
A: 8/SS-N-14 (IV × 2) with 8 missiles — 4/SA-N-3 (II × 2) with 44 Goblet missiles — 2/SA-N-4 with 36 missiles — 4/76-mm DP (II × 2) — 4 Gatling-type rapid-fire guns — 2/MBU 2500A rocket launchers — 2 MBU 4500A rocket launchers — 10/533-mm TT (V × 2) — 1 Hormone-A helicopter
Electron Equipt: Radars: 2 Don Kay, 2 Owl Screech, 1 Top Sail, 1 Head Net-C, 2 Head Lights, 2 Pop Groups, 2 Bass Tilt
Sonars: 1 low-frequency hull-mounted, 1 medium-frequency towed — ECM: numerous radomes and 2 chaff launchers
M: Gas turbines; 2 props; 120,000 hp **Man:** 550 men
Range: 2,000/30, 8,000/15

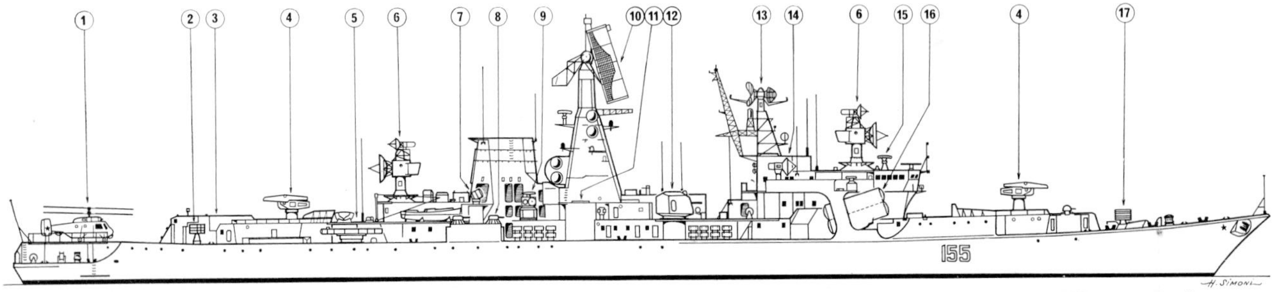

1: Hormone — 2: MBU 4500A — 3: helicopter hangar — 4: SA-N-3 — 5: TT (V × 1) — 6: Head Lights — 7: Bass Tilt — 8: Gatling-type guns — 9: Pop Group — 10: Top Sail — 11: SA-N-4 — 12: 76-mm guns (II × 1) — 12: Head Net C — 14: Owl Screech — 15: Don Kay — 16: SS-N-14 — 17: MBU 2500A.

GUIDED MISSILE CRUISERS (*continued*)

Ochakov (details) French Navy, 1977

Ochakov (details) French Navy, 1977

Nikolaev French Navy, 1974

GUIDED MISSILE CRUISERS (*continued*)

Nikolaev

♦ *10 Kresta-II class* — Bldr: Zhdanov, Leningrad

	In serv.
KRONSTADT	1970
ADMIRAL ISAKOV	1971
ADMIRAL NAKHIMOV	1972
ADMIRAL MAKAROV	1973
MARSHAL VOROSHILOV	1973
ADMIRAL OKTYABRSKY	1974
ADMIRAL ISACHENKOV	1975
MARSHAL TIMOSHENKO	1976
VASILY CHAPAEV	1977
ADMIRAL YUMASHEV	1978

D: 7,600 tons (fl) **S:** 34 kts **Dim:** 158.0 × 17.0 × 5.5 (avg)

A: 8/SS-N-14 (IV × 2) with 8 missiles — 4/SA-N-3 (II × 2) with 44 Goblet missiles — 4/57-mm AA (II × 2) — 2/MBU 2500A rocket launchers — 2/MBU 4500A rocket launchers — 10/533-mm TT (V × 2) — 4 Gatling-type 23-mm rapid-fire guns — 1 Hormone-A or -B helicopter

Electron Equipt: Radars: 2 Don Kay, 1 Top Sail, 1 Head Net-C, 2 Head Lights, 2 Muff Cob, 2 Bass Tilt

Sonars: 1 medium-frequency hull-mounted

Range: 1,500/32, 7,000/14

M: GT; 4 boilers; 2 props; 100,000 hp

Man: 380 men

Fuel: 1,100 tons

Remarks: Early units do not have Bass Tilt. Late units have larger bridge superstructure.

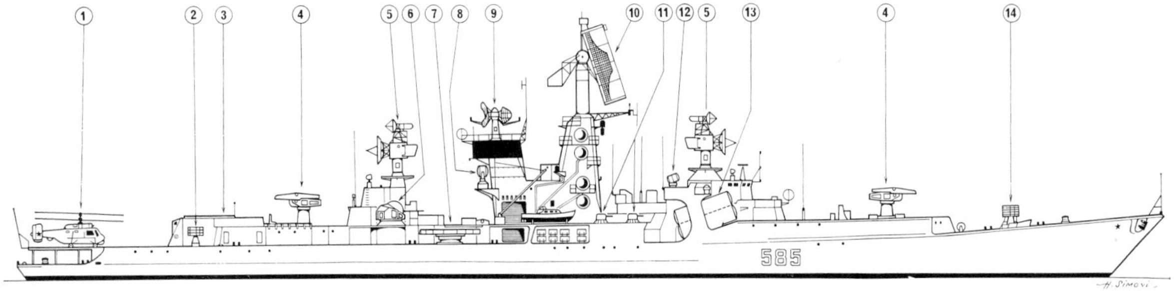

1: Hormone — 2: MBU 4500A — 3: helicopter hangar — 4: SA-N-3 — 5: Head Lights — 6: 57-mm AA (II × 1) — 7: TT (V × 1) — 8: Muff Cob — 9: Head Net-C — 10: Top Sail — 11: Gatling-type guns — 12: Bass Tilt — 13: SS-N-14 — 14: MBU 2500A.

GUIDED MISSILE CRUISERS (*continued*)

Vasily Chapaev 1977

Marshal Voroshilov French Navy, 1974

Marshal Voroshilov French Navy, 1974

GUIDED MISSILE CRUISERS (*continued*)

Kronstadt — Kresta-II class French Navy, 1970

Admiral Oktyabrsky — Kresta-II class French Navy, 1974

GUIDED MISSILE CRUISERS *(continued)*

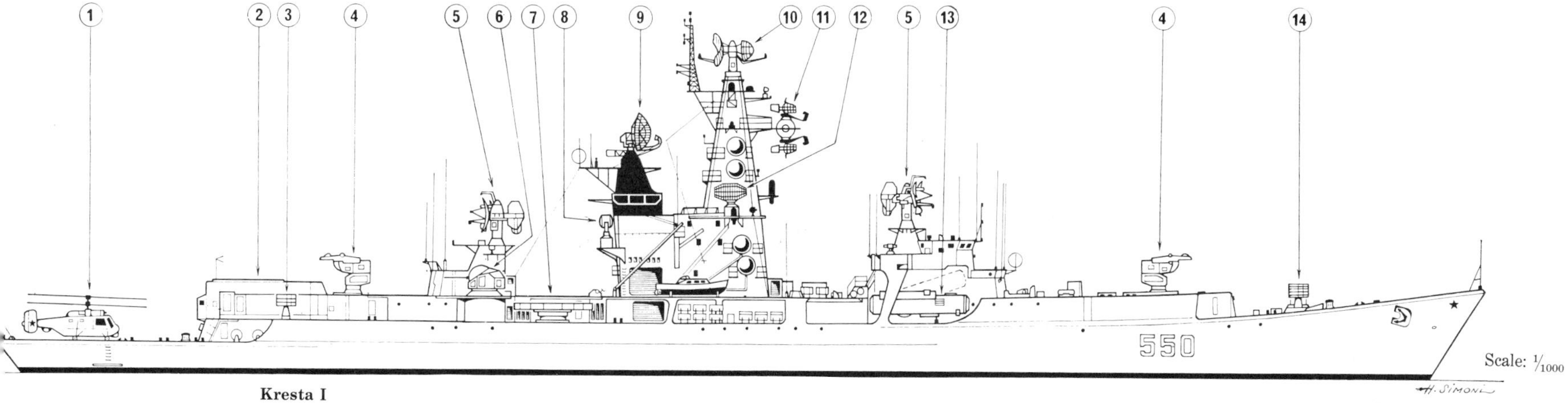

Kresta I

1: Hormone — 2: helicopter hangar — 3: MBU 4500A — 4: SA-N-1 — 5: Peel Group — 6: 57-mm AA (II × 2) — 7: TT (V × 2) — 8: Muff Cob — 9: Big Net — 10: Head Net-C — 11: Scoop Pair — 12: Plinth Net — 13: SS-N-3 — 14: MBU 2500A.

♦ 4 *Kresta-I class* — Bldr: Zhdanov, Leningrad — In serv. 1967-68

VITSE-ADMIRAL DROZD
SEVASTOPOL
ADMIRAL ZOZULYA
VLADIVOSTOK

D: 7,500 tons (fl) **S:** 34 kts **Dim:** 155.0 × 17.0 × 5.50 (avg)

A: 4/SS-N-3 (II × 2) with 4 Shaddock missiles — 4/SA-N-1 (II × 2) with 44 Goa missiles — 4/57-mm AA (II × 2) — *Vitse-Admiral Drozd:* 4/23-mm Gatling AA guns — 2/MBU 2500A rocket launchers — 2/MBU 4500A rocket launchers — 10/533-mm TT (V × 2) — 1 Hormone-A helicopter

Electron Equipt: Radars: 2 Don, 1 Big Net, 1 Head Net-C, 2 Plinth Net, 1 Scoop Pair, 2 Peel Group, 2 Muff Cob, *Vitse-Admiral Drozd:* 2 Bass Tilt
Sonar: 1 medium-frequency hull-mounted

M: GT; 4 boilers; 2 props; 10,000 hp

Range: 1,600/34, 7,000/14 **Man:** 380 men

REMARKS: Based on the Kynda class but has better mixture of weapons. Superstructure is built around the stack. The surface-to-surface launchers, fitted on each side of the superstructure, forward under the bridge wings, can be elevated, not trained. No Shaddock missile reloads. Installation of Gatling guns abaft the Shaddock launchers and construction of a new deckhouse between the Gatling guns has altered the silhouette of the *Vitse-Admiral Drozd* (see photos).

Vitse-Admiral Drozd French Navy, 1976

GUIDED MISSILE CRUISERS (*continued*)

Vitse-Admiral Drozd — Kresta-I class

French Navy, 1976

Admiral Zozulya — Kresta-I class

French Navy, 1968

GUIDED MISSILE CRUISERS (*continued*)

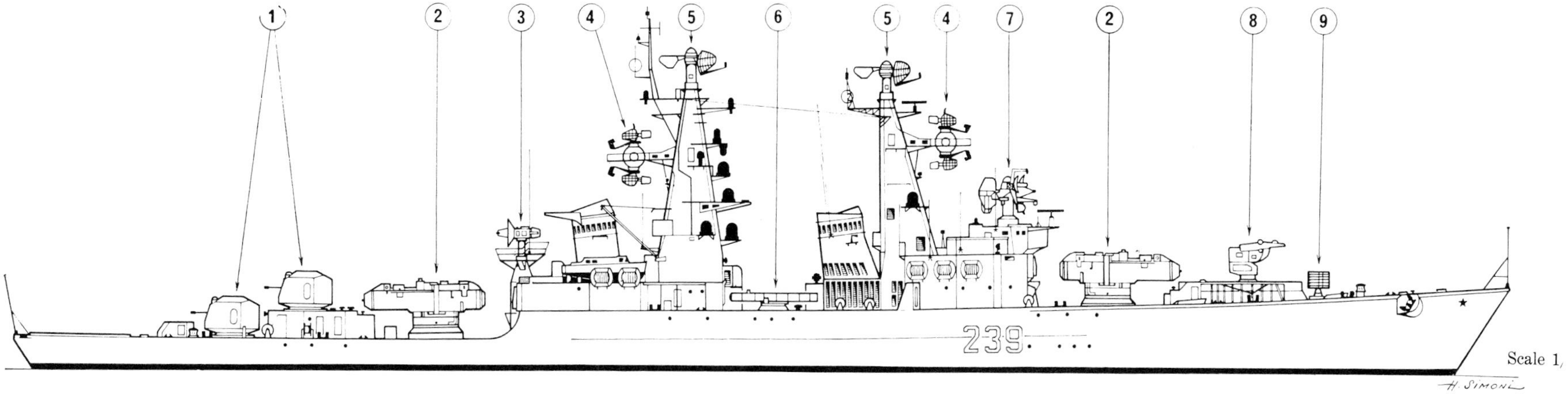

1: 76-mm DP (II × 1) — 2: SS-N-3 — 3: Owl Screech — 4: Scoop Pair — 5: Head Net-A — 6: TT (III × 2) — 7: Peel Group — 8: SA-N-1 — 9: MBU 2500A

♦ *4 Kynda class*

	Bldr	Laid down	L	In serv.
ADMIRAL FOKIN	Zhdanov (Leningrad)	1957	1959	1962
ADMIRAL GOLOVKO	Zhdanov (Leningrad)	1957	1959	1962
GROZNY	Zhdanov (Leningrad)	. . .	. . .	8-62
VARYAG	Zhdanov (Leningrad)	. . .	. . .	4-61

D: 5,700 tons (fl) **S:** 34 kts **Dim:** 142.0 × 16.0 × 5.0 (avg)

A: 8/SS-N-3 (IV × 2) with 16 Shaddock missiles — 2/SA-N-1 (II × 1) with 22 Goa missiles — 4/76-mm AA (II × 2) — 2/MBU 2500A rocket launchers — 6/533-mm TT (III × 2)

Electron Equipt: Radars: 2 Don, 2 Head Net, 2 Scoop Pair, 1 Peel Group, 1 Owl Screech *Grozny, Varyag:* 1 Plinth Net

Sonar: 1 high-frequency hull-mounted

M: GT; 2 props; 100,000 hp **Range:** 1,1000/32, 6,800/15 **Man:** 375 men

REMARKS: The eight Shaddock missiles are loaded in the tubes. Reloading the launchers from the handling rooms requires some time. *Varyag* now has 1 Head Net-A, one Head Net-C, and 2 Plinth Net; *Grozny* received Plinth Net around 1973.

Grozny French Navy, 1973

GUIDED MISSILE CRUISERS *(continued)*

Grozny J.C. Bellonne, 1973

Grozny J.C. Bellonne, 1973

GUIDED MISSILE CRUISERS *(continued)*

♦ *1 Dzerzhinsky class*

DZERZHINSKY — Bldr: Nikolaev, 1954

For characteristics of hull and machinery, see *Sverdlov* class.

A: 2/SA-N-2 (II × 1), with 30 Guideline missiles — 9/152-mm guns — 12/100-mm (II × 6) — 16/37-mm AA (II × 8)

Electron Equipt: Radars: 1 Neptune, 1 Low Sieve, 1 Big Net, 1 Slim Net, 1 Fan Song-E, 1 Top Bow, 2 Sun Visor, 6 Egg Cup

REMARKS: In 1961 the *Dzerzhinsky* completed refit with an SA-N-2 system (twin launcher aft) replacing her No. 3 152-mm turret. High Lune height-finder radar removed 1976.

Dzerzhinsky French Navy, 1976

COMMAND CRUISERS

♦ *2 modified Sverdlov class*

	Bldr	In serv. after refit
ADMIRAL SENYAVIN	Komsomolsk/Amur	1972
ZHDANOV	Nikolaev	1972

For characteristics of hull and machinery, see *Sverdlov* class.

A: 6 or 9/152-mm (III × 2 or 3) — 12/100-mm DP (II × 6) — 2/SA-N-4 (II × 1) — 16/37-mm AA — 8 or 16/30-mm AA (II × 4 or 8)

Electron Equipt: Radars: 2 Top Bow, 1 Top Trough, 2 Sun Visor, 6 Egg Cup, *Zhdanov:* 2 Drum Tilt, *Admiral Senyavin:* 4 Drum Tilt, 1 Pop Group

REMARKS: Excellent long-range communications, including a Vee Cone antenna, which can be seen on the after tripod mast. The 37-mm guns are divided on each side of the forward stack and on the after deckhouse as well on the *Admiral Senyavin.* The two after turrets on the *Admiral Senyavin* have been removed and replaced by a helicopter hangar and platform for at least two Hormone-A or -B.

Admiral Senyavin 1973

Zhdanov French Navy, 1973

♦ *9 Sverdlov class*

ADMIRAL LAZAREV
ADMIRAL USHAKOV
ALEXANDER NEVSKY (6-51)
ALEXANDER SOVOROV
DMITRI POZHARSKY
MIKHAIL KUTUZOV (5-56)
MURMANSK
OKTYABRSKAYA REVOLYUTSIYA (1958)
SVERDLOV (7-50)

Bldrs: Baltiski (Leningrad), Nikolaev (Black Sea), and Sevorodvinsk (Arctic)

D: 20,000 tons (fl) **Dim:** 210.00 (199.95 pp) × 21.60 × 8.50
S: 33/32 kts **Range:** 2,200/33, 8,400/15
A: 12/152-mm (III × 4) — 12/100-mm DP (II × 6) — 32/37-mm AA (II × 16) — *Oktyabrskaya Revolyutsiya:* also 16/30-mm AA (II × 8) — mines
Man: 70 officers, 940 men

COMMAND CRUISERS *(continued)*

Admiral Ushakov French Navy, 1972

Electron Equipt: Radars: 1 Neptune or Don, 1 Low Sieve or High Sieve, 1 Big Net on certain ships, 1 Knife Rest on others, 1 Top Trough, 1 Slim Net, 2 Top Bow, 2 Sun Visor, 8 Egg Cup

Armor: 152-mm turret: 76/100 Deck: 25/50 and 50/75 100-mm gun shields: 25

Fuel: 4,000 tons

M: GT; 2 props; 6 boilers; 100,000 hp

REMARKS: Based on the *Chapaev* class. Fourteen put in service from 1952 to 1958; others were laid down but construction was suspended in 1957 and canceled in 1960. Slight differences in profile, the merging of the forward stack with the bridge structure being noticeable. The *Admiral Nakhimov* was scrapped in 1961. In 1962 the *Ordzhonikidze* was transferred to Indonesia and has since been taken off the active list. The *Dzerzhinsky* was transformed into a guided-missile cruiser by 1961, and two others, the *Zhdanov* and *Admiral Senyavin*, completed conversion to command cruisers in 1972. In 1977, the *Oktyabrskaya Revolyutsiya* completed overhaul with eight twin 30-mm AA and four Drum Tilt radars added, and the Egg Cup radars removed from her 100-mm mounts; also her bridge was enlarged. The *Sverdlov* has 2 Don, 1 Top Trough, and no Egg Cup on the 100-mm turrets.

Alexandr Sovorov U.S. Navy, 1970

Oktyabrskaya Revolyutsiya 1977

COMMAND CRUISERS (*continued*)

Zheleznyakov (similar to Komsomolets) 1975

♦ *1 Chapaev class*

	Bldr	Laid down	L	In serv.
KOMSOMOLETS (ex-*Chlakov*)	Baltiski (Leningrad)	1939	1948	1950

D: 15,000 tons (fl) **S:** 34 kts **Dim:** 201.0 × 18.9 × 7.3 (mean)
A: 12/152-mm (III × 4) — 8/100-mm DP (II × 4) — 24/37-mm AA (II × 2) — 140 mines
Electron Equipt: Radars: 1 Neptune, 1 Low Sieve, 1 Slim Net, 1 Knife Rest, 1 Top Bow, 2 Sun Visor, 6 Egg Cup
M: GT; 2 props; 90,000 hp **Range:** 1,200/34, 5,400/15

REMARKS: Training ship. Survivor of a class of seven; sister *Zheleznyakov* discarded 1976. Old cruiser *Kirov* discarded 1975.

GUIDED MISSILE DESTROYERS

♦ *4 Krivak-II class*, 1976–77

REZKY, REZVY, RAZITELNY, GROZYASHCHY

♦ *14 Krivak-I class*, 1970-7 . . .

BDITEL'NY, BODRY, DEYATELNY, DOBLESTNY, DOSTOINY, DRUZHNY, LENINGRADSKY KOMSOMOLETS, RAZUMNY, RAZYASHY, RETIVY, SIL'NY, STOROZHEVOI, SVIREPY, ZHARKY

Bldrs: Kaliningrad, Kamysch-Burun, and Zhdanov (Leningrad)

D: 3,600 tons (fl) **S:** 30 kts **Dim:** 122.0 × 14.3 × 5.0 (avg)
A: 4/SS-N-14 (IV × 1) and 4 missiles — 4/SA-N-4 (II × 2) — 4/76-mm DP (II × 2) Krivak-II: 2/85-mm DP (I × 2) vice 76-mm — 2/MBU 2500A rocket launchers — 8/533-mm TT (IV × 2) — mines
Electron Equipt: Radars: 1 Don, 1 Don Kay, 1 Head Net-C, 2 Eye Bowl, 2 Pop Group, 1 Owl Screech
Sonars: 1 hull-mounted, 1 medium-frequency towed
M: Gas turbines; 2 props; 50,000 hp **Range:** 4,500/18
Man: 250 men

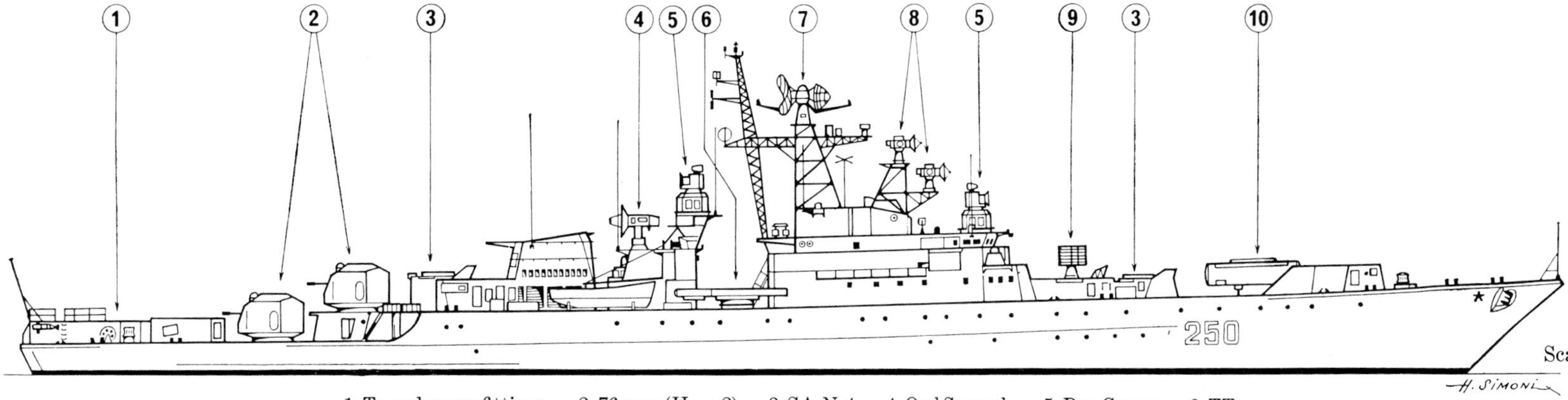

Scale 1/1000

1: Towed sonar fittings — 2: 76-mm (II × 2) — 3: SA-N-4 — 4: Owl Screech — 5: Pop Group — 6: TT (IV × 2) — 7: Head Net-C — 8: Eye Bowl — 9: MBU 2500A — 10: SS-N-14.

GUIDED MISSILE DESTROYERS *(continued)*

REMARKS: Construction rate is three per year. Have four 16-tubed chaff rocket launchers. In 1976, the first of a new version, designated Krivak-II, appeared with the hull lengthened by three meters, two single-barreled guns, a new fire-control radar for them, and an enlarged housing over the towed sonar equipment.

Rezky — Krivak-II class 1976

Doblestny — Krivak-I class 1974

Razyashy — Krivak-I class French Navy, 1976

Bditel'ny — Krivak-I class 1972

GUIDED MISSILE DESTROYERS *(continued)*

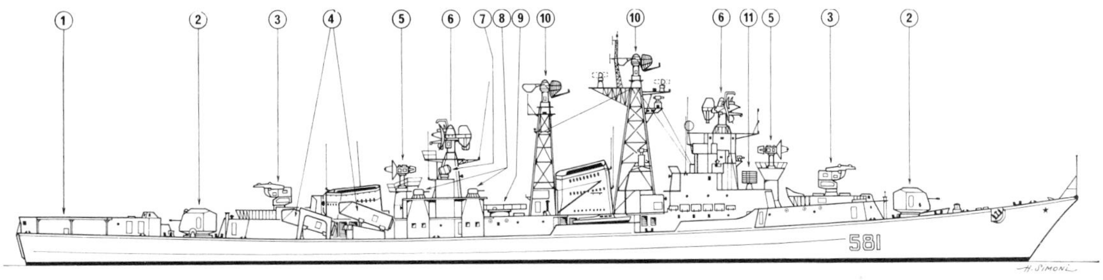

Scale 1/1000

1: Towed sonar fittings — 2: 76-mm (II × 2) — 3: SA-N-1 — 4: SS-N-11 — 5: Owl Screech — 6: Peel Group — 7: Bass Tilt — 8: Gatling guns — 9: TT (V × 1) — 10: Head Net-A — 11: MBU 2500A

♦ *5 modified Kashin class*

OGNEVOI (Zhdanov), **SLAVNY** (Zhdanov), **SDERZHANNY, SMELY, SMYSHLENNY** (Black Sea)

D: 4,900 tons (fl) **S:** 35 kts **Dim:** 146.0 × 15.8 × 6.0

A: 4/SS-N-11 (I × 4) — 4/SA-N-1 (II × 2) with 44 Goa missiles — 4/76-mm DP (II × 2) — 4/23-mm Gatling guns — 5/533-mm TT (V × 1) — 2 MBU 2500A rocket launchers — helicopter deck

Electron Equipt: Radars: 2 Don Kay, 2 Head Net-A or 1 Head Net-C and 1 Big Net, 2 Peel Group, 2 Owl Screech, 2 Bass Tilt
Sonars: 1 towed, 1 medium-frequency hull-mounted

M: See *Kashin* class

REMARKS: Conversions completed commencing in 1973. Additional units may be similarly altered later.

Ognevoi 1974

Sderzhanny French Navy, 1975

GUIDED MISSILE DESTROYERS (*continued*)

Kashin class

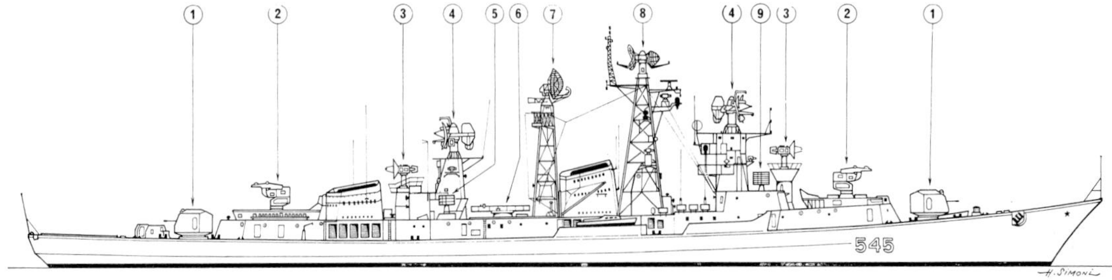

Scale: $^1/_{1000}$

1: 76-mm (II × 2) — 2: SA-N-1 — 3: Owl Screech — 4: Peel Group — 5: MBU 4500A — 6: TT (V × 1) — 7: Big Net — 8: Head Net-C — 9: MBU 2500A

♦ *14 Kashin class*

OBRAZTSOVY, ODARENNY, STEREGUSHCHY

Bldr: Zhdanov, Leningrad, 1963-66

KOMSOMOLETS UKRAINY, KRASNY KAVKAZ, KRASNY KRYM, PROVORNY, RESHITELNY, SKORY, SMETLIVY, SOOBRAZITELNY, SPOSOBNY, STROYNY, STROGY

Bldr: Nikolaev, 1963-72

D: 4,750 tons (fl) **S:** 35/36 kts **Dim:** 144.0 × 15.8 × 5.8 (mean)

A: 4/SA-N-1 (II × 2) and 44 Goa missiles — 4/76-mm DP (II × 2) — 2/MBU 2500A rocket launchers — 2/MBU 4500A rocket launchers — 5/533-mm TT (V × 1) — mines

Electron Equipt: Radars: 2 Don, 2 Head Net-A or 1 Head Net-C and 1 Big Net, 2 Peel Group, 2 Owl Screech

Sonar: 1 high-frequency hull-mounted

M: 4 gas turbines; 2 props; 94,000 hp **Range:** 900/35, 4,500/18

Man: 280 men

REMARKS: The *Otvazhny* of the same class was sunk 31-8-74 following an explosion. Five others have been converted to Modified Kashin configuration. All have a helicopter pad on the fantail.

Steregushchy 1973

Reshitelny

Komsomolets Ukrainy 1972

GUIDED MISSILE DESTROYERS *(continued)*

Provorny J. C. Bellonne, 1973

Obraztsovy (detail) 1974

Obraztsovy (detail) 1974

Krasny Krym French Navy, 1976

♦ *8 Kanin class*

BOIKY, DERZKY, GNEVNY, GORDY, GREMYASHCHY, UPORNY, ZHGUCHY, ZORKY

Bldrs: Various, 1958-60

Zhguchy 1977

D: 4,500 tons (fl) **S:** 34 kts **Dim:** 141.0 × 14.6 × 5.0 (avg)
A: 2/SA-N-1 (II × 1) and 22 Goa missiles — 8/57-mm AA (IV × 2) — 8/30-mm AA (II × 4) — 3/MBU 2500A rocket launchers — 10/533-mm TT (V × 2)
Electron Equipt: Radars: 2 Don Kay, 1 Head Net-C, 1 Peel Group, 1 Hawk Screech, 2 Drum Tilt
Sonar: 1 medium-frequency hull-mounted
M: GT; 2 props; 80,000 hp **Range:** 1,000/30, 4,500/18 **Man:** 350 men

Remarks: Modifications from the Krupny class completed 1967-68. The *Gremashchy* does not have 30-mm AA. Helicopter platform.

GUIDED MISSILE DESTROYERS (*continued*)

Zhguchy 1977

♦ *3 modified Kildin class*

BEDOVY, NEUDERZHIMY, PROZORLIVY

Bldrs: Zhdanov (Leningrad) and Nikolaev, 1958

Bedovy French Navy, 1977

D: 3,800 tons (fl) **S:** 34 kts **Dim:** 126.5 × 12.9 × 4.6 (avg)
A: 4/SS-N-11 (I × 4) — 4/76-mm AA (II × 2) — 16/57-mm AA (IV × 4) except *Bedovy:* 16/45-mm AA (IV × 4) — 2/MBU 2500 rocket launchers — 4/533-mm TT (II × 2)
Electron Equipt: Radars: 1 Head Net-C, 1 Owl Screech, 2 Hawk Screech
Sonar: 1 high-frequency hull-mounted
M: GT; 2 props; 72,000 hp **Range:** 1,000/30, 4,000/18

REMARK: The *Bedovy* has Strut Pair radar in place of Head Net-C.

♦ *1 Kildin class*

NEULOVIMY

D: 3,800 tons (fl) **S:** 34 kts **Dim:** 126.5 × 12.9 × 4.6 (avg)
A: 1/SS-N-1 (I × 1) and 6 Scrubber missiles — 16/57-mm AA (IV × 4) — 2/MBU 2500 rocket launchers — 4/533-mm TT (II × 2)
Electron Equipt: Radars: 3 Slim Net, 1 Flat Spin, 1 Top Bow, 2 Hawk Screech
M: GT; 2 props; 72,000 hp **Range:** 1,000/30, 4,000/18

REMARK: Probably will be converted to Modified Kildin class.

♦ *8 Sam Kotlin class*

BRAVY, NAKHODCHIVY, NASTOYCHIVY, NESOKRUSHIMY, SKROMNY, SKRYTNY, SOZNATEL'NY, VOZBUZHDENNY

Bldrs: Various, 1955–57

Bravy (conversion prototype) U.S. Navy, 1970

Skromny 1974

GUIDED MISSILE DESTROYERS (*continued*)

Skromny French Navy, 1973

D: 3,500 tons (fl) **S:** 34 kts **Dim:** 126.5 × 12.9 × 4.6 (avg)
A: *Bravy:* 2/SA-N-1 (II × 1) — 2/130-mm DP (II × 1) — 12/45-mm AA (IV × 3) — 5/533-mm TT (V × 1) — 2 MBU 2500 rocket launchers
Others: 2/SA-N-1 (II × 1) — 2/130-mm DP (II × 1) — 4/45-mm AA (IV × 1) — 5/533 mm TT (V × 1) — 2/MBU 2500A rocket launchers (two have MBU 2500)
Electron Equipt: Radars: 1 or 2 Don, 1 Head Net-C, 1 Peel Group, 1 Sun Visor, 1 Hawk Screech, 1 Egg Cup; ships with 30-mm: 2 Drum Tilt
Sonar: 1 high-frequency
M: GT; 2 props; 72,000 hp **Range:** 1,000/30, 4,000/18 **Man:** 300 men

REMARKS: The *Nesokrushimy, Skrytny,* and *Soznatelny* have 8/30-mm AA (II × 4) as well, with Drum Tilt fire-control radar. The *Nastoychivy* has no Egg Cup radar. The *Bravy* has Head Net-A, two extra quadruple 45-mm AA mounts, and (as does the *Skromny*) MBU 2500 vice MBU 2500A.

Nakhodchivy

Nastoychivy French Navy, 1974

DESTROYERS

♦ *19 Kotlin and Modified Kildin class*

BESSLEDNY, BLAGORODNY*, BLESTYASHCHY*, BURLIVY*, BYVALY*, DALNEVOSTOCHNY KOMSOMOLETS, MOSKOVSKY KOMSOMOLETS*, NAPORISTY*, PLAMENNY*, SPESHNY, SPOKOINY, SVEDUSHCHY*, SVETLY, VESKY, VDOKHNOVENNY*, VLIYATELNY, VOZMUSHCHENNY, VYDERZHANNY*, VYSYVAYUSHCHY*

*Modernized units

Bldrs: Leningrad and Nikolaev, 1955-57

D: 2,850 tons (3,800 fl) **S:** 34 kts **Dim:** 126.5 × 12.9 × 4.6
A: 4/130-mm DP (II × 2) — 16/45-mm AA (IV × 4) — 10/533-mm TT (V × 2) — 6 depth-charge projectors — 2 depth-charge racks — 70 mines may be carried

Kotlin class 1970

DESTROYERS (*continued*)

Electron Equipt: Radars: 1 Neptune or Don, 1 Slim Net, 1 Sun Visor, 2 Hawk Screech (45-mm AA), 2 Egg Cup, 1 Post Lamp or Top Bow
Sonar: 1 high-frequency
Man: 36 officers, 300 men **Range:** 1,000/32, 4,000/18
M: GT; 2 props; 4 boilers; 72,000 hp

REMARKS: Eleven were modified 1960-62 with 2/MBU 2500 forward and 2/MBU 4500 in place of the depth-charge equipment, the after bank of 5/533-mm TT being removed; later, most of these ships got 8/25-mm AA (II × 4) additional. The *Moskovsky Komsomolets* got MBU 2500A forward, nothing aft. Most of those remaining unmodified received 4/25-mm AA (II × 2) additional; the *Svetly* has a helicopter platform in place of depth-charge gear and thus has no ASW armament. Helo decks were removed from the other two ships that had them. Many have had their Egg Cup radar removed.

Svetly French Navy, 1974

Dalnevostochny Komsomolets French Navy, 1974

Speshny French Navy, 1974

♦ *20 Skory and Modified Skory class(*)*

Possible names:

BESSMENNY
BESSTRASHNY
BEZUDERZHNY
BEZUKORIZNENNY
BUINY
OKRYLENNY
OGNENNY*
OTCHAYANNY
OTCHETLIVY*
OTVETSTVENNY
OZHESTOCHENNY
OZHIVLENNY
OSTOROZHNY*
SERDITY
SERIOZNY
SMOTRYASHCHY
SOKRUSHITELNY
STATNY
STEPENNY
STOIKY*
SUROVY
SVOBODNY*
VDUMCHIVY
VOL'NY*
VRAZUMITELNY

*Modified units

In service, 1949-1954

Bldr: Severodvinsk, Zhdanov (Leningrad), Nikolaev, Komsomolsk

D: 3,200 tons (fl) **S:** 34 kts **Dim:** 121.5 × 12.5 × 4.6
A: *Standard:* 4/130-mm (II × 2) — 2/85-mm AA (II × 1) — 7/37-mm AA (I × 7) or 8 (II × 4) — 4 or 6/25-mm AA (II × 2 or 3) on a few — 10/533-mm TT (V × 2) — 2 depth-charge projectors — 2 depth-charge racks — 50 mines
Modified: 4/130-mm DP (II × 2) — 5/57-mm AA (I × 5) — 2/MBU 2500 rocket launchers — 5/533-mm TT (V × 1) — 50 mines

Modified Skory class 1961

DESTROYERS *(continued)*

Modified Skory class 1961

Skory class 1968

Electron Equipt: Radars: *Standard:* 1 High Sieve, 1 Top Bow or Half Bow or Post Lamp, 1 Cross Bird, 1-2 Don (Knife Rest on a few)
Modified: 1 Slim Net, 1 Top Bow, 1-2 Don, 2 Hawk Screech
Sonar: 1 high-frequency

M: GT; 2 props; 62,000 hp **Range:** 906/32, 3,500/15 **Man:** 280 men

REMARKS: Survivors from among 72 built, derived from prewar *Ognevoy* design. A small number were modernized around 1960 to Modified Skory configuration. Several Skory class were transferred to Egypt, Poland, and Indonesia (only 4 Egyptian remain). Of little further value.

FRIGATES

♦ *1 or more Koni class* — Bldr: . . . , 1977-. . .

D: 1,800 tons (fl) **S:** . . . **Dim:** 95.0 × . . . × . . .
A: 2/SA-N-4 (II × 1) — 4/76-mm DP (II × 2) — 4/30-mm AA (II × 2) — 2/MBU 2500A

Electron Equipt: Radars: 1 Strut Curve, 1 Pop Group, 1 Drum Tilt
Sonar: . . .
M: GT and diesels

REMARK: Possibly to replace the Riga class

♦ *7 Modified Petya-I class* — Converted, 1973-7 . . .

A: 4/76-mm DP (II × 2) — 2/MBU 2500 — 5/400-mm ASW TT (V × 1)

Modified Petya-I class 1973

REMARK: Petya-I class altered with a medium-frequency towed sonar in a new stern deckhouse.

♦ *24 Petya-II class* — Bldrs: Various, 1964-69

Petya II

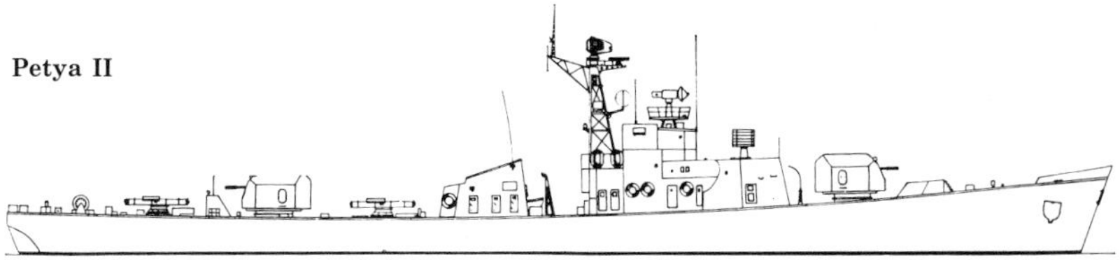

Petya II 1976

FRIGATES *(continued)*

Petya II 1976

♦ *16 Petya-I class* — Bldr: Various, 1962-64

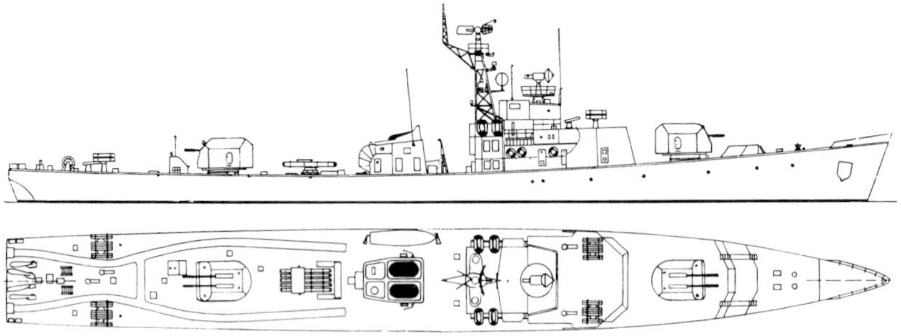

D: 1,100 tons (fl) **S:** 30 kts **Dim:** 82.0 × 9.1 × 3.2
A: 4/76-mm DP (II × 2) — 4/MBU 2500 rocket launchers and 10/400-mm ASW TT on Petya-II — depth charges and mines on both
Electron Equipt: Radars: 1 Neptune or Don, 1 Slim Net (Strut Curve on Petya-II), 1 Hawk Screech
Sonar: 1 high-frequency
M: CODAG propulsion: 2 gas turbines (30,000 hp) + 1 diesel (6,000 hp); 3 props
Range: 4,000/10 (diesel), 500/34 (diesel + gas turbine)
Man: 80-90 men

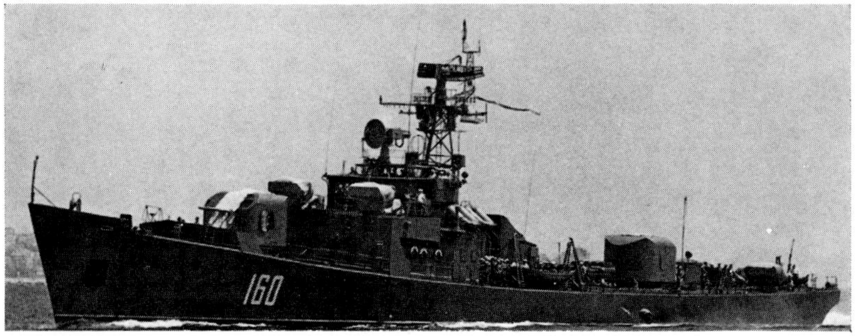

Petya I class 1973

♦ *20 Mirka I and II* — Bldrs: Various, 1964-66

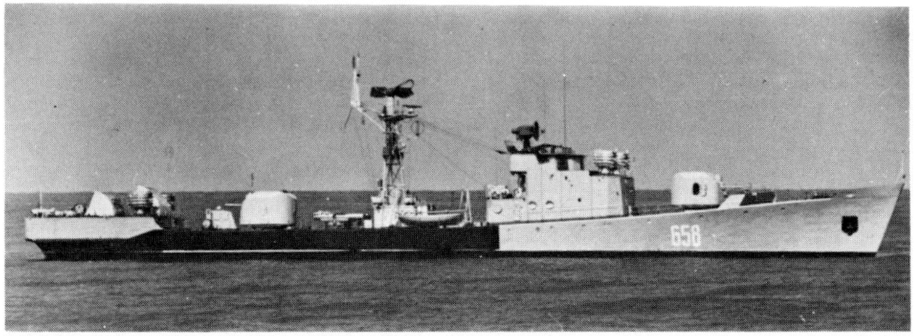

Mirka-I class

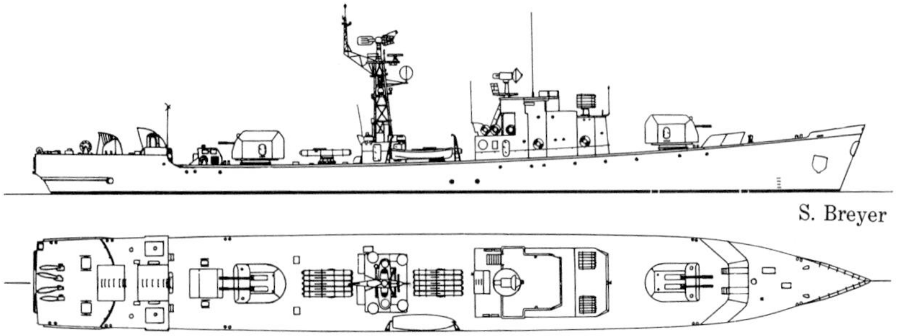

S. Breyer

D: 1,100 tons (fl) **S:** 34 kts **Dim:** 82.0 × 9.1 × 3.2
A: 4/76-mm DP (II × 2) — 2 or 4/MBU 2500A rocket launchers — 5 or 10/400-mm ASW TT (V × 1 or 2)
Electron Equipt: Radars: 1 Don, 1 Slim Net or Strut Curve, 1 Hawk Screech
Sonars: 1 high-frequency plus (on many) a dipping sonar of the type used by the Hormone helicopter
M: CODAG propulsion: 2 gas turbines (15,000 hp each) + 2 diesels (6,000 hp each); 2 props
Range: 4,000/10 (diesel), 500/34 (gas turbine) **Man:** 80-90 men

Mirka-II class 1970

REMARKS: Mirka-I has 4/MBU 2500A, 5 TT (V × 1). Mirka-II has 2/MBU 2500A, 10 TT (V × 2).

FRIGATES (*continued*)

♦ *35 Riga class* — Bldrs: Various, 1955–58

Riga class 1974

Possible names:
ASTRAKHANSKY KOMSOMOLETS, BARS, BARSUK, BOBR, BYK, GIENA, GOBCHIK, KOMSOMOLETS GRUZY, KOMSOMOLETS LITVY, KRASNODARSKY KOMSOMOLETS, KUNITSA, LEOPARD, LEV, MEDVED, ROSOMAKHA, SCHAKAL, TIGR, VOLK, VORON, YAGUAR, etc.

Riga class (unique unit with extra radomes) French Navy, 1972

D: 1,450 tons (fl) **S:** 28 kts **Dim:** 91.0 × 11.0 × 3.4
A: 3/100-mm DP (I × 3) — 4/37-mm AA (II × 2) — 4/25-mm AA (II × 2) — 2 or 3/533-mm TT (II or III × 1) — 2 depth-charge racks — 2/MBU 2500 rocket launchers (a few have 1/MBU 600 hedgehog, 4 depth-charge projectors vice MBU 2500)
Electron Equipt: Radars: 1 Neptune or 1 Don, 1 Slim Net, 1 Sun Visor
Sonar: 1 high-frequency
M: GT; 2 props; 20,000 hp **Range:** 2,000/10 **Man:** 180 men

REMARKS: One ship has a Hawk Screech forward and the main gun director aft. Some of the Riga class have been transferred to other navies (Indonesia, Finland, Bulgaria, China, East Germany).

♦ *3 Kola class* — Bldr: Kaliningrad, 1953–57

SOVETSKY AZERBAIZHAN, SOVETSKY DAGESTAN, SOVETSKY TURKMENISTAN

Kola class

D: 1,700 tons (fl) **S:** 27 kts **Dim:** 100.0 × 10.7 × 3.5
A: 4/100-mm DP (I × 4) — 4/37-mm AA (II × 2) — 4/25-mm AA (II × 2) — 3/533-mm TT (III × 1) — 2 MBU 900 — 4 depth-charge projectors — 2 depth-charge racks
M: GT; 2 boilers; 2 props; 30,000 hp **Man:** 213 men

REMARKS: Based on the German *Elbing* class of World War II. All now in Caspian Sea Flotilla.

GUIDED MISSILE CORVETTES

♦ *12 Nanuchka class* — Bldr: Petrovsky (Leningrad), 1969–7 . . .

Nanuchka class (note blast marks from missile firing) 1975

D: 780 tons (930 fl) **S:** 34 kts **Dim:** 60.3 × 12.2 × 3.1
A: 6/SS-N-9 (II × 3) — 2/SA-N-4 (II × 1) — 2/57-mm AA (II × 1)
Electron Equipt: 1 Peel Pair, 1 Pop Group, 1 Muff Cob, 1 Band Stand
M: 6 diesels; 3 props; 24,000 hp **Man:** 60 men

GUIDED MISSILE CORVETTES *(continued)*

Nanuchka class guided missile patrol boat 1975

Nanuchka class

REMARKS: These ships are reported to be poor sea boats with very unreliable engines (paired M503A diesels). Three, modified with 4/SS-N-11 missiles, have been sold to India.

CORVETTES

♦ *5 Grisha-II class*

AMETIST, BRILLIANT, IZUMRUD, RUBIN, ZHEMCHUG

Grisha-II class U.S. Navy, 1974

Identical to the Grisha I and III classes except for a second 57-mm mount in place of the SA-N-4 system and no Pop Group radar. Thus, the armament consists of 4/57-mm AA (II × 2), 2/MBU 2500A rocket launchers, 4/533-mm TT (II × 2), 2 depth-charge racks, and mines. The class is manned by the maritime section of the KGB.

♦ *20-22 Grisha-I and Grisha-II classes* — Bldrs: Various, 1968-7 . . .

Grisha-I class French Navy, 1971

Grisha-I class French Navy, 1972

CORVETTES (*continued*)

D: 900 tons (fl) **S:** 33 kts **Dim:** 75.0 × 9.0 × 2.8
A: 2 SA-N-4 (II × 1) (18/20 missiles) — 2/57-mm AA (II × 1) — *Grisha-III:* 1/23-mm Gatling AA — 2/MBU 2500A rocket launchers — 4/533-mm TT (II × 2) — 2 depth-charge racks — mines
Electron Equipt: Radars: 1 Don, 1 Strut Curve, 1 Pop Group, 1 Muff Cob (*Grisha-III:* Bass Tilt vice Muff Cob)
Sonar: 1 medium-frequency(?)
M: CODAG propulsion: 2 diesels + 1 gas turbine; 3 props; 24,000 hp
Range: 450/30, 4/000/12 **Man:** 60 men

Grisha-III class (Gatling gun added) 1976

REMARKS: The latest version, *Grisha III*, substitutes a 23-mm Gatling gun in the Muff Cob fire-control radar position and has a Bass Tilt on a deckhouse atop the after superstructure to control both the Gatling gun and the twin 57-mm AA. The depth-charge racks are portable and are mounted on the mine rails when needed.

♦ *65 Poti class* — Bldrs: Various, 1961-67

Poti class

D: 500 tons (fl) **S:** 34 kts **Dim:** 60.3 × 8.0 × 3.0
A: 2/57-mm AA (II × 1) — 2/MBU 2500A rocket launchers — 4/533-mm TT (I × 4)
Electron Equipt: Radars: 1 Don, 1 Strut Curve, 1 Muff Cob
Sonar: 1 high-frequency
M: CODAG propulsion: 2 M503A diesels (8,000 hp) + 2 gas turbines; 2 props; 20,000 hp

♦ *17 or less Kronstadt class*, 1948-56

D: 300 tons (fl) **S:** 18 kts (cruising) **Dim:** 52.1 × 6.5 × 2.2
A: 1/85-mm DP — 2/37-mm AA (I × 2) — 6/12.7-mm AA (II × 3) — 2 depth-charge projectors — 2 depth-charge racks — mines
Man: 50 men **Range:** 3,500/14
M: 3 diesels; 3 props; 3,300 hp **Fuel:** 20 tons

REMARKS: Obsolete. Some of this class have been modified as command ships for small gunboats (see Libau-class communications ships). Kronstadt ships have been transferred to Poland, East Germany, Indonesia, People's Republic of China, Romania, Bulgaria, and Albania, but many have been removed from active service in those navies.

GUIDED MISSILE PATROL BOATS

♦ *1 Sarancha class* — Bldr: Petrovsky (Leningrad), 1977

D: 300 tons (fl) **S:** 50 kts (?) **Dim:** 43.0 × 10.0 × 2.0 (hull)
A: 4/SS-N-9 (II × 2) — 2/SA-N-4 (II × 1) — 1/23-mm Gatling AA
Electron Equipt: Radars: Peel Pair, Band Stand, Pop Group, Bass Tilt
M: GT; 4 props; 30,000 hp (?)

REMARKS: Too large and complex to be an Osa successor; essentially a reduced high-speed Nanuchka. Folding-foil system like U.S. Navy PHM. Stepped hydroplane hull bottom.

♦ *40 to 45 Osa II class*

Osa II class 1971

GUIDED MISSILE PATROL BOATS *(continued)*

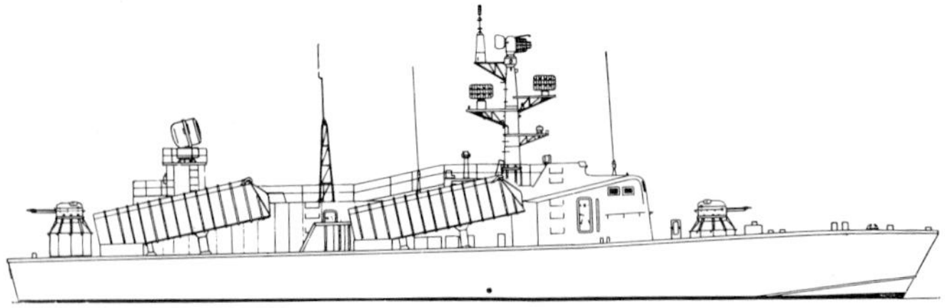

Siegfried Breyer

Osa II 1971

Osa-II (with SA-N-5 aft) 1976

♦ *70 Osa-I class* — Bldrs: Various, post 1960

D: 175 tons (fl) **S:** 36 kts max. **Dim:** 39.0 × 7.7 × 1.8
A: 4/SS-N-2 Styx — 4/30-mm AA (II × 2)
Electron Equipt: Radars: 1 Square Tie, 1 Drum Tilt
M: 3 M503A diesels; 3 props; 12,000 hp **Range:** 450/34, 700/20

Osa I class 1970

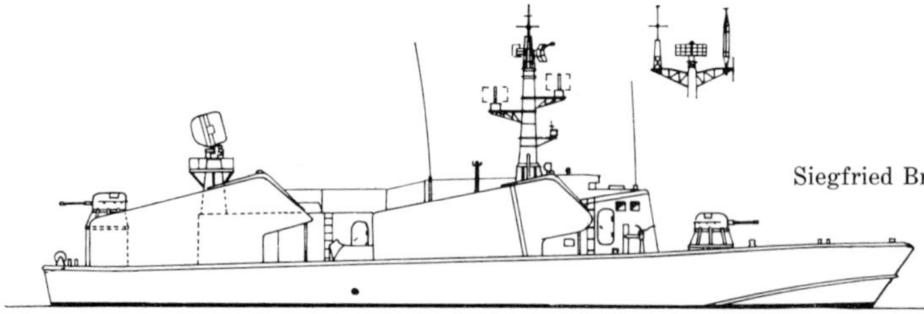

Siegfried Breyer

REMARKS: These small craft can launch their missiles in a Force-4 sea (2-m waves). Many Osa-I class have been transferred to other navies. Iraq, Finland, Cuba, and Algeria have received some Osa-II. No doubt the Osa I and II are fitted with some SS-N-2 missiles which carry an infrared homing device. Some are now receiving SA-N-5 (naval SA-7 Grail) systems aft. Osa-II is 240 tons (fl) and has 3 M504 engines totaling 15,000 hp; performance is probably similar to Osa-I. Some have been built as, or converted to, targets, while the Stenka, Turya, and MOL (an export model torpedo boat — see Somalia and Sri Lanka) all use Osa hulls and propulsion plants.

PATROL BOATS

♦ *60 Stenka class* — Bldrs: Various, 1967–7 . . .

Stenka class Siegfried Breyer

PATROL BOATS (*continued*)

D: 205 tons (fl) **S:** 38 kts **Dim:** 39.5 × 7.7 × 1.8
A: 4/30-mm AA (II × 2) — 4/400-mm ASW TT — 2 depth-charge racks
Electron Equipt: Radars: 1 Pot Drum, 1 Drum Tilt
Sonar: 1 dipping sonar from a Hormone helicopter
M: 3 M503A diesels; 3 props; 12,000 hp

Stenka class

REMARKS: Manned by the maritime contingent of the KGB.

♦ *65 SO-I class* — Bldrs: Various, 1958-64

SO-1 class Siegfried Breyer

D: 215 tons (fl) **S:** 28 kts **Dim:** 42.0 × 6.1 × 1.9
A: 4/25-mm AA (II × 2) — 4/MBU 1800 rocket launchers — some have 2/400-mm TT to replace the 25-mm mount aft — 2 depth-charge racks — mines
Electron Equipt: Radar: 1 Pot Head
M: 3 diesels; 3 props; 7,500 hp **Man:** 3 officers, 27 men

REMARKS: Several have been transferred to East Germany, North Vietnam, Algeria, Iraq, Cuba, South Yemen, etc. Obsolete. Poor sea boats.

HYDROFOIL TORPEDO BOATS

♦ *26 Turya class* — Bldr: . . . , 1974-7 . . .

Turya class

D: 240 tons (fl) **S:** 40 kts **Dim:** 39.0 × 7.7 × 1.8 (without foils)
A: 2/57-mm AA aft (II × 1) — 2/25-mm AA (II × 1) — 4/533-mm TT (I × 4)
Electron Equipt: Radars: 1 Pot Drum, 1 Muff Cob
Sonar: 1 dipping sonar from a Hormone helicopter
M: 3 M504 diesels; 3 props; 15,000 hp **Man:** 16 men

REMARKS: Fitted with fixed foils forward only; stern planes on water surface. Uses Osa-II hull and propulsion.

Turya class

HYDROFOIL TORPEDO BOATS *(continued)*

Turya class (dipping sonar on starboard quarter)

Turya class

TORPEDO BOATS

♦ *50 Shershen class* — Built 1963–70

D: 180 tons (fl) **S:** 45 kts **Dim:** 34.0 × 7.2 × 1.5
A: 4/30-mm AA (II × 2) — 4/533-mm TT (I × 4) — 2 depth-charge racks

Shershen class (East German unit) 1970

Electron Equipt: Radars: 1 Pot Drum, 1 Drum Tilt **Range:** 450/34, 700/20
M: 3 M503A diesels; 3 props; 12,000 hp

REMARKS: Contemporaneous with Osa-I and have same propulsion, but a smaller hull. Have been exported to Egypt, North Korea, and East Germany. Yugoslavia built some under license.

NOTE: MOL, new torpedo boat design, based on Osa but with Shershen armament, has been built only for export — with examples going to Sri Lanka (no TT) and Somalia (TT and no TT) to date.

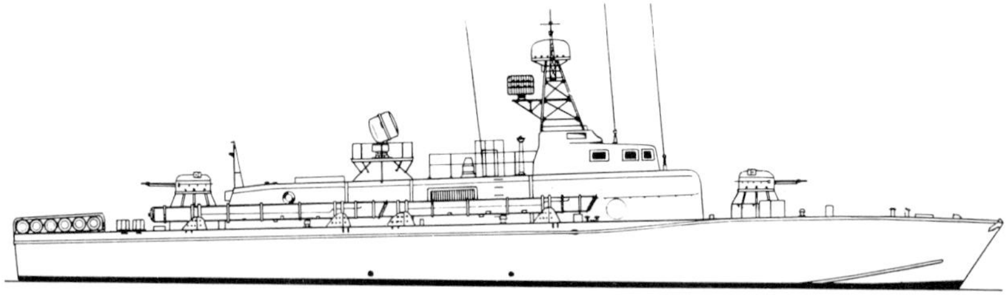

Siegfried Breyer

Shershen class (East German unit)

TORPEDO BOATS *(continued)*

♦ *35 or less P-6 class* — Bldrs: Various, 1952–59

P 6 torpedo boat 1969

D: 66.5 tons (fl) **S:** 43 kts **Dim:** 25.3 × 6.1 × 1.7
A: 4/25-mm AA (II × 2) — 2/533-mm TT (I × 2) — 6 depth charges on some
Electron Equipt: Radar: 1 Skin Head **Man:** 12 men
M: 4 M50 diesels, 4 props, 4,800 hp **Range:** 400/32, 700/15

REMARKS: All may have been discarded. The P-8 hydrofoil and P-10 CODAG variants had disappeared by the mid-1960s. Wooden hull. Many adapted as targets, yachts, patrol craft, etc. Large numbers exported.

NOTE: All examples of the earlier aluminum-hull hydroplane P-4 class are believed to have been discarded some time ago.

PATROL CRAFT

♦ *20 or more Zhuk class*

D: 60 tons (fl) **S:** 30 kts **Dim:** 26.0 × 4.9 × 1.5
A: 2/14.5-mm AA (II × 1) **Electron Equipt:** Radar: 1 set
M: 2 M50 diesels; 2 props; 2,400 hp

REMARKS: Probably manned by KGB or Port Police. A number have been exported to Cuba, North Vietnam, and several African states.

♦ *20 Pchela-class hydrofoils, 1964–65*

Pchela class

Pchela class

D: 83 tons (fl) **Dim:** 25.3 × 5.8 × 1.3 (without foils)
S: 42 kts **A:** 4/14.5-mm AA (II × 2)
Electron Equipt: Radar: 1 Pot Drum
Sonar: 1 dipping sonar from a Hormone helicopter on a few
M: Diesels; 2 props; 4,000 hp

REMARKS: Simple, fixed, surface-piercing hydrofoils; aircraft type machine-gun mountings. Manned by the KGB.

♦ *34 Poluchat-I class,* 1953–56

Poluchat-1-class torpedo retriever (patrol version similar)

PATROL CRAFT (*continued*)

D: 90 tons (fl) **S:** 18 kts **Dim:** 29.6 × 5.8 × 1.5
A: 2/14.5-mm AA (II × 1) **Man:** 20 men
M: 2 M50 diesels; 2 props; 2,400 hp **Range:** 450/17, 900/10

REMARKS: Modified version of standard Soviet Navy torpedo-retriever with stern ramp decked over, a boat carried aft, and a twin machine-gun mount. Probably operated by the KGB.

RIVERINE CRAFT

NOTE: The U.S.S.R. maintains a number of river gunboats on the Lower Danube, on the Amur and Ussuri river systems in the Far East, and possibly elsewhere. In addition to gunboats, the riverine forces have a few support craft, including the administrative craft PS-10 on the Danube.

♦ *75-80 Shmel-class patrol gunboats (BKL)*, 1967-74

Shmel class (Austrian gunboat in background) Jürg Meister, 1975

D: 60 tons (fl) **S:** 22 kts **Dim:** 28.3 × 4.6 × 1.0
A: 1/76-mm, 48 cal., fwd in a tank turret — 2/25-mm AA (II × 1) aft — 2/18-tube, 122-mm rocket launchers — mines
M 2 M50 diesels; 2 props; 2,400 hp **Man:** 15 men

REMARKS: Not all these craft have the rocket launchers. An earlier version has a twin machine-gun mount aft that resembles a tank turret. A few of the older BK-IV-class river monitors may still be in service; similar in size to the Shmel, they had an undulating deckline, were more heavily armed, slower, and carried 1/85-mm and 4/14.5-mm AA (II × 2).

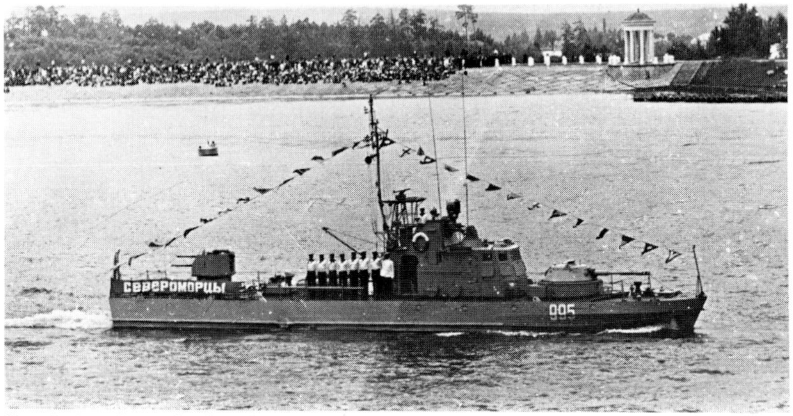

Shmel class (no rocket launcher)

MINE WARFARE SHIPS

♦ *3 Alesha-class minelayers*, 1967-69

Alesha class 1969

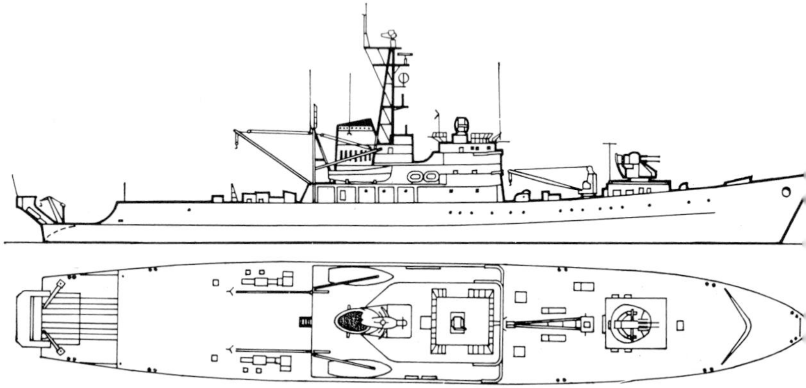

Siegfried Breyer

MINE WARFARE SHIPS *(continued)*

D: 2,900 tons (fl) **S:** 20 kts **Dim:** 98.0 × 14.5 × 4.8
A: 4/57-mm (IV × 1) **Man:** . . . men
Electron Equipt: Radars: 1 Don-2, 1 Strut Curve, 1 Muff Cob
M: 4 diesels; 2 props; 8,000 hp

REMARKS: Have also been described as netlayers, but mine rails over the stern are clearly visible. May also serve as minesweeper tenders and command ships.

♦ *20 Natya-class fleet minesweepers,* 1970-7 . . .

Natya class French Navy, 1972

D: 750 tons (fl) **S:** 20 kts **Dim:** 61.0 × 9.6 × 2.7
A: 4/30-mm AA (II × 2) — 4/25-mm (II × 2) — 2/MBU 1800 rocket launchers — mines
Electron Equipt: Radars: 1 Don, 1 Drum Tilt
M: 2 diesels; 2 props; 8,000 hp **Man:** 50 men

REMARK: Equipped to serve as ASW escorts.

♦ *40 to 45 Yurka-class fleet minesweepers,* 1964-70

Yurka class French Navy, 1972

D: 460 tons (fl) **S:** 18 kts **Dim:** 52.0 × 8.8 × 2.0
A: 4/30-mm AA (II × 2) — mines
Electron Equipt: Radars: 1 Don, 1 Drum Tilt **Man:** 45 men
M: 2 diesels; 2 props; 4,000 hp

REMARKS: Aluminum hull. Four transferred to Egypt.

♦ *19 T-58-class fleet minesweepers,* 1957-61

T-58 class French Navy, 1974

D: 900 tons (fl) **S:** 18 kts **Dim:** 70.0 × 9.1 × 2.5
A: 4/57-mm AA (II × 2) — 2/MBU 1800 rocket launchers — mines
Electron Equipt: Radars: 1 Don, 1 Muff Cob
M: 2 diesels; 2 props; 4,000 hp

REMARKS: Steel hull. Can be used as coastal escorts. Others were built as submarine-rescue ships (one of which is used for intelligence-collecting).

♦ *84 T-43-class fleet minesweepers,* 1947-57

T-43 class (short-hull version)

D: 580 tons (fl) **S:** 14 kts **Dim:** 58.0 × 8.4 × 2.3
A: 4/37-mm AA (II × 2) — 4/25-mm AA (II × 2) or 4-8/14.5-mm or 12.7-mm AA (II × 2 or 4) — 2 depth-charge projectors — mines
M: 2 diesels; 2 props; 2,200 hp **Range:** 3,200/10 **Man:** 75 men

MINE WARFARE SHIPS (*continued*)

REMARKS: Many of the T-43 class have been transferred to Poland, Egypt, Algeria, China, etc. The version armed with 4/25-mm AA amidships is 60 m long and displaces 600 tons (fl). Most Soviet units have no machine guns. A few have 2/45-mm AA (I × 2) vice 4/37-mm AA. Also built on the T-43 hull were radar pickets, noise-measurement ships, diving tenders, and trials ships. Well over 200 were built.

♦ *10 Sonya-class coastal minesweepers,* 1973-7 . . .

Sonya class

D: 400 tons (450 fl) **S:** 14 kts **Dim:** 48.5 × 8.8 × 2.1
A: 2/30-mm AA (II × 1) — 2/25-mm AA (II × 1) — mines **Man:** 43 men
Electron Equipt: Radar: 1 Don-2 **M:** 2 diesels; 2,400 hp

REMARK: Wooden hull with plastic sheathing.

♦ *4 Zhenya class coastal minesweepers,* 1972-73

Zhenya class

D: 300 tons (fl) **S:** 14 kts **Dim:** 42.7 × 7.5 × 1.8
A: 2/30-mm AA (II × 1) — mines
Electron Equipt: Radar: 1 Spin Trough
M: 2 diesels; 2 props; 2,400 hp
Man: 30 men

REMARKS: Plastic hull. Apparently not successful, as similar but larger, wooden-hulled Sonya class went into production instead.

♦ *70 Vanya-class coastal minesweepers,* 1961-73

Vanya class

D: 245 tons (fl) **S:** 18 kts **Dim:** 40.0 × 7.6 × 1.8
A: 2/30-mm AA (II × 1) — mines **Man:** 30 men
M: 2 diesels; 2 props; 2,200 hp
Electron Equipt: Radar: 1 Don-2

REMARKS: Wooden construction. At least one was built or has been converted as a minehunter, armed with 2/25-mm AA (II × 1) (more accurate than 30-mm for mine disposal?) and with 1 Don Kay in place of Don-2; has two boats in davits on fantail.

♦ *15 Sasha-class coastal minesweepers,* 1954-5 . . .

D: 250 tons (280 fl) **S:** 18 kts **Dim:** 45.7 × 6.2 × 1.8
A: 1/45 or 57-mm AA — 4/25-mm AA (II × 2) — mines **Man:** 25 men
M: 2 diesels; 2 props; 2,200 hp
Electron Equipt: Radar: 1 Ball End

REMARKS: Steel hull; also used as patrol boats.

MINE WARFARE SHIPS (*continued*)

Sasha class

♦ *14 Yevgenya-class inshore minesweepers*, 1970-7 . . .

Yevgenya class 1976

D: 80 tons (90 fl) **S:** 12 kts **Dim:** 26.0 × 6.0 × 1.5
A: 2/14.5-mm (II × 1) **Man:** 12 men
Electron Equipt: Radar: 1 Spin Trough
M: 2 diesels; 2 props; 600 hp

REMARKS: Plastic hull. Several transferred to Iraq.

♦ *3 Olya-class minesweeping boats*, 1976-7 . . .

D: 50 tons (fl) **S:** 15 kts **Dim:** 25.5 × 4.5 × 1.4
A: 2/25-mm AA **Electron Equipt:** Radar: 1 Spin Trough
M: 2 diesels; 600 hp **Man:** 15 men

♦ *6 Ilyusha-class minesweeping boats*

D: 70 tons (fl) **S:** 12 kts **Dim:** 24.4 × 4.9 × 1.4
A: None **Electronic Equipt:** Radar: 1 Spin Trough
M: 1 diesel; 450 hp **Man:** 10 men

REMARK: Apparently a drone, but can be manned for transit.

♦ *70 K-8-class minesweeping boats* — Bldr: Poland, 1954-59

D: 26 tons (fl) **S:** 12 kts **Dim:** 16.9 × 3.2 × 0.8
A: 2/14.5-mm (II × 1) **Electron Equipt:** None
M: 2 diesels; 2 props; 300 hp **Man:** 6 men

♦ *a few TR-40-class minesweeping boats* — Bldr: Poland, 1954-60

D: 50 tons (fl) **S:** 18 kts **Dim:** 27.7 × 4.1 × 0.6
A: 2/25-mm AA (II × 1) — 2/14.5-mm (II × 1) — mines **Man:** 16 men
Electron Equipt: None **Range:** 500/10
M: 2 3D6 diesels; 2 props; 600 hp

REMARKS: Wooden hull. For riverine use.

RADAR PICKET SHIPS

♦ *20 T-43-class*, 1952-54

T-43-class radar picket with Big Net aft 1966

D: 580 tons (fl) **S:** 14 kts **Dim:** 58.0 × 8.5 × 2.3
A: 4/37-mm AA (II × 2) — 2/25-mm AA (II × 1) — 2 depth-charge projectors — mines

RADAR PICKET SHIPS (*continued*)

Electron Equipt: Radars: 1 Ball End, 1 Big Net or 2 Knife Rest
M: 2 diesels; 2 props; 2,200 hp **Man:** 77 men

REMARKS: Configured as radar pickets; otherwise similar to the mine-sweeper version. Not likely to last much longer.

COMMUNICATION SHIPS

♦ *20 Libau-class,* late 1950s

Libau class

D: 330 tons (fl) **S:** 18 kts **Dim:** 52.1 × 6.5 × 2.2
A: 4/25-mm AA (II × 2), but usually removed **Man:** 50 men
M: 3 diesels; 3 props; 3,300 hp

REMARKS: Hull and propulsion the same as the Kronstadt-class corvettes. Believed originally intended to control groups of torpedo boats, etc., but now used as general-purpose patrol boats or training tenders. Not likely to last much longer.

AMPHIBIOUS WARFARE SHIPS

♦ *6 Ropucha-class tank landing ships* — Bldr: Gdansk, Poland, 1975-7 . . .

Ropucha class 1976

Ropucha class 1976

Ropucha class

D: 3,450 tons (4,400 fl) **Dim:** 110.0 × 14.5 × 3.6 (aft) 2.0 (fwd)
S: 17 kts **Man:** 70 men
A: 4/57-mm AA (II × 2)
Electron Equipt: Radars: 1 Don-2, 1 Strut Curve, 1 Muff Cob
M: 4 diesels; 2 props; 10,000 hp

REMARKS: Bow and stern doors to permit roll-on/roll-off loading. Mounting positions forward for two bombardment rocket launchers.

AMPHIBIOUS WARFARE SHIPS (*continued*)

♦ *14 Alligator-class tank landing ships* — Bldr: U.S.S.R., 1964-197 . . .

ALEKSANDR TORTSEV	SERGEI LAZO
DONETSKY SHAKTER	TOMSKY KOMSOMOLETS
KRASNAYA PRESNAYA	TOPAZ
KRYMSKY KOMSOMOLETS	VORONEZHSKY KOMSOMOLETS
NIKOLAI FILCHENKOV	50 LET SHEFSTVA V.L.K.S.M.
NIKOLAI VILKHOV	N . . .
PETR ILICHEV	N . . .

Alligator class French Navy, 1969

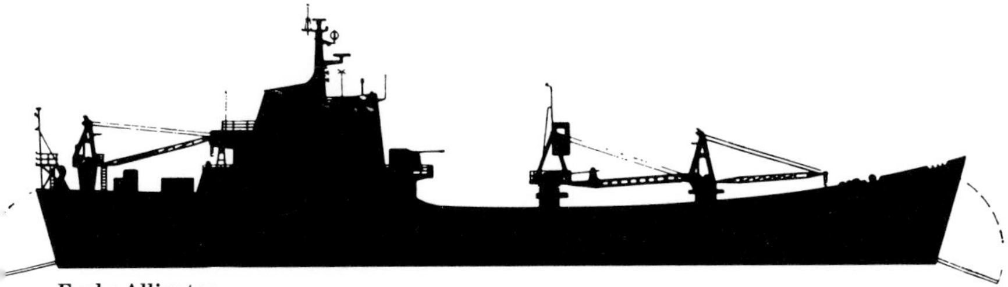

Early Alligator

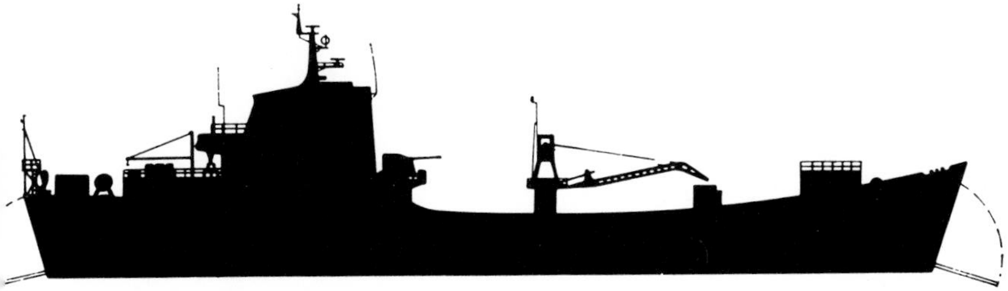

Later Alligator

Alligator class U.S. Navy, 1971

Alligator class (early unit) U.S. Navy, 1971

Alligator class (with rocket launcher forward) 1975

AMPHIBIOUS WARFARE SHIPS (*continued*)

D: 4,500 tons (fl) **S:** 18 kts **Dim:** 114.0 × 15.6 × 3.7 (aft)
A: 2/57-mm AA (II × 1) see remarks **Electron Equipt:** Radars: 2 Don-2
M: 2 diesels, 9,000 hp **Man:** 70 men **Range:** 6,000/16

REMARKS: The design has evolved continually over the long span during which these ships have been built. Ramps fore and aft. Variations in armament and hoisting equipment (1 or 2 cranes of 5 tons, 1 crane of 15 tons). Later ships also have a rocket launcher forward for shore bombardment and 2/25-mm AA aft.

♦ *60 Polnocny-class medium landing ships* — Bldr: Gdansk, Poland, 1961–1973

A version:

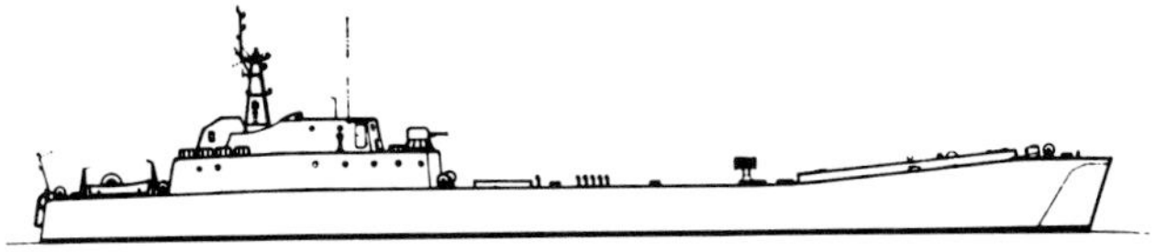

D: 900 tons (fl) **S:** 18 kts **Dim:** 72.5 × 8.5 × 2.0 (fl)
A: 2/14.5-mm AA (II × 1) or 2/30-mm AA (II × 1) or none — 2/140-mm multiple rocket launchers (XVIII × 2)
M: 2 diesels; 2 props; 4,000 hp **Man:** 40 men

B version:

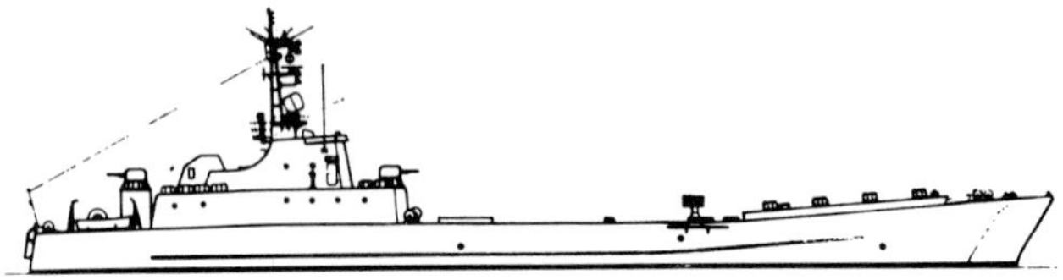

D: 950 tons (fl) **S:** 18 kts **Dim:** 74.0 × 8.5 × 2.0
A: 2 or 4/30-mm AA — 2/140-mm multiple rocket launchers (XVIII × 2)
M: 2 diesels; 2 props; 4,000 hp **Man:** 40 men

C version:

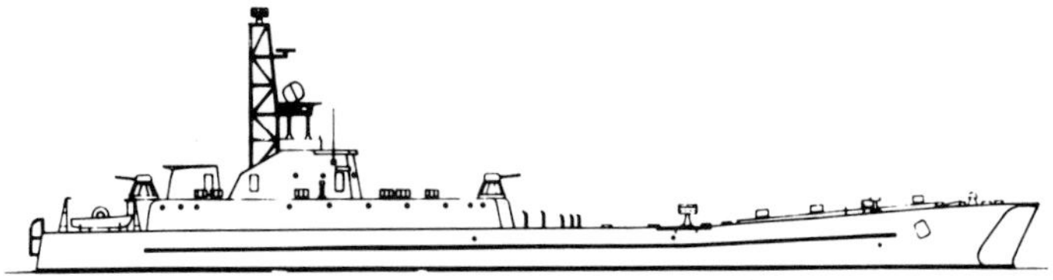

D: 1,150 tons (fl) **S:** 18 kts **Dim:** 82.0 × 10.0 × 2.0
A: 4/30-mm AA (II × 2) — 2/140-mm multiple rocket launchers (XVIII × 2)
M: 2 diesels; 2 props; 5,000 hp **Man:** 60 men

REMARKS: A few have been equipped with two or four SA-N-5 systems. B version with 30-mm aft has heightened stacks. This class also delivered to India, Iraq, Indonesia, Egypt, etc.

Polnocny-B (with high stack, aft 30-mm AA) 1971

Polnocny-A (with twin 14.5-mm AA) 1974

Polnocny-B (with low stack, no aft 30-mm) 1974

AMPHIBIOUS WARFARE SHIPS *(continued)*

Polnocny-C 1974

♦ *18 MP-4-class medium landing ships* — Bldr: U.S.S.R., 1950s

D: 780 tons (fl) **S:** 10 kts **Dim:** 56.0 × 9.0 × 2.7
A: 4/25-mm AA (II × 2) **M:** 2 diesels; 2 props; 1,200 hp

NOTE: All MP-6-class landing ships were converted to cargo ships in the early 1960s, and most are still in service as auxiliaries. The small MP-2-class ships are out of service.

♦ *36 Vydra-class utility landing craft* — Bldr: U.S.S.R., 1967

D: 750 tons (fl) **S:** 10.5 kts **Dim:** 55.0 × 7.6 × 2.7
A: None **M:** 2 diesels; 2 props; 600 hp

♦ *40 SMB-I-class utility landing craft* — Bldr: U.S.S.R., 1959-64

SMB I class Siegfried Breyer

D: 335 tons (fl) **S:** 10 kts **Dim:** 48.2 × 6.5 × 2.0
A: None **Cargo:** 180 tons
M: 2 diesels; 2 props; 600 hp **Range:** 400/8

♦ *several Lebed-class surface-effect landing craft*

D: 85 tons (fl) **S:** 60 kts **Dim:** 24.0 × 12.0 × . . .
M: 4 turbofans; 2 props **A:** . . .

REMARK: Can carry 1-2 PT-76 light tanks or 120 troops or about 45 tons of cargo.

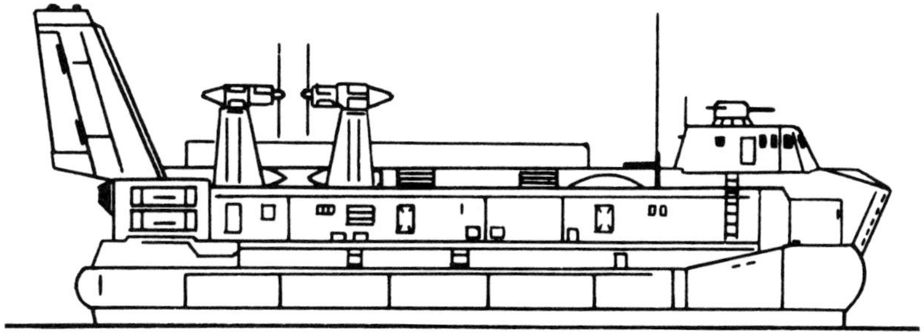

♦ *3 Aist-class surface-effect landing craft*

D: 220 tons (fl) **S:** 65 kts **Dim:** 47.8 × 17.5 × . . .
A: 2/30-mm AA (II × 1) **M:** 4 turbofans; 4 props; 2 lift fans

REMARK: Can carry 5 PT-76 light tanks or 4 PT-6 and 150 troops.

♦ *26 Gus-class surface-effect landing craft*

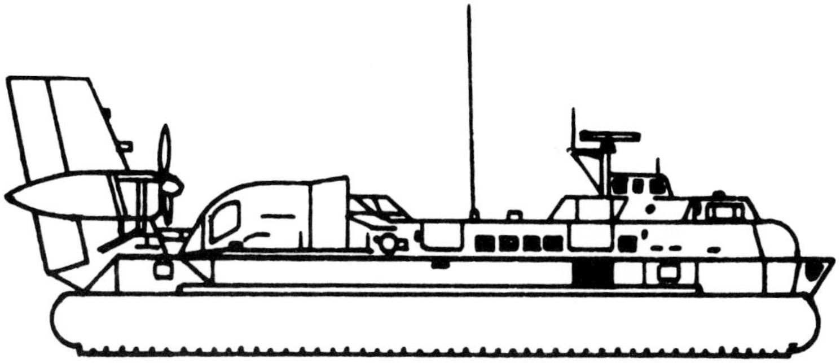

D: 27 tons (fl) **S:** 57.5 kts **Dim:** 21.3 × 8.2 × . . .
A: None **M:** 2 turbofans; 2 props; 1 lift fan; 2,340 hp

REMARKS: Can carry 24 troops. Drawing shows training version with two pilot positions.

SUBMARINE TENDERS

♦ *8 Ugra-class command tenders, 1963-72*

BORODINO, GANGUT, IVAN KOLYSHKIN, IVAN KUCHERENKO, IVAN VAKHRAMEYEV, TOBOL, VOLGA, N . . .

SUBMARINE TENDERS (*continued*)

Volga (with Vee Cone antenna aft) 1976

D: 9,000 tons (fl) **S:** 20 kts **Dim:** 141.4 × 17.7 × 6.5
A: 8/57-mm AA (II × 4) **Man:** 300 men **Range:** 10,000/12
Electron Equipt: Radars: 1-3 Don-2, 1 Strut Curve, 1 Muff Cob
M: 4 diesels; 2 props; 8,000 hp

Gangut 1974

REMARKS: One modified version of this was built for India as *Amba. Ivan Kolyshkin* has a tall helicopter hangar. The *Volga* is equipped with a Vee Cone communications antenna. The *Gangut* and *Borodino* are configured as training ships for naval officer cadets and do not serve submarines. The others can support 8 to 12 submarines at sea with supplies, fuel, provisions, water, and spare torpedoes as well as offer repair services. This class and the Don class are frequently used as flagships.

♦ *6 Don-class command tenders, 1958–61*

MAHOMET GADZHIEV
DMITRI GALKIN
VIKTOR KOTELNIKOV
FEDOR VIDYAEV
KAMCHATSKY KOMSOMOLETS
MAGADANSKY KOMSOMOLETS

Don class 1970

D: 6,700 tons (fl) **S:** 21 kts **Dim:** 137.0 × 16.8 × 5.2
A: 4/100-mm AA (I × 4) — 4/57-mm AA (II × 2) **Man:** 300 men
Electron Equipt: Radars: 1 Slim Net, 1 Sun Visor, 1-2 Don-2, 2 Hawk Screech
M: 4 diesels; 2 props; 8,000 hp

Dmitri Galkin with Vee Cone antenna 1974

REMARKS: Can serve as logistic support for a flotilla of 8 to 12 submarines. The *Viktor Kotelnikov*'s after 100-mm has been removed and replaced with a helicopter platform, while the *Magadansky Komsomolets* never had any 100-mm. The *Dmitri Galkin* and one other have 8/25-mm (II × 4) also, but no Hawk Screech. Two or three have been fitted with a Vee Cone radar for long-range communication. All are used as flagships. One unit was transferred to Indonesia.

SUBMARINE TENDERS (*continued*)

♦ *6 Atrek class* — Bldr: East Germany, 1955–57

ATREK, AYAT, BAKHMUT, DVINA, MURMAT, EVGENI OSIPOV

Atrek 1970

D: 4,000 tons (5,450 fl) **S:** 13 kts **Dim:** 102.4 × 14.4 × 5.5
M: 1 triple-expansion engine and 1 turbine; 1 prop; 2,000 hp
Range: 6,900/13

REMARKS: Modified Kolomna-class cargo ships. Bow reinforced for ice. Several carry 6/37-mm AA (II × 3).

MISSILE TRANSPORTS

♦ *2 Amga class* — Bldr: U.S.S.R.

AMGA (1973), **VETLUGA** (1976)

Amga 1973

D: 5,800 tons (fl) (?) **S:** 12 kts **Dim:** 110.0 × 17.0 × 4.4
A: 4/25-mm AA (II × 2) **M:** 2 diesels; 2 props; 4,000 hp

REMARKS: One 50-ton-capacity crane (reach: 34 m). Intended to transport SS-N-8 ballistic missiles for Delta-class submarines. Icebreaker bow.

♦ *6 Lama class*, 1963–72

Lama class

D: 6,000 tons (fl) **S:** 14 kts **Dim:** 113.0 × 15.0 × 5.0
A: 4 or 8/57-mm AA (IV × 1 or 2, or II × 2)
Electron Equipt: Radars: 1 Don-2, 1 Slim Net or Strut Curve, 1 or 2 Hawk Screech or 2 Muff Cob

REMARKS: Vary greatly in equipment. Intended to transport cruise missiles for submarines and surface ships. Two have larger missile-stowage areas and smaller cranes, and carry 4/25-mm AA (II × 2) additional; these apparently serve Nanuchka-class corvettes and Osa-class patrol boats. Two 20-ton precision cranes.

♦ *2 Modified Andizhan class*, 1950s

VENUTA, UILYUI

D: 6,800 tons (fl) **S:** 13.5 kts **Dim:** 104.0 × 14.4 × 6.6
A: None **Electron Equipt:** Radars: 2 Don-2
M: 1 diesel; 1,890 hp **Range:** 6,000/13

REMARKS: Converted from cargo ships. Large crane forward, two small cranes and helicopter deck aft.

REPAIR SHIPS

♦ *14 Amur class* — Bldr: Szczecin, Poland, 1968–74

Amur class 1970

REPAIR SHIPS (*continued*)

D: 6,000 tons (fl) **S:** 18 kts **Dim:** 120.0 × 17.4 × 5.2
A: None **Man:** 140 men
M: 2 diesels; 1 prop; 9,000 hp

REMARK: Enlarged version of the Oskol class.

♦ *12 Oskol class* — Bldr: Szczecin, Poland, 1964–67

Oskol class (flush-decked version) 1970

D: 3,000 tons (fl) **S:** 18 kts **Dim:** 91.4 × 12.2 × 4.0
Electron Equipt: Radar: 1 Don-2 **Man:** 60 men
M: 2 diesels; 1 prop; 4,000 hp

REMARKS: Most have well-deck forward of bridge. One unit has 2/57-mm AA (II × 1), 4/25-mm AA (II × 2). All have one 3.4-ton crane.

♦ *5 Dnepr class* — Bldr: U.S.S.R., 1960–64

Dnepr class (early version) 1960

D: 4,500 tons (fl) **S:** 11 kts **Dim:** 113.3 (100.0 pp) × 16.5 × 4.4
M: 1 diesel; 2,000 hp **Range:** 6,000/8.3 **Man:** 420 men

REMARKS: Hoisting equipment: 1/150-ton bow hoist, 1 kingpost, 1 crane; equipment varies from ship to ship. The two final units were flush-decked (Dnepr-II).

♦ *1 Tovda class* — Bldr: Gdansk, Poland, 1958

Tovda class 1959

D: 4,000 tons (fl) **S:** 11.5 kts **Dim:** 87.0 × 12.5 × 5.2
A: Removed **Man:** 100 men **Range:** 3,200/10
M: Reciprocating, 2 boilers; 1,350 hp

REMARKS: Converted collier, last of five. Possibly scrapped.

♦ *3 Tomba class* — Bldr: Sczcecin, Poland, 1975–7 . . .

Tomba class 1976

D: 6,000 tons (fl) **S:** 14 kts **Dim:** 107.0 × 17.0 × 5.0
A: None **Electron Equipt:** Radar: 1 Don-2
M: Diesels; 1 prop; 4,500 hp

REMARKS: Apparently intended to supply electrical power and steam in remote locations. Two funnels and "mack" on the forecastle. Two 3-ton cranes.

SUBMARINE RESCUE SHIPS

♦ *1 Nepa class* — Bldr: U.S.S.R.

KARPATY (1970)

D: 9,500 (fl) **S:** 18 kts **Dim:** 130.0 × 19.0 × 6.5
M: 2-4 diesels; 2 props; 8,000 hp **Man:** 270 men

SUBMARINE RESCUE SHIPS (*continued*)

Karpaty 1971

Remarks: 600-ton lift hook, some aft, others beneath hull. Very large all-purpose salvage ship with submarine-rescue equipment, including several rescue bells and observation chambers.

♦ *9 Prut class* — Bldr: U.S.S.R., post-1960

ALTAI, BESHTAV, VLADIMIR TREFOLEV, ZHIGULI, others with SS . . . numbers only

Beshtav 1969

D: 2,120 tons (2,640 fl) **S:** 18 kts **Dim:** 90.0 × 14.3 × 5.5
M: 4 diesels; 2 props; 8,000 hp **Electron Equipt:** Radars: 1-2 Don-2

Remark: One kingpost, two special carriers for rescue chambers.

♦ *14 Modified T-58-class minesweepers*, late 1950s

KAZBEK, KHIBINY, VALDAI, ZANGEZUR, others with SS . . . numbers only

D: 725 tons (840 fl) **S:** 18 kts **Dim:** 72.0 × 9.1 × 2.5
Electron Equipt: Radar: 1 Ball End or Don-2 **Man:** 60 men
M: 2 diesels; 2 props; 4,000 hp

Remarks: Lift rig overhanging stern to handle divers' gear. Rescue diving chamber to port.

♦ *9 Modified T-43-class minesweepers*, 1950s

D: 500 tons (580 fl) **S:** 14 kts **Dim:** 58.0 × 8.4 × 2.3
Electron Equipt: Radar: 1 Neptune **Man:** 77 men
M: 2 diesels; 2 props; 2,200 hp

Remark: Lift rig overhanging stern but no rescue chamber.

FLEET REPLENISHMENT SHIPS

♦ *5 Boris Chilikin class* — Bldr: Baltic Yd., Leningrad, 1971-7 . . .

BORIS CHILIKIN, DNESTR, GENRIKH GASANOV, IVAN BUBNOV, VLADIMIR KOLYACHITSKY

Boris Chilikin French Navy, 1972

Boris Chilikin (armed) French Navy, 1975

Ivan Bubnov 1975

FLEET REPLENISHMENT SHIPS (*continued*)

D: 24,450 tons (fl) **S:** 17 kts **Dim:** 162.3 × 21.4 × 8.9
A: 4/57-mm AA (II × 2)
Electron Equipt: Radars: 2 Don-Kay, 1 Muff Cob, 1 Strut Curve
M: 1 diesel; 9,600 hp **Range:** 10,000/16.6

Remarks: Navy version of merchant *Velikiv Oktubr* class. 16,300 dwt. Equipment varies: early units had solid stores, constant-tension rigs on both sides forward; later units only to starboard, with liquids to port. All have port and starboard liquid replenishment stations amidships and can replenish liquids over the stern. Cargo: 13,000 tons liquid (fuel oil, diesel, water); 400 tons ammunition; 400 tons provisions; 400 tons stores. The *Ivan Bubnov* and *Genrikh Gasanov* were completed in merchant colors, without guns, Strut Curve, or Muff Cob; the same equipment is being removed from the other ships.

♦ *2 (+2) Dubna class* — Bldr: Rauma-Repola, Finland, 1975-7 . . .

DUBNA, IRKUT, N . . ., N . . .

Irkut (refueling over stern, below) 1976

Irkut

D: 13,500 tons (fl) **S:** 16 kts **Dim:** 130.0 × 20.0 × 7.2
A: None **Man:** 80 men **M:** 1 diesel; 6,000 hp

Remarks: 6,022 grt/6,500 dwt. Two additional ordered spring 1977. Carry fuel, lube oil, fresh water, provisions, and spares. Can transfer 1-ton loads from constant-tension stations forward. Liquid replenishment from one station on port and starboard amidships and over stern. Painted merchant colors.

♦ *6 Uda class,* 1962-64

DUNAI, KOIDA, LENA, SHEKSNA, TEREK, VISHERA

Terek

D: 7,100 tons (fl) **S:** 17 kts **Dim:** 122.0 × 16.0 × 6.3
A: Removed **M:** 2 diesels; 2 props; 8,000 hp

Remarks: Three transferred to Indonesia. Equipped to carry 8/57-mm AA (IV × 2).

♦ *3 Kazbek class,* post-1954

ALATYR, DESNA, VOLKHOV

Note: In addition to these specially configured units of the class, the following merchant marine units have served the Soviet Navy from time to time: **ELBRUS, KAZBEK, KURSK, KAUNAS, LENINGRAD, ZITOMIR,** and others.

Desna (replenishing the cruiser *Nikolaev* and, aft a Kashin-class destroyer) 1973

FLEET REPLENISHMENT SHIPS (*continued*)

Desna 1971

D: 16,250 tons (fl) **S:** 14 kts **Dim:** 145.50 × 19.24 × 8.50
Man: 44 men **Range:** 18,000/14
M: 2 diesels; 2 props; 4,000 hp

REMARKS: 8,230 grt/11,800 dwt. Carry 11,600 tons fuel. The three naval units can be distinguished from their civilian sisters by two tall kingposts and an A-frame kingpost to support fueling hoses before the bridge and the working decks added over the cargo decks before and abaft the bridge.

♦ *1 ex-German, ex-Dutch* — Bldr: The Netherlands, 1940

POLYARNIK (ex-*Karnten*)

D: 12,500 tons (fl) **S:** 15.2 kts **Dim:** 132.1 × 16.2 × 7.6
M: 2 diesels; 2 props; 7,000 hp **Man:** 57 men

REMARKS: War reparations, 1946. Oldest oiler in any navy. 6,640 dwt. 5,600 tons liquid cargo, plus solid stores and provisions.

OILERS

♦ *6 Altay class* — Bldr: Rauma-Repola, Finland, 1969–73

ELNIA, ILIM, IZHORA, KOLA, EGORLYK

Izhora U.S. Navy, 1975

D: 7,400 tons (fl) **S:** 14.2 kts **Dim:** 106.0 × 15.0 × 6.7
M: 1 Burmeister & Wain diesel; 2,900 hp **Man:** 60 men
Range: 8,600/12

REMARKS: 3,670 grt/5,045 dwt. Able to replenish over stern. More than two dozen sisters in Soviet merchant marine.

♦ *1 Sofia class* — Bldr: U.S.S.R., 1969

AKHTUBA (ex-*Khanoi*)

Akhtuba (as merchant Khanoi) French Navy, 1969

D: 62,600 tons (fl) **S:** 17 kts **Dim:** 230.6 × 31.0 × 11.8
M: Steam turbine; 1 prop; 19,000 hp **Man:** 70 men
Range: 20,900/17

REMARKS: 32,840 grt/49,385 dwt. Largest ship in Soviet Navy. Carries 44,500 tons liquid cargo. Can refuel over stern.

♦ *4 Olekhma and Pevek classes* — Bldr: Rauma-Repola, Finland, mid-1960s

AKSAI, OLEKHMA, IMAN — and **ZOLOTOI ROG** (*Pevek* class)

D: 6,700 tons (fl) **S:** 14 kts **Dim:** 105.0 × 14.8 × 6.8
M: 1 diesel; 2,900 hp **Range:** 7,900/13.6 **Man:** 40 men

REMARKS: 3,300 grt/4,400 dwt. Predecessor to *Altai* design but with conventional "3-island" tanker layout. The *Zolotoi Rog* differs slightly. All can refuel over stern.

♦ *2 or more Baskunchak class* — Bldr: U.S.S.R.

SILVET, UKHTA, N . . .

D: 2,920 tons (fl) **S:** 13 kts **Dim:** 83.6 × 12.0 × 4.9
M: 2 diesels; 2,000 hp **Range:** 5,000/13

REMARKS: 1,756 grt/1,660 dwt. Sister *Usedom* in East German Navy; others in Soviet merchant marine.

♦ *5 Konda class* — Bldr: Sweden, 1950s

KONDA, ORSK, ROSSOSH, SOYANA, IAKHROMA

D: 1,980 tons (fl) **S:** 12 kts **Dim:** 69.0 × 10.0 × 4.3
M: 1 diesel; 1,600 hp **Range:** 2,470/10

REMARKS: 1,117 grt/1,265 dwt.

♦ *3 Nertcha class* — Bldr: Finland, 1950s

KLIASMA, NARA, NERTCHA

D: 1,800 tons (fl) **S:** 11.3 kts **Dim:** 63.5 × 10.0 × 4.5
M: 1 diesel; 1,000 hp **Range:** 2,000/10

REMARKS: 1,081 grt/1,127 dwt.

OILERS (*continued*)

♦ *approx. 18 Khobi class* — Bldr: U.S.S.R., early 1950s

Possible names:

ALAZAN, BRIMAK, CHEREMSHAN, GORYN, INDIGA, KHOBI, LOVAT, METAN, MOKSHA, ORSHA, SHACHA, SEIMA, SHELON, SOSVA, SYSOLA TARTU, TITAN, TUNGUSKA

D: 1,525 tons (fl) **S:** 12 kts **Dim:** 62.0 × 10.0 × 4.4
M: 2 diesels; 2 props; 1,600 hp **Man:** 37 men

REMARKS: Being discarded. 795 grt. Refuel over bows while being towed by receiving ship. *Linda* and one other to Albania 1959; others to Indonesia.

WATER TANKERS

♦ *2 Manych class* — Bldr: U.S.S.R.

MANYCH (1971) — **TAGIL** (1977)

Manyeh 1972

D: 8,600 tons (fl) **S:** 18 kts **Dim:** 115.0 × 15.5 × 7.0
A: 4/57-mm AA (II × 2) — removed from *Manych*
Electron Equipt: Radars: 2 Don Kay, 1 Strut Curve, 2 Muff Cob
M: 2 diesels; 2 props; 9,000 hp **Man:** 90 men

REMARKS: Originally intended as a small replenishment oiler to carry fuel and solid stores for submarines. Reported in Soviet press as unsuccessful, *Manych* was assigned as a water tender to support the Mediterranean Squadron; her guns were removed, but her fire-control equipment remains. The appearance of a second unit may indicate the earlier difficulties with the design have been overcome.

♦ *14 Voda class,* 1950s

ABAKAN, SURA

Voda class 1972

D: 3,100 tons (fl) **S:** 12 kts **Dim:** 81.5 × 11.5 × 4.3
M: 2 diesels; 2 props; 1,600 hp **Man:** 40 men

SPECIAL LIQUIDS TANKERS

♦ *1 Ural class,* 1970(?)

D: 2,000 tons (fl) **S:** 12 kts **Dim:** 80.0 × 12.0 × 4.5
M: 2 diesels; 1 prop; 1,200 hp

REMARK: Nuclear-waste transporter.

♦ *9 Luza class,* 1960s

ALAMBAI, ARAGUI, BARGUZIN, DON, KANA, OKA, SASIMA, SELENGA, ENISEI

D: 2,000 tons (fl) **S:** 11 kts **Dim:** 63.0 × 11.0 × 4.3
M: 1 diesel; 1,000 hp

REMARK: Volatile-fuels carriers.

♦ *5 Vala class*

REMARK: Carry waste from nuclear-propulsion plants.

TRANSPORT

♦ *1 Mikhail Kalinin class* — Bldr: East Germany

KUBAN (ex-*Nadezhdia Krupsaya*)

D: 6,400 tons (fl) **S:** 18 kts **Dim:** 122.2 × 16.0 × 5.1
M: 2 M.A.N. diesels; 2 props; 8,000 hp **Range:** 8,100/17

REMARKS: Former passenger-cargo ship used to rotate crews on ships in the Mediterranean Squadron. 5,260 grt/1,354 dwt. Can carry 340 passengers, 1,000 tons cargo.

CARGO SHIPS

♦ *1 Amguema class* — Bldr: U.S.S.R., 1975

YAUZA

D: 15,100 tons (fl) **S:** 15 kts **Dim:** 133.1 × 18.9 × 9.1

CARGO SHIPS *(continued)*

Yauza 1976

Electron Equipt: Radars: 2 Don-2 **Range:** 10,000/15
M: 4 diesels (1,800 hp each), electric drive; 1 prop; 7,200 hp

REMARKS: 7,900 grt/9,045 dwt. Icebreaking passenger-cargo ship. Numerous merchant sisters. 6,600 tons cargo.

♦ *3 Yuny Partizan class* — Bldr: Romania, 1975-7 . . .

TURGAY, PECHORA, PINEGA

D: 2,840 tons (fl) **S:** 12.9 kts **Dim:** 88.7 × 12.8 × 5.2
M: 1 diesel; 2,080 hp **Range:** 4,000/12 **Man:** 25 men

REMARKS: 2,079 grt/2,150 dwt. Small container ship; 21 sisters are civilian. Three 10-ton cranes.

♦ *10 Keyla class* — Bldr: Hungary, 1960-66

BEREZINA, MEZEN, ONEGA, PONOI, RITSA TEREBERKA, TULOMA, UNZHA, YERUSLAN

D: 2,000 tons (fl) **S:** 12 kts **Dim:** 78.5 × 10.5 × 4.6
M: 1 diesel; 1,000 hp **Range:** 4,200/10.7 **Man:** 26 men

REMARKS: 1,296 grt/1,280 dwt. Carry 1,100 tons cargo. The *Ritsa* has a deckhouse over her after hatch, numerous communications antennas.

♦ *5 MP-6 class, former landing ships* — Bldr: Hungary, 1959-60

BIRA, BUREYA, IRGIZ, KHOPER, VOLOGDIA

D: 2,100 tons (fl) **S:** 12 kts **Dim:** 75.0 × 11.3 × 4.4
M: 1 diesel; 1,000 hp

REMARKS: Unsuccessful as landing ships, bow doors welded closed.

♦ *1 Andizhan class* — Bldr: East Germany, 1959

ONDA

D: 6,739 tons (fl) **S:** 13.5 kts **Dim:** 104.2 × 14.4 × 6.6
M: 1 diesel; 1,890 hp **Range:** 6,000/13.5 **Man:** 44 men

REMARKS: 3,368 grt/4,324 dwt. 3,954 tons cargo. Two naval sisters are now missile transports; others are in merchant service.

♦ *5 Chulym class* — Bldr: Poland, 1950s

INSAR, KAMCHATKA, LENINSK, KUZNETSKY, PECHENGA, SEVERODONETSK

D: 7,200 tons (fl) **S:** 12 kts **Dim:** 108.2 × 14.6 × 7.2
M: Reciprocating plus TG; 1 prop; 1,650 hp **Range:** 8,500/11.5

REMARKS: 2,135 grt/3,120 dwt. 2,240 tons cargo. Coal-burners.

♦ *2 Donbass class* — Bldr: East Germany, 1950s

ANADYR, SVIR

D: 7,200 tons (fl) **S:** 12 kts **Dim:** 108.2 × 14.6 × 7.2
M: Reciprocating steam; 1 prop; 2,300 hp **Range:** 9,800/12

REMARKS: 3,561 grt/4,864 dwt. 3,570 tons cargo. Coal-burners.

♦ *4 Kolomna class* — Bldr: East Germany, 1950s

KRASNOARMESK, KUZNETSK, MEGRYA, SVANETYA

D: 6,700 tons (fl) **S:** 13 kts **Dim:** 102.3 × 14.4 × 6.6
M: Reciprocating steam plus TG; 1 prop; 2,450 hp **Man:** 44 men
Range: 6,890/13

REMARKS: 3,758 grt/4,355 dwt. 3,634 tons cargo. Six sisters serve as *Atrek*-class submarine tenders. Coal-burners.

♦ *4 Telnovsk class* — Bldr: Hungary, 1949-57

BUREVESTNIK, ISHIM, LAG, MANOMETR

D: 1,700 tons (fl) **S:** 11 kts **Dim:** 70.0 × 10.0 × 4.2
M: 1 diesel; 800 hp **Range:** 3,300/9.7 **Man:** 40 men

REMARKS: 1,194 grt/1,133 dwt. Several others serve as survey ships. Being discarded.

♦ *up to 25 Khabarovsk class* — Bldr: U.S.S.R., 1950s

D: 600 tons (fl) **S:** 10 kts **Dim:** 46.0 × 8.0 × 3.0

REMARKS: Some are civilian, others may be degaussing tenders.

PROVISIONS SHIPS

♦ *8 Mayak class, former trawlers* — Bldr: U.S.S.R., 1970s

BUZULUK, ISHIM, LAMA, MIUS, NEMAN, RIONI, ULMA, VITEGRA

D: 1,050 tons (fl) **S:** 11 kts **Dim:** 54.3 × 9.3 × 3.6
M: 1 diesel; 800 hp **Range:** 9,400/11 **Man:** 29 men

REMARKS: 690 grt. Naval sisters operate as intelligence collectors.

♦ *up to 15 Lentra class* — Bldr: East Germany, 1949-57

ALMA, KASHA, UGRA, RUZA, etc.

D: 250 tons (266 fl) **S:** 11 kts **Dim:** 39.2 × 7.4 × 3.4
M: 1 diesel; 300 or 400 hp

REMARKS: Being discarded; several sisters serve as intelligence collectors.

AMMUNITION SHIPS

♦ *9 Muna class*

Muna class

D: 750 tons (fl) **S:** 11 kts **Dim:** 50.0 × 9.0 × 3.8
M: 1 diesel; 600 hp

REMARKS: Specialized transports for torpedoes and perhaps also surface-to-air missiles.

MOORING TENDERS

♦ *10 Sura class* — Bldr: East Germany, 1965-7 . . .

Sura class

D: 3,150 tons (fl) **S:** 13 kts **Dim:** 87.0 (68.0 pp) × 14.8 × 5.0
M: 4 diesels, electric drive; 2 props; 2,240 hp **Range:** 4,000/10

REMARKS: 2,366 grt. 890 tons cargo in hold amidships. Stern rig, which can lift 60 tons, is used to lift mooring buoys and for salvage. Construction recently resumed.

♦ *14 Neptun class* — Bldr: East Germany, 1957-60

Neptun class

D: 1,240 tons (fl) **S:** 12 kts **Dim:** 57.3 (46.5) × 11.4 × 3.4
M: 2 triple-expansion; 1,000 hp **Range:** 1,000/11 **Man:** 41 men

REMARKS: Most burn coal. 80-ton bow lift for buoy-handling and salvage.

CABLE LAYERS

♦ *6 Klazma class* — Bldr: Wärtsilä, Finland, 1962-7 . . .

DONETS, INGUL, KATUN, TSNA, ZEYA, YANA

Klazma class (later unit)

D: 6,900 tons (fl) **S:** 16 kts **Dim:** 130.4 (120.0 pp) × 16.0 × 5.2
M: 4 or 5 diesels, electric drive; 4,238 hp **Range:** 12,000/14

REMARKS: Two more under construction. 5,645 grt/3,400 dwt. The *Ingul* and *Yana* have 5 diesels and a longer forecastle.

CABLE LAYERS (*continued*)

♦ *3 or 4 Kalar class* — Bldr: Hungary, 1954-56

D: 4,000 tons **S:** 11 kts **Dim:** 87.0 × 12.5 × 5.2
M: Reciprocating steam, 1 prop; 1,350 hp **Range:** 3,200/10

REMARKS: Former colliers; same original design as *Tovda* class.

FLEET OCEAN TUGS

♦ *4 Goryn class* — Bldr: Rauma-Repola, Finland, 1977-78

D: 2,600 tons (fl) **S:** 13.5 kts **Dim:** 63.5 × 14.3 × 5.1
M: 1 diesel; 3,500 hp

REMARKS: For ocean towing, salvage, and fire-fighting; 35-ton pull.

♦ *5-6 Sorum class* — Bldr: U.S.S.R., 1974-7 . . .

KAMCHATKA, SAKHALIN, others with "MB" hull numbers

Sakhalin 1975

D: 1,210 tons (1,656 fl) **S:** 14 kts **Dim:** 58.3 × 12.6 × 4.6
A: 4/30-mm (II × 2) — named units only **Man:** 35 men
Electron Equipt: Radars: 2 Don-2 **Range:** 6,720/13
M: 2 5-2D42 diesels, electric drive; 1 prop; 1,500 hp **Fuel:** 322 tons

REMARKS: Units with names apparently manned by the KGB.

♦ *57 Okhtensky class* — Bldr: U.S.S.R., 1960s

D: 700 tons (950 fl) **S:** 13.3 kts **Dim:** 47.3 × 10.3 × 5.5
M: 2 diesels; 1 prop; 1,500 hp **Range:** 7,800/7

REMARKS: Several have 2/57-mm AA (II × 1) and are probably manned by the KGB and used as patrol ships. Units of this class with names are civilian; naval units have "MB" (ocean tug) or "SB" (rescue tug) hull numbers.

Okhtensky class 1965

♦ *12-16 Roslavl class* — Bldr: U.S.S.R., 1950s

D: 750 tons (fl) **S:** 11 kts **Dim:** 44.5 × 9.5 × 3.5
M: Diesel-electric; 2 props; 1,200 hp **Man:** 28 men

♦ *10-12 Priboi or Zenit class* — Bldr: Finland, 1948-55

D: 800 tons (fl) **S:** 10 kts **Dim:** 47.9 × 10.0 × 4.3
M: Reciprocating steam; 2 props; 800 hp **Range:** 10,000/8

RESCUE TUGS

♦ *2 Ingul class* — Bldr: Admiralty, Leningrad, 1975-7 . . .

PAMIR, MASHUK

Ingul class

RESCUE TUGS (*continued*)

D: 4,000 tons (fl) **S:** 20 kts **Dim:** 92.8 × 15.4 × 5.8
Electron Equipt: Radars: 2 Don-2 **Man:** 120 men
M: 2 type 58D-4R diesels; 2 props; 9,000 hp **Range:** 9,000/18.7

REMARKS: Two sisters, *Yaguar* and *Bars,* are in the merchant marine. Very powerful tugs with constant-tension highline personnel rescue systems, salvage pumps, fire-fighting equipment and very complete diving gear.

♦ *2 Pamir class* — Bldr: Gäyle, Sweden, 1958

AGATAN, ALDAN

Agatan

D: 2,300 tons (fl) **S:** 17.5 kts **Dim:** 78.0 × 12.8 × 4.0
Range: 15,200/17.5, 21,800/12
Electron Equipt: Radar: 1-2 Don or Don-2
M: 2 M.A.N. G10V 40/60 diesels; 2 controllable-pitch props; 4,200 hp

REMARKS: Two sisters, *Gidrograf* and *Peleng,* are intelligence collectors.

♦ *3 Orel class* — Bldr: Finland

Orel class

D: 1,700 tons (fl) **S:** 15 kts **Dim:** 61.3 × 11.9 × 4.5
M: 1 M.A.N. G5Z52/70 diesel; 1,700 hp **Man:** 37 men
Range: 13,000/13.5

REMARK: Several civilian sisters.

SEAGOING FIREBOATS

♦ *5 Katun class* — Bldr: U.S.S.R., 1970-7 . . .

Katun class

D; 1,016 tons (fl) **S:** 17 kts
M: 2 40DM diesels; 4,000 hp
Dim: 62.6 × 10.2 × 3.6
Man: 32 men
Range: 2,200/16

REMARKS: Extensive fire-fighting gear, including extendable boom. Powerful pumps. Several civilian sisters, one of which is the *General Gamidov.*

INTELLIGENCE COLLECTORS

NOTE: The Soviets man many ships, often designated ELINT (Electronic Intelligence) or SIGINT (Signal Intelligence), that look like trawlers; others, such as the *Primorye* class, are obviously configured for their roles. No longer is any pretense made that the AGIs are anything but intelligence collectors, which detect and analyze radio-electric and electro-magnetic signals. Some patrol the offshore stations of strategic submarines, others follow Western fleets.

♦ *6 Primorye class*

KAVKAZ, KRYM, PRIMORYE, ZABAYKALE, ZAKAPAT'E, ZAPOROZHE

D: 3,400 tons (4,500 fl) **S:** 12 kts
M: 2 diesels; 1 prop; 2,000 hp
Dim: 84.7 × 14.0 × 7.0
Man: 117 men

INTELLIGENCE COLLECTORS (*continued*)

Primorye

Zaporozhe

REMARKS: Although these ships resemble small passenger liners, they are in fact modified versions of *Mayakovsky*-class stern-haul factory trawlers. Have the most extensive arrays and are the newest and largest of the Soviet ELINT/SIGINT ships.

♦ *6 Moma class, ex-survey ship/buoy tenders* — Bldr: Poland

ARKHIPELAG, IL'MEN, NAKHODKA, PELORUS, SELIGER, YUPITR

D: 1,260 tons (1,540 fl) **S:** 17 kts **Dim:** 73.3 × 10.8 × 3.8
M: 2 Sgoda 6TD48 diesels; 2 props; 3,600 hp **Range:** 8,000/11

Yupitr — Moma class 1976

REMARKS: The *Yupitr* (see photo) and *Arkhipelag* have new superstructures in the area forward of the bridge and new masts (deckhouse larger in the *Arkhipelag*); the others are much less modified, most merely having a few canvas-covered antennas atop the bridge.

♦ *8 Mayak class, ex-trawlers*

ANEROID, GIRORULEVOY, KHERSONES, KURS, KURSOGRAF, LADOGA, GS 239, GS 242

Kurs — Mayak class 1975

INTELLIGENCE COLLECTORS (*continued*)

D: 1,050 tons (fl) **S:** 11 kts **Dim:** 54.2 × 9.3 × 3.6
M: 1 8NVD48 diesel; 800 hp **Range:** 9,400/11

REMARK: Vary greatly in appearance and equipment.

GS 239 — Mayak class 1975

♦ *2 Nikolai Zubov class, ex-oceanographic ships* — Bldr: Poland

KHARITON LAPTEV, GAVRIL SARYCHEV

Gavril Sarychev — Nikolay Zubov class U.S. Navy, 1970

D: 2,200 tons (3,100 fl) **S:** 16.5 kts **Dim:** 90.0 × 13.0 × 4.7
M: 2 Sgoda 85D48 diesels; 2 props; 4,800 hp **Range:** 11,000/14

REMARKS: Similar to oceanographic-research ship sisters but have collection of antenna arrays.

♦ *2 Pamir class, ex-rescue tugs* — Bldr: Sweden

GIDROGRAF, PELENG (ex-*Pamir*)

Gidrograf — Pamir class

REMARKS: Data as for rescue tug sisters *Agatan* and *Aldan*. Both heavily modified with extra deckhouse levels, extended forecastle, numerous collection antenna arrays, etc. Extremely long range (21,000 nautical miles at 12 knots) makes them invaluable in the Pacific and Indian oceans.

♦ *4 Mirny class, ex-whalers*

BAKAN, LOTSMAN, VAL, VERTIKAL

Val — Mirny class French Navy, 1972

INTELLIGENCE COLLECTORS (*continued*)

D: 1,300 tons (fl) **S:** 17.5 kts **Dim:** 63.0 × 9.5 × 4.5
M: 4 diesels, electric drive; 1 prop; 4,000 hp **Range:** 18,700/11

REMARKS: Differ in detail; very low freeboard amidships.

♦ *15 Okean trawler class* — Bldr: East Germany

ALIDADA	**DEFLEKTOR**	**LINZA**	**TEODOLIT**
AMPERMETR	**EKHOLOT**	**LOTLIN**	**TRAVERZ**
BAROGRAF	**GIDROFON**	**REDUKTOR**	**ZOND**
BAROMETR	**KRENOMETR**	**REPITR**	

Zond — Okean trawler class French Navy, 1976

Alidada — Okean trawler class 1975

D: 700 tons (fl) **S:** 11 kts **Dim:** 50.8 × 8.9 × 3.7
M: 1 diesel; 540 hp **Range:** 7,900/11

REMARK: Appearances vary greatly.

♦ *2 Dnepr class, ex-tuna boats* — Bldr: Japan

IZERMETEL, PROTRAKTOR

D: 750 tons (fl) **S:** 11 kts **Dim:** 52.7 × 9.2 × 3.5
M: 2 Burmeister & Wain diesels; 1 prop; 1,210 hp

♦ *1 T-58 class, ex-submarine rescue ship*

GIDROLOG

REMARKS: For details, see T-58-class submarine rescue ships. Very few external differences, even retaining full rescue and diving capability.

♦ *6-8 Lentra class* — Bldr: East Germany

D: 250 tons (266 fl) **S:** 11 kts **Dim:** 39.2 × 7.4 × 3.4
M: 1 diesel; 300 or 400 hp

REMARKS: Actually three different classes, length varies by 3-5 m. No longer sighted and may have been scrapped.

OCEANOGRAPHIC RESEARCH SHIPS

NOTE: The only units included are those known to be subordinate to the Soviet Navy. There are in addition nearly 300 research ships under the control of civilian agencies, primarily the Ministry of Science and the Ministry of Fisheries. Some of the civilian ships may from time to time perform research in support of military aims, but their purpose is primarily peaceful and, because of their number and variety, they cannot be described here. Such ships include the seven-unit *Akademik Kurchatov* expeditionary ships, the nine *Passat*-class weather ships, and the large and complex *Yuri Gagarin, Kosmonaut Vladimir Komorov, Akademik Sergei Korolev*, as well as the 17 or more Finnish-built *Dmitri Ovtslin* arctic oil survey ships, which operate under the Ministry of the Merchant Marine. All naval units are painted white.

♦ *4 Akademik Krylov class* — Bldr: Poland, 1974-75

ADMIRAL VLADIMIRSKY, AKADEMIK KRYLOV, IVAN KRUZHENSTERN, LEONID SOBELYEV

Akademik Krylov 1975

OCEANOGRAPHIC RESEARCH SHIPS (*continued*)

D: 9,100 tons (fl) **S:** 20.4 kts **Dim:** 147.0 × 18.6 × 6.3
Endurance: 90 days **Man:** 90 men
M: 4 diesels; 2 props; 16,000 hp **Range:** 23,000/15.4

REMARKS: Largest ships of their type in any navy. Helicopter hangar and flight deck, 2 survey launches, 26 laboratories totaling 900 m^2.

♦ *2 Vladimir Kavraysky class* — Bldr: Leningrad

VLADIMIR KAVRAYSKY (1973), **OTTO SCHMIDT** (1978)

D: 3,900 tons (fl) **S:** 15.4 kts **Dim:** 70.0 × 18.0 × 6.4
Endurance: 60 days **Range:** 13,900/9.4
M: 3 13D100 diesels, electric drive; 2 props; 4,800 hp

REMARKS: Greatly modified version of *Dobrynya Nikitich* icebreaker class for arctic research. Helicopter deck but no hangar. Carry survey launch and have 9 laboratories totaling 180 m^2. The *Otto Schmidt* may differ in appearance.

♦ *4 Abkhazia class* — Bldr: East Germany

ABKHAZIA, ADZHARYA, BASHKIRYA, MOLDAVYA

Abkhazia

D: 7,500 tons (fl) **S:** 21 kts **Dim:** 124.2 × 17.0 × 6.4
Man: 85 men **Range:** 20,000/16 **Endurance:** 60 days
M: 2 M.A.N. K6Z 57/80 diesels; 2 props; 8,000 hp

REMARKS: Military version of *Akademik Kurchatov* class with helicopter deck, telescoping hangar, Vee Cone communications antenna, stern-mounted A-frame lift gear, 2 survey launches, and 27 laboratories totaling 460 m^2.

♦ *9 Nikolai Zubov class* — Bldr: Poland, 1963-68

**ALEKSEI CHIRIKOV FADDEI BELLINCGAUZEN SEMEN CHELYUSKIN
ANDREI VILKITSKI FEDOR LITKE SEMEN DEZHNEV
BORIS DAVIDOV NIKOLAI ZUBOV VASILY GOLOVNIN**

Andrei Vilkitski — Nikolai Zubov class

D: 2,200 tons (3,020 fl) **S:** 16.5 kts **Dim:** 90.0 × 13.0 × 4.7
M: 2 Sgoda 85D48 diesels; 4,800 hp **Range:** 11,000/14
Endurance: 60 days **Man:** 50 men

REMARKS: Considerable variation from ship to ship. Can carry four survey launches but usually have only two. Small deck aft for weather balloons, not helicopters. Nine laboratories totaling 120 m^2.

♦ *1 Nevelskoy class* — Bldr: U.S.S.R., 1962

NEVELSKOY

Nevelskoy

OCEANOGRAPHIC RESEARCH SHIPS (*continued*)

D: 2,350 tons (fl) **S:** 18 kts **Dim:** 83.0 × 15.2 × 3.6
M: 2 diesels; 2 props; 4,000 hp **Man:** 45 men

REMARKS: The *only* naval oceanographic research ship of Soviet origin; apparently a prototype for the *Nikolai Zubov* design.

♦ *3 Polyus class* — Bldr: East Germany, 1962-64
BAIKAL, BAL'KHASH, POLYUS

Baikal

D: 6,700 tons **S:** 14.2 kts **Dim:** 111.6 × 14.4 × 6.3
M: 4 diesels, electric drive; 2 props; 4,000 hp
Endurance: 75 days **Range:** 25,000/12.3

REMARK: Seventeen laboratories totaling 290 m^2.

HYDROGRAPHIC SURVEY SHIPS

NOTE: Ships of the Moma, Biya, Kamenka, and Samara classes perform the combined duties of hydrographic survey ships and navigational tenders, handling buoys and marking channels, etc. Most can carry and emplace two to six navigational buoys. In addition, they are equipped to take basic oceanographic and meteorological samplings.

♦ *23 Moma class* — Bldr: Poland, 1967-74
ALTAIR, ANADYR, ANDROMEDA, ANTARES, ANTARKTYDA, ARKTIKA, ASKOLD, BEREZEN, CHELEKEN, EKVATOR, ELTON, KILDIN, KOLGUEV, KRILON, LIMAN, MARS, MORZHOVETS, ODOGRAF, OKEAN, SEVER, TAYMYR, VEGA, ZAPOLYARE

D: 1,260 tons (1,540 fl) **S:** 17 kts **Dim:** 73.3 × 10.8 × 3.8
Man: 56 men **Electron Equipt:** Radar: 2 Don-2
M: 2 Sgoda 6 TD48 diesels; 2 controllable-pitch props; 3,600 hp
Range: 8,700/11 **Endurance:** 35 days

REMARKS: Carry one survey launch, 5-ton crane. Four laboratories totaling 35 m^2. Sisters in Polish and Yugoslav navies.

Elton — Moma class French Navy

♦ *10 Biya class* — Bldr: Poland, 1972-7 . . .

D: 750 tons (fl) **S:** 13 kts **Dim:** 55.0 × 9.2 × 2.6
Man: 25 men **Electron Equipt:** Radar: 1 Don-2
Endurance: 15 days
M: 2 diesels; 2 controllable-pitch props; 1,200 hp **Range:** 4,700/11

REMARKS: Similar to Kamenka class but with longer superstructure, less buoy-handling space; one survey launch. All ships have "GS" series hull numbers. Laboratory 15 m^2.

♦ *10 Kamenka class* — Bldr: Poland, 1968-7 . . .
BEL'BEK, SIMA, VERNER, others with "GS" numbers

GS-108 — Kamenka class

HYDROGRAPHIC SURVEY SHIPS (*continued*)

D: 703 tons (fl) **S:** 13.7 kts **Dim:** 53.5 × 9.1 × 2.6
M: 2 diesels; 2 controllable-pitch props; 1,765 hp **Range:** 4,000/10

REMARKS: Similar to Biya class but more facilities devoted to stowing and handling buoys. No survey launch. One sister in East German Navy.

♦ *16 Samara class* — Bldr: Poland, 1962-64

AZIMUT, GLOBUS, GLUBOMETR, GORIZONT, GRADUS, GIGROMETR, KOLESNIKOV, KOMPAS, PAMYAT MERKURIYA, RUMB, TROPIK, VAYGACH, VOSTOK, YUG, ZENIT

Gorizont — Samara class 1976

D: 1,050 tons (1,276 fl) **S:** 15.5 kts **Dim:** 59.0 × 10.4 × 3.8
Man: 45 men **Electron Equipt:** Radars: 2 Don-2
M: 2 Sgoda 5TD48 diesels; 2 controllable-pitch props; 3,000 hp
Range: 6,200/11 **Endurance:** 25 days

REMARKS: Survey launch. 15 m^2 laboratory space.

♦ *5 Telnovsk class* — Bldr: Hungary, 1949-57

AITODOR, SIRENA, STVOR, SVIYAGA, ULYANA GROMOVA

D: 1,700 tons (fl) **S:** 11 kts **Dim:** 70.0 × 10.0 × 4.2
M: 1 Ganz diesel; 800 hp **Range:** 3,300/9.7 **Man:** 50 men

REMARKS: Similar in most respects to cargo-ship version. The *Stvor* and *Ulyana Gromova* have lengthened poop decks. All carry one survey launch.

♦ *3 Melitopol class* — Bldr: U.S.S.R., 1950s

MAYAK, NIVILER, PRIZMA

D: 1,200 tons (fl) **S:** 11.3 kts **Dim:** 57.6 × 9.0 × 4.3
M: 1 6DR30/40 diesel; 600 hp **Range:** 2,500/10.5

Prizma — Melitopol class

REMARKS: Converted small 2-hatch cargo ships with few modifications; 673 grt/776 dwt. Carry one survey launch on deck.

♦ *up to 15 Lentra class* — Bldr: East Germany, 1948-57

GIDROSTAT, GROT, POLYARNIK, TAYFUN, others with "GS" numbers

D: 261 tons (fl) **S:** 11 kts **Dim:** 39.2 × 7.4 × 3.4
M: 1 diesel; 300 or 400 hp

MISSILE-RANGE SHIPS

♦ *8 Vytegrales class*

APSHERON, BASKUNCHAK, DIKSON, DAURIYA, DONBAS, SEVAN, TAMAN, YAMAL (1966)

D: 9,650 tons (fl) **S:** 16 kts **Dim:** 121.9 × 16.7 × 7.3
Range: 7,380/14.5 **Man:** 90 men
M: 1 Burmeister & Wain 950VTBF110 diesel; 1 prop; 5,200 hp

REMARKS: Former timber carriers converted for naval missile-associated duties. Few alterations; helicopter deck added over former after hold. Three holds and cargo cranes retained forward. Seven sisters converted as Academy of Sciences satellite tracking ships (3 *Borovichy*/4 *Kosmonaut* class).

MISSILE-RANGE SHIPS (*continued*)

Dauriya — Vytegrales class French Navy, 1972

♦ *2 Desna class* — Bldr: Poland, 1963

CHAZMA, CHUMIKAN

Chazma (hull now gray)

D: 14,065 tons (fl) **S:** 15 kts **Dim:** 139.9 × 18.0 × 7.9
Electron Equipt: Radars: 1 Head Net-B, 2 Don-2
M: 1 M.A.N. diesel; 5,400 hp

REMARKS: Heavily modified cargo ships. Tracking radar in large dome atop bridge, with three tracking directors mounted forward. Hormone helicopter with hangar aft. Vee Cone communications antennas atop deck.

♦ *4 Sibir class* — Bldr: East Germany, post-1958

CHUKOTKA, SAKHALIN, SIBIR, SPASSK (ex-*Suchan*)

D: 7,800 tons (fl) **S:** 12 kts **Dim:** 108.2 × 14.6 × 7.2
M: Triple-expansion; 1 prop; 2,300 hp **Range:** 11,800/12

Spassk (as Suchan) — **Sibir class** (hull now gray)

REMARKS: Converted Donbas-class cargo ships. Carry Big Net radar for tracking, plus three tracking directors forward. The *Chukotka* is flush-decked; others have well deck forward. All carry one Hormone helicopter; no hangar.

NOISE-MEASUREMENT SHIPS

♦ *2 or more Onega class,* 1973-7 . . .

D: 2,500 tons (fl) **S:** 20 kts **Dim:** 86.0 × 10.5 × 4.5
M: Gas turbines **Man:** 45 men

REMARKS: "GKS" in hull number indicates these ships are successors to the T-43-class noise-monitoring ships. Helicopter deck aft, long forecastle, two pylon masts, and a low stack.

♦ *20 Modified T-43 class,* 1950s

GKS-15

NOISE-MEASUREMENT SHIPS (*continued*)

D: 570 tons (fl) **S:** 14 kts **Dim:** 58.0 × 8.5 × 2.3
M: 2 diesels; 2 props; 2,200 hp **Man:** 77 men
Electron Equipt: Radar: 1 Neptune

REMARKS: "GKS" in hull number indicates use as noise-monitoring ships, presumably meaning that they measure the radiated noise of other ships, including submarines, by laying hydrophone arrays via the numerous small davits aft.

ICEBREAKERS

NOTE: The Soviet Union has far and away the largest and most powerful icebreaker fleet in the world. Its civilian component includes the first atomic-powered surface ship ever built, the *Lenin,* as well as the *Arktika* and her soon-to-be-completed sister *Sibir,* also nuclear-powered and the world's most powerful icebreakers. The Soviet Navy operates two types of icebreakers, patrol and support, both based on the same civilian design; these are among the very few conventionally driven icebreakers in service that were actually designed and built in the U.S.S.R., the remainder being of Finnish origin.

♦ *4 Ivan Susanin-class patrol icebreakers*

AYSBERG, IMENI XXV'S EZDA KPSS, IVAN SUSANIN, RUSLAN

Ivan Susanin 1975

D: 3,400 tons (fl) **S:** 14.5 kts **Dim:** 67.6 × 18.1 × 6.0
A: 2/76-mm DP (II × 1) — 2/23-mm Gatling AA (VI × 2)
Electron Equipt: Radars: 2 Don Kay, 1 Strut Curve, 1 Owl Screech
M: 3 diesels, electric drive; 2 props; 5,400 hp **Range:** 13,000/9.4

REMARKS: Based on the *Dobrynya Nikitich* and *Vladimir Kavraysky* designs. At least one is manned by the KGB. Helicopter deck aft, but no hangar. Gatling guns do not have Bass Tilt radar directors, as do other classes with that weapon.

♦ *7 or more Dobrynya Nikitich-class support icebreakers*

BURAN, DOBRYNYA NIKITICH, ILYA MUROMETS, PERESVET, PURGA, SADKO, VYUGA . . .

D: 2,940 tons (fl) **S:** 14.5 kts **Dim:** 67.7 × 18.3 × 6.1
A: 2/57-mm AA (II × 1) — 2/25-mm AA (II × 1) in several
Range: 5,500/12 **Man:** 100 men
Electron Equipt: Radar: 1-2 Don-2
M: 3 13D100 diesels, electric drive; 3 props (1 fwd); 5,400 hp

REMARKS: More than 20 of this class were built 1959-74 at Leningrad. The *Peresvet, Purga, Sadko,* and *Vyuga* are armed. Resemble *Ivan Susanin* class, but have much less superstructure and open fantail rigged for ocean towing.

TRAINING SHIPS

♦ *2 Smol'ny class* — Bldr: Warski SY, Szczecin, Poland

PEREKOP (1977), **SMOL'NY** (1976)

Smol'ny class 1977

Smol'ny class 1977

TRAINING SHIPS (*continued*)

D: 6,500 tons (fl) **S:** 20 kts (?) **Dim:** 137.5 × 16.7 × 6.3
A: 4/76-mm DP (II × 2) — 4/30-mm AA (II × 2) — 2/MBU 2500
Electron Equipt: Radars: 4 Don-2, 1 Head Net-C, 1 Owl Screech, 1 Drum Tilt
Sonar: 1 medium-frequency (?)
M: Diesels

REMARKS: Presumably to relieve the *Sverdlov*-class cruisers that were formerly used as cadet training ships. Can carry more than 270 cadets.

♦ *2 Ugra class*

BORODINO, GANGUT

REMARKS: See Ugra-class submarine tenders. Modified to carry more than 400 cadets on worldwide training cruises.

♦ *2 Modified Wodnik class* — Bldr: Poland, 1977

OKA, N . . .

D: 1,800 tons (fl) **S:** 17 kts **Dim:** 74.0 × 12.0 × 4.2
M: 2 diesels; 2 controllable-pitch props; 3,600 hp

REMARKS: Similar to Polish and East German units of the Wodnik class, but lack armament and have slightly larger superstructures. Based on the Moma design.

VARIOUS CRAFT

♦ *9 target-control boats*

Osa target

REMARKS: Have Osa hull and propulsion. Used to operate craft shown below by remote control. Square Tie radar.

♦ *8 missile targets, Modified Osa class*

Osa target controller

REMARKS: Have Osa hull and propulsion. Equipped with radar corner reflectors to enhance target strength and two heat-generator chimneys to attract infrared homing missiles.

♦ *9 missile targets, Modified P-6 class*

P-6 target-radar

REMARK: Former torpedo boats equipped with radar corner reflectors.

SERVICE CRAFT

The Soviet Navy operates more than 1,000 service craft in many categories. Space prohibits their description here.

Personnel: 63,600 officers, 476,000 enlisted

Merchant Marine (1976) — 4,616 ships — 14,900,445 grt
(Tankers: 319 ships — 5,601,607 grt).
Note: It should be remembered that ships flying flags of convenience (Liberia, Panama, etc.) carry a great deal of cargo and many are owned by American companies.

Naval Program

Five-Year Construction Plan 1978-82 (revised annually)
The U.S. Navy plans to request funding for the following new ships:

	FY 78*	FY 79	FY 80	FY 81	FY 82	Total
SSBN, *Ohio* class	2	1	2	1	2	8
SSN, *Los Angeles* class	2(1)	2	1	2	2	9
Aircraft carriers		1		1		
Destroyers, DDG-47 class	1		3	3	3	10
Destroyers, DD-997 class	(1)					1
Frigates, FFG-7 class	11(8)	8	8	8	8	43
Frigates, FFG-X class				1	1	2
Oilers, AO-177 class	4(2)	4	2	2	2	14
Fast oilers, AOE type				1		1
Destroyer tenders AD-39 class		1	1			2
Oceanographic ships, T-AGOS type		3	5	4		12
Fleet tugs, T-ATF type	5(3)	4				9
Cable-layer, T-ARC type		1				1
Salvage ships, T-ARS type			22		4	26
Total	25(17)	25	24	25	18	138

*Numbers in parentheses indicate units authorized and funded by Congress. A single DD-963(N) (not listed) is not likely to be built because the Navy did not request it and does not want it.

The Five-Year Plan also provides for SLEP (Service Life Extension) modernization on the carriers *Forrestal* and *Saratoga* to prolong their careers by 15 years and for modernization of the first 18 ships of the *Charles F. Adams*-class guided-missile destroyers, modernization of the remainder to be requested for the following year.

A new aircraft carrier called the "CVV," whose characteristics have yet to be worked out in detail, will not be nuclear-propelled.

Plans to build a new class of 6 amphibious landing ships (LSD-41) and a new class of 19 mine-warfare ships (MCM) have been canceled. They may be reintroduced at a later date.

FY 1976 Construction Program: 1 *Ohio*-class SSBN (SSBN-729), 2 SSN (SSN-714 and SSN-715), 6 FFG-7-class frigates (FFG-11 to FFG-16), 1 destroyer tender (AD-42), 2 oilers (AO-177 and AO-178).

FY 1977 Construction Program: 1 *Ohio*-class SSBN (SSBN-738), 3 SSN (SSN-716 to SSN-718), 8 FFG-7-class frigates (FFG-19 to FFG-26), 1 destroyer tender (AD-43), 1 submarine tender (AS-41), and one oiler (AO-179).

FY 1978 Construction Program: 2 *Ohio*-class SSBN (SSBN-731 and SSBN-732), 1 SSN (SSN-719), 1 DD-963(N), 1 DDG (DDG-47), 8 FFG-7-class frigates (FFG-27 to FFG-34), 2 oilers (AO-180 and AO-181), and 3 ocean tugs (ATF-170 to ATF-172). Plus long-lead items for the first Aegis cruiser (CGN-42) and modernizations for 6 DDG-2 class and one carrier.

END YEAR ACTIVE FLEET STATISTICS

	1976	1978
SSBN	41	41
Aircraft carriers (CVN, CV)	14	13
Cruisers (CG, CGN, CA)	27	27
Guided-missile destroyers (DDG)	39	39
Destroyers (DD)	29	31
Frigates (FF, FFG)	64	65
Nuclear-powered attack submarines (SSN)	68	71
Conventionally powered submarines (SS)	12	5
Patrol boats	13	4
Amphibious command ships (LCC)	2	2
Amphibious assault ships (LPH)(LHA)	7	7
Amphibious transports, dock (LPD)	14	14
Amphibious cargo and dock landing ships (LKA, LSD)	18	18
Tank landing ships (LST)	20	20
Minesweepers, fleet (MSO)	3	3
Auxiliary ships	117	100

Roughly half of these ships are in the Pacific (Third and Seventh Fleets) and half in the Atlantic (Second and Sixth Fleets). Only the Seventh and the Sixth Fleets — the latter assigned to the Mediterranean — are fully operational. The table does not include units assigned to Naval Reserve training (25 destroyers, 3 amphibious warfare ships, 20 minesweepers, approx. 46 small combatants, and 3 fleet tugs), or to the Military Sealift Command (67 ships).

MARINE CORPS

Created in 1775, the Marine Corps, which gives the Navy a distinctive quality, has three missions:

- to seize and/or defend advanced bases as needed for the operations of the fleet
- to furnish security detachments on board ships and at land bases
- to carry out any other operations that the president of the United States may assign.

The third mission permits the Corps to be used in operations that are not purely naval (e.g., Belleau Wood in 1918 and Vietnam in the 1960s and 1970s).

Its total strength is about 196,500 men, and they form three divisions (1 stationed in Okinawa/Japan, 2 in the United States), each of 18,000 men and three air wings, organized under two Fleet Marine Forces (FMF). These last also maintain heavy support elements for the divisions. A fourth division-wing team constitutes a reserve cadre.

The Marine Corps has approximately 400 fighter and attack aircraft (A-4M, A-6, AV-8, F-4), 600 assault and utility helicopters, over 500 tanks, and some 450 amphibious landing vehicles.

MARINE CORPS (*continued*)

The major operational unit is the Marine Amphibious Force (MAF), which consists of one division, one air wing, and Fleet Marine Forces augmentation, for a total of about 45,000 men.

Amphibious ships presently in service do not permit the rapid overseas deployment of MAFs, but only of two Marine Amphibious Brigades (MAB). An MAB consists of one Regimental Landing Team, a strong unit with two or more battalion landing teams of about 1,500 men each; one mixed air group of fighter, attack fixed-wing aircraft and/or helicopter squadrons; and some augmentation from the Fleet Marine Force.

The position of importance in U.S. military forces occupied by the Marines is illustrated by the following percentages:

15% of all land forces
12% of general warfare forces
9% of the total military force
3.5% of the military budget.

WARSHIPS IN SERVICE, UNDER CONSTRUCTION, OR PROJECTED AS OF 1 OCTOBER 1977

N = nuclear propulsion
H = ASW helicopter hangar and flight deck

	L	Tons	Main armament
♦ *14 attack carriers* (CVN, CV)			
3 NIMITZ (CVN)	1972–79	81,600	90/100 aircraft, 3 missile launchers
1 ENTERPRISE (CVN)	1960	75,700	80/100 aircraft, 3 missile launchers
1 JOHN F. KENNEDY	1967	61,000	70/90 aircraft, 3 missile launchers
3 KITTY HAWK	1960–64	60,100	70/90 aircraft, 3 missile launchers
4 FORRESTAL	1954–58	59,600	80/90 aircraft, 2/3 missile launchers
2 MIDWAY	1945–46	51,000	60/75 aircraft, 3/127 mm DP

♦ *12 helicopter carrier and amphibious assault ships* (LHA and LPH)

5 TARAWA (LHA)	1972–78	39,000 (fl)	3/127-mm DP, 2 missile launchers, 26 helicopters
7 IWO JIMA (LPH)	1960–69	17,000	4/76-mm, 2 missile launchers, 20 helicopters

* = "tear-drop" hulls and a single propeller
** = can also launch conventional torpedoes

♦ *144 nuclear-powered submarines* (SSBN, SSN)

		Tons (surfaced)	
7 OHIO* (SSBN)	1978–8 . . .	15,750	24 Trident-1, 4 TT
31 LAFAYETTE* (SSBN)	1962–66	7,250	16 Poseidon, 4 TT
5 ETHAN ALLEN* (SSBN)	1960–62	6,955	16 Polaris, 4 TT
5 GEORGE WASHINGTON* (SSBN)	1959–60	6,019	16 Polaris, 6 TT
32 LOS ANGELES*	1973– . . .	6,000	4/TT (Subroc)**
1 GLENARD P. LIPSCOMB*	1973	5,813	4/TT (Subroc)**
37 STURGEON*	1966–74	3,640	4/TT (Subroc)**
1 NARWHAL	1967	4,550	4/TT (Subroc)**
13 PERMIT*	1961–66	3,526	4/TT (Subroc)**
1 TULLIBEE*	1960	2,317	4/TT
5 SKIPJACK*	1958–60	3,075	6/TT
4 SKATE	1957–58	2,750	8/TT
1 SEAWOLF	1955	3,765	6/TT
1 NAUTILUS	1954	3,764	6/TT

♦ *9 diesel/electric-powered submarines* (SS)

3 BARBEL	1958–59	2,146	6/TT
1 SAILFISH	1955	2,625	6/TT
1 DARTER	1956	1,720	8/TT
3 TANG	1951–52	2,100	8/TT
1 GRAYBACK	1957	2,670	8/TT

♦ *2 diesel/electric-powered submarines* (AGSS)

1 DOLPHIN*	1968	800	. . .
1 TANG	1951	2,100	8/TT

♦ *30 cruisers*

		Tons	
10 guided-missile, nuclear-powered (CGN)			
1 CGN-42	. . .	12,000 (fl)	2 missile launchers, 2/127-mm DP, ASW TT, H
4 VIRGINIA	1974–78	11,260 (fl)	2 missile launchers 2/127-mm DP, ASW TT, H
2 CALIFORNIA	1971–72	9,560 (fl)	2 missile launchers, 2/127-mm DP, ASW TT
1 TRUXTUN	1964	8,200	1 missile launcher, 1/127-mm DP, 2/76-mm AA, ASW TT
1 BAINBRIDGE	1961	7,600	2 missile launchers, Asroc
1 LONG BEACH	1959	14,200	3 missile launchers, Asroc
20 guided-missile (CG)			
9 BELKNAP	1963–65	6,570	1 missile launcher, 1/127-mm DP, 2/76-mm AA, ASW TT, H
9 LEAHY	1961–63	5,670	2 missile launchers, 4/76-mm AA, ASW TT
2 ALBANY	1944–45	13,000	4 missile launchers, 2/127-mm DP, Asroc, H

CRUISERS (*continued*)

♦ *123 destroyers*

10 DDG-47	1981- . . .	9,010 (fl)	2 missile launchers, Harpoon, 2/127-mm, ASW TT, H
30 SPRUANCE	1973–79	8,010	1 missile launcher, 2/127-mm DP, Asroc, ASW TT, H
23 CHARLES F. ADAMS	1959–63	3,370	1 missile launcher, 2/127-mm DP, Asroc, ASW TT
10 COONTZ	1968–60	4,700	1 missile launcher, 1/127-mm DP, Asroc, ASW TT
4 DECATUR	1955–58	2,850	1 missile launcher, 1/127-mm DP, Asroc, ASW TT
2 MOD. MITSCHER	1952	3,680	1 missile launcher, 2/127-mm DP, Asroc, ASW TT
8 BARRY	1955–58	2,850	2/127-mm DP, Asroc, ASW TT
6 FORREST SHERMAN	1955–58	2,780	3/127-mm DP, ASW TT
2 CARPENTER	1945–46	2,400	2/127-mm DP, Asroc, ASW TT
28 GEARING	1944–46	2,400	4/127-mm DP, Asroc, ASW TT

♦ *86 frigates*

21 OLIVER HAZARD PERRY	1976- . . .	3,605 (fl)	1 missile launcher, 1/76-mm, ASW TT, H
46 KNOX	1966–73	3,011	1 or 2 missile launchers, 1/127-mm, ASW TT
6 BROOKE	1963–66	2,643	1 missile launcher, 1/127-mm, Asroc, ASW TT
10 GARCIA	1963–65	2,624	2/127-mm, Asroc, ASW TT
1 GLOVER	1965	2,650	1/127-mm, Asroc, ASW TT
2 BRONSTEIN	1962	2,360	2/76-mm, Asroc, ASW TT

WEAPONS AND SYSTEMS

(A) MISSILES

♦ *fleet ballistic missiles*

NOTE: All are launched from submerged submarines.

Polaris A2 (UGM 27B A2)

Length: 9.340 m
Diameter: 1.370 m
Weight: 14,500 kg at launch
Propulsion: solid propellant, two stages
Guidance: inertial
Warhead: 800 kt
Range: 1,500 nautical miles

Polaris A3 (UGM 27C A3)

Length: 9.520 m
Diameter: 1.370 m
Weight: 15,860 kg at launch
Propulsion: solid propellant, two stages
Guidance: inertial (same precision as the Polaris A2 but at a longer range)
Range: 2,500 nautical miles
Warhead: 1 MT or 3 independent but not individually controllable (MRV) of 200 kt each

Poseidon (UGM 73A)

Length: 10.400 m
Diameter: 1.830 m
Weight: about 30 tons at launch
Propulsion: solid propellant, two stages
Guidance: inertial
Range: 2,500 or 3,200 nautical miles
Warhead: 14 warheads with independent and controllable trajectory, each of 50 kt (MIRV) to 2,500 nautical miles or 10 of 50 kt to 3,200 nautical miles

Trident 1 (UGM-96A) C4

New type missile, operational in 1978 and designed for the *Ohio*-class SSBN which will carry 24 of them.

Length: 10.400 m
Weight: more than 30 tons at launch
Propulsion: solid propellant, three stages
Guidance: inertial
Range: about 4,000 miles
Warhead: 8 MIRV of 100 kt (Mk 4)

Trident 2 D5

Now under study

Length: 13.900 m
Weight: 57 tons
Propulsion: solid propellant, three stages
Range: 6,000 nautical miles
Warhead: 14 MIRV of 150 kt each or 7 MARV (Maneuverable Re-entry Vehicles) of 300 kt each

♦ *surface-to-surface missiles*

Tomahawk (BGM 109)

Two versions are projected: strategic and tactical. The characteristics of the former are:

Length: 6.170 m
Diameter: 0.517 m
Weight: 1,360 kg at launch
Propulsion: solid booster, turbojet sustainer
Navigation/Guidance: TAINS (Tercom-Aided Inertial Navigation System) using

WEAPONS AND SYSTEMS *(continued)*

pre-programmed data plus TERCOM (Terrain Contour Matching)

Range: *Strategic version:* 1,300 nautical miles, operating at an altitude between 15 and 100 meters, at a speed of Mach 0.7. For launching from submarines, the weapon will be fired from torpedo tubes in a special container, jettisoned on leaving the water. *Tactical version:* around 350 nautical miles, thus requiring an external means of target designation.

Harpoon (RGM-84)

An all-weather cruise missile that can be launched by aircraft, surface ship, or submarine.

Propulsion:	turbojet with a rocket booster added to the ship and submarine version
Weight:	225 kg
Length:	3.20 m
Diameter:	0.350 m
Rocket booster:	weight 118 kg
Length:	0.75 m
Trajectory:	between 15 and 60 miles, descending to a few miles prior to impact
Guidance:	inertial, then active homing on J Band in the final trajectory
Range:	70 nautical miles

Warhead: 225 kg. The submarine version is shrouded and may be launched from the TT while submerged. In order to reach the maximum range, it is necessary to use designation systems external to the launching unit — helicopters, for example. AGM-84 is the air-dropped version.

Standard (RGM-66D/E)

In order to give small ships such as the now-stricken *Asheville*-class patrol gunboats and *Knox*-class escort ships an anti-surface capability, the U.S. Navy has developed a surface-to-surface missile based on the Standard RIM-66; it can be fired from the Mk 112 Asroc system launcher. Being phased out.

♦ *surface-to-air missiles*

Talos (RIM-8) — Bldr: Bendix and RCA.

Propulsion system on launch is by a 4,000-pound solid booster; then by a McDonnel ramjet sustainer engine.

Weight: 2.7 tons
Length: 9.70 m
Speed: Mach 3
Range: 65 nautical miles. Beam-riding guidance system, then semi-active homing. Proximity fuse. Can carry a nuclear warhead. Produced in series until 1968. Twin launcher, with the number of missile reloads varying according to the ship class. Guidance system includes an air-search radar, an elevation radar, two SPW 2 radars for target acquisition, and 2 SPG 49 tracking radars. To be discarded shortly.

Terrier (RIM-2) — Bldrs: Convair

Solid-propellant booster.

Length:	4.57 m without the booster, 8 m with
Diameter:	0.356 m
Weight:	at launch 500 kg + 1,350 kg with booster
Speed:	Mach 2.5

Built in series until 1968. One version of the Terrier missile enables it to attack low-flying aircraft and surface-to-surface missiles. System consists of twin Mk 10 launcher with 2 or 4 horizontal ready-service magazines, each with 20 missiles, a computer, an air-search radar, a three-dimensional radar (SPS 39, SPS 48, or SPS 52 on modernized or recently built ships) and two guidance radars SPG 55 or SPG 55B. Terrier has been replaced by Standard-ER (SM 1), which will in turn be replaced by SM-2.

Tartar (RIM 24B, C) — Bldr: Convair and General Dynamics.

Dual-thrust rocket motor with solid propellant.

Length:	4.54 m
Diameter:	0.356 m
Weight:	590 kg.
Guidance:	semi-active homing
Range:	15 nautical miles, 150 to 60,000 ft

System comprises Mk 11 twin launcher or Mk 13 single launcher with a vertical ready-service magazine containing 40 missiles (or, on the FFG-1 class, Mk 22 with 16 missiles), a computer, an air-search radar, a three-dimensional SPS 39, SPS 48 or SPS 52 radar, and two SPG 51 guidance radars. A series of missiles of approximately the same size as the first RIM 24 Mod 0 (U.S. military designation) but constantly improved propulsion, miniaturization of components, and missile-flight profile.

Standard SM-1 MR (RIM-66B)

Single-stage missile to replace Tartar.

Length:	4.54 m
Diameter:	0.356 m
Weight:	603 kg
Range:	20 nautical miles, 150–60,000 ft.
Guidance:	semi-active homing

Standard SM-1 ER (RIM-67)

Standard with booster stage added for use with Terrier-type missiles.

Length: 8.0 m
Weight: 1,305 kg
Range: 35 nautical miles

Standard SM-2 MR (RIM 67B-1)

Replacement missile for SM-1 ER, initial procurement under FY 78.

Range: in excess of 60 nautical miles

Aegis (ex-Advanced Surface Missile System — ASMS)

Under study since 1964. A fire-control system based on a "billboard" fixed-array radar to provide 360° coverage. It will employ SM-2 ER missiles to simultaneously repel a number of targets under the most adverse electronic countermeasures, including targets at extremely low altitude (sea skimmers). For precise response to threats, the Aegis system will be made of various components permitting the control of all necessary steps from target acquisition to missile detonation against the target. Three clusters of four AN/UYK-7 computer systems will direct all these functions automatically, especially the detection and tracking of the closing targets, data distribution for target evaulation and designation through pre-programmed information retained in the system, integration of radar and other information sources in the ship, and the selection of missiles and distribution of fire.

The AN/SPY-1 radar is the most important element in the system. The missile to be used is the Standard SM 2. A Mk 26 twin launcher will be used. This launcher can also handle the ASW Asroc system and Harpoon surface-to-surface missile. The various types of missiles are stowed vertically in ready-service magazines below the

WEAPONS AND SYSTEMS (*continued*)

launcher. The Aegis system has been undergoing trials in the USS *Norton Sound* since 1974 and will first be operational in DDG-47 in 1982.

Sea Sparrow (RIM-7) — Bldr: Raytheon-Northrop

Known at first as BPDMS (Basic Point Defense Missile System). Initial installations employed fixed-fin missiles launched from the 8-celled Mk 25 launcher and controlled by the Mk 115 radar-equipped fire-control system. A lightweight launcher, Mk 29, employing eight RIM-7F folding-fin missiles and the Mk 91 radar fire-control system, is now coming into use; in Europe, this later system is known as NATO Sea Sparrow and was first tested in the *Downes* (FF-1070).

Length: 3.657 m
Weight: 171 kg
Range: 8 nautical miles

APDMS (Advanced Point Defense Missile System).

This system is still under study and will use a new missile.

♦ *antisubmarine warfare missiles*

Asroc (RUR-5)

A solid-fuel rocket that can be used with a Mk 44 or Mk 46 torpedo with a parachute that decelerates the torpedo to a safe re-entry speed to prevent damaging its highly sensitive transducer head. Range is regulated by the combustion time of the rocket motor. Rocket-torpedo separation is timed. The Mk 112 launcher carries eight rockets that can be trained together and elevated in pairs. Fire control is made up of a computer linked with an SQS 23 or SQS 26 sonar.

Length:	4.70 m
Diameter:	0.3 m
Weight:	450 kg
Warhead:	Mk 44 or Mk 46 torpedo
Range:	9,800 m (Mk 44)
	9,200 m (Mk 46)
Rate of fire:	2 rockets/minute
Arc of elevation:	3° to 85° — rockets usually launched at 45°

A nuclear depth charge can replace the torpedo. On some *Knox*-class escorts the launcher has been modified to permit the launching of Standard SSM missiles in place of some ASW weapons. The loading system is slow because the rockets have to be manually transferred from the magazines; however, on the most recently built escorts, a hoist brings the rocket up forward of the bridge for semiautomatic loading, while missiles are vertically-reloaded in the *Spruance* class.

Asroc may also be launched from the Mk 10 missile launchers in the CG-26 and CGN-35, and from the Mk 26 launchers in the CGN-38 and DDG-47.

Subroc

This missile has a nuclear warhead and is fired through torpedo tubes by submerged submarines. After launch, the missile follows an aerial trajectory that is regulated by the range to the target. The second stage of the rocket carries the warhead, follows a ballistic trajectory, and enters the water where the warhead explodes at a pre-determined depth. The Mk 113 fire-control system is used with BQQ 2 and BQQ 5 sonars.

Length:	5.950 m
Diameter:	0.533 m
Weight:	1,800 kg
Maximum range:	35 nautical miles
Speed:	Supersonic Mach 1.0+

First stage: solid fuel missile motor with 3,400 m firing distance. Second stage: nuclear depth charge with feathering vanes and a protection cone for re-entry into the water. The weapon can be used against submarines or surface ships.

♦ *air-to-surface missiles*

Bullpup — Bldr: Martin Marietta

Fixed cruciform wings and 4 control ailerons forward. There are several versions, the most common being the AGM 12B, or Bullpup A, and the AGM 12C, or Bullpup B.

Bullpup A (AGM-12B)

Propulsion:	solid propellant grains
Length:	3.200 m
Diameter:	0.305 m
Wingspan:	0.952 m
Weight at launch:	258 kg
Range:	11,000 m
Warhead:	115 kg

Bullpup B (AGM-12C/D)

Propulsion:	liquid propellant
Length:	4.070 m
Diameter:	0.439 m
Wingspan:	1.177 m
Weight at launch:	812 kg
Range:	17,000 m
Warhead:	453.6 kg

Standard-ARM (AGM-78)

Air-launched version of Standard that homes on electromagnetic radiation.

Length: 4.572 m
Range: 35 nautical miles. More versatile than Shrike

Shrike (AGM-45)

An anti-radar missile

Length:	3.048 m
Diameter:	0.200 m
Wingspan:	0.914 m
Weight:	117 kg.
Propulsion:	solid-propellant rocket motor
Speed:	Mach 2
Range:	12,000 to 16,000 m

Walleye (AGM-62)

Glide bomb guided by television

Length:	0.344 m
Diameter:	0.325 m
Wingspan:	1.160 m
Weight:	499 kg
Warhead:	conventional

Harpoon (AGM-84)

See under surface-to-surface missiles.

Condor

This missile has been canceled.

WEAPONS AND SYSTEMS (*continued*)

♦ *air-to-air missiles*

Sparrow III (AIM 7H) — Bldr: Raytheon-Northrop
- Propulsion: solid propellant grains
- Length: 3.650 m
- Diameter: 0.200 m
- Weight: 204 kg
- Speed: Mach 2.5
- Range: 15,000 m (AIM 7D version), 26,000 m (AIM 7E version)
- Warhead: 27 kg, proximity fuse
- Guidance: semi-active homing

Sidewinder (AIM 9) — Bldr: Raytheon-Northrop

Sidewinder 1A
- Propulsion: solid propellant grains
- Length: 2.840 m
- Diameter: 0.127 m
- Wingspan: 0.609 m
- Weight: 75 kg
- Speed: Mach 2.5
- Range: 6,000 m (3,500 m practical)
- Guidance: infrared

Sidewinder 1C
- Propulsion: solid propellant grains
- Length: 2.950 m
- Weight: 85 kg
- Speed: Mach 3
- Range: 18,000 m
- Guidance: semi-active homing

Phoenix (AIM 54A) — Bldr: Hughes Aircraft Co.
- Propulsion: solid propellant grains
- Length: 3.960 m
- Diameter: 0.380 m
- Wingspan: 0.914 m
- Weight: 380 kg
- Range: over 80,000 m

HARM (AGM-88)

High-speed anti-radiation missile. To replace Shrike. In development.

(B) GUNS

406-mm, Model 1936

Fitted in triple turrets in *New Jersey*-class battleships
- Length: 50 calibers
- Muzzle velocity: 850 m/sec
- Rate of fire: 2 rounds/minute/barrel
- Maximum range: 39,000 m
- Weight of projectile: 1,230 kg
- Cartridge bags: 6 weighing 300 kg

203-mm, Model 1944 (Mk 16)

Automatic weapon fitted in triple turrets on the *Des Moines*-class cruisers
- Length: 55 calibers
- Muzzle velocity: 900 m/sec
- Elevation: −5° to +41°
- Rate of fire: 10 rounds/min/barrel
- Maximum range: 30,000 m
- Maximum effective range: 23,000 to 24,000 m
- Projectile: 125 kg
- Fire control: Mk 54 director with Mk 13 radar

203-mm, Model 1927 (Mk 15)

Fitted in triple turrets in *Baltimore*-class cruisers
- Length: 55 calibers
- Muzzle velocity: 830 m/sec
- Elevation: −5° to +30°
- Rate of fire: 2 rounds/minute/barrel
- Maximum range: 30,000 m
- Maximum effective range: 23,000 to 24,000 m
- Projectile: 127 kg. A 51-kg projectile fitted with a rocket was fired in Vietnam by the *Saint Paul* (CA-73) and reached a target 51 km away
- Fire control: Mk 54 director with Mk 13 radar

203-mm, Model 1971 (MK 71)

This model, which has been undergoing tests since the mid-1960s, can fire 75 projectiles in sequence without interference at a rate of 12 rounds per minute. Evaluation ship is the destroyer *Hull*. Planned for installation in some *Spruance*-class destroyers during first overhauls in the early 1980s.

152-mm, Model 1933 (Mk 16)

Fitted in one triple turret on CG-5, CG-6, and CG-7.
- Length: 47 calibers
- Muzzle velocity: 915 m/sec
- Rate of fire: 3 rounds/min/barrel
- Maximum range: 23,500 m
- Maximum effective range: 19,000 m
- Projectile: 46.4 kg
- Fire control: 1 Mk 34 director with Mk 13 radar (CG-5: Mk 37 director)

127-mm twin barrel, Model 1935

Semi-automatic, triple-purpose (air, sea, and land targets) gun fitted in the mounts of the *New Jersey*, *Galveston*, *Providence*-class, *Des Moines*-class, and *Baltimore*-class cruisers, and *Gearing*-class destroyers.
- Length: 38 calibers
- Muzzle velocity: 792 m/sec
- Elevation: −15° to +85°
- Rate of fire: 17 rounds/min/barrel with a well-trained crew
- Maximum range on a surface target: 16,500 m
- Maximum effective range on a ship target: 12,000 to 13,000 m
- Maximum range in anti-aircraft fire: 11,400 m
- Maximum effective range in anti-aircraft fire: 8,000 m
- Projectile: 25 kg
- Fire control: Mk 37 director with Mk 25 radar; Mk 56 director in a few ships

127-mm, Mk 39

Single-barrel, semi-automatic, triple-purpose (air, sea, and land targets) gun installed on *Midway*-class aircraft carriers.
- Length: 54 calibers

WEAPONS AND SYSTEMS *(continued)*

Muzzle velocity: 900 m/sec
Elevation: similar to the Mk 32
Rate of fire: 17 rounds/min
Maximum range on a surface target: 22,000 m
Maximum effective range on a surface target: 20,000 m
Maximum effective range in anti-aircraft fire: 10,000 m
Projectile: 32 kg
Fire control: Mk 37 and Mk 56 directors

127-mm, Mk 42

Single-barrel, triple-purpose (air, sea, and land targets) gun fitted on most recently built ships.

Mount weight: 58.7 tons
Length: 45 calibers
Muzzle velocity: 810 m/sec
Arc of elevation: $-5°$ to $+80°$
Rate of train: 50°/sec
Rate of elevation: 80°/sec
Rate of fire: 40 rounds/minute
Projectile: 46 kg

Loading entirely automatic from two ammunition drums in the handling room up to the loading tray by means of a rotating hoist. Each drum contains 20 rounds. The rate of fire can be maintained for only one minute, inasmuch as it is necessary to reload the drums.

Personnel: 13 with 2 in the turret
Fire control: Mk 68 fire-control system in most ships

127-mm, Mk 45

Single-barrel mount fitted on *California* and *Virginia*-class cruisers, *Spruance*-class destroyers, and *Tarawa*-class LHAs.

Weight of the turret: 20 tons
Length: 54 calibers
Muzzle velocity: 810 m/sec
Elevation: $-5°$ to $+65°$
Rate of fire: 20 rounds/min
Personnel: none, except in the handling room to reload the ammunition drums
Fire control: 1/SPQ 9 search radar, 1/SPQ 60 tracking radar

76-mm, Mk 33 and Mk 34

Automatic anti-aircraft gun in single (Mk 34) or twin (Mk 33) mounts.

Length: 50 calibers
Rate of fire: 45 rounds/min/barrel
Maximum effective range on surface target: 7,000 m
Maximum effective range on aerial target: 6,000 m
Fire control: Mk 51, Mk 56, or Mk 63 control systems

76-mm, Mk 75

Single-barreled, license-built version of OTO Melara Compact, tested in the frigate *Talbot* and used in PHM and FFG-7 classes. Rate of fire: 85 rounds/min

Vulcan/Phalanx System, Mk 15

"Close-in weapon system" designed to destroy missiles such as the Styx and sea-skimmer missiles such as the French Exocet and the Israeli Gabriel.

It consists of a multi-barrel 20-mm gun with a very high rate of fire (3,000 rounds/minute). The gun is linked with two radars, one of which follows the target and the other the projectile burst. A computer furnishes the necessary corrections for train and elevation so that the two radar targets coincide, bringing heavy fire to bear on the target.

(D) TORPEDOES

♦ *submarine torpedoes*

Mk 37 Mod 0

Electric torpedo with an active-passive guidance system. Used against surface and submarine targets.

Length: 3.450 m
Diameter: 0.485 m
Weight: 650 kg
Speed: 25 knots
Run duration: 20,000 m

Mk 37 Mod 1

Similar to the Mk 37 Mod 0 but is wire-guided. Can be used against submarines.

Length: 4.100 m
Weight: 770 kg

MK 45 Astor

Heavy wire-guided torpedo. Corrective commands are transmitted to the torpedo through the wire. Can be used against surface targets and submarines. Carried by SSN classes.

Length: 5.760 m
Weight: 1,090 kg
Speed: 40 knots (?)
Run duration: 20,000 m (?)
Warhead: nuclear.

Mk 48

Will replace or supplement the Mk 37 Mod 0 and Mod 1 torpedoes. Can be launched from a submarine against a surface target or a submarine. No surface ships are currently equipped to launch Mk 48, although that capability was originally intended.

Length: 5.800 m
Diameter: 0.533 m
Weight: 1,506 kg

Can be launched with its own guidance system or with a wire-guidance system. High speed (40 knots?) and long run duration (25,000 m). Active-passive guidance.

♦ *surface-launched torpedoes*

Mk 44 Mod 1

Electric torpedo with an active-passive guidance system for use against submarines. Being phased out.

Length: 2.540 m
Diameter: 0.324 m
Weight: 195 kg

Mk 46 Mod 0 and Mod 1

ASW torpedo using solid fuel (Monergol). Active-passive guidance.

Length: 2.570 m
Diameter: 0.324 m
Weight: 258 kg

WEAPONS AND SYSTEMS (*continued*)

♦ *aircraft torpedoes*

Mk 44 Mod 0

Similar to surface-launched Mod 1 but no run-out prior to helical search.

Mk 46 Mod 0 and Mod 1

(E) MINES

Mk 52 Mod 2

Weight: 500 kg with 315 kg of explosive. Its magnetic adjustment is highly sensitive, which makes it a very difficult mine to sweep.

Mk 36 "Destructor"

Weight: 226 kg with 87 kg of explosive. Also a magnetic mine and very difficult to sweep.

These mines have devices that automatically neutralize them at the end of a preselected period.

(F) RADARS

The principal radars of many models in the AN nomenclature are:

♦ *surface search and target designation*

SPS 10:
SPS 55: On *Spruance*-class destroyers and planned for the FFG-7 and others of this class; will eventually replace the SPS 10.

♦ *air search*

SPS 6: Being replaced.
SPS 12: On CGN-9, CVN-65, and several amphibious-warfare ships.
SPS 29: On some of the older DDs. A Band
SPS 37: On CGN-25, some CGs, and DDGs. A Band
SPS 32: "Billboard" fixed-array radar (bearing/range) used only on CVAN-65 and CGN-9. Looks like four rectangular surfaces mounted on the four sides of the superstructure of these ships. SPS 32 uses the horizontal component, SPS 33 the vertical. A Band
SPS 40: The most widely used air-search radar. Range against medium bombers: 150 to 180 miles. Earlier "A" models being modernized to **SPS-40D.** B Band
SPS 43: Mounted in all aircraft carriers and 3 cruisers. A Band
SPS 49: New type of search radar for the FFG-7 class and others. Will eventually replace SPS-37 in all ships so fitted. C Band
SPS 58: Combined air-surface search radar

♦ *height-finding*

SPS 8A:
SPS 30: Mounted on aircraft carriers and cruisers. F Band
SPS 33: "Billboard" fixed-array radar. Mounted on CVN-65 and CG-9. Looks like four vertical rectangular surfaces mounted on the four sides of the superstructure of these ships. E Band
SPS 39: E Band
SPS 39A: (MT1 digital) Mounted on some aircraft carriers, cruisers, and DDGs.
SPS 48A: Mounted on CG classes. E Band
SPS 48B: Electronic frequency sweeping radar. Will replace the SPS 48A
SPS 52A: Mounted on DDGs. E and F Bands
SPS 52B: Electronic frequency sweeping radar. Will replace the SPS 52A
SPY 1: The most important segment of the Aegis system. Obtaining a directional effect by dipole radiation to secure an electronic sweep, it will have four fixed aerials that will provide an instant 360° coverage. Long-range air search, target tracking, and missile guidance. F Band

♦ *guidance*

SPG 49 + SW 2: Guidance for Talos missiles. Mounted on CG-5, CG-9, CG-10 and CG-11. I Band
SPG 51: Illumination for Standard SM-1 missiles. G Band
SPG 55: Illumination for Standard SM1-ER missiles. G Band

(G) SONARS

The principal types of sonar in the AN nomenclature are:

♦ *on surface ships*

SQS 23: Bow sonar, LF, mounted on many destroyers, on one aircraft carrier, and eleven guided-missile cruisers.
SQS 26: The most widely used LF sonar. Several types. It is mounted in a dome in the stem of cruisers and guided-missile destroyers as well as in the *Bronstein, Garcia, Brooke,* and *Knox* frigates. An improved SQS 26, the SQS 53, is used in *Spruance*-class destroyers.
SQS 35: Towed sonar, MF
SQS 56: New sonar designed for the FFG-7 class, MF
SQR 15: Passive towed sonar. An improved version known as SQR 19 is in development. Also known as TACTAS (Tactical Towed Array System).

♦ *on submarines*

BQS 4, BQS 6, BQS 11, BQS 12, and **BQS 13:** Active-passive sonars
BQR 2, BQR 7, BQR 15 towed, **BQH 4** replacing BQR 15: Passive sonars
BQQ 1 (1958): Multi-function sonar including: BQR 2, BQR 7, BQS 4 or BQS 6. Mounted in the SSN *Skate* and *Skipjack* classes.
BQQ 1: Retrofit III (1964): Multi-function sonar including new versions of the BQR 2 and BQR 7, BQS 11 or BQS 12. Mounted in the SSN *Permit* and *Sturgeon* classes.
SSBN Sonar Unit (1973): Multi-function sonar of the SSBN classes, BQR 15 included.
BQQ 5 (1975): Multi-function sonar including especially the BQR 7 and BQS 13, and a towed passive linear array now under development. Mounted in the *Los Angeles* class and later in the *Permit* and *Sturgeon* classes.
BQG 4 PUFFS: (Passive Underwater Fire Control System). USCS hydrophone arrays mounted within three fin-like domes to provide a triangulated fix on a target. Now mounted in only a few old submarines.

♦ *fixed listening systems for submarine detection*

SOSUS (Sound Surveillance System): This system has two networks:
CAESAR: Surveillance of the Northwest Atlantic
COLOSSUS: Surveillance of the Northeast Pacific along the coast of the U.S.A.

These networks are made up of fixed hydrophones suspended under water and connected by cable to about 20 land stations which receive and interpret the signals.

MSS (Moored Surveillance System): This semi-fixed system, now under study, is made up of long-life buoys transmitting to patrol aircraft.

WEAPONS AND SYSTEMS (*continued*)

(H) PROCESSING OF TACTICAL DATA

The system now in use is the NTDS (Naval Tactical Data System). Thanks to its digital calculators (AN/USQ 20 and Univac AN/UYK 7), it instantaneously gives an overall picture of a tactical situation — air, surface, and underwater — and enables the commander to employ the means necessary to oppose the enemy. Excellent automatic data transmission systems (Links 11 and Links 14) permit the exchange of tactical information with similarly equipped ships and aircraft carrying the ATDS (P3C Orion and S3A Viking) and amphibious landing forces equipped with NTDS.

NUCLEAR-POWERED AIRCRAFT CARRIERS

NOTE: The future of aircraft carrier construction for the U.S. Navy is in a confused state. Although it is planned to request funds for the first 50,000-ton-plus, conventionally powered "CVV" in FY 79, and another in FY 81, the characteristics for the class have in no way been determined. What seems certain is that they will be more expensive to build than the current *Nimitz* class, and being smaller, non-nuclear, and more austerely equipped, they will be far less effective.

Also planned is a very comprehensive SLEP modernization to be applied to CV-59 through CV-67 between 1981 and 1999. Two years and several hundred million current dollars will be required to rejuvenate each ship, permitting at least 15 years additional active operations. Of the other carriers, the *Franklin D. Roosevelt* was stricken in October 1977, while the *Coral Sea* will decommission in 1981 on completion of the *Carl Vinson*, and the *Midway* in 1984-85 on completion of the first CVV.

Construction of smaller carriers (VSS) for V/STOL (Vertical or Short Takeoff aircraft) operations is stymied for lack of adequate aircraft technology and a very-low-key V/STOL research and development effort. The chief of naval operations has testified that the first operational V/STOL aircraft, a utility design, will not be available until the early 1990s and a supersonic V/STOL fighter until the late 1990s.

♦ *3 Nimitz class*

	Laid down	L	In serv.
CVN 68 NIMITZ	6-68	13-5-72	7-75
CVN 69 DWIGHT D. EISENHOWER	8-70	11-10-75	10-77
CVN 70 CARL VINSON	11-10-75	-79	1980-81

Authorized: CVN-68: 1966-67; CVN-69: 1970-71; CVN-70: 1973-74 — Bldr: Newport News SB & DD

D: 81,600 tons (91,400 fl) **S:** over 30 kts
Dim: 332.84 (317 pp)* × 40.85 (flight deck, 77.11) × 10.90
Man: 5,758 (446 officers), including aviation personnel (2,626 with 304 officers)
A: About 100 airplanes and helicopters — 2 Mk 25 launchers for Sea Sparrow
Electron Equipt: Radars: 1/SPS 10F, 1/SPS 43A, 1/SPS 48B, 1/SPN 42, 1/SPN 43A, 1/SPN 44 — NTDS
M: 2 pressurized-water nuclear reactors; 4 sets GT; 4 props; 280,000 hp
Electric: 64,000 kw + 4 emergency generators (8,000 kw)

*326, excluding catapult bridle retrieval horns

REMARKS: The *Nimitz* cost $685,800,000 to build, while her air wing and equipment cost $710,600,000. The offensive potential of these ships is remarkable; they carry 90% more aviation fuel and 50% more ammunition (3,000 tons) than the *Forrestal* class. They have an ASCAC (Antisubmarine Classification and Analysis Center), which permits instant sharing of target data between the carrier, its ASW aircraft, and escorting ships.

Dwight D. Eisenhower (CVN 69)

NUCLEAR-POWERED AIRCRAFT CARRIERS (*continued*)

Nimitz (CVN 68)

Armor: Decks and hull are of extra-strong, high-tensile steel that can limit the impact of semi-armor-piercing bombs. Apart from the longitudinal bulkheads, there are 23 watertight transverse bulkheads (more than 2,000 compartments) and 10 firewall bulkheads. Foam devices for fire-fighting are very well developed, and pumping equipment is excellent, a 1.5° list being correctable in 20 minutes. Thirty damage-control teams are available at all times. *Nimitz*-class ships can withstand three times the severe pounding taken by the *Essex*-class aircraft carriers in 1944–45, and they can take impacts and shock waves in the same proportion.

Machinery: The cores of these ships are expected to last 13 years in normal usage, for a cruising distance of 800,000 to 1,000,000 miles.

Aircraft-handing installations: There are four side elevators: two forward, one aft of the island to starboard, and one on the stern to port. There are also four Mk C13 Mod 1 steam catapults, three of which are 94.5 m long, and the fourth is considerably longer. The *Dwight D. Eisenhower* has only the forward starboard catapult bridle retrieval horn, because most aircraft in service do not require the bridle for launching.

Nimitz (CVN 68) 1975

NUCLEAR-POWERED AIRCRAFT CARRIERS (*continued*)

♦ *1 Enterprise class (SCB 160 type)*

	Bldr	Laid down	L	In serv.
CVN 65 ENTERPRISE	Newport News SB	2-58	24-9-60	25-11-61

Authorized: 1957-58

D: 75,700 tons (91,000 fl) **S:** 33 kts

Dim: 335.75* × 40.54 (hull)
317 (pp) 78.40 (flight deck) × 11.30 (draft) 19.60 (freeboard)

A: 80 to 100 airplanes and helicopters — 3 Mk 25 launchers for Sea Sparrow

Electron Equipt: Radars: 1/SPS 10, 1/SPS 32, 1/SPS 33, 1/SPS 12, 1/SPS 58, 2 aircraft landing radars SPN 12 — NTDS

M: 8 Westinghouse A2 nuclear reactors, 35,000 hp each (max: 45,000 hp), supplying in pairs 32 Foster-Wheeler heat exchangers; 4 Westinghouse GT; 4 props

Electric: 40,000 kw

Electricity: 16 turbo-dynamo generators, 2,500 kw each

Range: 140,000/30, 400,000/20 (From 21-7 to 2-10-64 circumnavigated the globe without replenishment, a total of 30,126 miles)

Man: 451 officers, 5,237 men (including 304/2,323 aviation personnel)

*342.30 over the catapult bridle horn

REMARKS: The island superstructure is comparatively small; four Mk C13 steam catapults; four elevators, one on the port side aft of the angled deck, three to starboard, two of which are forward of the island, one aft. Elevators are steel and alloy and weigh 105 rather than 135 tons, 26 m. long, 16 m. wide, lift 45 tons. The hangar is 7.62 m. high and the flight deck is over 20,000 m^2. Carries half again as much aviation fuel as the *Forrestal* class, which permits 12 days' of intensive aerial operations without replenishment. Carries fuel oil as ballast to replenish other ships. Now has ASCAC like *Nimitz.*

Enterprise (CVN 65) 1975

Enterprise (CVN 65) G. Arra, 1976

NUCLEAR-POWERED AIRCRAFT CARRIERS *(continued)*

Enterprise (CVN 65) G. Arra, 1976

CONVENTIONALLY PROPELLED AIRCRAFT CARRIERS

♦ *1 John F. Kennedy class (SCB 127C type)*

	Laid down	L	In serv.
CV 67 JOHN F. KENNEDY	22-10-64	27-5-67	7-9-68

Bldr: Newport News SB & DD Co.

John F. Kennedy (CV 67) 1975

John F. Kennedy (CV 67) 1975

John F. Kennedy (CV 67) 1976

CONVENTIONALLY PROPELLED AIRCRAFT CARRIERS (*continued*)

D: 61,000 tons (82,000 fl) **S:** over 30 kts
Dim: 320.7 (301.8 wl) × 39.60 (wl) (flight deck: 76.90) × 10.90
Man: 420 officers, 4,842 men (including 285/2,113 aviation personnel)
A: 3 Mk 25 launchers for Sea Sparrow — 70 to 90 aircraft
Electron Equipt: Radars: 1/SPS 10, 1/SPS 43, 1/SPS 48, 1/SPS 58, 1/SPN 10, 2/SPN 42
Sonar: 1/SQS 23 — NTDS
M: General Electric GT; 4 props; 280,000 hp **Electric** . . . kw
Boilers: 8 Foster-Wheeler, 83.4 kg/cm^2

REMARKS: Four side elevators, three to starboard (two forward and one aft of the island), and one on the port quarter. Completely automatic landing system, permitting all-weather operation. Three 90-m Mk C13 catapults and one 94.5-m Mk C13-1. Flight deck allows 40-ton plane operation. Has PLAT (Pilot Landing Air Television), which facilitates the control of launching and recovery operations. Stack angled to starboard.

Kitty Hawk (CV 63) — prior to removal of missiles 1975

♦ *3 Kitty Hawk class (SCB 127A and SCB 127B types)*

	Bldr	Laid down	L	In serv.
CV 63 KITTY HAWK	New York SB	27-12-56	21-5-60	29-4-61
CV 64 CONSTELLATION	Brooklyn NSY	14-9-47	8-10-60	27-10-61
CV 66 AMERICA	Newport News SB	9-1-61	1-2-64	23-1-65

Authorized: CV-63: 1955-56; CV-64: 1956-57; CV-66: 1960-61

D: 60,100 tons (80,300 fl) (CV-66: 81,700 fl) **S:** 33 kts
Dim: 318.8 (CV-66: 319.25) (301.76 pp) × 39.62 (wl) (flight deck: 76.81) × 11.20 (CV-66: 11.30)
A: Up to 90 aircraft — 2 Mk 25 launchers for Sea Sparrow
Electron Equipt: Radars: 1/SPS 10, 1/SPS 58, 1/SPS 43, 1/SPS 30, 1/SPS 52, 1/SPN 10, 1/SPN 42, 3 or 4/SPG 55 — NTDS (CV-64 and CV-66 only)
Sonar: CV-66 only: 1/SQS 23
M: 280,000 hp Westinghouse GT; 4 props (CV-66: 2 × 4, CV-63: 2 × 5, CV-64: 4 × 5)
Electric: . . . kw **Boilers:** 8 Foster-Wheeler 83.4/cm^2
Fuel: 7,800 tons **Range:** 4,000/30, 8,000/20
Man: CV-63: 443 officers, 5,044 enlisted men (including 303/2,306 aviation personnel)
CV-64: 431 officers, 4,944 enlisted men (including 294/2,180 aviation personnel)
CV-66: 429 officers, 4,940 enlisted men (including 285/2,130 aviation personnel)
Aviation fuel: 5,882 tons

REMARKS: These ships are a great improvement over the *Forrestal* class, on which they are based, and have one essential difference: they have three elevators on the starboard side, two forward and one abaft the island, and one to port, abaft the angled flight deck. Aircraft can be landed and catapulted simultaneously, a difficult operation on the earlier ships. Four Mk C 13 steam catapults. CV-63 and CV-64 will receive 3/20-mm Vulcan/Phalanx. CV-66 will keep her Standard system and will also receive 3 Vulcan/Phalanx; she has ASCAC.

America (CV 66) 1977

CONVENTIONALLY PROPELLED AIRCRAFT CARRIERS (*continued*)

Constellation (CV 64) 1974

♦ *4 Forrestal class (CV-59: SCB 80 type, CV-60 to CV-62 SCB 80M type)*

	Bldr	Laid down	L	In serv.
CV-59 FORRESTAL	Newport News SB & DD	14-7-52	11-12-54	1-10-55
CV-60 SARATOGA	Brooklyn NSY	16-12-52	8-10-55	14-4-56
CV-61 RANGER	Newport News SB & DD	2-8-54	29-9-54	10-8-57
CV-62 INDEPENDENCE	Brooklyn NSY	1-7-55	9-6-58	10-1-59

Authorized: CV-59: 1951-52; CV-60: 1952-53; CV-61: 1953-54; CV-62: 1954-55

D: CV-59: 59,600 tons (79,250 fl); CV-60, CV-61: 60,000 tons (80,250 fl) CV-62: 60,000 tons (79,650 fl)

Dim: CV-59: 331.0; CV-60: 324; CV-61: 326.4; CV-62: 326.1 (319.13 flight deck, 301.8 pp) × 39.47; CV-59, CV-60: 78.9; CV-61, CV-62: 77.7 flight deck) × 11.2

S: 33 kts **Range:** 4,000/30, 8,000/20

A: 60 to 90 planes and helicopters — 2 Mk 25 launchers for Sea Sparrow (except CV-61: 3 Mk 29 launchers for Sea Sparrow)

Electron Equipt: Radars: 1/SPS 10, 1/SPS 43, 1/SPS 30, 1/SPN 10, 1/SPS 58 — NTDS — Mk 28 chaff launchers

M: General Electric or Westinghouse GT; 4 props; CV-59: 260,000 hp; others: 300,000 hp

Boilers: 8 Babcock & Wilcox, 41.7 kg/cm² on the CV-59, 84 kg/cm² on the others; superheat 520°C

Independence (CV 62) Pradignac & Leo, 1974

Forrestal (CV 59) Terzibaschitsch, 1976

Fuel: 12,000 tons

Man: CV-59: 420 officers, 4,796 enlisted (including 285/2,063 aviation personnel)
CV-60: 415 officers, 4,789 enlisted (including 280/2,035 aviation personnel)
CV-61: 434 officers, 5,005 enlisted (including 304/2,273 aviation personnel)
CV-62: 433 officers, 4,931 enlisted (including 295/2,206 aviation personnel)

CONVENTIONALLY PROPELLED AIRCRAFT CARRIERS (*continued*)

Independence (CV 62) 1975

Saratoga (CV 60) 1975

Saratoga (CV 60) 1975

Forrestal (CV 59) 1976

REMARKS: Hangar: 7.60 m in height, 234 to 240 m in length; flight deck: 315.75 m long. The landing system permits safe landing in the darkest of nights. Four side elevators (15.95 × 18.90) and four steam catapults: two forward on the main flight deck, two on the angled flight deck. With the four catapults, 32 planes can be launched in four minutes. Deck angled at 8°. Armored flight deck. Six-cable arresting gear. CV-59 and CV-60 have 2 Mk C7 (75 m) and 2 Mk C11 (65 m) catapults; the others have 4 Mk C7.

CONVENTIONALLY PROPELLED AIRCRAFT CARRIERS (*continued*)

Independence (CV 62) G. Arra, 1976

Coral Sea (CV 43) 1975

Coral Sea (CV 43) 1968

CV-59 has three rudders and four propellers, the two outboard with five blades and the two inboard with four blades. Deck protection and internal compartmentation are extensive (1,200 watertight compartments): two longitudinal bulkheads are fitted from keel to waterline from stem to stern; there are transverse bulkheads at about every 10 meters.

CV-60, CV-61, and CV-62 are slightly larger and faster than CV-59. They all have the same machinery, reaching about 300,000 hp, and carry 5,880 tons of jet fuel.

CV-59 will be the first to receive a major SLEP modernization, beginning in FY 81. The others will follow in order of their construction, the yard periods lasting about two years and adding 15 years to their service lives. All will ultimately be armed with 3 Mk 29 Sea Sparrow launchers and 3 Mk 15 Vulcan/Phalanx Gatling guns. All originally carried eight 127-mm/54 Mk 42 guns. CV-61 retains her forward gun sponsons and was the last to relinquish her last two guns (1977).

♦ *2 Midway class*

	Laid down	L	In serv.
CV 41 MIDWAY	27-10-43	20-3-45	10-9-45
CV 43 CORAL SEA	10-7-44	2-4-46	1-10-47

Bldr: Newport News SB & DD

D: CV-41: 51,000 tons (64,100 fl) CV-43: 52,500 tons (63,800 fl)
Dim: 298.38 (293.91 pp) × 41.45 (wl) (flight deck: 72.54) × 10.90
S: 33 kts
A: 3/127-mm DP 54 cal. (I × 3) — 60 to 75 planes
Electron Equipt: Radars: 1/SPS 10, 1/SPS 43, 1/SPS 30, 1/SPS 58 (CV-41), 1/SPN 6, 1/SPN 10 — NTDS
Armor: Horizontal protection on several decks for a total of about 40 cm; excellent compartmentation

CONVENTIONALLY PROPELLED AIRCRAFT CARRIERS (*continued*)

Midway (CV 41) G. Arra, 1977

Midway (CV 41) G. Arra, 1977

Man: CV-41: 338 officers, 4,253 enlisted men (including 222/1,724 aviation personnel)
CV-43: 317 officers, 4,058 enlisted men (including 201/2,063 aviation personnel)
M: Westinghouse GT; 212,000 hp **Electric:** . . . kw
Boilers: 12 Babcock & Wilcox, 41.7 kg/cm² pressure

REMARKS: Machinery and ships' bottoms very similar to the *Iowa*-class battleships. The original number of AA guns has been considerably reduced: the 127-mm are semi-automatic Mk 39. Fire control is by one Mk 37 and one Mk 56 director. The *Franklin D. Roosevelt* (CV-42) was stricken 1 October 1977. CV-43 is to be stricken on completion of *Carl Vinson* (1980-81) and CV-41 about 1985. CV-43 may replace the *Lexington* (CVT-16) as training carrier.

Elevators: Two side elevators to starboard, one forward and one aft of the island; one side elevator to port aft of the angled flight deck. The elevator platforms are of alloy construction.

Refits: From 1954 to 1963, the ships underwent several overhauls: angled flight deck installed; flight deck lengthened; hydraulic catapults replaced with steam ones; side armor removed and "bulges" added; reinforced arresting gear and barriers installed; centerline elevators replaced with side ones; aviation gasoline capacity increased; new jet fuel bunkers installed.

In October 1967 CV-41 entered another major overhaul period. She was returned to service in 1-70. Her angled flight deck was extended to port; her three elevators were enlarged; her forward port elevator was moved aft; her catapults were replaced by a more powerful model; and all her electronic equipment was replaced. She can launch the all-weather F 14 Tomcat interceptor.

RESERVE AIRCRAFT CARRIERS (CV, CVA, CVS)
TRAINING AIRCRAFT CARRIER (CVT)

♦ *5 Hancock and Intrepid class*

♦ *2 Essex class**

	Bldr	Laid down	L	In serv.
CVS 11 INTREPID	Newport News	1-12-41	26-4-43	16-8-43
CVS 12 HORNET*	Newport News	3-8-42	29-8-43	29-11-43
CVT 16 LEXINGTON	Bethlehem, Quincy	16-7-41	26-9-42	17-2-43
CVS 20 BENNINGTON*	N.Y. Navy Yd.	15-12-42	26-2-44	6-8-44
CVA 31 BON HOMME RICHARD	N.Y. Navy Yd.	1-2-43	29-4-44	26-11-44
CV 34 ORISKANY	N.Y. Navy Yd.	1-5-44	13-10-45	25-9-50
CVS 38 SHANGRI-LA	Norfolk N.Yd.	15-1-43	24-2-44	15-9-44

D: approx. 33,000 tons (40,600 to 41,900 fl) **S:** over 30 kts
Dim: 274.01 (except CVT-16, CVS-38: 270.97) (249.94 wl) × 31.39 wl (CV-34: 32.46) (flight deck: approx. 58.5 × 9.45
A: CV/CVA: 75 aircraft; CVS: 40 to 45 aircraft; CVT-16: none — 4/127-mm DP (I × 4), except CV-34: 2, CVT-16: none
Electron Equipt: Radars: 1/SPS 10, 1/SPS 30, 1/SPS 43 (CVS-11: SPS 37), 1/SPN 10, 1/SPN 43 (CVT-16: 1/SPS 10, 1/SPS 12, 1/SPS 43, 1/SPN 10)
Sonars: CVS only: SQS-23 (bow-mounted)
Man: CVT-16: 75 officers, 1,365 enlisted (no aviation personnel)
M: Westinghouse GT; 4 props; 150,000 hp **Fuel:** 6,750 tons
Boilers: 8 Babcock & Wilcox, 41.7 kg/cm² **Range:** 18,000/12

REMARKS: CVT-16, the only one of the above in commission, is used for carrier flying training at Pensacola; she has no embarked air group or aircraft support facilities, merely supplying a seagoing platform for takeoffs and landings. CV-34, the only unit sufficiently modern in equipment to be worth reactivating, was placed in reserve 30-9-75; she is equipped with NTDS.

CVS-12 and CVS-20 retain Mk H-8 hydraulic catapults; the other ships have

RESERVE AIRCRAFT CARRIERS (*continued*)

steam catapults. All have three elevators: one centerline between the catapults, one at the forward end of the angled deck, and one (vertically-stowable) to starboard, abaft the island. Four arrester wires. CV-34 has 2 Mk 37 gun directors. The others have one Mk 37 and two or three Mk 56 directors.

Lexington (CVT 16) — training carrier 1975

Shangri-La (CVS 38) — *Intrepid* class 1966

Bennington (CVS 20) — *Essex* class 1967

Oriskany (CV 34) — *Hancock* class 1969

NAVAL AVIATION

ASW aircraft, S-3A Viking

NAVAL AVIATION

Aviation is an integral part of the U.S. Navy and Marine Corps. The approximately 6,100 aircraft (budget 1976–77) assigned to it include:

1,230 attack planes
727 fighters
136 ship-based ASW planes
377 patrol aircraft
1,163 helicopters
1,101 training aircraft

The aircraft are divided as follows:

Navy

62 attack and fighter squadrons
8 reconnaissance squadrons
4 helicopter squadrons
21 ASW (VS/HS) squadrons
24 patrol squadrons (VP)
41 various

Marine Corps

25 attack and fighter squadrons (VMA/VMF)
24 helicopter squadrons
8 various (transport, liaison, etc.)

♦ *Ship-based*

The combination of all the aircraft on board an aircraft carrier is called a Carrier Air Wing (CAW), whose composition varies according to the carrier's mission. When all the antisubmarine aircraft carriers (CVSs) had been withdrawn from service, attack carriers (CVAs) were converted to perform any mission and were designated CVs.

There are three basic types of air wing: one whose mission is to project power, or support landing operations; one to control the sea, with emphasis on antisubmarine warfare and the protection of ships; and one that consists of a combination of the aircraft needed to perform the two previously mentioned missions at the same time. The following is a typical breakdown of the types of aircraft assigned:

Projection: 24 all-weather fighters, 34 attack planes, 3 ASW helos, 3 reconnaissance aircraft, 8 electronic warfare aircraft (AEW), 2 utility aircraft (COD)
Sea Control: 24 all-weather fighters, 12 attack aircraft, 24 ASW fixed-wing aircraft, 16 ASW helos, 4 AEW, 2 COD
Composite: 24 all-weather fighters, 24 attack aircraft, 10 ASW fixed-wing aircraft, 8 ASW helos, 8 AEW, 2 COD

♦ *Land-based* — search, ASW patrol, minesweeping, utility

Organized in squadrons of nine aircraft (Orion P-3B and P-3C) each. The squadrons are operational and administrative commands. These formations make up fleet air wings, three of which are usually on the Atlantic seaboard and six in the Pacific. Reserve formations are equipped with Orion P-3s and Neptune P-2s.

♦ *Marine Corps*

Marine Corps aviation is composed of three air wings. Each Marine Air Wing (MAW) is divided into groups. A group may be made up of one attack squadron (VMA) of 20 aircraft, 1 all-weather attack squadron (VMA-AW) of 12 aircraft, 1 squadron of fighter-bombers (VMFA) of 15 aircraft, 1 squadron of all-weather fighters (VMF-AW) of 15 aircraft. A helicopter group is made up of 1 observation squadron, 2 medium helicopter squadrons, and 2 heavy helicopter squadrons.

Marine pilots, who are trained to operate from aircraft carriers, man the aircraft of the LPHs (Amphibious Assault Ships).

♦ *Aircraft Designations*

Besides the name given to an aircraft — Phantom, Intruder, Orion, etc. — each type is designated by a group of letters and figures divided by a hyphen and made up in the following manner:

1. The letter immediately preceding the hyphen indicates the principal mission:

A — attack
B — bomber
C — cargo/transport
E — airborne early warning
F — fighter
K — tanker, inflight refueling
O — observation
P — patrol
S — antisubmarine
T — training
U — utility
V — VTOL/STOL, vertical or short takeoff and landing
X — research

2. The figure that comes immediately after the hyphen is the design sequence number. When a letter follows this figure, its position in the alphabet indicates that the aircraft is the first, second, third, etc. modification to the original design.

Example: A-4E = an attack aircraft, the fourth attack plane design, the fifth modification

3. When an aircraft is assigned to duty that is not its principal mission, a second letter precedes the letter of that mission (see para. 1 above):

A — attack
C — cargo/transport
D — direction or control of drones, aircraft, or missiles
E — special electronic installation
H — search and rescue
K — tanker, inflight refueling
L — cold weather; for arctic regions
M — missile carrier
Q — drone aircraft
R — reconnaissance
S — antisubmarine
T — trainer
U — utility, general service
V — staff
W — weather, meteorology

NAVAL AVIATION *(continued)*

All-weather fighter, F-14A Tomcat

Attack aircraft, A-6E Intruder 1972

Attack aircraft, AV-8A Harrier (Marine Corps) 1971

All-weather fighter, F-4B Phantom

Attack aircraft, A-4E Skyhawk 1974

NAVAL AVIATION (*continued*)

The following letters may be placed in front of the letter or letters that indicate the mission:

G — permanently grounded
J — special test, temporarily
N — special test, permanently
X — experimental
Y — prototype
Z — planning

Reconnaissance configured RF-4B Phantom

Attack aircraft, A-7A Corsair

RA-5C Vigilante tactical reconnaissance aircraft

RA-5C Vigilante refueling in flight from a KA-3D Skywarrior

All-weather ASW helicopter, SH-3D Sea King 1975

SH-3G Sea King ASW helicopter

NAVAL AVIATION *(continued)*

ASW helicopter SH-2D Sea Sprite [LAMPS program] 1971

EA-6B Prowler

Attack aircraft, A-6A Intruder

E-2A Hawkeye

ASW aircraft, S-2E Tracker

PRINCIPAL COMBAT AIRCRAFT

SHIP-BASED FIXED-WING

Class, builder	Mission	Wingspan in m	Length in m	Height in m	Weight in kg	Engine	Max speed mach/knots	Ceiling in feet	1) Ferry range (nautical miles) 2) Combat radius (nautical miles) 3) Range (hours)
F-18 HORNET (McDonnell-Douglas) (In service 1981)	Multi-rôle fighter (Navy)	11.43	16.94	4.51	19,960	2 GE F 404 GE 400 8,200 kg thrust	M 1.8	50,000	2,303 460 3
	Armament: 13,000 pounds of conventional or tactical nuclear bombs; 2 Sidewinder; 4 Sparrow III; 1/20-mm M61 cannon.								
	REMARKS: First aircraft to have a system using a microprocessor to control the various weapons. An A-18 version is being developed to replace the A-7.								
F-14 TOMCAT (Grumman)	Two-man, all-weather fighter with variable-geometry wing	19.60/ 10.10	18.85	4.87	30,000 26,000	2 PW TF 30 P 412 9,350 kg thrust with after burners	M 2.34	60,000	2,000 500 2½ to 3
	Armament: 1/20-mm Vulcan gun; 6 Phoenix, 2 Sidewinder missiles (standard weapons) or 8,500 pounds of Sparrow and Sidewinder missiles or bombs, including tactical atomic bombs.								
	REMARKS: Max. landing speed: 120 knots. The attack version of the F-14 could, for certain missions, be equipped with the air-to-surface anti-radar Shrike.								
F-4 PHANTOM (McDonnell-Douglas)	All-weather fighter (Navy) fighter-bomber (Marine Corps)	11.70	17.75	4.95	24,750	2 GE J 79 10 8,120 kg thrust with afterburners	M 2.3	60,000	1,800 520 2¼
	Armament: 4 Sparrow III and 4 Sidewinder missiles (standard weapons) or 6 Sparrow III or 16,000 pounds of missiles, rockets or bombs, usually 18 bombs of 750 pounds, 15 of 680 pounds, 11 of 1,000 pounds; 7 smoke bombs; 11 napalm bombs; 4 Bullpup missiles; 15 pods of air-to-surface rockets. Can carry an atomic bomb.								
	REMARKS: Max. landing speed: 140 knots. Several versions: B, J, G, and RF-4 B (reconnaissance).								
F-8 CRUSADER (Ling-Temco-Vought)	All-weather interceptor	10.90	16.60	4.80	13,500	1 PW J 57 P 20 8,100 kg thrust with afterburner	M 1.7	53,000	. . . 400 2
	Armament: 4/20-mm guns; 4 Sidewinder missiles.								
	REMARKS: Several versions: E, H, I, J, K, L, and RF-8 (reconnaissance). Other than RF-8, few left in service.								
A-4 SKYHAWK (McDonnell-Douglas)	Attack (Navy and Marine Corps)	8.40	12	4.60	8,000	1 PW J 52 P 408 A 5,000 kg thrust	560 kts	42,000	1,600 400 2 h 5
	Armament: 2/20-mm Mk 12 guns; 6,500 pounds of bombs or 127-mm rockets or Mighty Mouse; Sidewinder or Bullpup missiles.								
	REMARKS: Non-folding wings. Very strong; versatile. Can carry a tactical atomic bomb. Several versions: A, B, C, E, F, M.								
A-6 INTRUDER (Grumman)	All-weather attack (Navy and Marine Corps)	16.15	16.65	4.75	27,350	2 PW J 52 P 8 A 4,200 kg thrust	530 kts	42,000	2,400 300 2
	Armament: 18,000 pounds of conventional bombs or tactical atomic bombs, rockets, etc. Examples of ordnance: 46 bombs of 250 pounds, 30 of 450 pounds, 15 of 900 pounds, 5 of 2,000 pounds; 13 pods with 247 rockets; 52 Zuni rockets; 4 Sidewinder or 4 Bullpup missiles.								
	REMARKS: Very strong; versatile. Several versions: A, B and C, EA-6A, and EA-6B are fitted for electronic warfare. The latter have a four-man crew (EA-6B) and a minimum of 30 sensors of various types.								

SHIP-BASED FIXED-WING (cont.)

Class, builder	Mission	Wingspan in m	Length in m	Height in m	Weight in kg	Engine	Max speed mach/knots	Ceiling in feet	1) Ferry range (nautical miles) 2) Combat radius (nautical miles) 3) Range (hours)
A-7 CORSAIR II (Ling-Temco-Vought)	Attack	11.80	14.05	4.90	19,000	1 Allison TF 41.A.1 6,800-kg thrust	595 kts	40,000	3,050 500 2 h 15

Armament: 2/20-mm guns; 4,000 to 15,000 pounds of bombs, rockets or missiles, according to the mission and the target distance. Examples of weapons: 24 Mk 81 bombs of 250 pounds; 4 Zuni rockets; 28/2.75-inch rockets; 1 Shrike missile and one Walleye diffusion bomb; 12 Snakeye bombs; 4 Bullpup-A missiles; 2 Shrike missiles; 2 bombs of 2,000 pounds.

Remarks: Excellent machine, very strong versatile. Several versions: A, B, C, D, E.

Class, builder	Mission	Wingspan in m	Length in m	Height in m	Weight in kg	Engine	Max speed mach/knots	Ceiling in feet	1) Ferry range 2) Combat radius 3) Range (hours)
S-2 TRACKER (Grumman)	ASW	22.10	13.25	5.05	11,800	2 Wright R 1 820-82 A 1,525 hp	Max 210 kts Cruise 140 kts Patrol 130 kts	22,000	1,150 . . . 8 h 15

Armament: 10 sonobuoys; 6/127-mm rockets, conventional or atomic; ASW depth charges or 1 Mk 13 torpedo or 2 Mk 44 or Mk 46 torpedoes.

Remarks: Retracting belly radome aft, radome in the nose; MAD. Four-men crew. Few left in service.

Class, builder	Mission	Wingspan in m	Length in m	Height in m	Weight in kg	Engine	Max speed mach/knots	Ceiling in feet	1) Ferry range 2) Combat radius 3) Range (hours)
S-3 VIKING (Lockheed)	ASW	20.90	16.25	6.95	19,700	2 TF 34. GE2 4,080-kg thrust	Max 440 kts Cruise 350 kts Patrol 160 kts	35,000	3,000 . . . 6

Armament: 60 sonobuoys, LOFAR (SSQ 41), R/O (SSQ 47), DIFAR (SSQ 53), CASS (SSQ 50), DICASS (SSQ 62) or BT (SSQ 36) types; 4 Mk 32 bombs; 4 Mk 57 depth charges; 4 Mk 53 depth charges or 4 Mk 53 mines or 2 Mk 46 torpedoes.

Remarks: Fitted with a Univac digital computer to apply the information from the different sensors on board. Four-man crew.

Class, builder	Mission	Wingspan in m	Length in m	Height in m	Weight in kg	Engine	Max speed mach/knots	Ceiling in feet	1) Ferry range 2) Combat radius 3) Range (hours)
RA-5 C VIGILANTE (North American)	Reconnaissance	16.15	23.25	5.90	30,000	2 J 79 GE 10 5,395-kg thrust and 8,120 with after-burner	M 2	64,000	. . . 1,000 4

Remarks: Carries cameras, etc. Being phased out.

Class, builder	Mission	Wingspan in m	Length in m	Height in m	Weight in kg	Engine	Max speed mach/knots	Ceiling in feet	1) Ferry range 2) Combat radius 3) Range (hours)
AV-8 HARRIER (Hawker-Siddeley)	Attack (Marine Corps)	7.70	13.87	3.43	VTOL 8,200 STOL 11,900	1 RR Pegasus 108 9,750-kg thrust	640 kts	50,000	2,000 VTOL 50/STOL 200

Armament: 2/30-mm guns; bombs to a total of 5,000 pounds.

Remarks: Improved B version in development.

Class, builder	Mission	Wingspan in m	Length in m	Height in m	Weight in kg	Engine	Max speed mach/knots	Ceiling in feet	1) Ferry range 2) Combat radius 3) Range (hours)
A-3 SKYWARRIOR (McDonnell-Douglas)	Inflight fueling	22.10	22.65	7.28	38,000	2 PW-J 57-P 10 4,535-kg thrust	500 kts	45,000	5,000 1,200 6
E-2 HAWKEYE (Grumman)	Airborne Electronic Warfare radar search	24.55	17.55	5.60	23,000	2 Allison T 56 A 8 turboprops 4,050 hp	315 kts	28,000	1,500 . . . 6

Remarks: The A version has a radome and an Air Tactical Data System (for the transmission of tactical information). The B version has an L304F computer as well, and the C version has a CAINS inertial navigation computer is fitted.

NAVAL AVIATION (*continued*)

Minesweeping helicopter, CH-53 Sea Stallion, preparing to take off with the MK 105 mine sled attached from the *Raleigh* (LPD 1) 1975

Utility Helicopter, UH-46 Sea Knight

ASW patrol aircraft, P3 Orion

PATROL

Class, builder	Mission	Wingspan in m	Length in m	Height in m	Weight in kg	Engine	Max speed mach/knots	Ceiling in feet	1) Ferry range (nautical miles) 2) Combat radius (nautical miles) 3) Range (hours)
P-3 ORION (Lockheed)	ASW	30.35	35.60	10.29	64,000	4 Allison T 56 A 14 turboprops, 4,910 hp	410 kts max 205 kts patrol	27,000	. . . 2,000 without patrol time 16

Armament: 6 mines of 2,000 pounds; 2 Mk 101 nuclear depth charges; 4 Mk 44 or 46 torpedoes; 87 sonobuoys, etc. Weapons can vary and consist, for instance, of 1 mine of 2,000 pounds; 3 mines of 1,000 pounds; 3 Mk 57 depth charges; 8 Mk 54 depth charges; 8 Mk 44 or 46 torpedoes; sonobuoys and markers. Can carry a total of 17,000 pounds of arms and equipment that can be dropped.

REMARKS: Several versions. The P-3C is fitted with an A-NEW central operations module built around the ASQ 114 miniaturized computer and with an Air Tactical Data System.

HELICOPTERS

	Mission	Diameter (rotor)	Length	Height	Weight in kg	Engine	Max speed in knots	Ceiling in feet	1) Range (nautical miles) 2) Endurance (hours)
SH-3 A, D, G, H SEA KING (Sikorsky)	ASW	18.90	22.15	4.72	8,450	2 T 58 GE 10 turboshaft, 1,400 hp	144	14,700	542 . . .

Armament: Depth charges or Mk 44 or 46 torpedoes, 840 pounds.

REMARKS: On CV aircraft carriers or land-based; can be carried on *Spruance*-class DD. SH-3H is a multi-purpose version of the SH-36 utility model. Fitted with AQS 10 dipping sonar. There is an HH-3 A, for rescue duties.

	Mission	Diameter (rotor)	Length	Height	Weight in kg	Engine	Max speed in knots	Ceiling in feet	1) Range 2) Endurance
SH-2 D SEA SPRITE (Kaman)	ASW	13.41	16.05	4.72	5,700	1 T 58 GE 8B turboshaft, 1,250 hp	146	22,500	387 2½

Armament: Sonobuoys; 1 torpedo.

REMARKS: Found on FF, DD, and CG types.

	Mission	Diameter (rotor)	Length	Height	Weight in kg	Engine	Max speed in knots	Ceiling in feet	1) Range 2) Endurance
CH-46 A/D SEA KNIGHT (Boeing Vertol)	Troop-carrying assault (Marine Corps)	15.25	15.50	5.10	10,400	2 T 58 GE 8 turboshaft, 1,250 hp	155 (CH-46 A) 161 (CH-46 D)	14,000	230 (CH-46 A) 248 (CH-46 D)

REMARKS: Can carry 33 fully equipped troops. The two cargo versions (UH-46A and 46D) are usually assigned to vertical replenishment duties in modern underway replenishment ships.

	Mission	Diameter (rotor)	Length	Height	Weight in kg	Engine	Max speed in knots	Ceiling in feet	1) Range 2) Endurance
CH-53 SEA STALLION (Sikorsky)	Minesweeping (Navy). Assault transport (Marine Corps)	22.02	26.90	5.22	22,650	2 T 64 GE 6 turboshaft, 2,850 hp	170	21,000	223 . . .

REMARKS: Version A can carry 38 fully equipped troops or 24 occupied stretchers with 4 hospital corpsmen or 4 tons of freight (2 Hawk missiles for example). CH-53E (three turboshafts totalling 11,570 hp) first flew in 1974 and will be used for amphibious support. The RH-53D version is equipped for aerial minesweeping.

HELICOPTERS (cont.)

	Mission	Diameter (rotor)	Length	Height	Weight in kg	Engine	Max speed in knots	Ceiling in feet	1) Range (nautical miles) 2) Endurance (hours)
UH-1E IROQUOIS (Bell)	Assault and attack (Marine Corps)	13.41	12.98	3.87	2,155 (empty)	1 Lycoming T 53 L 5 turbine, 1,100 hp	140	14,000	240 ...

Armament: 2/7.62 machine guns and rockets.

REMARKS: Can carry 7 troops. The AH-1G Huey Cobra (different design) is especially armed for ground support (3-barrel 20-mm cannon, 48/70-mm rockets or six TOW anti-tank missiles).

NOTE: The SH-2 Sea Sprite will be replaced beginning in 1980 by a new shipboard helicopter, the LAMPS MK III. Systems under development for use with it include: AN/APS-24 radar, AN/SSQ-53 DIFAR sonobuoys, AN/SSQ-50 CASS active sonobuoys, and AN/ASQ-81 towed MAD. IBM Electronics System Center integrates the electronics systems. Sikorsky will build the helicopter, a navalized version of its UTTAS competition-winner, UH-60A.

NUCLEAR-POWERED SUBMARINES

Nuclear reactors maintain (by means of a heat exchanger circulating water under pressure) a steam cycle that drives one or several conventional turbines, or, in some submarines, turbo-generators, which furnish the current required for an electric motor directly linked to the propeller.

There are two types of American nuclear submarines:

SSBN Strategic submarines armed with Polaris A-3 type ballistic missiles, Poseidon (since 1971), and eventually Trident.

SSN Attack submarines armed with mines, torpedoes and/or Subroc (and in the future Harpoon and Tomahawk).

Henry L. Stimson (SSBN 655) 1966

SSBN classes carry the DATICO (Digital Automatic Tape Intelligence Checkout) system for trial and control. DATICO is controlled by a magnetic tape carrying an arithmetic code that constantly checks the missiles' circuits and rejects unsuitable missiles. This appears to be the system that maintains continually required data on the target and on the launching boat, thus ensuring that the weapons are ready to be fired towards the assigned target or targets.

SSBN submarines are fitted with SINS (Ship's Inertial Navigation System) and can also use the Transit satellite navigation system. Signals sent by satellite are received by a special computer at regular intervals and are then compared with information received from other navigational systems.

Although SSBNs can cruise submerged at 20 knots, on station they usually maintain 5 knots, at which slow speed they can fire approximately one missile per minute. The ballistic missiles are launched while the submarine is submerged and are armed automatically after emergence from the sea, about 30 m above the surface.

TRIDENT PROJECT

In keeping with the demands of technological progress, the United States has for some years been studying a strategic missile of extremely long range to be launched from a submerged nuclear submarine. Known in the beginning as ULMS (Underwater Long-Range Missile System), the project has made great strides and is now known as Trident.

There will be two models of the Trident missile: Trident-I and Trident-II.

Trident-I has three propulsion stages and a "bus" re-entry system carrying 8 nuclear warheads. This system, called MIRV (Multiple Independently Targetable Re-entry Vehicle), is fitted, 24 to a boat, on very large SSBN submarines, whose characteristics are outlined below.

Trident-I has a range of 4,000 miles, giving it a great advantage over the Poseidon missile, whose range is 2,500 miles.

It is hoped that Trident-II, which will follow, will be able to reach a target 6,000 miles from the launching submarine. It might be fitted with 7 MARV (Maneuverable Re-entry Vehicle) or 14 MIRV.

NUCLEAR-POWERED SUBMARINES *(continued)*

Ethan Allen (SSBN 608) — Ethan Allen class

John C. Calhoun (SSBN 630) 1972

Daniel Webster (SSBN 626) — Note the unique position of the diving planes in this ship on the dome on the bow at the extreme lower right of the photograph

James Monroe (SSBN 622) — Lafayette class 1970

George Washington (SSBN 598)

BALLISTIC-MISSILE SUBMARINES

♦ *7 Ohio class*

	Bldr	Laid down	L	In serv.
SSBN 726 OHIO	General Dynamics	10-4-76	5-78	10-79
SSBN 727 MICHIGAN	General Dynamics	4-4-77	. . .	10-80
SSBN 728 N . . .	General Dynamics	. . .	. . .	11-81
SSBN 729 N . . .	General Dynamics	. . .	. . .	7-82
SSBN 730 N . . .	General Dynamics	. . .	. . .	. . .
SSBN 731 N . . .	. . .	. . .	. . .	. . .
SSBN 732 N . . .	. . .	. . .	. . .	. . .

Authorized: 1 in FY 74, 2 in FY 75, 1 in FY 76, 1 in FY 77, 2 in FY 78

BALLISTIC-MISSILE SUBMARINES *(continued)*

Ohio (SSBN-726) — (Artist's concept) 1976

D: 15,750 tons surfaced, 18.750 submerged **S:** 25 kts (submerged)
Dim: 170.7 × 12.8 × 10.8 **Man:** 16 officers, 117 men
A: 24 Trident-I missiles — 4/533-mm TT Mk 68
Electron Equipt: Sonar: BQQ 6
M: 1 General Electric S8G pressurized-water cooled reactor

REMARKS: The reactor will have a 9-year life span. A more advanced and more precise inertial navigation system than the SINS of the SSBNs now in service will be carried. Very quiet operation. Submersion depth is more than 300 m. At least 13 are planned, the remaining six in the following sequence: 1 in FY 79, 2 in FY 80, 1 in FY 81, and 2 in FY 82.

♦ *31 Lafayette and Benjamin Franklin classes (SCB 216 and SCB 216A types)*

	Bldr	Laid down	L	In serv.
SSBN 616 LAFAYETTE	Gen. Dynamics	1-61	8-5-62	23-4-63
SSBN 617 ALEXANDER HAMILTON	Gen. Dynamics	6-61	18-8-62	27-6-63
SSBN 619 ANDREW JACKSON	Mare Island NSY	4-61	15-9-62	3-7-63
SSBN 620 JOHN ADAMS	Portsmouth NSY	1-62	12-1-63	12-5-64
SSBN 622 JAMES MONROE	Newport News	7-61	4-8-62	7-12-63
SSBN 623 NATHAN HALE	Gen. Dynamics	10-61	12-1-63	23-11-63
SSBN 624 WOODROW WILSON	Mare Island NSY	9-61	22-2-63	27-12-63
SSBN 625 HENRY CLAY	Newport News	10-61	30-11-62	20-2-64
SSBN 626 DANIEL WEBSTER	Gen. Dynamics	12-61	27-4-63	9-4-64
SSBN 627 JAMES MADISON	Newport News	2-62	15-3-63	28-7-64
SSBN 628 TECUMSEH	Gen. Dynamics	6-62	22-6-63	29-5-64
SSBN 629 DANIEL BOONE	Mare Island NSY	2-62	22-6-63	23-4-64
SSBN 630 JOHN C. CALHOUN	Newport News	6-62	22-6-63	15-9-64
SSBN 631 ULYSSES S. GRANT	Gen. Dynamics	8-62	2-11-63	17-7-64
SSBN 632 VON STEUBEN	Newport News	9-62	18-10-63	30-9-64
SSBN 633 CASIMIR PULASKI	Gen. Dynamics	1-63	1-2-64	14-8-64
SSBN 634 STONEWALL JACKSON	Mare Island NSY	7-62	30-11-63	26-8-64
SSBN 635 SAM RAYBURN	Newport News	12-62	20-12-63	2-12-64
SSBN 636 NATHANAEL GREENE	Portsmouth NSY	5-62	12-5-64	19-12-64
SSBN 640 BENJAMIN FRANKLIN	Gen. Dynamics	5-63	5-12-64	22-10-65
SSBN 641 SIMON BOLIVAR	Newport News	4-63	22-8-64	29-10-65
SSBN 642 KAMEHAMEHA	Mare Island NSY	5-63	16-1-65	10-12-65
SSBN 643 GEORGE BANCROFT	Gen. Dynamics	8-63	20-3-65	22-1-66
SSBN 644 LEWIS AND CLARK	Newport News	7-63	21-11-64	22-12-65
SSBN 645 JAMES K. POLK	Gen. Dynamics	11-63	22-5-65	16-4-66
SSBN 654 GEORGE C. MARSHALL	Newport News	3-64	21-5-65	29-4-66
SSBN 655 HENRY L. STIMSON	Gen. Dynamics	4-64	13-11-65	20-8-66
SSBN 656 GEORGE WASHINGTON CARVER	Newport News	8-64	14-8-65	15-6-66
SSBN 657 FRANCIS SCOTT KEY	Gen. Dynamics	8-64	23-4-66	3-12-66
SSBN 658 MARIANO G. VALLEJO	Mare Island NSY	7-64	23-10-65	16-12-66
SSBN 659 WILL ROGERS	Gen. Dynamics	3-65	21-7-66	1-4-67

Authorized: SSBN-616 to SSBN-626 in FY 61, SSBN-627 to SSBN-636 in FY 62, 6 + 6 in FY 63

D: 7,250 tons surfaced, 8,250 submerged
S: 15 kts (surfaced), 25 kts (submerged)
Dim: 129.54 × 10.05 × 9.0 **Man:** 20 officers, 148 men
A: 16 Poseidon missiles — 4/533-mm TT fwd (can launch Subroc missile)
Electron Equipt: Sonar: SSBN Unit
M: 1 Westinghouse SW5 pressurized-water reactor; 1 7-bladed prop; 15,000 hp

REMARKS: Conversion of both classes from Polaris A-3 to Poseidon missiles completed 1970-77. Submersion depth is more than 300 m. Mk 84 computer for analysis, display, and transmission of tactical information. After the SSBN-640 more silent propulsion machinery. Three Mk 2 SINS were installed during conversion. Poseidon missile may be replaced by Trident-I. Funds will be requested FY 79 for conversion of the first SSBN and for three each year thereafter through FY 82. SSBN-657 will be the first to be converted.

BALLISTIC-MISSILE SUBMARINES (*continued*)

♦ *5 Ethan Allen class (SCB 180 type)*

	Bldr	Laid down	L	In serv.
SSBN 608 ETHAN ALLEN	Gen. Dynamics	9-59	22-11-60	8-8-61
SSBN 609 SAM HOUSTON	Newport News	12-59	2-2-61	6-3-62
SSBN 610 THOMAS A. EDISON	Gen. Dynamics	3-60	15-6-61	10-3-62
SSBN 611 JOHN MARSHALL	Newport News	4-60	15-7-61	21-5-62
SSBN 618 THOMAS JEFFERSON	Newport News	2-61	24-2-62	4-1-63

Authorized: SSBN-608 to SSBN-611 in FY 59, SSBN-618 in FY 61

D: 6,300 tons surfaced, 7,880 submerged (6,955 avg)
Dim: 124.96 × 10.05 × 9.00
S: 15/20 kts **Man:** 15 officers, 127 men
A: 16 Polaris A-3 — 4/533-mm TT fwd, four conventional or eight ASW torpedoes as reloads
Electron Equipt: SSBN sonar unit **M:** As preceding classes

REMARK: Mk 80 computer, Mk 2 Mod 3 SINS.

♦ *5 George Washington class (SCB 180A type)*

	Bldr	Laid down	L	In serv.
SSBN 598 GEORGE WASHINGTON	Gen. Dynamics	1-57	9-6-59	30-12-59
SSBN 599 PATRICK HENRY	Gen. Dynamics	6-58	22-9-59	9-4-60
SSBN 600 THEODORE ROOSEVELT	Mare Island NSY	5-58	3-10-59	13-2-61
SSBN 601 ROBERT E. LEE	Newport News SB	8-58	18-12-59	16-9-60
SSBN 602 ABRAHAM LINCOLN	Portsmouth NSY	11-58	14-5-60	11-3-61

Authorized: SSBN-598 to SSBN-600 in FY 58, SSBN-601 and SSBN-602 in FY 59

D: 6,019 tons surfaced, 6,888 submerged **S:** 15/20 kts
Dim: 115.82 × 10.05 × 8.80 **Man:** 10/12 officers, 90/100 men
A: 16 Polaris A-3, 6/533-mm TT fwd
Electron Equipt: Sonar: SSBN sonar unit **M:** As preceding classes

REMARKS: During her first cruise (30-12-60 to 8-3-61), SSBN-599 remained submerged for 66 days and 22 hours, traveled 11,000 miles (20,400 km) and, in exercises, successfully launched 8 Polaris missiles. The SSBN-598 cruised from 12-59 to 3-65 with her original nuclear core. From 6-64 to 6-67 SSBN-598 to SSBN-602 were overhauled; a new core and a Mk 84 computer were added, and launching wells were modified to permit launch by steam of the A-3 missiles in place of the original A-1.

NUCLEAR-POWERED ATTACK SUBMARINES

♦ *32 Los Angeles class*

	Bldr	Laid down	L	In serv.
SSN 688 LOS ANGELES	Newport News	8-1-72	6-4-74	13-11-76
SSN 689 BATON ROUGE	Newport News	18-11-72	18-4-75	25-6-77
SSN 690 PHILADELPHIA	Gen. Dynamics	12-8-72	19-10-74	25-6-77
SSN 691 MEMPHIS	Newport News	23-6-73	3-4-76	12-30-77
SSN 692 OMAHA	Gen. Dynamics	27-1-73	21-2-76	12-30-77
SSN 693 CINCINNATI	Newport News	6-4-74	19-2-76	5-78
SSN 694 GROTON	Gen. Dynamics	3-8-73	9-10-76	4-78
SSN 695 BIRMINGHAM	Newport News	26-4-75	15-10-77	12-78
SSN 696 NEW YORK CITY	Gen. Dynamics	15-12-73	18-6-77	78
SSN 697 INDIANAPOLIS	Gen. Dynamics	19-10-74	30-7-77	79
SSN 698 BREMERTON	Gen. Dynamics	8-5-76	11-77	79
SSN 699 JACKSONVILLE	Gen. Dynamics	21-2-76	6-78	79
SSN 700 DALLAS	Gen. Dynamics	9-10-76	5-78	79
SSN 701 LA JOLLA	Gen. Dynamics	16-10-76	-78	79
SSN 702 PHOENIX	Gen. Dynamics	30-7-77	-78	80
SSN 703 BOSTON	Gen. Dynamics	11-77	. . .	80
SSN 704 BALTIMORE	Gen. Dynamics	. . .	. . .	80
SSN 705 N . . .	Gen. Dynamics	. . .	. . .	80
SSN 706 N . . .	Gen. Dynamics	. . .	. . .	. . .
SSN 707 N . . .	Gen. Dynamics	. . .	. . .	. . .
SSN 708 N . . .	Gen. Dynamics	. . .	. . .	. . .
SSN 709 N . . .	Gen. Dynamics	. . .	. . .	. . .
SSN 710 N . . .	Gen. Dynamics	. . .	. . .	. . .
SSN 711 N . . .	Newport News	26-5-77	. . .	7-80
SSN 712 N . . .	Newport News	. . .	. . .	6-81
SSN 713 N . . .	Newport News	. . .	. . .	2-82
SSN 714 N . . .	Newport News	. . .	. . .	9-82
SSN 715 N . . .	Newport News	. . .	. . .	3-83
SSN 716 N . . .	Newport News	. . .	. . .	. . .
SSN 717 N . . .	Newport News	. . .	. . .	. . .
SSN 718 N . . .	Newport News	. . .	. . .	. . .
SSN 719 N . . .	. . .	. . .	. . .	. . .

Authorized: SSN-688 to SSN-690 in FY 70, SSN-691 to SSN-694 in FY 71, SSN-695 to SSN-700 in FY 72, SSN-701 to SSN-705 in FY 73, SSN-706 to SSN-710 in FY 74, SSN-711 to SSN-713 in FY 75, SSN-714 and SSN-715 in FY 76, SSN-716 to SSN-718 in FY 77, SSN-719 in FY 78

Los Angeles (SSN 688) 1976

D: 6,000 tons surfaced, 6,900 submerged **S:** over 30 kts (submerged)
Dim: 109.73 × 10.06 × 9.75 **Man:** 12 officers, 115 men
A: 4/533-mm TT (torpedoes, Subroc, Harpoon)
Electron Equipt: Radars: 1/BPS 15
Sonars: 1/BQQ 5, BQS-15, towed array-Computer: UYK-7
M: General Electric S6G reactor; 2 GT; 1 prop; 30,000 hp

NUCLEAR-POWERED ATTACK SUBMARINES (*continued*)

REMARKS: At least six additional programmed. Mk 113 Mod 10 torpedo fire control in SSN-688 to SSN-699, Mk 117 in later units. Harpoon to be carried beginning in 1978. Maximum diving depth 450 m. Described as the finest ASW platforms now afloat. Bow is constructed of fiberglas, a streamlined cover over the spherical BQQ5 sonar array. There are two inertial guidance systems (SINS). Construction program far behind schedule due to labor problems and lack of shipyard capacity. An improved version of this class will be introduced in the early 1980s.

♦ *1 Glenard P. Lipscomb class*

	Bldr	Laid down	L	In serv.
SSN 685 GLENARD P. LIPSCOMB	Gen. Dynamics	5-6-71	4-8-73	21-12-74

Authorized: FY 68

Glenard P. Lipscomb (SSN 685) 1973

D: 5,813 tons standard, 6,480 submerged **S:** 25 kts (submerged)
Dim: 111.3 × 9.7 × 8.8 **Man:** 12 officers, 108 men
A: 4/533-mm TT (Subroc)
M: 1 Westinghouse S5W reactor and General Electric turboelectric drive

REMARKS: The TEDS (Turbo-Electric Drive Submarine) was an effort to make an exceptionally quiet submarine at the expense of some speed. Most other equipment is similar to the *Sturgeon* class.

♦ *37 Sturgeon class (SCB 188M and SCB 188A types)*

	Bldr	Laid down	L	In serv.
SSN 637 STURGEON	Gen. Dynamics	8-63	26-2-66	3-3-67
SSN 638 WHALE	Gen. Dynamics	5-64	14-10-66	12-10-68
SSN 639 TAUTOG	Ingalls	1-64	15-4-67	17-8-68
SSN 646 GRAYLING	Portsmouth NSY	5-64	22-6-67	11-10-69
SSN 647 POGY	New York SB	5-64	3-6-67	15-5-71
SSN 648 ASPRO	Ingalls	11-64	29-11-67	20-2-69
SSN 649 SUNFISH	Gen. Dynamics	1-65	14-10-66	15-3-69
SSN 650 PARGO	Gen. Dynamics	6-64	17-9-66	1-5-68
SSN 651 QUEENFISH	Newport News	5-64	25-2-66	6-12-66
SSN 652 PUFFER	Ingalls	2-65	30-3-68	9-8-69
SSN 653 RAY	Newport News	1-65	21-6-66	12-4-67
SSN 660 SANDLANCE	Portsmouth NSY	1-65	11-11-69	25-9-71
SSN 661 LAPON	Newport News	7-65	16-12-66	14-12-67
SSN 662 GURNARD	Mare Island NSY	12-64	20-5-67	6-12-68
SSN 663 HAMMERHEAD	Newport News	11-65	14-4-67	28-6-68
SSN 664 SEA DEVIL	Newport News	4-66	5-10-67	30-1-69
SSN 665 GUITARRO	Mare Island NSY	12-65	27-7-68	9-9-72
SSN 666 HAWKBILL	Mare Island NSY	9-66	12-4-69	4-2-71
SSN 667 BERGALL	Gen. Dynamics	4-66	17-2-69	13-6-69
SSN 668 SPADEFISH	Newport News	12-66	15-5-68	14-8-69
SSN 669 SEA HORSE	Gen. Dynamics	8-66	15-6-68	19-9-69
SSN 670 FINBACK	Newport News	6-67	7-12-68	4-2-70
SSN 672 PINTADO	Mare Island NSY	10-67	16-8-69	11-9-71
SSN 673 FLYING FISH	Gen. Dynamics	10-67	17-5-69	29-4-70
SSN 674 TREPANG	Gen. Dynamics	3-68	27-9-69	14-8-70
SSN 675 BLUEFISH	Gen. Dynamics	3-68	10-1-70	8-1-71
SSN 676 BILLFISH	Gen. Dynamics	9-68	1-5-70	12-3-71
SSN 677 DRUM	Mare Island NSY	8-68	23-5-70	15-4-72
SSN 678 ARCHERFISH	Gen. Dynamics	6-69	16-1-71	24-12-71
SSN 679 SILVERSIDES	Gen. Dynamics	12-69	4-6-71	5-5-72
SSN 680 WILLIAM H. BATES	Ingalls	8-69	12-71	5-5-73
SSN 681 BATFISH	Gen. Dynamics	2-70	9-10-71	1-9-72
SSN 682 TUNNY	Ingalls	5-70	10-6-72	26-1-74
SSN 683 PARCHE	Ingalls	12-70	12-72	17-8-74
SSN 684 CAVALLA	Gen. Dynamics	6-70	19-2-72	9-2-73
SSN 686 L. MENDEL RIVERS	Newport News	6-71	2-6-73	31-12-74
SSN 687 RICHARD B. RUSSELL	Newport News	10-71	12-1-74	16-8-75

Authorized: SSN-637 to SSN-639 in FY 62, SSN-646 to SSN-653 in FY 63, SSN-660 to SSN-664 in FY 64, SSN-665 to SSN-670 in FY 65, SSN-672 to SSN-677 in FY 66, SSN-678 to SSN-682 in FY 67, SSN-683 and SSN-684 in FY 68, SSN-686 and SSN-687 in FY 69

D: 3,640 tons surfaced, 4,640 submerged **S:** 15/30 kts
Dim: 89.0 (SSN-678 and later: 92.1) × 9.65 × 8.80
A: 4/533-mm TT (Subroc, Harpoon) **Man:** 12 officers, 95 men
Electron Equipt: Radar: 1/BPS 14
Sonars: BQQ 1, Retrofit III: 1/BQS 8, 1/BQS 13
M: 1 S5W2 Westinghouse reactor; General Electric or de Laval GT; 1 prop; 20,000 hp

NUCLEAR-POWERED ATTACK SUBMARINES *(continued)*

Billfish (SSN 676) — Note new sonar domes Terzibaschitsch, 1977

Richard B. Russell (SSN 687) 1976

Hawkbill (SSN 666) with a DSRV 1971

REMARKS: The construction contract of SSN-647 with New York Shipbuilding, Camden, was canceled in 4-67 and completion of the ship was given to Ingalls, Pascagoula. Completion of SSN-665 was delyaed 28 months. Two counterrotating propellers mounted on a single shaft. Torpedo tubes are amidships. The width of the diving planes is 11.60 m. Maximum depth about 400 m. SSN-666 has been modified (as have other submarines of this class) to carry a DSRV (salvage submarine), which can be launched and recovered while submerged. The after hatch is so constructed that people can be transferred between the two ships while submerged.

♦ *1 prototype based on the Sturgeon class (project SCB-245)*

	Bldr	Laid down	L	In serv.
SSN 671 NARWHAL	Gen. Dynamics	1-66	9-9-67	12-7-69

Narwhal (SSN 671) General Dynamics, 1961

NUCLEAR-POWERED ATTACK SUBMARINES (*continued*)

Authorized in FY 64

D: 4,550 tons surfaced, 5,350 submerged **S:** 20/25 kts
Dim: 95.7 × 11.5 × 7.9
Man: 12 officers, 95 men **A:** 4/533-mm TT (Subroc, Harpoon)
Electron Equipt: Sonar: BQQ-2 (BQS-6 active/BQR-7 passive), BQS-8
M: 1 General Electric S5G reactor; 2 GT; 1 prop; 17,000 hp

REMARKS: Prototype seagoing reactor designed to study the cooling of the S5G reactor by free circulation, thus eliminating circulation pumps and their noise. Essentially a lengthened *Sturgeon* in most other respects. Will receive Harpoon when available.

♦ *13 Permit class (SCB 188 type: SSN-594 to SSN-612 and SSN-621; SCB 188M type: SSN-613 to SSN-615)*

	Bldr	Laid down	L	In serv.
SSN 594 PERMIT	Mare Island NSY	7-59	1-7-61	29-5-62
SSN 595 PLUNGER	Mare Island NSY	3-60	12-9-61	21-11-62
SSN 596 BARB (ex-*Pollack*)	Ingalls	11-59	12-2-62	24-8-63
SSN 603 POLLACK (ex-*Barb*)	New York SB	3-60	17-3-62	26-5-64
SSN 604 HADDO	New York SB	9-60	18-8-62	16-12-64
SSN 605 JACK	Portsmouth NSY	9-60	24-4-63	31-3-67
SSN 606 TINOSA	Portsmouth NSY	11-59	9-12-61	17-10-64
SSN 607 DACE	Ingalls	6-60	18-8-62	4-4-64
SSN 612 GUARDFISH	New York SB	2-61	15-5-65	20-12-66
SSN 613 FLASHER	Gen. Dynamics	4-61	22-6-63	22-7-66
SSN 614 GREENLING	Gen. Dynamics	8-61	4-4-64	3-11-67
SSN 615 GATO	Gen. Dynamics	12-61	14-5-64	25-1-68
SSN 621 HADDOCK	Ingalls	4-61	21-5-66	22-12-67

Tinosa (SSN 606) — 4.6 m sail 1964

Gato (SSN 615) — 6.1 m sail 1967

Authorized: SSN-594 to SSN-596 in FY 58, SSN-603 to SSN-607 in FY 59, SSN-612 to SSN-615 in FY 60, SSN-621 in FY 61

SSN-594 to SSN-604, SSN-606 to SSN-612, and SSN-621:
D: 3,526 tons surfaced, 4,310 submerged **Dim:** 84.88 × 9.75 × 8.80
SSN-606:
D: 3,526 tons surfaced, 4,465 submerged **Dim:** 90.11 × 9.65 × 8.80
SSN-613 to SSN-615:
D: 3,836 tons surfaced, 4,650 submerged **Dim:** 89.0 × 9.65 × 8.80
A: 4/533-mm TT (Subroc, Harpoon) **S:** 15/30 kts
Man: 12 officers, 91 men
Electron Equipt: Sonar: BQQ 2 (BQS 6 active/BQR 7 passive)
M: 1 S5W2 Westinghouse reactor; General Electric or de Laval GT; 1 prop

REMARKS: The *Thresher* (SSN-593) was lost 10-4-63. SSN-605 has contrarotating props with a contrarotating turbine and no reduction gearing. SSN-613 to SSN-615 have taller sails (6.1 m vice 4.2 or 4.6 in other ships) heavier machinery, and had safety features built in that were later backfitted in the others. The BQR-7 special array is in the bow, necessitating placement of the tubes abreast the sail. These ships will carry Harpoon when it is available. SSN-594 conducted sub-launched Harpoon trials during 1976.

♦ *1 special submarine (SCB 178 type)*

	Bldr	Laid down	L	In serv.
SSN 597 TULLIBEE	Gen. Dynamics	5-58	27-4-60	8-60

Authorized: FY 58

NUCLEAR-POWERED ATTACK SUBMARINES (*continued*)

Tullibee (SSN 597) 1975

D: 2,317 tons surfaced (2,490 normal), 2,640 submerged **S:** 15/20 kts
Dim: 83.15 × 7.31 × 6.10 **Man:** 6 officers, 50 men
A: 4/533-mm TT
Electron Equipt: Sonar: BQQ 2 (BQS 6/BQR 7) BQG 4 (PUFFS)
M: 1 Combustion Engineering S2C; turbo-electric propulsion; 1 prop

Remarks: The torpedo tubes, amidships, have a 10° angle from the centerline. Turbo-electric propulsion with GTs. Original nuclear core changed in 1965. PUFFS (Passive Underwater Fire Control System) hydrophones are mounted in three fins along the top of the hull.

♦ *1 Halibut class (SCB 137A type) ex-SSGN*

	Bldr	Laid down	L	In serv.
SSN 587 HALIBUT	Mare Island NSY	4-57	9-1-59	4-1-60

Authorized: FY 57

D: 3,850 tons surfaced, 5,000 submerged **S:** 15/20 kts
Dim: 106.70 × 8.85 × 8.80 **Man:** 10 officers, 88 men
A: 6/533-mm TT (2 aft) **Electron Equipt:** Sonar: BQS 4
M: 1 S3W Westinghouse reactor; 2 GT; 2 props; 12,000 hp

Remarks: Forward compartment 27 m long and 7.60 m high, where four Regulus missiles were stowed. The missiles and their launchers were removed in 1965 when the ship was reclassified as an SSN. Placed in reserve 30-6-76. Equipped to carry DSRV rescue vehicle.

Halibut (SSN 587) 1970

♦ *1 Triton class (SCB 132 type) ex-SSRN*

	Bldr	Laid down	L	In serv.
SSN 586 TRITON	Gen. Dynamics	5-56	19-8-58	10-11-59

Authorized: FY 57

D: 5.940 tons surfaced, 7,780 submerged **S:** 27/20 kts
Dim: 136.25 × 11.30 × 7.60 **Man:** 14 officers, 156 men
A: 6/533-mm TT (4 fwd, 2 aft) **Electron Equipt:** Sonar: BQS 4
M: 2 S4G General Dynamics reactors; 2 props; 34,000 hp

Triton (SSN 586) 1959

NUCLEAR-POWERED ATTACK SUBMARINES (*continued*)

REMARKS: First submarine with three decks. In 1960 made a round-the-world cruise submerged, sailing 41,519 miles in 84 days at an average speed of 18 knots. In 1962 the original nuclear core, with which she had run 125,000 miles (231,500 km), was replaced. Unlike other submarines, her speed on the surface is greater than her submerged speed, and, because of her conventional hull configuration, she has good seagoing qualities. It was hoped that she would be able to operate easily as a radar picket with large surface-ship task forces. Reclassified SSN on 1-3-61. Decommissioned since 3-5-69 as too unwieldy and uneconomical to operate.

♦ *5 Skipjack class (SCB 154 type)*

	Bldr	Laid down	L	In serv.
SSN 585 SKIPJACK	Gen. Dynamics	5-56	26-5-58	15-4-59
SSN 588 SCAMP	Mare Island, NSY	1-59	15-2-60	5-6-61
SSN 590 SCULPIN	Ingalls	2-58	31-3-60	1-6-61
SSN 591 SHARK	Newport News SB	2-56	16-3-60	9-2-61
SSN 592 SNOOK	Ingalls	4-58	31-10-60	24-10-61

Authorized: SSN-585 in FY 56, SSN-588 and SSN-590 to SSN-592 in FY 57

Scamp (SSN 588) G. Arra, 1976

D: 3,075 tons surfaced, 3,513 submerged **S:** 15/30 kts
Dim: 76.80 × 9.75 × 8.50 **Man:** 8 officers, 85 men
A: 6.533-mm TT, 24 torpedoes (all fwd)
M: 1 Westinghouse S5W reactor; 1 Westinghouse GT (SSN-585) or General Electric (the others); 1 prop; 15,000 hp

REMARKS: The reactor compartment takes up 6.10 m. Between the reactor and the propeller, all engine fittings are duplicated (two heat exchangers, two pressurized-water coolers; two groups of turbines, two groups of turbo-generators). In case of emergency, submerged propulsion can take over by means of two electric motors linked directly on the propeller shaft and feeding off two electric batteries or two small diesel generators. Better hull form than later SSN. Still considered first-line submarines. The *Scorpion* (SSN-589) disappeared in the Atlantic about 27-5-68.

♦ *4 Skate class (SCB 121 type)*

	Bldr	Laid down	L	In serv.
SSN 578 SKATE	Gen. Dynamics	7-55	16-5-57	22-12-57
SSN 579 SWORDFISH	Portsmouth NSY	1-56	27-8-57	15-9-58
SSN 583 SARGO	Mare Island NSY	2-56	10-10-57	1-10-58
SSN 584 SEADRAGON	Portsmouth NSY	6-56	16-8-58	5-12-59

Authorized: SSN-578 and SSN-579 in FY 55, SSN-583 and SSN-584 in FY 56

Skate (SSN 578)

D: 2,570 tons surfaced, 2,860 submerged **S:** 15/19 kts
Dim: 81.40 × 7.62 × 6.10 **Man:** 8 officers, 87 men
A: 8/533-mm TT (6 fwd, 2 aft) **Electron Equipt:** Sonar: BQS 4
M: 1 Westinghouse S3W reactor in SSN-578 and SSN-583; S4W reactor in SSN-579 and SSN-584; 2 GT; 2 props; 13,200 hp

REMARKS: SSN-578 passed under the North Pole twice (8-58), coming to the surface nine times while in ice-capped waters during this cruise. She ran 120,862 miles in 39 months with her first core.

♦ *1 Seawolf class (SCB 64A type)*

	Bldr	Laid down	L	In serv.
SSN 575 SEAWOLF	Gen. Dynamics	9-53	21-7-55	30-3-57

Authorized: FY 53

Seawolf (SSN 575) General Dynamics

NUCLEAR-POWERED ATTACK SUBMARINES *(continued)*

D: 3,765 tons surfaced, 4,287 submerged **S:** 20/20 kts
Dim: 102.87 × 8.45 × 6.70 **Man:** 11 officers, 90 men
A: 6/533-mm TT (fwd)
M: 1 Westinghouse S2WA reactor; 2 GT; 2 props; 15,000 hp

REMARK: The original propulsion, which was by an S2G reactor with sodium cooling, did not prove satisfactory and was replaced by 1 S2WA.

♦ *1 Nautilus class (SCB 64 type)*

	Bldr	Laid down	L	In serv.
SSN 571 NAUTILUS	Gen. Dynamics	6-52	21-1-54	30-9-54

Authorized: FY 52

Nautilus (SSN 571) 1975

D: 3,764 tons surfaced, 4,091 submerged **S:** 20/20 kts
Dim: 97.3 × 8.45 × 6.70 **Man:** 13 officers, 92 men
A: 6/533-mm TT (fwd)
M: 1 S3W Westinghouse reactor; 2 GT; 2 props; 15,000 hp

REMARKS: World's first nuclear submarine. Overhaul from 1972-74. Second-line ship, used in communications research. May decommission during FY 79.

CONVENTIONAL SUBMARINES

♦ *3 Barbel class (SCB 150 type)*

	Bldr	Laid down	L	In serv.
SS 580 BARBEL	Portsmouth NSY	18-5-56	19-7-58	17-1-59
SS 581 BLUEBACK	Ingalls	15-4-57	16-5-69	15-10-59
SS 582 BONEFISH	New York SB	3-6-57	22-11-58	9-7-59

Authorized: FY 56

D: 1,740 tons standard, 2,146 surfaced, 2,895 submerged **S:** 15/25 kts
Dim: 66.75 × 8.84 × 5.80 **Man:** 8 officers, 70 men

Barbel (SS 580) 1962

A: 6/533-mm TT (fwd)
M: Diesel-electric drive (3 1,600-hp Fairbanks-Morse diesels, 1 Westinghouse electric motor); 1 prop; 3,150 hp

REMARKS: Teardrop hull design as on the *Albacore*. Diving planes were moved to the sail structure in 1961-62. Dutch *Tijgerhaai* class based on this design.

♦ *1 Sailfish class, ex-SSR*

	Bldr	Laid down	L	In serv.
SS 572 SAILFISH	Portsmouth NSY	8-12-53	7-9-55	14-4-56

Authorized: FY 52

Sailfish (SS 572) 1968

D: 2,045 tons standard, 2,625 surfaced, 3,168 submerged **S:** 19.5/14 kts
Dim: 106.80 × 8.84 × 4.98 **Man:** 12 officers, 96 men
A: 6/533-mm TT (fwd)
M: 4 1,500-hp Fairbanks-Morse diesels; 2 Elliot electric motors; 2 props; 8,200 hp

REMARKS: FRAM-II modernization. Radar picket radars removed 1961. Equipped with BQG-4 (PUFFS) passive fire-control sonar. The *Salmon* (SS-573) was stricken 1 October 1977; *Sailfish* to follow at end of FY 78.

CONVENTIONAL SUBMARINES (*continued*)

♦ *1 Darter class (SCB 116 type)*

	Bldr	Laid down	L	In serv.
SS 576 DARTER	Electric Boat Co.	1-11-54	28-5-56	20-1-56

Authorized: FY 54

Darter (SS 576)

D: 1,590 tons standard, 1,720 surfaced, 2,372 submerged **S:** 20/20 kts
Dim: 81.68 × 8.23 × 5.80 **Man:** 10 officers, 75 men
A: 8/533-mm TT (6 fwd, 2 aft) **Electron Equipt:** Sonar: BQG 4 (PUFFS)
M: Diesel electric (3 Fairbanks-Morse diesels, 2 electric Westinghouse motors); 2 props; 5,500 hp

REMARKS: Very similar to ultimate configuration of the *Tang* class. To be stricken at end FY 79.

♦ *1 Grayback class (SCB 161 type)*

	Bldr	Laid down	L	In serv.
SS 574 GRAYBACK	Mare Island NSY	1-7-54	2-7-57	5-58

Authorized: FY 53

Grayback (SS 574) 1969

D: 2,670 tons surfaced, 3,650 submerged **S:** 20/16.7 kts
Dim: 101.8 × 8.20 × 5.8 **A:** 8/533-mm TT (2 aft)
Man: 10 officers, 78 men **Electron Equipt:** BSQ 2, BQG 4 (PUFFS)
M: Diesel-electric propulsion, (3 Fairbanks-Morse); 2 props; 5,500 hp

REMARKS: Designed as SSG carrying 2 Regulus-II surface-to-surface missiles. LPSS conversion, which took six years, finished 9-5-69. Redesignated SS in 1975, but retains capacity for 10 officers and 75 commandos with their equipment (including swimmer-delivery vehicles) stowed in the former missile hangars.

♦ *4 Tang class (SCB-2A type)*

	Bldr	Laid down	L	In serv.
AGSS 563 TANG	Portsmouth NSY	4-49	19-6-51	4-52
SS 565 WAHOO	Portsmouth NSY	10-49	16-10-51	30-5-52
SS 566 TROUT	Electric Boat Co.	12-49	21-8-51	27-6-52
SS 567 GUDGEON	Portsmouth NSY	5-50	11-6-52	21-11-52

Authorized: AGSS-563, SS-565, and SS-566 in FY 49, SS-567 in FY 50

Tang (AGSS 563) — The 3BQG-4 PUFFS arrays are visible on the deck

Gudgeon (SS 567) 1971

D: 2,100 tons surfaced, 2,700 submerged **S:** 15.5/16 kts
Dim: 84.73 × 8.30 × 5.70 **Man:** 11 officers, 75 men
A: 8/533-mm TT (6 fwd, 2 aft)
Electron Equipt: Sonar: BQG 4 (PUFFS)
M: Diesel-electric propulsion (see Remarks); 2 props; 5,600 hp
Fuel: 350 tons

REMARKS: Forward diving planes retractable. The pancake engines of the first four proved unsatisfactory and were replaced by the same Fairbanks-Morse high-speed diesels that were used in the last two built, which necessitated lengthening of the ship by 2.75 m. (1957-58). SS-567 was used for trials of a plastic bridge in the sail structure (1964-65). FRAM-II modernization. The *Trigger* (SS-564) and *Harder*

CONVENTIONAL SUBMARINES *(continued)*

(SS-568) were transferred to Italy in 7-73 and 3-74, respectively. The *Tang* replaced the AGSS *Tigrone* in 1975 as a trials ship. The other three submarines of this class will be transferred to the Iranian Navy in 1979-81 after extensive overhauls, one per year.

GUIDED MISSILE SUBMARINE

♦ *1 Grayback class*

	Bldr	Laid down	L	In serv.
SSG 577 GROWLER	Portsmouth NSY	10-11-54	28-5-56	30-8-58

Authorized: FY 55

Growler (SSG 577) 1958

D: 2,540 tons surfaced, 3,515 submerged **Dim:** 96.8 × 8.2 × 5.8
S: 20/12 kts **Man:** 9 officers, 87 men **A:** 6/533-mm TT (2 aft)
M: Diesel-electric: 3 Fairbanks-Morse, 1,500-hp diesels, 2 motors; 2 props; 5,500 hp

Remarks: Intended for Regulus-II cruise missiles, two of which were carried in her two hangars forward. Design is essentially a lengthened *Darter,* cut in two to add missile features. Decommissioned 25-5-64. Planned conversion to LPSS canceled 1968 but still retained because of her low usage and potential for conversion.

RESEARCH SUBMARINES

♦ *1 Dolphin class (SCB 207 type)*

	Bldr	Laid down	L	In serv.
AGSS 555 DOLPHIN	Portsmouth NSY	11-62	8-6-68	8-69

Authorized: FY 61

D: 800 tons surfaced, 930 submerged **S:** . . ./12 kts
Dim: 46.33 × 5.79 × 4.90 **Man:** 3 officers, 21 men
M: Diesel-electric propulsion, 2 G.M. 12V71 diesels; 1 prop; 1,650 hp

Remarks: The hull is a perfect cylinder, 5.49 m in diameter, strongly braced and closed at the forward and after ends by two hemispheric bulkheads, with minimum compartmentation. Used for deep-diving tests as well as acoustic and oceanographic experiments. Extensive use of alloys and plastics. Single torpedo tube removed in 1970.

Dolphin (AGSS 555) 1969

♦ *1 Albacore class (SCB 182A)*

	Bldr	Laid down	L	In serv.
AGSS 569 ALBACORE	Portsmouth NSY	15-3-52	1-8-53	12-53

Authorized: FY 62

D: 1,265 tons surfaced, 1,517 normal, 1,810 submerged **S:** 25/33 kts
Dim: 60.95 × 8.33 × 5.65 **Man:** 5 officers, 47 men
M: 1 diesel; 1,700 hp; 1 electric motor (see Remarks); 1 5-bladed prop

Remarks: Hydrodynamic (teardrop) hull. Fittings reduced to a minimum. Forward planes non-retractable; after planes in cruciform configuration. At 18 knots and an angle of 20° can submerge 105 m per minute. In 1963 she was fitted with a new type of electric motor that drives counterrotating propellers. Batteries of a new type have permitted higher speed and greater distances while submerged. In reserve since 9-72.

♦ *1 nuclear research submarine for deep diving*

	Bldr	Laid down	L	In serv.
NR 1	Electric Boat Co.	6-67	21-1-69	27-10-69

Authorized: FY 66

NR1

RESEARCH SUBMARINES (*continued*)

D: 400 tons surfaced, 700 submerged **Dim:** 42.67 × 3.75 × 4.45
Man: 3 officers, 9 men, 2 scientists
M: 1 reactor; turbo-electric drive; 2 props

REMARKS: Project approved 18-4-65. Designated as a Deep Submergence Rescue Vehicle. Fitted for all oceanographic missions, military and civilian. Thick cylindrical hull. Wheels for moving on ocean bottom. A very successful vehicle, but cost three times original estimate.

DEEP-SUBMERGENCE VEHICLES

♦ **DSRV 1, DSRV 2** — Bldr: Lockheed Missile and Space Co., 1970-71

D: 30.5 tons **S:** 5 kts **Dim:** 15 × 2.50 × . . .
M: Electric

REMARKS: The impossibility of bringing help to the submarine *Thresher,* which disappeared 10-4-63 in 1,400 fathoms, and an interest in oceanographic studies led the United States to develop small submersibles that could operate at great depths and rescue the crews of sunken submarines. Various types were tried and the U.S. Navy undertook a project called DSSP (Deep Submergence System Project) and brought into service several vehicles designated DSRV (Deep Submergence Rescue Vehicle), which can:
— operate at a maximum depth of 3,500 feet (1,070 m)
— stand a pressure equal to 9,000 feet (2,750 m)
— dive or rise at 100 feet a minute
— make a maximum speed of 5 knots while submerged
— remain submerged for 30 hours at 3 knots
— maintain station in a 1-knot current
— operate all machinery submerged at a 45° angle.

Three men, including one hospital corpsman, are carried by DSRVs, which can bring to the surface as many as 24 men at one time. Motors energized by a zinc battery can turn a regular propulsion propeller and two types of rotor (one forward, one aft) or two variable-pitch propellers (one forward, one aft) which can be positioned to permit a close approach to a sunken object. The vehicles have an articulated arm with pincers for removing debris. Their size and weight were determined by the possible need to airlift them in the Starlifter (Lockheed C-141A) cargo plane. Additional equipment, especially a truck transport for the DSRV, would be carried in a second Starlifter. In addition, the SSN nuclear submarines have received or will receive the equipment necessary to fasten a DSRV to their deck (see photograph of the *Hawkbill,* SSN-666, with a DSRV secured to her deck) and carry it at 15 knots. The SSN will serve as a base for the DSRV while it awaits the arrival of a submarine rescue ship (ASR). A new class of ASR with a double (catamaran) hull has been designed for use with the DSRV. See the *Halibut* (SSN-587).

A cost overrun of nearly 1,500 per cent has prevented the procurement of any additional DSRV and ensured that the existing pair would not be sufficient to equip more than one of the two ASRs built to carry them.

♦ **DSV 1 TRIESTE II**

D: 220 tons, submerged **S:** 2 kts **Dim:** 22.86 × 4.58
Man: 3 men **M:** Electric propulsion
Range: 5 hours at 2 kts

REMARKS: The U.S. Navy bought Professor Piccard's *Trieste,* modified it, and renamed it *Trieste II.* Can dive as deep as 6,100 m.

♦ **DSV 3 TURTLE, DSV 4 SEA CLIFF**

DSV4 Sea Cliff and DSV3 Turtle 1970

D: 32 dwt **S:** 5 kts **Dim:** 14.95 × 2.43
M: 1 electric motor

REMARK: *Alvin* (DSV-2) — D: 13 dwt, S: 4 kts, Dim: 6.70 × 7.44 — sank in 1,500 m of water.

BATTLESHIPS

♦ *4 Iowa class*

	Bldr	Laid down	L	In serv.
BB 61 IOWA	New York NSY	27-6-40	27-8-42	22-2-43
BB 62 NEW JERSEY	Philadelphia NSY	16-9-40	7-12-42	23-5-43
BB 63 MISSOURI	New York NSY	6-1-41	29-1-44	11-6-44
BB 64 WISCONSIN	Philadelphia NSY	25-1-41	7-12-43	16-4-44

New Jersey (BB 62) 1968

BATTLESHIPS *(continued)*

D: 47,000 tons (57,840 fl)
S: 30.5 kts **Dim:** 270.57 (262.13 pp) × 33.00 × 11.43
Man: 70 officers, 1,556 men (after reactivation)
A: 9/406-mm (III × 3) — 20/127-mm AA (II × 10) — BB-63 only: 80/40-mm AA (IV × 20)
Electron Equipt: Radars: 1/SPS 10, 1/SPS 6 — 4 chaff launchers
Armor: Belt: 406 — 3 armored decks with a total of 285 (one of 200) — Turrets and bridge: 457
M: 4 GT; 4 props; 212,000 hp
Boilers: 8 Babcock & Wilcox, 42 kg/cm^2 **Fuel:** 8,800 tons

New Jersey (BB 62) 1969

REMARKS: Data above apply to BB-62. The above battleships are being maintained in inactive reserve (2 at Philadelphia and 2 at Bremerton) as potential fire support ships. BB-62, reactivated from 1966 to December 1969, underwent a partial overhaul that permitted her to be used in bombardment operations in Vietnam, where her 406-mm guns were very effective. Of these lone survivors of a long line of dreadnoughts, which for several decades were the keystone of the fleet, only BB-62 could be returned to service. BB-63 went aground in 1950 and was not restored to her original condition and speed. A fire broke out near the 406-mm No. 1 and No. 2 turrets of BB-64 during her last inactivation overhaul and her circuitry was not repaired. The electronic equipment of BB-61 is completely out of date, and she and BB-64 were cannibalized to refurbish BB-62. The superstructure and fittings of the latter have been completely overhauled and the most modern electronic warfare equipment has been installed. All the original 40-mm anti-aircraft guns were removed in the 1950s, except from BB-63.

NUCLEAR-POWERED GUIDED MISSILE CRUISERS

♦ *1 CGN-42 class*

CGN 42 N . . .

Proposed FY 79 budget

CGN 42 — (Artist's concept)

D: 12,000 tons (fl) **S:** over 30 kts **Dim:** 177.3 × 18.9 × 9.0
A: 2 twin Mk 26 launchers for Standard SM-2 MR and Asroc — 8 Harpoon ASM (IV × 2) — 2/127-mm DP Mk 45 (I × 2) — 2/20-mm Vulcan/Phalanx AA — 6 ASW TT Mk 32 (III × 2) — LAMPS III ASW helicopters
Electron Equipt: Radars: 1/SPY 1 (Aegis), 1/SPS 49, 1/SPS 55, 1 Mk 86 fire control (1/SPQ 9), 4/Mk 99 illuminators
Sonar: 1/SQS 53A — Mk 36 RBOC
M: 2 General Electric D2G reactors; 2 props; . . . hp **Man:** . . . men

REMARKS: With the cancelation of the Strike Cruiser (CSGN) program, it was decided to proceed with a modified version of the *Virginia* (CGN-38) class to be equipped with the Aegis Mk 13 weapon system. The ships will probably also carry Tomahawk cruise missiles when these become available. Long-lead items for the construction of CGN-42 (which would have to be built either at Newport News or General Dynamics, Quincy) were appropriated under the FY 78 budget. Aegis aboard the *Virginia* class was proposed in the early 1970s, but was rejected as being too large, heavy, and expensive.

NUCLEAR-POWERED GUIDED MISSILE CRUISERS (*continued*)

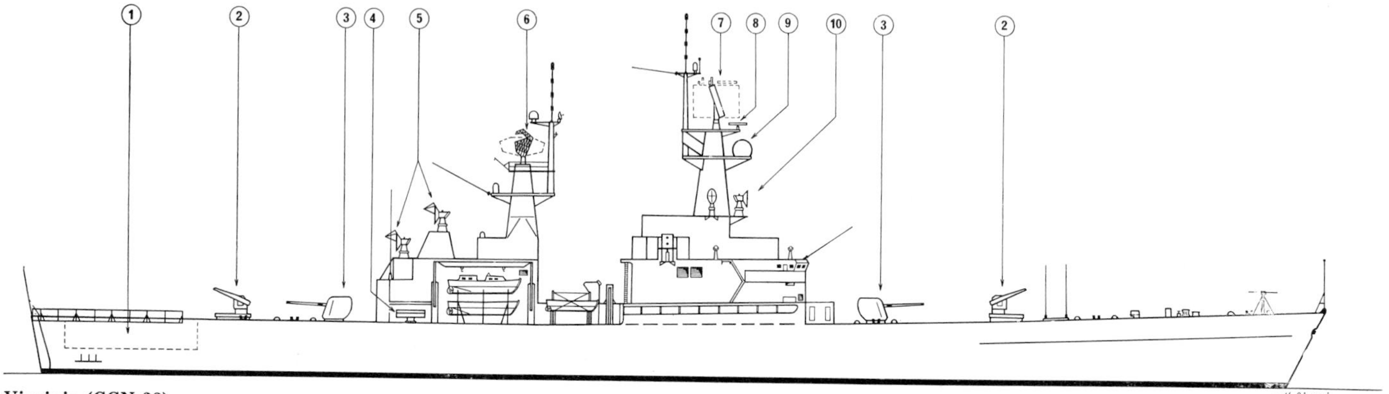

Virginia (CGN 38)

Scale 1/1000

1: Helicopter hangar — 2: Mk 26 launcher — 3: 127-mm Mk 45 mount — 4: Mk 32 TT — 5: SPG 51 D radar — 6: SPS 40 B radar — 7: SPS 48 A radar — 8: SPS 55 radar — 9: SPQ 9 radar — 10: SPG 60 radar

♦ *4 Virginia class*

	Bldr	Laid down	L	In serv.
CGN 38 VIRGINIA	Newport News SB	19-8-72	14-12-74	11-9-76
CGN 39 TEXAS	Newport News SB	18-8-73	9-8-75	10-9-77
CGN 40 MISSISSIPPI	Newport News SB	22-2-75	31-7-76	9-78
CGN 41 ARKANSAS	Newport News SB	9-76	. . .	5-80

Authorized: CGN-38 in FY 70, CGN-39 in FY 71, CGN-40 in FY 72, and CGN-41 in FY 75

D: 11,260 tons (fl) **S:** over 30 kts
Dim: 177.30 × 19.20 × 9.0 (fwd)
Man: 27 officers, 415 men
A: 2 Mk 26 twin launchers (1 fwd, 1 aft) permit the selection at will of SM-1 ER surface-to-air missiles or Asroc ASW missiles — 2/127-mm DP Mk 45 (I × 2) — 2 Mk 32 triple TT (Mk 46 torpedoes) — 2 LAMPS ASW helicopters
Electron Equipt: Radars: 1/SPS 40B, 1/SPS 48A, 1/SPS 55, 2 SPG 51D, 1 Mk 86 fire control (1/SPQ 9, 1/SPG 60)
Sonar: 1/SQS 53A — NTDS — TACAN
M: 2 General Electric D2G reactors; 2 props; . . . hp

REMARKS: The Mk 26 launchers will initially have Standard SM1 ER anti-aircraft missiles and Asroc ASW missiles, stowed vertically. The magazines can hold 80 SM1 ER and 20 Asroc. These magazines will also be able to accommodate the SM-2 when it comes into service around 1980, as well as the Harpoon ASM (although the latter may be carried in topside canister launchers because magazine capacity is restricted). It is also planned to add 2/20-mm Vulcan/Phalanx Gatling AA guns on the forward superstructure. The helicopter hangar is beneath the fantail, aircraft being raised to the main deck by an elevator. The ships will eventually carry the Mk 36 RBOC chaff/flare rocket system (four launchers). The missile fire-control system is Mk 74; ASW fire control is Mk 116. The SQS-53 sonar is a greatly improved version of the SQS-26. CGN-41 had not officially been named as of October 1977; she may not be named *Arkansas* as has been widely published.

Virginia (CGN 38) 1976

NUCLEAR-POWERED GUIDED MISSILE CRUISERS *(continued)*

Texas (CGN 39) 1977

Texas (CGN 39) 1977

Virginia (CGN 38) G. Arra, 1976

NUCLEAR-POWERED GUIDED MISSILE CRUISERS *(continued)*

♦ *2 California class*

	Bldr	Laid down	L	In serv.
CGN 36 CALIFORNIA	Newport News SB	23-1-70	22-9-71	16-2-74
CGN 37 SOUTH CAROLINA	Newport News SB	1-12-70	1-7-72	25-1-75

Authorized: CGN-36 in FY 67, CGN-37 in FY 68

D: 9,566 tons (fl) **S:** over 30 kts

Dim: 181.66 × 18.60 × 9.60 (fwd)

Man: 28 officers, 512 men

A: 2 missile launchers Mk 13 (II × 1) for SM-1 (80 missiles) with Mk 74 digital fire-control systems — 2/127-mm DP Mk 45 automatic — 1 ASW Asroc system — 4/ASW TT Mk 32 (II × 2)

Electron Equipt: Radars: 1/SPS 10, 1/SPS 40B, 1/SPS 48A, 4/SPG 51D, 1 Mk 86 fire control (1/SPQ 9 + 1/SPG 60)
Sonar: 1/SQS 26CX — NTDS — TACAN

M: 2 General Electric D2G reactors; 2 GT; 2 props; . . . hp

Remarks: It appears from photographs that the stern tubes for the wire-guided torpedoes have not been installed. Eventually will have the SM-2 missile system. Each Mk 13 launcher magazine holds 40 missiles. The ships will eventually receive 2/20-mm Vulcan/Phalanx AA and Harpoon ASM, as well as four Mk 36 RBOC chaff/flare rocket launchers. There is no helicopter hangar. Weapons are controlled by the Mk 11 Mod 3 weapons direction system, ASW being controlled by a Mk 114 fire-control system.

California (CGN 36) 1973

NUCLEAR-POWERED GUIDED MISSILE CRUISERS *(continued)*

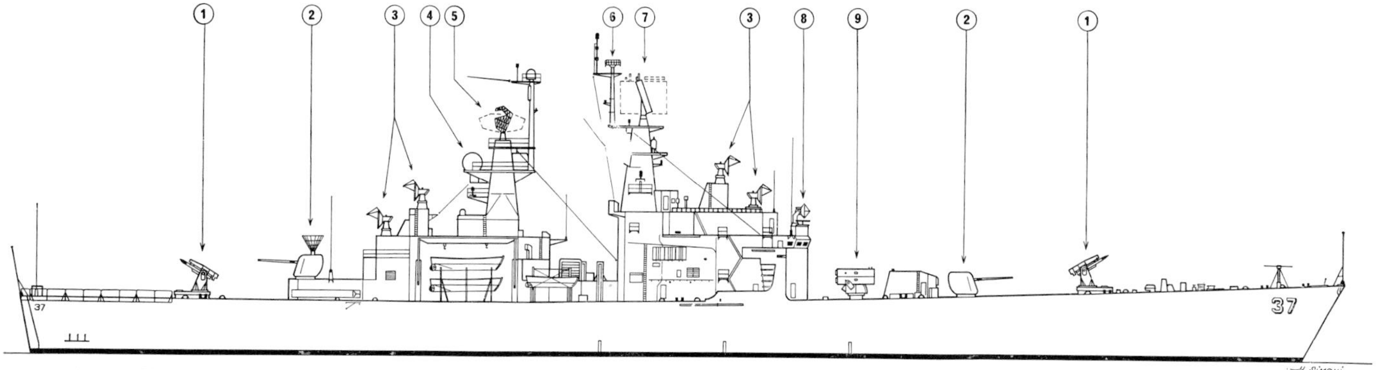

1: MK 13 launcher — 2: 127-mm MK 45 mount — 3: SPG 51 radar — 4: SPQ 9 radar — 5: SPS 40B radar — 6: SPS 10 radar — 7: SPS 48A radar — 8: SPG 60 radar — 9: Asroc

South Carolina (CGN 37) 1975

♦ *1 Truxtun class*

	Bldr	Laid down	L	In serv.
CGN 35 TRUXTUN	New York SB	6-63	19-12-64	27-5-67
Authorized: FY 62				

Truxtun (CGN 35) 1970

D: 8,200 tons (9,127 fl) **S:** Over 30 kts
Dim: 171.91 × 17.67 × 9.45 (fwd)
A: 1 Aster system (Mk 10 twin launcher for Standard SM-1 ER (40) and Asroc (20)) — 1/127-mm DP 54-cal. (fwd) Mk 42 — 2/76-mm AA Mk 34 (I × 2) — 4 ASW TT Mk 32 (II × 2)

NUCLEAR-POWERED GUIDED MISSILE CRUISERS (*continued*)

Electron Equipt: Radars: 1/SPS 10, 1/SPS 40, 1/SPS 48, 2/SPG 55
Sonar: 1/SQS 26 — NTDS — TACAN — Mk 28 chaff launchers

M: 2 General Electric D2G reactors; 2 GT; 2 props; . . . hp
Electric: 10,000 kw **Man:** 36 officers, 465 men

REMARKS: Will receive 2/20-mm Vulcan/Phalanx AA in place of the 76-mm AA. Two Mk 25 torpedo tubes at stern de-activated. Eventually will carry the SM-2 ER missile, and probably the Harpoon system, using canister launchers (III × 2). Has flag accommodations for 6 officers, 12 enlisted, in addition to crew. Mk 16 Mod 6 missile control system. 1 Mk 68 fire-control system for the 127-mm gun, two Mk 51 (no radar) directors for the 76-mm. Mk 114 ASW fire-control system.

Truxtun (CGN 35) 1975

♦ *1 Bainbridge class*

	Bldr	Laid down	L	In serv.
CGN 25 BAINBRIDGE	Bethlehem Steel (Quincy)	5-59	15-4-61	6-10-62

Authorized: FY 59

D: 7,600 tons (8,580 fl) **S:** 34 kts
Dim: 172.21 (167.65 wl) × 17.57 × 9.45
A: 2 Mk 10 Standard SM-1 ER missile launchers (II × 2, 1 fwd, 1 aft, 80 missiles) — 2/20-mm AA Mk 67 (I × 2) — 1 Asroc ASW system — 6 ASW TT Mk 32 (III × 2)
Electron Equipt: Radars: 1/SPS 10, 1/SPS-48A, 1/SPS 37, 4/SPG 55
Sonar: 1/SQS 23 — NTDS — TACAN
M: 2 General Electric D2G reactors; 2 GT; 2 props, over 60,000 hp
Electric: 10,000 kw **Man:** 34 officers, 436 men

REMARKS: In refit/modernization at Puget Sound NSY from 6-74 to 9-76 to improve AAW; refit completed at San Diego 4-77. Obsolete 76-mm AA removed, temporarily replaced with 2/20-mm AA (to be in turn replaced by 2/20-mm Vulcan/Phalanx when available). Large deckhouse added aft to house NTDS. SPS 37 radar will be replaced by SPS 49 later. Still to be fitted with Harpoon and Mk 36 RBOC chaff/flare system. Helicopter platform but no hangar. Will eventually carry Standard SM-2 ER SAM. Mk 111 ASW fire-control system, Mk 76 missile fire-control system.

Bainbridge (CGN 25) 1977

Bainbridge (CGN 25) 1977

NUCLEAR-POWERED GUIDED MISSILE CRUISERS (*continued*)

♦ *1 Long Beach class (SCB 169 type)*

	Bldr	Laid down	L	In serv.
CGN 9 LONG BEACH	Bethlehem Steel (Quincy)	2-12-57	14-7-59	9-9-61

Authorized: FY 57

Long Beach (CGN 9) 1968

D: 14,200 tons (17,100 fl) **S:** 30.5 kts (trials: 33)
Dim: 219.75 × 22.35 × 9.45 (fwd) **Man:** 79 officers, 1,081 men
A: 1 Mk 12 Talos twin launcher (II × 1, aft) — 2 Mk 10 Standard SM-1 ER twin launchers (II × 2, fwd) — 2/127-mm DP 38-cal. (I × 2) — 1 Asroc ASW system — 6 ASW TT Mk 32 (III × 2)
Electron Equipt: Radars: 1/SPS 10, 1/SPS 12, 1/SPS 32, 1/SPS 33, 4/SPG 55, 2/SPG 49, 4/SPG 55
Sonar: 1/SQS 23 — NTDS — TACAN
M: 2 Westinghouse C1W reactors; 8 Foster-Wheeler heat exchangers; 2 General Electric GT; 2 props; 80,000 hp
Electric: 15,000 kw

REMARKS: CGN-9 was the first U.S. surface ship to have nuclear propulsion. She was planned at first as a 7,800-ton frigate, but revised plans increased her armament and called for the installation of extremely sophisticated radar and sonar equipment. Having been fitted with a modular type CIC and with NTDS, she has the qualifications for a command ship of a large fleet. The plan to mount eight Polaris missiles was canceled. She has a bow freeboard of 9.20 m. The Talos missile-launching system weighs 350 tons and the CGN-9 carries 46 Talos and 120 Terrier missiles. Her armament was augmented with 2 127-mm DP guns in single Mk 30 mounts, one on each side, amidships, with 2 Mk 56 gun FCS.

Under FY 77 Congress authorized long-lead funds to modernize CGN-9 to Aegis configuration. Despite plans to keep her in service until at least 2002, this major reconstruction was canceled in 1977. She will now be given an interim modernization from 1979 to 1981, during which the Talos system and the SPS 32/33 and SPS 12 radars will be removed. She will receive SPS 48C and SPS 49 radars, 2 Vulcan/Phalanx Gatling AA guns, and Harpoon ASM in canister launchers (IV × 2 or 4); the space vacated by Talos may be rebuilt as a helicopter hangar. Her appearance should thus be greatly altered.

Long Beach (CGN 9) 1976

Long Beach (CGN 9) 1976

GUIDED MISSILE CRUISERS

♦ *9 Belknap class (SCB 212 type)*

	Bldr	Laid down	L	In serv.
CG 26 BELKNAP	Bath Iron Works	2-62	20-7-63	7-11-64
CG 27 JOSEPHUS DANIELS	Bath Iron Works	4-62	2-12-63	8-5-65
CG 28 WAINWRIGHT	Bath Iron Works	7-62	25-4-64	8-1-66
CG 29 JOUETT	Puget Sound NSY	9-62	30-6-64	3-12-66
CG 30 HORNE	San Francisco NSY	9-62	30-10-64	15-4-67
CG 31 STERRETT	Puget Sound NSY	9-62	30-6-64	8-4-67
CG 32 WILLIAM H. STANDLEY	Bath Iron Works	7-63	19-12-64	9-7-66
CG 33 FOX	Todd SY (San Pedro)	1-63	21-11-64	28-5-66
CG 34 BIDDLE	Bath Iron Works	12-63	2-7-65	21-1-67

Authorized: Three in FY 61 and six in FY 62

William H. Standley (CG 32) Martinelli, 1976

D: 6,570 tons (8,500 fl) **S:** 34 kts
Dim: 166.72 × 16.76 × 8.80 (fwd)
A: 1 Aster Mk 10 Mod 7 system (Standard SM-1 ER/Asroc) (II × 1 aft, 60 missiles, including 20 Asroc) — 1/127-mm DP Mk 42 aft — 2/76-mm AA (II × 1) — 6 ASW TT Mk 32 (III × 2) — 1 piloted ASW helicopter (SH-2D Sea Sprite)
Electron Equipt: Radars: 1/SPS 10, 1/SPS 40A (except CG-27 and CG-28, which have 1/SPS 37), 1/SPS 48, 2/SPG 55
Sonar: 1/SQS 26 — NTDS — TACAN
Range: 2,500/30, 8,000/14 **Man:** 31 officers, 387 men
M: 2 GT; 2 6-bladed props; 85,000 hp **Electric:** 6,900 kw
Boilers: 4 Foster-Wheeler, 84 kg/cm² pressure, superheat 520°C

Biddle (CG 34) 1976

REMARKS: First ships equipped with the Aster system. Ex-DLG, classified CG on 1-7-75. CG-26, severely damaged in collision with CV-67 in the Mediterranean in November 1975, will be out of commission for repairs at Philadelphia until 1980. She will have her 76-mm guns replaced by 2/20-mm Vulcan/Phalanx Gatling AA and will receive SPS 48C radar, Harpoon, SM-2 MR missiles, and improved electronics (including NTDS Mod 4) and communications gear. CG-31 lost her 76-mm in 1976 to make way for 8 Harpoon ASM (IV × 2). The others will all receive Vulcan/Phalanx and Harpoon. CG-28 has been used as trials ship for SM-2 MR. SPS 49 will replace SPS 37 in CG-27 and CG-28. The 127-mm gun is controlled by a Mk 68 director; the 76-mm by two Mk 51 directors (no radars). Mk 114 ASW fire-control system; Mk 11 weapon-direction system. Two Mk 25 ASW TT have been removed from all.

Josephus Daniels (CG 27) Pradignac & Leo, 1976

GUIDED MISSILE CRUISERS (*continued*)

♦ *9 Leahy class (SCB 172 type)*

	Bldr	Laid down	L	In serv.
CG 16 LEAHY	Bath Iron Works	3-12-59	1-7-61	4-8-62
CG 17 HARRY E. YARNELL	Bath Iron Works	31-5-60	9-12-61	2-2-63
CG 18 WORDEN	Bath Iron Works	19-9-60	2-6-62	3-8-63
CG 19 DALE	New York SB	6-9-60	28-7-62	23-11-63
CG 20 RICHMOND K. TURNER	New York SB	9-1-61	6-4-63	13-6-64
CG 21 GRIDLEY	Puget Sound B & DD Co.	15-7-60	31-7-61	25-5-63
CG 22 ENGLAND	Todd SY (Los Angeles)	4-10-60	6-3-62	7-12-63
CG 23 HALSEY	San Francisco NSY	26-8-60	15-1-62	20-7-63
CG 24 REEVES	Puget Sound NSY	1-7-60	12-5-62	15-5-64

Authorized: 3 in FY 58, 6 in FY 59

D: 5,670 tons (7,800 fl) **S:** 34 kts
Dim: 162.46 × 16.15 × 5.80 (7.90 fwd)
A: 2 Mk 10 twin Standard SM-1 ER missile launchers (1 fwd, 1 aft, 80 missiles) — 4/76-mm AA (II × 2) — 1 Asroc ASW system — 6 ASW TT Mk 32 (III × 2)

Leahy (CG 16) 1976

Electron Equipt: Radars: 1/SPS 10, 1/SPS 37 (CG-19: SPS 49), 1/SPS 48, 4/SPG 55
Sonar: 1/SQS 23 — NTDS — TACAN
M: 2 General Electric, de Laval (CG-20 to CG-22), or Allis Chalmers (CG-23 and CG-24) GT; 2 5-bladed props; 85,000 hp
Boilers: 4 84 kg/cm² pressure, superheat 520°C **Electric:** 5,100 kw
Range: 2,500/30, 8,000/14 **Man:** 32 officers, 381 men

Dale (CG 19) with SPS-49 radar A.D. Baker, 1976

Richmond K. Turner (CG 20) A.D. Baker, 1976

GUIDED MISSILE CRUISERS *(continued)*

REMARKS: The stacks are inside the radar-supporting towers (macks). During their overhaul, the *Leahy*-class ships received an advanced version of the Mk 76 missile fire-control system that permits firing of the SM-1 ER missile. CG-16, the first ship ready after this overhaul, returned to active service on 17-8-68. These are former DLGs, classified CG on 1-7-75. All will receive SM-2 ER missiles, commencing with CG-17. Two 20-mm Vulcan/Phalanx Gatling AA will replace the obsolete 76-mm AA, and Harpoon ASM will be carried. CG-19 received SPS 49 in place of SPS 37 in 1976; the others will be similarly reequipped and all will get Mk 36 RBOC chaff/flare rocket launchers. Four Mk 76 missile fire-control systems; Mk 114 ASW fire-control; two Mk 63 gun fire control.

♦ *2 Albany class (SCB-002-66 conversions)*

	Bldr	L	In serv. after refit
CG 10 ALBANY	Bethlehem, Quincy	30-6-45	2-11-62
CG 11 CHICAGO	Philadelphia NSY	20-8-44	2-5-64

Albany (CG 10) — satellite antenna aft 1977

D: 13,000 tons (17,800 fl) **S:** 32 kts
Dim: 205.25 (202.40 wl) × 21.27 × 7.80 (9.10 fwd)
A: 2 Mk 12 Talos twin launchers (II × 2, 92 missiles) — 2 Mk 11 Standard SM-1 twin launchers (II × 2, 80 missiles) — 2/127-mm DP Mk 24 (I × 2) — 1 Asroc ASW system — 6 ASW TT Mk 32 (III × 2) — 2 helicopters
Electron Equipt: Radars: 1/SPS 10, 1/SPS 43, 1/SPS 48, 4/SPG 49B, 4/SPG 51C
Sonar: SQS-23 — TACAN — NTDS — Mk 28 chaff launchers
Armor: Belt: 152 to 203 — Upper deck: 100 — Lower deck: 62
Man: 72 officers, 1,150 men **Fuel:** 2,500 tons **Range:** 7,000/15
M: Westinghouse or General Electric GT; 4 props; 120,000 hp
Boilers: 8 Babcock & Wilcox, 43 kg/cm^3; superheat; 465°C

Chicago (CG 11) 1975

REMARKS: Former *Baltimore*-class heavy cruisers. Reconversion took four years. Alloy superstructure; living spaces entirely air-conditioned. Old masts and stacks replaced by "macks," which allow the stack gases to vent through lateral conduits in the same structures on which the radar antennas are mounted; this method prevents corrosion of the radars by hot gases. Two single-barrel 127-mm semi-automatic, 38-caliber, gun mounts were added in 1963, one on each side; each has a Mk 56 director. The *Columbus* (CG-12) was decommissioned at Norfolk on 31

Albany (CG 10) — still with SPS-30 aft G. Arra, 1973

GUIDED MISSILE CRUISERS (*continued*)

January 1975 and was struck on 9 August 1976. CG-10 and CG-11 will undergo extensive overhauls 1978-79, costing over $22 million each, to enable them to continue their flagship duties into the 1980s. Two 20-mm Vulcan/Phalanx Gatling AA will be added (probably replacing the open 127-mm mounts), Harpoon will be carried, Mk 36 RBOC will replace the Mk 28 chaff launchers, and electronics will be extensively updated. A satellite communications antenna replaced the remaining SPS-30 height-finder in 1975-76; the ships originally had 2/SPS-30. CG-10 has operated as flagship of the Sixth Fleet; CG-11 is in the Pacific.

♦ *1 Galveston class (SCB 140A conversion)*

	Bldr	L	In serv. after refit
CG 5 OKLAHOMA CITY	Wm. Cramp SB, Philadelphia	20-2-44	7-9-60

Oklahoma City (CG 5) 1971

D: 10,670 tons (14,400 fl) **S:** 31 kts
Dim: 185.93 (189.90 wl) × 20.11 × 7.6 **Range:** 7,000/15
Man: 90 officers, 1,288 men **Fuel:** 2,000 tons
A: 1 Mk 7 Talos missile launcher (II × 1, aft, 46 missiles) — 3/152-mm (III × 1, fwd) — 2/127-mm DP (II × 1, fwd)
Electron Equipt: Radars: 1/SPS 10, 1/SPS 43, 1/SPS 30, 2/SPG 49, 2/SPW 2 — TACAN
Armor: Belt: 37 to 127 — Decks: 76 + 52 — Turret: 127/76
M: General Electric GT; 4 props; 100,000 hp
Boilers: 8 Babcock & Wilcox

REMARKS: Former *Cleveland*-class light cruiser. Sister *Little Rock* (CG-4) decommissioned and struck 22 November 1976; the differently armed *Galveston* (CG-3) was stricken 21-12-73. CG-5 is flagship of the Seventh Fleet and is home-ported in Japan. In addition to her crew, she carries 50 officers and 166 men. Despite her great age, it is planned to retain her into the 1980s and to improve her minimal defensive capabilities by adding 2/20-mm Vulcan/Phalanx Gatling AA and the Mk 36 RBOC chaff/flare rocket system. The Mk 34 main battery director was removed around 1970, leaving only a single Mk 37 director to control both the 152-mm and 127-mm mounts. An SH-3 liaison helicopter is normally carried aft; there is no hangar. There is a satellite communications antenna atop the mast amidships.

♦ *2 Providence class*

	Bldr	L	In serv. after refit
CG 6 PROVIDENCE (ex-CL-82)	Bethlehem Steel (Quincy)	28-12-44	17-9-59
CG 7 SPRINGFIELD (ex-CL-66)	Bethlehem Steel (Quincy)	9-3-44	2-7-60

Springfield (CG 7) G. Arra, 1972

D: 10,670 tons (14,400 fl) **S:** 31 kts
Dim: 185.93 (189.90 wl) × 20.11 × 7.60 **Range:** 7,000/15
A: 1 Mk 10 Terrier twin missile launcher (II × 1, aft, 120 missiles) — 3/152-mm (III × 1) — 2/127-mm DP (II × 1)
Electron Equipt: 1/SPS 10, 1/SPS 43, 1/SPS 30, 1/SPS 52, 2/SPQ 5
Armor: Belt: 35 to 127 — Decks: 76 + 52 — Turrets: 127/76
Man: 1,680, with flagship personnel **Fuel:** 2,000 tons
M: General Electric **Boilers:** 8 Babcock & Wilcox

REMARKS: CG-6 in reserve since 31 August 1973; CG-7 since 15 June 1974. Fitted as flagships. Can carry a liaison and support helicopter. Reclassified CG on 1-7-75; sister *Topeka* (CLG-8) in 12-73. Mk 34 radar director for 152-mm; Mk 37 for 127-mm. Unlikely to see further service. Terrier system not updated to handle Standard SM-1 ER missiles.

HEAVY CRUISERS

♦ *3 Des Moines class*

	Bldr	Laid down	L	In serv.
CA 134 DES MOINES	Bethlehem, Fore River	28-5-45	27-9-46	16-11-48
CA 139 SALEM	Bethlehem, Fore River	4-7-45	25-3-47	14-5-49
CA 148 NEWPORT NEWS	Newport News SB	1-10-45	6-3-47	29-1-49

D: 17,000 tons (21,470 fl) **S:** 32 kts
Dim: 218.42 × 22.96 × 7.50 **Range:** 8,000/15
Man: 105 officers, 1,745 men (wartime)

HEAVY CRUISERS (*continued*)

Newport News (CA 148) 1974

Newport News (CA 148) 1974

A: 9/203-mm (III × 3, CA-148: III × 2) — 12/127-mm DP (II × 6) — 20-22/76-mm AA (II × 10 or 11, CA-148: none)
Electron Equipt: Radars: 1/SPS 10, 1/SPS 6E, 1/SPS 8A, 1/SPS 29 — TACAN
Armor: Belt: 152/203 — Upper deck: 76 — Lower deck: 52
M: GT; 4 props; 120,000 hp **Boilers:** Babcock & Wilcox
Fuel: 2,600 tons

Remarks: All in reserve fleet. CA-148 fitted out as a flagship. Her No. 2 turret has only two barrels, the center gun having been destroyed in an explosion and not replaced; its embrasure has been plated over, and the turret can no longer rotate. Radars listed are for CA-148, which decommissioned 27 June 1975. CA-139 decommissioned 30-1-59 and CA-134 on 14-7-61; both had 1/SPS 10, 1/SPS 6, 1/SPS 9A radars and retain their 76-mm twin mounts (10 on CA-134, 11 on CA-139). Directors on CA-148 include 2 Mk 54 for 203-mm and 4 Mk 37 and 2 Mk 56 for 127-mm; the others have 4 Mk 56 and 2 Mk 63 fire control for their 76-mm.

♦ *2 Baltimore class*

	Bldr	Laid down	L	In serv.
CA 70 CANBERRA	Bethlehem, Fore River	3-9-41	19-4-43	14-10-43
CA 73 SAINT PAUL	Bethlehem, Fore River	3-2-43	16-9-44	17-2-45

D: 13,300 tons (17,750 fl) **S:** 33 kts **Dim:** 202.4 × 21.6 × 7.9
Range: 7,500/15 **Fuel:** 2,500 tons
A: 9 (CA-70: 6)/203-mm 55-cal. (III × 2 or 3) — 10 (CA-70: 8)/127-mm DP (II × 4 or 5) — 8 (CA-70: 4)/76-mm AA (II × 2 or 4)
Electron Equipt: Radar: 1/SPS 10, CA-70:1/SPS 30, 1/SPS 43; CA-73:1/SPS 8A, 1/SPS 37 — TACAN — Mk 28 Chaffroc launchers
M: 4 General Electric GT; 4 props; 120,000 hp
Boilers: 4 Babcock & Wilcox
Man: CA-70: 110 officers, 1,620 men (plus flag staff: 10 officers, 62 men)
CA-73: 106 officers, 1,671 men (plus flag staff: 37 officers, 160 men)

Canberra (CA 70) — prior to removal of Terrier system 1968

HEAVY CRUISERS *(continued)*

Saint Paul (CA 73) 1966

Saint Paul (CA 73) 1966

Remarks: CA-73, former flagship of the Seventh Fleet, decommissioned to reserve on 30-4-1971. CA-70, equipped as a guided missile cruiser, served from 1956 to 1969 (as CAG-2), decommissioned to reserve on 16-2-70 after a refit. Two twin Terrier launchers and their directors were removed from CA-70, the former magazines being used as storerooms, offices, and for accommodations. Both have a helicopter platform aft (raised on CA-70). Fire control for the 203-mm guns is by 2 Mk 34 directors (CA-70: 1). CA-70 has 1 Mk 37 and 4 Mk 56 fire-control systems for the 127-mm and 76-mm; CA-73 has 2 Mk 37 and 4 Mk 56.

COMMAND SHIPS

♦ *1 Raleigh class (ex-LPD, modified 1972)*

	Bldr	Laid down	L	In serv.
AGF 3 LA SALLE	New York NSY	2-4-62	3-8-63	22-2-64

La Salle (AGF 3) 1972

D: 8,040 tons (13,900 fl) **Dim:** 158.40 (155.4 pp) × 25.6 × 6.4
S: 21 kts **Man:** 18 officers, 369 men (plus 12/47 staff)
A: 8/76-mm Mk 33 AA (II × 4) — 2 SH-3 helicopters
Electron Equipt: Radars: 1/SPS 10, 1/SPS 40 — TACAN
M: 2 de Laval GT; 2 props; 24,000 hp **Boilers:** 2 Foster-Wheeler

Remarks: Former LPD-3, employed since 1972 as the flagship for Commander, Mid-East Force, replacing *Valcour* (AGF-1). Painted white. Helicopter hangar and ceremonial shelter built on flight deck. Has 1 Mk 56 and 2 Mk 63 fire control for guns. Will eventually receive 2 Vulcan/Phalanx Gatling guns and Mk 36 RBOC.

♦ *1 Wright class (ex-light carrier, modified 1963)*

	Bldr	Laid down	L	In serv.
CC 2 WRIGHT	New York SB	21-8-44	1-9-45	9-2-47

COMMAND SHIPS (*continued*)

Wright (CC 2) 1968

D: 14,500 tons (19,750 fl) **Dim:** 208.35 × 23.41 × 8.50
S: 33 kts **Man:** 746 total (plus 522 staff)
A: 8/40-mm AA (II × 4) — 5 helicopters
Electron Equipt: Radars: 1/SPS 10, 1/SPS 6
Fuel: 2,400 tons **Boilers:** 4 Babcock & Wilcox
M: General Electric GT; 4 props; 120,000 hp

REMARKS: Decommissioned 27-5-70. Former light aircraft carrier (CVL-49, ex AVT-8) modified as a communications relay ship. Designed for theater commands requiring excellent radio communications. Was planned as a ship for the president and his staff in case of nuclear threats. In 1968 the flight deck was lengthened at the after end and a tall pylon mast was added amidships to support a circular tropospheric-scatter communications antenna. Extremely powerful and comprehensive communications installation. The 40-mm AA are controlled by 4 Mk 51 directors. Small hangar retained aft beneath flight deck. Scheduled to be stricken 1-12-77.

Northampton (CC 1)

♦ *1 Northampton class (begun as a Baltimore-class cruiser, CA-125)*

	Bldr	Laid down	L	In serv.
CC 1 NORTHAMPTON	Bethlehem, Quincy	31-8-44	27-1-51	7-3-53

D: 14,700 tons (17,700 fl) **Dim:** 205.25 × 21.27 × 8.84
S: 32 kts **Man:** 68 officers, 1,123 men (plus 191/197 staff)
Electron Equipt: Radars: 1/SPS 10, 1/SPS 37, 1/SPS 8A — TACAN
Armor: Belt: 152
M: General Electric GT; 4 props; 120,000 hp
Boilers: 4
Range: 8,000/15

REMARKS: In reserve fleet at Norfolk since 8-4-1970. Construction suspended after the war, begun again 1-7-48. Originally used as a tactical command ship, later as flagship of Second Fleet. Huge dish atop bridge is for a tropospheric-scatter communications system. Originally had 4/127-mm (I × 4), 8/76-mm AA (II × 4), reduced to one 127-mm aft at time of decommissioning; gun later removed. Hangar beneath fantail can hold 3 UH-34 Sea Sprite helicopters. Hull is one deck higher than normal in *Baltimore* class. Scheduled to be stricken 1-12-77.

GUIDED MISSILE DESTROYERS

♦ *1 DDG-47 class*

	Bldr	Laid down	L	In serv.
DDG 47 N . . .	Gen. Dynamics, Quincy	5-78	. . .	9-82

Authorized: FY 78

D: 9,055 tons (fl) **Dim:** 172.5 × 17.6 × 9.1
S: over 30 kts **Man:** 29 officers, 289 men
A: 2 Mk 26 Mod 1 twin launchers for Standard SM-2 MR (68 missiles) and Asroc (20 missiles) — 8 Harpoon ASM (IV × 2) — 2/127-mm Mk 45 (I × 2) — 2/20-mm Vulcan/Phalanx AA — 6 ASW TT Mk 32 (III × 2) — 2 LAMPS III ASW helicopters
Electron Equipt: Radars: Aegis system (SPY 1 plus 4/Mk 99 illuminators), 1/SPS 49, 1/SPS 55, 1/SPQ 9 (Mk 86 fire control)
Sonars: 1/SQS 53, 1/SQR 19 TACTASS (towed passive array), URN 26 TACAN — SLQ 32 ECM/ESM — Mk 36 RBOC
M: 4 General Electric LM 2500 TG; 2 props; 80,000 hp
Range: 6,000/20
Electric: 6,000 kw

REMARKS: The design is based on the hull and propulsion plant of the *Spruance*-class destroyer. At least ten are planned, with three each year programmed for FY 80–FY 82. Will have the same quieting features as the *Spruance* but will displace over 1,000 tons more. DDG-47 to cost $930 million. The 127-mm guns have no AA role because the MK 86 fire-control system has no SPG-61 AA fire-control radar. Each Mk 26 Mod 1 magazine holds 44 missiles, with all Asroc to be carried in the forward magazine. The SPY-1 phased-array radar uses four panel antenna arrays, asymmetrically arranged on the sides of the superstructure. Aegis uses UYK-7 computers and can track a very large number of targets simultaneously. The Mk 99 radars are used to illuminate the targets for the semi-active homing SM-2 MR missiles and are slaved to the Aegis fire-control computer.

GUIDED MISSILE DESTROYERS *(continued)*

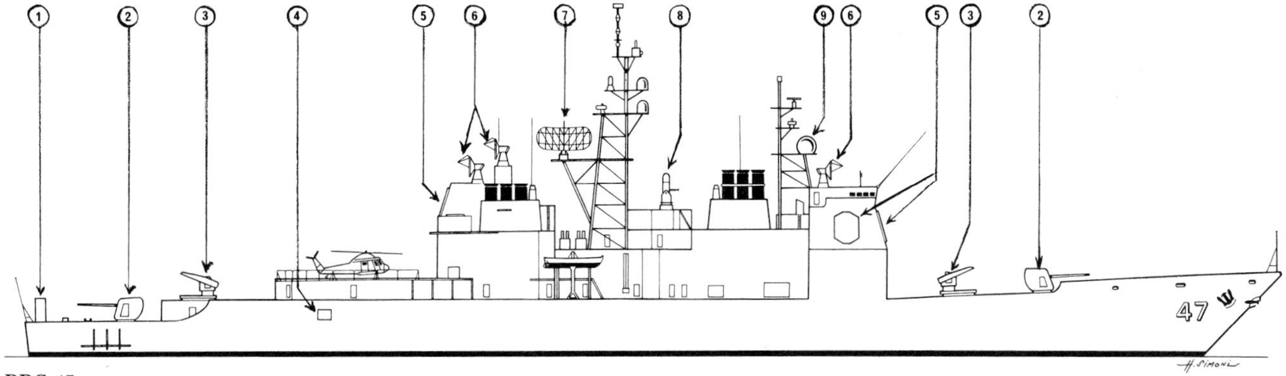

DDG 47
1: Quadruple Harpoon port & stbd. — 2: 127-mm Mk 45 gun mounts — 3: Mk 26 missile launchers — 4: ASW TT (behind door) — 5: SPY-1 radar — 6: Mk 99 illuminators — 7: SPS-49 radar — 8: Vulcan/Phalanx — 9: SPQ-9 radar (Mk 86 FCS)

DDG 47 (Artist's concept) R.C.A., 1977

♦ *23 Charles F. Adams class (SCB 155 type)*

	Bldr	Laid down	L	In serv.
DDG 2 CHARLES F. ADAMS	Bath Iron Works	16-6-58	8-9-59	10-9-60
DDG 3 JOHN KING	Bath Iron Works	25-8-58	30-1-60	4-2-61
DDG 4 LAWRENCE	New York SB	27-10-58	27-2-60	6-1-62
DDG 5 CLAUDE V. RICKETTS (ex-*Biddle*)	New York SB	18-5-59	16-4-60	5-5-62
DDG 6 BARNEY	New York SB	18-8-59	10-12-60	11-8-62
DDG 7 HENRY B. WILSON	Defoe SB	28-2-58	22-4-59	17-12-60
DDG 8 LYNDE McCORMICK	Defoe SB	4-4-58	28-7-59	3-6-61
DDG 9 TOWERS	Todd-Pacific	1-4-58	23-4-59	6-6-61
DDG 10 SAMPSON	Bath Iron Works	2-3-59	21-5-60	24-6-61
DDG 11 SELLERS	Bath Iron Works	3-8-59	27-9-60	28-10-61
DDG 12 ROBISON	Defoe SB	23-4-59	27-4-60	9-12-61
DDG 13 HOEL	Defoe SB	1-6-58	1-8-60	16-6-62
DDG 14 BUCHANAN	Todd-Pacific	23-4-59	11-5-60	7-2-62
DDG 15 BERKELEY	New York SB	1-6-60	29-7-61	15-12-62
DDG 16 JOSEPH STRAUSS	New York SB	27-12-60	9-12-61	20-4-63
DDG 17 CONYNGHAM	New York SB	1-5-61	19-5-62	13-7-63
DDG 18 SEMMES	Avondale SY	18-8-60	20-5-61	10-12-62
DDG 19 TATTNALL	Avondale SY	14-11-60	26-8-61	13-4-63

GUIDED MISSILE DESTROYERS (*continued*)

DDG 20 GOLDSBOROUGH	Puget Sound B & DD	3-1-61	12-12-61	9-11-63
DDG 21 COCHRANE	Puget Sound B & DD	31-7-61	18-7-62	21-3-64
DDG 22 BENJAMIN STODDERT	Puget Sound B & DD	11-6-62	8-1-63	12-9-64
DDG 23 RICHARD E. BYRD	Todd-Pacific	12-4-61	6-2-62	7-3-64
DDG 24 WADDELL	Todd-Pacific	6-2-61	26-2-63	28-8-64

Sampson (DDG 10) 1974

Authorized: FY 57, FY 58, FY 60, FY 61

D: 3,370 tons (4,500 fl) **S:** 31 kts **Dim:** 133.19 × 14.32 × 6.1
Man: 20/24 officers, 319/330 men **Range:** 1,600/30, 6,000/14
A: 1/Mk 11 twin missile launcher or, beginning with DDG-16, 1/Mk 13 single missile launcher (40 Standard SM-1 missiles) — 2/127-mm DP Mk 42 (I × 2) — 6/ASW Mk 32 TT (III × 2) — 1/Asroc ASW system
Electron Equipt: Radars: 1/SPS 10, 1/SPS 37 (SPS-40 in DDG-24), 1/SPS 39A or SPS 52, 2/SPG 51C
Sonars: 1/SQS 23 (hull-mounted in DDG-2 to DDG-15; bow-mounted in DDG-16 to DDG-24) — TACAN — JTDS in 4 ships
M: General Electric GT; 2 props; 70,000 hp **Fuel:** 900 tons
Boilers: 4 84 kg/cm^2 pressure; superheat; 520°C **Electric:** 2,000 kw

REMARKS: Although they have the lowest hull numbers, these are the newest of the DDGs. Sisters DDG-25, DDG-26, and DDG-27, built at the Defoe Shipbuilding Company, Bay City, Michigan, were ordered by Australia; DLG-28, DLG-29, and DLG-30 were built at the Bath Iron Works for the West German Navy.

These ships are all to be modernized at the rate of six per year, beginning with DDG-3, DDG-8, DDG-10, DDG-19, DDG-22, and DDG-23 in FY 80. All 23 are to be completed by 1984. The SPS 40 in DDG-14 to DDG-24 will be updated to SPS 40C or 40D, while SPS 37 in the earlier ships will be replaced by SPS 58. The Mk 68 gun director in all will be replaced by Mk 86 (with SPQ 9 in a radome on the mast and SPG-60 atop the bridge), permitting control of three missiles at a time, if need be. Harpoon ASM will be carried in the Mk 11 or Mk 13 missile-launcher magazines. Mk 13 weapons direction will replace Mk 4, while the CIC will be greatly modernized with a small computerized Tactical Data System. The SLQ 31/32 EW system will replace existing gear. Mk 36 RBOC will be added, and engineering and hull systems will be upgraded or overhauled. The original missile launchers and Mk 42 guns will be retained, as will the SQS-23 sonar.

Hoel (DDG 13) G. Arra, 1977

Richard E. Byrd (DDG 23) G. Arra, 1975

GUIDED MISSILE DESTROYERS (*continued*)

♦ *10 Coontz class (SCB 142/149 type)*

	Bldr	Laid down	L	In serv.
DDG 37 FARRAGUT (ex-DLG-6)	Bethlehem Steel (Quincy)	6-57	18-7-58	12-10-60
DDG 38 LUCE (ex-DLG-7)	Bethlehem Steel (Quincy)	10-57	11-12-58	20-5-61
DDG 39 MACDONOUGH (ex-DLG-8)	Bethlehem Steel (Quincy)	4-58	9-7-59	4-11-61
DDG 40 COONTZ (ex-DLG-9)	Puget Sound NSY	1-57	18-11-58	10-60
DDG 41 KING (ex-DLG-10)	Puget Sound NSY	1-57	18-11-58	15-7-60
DDG 42 MAHAN (ex-DLG-11)	San Francisco NSY	7-57	7-10-59	25-8-60
DDG 43 DAHLGREN (ex-DLG-12)	Philadelphia NSY	3-58	16-3-60	8-4-61
DDG 44 WILLIAM V. PRATT (ex-DLG-13)	Philadelphia NSY	3-58	16-3-60	4-11-61
DDG 45 DEWEY (ex-DLG-14)	Bath Iron Works	8-57	30-11-58	7-12-59
DDG 46 PREBLE (ex-DLG-15)	Bath Iron Works	12-57	23-5-59	9-5-60

Authorized: DDG-37 to DDG-42 in FY 57, DDG-43 to DDG-46 in FY 57

William V. Pratt (DDG 44) Terzibaschitsch, 1976

D: 4,700 tons (5,800 fl) **Dim:** 156.2 × 16.0 × 7.6 (max.)
S: 34 kts **Man:** 21 officers, 356 men (plus 7/12 flag staff)
A: 1 Mk 10 Mod 0 twin standard SM-1 ER missile launcher (aft) (40 missiles) — 1/127-mm DP automatic, Mk 42 (fwd) — 1 Asroc ASW system — 6/ASW TT Mk 32 (III × 2)
Electron Equipt: Radars: 1/SPS 10, 1/SPS 37, 1/SPS 48, 2/SPG 55
Sonar: SQS 23 — NTDS — TACAN
M: De Laval GT (DDG-37, DDG-38, DDG-39, DDG-45), Allis-Chalmers in the others; 2 props; 85,000 hp
Boilers: 4 84 kg/cm² pressure; superheat 520°C
Range: 1,500/30, 6,000/14 **Electric:** 4,000 kw

REMARKS: Reclassified DDG from DLG-6 to DLG-15 in 1975. All modernized 1970-77 with Standard SM-1 ER missiles, NTDS (fitted previously in DDG-40, DDG-41), SPS 48 radar, etc.; 4/76-mm AA (II × 2) removed. DDG-37, the first to be modernized, received an Asroc reload magazine forward of the bridge and a taller after mast; to save weight and cost, the others were not similarly equipped. Missile fire control is Mk 76. A Mk 68 fire-control system is carried for the 127-mm gun. DDG-40 carried 2/20-mm Vulcan Gatling guns (*not* Phalanx) in 1975. DDG-41 conducted Vulcan/Phalanx 20-mm Gatling AA gun sea trials in 1973-74, prior to modernization. All will eventually receive 2 Vulcan/Phalanx, Harpoon ASM, and Mk 36 RBOC.

Coontz (DDG 40) — Gatling gun abaft boats 1975

Farragut (DDG 37) — Asroc magazines, taller mast 1975

GUIDED MISSILE DESTROYERS (*continued*)

Macdonough (DDG 39) 1976

♦ *4 Decatur class (SCB 222-66 type)*

	Bldr	Laid down	L	In serv.	after refit
DDG 31 DECATUR (ex-DD-936)	Bethlehem Steel (Quincy)	9-54	15-12-55	12-56	29-4-67
DDG 32 JOHN PAUL JONES (ex-DD-932)	Charleston NSY	1-54	7-5-55	11-56	23-9-67
DDG 33 PARSONS (ex-DD-949)	Ingalls	6-57	19-8-58	10-59	3-11-67
DDG 34 SOMERS (ex-DD-947)	Bath Iron Works	3-57	30-5-58	4-59	2-10-68

D: 2,850 tons (4,200 fl) **Dim:** 127.40 × 13.70 × 6.1 (fl)
S: 32.5 kts **Man:** 25 officers, 339 men
A: 1 Mk 13 missile launcher (40 Standard SM-1 missiles) — 1/127-mm Mk 42 DP — 1 Asroc ASW system — 6 ASW TT Mk 32 (III × 2)
Electron Equipt: Radars: 1/SPS 10, 1/SPS 37 (DDG-34: SPS 40) 1/SPS 48, 1/SPG 51 — NTDS — TACAN
Sonar: 1/SQS 23
M: General Electric GT on DDG-31, DDG-33, DDG-34, Westinghouse on DDG-32; 2 props; 70,000 hp
Boilers: 4 Foster-Wheeler on DDG-31 and DDG-33, Babcock & Wilcox on DDG-32 and DDG-34

REMARKS: Originally *Forrest Sherman-* and *Hull*-class destroyers. Mk 68 director forward can control gun *or* Standard SM-1 missiles. DDG-33 and DDG-34 have higher freeboard forward. Alloy superstructure. All to receive Mk 36 RBOC chaff/flare rocket system.

Decatur (DDG 31) 1972

Somers (DDG 34) 1968

GUIDED MISSILE DESTROYERS (*continued*)

♦ *2 modified Mitscher class*

	Bldr	Laid down	L	In serv.
DDG 35 MITSCHER (ex-DL-2)	Bath Iron Works	1949	26-1-52	5-53
DDG 36 JOHN S. McCAIN (ex-DL-3)	Bath Iron Works	1949	29-2-52	10-53

D: 3,680 tons (5,200 fl) **Dim:** 150.56(137.16 pp) × 15.24 × 6.70
S: 33 kts **Man:** 29 officers, 349 men
A: 2/127-mm DP Mk 42 (I × 2) — 1 Mk 13 missile launcher (40 Standard SM-1 missiles) — 1 Asroc ASW system — 6 ASW TT Mk 32 (III × 2)
Electron Equipt: Radars: 1/SPS 10, 1/SPS 37, 1/SPS 48, 2/SPG 51C
Sonar: 1/SQS 23 — TACAN
M: General Electric GT; 2 props; 80,000 hp
Boilers: 4 Combustion Engineering, 86 kg/cm²

REMARKS: Overhaul begun in 1966, after which redesignated DL because of new armament. DDG-35 returned to service 29-6-68 and DDG-36 on 6-9-69. There is a reload magazine for the Asroc. Gun fire control is by a Mk 68.

Mitscher (DDG 35) J.C. Bellonne, 1973

DESTROYERS

♦ *30 Spruance class (SCN-275 type)*

Bldr: Ingalls SB, Pascagoula (Litton Ind.)

	Laid down	L	In serv.
DD 963 SPRUANCE	17-11-72	9-11-73	20-9-75
DD 964 PAUL F. FOSTER	6-2-73	23-2-74	21-2-76
DD 965 KINKAID	19-4-73	25-5-74	10-7-76
DD 966 HEWITT	23-7-73	24-8-74	25-9-76
DD 967 ELLIOT	15-10-73	19-12-74	22-1-76
DD 968 ARTHUR W. RADFORD	14-1-74	1-3-75	16-4-77
DD 969 PETERSEN	29-4-74	21-6-75	9-7-77
DD 970 CARON	1-7-74	23-6-75	1-10-77
DD 971 DAVID R. RAY	23-9-74	24-8-75	26-11-77
DD 972 OLDENDORF	27-12-74	21-10-75	4-3-78
DD 973 JOHN YOUNG	17-2-75	6-1-76	27-5-78
DD 974 COMTE DE GRASSE	4-4-75	26-3-76	19-8-78
DD 975 O'BRIEN	9-5-75	8-7-76	17-12-77
DD 976 MERRILL	16-6-75	1-9-76	15-4-78
DD 977 BRISCOE	21-7-75	28-12-76	8-7-78
DD 978 STUMP	22-8-75	21-3-77	30-9-78
DD 979 CONOLLY	29-9-75	3-6-77	11-11-78
DD 980 MOOSBRUGGER	3-11-75	23-7-77	12-78
DD 981 JOHN HANCOCK	16-1-76	10-9-77	2-79
DD 982 NICHOLSON	20-2-76	24-10-77	3-79
DD 983 JOHN RODGERS	12-8-76	1-78	5-79
DD 984 LEFTWICH	12-11-76	2-78	6-79
DD 985 CUSHING	2-2-77	3-78	7-79
DD 986 HARRY W. HILL	1-4-77	5-78	9-79
DD 987 O'BANNON	24-6-77	6-78	10-79
DD 988 THORN	29-8-77	7-78	12-79
DD 989 DEYO	10-77	9-78	1980
DD 990 INGERSOLL	11-77	10-78	1980
DD 991 FIFE	1-78	12-78	1980
DD 992 FLETCHER	2-78	1979	1980

Authorized: FY 70, FY 71, FY 72, FY 74

Spruance (DD 963) Litton, 1976

DESTROYERS (*continued*)

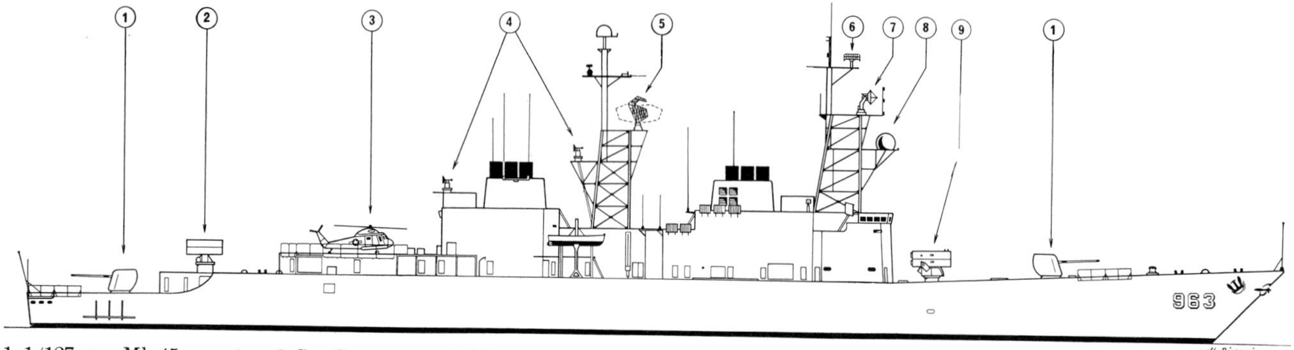

1: 1/127-mm Mk 45 mount — 2: Sea Sparrow — 3: ASW helicopter — 4: Sea Sparrow fire-control and helicopter-guidance radar — 5: SPS 40 radar — 6: SPS 55 radar — 7: SPG 60 radar — 8: SPQ 9 radar — 9: Asroc system

D: 8,010 tons (fl)
Dim: 171.70 (oa) (161.25 pp) × 16.76 × 8.84
S: Over 30 kts
Man: 24 officers, 272 men
Range: 6,000/20
A: 2/127-mm DP Mk 45 (I × 2) — 1 Mk 29 launcher for Sea Sparrow — 1 Asroc ASW system — 6 Mk 32 ASW TT (III × 2) — 2 ASW or 1 manned helicopter (LAMPS III or 1 SH-3 Sea King)
Electron Equipt: Radars: 1/SPS 40A, 1/SPS 55, 1 Mk 86 fire control — (SPQ 9, SPG 60)
Sonars: 1/SQS 53 — NTDS — TACAN
M: 4 General Electric LM 2500 gas turbines; 2 props; 80,000 hp
Electric: 6,000 kw

REMARKS: The design group of Litton Systems Incorporated was assigned this program in June of 1970 and began construction in a new shipyard in Pascagoula, Mississippi. The construction program is much behind schedule. Listed dates after 1 October 1977 are projections and may slip considerably, as in the past. After commissioning, the ships perform preliminary work-up and then enter a naval shipyard for installation of electronic warfare equipment, the Mk 29 Sea Sparrow launcher, the Mk 91 fire-control system and other gear. There are currently not enough helicopters to equip these ships and they will not begin to receive their full complement until LAMPS III deliveries begin in the early 1980s.

The hull is so constructed that standard prefabricated sections (modules) weighing 1,500 to 2,100 tons can be fitted out (small machinery and its components, piping, wiring, etc.) before they are joined. Once these elements are brought together, the ship is 92 per cent complete. The hull is transferred to a submerged pontoon for launching — there is no launching in the usual sense — and the ship is then finished alongside a pier.

Considerable attention was given to the propulsion machinery from the viewpoint of silent operation and flexibility. On each of the two shafts, two General Electric LM 2500 gas turbines are coupled to a reduction gear. Each shaft turns a controllable-pitch propeller (5.10 m in diameter, 168 rpm at 30 knots). Electric power is furnished by three gas turbines each powering one 2,000-kw alternator and mounted in separate compartments. All propulsion machinery is under the control of a single operator in a Central Control Station (CCS).

The hull conformations were carefully studied to minimize rolling and pitching. Habitability received particular attention, living spaces being divided by bulkheads and intended for no more than six men each, with a recreational area and good sanitary facilities. The crew is small for a ship the size of the *Spruance* class because all the machinery and systems have advanced automation.

The armament of these large destroyers will probably be augmented by the installation of 2 Vulcan/Phalanx systems, the Harpoon system, and the substitution of a 203-mm Mk 71 gun for the forward 127-mm gun on at least the first 6 or 8 units of the class during FY 81. All will be equipped with a four-launcher Mk 36 RBOC chaff/flare rocket system. ASW is handled by a Mk 116 fire-control system. The Mk 32 torpedo tubes are standard triple trainable mountings, fired through doors in the ships' sides. The Mk 91 Mod 0 fire-control system for Sea Sparrow uses a single radar-equipped, manned director. Four much more heavily armed ships of the same class have been ordered by Iran.

NOTE: Congress, under the FY 78 budget, appropriated more than $300 million for design and construction of an additional unit of the *Spruance* class to be equipped with an enlarged aircraft facility, ostensibly to increase the helicopter capacity, but also capable of handling a V/STOL ASW aircraft, should one be developed. The Navy did not request the ship, does not want it, and will probably attempt to have the money re-directed toward the repair and overhaul of existing ships. The notional design for this "DD-997" envisages enlarging the hangar and extending the flight deck aft to a point just forward of the after 5-inch gun.

DESTROYERS *(continued)*

Paul F. Foster (DD 964) — with SH-2F Sea Sprite 1976

Hewitt (DD 966) 1976

Elliot (DD 967) — on trials 1977

Hewitt (DD 966) — fitting out Litton, 1976

DESTROYERS (*continued*)

Spruance (DD 963) 1975

♦ *14 Forrest Sherman and Hull classes (SCB 240 type)*
8 ASW refits (1967-71) (SCB 221 modernization except DD-933: SCB 251)

	Bldr	Laid down	L	In serv.
DD 933 BARRY	Mare Island NSY	15-3-54	1-10-55	31-8-56
DD 937 DAVIS	Bethlehem Steel (Quincy)	1-2-55	28-3-56	28-2-57
DD 938 JONAS INGRAM	Bethlehem Steel (Quincy)	15-6-55	8-7-56	19-7-57
DD 940 MANLEY	Bath Iron Works	10-2-55	12-4-56	1-2-57
DD 941 DUPONT	Bath Iron Works	11-5-55	8-9-56	1-7-57
DD 943 BLANDY	Bethlehem Steel (Quincy)	29-12-55	19-12-56	8-11-57
DD 948 MORTON	Ingalls (Pascagoula)	4-3-57	23-5-58	26-5-59
DD 950 RICHARD S. EDWARDS	Puget Sound B & DD	20-12-56	21-9-57	5-2-59

Barry (DD 933) — ASW Mod, bow sonar, VDS 1971

6 that will not be modernized or ASW refitted

	Bldr	Laid down	L	In serv.
DD 931 FORREST SHERMAN	Boston NSY	27-10-53	5-2-55	9-11-55
DD 942 BIGELOW	Bath Iron Works	6-7-55	2-2-57	8-11-57
DD 944 MULLINIX	Bethlehem Steel (Quincy)	5-4-56	18-3-57	7-3-58
DD 945 HULL	Bath Iron Works	12-9-56	10-8-57	3-7-58
DD 946 EDSON	Bath Iron Works	3-12-56	1-1-58	7-11-58
DD 951 TURNER JOY	Puget Sound B & DD	30-9-57	5-5-58	3-8-59

Authorized: FY 53, FY 54, FY 55, FY 56

D: 2,780/2,850 tons (4,050 fl) **S:** 32.5 kts
Dim: 127.51 (DD-933: 129.54; DD-945 to DD-951: 127.40) × 13.70 × 6.10

DESTROYERS (*continued*)

Man: ASW refits: 17 officers, 287 men; others: 17 officers, 275 men
A: ASW refits: 2/127-mm DP Mk 42 (I × 2) — 1 Asroc ASW system — 6/ASW TT Mk 32 (III × 2); others: 3/127-mm DP (I × 3) DD-931, DD-946, DD-951: 2/76-mm AA (II × 1) — 6/324-mm ASW TT (III × 2)
Electron Equipt: On the ASW refits:
Radars: 1/SPS 10, 1/SPS 37 (SPS 40 on DD-940, DD-941, DD-943, DD-948, DD-950)
Sonar: 1/SQS 23 (bow-mounted in DD-933) and 1/SQS 35 towed
On the others:
Radars: 1/SPS 10, 1/SPS 37 (SPS 40 on DD-931, DD-944, DD-945)
Sonar: 1/SQS 23
M: General Electric GT except DD-931 and DD-933, which have Westinghouse; 2 props; 70,000 hp
Boilers: 4 Foster-Wheeler (DD-937, DD-938, DD-943, DD-944, DD-948) or Babcock & Wilcox, pressure 84 kg/cm²; superheat 520°C

Remarks: DD-946 is assigned to the Naval Reserve Force for reserve training and as training ship for the officer candidate school. From DD-937 on, the bows are somewhat higher than DD-931 and DD-933, while DD-945 and later are considered a separate class due to altered bow design. Four of the same series have been designated as DDGs (see preceding Remarks). DD-945 is used as trials ship for the 203-mm Mk 71 gun mounted forward; it will be retained. The 76-mm mounts remaining in DD-931, DD-946, and DD-951 will be removed soon. All 127-mm Mk 42 guns are being modernized to Mod 10 configuration. There are two gun fire-control systems, Mk 68 fwd and Mk 56 aft (positions reversed in DD-931, DD-937, DD-938, DD-944). ASW refits have Mk 114 ASW fire-control systems, the others Mk 105. All Hedgehog and depth charges removed in early 1970s.

Hull (DD 945) — with 203-mm Mk 71 forward 1975

Forrest Sherman (DD 931) 1972

♦ *2 Carpenter class (ex-DDE)*

	Bldr	Laid down	L	In serv.
DD 825 CARPENTER	Consolidated Steel	30-7-45	30-12-45	15-12-49
DD 827 ROBERT A. OWENS	Bath Iron Works	29-10-45	15-7-46	5-11-49

D: 2,425 tons (3,540 fl) **S:** 34 kts **Dim:** 119.0 × 12.4 × 5.8
A: 2/127-mm DP (II × 1) — 1 Asroc ASW system — 6 ASW TT Mk 32 (III × 2)
Man: 12 officers, 176 enlisted (plus 8/86 Naval Reserve)

Carpenter (DD 825) 1976

DESTROYERS *(continued)*

Electron Equipt: Radars: 1/SPS 10, 1/SPS 40
Sonar: SQS 23

M: As for *Gearing* class

REMARKS: Variants of the *Gearing* class, with higher bridge, Mk 56 gun fire-control system, tripod mainmast, and enlarged after superstructure. FRAM-I modernization completed 1962. Both assigned to Naval Reserve Force.

♦ *28 Gearing class FRAM-I*

NOTE: All of the following are assigned to the Naval Reserve Force for reserve training except DD-824, DD-845, and DD-873; the two latter were scheduled to be stricken 31-5-78 and 1-3-78, respectively, leaving DD-826 the sole unit of the class in the active fleet. All these ships are more than 30 years old, and, despite major modernizations in the early 1960s, would be of very little value in wartime. DD-714 is scheduled for striking on 1-7-78.

Bldrs: Federal SB&DD: DD-714, DD-718; Bath Iron Works: DD-743, DD-806, DD-826 to DD-845; Bethlehem Steel (San Francisco): DD-763; Bethelem Steel (Staten Island): DD-862 to DD-871; Todd Pacific Shipyards: DD-784 to DD-788; Consolidated Steel Corp.: DD-817 to DD-822, DD-873 to DD-890

	Laid down	L	In serv.
DD 714 WILLIAM R. RUSH	29-10-44	8-7-45	21-9-45
DD 718 HAMNER	23-4-45	24-11-45	11-7-46
DD 743 SOUTHERLAND	27-5-44	5-10-44	22-12-44
DD 763 WILLIAM C. LAWE	12-3-44	21-5-45	18-12-46
DD 784 MCKEAN	15-9-44	31-3-45	9-6-45
DD 785 HENDERSON	27-10-44	28-5-45	4-8-45
DD 788 HOLLISTER	27-12-44	9-10-45	26-3-46
DD 806 HIGBEE	26-6-44	12-11-44	27-1-45
DD 817 CORRY	5-4-45	28-7-45	26-2-46
DD 820 RICH	16-5-45	5-10-45	4-7-46
DD 821 JOHNSTON	6-5-45	19-10-45	10-10-46
DD 822 ROBERT H. MCCARD	20-6-45	9-11-45	26-10-46
DD 826 AGERHOLM	10-9-45	30-3-46	20-6-46
DD 829 MYLES C. FOX	14-8-44	13-1-45	20-3-45
DD 835 CHARLES P. CECIL	2-12-44	22-4-45	29-6-45
DD 842 FISKE	9-4-45	8-9-45	28-11-45
DD 845 BAUSELL	28-5-45	19-11-45	7-2-47
DD 862 VOGELGESANG	3-8-44	15-1-45	28-4-45
DD 863 STEINAKER	1-9-44	13-2-45	26-5-45
DD 864 HAROLD J. ELLISON	3-10-44	14-3-45	23-6-45
DD 866 CONE	30-11-44	10-5-45	18-8-45
DD 871 DAMATO	10-5-45	21-11-45	27-4-46
DD 873 HAWKINS	14-5-44	7-10-44	10-2-45
DD 876 ROGERS	3-6-44	20-11-44	26-3-45
DD 880 DYESS	17-8-44	26-1-45	21-5-45
DD 883 NEWMAN K. PERRY	10-10-44	17-3-45	26-7-45
DD 885 JOHN R. CRAIG	17-11-44	14-4-45	20-8-45
DD 886 ORLECK	28-11-44	12-5-45	15-9-45
DD 890 MEREDITH	27-1-45	28-6-45	31-12-45

D: 2,425 tons (3,480/3,520 fl) **Dim:** 119.1 × 12.4 × 5.8
S: 30 kts **Man:** 12 officers, 176 men (plus 7/112 Reserves)
Range: 2,400/25, 4,800/15

Higbee (DD 806) — guns fore and aft, SPS-40 1974

Bausell (DD 845) — guns forward, SPS-37 1970

A: 4/127-mm 38-cal DP (II × 2) — 1 Asroc ASW system — 6 ASW TT Mk 32 (III × 2)
Electron Equipt: Radars: 1/SPS 10, 1/SPS 29, 37, or 40
Sonar: 1/SQS 23
M: GT; 2 props; 60,000 hp **Boilers:** 4 Babcock & Wilcox **Fuel:** 650 tons

DESTROYERS (*continued*)

Henderson (DD 785) 1974

REMARKS: DD-826, DD-845, and DD-890 have 127-mm mounts fore and aft, as did others now stricken. Crew on DD-826 is 14 officers, 260 men. Some Naval Reserve Force ships have had their Asroc systems removed for installation in *Spruance*-class destroyers. Former drone helicopter decks used for underway replenishment stations.

FRIGATES

♦ *21+ Oliver Hazard Perry class (SCN 207/2001 type)*

	Bldr	Laid down	L	In serv.
FFG 7 OLIVER HAZARD PERRY	Bath Iron Works	6-12-75	9-25-76	30-11-77
FFG 8 MCINERNEY	Bath Iron Works	11-77	. . .	1980
FFG 9 WADSWORTH	Todd, San Pedro	13-7-77	. . .	1980
FFG 10 DUNCAN	Todd, Seattle	29-4-77	. . .	1980
FFG 11 N . . .	Bath Iron Works	. . .	. . .	1980
FFG 12 N . . .	Todd, San Pedro	. . .	. . .	1980
FFG 13 N . . .	Bath Iron Works	. . .	. . .	1980
FFG 14 N . . .	Todd, San Pedro	. . .	. . .	1980
FFG 15 N . . .	Bath Iron Works	. . .	. . .	1981
FFG 16 N . . .	Bath Iron Works	. . .	. . .	1981
FFG 19 N . . .	Todd, San Pedro	. . .	. . .	1981
FFG 20 N . . .	Todd, Seattle	. . .	. . .	1981
FFG 21 N . . .	Bath Iron Works	. . .	. . .	1981
FFG 22 N . . .	Todd, Seattle	. . .	. . .	1981
FFG 23 N . . .	Todd, San Pedro	. . .	. . .	1981
FFG 24 N . . .	Bath Iron Works	. . .	. . .	1981
FFG 25 N . . .	Todd, San Pedro	. . .	. . .	1982
FFG 26 N . . .	Bath Iron Works	. . .	. . .	1982
FFG 27 N . . .	. . .	. . .	. . .	1982
FFG 28 N . . .	. . .	. . .	. . .	1982
FFG 29 N . . .	. . .	. . .	. . .	1982
FFG 30 N . . .	. . .	. . .	. . .	1982
FFG 31 N . . .	. . .	. . .	. . .	1982
FFG 32 N . . .	. . .	. . .	. . .	1982
FFG 33 N . . .	. . .	. . .	. . .	1983

Authorized: 1 in FY 73, 3 in FY 75, 6 in FY 76, 8 in FY 77, 8 in FY 78

D: 3,537 tons (fl) **Dim:** 135.64 (125.9 pp) × 13.72 × 7.47
S: 30 kts **Man:** 11 officers, 152 men
A: 1 Mk 13 Mod 4 missile launcher (40 Harpoon and Standard SM-1 MR) — 1/76-mm DP Mk 75 — 6 ASW TT Mk 32 (III × 2) — 2 LAMPS III helicopters

Oliver Hazard Perry showing old hull number

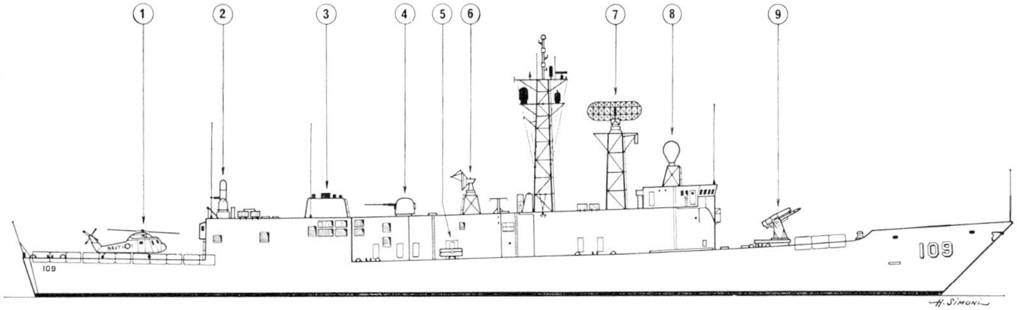

1: ASW helicopter — 2: Vulcan-Phalanx system — 3: Stack — 4: 76-mm Mk 75 — 5: ASW TT Mk 32 — 6: SPG-60 radar — 7: SPS 49 radar — 8: fire control Mk 92 — 9: Mk 13 missile launcher

FRIGATES (*continued*)

Electron Equipt: Radars: 1/SPS 55, 1/SPS 49, Mk 92 fire control system
Sonars: 1/SQS 56, 1/SQR 19 TACTAS

M: 2 General Electric LM 2500 gas turbines; 1 controllable-pitch prop, 5.50 m in diameter; 40,000 hp

Range: 5,000/18 **Electric:** 3,000 kw

REMARKS: This class will be fitted with two electrically driven drop-down screws for maneuvering in restricted waters; the 325-hp engines will provide 3 to 5 knots. FFG-34 and later will have fin stabilization, Vulcan/Phalanx 20-mm Gatling AA guns; earlier units will be backfitted. Will have URN 26 TACAN and SLQ 32 electronic warfare system. FFG-17 and FFG-18 are building at Todd, Seattle, for Australia. Speed on one turbine will be 22 knots. The Mk 92 Mod 4 fire-control system will control missile and 76-mm gun fire; it uses a STIR (modified SPG 60) antenna and a modified Hollandse Signaal Apparaten WM 28 radar forward, and can track four separate targets. The Mk 75 gun is a license-built version of the OTO Melara Compact. Mk 36 RBOC four-launcher chaff/flare rocket system to be carried.

Oliver Hazard Perry (FFG 7) 1977

Oliver Hazard Perry (FFG 7) 1977

FRIGATES (*continued*)

♦ *6 Brooke class (SCR 199B type)*

	Bldr	Laid down	L	In serv.
FFG 1 BROOKE	Lockheed SB (Seattle)	12-62	19-7-63	12-3-66
FFG 2 RAMSEY	Lockheed SB (Seattle)	2-63	15-10-63	3-6-67
FFG 3 SCHOFIELD	Lockheed SB (Seattle)	4-63	7-12-63	11-5-68
FFG 4 TALBOT	Bath Iron Works	5-64	6-1-66	2-4-67
FFG 5 RICHARD L. PAGE	Bath Iron Works	11-64	4-6-66	5-8-67
FFG 6 JULIUS A. FURER	Bath Iron Works	7-65	22-7-66	11-11-67

D: 2,643 tons (3,425 fl) **Dim:** 126.33 (121.90 pp) × 13.47 × 7.90 (sonar)
S: 27 kts **Man:** 17 officers, 231 men
A: 1/127-mm 38-cal DP (fwd) — 1 Mk 22 single launcher (16 Standard SM-1 MR missiles, aft) — 1 Asroc ASW system — 6/ASW TT Mk 32 (III × 2) — ASW helicopter
Electron Equipt: Radars: 1/SPS 10, 1/SPS 52, 1/SPG 51C
Sonar: 1/SQS 26
Range: 4,000/20 **M:** GT; 1 prop; 35,000 hp
Boilers: 2 Foster-Wheeler

Julius A. Furer (FFG 6) 1975

Richard L. Page (FFG 5) A.D. Baker, 1976

Julius A. Furer (FFG 6) — with Sea Sprite A.D. Baker, 1976

Talbot (FFG 4) — with the same weapons and equipment intended for the patrol frigates. She is now restored to standard configuration. 1975

Remarks: Differ from the *Garcia* class in having their 127-mm aft replaced by a missile launcher. Excellent sea-keeping qualities. Anti-rolling stabilizers. Hangar enlarged for the SH-2D Sea Sprite helicopter. The FFG-4, FFG-5, and FFG-6 have an Asroc system with a reloading magazine. Boilers with pressure combustion. The FFG-4 was used as an experimental ship for the weapons and systems of the patrol frigates but has now been restored to standard configuration.

FRIGATES (*continued*)

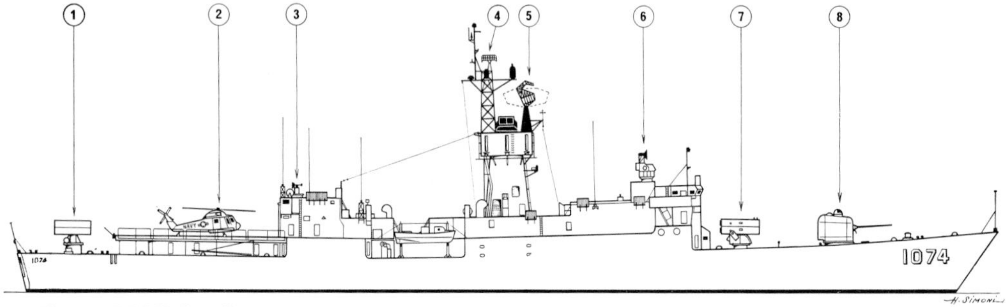

Scale 1/1000

1: Mk 25 BPDMS Sea Sparrow — 2: Sea Sprite ASW Helicopter — 3: Mk 74 Sea Sparrow director atop telescoping hangar — 4: SPS 10 Radar — 5: SPS 40 Radar — 6: Mk 68 fire control director — 7: Asroc ASW system — 8: 1/127-mm Mk 42 DP mount.

♦ *46 Knox class (SCN 200.65 and 200 types)*

	Bldr	Laid down	L	In serv.
FF 1052 KNOX	Todd-Pacific, Seattle	10-65	19-11-66	12-4-69
FF 1053 ROARK	Todd-Pacific, Seattle	2-66	24-4-67	22-11-69
FF 1054 GRAY	Todd-Pacific, Seattle	11-66	3-10-67	4-4-70
FF 1055 HEPBURN	Todd SY, San Pedro	6-66	25-3-67	3-7-69
FF 1056 CONNOLE	Avondale SY	3-67	20-7-68	30-8-69
FF 1057 RATHBURNE	Lockheed, Seattle	1-68	2-5-69	16-5-70
FF 1058 MEYERKORD	Todd SY, San Pedro	9-66	15-7-67	28-12-69
FF 1059 WILLIAM S. SIMS	Avondale SY	4-67	4-1-69	3-1-70
FF 1060 LANG	Todd SY, San Pedro	3-67	17-2-68	28-3-70
FF 1061 PATTERSON	Avondale SY	10-67	3-5-69	14-3-70
FF 1062 WHIPPLE	Todd-Pacific, Seattle	4-67	12-4-68	22-8-70
FF 1063 REASONER	Lockheed, Seattle	1-69	1-8-70	31-7-71
FF 1064 LOCKWOOD	Todd-Pacific, Seattle	11-67	5-9-68	5-12-70
FF 1065 STEIN	Lockheed, Seattle	6-70	19-12-70	8-1-72
FF 1066 MARVIN SHIELDS	Todd-Pacific, Seattle	4-68	23-10-69	10-4-71
FF 1067 FRANCIS HAMMOND	Todd SY, San Pedro	7-67	11-5-68	25-7-70
FF 1068 VREELAND	Avondale SY	3-68	14-6-69	13-6-70
FF 1069 BAGLEY	Lockheed, Seattle	9-70	29-5-71	6-5-72
FF 1070 DOWNES	Todd-Pacific, Seattle	9-68	12-69	28-8-71
FF 1071 BADGER	Todd SY, San Pedro	2-68	7-12-69	1-12-70
FF 1072 BLAKELY	Avondale SY	6-68	23-8-69	18-7-70
FF 1073 ROBERT E. PEARY (ex-*Conolly*)	Lockheed, Seattle	2-70	25-6-71	23-9-72
FF 1074 HAROLD E. HOLT	Todd SY, San Pedro	5-68	3-5-69	26-3-71
FF 1075 TRIPPE	Avondale SY	7-68	1-11-69	19-9-70
FF 1076 FANNING	Todd SY, San Pedro	12-68	24-1-70	23-7-71
FF 1077 OUELLET	Avondale SY	5-69	7-3-70	12-12-70
FF 1078 JOSEPH HEWES	Avondale SY	5-69	7-3-70	24-4-71
FF 1079 BOWEN	Avondale SY	7-69	2-5-70	22-5-71

Barbey (FF 1088) — telescoping hangar extended G. Arra, 1977

FRIGATES *(continued)*

Jesse L. Brown (FF 1089) J.C. Bellonne, 1976

Bowen (FF 1079) 1976

FF 1080	**PAUL**	Avondale SY	9-69	20-6-70	14-2-71
FF 1081	**AYLWIN**	Avondale SY	11-69	29-8-70	18-9-71
FF 1082	**ELMER MONTGOMERY**	Avondale SY	1-70	21-11-70	30-10-71
FF 1083	**COOK**	Avondale SY	3-70	23-1-71	18-3-72
FF 1084	**McCANDLESS**	Avondale SY	4-70	27-3-71	22-7-72
FF 1085	**DONALD B. BEARY**	Avondale SY	7-70	22-5-71	22-7-72
FF 1086	**BREWTON**	Avondale SY	2-70	24-7-71	8-7-72
FF 1087	**KIRK**	Avondale SY	12-70	25-9-71	9-9-72
FF 1088	**BARBEY**	Avondale SY	2-71	4-12-71	72
FF 1089	**JESSE L. BROWN**	Avondale SY	4-71	18-3-72	17-2-73
FF 1090	**AINSWORTH**	Avondale SY	6-71	15-4-72	27-3-73
FF 1091	**MILLER**	Avondale SY	8-71	3-6-72	30-6-73
FF 1092	**THOMAS C. HART**	Avondale SY	10-71	2-8-72	28-7-73
FF 1093	**CAPODANNO**	Avondale SY	12-71	25-2-72	17-11-73
FF 1094	**PHARRIS**	Avondale SY	3-72	12-72	21-1-74
FF 1095	**TRUETT**	Avondale SY	4-72	2-73	1-6-74
FF 1096	**VALDEZ**	Avondale SY	6-72	24-3-73	27-7-74
FF 1097	**MOINESTER**	Avondale SY	8-72	12-7-73	2-11-74

Authorized: 10 in FY 64, 16 in FY 65, 10 in FY 66, 10 in FY 67

NOTE: Although they are very similar to FF-1052 through FF-1077, FF-1078 through FF-1097 are considered the *Joseph Hewes* class. They were built at the Avondale yards in Westwego, Louisiana, under the most modern conditions: very advanced prefabrication, assembly on only three shipbuilding stocks, broadside launch.

D: 3,011 tons (3,877 fl) **Dim:** 133.50 × 14.25 × 7.55 (sonar)
S: over 27 kts **Man:** 22 officers, 261 men
A: 1/127-mm DP Mk 42 — 1 Mk 25 Sea Sparrow on FF-1052 to FF-1069, FF-1071 to FF-1083 — 1 Asroc ASW system — 4/324-mm Mk 32 TT fixed amidships at a 45° angle, 2 on each side — 1 SH-2D ASW helicopter (not in FF-1061, FF-1070)
Electron Equipt: Radars: 1/SPS 10, 1/SPS 40
Sonars: 1/SQS 26CX, SQS 35 on 35 ships
M: Westinghouse GT; 1 prop; 35,000 hp **Range:** 4,000/20
Boilers: 2 Babcock & Wilcox or Foster-Wheeler

Badger (FF 1071) 1975

FRIGATES *(continued)*

Harold E. Holt (FF 1074) 1975

Moinester (FF 1097) — the final Knox 1975

REMARKS: The Asroc system has an automatic reloading magazine beneath the bridge; it will be used to stow Harpoon missiles, which will be launched from two of the eight launcher cells (FF-1091 first to receive Harpoon, 1976). FF-1084 to FF-1097 are not to receive Sea Sparrow but may later get a 24-missile General Dynamics ASMD infrared-homing SAM launcher. FF-1070 has been used as a Sea Sparrow trials ship; she carries a Mk 29 NATO Sea Sparrow launcher and the two-director Mk 91 Mod 1 fire-control system. FF-1070 tested SPS 58 (on a lattice mast aft) in 1973 but since 1975 has carried SPS 40 aft and has the prototype radar for the Mk 23 Target Acquisition System on her mack. FF-1053 to FF-1055, FF-1057 to FF-1062, FF-1072, and FF-1077 do not have SQS 35 independent VDS; they may carry the SQR 15 TACTAS towed passive array. FF-1088 has acted as a trials ship and has a controllable-pitch prop; the large inflatable radome atop her hangar has been removed. All carry a Mk 68 gun fire-control system with SPG 53A radar. In those ships not already equipped with Mk 33 RBOC, Mk 36 will be fitted. FF-1078 to FF-1097 have a TEAM (SM 5) system for the continual monitoring of ship's electronic equipment. Telescoping hangar fitted in all this class, except FF-1061 and FF-1070. Antirolling fin stabilizers fitted in all. Bubble system fitted to hulls to reduce radiated noise.

♦ *10 Garcia class (SCB 199A type)*

	Bldr	Laid down	L	In serv.
FF 1040 GARCIA	Bethlehem, San Francisco	10-62	31-10-63	21-12-64
FF 1041 BRADLEY	Bethlehem, San Francisco	1-63	26-3-64	15-5-65
FF 1043 EDWARD McDONNELL	Avondale SY	4-63	15-2-64	15-2-65
FF 1044 BRUMBY	Avondale SY	8-63	6-6-64	5-8-65
FF 1045 DAVIDSON	Avondale SY	9-63	3-10-64	7-12-65
FF 1047 VOGE	Defoe SB, Michigan	11-63	8-2-65	25-11-66
FF 1048 SAMPLE	Lockheed, Seattle	7-63	28-4-64	23-3-68
FF 1049 KOELSH	Defoe SB, Michigan	2-64	8-6-65	10-6-67
FF 1050 ALBERT DAVID	Lockheed, Seattle	4-64	19-12-64	19-10-68
FF 1051 O'CALLAHAN	Defoe SB, Michigan	2-64	2-10-65	13-7-68

Authorized: 2 in FY 61, 3 in FY 62, 5 in FY 63

D: 2,624 tons (3,403 fl) **Dim:** 126.33 × 13.47 × 7.90 (sonar)
S: 27 kts **Man:** 16 officers, 231 men
A: 2/127-mm 38-cal DP (1 fwd, 1 aft) — 1 Asroc ASW system — 6 ASW TT Mk 32 (III × 2) — SH-2D ASW helicopter (except FF-1048 and FF-1050)
Electron Equipt: Radars: 1/SPS 10, 1/SPS 40
Sonar: 1 SQS 26, FF-1048 and FF-1050: SQR 15 towed array
M: General Electric GT; 1 prop; 35,000 hp **Range:** 4,000/20
Boilers: 2 Foster-Wheeler, 83.4 kg/cm² pressure; superheat 528°C

Albert David (FF 1050) — no LAMPS capability 1975

REMARKS: Anti-rolling stabilizers. FF-1047 and FF-1049 have a special ASW NTDS. The boilers are vertical and have pressure combustion. Hangar enlarged for SH-2D Sea Sprite helicopter during early 1970s, except for FF-1048 and FF-1050, which conduct trials for towed passive sonar array. Gun fire control is by a Mk 56 radar director. FF-1047 and later have an Asroc reload magazine beneath the bridge. Twin Mk 25 torpedo tubes at the stern have been removed from the ships that had them.

FRIGATES *(continued)*

Garcia (FF 1040) 1977

♦ *1 experimental escort ship (SCB 198 type)*

	Bldr	Laid down	L	In serv.
AGFF 1 GLOVER	Bath Iron Works	7-63	17-4-65	11-65

Authorized: FY 61

Glover (AGFF 1) G. Arra, 1976

D: 2,650 tons (3,500 fl) **Dim:** 126.33 × 13.47 × 7.90
S: 27 kts **Man:** 14 officers, 211 men, up to 38 technicians
A: 1/127-mm 38-cal DP — 1 Asroc ASW system — 6 ASW TT Mk 32 (III × 2)
Electron Equipt: Radars: 1/SPS 10, 1/SPS 40
Sonars: SQS 26, SQS 35 VDS
M: Westinghouse GT; 1 prop; 35,000 hp
Boilers: 2 Foster-Wheeler 83.4 kg/cm² pressure

REMARKS: Basically a *Garcia*-class unit but with a pump-jet propeller and the after 127-mm gun removed to provide accommodations for civilian technicians. Extreme stern raised during SQS 36 IUDS trials.

♦ *2 Bronstein class*

	Bldr	Laid down	L	In serv.
FF 1037 BRONSTEIN	Avondale SY	5-61	31-5-62	15-6-63
FF 1038 MCCLOY	Avondale SY	9-61	4-6-62	21-10-63

Authorized: FY 60

Bronstein (FF 1037) 1975

D: 2,360 tons (2,650 fl) **S:** 26 kts **Dim:** 113.23 × 12.34 × 7.00
A: 2/76-mm Mk 33 AA (II × 1, fwd) — Asroc ASW system — 6 ASW TT Mk 32 (III × 2)
Electron Equipt: Radars: 1/SPS 10, 1/SPS 40
Sonars: 1/SQS 26, 1/SQR 15 TASS
Man: 16 officers, 180 men
M: 1 de Laval GT; 1 prop; 20,000 hp
Boilers: 2 Foster-Wheeler, 83.4 kg/cm²

McCloy (FF 1038) 1974

REMARKS: Only remaining U.S. frigates with 76-mm guns, controlled by a Mk 56 radar director. Single 76-mm aft replaced by towed passive sonar array equipment.

GUIDED MISSILE PATROL BOATS

♦ *6 PHM (Patrol Hydrofoil Missile) class (SCB 602 type)*

	Bldr	Laid down	L	In serv.
PHM 1 PEGASUS	Boeing, Seattle	10-5-73	9-11-74	9-7-77
PHM 2 HERCULES	Boeing, Seattle	30-5-74	. . .	. . .
PHM 3 N . . .	Boeing, Seattle	. . .	. . .	. . .
PHM 4 N . . .	Boeing, Seattle	. . .	. . .	. . .
PHM 5 N . . .	Boeing, Seattle	. . .	. . .	. . .
PHM 6 N . . .	Boeing, Seattle	. . .	. . .	. . .

Authorized: 2 in FY 73, 4 in FY 75

Pegasus (PHM 1) — Note the Harpoon canisters on the stern 1975

D: 218 tons (239 fl) **S:** 48 kts (12 kts on diesels)
Dim: 40.20 (45.0 with foils retracted) × 8.60 × 7.1 (1.9, foils retracted)
Man: 4 officers, 17 men
A: 8 Harpoon ASM (IV × 2) — 1/76-mm Mk 75 DP (OTO Melara Compact)
Electron Equipt: Radar: 1/LN-66, 1 Mk 92 Mod 1 radar fire-control system
M: CODOG: 1 General Electric LM-2500 gas turbine; waterjets; 18,000 hp; 2 MTU 8V331TC80 diesels; 2 waterjets; 1,340 hp

REMARKS: PHM-1 began her protracted trials 2-25-75. PHM-2 suspended 8-75 prior to launch. PHM-2 through PHM-6 were canceled 15-4-77, then reinstated 14-8-77 at the insistence of Congress, the contract going to Boeing shortly thereafter to complete the series. No more likely to be built. One of the series PHM-2 to PHM-6 will be unarmed as yet another hydrofoil trials craft; the others will operate in the Mediterranean with the tender *Wood County* (AGP-1178), whose conversion will now also be undertaken. The Mk 92 Mod 1 fire-control system is an Americanized version of the Hollandse Signaal Apparaten WM-28 system. It was planned at one time to carry 8 reload Harpoons, for a total of 16.

Pegasus (PHM 1) 1975

PATROL BOATS

♦ *2 Asheville class (SCB 229/600 type)*

	Bldr	L	In serv.
PG 92 TACOMA	Tacoma Boatbuilding	13-4-68	14-7-69
PG 93 WELCH	Peterson Builders	25-7-68	8-9-69

Authorized: FY 66

Tacoma (PG 92) 1969

D: 225 tons (240 fl) **S:** 40 kts (16 cruising)
Dim: 50.14 (46.94 pp) × 7.28 × 2.90 **Man:** 3 officers, 22 men
A: 1/76-mm — 1/40-mm AA — 4/12.7-mm machine guns (II × 2)
M: CODOG propulsion; 1 General Electric Mk 7 LM 1500 GT, 12,500 hp (14,000 max); 2 Cummins Mk 875 V-12 diesels, 725 hp each (875 maximum); 2 props
Range: 325/37, 1,700/16 **Fuel:** 50 tons

PATROL BOATS (*continued*)

REMARKS: Designed by Gibbs & Cox of New York. Mk 63 gun fire control, with SPG 50 mounted on the 76-mm mount and the director atop the bridge. Propellers have controllable pitch. Survivors of a class of 17, employed in training Saudi Arabian personnel at Norfolk. Of the others, PG-84, PG-87 and PG-89 transferred to the Massachusetts Maritime Academy in 1977; PG-85, PG-86, and PG-90, stricken 1977, are available for sale abroad; PG-88, with gas turbines removed, was transferred to the Environmental Protection Agency in 1977; PG-94 (now named *Athena*) and PG-98 are operated as "boats," disarmed by the Naval Ships R&D Center (1975 and 1977, respectively); PG-95 and PG-97 transferred to Turkey 1973; PG-96 to South Korea in 1971, and PG-99 and PG-101 were laid up 1-4-77 for eventual transfer to Greece. PG-92 and PG-93 will probably be sold abroad in the near future. None of these ships served more than 10 years.

♦ *4 PTF-23 class* — Bldr: Sewart, Berwick, Louisiana, 1967-68

PTF 23 **PTF 24** **PTF 25** **PTF 26**

PTF 23 class 1969

D: 72 tons (109 fl) **S:** 40 kts **Dim:** 28.86 × 7.06 × 2.10
A: 1/40-mm AA — 2/20-mm AA (I × 2) — 1/81-mm mortar/12.7-mm machine gun combined mounting
M: 2 Napier Deltic T18-37K diesels; 2 props; 6,200 hp (2 units to receive gas turbines in lieu of diesels)
Man: 1 officer, 18 men **Range:** 1,000/35

REMARKS: For Naval Reserve training. Aluminum alloy construction.

NOTE: All wooden-hulled PTFs of Norwegian design have been stricken.

♦ *1 High Point-class hydrofoil*

	Bldr	Laid down	L	In serv.
PCH 1 HIGH POINT	Boeing, Seattle	27-2-61	17-8-62	3-9-63

Authorized: FY 62

High Point (PCH 1)

D: 110 tons (fl) **Dim:** 35.0 × 9.0 × 5.2 (1.8 foils retracted)
S: 48 kts **A:** None **Man:** 1 officer, 12 men
M: CODOG: 2 Rolls-Royce Proteus gas turbines; 4 props (paired); 6,200 hp; 2 diesels; 1 prop; 600 hp

REMARKS: Never was anything but an experimental craft but continues to carry an operational hull number. Has served in Harpoon trials and was briefly loaned to the Coast Guard in 1975. New foils 1973.

PATROL CRAFT

♦ *3 PB Mk III class* — Bldr: Peterson Bldrs., 1975

PB Mk III class G. Arra, 1975

PATROL CRAFT (*continued*)

D: 28 tons (36.7 fl) **S:** 30 kts **Dim:** 19.78 × 5.50 × 1.80
A: 5/12.7-mm machine guns (II × 1, I × 3) **Man:** 1 officer, 4 men
M: 3 G.M. 8V71 TI diesels; 3 props; 1,950 hp **Range:** 500/30

REMARKS: For evaluation and Naval Reserve training. Winner in competition with Mk I; more may be built for U.S. Navy. Many under construction for Iran.

♦ *2 PB Mk I class* — Bldr: Sewart, Berwick, Louisiana, 1972

D: 30 tons (fl) **S:** 25 kts **Dim:** 19.78 × 5.25 × 1.37
A: 2/20-mm AA (II × 1) — 4/12.7-mm machine guns — 1/81-mm mortar/12.7-mm machine gun combination
M: 2 G.M. 12V71 TI diesels; 2 props; 1,200 hp
Man: 2 officers, 6 men **Range:** 30/26

REMARKS: Used for Naval Reserve training.

♦ *5 PCF Mk I class* — Bldr: Swiftships, Louisiana, 1965–68

PCF Mk I class

D: 22.5 tons (fl) **S:** 22 kts **Dim:** 15.30 × 4.55 × 1.10
A: 1/81-mm mortar/12.7-mm machine gun combination — 2/12.7-mm machine guns
Man: 6 men **Range:** 400/22
M: 2 G.M. 12V71 TI diesels; 2 props; 850 hp

REMARKS: Survivors of some 125 built. Aluminum alloy construction. Used for Naval Reserve training.

RIVERINE WARFARE CRAFT

♦ *20 PBR (Patrol Boat, Riverine) Mk II* 1967–1973

D: 8 tons (fl) **S:** 24 kts **Dim:** 9.73 × 3.53 × 0.81
A: 3/12.7-mm machine guns (II × 1, I × 1) — 1/60-mm mortar
M: 2 G.M. 6V53N diesels; 2 Jacuzzi water jets; 430 hp
Man: 4 men **Range:** 150/23

REMARKS: Fiberglass hull, plastic armor. Used for Naval Reserve training.

♦ *2 ASPB (Assault Support Patrol Boat) Mk 1* 1967–68

D: 29.7 tons (35.1 fl) **S:** 14 kts **Dim:** 15.30 × 5.32 × 1.10
A: 2/20-mm AA (I × 2) — 2/7.62-mm machine guns **Man:** 5 men
M: 2 G.M. 12V71N diesels; 2 props; 1,050 hp **Range:** 200/12

REMARKS: Lightly armored, 20-mm in turrets. Used for Naval Reserve training.

♦ *1 CCB (Command and Control Boat) Mk 1* 1965–66

D: 60 tons (74.5 fl) **S:** 8.5 kts **Dim:** 18.29 × 5.33 × 1.00
A: 1/20-mm AA — 1/12.7-mm machine gun — 3/7.62-mm machine guns (I × 3)
M: 2 Gray Marine 64HN9 diesels; 2 props; 330 hp **Man:** 11 men

REMARKS: Greatly-modified LCM(6) landing craft. Naval Reserve training.

♦ *14 Mini ATC (Armored Troop Carrier)*

D: 14.7 tons (fl) **S:** 28 kts **Dim:** 10.97 × 3.89 × . . .
A: 12.7-mm machine guns **Man:** 2 men plus 15 troops
M: 2 G.M. 8V53N diesels; 2 Jacuzzi water jets; 566 hp

REMARKS: One has gas turbine propulsion. Planing hull. Aluminum construction; ceramic armor. Naval Reserve training.

MINE WARFARE SHIPS

NOTE: Except for MSO-443, MSO-448, and MSO-490, all minesweepers are assigned to the Naval Reserve Force.

♦ *19 MCM-class fleet minesweepers (programmed)*

Authorized: 1 in FY 79, 6 in FY 80, 6 in FY 81, 6 in FY 82

D: 1,640 tons (2,200 fl) **S:** 18 kts **Dim:** 80.00 × 12.10 × 3.40
A: 1/20-mm AA **Man:** . . .
Electron Equipt: Radar: SPS 55 — Sonar: SQQ 14 Deep Mod
M: 2 diesels; 2 controllable-pitch props; 6,800 hp

MCM class (Artist's concept) 1977

MINE WARFARE SHIPS (*continued*)

REMARKS: Although this class was programmed for FY 79–82, it may be deferred or deleted because the Department of Defense places a low priority on mine warfare defense. The MCMs would use a remote-controlled minehunting device similar to the French PAP 104 but have much greater range and depth capability. They would be steel-hulled, and have bow and stern side-thrusters for precision maneuvering at low speed. An SSN-2 precise navigation system would be installed. These ships, if built, would be operated mainly by the Naval Reserve Force.

♦ *24 Aggressive/Acme*-class fleet minesweepers, 1952–56*

MSO 427 CONSTANT
MSO 428 DASH
MSO 429 DETECTOR
MSO 431 DOMINANT
MSO 433 ENGAGE
MSO 437 ENHANCE
MSO 438 ESTEEM
MSO 439 EXCEL
MSO 440 EXPLOIT
MSO 441 EXULTANT
MSO 442 FEARLESS
MSO 443 FIDELITY
MSO 446 FORTIFY
MSO 448 ILLUSIVE
MSO 449 IMPERVIOUS
MSO 455 IMPLICIT
MSO 456 INFLICT
MSO 464 PLUCK
MSO 488 CONQUEST
MSO 489 GALLANT
MSO 490 LEADER
MSO 492 PLEDGE
MSO 509 ADROIT*
MSO 511 AFFRAY*

Authorized: FY 51 and FY 52

Direct (MSO 430) G. Arra, 1976

D: 665 tons (777 fl) **S:** 14 kts **Dim:** 52.4 × 4.0 × 4.2
A: 2/12.7-mm machine guns (I × 2) **Range:** 2,400/10
Electron Equipt: Sonar: SQQ 14 (except MSO-509, MSO-511 UQS 1)
Man: 8 officers, 70 men (Naval Reserve Force ships: 3 officers, 36 men plus 3/44 Reserves)
M: 4 Packard diesels; 2 controllable-pitch props; 2,280 hp (MSO-428 to MSO-431: 2 G.M. diesels; 2 controllable-pitch props; 1,520 hp)

REMARKS: Wooden construction; non-magnetic machinery. Eight units in reserve fleet stricken 1-9-77: MSO-421, MSO-461, MSO-462, MSO-471, MSO-474, MSO-494 to MSO-496. The remainder are operated for the Naval Reserve Force, except MSO-443, MSO-448, and MSO-490, which are employed in experimental mine-warfare-related duties. Ninety-three of the MSO-421 to MSO-508 classes were built; many transferred abroad. MSO-509 and MSO-511 are slightly different: **D:** 720 tons (750 fl) and **Dim:** 52.7 × 10.7 × 4.3. The hoist machinery for the SQQ 14 minehunting sonar occupies the position of the former 40-mm gun (a 20-mm AA mounted to starboard on the forecastle seems to have been removed from all the others). MSO-433, MSO-437, MSO-438, MSO-442, MSO-446, MSO-449, MSO-456, MSO-488, and MSO-490 were given very thorough rehabilitations; they have Waukesha diesels, improved accommodations, and new communications gear. All surviving units have received SQQ 14 and have new, semi-enclosed bridges and enlarged superstructures abaft the bridge.

NOTE: The larger, former MSO-520 and MSO-521 (*Alacrity* and *Assurance*) recently operating as AG-520 and AG-521, were stricken on 30-9-77.

Leader (MSO 490) — one of three in the active fleet 1972

MINESWEEPING BOATS

♦ *1 MSB-29 class* — Bldr: Trumpy, Annapolis, 1954

D: 80 tons (fl) **S:** 12 kts **Dim:** 25.0 × 5.8 × 1.7

REMARKS: Enlarged MSB-5; only one built. At Charleston.

♦ *7 MSB-5 class, 1952–56*

MSB 15, MSB 16, MSB 25, MSB 28, MSB 41, MSB 51, MSB 52

D: 30 tons (39 fl) **S:** 12 kts **Dim:** 17.45 × 4.83 × 1.2
A: 1/12.7-mm machine gun **Man:** 6 men
M: 2 Packard diesels; 2 props; 600 hp

REMARKS: Survivors of a class of 47; wooden hulls; non-magnetic machinery (including 2 sweep generators). All based at Charleston.

MINESWEEPING BOATS (*continued*)

MSB 15 (in Vietnam) 1970

AMPHIBIOUS WARFARE SHIPS

♦ *2 Blue Ridge-class amphibious command ships (SCN 400-65-type)*

	Bldr	Laid down	L	In serv.
LCC 19 BLUE RIDGE	Philadelphia NSY	27-2-67	4-1-69	14-11-70
LCC 20 MOUNT WHITNEY	Newport News SB & DD	8-1-69	8-1-70	16-1-71

Authorized: FY 65 and FY 66

Mount Whitney (LCC 20) 1976

Mount Whitney (LCC 20) A.D. Baker, 1976

D: 19,290 tons (fl) **S:** 21.5 kts
Dim: 213.60 (183.20 pp) × 25.30 × 8.20
A: 4/76-mm AA (II × 2) — 2 Mk 25 launchers for Sea Sparrow (VIII × 2)
Electron Equipt: 1/SPS 10, 1/SPS 48, 1/SPS 40 — NTDS — TACAN
Man: 40 officers, 680 men plus 200/500 flag staff
M: General Electric GT; 1 prop, 22,000 hp **Boilers:** 2 Foster-Wheeler

REMARKS: Like all recent amphibious-force ships, these have a good crusing speed (20 knots) and excellent communication, transmission, and analysis systems: ACIS (Amphibious Command Information System), NIPS (Naval Intelligence Processing System). Same machinery and basic hull form as the *Iwo Jima*-class LPH. Photographic laboratories and document-publication facilities. LCP and LCVP small craft are carried in davits. Liaison and transport helicopters (two UH-2, one CH-46A). Air-conditioned, and anti-rolling stabilizers. Two Mk 56 fire-control systems for 76-mm guns; 2 Mk 76 directors for Sea Sparrow. They will eventually receive two Vulcan/Phalanx.

♦ *5 Tarawa-class amphibious assault ships*

Bldr: Ingalls SB., Litton Ind., Pascagoula, Mississippi

	Laid down	L	In serv.
LHA 1 TARAWA	15-11-71	1-12-73	29-5-76
LHA 2 SAIPAN	21-7-72	18-7-74	15-10-77
LHA 3 BELLEAU WOOD (ex-*Philippine Sea*)	5-3-73	11-6-77	1978
LHA 4 NASSAU (ex-*Leyte Gulf*)	13-8-73	1-78	1979
LHA 5 DA NANG (ex-*Khe Sanh*)	12-11-76	1978	1980

Authorized: 1 in FY 69, 2 in FY 70, 2 in FY 71

D: 39,300 tons (fl) **S:** 24 kts
Dim: 249.94 (237.14 pp) × 32.30 × 8.40
Man: 90 officers, 812 men (plus 172/1,731 troops)
A: 2 Mk 25 Sea Sparrow launchers (VIII × 2) — 3/127-mm 54-cal DP Mk 45 (I × 3) — 6/20-mm Mk 68 AA (I × 6) — 19 CH-53 or 30 CH-46 helicopters
Electron Equipt: Radars: 1/SPS 10, 1/SPS 40, 1/SPS 52, 1/SPN 35 Mk 86 fire control (SPQ 9, SPG 60) — ITAWDS (Integrated Tactical Amphibious Warfare Data System) — TACAN
M: 2 Westinghouse GT; 2 props; 140,000 hp
Boilers: 2 Combustion Engineering **Range:** 10,000/20

AMPHIBIOUS WARFARE SHIPS (*continued*)

Tarawa (LHA 1) 1975

Tarawa (LHA 1) 1976

REMARKS: The LHA is a multi-purpose assault transport, a combination of LPH and LPD. It has the general profile of an aircraft carrier, with its superstructure to starboard, flight deck, helicopter elevators to port and aft, and an 80 × 23.4-m well deck for landing craft (up to four LCU 1610 class). Two LCM(6) and two LCP are stowed on deck. Advanced automation; can carry AV-8A Harrier VTOL/STOL aircraft as well as the usual transport helicopters; eventually will carry surface-effect landing craft of the JEFF A/B type. Very complete hospital and mortuary facilities are fitted. All troops have bunks. Completely air-conditioned. Four additional units were canceled in 1971; the remainder are far behind schedule. The 127-mm guns are aboard primarily to provide shore fire support.

Tarawa (LHA 1) 1975

AMPHIBIOUS ASSAULT HELICOPTER CARRIERS

♦ *7 Iwo Jima class (SCB P57, LPH-12: SCB 401-66)*

	Bldr	Laid down	L	In serv.
LPH 2 IWO JIMA	Puget Sound NSY	4-59	30-9-60	26-8-61
LPH 3 OKINAWA	Philadelphia NSY	4-60	19-8-61	14-4-62

AMPHIBIOUS ASSAULT HELICOPTER CARRIERS (*continued*)

LPH 7 GUADALCANAL	Philadelphia NSY	9-61	16-3-63	20-7-63
LPH 9 GUAM	Philadelphia NSY	11-62	22-8-64	16-1-65
LPH 10 TRIPOLI	Ingalls, Pascagoula	6-64	31-7-65	6-8-66
LPH 11 NEW ORLEANS	Philadelphia NSY	3-66	3-2-68	16-11-68
LPH 12 INCHON	Ingalls, Pascagoula	4-68	5-4-69	20-6-70

Authorized: 1 each year in FY 59-63, FY 65, FY 66

Inchon (LPH 12) J.C. Bellonne, 1972

Iwo Jima (LPH 2) 1973

D: 17,000 tons (18,300 fl) **S:** 23 kts
Dim: 179.83 (180.18 pp) × 31.70 (25.60 wl) × 7.92
Man: 47 officers, 605 men + 143/1,581 troops
A: 4/76-mm DP (II × 2) — 2 Mk 25 Sea Sparrow launchers (VIII × 2) — 20 to 24 CH-46 helicopters — 4 CH-53 heavy helicopters — 4 HU-1 observation helicopters (LPH-3: 12 AV-8A Harrier V/STOL aircraft)
Electron Equipt: Radars: 1/SPS 10, 1/SPS 40, 1/SPN 10, 1/SPN 35 — TACAN
M: GT; 1 prop; 23,000 hp
Boilers: 4 Combustion Engineering (LPH-9: Babcock & Wilcox)

REMARKS: Specially built for the transportation and vertical landing of fully equipped Marines. One side elevator forward to port, one to starboard aft of the island, 70-m hangar. Up to seven helicopters can be operated simultaneously on the flight deck. Excellent medical facilities (300 beds). LPH-9 has an ASCAC (Air-Surface Classification and Analysis Center). LPH-12, to a slightly different design, carries two LCM(6) in davits. Two Mk 63 gun fire control being removed in expectation of adding 2/20-mm Vulcan/Phalanx AA.

AMPHIBIOUS TRANSPORTS, DOCK

♦ *12 Austin class*

	Bldr	Laid down	L	In serv.
LPD 4 AUSTIN	New York NSY	2-63	27-6-64	6-2-65
LPD 5 OGDEN	New York NSY	2-63	27-6-64	19-6-65
LPD 6 DULUTH	New York NSY	12-63	14-8-65	18-12-65
LPD 7 CLEVELAND	Ingalls, Pascagoula	11-64	7-5-65	21-4-67
LPD 8 DUBUQUE	Ingalls, Pascagoula	1-65	6-8-66	1-9-67
LPD 9 DENVER	Lockheed SB, Seattle	2-64	23-1-65	26-10-68
LPD 10 JUNEAU	Lockheed SB, Seattle	1-65	12-2-66	12-7-69
LPD 11 CORONADO	Lockheed SB, Seattle	5-65	30-7-66	23-5-70
LPD 12 SHREVEPORT	Lockheed SB, Seattle	12-65	22-10-66	14-2-70
LPD 13 NASHVILLE	Lockheed SB, Seattle	3-66	7-10-67	12-7-70
LPD 14 TRENTON	Lockheed SB, Seattle	8-66	3-8-70	6-3-71
LPD 15 PONCE	Lockheed SB, Seattle	10-66	20-5-70	10-7-71

Authorized: 3 in FY 62, 4 in FY 63, 3 in FY 64, 2 in FY 65

Ponce (LPD 15) — Enclosed forward gun mounts 1976

D: 11,050 tons (17,150 fl) **S:** 21 kts
Dim: 173.4 × 32.3 × 7.0-7.2
Man: 27 officers, 446 men + 90 staff in LPD-7 to LPD-13 + 940 troops (840 in LPD-7 to LPD-13)

AMPHIBIOUS TRANSPORTS, DOCK (*continued*)

A: 8/76-mm AA (II × 4) — 2 to 4 CH-46 helicopters
Electron Equipt: Radars: 1/SPS 10, 1/SPS 40 — TACAN
M: 2 de Laval GT; 2 props; 24,000 hp **Boilers:** 2 Babcock & Wilcox

Nashville (LPD 13) — Flagship configuration A.D. Baker, 1976

Coronado (LPD 11) — Flagship configuration 1970

REMARKS: Lengthened version of the *Raleigh* class. Combination LSD and assault transport APA; well deck 120 × 15.24; helicopter platform. Either one LCU and three LCM(6) or nine LCM(6) or four LCM(8) or 28 LVT can be carried in the well deck. Six cranes, one 8.15-ton elevator, two forklifts. Small telescoping hangar on the flight deck.

LPD-7 to LPD-13 are fitted for flagship duty and have one additional superstructure deck. All those ships will lose 4/76-mm (II × 2) in favor of 2/20-mm Vulcan/Phalanx AA; LPD-5 had two mounts removed in 1977. They will also lose their one Mk 56 and two Mk 63 gun fire control, leaving the 76-mm guns locally controlled.

♦ *2 Raleigh class*

	Bldr	Laid down	L	In serv.
LPD 1 RALEIGH	New York NSY	6-60	17-3-62	8-9-62
LPD 2 VANCOUVER	New York NSY	11-60	15-9-62	11-5-63

Vancouver (LPD 2) G. Arra, 1977

D: 8,040 tons (13,600 fl) **Dim:** 159.0 (152.4 pp) × 32.3 × 6.7
S: 21 kts **Man:** 30 officers, 460 men, plus 930 troops
A: 8/76-mm AA (II × 4) — 2 to 4 CH-46 helicopters
Electron Equipt: Radars: 1/SPS 10, 1/SPS 40
M: 2 de Laval GT; 2 props; 24,000 hp **Boilers:** 2 Babcock & Wilcox

REMARKS: Sister *La Salle* (LPD-3), modified as flagship for CoMideastFor in the Indian Ocean and reclassified AGF-3, had an additional superstructure deck like LPD-7 to LPD-13 (see above). Docking well, 51.2 × 15.2 m, is shorter than on *Austin* class. Emphasis in LPD is on personnel capacity, in LSD on dock capacity; the flight deck, which forms the top of the well deck, can handle up to 6 CN-46 helicopters; there is no hangar. LPD-1 and LPD-2 are to be rearmed the same as the *Austin* class; they now have 1 Mk 56 and 2 Mk 51 gun fire-control systems.

DOCK LANDING SHIPS

♦ *1 LSD-41 class* (proposed)

REMARKS: It was planned to request LSD-41 under the FY 79 budget, but this may be postponed or canceled because of congressional objections to the essential obsolescence of the design concept. The LSD-41 class was to be a near-repeat of the *Anchorage* class, with updated armament and electronics. A total of eight is required to replace the *Thomaston* class, some of which will have been 25 years in service by 1979.

DOCK LANDING SHIPS (*continued*)

♦ *5 Anchorage class (SCN 404-65 and 66 types)* — Bldr: General Dynamics, Quincy (except LSD-36: Ingalls, Pascagoula)

	L	In serv.
LSD 36 ANCHORAGE	5-5-68	15-3-69
LSD 37 PORTLAND	20-12-69	3-10-70
LSD 38 PENSACOLA	11-7-70	27-3-71
LSD 39 MOUNT VERNON	20-2-71	13-5-72
LSD 40 FORT FISHER	24-4-72	12-9-72

Authorized: 1 in FY 65, 3 in FY 66, 1 in FY 67

Portland (LSD 37) G. Arra, 1973

Portland (LSD 37) 1970

D: 13,650 tons (fl) **Dim:** 168.6 (162.8 pp) × 25.6 × 5.7
S: 22/20 kts **Man:** 21 officers, 376 men plus 28/348 troops
A: 6-8/76-mm AA (II × 3 or 4)
Electron Equipt: Radars: 1 SPS 10, 1 SPS 40
M: de Laval GT; 2 props; 24,000 hp **Boilers:** 2

Pensacola (LSD 38) G. Arra, 1976

REMARKS: Carry assault landing craft in the well deck (113.28 × 15.24); can accommodate 3 LCU or 29 LCM(6) and many LVT. One or two LCM(6) stowed on deck. The helicopter deck is removable. One twin 76-mm removed from LSD-37, LSD-40; others to follow to allow mounting 2/20-mm Vulcan/Phalanx. Mk 56 and Mk 63 directors now removed.

♦ *8 Thomaston class* — Bldr: Ingalls, Pascagoula

LSD 28 THOMASTON	9-2-54	**LSD 32 SPIEGEL GROVE**	10-11-55
LSD 29 PLYMOUTH ROCK	7-2-54	**LSD 33 ALAMO**	20-1-56
LSD 30 FORT SNELLING	6-7-54	**LSD 34 HERMITAGE**	12-6-56
LSD 31 POINT DEFIANCE	28-9-54	**LSD 35 MONTICELLO**	10-8-56

Plymouth Rock (LSD 29) G. Arra, 1975

DOCK LANDING SHIPS (*continued*)

D: 6,880 tons (11,270 fl) **Dim:** 155.45 × 25.60 × 5.80
S: 23 kts **Man:** 21 officers, 379 men, 340 troops
A: 8/76-mm AA (II × 4) (LSD-28, LSD-31: II × 3)
Electron Equipt: Radars: SPS 10, SPS 6
M: GT; 2 props; 23,000 hp **Boilers:** 2 Babcock & Wilcox

REMARKS: Portable helicopter platform can carry 3 LCU or 21 LCM(6) in 119.2 × 14.6-m well deck. Originally had 16/76-mm AA (II × 8). Two Mk 56 and Mk 63 gun fire-control systems being removed; will receive two Vulcan/Phalanx.

NOTE: The remaining units of the *Casa Grande* class, built in World War II, were stricken in October/November 1976.

TANK LANDING SHIPS

♦ *20 Newport class (SCN 405-66 type)*

Bldrs: LST-1179: Philadelphia NSY Others: National Steel SB, San Diego

	Laid down	L	In serv.
LST 1179 NEWPORT	1-11-66	3-2-68	7-6-69
LST 1180 MANITOWOC	1-2-67	4-6-69	24-1-70
LST 1181 SUMTER	14-11-67	13-12-69	20-6-70
LST 1182 FRESNO	16-12-67	28-9-68	22-11-69
LST 1183 PEORIA	22-2-68	23-11-68	21-2-70
LST 1184 FREDERICK	13-4-68	8-3-69	11-4-70
LST 1185 SCHENECTADY	2-8-68	24-5-69	13-6-70
LST 1186 CAYUGA	28-9-68	12-7-69	8-8-70
LST 1187 TUSCALOOSA	23-11-68	6-9-69	24-10-70
LST 1188 SAGINAW	24-5-69	7-2-70	23-1-71
LST 1189 SAN BERNARDINO	12-7-69	28-3-70	27-3-71
LST 1190 BOULDER	6-9-69	22-5-70	4-6-71
LST 1191 RACINE	13-12-69	15-8-70	9-7-71
LST 1192 SPARTANBURG COUNTY	7-2-70	11-11-70	1-9-71
LST 1193 FAIRFAX COUNTY	28-3-70	19-12-70	16-10-71
LST 1194 LA MOURE COUNTY	22-5-70	13-2-71	18-12-71
LST 1195 BARBOUR COUNTY	15-8-70	15-5-71	12-2-72
LST 1196 HARLAN COUNTY	7-11-70	24-7-71	8-4-72
LST 1197 BARNSTABLE COUNTY	19-12-70	2-10-71	27-5-72
LST 1198 BRISTOL COUNTY	13-2-71	4-12-71	5-8-72

Authorized: 1 in FY 65, 8 in FY 66, 11 in FY 67

Saginaw (LST 1188) — with pontoon sections G. Arra, 1972

Saginaw (LST 1188) G. Arra, 1972

D: 8,450 tons (fl) **S:** 20 kts
Dim: 159.2 (171.3 over horns) × 21.18 × 5.3 (aft) × 1.80 (fwd)
Man: 12 officers, 174 men + 20/411 troops
A: 4/76-mm AA (II × 2) **Electron Equipt:** Radar: 1/SPS 10
M: 6 Alco (LST-1179 to LST-1181: G.M.) diesels; 2 controllable-pitch props; 16,500 hp

La Moure County (LST 1194) 1972

REMARKS: Can carry 500 tons of cargo and 431 troops. A side-thruster propeller forward helps when marrying to a causeway. There is a mobile aluminum ramp forward (34.15 tons), which is linked to the tank deck by a second ramp. These ramps can carry 75 tons. Aft is a helicopter platform and a stern door for loading and unloading vehicles. Four pontoon causeway sections can be carried on the hull sides.

TANK LANDING SHIPS (*continued*)

♦ *2 de Soto County class (SCB 119 type)*

	Bldr	L	In serv.
LST 1173 SUFFOLK COUNTY	Boston NSY	5-9-56	15-8-57
LST 1177 LORAIN COUNTY	Amer.SB., Lorain	22-6-57	3-10-59

D: 4,164 tons (7,100 fl) **S:** 16 kts **Dim:** 135.7 × 18.9 × 5.3
A: 6/76-mm 50-cal (II × 3) **Man:** 15 officers, 173 men
M: 6 diesels; 2 controllable-pitch props; 14,000 hp

Lorain County (LST 1177)

REMARKS: Air-conditioned. Can carry 700 troops. Special tanks for vehicle fuel. Four LCVP carried in davits; one LCU and two pontoons can be carried on board. Helicopter platform. *De Soto County* (LST-1171) and *York County* (LST-1175) transferred to Italy, *Grant County* (LST-1174) to Brazil. *Graham County* (LST-1176) served as a tender to the *Asheville*-class patrol boats until 1976. *Wood County* (AGP-1178, ex-LST) will be converted as a tender to the *Pegasus*-class PHM. The two others have been in reserve since 1972.

AMPHIBIOUS CARGO SHIPS

♦ *5 Charleston class*

	Bldr	Laid down	L	In serv.
LKA 113 CHARLESTON	Newport News	5-12-66	2-12-67	14-12-68
LKA 114 DURHAM	Newport News	10-7-67	29-3-68	24-5-69
LKA 115 MOBILE	Newport News	15-1-68	19-10-68	20-9-69
LKA 116 St. LOUIS	Newport News	3-4-68	4-1-69	22-11-69
LKA 117 EL PASO	Newport News	22-10-58	5-69	12-69

Authorized: 4 in FY 65, 1 in FY 66

D: 18,600 tons (fl) **S:** 20 kts **Dim:** 175.4 × 18.9 × 7.8
A: 8/76-mm AA (II × 4) **Electron Equipt:** Radar: 1/SPS 10
Man: 24 officers, 310 men + 15/211 troops
M: 1 GT; 1 prop; 22,000 hp **Boilers:** 2

REMARKS: Air-conditioned. Machinery control is automatic. Helicopter platform. Fittings include 2/40-ton lifting booms, 8 of 15 tons, and 50 lifting nets, which are hydraulically controlled by 50 winches. This class of LKA carries four LCM(8), four LCM(6), two LCVP, and 2 LCP.

Charleston (LKA 113) G. Arra, 1974

Charleston (LKA 113) G. Arra, 1974

St. Louis (LKA 116)

AMPHIBIOUS CARGO SHIPS (*continued*)

♦ *1 Tulare class* — Bldr: Bethlehem Steel, San Francisco

	Laid down	L	In serv.
LKA 112 TULARE (ex-*Evergreen Mariner*)	16-2-53	22-12-53	12-1-56

Tulare (LKA 112)

D: 16,800 tons (fl) **S:** 22 kts **Dim:** 171.9 × 23.2 × 8.5
Man: 10 officers, 154 men + 21/208 Reserves + 18/301 troops
A: 12/76-mm AA (II × 6)
Electron Equipt: Radars: 1/SPS 10, 1/SPS 6
M: 1 General Electric GT; 1 prop; 22,000 hp
Boilers: 2 Combustion Engineering

REMARKS: Helicopter platform. Loading rigging for 60 tons. Carries nine LCM(6) and eleven LCVP. Assigned to the Naval Reserve Force 1-7-75 for active service in training.

AMPHIBIOUS TRANSPORTS

♦ *2 Paul Revere class* — Bldr: New York SB, Camden, N.J.

	L	In serv.
LPA 248 PAUL REVERE (ex-*Diamond Mariner*)	13-2-54	3-9-58
LPA 249 FRANCIS MARION (ex-*Prairie Mariner*)	11-4-53	6-7-61

D: 10,709 tons (16,838 fl) **Dim:** 171.9 × 23.2 × 7.3
S: 22 kts **A:** 8/76-mm AA (II × 4)
Electron Equipt: Radars: 1/SPS 10, 1/SPS 40
Man: 13 officers, 187 men + 15/237 Reserve + 96/1,561 troops
M: General Electric GT; 22,000 hp **Boilers:** 2 Combustion Engineering

REMARKS: Assigned to the Naval Reserve Force 1-7-75 for active training. Can carry nine LCM(6), eleven LCVP. Four Mk 63 radar directors removed from LPA-248. Helicopter platform aft. Unusually complete communications equipment and electronics warfare gear.

Francis Marion (LPA 249) Terzibaschitsch, 1977

UTILITY LANDING CRAFT

♦ *60 LCU-1610 class* — Bldrs: Various, 1960-1976

LCU 1653 G. Arra, 1975

D: 190 tons (390 fl) **S:** 11 kts **Dim:** 41.07 × 9.07 × 2.08
A: 2/12.7-mm machine guns **Man:** 6 men + 8 troops
M: 4 G.M.6-71 diesels; 2 props; 1,200 hp

REMARKS: Includes LCU-1613, LCU-1614, LCU-1616 to LCU-1619, LCU-1621, LCU-1623, LCU-1624, LCU-1626 to LCU-1635, LCU-1637, LCU-1641 to LCU-1680.

UTILITY LANDING CRAFT (*continued*)

LCU-1637 (aluminum hull): **D:** 135 tons (357 fl). LCU-1621 has cycloidal props. Missing numbers are units reclassified as service craft, YFB or YFU. Can carry three M-48 tanks.

♦ *24 LCU-1466 class, 1953–*

LCU 1468 1969

D: 180 tons (347 fl) **S:** 8 kts **Dim:** 35.1 × 10.4 × 1.6 (aft)
A: 2/20-mm AA (I × 2) **Man:** 6 men + 8 troops
M: 3 Gray Marine 64YTL diesels; 3 props; 675 hp

Remarks: Can carry 167 tons. Engines and bridge aft; improved version of LCU-501 class. In service are LCU-1466 to LCU-1470, LCU-1472, LCU-1477, LCU-1482, LCU-1484 to LCU-1490, LCU-1492, LCU-1525, LCU-1535 to LCU-1537, LCU-1539, LCU-1547, LCU-1548, LCU-1559. Missing numbers have been either transferred, sunk, or converted to service craft (YFU).

♦ *22 LCU-501 class, 1943–45*

D: 143 tons (309 fl) **S:** 10 kts **Dim:** 36.3 × 9.8 × 1.2 (aft)
A: 2/20-mm AA (I × 2) **Man:** 6 men
M: 3 Gray Marine 64YTL diesels; 3 props; 675 hp

Remarks: Survivors of a class of more than 900, originally called LCT(6) class. In service are: LCU-539, LCU-588, LCU-599, LCU-608, LCU-654, LCU-660, LCU-666, LCU-667, LCU-674, LCU-742, LCU-768, LCU-803, LCU-871, LCU-893, LCU-1045, LCU-1124, LCU-1241, LCU-1348, LCU-1387, LCU-1430, LCU-1451, LCU-1462.

LCU 608

MINOR LANDING CRAFT (Exact totals not available)

♦ *over 300 LCM(8) class, 1949–76*

D: 95–115 tons (fl) **S:** 9–12 kts **Dim:** 22.7 × 6.4 × 1.4
M: 4 G.M. 6-71 diesels; 2 props; 600 hp

LCM(8) class

Remarks: Latest version, Mk 2, has aluminum hull. U.S. Army also uses large numbers of this class, which has been in production for nearly 30 years.

♦ *over 600 LCM(6) class, 1952–1977*

D: 56 tons (fl) **S:** 10 kts **Dim:** 17.1 × 4.4 × 1.2 (aft)
M: 2 Gray Marine 64NN9 diesels; 2 props; 330 hp

Remarks: Designed during World War II. Many used in utility roles.

♦ *. . . LCVP class*

D: 13 tons (fl) **S:** 9 kts **Dim:** 11.0 × 3.2 × 1.1 (aft)
M: 1 Gray Marine 64HN9 diesel; 225 hp

MINOR LANDING CRAFT (*continued*)

REMARKS: 1,552 built, 1950-62. Wooden or plastic hulls. Can carry 36 troops or 3.5 tons cargo.

♦ *LCP(L) Mk 4 and Mk 11 classes*

D: 9.2-10.2 tons (fl) **S:** 17 kts **Dim:** 11.0 × 4.0 × 1.1
M: 1 G.M. diesel; 270-350 hp

REMARKS: For use as control craft; carried aboard are LHA, LPD, LSD, LST classes, etc.

EXPERIMENTAL LANDING CRAFT

NOTE: The best features of the two designs listed below will be combined into a new production air cushion vehicle intended to supplement the LCU classes beginning in the 1980s. They will be carried in the *Tarawa*-class LHA. The goal is to carry a 54,446-kg payload at 50 kts.

♦ **JEFF-A** — Bldr: Aerojet General (del. 2-77)
Weight: 85.8 tons (166 loaded) **Dim:** 31.5 × 15.7 × 7.5 (high)
S: 50 kts **Range:** 200/50 **Man:** 6 men
M: 6 Avco T40 gas turbines (2 for lift); 4 shrouded airscrews; 11,200 hp

REMARKS: Actually built at Todd Shipyards, Seattle. Aluminum construction.

♦ **JEFF-B** — Bldr: Bell Aerosystems, New Orleans (del. 1976)

Weight: 93 tons (147 loaded) **Dim:** 26.4 × 14.3 × 7.1 (high)
S: 70 kts **Range:** 200/50 **Man:** 6 men
M: 6 Avco T40 gas turbines (4 for lift); 2 shrouded propellers; 16,080 hp

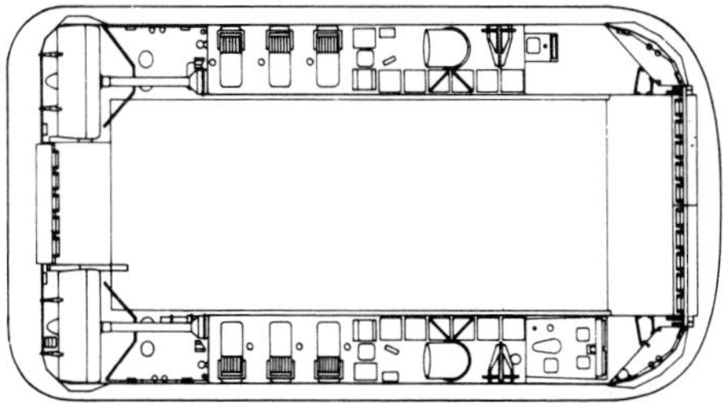

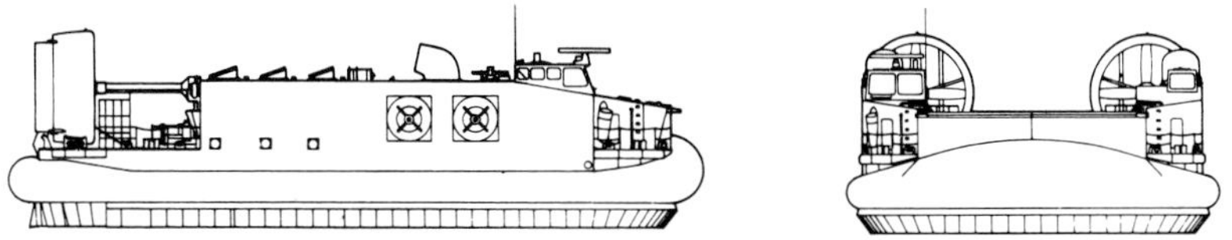

JEFF B Bell Aerosystems

REMARKS: In this design, all six turbines are interconnected to provide power simultaneously to the two propellers and four lift fans.

AUXILIARY SHIPS

NOTE: This section includes only ships that are subordinate to the U.S. Navy proper. Ships assigned to the civilian-manned Military Sealift Command are listed separately in a following section. Below, ships are listed alphabetically by their U.S. Navy type designation i.e., AD, AF, AG, etc.

♦ *5 Samuel Gompers-class destroyer tenders (SCB 244 type)*

Bldrs: AD-37 and AD-38, Puget Sound NSY; AD-41 to AD-43, National Steel, San Diego

	Laid down	L	In serv.
AD 37 SAMUEL GOMPERS	7-64	14-5-66	1-7-67
AD 38 PUGET SOUND	2-65	16-9-66	27-4-68
AD 41 YELLOWSTONE	27-6-77	10-78	1980
AD 42 ACADIA	2-78	1979	1980
AD 43 N . . .	. . .	. . .	1981

Authorized: 1 in FY 64, 1 in FY 65, 1 in FY 75, 1 in FY 76, 1 in FY 77

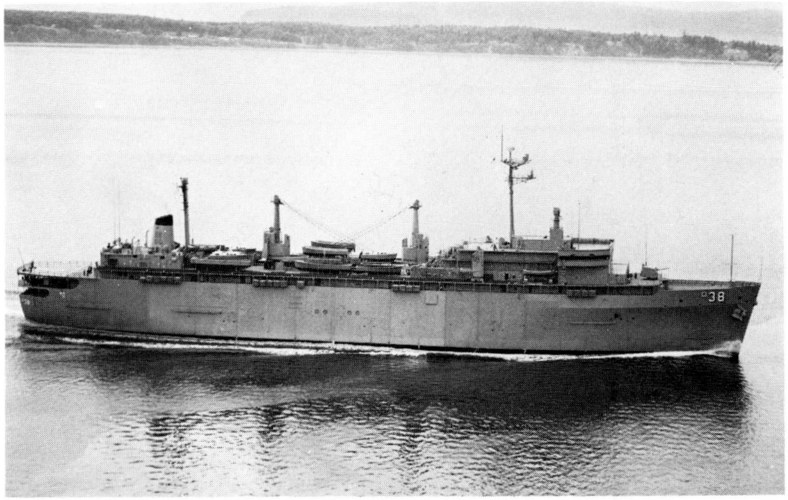

Puget Sound (AD 38) 1968

D: 20,500 tons (fl) **Dim:** 196.3 × 25.9 × 6.9
S: 20 kts **Man:** 135 officers, 1,671 men
A: 1/127-mm 38-cal (AD-38 only) — 4/20-mm AA (I × 4)
Electron Equipt: Radar: 1/SPS 10
M: de Laval GT; 1 prop; 20,000 hp **Boilers:** 2 Combustion Engineering

REMARKS: Maintenance ships for guided-missile cruisers and destroyers, six of which can come alongside at one time. Two 30-ton cranes; two 3.5-ton traveling cranes. Helicopter deck. Excellent workshops for electronic equipment and surface-to-air missiles. No longer planned to carry Sea Sparrow in AD-41 and later, which will carry only 2/20-mm AA (I × 2). Funds for AD-44 and AD-45 will be requested under FY 79 and FY 80.

AUXILIARY SHIPS (*continued*)

♦ *3 Klondike/Shenandoah-class destroyer tenders*

	Bldr	Laid down	L	In serv.
AD 24 EVERGLADES	L.A. SB	26-6-44	28-1-45	25-5-51
AD 26 SHENANDOAH	Todd, Tacoma	16-9-44	29-3-45	13-8-45
AD 36 BRYCE CANYON	Charleston NSY	. . .	. . .	15-9-50

Everglades (AD 24) 1967

D: 8,165 tons (14,700 fl) **Dim:** 149.96 × 21.25 × 8.30
S: 18 kts **Man:** 800-918 men
A: AD-24: 2/76-mm (I × 2) — AD-26: 4/20-mm AA (I × 4) — AD-36: 1/127-mm 38 cal
Electron Equipt: Radar: 1/SPS 10 **Boilers:** 2 Foster-Wheeler
M: Westinghouse GT; 1 prop; 8,500 hp

REMARKS: AD-24 is in reserve as an accommodations ship. The others, both FRAM II, are active. Built on C-3 cargo hull. Helicopter deck; hangar for DASH, now not used.

♦ *5 Dixie-class destroyer tenders*

	Bldr	Laid down	L	In serv.
AD 14 DIXIE	New York SB	17-3-38	27-5-39	25-4-40
AD 15 PRAIRIE	New York SB	7-12-38	9-12-39	5-8-40
AD 17 PIEDMONT	Tampa SB	1-12-41	7-12-42	5-1-44
AD 18 SIERRA	Tampa SB	31-12-41	23-2-43	20-3-44
AD 19 YOSEMITE	Tampa SB	19-1-42	16-5-43	25-3-44

D: 9,450 tons (17,190 fl) **S:** 18 kts (19.6 during trials)
Dim: 161.70 × 22.33 × 7.80 **Man:** 1,131 to 1,271 men
A: 4/20-mm AA (I × 4) **Electron Equipt:** Radar: 1/SPS 10
M: GT; 2 props; 12,000 hp **Boilers:** 4 Babcock & Wilcox

Dixie (AD 14) — oldest active ship in the U.S. Navy 1976

Prairie (AD 15) 1975

REMARKS: The design of these support ships goes back to pre-1939 programs. Modernized under the FRAM program from 1959 to 1963 to serve as maintenance vessels for guided-missile ships, they have workshops, spare parts for missiles, and two 20-ton rotating cranes. Helicopter deck. 127-mm guns removed 1974-75.

♦ *8 Kilauea class ammunition ships*

	Bldr	Laid down	L	In serv.
AE 26 KILAUEA	Gen. Dynamics	10-3-66	9-8-67	10-8-68
AE 27 BUTTE	Gen. Dynamics	21-7-66	9-8-67	29-11-68
AE 28 SANTA BARBARA	Bethlehem, Sparrows Pt	20-12-66	23-1-68	2-70
AE 29 MOUNT HOOD	Bethlehem, Sparrows Pt	8-5-67	17-7-68	1-5-71
AE 32 FLINT	Ingalls, Pascagoula	4-8-69	9-11-70	20-11-71
AE 33 SHASTA	Ingalls, Pascagoula	10-11-69	3-4-71	26-2-72

UXILIARY SHIPS *(continued)*

E 34 MOUNT BAKER	Ingalls, Pascagoula	10-5-70	23-10-71	22-7-72
E 35 KISKA	Ingalls, Pascagoula	4-8-71	11-3-72	16-12-72

Authorized: 2 in FY 65, 2 in FY 66, 2 in FY 67, 2 in FY 68

utte (AE 27) 1970

D: 18,088 tons (fl) **S:** 20 kts **Dim:** 171.9 × 24.7 × 8.5
A: 8/76-mm AA (II × 4) AE-32 and AE-33: 4/76-mm (II × 2) — 2 UH-46 helicopters
Electron Equipt: Radar: 1/SPS 10 **Man:** 28 officers, 373 men
M: General Electric GT; 1 prop; 22,000 hp
Boilers: 3 Foster-Wheeler

EMARKS: Sophisticated FAST rapid replenishment system. Hangar and flight deck aft. Two twin 76-mm mounts and both Mk 56 directors being removed; 2/20-mm Vulcan/Phalanx AA and 2 Mk 36 RBOC chaff/flare launchers to be added.

utte (AE 27) G. Arra, 1972

♦ *3 Nitro-class ammunition ships*

Bldr: Bethlehem Steel Corporation, Sparrows Point, Maryland

	Laid down	L	In serv.
AE 23 NITRO	20-5-57	26-6-58	1-5-59
AE 24 PYRO	21-10-57	5-11-58	24-7-59
AE 25 HALEAKALA	10-3-58	17-2-59	3-11-59

D: 10,000 tons (16,083 fl) **Dim:** 156.1 × 22.0 × 8.8
S: 20 kts **Man:** 18 officers, 298 men
A: 4/76-mm AA (II × 2) **M:** GT; 1 prop; 16,000 hp

Nitro (AE 23) 1968

REMARKS: All had platforms for cargo helicopters added during the 1960s. Gun directors being removed. Mk 36 RBOC to be added.

♦ *2 Suribachi-class ammunition ships*

Bldr: Bethlehem Steel Corporation, Sparrows Point, Maryland

	Laid down	L	In serv.
AE 21 SURIBACHI	16-5-55	3-5-56	30-3-57
AE 22 MAUNA KEA	31-1-55	2-11-55	17-11-56

Mauna Kea (AE 22) 1970

AUXILIARY SHIPS (*continued*)

D: 10,000 tons (15,500 fl) **S:** 20 kts **Dim:** 153.6 × 22.0 × 8.8
A: 4/76-mm (II × 2) **Man:** 18 officers, 298 men
M: GT; 1 prop; 16,000 hp **Boilers:** 2 Combustion Engineering

REMARKS: SPS 6 radar removed; retain SPS 10. Gun mounts superfiring, whereas AE-23 to AE-25 have them side by side. Have Mk 63 gun fire-control system.

♦ *7 Mars-class combat stores ships (SCB 208 type)*

Bldr: National Steel & SB Co., San Diego

	Laid down	L	In serv.
AFS 1 MARS	5-5-62	15-6-63	21-12-63
AFS 2 SYLVANIA	18-8-62	10-8-63	11-7-64
AFS 3 NIAGARA FALLS	22-5-65	25-3-66	29-4-67
AFS 4 WHITE PLAINS	2-10-65	23-7-66	23-11-68
AFS 5 CONCORD	26-3-66	17-12-66	27-11-68
AFS 6 SAN DIEGO	11-3-67	13-4-68	24-5-69
AFS 7 SAN JOSE	8-3-69	13-12-69	23-10-70

Authorized: 1 in FY 61, 1 in FY 62, 1 in FY 64, 2 in FY 65, 1 in FY 66, 1 in FY 67

D: 16,240 tons (fl) **Dim:** 177.08 (161.54 pp) × 24.08 × 7.32
S: 20 kts **Man:** 45 officers, 441 men
A: 8/76-mm AA (II × 4) **Electron Equipt:** Radar: 1/SPS 10 — TACAN
M: GT; 1 prop; 22,000 hp **Boilers:** 3 Babcock & Wilcox

San Jose (AFS 7) 1971

REMARKS: Two UH-46A (Sea Knight) cargo helicopters with platform and hangar. Four M-shaped cargo masts with constant-tension equipment; transfer from the supply ship to the receiving ship takes 90 seconds. Five holds (1 and 5 for spare parts, 3 and 4 for provisions, 2 for aviation parts) have only two hatches. Eleven hoists, which raise up to 5.5 tons, link the decks; several others feed into the helicopter area. Ten loading areas (five on each side) and palletized cargo help in the control of replenishment. There are four refrigerated compartments, three for the storage of dried provisions. Some 35,000 types of spare parts are divided between 40,000 bins and racks and are accounted for by five data-processing machines, one of which is a Univac 1104 computer. Quarters air-conditioned. Draw 2.70 m more aft than forward. One boiler always in reserve. Three additional units no longer planned. SPS 40 radar removed. Fire-control directors being removed.

♦ *5 AO-177-class oilers*

	Bldr	Laid down	L	In serv.
AO 177 N . . .	Avondale SY	5-78	. . .	1979
AO 178 N . . .	Avondale SY	. . .	. . .	1980
AO 179 N . . .	Avondale SY	. . .	. . .	1980
AO 186 N . . .	. . .	. . .	. . .	1981
AO 187 N . . .	. . .	. . .	. . .	1981

AO 177 (Artist's impression)

D: 27,500 tons (fl) **Dim:** 180.2 (167.7 pp) × 26.8 × 10.7
S: 20 kts **Man:** 135 men
A: 2/20-mm Vulcan/Phalanx Gatling AA **Electric:** 5,000 kw
M: GT; 1 prop; 24,000 hp; 2 boilers (40 kg/cm², 440°C)

REMARKS: Will carry 72,000 barrels fuel oil, 48,000 barrels JP-5 gas turbine fuel, and will be able to replenish ships while making 15 knots. Mk 36 RBOC chaff/flare rocket system will be carried, and there will be a helicopter hangar and platform aft. Four constant-tension replenishment stations to port, three to starboard. Will be able to transfer 408,000 liters of fuel oil and 245,000 liters JP-5 per hour. Four requested under FY 78, 2 funded; 12 more programmed (AO-188 to AO-199).

♦ *5 Neosho-class oilers*

	Bldr	L	In serv.
AO 143 NEOSHO	Bethlehem, Quincy	10-11-53	24-9-54
AO 145 HASSAYAMPA	New York SB	12-9-54	19-4-55
AO 146 KAWISHIWI	New York SB	11-12-54	6-7-55

AUXILIARY SHIPS (*continued*)

AO 147 TRUCKEE	New York SB	10-3-55	23-11-55
AO 148 PONCHATOULA	New York SB	9-7-55	12-1-56

Neosho (AO 143) J.C. Bellonne, 1977

Truckee (AO 147) 1975

D: 11,600 tons light (38,000 fl) **S:** 20 kts
Dim: 199.6 × 26.2 × 10.7 **Man:** 21 officers, 303 men
A: 8/76-mm AA (AO-145: 4) (II × 4 or 2)
Electron Equipt: Radar: 1/SPS 10
M: General Electric GT; 2 props; 28,000 hp
Boilers: 2 Babcock & Wilcox

REMARKS: Carry 180,000 barrels of liquid cargo. Helicopter platform aft (not in AO-148). Sister *Mississinewa* (T-AO-144), disarmed, operates under the Military Sealift Command.

♦ *3 T3-S2-AL-class (jumboized) oilers*

Bldr: Bethlehem Steel, Sparrows Point, Maryland

	L	In serv.
AO 51 ASHTABULA	22-5-43	7-8-43
AO 98 CALOOSAHATCHEE	6-7-45	3-12-45
AO 99 CANISTEO	2-6-45	10-10-45

Canisteo (AO 99) 1970

D: 34,750 tons (fl) **S:** 18 kts **Dim:** 196.3 × 22.9 × 9.6
A: 4/76-mm AA (I × 4) **Man:** 13 officers, 287 men
Electron Equipt: Radar: 1/SPS 10
M: GT; 2 props; 13,500 hp **Boilers:** 4 Foster-Wheeler

REMARKS: Lengthened 27 m by insertion of new mid-body during 1960s. Two 76-mm being removed, and probably the 1 Mk 52 and 2 Mk 51 directors as well. Carry 143,000 barrels of fuel, 175 tons of ammunition, and 100 tons of provisions. No helicopter deck.

♦ *4 Sacramento-class fast combat support ships (SCB-196 type)*

	Bldr	Laid down	L	In serv.
AOE 1 SACRAMENTO	Puget Sound NSY	30-6-61	14-9-63	14-3-64
AOE 2 CAMDEN	New York SB	17-2-64	29-5-65	1-4-67
AOE 3 SEATTLE	Puget Sound NSY	1-10-65	2-3-68	5-4-69
AOE 4 DETROIT	Puget Sound NSY	29-11-66	21-6-69	28-3-70

Authorized: 1 in FY 61, 1 in FY 63, 1 in FY 65, 1 in FY 66

D: 19,200 tons light (53,600 fl) **Dim:** 241.4 (215.8 pp) × 32.9 × 11.6
S: 26 kts **Man:** 33 officers, 567 men
A: 1 Mk 29 launcher for Sea Sparrow (VIII × 1) — 6/76-mm AA (II × 3)
Electronic Equipt: Radars: 1/SPS 10, 1/SPS 6 (AOE-1 and AOE-2: SPS 40) — TACAN
M: General Electric GT; 2 props; 100,000 hp **Range:** 10,000/17
Boilers: 4 Combustion Engineering (42.2 kg/cm², 480°C)

REMARKS: Sea Sparrow launcher and Mk 91 control system replacing one twin 76-mm AA; 2 Mk 56 directors to be removed. Will also receive 2/20-mm Vulcan/Phalanx and Mk 36 RBOC chaff/flare rocket system. Carry 177,000 barrels fuel plus 2,150 tons ammunition, 750 tons provisions. Helicopter hangar and flight deck for two UH-46 (Sea Knight) Vertical Replenishment (VERTREP) helicopters. Plans announced 1976 to build AOE-5 under FY 80 program. Turbines in AOE-1 and AOE-2 are from battleship *Kentucky* (BB-66).

AUXILIARY SHIPS (*continued*)

Seattle (AOE 3) G. Arra, 1976

Detroit (AOE 4) 1972

♦ *7 Wichita-class replenishment oilers*

Bldr: General Dynamics, Quincy

	Laid down	L	In serv.
AOR 1 WICHITA	18-6-66	18-3-68	7-6-69
AOR 2 MILWAUKEE	29-11-66	17-1-69	1-11-69
AOR 3 KANSAS CITY	20-4-68	28-6-69	6-6-70
AOR 4 SAVANNAH	22-1-69	25-4-70	5-12-70
AOR 5 WABASH	21-1-70	6-2-71	20-11-71
AOR 6 KALAMAZOO	28-10-70	11-11-72	11-8-73
AOR 7 ROANOKE	19-1-74	7-12-74	30-10-76

Authorized: 2 in FY 66, 2 in FY 67, 2 in FY 68, 1 in FY 73

Kalamazoo (AOR 6) — no hangar A.D. Baker, 1976

Roanoke (AOR 7) 1976

D: 37,360 tons (fl) **S:** 20 kts **Dim:** 200.9 × 29.3 × 10.1

A: AOR-1, AOR-4 to AOR-6: 4/76-mm AA (II × 2); AOR-2: 4/20-mm AA (I × 4); AOR-3 and AOR-7: 1 Mk 29 launcher for Sea Sparrow (VIII × 1) — 4/20-mm AA (I × 4)

Electron Equipt: Radar: 1/SPS 10 (AOR-7: SPS 58 also)

AUXILIARY SHIPS *(continued)*

Man: 27 officers, 363 men **Range:** 6,500/20, 10,000/17
M: General Electric GT; 2 props; 32,000 shp **Boilers:** 3 Foster-Wheeler

Milwaukee (AOR 2) 1976

REMARKS: Carry 175,000 barrels fuel (90,000 distillate fuel), 600 tons ammunition, 575 tons provisions. AOR-1 and AOR-4 to AOR-6 have no hangars; others have hangars flanking stack (2 UH-46 VERTREP helicopters). AOR-3 and AOR-7 have single Sea Sparrow launcher with two Mk 76 directors on lattice towers abreast the stack (AOR-2 may be similarly armed shortly). All are to receive 2/20-mm Vulcan/Phalanx Gatling AA and the Mk 36 RBOC system. Ships with 4/76-mm AA have 2 Mk 56 directors. There are 4 stations for liquid transfer and 2 for solid transfer to port, 3 liquid and 2 solid to starboard; all have constant-tension devices.

♦ *4 Vulcan-class repair ships*

	Bldr	Laid down	L	In serv.
AR 5 VULCAN	New York SB	26-12-39	14-12-40	16-6-41
AR 6 AJAX	Los Angeles SB & DD	7-5-41	22-8-42	30-10-42
AR 7 HECTOR	Los Angeles SB & DD	28-7-41	11-11-42	7-2-44
AR 8 JASON	Los Angeles SB & DD	9-3-42	3-4-43	19-6-44

Hector (AR 7) 1975

D: 9,140 tons (16,380 fl) **S:** 19.2 kts **Dim:** 161.3 × 22.3 × 7.1
A: 4/20-mm AA (I × 4) **Man:** 63 officers, 1,273 men
M: GT; 2 props; 11,000 hp **Boilers:** 4 Babcock & Wilcox

REMARKS: Very elaborately equipped repair facilities. 4/127-mm DP (I × 4) removed from all. *Jason,* typed ARN-1 (heavy hull repair ship), redesignated in 1957 as AR-8.

NOTE: *Delta* (AR-9) stricken 1-10-77; *Markab* (AR-23) stricken 3-12-76. *Grand Canyon* (AR-28, ex-AD-28) scheduled to be stricken 1-8-78. A new class of repair ship, ARX, is planned for construction in the 1980s.

Landing Craft Repair Ships *Egeria* (ARL-8) and *Bellerophon* (ARL-31) were both stricken on 1-10-77. *Sphinx* (ARL-24) was being considered for sale to Spain late in 1977, and *Indra* (ARL-37) may be stricken by the time of publication. These four LST-hulled ships were all in the reserve fleet.

♦ *11 Diver- and Bolster-class salvage ships*

Bldr: Basalt Rock Co., Napa, California

	Laid down	L	In serv.
ARS 8 PRESERVER	26-10-42	1-4-43	11-1-44
ARS 23 DELIVER	2-4-43	25-9-43	18-7-44
ARS 25 SAFEGUARD	5-6-43	20-11-44	31-10-44
ARS 33 CLAMP	2-3-42	24-10-42	23-8-43
ARS 34 GEAR	2-3-42	24-10-42	24-9-43
ARS 38 BOLSTER	20-7-44	23-12-44	1-5-45
ARS 39 CONSERVER	10-8-44	27-1-45	9-6-45
ARS 40 HOIST	13-9-44	31-3-45	21-7-45
ARS 41 OPPORTUNE	13-9-44	31-3-45	5-10-45
ARS 42 RECLAIMER	11-11-44	25-6-45	20-12-45
ARS 43 RECOVERY	6-1-45	4-8-45	15-5-46

D: 1,530 tons (1,970 fl; ARS-38 to ARS-43; 2,040 fl)
Dim: 65.1 × 12.5 × 4.0 (ARS-38 to ARS-43: 13.4 beam)
S: 14.8 kts **Man:** 6 officers, 77 enlisted men

Opportune (ARS 41) G. Arra, 1974

AUXILIARY SHIPS *(continued)*

A: ARS-39, ARS-41, ARS-42: 1/40-mm AA; ARS-8, ARS-23, ARS-25, ARS-38, ARS-43: 2/20-mm AA (I × 2)
M: 2 Cooper-Bessemer diesels, electric drive; 2 props; 2,440 hp

REMARKS: Equipped for diver support, salvage, and towing. ARS-33 is in Maritime Administration Reserve Fleet. ARS-34 is operated for the Navy by a private company. Two others, *Cable* (ARS-19) and *Curb* (ARS-21) are on loan to private companies for commercial use. *Grapple* (ARS-7) stricken 1-12-77. *Grasp* (ARS-24) stricken 24-2-78. *Escape* (ARS-6) scheduled to be stricken 1-9-78.

♦ *5 L. Y. Spear-class submarine tenders (SCB 702-66 and 737-72 types)*

	Bldr	Laid down	L	In serv.
AS 36 L. Y. SPEAR	Gen. Dynamics, Quincy	5-5-66	7-9-67	28-2-70
AS 37 DIXON	Gen. Dynamics, Quincy	7-9-67	20-6-70	7-8-71
AS 39 EMORY S. LAND	Lockheed SB, Seattle	2-3-76	4-5-77	1979
AS 40 FRANK CABLE	Lockheed SB, Seattle	2-3-76	1-78	1979
AS 41 McKEE	Lockheed SB, Seattle	. . .	. . .	1981

Authorized: 1 in FY 65, 1 in FY 66, 1 in FY 72, 1 in FY 73, 1 in FY 77

L. Y. Spear (AS 36) 1975

D: 13,000 tons (AS-36 and AS-37: 22,640 fl; AS-39 to AS-41: 24,000 fl)
S: 20 kts **Dim:** 196.2 × 25.9 × 8.7
Man: AS-36 and AS-37: 96 officers, 1,252 men
AS-39 to AS-41: 50 officers, 1,108 men (plus 75/44 flag staff)
A: 4/20-mm AA (I × 4) **M:** General Electric GT; 1 prop; 20,000 hp
Boilers: 2 Foster-Wheeler

REMARKS: Provide support to submarines (SSN), AS-39 to AS-41 being specifically tailored to the needs of the *Los Angeles* class. One 60-ton crane and two 7-ton traveling cranes. Helicopter deck, but no hangar. Radar: AS-36 and AS-37: SPS 10; AS-39 to AS-41: SPS 55. No longer planned to fit Vulcan/Phalanx or Sea Sparrow in later ships; 2/127-mm DP (I × 2) removed from AS-36 and AS-37. AS-38 (FY 69) canceled 27-3-69. No other submarine tenders currently programmed.

♦ *2 Simon Lake-class submarine tenders*

	Bldr	Laid down	L	In serv.
AS 33 SIMON LAKE	Puget Sound NSY	7-1-63	8-2-64	7-11-64
AS 34 CANOPUS	Ingalls, Pascagoula	2-3-64	12-2-65	4-11-65

Authorized: 1 in FY 63, 1 in FY 64

Canopus (AS 34) 1966

D: 12,000 tons (AS-33: 19,934 fl; AS-34: 21,089 fl)
Dim: 196.2 × 25.9 × 8.7 **S:** 18 kts
Man: AS-33: 90 officers, 1,338 men
AS-34: 95 officers, 1,326 men
A: 4/76-mm AA (II × 2) **Boilers:** 2 Combustion Engineering
M: de Laval GT; 1 prop; 20,000 hp

REMARKS: Specifically equipped to support nuclear-powered ballistic-missile submarines, with reload missiles stowed vertically amidships. Converted to carry Poseidon missiles, 1969-71. Two 60-ton cranes and four 7-ton traveling cranes. Helicopter deck aft, but no hangar. Guns will probably be removed and replaced by 4/20-mm (I × 4).

♦ *2 Hunley-class submarine tenders*

	Bldr	Laid down	L	In serv.
AS 31 HUNLEY	Newport News SB	28-11-60	28-9-61	16-6-62
AS 32 HOLLAND	Ingalls, Pascagoula	5-3-62	19-1-63	7-9-63

Authorized: 1 in FY 60, 1 in FY 62

D: 10,500 tons (19,300 fl) **Dim:** 182.6 × 25.3 × 7.4
S: 19 kts **Man:** 144 officers, 2,424 men
A: 4/20-mm AA (I × 4)
M: Diesel-electric (10 Fairbanks-Morse diesels); 1 prop; 15,000 hp

AUXILIARY SHIPS (*continued*)

Holland (AS 32) 1971

REMARKS: Intended to support SSBNs; converted to carry Poseidon missiles, 1973-75. The propulsion groups develop 12,000 kw; in addition, there are four auxiliary generator groups (3,000 kw). Air-conditioned. Helicopter platform. Original 32.5-ton rotating crane removed around 1970 and replaced by two 60-ton cranes.

♦ *1 Proteus-class submarine tender*

Bldr: Moore SB & DD, Oakland, California

	Laid down	L	In serv.	Conv.
AS 19 PROTEUS	15-9-41	12-11-42	31-1-44	8-7-60

Proteus (AS 19) — 127-mm gun now gone 1963

D: 10,250 tons (19,200 fl) **Dim:** 175.1 × 27.3 × 8.2
S: 15.4 kts **Man:** 86 officers, 1,214 men
A: 4/20-mm AA (I × 4)
M: 8 G.M. 16-248 diesels, electric drive; 2 props; 11,200 hp

REMARKS: Lengthened 13.4 m, 1959-60, as the first SSBN tender, carrying Polaris missiles in the new section, handled by an extendable gantry crane. Superstructure enlarged over that of former sisters in the *Fulton* class.

♦ *6 Fulton-class submarine tenders*

	Bldr	L	In serv.
AS 11 FULTON	Mare Island NSY	27-12-40	12-12-41
AS 12 SPERRY	Mare Island NSY	17-12-41	1-5-42
AS 15 BUSHNELL	Mare Island NSY	14-9-42	10-4-43
AS 16 HOWARD W. GILMORE	Mare Island NSY	16-9-43	24-5-44
AS 17 NEREUS	Puget Sound NSY	12-2-45	27-10-45
AS 18 ORION	Moore SB, Oakland	14-10-42	30-9-43

Howard W. Gilmore (AS 16) G. Arra, 1975

D: 9,734 tons (18,000 fl) **Dim:** 161.4 × 22.3 × 7.8
S: 15.4 kts **Man:** 1,286 to 1,937 men
A: AS-15 and AS-17: 2/127-mm DP (I × 2), AS-17 also: 4/20-mm AA (II × 2)
Others: 4/20-mm AA (I × 4)
Electric: 6,700 kw **Range:** 15,600/10 **Fuel:** 3,760 tons
M: 8 G.M. 16-248 diesels, electric drive; 2 props; 11,200 hp

REMARKS: AS-15, used as an accommodations ship at Norfolk, and AS-17 are in reserve. All received FRAM II modernization and can support nuclear submarines. Foundry can cast pieces up to 250 kg. Two 20-ton rotating cranes (as in *Dixie* class ADs) are fitted to all but AS-16, which has two kingposts and booms. AS-16 was originally named *Neptune*.

♦ *2 Pigeon-class submarine-rescue ships (SCB 721-67 type)*

Bldr: Alabama DD & SB, Mobile

	Laid down	L	In serv.
ASR 21 PIGEON	17-7-68	13-8-69	28-4-73
ASR 22 ORTOLAN	22-8-68	10-9-69	14-7-73

Authorized: 1 in FY 67, 1 in FY 68

AUXILIARY SHIPS (*continued*)

Pigeon (ASR 21) Alabama DD&SB, 1972

Ortolan (ASR 22) 1973

D: 3,411 tons (fl) **S:** 15 kts **Dim:** 76.5 × 26.2 × 6.5
A: 2/20-mm AA (I × 2) **Range:** 8,500/13
Man: 6 officers, 109 men plus 4/10 staff and 4/20 DSRV crew
M: 4 Alco high-speed diesels; 2 props; 6,000 hp

REMARKS: The catamaran hulls (7.925-m beam) are separated by 10.36 m. Diving bells and other salvage equipment are lowered between the two hulls by a moving crane. The ships can carry two small DSRV (Deep Submergence Rescue Vehicle) submarines, but as only two DSRV have been built, they normally have only one each. Excellent lowering and handling equipment for up to 60 tons; divers to 250 m.

♦ *4 Chanticleer-class submarine-rescue ships*

Bldr: Savannah Machine Foundry (ASR-9: Moore SB & DD, Oakland)

	Laid down	L	In serv.
ASR 9 FLORIKAN	30-9-41	14-6-42	5-4-43
ASR 13 KITTIWAKE	5-1-45	10-7-45	18-7-46
ASR 14 PETREL	26-2-45	29-9-45	24-9-46
ASR 15 SUNBIRD	2-4-45	3-4-46	28-1-47

Petrel (ASR 14) 1968

D: 1,653 tons (2,320 fl) **S:** 14.9 kts **Dim:** 76.7 × 13.4 × 4.9
A: 2/20-mm AA **Man:** 116 to 221 men
M: 2 G.M. 12-278A diesels, electric drive; 1 prop; 3,000 hp

REMARKS: Carry rescue diving bells. *Coucal* (ASR-8) stricken 15-9-77; *Tringa* (ASR-16) stricken 30-9-77 for transfer to Turkey, which also received *Greenlet* (ASR-10) in 6-70.

♦ *6 Abnaki and Achomawi classes fleet ocean tugs*

	Bldr	L	In serv.
ATF 105 MOCTABI	Charleston SB&DD	25-3-44	25-7-44
ATF 110 QUAPAW	United Eng., Alameda	15-5-43	6-5-44
ATF 113 TAKELMA	United Eng., Alameda	18-9-43	3-8-44
ATF 159 PAIUTE	Charleston SB&DD	4-6-45	27-8-45
ATF 160 PAPAGO	Charleston SB&DD	21-6-45	3-10-45
ATF 162 SHAKORI	Charleston SB&DD	9-8-45	20-12-45

D: 1,235 tons (1,640 fl) **S:** 15 kts **Dim:** 62.5 × 11.7 × 4.7
A: ATF-110, ATF-113, ATF-160, ATF-162: 1/76-mm
Man: 5 officers, 70 men
M: 2 diesels, electric drive; 1 prop; 3,000 hp

REMARKS: Developed from pre-World War II *Apache* class. ATF-105, ATF-110, and ATF-113 have 4 Busch-Sulzer BS-539 diesels and a small-diameter funnel; the others have G.M. 12-278A diesels and a large funnel. ATF-105, ATF-110, and ATF-159 are operated by the Naval Reserve Force. Also operational are *Ute* (T-ATF-76) and *Lipan* (T-ATF-85) of the *Cherokee* class, and *Atakapa* (T-ATF-149) and *Mosopelea* (T-ATF-158) of the *Achomawi* class — manned by the Military Sealift Command. Available in the Maritime Commission Reserve Fleet is *Seneca* (ATF-91). This group of tugs, once very numerous, is rapidly being eliminated: *Mataco* (ATF-86) and *Chowanoc* (ATF-100) were stricken 1-10-77; *Cree* (ATF-84),

AUXILIARY SHIPS (*continued*)

Papago (ATF 160) A.D. Baker, 1976

Abnaki (ATF-96), *Cocopa* (ATF-101), *Hitichi* (ATF-103), *Molala* (ATF-106), *Tawakoni* (ATF-114), *Nipmuc* (ATF-157), and *Salinan* (ATF-161) were due for disposal between 1-6-78 and 30-9-78.

NOTE: The new construction fleet ocean tugs of the *Powhatan* class are to be operated by the Military Sealift Command.

♦ *3 Edenton-class salvage and rescue ships* — Bldr: Brooke Marine, G.B.

Authorized: 1 in FY 66; 2 in FY 67

	Laid down	L	In serv.
ATS 1 EDENTON	1-4-67	15-5-68	23-1-71
ATS 2 BEAUFORT	19-2-68	20-12-68	22-1-72
ATS 3 BRUNSWICK	5-6-68	14-10-69	19-12-72

Beaufort (ATS 2) 1974

D: 2,650 tons (2,929 fl) **S:** 16 kts **Dim:** 88.0 (80.5 pp) × 1.53 × 4.6
A: 4/20-mm AA (II × 2) **Man:** 9 officers, 91 men
Range: 12,000/ . . .
M: 4 Paxman 12 YLCM (900 rpm) diesels: 2 Escher-Wyss controllable-pitch props; 6,000 hp

REMARKS: ATS-4 (FY 72) and ATS-5 (FY 73) canceled in favor of *Powhatan* class T-ATF. Can tow ships up to AOE-1-class size. 272-ton dead lift over the bow. 20-ton crane aft; 10-ton boom forward. Can conduct dives to 260 m. Powerful pumps and complete fire-fighting equipment. Equipped with bow-thruster.

♦ *1 Currituck-class guided-missile ship (ex-seaplane tender)*

Bldr: Los Angeles SB & DD Co., San Pedro

	Laid down	L	In serv.
AVM 1 NORTON SOUND	7-9-42	28-11-43	8-1-45

Norton Sound (AVM 1) 1975

D: 9,106 tons (15,170 fl) **S:** 19 kts **Dim:** 165.6 × 21.8 × 7.2
A: 1 Mk 26 twin launcher for Standard SM-1 ER missiles
Electron Equipt: Radars: 1/SPS 10, 1/SPS 40, Aegis fire-control system (SPG 51, SPY 1) — TACAN
M: Allis-Chalmers GT; 2 props; 12,000 hp
Boilers: 4 Babcock & Wilcox

REMARKS: Has served as guided-missile trials ship since 1948. Prototype AEGIS system installed 1974, with only forward starboard "face" of the SPY-1 phased array radar operational. SPS 40 replaced the unique, large-antenna SPS 52 variant radar in 1975. Will probably also test SM-2 series missiles.

EXPERIMENTAL AUXILIARY SHIPS

NOTE: Experimental craft not covered by letter designators are listed at the end of this section. Many other experimental or research ships are operated by the Military Sealift Command (T-AGOR, T-AGM, T-AGS, etc.).

♦ *1 former salvage ship* — Bldr: Sun Ship, Chester, Pa.

	L	In serv.
AG 193 N . . . (ex-*Hughes Glomar Explorer*)	7-73	9-76

EXPERIMENTAL AUXILIARY SHIPS *(continued)*

D: 63,300 tons (fl) **S:** . . . kts
Dim: 188.6 (169.8 pp) × 35.3 × 11.6
M: 5 Nordberg 16-cyl. diesels, 6 General Electric motors; 13,200 hp

REMARKS: Transferred from the Central Intelligence Agency to U.S. Navy ownership in 9-76 and laid up in reserve at Suisun Bay. Official "name" is *ex-Hughes Glomar Explorer.* 27,455 grt. Could eventually be chartered and used for its original "cover" purpose: sea-bottom mining. The associated salvage barge is now owned by the Environmental Protection Agency.

♦ *2 Mariner class* — Bldr: New York SB, Camden, N.J.

	L	In serv.
AG 153 COMPASS ISLAND (ex-*Garden Mariner*)	24-10-53	3-12-56
AG 154 OBSERVATION ISLAND (ex-*Empire State Mariner*)	15-8-53	5-12-58

Observation Island (AG 154) 1972

Compass Island (AG 153) 1956

D: AG-153: 17,600 fl; AG-I54: 16,076 fl **S:** 20 kts
Dim: 171.6 × 23.0 × 8.8
Man: AG-153: 18 officers, 232 men; AG-154: 35/393
M: General Electric GT; 1 prop; 19,250 hp
Boilers: 3 Combustion Engineering

REMARKS: AG-153 tests navigation systems for SSBNs. AG-154, in reserve fleet since 29-9-72, tested ballistic missiles; plans call for her conversion and recommissioning as T-AGM-23 in support of Air Force missile programs. *Alacrity* (AG-520) and *Assurance* (AG-521) were stricken 30-9-77.

♦ *1 auxiliary deep-submergence support ship*

	L	In serv.
AGDS 2 POINT LOMA (ex-*Point Barrow,* AKD-1)	25-5-57	28-2-58

Point Loma (AGDS 2) as Point Barrow 1965

D: 9,415 tons (14,094 fl) **Dim:** 150.0 × 23.8 × 6.7
S: 18 kts **Man:** 160 men
M: GT; 2 props; 6,000 hp; 2 boilers

REMARKS: Built for Arctic supply and configured like a Dock Landing Ship (LSD). Served in MSC until 1972, in later years as a transport for Saturn rocket booster stages (hence white cover over dock in above photo). Converted 1974-75 to serve as mother ship to submersible *Trieste II,* recommissioning 30-5-75.

EXPERIMENTAL AUXILIARY SHIPS (*continued*)

♦ *1 auxiliary hydrofoil research ship* — Bldr: Lockheed, Seattle

	Laid down	L	In serv.
AGEH 1 PLAINVIEW	8-5-64	28-6-65	1-5-69

Plainview (AGEH 1)

D: 309 tons (fl) **Dim:** 67.1 × 12.3 × 3.0 (7.9 foils extended)
S: 50 kts **Man:** 4 officers, 16 men
A: 6/ASW TT Mk 32 (III × 2)
M: CODOG propulsion: 2 General Electric J-79 gas turbines; 2 props on fwd foils; 30,000 hp; 2 G.M. diesels; 2 retractable props; 1,200 hp

REMARKS: Remains a prototype, despite armament. Plans to increase speed to 80 kts by doubling power never carried out.

♦ *1 de Soto County-class patrol combatant support ship*

	Bldr	L	In serv.
AGHS 1178 WOOD COUNTY	American SB, Lorain	14-12-57	5-8-69

D: 4,164 tons (7,100 fl) **S:** 16.5 kts **Dim:** 135.7 × 18.9 × 5.3
A: 6/76-mm AA (II × 3) **Man:** . . .
M: 6 Cooper-Bessemer diesels; 2 controllable-pitch props; 13,700 hp

REMARKS: Former LST re-acquired from the Maritime Commission Reserve Fleet 12-15-76 to replace sister *Graham County* (AGP-1176) as small combatant tender in Mediterranean. As a result of the striking of the *Asheville* class and the reaffirmation of construction of all six of the *Pegasus* class PGH on 14-8-77, she will be converted (FY 78) to support the latter, using some equipment from *Graham County.*

Graham County (AGP 1176) with PG-98 (both now stricken) G. Arra, 1976

♦ *1 Haven-class hospital ship* — Bldr: Sun SB & DD, Chester, Pa.

	L	In serv.
AH 17 SANCTUARY	15-8-44	20-6-45

Sanctuary (AH 17) 1967

EXPERIMENTAL AUXILIARY SHIPS (*continued*)

D: 11,141 tons (15,100 fl) **S:** 18 kts **Dim:** 158.5 × 21.8 × 7.3
Man: 20 officers, 330 men plus 50/120 medical
M: General Electric GT; 1 prop; 9,000 hp; 2 boilers

REMARKS: In reserve fleet since 28-3-74. Built on C4-S-B2 cargo ship hull. Last of six sisters. Modified 15-12-71 to 18-11-72 as a "dependents' ship" for service at Piraeus, Greece, with shops, stores, recreation facilities, as well as a 74-bed sick bay. First (and only) U.S. Navy ship to include women in regular crew.

VARIOUS UNCLASSIFIED SHIPS

♦ *1 former medium harbor tug*

IX 505 (ex-YTM-759) (no name). Reclassified 9-11-76 as tender to NAVSEACTR, San Diego.

♦ *3 Benewah-class barracks craft* — Bldr: Boston NSY

	Laid down	L	In serv.
IX 502 MERCER (ex-APB-39)	25-8-44	17-11-44	19-9-45
IX 503 NUECES (ex-APB-40)	2-1-45	6-5-45	30-11-45
IX 504 ECHOLS (ex-APB-37)	. . .	30-7-45	1-1-47

D: 2,189 tons light (4,080 fl) **Dim:** 100.0 × 15.2 × 3.4
A: 8/40-mm AA (IV × 2) **S:** 10 kts
Man (when operational): 13 officers, 180 men plus 26/1,200 troops
M: 2 G.M. 12-267ATL diesels; 2 props; 1,600 hp

REMARKS: IX-502 and IX-503 recommissioned 1968 for service in Vietnam, placed back in reserve 1969-71; activated again in 1975 as barracks ships at Puget Sound NSY. IX-504, in reserve since completion in 1947, activated in 1976 as a barracks ship for *Ohio*-class SSBN crews at General Dynamics, Groton. *Kingman* (APB-47) stricken 1-10-77. *Benewah* to Philippines; nine others scrapped.

♦ *1 test range support ship (ex-LSMR)* — Bldr: Brown SB, Houston

	L	In serv.
IX 501 ELK RIVER (ex-LSMR-501)	21-4-45	27-5-45

Elk River (IX 501) 1968

D: 1,785 tons (fl) **Dim:** 70.0 × 15.2 × 2.8
S: 11 kts **Man:** 25 men plus 20 technicians
M: 2 G.M. 16-278A diesels; 2 props; 2,800 hp

REMARKS: Former fire-support rocket ship converted 1967-68 at Avondale Shipyards, Westwego, Louisiana, to act as support ship at the San Clemente Island Range for the Navy deep-submergence diving program. 2.4-m bulges were added to her hull sides and a center well cut for lowering equipment through the hull. The well is straddled by a 65-ton traveling gantry crane. Thrusters added to allow accurate dynamic mooring. Tests diving procedures, equipment, and small diving vehicles.

♦ *1 sonar test barge*

IX 310 (no name) Actually, two barges moored in Lake Seneca, New York; subordinated to the Naval Underwater Sound Laboratory, Newport, Rhode Island. In service in 1971. IX-309, Monob I, is now numbered YAG-61.

♦ *2 U.S. Army FS-class cargo ships* — Bldr: Higgins, New Orleans, 1944-45

IX 306 (ex-FS-221) (no name)
IX 308 NEW BEDFORD (ex-AKL-17, ex-FS-289)

D: 520 tons (906 to 935 fl) **S:** 10 kts
Dim: 53.8 × 10.1 × 3.1
A: 1/533-mm TT **M:** 2 G.M. diesels; 2 props; 1,000 hp

REMARKS: IX-306 acquired 1-69, operates at Atlantic Underwater Test and Evaluation Center (AUTEC) in the Bahamas. IX-308 acquired from the Army on 1-3-50 as a cargo ship. Converted 1963 as trials ship for Naval Torpedo Station, Keyport, Washington.

♦ *1 former Coast Guard inland buoy tender*

IX-307 BRIER (ex-WLI-299) (1943)

D: 178 tons (fl) **S:** 10.5 kts **Dim:** 32.8 × 7.8 × 1.6
M: 2 diesels, electric drive; 2 props; 600 hp

REMARK: Acquired 10-3-69, and used as instrumentation ship for testing explosives.

♦ *1 "3,000-ton" surface-effect ship*

	Bldr	Laid down	L	In serv.
N . . .	Rohr Marine, San Diego	1978	. . .	1981

Rohr 3,000-ton SES design 1977

VARIOUS UNCLASSIFIED SHIPS (*continued*)

D: 2,200 tons (3,000 fl) **S:** 80–100 kts **Dim:** 81.5 × 32.9 × . . .
A: See remarks **Man:** 125 men
M: 4 LM-2500A gas turbines; 4 pump-jets; 80,000 hp (plus 2 LM-2500A gas turbines to drive lift fans)

REMARKS: Rohr won a competition with Bell Aerospace to design and construct a prototype surface-effect ship of nearly 3,000 tons. Although it was originally to have been armed, the Secretary of Defense announced in 1977 that only limited military sensors and armament would be fitted — effectively making the ship into yet another systems prototype. The armament originally proposed included two SH-3 Sea King helicopters, 2/20-mm Vulcan/Phalanx Gatling AA guns, 6/Mk 32 ASW TT (III × 2), and four twin Harpoon launchers. The design has rigid side walls with flexible skirts fore and aft to trap the air-cushion "bubble."

♦ *1 Aerojet General prototype surface-effect ship*

	Bldr	In serv.
SES 100A	Tacoma Boatbuilding	7-72

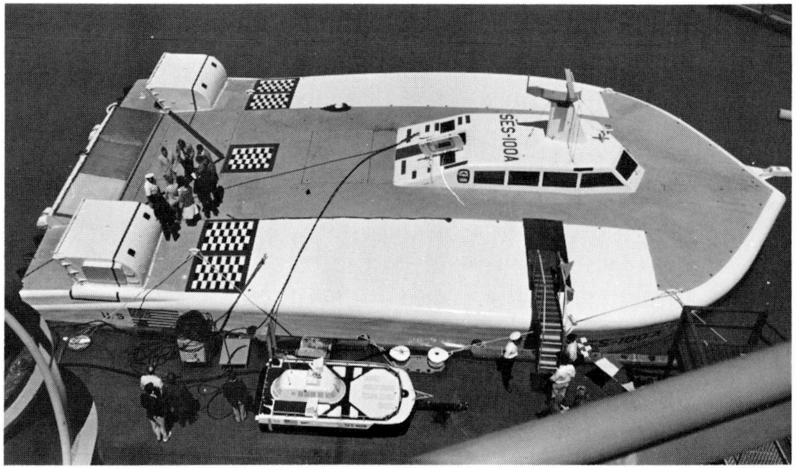

SES 100A (with SES 100B model in foreground) A.D. Baker, 1976

D: 100 tons **S:** 76 kts **Dim:** 25.0 × 12.5 × . . .
M: 4 Avco TF-35 gas turbines (12,000 hp) driving two water jets and 3 lift fans
Man: 1 officer, 3 men, plus 6 technicians

REMARKS: A rigid-side-wall design developed in competition with Bell's SES-100B. Can carry 10 tons of test equiptment.

♦ *1 Bell Aerospace prototype surface-effect ship*

	Bldr	In serv.
SES 100B	Bell, Michoud, Louisiana	2-72

D: 100 tons **S:** 82.3 kts **Dim:** 23.8 × 10.7 × . . .

SES 100B at 40 knots 1973

M: 3 Pratt & Whitney FT-12 gas turbines; 2 props; 13,500 hp (with United Aircraft of Canada ST-6J-70 gas turbines (1,500 hp) driving 8 lift fans)
Man: 1 officer, 3 men, plus 6 technicians

REMARKS: Employed in 1976 in trials with vertically launched Standard-ARM anti-ship missiles while under way at 80 kts.

♦ *1 SWATH (Small Waterplane Area, Twin Hull) prototype*

SSP 1 KAIMALINO — Bldr: U.S. Coast Guard, Curtis Bay, Maryland

D: 190 tons (fl) **S:** 25 kts **Dim:** 27.1 × 13.7 × . . .
M: 2 T-64 gas turbines; 2 props; 5,000 hp

REMARKS: Catamaran hull with cigar-shaped flotation pontoons. Helicopter deck. Operated by the Naval Ocean Systems Center, Hawaii Laboratory. The SWATH type shows great promise as an economical, high-performance/high-endurance ASW ship.

♦ *2 Asheville-class engineering trials ships* — Bldr: Tacoma Boatbuilding

	In serv.
ATHENA (ex-*Chehalis*, PG-94)	11-8-69
. . . (ex-*Grand Rapids*, PG-98)	9-5-70

D: 225 tons (235 fl) **S:** 40 kts **Dim:** 50.1 × 7.3 × 2.9
M: CODOG: 1 General Electric LM 1500 gas turbine (13,300 hp), 2 Cummins diesels (1,400 hp); 2 controllable-pitch props

REMARKS: These craft are considered to be "boats" and therefore do not have USN hull numbers. Operate from Mayport, Florida, for the Naval Ships Research & Development Center, Annapolis; civilian crews, disarmed. *Athena* reclassified 21-8-75; ex-PG-98 on 1-10-77.

VARIOUS UNCLASSIFIED SHIPS (*continued*)

♦ *2 Cove-class former inshore minesweepers* — Bldr: Bethlehem, Bellingham

	Laid down	L	In serv.
MSI 1 COVE	1-2-57	8-2-58	20-11-58
MSI 2 CAPE	1-5-57	5-4-58	27-2-59

Cape (MSI 2) 1959

D: 200 tons (240 fl) **S:** 12 kts **Dim:** 34.1 × 7.1 × 3.0
M: 2 G.M. diesels; 2 props; 650 hp **Man:** . . . (civilians)

REMARKS: Wooden construction; sweep gear removed. MSI-1 has been operated by the Applied Physics Laboratory of Johns Hopkins University since 31-7-70. MSI-2 serves the Naval Ocean Systems Center, San Diego. Sisters operate as minesweepers in the Iranian and Turkish navies.

♦ *4 deep-submergence research craft*

	Bldr	In serv.	Weight	Depth
DSV 1 TRIESTE II	Mare Island NSY	1966	84 tons	3,658 m
DSV 2 ALVIN	General Mills	1968	16 tons	3,658 m
DSV 3 TURTLE	Gen. Dynamics	1968	21 tons	1,980 m
DSV 4 SEA CLIFF	Gen. Dynamics	1968	21 tons	1,980 m

REMARKS: *Nemo* (DSV-5) is on loan to a private company. DSV-1 is carried and attended by *Point Loma* (AGDS-2).

SERVICE CRAFT

NOTE: As of 1 October 1977, the U.S. Navy had 859 active service craft, with another 210 in reserve or on loan or lease. Few service craft, other than waste-disposal barges and some open-hopper barges, are being built, and the majority of the force consists of craft built during World War II (exceptions being 81 large harbor tugs built 1959-75 to a standard design). Craft currently operational are listed below alphabetically by U.S. Navy hull type.
* = non-self-propelled

♦ 6 AFDB Large Auxiliary Floating Dry Dock* (1 active, in 3 sections)

♦ 9 AFDM Medium Auxiliary Floating Dry Docks* (3 active)

♦ 4 ARD Auxiliary Repair Docks* (3 active)

♦ 4 ARDM Medium Auxiliary Repair Docks* (all active)

♦ 16 Barracks craft* (12 active)

♦ 1 YAG Miscellaneous Auxiliary (active; this is YAG-1, Monob-I, ex-YW-87, used as a mobile noise barge)

♦ 218 YC Open Lighters* (194 active; YC-1517 to YC-1522 built 1976-77)

♦ 1 YCF Car Float* (active; for railroad cars)

♦ 6 YCV Aircraft Transportation Lighters* (all active)

♦ 72 YD Floating Cranes (60 active)

♦ 4 YDT Diving Tenders* (all active)

♦ 3 YF Covered Lighters (2 active)

♦ 6 YFB Ferry Boats (all active; ex-LCUs)

♦ 10 YFD Yard Floating Dry Docks* (1 active)

♦ 173 YFN Covered Lighters* (156 active)

♦ 19 YFNB Large Covered Lighters* (13 active)

♦ 5 YFND Dry Dock Companion Craft* (2 active)

♦ 10 YFNX Special Purpose Lighters* (9 active)

♦ 4 YFP Floating Power Barges* (all active; YFP-14 from Army, 1-10-77)

♦ 3 YFR Refrigerated Covered Lighters (none active)

♦ 4 YFRN Refrigerated Covered Lighters* (1 active)

♦ 6 YFRT Covered Lighters (Range Tenders) (4 active)

♦ 22 YFU Harbor Utility Craft (10 active; 10 are ex-LCUs)

♦ 7 YNG Garbage Lighters* (5 active)

♦ 2 YHLC Heavy Salvage Lift Craft* (none active)

♦ 8 YM Dredges* (all active)

♦ 2 YNG Gate Craft* (both active)

♦ 24 YO Fuel Oil Barges (13 active)

♦ 10 YOG Gasoline Barges (4 active; i.e., aircraft fuel)

♦ 10 YOGN Gasoline Barges* (all active; i.e., aircraft fuel)

♦ 53 YON Fuel Oil Barges* (48 active, 5 under construction)

♦ 12 YOS Oil Storage Barges* (11 active)

♦ 20 YP Patrol Craft (19 active; all used for maneuvering training)

♦ 6 YPD Floating Pile Drivers* (4 active)

SERVICE CRAFT *(continued)*

San Onofre (ARD 30) with YFND-27 alongside 1970

- ♦ 31 YR Floating Workshops* (21 active)
- ♦ 2 YRB Repair and Berthing Barges* (both active)
- ♦ 22 YRBM Repair, Berthing, and Messing Barges* (21 active)
- ♦ 4 YRDH Floating Dry Dock Workshops (Hull)* (1 active)
- ♦ 4 YRDM Floating Dry Dock Workshops (Machinery)* (2 active)
- ♦ 14 YRR Radiological Repair Barges* (all active)

YOG 89 (YO and YW nearly identical)

YP 668 1967

- ♦ 5 YRST Salvage Craft Tenders* (3 active)
- ♦ 8 YSD Seaplane Wrecking Derricks (all active; used as general-purpose self-propelled cranes)
- ♦ 25 YSR Sludge Removal Barges* (21 active)
- ♦ 81 YTB Large Harbor Tugs (all active)

D: 290 tons (350 fl) **S:** 12 kts **Dim:** 33.1 × 9.3 × 4.1
M: 2 diesels; 1 controllable-pitch prop; 2,000 hp

Nanticoke (YTB 803) 1970

SERVICE CRAFT (*continued*)

REMARKS: YTB-752 to YTB-836 have Indian tribal names. YTB-837 and YTB-838 of same class completed 1975 for Saudi Arabia.

♦ 23 YTL Small Harbor Tugs (6 active; unnamed)

♦ 69 YTM Medium Harbor Tugs (49 active; all but YTM-496 have Indian tribal names)

♦ 13 YW Water Barges (3 active)

♦ 8 YWN Water Barges* (7 active)

YR 26 1969

MILITARY SEALIFT COMMAND

This quasi-military organization was founded in 1949 as the Military Sea Transportation Service, and given its current name on 1-8-70. Its ships are unarmed, considered to be non-commissioned, and are manned by civilians: they are described below in the order of their hull type numbers. The prefix "T" is appended to the hull numbers of its ships, whose missions are fleet support, transportation of bulk military cargo, and scientific research and survey.

NOTE: MSC ships are painted gray (AGOR/AGS: white) and have blue and gold-yellow stack bands. They do *not* display hull numbers.

STORES SHIP

♦ *1 Rigel class* — Bldr: Ingalls, Pascagoula

	L	In serv.
T-AF-58 RIGEL	15-3-55	2-9-55

D: 7,950 tons (15,540 fl) **S:** 20 kts **Dim:** 153.0 × 22.0 × 8.8
M: G.E. GT; 1 prop; 16,000 hp; 2 Combustion Engineering boilers
Range: 11,000/18

REMARKS: 10,781 grt/8,112 dwt. Twelve 10-ton booms. Cargo: 5,975 cu. m. dry/5,400 cu. m. refrigerated. Provides fleet support.

Rigel (T-AF 58) 1968

HYDROGRAPHIC RESEARCH SHIP

♦ *1 Victory class* — Bldr: California SB Corp., 1-44

T-AG 164 KINGSPORT (ex-*Kingsport Victory*, AK-239)

Kingsport (T-AG 164) dome removed 1966

HYDROGRAPHIC RESEARCH SHIP *(continued)*

D: 7,190 tons light (10,680 fl) **Dim:** 138.7 × 18.9 × 6.7
S: 16.5 kts **Man:** 13 officers, 42 men, 15 technicians
M: GT; 1 prop; 8,500 hp; 2 boilers **Fuel:** 2,824 tons
Range: 20,000/16.5

REMARKS: 7,607 grt/6,123 dwt. Modified 1961-62 as a satellite communications relay ship; reassigned to hydrographic research 1966. Operated for Naval Electronics Systems Command. Helo deck aft.

RANGE INSTRUMENTATION SHIPS

NOTE: *Observation Island* (AG-154) now in reserve, is expected to be recommissioned and reconfigured as T-AGM-23.

♦ *1 converted Haskell-class former attack transport* — Bldr: Permanente Metals, Richmond, Cal.

T-AGM 22 RANGE SENTINEL (ex-*Sherburne*, APA-205) In serv. 20-9-44

D: 11,860 tons (fl) **S:** 15.5 kts **Dim:** 138.7 × 18.9 × 8.8
Man: 14 officers, 54 men, 27 technicians **Fuel:** 1,197 tons
M: GT; 1 prop; 8,500 hp; 2 boilers **Range:** 10,000/15.5

REMARKS: 8,306 grt/5,301 dwt. Converted 10-69 to 14-10-71 as support ship for the Poseidon (and later, Trident) program. "Victory" type hull and propulsion; forecastle deck now extends three-quarters of her length and she has four large tracking radars forward.

♦ *2 Vanguard class* — Bldr: Marine Ship, Sausalito, Cal.

T-AGM 19 VANGUARD (ex-*Muscle Shoals*, ex-*Mission San Fernando*) (1944)
T-AGM 20 REDSTONE (ex-*Johnstown*, ex-*Mission de Pala*) (1944)

Vanguard (T-AGM 19) 1967

D: 21,626 tons (fl) **S:** 16 kts **Dim:** 181.4 × 22.9 × 7.6
Man: T-AGM-19: 19 officers, 71 men, 108 technicians; T-AGM-20: 20/71/120
M: GT, electric drive; 1 prop; 10,000 hp; 2 boilers **Range:** 28,000/16
Fuel: T-AGM-19: 4,158 tons; T-AGM-20: 3,995 tons

REMARKS: 16,060 grt/16,255 dwt. Former T2-SE-A2-type tankers converted 1964-66 to serve as tracking and communications ships for NASA manned space flights; 22 meters added amidships. T-AGM-20 has a much larger forward superstructure than her sister. Third sister *Mercury* (T-AGM-21) stricken 1969 after very little use.

♦ *2 General H. H. Arnold class* — Bldr: Kaiser, Richmond, Cal.

	In serv.	Conv.
T-AGM 9 GENERAL H. H. ARNOLD (ex-*General R. E. Callan*, T-AP-139)	17-8-44	1963
T-AGM 10 GENERAL HOYT S. VANDENBERG (ex-*General Harry Taylor*, T-AP-145)	1-4-44	1963

General Hoyt S. Vandenberg (T-AGM 10)

D: 16,600 tons (fl) **S:** 17 kts **Dim:** 168.5 × 21.8 × 7.9
Man: 21 officers, 71 men, 113 technicians **Fuel:** 2,685 tons
M: GT; 1 prop; 9,000 hp; 2 boilers **Range:** 18,000/17

REMARKS: 12,848 grt/3,950 dwt; converted C4-S-Al-class troop transports, originally under Air Force but assigned to MSC in 7-64.

♦ *1 converted "Victory" class (VC2-S-AP3-type)* — Bldr: Oregon SB, Portland

	In serv.	Conv.
T-AGM 8 WHEELING (ex-*Seton Hall Victory*)	1944	1964

D: 10,680 tons (fl) **S:** 16.5 kts **Dim:** 138.7 × 18.9 × 8.8
Man: 13 officers, 46 men, 62 technicians **Fuel:** 2,824 tons
M: GT; 1 prop; 8,500 hp **Range:** 20,000/16.5

REMARKS: 8,319 grt/10,650 dwt. Now in ready reserve; only survivor of six "Victory"-class cargo ships converted to AGM. Hangar and flight deck for two helicopters.

OCEANOGRAPHIC RESEARCH SHIPS

♦ *2 Gyre class* — Bldr: Halter Marine, New Orleans

	Laid down	L	In serv.
AGOR 21 GYRE	9-10-72	7-6-73	14-11-73
AGOR 22 MOANA WAVE	9-10-72	23-6-73	16-1-74

D: 950 tons (1,190 fl) **S:** 12.5 kts **Dim:** 53.14 × 11.05 × 3.05
Man: 10 men plus 11 researchers
M: 2 Caterpillar diesels; 2 controllable-pitch props; 1,700 hp (plus 170 hp retractable maneuvering prop)

Remarks: Not under MSC control but listed here for simplicity; on completion, assigned to Texas A&M University and University of Hawaii. Modified oil-field supply ships using modular equipment vans on long open fantail.

♦ *1 converted Diver-class salvage ship* — Bldr: Basalt Rock Co., Napa, Cal.

	Laid down	L	In serv.	Conv.
AGOR 17 CHAIN (ex-ARS-20)	21-7-42	3-6-43	31-3-44	1958

D: 1,800 tons (2,100 fl) **S:** 14 kts **Dim:** 65.1 × 11.9 × 4.7
Man: 29 men plus 26 researchers
M: 4 Cooper-Bessemer GSB-8 diesels, electric drive; 2 props; 3,000 hp (plus 250-hp maneuvering motor)

Remarks: Under Navy control (not MSC), assigned to Woods Hole Oceanographic Institute, Massachusetts.

♦ *1 Hayes class* — Bldr: Todd SY, Seattle

	Laid down	L	In serv.
T-AGOR 16 HAYES	12-11-69	2-7-70	21-7-71

Hayes (T-AGOR 16) 1974

D: 3,080 tons (fl) **S:** 15 kts **Dim:** 75.1 (67.0 pp) × 22.9 × 6.6
Man: 11 officers, 33 men, 30 researchers **Range:** 6,000/13.5
Electric: 850 kw **Fuel:** 368 tons

Electron Equipt: Sonars: 1/3.5 kHz mapping, 1/16 kHz
M: 4 high-speed diesels; 2 controllable-pitch props; 5,400 hp (plus 2 165-hp diesels for low-speed operations, 2 to 4 kts)

Remarks: 3,677 grt/393 dwt. Catamaran, each hull 7.3-m beam. Suffered at first from severe pitching problems. Numerous equipment-handling gallows up to 15-ton capacity. Extremely well equipped.

♦ *2 Melville class* — Bldr: Defoe SB, Bay City, Mich.

	Laid down	L	In serv.
AGOR 14 MELVILLE	12-7-67	10-7-68	27-8-69
AGOR 15 KNORR	9-8-67	21-8-68	14-1-70

Melville (AGOR 14) 1970

D: 1,915 tons (2,080 fl) **S:** 12.5 kts
Dim: 74.7 (67.0 pp) × 14.1 × 4.6
Man: 9 officers, 16 men, 25 researchers **Range:** 10,000/12
M: 2 diesels; Voith-Schneider cycloidal props; 2,500 hp

Remarks: One vertical cycloidal propeller forward, larger unit aft; intended for precise maneuvering but, as mechanical rather than electric drive was used, have proven troublesome. AGOR-19 and AGOR-20 of this class therefore canceled. AGOR-14 and AGOR-15 under Navy control: the former operated by Scripps Institute, the latter by Woods Hole for Office of Naval Research.

♦ *7 Robert D. Conrad class*

	Bldr	L	In serv.
AGOR 3 ROBERT D. CONRAD	Gibbs, Jacksonville	26-5-62	29-11-62
T-AGOR 4 JAMES M. GILLIS	Christy Corp., Wisc.	19-5-62	5-11-62
T-AGOR 7 LYNCH	Marinette, Wisc.	17-3-65	27-3-65
AGOR 9 THOMAS G. THOMPSON	Marinette, Wisc.	18-7-64	24-8-65
AGOR 10 THOMAS WASHINGTON	Marinette, Wisc.	1-8-64	27-9-65
T-AGOR 12 DE STEIGUER	N.W. Marine, Portland	3-6-66	28-2-69
T-AGOR 13 BARTLETT	N.W. Marine, Portland	24-5-66	31-3-69

OCEANOGRAPHIC RESEARCH SHIPS (*continued*)

Thomas Washington (AGOR 10) 1965

De Steiguer (T-AGOR 12) 1969

D: 1,200 tons (1,380 fl) **S:** 13.5 kts **Dim:** 63.7 × 11.4 × 4.7
Man: 9 officers, 17 men, 18 researchers **Range:** 12,000/12
M: 2 Caterpillar diesels, electric drive; 1 prop; 1,000 hp **Fuel:** 211 tons

REMARKS: All civilian crews; 3 under Navy control, 4 under MSC. Assigned: AGOR-3: Lamont Geophysical Lab., Columbia U.; T-AGOR-4: U. of Miami for Navy research; T-AGOR-7: MSC for Oceanographer of the Navy; AGOR-9: U. of Washington for Navy; AGOR-10: Scripps Inst. of Oceanography; T-AGOR-12 and T-AGOR-13: MSC for Oceanographer of the Navy. Vary in details and paint (see photos). *Sands* (T-AGOR-6) on loan to Brazil, *Charles H. Davis* (T-AGOR-5) to New Zealand.

♦ *1 Eltanin class* — Bldr: Avondale Marine, New Orleans

	L	In serv.	Conv.
T-AGOR 11 MIZAR (ex-T-AK-272)	7-10-57	22-11-57	1962

Mizar (T-AGOR 11) J.C. Bellonne, 1971

D: 2,040 tons light (4,942 fl) **S:** 13 kts **Dim:** 79.9 × 15.7 × 6.9
Man: 11 officers, 30 men, 15 technicians **Range:** 14,000/12
M: 4 Alco diesels, Westinghouse motors; 2 props; 3,200 hp
Fuel: 675 tons

REMARKS: 2,486 grt/1,850 dwt. Former sister to *Mirfak* (T-AK-271). Operates for the Naval Electronics Command. Icebreaker hull; covered well on centerline for lowering equipment.

OCEAN SURVEILLANCE SHIPS

♦ *12 ships programmed* (*T-AGOS*) — Authorized: 3 in FY 79, 5 in FY 80, 4 in FY 81

D: 2,400 tons (fl) **S:** 15 kts **Dim:** 73.2 × 14.6 × 5.2
M: 2 G.M. diesels; 2 controllable-pitch props; 4,500 hp

REMARKS: Intended to perform ASW detection employing long towed passive sonar arrays (SURTASS), remaining at sea 300 days per year. Design based on that of the *Powhatan*-class tug (T-ATF-166 class).

SURVEYING SHIPS

♦ *1 converted cargo ship* (*C4-SA type*) — Bldr: National Steel, San Diego

	L	In serv.
T-AGS 38 H. H. HESS (ex-*Canada Mail*)	1965	1-3-77

D: . . . tons **S:** 20 kts **Dim:** 171.9 × 23.2 × 10.0
Man: . . . **Fuel:** 3,223 tons **Range:** 14,000/20
M: GT; 1 prop; 19,250 hp; 2 boilers

REMARKS: 12,440 grt/14,747 dwt. Acquired from Maritime Commission 9-7-75 for conversion to replace *Michelson* (T-AGS-23) in SSBN navigational support program.

♦ *2 Chauvenet class* — Bldr: Upper Clyde SB, Glasgow, G.B.

	Laid down	L	In serv.
T-AGS 29 CHAUVENET	24-5-67	13-5-68	13-11-70
T-AGS 32 HARKNESS	30-6-67	12-6-68	29-1-71

D: 4,200 tons (fl) **S:** 15 kts **Dim:** 119.8 (101.8 pp) × 16.5 × 4.9
Man: 13 officers, 150 men, 12 scientists **Fuel:** 824 tons
M: 2 Alco diesels, Westinghouse motor; 1 controllable-pitch prop; 3,600 hp
Range: 15,000/12

SURVEYING SHIPS (*continued*)

Chauvenet (T-AGS 29) 1971

REMARKS: 2,890 grt/1,030 dwt. Can carry four small survey launches; hangar and flight deck for two helicopters. Operated for the Oceanographer of the Navy; some naval personnel aboard.

♦ *4 Silas Bent class (SCB 226 type)*

	Bldr	L	In serv.
T-AGS 26 SILAS BENT	American SB, Lorain	16-5-64	23-7-65
T-AGS 27 KANE	Christy, Sturgeon Bay	20-11-65	19-5-67
T-AGS 33 WILKES	Defoe, Bay City, Mich.	31-7-69	28-6-71
T-AGS 34 WYMAN	Defoe, Bay City, Mich.	30-10-69	3-11-71

Wilkes (T-AGS 33) 1971

D: 1,935 tons (2,420 to 2,558 fl) **Dim:** 86.9 × 14.6 × 4.6
S: 15 kts **Man:** 12 officers, 35 men, 30 scientists
Range: 14,000/15 **Fuel:** 461 tons
M: 2 Alco diesels, Westinghouse motor; controllable-pitch prop; 3,600 hp (plus 350-hp bow propulsor)

REMARKS: Operated for Oceanographer of the Navy. T-AGS-33 has been in ready reserve since shortly after completion.

♦ *2 Bowditch class* (*converted Victory-class cargo ships*) — Bldr: Oregon SB, Portland, South Coast Co.

	L	Conv.
T-AGS 21 BOWDITCH (ex-*South Bend Victory*)	7-45	30-9-58
T-AGS 22 DUTTON (ex-*Tuskegee Victory*)	6-45	16-11-58

Dutton (T-AGS 22)

D: 14,512 tons (fl) **S:** 16.5 kts **Dim:** 138.7 × 18.9 × 7.6
Man: 14 officers, 47 men, 40 technicians **Fuel:** 2,824 tons
M: GT; 1 prop; 8,500 hp; 2 boilers **Range:** 20,000/16.5

REMARKS: 7,783 grt/8,350 dwt. Converted to support SSBN program. Sister *Michelson* (T-AGS-23) stricken 1975.

CARGO SHIPS

♦ *1 Andromeda class* — Bldr: Moore DD, Oakland

	L	In serv.
T-AK 283 WYANDOT (ex-T-AKA-92)	28-6-44	30-9-44

D: 7,430 tons light (14,000 fl) **Dim:** 140.0 × 19.2 × 7.3
S: 16.5 kts **M:** G.E. GT; 1 prop; 6,000 hp; 2 boilers

REMARKS: Built as an attack cargo ship. Winterized for Arctic service; renumbered T-AK-283 in 1969. In Maritime Administration Reserve.

♦ *4 Norwalk class* — Bldr: Oregon SB, Portland (T-AK-281: Permanente, Richmond, Cal.)

CARGO SHIPS *(continued)*

	L	Conv.
T-AK 279 NORWALK (ex-*Norwalk Victory*)	8-45	30-12-63
T-AK 280 FURMAN (ex-*Furman Victory*)	4-45	7-10-64
T-AK 281 VICTORIA (ex-*Ethiopia Victory*)	7-44	15-10-65
T-AK 282 MARSHFIELD (ex-*Marshfield Victory*)	6-44	28-5-70

Norwalk (T-AK 279) N. Friedman, 1976

D: 6,700 tons light (11,150 fl) **S:** 16.5 kts
Dim: 138.7 × 18.9 × 7.3
Man: 80 to 90 men **Fuel:** 2,824 tons **Range:** 20,000/16.5
M: GT; 1 prop; 8,500 hp; 2 boilers

REMARKS: 7,491 grt/9,649 dwt. Hold No. 3 accommodates 16 vertically stowed Poseidon SLBM. Ships support SSBN activities. Carry torpedoes, submarine spares etc.; also carry 18,000 barrels cargo fuel (7,566 bbl diesel/10,434 bbl fuel oil). 40-ton cargo booms. Small Navy security detachment aboard.

♦ *1 C3-S-DX1 type, 1-51*

T-AK 277 SCHUYLER OTIS BLAND

D: 15,910 tons (fl) **S:** 18.5 kts **Dim:** 145.7 × 20.1 × 9.1
M: G.T.; 1 prop; 13,750 hp; 2 boilers
Range: 12,000/18.5 **Fuel:** 2,208 tons

REMARKS: 8,918 grt/10,516 dwt. Cargo: 15,066 cu. m. dry cargo, 76,000 barrels liquid. In reserve as of 1-1-77. Prototype for later Mariner class.

♦ *1 Eltanin class (C1-M-E2-13a type)*

T-AK 271 MIRFAK — Bldr: Avondale, New Orleans — L: 5-8-57

D: 2,036 tons light (4,942 fl) **Dim:** 79.9 × 15.7 × 5.7
S: 13 kts **Man:** 48 men
Range: 14,000/13 **Fuel:** 612 tons
M: Alco diesels, Westinghouse motors; 2 props; 3,200 hp

REMARKS: 2,486 grt/1,850 dwt. Icebreaker hull for Arctic operations. Cargo: 2,634 cu. m. dry/2,350 cu. m. refrigerated. Sister *Eltanin* (AGOR-8) loaned to Argentina. *Mizar* (ex-T-AK-272) is now T-AGOR-11.

♦ *5 Victory class (VC2-S-AP3 and AP2 types)*

	L
T-AK 237 GREENVILLE VICTORY	7-44
T-AK 240 PVT. JOHN R. TOWLE (ex-*Appleton Victory*)	3-45
T-AK 242 SGT. ANDREW MILLER (ex-*Radcliffe Victory*)	4-45
T-AK 254 SGT. TRUMAN KIMBRO (ex-*Hastings Victory*)	12-44
T-AK 274 LT. JAMES E. ROBINSON (ex-T-AG-170, ex-T-AK-174 ex-AKV-3, ex-*Czechoslovakia Victory*)	3-44

D: 6,700 tons light (12,450 fl) **S:** 17 kts (T-AK-254: 15)
Dim: 138.7 × 18.9 × 8.9 **Fuel:** 2,824 tons
M: GT; 1 prop; 8,500 hp (T-AK-254: 6,000 hp); 2 boilers
Range: 20,000/16.5

REMARKS: 7,607 grt/10,681 dwt. All in Maritime Administration Reserve Fleet, remaining on Navy list. Cargo: approx. 12,600 cu. m. dry cargo (varies). T-AK-254 is a VC2-S-AP2 type. T-AK-274 was the second Victory ship to be completed.

♦ *1 CA-S-B1 type*

T-AK 255 PVT. LEONARD C. BROSTROM (ex-*Marine Eagle*), 1-43

D: . . . **S:** 17 kts **Dim:** 158.5 × 21.8 × 10.1
Man: 14 officers, 43 men **Fuel:** 2,052 tons
M: GT; 1 prop; 9,000 hp; 2 boilers **Range:** 10,000/15.8

REMARKS: 11,164 grt/13,504 dwt. Cargo: 19,512 cu.m. dry cargo plus 38,000 barrels fuel oil. Heavy-lift ship, with 150-ton boom capacity.

VEHICLE CARGO SHIPS

♦ *1 chartered ship* — Bldr: Sun SB & DD, Chester, Pa., 17-10-67

AKR . . . ADMIRAL WILLIAM M. CALLAGHAN

D: 24,500 tons (fl) **S:** 26 kts **Dim:** 211.5 × 28.0 × 8.8
M: 2 G.E. LM-2500 gas turbines; 2 props; 50,000 hp

REMARKS: On charter since completion and never officially put on Navy list, hence no number. Can carry 750 military vehicles, with Ro-Ro loading/unloading via stern ramp and four side ramps.

♦ *1 Meteor class (C4-ST-67a type)* — Bldr: Puget Sound Bridge & DD

	Laid down	L	In serv.
T-AKR 9 METEOR (ex-*Sea Lift*)	19-5-64	18-4-64	25-5-67

D: 11,130 tons light (21,700 fl) **Dim:** 164.7 × 25.5 × 8.8
S: 20 kts **Man:** 62 men
Fuel: 2,511 tons **Range:** 10,000/20
M: GT; 2 props; 19,400 hp; 2 boilers

REMARKS: 16,467 grt/12,326 dwt. Cargo: 26,819 cu.m. vehicle parking volume. Stern and four side ramps for Ro-Ro loading/unloading. Can carry 12 passengers.

VEHICLE CARGO SHIPS (*continued*)

Meteor (T-AKR 9) 1968

♦ *1 Comet class* (*C3-ST-14A type*) — Bldr: Sun SB & DD, Chester, Pa.

	Laid down	L	In serv.
T-AKR 7 COMET	15-5-56	31-7-57	27-1-58

D: 7,605 tons light (18,150 fl) **Dim:** 152.1 × 23.8 × 8.9
S: 18 kts **Man:** 73 men
Fuel: 2,423 tons **Range:** 12,000/18
M: G.E. GT; 2 props; 13,200 hp; 2 boilers

REMARKS: 13,792 grt/10,111 dwt. Cargo: over 700 military vehicles in holds totaling 19,370 cu.m. volume. Side and stern ramps. Denny-Brown fin stabilizers. Similar to *Meteor,* but smaller.

OILERS

♦ *4 Falcon class* — Bldr: Ingalls SB, Pascagoula, Mississippi

	L	In serv.
T-AO 182 COLUMBIA (ex-*Falcon Lady*)	1971	15-1-76
T-AO 183 NECHES (ex-*Falcon Duchess*)	1971	11-2-76
T-AO 184 HUDSON (ex-*Falcon Princess*)	1972	23-4-76
T-AO 185 SUSQUEHANNA (ex-*Falcon Countess*)	1972	11-5-76

D: 42,000 tons (fl) **S:** 16.5 kts **Dim:** 204.9 × 27.1 × 11.0
Man: . . . men **Fuel:** 2,620 tons **Range:** 16,000/16.5

REMARKS: 20,571 grt/37,276 dwt. Cargo: 310,000 barrels fuels.

♦ *1 Potomac class* — Bldr: Ingalls SB, Pascagoula, Miss.

	Laid down	In serv.
T-AO 181 POTOMAC (ex-*Shenandoah,* ex-*Potomac,* T-AO-150)	9-6-55	1-57

D: 35,000 tons (fl) **S:** 18 kts **Dim:** 189.0 × 25.5 × 10.4
Man: . . . men **Fuel:** 4,321 tons
M: GT; 1 prop; 20,460 hp; 2 boilers **Range:** 18,000/18

REMARKS: 15,739 grt/27,467 dwt. Cargo: 200,000 barrels fuel plus 878 cu.m. dry cargo. Originally a unit of the *Maumee* class, she was heavily damaged in 1961. Rebuilt (only stern salvaged) and operated on charter to MSC as *Shenandoah* from 1964 until taken over in 1976.

♦ *9 Sealift class* — Bldrs: First four: Todd, Los Angeles; others: Bath Iron Works

	L	In serv.
T-AO 168 SEALIFT PACIFIC	13-10-73	14-8-74
T-AO 169 SEALIFT ARABIAN SEA	26-1-74	6-5-75
T-AO 170 SEALIFT CHINA SEA	20-4-74	9-5-75
T-AO 171 SEALIFT INDIAN OCEAN	27-7-74	29-8-74
T-AO 172 SEALIFT ATLANTIC	26-1-74	26-8-74
T-AO 173 SEALIFT MEDITERRANEAN	9-3-74	6-11-74
T-AO 174 SEALIFT CARIBBEAN	8-6-74	10-2-75
T-AO 175 SEALIFT ARCTIC	31-8-74	22-5-75
T-AO 176 SEALIFT ANTARCTIC	26-10-74	1-8-75

Sealift Pacific (T-AO 168) 1974

D: 33,000 tons (fl) **Dim:** 178.9 (170.8 pp) × 25.6 × 10.5
S: 16 kts **Man:** 10 officers, 20 men, 2 cadets
Range: 12,000/16 **Fuel:** 3,444 tons
M: 2 Colt-Pielstick 14-cyl., 520-rpm diesels; 1 controllable-pitch prop; 14,000 hp

REMARKS: 17,157 grt/27,217 dwt (vary slightly). Cargo: 225,000 barrels fuel oil, diesel, etc. Equipped with bow-thruster. MSC chartered these ships for 20 years and has commercial contractors operating them.

OILERS (*continued*)

♦ *1 American Explorer class (T5-S-RM2A type)* — Bldr: Ingalls, Pascagoula

	Laid down	L	In serv.
T-AO 165 AMERICAN EXPLORER	9-7-57	11-5-58	27-10-59

D: 30,000 tons (fl) **S:** 20 kts **Dim:** 187.5 × 24.4 × 9.8
Man: 53 men **Fuel:** 3,482 tons
M: GT; 1 prop; 22,000 hp; 2 boilers **Range:** 14,000/20

REMARKS: 14,984 grt/24,226 dwt. Cargo: 174,000 barrels fuel oil, diesel, etc. plus 878 cu.m. dry cargo. Commercial operator.

♦ *3 Maumee class (T5-S-12A type)*

	Bldr	Laid down	L	In serv.
T-AO 149 MAUMEE	Ingalls SB	8-3-55	16-2-56	12-56
T-AO 151 SHOSHONE	Sun SB, Chester	15-8-55	17-1-57	4-57
T-AO 152 YUKON	Ingalls SB	16-5-55	16-3-56	5-57

D: 32,000 tons (fl) **S:** 18 kts **Dim:** 189.0 × 25.5 × 9.8
Man: 62 men **Fuel:** 4,321 tons
M: GT; 1 prop; 20,460 hp; 2 boilers **Range:** 18,000/18

REMARKS: 15,626 grt/26,943 dwt. Cargo: 187,000 barrels fuel oil, diesel, etc., plus 878 cu.m. dry cargo. T-AO-149 has ice-reinforced bow. Sister *Potomac* (T-AO-150, now T-AO-181) rebuilt to different design.

♦ *1 Neosho class* — Bldr: New York SB, Camden, N.J.

	L	In serv.
T-AO 144 MISSISSINEWA	12-6-54	18-1-55

REMARKS: Data as for naval sisters; disarmed. Transferred to MSC on 15-11-76; other units of the class may follow. Still capable of underway replenishment; fleet support unit.

♦ *5 Mispillion class (jumboized T3-S2-A3 type)* — Bldr: Sun SB, Chester, Pa.

	L	In serv.
T-AO 105 MISPILLION	10-8-45	29-12-45
T-AO 106 NAVASOTA	30-8-45	27-2-46
T-AO 107 PASSUMPSIC	31-10-45	1-4-46
T-AO 108 PAWCATUCK	19-2-46	10-5-46
T-AO 109 WACCAMAW	30-3-46	25-6-46

Waccamaw (T-AO 109) 1976

D: 11,000 tons light (33,750/34,179 fl) **Dim:** 196.9 × 22.9 × 10.8
S: 16 kts **Man:** . . . **Fuel:** 2,250 tons
M: GT; 2 props; 13,500 hp; 4 boilers (30 kg/cm², 380°C)

REMARKS: 19,294 grt/23,250 dwt. Cargo: 107,000 barrels fuel oil, diesel, etc. plus dry cargo. Transferred from Navy beginning in 1973. Fleet support units, intended for underway replenishment. Disarmed (had 4/76-mm single). Helo deck forward.

♦ *2 Cimarron class (T3-S2-A1 type)* — Bldr: Bethlehem, Sparrows Point, Md.

	L	In serv.
T-AO 57 MARIAS	21-12-43	12-2-44
T-AO 62 TALUGA	10-7-44	25-8-44

Marias (T-AO 57) 1975

D: 24,450 tons (fl) **S:** 18 kts **Dim:** 168.6 × 22.9 × 10.1
Man: . . . **Fuel:** 2,205 tons
M: GT; 2 props; 13,500 hp; 4 Babcock & Wilcox boilers (30 kg/cm², 380°C)

REMARKS: 12,000 grt/18,400 dwt. Cargo: 87,000 barrels fuel oil, diesel, etc. Transferred from Navy 2-10-73 and 4-5-72. Fleet support units, intended for underway replenishment.

♦ *4 Suamico class (T2-SE-A1 type)* — Bldr: Sun SB, Chester, Pa.

	L	In serv.
T-AO 50 TALLULAH (ex-*Valley Forge*)	25-6-42	5-9-42
T-AO 73 MILLICOMA (ex-*Conestoga*, ex-*King's Mountain*)	21-1-43	5-3-43
T-AO 75 SAUGATUCK (ex-*Newton*)	7-12-42	19-2-43
T-AO 76 SCHUYLKILL (ex-*Louisburg*)	16-2-43	9-4-43

D: 5,730 tons light (22,380 fl) **S:** 15 kts
Dim: 159.6 (153.3 pp) × 20.7 × 9.2
Man: . . . **Range:** 13,000/14.5 **Fuel:** 1,455 tons
M: GT, electric drive; 1 prop; 6,000 hp; 2 boilers

REMARKS: 10,296 grt/16,500 dwt (vary). Cargo: 141,000 barrels fuel oil, etc. All in reserve, having been replaced in 1975 by Sealift-class tankers.

GASOLINE TANKERS

♦ *3 Peconic class (T1-M-BT2 type)* — Bldr: Todd SY, Houston

	L	In serv.
T-AOG 77 RINCON (ex-*Tarland*)	5-1-45	1-7-50
T-AOG 78 NODAWAY (ex-*Belridge*)	15-5-45	7-9-50
T-AOG 79 PETALUMA (ex-*Raccoon Bend*)	9-8-45	7-9-50

D: 2,060 tons light (6,000 fl) **Dim:** 99.1 × 14.7 × 5.8
S: 10 kts **Range:** 6,000/10 **Fuel:** 154 tons
M: 2 diesels; 1 prop; 1,400 hp

REMARKS: 3,160 grt/3,933 dwt. Cargo: 31,000 barrels light fuels (diesel, JP-5, gasoline). Two sisters now scrapped.

CABLE SHIPS

NOTE: Two units of a new class of cable ships to be manned by the MSC are to be requested under the FY 79 and FY 80 budgets. In addition, the Canadian Coast Guard's icebreaking cable-layer *Cabot* is frequently chartered by the U.S. Navy.

♦ *2 Neptune class (S3-S2-BP1 type)* — Bldr: Pusey & Jones, Wilmington, Delaware

	L	In serv.
T-ARC 2 NEPTUNE (ex-*Wm. H. G. Bullard*)	1945	1-6-53
T-ARC 6 ALBERT J. MEYER	1945	13-5-63

D: 7,080 tons (fl) **Dim:** 112.8 (98.1 pp) × 14.3 × 5.5
S: 14 kts **Man:** . . . **Range:** 10,000/12.5
Fuel: 1,129 tons (T-ARC-2: 980)
M: 2 Skinner Uniflow reciprocating steam; 2 props; 4,800 hp; 2 boilers

REMARKS: T-ARC-2: 3,929 grt/2,000 dwt; T-ARC-6: 4,012 grt/4,332 dwt. Differ in detail. Last reciprocating steam-propelled ships in USN/MSC service. T-ARC-2 to MSC from Navy 8-11-73. T-ARC-6 from U.S. Army in 1953. T-ARC-2 has a helicopter deck aft; T-ARC-6 does not. Both have been modernized.

♦ *1 Aeolus class (converted S4-SE2-BE1 attack cargo ship)*
Bldr: Walsh Kaiser, Providence, R.I.

	L	In serv.	Conv.
T-ARC 3 AEOLUS (ex-*Turandot*, AKA-47)	1945	18-6-45	14-5-55

Aeolus (T-ARC 3) 1970

D: 7,080 tons (fl) **Dim:** 133.5 (121.9 pp) × 17.7 × 5.9
S: 16.9 kts **Man:** . . . **Range:** 9,000/15
Fuel: 1,407 tons
M: GT, electric drive; 2 props; 6,000 hp; 2 Wickes boilers (30 kg/cm^2)

REMARKS: 6,063 grt/2,958 dwt. Converted by Bethlehem Steel to cable-layer 1955-56. Sister *Thor* (T-ARC-4) stricken 17-7-75, transferred to Maritime Commission and placed in reserve. T-ARC-3 is in poor condition but must be retained until the projected FY 79 ship is completed.

FLEET TUGS

♦ *7 Powhatan class* — Bldr: Marinette Marine, Wisconsin

	Laid down	L	In serv.
T-ATF 166 POWHATAN	30-9-76	. . .	7-78
T-ATF 167 NARRAGANSETT	. . .	. . .	. . .
T-ATF 168 CATAWBA	. . .	. . .	. . .
T-ATF 169 NAVAJO	. . .	. . .	. . .
T-ATF 170 N . . .	. . .	. . .	. . .
T-ATF 171 N . . .	. . .	. . .	. . .
T-ATF 172 N . . .	. . .	. . .	. . .

Authorized: 1 in FY 75, 3 in FY 76, 3 in FY 78

D: 2,000 tons (2,400 fl) **S:** 15 kts
Dim: 73.2 (68.9 pp) × 12.8 × 4.6
Man: 4 officers, 12 men, plus 4 Navy communications team
M: 2 G.M. diesels; 2 kort-nozzle, controllable-pitch props; 4,500 hp

REMARKS: Modified oil-field supply-boat design built to merchant marine specifications. If required, could mount 2/20-mm AA (I × 2) and 2/12.7-mm machine guns (I × 2). Five were requested under FY 78, three approved. Five will probably be requested under FY 79. Later units may be Navy-manned. This class has been subjected to serious delays because of a strike at the shipyard; only one had been laid down by 1-9-77.

♦ *4 Cherokee and Achomawi classes*

	Bldr	L	In serv.
T-ATF 76 UTE	United Eng., Alameda, Cal.	24-6-42	31-12-42
T-ATF 85 LIPAN	United Eng., Alameda, Cal.	17-9-42	29-4-43
T-ATF 149 ATAKAPA	Charleston SB, S. Carolina	11-7-44	8-12-44
T-ATF 158 MOSOPELEA	Charleston SB, S. Carolina	7-3-45	28-7-45

REMARKS: Data as for *Abnaki* and *Achomawi* classes of ATF in Navy section, except that T-ATF-76 and T-ATF-85 have G.M. 12-278A diesels. ATF-85 and ATF-158 to MSC in 7-73, others in 1974. Will probably be stricken when the *Powhatan* class becomes available.

COAST GUARD

GENERAL

The Revenue Marine, which was created in 1790, became the Coast Guard on 28 January 1915 by act of Congress. Until 1 April 1967 the Coast Guard was part of the Department of the Treasury; at that time it was transferred to the Department of

Transportation. The act that created the service calls for it to operate in time of crisis under the control of the Navy. The principal responsibilities of the Coast Guard are:
— preparation and training for combat in cooperation with the Navy;
— enforcement of the laws of the sea and the policing of navigation;
— control of territorial waters, suppression of smuggling, and policing and assisting the fishing industry;
— surveillance of the coasts and protection of access to ports and bases;
— search and rescue at sea, including transocean air routes;
— manning and maintaining aids to navigation: lighthouses, beacons, buoys, lightships, and Loran stations (46,000 in all);
— control of piloting and the investigation of accidents at sea;
— control of the safety and seaworthiness aspects of shipbuilding;
— international ice patrols (keeping track of drifting icebergs);
— protection of offshore oil installations;
— pollution control and protection of the environment;
— meteorologic, oceanographic, and hydrographic surveying.

The Coast Guard played an active part in the war in Vietnam (patrolling the coasts, inspecting junks, protecting convoys, port security, maritime salvage, and shore fire support).

ORGANIZATION

The Coast Guard is divided into two main components, one for the Pacific and one for the Atlantic. Each of these area commands is headed by a rear admiral. Just as the Navy is divided into Naval Districts, the Coast Guard is further divided into twelve Coast Guard Districts in order to fulfill its responsibilities along the U.S. coastline (more than 10,000 nautical miles, not including Hawaii).

A four-star admiral heads the Coast Guard. He is appointed for four years and is assisted by a general staff, whose headquarters are in the Department of Transportation building. The commandant reports to the Secretary of Transportation and not the Joint Chiefs of Staff.

COMPOSITION OF THE FLEET

Coast Guard patrol ships have their names preceded by USCGC (United States Coast Guard Cutter). Cutters and patrol craft are white, icebreakers have red hulls, buoy tenders, black. All ships carry a diagonal red stripe and the USCG shield on the hull.

As of 1-10-77 the seagoing USCG fleet was composed of the following:

♦ *19 high-endurance cutters* (WHEC):
12 *Hamilton* class, 3,050 tons (fl)
6 Secretary class, 2,656 tons (fl) (1 in reserve)
1 Casco class, 2,800 tons (fl)

♦ *23 medium-endurance cutters* (WMEC) from 860 to 1,745 tons (fl)

♦ *7 icebreakers* (WAGB)

♦ *22 patrol boats* (WPB), 105-tons (fl)

♦ *53 Point-class patrol boats,* 67 to 69 tons (fl)

♦ *29 tugs* (WYTM and WYTL)

♦ *3 oceanographic research ships* (WAGO)

♦ *53 seagoing buoy tenders* (WLB and WLM)

♦ *36 inland and river buoy tenders* (WLI and WLR)

♦ *14 construction tenders* (WLI)

♦ *2 officer training ships* (WIX)

♦ *1 reserve training ship* (WTR)

♦ *3 lightships* (WLV)

AVIATION

The USCG operates 64 fixed-wing aircraft and 117 helicopters: 34 HC-130 Hercules, 18 HU-16 Albatross amphibians, 1 VC-4A Gulfstream I, and 11 VC-11A Gulfstream II transports, 38 HH-3F Pelican (Sea King variant), and 79 HH-52A Sea Guard rescue helicopters.

PROJECTS

A program to rejuvenate the Coast Guard so that it will be able to meet its new commitments covers the period 1977–1986 and includes plans to construct:
— 11 to 25 *Bear*-class WMEC, 1,722 tons (fl)
— 10 *Katmai Bay*-class icebreaking tugs (WYTM), 662 tons (fl)

Plans to build up to 30 33-meter patrol boats have been canceled in favor of modernizing the Cape class.

A contract was announced in January 1977 to construct 41 twin-jet patrol aircraft of the Falcon-20G type, a license-built Dassault-Bréguet Mystère-20. The Air Force is transferring a number of mothballed Convair-240 piston-engined transports to act as patrol aircraft to replace worn-out HU-16 Albatross amphibians.

The Coast Guard's expanded role in patrolling out to a 200-mile limit may require even more ships than the projected WMECs. The new ships could be equipped with towed passive sonar arrays (like SQR 15 or SQR 19) to allow participation in ASW patrol as well.

HIGH-ENDURANCE CUTTERS

♦ *12 378-ft Hamilton class*

Bldr: Avondale Shipyards, Westwego, Louisiana

	Laid down	L	In serv.
WHEC 715 HAMILTON	1-65	18-12-65	20-2-67
WHEC 716 DALLAS	2-66	1-10-66	1-10-67
WHEC 717 MELLON	7-66	11-2-67	22-12-67
WHEC 718 CHASE	10-66	20-5-67	1-3-68
WHEC 719 BOUTWELL	12-66	17-6-67	14-6-68
WHEC 720 SHERMAN	2-67	23-9-67	23-8-68
WHEC 721 GALLATIN	4-67	18-11-67	20-12-68
WHEC 722 MORGENTHAU	7-67	10-2-68	14-2-69
WHEC 723 RUSH	10-67	16-11-68	3-7-69
WHEC 724 MUNRO	2-70	5-12-70	10-9-71
WHEC 725 JARVIS	9-70	24-4-71	30-12-71
WHEC 726 MIDGETT	4-71	4-9-71	17-3-72

D: 2,716 tons (3,050 fl) **S:** 29 kts (19 cruising)
Dim: 115.2 (106.7 pp) × 13.0 × 6.1 **Man:** 15 officers, 149 men
A: 1/127-mm 38-cal, semi-automatic — 2/20-mm — 2/12.7-mm machine guns — 6 ASW TT Mk 32 (III × 2)
Electron Equipt: Radars: SPS 64 surface-search, SPS 29 air-search, Mk 56 gun fire-control system
Sonar: SQS 38
Range: 2,300/29, 9,600/19 on gas turbines **Electric:** 1,500 kw

HIGH-ENDURANCE CUTTERS *(continued)*

Morgenthau (WHEC 722) with "40-foot utility boat" in foreground A.D. Baker, 1976

Midgett (WHEC 726) 1972

M: CODOG propulsion: 2/12-cyl. Fairbanks-Morse diesels, each of 3,500 hp; 2 Pratt & Whitney FT 4A gas turbines, each 18,000 hp; 2 props; 36,000 hp

REMARKS: Remote-control, variable-pitch propellers, 3.90 m in diameter. Same gas turbines as B-52, F-105, and Boeing 707 aircraft. A single 1.20-m-diameter, 360-degree, trainable bow propeller linked to a 350-hp electric motor, used for close-quarters maneuvering at slow speeds, retracts into the hull. Bilge keels. Helicopter platform, 26.82 × 12.20 m, carried; weather balloon shelter at forward end of flight deck is used as a helicopter shop/storage area when a helicopter is embarked. An HH-52A turboshaft helicopter (8 passengers) can be carried. Living spaces air-conditioned. Laboratories for weather and oceanographic research. Welded hull; aluminum superstructure. Named after secretaries of the Treasury and Coast Guard heroes. Thirty-six planned, only twelve built.

♦ *6 327-ft Secretary class*

	Bldr	Laid down	L	In serv.
WHEC 31 BIBB	Charleston NSY	18-5-35	14-1-37	19-3-37
WHEC 32 CAMPBELL	Philadelphia NSY	1-5-35	3-6-36	22-10-36
WHEC 33 DUANE	Philadelphia NSY	1-5-35	3-6-36	16-10-36
WHEC 35 INGHAM	Philadelphia NSY	1-5-35	3-6-36	6-11-36
WHEC 36 SPENCER	New York NSY	11-9-35	6-1-37	13-5-37
WHEC 37 TANEY	Philadelphia NSY	1-5-35	3-6-36	19-12-36

Taney (WHEC 37) with weather radome 1973

Duane (WHEC 33) 1968

HIGH-ENDURANCE CUTTERS (*continued*)

D: 2,216 tons (2,656 fl) **Dim:** 99.7 (94.2 wl) × 12.6 × 4.6
S: 19.8 kts **Man:** 13 officers, 131 men
Range: 4,000/18, 8,000/12.5, 12,300/11
A: 1/127-mm 38-cal semi-automatic — 2/20-mm AA **Fuel:** 572 tons
Electron Equipt: Radars: SPS 53, SPS 29, Mk 52 gun fire-control system
Sonar: SQS 36A
M: Westinghouse GT; 2 props; 6,200 hp **Boilers:** 2 Babcock & Wilcox

REMARKS: WHEC-36 has been in reserve since 1-2-74. WHEC-37 has a dome above her bridge for WSR-S1 weather radar.

♦ *1 Casco class*

	Laid down	L	In serv.
WHEC 379 UNIMAK (ex-WTR, ex-WHEC, ex-AVP-31)	12-2-42	27-5-43	31-12-43

Bldr: Associated SB, Seattle

D: 1,766 tons (2,800 fl) **Dim:** 94.70 (94.63 wl) × 12.52 × 3.65
S: 17 kts **Man:** 13 officers, 137 men
A: 1/127-mm — 2/12.7-mm machine guns **Range:** 8,000/17
M: 2 Fairbanks-Morse 38D8 1/8 diesels; 2 props, 6,080 hp
Fuel: 400 tons **Electric:** 600 kw

REMARKS: The last of a series of small seaplane tenders (AVP), 18 of which were transferred to the Coast Guard in 1947-48; seven were given to South Vietnam beginning in 1970 and eight have been taken out of service since 1968. WHEC-379 was a training ship from 11-69 until placed in reserve on 30-5-75; she is being recommissioned to replace the *Spencer* (WHEC-36), which is in worse condition. Mk 52 fire-control director; ASW TT removed.

MEDIUM-ENDURANCE CUTTERS

♦ *11 or more Bear class* — programmed

WMEC 630 BEAR
WMEC 631 TAMPA
WMEC 632 HARRIET LANE
WMEC 633 NORTHLAND
WMEC 634 SENECA
WMEC 635 PICKERING
WMEC 636 ESCABANA
WMEC 637 LEGARE
WMEC 638 ARGUS
WMEC 639 . . .
WMEC 640 . . .

Authorized: 2 in FY 77, 2 in FY 78, . . . in FY 79

D: 1,722 tons (fl) **Dim:** 82.3 × 11.6 × 4.1
S: 19.5 kts **Man:** 15 officers, 94 men
A: 1/76-mm DP OTO-Melara — 1 HH-52A or LAMPS III helicopter
Electron Equipt: Radar: Mk 92 fire-control system
Sonar: SQR 19 TASS
M: 2 diesels; 2 controllable-pitch props; 7,000 hp **Range:** 6,800/13.5

REMARKS: Builder not yet assigned; names listed will be used as ships are authorized. Intended to be able to act as ASW escorts in wartime, using LAMPS III ASW helicopter. No hull-mounted sonar or on-board ASW weapons. Space and weight reserved for Vulcan/Phalanx 20-mm Gatling AA gun and Harpoon missile-launch canisters. Can carry van-mounted towed passive sonar array on fantail. Telescoping hangar, fin stabilization.

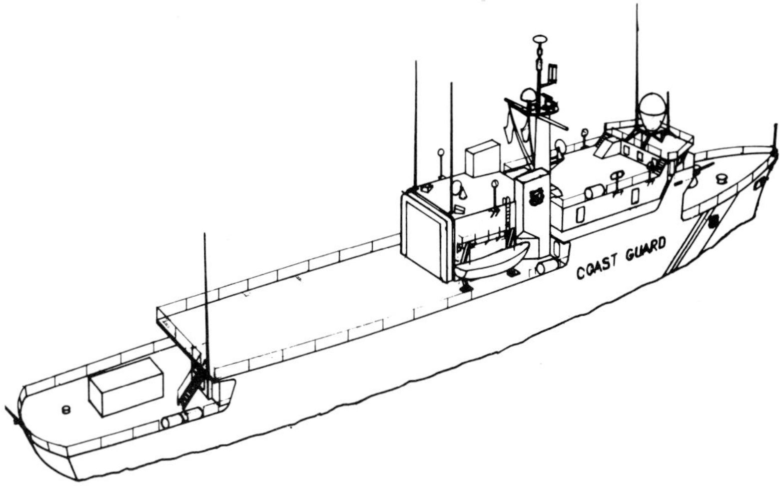

Bear-class WMEC 1977

♦ *16 210-ft Reliance class*

	Bldr	L	In serv.
WMEC 615 RELIANCE (WTR)	1	25-5-63	20-6-64
WMEC 616 DILIGENCE	1	20-7-63	26-8-64
WMEC 617 VIGILANT	1	24-12-63	3-10-64
WMEC 618 ACTIVE	2	31-7-65	17-9-66
WMEC 619 CONFIDENCE	3	8-5-65	19-2-66
WMEC 620 RESOLUTE	3	30-4-66	8-12-66
WMEC 621 VALIANT	4	14-1-67	28-10-67
WMEC 622 COURAGEOUS	4	18-5-67	10-4-68
WMEC 623 STEADFAST	4	24-6-67	25-9-68
WMEC 624 DAUNTLESS	4	21-10-67	10-6-68
WMEC 625 VENTUROUS	4	11-11-67	16-8-68
WMEC 626 DEPENDABLE	4	16-3-68	27-11-68
WMEC 627 VIGOROUS	4	4-5-68	2-5-69
WMEC 628 DURABLE	3	29-4-67	8-12-67
WMEC 629 DECISIVE	3	14-12-67	23-8-68
WMEC 630 ALERT	3	19-10-68	4-8-69

Bldrs: 1. Todd Shipyards — 2. Christy Corp., Sturgeon Bay, Wis. — 3. Coast Guard SY, Curtis Bay, Md. — 4. American SB, Lorain, Ohio.

D: 759 tons (970 or 1,007 fl) **Dim:** 64.2 (61 pp) × 10.4 × 3.2
S: 18 kts **Man:** 7 officers, 54 men
Range: 2,000/18, 5,000/15, 6,100/13 **Endurance:** 15 days
A: 1/76-mm — 1 HH-52-A helicopter
M: 2 Alco 251B 16-cyl. diesels, each 2,500 hp; 2 controllable-pitch props; (WMEC-615 to WMEC-619 also: 2 gas turbines, each of 2,000 hp)

REMARKS: WMEC-615 replaced WHEC-379 as reserve personnel training cutter in 1974; she retains full WMEC capabilities. CODOG propulsion in WMEC-615 to

MEDIUM-ENDURANCE CUTTERS (*continued*)

Dauntless (WMEC 624) with HH-52A helicopter 1972

WMEC-619. No hangar. Designed to operate up to 500 miles off the coast. High superstructure permitting 360° visibility. No stack, exhaust is at stern. Can tow a 10,000-ton ship. Air-conditioned.

♦ *1 Diver class* — Bldr: Basalt Rock Co., Napa, Cal.

	L	In serv.
WMEC 168 YOCONA (ex-WAT-168, ex-*Seize*, ARS-26)	8-4-44	3-11-44

D: 1,557 tons (1,745 fl) **Dim:** 70.0 × 12.8 × 4.9
S: 15.5 kts **Man:** 7 officers, 65 men
M: 2 Cooper-Bessemer GSB-8 diesels; 2 props; 3,000 hp

Remarks: Former salvage ship, taken over from the Navy in 1946. No guns. Sister *Acushnet* serves as WAGO-167, which see for appearance.

♦ *2 Sotoyoma class* — Bldrs: Levingston SB, Orange, Texas; Gulfport Boiler, Port Arthur, Texas

	L	In serv.
WMEC 194 MODOC (ex-*Bagaduce*, ATA-194)	4-12-44	14-2-45
WMEC 202 COMANCHE (ex-*Wampanoag*, ATA-202)	10-10-44	8-12-44

D: 534 tons (860 fl) **S:** 13.5 kts **Dim:** 46.8 × 11.0 × 4.9
A: 2/12.7-mm machine guns **Man:** 5 officers, 42 men
M: 2 G.M. 12-278A diesels; 1 prop; 1,500 hp **Fuel:** 178 tons

Comanche (WMEC 202) 1969

♦ *1 Storis class* — Bldr: Toledo SB, Ohio

	Laid down	L	In serv.
WMEC 38 STORIS (ex-*Eskimo*)	14-7-41	4-4-42	30-9-42

Storis (WMEC 38) 1971

D: 1,715 tons (1,925 fl) **Dim:** 70.1 × 13.1 × 4.6
S: 14 kts **Man:** 10 officers, 96 men
A: 1/76-mm — 2/12.7-mm machine guns (I × 2)
Range: 12,000/14, 22,000/8
M: 2 diesels, electric drive; 1 prop; 1,800 hp

MEDIUM-ENDURANCE CUTTERS (*continued*)

REMARKS: Rated as WAG until 1966, then WAGB until 1-7-72, when she was retyped WMEC. Resembles a *Balsam*-class buoy tender, but is larger. Has an icebreaker hull but is no longer considered capable of acting as such.

♦ *3 Cherokee and Achomawi classes*

	Bldr	L	In serv.
WMEC 153 CHILULA (ex-ATF-153)	Charleston SB	1-12-44	5-4-45
WMEC 165 CHEROKEE (ex-ATF-66)	Bethlehem, Staten I.	10-11-39	26-4-40
WMEC 166 TAMAROA (ex-*Zuni*, ATF-95)	Commercial Iron Works, Portland, Oregon	13-7-43	9-10-43

Cherokee (WMEC 165) Terzibaschitsch, 1976

D: 1,731 tons (fl) **S:** 16.2 kts **Dim:** 62.5 × 11.7 × 5.2
A: 1/76-mm — 2/12.7-mm machine guns **Man:** 7 officers, 65 men
M: 4 G.M. 12-278A diesels, electric drive; 1 prop; 3,000 hp
Fuel: 315 tons

REMARKS: WMEC-165 and WMEC-166 were the first and last of their numerous class to be built; WMEC-153 is one of a later version with similar appearance.

ICEBREAKERS

♦ *2 Polar Star class* — Bldr: Lockheed SB, Seattle

	Laid down	L	In serv.
WAGB 10 POLAR STAR	15-5-72	17-11-73	17-1-76
WAGB 11 POLAR SEA	27-11-73	24-6-75	7-2-77

D: 10,863 tons (13,190 fl) **Dim:** 121.9 (102.8 pp) × 25.5 × 9.2
S: 21 kts **Man:** 13 officers, 125 men, 10 scientists
Range: 28,275/13 **Fuel:** 3,555 tons

Polar Star (WAGB 10) 1975

M: CODAG: 6 Alco 16V-251 diesels (3,000 hp each), 3 Pratt & Whitney FT-4A12 gas turbines (25,000 hp each, down-rated), electric drive; 3 controllable-pitch props; 60,000 to 66,000 hp

REMARKS: No additional units planned. Carry two HH-52A helicopters. Can break 2-meter ice at 3 knots, 6.4-meter ice maximum. Propulsion plant completely cross-connected and automatic. Controllable-pitch propellers have not been reliable and are being replaced by newer version. 4/20-mm AA (I × 4) to be installed.

ICEBREAKERS (*continued*)

Polar Star (WAGB 10) 1976

♦ *1 Glacier class* — Bldr: Ingalls SB, Pascagoula

	Laid down	L	In serv.
WAGB 4 GLACIER	8-53	27-8-54	5-55

Glacier (WAGB 4) 1972

D: 5,100 tons (8,449 fl) **Dim:** 94.5 (88.4 pp) × 22.6 × 8.8
S: 17 kts **Man:** 14 officers, 215 men
Range: 12,000/17, 29,000/12
A: Removed in 1969 — 1 HH-52A helicopter
Electron Equipt: Radars: SPS 6, SPS 53
M: Diesel-electric propulsion: 10 Fairbanks-Morse diesels and 2 Westinghouse electric motor-generators; 21,000 hp

♦ *3 Wind class* — Bldr: Western Pipe & Steel, San Pedro, Cal.

	L
WAGB 281 WESTWIND (ex-AGB-6, ex-*Severniy Polyus*)	31-7-43
WAGB 282 NORTHWIND	22-5-45
WAGB 283 BURTON ISLAND (ex-AGB-1, ex-AG-88)	30-4-46

Westwind (WAGB 281) 1974

D: 3,500 tons (6,515 fl) **Dim:** 82.0 (76.2 pp) × 19.5 × 8.8
S: 16 kts **Man:** 135 men
A: 4/12.7-mm machine guns (I × 4) **Range:** 16,000/16, 38,000/10.5
M: 6 Fairbanks-Morse, 10 cyl. diesel engines, each of 2,000 hp and linked to a Westinghouse generator of 1,375 kw; 2 props; 10,000 hp

REMARKS: Can make way in 2.70-m ice. Double hull entirely welded. Telescoping hangar of alloy metal for the two helicopters carried. WAGB-281 and WAGB-282 have been fitted with four new Enterprise diesel engines. WAGB-283 is performing Arctic trials for the Navy and is no longer acting as an icebreaker. WAGB-281, which was in the Soviet Navy from 1945 to 1951, is in the Great Lakes. Four sisters discarded.

♦ **WAGB-83 MACKINAW** (ex-*Manitowoc*) — Bldr: Toledo SB, 6-3-44

D: 5,252 tons (8,775 fl) **Dim:** 88.4 × 22.8 × 5.8
S: 18.7 kts **Man:** 10 officers, 117 men
Range: 10,000/18.7, 60,000/12
M: 4 Fairbanks-Morse diesels, electric drive; 3 props (2 aft, 1 fwd); 10,000 hp

REMARKS: Built for use on the Great Lakes. Helicopter platform. Fitted with 2/12-ton cranes. Can break 1.2-m solid ice or 11-m broken ice.

ICEBREAKERS *(continued)*

Mackinaw (WAGB 83) — now has red hull 1971

HYDROFOIL GUNBOAT

♦ *1 Flagstaff class* — Bldr: Grumman, Stuart, Florida

	Laid down	L	In serv.
WPGH 1 FLAGSTAFF (ex-PGH-1)	15-7-66	9-1-68	14-9-68

Flagstaff (WPGH 1) 1974

D: 56.8 tons (fl) **Dim:** 22.7 × 6.2 × 1.4 (4.1 foils down)
S: 45 kts **Man:** 1 officer, 12 men
A: 1/81-mm mortar — 2/12.7-mm machine guns (I × 2)
Range: 300/40
M: CODOG: 1 Rolls-Royce Tyne 621 gas turbine; 1 prop; 3,620 hp; 2 Packard diesels; 2 water jets; 300 hp (8 kts)

REMARKS: Loaned to the Coast Guard by the Navy in 1974; permanently transferred 29-9-76. Operates from Woods Hole, Massachusetts.

NOTE: The Coast Guard's two hovercraft have been stricken.

PATROL CRAFT

♦ *22 95-ft Cape class* — Bldr: Coast Guard Yard, Curtis Bay, Maryland, 1953-59

WPB 95300 CAPE SMALL
WPB 95301 CAPE CORAL
WPB 95306 CAPE GEORGE
WPB 95307 CAPE CURRENT
WPB 95308 CAPE STRAIT
WPB 95309 CAPE CARTER
WPB 95310 CAPE WASH
WPB 95311 CAPE HEDGE
WPB 95312 CAPE KNOX
WPB 95313 CAPE MORGAN
WPB 95314 CAPE FAIRWEATHER
WPB 95316 CAPE FOX
WPB 95317 CAPE JELLISON
WPB 95318 CAPE NEWAGEN
WPB 95319 CAPE ROMAIN
WPB 95320 CAPE STARR
WPB 95321 CAPE CROSS
WPB 95322 CAPE HORN
WPB 95324 CAPE SHOALWATER
WPB 95326 CAPE CORWIN
WPB 95328 CAPE HENLOPEN
WPB 95332 CAPE YORK

Cape Fairweather (WPB 95314) A.D. Baker, 1976

D: 105 tons (fl) **Dim:** 28.9 × 5.8 × 1.8
S: 18 kts (cruising fl) **Man:** 1 officer, 13 men
A: 1/81-mm mortar — 2/12.7-mm machine guns (I × 2) or none
Range: WPB-95300 to WPB-95311: 2,600; WPB-95312 to WPB-95320: 3,000; WPB-95321 to WPB-95332: 2,800/all 9 kts
M: 4 Cummins high-speed diesels; 2 props; 2,324 hp

PATROL CRAFT *(continued)*

REMARKS: Two transferred to Haiti (1956), two to Ethiopia (1958), four to Thailand, one to Saudi Arabia. Nine were given to South Korea (1969-70). Others have been scrapped. The 22 remaining are to be re-engined and rehabilitated 1977-81 in lieu of constructing 30 new WPBs.

♦ *53 83-ft Point class* — Bldr: Coast Guard Yard, Curtis Bay, Maryland

In serv: WPB-82302 to WPB-82314: 1960-61; WPB-82318 to WPB-82370: 1961-67; WPB-82371 to WPB-82379: 1970

WPB 82302 POINT HOPE
WPB 82311 POINT VERDE
WPB 82312 POINT SWIFT
WPB 82314 POINT THATCHER
WPB 82318 POINT HERRON
WPB 82332 POINT ROBERTS
WPB 82333 POINT HIGHLAND
WPB 82334 POINT LEDGE
WPB 82335 POINT COUNTESS
WPB 82336 POINT GLASS
WPB 82337 POINT DIVIDE
WPB 82338 POINT BRIDGE
WPB 82339 POINT CHICO
WPB 82340 POINT BATAN
WPB 82341 POINT LOOKOUT
WPB 82342 POINT BAKER
WPB 82343 POINT WELLS
WPB 82344 POINT ESTERO
WPB 82345 POINT JUDITH
WPB 82346 POINT ARENA
WPB 82347 POINT BONITA
WPB 82348 POINT BARROW
WPB 82349 POINT SPENCER
WPB 82354 POINT EVANS
WPB 82355 POINT HANNON
WPB 82356 POINT FRANCIS
WPB 82357 POINT HURON
WPB 82358 POINT STUART
WPB 82359 POINT STEELE
WPB 82360 POINT WINSLOW
WPB 82361 POINT CHARLES
WPB 82362 POINT BROWN
WPB 82363 POINT NOWELL
WPB 82364 POINT WHITEHORN
WPB 82365 POINT TURNER
WPB 82366 POINT LOBOS
WPB 82367 POINT KNOLL
WPB 82368 POINT WARDE
WPB 82369 POINT HEYER
WPB 82370 POINT RICHMOND
WPB 82371 POINT BARNES
WPB 82372 POINT BROWER
WPB 82373 POINT CAMDEN
WPB 82374 POINT CARREW
WPB 82375 POINT DORAN
WPB 82376 POINT HARRIS

Point Huron (WPB 82357) G. Arra, 1976

WPB 82350 POINT FRANKLIN
WPB 82351 POINT BENNETT
WPB 82352 POINT SAL
WPB 82353 POINT MONROE
WPB 82377 POINT HOBART
WPB 82378 POINT JACKSON
WPB 82379 POINT MARTIN

D: 64 tons (67-69 fl) **Dim:** 25.3 × 5.25 × 1.95 (fl)
S: 23.5 kts (see Remarks) **Man:** 1 officer, 7 men
A: 1/81-mm mortar — 2/12.7-mm machine guns (some none)
M: 2 Cummins diesels; 2 props; 1,600 hp **Range:** 1,400 to 1,500/8 to 9 kts

REMARKS: Hull in mild steel. High-speed diesels controlled from the bridge. WPB-82301 and WPB-82317 had two 600-hp diesels (**S:** 17 kts); the others have 800-hp diesels and 23.5 knots, except that the heavier WPB-82371 and later make 22.6 kts. WPB-82314 has two gas turbines with 1,000 hp (27-knot potential) and controllable-pitch propellers. Well equipped for salvage and towing. Beginning in 6-65, twenty-six were sent to Vietnam.

OCEANOGRAPHIC CUTTERS

♦ *1 Diver class* — Bldr: Basalt Rock Co., Napa, California

	L	In serv.
WAGO 167 ACUSHNET (ex-*Shackle*, ARS-9)	1-4-43	5-2-44

Acushnet (WAGO 167) 1975

REMARKS: Data as for WMEC sister, *Yocona*, except **Man:** 7 officers, 57 men. Large oceanographic crane on port side of fantail.

♦ *1 Balsam class*

WAGO 295 EVERGREEN (1944)

OCEANOGRAPHIC CUTTERS (*continued*)

Evergreen (WAGO 295) 1973

REMARKS: Data as for *Balsam*-class buoy tenders. Reconstruction completed 2-73 for service as an oceanographic research ship. Equipped with COGLAD (Coast Guard Loran Assist Device) which gives a continuous real-time plot of ship's position. Bow-thruster fitted, also enlarged superstructure. Operates on International Ice Patrol when not doing research.

TRAINING CUTTERS

♦ *1 Horst Wessel class* — Bldr: Blohm & Voss, Hamburg

	L	In serv.
WIX 327 EAGLE (ex-*Horst Wessel*)	13-6-36	1-46

Eagle (WIX 327) 1976

D: 1,784 tons (fl) **Dim:** 89.9 (70.4 wl) × 11.9 × 5.2
S: 18 kts **Man:** 19 officers, 46 men, 180 cadets
M: 1 M.A.N. diesel; 1 prop; 728 hp (10.5 kts); 2,355 m^2 sail area

REMARKS: Training ship at the Coast Guard Academy, New London. Sisters operate in the Brazilian Navy and Soviet merchant marine.

♦ *1 Active class*

WIX 157 CUYAHOGA (ex-WMEC-157, ex-WPC-157, ex-WAG-26) (1926)

Cuyahoga (WIX 157) 1974

D: 290 tons (fl) **S:** 13.2 kts **Dim:** 38.1 × 7.3 × 2.4
M: 2 diesels; 2 props; 8,000 hp **Man:** 1 officer, 10 men

REMARKS: Reserve officer candidate training ship at Yorktown, Virginia. Last of a class of 33 patrol boats.

BUOY TENDERS, SEAGOING

♦ *35 Balsam class* — Bldrs: WLB-297: Coast Guard Yard; others: Marine Iron SB, Duluth, or Zenith Dredge Co., Duluth, Minnesota, 1942-44

WLB 62 BALSAM	**WLB 306 BUTTONWOOD**	**WLB 396 MALLOW**
WLB 277 COWSLIP	**WLB 307 PLANETREE**	**WLB 397 MARIPOSA**
WLB 290 GENTIAN	**WLB 308 PAPAW**	**WLB 399 SAGEBRUSH**
WLB 291 LAUREL	**WLB 309 SWEETGUM**	**WLB 400 SALVIA**

BUOY TENDERS, SEAGOING (*continued*)

WLB 292 CLOVER
WLB 296 SORREL
WLB 297 IRONWOOD
WLB 300 CITRUS
WLB 301 CONIFER
WLB 302 MADRONA
WLB 303 TUPELO
WLB 305 MESQUITE
WLB 388 BASSWOOD
WLB 389 BITTERSWEET
WLB 390 BLACKHAW
WLB 391 BLACKTHORN
WLB 392 BRAMBLE
WLB 393 FIREBUSH
WLB 394 HORNBEAM
WLB 395 IRIS
WLB 401 SASSAFRAS
WLB 402 SEDGE
WLB 403 SPAR
WLB 404 SUNDEW
WLB 405 SWEETBRIER
WLB 406 ACACIA
WLB 407 WOODRUSH

Madrona (WLB 302) 1970

D: 935 tons (1,025 fl) **Dim:** 54.9 × 11.3 × 4.0
S: 12.8/15 kts **Man:** 6 officers, 47 men
A: WLB-277, WLB-296, WLB-300, and WLB-394: 1/76-mm; WLB-402: 2/20-mm (I × 2); others: 2/12.7-mm machine guns or none
Fuel: 90 to 96 tons
M: 2 diesels, electric drive; WLB-62 to WLB-303: 1,000 hp; WLB-297, WLB-305 to WLB-407: 1,200 hp

REMARKS: *Evergreen* (WAGO-295) converted to oceanographic research ship. WLB-62, WLB-296, WLB-300, WLB-390, WLB-392, WLB-402, and WLB-403 have strengthened hulls for icebreaking, but all have icebreaker hull form. All have 20-ton derrick.

BUOY TENDERS, COASTAL

♦ *5 Red class* — Bldr: Coast Guard Yard, Curtis Bay, Maryland, 1964–71

WLM 685 RED WOOD
WLM 686 RED BEECH
WLM 687 RED BIRCH
WLM 688 RED CEDAR
WLM 689 RED OAK

D: 471 tons (512 fl) **S:** 12.8 kts **Dim:** 47.9 × 10.1 × 1.9

Red Cedar (WLM 688) G. Arra, 1976

Man: 4 officers, 27 men **Range:** 3,000/11.6
M: 2 diesels; 2 controllable-pitch props; 1,800 hp

REMARKS: Can break light ice. 10-ton derrick. Bow-thruster.

♦ *3 Hollyhock class, 1937–1939*

WLM 212 FIR **WLM 220 HOLLYHOCK** **WLM 252 WALNUT**

Fir (WLM 212) 1974

BUOY TENDERS, COASTAL (*continued*)

D: 989 tons (fl) **S:** 12 kts **Dim:** 53.4 × 10.4 × 3.7
M: 2 diesels; 2 props; 1,350 hp **Man:** 5 officers, 35 men

♦ *1 Juniper class*

WLM 224 JUNIPER (18-5-40)

D: 794 tons (fl) **S:** 10.8 kts **Dim:** 54.0 × 10.1 × 2.8
M: 2 diesels, electric drive; 2 props; 900 hp **Man:** 4 officers, 34 men

♦ *7 White class (former U.S. Navy YF)*

WLM 540 WHITE SUMAC
WLM 542 WHITE BUSH
WLM 543 WHITE HOLLY
WLM 544 WHITE SAGE
WLM 545 WHITE HEATH
WLM 546 WHITE LUPINE
WLM 547 WHITE PINE

White Sage (WLM 544) 1976

D: 435 tons (600 fl) **S:** 9.8 kts **Dim:** 40.5 × 9.4 × 2.7
M: 2 diesels; 2 props; 600 hp **Man:** 1 officer, 20 men

BUOY TENDERS, INLAND

♦ *1 Tern class* — Bldr: Coast Guard Yard, Curtis Bay (A)

WLI 80801 TERN

♦ *1 Buckthorn class* (B)

WLI 642 BUCKTHORN

♦ *1 Azalea class* (C)

WLI 641 AZALEA

♦ *2 Bayberry class* (D)

WLI 65400 BAYBERRY **WLI 65401 ELDERBERRY**

♦ *3 Blackberry class* (E)

WLI 65303 BLACKBERRY
WLI 65304 CHOKEBERRY
WLI 65305 LOGANBERRY

♦ *6 Cosmos class* (F)

WLI 293 COSMOS
WLI 298 RAMBLER
WLI 313 BLUEBELL
WLI 315 SMILAX
WLI 316 PRIMROSE
WLI 317 VERBENA

	Tons (fl)	Dim	S kts	HP	Officers/ Men	Built
A:	168	24.4 × 7.6 × 1.5	10	450	0/7	1969
B:	200	30.5 × 7.3 × 1.3	7.3	600	1/13	1963
C:	200	30.5 × 7.3 × 1.5	9.0	440	1/13	1958
D:	68	19.8 × 5.2 × 1.3	11.3	400	0/5	1954
E:	68	19.8 × 5.2 × 1.3	9.0	220	0/5	1946
F:	178	30.5 × 7.3 × 1.5	10.5	600	1/14	1942-45

REMARKS: Several equipped with pile drivers.

BUOY TENDERS, RIVER

♦ *9 75-ft Gasconade class* (A)

WLR 75401 GASCONADE
WLR 75402 MUSKINGUM
WLR 75403 WYACONDA
WLR 75404 CHIPPEWA
WLR 75405 CHEYENNE
WLR 75406 KICKAPOO
WLR 75407 KANAWHA
WLR 75408 PATOKA
WLR 75409 CHENA

♦ *6 65-ft Ouachita class* (B)

WLR 65501 OUACHITA
WLR 65502 CIMARRON
WLR 65503 OBION
WLR 65504 SCIOTO
WLR 65505 OSAGE
WLR 65506 SANGAMON

♦ **WLR 285 FOXGLOVE** (C)

♦ **WLR 311 SUMAC** (D)

♦ **WLR 80310 LANTANA** (E)

♦ **WLR 259 DOGWOOD, WLR 263 FORSYTHIA, WLR 268 SYCAMORE** (F)

♦ **WLR 7364 OLEANDER** (G)

	Tons (fl)	Dim	S kts	HP	Officers/ Men	Built
A:	145	22.9 × 6.7 × 1.2	10.8	600	0/12	1964-71
B:	139	20.0 × 6.4 × 1.5	12.5	600	0/10	1960-62
C:	350	34.8 × 9.1 × 1.8	13.5	1,500	1/20	1945
D:	404	35.1 × 9.1 × 1.8	10.6	960	1/22	1943
E:	235	34.4 × 9.1 × 1.5	10.0	1,000	1/19	1943
F:	230	34.7 × 7.9 × 1.2	11.0	2,800	1/20	1940-43
G:	90	22.3 × 5.4 × 1.5	12.0	300	0/10	1940

REMARKS: Flat-ended, barge-like hulls; each has an associated push-barge.

CONSTRUCTION TENDERS

♦ *4 Pamlico class* — Bldr: Coast Guard Yard, Curtis Bay, Maryland

CONSTRUCTION TENDERS (*continued*)

WLIC 800 PAMLICO (1976)
WLIC 801 HUDSON (1976)
WLIC 803 KENNEBEC (1977)
WLIC 804 SAGINAW (1977)

Pamlico (WLIC 800) 1976

D: 413 tons (459 fl) **S:** 11.5 kts **Dim:** 49.1 × 9.1 × 1.2
Man: 1 officer, 13 men **Range:** 1,300/11
M: 2 Cummins D379, 8-cyl. diesels; 2 props; 1,000 hp

REMARKS: Design combines capabilities of the *Anvil* class and their associated equipment barges.

♦ *10 Anvil class, 1962–65*

WLIC 75301 ANVIL
WLIC 75302 HAMMER
WLIC 75303 SLEDGE
WLIC 75304 MALLET
WLIC 75305 VISE
WLIC 75306 CLAMP
WLIC 75307 WEDGE
WLIC 75308 SPIKE
WLIC 75309 HATCHET
WLIC 75310 AXE

D: 145 tons (fl) **S:** 10 kts **Dim:** 22.9 × 6.7 × 1.2
M: 2 diesels; 2 props; 600 hp **Man:** 0 or 1 officer, 9 men

REMARKS: Each has an associated work barge with a crane. WLIC-75306 to WLIC-75310 are 23.2 m overall.

HARBOR TUGS, MEDIUM

♦ *10 Bay class* — Bldr: Tacoma BB, Washington (WYTM-101 to WYTM-104)

WYTM 101 KATMAI BAY
WYTM 102 BRISTOL BAY
WYTM 103 MOBILE BAY
WYTM 104 BISCAYNE BAY
WYTM 105 NEAH BAY
WYTM 106 MORRO BAY
WYTM 107 PENOBSCOT BAY
WYTM 108 THUNDER BAY
WYTM 109 STURGEON BAY
WYTM 110 N . . .

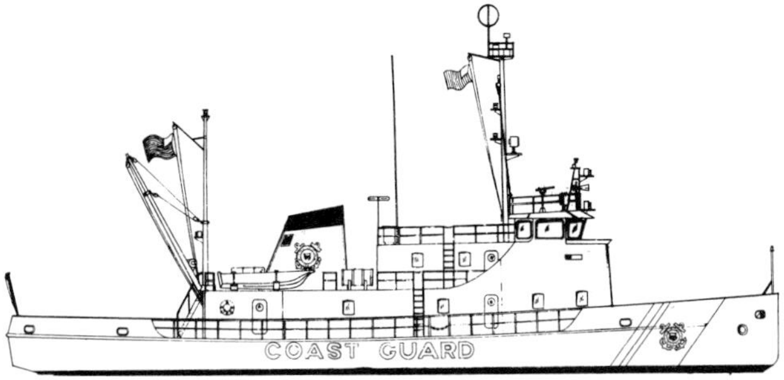

Bay-class icebreaking tug 1975

D: 662 tons (fl) **S:** 14 kts **Dim:** 42.7 × 11.5 × 3.7
Man: 3 officers, 14 men **Range:** 4,000/12
M: Diesel-electric; 1 prop; 2,500 hp

REMARKS: WYTM-101 to be delivered 11-78. Names listed are for use as these ships are authorized. Icebreaker hulls; first units will operate on the Great Lakes. To replace existing WYTMs.

♦ *13 110-ft class* (1943, except WYTM-90 to WYTM-93: 1939)

WYTM 60 MANITOU
WYTM 61 KAW
WYTM 71 APALACHEE
WYTM 72 YANKTON
WYTM 73 MOHICAN
WYTM 90 ARUNDEL
WYTM 91 MAHONING
WYTM 92 NAUGATUCK
WYTM 93 RARITAN
WYTM 96 CHINOOK
WYTM 97 OJIBWA
WYTM 98 SNOHOMISH
WYTM 99 SAUK

Chinook (WYTM 96) 1977

HARBOR TUGS, MEDIUM (*continued*)

D: 370 tons (fl) **S:** 11.2 kts **Dim:** 33.5 × 8.2 × 3.3
M: Diesel-electric; 1 prop; 1,000 hp **Man:** 1 officer, 19 men

♦ **WYTM 85009 MESSENGER** (1944)

D: 230 tons (fl) **S:** 9.5 kts **Dim:** 25.9 × 7.0 × 2.7
M: 1 diesel; 1 prop; 700 hp **Man:** 10 men

HARBOR TUGS, SMALL

♦ *15 65-ft class, 1961–67*

WYTL 65601 CAPSTAN
WYTL 65602 CHOCK
WYTL 65603 SWIVEL
WYTL 65604 TACKLE
WYTL 65609 SHACKLE
WYTL 65610 HAWSER
WYTL 65611 LINE
WYTL 65612 WIRE
WYTL 65605 TOWLINE
WYTL 65606 CATENARY
WYTL 65607 BRIDLE
WYTL 65608 PENDANT
WYTL 65613 BITT
WYTL 65614 BOLLARD
WYTL 65615 CLEAT

D: 72 tons (fl) **S:** 9.8–10.5 kts **Dim:** 19.8 × 5.8 × 2.1
M: 1 diesel; 1 prop; 400 hp **Man:** 10 men

LIGHTSHIPS

♦ **WLV 604 LIGHTSHIP COLUMBIA** **WLV 605 LIGHTSHIP RELIEF**
WLV 612 LIGHTSHIP NANTUCKET 1950

D: 617 tons (fl) (WLV-612: 607 tons) **Dim:** 39.0 × 9.1 × 3.4
S: 11 kts **M:** 1 diesel; 1 prop; 550 hp

REMARKS: Most lightships have now been replaced by fixed installations. WLV-604 assigned to Astoria, Oregon; other pair at Boston, Massachusetts.

VENEZUELA

PERSONNEL: 7,500 men, including 4,000 marines

MERCHANT MARINE (1976): 165 ships — 543,446 grt
(tankers: 18 ships — 300,870 grt)

SHIPS IN SERVICE OR UNDER CONSTRUCTION AS OF 1 OCTOBER 1977

	L	Tons (surfaced)	Main armament
♦ *5 submarines*			
2 209 TYPE	1975	980	8/533-mm TT
2 GUPPY II	1944-45	1,870	10/533-mm TT
1 BALAO	1943	1,825	10/533-mm TT
		Tons	
♦ *4 destroyers*			
2 BATTLE CLASS	1952-53	2,600	6/114-mm
2 ALLEN M. SUMNER	1944	2,200	6/127-mm, 6/ASW TT
♦ *8 frigates*			
6 MARISCAL SUCRE	. . .	2,500 (fl)	4 Otomat, 1/127-mm, 1 Albatros, 1 helicopter
2 ALMIRANTE CLEMENTE	1954-55	1,300	4/102-mm

SUBMARINES

♦ *2 209 type* — Bldr: Howaldtswerke, Kiel — Ordered: 1971

	L	In serv.		L	In serv.
S 21 SABALO	21-8-75	1977	**S 22 CONGRIO**	16-12-75	1977

D: 980 tons surfaced, 1,230 submerged **S:** 21 kts
Dim: 55.0 × 6.6 × 5.9 **Man:** 5 officers, 26 men
A: 8/533-mm TT — 6 reserve torpedoes
M: Diesel-electric propulsion: 4 MTU Type 12V-492-Ty-60 diesels; Siemens electric motor, 3,600 hp

♦ *2 ex-U.S. Guppy II* — Transferred: 1972 and 1973

	Bldr	L
S 12 TIBURON (ex-*Cubera*, SS-347)	Electric Boat Co.	17-6-45
S 13 PICUDA (ex-*Grenadier*, SS-525)	Boston NSY	15-12-44

D: 1,517 tons, 1,870 surfaced, 2,240 submerged **S:** 18/13-15 kts
Dim: 93.8 × 8.2 × 5.2 **Man:** 82 men **Range:** 10,000/10
A: 10/533-mm TT (6 fwd, 4 aft)
M: Diesel-electric propulsion: 3 groups of generators; 2 electric motors; 2 props; 4,800/5,200 hp
Fuel: 300 tons

REMARKS: The *Balao* class, to which these boats originally belonged, was modernized from 1952-54; a fourth generator group was removed to permit enlargement of the sonar compartment. Two 126-cell batteries.

♦ *1 ex-U.S. Balao class* — Bldr: Mare Island NSY — Purchased: 5-60

	L	In serv.
S 11 CARITE (ex-*Tilefish*, SS-307)	25-10-43	12-43

D: 1,525 tons, 1,825 surfaced, 2,300 submerged **S:** 19/10 kts
Dim: 95.0 × 8.25 × 5.2 **Man:** 9 officers, 66 men
A: 10/533-mm TT (6 fwd, 4 aft) **Fuel:** 300 tons
M: Diesel-electric propulsion; 2 props; 6,500/5,400 hp

REMARK: Serves as a pierside training ship.

DESTROYERS

♦ *2 modified British Battle class* — Bldr: Vickers-Armstrong

	Laid down	L	In serv.
D 11 NUEVA ESPARTA	24-7-51	19-11-52	11-53
D 12 ZULIA	24-7-51	29-6-53	1955

Nueva Esparta (D 11) 1972

D: 2,600 tons (3,670 fl) **Dim:** 122.52 (117 pp) × 12.8 × 5.8
S: 34.5 kts **Man:** 20 officers, 236 men **Range:** 5,000/10
A: 6/114-mm AA automatic (II × 3) — 16/40-mm AA (II × 8) — D-12: 3/533-mm TT — 2 depth-charge projectors — 2 depth-charge racks — D-11: 2 squids
Electron Equipt: Radars: D-11: 1 AW 52; D-12: 1 SPS 6
M: Parsons GT; 2 props; 50,000 hp **Boilers:** 2

REMARKS: Refit in Great Britain in 1959. Living spaces air-conditioned. D-11 modernized by Cammell Laird, 1968-69: Sea Cat missile launcher installed and has only 4/40-mm guns. D-12 modernized by the Puerto Cabello navy yard with the technical assistance of Cammell Laird; returned to service in 1973. The *Aragua* (D-31) was scrapped in 1975.

♦ *2 ex-U.S. Allen M. Sumner class* — Transferred: 14-7-72 and 31-10-73

	Bldr	L
D 41 CARABOBO (ex-*Beatty*, DD-756)	Bethlehem, Staten I.	30-11-44
D 51 FALCON (ex-*Robert K. Huntington*, DD-781)	Todd Pacific	5-12-44

D: 2,200 tons (3,320 fl) **S:** 30 kts **Dim:** 114.75 × 10.45 × 5.8
Man: 14 officers, 260 men **Range:** 1,260/30, 4,800/15
A: 6/127-mm AA 38-cal. (II × 3) — 2/76-mm AA — 6/324-mm Mk 32 ASW TT (III × 2)

DESTROYERS (*continued*)

Electron Equipt: Radars: 1 SPS 10, 1 SPS 40
Sonar: 1 SQS 29
M: GT; 2 props; 60,000 hp **Boilers:** 4 Babcock **Fuel:** 650 tons

REMARK: The D-51 has been modernized in the FRAM-II program.

FRIGATES

♦ *6 Mariscal Sucre class*

MARISCAL SUCRE N . . . N . . .
ALMIRANTE BRION N . . . N . . .

D: 2,500 tons (fl) **S:** 35 kts **Dim:** 111.6 × 12.0 × 3.6
A: 4/Otomat (I × 4) — 1/127-mm DP — 1 Albatros SAM — 4/40-mm AA — 1 AB-212 helicopter
Electron Equipt: Radars: 1 SPS 74 Selenia surface-search, 1 Mk 10 Elsag fire-control, 1 ex-77 missile-guidance, 1 SPQ-2F navigation
Sonar: 1 SQS 29
M: CODAG; 2 General Electric-Fiat LM 2500 gas turbines, 34,400 hp; 2 Fiat diesels, 7,800 hp; 2 props

REMARKS: Based on the Italian *Lupo* class. Four were ordered from C.N.T. Riva Trigoso, Castellammare, 10-75. Two others will be built by the Ancona shipyard with the assistance of Riva Trigoso. The ships' maximum speed on diesels alone is 21 knots.

♦ *2 Almirante Clemente class* — Bldr: Ansaldo, Livorno

	L		L
F 12 ALMIRANTE CLEMENTE	12-54	**F 22 GENERAL JOSÉ MORAN**	5-2-55

D: 1,300 tons (1,550 fl) **S:** 32 kts (see Remarks)
Dim: 97.6 × 10.84 × 2.6 **Man:** 12 officers, 150 men
A: 4/102-mm AA (II × 2) — 4/40-mm AA (II × 2) — 8/20-mm AA (II × 4) — 2 hedgehogs (fwd) — 4 depth-charge projectors — 1 depth-charge rack — 3/533-mm TT (III × 1)
M: GT; 2 props; 24,000 hp **Boilers:** 2 Foster-Wheeler
Range: 2,500/18, 4,000/15 **Fuel:** 350 tons

REMARKS: Heavily armed. In normal service, they do not exceed 29 knots. The 102-mm guns may have been replaced by 76-mm OTO Melara Compacts. The ships are air-conditioned and have Denny-Brown stabilizers. They were refitted at Cammell Laird from 1968 to 1975.

PATROL BOATS AND CRAFT

♦ *6 Constitucion class* — Bldr: Vosper Thornycroft

	L		L
P 11 CONSTITUCIÓN	1-6-73	**P 14 FEDERACIÓN**	26-2-74
P 12 INDEPENDENCIA	24-7-73	**P 15 LIBERTAD**	5-3-74
P 13 PATRIA	27-9-73	**P 16 VICTORIA**	5-74

D: 150 tons **S:** 27 kts **Dim:** 36.88 × 3.7 × . . .
A: P-11 to P-13: 1/76-mm OTO Melara Compact — P-14 to P-16: 2/Otomat SSM missiles — 1/40-mm
M: MTU diesels; 2 props; 3,600 hp

Constitución Vosper, 1975

REMARKS: P-11, P-12, and P-13, armed as gunboats, have an SPQ-2D search radar, an RTN 10 X Orion fire-control radar made by Selenia, and an Elsag computer. The other three also carry the Selenia SPQ-2D search radar.

♦ *2 ex-U.S. coastal escorts* — Bldr: U.S.A., 1943-44

P 02 CALAMAR (ex-PC-566) **P 04 ALBATROS** (ex-PC-582)

D: 280 tons (420 fl) **S:** 18 kts **Dim:** 53.0 × 7.0 × 3.25
A: 1/76-mm — 1/40-mm **Man:** 60-65 men
M: 2 General Motors diesels; 2 props; 2,800 hp

REMARKS: Bought from surplus and overhauled in Venezuela. Assigned to coastal surveillance in 1961.

♦ *4 ex-U.S. landing ships* — Bldr: U.S.A., 1943-44

T 13 LOS MONJES (ex-LSM-548) **T 15 LOS FRAILES** (ex-LSM-544)
T 14 LOS ROQUES (ex-LSM-543) **T 16 LOS TESTIGOS** (ex-LSM-545)

D: 743 tons (1,095 fl) **S:** 12 kts **Dim:** 61.87 × 10.36 × 2.4 (aft)
A: 1/40-mm AA — 4/20-mm AA **Man:** 59 men **Range:** 9,000/11
M: 2 diesels; 2 props; 2,800 hp

REMARK: In service with the Venezuelan Navy since 1961.

♦ *8 patrol craft* — Bldr: Estérel, Cannes, 1954

RIO APURE **RIO CABRALES** **RIO GUARICO** **RIO NEVERI**
RIO ARAUCA **RIO CARONI** **RIO NEGRO** **RIO TUY**

D: 38.5 tons **S:** 27-28 kts **Dim:** 28.0 (25 pp) × 4.65 × 1.25
A: Machine gun **Man:** 12 men **Range:** 750/24 (cruising speed)
M: 2 Mercedes-Benz 820 MB diesels, 675 hp each

REMARK: Manned by the National Police.

VENEZUELA (*continued*)

PATROL BOATS AND CRAFT (*continued*)

♦ *2 patrol craft*

RIO SANTO DOMINGO

D: 40 tons **S:** 23 kts **Dim:** 22.0 × 4.61 × 1.9
M: 2 General Motors diesels; 1,250 hp

GOLFO DE CARIACO

D: 37 tons **S:** 19 kts **Dim:** 20.0 × 5.5 × 2.8

REMARK: Manned by the National Police.

AMPHIBIOUS WARFARE SHIP

♦ *1 ex-U.S. landing ship* — Bldr: Ingalls, Pascagoula, 1952. Transferred: 6-73

AMAZONAS (ex-*Vernon County*, LST-1161)

D: 2,590 tons (5,786 fl) **S:** 13 kts **Dim:** 117.35 × 16.76 × 3.7
A: 4/76-mm AA **Man:** 116 men
M: 4 General Motors diesels; 2 variable-pitch props; 6,000 hp

AUXILIARY SHIPS

♦ *3 transports*

T 12 LAS AVES (ex-*Dos de Diciembre*) — Bldr: Dubigeon — L: 29-12-54

Las Aves (T 12)

D: 944 tons (fl) **S:** 15 kts **Dim:** 71.4 (64.5 pp) × 10.2 × 3.0
A: 4/20-mm AA (II × 2) **Range:** 2,520/14
Cargo capacity: 215 tons
M: Diesels; 2 props; 1,600 hp

REMARK: Also fitted as the presidential yacht.

T 17 PUNTA CABANA **T 20 N . . .** — Bldr: Uraga DD, Japan

D: 3,000 tons **S:** 17 kts

♦ *2 ex-U.S. netlayers* — Transferred: 1962-63

H 01 PUERTO SANTO (ex-*Marietta*, AN-82) — L: 27-4-45
H 03 PUERTO MIRANDA (ex-*Waxsaw*, AN-91) — L: 15-9-44

D: 650 tons (785 fl) **S:** 12 kts **Dim:** 51.35 × 10.25 × 3.25
A: None **Man:** 46 men **M:** Diesel-electric propulsion; 1,500 hp

REMARK: H-01 is assigned to the buoy and lighthouse service, and also serves as a hydrographic ship.

♦ *1 ex-U.S. repair ship* — Bldr: U.S.A., 1946 — Transferred: 6-62

T 18 GUYANA (ex-*Quirinus*, ex-ARL-39, ex-LST-1151)

D: 1,625 tons (4,100 fl) **S:** 10 kts (8 cruising)
Dim: 99.98 × 15.24 × 4.36 **Range:** 6,000/8
A: 8/40-mm AA (IV × 2) **M:** Diesels; 2 props; 1,800 hp

♦ *1 ex-U.S. floating workshop* — Transferred: 1965

DF 01 (ex-YR-48)

♦ *3 ex-U.S. tugs*

R 12 FERNANDO GOMEZ (ex-YTM-744)

D: 160 tons **S:** 10 kts **Dim:** 24.5 × 5.8 × 2.5
Man: 10 men **M:** Clark diesel; 1 prop; 560 hp

R 13 JOSÉ FELIX RIBAS (ex-YTB-515) (1945)

D: 450 tons

R 21 FELIPE LARRAZABAL (ex-*Utina*, ATF-163)

D: 1,280 tons (1,700 fl) **S:** 16 kts **Dim:** 61.7 × 11.6 × 4.7
A: 1/76-mm — 4/40-mm AA **Man:** 85 men
M: 4 diesel-electric groups; 2 props; 3,000 hp

REMARK: Transferred in 9-72.

VIETNAM

MERCHANT MARINE (1976): 64 ships — 107,456 grt
(tankers: 9 ships — 31,074 grt)

In the absence of exact information on the Vietnamese Navy, only a few remarks can be made.

Such South Vietnamese ships as managed to escape to Thailand and The Philippines before the fall of the government in Saigon reverted to the U.S. Navy, which, in turn, transferred them to the navies of those two nations.

Some ships were scuttled at sea, viz.: the landing ship *Lam Giang* (LSM-402), the patrol boat *Keon Ngua* (HQ-604), and the small gasoline tanker, HQ-474.

The LSILs *Tam Sat* (HQ-331) and *Loi Cong* (HQ-330), the LSSL *Nguyen Duc Dong*, and the patrol boat *Minh Hoa* (HQ-602) took refuge in Singapore but subsequently returned to Saigon. The frigate *Tran Khanh Du* (HQ-04) was captured by the Vietcong while she was undergoing overhaul in the Saigon shipyard. Presumably, these ships have been incorporated into the Vietnamese Navy. The same fate probably overtook the numerous small riverine units that the South Vietnamese government owned before its defeat (see the section on South Vietnam in *Combat Fleets 1976/77*).

Besides the ships referred to above, the Vietnamese Navy includes the following:

♦ *2 ex-Soviet SO-I-class patrol boats*

D: 190 tons (215 fl) **S:** 28 kts **Dim:** 42.0 × 6.1 × 1.9

VIETNAM (*continued*)

A: 4/25-mm AA (II × 2) — 2/ASW MBU-1500 rocket launchers — 2 depth-charge racks
M: 3 diesels; 3 props; 6,000 hp **Man:** 30 men

♦ *2 ex-Soviet Komar-class guided-missile patrol boats*

D: 71 tons (82 fl) **S:** 40 kts **Dim:** 25.3 × 7.0 × 2.0
A: 2/SS-N-2 Styx (I × 2) — 2/25-mm AA (II × 1) **Man:** 19 men
M: 4 M 50 diesels; 4 props; 4,800 hp

REMARK: It is doubtful that these two boats are operational.

♦ *6 ex-Soviet P-6-class torpedo boats*

♦ *4 ex-Soviet P-4-class torpedo boats*

♦ *8 ex-Chinese Shanghai-class patrol boats*

D: 155 tons (fl) **S:** 28 kts **Dim:** 38.8 × 5.4 × 1.6
A: 4/37-mm AA (II × 2) — 4/25-mm AA (II × 2)
M: 4 diesels; 4 props; 4,800 hp

♦ *14 ex-Chinese Swatow-class patrol boats*

D: 480 tons (fl) **S:** 28 kts **Dim:** 25.1 × 6.0 × 1.8
A: 4/37-mm (II × 2) — 2/25-mm (II × 1) — 2 depth charges
M: 4 diesels; 3,000 hp **Man:** 25 men

YEMEN

Southern

PERSONNEL: 150 men

MERCHANT MARINE (1976): 15 ships — 6,654 grt

PATROL BOATS

♦ *2 ex-Soviet SO-I class*

D: 190 tons (215 fl) **S:** 28 kts **Dim:** 42.0 × 6.1 × 1.9
A: 4/25-mm AA (II × 2) — 2/ASW MBU-1500 rocket launchers — 2 depth-charge racks
M: 3 diesels; 3 props; 6,000 hp **Man:** 30 men

REMARK: Transferred in 4-72 in bad condition.

♦ *2 ex-Soviet Zhuk class* — Transferred: 2-75

D: 50 tons (60 fl) **S:** 30 kts **Dim:** 26.0 × 4.9 × 1.5
A: 2/14.5-mm machine guns (II × 1)
M: 2 M 50 diesels; 2 props; 2,400 hp

♦ *1 ex-Soviet Poluchat class*

D: 80 tons (90 fl) **S:** 18 kts **Dim:** 29.6 × 5.8 × 1.5
A: 2/14.5-mm machine guns (II × 1) **Man:** 20 men
M: 2 M 50 diesels; 2 props; 2,400 hp

♦ *2 P-6-class torpedo boats*

111 **112**

♦ *3 ex-British "-ham"-class minesweepers*

AL SAQR (ex-*Bodenham*) **AL DAIRAK** (ex-*Blunham*) **AL GHAZALA** (ex-*Elsenham*)

D: 120 tons (159 fl) **Dim:** 32.43 (30.48 pp) × 6.45 × 1.7
S: 13 kts **Man:** 2 officers, 13 men
A: 1/20-mm AA **Range:** 1,500/12
M: Davey-Paxman diesels; 2 props; 1,000 hp **Fuel:** 15 tons

REMARK: In very poor condition, will probably soon be scrapped.

AMPHIBIOUS WARFARE SHIPS

♦ *2 ex-Soviet Polnocny-class landing ships* — Transferred: 8-73

A: 4/25-mm AA (II × 2) — 2/140-mm rocket launchers (XVIII × 2) for shore bombardment

♦ *3 ex-Soviet landing craft* — Transferred: 11-70

VARIOUS CRAFT

♦ *3 Spear-class patrol craft* — Bldr: Fairey Marine, Great Britain

D: 4.5 tons **S:** 26 kts **Dim:** 12.0 × 2.0 × 0.7
A: 2 machine guns **M:** 2 Sabre diesels; 290 hp

♦ *2 rescue boats* — Bldr: Fairey Marine, Great Britain

YEMENITE ARAB REPUBLIC

PERSONNEL: Approximately 150 men

MERCHANT MARINE (1976): 3 ships — 1,260 grt

♦ *4 Soviet Poluchat-class patrol boats*

♦ *3 Soviet P-4-class patrol torpedo boats*

♦ *3 small landing craft*

YUGOSLAVIA

PERSONNEL: 17,000 men

MERCHANT MARINE (1976): 423 ships — 1,943,750 grt
(tankers: 28 ships — 226,487 grt)

NAVAL AVIATION: A few Soviet Hound and Hormone helicopters

WARSHIPS IN SERVICE OR UNDER CONSTRUCTION AS OF 1 OCTOBER 1977

	L	Tons	Main armament
♦ *6 submarines*			
1 NEW TYPE	. . .	964 (submerged)	6/533-mm TT
3 HEROJ	1966-67	1,170 (surfaced)	6/533-mm TT
2 SUTJESKA	1958-59	820 (surfaced)	6/533-mm TT
♦ *1 destroyer*			
SPLIT	1950	2,400	4/127-mm, 5/533-mm TT
♦ *1 frigate* (planned)	. . .	2,000 (min.)	. . .
♦ *14 guided-missile patrol boats*			
4 KONČAR	1976-	250 (fl)	2/MM-30 Exocets, 1/57-mm AA
10 OSA-I	. . .	175	4/SS-N-2, 4/30-mm AA

SUBMARINES

♦ *1 new type submarine*

	Bldr	Laid down	L	In serv.
N . . .	Split	. . .	. . .	. . .

D: 964 tons, submerged **S:** 16 kts, submerged
Dim: 55.8 × 5.05 × . . . **Man:** 35 men **Endurance:** 28 days
A: 6/533-mm TT — 10 torpedoes in reserve or 20 mines
M: Diesel-electric

REMARKS: First of a series that could eventually consist of four units. Maximum diving depth: 300 m.

♦ *3 Heroj class* — Bldr: Uljanik, Pula

	Laid down	L	In serv.
821 HEROJ	1965	1966	1968
822 JUNAK	1966	1967	1969
823 USKOK	. . .	. . .	. . .

Heroj (821) 1968

D: 1,068 tons standard, 1,170 surfaced, 1,350 submerged **S:** 16/10 kts
Dim: 64.0 × 6.6 × 5.0 **Man:** 55 men **Range:** 9,700/8
A: 6/533-mm TT **M:** 2 diesels and electric motors; 2,400 hp

♦ *2 Sutjeska class* — Bldr: Uljanik, Pula

	Laid down	L	In serv.
811 SUTJESKA	1957	28-9-58	9-60
812 NERETVA	1957	1959	1962

Neretva (812) G. Arra

D: 700 tons standard, 820 surfaced, 945 submerged **Dim:** 55.0 × 6.6 × 4.8
S: 18/12 kts **Man:** 38 men **Range:** 4,400/8.6
A: 6/533-mm TT **M:** 2 Sulzer diesels and electric motors; 2,800 hp

REMARK: First submarines built in Yugoslavia.

DESTROYER

♦ *1 French type* — Bldr: "3 Maj" Brodogradiliste, Rijeka

	Laid down	L	In serv.
11 SPLIT	7-39	3-50	4-7-58

Split (D 11)

DESTROYER (*continued*)

D: 2,400 tons (3,000 fl) **S:** 24 kts
Dim: 120.0 (114.7 pp) × 12.0 × 3.7
A: 4/127-mm (I × 4) — 12/40-mm AA (II × 6) — 4/20-mm AA — 5/533-mm TT (V × 1) — 2 hedgehogs or Squids — 6 depth-charge projectors — 2 depth-charge racks
M: GT; 2 props; 50,000 hp **Fuel:** 590 tons

REMARKS: Plans from the Loire Shipyards. Equipped to lay 40 mines. U.S. radars and weapons.

FRIGATE

♦ *1 planned*

D: 2,000 tons (min.)

REMARK: Will replace the destroyer *Split*.

GUIDED-MISSILE PATROL BOATS

♦ *4 Končar (211) class* — Bldr: Kraljevica

	L	In serv.
401 KONČAR	15-10-76	8-77
... VLADO ČETKOVIĆ	1977	...

D: 250 tons (fl) **S:** 40 kts **Dim:** 45.0 × 8.4 × 1.8
A: 2/mm-30 Exocet — 1/57-mm Bofors — 2/illumination rocket launchers
Man: 30 men **Range:** 500/35
M: 2 Rolls-Royce gas turbines, 11,600 hp; 2 MTU diesels, 3,600 hp; 4 variable-pitch props

♦ *10 ex-Soviet Osa-I class* — Transferred: 1965-69

RC 301 M. ACEV
RC 302 V. BAGAT
RC 303 P. DRAPSIN
RC 304 S. FILIPOVIC
RC 305 Z. JOVANOVIC
RC 306 N. MARTINOVIC
RC 307 J. MAZAR
RC 308 K. ROJC
RC 309 F. ROZMAN
RC 310 V. SKORPIK

M. Acev (RC 301)

D: 175 tons (210 fl) **S:** 36 kts **Dim:** 39.0 × 7.7 × 1.8
A: 4/SS-N-2 Styx SSMs — 4/30-mm AA (II × 2) **Man:** 25 men
Electron Equipt: Radars: 1 Square Tie, 1 Drum Tilt, IFF High Pole
M: 3 M 503A diesels; 3 props; 12,000 hp

TORPEDO AND GUN BOATS

♦ *14 Soviet Shershen class*

TC 211 to **TC 224**

Known names: **CRVENA ZVIJEZDA, PARTIZAN II, BIOKOVAC, IVAN, KORNAT, PROLETER, STRELJKO**

D: 150 tons (180 fl) **S:** 45 kts **Dim:** 34.0 × 7.2 × 1.5
A: 4/30-mm AA (II × 2) — 4/533-mm TT (two fixed on each side)
Electron Equipt: Radars: 1 Pot Drum, 1 Drum Tilt, IFF High Pole
M: 3 diesels; 3 props; 12,000 hp

REMARK: Ten built in Yugoslavia under license, 1966-71.

♦ *6 158-type* — Bldr: Yugoslavia, 1951-60

D: 55-60 tons **S:** 26 kts **Dim:** 21.0 × 6.5 × 1.5
A: 2/40-mm — 4/13-mm machine guns (II × 2) — 2-4 mines
M: Packard motors; 3 props; 5,000 hp **Man:** 14 men

REMARK: Converted Higgins-108 boats, now considered obsolete.

PATROL BOATS

♦ *1 Udarnik class* — Bldr: Méditerranée, Le Havre

PBR 581 UDARNIK (ex-P-6) — L: 21-12-54

D: 325 tons (400 fl) **Dim:** 53.3 × 7.0 × 2.0 (light)

PATROL BOATS (*continued*)

Udarnik (PBR 581)

S: 18.7 kts **Man:** 60 men
A: 2/40-mm AA — 2/20-mm AA — 1 hedgehog — 4 ASW mortars — 1 depth charge
Range: 2,000/15, 3,000/12
M: 4 SEMT-Pielstick diesels; 2 props; 3,240 hp

REMARK: The same design as the French *Le Fougueux* class and as American PCs.

♦ *2 Mornar class* — Bldr: Yugoslavia

PBR 551 MORNAR — In serv. 9-59 **PBR 552 BORAC** — In serv. 1965

Mornar (PBR 551) 1970

D: 325 tons (400 fl) **S:** 18.7 kts **Dim:** 51.8 × 6.97 × 2.0 (light)
A: 1/76-mm — 2/40-mm — 4/20-mm — 2/MBU-1200 rocket launchers — depth charges
M: 4 SEMT-Pielstick diesels; 2 props; 3,240 hp
Range: 2,000/15, 3,000/12

REMARKS: Based on the *Udarnik*. Might have been modernized as follows: **M:** 3 Werkspoor diesels; 3 props, 2,100 hp — **A:** 2/40-mm Bofors AA — 2/20-mm — 4/ASW rocket launchers — 2 depth-charge racks — 2 mortars — 2/illumination rocket launchers.

♦ *13 Kraljevica class* — Bldr: Yugoslavia, 1953-60

PBR 501	**PBR 506** to **PBR 508**	**PBR 524**
PBR 503	**PBR 510** to **PBR 512**	
PBR 504	**PBR 519** to **PBR 521**	

PBR 512

D: 195 tons (225 fl) **S:** 19.2 kts **Dim:** 44.8 × 6.3 × 1.9
A: 1/76-mm — 1/40-mm AA — 4/20-mm AA — depth charges
M: 2 M.A.N. diesels; 2 props; 2,400 hp **Range:** 1,600/12

REMARK: Some units of this class have been transferred to Sudan, Ethiopia, and Bangladesh.

♦ *10 131-type coastal patrol craft* — Bldr: Yugoslavia, 1967-68

PC 131 to **PC 140**
Known names: **CER, DURMITOR, KALNIK, KOPAONIK, KOŽUF, ROMANIJA**

PC 135 1968

D: 120 tons **S:** 15 kts **Dim:** 32.0 × 5.5 × 2.5
A: 3/20-mm Hispano AA (III × 1) **M:** 2 diesels; 2 props; 900 hp

MINE WARFARE SHIPS

♦ *1 minelayer*

M 11 GALEB (ex-Italian *Ramb III*)

Galeb (M 11)

D: 5,182 tons **S:** 16 kts **Dim:** 117.3 × 15.6 × 5.6
M: Diesels; 2 props

REMARKS: Former banana boat armed as an auxiliary cruiser between 1940 and 1945. Rebuilt and rearmed in 1952. Now, she has had her armament removed and is used as a yacht by the head of state.

♦ *4 Sirius-class coastal minesweepers, 1956–60*

M 151 VUKOV KLANAC (ex-*Hrabri*) **M 153 BLITVENICA** (ex-*Slobodni*)
M 152 PODGORA (ex-*Smeli*) **M 161 GRADAC** (ex-*Snazhi*)

D: 365 tons (424 fl) **S:** 15 kts (sweeping: 11.5)
Dim: 46.4 (42.7 pp) × 8.55 × 2.5 **Man:** 40 men

A: 1/40-mm AA — 1/20-mm AA **Range:** 3,000/10
M: SEMT-Pielstick diesels; 2 props; 2,000 hp **Fuel:** 48 tons

REMARKS: M-151, M-152, and M-153 were built by the Augustin Normand yard, Le Havre, and transferred by France at the end of 1957. M-161 was built in Yugoslavia with the technical assistance of the Augustin Normand yard.

♦ *4 British "-ham"-type minesweepers* — Bldr: Yugoslavia, 1964–66

M 141 (ex-MSI-98) **M 143** (ex-MSI-100)
M 142 (ex-MSI-99) **M 144** (ex-MSI-101)

D: 120 tons **S:** 14 kts **Dim:** 32.4 × 6.3 × 1.7
A: 1/40-mm **Man:** 22 men **Range:** 2,000/9
M: Diesels; 2 props; 550 hp **Fuel:** 15 tons

REMARKS: Built under MAP. The numbers MSI-98 to MSI-101 are those assigned by American authorities.

♦ *6 inshore minesweepers* — Bldr: Yugoslavia, 1966–68

ML 117 to **ML 122**

D: 131 tons (fl) **S:** 12 kts **Dim:** 30.0 × 5.5 × 1.5
A: 1/40-mm — 2/12.7-mm machine guns
M: 2 General Motors diesels; 1,000 hp

REMARK: Also used for coastal patrol.

♦ *3 Nestin-class river minesweepers* — Bldr: Brodotelina, Belgrade

M 331 NESTIN (20-12-75) **M 333 BELEGIS** (1-77)
M 332 MOTAJICA (18-12-76)

D: 65 tons **S:** 20 kts **Dim:** 27.0 × 6.3 × . . .
A: 3/20-mm AA (III × 1) **M:** 2 diesels; 260 hp

REMARK: Hull of light-metal alloy.

♦ *14 small river minesweepers*

RML 301 to **RML 314**

D: 38 tons **S:** 12 kts **A:** 1/20-mm AA

AMPHIBIOUS WARFARE SHIPS

♦ *1 tank landing ship of new design* — Bldr: Yugoslavia

N . . .

D: 2,980 tons (fl) **S:** . . . **Dim:** 102.0 (95.0 pp) × 14.2 × 3.1
A: 2/40-mm Bofors **Cargo capacity:** 1,500 tons
M: 2 diesels; 3,400 hp

♦ *24 landing craft*

DTM 211 to **DTM 234**

D: 500 tons (approx.) **S:** . . . **Dim:** . . . × . . . × . . .
A: 4/20-mm AA **Cargo capacity:** 3 medium tanks

♦ *2 601-class landing craft* — Bldr: Yugoslavia

D: 35 tons **S:** 22 kts **Dim:** 21.4 × 4.6 × 0.6
A: 1/20-mm **M:** 2 diesels

AUXILIARY SHIPS

♦ *1 Soviet Moma-type hydrographic ship* — Bldr: Gdansk, Poland, 1971

PH 33 ANDRIJA MOHOROVIČIĆ

Andrija Mohorovičić (PH 33) 1971

D: 1,475 tons (fl) **S:** 15 kts **Dim:** 67.0 × 10.8 × 4.0
M: 2 diesels

♦ *4 small transports* — Bldr: Yugoslavia, 1961-62

PT 71 to **PT 74**

D: 310 tons (428 fl) **S:** 7 kts **Dim:** 43.1 × 6.8 × 4.85
M: 300 hp

REMARK: Resemble small coastal vessels.

♦ *4 PN-13-class oilers* — Bldr: Yugoslavia, 1951-53

D: 695 tons **S:** 8.5 kts

♦ *1 salvage vessel* — Bldr: Tito, Belgrade

PS 12 SPASILAC

REMARK: Replacement for a salvage ship of the same name that was built in 1929 and has now been scrapped.

♦ *6 tugs*

	L	S	Length	Hp
PR 52 (ex-*San Remo*)	1937	8 kts	173	350
PR 58 (ex-*Molara*)	1937	8 kts	120	250
PR 51 (ex-*Porto Conte*)	1936	11 kts	226	600
PR 55 (ex-*Snazni*)	1917	10 kts	100	300
PR 54 (ex-*Ustrajni*)	1917	9 kts	160	250
LR 11 (ex-*Basiluzzo*)	1915	5 kts	110	180

♦ *3 water carriers*

PV 6 **PV 11** **PV 13**

VARIOUS SHIPS

♦ *1 admiralty yacht* — Bldr: C.R.D.A., Monfalcone

Jadranka

	Laid down	L	In serv.
JADRANKA (ex-*Biokovo*, ex-*Beli Orao*)	23-12-38	3-6-39	10-39

D: 567 tons (660 fl) **S:** 17 kts (trials: 18.5)
Dim: 60.45 × 7.93 × 2.7 **A:** 2/40-mm AA — 2/20-mm AA
M: Sulzer diesels; 2 props; 1,900 hp

ADDITIONAL SHIPS

♦ *1 topsail training schooner* — Bldr: Blohm & Voss, 1932

JADRAN

D: 720 tons **S:** 8 kts **Dim:** 58.0 × 8.8 × 4.2
M: 1 Linke-Hoffman diesel; 375 hp **Sail area:** 800 m²

REMARK: Accommodations for 150 cadets.

♦ *2 command ships*

VIS

REMARKS: Built in Yugoslavia in 1956. Serves as flagship for missile boats.

KOZARA

REMARKS: Former presidential yacht, now reportedly flagship of the River Flotilla.

♦ *2 PN-24-class tankers*
♦ *4 PN-13-class tankers* **D:** 695 tons **S:** 12 kts
♦ *6 PT-61-type transports*

PT 61 to **PT 66**

♦ *3 water carriers*
♦ *4 ammunition transports*

PO 52 to **PO 55**

ZAIRE

PERSONNEL: 300 men

MERCHANT MARINE (1976): 32 ships — 107,278 grt

♦ *6 20-meter Swift boats* — Delivered: 1972

♦ *3 12-ton boats*

♦ *other boats and supply barges*

NOTE: In 7-74 a contract was signed with a French group for 12 security and lake patrol boats

ZANZIBAR

Although part of the United Republic of Tanzania, Zanzibar has internal autonomy and its own armed forces.

♦ *4 75-foot Vosper boats*

D:	70 tons	**S:**	24.5 kts	**Dim:**	22.9 × 6.0 × 1.5
A:	2/20-mm	**Range:**	800/20	**M:**	2 diesels; 1,840 hp

REMARK: The first two units were delivered in 7-73, the last two in 1974.

INDEX OF SHIPS

All ships are indexed by their full names, e.g., Almirante Domecq Garcia.

NAME — Pages

NAME — Pages

N